Sixth Edition

PSYCHOLOGY

The SCIENCE *of* BEHAVIOR

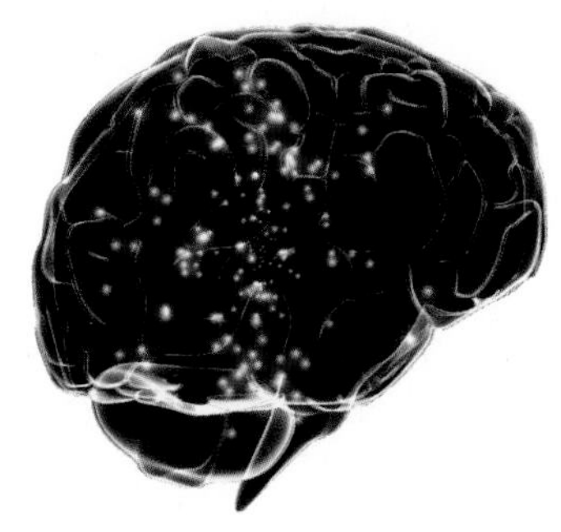

R. H. Ettinger

BVT Publishing
Better textbooks, better prices
www.BVTPublishing.com

Publisher and Managing Director: Richard Schofield

Product Development Manager: Shannon Conley

Production and Fulfillment Manager: Janai Escobedo

Senior Designer: Esther Scannell

Designer/Typesetter: Rhonda Minnema

Ancillary Coordinator: Tiffany Koopal

Copyeditor: Tara Joffe

Reference Editor: Tiffany Koopal

Proofreader: Teresa Daly

Permissions Coordinators: Logan McDonald and Jade Elk

eBook Value Pack ISBN: 978-1-5178-0394-0

Textbook^{Plus} (Loose-Leaf Bundle) ISBN: 978-1-5178-0150-2

eBook^{Plus} ISBN: 978-1-5178-0149-6

Loose-Leaf ISBN: 978-1-5178-0147-2

Soft Cover ISBN: 978-1-5178-0148-9

Cover Photo: Shutterstock

Brief Contents

Table *of* Contents

PART 1: *Origins and Methods of Psychology*

Chapter 1

The Origins of Psychology 1

Chapter 2

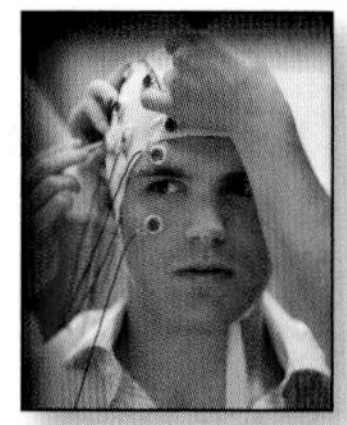

The Methods of Psychology 31

PART 2: *Biological Foundations, Perception, and Sleep*

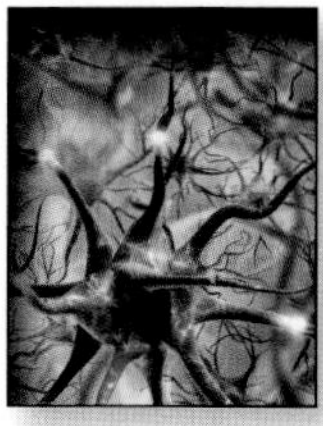

Chapter 3

Chapter 4

Chapter 7

Memory 265

Chapter 8

Motivation 311

Chapter 9

Emotion and Stress 345

Chapter 10

Cognition: Thinking and Language 379

PART 4: *Developmental Processes and Individual Differences*

Chapter 11

Development 1: Conception Through Childhood 429

Chapter 12

Development 2: Adolescence to the End of Life 483

Chapter 13

Intelligence 515

Chapter 16

Chapter 17

Social Psychology 677

Appendix 721

Glossary 747

References 777

Index 814

Preface

If psychology is a science, then it should be presented as a science.

We live in an age in which science and technology have revolutionized the way we view the world, yet many students fail to realize that scientific methods can also be applied to the study of human behavior. While many students have no difficulty mastering numerous facts and principles, their behavior appears to be little changed by this experience—that is, there is little evidence that a first course in psychology has changed the way they interpret behavioral events. Perhaps this is because it is so difficult to remain objective about our behavior—and perhaps that is due, in part, to the ways in which texts present and support principles of psychology.

Throughout this text, we have attempted to actively involve students in the discovery process by inviting them to question assumptions and to participate in the scientific process of supporting or refuting ideas. Although the text is rich with content, it endeavors to bring students—and their own behavior—closer to the scientific process of observation and control.

The major goals of this textbook are to demonstrate to students how the science of psychology has evolved and how it continues to develop. We wanted to create a textbook that engages students in the scientific process by asking stimulating questions and demonstrating how scientific research proceeds in order to answer them. We believe it is important to show students how we know what we know by discussing principles of psychology in terms of the scientific context in which they are demonstrated. More important, we discuss the methods of research throughout the text as we present hundreds of classic and contemporary experiments in detail. Although we strive to present and interpret the most recent research available, we also discuss many older classic studies where they remain relevant.

Not all psychologists agree with a single approach to studying human behavior. Throughout this text, behavioral phenomena are discussed from different, and sometimes competing, perspectives. In cases in which the preponderance of evidence supports a particular perspective, we discuss the evidence for a stronger point of view. Psychology is a dynamic science, and other disciplines are continually adding to and changing our understanding. This is particularly evident in the rapidly evolving neural and biological sciences. Throughout this text we present the most recent and compelling biological perspectives when they are relevant.

Special Features

What makes this text different from others that are also well grounded in current research is the way in which research is presented. Throughout each chapter, we attempt to demonstrate how research evolves from simple questions about behavior, often by asking students to think about how answers to questions might be found. Then we show how research, using a variety of methods, answers these questions. In some cases, research does not lead to clear answers, and we discuss how to critically evaluate both sides of an issue. In many cases, we discuss how both the questions and the research are influenced by individual personalities and the political climate of the time. Psychology, like any other science, is a dynamic, social process within which our knowledge continually changes.

Because psychology can be presented from different theoretical perspectives, we have included several end-of-chapter interviews with prominent, influential psychologists to demonstrate these differences. These interviews also show students how researchers think about important issues and illustrate how controversy still surrounds much of this important discipline.

New to This Edition

The 6th edition of *Psychology: The Science of Behavior* is the most current introductory textbook available. It continues to present contrasting theoretical perspectives, while maintaining a strong scientific orientation to the study of psychology. For instance, while the text emphasizes a strong scientific perspective, it also presents competing points of view on several of the most important topics, including animal language, behavioral disorders and their treatment, and issues in social psychology. Some of the most noticeable changes to the 6th edition include the following:

- The addition of a section on sport psychology
- Updated statistics on drug use
- Research on hearing loss in teenagers from the use of ear buds
- New research on how sleep functions to maintain brain homeostasis
- New research on sensory memories and subliminal perception
- New research on eating disorders and their prevalence
- The role of epigenetics in the development of homosexuality
- New research on the neurobiology of emotions and the role of stress in disease
- New research on the development of telegraphic speech in infants
- Discussion of epigenetics and the nature-nurture argument
- Updated statistics on the prevalence of fetal alcohol syndrome and marriage in the United States
- Revised discussion of attention deficit/hyperactivity disorder, its pathology, and its treatment
- Revised discussion of the pathology and treatment of schizophrenia
- New research on stereotype threat and sex differences
- Updated discussion of facial symmetry and physical attractiveness

These enhancements help ensure a textbook that will provide the most current introduction to the science of psychology and behavior.

About the Author

Dr. R. H. Ettinger is professor of psychology at Eastern Oregon University. His research focuses on psychopharmacology and includes investigations of the neural mechanisms underlying feeding and addiction. Notably, his research has led to the development of an anticocaine antibody and the understanding of the role of Pavlovian conditioning in drug tolerance and addiction. In addition to this textbook, Ettinger is the author of a textbook on psychopharmacology. In addition to his research and writing, he is an avid cyclist and cross-country skier, and he enjoys flying a private airplane.

Supplements and Resources

Instructor Supplements

A complete teaching package is available for instructors who adopt this book. This package includes an **online lab**, **instructor's manual**, **test bank**, **course management software**, and **PowerPoint™ slides**.

BVT*Lab*	An online lab is available for this textbook at www.BVTLab.com, as described in the BVT*Lab* section below.
Instructor's Manual	The instructor's manual helps first-time instructors develop the course, while offering seasoned instructors a new perspective on the material. Each section of the instructor's manual coincides with a chapter in the textbook. The user-friendly format begins by providing learning objectives and detailed outlines for each chapter. The manual then presents lecture discussions, class activities, and sample answers to the end-of-chapter review questions. Lastly, additional resources—books, articles, websites—are listed to help instructors review the materials covered in each chapter.
Test Bank	An extensive test bank is available to instructors in both hard copy and electronic form. Each chapter has approximately 75 multiple choice, 25 true/false, 10 short answer, and 10 essay questions ranked by difficulty and style. Each question is referenced to the appropriate section of the text to make test creation quick and easy.
Course Management Software	BVT's course management software, Respondus, allows for the creation of tests and quizzes that can be downloaded directly into a wide variety of course management environments, such as Blackboard®, Web CT™, Desire2Learn®, Canvas™, and others.
PowerPoint Slides	A set of PowerPoint slides for each chapter, comprising a chapter overview, learning objectives, slides covering all key topics, key figures and charts, and summary and conclusion slides.

Student Resources

Student resources are available for this textbook at www.BVTLab.com. These resources are geared toward students needing additional assistance, as well as those seeking complete mastery of the content. The following resources are available:

Practice Questions	Students can work through hundreds of practice questions online. Questions are multiple choice or true/false in format and are graded instantly for immediate feedback.
Flashcards	BVT*Lab* includes sets of flashcards that reinforce the key terms from each chapter.
PowerPoint Slides	All instructor PowerPoint slides are available for convenient lecture preparation and for students to view online for a study recap.

BVT*Lab*

BVT*Lab* is an affordable online lab for instructors and their students. It includes an online classroom with a grade book and class forum, a homework grading system, extensive test banks for quizzes and exams, and a host of student study resources.

Course Setup	BVT*Lab* has an easy-to-use, intuitive interface that allows instructors to quickly set up their courses and grade books and to replicate them from section to section and semester to semester.
Grade Book	Using an assigned passcode, students register for the grade book, which automatically grades and records all homework, quizzes, and tests.
Class Forum	Instructors can post discussion threads and upload documents to a class forum and then monitor and moderate student replies.
Student Resources	All student resources for this textbook are available in digital form at BVT*Lab*.
eBook	Students who have purchased a product that includes an eBook can download the eBook from a link in the lab. A web-based eBook is also available within the lab for easy reference during online classes, homework, and study sessions.

Customization

BVT's Custom Publishing Division can help you modify this book's content to satisfy your specific instructional needs. The following are examples of customization:

- Rearrangement of chapters to follow the order of your syllabus
- Deletion of chapters not covered in your course
- Addition of paragraphs, sections, or chapters you or your colleagues have written for this course
- Editing of the existing content, down to the word level
- Customization of the accompanying student resources and online lab
- Addition of handouts, lecture notes, syllabus, and so on
- Incorporation of student worksheets into the textbook

All of these customizations will be professionally typeset to produce a seamless textbook of the highest quality, with an updated table of contents and index to reflect the customized content.

(Shutterstock)

Chapter 1

The Origins of Psychology

Are the things you see, feel, and hear every day only in your mind, or do they exist in the external world? How can you know for sure? How can you know anything for sure? As John Locke, a seventeenth-century philosopher, put it:

> The knowledge of the existence of any other thing we can have only by sensation. … For the having the idea of anything in our mind no more proves the existence of that thing than a picture of a man evidences his being in the world.

Questions about the mind were of great interest to philosophers of the seventeenth and eighteenth centuries and can actually be traced back to the Greek philosophers Aristotle and Plato. Although the philosophers' answers contribute relatively little to our current understanding of psychology, their methods of inquiry did. During the nineteenth century, philosophers became less reliant on theological and nonempirical explanations of mind and behavior, and more and more dependent on direct observation. However, as the following quote points out, mental philosophy (the term used before psychology became a discipline of its own) was making very little progress in understanding the mind.

> There is no department of knowledge in which so little progress has been made as in that of mental philosophy. … No attempt indeed has been made to examine its phenomena by the light of experiment and observation. (Brewster, 1854)

However, by the middle of the nineteenth century, psychological phenomena such as perception, thought, and learning would be studied scientifically. Rapid advances in the physical sciences using scientific methods suggested that the study of the mind, which had made relatively little progress, might also benefit from a new methodology. This dramatic shift in the way the mind was studied led the way for modern psychology.

We will trace these beginnings of psychology in this first chapter. An appreciation of where psychology has been will help you to see where it is going.

1.1 The Study of Psychology

For many of you, this text will be your first formal exposure to a science that is central to us. Perhaps you have wondered as you were taking some other courses, what has this to do with my life? Psychology has everything to do with your life.

Although we admit to some bias, we do believe that a knowledge of psychology is helpful even to people who do not plan to pursue it as a career. Studying psychology provides insights into why people behave as they do. It also helps us to better understand our own thoughts, feelings, behaviors, and attitudes; hopefully, it can strengthen our appreciation of, and tolerance for, the wide differences that exist among people.

Psychology investigates a wide variety of questions and attempts to answer them using scientific methods. Among the questions that will be explored in this book are these:

> Can something as complex as human behavior be studied scientifically?
>
> What is the relationship between the mind and the brain?
>
> How are our memories represented in the brain?

Psychology Scientific study of the behavior of humans and other animals

Are mental disorders caused by chemical or structural abnormalities in the brain?

What causes some people to overeat and to become obese?

Are dreams necessary? What happens if people are prevented from dreaming?

What do intelligence tests really measure?

Why are you less likely to be assisted in an emergency when there are many bystanders than when in the presence of only a few?

Can one person possess two or more distinct personalities at the same time?

How does psychological stress contribute to illnesses such as heart disease, hypertension, and the flu?

Does psychotherapy help people overcome psychological problems such as depression and anxiety?

Is punishment a more effective method for controlling behavior than the use of reinforcement?

Psychology also helps us evaluate the many so-called psychological facts we encounter every day in the popular media. When was the last time you read a newspaper or magazine article or heard a talk-show host present the latest findings on the meaning of dreams, how to become more successful, or why men behave differently than women? Many people accept such "scientifically based facts" without questioning whether they are founded on reliable evidence. We hope that an understanding of psychology will help you think critically and carefully evaluate such claims. You will see that many of your unquestioned assumptions about human behavior have no scientific basis.

1.2 Definition of Psychology

Formally defined, **psychology** is *the scientific study of the behavior of humans and other animals.* This definition can be separated into three parts: Psychology is a scientific study; it studies behavior; and it includes the study of other animals as well as humans.

1.2a Psychology as a Science

The first part of our definition states that psychology is a scientific study. Indeed, the theories and facts of psychology emerge from the careful application of scientific methods. This aspect of our definition may contradict many people's views of psychology, for it is often assumed that psychology is just a matter of common sense. After all, are we not applying psychology when we mix enough praise with criticism to make a child feel good about changing bad habits, or when we carefully discuss relationship problems with our partners rather than keeping those concerns to ourselves? If syndicated columnists in the daily paper can provide advice for dealing with people, what sets psychology apart as a science?

The purpose of psychology is to give us a completely different idea of the things we know best.

Paul Valéry, poet, essayist, and philosopher

(Shutterstock)

According to research conducted by Latané and Darley, the presence of other people affects our perception of an emergency situation.

Psychology certainly involves knowing how to deal with people effectively, but it involves a great deal more than this. In fact, dealing with people effectively is only a small part of the science of behavior. As you will soon see, it involves much more than commonsense explanations. For example, take a minute to consider the following question: Would you expect that the number of people present in an emergency could determine whether or not one of them responds with help?

Most people when asked this question immediately reply that the more people present, the more likely someone will help. After all, some individual in the crowd is bound to see the emergency and assist. However, numerous case studies and experiments conducted by psychologists tend to confirm the opposite: Assistance is more likely to be given if very few bystanders are present.

According to research conducted by Latané and Darley (1970), the presence of other people affects our perception of an emergency situation, and we tend to diffuse our responsibility to act in an emergency to others who are present. In a now classic experiment, subjects were asked to participate in an interview about urban life. While waiting to be called to the interview, they were instructed to wait in a specific room and fill out some forms. Some of the subjects waited alone, and others waited in groups of three. After working on the forms for several minutes, smoke began to infiltrate the room through a vent. Observations of the subjects revealed that 63 percent of the subjects working alone noticed the smoke within five seconds while only 26 percent of the subjects working with others noticed it. Subjects working alone also were more likely to report the smoke than subjects working with others.

This research, along with numerous other experiments, has helped to explain bystander apathy. It is only through carefully designed experiments such as these that our commonsense assumptions can be validated or refuted.

Psychological research using scientific methods often provides enlightening and reliable information about behavior that we might not otherwise learn. In contrast, relying

BVT Lab

Flashcards are available for this chapter at **www.BVTLab.com**.

on common sense produces subjective opinions that may have little basis in fact. One only has to look at the history of other sciences to see that psychology is not alone here. It was not all that long ago that stars were known as windows to the heavens and that diseases were believed to be caused by spirits invading the body. As science progresses, subjective opinions and folklore are either confirmed or left behind.

Psychology uses scientific methods to investigate its subject. Many of these methods are discussed in detail in Chapter 2. Despite its careful methodology, however, many questions about behavior remain unanswered by the science of psychology. Much of our understanding of people and behavior is subject to constant review and revision. You will learn that very few psychological principles are carved in stone; new theories as well as technological developments are constantly providing fresh directions and methods for expanding knowledge.

1.2b The Study of Behavior

The second part of our definition states that psychology is the study of behavior. There have been times in the history of psychology, as you will see later in this chapter, when psychology focused almost entirely on unobservable mental processes. At other times, psychologists have been concerned only with behavior that could be observed directly, strictly avoiding any reference to mental processes.

At present, psychologists are interested in studying both behavioral processes and mental processes. It is hoped by many that theories about mental processes can be based on direct observations of behavior. To illustrate how both behavior and mental processes can be the subject matter of psychology, imagine participating in a psychological experiment in which a psychologist displays a moving object on a computer screen. After the object has moved up (or down) the screen for several seconds, it disappears. Your task is to locate the exact spot on the screen where the object disappeared. The psychologist here is interested in both direct measurements (your reported estimate of position) and discovering something about how movement and velocity are represented internally (by developing a theory based on numerous observations). For example, psychologists have found that if the object is moving downward, people tend to exaggerate its velocity by overestimating how far it traveled before disappearing. When the object is moving upward, the velocity estimate is often too low (Hubbard, 1990). Interestingly, these observations are consistent with how "real" moving objects are affected by gravity. That is, as an object goes up, it slows down; when an object is going down, it accelerates *because of gravity*. Thus, it appears as though our mental representations of moving objects have some of the same characteristics as real moving objects. In this example, a theory about a mental process (our representation of movement) is developed through direct observation of observable behavior (placement of the cursor on the computer screen).

Thus, psychology does not solely study behaviors that can be observed directly by onlookers or research scientists (although those observations are an important part of psychology). Nor—contrary to some people's assumptions that all psychologists are interested in is analyzing dreams and probing for repressed memories—does psychology confine itself only to the inner workings of the mind. Instead, contemporary psychologists are often interested in both observable behavior and mental processes.

1.2c The Study of Humans and Other Animals

The third part of our definition states that psychology is the study of humans and other animals. Psychologists study rats, dogs, cats, and pigeons, among other animals; even insects have provided useful information about behavior.

Learning About Psychology from Nonhuman Animals

Students are often surprised to discover that the subject matter of psychology includes the behavior of all animals, not just humans. How can psychologists generalize from rats to people? Why study nonhuman animals when there are so many pressing problems threatening the quality of human lives? Try to formulate at least a few answers to this question before reading on.

There are at least five major reasons why psychology includes the study of animal behavior as well as human behavior. One is the need to find a simpler model. Scientists in all fields generally attempt to understand a particular phenomenon by first studying the simplest examples available in nature. For instance, to understand respiration, metabolism, and other cellular processes, a biologist might first examine them in a simple, one-celled amoeba, rather than in a more complex, multicelled organism. Similarly, scientists seeking to understand the neurological processes that underlie learning and memory can benefit from examining the nervous system of a relatively simple organism such as a sea slug, which may have about twenty thousand nerve cells, rather than by beginning their investigations with humans, who have about 200 billion nerve cells.

A second reason to study animal behavior is because such research can provide greater control. In a typical experiment, a number of different factors or variables may influence behavior. The more control the experimenter has over these variables, the more precise the conclusions can be. To illustrate, suppose you wanted to study the relationship between environmental noise levels and problem-solving behavior. You might anticipate that a number of variables (such as how rested, hungry, or relaxed a subject is) could also influence problem solving. If you were to use human subjects, it would be hard to control precisely the events occurring in their lives in the twenty-four-hour period before they arrived at your laboratory for testing. In contrast, the life of an experimental animal, such as a monkey, can be controlled twenty-four hours a day. Thus, by using animal subjects, you could carefully monitor important conditions such as levels of hunger, rest, and stress.

(Shutterstock)

What can we learn about behavior from pigeons?

Ethical considerations are a third reason for studying animals. Psychologists often ask questions that for ethical reasons cannot be addressed initially in research with humans. For example, over the last four decades, psychologists involved in brain research have conducted experiments in which they have placed electrodes into the brain to stimulate or record brain activity. You can imagine the ethical questions that would surface if we were limited to human subjects in these pioneering efforts. Just as medical researchers must test experimental drugs extensively with nonhumans before they can begin clinical testing on people, research psychologists cannot apply new laboratory procedures to human subjects until they have ruled out the possibility of harmful effects.

The fact that psychologists conduct experiments on nonhuman animals that may be unethical to conduct on humans does not mean that ethical guidelines are not followed in animal research. Quite the contrary, virtually everywhere that research is conducted in the United States, ethics committees (called Institutional Review Boards) review all proposed studies to ensure that the welfare of participants (human or otherwise) is safeguarded. The vast majority of scientists conducting animal research are aware of the responsibilities regarding humane treatment of their subjects and work within the confines of these limitations.

(Shutterstock)

Although psychologists conduct experiments on nonhuman animals, ethics committees review all studies to ensure the welfare of the subjects.

A fourth reason for using nonhuman subjects is a practical one. Animals are readily available for experimentation, often at minimal cost. White rats, for instance, are generally in plentiful supply at a price well within most researchers' budgets. In addition, some experiments require frequent testing of subjects, often over an extended period. Few humans would commit to any kind of research that required more than a few hours conveniently taken from their daily routines. Laboratory animals, on the other hand, are available night and day for as long as necessary.

Finally, psychologists study the behavior of animals simply to learn more about animal behavior. For example, psychologists and other scientists who study animal behavior have provided important information about the feeding, social, and reproductive behaviors of countless species. This information is critical when developing policy that may affect animal environments. In the northwest United States, there is a renewed discussion about the habitats of the spotted owl and wild salmon. What effects will extensive logging have on the populations of these species? Only research on the behavior of these species can answer this question.

Even if you acknowledge that animal research has some advantages, you may still be unconvinced that such research is worthwhile. If so, the findings of research psychologist James Olds (Olds & Milner, 1973) may persuade you to modify this view somewhat, for his research illustrates how animal studies can have direct value for humans. Olds identified an area within a rat's brain that produces intense pleasure when stimulated electrically (see Chapter 3). His pioneering work encouraged researchers to look for similar pleasure centers in human brains. Their discovery in humans has had many important applications, including pleasure center stimulation to provide relief for severely disturbed psychiatric patients and to counteract debilitating pain in terminally ill patients. Electrical stimulation has also been applied to treat severe seizures associated with epilepsy. More recent research on the neural structures that make up this "pleasure center" has led to a better understanding of drug and alcohol addictions. Without first experimenting on animals, it is unlikely that these treatments would now be available for humans.

We have defined psychology as the scientific study of behavior, yet this definition represents only a contemporary view of psychology. In its short history (the discipline had its formal beginnings only a little over a century ago), the answer to "What is psychology?" has varied considerably, depending on the era in which it was asked. The following section presents a brief overview of the history of psychology.

1.3 Psychology's History

Although psychology is a very young science, its roots go back to antiquity. Since the earliest recorded civilizations, people have been concerned about issues still considered central to present-day psychology. This focus was particularly true for philosophers such as Plato, Aristotle, Descartes, and Locke, who raised provocative questions about human thoughts, feelings, and behaviors.

(iStock)

Without first experimenting on animals, it is unlikely that there would be treatments or vaccines for diseases such as polio or lupus.

These philosophers speculated about the mind. Where was it located? How did ideas within the mind gain expression in physical actions? By what processes did events in our external environment become part of our awareness? Such questions reflected a fundamental interest in the relationship between mind and body. The early philosophers endeavored to understand this relationship by formulating assumptions and then applying logical thought processes as they reasoned their way to conclusions. While based on logic, this approach had an important limitation because it relied on subjective assumptions about how the world seemed to be, rather than scientific assessments about how the world really is. As a result, logical reasoning of early philosophers sometimes led to inaccurate conclusions.

For instance, the influential seventeenth-century philosopher René Descartes proposed that mind and body are distinct entities that interact at a point represented by the brain's tiny pineal gland. Descartes's position was known as dualism. He believed that the physical body was mechanical and obeyed known laws of physics. The mind or soul, however, was not physical but interacted in some way through the pineal gland to produce intentional behavior. Descartes's dualistic view is summarized in the following statement:

> I here remark, in the first place, that there is a vast difference between mind and body, in respect that body, from its nature, is always divisible, and that mind is entirely indivisible. ... This would be sufficient to teach me that the mind or soul of man is entirely different from the body.

As you might have guessed, Descartes's ideas have greatly influenced the way we commonly think of mind and body. For example, the concept of free will is central to our everyday assumption that our behavior is influenced by our wants, desires, and intentions. This is contrary to the position that behavior is caused or determined by *physical* events either within or outside of our bodies. This position, referred to as *determinism*, is central to the science of psychology. Determinism assumes that all physical events (including behavior and mental processes) are caused or determined by other physical events. These other physical events include the activity of our nervous system. Many contemporary scientists and philosophers even question whether we have free will at all (Harris, 2012; Wegner, 2002).

Psychology which explains everything explains nothing, and we are still in doubt.

Marianne Moore, American poet

Psychology also has roots in *physiology*, a division of biology concerned with the systematic study of bodily processes. An interest in how the bodies of humans and other animals function led a number of influential nineteenth-century physiologists to begin

(Portrait of René Descartes by Frans Hals, oil on canvas, Wikimedia Commons/Public Domain)

René Descartes (1596–1650)

exploring some of the same psychological issues as their philosopher counterparts. However, unlike the philosophers who relied on reasoning and speculation, the physiologists adhered to the concept of *empiricism*, the idea that knowledge is best acquired through observation. These early physiologists were well schooled in the **scientific method**, which involves careful observation of events in the world, the formation of predictions based on these observations, and then the testing of these predictions by further systematic observations.

The physiologists of the mid-nineteenth century provided important new insights into how the brain and the rest of the nervous system influence behavior. For example, in the mid-1800s, a group of German scientists led by Hermann von Helmholtz pioneered a series of experiments in which they measured the speed of conduction of a nerve impulse and assessed the nature of neural communication within the nervous system. By 1870, researchers at the University of Berlin had begun to study the exposed brains of laboratory animals and found that electrical stimulation of certain locations caused specific bodily movements. Studies such as these marked the way for later laboratory research that has helped reveal the relationship between brain processes and behavior.

Thus, while psychology has roots in philosophical questions about the relationship of mind and body, the empirical nature of contemporary psychology and its adherence to the scientific method also reflects the science of physiology, which provided the tools for careful examination of these questions. The next logical step in the evolution of psychology was to take the questions about behavior and mental process posed by philosophy into the laboratory.

1.3a Structuralism

Wilhelm Wundt (1832–1920)

Entering the laboratory is exactly what Wilhelm Wundt, a German scientist trained in physiology, did in the late 1800s. The establishment of Wundt's small laboratory at the University of Leipzig in 1879 marked the formal beginning of psychology as a scientific discipline.

Wundt defined the task of psychology as the systematic study of the structure of the conscious adult mind. He believed that the conscious mental processes involved in such things as perceiving colors, reacting to stimuli, and experiencing emotions could be understood best by breaking them down into their basic elements and then analyzing how the elements were connected with one another. In this sense, he hoped to pattern psychology after the physical sciences of chemistry, physics, and physiology.

Wundt borrowed a tool of philosophy, *introspection* (looking inward), for studying mental processes. For example, subjects listening to music might be asked to break their perceptual experience down into its basic elements of pitch, volume, timbre, and so forth. Subjects were trained in introspection so that they could provide clear reports of their sensations. Wundt also believed that introspection needed to be supplemented by experiments. Therefore, he would systematically vary some physical dimension of a stimulus, such as the volume of a particular sound, to see how sensations changed. This approach came to be known as *experimental self-observation*. Throughout Wundt's career, he continued to emphasize gaining information about the mind from observable, measurable events.

Scientific Method Careful observation of events in the world, the formation of predictions based on these observations, and the testing of these predictions by manipulation of variables and systematic observation

Many of the pioneers of American psychology received their training in Wundt's laboratory in Germany. One of these students, Edward Titchener, brought his mentor's particular brand of psychology to America when he established a psychology laboratory at Cornell University in 1892. Like Wundt, Titchener thought the proper goal of psychology was to describe mental structures. This approach to psychology was called **structuralism**.

Structuralism attempted to develop a kind of mental chemistry by breaking experience down into its basic elements—or structures—in the same way that a substance such as water could be broken down into molecules of hydrogen and oxygen. This approach seemed reasonable at the time because it was proving successful for the sciences of chemistry and physics.

(Wikimedia Commons/Public Domain)

Wilhelm Wundt (1832–1920)

Problems with Structuralism

Can you see any problems associated with trying to break an experience into its basic elements? Will an experience retain its essential character when subjected to this reductionist approach? Think about this question for a few moments before reading on.

Structuralism enjoyed only short-lived popularity. Psychologists soon discovered that introspection, the major research tool of structuralism, often altered the nature of the conscious mental processes they wished to analyze. The next time you find yourself entranced by an exquisite sunset or a haunting melody, stop and pay attention to your sensations, thoughts, and feelings. You will probably find, as did many of the early introspectionists, that analyzing what you are experiencing changes the experience. An even more damaging flaw became apparent when a number of researchers who were using introspection independently of one another discovered that their results were often different. Finally, many American psychologists criticized structuralism as impractical; they thought psychology should offer solutions to the problems of everyday life. This movement toward a more pragmatic psychology culminated in the functionalist school.

1.3b **Functionalism**

William James (1842–1910)

Perhaps one of the greatest of all American psychologists was William James. James distinguished himself as a writer of psychology, as a reactionist against the introspective method, and by his new approach to investigating the mind. He agreed with the structuralists that psychology should study mental processes. However, he felt that the science would be better served by attempting to understand the fluid, functional, continually changing, personal nature of conscious experience. He was particularly interested in trying to understand mental processes that helped humans and other animals adapt to their environments. Because of his emphasis on the functional, practical nature of the mind, his conception of psychology's proper task became known as **functionalism**. One of the most important events in psychology's history was the publication in 1890 of James's landmark text, *The Principles of Psychology*. This two-volume book, which detailed his view of the nature of psychology, is still considered to be one of the most important psychological texts of all time.

Charles Darwin's theory of evolution by natural selection greatly influenced James. According to Darwin, characteristics of a species change or evolve over time as environmental conditions change. Those characteristics that aid in the survival and reproduction of the species are maintained while others are eliminated. For instance, the protective

Structuralism Approach to psychology that attempted to break down experience into its basic elements, or structures, using a technique called introspection, in which subjects provided scientific reports of perceptual experiences

Functionalism Approach to psychology that emphasized the functional, practical nature of the mind; influenced by Darwin's theory of natural selection, functionalists attempted to learn how mental processes—such as learning, thinking, and perceiving—helped people adapt

coloration of some types of moths or the opposable thumbs of humans are traits that were preserved because they helped these species adapt to their environments. Similarly, functionalists concluded that psychological states or processes, such as consciousness, also evolved because they served particular functions, such as guiding the activities of the individual. Functionalists wanted to learn how various mental processes—such as perceiving, learning, and thinking—helped people adapt. To accomplish this purpose, they continued to use introspection in their research. However, they also introduced another research method—collecting data from observations of human and animal behavior.

Both structuralism and functionalism played important roles in the development of psychology as a science. Structuralism brought psychology into the laboratory by demonstrating that mental processes were a legitimate focus for scientific research. Functionalism broadened psychology to include the study of nonhuman animals, and it expanded the data of psychology to include observations of behavior. James's contributions have had enduring effects on both psychology and education.

1.3c Psychoanalysis

Sigmund Freud (1856–1939)

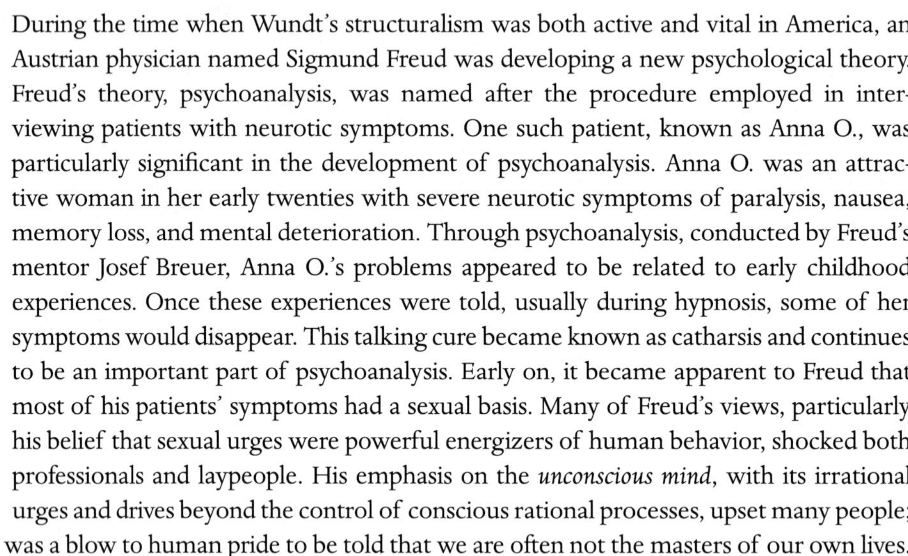

(Wikimedia Commons/ Public Domain)

Sigmund Freud (1856–1939)

During the time when Wundt's structuralism was both active and vital in America, an Austrian physician named Sigmund Freud was developing a new psychological theory. Freud's theory, psychoanalysis, was named after the procedure employed in interviewing patients with neurotic symptoms. One such patient, known as Anna O., was particularly significant in the development of psychoanalysis. Anna O. was an attractive woman in her early twenties with severe neurotic symptoms of paralysis, nausea, memory loss, and mental deterioration. Through psychoanalysis, conducted by Freud's mentor Josef Breuer, Anna O.'s problems appeared to be related to early childhood experiences. Once these experiences were told, usually during hypnosis, some of her symptoms would disappear. This talking cure became known as catharsis and continues to be an important part of psychoanalysis. Early on, it became apparent to Freud that most of his patients' symptoms had a sexual basis. Many of Freud's views, particularly his belief that sexual urges were powerful energizers of human behavior, shocked both professionals and laypeople. His emphasis on the *unconscious mind*, with its irrational urges and drives beyond the control of conscious rational processes, upset many people; it was a blow to human pride to be told that we are often not the masters of our own lives.

Freud's theories are more widely recognized among non-psychologists than are any other school of psychological thought. This is not to say that Freud's analytic approach has been at the forefront of scientific psychology since it was first introduced to America in the early 1900s. Quite the contrary, much of the impact of psychoanalysis lies in the critical reactions it has generated, not on the contributions it has made to modern psychology. Psychoanalysis has been widely criticized, in part because its assertions cannot be tested in the laboratory.

The most complicated achievements of thought are possible without the assistance of consciousness.

Sigmund Freud, "father" of psychoanalysis

Despite these criticisms, Freud's impact on psychology was profound. He provided important insights into understanding the emotional lives of people. He encouraged psychologists to consider the impact on behavior of processes not immediately available to conscious inspection. He also helped to legitimize the study of human sexuality. Although psychoanalysis is not a major force in contemporary psychology, the practice of psychoanalysis by psychiatrists treating emotionally disturbed patients continues. We discuss Freud's views in several places throughout the book, particularly in Chapters 14 and 16.

1.3d Behaviorism

The change in psychology from structuralism to functionalism in the United States was both gradual and incomplete. Certainly functionalism did not completely replace the methods of structuralism, and both schools agreed that mental processes were the subjects of psychology. However, in 1913 a revolution against both of these schools occurred. This revolution, initiated by John Watson, was both sudden and quite dramatic. The new and revolutionary approach to psychology was called **behaviorism**.

BVT *Lab*

Visit **www.BVTLab.com** to explore the student resources available for this chapter.

John Watson (1878–1958)

Behaviorism was founded in the first few decades of the twentieth century by John B. Watson. Although trained as a functionalist, Watson ultimately came to believe it was impossible to study the mind objectively. He especially opposed the use of introspection, which he considered unscientific, and he chastised the functionalists for not going far enough in their rebellion against structuralism. Watson proclaimed a new psychology, free of introspection, whose task was simply to observe the relationship between environmental events (stimuli) and an organism's responses to them. This stimulus-response (S-R) approach to psychology was a radical departure from Watson's predecessors' focus on mental processes.

The goal of behaviorism was (and still is) to identify the processes by which stimuli and responses become connected or associated—in other words, how we learn. Watson believed that complex human behavior could be analyzed in terms of simple learned associations. The early goal of behaviorism was to discover the rules of association and how combinations of simple associations lead to complex behavior. Watson's work was greatly influenced by the Russian physiologist Ivan Pavlov (1849–1936) and another American psychologist Edward Thorndike (1874–1949), both of whom provided Watson and later behaviorists with new ways of investigating behavior and clues to the rules of association. We will have much more to say about Pavlov and Thorndike in Chapter 6.

Behaviorism quickly caught on, and soon many younger American psychologists were calling themselves behaviorists. Behaviorism continues to exert a profound influence on contemporary American psychology, due mainly to the monumental contributions of Harvard's B. F. Skinner (1904–1990). Skinner's major contributions to psychology include his important work in operant conditioning, in which he systematically investigated the effects of reinforcement on behavior. In addition, Skinner's contributions include his extensive writings on language learning, programmed instruction, the philosophy of science, and politics.

Behaviorism is characterized by its insistence upon an empirical, objective science of behavior that has no need for theories of mind or free will. The behaviorist position on the free will–determinism controversy is well summarized in Skinner's statement:

> The issue of personal freedom must not be allowed to interfere with a science of behavior. … We cannot expect to profit from applying the methods of science to human behavior if for some extraneous reason we refuse to admit that our subject matter cannot be controlled. (Skinner, 1953, p. 322)

More recently psychologists and philosophers have begun to openly question whether free will exists or is merely a functional illusion (Harris, 2012; Wegner, 2002). The concept of free will is to be discussed more in Chapter 5, and Skinner and behavioral psychology will be discussed in more detail in Chapter 6. In fact, behaviorism and modern behaviorists will be discussed throughout this book.

Behaviorism Scientific approach to the study of behavior that emphasizes the relationship between environmental events and an organism's behavior

1.3e **Gestalt Psychology**

Wolfgang Köhler (1887–1967)

At about the same time as behaviorism was catching hold in the United States, a group of German psychologists was mounting its own opposition to Wundtian structuralism and the new behaviorism of American psychologists. These scientists, most notably Max Wertheimer, Wolfgang Köhler, and Kurt Koffka, disagreed with the principles and methods of both structuralism and behaviorism. They argued that it was a mistake to try to break psychological processes into basic components such as elementary sensations or simple associations. While structuralists claimed that the perception of objects results from the accumulation of elements into groups or collections, these German psychologists argued that when sensory elements are brought together, something new is formed. This something new is our perception of the stimulus. Put another way, the whole (our perception) is more than the sum of its parts (sensory elements). For example, put together a number of simple musical notes, and a melody emerges. The melody you hear did not exist in any of the individual notes. This new approach to the investigation of perception was called **Gestalt psychology**.

(Shutterstock)

Put together a number of simple musical notes, and a melody emerges. The melody you hear did not exist in any of the individual notes. Put another way, the whole is more than the sum of its parts. This new approach to the investigation of perception was called Gestalt psychology.

Consider a typical experiment in perception that demonstrates the Gestalt approach: Imagine sitting in front of a computer and being instructed to watch the screen carefully for the emergence of an object. Your task will be to accurately describe what you see during a very brief presentation of stimuli. The experimenter has programmed the computer to present a small red ball on the left side of your screen for about one hundred milliseconds (one-tenth of a second) followed immediately by the presentation of a larger yellow ball on the right side, again for about one hundred milliseconds. Before reading on, think about what you might report seeing. Remember both images were presented so quickly that you really don't recognize them individually.

What subjects typically report seeing in such an experiment is much more than was actually presented. Most likely you would have seen a small reddish orange circle moving across the screen from left to right. As it moved, it appeared to get larger or to move toward you while getting less red and more yellowish-orange. Both the movement and the change in color were constructed by perception and not characteristics of the stimuli themselves. Experiments like these clearly demonstrate that perception is an active, constructive process, not merely the passive detection of stimulus elements.

Gestalt Psychology
Approach to psychology that argues that the whole of an experience is different from the sum of its parts; an active force in current investigations of perceptual processes and learning, as well as therapy, where it emphasizes the whole person

Because many of our experiences as humans cannot be broken down into separate pieces, Gestalt psychology remains an active force in our present-day investigation of perceptual processes. For example, Gestalt psychologists discovered much of what we now know about producing the illusion of movement through film or through the successive illumination of lights. These and many other perceptual phenomena will be discussed in more detail in Chapter 4.

1.3f Humanistic Psychology

Abraham Maslow (1908–1970)

Although humanistic psychology is still too new to be viewed as a part of psychology's history, we consider it here because it developed out of strong criticism of behaviorism and psychoanalysis.

Humanistic psychology differs from both the psychoanalytic approach and behaviorism in that it does not view humans as being controlled either by events in the environment or by internal, unconscious forces. Humanistic psychologists, most notably Abraham Maslow and Carl Rogers, de-emphasize the influence of both environmental events and unconscious processes in determining human behavior. They argue that the images of man provided by both behavioral and psychoanalytic approaches are incomplete and inaccurate because they do not emphasize what is unique about being human. Instead, humanistic psychologists emphasize the role of *free will* and our ability to make conscious, rational choices about how we live our lives. Humanistic psychologists also believe that people have a natural inclination to fulfill their human potential, a process called *self-actualization*. A person's striving toward self-actualization is seen as the motivating force of behavior.

Although many of humanistic psychology's major tenets are just as difficult to test objectively as are the concepts of psychoanalysis, many psychologists respond favorably to this movement's optimism. Such optimism is in sharp contrast to Freud's psychology, which viewed the outlook for personal fulfillment very pessimistically. Humanistic psychology has increased psychologists' awareness of the importance of such things as love, feeling needed, personal fulfillment, and self-esteem; in this sense, its contributions are of value. While humanistic psychology has been criticized sharply for its reliance on a nonscientific approach to understanding human behavior, its proponents have steadily maintained that human behavior is not a subject to be investigated scientifically. As Maslow phrased it, "We are offered beautifully executed, precise, elegant experiments which, in at least half the cases, have nothing to do with enduring human problems" (Maslow, 1965).

1.4 Contemporary Psychology

The previous section briefly introduced the major historical contributions to modern psychology. Many of those approaches have endured and even thrived into the present. For example, modern behaviorism and Gestalt psychology are still quite influential. The methods of psychoanalysis are still taught and practiced widely throughout the United States, and the functional approach of William James is emphasized in contemporary education. Modern psychology, however, is not dominated by any single theoretical approach. Rather, there are many specialties within the field of psychology, and each emphasizes a particular theoretical approach. The following section describes several major areas of specialization that, together with the enduring historical perspectives, define modern psychology.

Humanistic Psychology
Approach to psychology that emphasizes the role of free choice and our ability to make conscious rational decisions about how we live our lives

1.4a Fields of Specialization in Psychology

Cognitive Psychology

Cognitive Psychology Approach to psychology that focuses on the ways in which organisms process information and investigates processes such as thinking, memory, language, problem solving, and creativity

Developmental Psychology Field of specialization in psychology concerned with factors that influence development and shape behavior throughout the life cycle, from conception through old age

Social Psychology Field of specialization concerned with understanding the impact of social environments and social processes on individuals

Personality Psychology Field of specialization that focuses on exploring the uniqueness of the individual, describing the elements that make up human personality, and investigating how personality develops and how it influences people's activities

Although internal mental processes were considered important in the days of structuralism and functionalism, these processes received little attention while psychology was dominated by behaviorism. Now **cognitive psychology** is refocusing our attention on processes such as thinking, memory, language, problem solving, and creativity. Although some of these are problems currently studied by behaviorists, cognitive psychologists are more interested in internal mental processes, as opposed to behavioral processes. For example, a cognitive psychologist might describe your ability to navigate through campus in terms of internal representations, or *cognitive maps,* of your environment. They are interested in how these "maps" are constructed and the characteristics of the representations. A behavioral psychologist, on the other hand, might explain this same ability to navigate in terms of stimulus control and learning. The major difference would be the cognitive psychologists' reference to internal, mental processes, as opposed to observable stimulus events and learned behavior. Both of these approaches are discussed throughout this text.

Developmental Psychology

Another important field is **developmental psychology**. Psychologists in this field are interested in factors that influence development and shape behavior throughout the life cycle, from conception through old age. These specialists typically focus on a particular phase of the growth process, such as adolescence or old age, and examine how a particular ability or trait unfolds during that phase of development. For example, a developmental psychologist might investigate how the viewing of television violence influences the development of aggressive behavior in children. Chapters 11 and 12 are devoted to the study of human development.

Social Psychology

Social psychology is concerned with understanding the impact of social environments on the individual. Social psychologists are interested in attitude formation and change, social perception, conformity, social roles, prejudice, interpersonal attraction, and aggression. These topics will be discussed in detail in Chapter 17.

Personality Psychology

Personality psychology explores the uniqueness of the individual and describes the key elements that provide the foundation for human personalities. There is considerable diversity of opinion among personality theorists as to what factors constitute the major components of personality. For example, do our personalities consist of three interacting and sometimes conflicting forces (the id, ego, and superego) described by Sigmund Freud, or are we better characterized as a composite of sixteen primary traits, as suggested by Raymond Cattell? Perhaps as you read Chapter 14, you will form your own opinion on this matter. Many personality psychologists devote their professional careers to investigating how personality develops, evolves, and influences people's activities.

Experimental Psychology

Psychologists in every area of specialization usually conduct experiments at some point in their careers. Thus, it may be a bit misleading to call **experimental psychology** a separate field. Nevertheless, approximately 4 percent of those in the profession classify themselves as experimental psychologists whose primary activity involves conducting research.

In Chapter 2 we discover that psychologists use a number of research methods in their efforts to understand the nature and causes of behavior. Most experimental psychologists prefer to conduct research in a laboratory setting where they have precise control over the varied factors that influence behavior. For example, an experimental psychologist might investigate the relationship between sexual response and alcohol consumption by precisely measuring sexual arousal to erotic stimuli at different levels of alcohol consumption (the results of these experiments are discussed in Chapter 2).

Experimental Psychology Field of specialization in which the primary activity is conducting research

Biological Psychology Branch of neuroscience, also known as *physiological psychology*, that focuses on the relationship between behavior and physiological events within the brain and the rest of the nervous system

Clinical Psychology Area of specialization involved in the diagnosis and treatment of behavioral problems

Counseling Psychology Area of specialization involved in the diagnosis and treatment of problems of adjustment (Counseling psychologists tend to focus on less serious problems than do clinical psychologists; they often work in settings such as schools.)

Biological Psychology

Still another field, **biological psychology** (also called *physiological psychology* or *neuroscience*), studies the relationship between physiological processes and behavior. Biological psychologists investigate such things as the brain structures and processes involved in emotion, learning, memory, and psychological disorders. Biological psychologists are also interested in the effects of drugs on behavior. Biological psychology is the topic of Chapter 3, but its contributions to psychology will be discussed throughout this text.

Clinical and Counseling Psychology

Many psychologists in the United States are engaged in either of two closely related fields: **clinical psychology** and **counseling psychology**. Both of these groups of psychologists are involved in the diagnosis and treatment of psychological problems, including such things as developmental disorders, substance abuse, relationship difficulties, vocational and educational problems, and behavior disorders.

While a great deal of overlap exists between counseling and clinical psychology, it is generally accurate to state that individuals specializing in counseling psychology tend to focus on less serious problems of adjustment than do their counterparts in clinical psychology. Thus, a counseling psychologist in a high school, college, or university setting might assist students with problems of social or academic adjustment or provide guidance in the area of career decisions. In contrast, clinical psychologists are more likely to work in mental health clinics, mental hospitals, juvenile and adult courts, medical schools, and prisons. Specialists in both areas often see clients in a private practice.

(Shutterstock)

More than half of psychologists in America engage in clinical or counseling psychology, which diagnose and treat psychological problems.

Clinical psychology and *psychiatry* are often confused, because professionals within these respective fields often perform comparable functions, such as providing psychotherapy. However, these occupations differ in several important ways.

Most clinical psychologists obtain a doctor of philosophy degree (PhD) that is likely to consist of three to five years of university graduate school

Educational Psychology Field of specialization in psychology concerned with the study and application of learning and teaching methods, focusing on areas such as improving educational curricula and training teachers

School Psychology Field of specialization concerned with evaluating students' interests and abilities and resolving learning and emotional problems

Industrial/Organizational (I/O) Psychology Field of specialization concerned with using psychological concepts to make the workplace a more satisfying environment for employees and management

Sport Psychology Field of specialization concerned with enhancing sport and exercise performance; focuses on helping people overcome psychological barriers that can impede performance and success in competition or performance

instruction in psychological theory, research methods, techniques of clinical diagnosis, and psychotherapy strategies, followed by a one-year internship in an institutional setting. In contrast, a psychiatrist is a medical doctor (MD) who undergoes several years of specialized training in psychiatry after earning a doctor of medicine degree. Of the two, psychiatrists are more likely to provide medical treatments, such as drugs, in treating psychological disorders. However, clinical psychologists can gain prescription privileges in some states.

Clinical psychologists and psychiatrists may also differ somewhat in their perspectives about the causes of psychological problems and appropriate treatment for such difficulties. For example, psychiatrists are more inclined to look for physical causes, such as abnormal brain chemistry or hormonal imbalances, and to use medical or biological therapies as remedies for disorders. In contrast, clinical psychologists tend to emphasize psychosocial causes, such as inappropriate learning, faulty attitudes, and disturbed interpersonal relationships, and to focus on psychotherapy as the best road to improvement. Exceptions to these generalizations are not uncommon, however, and clinical psychologists and psychiatrists sometimes meld their respective skills as they collaborate in the design and implementation of treatment strategies.

Educational and School Psychology

Many important discoveries in psychology have direct application to the educational process. **Educational psychology** involves the study and application of learning and teaching methods. Psychologists in this field conduct research on ways to improve educational curricula, and they often help train teachers. They may work in primary or secondary schools, but more often they are found in a university's school of education.

School psychology encompasses work in elementary and secondary schools, dealing primarily with the evaluation of student's abilities and interests. School psychologists use a variety of methods including personality, interest, and ability tests to evaluate students and to assist schools in developing programs for gifted and challenged students. School psychologists may also assist educators in attempts to resolve student learning and emotional problems. These psychologists are a valuable resource for students and teachers.

Industrial/Organizational Psychology

The field of **industrial/organizational (I/O) psychology** uses psychological concepts to make the workplace a more satisfying environment for both employees and management. I/O psychologists may work with businesses either as company employees or as consultants, designing programs to improve morale, increase job satisfaction, foster better communication within the corporation, enhance productivity, and increase workers' involvement in decision making. They are also frequently involved in designing job-training programs and in selecting the most suitable people for a particular job.

Sport Psychology

Sport psychology (sometimes called sport and performance psychology) focuses on how to apply psychological principles to enhance sport performance and increase participation in physical activities. Sport and performance psychologists help athletes and professionals overcome obstacles that impede performance. However, these psychologists do not work only with athletes. They may also help individuals who need to regain confidence after an injury or perhaps a surgeon who needs to regain confidence after losing a patient. Actors and musicians may also consult performance psychologists to overcome stage fright or regain confidence after a poor performance.

Health Psychology Area of specialization concerned with the interaction between behavioral factors and physical health

Positive Psychology The study of human behavior aimed at discovering and promoting the positive strengths and attributes that enable individuals to thrive and succeed

Health Psychology

In recent years there has been a mounting interest in achieving and maintaining good health, both physical and psychological. Psychologists have known for many years that emotional conditions such as stress or depression often play a major role in the development of physical ailments such as ulcers, skin diseases, stomach disorders, infectious diseases, and probably even cancer. Increasing evidence also indicates that psychological factors have a great deal to do with prevention of and recovery from illness. This growing body of data on the interaction between physical and psychological health factors has led to the emergence of a dynamic new area of specialization known as **health psychology**. In recognition of the importance of this new field of study, the National Institutes of Health (NIH) recently designated health psychology as a priority training area and allocated funds for developing training programs within psychology departments throughout the country.

(Shutterstock)

Health psychologists are active in areas such as developing programs to help people reduce stress.

Health psychologists are currently active in such diverse areas as assessing the psychological and physical effects of stress; developing programs to help people reduce stress in their lives; studying coping strategies for dealing with serious or catastrophic illness; evaluating the impact of psychological factors on diseases such as cancer and cardiovascular illness; devising ways to test people for susceptibility to disease; and seeking to identify the factors that motivate people to engage in health-threatening activities such as smoking, overeating, and undereating (Brannon, Feist, & Updegraff, 2014). Throughout this text we will comment on current research related to our health.

Positive Psychology

In his 1998 address as president of the American Psychological Association (APA), Martin Seligman proposed that scientific psychology investigate "the understanding and building of the most positive qualities of an individual: Optimism, courage, work ethic, future-mindedness, interpersonal skill, the capacity for pleasure and insight, and social responsibility." This address marked a movement that would become known as **positive psychology**, focused on understanding factors contributing to self-fulfillment and happiness. While it is far too early to evaluate the success of these research efforts, it is clear that psychology as a scientific endeavor has focused most of its attention on understanding pathology and abnormal behavior, and not nearly enough of its efforts toward understanding characteristics of healthy people. Can adopting an optimistic, future-oriented attitude toward life contribute to greater happiness, life satisfaction, and health? Although there is no lack of speculation here, science is only just beginning to investigate questions like these.

Forensic Psychology

Forensic Psychology Field of specialization that works with the legal, court, and correctional systems to develop personality profiles of criminals, make decisions about disposition of convicted offenders, and help law enforcers understand behavioral problems

Artificial Intelligence (AI) Field of specialization in which researchers develop computer models to simulate human cognitive processes and to solve problems

Connectionism The learning theory that says learning is the result of forming associations or connections between stimuli and responses (Modern connectionism is focused on discovering the neurobiological mechanisms underlying learned associations.)

Evolutionary Psychology A recent approach to both investigating and explaining human behavior in terms of natural selection

Forensic psychology is another specialty. It works hand in hand with the legal, court, and correctional systems. Forensic psychologists assist police in a variety of ways, from developing personality profiles of criminal offenders to helping law-enforcement personnel understand problems such as family conflict and substance abuse. They may also assist judges and parole officers in making decisions about the disposition of convicted offenders. The 1991 case of Jeffrey Dahmer, who murdered, dismembered, and apparently ate body parts from numerous victims, attracted the attention of both the public and forensic psychologists. Before reading on, you might consider whether Dahmer was competent to stand trial, or whether he was insane and thus didn't understand the nature of his crimes.

Artificial Intelligence and Connectionism

Artificial intelligence (**AI**) captured the interest of many in 1997 as they witnessed IBM's chess-playing computer Deep Blue defeat Garry Kasparov, the world chess champion. Although chess-playing computers have gained our attention, AI researchers attempt to develop models that simulate a variety of complex human cognitive processes such as perceiving stimuli, solving problems, learning, and making decisions. AI theorists are hopeful that as they become more proficient in designing sophisticated computer models of cognitive processes, they will achieve a better understanding of how we think, learn, and perceive our surroundings. AI has a practical side as well, as evidenced by its successful application to such varied pursuits as the diagnosis of illness and the location of deposits of valuable resources such as oil.

Connectionism is a relatively new approach to studying complex human abilities such as learning, problem solving, and perception. Like artificial intelligence, it too employs computer models to help solve these problems. However, connectionist researchers are attempting to design computer hardware that simulates the kinds of parallel connections among neurons in the brain. These connectionist machines have proven to be much more powerful than their predecessors for certain kinds of tasks, including pattern recognition, perception, problem solving, and learning.

Evolutionary Psychology

Evolutionary psychology is a recent approach to both investigating and explaining human behavior in terms of natural selection. Modern evolutionary psychology can be traced to early writings of Charles Darwin, including *The Descent of Man* (Darwin, 1871/2004) and *The Expression of the Emotions in Man and Animals* (Darwin, 1872/1955). In these writings, Darwin expressed his views about sexual selection and the adaptive significance of human and animal traits. As you might expect, these works, along with his others, have been hotly debated since their original writing.

Evolutionary psychologists argue that traits that tend to occur across many cultures may be a result of selection pressures. Some examples of these traits include our perceptions of sexual attractiveness, marriage patterns, cooperation, facial expressions of emotion, specific fears, and perhaps even religious beliefs. These universal traits, according to evolutionary psychologists, are rooted in our genes and provided our ancestors with reproductive and survival advantages. For example, evolutionary psychologist David Buss (1989) has proposed that the features we find sexually attractive in the opposite sex are universal and genetically based. Men, he argues, find women attractive when they are healthy and appear fertile. This includes features such as a narrow waist (about one-third the width of their hips), luscious hair, large breasts, and a youthful appearance. Women, on the other hand, prefer features that predict a potential for longer-term mating, and an investment (time and resources) in them and their offspring. These features include maturity, dominance, and affluence. In a recent study, men found women to be equally attractive regardless of whether they were pictured in a modest or an expensive-looking car. Women, however, found men to be more attractive if they were pictured in the expensive-looking car (Dunn & Searle, 2010). The authors suggest that perceived wealth and status enhance male attractiveness, much as perceived youth and fertility enhance female attractiveness. There will be more discussion of evolutionary psychology and attractiveness in Chapter 17.

Cultural Psychology

Cultural psychology investigates how cultural and religious traditions and practices shape and contribute to differences in human behavior. Of recent concern to cultural psychologists is how Western and Islamic cultural traditions contribute to significant differences in ways of life. These differences in tradition may continue to be roadblocks to peace and democracy building in Iraq and Afghanistan. For example, Islamic culture has vastly different views than the West about the purpose of life and the role of women in society. In Islam, life's purpose is to serve Allah Ta'ala by sacrificing wealth, personal pleasure, and time. In contrast, the purpose of life in Western culture is prosperity, worldly enjoyment, and self-fulfillment. These cultural differences contribute to distrust, misunderstanding, and strife. Western travelers are often unwelcome in foreign countries because of stereotypes about Western cultural insensitivities. Cultural psychologists hope to not only create greater cultural awareness, but to incorporate cultural differences into modern psychological theory.

(Shutterstock)

A part of cultural psychology is to investigate how religious traditions and practices influence human behavior.

1.4b Careers in Psychology

Many beginning psychology students believe that most psychologists work in counseling or clinical settings dealing with people adjusting to problems of living. The previous section on areas of specialization in psychology suggests psychologists do a wide variety of things. While many psychologists do work as counselors or therapists, most do not. Figure 1-1 illustrates where most psychologists work.

Psychological Associations

During its brief history, psychology has grown by leaps and bounds. The **American Psychological Association** (APA), the major professional organization of psychologists in the United States, was founded in 1892 by thirty-one charter members. The APA now has more than 122,500 members, and there are countless professional psychologists who are not listed in its membership (American Psychological Association, 2017). As the APA's ranks have increased, so has the number of fields within the profession. There are some generalists, just as there are general practitioners in medicine. However,

Cultural Psychology A field that investigates how cultural and religious traditions and practices shape and contribute to differences in human behavior

American Psychological Association (APA) The major professional organization of psychologists in the United States

Figure 1-1 Where Most Psychologists Work

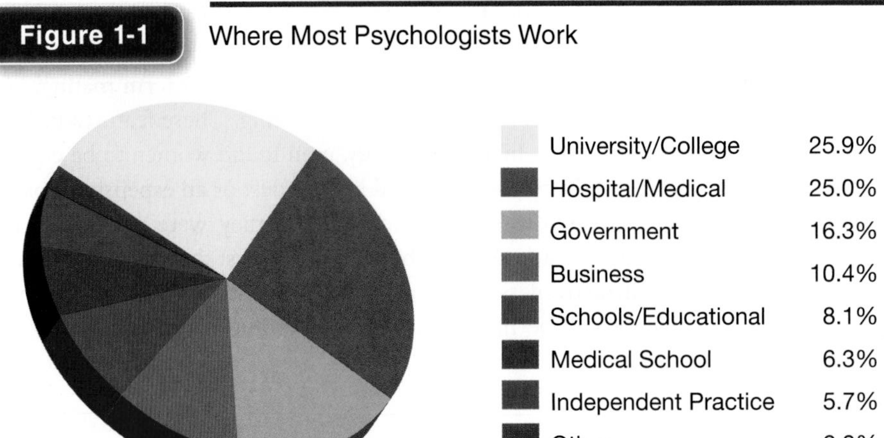

Data from the American Psychological Association (2011), Careers in Psychology. Washington, D.C.: Author. Available online at http://www.apa.prg/careers/resources/guides/careers.aspx

most psychologists find that as their careers evolve, they become increasingly specialized in both their interests and their professional activities. The APA presently recognizes fifty-four divisions or specialties within psychology. Even with an increasing number of divisions within the APA, many members believe that the organization's mission is directed more toward clinical applications than toward basic research. As a result, a separate psychological association was organized.

In 1988 the **Association for Psychological Science (APS)** was founded with the stated purpose of better representing the academic and research interests of psychology and to more effectively promote psychology as a science. Today there are more than thirty-three thousand members of the APS (Association for Psychological Science, 2017).

1.5 The Goals of Psychology

Essentially all scientists, psychologists included, share the common goals of *understanding, predicting,* and *controlling* or *influencing* the phenomena that constitute the subject matter of their respective disciplines. A biologist, for example, after first acquiring an understanding of how the SARS virus invades a healthy body, might then seek to predict conditions under which infection is likely to occur and follow this with efforts to control or influence the infectious process in a manner that minimizes transmission of the virus. Similarly, a psychologist might seek to understand the mechanisms whereby our psychological and physiological responses to stress increase our susceptibility to disease, in order to predict which of us are likely to develop coronary heart disease, hypertension, or other stress-related diseases. The psychologist might also try to apply this knowledge to influence or modify certain behaviors that make people susceptible to the ravages of stress.

Association for Psychological Science (APS) Professional group of academic and research psychologists founded in 1988

While many people accept the goal of using psychological knowledge to understand and predict behavior, the idea of applying psychology to control people's behavior is more controversial. What do you think of this goal? Is it a legitimate aim of psychology? Always? Sometimes? Never? Give some thought to this complex issue before reading on.

People often react with concern or skepticism to the notion that behavioral control is a legitimate goal of psychology. Indeed, it would be misleading to imply that all the knowledge acquired through psychological research leads directly to behavioral control. Nevertheless, psychologists have been able to influence behavior under a wide variety of situations. For example, understanding the processes and predicting the circumstances under which prejudices are formed has resulted in the development of educational programs that have reduced the formation and expression of prejudicial behavior in some schoolchildren (see Chapter 17). Similarly, knowledge about the psychobiological causes of certain severe psychological disorders has provided the impetus for developing various therapies effective in controlling certain disruptive symptoms, as we will see in Chapter 15.

People seldom object to such examples of legitimate and helpful behavioral control. However, there are many gray areas in which the wielding of psychological influence over various behaviors is more controversial; such situations raise important questions. For instance, is it appropriate for industrial psychologists to manipulate work conditions in a manner known to increase worker productivity, or for forensic/clinical psychologists to subject imprisoned sexual offenders to extremely aversive or negative stimuli in order to reduce inappropriate sexual arousal patterns? Such questions suggest that the pursuit of the goal of controlling behavior is often modified or tempered by complex ethical issues.

Although psychology in its relatively short history has managed to accumulate in-depth knowledge about many important areas of human behavior, a vast array of questions remains to be answered. All sciences, however, rarely complete the pursuit of their ultimate goals. However, most disciplines are much further along in their journeys toward understanding, prediction, and control than is the infant science of psychology. Nevertheless, this incompleteness of knowledge is in many ways parent to much of the excitement, anticipation, and vitality of contemporary psychology.

Most of our present understanding of behavior and mental processes must be evaluated cautiously, with a healthy realization that little in this developing discipline should be considered absolute. Thus, for the most part, our understanding of varied behavioral phenomena is couched in the language of theories. Theories are testable and logical explanations for all of the relevant data or facts scientists have observed regarding certain natural phenomena. For example, psychologists who study sleep and dreaming might formulate theories about why we need sleep or why we dream. Some dream researchers have noted that people spend more time dreaming when they are experiencing relationship conflicts, problems at work, or other emotionally stressful situations. These and similar observations have generated a theory of dreaming that views dreams as a relatively safe, low-stress way to deal with problems that occur during waking hours.

A good psychological **theory** generates predictions, or **hypotheses**, which are assumptions about how people should respond under certain conditions, assuming the overall theory is correct. Hypotheses can be subjected to empirical tests in which scientists manipulate conditions or behaviors and observe the results. Thus, a psychologist who adheres to the theory that dreaming allows people to deal with emotional problems might set up an experiment to test the following hypothesis: People who are presented with waking-state problems and then deprived of nighttime dreaming will be less likely to suggest reasonable solutions the following morning than are subjects who are allowed a normal night's rest (see Chapter 5 for a discussion of research supporting this hypothesis).

This scientific approach to understanding human behavior differs from some of our common conceptions and practices. For instance, how often do we hear post hoc

Theory A logical explanation for all the relevant data or facts scientists have observed regarding certain natural phenomena (An essential aspect of scientific theories is that they must be both testable and refutable, not to be confused with the common usage of the term used to signify a hunch, a speculation, or an opinion.)

Hypothesis Statement proposing the existence of a relationship between variables, typically as a tentative explanation for cause and effect; often designed to be tested by research

Hindsight Bias The tendency to believe we could have foreseen an event after it has occurred

explanations of a variety of phenomena? Consider the newswoman who tells us a murderer was himself the victim of child abuse and this caused his behavior. Consider also finding out a relationship failure was a consequence of a recently disclosed affair, or a bout of depression was the cause of a recent financial loss. It's far too easy to explain an event after the fact. It is far more difficult to predict it. This tendency to explain events after they have occurred, as if we could have foreseen them, is referred to as **hindsight bias**. With the aid of hindsight it is easy to explain a wide variety of behavioral phenomena. The problem is, we will never really know for sure what caused the man to murder, the relationship failure, or the bout of depression. We will see throughout this book that hindsight biases and intuition may be right occasionally, but they are far more often wrong. You will learn that testing hypotheses with experimental methods has refuted many common assumptions about human behavior and that psychology as a scientific endeavor is progressing rapidly. We will say more about scientific theories and hypothesis testing in Chapter 2.

We have considered in some detail the history, scope, and goals of the science of psychology. In Chapter 2, we will look more closely at some of the methods psychologists have developed for exploring the many questions posed by the richly varied behaviors of humans and other animals. An appreciation of the methods used by psychologists will help you to critically evaluate the numerous facts and opinions presented throughout this book.

CHAPTER REVIEW

Definition of Psychology

1. Formally defined, psychology is the scientific study of the behavior of humans and other animals.
2. The theories and facts of psychology emerge from the careful application of scientific methods.
3. Psychology includes the study of animal behavior as well as human behavior. Nonhuman animal research offers several advantages, including providing a simpler model, the benefits associated with greater control afforded by nonhuman subjects, ethical considerations, time and cost factors, and the advantages of short life spans in assessing genetic contributions to behavior.

Psychology's History

4. Psychology has roots in both philosophy, which posed many of the important questions, and physiology, which provided the tools for careful, scientific examination of these questions.
5. The establishment of Wilhelm Wundt's laboratory at the University of Leipzig in 1879 marks the formal beginnings of psychology as a scientific discipline.
6. Wundt employed the methods of introspection and experimental self-observation to pursue what he considered to be the task of psychology: The systematic study of the structure of the conscious adult mind.
7. Edward Titchener, who brought Wundt's brand of psychology to the United States, introduced the label structuralism to describe his attempt to develop a kind of mental chemistry by breaking experience down into its basic elements or structures.
8. Structuralism soon gave way to the more practical psychology of William James, who emphasized the functional, practical nature of the mind. His conception of psychology's proper task became known as functionalism.
9. During the period when psychology was struggling to become more scientific and objective, Sigmund Freud traveled a different road as he developed his highly subjective psychoanalytic approach with its emphasis on the unconscious mind and repressed irrational urges and drives.
10. In the first few decades of the twentieth century, a new force in psychology, called behaviorism, emerged. This approach, championed by John B. Watson, defined the task of psychology as one of simply observing the relationship between environmental events (stimuli) and an organism's response to them. Modern behaviorism continues to be a powerful force within psychology today.

CHAPTER REVIEW

11. At the same time that behaviorism was catching hold in the United States, a group of German psychologists decried the principles of both structuralism and behaviorism. They argued that it was a mistake to try to break psychological processes into basic components such as elementary sensations or stimuli and responses because the whole of an experience is different than the sum of its parts. This approach became known as Gestalt psychology.
12. Humanistic psychology de-emphasizes the impact of both stimulus-response events and unconscious processes in determining human behavior. Instead, it focuses on the role of free choice and our ability to make conscious rational choices about how we live our lives.

Contemporary Psychology

13. In recent years the emergence of cognitive psychology as an important force in psychology has led to a refocusing of attention on processes such as thinking, memory, language, problem solving, and creativity.
14. Two other important areas in psychology that are achieving increasing prominence in the field are connectionism, which uses computers to help develop models of cognitive processes and learning, and biological psychology, the study of the relationship between behavior and physiological events that occur within the brain and the rest of the nervous system.
15. Both clinical and counseling psychologists are involved in the diagnosis and treatment of psychological problems. Individuals specializing in counseling psychology tend to focus on less serious problems of adjustment than do their counterparts in clinical psychology.
16. While psychologists in every area of specialization usually conduct experiments at some point in their careers, individuals who classify themselves as experimental psychologists devote their primary efforts to conducting research.
17. Biological psychologists study the relationship between physiological processes and behavior.
18. Educational psychologists focus their efforts on the study and application of learning and teaching methods.
19. School psychologists work in elementary or secondary schools, where they seek to evaluate and resolve learning and emotional problems of students.
20. Industrial/organizational psychology is concerned with using psychological concepts to make the workplace a more satisfying environment for both employees and management.
21. Sport and performance psychologists focus on enhancing performance in athletics, as well as in careers in acting, music, and other professions requiring peak human performance.

CHAPTER REVIEW

22. Developmental psychologists investigate the factors that influence development and shape behavior throughout the life cycle.
23. Social psychologists seek to understand the impact of social environments and social processes on the individual.
24. Personality psychologists focus on exploring the uniqueness of the individual and describing the key elements that provide the foundation for human personalities.
25. Health psychologists are interested in behavioral contributions to disease such as smoking, drinking, lack of exercise, social isolation, and stress.
26. Positive psychology emphasizes the positive characteristics of individuals. Research includes the study of happiness, self-fulfillment, future orientation, and optimism and how these characteristics lead to an improvement in life outlook and productivity.
27. Forensic psychology is the study of criminal behavior and the law.
28. Evolutionary psychology examines the adaptive value of universal traits and how they may be a consequence of natural selection.
29. Cultural psychologists examine the role of cultural and religious traditions in shaping differences in human behavior.

The Goals of Psychology

30. The goals of psychology include understanding, predicting, and controlling behavior.
31. For the most part, our understanding of behavioral phenomena is expressed in the language of theories. Theories are tentative attempts to organize and fit into a logical framework all relevant data or facts regarding certain phenomena.
32. Good psychological theories generate hypotheses, which are assumptions about how people should respond under certain conditions, assuming the overall theory is correct.

TERMS AND CONCEPTS

American Psychological Association (APA), pg. 19
Artificial Intelligence (AI), pg. 18
Association for Psychological Science (APS), pg. 20
Behaviorism, pg. 11
Biological Psychology, pg. 15
Clinical Psychology, pg. 15
Cognitive Psychology, pg. 14
Connectionism, pg. 18
Counseling Psychology, pg. 15
Cultural Psychology, pg. 19
Developmental Psychology, pg. 14
Educational Psychology, pg. 16
Evolutionary Psychology, pg. 18
Experimental Psychology, pg. 15
Forensic Psychology, pg. 18
Functionalism, pg. 9
Gestalt Psychology, pg. 12
Health Psychology, pg. 17
Hindsight Bias, pg. 22
Humanistic Psychology, pg. 13
Hypothesis, pg. 21
Industrial/Organizational (I/O) Psychology, pg. 16
Personality Psychology, pg. 14
Positive Psychology, pg. 17
Psychology, pg. 2
School Psychology, pg. 16
Scientific Method, pg. 8
Social Psychology, pg. 14
Sports Psychology, pg. 16
Structuralism, pg. 9
Theory, pg. 21

POP QUIZ

True or False

___ 1. Psychology is a science because it deals with both animal and human behavior.

___ 2. One of the main benefits that the science of psychology received from its roots in philosophy is that philosophy emphasizes the use of observation to acquire knowledge.

___ 3. Although they were in general agreement with the principles of behaviorism, Gestalt psychologists had major disagreements with the principles of structuralism.

___ 4. Biological psychologists might investigate the effects of both drugs and brain damage on behavior.

___ 5. The goals of psychology are to understand, predict, and control (or influence) behavior and mental processes.

Multiple Choice

6. What are psychologists interested in studying today?
   a. Behavior
   b. Mental processes
   c. Both behavior and mental processes
   d. Neither behavior nor mental processes
7. What was an approach to psychology that attempted to break down experience into its basic elements?
   a. Structuralism
   b. Psychoanalysis
   c. Functionalism
   d. Behaviorism
8. What was the approach to psychology that emphasized the practical nature of the mind and believed that processes such as consciousness helped people adapt?
   a. Gestalt psychology
   b. Functionalism
   c. Humanistic psychology
   d. Structuralism
9. Why has the psychoanalytic approach been widely criticized?
   a. Psychoanalysis does not help patients.
   b. Its assertions cannot be tested with scientific methods.
   c. It ignores mental processes.
   d. It does not include the study of animals.

POP QUIZ

10. "An empirical, objective science of behavior that has no need for theories of mind or personal freedom" characterizes which of the following?
    a. Gestalt psychology
    b. Humanistic psychology
    c. Structuralism
    d. Behaviorism

11. On what does Gestalt psychology focus?
    a. The most basic elements of our experiences
    b. Gaining an understanding of the unconscious mind
    c. The relationship between environmental stimuli and an organism's response to them
    d. The constructive processes of perception

12. Which of the following is a false statement?
    a. Humanistic psychologists emphasize the role of free choice.
    b. Humanistic psychologists view people as being controlled by events in their environment.
    c. Humanistic psychologists have an interest in topics such as self-esteem and personal fulfillment.
    d. Humanistic psychologists de-emphasize the influence of unconscious processes.

13. A(n) ________ psychologist would be concerned with enhancing human performance in a variety of settings, including athletic competition, acting, music, or surgery.
    a. Environmental
    b. Health
    c. Sports performance
    d. Personality

14. John Hinkley's (President Reagan's attempted assassin) psychological profile would probably have been created by a(n) ________ psychologist.
    a. Personality
    b. Forensic
    c. Social
    d. Organizational

15. The goal of psychology, which is sometimes perceived as controversial, is which of the following?
    a. Understanding behavior
    b. Generating behavior
    c. Controlling behavior
    d. Predicting behavior

Answer Key: 1.F 2.F 3.F 4.T 5.T 6.c 7.a 8.b 9.b 10.d 11.d 12.b 13.c 14.b 15.c

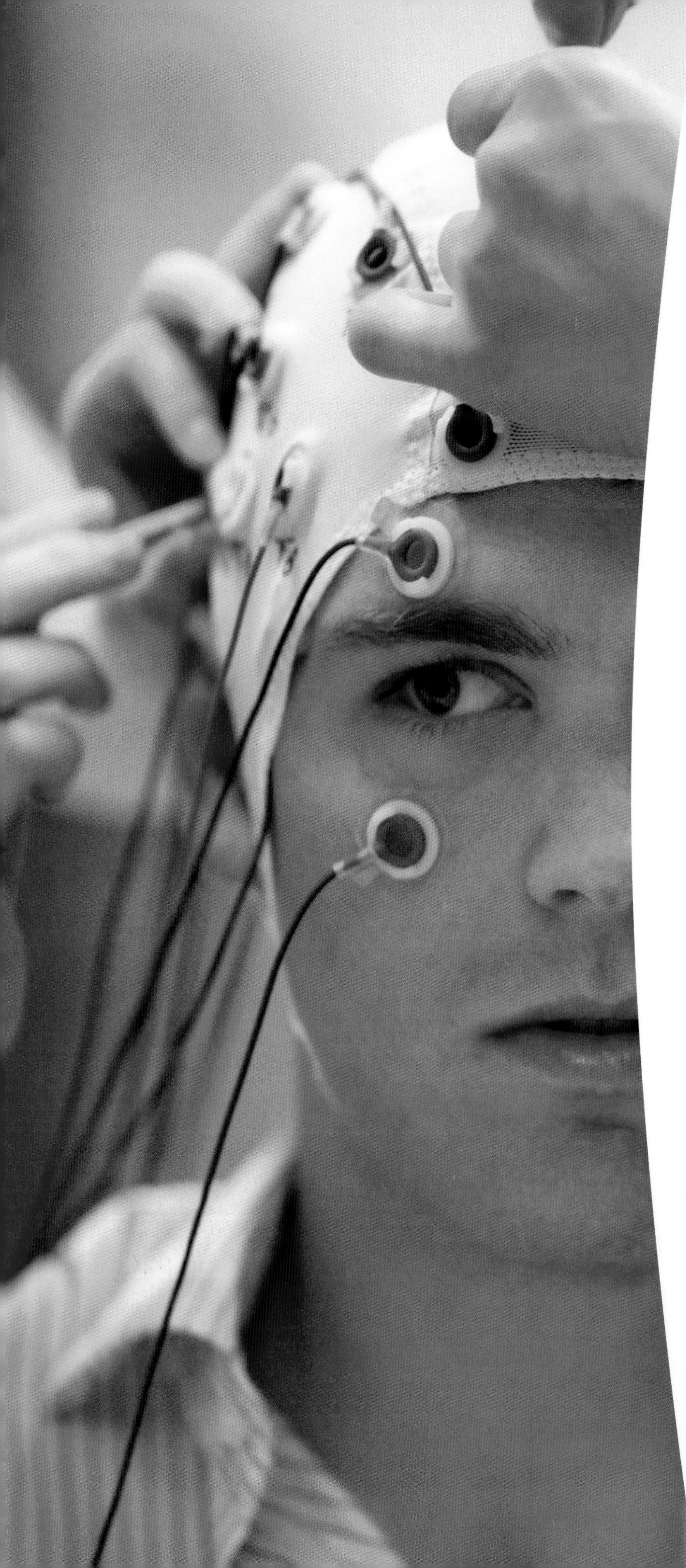

(Shutterstock)

The Methods of Psychology

Examine the following statements and decide whether they are typically true or false. Base your conclusions on both your personal experiences and your assumptions about human behavior. If you want to examine any of these questions more fully later, chapter references are provided for each.

- Sleepwalking most often occurs during a dreaming phase of sleep. (Chapter 5)
- Under hypnosis, people can perform feats of physical strength or mental prowess that they could not otherwise perform. (Chapter 5)
- Punishment is not as effective as reinforcement in bringing about changes in behavior. (Chapter 6)
- Memory of traumatic events is more accurate than for normal life events. (Chapter 7)
- Humans are the only organisms that use symbolic language to communicate. (Chapter 10)
- Couples who cohabit (live together) before marriage generally experience happier and more stable marriages than couples who do not live together before getting married. (Chapter 12)
- Evidence suggests that the wide variation in human intelligence is due more to environmental factors than to heredity. (Chapter 13)
- The most beneficial way to treat severe psychological disorders is to have people relive traumatic childhood experiences through psychoanalysis. (Chapter 16)
- One is more likely to be assisted in an emergency when many observers are present than when only one or two are present. (Chapter 17)

Most students evaluate all or most of the preceding statements incorrectly when they first begin studying psychology; you may also be surprised to find that they are all false. Indeed, many of the things people presume to be true about behavior are fallacies. To safeguard against the fallibility of common sense, folklore, and self-observation, psychologists have developed a number of tools or methods for systematically investigating behavior. These scientific methods have disproven many widely held beliefs about human behavior; they have also verified some other common assumptions. In this chapter we discuss the reasons for psychological research and outline the methods that psychologists use.

2.1 The Scientific Method and Behavior

Chapter 1 discussed an important research finding of the 1950s, but it did not tell you the story of how that finding was made. James Olds and a fellow researcher at McGill University, Peter Milner, were investigating the ways in which electrical stimulation of the brain affected exploratory behavior in rats. As they implanted electrodes in the rats' brains, one electrode was placed incorrectly, and Olds and Milner stumbled onto an important finding (Olds, 1956). When electrodes were placed in sites near the hypothalamus and the septal areas (discussed in Chapter 3), the rats seemingly could not get enough stimulation. They preferred stimulation of these brain areas even to food when they were hungry. This unexpected

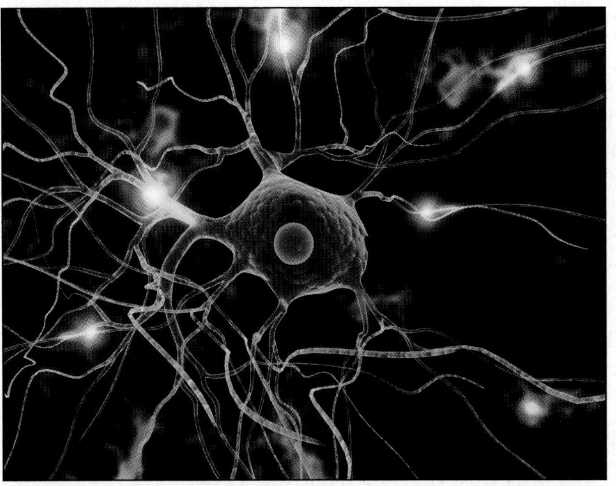
(iStock)

The study of electrical stimulation of the brain led to a series of experiments with animals and humans. These findings clearly indicated that there are pleasure centers within the brain.

finding led to a series of experiments with animals and humans that clearly indicated that there are pleasure centers within the brain. Since their finding, much has been learned about these structures and how they contribute to behavior.

2.1a The Purpose of Psychological Research

Although some psychological studies have their origins in serendipity, or a lucky discovery such as this one, Olds's and Milner's situation is hardly typical. Most psychological research is carefully planned and conducted with a specific end in mind. In this section we look at three of the most common reasons why psychologists conduct research: To test a hypothesis, to solve a problem, and to confirm findings of previous research.

Basic Research: Research to Test Theories or Hypotheses

As mentioned in the previous chapter, a scientific **theory** is a testable generalization that accounts for a number of facts and is capable of making predictions about future observations. There are very few scientific theories in the field of psychology. Several, however, will be explored later in this text. Examples of scientific theories in other disciplines would certainly include Newton's Theory of Universal Gravitation, Darwin's Theory of Evolution by Natural Selection, and Einstein's General Theory of Relativity. The scientific definition of theory is quite different from the common usage that signifies an opinion, a conjecture, or speculation. Unfortunately, we do not have a term to make this distinction more clear.

A **hypothesis**, on the other hand, is a statement proposing the existence of a relationship between variables. Hypotheses are typically offered as tentative explanations for relationships or events, and they can be tested by research. For example, a psychologist may hypothesize that there is an increase in violent tendencies among individuals who listen to music with violent lyrics. This hypothesis suggests a relationship (perhaps a causal one) between lyrics in music and the expression of violence. Hypotheses frequently emerge from psychologists' observations of behavior or from the results of previous investigations. To test this hypothesis, college students listened to music containing both violent and nonviolent content. Researchers controlled for song style by using violent and nonviolent samples from the same artists. After listening to the violent music, students gave more aggressive interpretations of ambiguous words and completed word fragments (such as "h_t") with aggressive words more frequently than they did after listening to nonviolent material. The authors concluded that the content of media does matter and may contribute to violent tendencies (Anderson et al., 2003b).

Applied Research: Research to Solve a Problem

A second reason to conduct research is to find a solution to a problem. While some applied research is initiated to address specific human problems, not all applied research starts out with this goal. For example, results from basic research often lead to solutions to problems, even though the resolution of the problem was not the original intent of the research. Quite often basic research helps us understand "normal" behavior and function, which leads to procedures that allow for the assessment of abnormal or impaired behavior. This is exactly how Smith and Langolf (Smith, Langolf, & Goldberg, 1981) discovered that exposure to low levels of mercury in certain chemical industries was neurotoxic to workers.

Although exposure to certain chemicals has long been suspected to cause certain diseases and possibly impairments in behavior, the identification of subtle behavioral

Theory A scientific theory is a logical explanation for all the relevant data or facts scientists have observed regarding certain natural phenomena. An essential aspect of scientific theories is that they must be both testable and refutable, not to be confused with the common usage of the term used to signify a hunch, a speculation, or an opinion.

Hypothesis Statement proposing the existence of a relationship between variables, typically as a tentative explanation for cause and effect and often designed for research testing

deficits following chemical exposure has been difficult. This is either because the behavioral measures used to assess performance are too insensitive to detect behavioral deficits or, quite possibly, because people exposed to toxic chemicals gradually adjust to these deficits, making them even more difficult to find. The assessment of behavioral changes produced by drugs and environmental toxins is of utmost importance to human welfare, and procedures used in basic research have proven valuable in identifying them. By using a well-understood memory-scanning procedure, Smith and Langolf found clear signs of memory impairment in workers exposed to mercury. In addition, this impairment increased corresponding to increased levels of mercury in workers' urine. These impairments were not previously identified by the workers' job performance or by other methods of psychological testing. In this case, basic research in human memory provided psychologists with sensitive methods to detect subtle changes in performance caused by toxic chemical exposure.

BVT Lab

Flashcards are available for this chapter at www.BVTLab.com.

In other cases, applied research sets out to solve a particular problem. In the last several years, increasing attention has been given to the relationship between stress in our lives and our ability to ward off disease. While stress has long been suspected to play a role in diseases such as heart disease, little evidence supported its role in infectious diseases (colds and flu) and cancer. Recently, however, studies have shown that stress can directly suppress the immune response, making us more susceptible to disease and making it more difficult for us to fight existing diseases such as cancer (Ben-Eliyahu, Yirmiya, Liebeskind, Taylor, & Gale, 1991; Palermo-Neto, de Oliveira Massoco, & Robespierre de Souza, 2003). Applied research conducted by psychologists and other scientists is now helping us understand how stress affects our immune system and how we can learn to manage stress to reduce these debilitating effects. We will have more to say about this research in Chapter 9.

Replication Research: Research to Confirm Previous Findings

Another reason for conducting research is to verify previous findings. When psychologists publish new research findings, they typically publish details about their work so that others may repeat the experiment to verify their results. This replication of prior research is the backbone of good science. Sometimes an especially controversial experiment is repeated in laboratories all over the world. This replication occurred many years ago when researcher James McConnell (1962) published a study suggesting that memory could be transferred from one organism to another by cannibalism; that is, one organism eating the other! This amazing experiment generated countless replication efforts—some successful and others not. Because the results of these follow-up investigations were inconsistent, and most laboratories failed to find a transfer effect, psychologists have abandoned this line of research.

In many cases, the results of **replication studies** are less ambiguous. For example, a number of studies conducted more than thirty years ago revealed that *identical twins* (siblings with identical genes) raised in different environments are more similar in intelligence as measured by IQ scores than are *fraternal twins* (siblings born at the same time whose genes are not identical) who are raised in the same environment (Erlenmeyer-Kimling & Jarvik, 1963). These early findings met with considerable criticism from a number of psychologists, particularly those who believed that environment is more important than heredity in shaping human intelligence. As a result, numerous replication studies were conducted. A sizable number of these more recent studies have confirmed the early findings (Bouchard, Lykken, McGue, Segal, & Tellegen, 1990; Devlin, Daniels, & Roeder, 1997); because of these successful replications, most psychologists consider the IQ data obtained from twin studies to be reliable. However, not all psychologists interpret the data in the same way. (See Chapter 13 for a discussion of the relative impact of heredity and environment on intelligence.)

Replication Studies
Research conducted for the purpose of verifying previous findings

Replication is an important part of all scientific research, not just psychological research. This is well illustrated in a highly publicized report in March 1989 by two physicists (Fleischmann & Pons, 1989) who claimed to have discovered a process for cold fusion. This report excited the scientific world with both suspicion and hope. An inexpensive cold fusion procedure could, theoretically, solve worldwide energy problems with a clean, unlimited energy source. On the other hand, since previous attempts to demonstrate fusion required more energy than they produced, many scientists were quite skeptical of the physicists' report. Scientists all over the world initiated replication efforts, and within a few months most agreed that the process observed by Fleischmann and Pons was not cold fusion but rather some other chemical reaction.

(Shutterstock)

A number of studies revealed that identical twins raised in different environments are more similar in intelligence than fraternal twins who are raised in the same environment.

Replication is important because the results of a study can vary considerably depending on experimental conditions and the research method used. As we will see in the following section, psychologists use a number of techniques to collect data, and a specific research method may not always be appropriate for a specific problem.

2.2 Research Methods

As we learned in Chapter 1, the goals of psychological research are to understand behavior (explain its causes) and, hopefully, to predict and possibly control the circumstances under which certain behaviors are likely to occur. Although a researcher may ultimately be interested in accomplishing all of these goals, such goals often require different research methods. For example, a researcher interested in understanding the role of aggression in children's play might begin by carefully observing children at play in a variety of natural settings. Later, the investigator might test some hypotheses arising from those observations by modifying the setting or circumstances in specific ways. For instance, does denying children access to favored toys increase their tendency to become more aggressive? This kind of research might reveal a certain cause-and-effect relationship between a specific condition (toy removal) and aggression, allowing the researcher to predict circumstances under which aggression is likely to occur.

Psychologists use a number of methods to study behavior, ranging from measuring behavior in highly controlled laboratory environments to producing detailed case studies of specific individuals. Other research methods include conducting surveys based on questionnaires or interviews; observing behavior in a natural setting; and assessing statistical relationships between two traits, events, or behaviors. For example, is there a relationship between the amount and/or intensity of exercise and stress levels?

Table 2-1 summarizes the major research methods used by psychologists. Each of these strategies has advantages and limitations for investigating different types of questions about behavior. We begin by discussing methods that involve the least control over circumstances surrounding behavior and progress through more highly controlled methods. We will also show how some of these methods have been used to understand the relationship between alcohol consumption and sexual behavior.

Table 2-1 A Summary of Research Methods

Method	Brief Description	Advantages	Limitations
Experimental Method	Subjects are confronted with specific stimuli under precisely controlled conditions. Researchers using this method directly manipulate a particular set of conditions (independent variables), and then observe the effect on behavior (dependent variable).	Design of laboratory experiments provides control over relevant variables and opportunities to draw conclusions about cause-and-effect relationships.	Artificial nature of the laboratory setting may influence subjects' behaviors, and some questions posed by psychologists do not lend themselves to experimental investigation.
Surveys	A representative group of people is questioned, using interviews or written questionnaires, about their behaviors and attitudes.	Surveys allow researchers to obtain information from more people than is practical to study in the laboratory and may require less investment of time and financial resources than laboratory research.	Demographic and sex bias, improperly worded questions that bias responses, and a tendency to provide only limited insights about factors that contribute to behaviors and attitudes of specific individuals.
Observational Method	Researchers observe their subjects as they go about their usual activities, which often take place in a natural setting.	This often provides a wealth of information, which may generate hypotheses for further research in a more controlled environment. Also, there are some clear advantages to seeing and recording behavior firsthand instead of relying either on subjective reports of past experiences (surveys) or on the possibly biased behaviors occurring in artificial laboratory settings.	Subjects' behavior may be altered by the presence of an observer. Furthermore, the reliability of recorded observations may sometimes be compromised by preexisting observer biases.
Case Studies	Involve in-depth explorations of either a single case or a small group of subjects who are examined individually.	Many different methods can be used to gather data (direct observation, testing, etc.), and this flexibility provides researchers excellent opportunities for acquiring insight into specific behaviors. Furthermore, because of the clinical nature of case studies, and because they may continue for long periods of time, the researcher is able to explore important variables, and possible relationships among them, in some detail.	Lack of investigative control of important variables, potential for subjective observer bias, poor sampling techniques that often limit generalization of finding to other people in the clinical category being investigated, and tendency for subjects to report earlier experiences inaccurately.
Correlational Methods	Statistical methods are used to assess and describe the amount and type of relationship between variables of interest.	This can be used to answer questions about some kinds of relationships that cannot be clarified by other research methods. Findings expressed in mathematical values provide a strong basis for making predictions about behavior.	This technique, by itself, does not allow researchers to conclude that a demonstrated relationship between two variables means that one is causing the other.

2.2a Nonexperimental Research Methods

Research About the Effects of Alcohol on Sexual Behavior

Many people believe that a few drinks get them in the mood and enhance sexual pleasure. If you were a psychologist trying to determine whether alcohol really does have a positive effect on sexual response, what method would you use to test this relationship? See what you can come up with before reading on.

Case Studies

Our first approach might be to conduct case studies of people who drink considerable amounts of alcohol. A **case study** is an in-depth exploration of either a single participant or a small group of participants who are examined individually. Many case studies of chronic alcoholics have revealed that these people often report reduced sexual interest and arousal. Here again, the evidence is difficult to interpret. It is unclear whether this reduced sexual interest is a direct result of drinking or a generalized side effect of the physical deterioration often associated with chronic alcoholism.

A related approach would be to have people keep personal diaries in which they record their daily alcohol intake along with some measure of sexual interest, such as frequency of orgasm or occurrence of sexual fantasies. We might then determine whether a relationship exists between these two measures.

Assume that an analysis of people's personal diaries did indicate an apparent relationship between sexual interest and alcohol consumption. Could this finding be interpreted as clear evidence that alcohol has a positive or stimulating effect on sexual response? Can you think of any factors that might call this conclusion into question? Give these questions some thought before reading on.

As tempting as it might be to jump to conclusions, the results of such an analysis might be clouded by a number of factors. One potential problem is inconsistent record keeping, because different individuals might take different approaches to making diary entries. In addition, some people might alter their normal behavior patterns simply because they are keeping records. Again, even if alcohol intake was found to be related to sexual response, could we be certain that it represented a cause-and-effect relationship? For example, if sexual activity and drinking both increase during the summer, is the increased drinking the cause of the sexual activity? It might be, but it is also possible that the summer heat is the cause of both of these phenomena. People are thirstier in hot weather; they may also sleep less on hot nights, so there are additional opportunities for sexual activity.

A number of methods can be used to gather data in a case study, including direct observation, testing and experimentation, and interviews or questionnaires. Because of this flexibility, case studies often provide opportunities to acquire insight into specific behaviors. Highly personal, subjective information about how individuals actually feel regarding their behavior represents an important step beyond simply recording activities. Case studies have another advantage. Because of the clinical nature of case studies, and because they may continue for long periods of time (months or even years), the researcher is able to explore important variables and the possible relationships among them in some detail.

Case Study Method of research that involves in-depth study of one or more participants who are examined individually using direct observation, testing, experimentation, and other methods

Limitations of the Case Study

There are some important limitations to the case study method, however. One of these is lack of investigative control. In case studies, a set of circumstances typically gives rise to the research investigation, rather than the other way around. Thus, the researcher's role is to gather as much information as possible from a given situation, but the variables are beyond his or her control. For instance, people often become participants for case studies because they have some physical or emotional disorder or because they have manifested a specific atypical behavior. Much of our current information about criminal behavior, incest victims, disorders such as multiple personalities, and other unusual conditions has been obtained using this approach. Case studies have provided valuable insights into such conditions and have led to other methods of studying them.

(Shutterstock)

A nonexperimental research method, such as a case study, might be used to determine whether alcohol has a positive effect on sexual response.

A second limitation is the potential for subjective bias on the researcher's part. Since the case study usually arises from a rare case, it is often impossible to obtain objective verification such as is provided when experiments are replicated. For instance, it is often difficult to verify someone's recollections of a particularly traumatic event from childhood. As you will see in later chapters, our memory of events can be greatly influenced by subsequent events.

Because an individual's past usually does not become a target of research interest until that person develops some sort of problem later in life, the researcher must often reconstruct the participant's earlier history in order to gather data. For example, suppose we want to evaluate Sigmund Freud's hypothesis that agoraphobia (an intense fear of being in open, public places) is related to separation anxiety, which is an underlying fear of being separated from parents. According to this view, certain individuals are predisposed to develop agoraphobia as a result of incidents of traumatic separation from their parents during early childhood. The case study method would be a logical way to evaluate this hypothesis. People with agoraphobia might be asked to recall events from early childhood in which they were separated from their parents. Then the frequency of these experiences could be compared to a control sample of nonagoraphobic people matched with the agoraphobic group on other variables. Unfortunately, however, many participants might have trouble remembering these early experiences accurately, especially if they are inclined to repress or block them from conscious memory. Thus, the recall of past events in the case study method is subject to errors in memory and sometimes to intentional efforts to distort or repress facts.

A third limitation of case studies is that, because they tend to focus on small samples of particularly interesting or unusual cases, the findings are often difficult to generalize to other people. This potential source of error is illustrated in the writings of investigators in the 1960s and 1970s who explored and reported on motivations for committing rape. Most of these earlier studies used small clinical samples of imprisoned rapists as their primary participants; their findings suggested that rape represents an act of domination, power, and violence that has little to do with sexual urges. More recent data, obtained from multiple large-scale surveys, contradicts this notion. Instead, these findings have revealed that a majority of rapes are committed by someone who knows the victim (acquaintance or date rapes) and whose motivation for committing rape is largely sexual gratification (Crooks & Baur, 2014; Dudley, 2005).

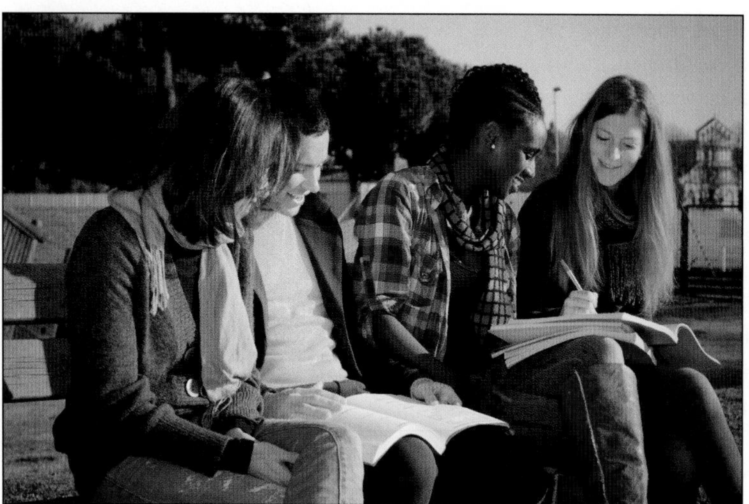
(Shutterstock)

The survey method can produce misleading results when it is limited to a specific population, such as college students, that does not accurately represent the overall general population.

Surveys and Questionnaires

A second important research method is the **survey**, in which a representative group of people is questioned about their behaviors or attitudes. Psychologists use this method when they are interested in obtaining information from more people than it is practical to study in the laboratory. Two examples of such research might be to find out how college students feel about men and women sharing domestic chores at home or to determine whether publicity about AIDS (acquired immune deficiency syndrome) has changed people's sexual practices in recent years.

Since such questions cannot be put to every person in a certain population, psychologists may elect to survey a representative sample group. A carefully constructed questionnaire may reveal trends that exist in the general population even though only a relatively small percentage of that population is surveyed.

How Samples Are Selected for Surveys

Most research questions relate to a population much too large to be studied in its entirety. For example, if you wished to find out how the use of marijuana affects adolescent problem-solving ability and scholastic achievement, your relevant population would include teenagers from all over the world. Even if you decided to limit your observations to American adolescents, your target group would still be prohibitively large; you could never evaluate all of its members.

Psychologists get around this difficulty by gathering data from a relatively small **sample**, or selected segment, of the entire population that interests them. Our ability to draw inferences or conclusions confidently about a much larger population rests chiefly on the techniques we use for selecting participants for the sample study group. We will review two important concepts regarding sampling.

Survey Research method that provides descriptive information in which a representative sample of people is questioned about their behaviors or attitudes

Sample Selected segment of a larger population that is being studied in psychological research; two kinds of samples are the representative sample and the random sample

Representative Sample Sample in which critical subgroups are represented according to their incidence in the larger population that the researcher is studying

Representative Samples

The ideal sample is called a **representative sample**. In such a sample, the participants chosen accurately represent the larger population about which we wish to draw conclusions. A representative sample closely matches the characteristics of the population of interest. If it does not, it is considered a biased sample.

How would you go about selecting a representative sample to investigate the effects of alcohol on sexual arousal? In order to draw broad conclusions about college students, your sample would need to be representative of that group. How could you ensure this? Take a few moments to consider what procedures you might use before reading on.

You might begin selecting your representative sample by obtaining the registration lists of college students in a variety of geographic areas throughout the United States. You would need to select these regions very carefully in order to reflect the actual distribution of the population you are studying. For instance, you wouldn't want to select either all private colleges or only colleges and universities from a particular state. Provided that your final sample was sufficiently large, you could be reasonably confident in generalizing your findings to all American college students.

Random Sample Sample group of a larger population that is selected by using randomization procedures

Random Samples

Another consideration for survey research is whether it is possible to select a **random sample**. A random sample is selected by randomization procedures, which assure that every member of the population (or representative sample) of interest has an equal chance of being selected. For example, suppose you have an opportunity to buy into a café on campus. The café has been only marginally profitable, and you think converting to a health food–oriented menu may help to increase profitability. You decide to survey students' attitudes about patronizing a health food restaurant on campus. Since summer provides you with more free time, you decide to conduct your poll during this period. A friend who works in the registrar's office supplies you with the roster of summer session enrollees, and you select your representative survey sample from this group as opposed to a nonstudent sample.

Assuming that your question about patronizing a health food restaurant is clearly stated, and that a large percentage of the sample responds to your poll, can you be confident that your findings reflect the views of the entire student body at your school? Consider this question before reading on.

For two reasons that you may already have guessed, the answer to the question just posed is no. First, students enrolled in summer classes are not necessarily representative of all students at your college or university. For example, if more graduate students enroll in the summer program, the average age will be higher than that of students in the fall and winter sessions. Second, your sample was not random because all students did not have an equal chance of being selected. Remember, your list was only for summer session students, and you wish to generalize your results to all students.

Once an unbiased random, representative sample is selected, survey data may be obtained in two major ways: either orally, through a face-to-face interview or by telephone, or in written form, using a paper-and-pencil questionnaire. Questionnaire designs can vary tremendously. Questionnaires may range from a few questions to over a thousand; they may be multiple-choice, true/false, or discussion questions. In addition, respondents may fill out the questionnaire either alone or in the presence of a researcher.

Each of the two major survey methods has both advantages and shortcomings. Because questionnaires are more anonymous, some people may be less likely to distort information about their lives by boasting, omitting facts, and so forth. (The presence of an interviewer sometimes encourages such false responses.) Questionnaires have another advantage in that they are usually cheaper and quicker than interview surveys. However, interviews have the advantage of flexibility. The interviewer may clarify confusing questions and vary the question sequence in order to meet the needs of the participant. A competent interviewer can establish a sense of rapport that may encourage more candor than would be produced by an impersonal questionnaire.

Limits of the Survey Method

The survey is effective for gathering a large amount of data, however, like any method, it has limitations. An important caution has to do with sample selection: Researchers need to be wary of demographic bias. A famous example illustrating the danger of demographic bias was the 1936 survey poll of more than two million people that led to a prediction that Republican presidential candidate Alf Landon would defeat Democratic incumbent Franklin Roosevelt by a landslide. In fact, the reverse happened.

The poll was dead wrong because the survey sample was selected by picking names from telephone directories. In the Depression years, only the well-to-do had telephones, and the wealthy tended to be in favor of Landon. Political survey techniques have been refined so that such errors rarely happen nowadays.

Consider the political polls prior to the 2008 presidential election that indicated during the final week before the election that Barack Obama would win by about 6 to 7 percentage points. Obama's actual margin of victory was indeed 7 percent of the popular vote. These polls were representative polls in that they only included registered voters who were likely to vote, and the participants were randomly selected from that representative group. Therefore, when polls and surveys use representative, random sampling techniques, accurate predictions about the underlying population can be made with relatively small samples. On the other hand, when samples are not representative and random, survey results can be very misleading.

For instance, much of what we know about human behavior is gathered from college students. This population is hardly representative of the general population in terms of age, socioeconomic status, and education—all variables that might well influence a participant's responses. Although the segment of the population from which participants are drawn may have little impact on some types of research (for instance, the study of how receptors in the eye respond to different colors), it may have an important influence on other types of research. Thus, we need to be very careful in generalizing from a sample of college students to a broader population. This caution applies to experiments and some other research methods, as well as to surveys.

Another potential bias in sample selection is gender bias. Males are used as participants for psychological investigation far more commonly than are females (Holmes & Jorgensen, 1971; McHugh, Koeske, & Frieze, 1986; Rohrbaugh, 1979; Rothblum, 1988). Females are not widely represented in medical research, either. This bias has led some people to suggest that our data reflect a psychology (or medicine) of men more than of people in general. Preference for male or female participants can have a serious biasing effect on research. For example, a substantial majority of investigations of human aggressive behavior have studied only male participants, suggesting that psychologists may have been influenced by our society's tendency to view males as more active and aggressive than females. This assumption would have little chance of being proven false by research that systematically ignored women.

Fortunately, research psychologists are becoming more aware of the implications of gender bias in research. Recent investigations of aggressive behavior, using participants of both sexes, have revealed that under some circumstances women may behave just as aggressively as men (Jacquin, Harrison, & Alford, 2006; Snethen & Puymbroeck, 2008). Unbiased sampling procedures will allow us to make accurate conclusions about both the similarities and differences between males and females.

Still another caution in using the survey method concerns the design of the actual questions. Psychologists have learned, often to their dismay, that even very minor changes in the wording of a question can alter people's responses. For example, Elizabeth Loftus (1975) asked participants, "Do you get headaches *occasionally*, and if so how often?" Those participants reported an average of 0.7 headaches a week. A comparable group of participants was asked, "Do you get headaches *frequently*, and if so how often?" That comparable group reported a weekly average of 2.2 headaches. Clearly, a considerable amount of thought and careful attention must be applied in constructing survey questions.

Finally, surveys are not appropriate for every research project. A survey can provide a broad profile of attitudes and behaviors of a large group, but it cannot look closely at specific individuals to understand their behaviors or attitudes. Psychologists must use other methods to provide that kind of information.

Survey Methods: Alcohol and Sexual Behavior

Let us return to our question about the relationship between alcohol and sexual arousal and see how this kind of research question might incorporate the survey method. In fact, this method was used in the early 1970s. In a survey of twenty thousand middle-class and upper-middle-class Americans, 60 percent of respondents reported that drinking increased their sexual pleasure (Athanasiou, Shaver, & Tavris, 1970). There was a pronounced difference between men and women, with significantly greater numbers of women reporting this effect. However, this research might be questioned because it relies on subjective reports. What people believe to be true may not always be the case: There is sometimes considerable discrepancy between actual behavior and the way people report it. In fact, alcohol is known to decrease sexual arousal, but leads to an increase in one's perception of a potential partner's willingness to engage in sexual activity (Abbey, Buck, Zawacki, & Saenz, 2003; George et al., 1997). Perhaps this change in perception leads one to believe they are more aroused.

Observational Method Method of psychological research, providing descriptive information, in which participants are observed as they go about their usual activities

Naturalistic Observation Psychological research using the observational method that takes place in a natural setting, such as a participant's home or school environment

Observer Bias Tendency of an observer to read more into a situation than is actually there or to see; what he or she expects to see a potential limitation of the observational method

The Observational Method

A third research method is the **observational method**, wherein researchers observe their participants as they go about their usual activities. This research method often takes place in a natural setting; when it does, it is called **naturalistic observation**.

Like the survey method, the observational method provides descriptive information. For instance, in the study of children's aggressive behavior discussed earlier in this chapter, researchers might observe that when children become aggressive, adults pay more attention to them. This observation might lead to the hypothesis that aggressive behaviors in children are likely to increase commensurate with the amount of adult attention they produce. This hypothesis could not be tested using the observational method since it does not provide any way of controlling variables. Nevertheless, such observations could serve as an excellent starting point for further research in a more controlled environment.

Other recent examples of the observational method are studies by Crockenberg and Smith (1982) and Crockenberg and Leerkes (2006), who observed the interactions between mothers and their newborn infants to determine how mother responsiveness contributes to infant irritability. Observations revealed that irritability in infants was not associated with neonatal irritability as expected, but with unresponsive mothering and longer delays to calm crying infants.

Limitations of the Observational Method

Just as with the case study and the survey, direct observation is not appropriate for every research question. Take a minute or two and try to anticipate some potential drawbacks of the observational method. See if you can list one or two limitations before reading on.

One potential problem of the observational method is the risk of subjectivity, or **observer bias**: An observer may read more into a situation than is actually there. For instance, a teacher observing a student may be tempted to record that he is more disruptive upon finding that the student was recently diagnosed with attention deficit hyperactivity disorder (ADHD). In one such study, for instance, both parents and teachers were asked to rate the occurrence of disruptive behaviors of fifty-five students ranging in age from six to twelve years old. The researchers found considerable disagreement between parents and teachers in their ratings of ADHD symptoms. These differences were attributed to different perceptions teachers and parents held about problem behaviors and the effects of medication (Antrop, Roeyers, Oosterlaan, & Van Oost, 2002). This finding is rather sobering, considering the widespread tendency of American educators to evaluate students as disruptive, uncooperative, and so forth, and then enter these evaluations into permanent records on

(Getty Images)

Dr. Jane Goodall observing a family of chimpanzees is an example of naturalistic observation.

Observer Effect Tendency of participants to modify behavior because they are aware of being observed

Correlational Method Research method that uses statistical techniques to determine the degree of relationship between variables

Coefficient of Correlation Statistic used to describe the degree of relationship between two or more variables in which positive correlations indicate that variables vary together in the same direction and negative correlations indicate the opposite

which future teachers rely. Psychologists conducting observational research generally try to avoid making biased interpretations by keeping very careful records of their observations. Sometimes audiovisual records that can be evaluated by independent observers are also used in the effort to minimize observer bias.

Another potential problem is that the presence of a human observer may affect the behavior being observed. For example, children on a playground may behave less aggressively simply because they are being watched by a strange adult. This problem of **observer effect** may require special attention when researchers take the observational method into the laboratory. For instance, when William Masters and Virginia Johnson (1966) used direct observation to document male and female sexual response patterns in the laboratory, many people questioned the validity of their findings.

Actually, in much of Masters's and Johnson's work, no one directly observed the participants. When investigators did use direct observation, they were as unobtrusive as possible—observing from a peripheral location or from behind one-way glass, or using videotapes to be viewed later, and so forth. According to a subsequent report, the vast majority of volunteers found it surprisingly easy to respond sexually in the laboratory in much the same way as they responded at home in private (Brecher & Brecher, 1966). Although there may be some merit to the concern about the artificial nature of Masters's and Johnson's laboratory observations, time has demonstrated that their research findings are accurate enough to be applied beneficially in such areas as sex therapy, infertility counseling, birth control, and general sex education.

Thus, despite its potential disadvantages, direct observation often produces valuable information when it is carefully conducted. In addition, there are some clear advantages to seeing and measuring behavior firsthand instead of relying on subjective reports of past experiences. Firsthand, direct observation virtually eliminates the possibility of data falsification, either through a participant's inaccurate recollections or through deceptive reporting. In addition, direct observation can provide some important insights into relationships that may exist in a particular behavioral area.

Correlational Method

Some types of questions cannot be answered by surveys, direct observation, or case studies. For instance, suppose that you wanted to determine how high school seniors' Scholastic Aptitude Test (SAT) scores related to their grade point averages (GPAs) during the first year of college. The best approach would be simply to collect the SAT scores and first-year GPAs of a large sample of college freshmen and use a statistical technique to determine the relationship between these two variables. This research technique is called the **correlational method**, and the statistic used to describe the amount and type of relationship is a **coefficient of correlation**.

A coefficient of correlation always falls somewhere between +1.00 and –1.00. A minus sign is used to signify negative correlations. A correlation of around 0 indicates a weak or nonexistent relationship between the two variables in question. A positive correlation indicates that the variables vary together in the same direction, so that increases in one measure are accompanied by increases in the other. For instance, it is known that SAT scores are positively correlated with college GPA because students who obtain high SAT scores tend to achieve high GPAs, and those with low SAT scores tend to have lower grades. This relationship is far from a perfect 1.00, however. In the real world, correlations between variables are virtually never perfect.

It is important to note that a high positive correlation between two variables does not mean that the matched scores are nearly identical in value. It simply means that a

Table 2-2 Positive Correlation Between SAT Scores and Freshman GPA for Five Students

Subject	SAT Score	GPA
1	595	2.15
2	621	2.67
3	650	3.45
4	652	3.20
5	712	3.85

generally consistent proportional relationship exists. For example, suppose we find a strong positive correlation of 0.90 between students' scores on SATs and their freshman GPAs at a particular college. In Table 2-2, it is clear that the two scores are far from identical, as SAT scores range from about 200 to 800, while GPAs range from 0 to 4.0.

This is what we mean by a generally consistent proportional relationship. As SAT scores increase, we see a corresponding increase in GPA. This is best illustrated in Figure 2-1. Had all the points fallen directly on the straight line, the correlation would have been 1.00. As the points get farther from the line, the correlation gets closer to 0.

Interpreting a Negative Correlation Between Variables Based on what you have just learned about positive correlation, take a moment to consider what kind of relationship must exist between variables to yield a negative correlation.

A negative correlation indicates that increases in one measure are associated with decreases in the other. If you have ever followed the stock market, you may have noted that as interest rates go up, market averages tend to come down. This relationship is by no means a perfect −1.00, but it does indicate a definite trend. Another example of a negative correlation is the well-known relationship between outdoor temperature and the incidence of colds. The data in Table 2-3 represent what we might find on a typical college campus during several weeks of the winter.

Figure 2-1 Positive Correlation Between SAT Scores and Freshman GPA for Five Students

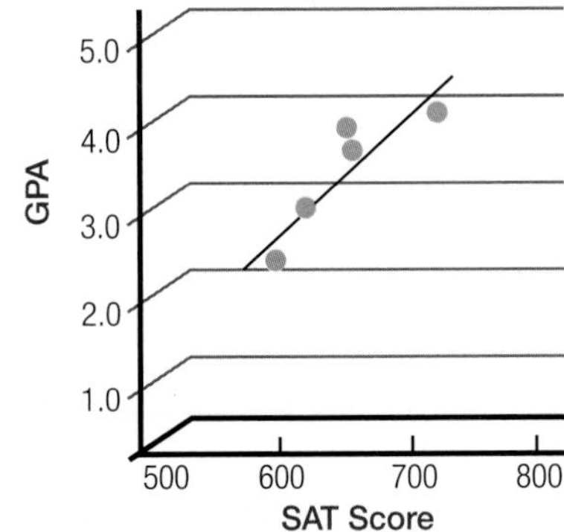

Table 2-3 Negative Correlation Between Average Daily Temperature and Students with Colds over a Five-Week Period

Week #	Average Daily Temperature	Students with Colds
1	63	9
2	57	26
3	46	32
4	42	40
5	38	55

These data are graphically presented in Figure 2-2. As you can see, the straight line through these points is negatively sloped, indicating a negative correlation. That is, as temperature goes down, the incidence of colds goes up. The correlation in this case is –0.94. Again, because the points don't always fall on the line, the correlation is not exactly –1.00.

Knowing the type and degree of relationship that exists between variables may be especially helpful to psychologists and others who wish to make predictions about behavior. For example, if you know that a high school senior scored high on the SAT, you can predict with some confidence that they are likely to earn good grades in college. Using Figure 2-1, can you predict the GPA of a student with an SAT score of 700?

Figure 2-2 Negative Correlation Between Average Daily Temperature over a Five-Week Period and the Incidence of Colds During the Same Five-Week Period

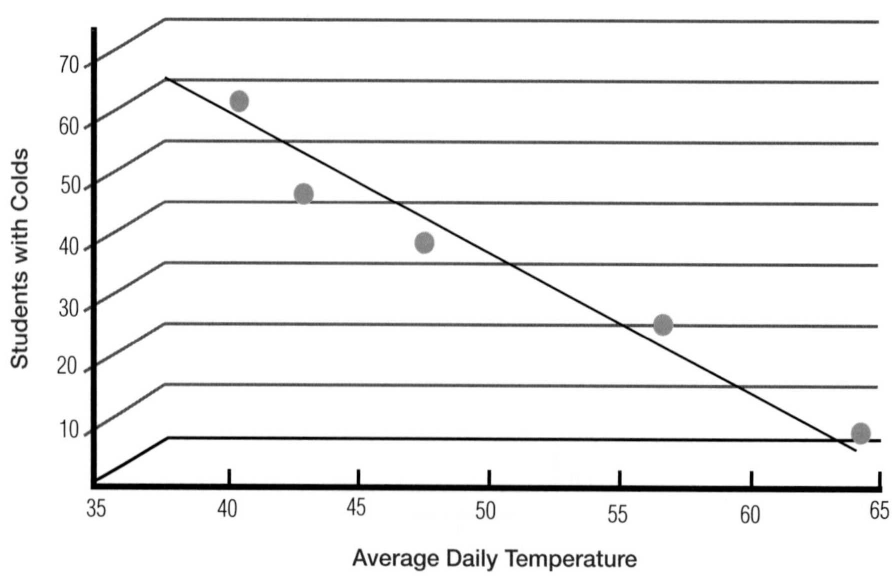

Limitations of Correlational Studies Correlational studies help us discover relationships between variables, but it is important not to read more into them than is there. One of the most common mistakes people make in interpreting correlational studies is to conclude that because two factors are related, one causes the other. Certainly, this is sometimes the case. Observations of drivers negotiating obstacle courses under the influence of alcohol, for instance, reveal a positive correlation between error scores and blood alcohol levels (the higher the level, the greater the number of errors). This correlational relationship is a causal one since alcohol is known to impair the brain's ability to perceive, interpret, and respond to stimuli.

On the other hand, a consistent relationship between two factors is not always causal. In some cases a third factor, related to each of the other two, may account for the apparent causal relationship. For example, upon examining our data about the relationship between outside temperature and the incidence of colds, one might be tempted to make the conclusion that getting a cold is caused by being cold (a misconception that actually led to naming the disease *cold*). The fact is that getting a cold is probably more related to drier cold air and being indoors among many others than *being* cold. Being indoors increases your exposure to the cold virus and, therefore, your likelihood of getting a cold. In sum, it is dangerous to read causal effects into correlational studies. You will find a more in-depth discussion of statistical correlation in the Appendix.

The problem with the research methods just discussed is that they do not allow for precise control over the various factors that may influence the behavior being studied. One research technique that *does* allow this control is the experimental method. All things considered, this is often the research approach preferred by psychologists. Also, as we shall see, it is the method that provides us with a clear answer to the question: Does alcohol affect sexual behavior?

Experimental Research
Research conducted in precisely controlled laboratory conditions in which participants are confronted with specific stimuli and their reactions are carefully measured to discover relationships among variables

Independent Variable
Condition or factor that the experimenter manipulates in order to determine whether changes in behavior (the dependent variable) result

Dependent Variable In experimental research, the behavior that results from manipulation of an independent variable

2.2b Experimental Research Methods

The Experimental Method

In **experimental research**, participants are confronted with specific stimuli under precisely controlled conditions that allow their reactions to be reliably measured. The major advantage of the experimental method is that it allows the researcher to control conditions, ruling out all possible influences on participants' behaviors other than the factors that are being investigated. A research psychologist using this method directly manipulates a particular set of conditions and then observes the effect on behavior. The purpose of the experimental method is to discover causal relations between variables—for example, whether the consumption of alcohol causes a change in sexual behavior.

Independent and Dependent Variables There are two kinds of variables in scientific experiments: independent and dependent. An **independent variable** is a condition or factor that the experimenter manipulates; the resulting behavior that is measured and recorded is called the **dependent variable**. In our alcohol study, the independent variable would be the amount of alcohol consumed, while the dependent variable would be any measurable change in sexual behavior.

Experimental and Control Groups

To determine the effects of alcohol on sexual behavior a researcher might compare sexual responsiveness in several groups of participants, with participants in each group receiving different amounts of alcohol (including no alcohol) before measurements of arousal are

Experimental Group In experimental research, a group of participants who are exposed to different varieties of independent variables, so that resulting behaviors can be compared

Control Group In experimental psychology, a group of participants who experience all the same conditions as participants in the experimental group except for the key factor (independent variable) the researcher is evaluating

taken. In this case, the groups of participants receiving alcohol are called **experimental groups**, and the group of participants receiving no alcohol would be the **control group**. Differences in sexual responsiveness (the dependent variable) between the experimental groups and the control group could then be attributed to the effects of alcohol (the independent variable).

Not all experiments involve comparisons between experimental and control groups, however. In some cases it is more desirable to compare an individual participant with himself or herself under different conditions. For example, a psychologist might compare a participant's sexual arousal after receiving alcohol to the level of arousal without alcohol. In this case the same participant serves in both the experimental and control conditions, but at different times.

Examples of the Experimental Method

Now that we have some understanding of the experimental method, let us examine how alcohol affects sexual behavior. Recall that in an earlier survey, a majority of respondents had reported that alcohol enhanced their sexual pleasure. However, a survey is limited to asking people what they think happens when they drink, and these subjective assessments may not match up with what actually happens. Two subsequent experimental studies revealed that there was good cause to be wary of the survey's findings. Both investigations were conducted at Rutgers University's Alcohol Behavior Research Laboratory.

The first experiment involved forty-eight male college students between the ages of eighteen and twenty-two (Briddell & Wilson, 1976). During an initial session the researchers obtained baseline data on flaccid (nonerect) penis diameter for all participants. The participants were then shown a ten-minute erotic film of explicit sexual interaction between male and female partners. Penile tumescence (engorgement) was measured continuously during the film, using a flexible rubber band-like device. This measurement provided information about these men's level of sexual arousal when they were not under the influence of alcohol. Thus, in this phase of the experiment, participants served as their own controls.

A second session was held a week later. In this session, participants drank measured amounts of alcohol prior to viewing a somewhat longer version of the erotic film. The forty-eight men were assigned to four experimental groups, with twelve participants in each group. Depending on his group assignment, each participant consumed 0.6, 3.0, 6.0, or 9.0 ounces of alcohol. After a forty-minute rest period, the participants viewed the film, during which sexual arousal was again precisely measured.

The results of the experiment indicated that alcohol significantly reduced sexual arousal in participants, as compared to their control levels. In addition, the arousal-reducing effects of alcohol were greater at higher intake levels.

A second investigation of alcohol effects was conducted with sixteen college women between the ages of eighteen and twenty-two (Wilson & Lawson, 1976). In this experiment, the group of sixteen women participated in weekly experimental sessions under varying conditions. Each received four different doses of alcohol (0.3, 1.4, 2.9, and 4.3 ounces) on different occasions and then watched either a control film or an erotic film. The control film was a boring twelve-minute review of the computer facilities at Rutgers University; the erotic film portrayed explicit heterosexual interaction. Sexual arousal was measured continuously during the film by use of a vaginal photoplethysmograph, a device designed to measure increased vaginal blood volume in a sexually aroused female. As expected, participants showed significantly more arousal in response to the erotic than the nonerotic film. More important, there was clear evidence that alcohol reduced sexual arousal, especially in higher dosages.

Both of these experiments tend to refute the belief that alcohol enhances erotic experiences; they also reveal the advantages of controlled laboratory conditions for measuring behavior. Clearly, the experimental method provided a more accurate indication of how alcohol affects sexual arousal than did the survey.

Laboratory experiments offer researchers a number of advantages, including the ability to control variables and, frequently, the ability to draw direct conclusions about cause-and-effect relationships between variables. None of the previously described methods allow for conclusions about cause-and effect.

BVT*Lab*

Visit **www.BVTLab.com** to explore the student resources available for this chapter.

How Samples Are Selected for Experiments

Sample selection is not just important for survey research. Because the results from experiments are often generalized to larger populations, the appropriate sampling considerations discussed under survey research apply to experimental research as well. That is, for the results of the experiment on the effects of alcohol on sexual arousal to be generalized to all college students, the sample selected for the experiment must be representative of all college students. If a representative sample cannot be obtained, the results of experiments are greatly limited.

Likewise, researchers attempt to obtain random samples from a population to avoid restricting the experiment to a select group of participants. Also, participants (once selected) are often randomly assigned to different treatment conditions to avoid further bias. For example, in the alcohol study conducted on forty-eight males, the participants were randomly assigned to groups receiving different amounts of alcohol. Consider for a moment how the results might have differed had the experimenter allowed the participants to choose to which group they were assigned, or if group selection was determined by the amount of prior alcohol experience participants had.

Limitations of the Experimental Method

We have discussed some of the positive aspects of experimental laboratory research. Before reading on, take a couple of minutes to look at the other side of the coin. Can you think of any potential drawbacks associated with this research method?

The experimental method also has some limitations. First, the somewhat artificial nature of the laboratory setting may influence participants' behaviors. The very fact that people know they are in an experiment can cause them to respond differently from the way they might normally behave. For instance, the artificial nature of the laboratory might limit our interpretations of the research previously discussed on the effects of alcohol on sexual arousal. Although both experiments measured differences in sexual arousal that could be attributed to alcohol, it may be that in a more natural setting with a sexual partner these differences wouldn't show up. Further research in a variety of settings would be necessary to confirm this.

A second limitation of the experimental method is simply that not all questions posed by psychologists lend themselves to experimental investigation. For instance, you might be interested in finding out whether children of divorced parents are as emotionally secure as children from two-parent families. Similarly, we might be interested in the effects of severe malnutrition on learning and memory. These kinds of data could not be gathered by manipulating variables in a laboratory setting. Instead, you would need to take your investigation to real families or natural settings.

The appropriateness of the experimental method has sometimes been questioned for a reason other than its artificial nature: A number of experimental studies have been criticized on ethical grounds.

2.2c Ethics in Psychological Experiments

In past years, several controversial studies have prompted serious questions about the ethics of some psychological experiments. Consider the following four examples, and decide whether you think any ethical principles were violated.

The Milgram Obedience to Authority Study

In the 1960s, social psychologist Stanley Milgram (1963) used deception in a widely discussed study of obedience to authority. Milgram's goal was to determine whether participants would administer painful electric shocks to others merely because an authority figure instructed them to do so. Milgram's participants, all male, thought they were participating in a study of how punishment affects learning. They were told to use an intercom system to present problems to a learner who was strapped in a chair in another room, out of sight, and to administer a shock each time the learner gave a wrong answer to a problem. Labeled switches on the shock apparatus ranged from a low of 15 volts to a high of 450 volts; participants were instructed to increase the voltage with each successive error the learner made.

In spite of protests and cries from the other room, most of the participants delivered what they believed were a full range of these painful shocks. Although they followed the experimenter's instructions, the task was not easy for them. Virtually all of the participants exhibited high levels of stress and discomfort as they administered the shocks. Later, these participants were told that the experiment was merely a contrived situation in which they had been deceived, and that no shocks had actually been given. How would you feel about yourself if you had been one of Milgram's participants? Do you think Milgram violated ethical principles by placing people in a position in which they might feel compelled to engage in hurtful behavior? Was deception appropriate in this experiment? For that matter, is it acceptable in any psychological research with human participants?

The Stanford University Prisoner Study

A second controversial study, the now famous Stanford University prisoner study, was conducted some years ago by social psychologist Philip Zimbardo and his colleagues (Haney & Zimbardo, 1974; Zimbardo, 1975). These investigators created a simulated prison environment to study how incarceration influenced the behavior of healthy, well-adjusted people. Student recruits played the roles of either guards or inmates.

No one anticipated the profoundly disturbing impact of this experience on students cast in either of the roles. The guards soon became so cruel that several of the prisoners suffered emotional reactions ranging from depression to anxiety and even extreme rage (not unlike the responses of many inmates in genuine penal institutions). As soon as Zimbardo and his associates became aware of the severe impact their study was having on their participants, they terminated the experiment—even before it had run its course. Should this experiment have been conducted? Was it unethical to place humans in a situation the researchers might have anticipated could lead to hostile confrontations?

Replication of the Stanford Prisoner Study

In 1983 the press widely reported a repeat of the Zimbardo research conducted by a high school teacher who used volunteer students. This researcher obtained permission from both parents and school officials to conduct the investigation. The results were similar to those obtained by the Stanford group a decade earlier, and many of the students were severely upset by their participation in this follow-up study. Needless to say, parents were irate, school officials were chagrined, and the press had a field day. Were ethical principles violated in this repeat of Zimbardo's earlier research?

Lost in a Shopping Mall

In 1992 the press began reporting on studies conducted by Elizabeth Loftus at the University of Washington. Loftus was attempting to demonstrate that recovered memories of past child abuse may be false memories induced by psychotherapists' suggestions. To demonstrate how false memories might be implanted, Loftus designed the "lost in a shopping mall" experiment, where participants were provided false information about being lost in a mall as a child. In Loftus's words, "I wanted to 'scar' the brain with something that never happened, creating a vivid but wholly imagined impression" (Loftus & Ketcham, 1994, p. 92). These planted memories apparently became real memories in some of her participants. As it turns out, Loftus may not have received appropriate approval for conducting these false memory experiments from either her participants or the university review board (Crook & Dean, 1999). As a university student, do you believe participants should have been given the opportunity to provide informed consent? Would knowing the nature of the experiments bias the outcome? Is deception in psychological research both necessary and justifiable?

2.2d **Ethical Guidelines for Research**

The four examples we have described present complex ethical issues. Perhaps the most controversial was Milgram's research, which generated a great deal of criticism. Many psychologists questioned the ethics of exposing unsuspecting people to a situation that might cause them considerable stress and might even have lasting harmful effects. Psychologist Diana Baumrind (1964), for example, argued that participants' feelings and rights had been abused. She suggested that many would have trouble justifying their willingness to administer high levels of shock and that their self-respect would be damaged. Milgram pointed out, however, that after the study all participants went through extensive debriefing, in which they were told that they had not actually shocked anyone and were reassured that many other participants had responded in the same way. He documented the success of these debriefing sessions, citing results from a follow-up questionnaire returned by 92 percent of the original participants. A large majority, 84 percent, said they were glad to have participated in the study. Fifteen percent indicated neutral feelings, and only 1 percent of the participants reported being sorry they had participated in the experiment (Milgram, 1964).

Some researchers seemed relatively satisfied with Milgram's response to his critics. One psychologist recently commented that Milgram seems to have employed little more deception in his work than is used regularly on TV programs such as *Candid Camera* (McConnell, 1983, p. 629). Nevertheless, such studies generated a debate about ethics in research that ultimately culminated in the American Psychological Association (APA) adopting in 1973 (the most recent revision in 2008) a list of ethical guidelines requiring, among other things, that researchers avoid procedures that might cause serious physical or mental harm to human participants. If an experiment involves even the slightest risk of harm or discomfort, investigators are required to obtain informed consent from their participants. Researchers must also respect a participant's right to refuse to participate at any time during the course of a study, and special steps must be taken to protect the confidentiality of the data and maintain participants' anonymity unless they agree to be identified.

The issue of deception in research remains controversial. Some studies would lose their effectiveness if participants knew in advance exactly what the experimenter was studying. The APA's guideline provides that if deception must be used, a postexperiment debriefing must thoroughly explain to participants why it was necessary. At such time, participants must be allowed to request that their data be removed from the study and destroyed.

Were ethical principles violated in the prison and the false memory studies? Keeping the APA's ethical guidelines in mind, how would you now evaluate the research examples in the preceding discussion? Take a few moments to think critically about the ethics of these studies before reading on.

Most psychologists believe that Zimbardo's simulated prison study did not violate ethical principles. The researchers were as shocked as anyone by their experiment's effects, and they terminated the study as soon as it became clear that some participants were experiencing severe emotional reactions. Also, all participants had voluntarily participated in the study after being carefully informed of its nature.

The second prisoner study is a different case entirely. Unlike Zimbardo's group, the high school teacher who replicated the prisoner study had access to previous research findings that strongly indicated the possibility of psychological harm to participants. These findings were ignored, however, and the experiment was re-created in clear violation of research ethics.

Sometimes it is hard for researchers to objectively weigh the potential benefits of a study against the possibility of harming its participants. Recognizing the difficulty of this task, virtually every institution conducting research in the United States has established ethics committees or Institutional Review Boards (IRBs) that review all proposed studies. If they perceive that the participants' (humans or other animals) welfare is insufficiently safeguarded, the proposal must be modified or the research cannot be conducted. Many students taking an introductory psychology class have opportunities to participate in psychological research. In fact, much of the human research discussed in this text comes from psychology students like you from across the country. Before participants can be recruited, however, the researchers submitted a research proposal to the institution's IRB for consideration. The IRB carefully weighs the benefits of knowledge gained from the research with potential risks to students. These risks include both physical risks (pain and injury) as well as psychological risks (emotional trauma). Once a proposal is approved, researchers must provide participants with an assurance of confidentiality. That is, any data collected from a participant cannot be later identified with a particular student. Participants must also be advised that they may withdraw from an experiment at any time without repercussions (loss of points, money, etc.).

Research proposals requesting to use animal subjects must also be approved by a similar university ethics committee. Typically, this committee is called an Institutional Animal Care and Use Committee (IACUC). It is the responsibility of an IACUC to assure that animals used in research studies are adequately housed and maintained as well as treated humanely during the experiment.

The APA's list of ethical principles, together with the activities of IRBs and IACUCs, makes it very unlikely that research along the lines of Stanley Milgram's study could be conducted today. Researchers who do not adhere to strict codes of ethics risk serious professional and legal consequences.

2.3 Statistical Concepts for Research

Regardless of the research method used, psychologists generally end up with data that must be described and interpreted. Usually the data are in the form of numbers that can be analyzed by **statistics**, mathematical methods for describing and interpreting data. There are essentially two kinds of statistics: descriptive and inferential. The Statistics Appendix provides detailed information about using statistics to make sense out of research findings; therefore, our discussion in this section provides only a brief overview.

Statistics Mathematical methods for describing and interpreting data; two kinds of statistics are descriptive and inferential statistics

Descriptive Statistics Mathematical and graphical methods for reducing data to a form that can be readily understood

Measure of Central Tendency In descriptive statistics, a value that reflects the middle or central point of a distribution of scores; the three measures of central tendency are the mean, the median, and the mode

Mean In descriptive statistics, the arithmetic average obtained by adding scores and dividing by the number of scores

Median In descriptive statistics, the score that falls in the middle of a distribution of numbers arranged from the lowest to the highest

Mode In descriptive statistics, the score that occurs most frequently in a distribution of numbers

2.3a Descriptive Statistics

Suppose you are enrolled in a psychology class attended by 130 students, the size of a class actually taught by one of the authors. On the first exam, you receive 51 points out of a possible 60. Naturally, you want to know how your score compares with the class as a whole—for example, were you among the top 10 percent or the bottom 25 percent of your class? Your instructor announces that the top score is 58 points. This information still does not provide sufficient data for you to evaluate your score. Your score of 51 may be well above average, but it is also possible that most of the class scored higher than you. What you need is a statistical description of overall class performance that will allow you to make sense of your score. This is what **descriptive statistics** is about: summarizing large amounts of data into a form that is easily interpreted. There are three major ways of describing data such as the class scores on a psychology exam: graphs, measures of central tendency, and measures of variation.

Using Graphs to Describe Data

A graph is particularly useful to present data because the way scores are distributed can be interpreted at a glance. Figure 2-3 shows a graph of actual scores from 130 students taking General Psychology. The highest score possible was 60 points. This particular type of graph is called a histogram, or bar graph. Each bar on the graph represents an interval width of 5 points on the test. The vertical axis (frequency) represents the number of students who received scores within each interval. If your score was 51 points, it is included in the interval 50 to 54 points.

Normal Distributions This distribution of scores represents an approximation of a normal distribution. A normal distribution is a bell-shaped distribution of scores that is symmetrical in shape. The dashed line in Figure 2-3 represents the shape of a normal distribution. As you can see, the scores from your test approximate this shape, with your score of 51 points falling among those of the top half of the class.

Measures of Central Tendency A **measure of central tendency** is a value that reflects the middle or central point of a distribution of scores. There are three measures of central tendency: The **mean**, the **median**, and the **mode**. The mean is an arithmetic average obtained by adding all of the scores and dividing by the number of scores (130). For our test scores, the mean was 43 points.

Figure 2-3 Bar Graph (Histogram) for 130 Scores from One of the Authors' General Psychology Classes

The numbers below each bar indicate how many scores fall within each interval. The dashed line represents the shape of a normal distribution of scores.

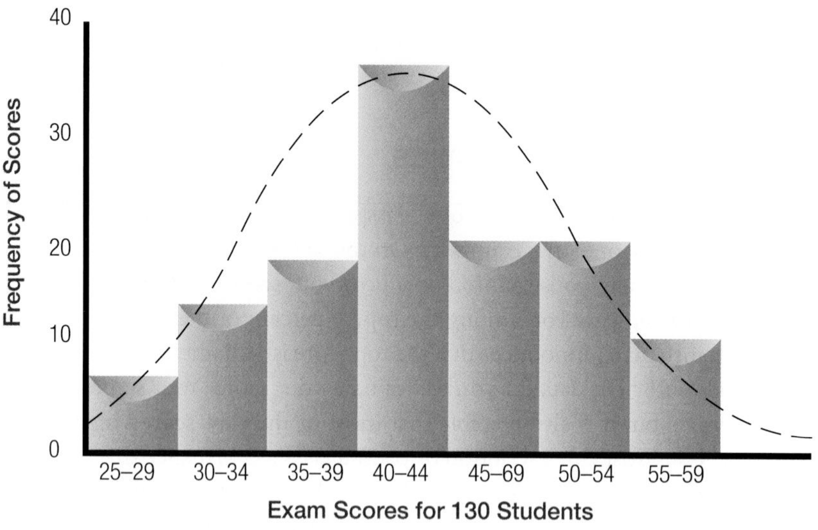

The median is the score that falls in the middle of a distribution of numbers that are arranged from the lowest to the highest. If we were to arrange our test scores from the lowest (27 points) to the highest (58 points), the middle value (the sixty-fifth score) of these 130 scores would have been 44 points. The median is especially useful as a descriptor of data when there are extreme values at either end of the distribution. For this reason, the median is often used to represent annual incomes since it won't be inflated by a few excessive values like the mean could be.

The mode is the score in the distribution that occurs most frequently. In this case, the most frequent score on our psychology exam was 42 points. In some cases, distributions can have several modes. When this occurs, the distribution is said to be multimodal.

Had the distribution of test scores been exactly normal, all three measures of central tendency (the mean, median, and mode) would have been the same value. In our distribution of test scores these values were quite similar, suggesting that our distribution approximates a **normal distribution**. When these values are very different, the distribution is skewed or unbalanced. This might have occurred if our test had been either too easy or too difficult. For instance, if the test was too difficult, the distribution would have been **skewed** to the right, or weighted toward lower scores. In such situations, a person needs to decide which measure most accurately reflects central tendency. All things considered, the mean is generally the most commonly used measure of central tendency.

Normal Distribution In descriptive statistics, a distribution in which scores are distributed similarly on both sides of the middle value, so that they have the appearance of the bell-shaped curve when graphed

Skewed In descriptive statistics, an unbalanced distribution of scores

Returning to our previous example, suppose you find out that the score 43 is the mean score on the psychology exam? You now know that your score of 51 is at least above average. With only this information, however, you still do not have a sense of how your score ranks. That average of 43 could result from the fact that, aside from your 51, half of the class scored 58 and the other half scored 35 (all A's and F's); or it could result from most of the class scoring in the 40–47 range. Your class position would be very different in these two situations. What you need to know in addition to the mean is how variable the scores were.

Measures of Variability The histogram in Figure 2-3 shows you that scores were quite variable, ranging from the upper 20s to the upper 50s. One **measure of variability** is the range, which is the difference between the highest and lowest score. The **range** is the easiest measure of variability to calculate. However, it may provide a misleading indication of how dispersed scores are. For example, suppose that all but one student in your psychology class received a test score somewhere between 36 and 58. Excluding this one exception, the range would be 22 (58 to 36). However, the one score outside the spread, a 14, had the effect of doubling the range to 44 (58 to 14). As you can see, whenever there are extreme scores at either end of a distribution, the range will provide a biased, inflated estimate of variation.

A much better measure of variability is provided by the **standard deviation**. This measure is an indication of the extent to which the scores in a distribution vary from the mean. The standard deviation is much more accurate than the range because it takes into account all the scores in a data set, not just the extreme values at either end. The standard deviation effectively describes whether a distribution of scores varies widely or narrowly around the mean. If the standard deviation is small, we know that individual scores tend to be very close to the mean. If it is large, we know that the mean is less representative because the scores are much more widely dispersed around it. For our distribution of test scores the standard deviation was 8. This means that the average amount scores deviated from the mean was 8 points.

Knowing the mean and standard deviation allows us to make relatively precise judgments about how a particular score relates to other scores. Since the standard deviation on your psychology test was 8, this would place you exactly one standard deviation unit above the mean, which was 43. Because your class's test scores were fairly normally distributed, you would know that roughly 85 percent of your classmates (110 out of 130) scored below your score of 51. This conclusion is derived from known properties of the normal distribution that are described in the Statistics Appendix.

Applying Standard Deviation Assume that two classes with an equal number of students take the psychology exam. The mean is 46 in both classes, and the distributions of scores are approximately normal. However, the standard deviations are different: In class *A* the standard deviation is 8; in class *B* it is 4. Assuming that your score is 4 points above the mean and that your instructor grades on a curve (i.e., assigns grades based on relative standing in the overall distribution of scores), in which class would you prefer to be enrolled? Think about your answer before reading on.

If you selected class *B*, you are correct. In this class a standard deviation of 4 indicates scores are clustered much more closely around the average than in class *A*, where the variation is much greater. This greater dispersion of scores would place more people above you in class *A*, and thereby lower your relative rank.

Graphs, central tendency, and variability are just three kinds of statistics psychologists use to summarize and characterize data. The coefficient of correlation, discussed earlier, is another important descriptive statistic. Other descriptive statistics include percentiles and standard scores. The **percentile** represents the percentages of scores that lie below a particular score. For example, your percentile score was 85, because 85 percent of the class had a score lower than yours. A **standard score** measures how far a score deviates from the average in standard deviation units. Your standard score for the psychology test would have been 1, because 51 was 1 standard deviation (8 points) above the mean. These and other descriptive measures are discussed in more detail in the Statistics Appendix.

Measure of Variability In descriptive statistics, a measure that indicates whether distribution scores are clustered closely around their average or widely spread out; two measures of variability are the range and the standard deviation

Range In descriptive statistics, a measure of variability that indicates the difference between the highest and lowest scores

Standard Deviation In descriptive statistics, a measure of variability that indicates the average extent to which all the scores in a distribution vary from the mean

Percentile Numbers from a range of data indicating percentages of scores that lie below them

Standard Score In descriptive statistics, a measure that indicates how far a score deviates from the average in standard units

2.3b Inferential Statistics

Inferential Statistics
Process of using mathematical procedures to draw conclusions about the meaning of research data

Operational Definition
Definition specifying the operations that are used to measure or observe a variable, such as a definition of obesity specifying a certain weight-height relationship

Statistical Significance
Term used to describe research result in which changes in the dependent variable can be attributed with a high level of confidence to the experimental condition (or independent variable) being manipulated by the researcher

Using descriptive statistics is often just the first step in analyzing and interpreting research results. Once data have been described, psychologists often wish to draw inferences or conclusions about their findings. The process of using statistical procedures to draw conclusions about the meaning of data is called **inferential statistics**.

As we have seen in this chapter, research often begins with some type of hypothesis about how things are related. For example, you may believe that people who use special relaxation techniques are likely to have lower anxiety levels than those who do not use such techniques. To test this hypothesis, you might begin by selecting a group of participants, none of whom have been trained in relaxation techniques, who are matched on a number of important variables that might influence anxiety (things such as age, socioeconomic status, profession, health factors, etc.). Participants might then be randomly assigned to one of two groups (the independent variable), one group trained in relaxation techniques and the other receiving no training. You would then collect data on the participants' anxiety levels for a number of weeks or months.

Anxiety, the dependent variable, could be measured in a number of ways, depending on how you define it for the purpose of your study. Many of the variables studied by psychologists (such as anxiety, hunger, intelligence, or aggression) cannot be investigated until we specify precisely what we mean by the term. This is accomplished by providing an **operational definition** that specifies the operations we use to measure or observe the variable in question. For instance, you might use physical measures such as blood pressure or muscle tension to measure anxiety, or you could use a score on a psychological test that measures anxiety levels.

At the completion of your experiment you would have lots of data to analyze. Suppose you find that after eight weeks the relaxation training group scores markedly lower on your measure of anxiety than does the control group. This difference seems meaningful. However, whenever you evaluate the performance or characteristics of two or more groups of participants, it is likely there will be some differences based on chance alone. The problem for the researcher is to determine whether differences between research groups are due to the experimental condition (your independent variable) or simply a chance result.

How can you assess whether the difference in anxiety levels (your dependent variable) of the two groups is genuine rather than a chance result? A variety of tests have been devised to answer this question. Such procedures are called tests of **statistical significance**. When scientists conclude that a research finding is statistically significant, they are merely stating, at a high level of confidence, that the difference is attributable to the experimental condition being manipulated by the researcher. This topic will be discussed in greater detail in the Statistics Appendix.

2.3c Evaluating Opinions, Beliefs, and Scientific Evidence

We have seen in this chapter that psychological research can be hindered by a number of factors, including difficulties in obtaining representative samples, ethical considerations, experimenter bias, participant bias, and a variety of other problems. We have also seen that research psychologists have shown remarkable versatility in their efforts, collecting data in many different ways. Thus, a major strength of psychological research is its reliance on a wide assortment of methodological techniques.

It is important that any serious student of psychology learns to differentiate between nonscientific polls and opinions and the results of scientific research conducted by serious investigators. A major goal of this text is to teach you to think critically and to ask questions about how we have come to conclusions about behavior. Even research conducted by reputable scientists must be critically evaluated according to the following criteria:

Are the researchers considered to be unbiased regarding the outcome, or do they have special interests in supporting a particular conclusion?

Were the results of the research published in scientific journals where peer review occurs prior to publication, or were the results published in popular magazines, newspapers, or on the Internet?

What type of methodology was used? Were the results based on experiments?

Is there any reason to suspect bias in the selection of participants?

Can the results be applied to individuals other than those in the sample group? How broad can these generalizations be and still remain legitimate?

Is it possible that the method used to obtain information may have biased the findings? For instance, did the questionnaire promote false replies? Is it likely that the artificial nature of the laboratory setting influenced participants' responses?

Have there been any other published reports that confirm or contradict the particular study in question?

Keeping questions such as these in mind is helpful in finding a middle ground between absolute trust and offhand dismissal of a given research study.

Throughout this text we will be discussing research findings related to a wide variety of topics. It will be useful for you to remember some of the advantages and limitations of different research methods as we discuss this research. In addition, this brief review of statistical methods will provide you with a better understanding of how research is interpreted to be either supportive of, or contradictory to, a particular hypothesis or theory.

CHAPTER REVIEW

The Scientific Method and Behavior

1. Three of the most common reasons why psychologists conduct research are to test a hypothesis, to solve a problem, and to confirm findings of previous research.
2. A hypothesis is a statement proposing the existence of a relationship between variables. Hypotheses are typically offered as tentative explanations for relationships or events, and they are often designed to be tested by research.
3. When psychologists publish new research findings, they include details so that others may repeat the experiment to verify the results. The replication of prior research is the backbone of good science.

Research Methods

4. Psychologists use a number of methods to study behavior. These techniques include surveys, the observational method, case studies, the correlational method, and the experimental method.
5. An important research method is the survey, in which a representative group of people is questioned, in face-to-face interviews or using written questionnaires, about their behaviors or attitudes.
6. Surveys are often conducted with a representative sample, that is, a sample in which critical subgroups are represented according to their incidence in the larger population about which one wishes to draw conclusions.
7. Another kind of sample, called a random sample, is selected by randomization procedures that alone do not ensure a representative sample.
8. Potential limitations of the survey method include demographic and gender bias, improperly worded questions that bias responses, and a tendency to provide only limited insights about factors that contribute to behaviors and attitudes of specific individuals.
9. Researchers employing the observational method observe their participants as they go about their usual activities. When this research takes place in a natural setting, it is called naturalistic observation.
10. A potential problem with the observational method is the risk that an observer may read more into a situation than is actually there. This phenomenon is called observer bias.
11. Another possible limitation of the observational method is the problem of observer effect, where the presence of a human observer may affect the behavior being observed.
12. The case study is an in-depth exploration of either a single participant or a small group of participants who are examined individually.

CHAPTER REVIEW

13. Shortcomings of the case study method include lack of investigative control of important variables, a potential for subjective observer bias, a lack of proper sampling techniques that limits generalization of findings to other people in the clinical category being investigated, and a tendency for participants to report earlier experiences inaccurately.
14. The correlational method utilizes statistical methods to assess and describe the amount and type of relationship between two variables of interest, such as the SAT scores of high school seniors and their GPAs during the first year of college.
15. One major limitation of the correlational method is that this technique, considered alone, does not provide sufficient evidence to determine whether a demonstrated correlational relationship between two variables is reflective of a causal relationship or merely indicative of another factor (or factors) related to each of the variables.
16. In experimental research, participants are confronted with specific stimuli under precisely controlled conditions that allow their reactions to be reliably measured. The purpose of the experimental method is to discover causal relationships among independent and dependent variables.
17. An independent variable is a condition or factor that the experimenter manipulates; the resulting behavior that is measured and recorded is called the dependent variable.
18. Many experiments utilize both experimental groups, which consist of various groups of participants exposed to different varieties of independent variables, and a control group composed of participants who experience all the same conditions as participants in the experimental group—except for the key factor the researcher is evaluating (the dependent variable).
19. Special advantages of the experimental method include control over relevant variables and opportunities to draw conclusions about cause-and-effect relationships.
20. Limitations of the experimental method include the artificial nature of the laboratory setting, which may influence participants' behaviors, and the fact that some questions posed by psychologists do not lend themselves to experimental investigation.
21. The APA has adopted ethical guidelines for research that require, among other things, that researchers avoid procedures that might cause serious physical or mental harm to human participants, that they protect confidentiality of the data, and that they respect a participant's right to refuse to participate at any time during the course of a study. Institutions conducting research use an IRB to evaluate research proposals involving human participants and IACUCs to evaluate proposals using animal subjects.

CHAPTER REVIEW

Statistical Concepts for Research

22. There are two kinds of statistics: descriptive and inferential. Descriptive statistics provide succinct descriptions by reducing a quantity of data to a form that is more understandable. Inferential statistics include a variety of mathematical procedures to draw conclusions about the meaning of data.
23. Measures of central tendency (descriptive statistics that reflect the middle or central point of a distribution) include the mean, median, and mode. The mean is the arithmetic average; the median is the score that falls in the middle of a distribution; and the mode is the most frequent score.
24. Measures of variability (descriptive statistics that indicate the spread of a distribution of scores) include the range and the standard deviation. The range is the difference between the highest and lowest score, and the standard deviation is an approximate indication of the average extent to which all scores in a distribution vary from the mean.
25. Inferential statistics allows researchers to make judgments about whether their research findings are statistically significant. When scientists conclude that a research finding is statistically significant, they are merely stating, at a high level of confidence, that obtained differences in the performances of different groups of participants are attributable to the experimental condition being manipulated by the researcher.

TERMS AND CONCEPTS

Case Study, pg. 36
Coefficient of Correlation, pg. 42
Control Group, pg. 46
Correlational Method, pg. 42
Dependent Variable, pg. 45
Descriptive Statistics, pg. 51
Experimental Group, pg. 46
Experimental Research, pg. 45
Hypothesis, pg. 32
Independent Variable, pg. 45
Inferential Statistics, pg. 54
Mean, pg. 51
Measure of Central Tendency, pg. 51
Measure of Variability, pg. 53
Median, pg. 51
Mode, pg. 51
Naturalistic Observation, pg. 41
Normal Distribution, pg. 52
Observational Method, pg. 41
Observer Bias, pg. 41
Observer Effect, pg. 42
Operational Definition, pg. 54
Percentile, pg. 53
Random Sample, pg. 39
Range, pg. 53
Replication Studies, pg. 33
Representative Sample, pg. 38
Sample, pg. 38
Skewed, pg. 52
Standard Deviation, pg. 53
Standard Score, pg. 53
Statistical Significance, pg. 54
Statistics, pg. 51
Survey, pg. 38
Theory, pg. 32

POP QUIZ

True or False

___ 1. The research method that allows the researcher the greatest amount of control over relevant factors is the case study method.

___ 2. The ethical guidelines for conducting research with humans state that it is never appropriate to deceive the participant.

___ 3. Observer bias relates to the potential drawback of observational studies characterized by participants altering their behavior as a result of the researcher's presence.

___ 4. If you are interested in uncovering cause-and-effect relationships between two variables, you would use the correlational method.

___ 5. The standard deviation is a more sensitive measure of variability than the range.

Multiple Choice

6. The results of previous research and the psychologist's observations of behavior are two common sources of which of the following?
   a. Operational definitions
   b. Serendipity
   c. Hypotheses
   d. Theories
7. Normally, which scientific method of research is used to learn about people's opinions, attitudes, and values?
   a. Survey
   b. Experimental
   c. Naturalistic observation
   d. Case study
8. Experimental research, as opposed to correlational research, is characterized by which of the following?
   a. Measuring more than two variables
   b. Correlations between independent and dependent variables
   c. How behavior is measured
   d. The manipulation and control of variables
9. What is the most controversial concern of the ethical guidelines for conducting research with humans?
   a. Debriefing
   b. Deception
   c. The protection of confidentiality
   d. Informed consent

POP QUIZ

10. Which type of sample would *least* likely be demographically biased?
    a. Representative sample
    b. Natural sample
    c. Random sample
    d. All of the above would show demographic bias.
11. If correctly used, the observational method frequently has which result for the researcher?
    a. Calculating the coefficient of correlation
    b. Developing hypotheses to be examined more completely through the use of other research methods
    c. Interpreting why the observed behaviors occurred
    d. Concluding that his or her original hypothesis was correct
12. Which of the following is not a limitation of the case-study method?
    a. The research project may last for months or even years.
    b. The researcher lacks investigative control over all potentially relevant variables.
    c. Not all relevant data or information are directly observed by the researcher.
    d. There is a potential of bias by the researcher.
13. In addition to your test score, your professor will give you only one piece of information concerning your test performance relative to that of your classmates. Which of the following statistics would give you the most useful information?
    a. Mean
    b. Percentile
    c. Standard deviation
    d. Median
14. In the following distribution of scores—1, 4, 4, 5, 6, 8, 8, 8, 10—what is the median score?
    a. 6
    b. 7
    c. 8
    d. 9
15. What is the most important question to ask when evaluating a survey study?
    a. Was there a control group?
    b. Was there bias in the selection of subjects?
    c. Have there been other surveys that confirm the results of this study?
    d. Did a reputable professional conduct the survey?

Answer Key: 1.F 2.F 3.F 4.F 5.T 6.c 7.a 8.d 9.b 10.a 11.b 12.a 13.b 14.a 15.b

(Shutterstock)

The Biology of Behavior

Until fairly recently, both laypersons and psychologists viewed behaviors such as thinking, feeling, and remembering as something more than complex interactions between cells in the brain. For example, the mind was thought to consist of nonphysical entities such as a spirit or soul. However, most researchers are now convinced that the mind consists of a collection of processes that will eventually be explained in terms of molecular events in the brain. In fact, neuroscientists are making remarkable progress toward this end.

This chapter provides a very broad overview of what we know about the biology of behavior. Biological structures including individual neurons, the central and peripheral nervous systems, and the endocrine systems are examined to see how they influence or regulate behaviors. We begin with a look at the nervous system.

3.1 Overview of the Nervous System: Organization and Function

All of our activities—sensing, perceiving, moving, feeling, thinking, and remembering—depend on the functioning of our nervous systems. Although the brain is the hub of the **nervous system**, it is by no means the sole component. The nervous system of humans and all other vertebrates (organisms with a spinal cord encased in bone) consists of two major parts: the central nervous system and the peripheral nervous system. The peripheral nervous system has two subdivisions: the somatic and autonomic nervous systems. These components are all shown in Figure 3-1. We shall examine each of these parts in depth after a preliminary overview.

The **central nervous system (CNS)** consists of the brain and the spinal cord, which are the most protected organs of the body. Both are encased in bones and surrounded by protective membranes called meninges. The CNS plays a central role in coordinating and integrating all bodily functions. It acts as an intermediary between the stimuli we receive and our responses to those stimuli. For example, if your bare foot comes in contact with something hairy and wiggly when you put on a shoe, a message of alarm will travel through nerves in your legs, enter your spinal cord, reach your brain, and trigger a rapid response.

In the situation just described, the CNS acts as a processor of incoming and outgoing messages; however, the brain also sends commands directly to various parts of our bodies without first receiving an incoming stimulus. For instance, the decision to put on your shoes in the first place may have been the result of a decision to go outdoors—a decision that was unrelated to any immediate stimulus.

Our brains can also send commands to glands or organs. If you are dressed too warmly in an overheated classroom, for example, you will probably begin to perspire. This response is mediated by the hypothalamus, a small structure in the brain that serves many critical functions—including temperature regulation. When our bodies become too hot, the hypothalamus signals our sweat glands to perspire, which helps us regulate body temperature.

Although the CNS occupies the commanding position in the nervous system, it could neither receive stimuli nor carry out its own directives without the **peripheral nervous system (PNS)**. The peripheral nervous system transmits messages to and from the central nervous system. It is subdivided into two functional parts, the somatic nervous system and the autonomic nervous system—both of which are discussed later in this chapter. Before looking further at both the central and peripheral nervous systems, it is helpful to have an understanding of the building blocks that are the basis of the entire nervous system. The individual cells that make up the nervous system are called neurons.

Nervous System A network of specialized cells called neurons and glia that coordinate action and transmit signals between different parts of the body; consists of the central nervous system and the peripheral nervous system

Central Nervous System (CNS) The part of the nervous system that consists of the brain and the spinal cord

Peripheral Nervous System (PNS) Portion of the nervous system that transmits messages to and from the central nervous system that consists of the somatic nervous system and the autonomic nervous system

Figure 3-1 Divisions of the Nervous System

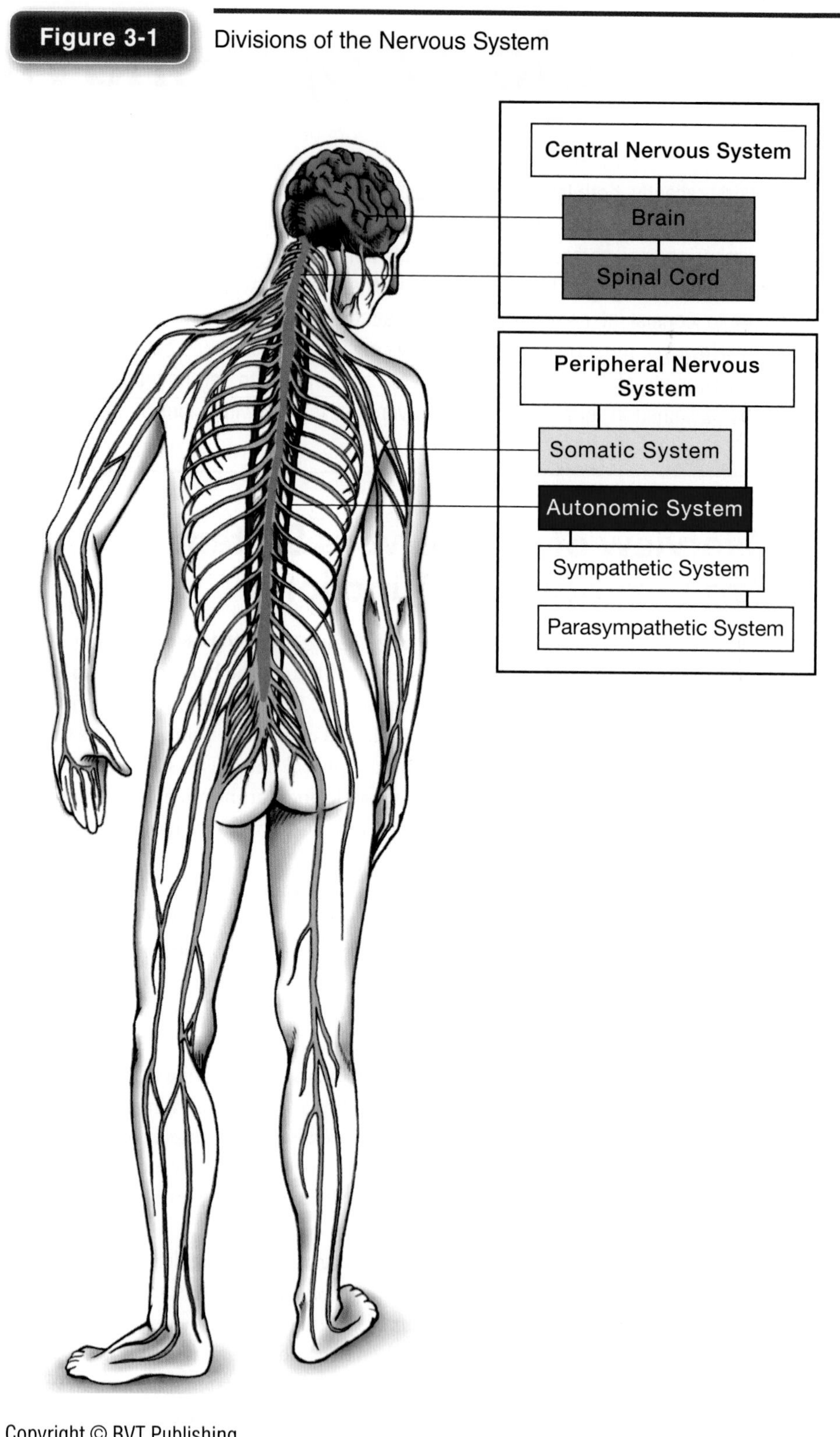

3.2 Neurons: Basic Units of the Nervous System

Our bodies are made up of trillions of living cells including blood cells, skin cells, muscle cells, and bone cells. The cells of particular interest in this chapter are the cells of the nervous system called **neurons**. Neurons are the basic units of the brain and the rest of the nervous system. They vary in shape, size, and other characteristics according to their location and function in the nervous system. The brain, for instance, contains the most concentrated mass of neurons. It is impossible to say how many neurons it contains, but estimates range between 100 and 200 billion. Although this is an extraordinarily large number, sheer number alone does not account for the extreme complexity of the brain. Neurons throughout the nervous system are supported and protected by an even larger number of non-neuronal cells called **glia**. Although glial cells do not transmit electrical signals, they do provide essential functions to surrounding neurons. Several of these are discussed below.

There are three major classes of neurons. One class, called **sensory** or **afferent neurons**, carries messages to the CNS from receptors in the skin, ears, nose, eyes, and so forth. The brain and sometimes the spinal cord interpret these messages and send appropriate responses through a second type of neuron called **motor** or **efferent neurons**, which lead to muscles and glands. A third class of neurons, **interneurons**, resides only within the central nervous system. Since motor and sensory neurons rarely communicate directly, interneurons play a critical intermediary role. Without these connecting neurons, sensory messages would never result in the appropriate bodily responses. Interneurons also communicate directly with each other.

3.2a Neuron Structure

Although neurons vary in size, shape, and function, they share four common structures: the cell body, the dendrites, the axon, and the terminal buttons (see Figure 3-2).

The Cell Body or Soma

The **cell body**, or soma, is the largest part of the neuron. It contains structures that handle metabolic functions; it also contains the nucleus, which holds genetic information encoded in the cell's DNA. The cell body can receive impulses from other neurons, although the cell body is not the primary receptor.

The Dendrites

Neurons typically receive neural messages at one end and pass them on at the other end. The part of the neuron that receives most transmitted signals is a collection of fibers called **dendrites**, which extend out from the cell body like branches of a tree. (The word *dendrite* comes from the Greek word for tree.) Dendrites may receive information from a few to thousands of surrounding neurons. The more extensive the neuron's network of dendrites, the more connections can be made with other neurons. (Interneurons in the brain typically contain far more dendritic fibers than neurons in the spinal cord, or the peripheral nervous system.) Signals received by the dendrites are passed on to the cell body, which in turn passes them through the axon.

Neuron Type of cell that is the basic unit of the nervous system (A neuron typically consists of a cell body, dendrites, and an axon. Neurons transmit messages to other neurons and to glands and muscles throughout the body.)

Glia Non-neuronal cells that provide support and protection for neurons throughout the nervous system (The name glia comes from the Greek term for glue.)

Sensory Neuron Neuron or nerve cell that carries messages to the CNS from receptors in the skin, ears, nose, eyes, and other receptor organs—also known as afferent neuron

Motor Neuron Neuron that transmits messages from the central nervous system to muscles or glands—also known as efferent neuron

Interneuron Neuron of the central nervous system that functions as an intermediary between sensory and motor neurons

Cell Body The largest part of a neuron, containing the nucleus as well as structures that handle metabolic functions

Dendrite Branch-like extensions from a neuron with the specialized function of receiving messages from surrounding neurons

Figure 3-2 Neuron Structure

Neural messages from surrounding neurons are received by the dendrites and then passed down to the cell body, the portion of the neuron in which metabolic functions take place. The neural signal then moves along the axons, which are the transmitting fibers of the neuron. Terminal buttons at the end of each axon release chemicals called neurotransmitters, which activate adjacent neurons, thereby allowing the messages to continue. This activation can take the form of either excitation or inhibition. Neural excitation facilities the transmission of neural messages, while neural inhibition retards or prevents the transmission of these signals.

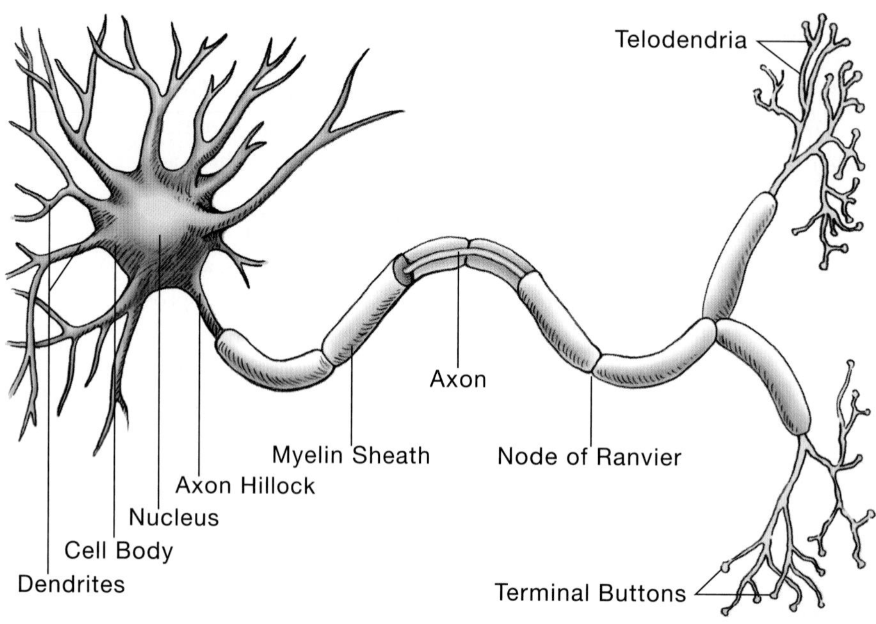

The Axon

The **axon** is a slender, extended fiber that takes a signal from the cell body at a point called the axon hillock and transmits the signal along its entire length, which may range from two or more feet in spinal cord and PNS neurons to a tiny fraction of an inch in brain neurons. The axon may divide into two or more major branches called collaterals, thereby increasing its capacity to communicate with other neurons. Axons may be myelinated or unmyelinated. Myelin is a type of glial cell that wraps around the axon, providing it with insulation. Most peripheral axons are myelinated, and most (but not all) of the axons in the brain are unmyelinated. Myelin serves both to insulate the axon, much like insulation on a wire, and to increase the speed of conduction along the axon. It is myelin that gives brain tissue, which is normally grayish brown, a white color (white vs. gray matter).

Axon Extension of a neuron that transmits an impulse from the cell body to the terminal buttons on the tip of the axon

Terminal Button Swollen bulb-like structure on the end of a neuron's axon that releases chemical substances known as neurotransmitters

The Terminal Buttons

The transmitting end of the axon consists of small bulblike structures known as terminal buttons. The **terminal buttons** store and release chemical substances (called neurotransmitters) that enable nerve impulses to cross from one neuron to adjacent neurons. In the next section we will look at this complex process.

3.2b Neural Transmission

People often think of the nervous system as a vast, complex network of interconnected wire-like structures. However, the multitudes of neural circuits or pathways within the central nervous system are not at all like electrical wires. Instead of a continuous filament, these circuits are made up of perhaps hundreds of thousands of individual neurons. In order for a message to travel from neuron to neuron, it must move from the terminal buttons at the end of one neuron's axon to the dendrites or cell body of an adjacent neuron. The process by which impulses are transmitted in the CNS is not just electrical, as it is in the wiring system of a house; it also involves chemical substances called neurotransmitters. The entire process is called neural transmission.

BVT*Lab*

Flashcards are available for this chapter at **www.BVTLab.com.**

Within the peripheral nervous system, messages are transmitted along the extended axonal fibers of both motor and sensory neurons that are contained within bundles of neural fibers called *nerves*. These fibers extend as continuous structures from sensory receptors or muscles to the CNS. For example, a sensory message from a pain receptor in the skin of your finger is transmitted along a single axonal fiber that extends the length of your arm to a point at which it enters the spinal cord and transfers its message to an interneuron.

3.2c Neuron Electrical Activity

Like all other cells, a neuron is surrounded by a membrane. This membrane acts as a kind of skin that permits the cell to maintain an internal environment different from the fluid outside the membrane. On both sides of the cell membrane are many particles called ions, which carry either a positive or a negative electrical charge. Ions that are particularly important in electrical conduction are negatively charged organic ions (An^-) and chloride ions (Cl^-), and positively charged sodium ions (Na^+) and potassium ions (K^+). If the cell membrane did not act as a barrier, these ions would be equally distributed both inside and outside of the neuron. However, some charged particles, such as the negative organic ions, do not pass through the cell membrane to the surrounding fluid. The membrane is only semipermeable to other ions. For instance, sodium and potassium ions pass through only when ion channels, or "gates," are open for them.

Resting Potential

Thus, the negative and positive charges are unequal on either side of the membrane, and its interior has a negative electrical potential with respect to its exterior. This phenomenon is due primarily to a high concentration of positively charged sodium ions outside the membrane and more negatively charged organic ions on the inside. A neuron at rest (that is, not transmitting a nerve impulse) contains a net negative charge of about –70 millivolts (0.07 of a volt) relative to the outside environment. The membrane is said to be in a polarized state when the neuron is at rest.

This differential charge gives the resting neuron a state of potential energy known as the **resting potential**. In other words, it is in a constant state of readiness to be activated by an impulse from an adjacent neuron. Maintaining this resting potential allows the neuron to store the energy that it utilizes when it transmits an impulse. The resting potential is maintained because the membrane is impermeable to the positively charged sodium (Na^+) ions concentrated on the outside of the neuron (see Figure 3-3).

Resting Potential State in which a neuron is not transmitting a nerve impulse; a neuron in this state has a net negative charge relative to its outside environment, and this state of potential energy prepares it to be activated by a signal from an adjacent neuron

Figure 3-3 Neuron Electrical Activity

A. Neuron at rest: Resting membrane potential is maintained by distribution of charged ions on either side of the membrane.

B. Initiation of action potential: Action potential is initiated at axon hillock by movement of sodium (Na^+) ions to inside of cell.

C. Movement of action potential: Action potential moves (propagates) along axon as Na^+ ions enter cell. After an action potential occurs, membrane potential is restored by movement of both potassium (K^+) and sodium (Na^+) ions to their resting potential positions.

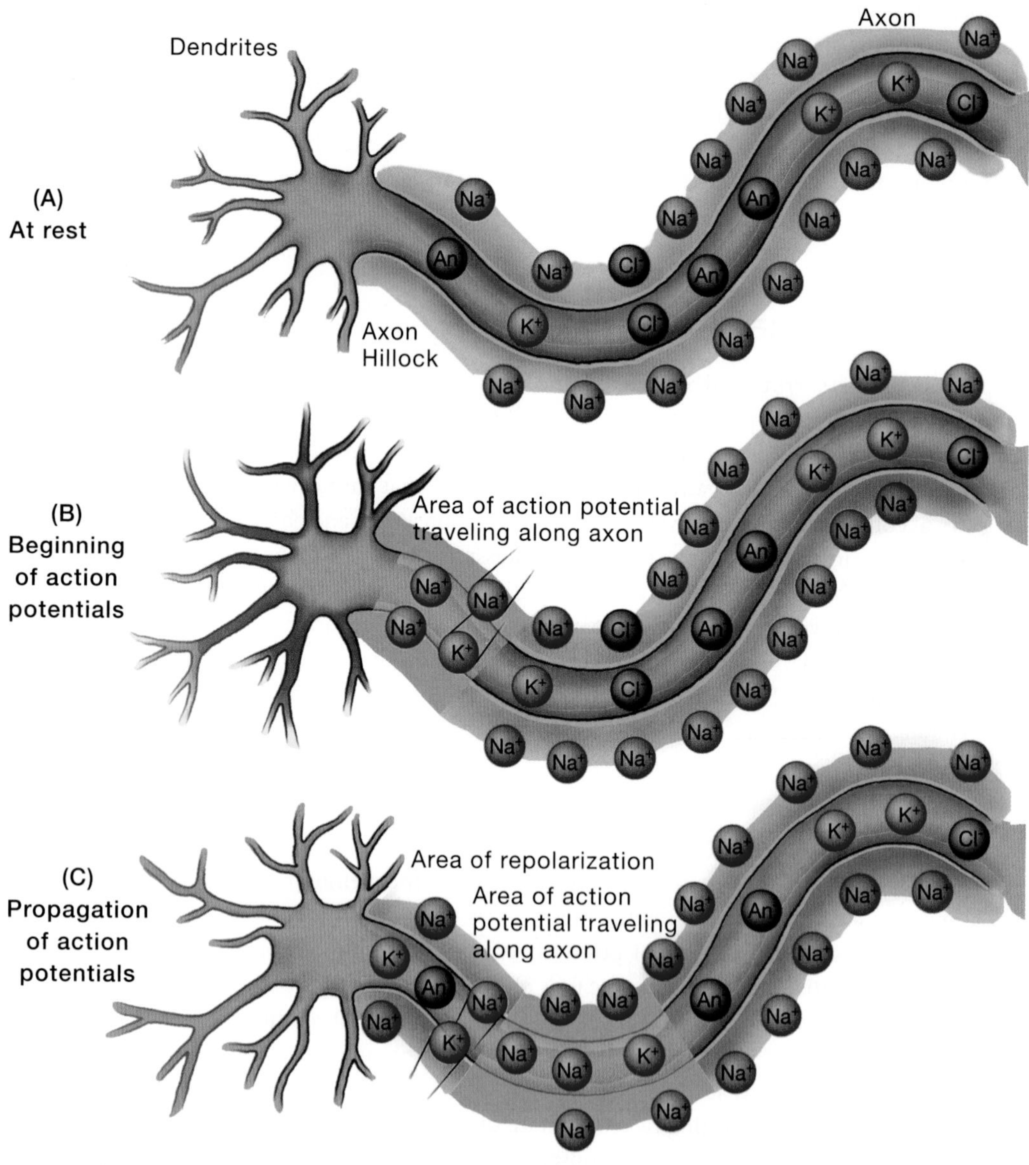

Graded Potentials

The resting potential is disturbed when an impulse is received from another neuron. This disturbance is referred to as a **graded potential**, and its strength varies with the intensity of stimulation. If we were to measure the charge on the axon during a graded potential, we would observe a change from –70 millivolts to perhaps –60 millivolts, depending on the amount of stimulation the cell receives. A graded potential by itself is of little consequence. However, when several graded potentials occur simultaneously or in rapid succession, together they may be sufficient enough to depolarize the neuron to a threshold value (the minimum voltage change sufficient to activate a response) of about –55 millivolts.

The determination of whether or not a graded potential is sufficient to bring the axon to its threshold level is made at the **axon hillock**, a specialized region of the cell body near the base of the axon (refer back to Figure 3-2). Like a tiny computer, the axon hillock combines and totals all the graded potentials that reach it. If the sum of these graded potentials reaches a sufficient magnitude or threshold, a sudden depolarization begins at the axon hillock. This depolarization is referred to as an action potential.

Action Potentials

An **action potential** is initiated when the axon is depolarized to its threshold level (approximately –55 millivolts). When the membrane reaches this threshold level, a sudden complete depolarization results—that is, the axon goes from about –55 millivolts to approximately +40 millivolts. This rapid depolarization is the result of the membrane changing its permeability to sodium (Na^+) ions. When the membrane is no longer impermeable to Na^+, it enters the cell, bringing the charge on the inside of the membrane to a positive value (about +40 millivolts). Some potassium ions begin to leave the axon at this time because the electrical gradient inside the axon becomes weakened as sodium ions enter. However, the number of potassium ions that leave the inside of the axon is far outweighed by the number of sodium ions that enter.

The change in permeability to Na^+ is extremely brief, and the closing of the Na^+ gates and the rapid expulsion of Na^+ from within the axon quickly restore the resting potential. Sodium ions are repelled because of the positive charge now inside the membrane. As sodium ions leave, the charge across the membrane returns to its resting state. In fact, an excess of sodium outflow briefly hyperpolarizes the membrane. This complete process for an action potential takes about one millisecond (0.001 of a second).

The action potential is an electrical signal that flows (or propagates) along the entire surface of the axon to the terminal button. Once the action potential reaches the terminal button, it initiates the release of neurotransmitter substances that carry the message to adjacent neurons.

The All-or-None Law

Unlike the graded potential, the strength of an action potential does not vary according to the degree of stimulation. Once a nerve impulse is triggered within an axon, it is transmitted the entire length of the axon with no loss of intensity. Partial action potentials or nerve impulses do not occur; thus, an axon is said to conduct without decrement. Because of this, the nerve impulse in the axon is said to follow the **all-or-none law**: If the sum of the graded potentials reaches a threshold, there will be an action potential; if the threshold is not reached, however, no action potential will occur.

Graded Potential Voltage change in a neuron's dendrites that is produced by receiving a signal from another neuron or neurons

Axon Hillock A specialized region of the cell body near the base of the axon

Action Potential Electrical signal that flows along the surface of the axon to the terminal buttons, initiating the release of neurotransmitters

All-or-None Law An action potential will be passed through a neuron's axon as long as the sum of the graded potentials reaches a threshold (The strength of an action potential does not vary according to the degree of stimulation.)

According to the all-or-none law, a neuron fires at only one level of intensity. How, then, is it possible to distinguish between different levels of stimulus intensity—for instance, a loud noise and a soft sound, or a light or heavy touch? Consider this question before reading on.

The answer to our question lies in the fact that, even though a single neuron's impulse level is always the same, two important variables may still change the number of neurons affected by an impulse and the frequency with which neurons fire. Very weak stimuli may trigger impulses in only a few neurons, whereas very strong stimuli may cause thousands of neurons to fire. The frequency in which neurons fire can also vary greatly, from fewer than one hundred times per second for weak stimuli to as often as one thousand times per second for strong stimuli. Thus, the combination of how many neurons fire and how often they fire allows us to distinguish different intensities of stimuli.

The speed with which an impulse travels through a neuron varies with the properties of the axon, ranging from less than 1 meter per second to as fast as 100 meters per second (roughly 224 miles per hour). At least two important factors affect speed. One is the resistance to current along the axon; there is an inverse relationship between resistance and impulse speed, so that speed is reduced as resistance increases. Resistance is most effectively decreased by an increase in axon size, which helps explain why large axons, such as those in PNS neurons, tend to conduct impulses at a faster rate than do small axons.

However, if the nervous system had to depend only on axon size to transmit impulses quickly, there would not be enough room in our bodies for all the large axons we would need. Fortunately, a second property also helps to increase the speed of transmission of nerve impulses. Glial cells wrap around some axons, forming an insulating cover called a **myelin sheath**. One type of glial cell, the oligodendrocyte, forms the myelin within the CNS. In the PNS the insulating sheaths are built from another type of glial cell known as the Schwann cell. Between each glial cell the axon membrane is exposed by a small gap called a **node of Ranvier**, as shown in Figure 3-2.

In these myelinated neurons, nerve impulses do not travel smoothly down the axon. Instead, they jump from node to node, in a process called *saltatory conduction* (from the Latin *saltare*, meaning to leap). Saltatory conduction is so efficient that a small myelinated axon can conduct a nerve impulse just as quickly as an unmyelinated axon 30 times larger. Because myelin plays such a critical role in the nervous system, it follows that the effects of certain diseases (such as *multiple sclerosis [MS]*) that involve progressive breakdown in these insulating sheaths can be devastating. In MS, the loss of myelination may short-circuit or delay the transmission of signals from the brain to the muscles of the arms and legs. As a consequence, a person with MS often experiences a weakness or loss of control over the limbs.

Myelin Sheath Insulating cover around some axons that increases a neuron's ability to transmit impulses quickly; made of specialized cells called glial cells

Node of Ranvier Small gap or exposed portion of the axon of a neuron between the glial cells that form the myelin sheath

Synapse Includes the synaptic gap and a portion of the presynaptic and postsynaptic membranes that are involved in transmitting a signal between neurons

3.2d Neurotransmitters and the Synapse

The transmission of an electrical impulse from one end of a neuron to the other provides only a partial explanation of how messages are transmitted. When an electrical nerve impulse reaches the end of an axon, it cannot flow directly into other neurons. This is because there is a space between neurons known as the synaptic gap. The space is minuscule—generally no more than five-millionths of an inch across—but the electrical impulse does not bridge it alone. A chemical process is necessary in bridging the synaptic gap. Figure 3-4 illustrates a **synapse**, which includes the membrane on the terminal button (the presynaptic membrane), the synaptic gap, and the membrane on the dendrite or receiving neuron (the postsynaptic membrane).

Figure 3-4 Synapse

Illustration of an active synapse with neurotransmitter being released into the synaptic gap

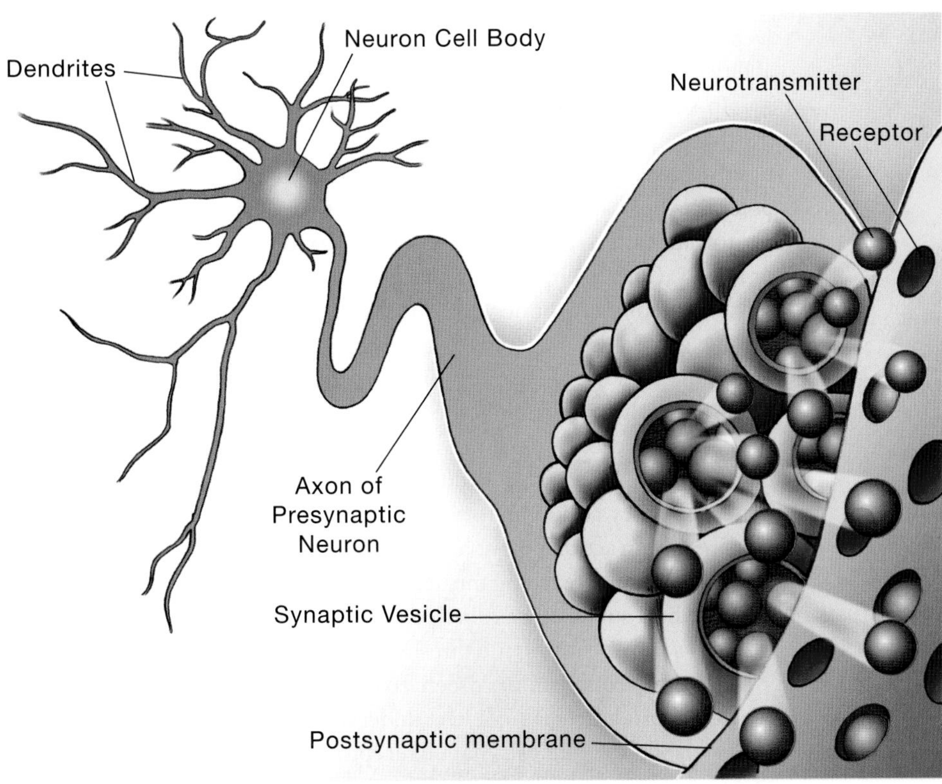

Many years ago, some scientists speculated that impulses were transmitted from neuron to neuron when something like an electric spark jumped the synaptic gap. We now know that this explanation is incomplete. Neurons communicate primarily through the release of chemicals. These chemical messengers, called **neurotransmitters**, are contained within tiny sacs in the axon terminal buttons called synaptic vesicles. Far less common is the electrical synapse, in which an electrical potential is conducted from one neuron to the next because of a tight junction between them. These rare electrical synapses will not be discussed here.

Steps in Neural Transmission

When the axon fires, the action potential travels along the axon to the terminal button. When it arrives at the terminal button, the membrane there changes its permeability to another ion, calcium (Ca^{++}). Calcium then enters the terminal button and allows the synaptic vesicles to migrate to the presynaptic membrane, where they release their contents into the synapse. The total amount of neurotransmitter released depends on how much Ca^{++} enters the terminal button. More intense stimulation produces a greater frequency of action potentials, which in turn allows more Ca^{++} to enter, thus increasing the amount of neurotransmitter released.

Neurotransmitter Chemical substance produced and secreted by neurons that causes a change in the receiving neuron's resting potential

Excitatory and Inhibitory Synaptic Events

The postsynaptic membrane of the receiving neuron contains specialized receptor sites that respond to a variety of neurotransmitters. Neurotransmitters act on these receptor sites to produce a rapid change in the permeability of the postsynaptic membrane. Depending on the receptor site and the type of neurotransmitter, this change in permeability can either excite or inhibit action potentials in the receiving neuron.

In simplified terms, neurotransmitters exert their effects by opening gates or channels in the postsynaptic membrane, letting ions of one kind or another pass through. If positively charged sodium ions enter, the membrane is excited or depolarized, and graded potentials are caused. Neurotransmitters that cause these changes are called excitatory neurotransmitters, and their effects are referred to as **excitatory postsynaptic potentials**, or **EPSPs**. Conversely, if positively charged potassium ions pass to the outside of the postsynaptic membrane, or negatively charged chloride ions enter, the membrane is inhibited and the graded potential results in making the membrane more negative (a process called hyperpolarization). Neurotransmitters that act in this way are called inhibitory neurotransmitters, and their effects are called **inhibitory postsynaptic potentials**, or **IPSPs**.

Since hundreds or even thousands of axon terminals may form synapses with any one neuron, EPSPs and IPSPs may be present at the same time. The combination of all these excitatory and inhibitory signals determines whether or not the receiving neuron will fire. For an action potential to occur, EPSPs must not only predominate, they must do so to the extent of reaching the neuron's threshold. To prevent this from happening, there needs to be a sufficient number of IPSPs present to prevent the algebraic sum of EPSPs and IPSPs from reaching the threshold of depolarization.

Some neurotransmitters seem to be exclusively excitatory or inhibitory; others seem capable of producing either effect under different circumstances. When transmitters have both capabilities, the postsynaptic receptor site determines what the effect will be. Thus, these neurotransmitters may have an inhibitory effect at one synapse and an excitatory effect at another.

Neurotransmitters interact with receptors on the postsynaptic cell membrane to change its electrical potential. If the change is sufficient to depolarize the cell membrane, a graded potential is initiated, thus beginning the cycle outlined earlier in Figure 3-3.

Neurotransmitter Breakdown and Reuptake

What keeps the supply of neurotransmitters from being exhausted? There are several answers to this question. First, the raw materials used in the manufacture of neurotransmitters are constantly being replenished by the cell body. Second, some neurotransmitters are broken down by enzyme action once they have accomplished their function. Their breakdown products then reenter the terminal buttons to be recycled for further use. Third, in many cases the transmitter substance is retrieved intact in a process called reuptake. The breakdown and reuptake processes, which are essential for normal neuronal functioning, can be influenced by a number of drugs. For example, drugs such as amphetamine and cocaine inhibit the reuptake of several neurotransmitters, resulting in heightened alertness and activity. Finally, neurons contain regulatory mechanisms that prevent depletion and regulate their sensitivity to neurotransmitters.

Excitatory Postsynaptic Potentials (EPSPs) Effects that result from excitatory neurotransmitters causing a depolarizing graded potential to occur on the dendrite or cell body of a receiving neuron, making the receiving neuron more likely to fire

Inhibitory Postsynaptic Potentials (IPSPs) Effects that occur when inhibitory neurotransmitters cause a hyperpolarizing graded postsynaptic potential on a receiving neuron, making the receiving neuron less likely to fire

Identifying Neurotransmitter Substances

As much as scientists know about the electrochemical process of transmitting nerve impulses, the neurotransmitters themselves have been hard to identify because they often

Table 3-1 Chemicals Known to Be Major Neurotransmitters

Neurotransmitter Effects	Location	Functions
Acetylcholine (ACh) Excitatory	Cortex, spinal cord, target organs activated by parasympathetic nervous system.	Excitation in brain. Either excitations or inhibition in target organs of PNS. Involved in learning, movement, memory.
Norepinephrine (NE) Excitatory	Spinal cord, limbic system, cortex, target organs of sympathetic nervous system	Arousal of reticular system. Involved in eating, emotional behavior, learning, memory.
Dopamine (DA) Inhibitory	Limbic system, basal ganglia, cerebellum	Involved in movement, emotional behavior, attention, learning, memory, and reward.
Serotonin (SE) Inhibitory	Brain stem, most of the brain	Involved in emotional behavior, arousal, and sleep.
Gamma-amino-butyric acid (GABA) Inhibitory	Most of the brain and spinal cord	Involved in regulating arousal: Major inhibitory neurotransmitter in brain.
Endorphins Inhibitory	Spinal cord, most of the brain	Functions as a natural analgesic for pain reduction; involved in emotional behavior, eating, and learning.
Glutamate Excitatory	Brain and spinal cord	Major excitatory neurotransmitter in the brain. Involved in learning.

occur in very small quantities. Table 3-1 presents a list of several important substances known to be neurotransmitters, as well as the functions they are thought to perform. For a substance to be considered a neurotransmitter it must meet the following criteria: (a) It must be contained in the axon terminal buttons; (b) it must be released into the synapse when the neuron fires; and (c) it must cause a postsynaptic effect after it interacts with the receptor.

Neurotransmitter Substances

What are some of the chemicals that are known to serve as neurotransmitters? Although the list of substances so far identified as neurotransmitters is quite large, we will discuss a few neurotransmitters that are well understood and play important roles in our behavior.

Acetylcholine (ACh) **Acetylcholine** was the first neurotransmitter discovered. It plays an important role in motor movement because it is the neurotransmitter released from motor neurons onto muscle fibers to make them contract. In addition, acetylcholine appears to be involved in both learning and memory. Several toxins such as botulism, nerve gas, and black widow spider venom interfere with acetylcholine transmission and produce paralysis in their victims. A common disorder that involves acetylcholine is Alzheimer's disease, which involves a degeneration of acetylcholine neurons in the brain. Although the causes of Alzheimer's disease are not well understood, and at the present

Acetylcholine (ACh) The neurotransmitter that is released from motor neurons onto muscle fibers to make them contract; also involved in learning, memory, and cognition

there is no cure, drugs that increase the availability of acetylcholine are being used to treat the symptoms of this debilitating disease (Tabet, 2006; Hernandez & Dineley, 2012).

Norepinephrine **Norepinephrine** is distributed throughout the central and peripheral nervous systems. It is important in emotional arousal, stress, and perhaps learning and memory. Norepinephrine is a major excitatory neurotransmitter in the brain. Deficiencies in norepinephrine activity are linked to depression and attention deficit disorders (Arnsten & Pliszka, 2011; Haenisch, Bilkei-Gorzo, Caron, & Bönisch, 2009).

Dopamine **Dopamine** is located primarily in the brain; it is involved with the initiation of motor movement, attention, and learning and memory. In addition, the dopamine system mediates reward and pleasure, and it is the substance of addiction. We will see later in this chapter that all addictive drugs increase the activity of the dopamine system. Degeneration of dopamine neurons results in Parkinson's disease, which is a severe motor disorder. Parkinson's disease is, at the present, most effectively treated with a drug (l-DOPA) that is converted into dopamine in the brain (Hurley & Jenner, 2006; Nandhagopal et al., 2011; Volkow et al., 2007). In addition, the major psychotic disorder, schizophrenia, appears to be associated with an excess of dopamine activity in certain regions of the brain. We will examine this more closely in Chapter 16.

Serotonin **Serotonin**, distributed throughout the brain and spinal cord, is involved in the control of the sleep/wake cycle, mood, and appetite. Deficiencies in serotonin are associated with sleep disorders, aggression, eating disorders, and depression (Leu-Semenescu et al., 2010; Carrillo, Ricci, Coppersmith, & Melloni, Jr., 2009). The most widely prescribed antidepressants are a class of drugs called serotonin uptake inhibitors; Prozac® is an example of such an antidepressant. We discuss depression and its treatment in more detail in Chapter 16.

Gamma-Amino-Butyric Acid (GABA) **GABA** is the major inhibitory neurotransmitter in the brain and spinal cord. It plays an important role in regulating arousal and anxiety (Möhler, 2012). Drugs such as Valium® and Xanax® increase the activity of GABA, producing a calming effect and even sleep (Greiss & Fogari, 1980). Alcohol also increases GABA activity, contributing to its relaxing and sedative effects, as well as its disruptive effects on motor control and movement.

Endorphins **Endorphins** are a family of neurotransmitters chemically similar to opiates such as morphine. They are widely distributed throughout most of the brain. Extensive research has linked endorphins to an array of behavioral and mental processes, including inducing a sense of well being and euphoria, counteracting the influence of stress, modulating food and liquid intake, facilitating learning and memory, and reducing pain. Medical science is particularly interested in the pain-reducing properties of endorphins, some of which may be as much as one hundred times stronger than morphine. Researchers are hopeful that one day a synthetic version of these powerful brain chemicals will be developed for use in pain management (Janecka, Perlikowska, & Fichna, 2007).

Glutamate **Glutamate**, or **glutamic acid**, is an amino acid derived from glucose. Glutamate is one of the most important excitatory neurotransmitters in the brain. It is believed to play an important role in a process called long-term potentiation, which is a change in neuronal functioning that mediates some forms of learning and memory (Robbins & Murphy, 2006). In fact, recent research suggests that learning and memory

Norepinephrine A major excitatory neurotransmitter in the brain that is distributed throughout the central and peripheral nervous systems and is important in emotional arousal and stress

Dopamine A neurotransmitter involved with the initiation of motor movement, attention, and learning and memory; the dopamine system mediates reward and pleasure and is the substance of addiction

Serotonin A neurotransmitter involved in the control of the sleep/wake cycle, mood, and appetite; deficiencies in serotonin are associated with sleep disorders, aggression, and depression

Gamma-Amino-Butyric Acid (GABA) The major inhibitory neurotransmitter in the brain and spinal cord that plays an important role in regulating arousal and anxiety

Endorphins A class of neurotransmitter substances that function to inhibit the transmission of pain information; morphine and other opiates act by facilitating endorphin transmission

Glutamate (Glutamic Acid) An amino acid derived from glucose that plays an important excitatory function (found in MSG)

formation can be enhanced by drugs that facilitate glutamate activity (Kanno et al., 2012). The food additive monosodium glutamate (MSG) contains glutamate, and eating foods containing large amounts of MSG may produce symptoms of dizziness and numbness and actually impair learning and memory. This result is likely to be a consequence of overexciting glutamate neurons with excessive amounts of glutamate (González-Burgos, Velázquez-Zamora, & Beas-Zárate, 2009).

The above discussion is only a brief review of several of the most important neurotransmitter substances. New neurotransmitters and other neuroactive chemicals are still being discovered and investigated. Such discoveries have been central to the development of the science of molecular neurobiology, a field devoted in part to a study of the molecular bases of behavior. At present, the number of substances identified and believed to be neurotransmitters exceeds fifty.

(Shutterstock)

As its name implies, the food additive monosodium glutamate (MSG) contains glutamate. Eating foods containing large amounts of MSG, such as most fast foods like pizza, may produce symptoms of dizziness and numbness.

You may have noticed in Table 3-1 that different neurotransmitter substances seem to have different effects. Instead of transmission of a signal from one neuron to another, the function of some neurotransmitters is inhibitory (that is, instrumental in restraining or suppressing the transmission of neural impulses). This label may seem contrary to logic, especially since we have just seen that neurotransmitters are essential for the transmission of neural impulses. Sometimes, however, neurotransmitters have just the opposite effect.

3.2e Neurotransmitters and Behavior

Although the information about cell structures may seem like a collection of dry facts, it relates directly to our behavior. The most striking examples are associated with schizophrenia, depression, and the use of certain drugs.

Schizophrenia

Schizophrenia is a severe psychological disorder characterized by disturbed thought processes, delusions, hallucinations, and exaggerated inappropriate emotions. In many cases, drugs such as chlorpromazine, haloperidol, and clozapine, which have similar effects, can control the most bizarre symptoms of schizophrenia. Antipsychotic drugs inhibit the effects of dopamine in the brain, which has led some psychologists to hypothesize that the disorder may be linked to excessive levels of dopamine or above-normal reactivity to this neurotransmitter (Carlsson & Carlsson, 2006; Cooper, Bloom, & Roth, 2003; Sillitoe & Vogel, 2008). This argument has been supported by numerous studies that have found abnormalities in dopamine system functioning in schizophrenics.

Neurotransmitter systems are complex, and conclusions about the relationship between schizophrenia and dopamine are incomplete. Nevertheless, it seems probable that this disorder is related to the neurotransmitter dopamine and dopamine neurons in several brain regions.

(iStock)

Depression has been linked to the neurotransmitters norepinephrine and serotonin.

Depression

Numerous other studies have linked another disorder, depression, to two neurotransmitters: norepinephrine and serotonin. A group of drugs called tricyclics, among the most successful in relieving depression, are believed to increase the availability of both these neurotransmitters in certain areas of the brain. Another drug that has been quite successful in alleviating depression is Prozac, which appears to specifically increase serotonin activity in the brain by preventing its reuptake into the nerve terminal. Since studies have linked norepinephrine and serotonin to people's positive feelings, it seems possible that either insufficient brain levels of these chemicals or decreased responsiveness to these neurotransmitters may be related to depression. Research suggests that the antidepressant effects of drugs are much more complicated than merely increasing the levels of neurotransmitters in the brain. It appears that drug treatment for depression changes both the number and sensitivity of specific receptor sites, resulting in increases in norepinephrine and serotonin activity (Cooper et al., 2003; Nutt, 2008). As with research about dopamine and schizophrenia, however, research on depression is not yet conclusive. Chapter 16 explores the evidence linking neurotransmitter abnormalities to depression, schizophrenia, and some other psychological disorders.

As stated at the outset of the chapter, the nervous system is divided into two major divisions: The peripheral nervous system and the central nervous system. We will now examine these systems in some detail.

3.3 The Peripheral Nervous System

The peripheral nervous system (PNS) consists of all the nervous system structures located outside the central nervous system (CNS). Its primary purpose is to serve the CNS by transmitting information to and from the spinal cord and brain. Signals are carried to and from various structures to the spinal cord and the brain along bundles of myelinated axons called **nerves**. The PNS has two divisions: the somatic nervous system and the autonomic nervous system (see Figure 3-5).

Nerve A cable-like bundle of myelinated axons that transmits signals from various structures of the body to the spinal cord and the brain

Somatic Nervous System A part of the peripheral nervous system that transmits messages to and from major skeletal muscles and from sensory organs to the central nervous system

Autonomic Nervous System (ANS) A part of the peripheral nervous system that transmits messages between the central nervous system and the endocrine system, as well as to the smooth muscles of the heart, lungs, stomach, and other internal organs that operate without intentional control

3.3a The Somatic Nervous System

The **somatic nervous system** contains nerves that serve the major skeletal muscles, such as the arm and leg muscles. These muscles, often called striated because they appear striped or striated when seen under a microscope, carry out intentional movements directed by messages from higher brain centers. The somatic nervous system also contains nerves that transmit sensory information from the skin, muscles, and various sensory organs of the body to the spinal cord and brain.

3.3b The Autonomic Nervous System

The other division of the PNS, the **autonomic nervous system (ANS)**, controls the glands and the smooth muscles of the heart, lungs, stomach, intestines, blood vessels,

Figure 3-5 Functions of the Sympathetic and Parasympathetic Nervous Systems

These two systems work together to allow our bodies to react quickly to our environments and to relax.

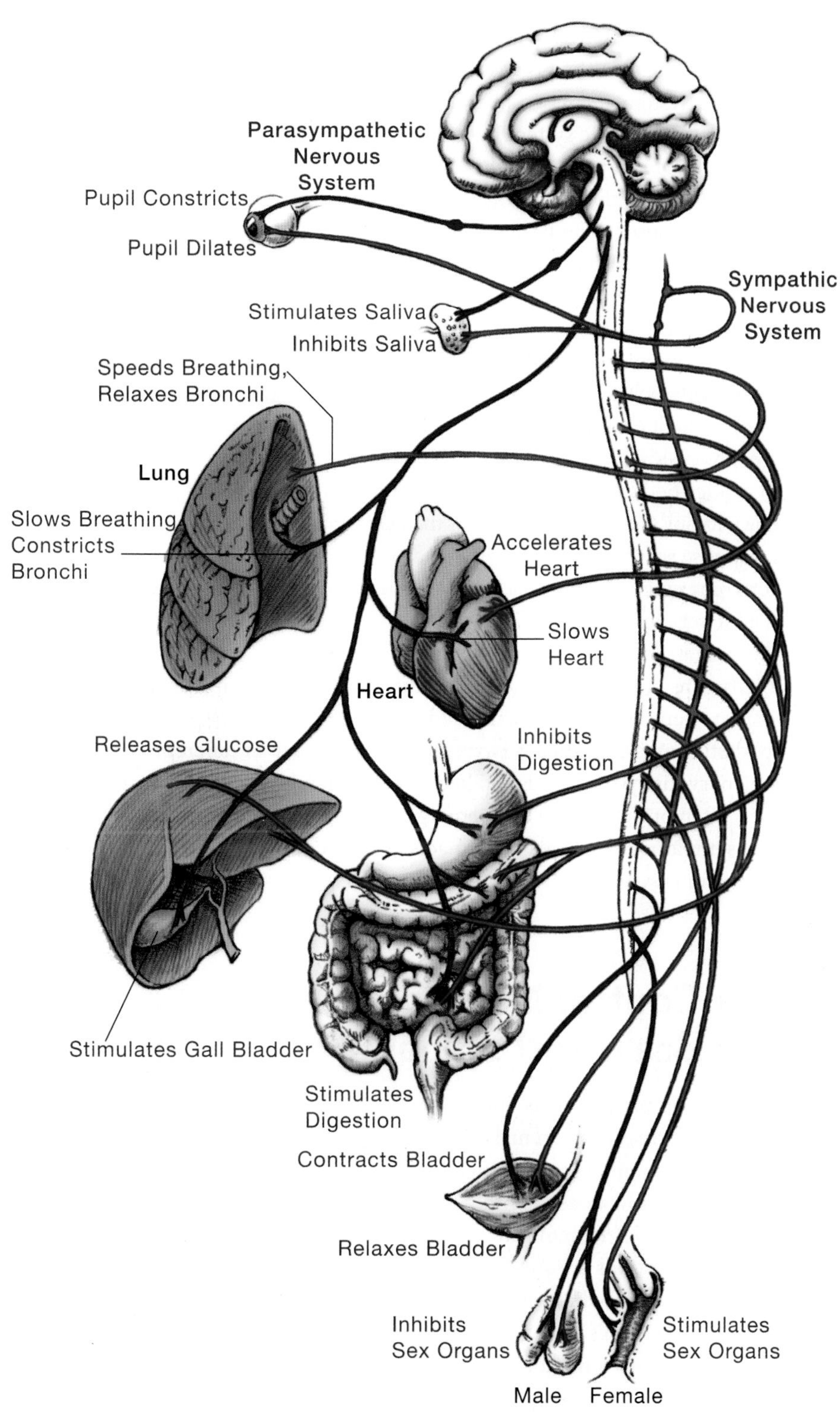

and various other internal organs. The ANS is named for the fact that the muscles and glands it serves operate reflexively without intentional or voluntary control. Thus they are autonomous, or self-regulating.

The autonomic nervous system is itself subdivided into two branches, the **sympathetic** and the **parasympathetic**. In most cases, each internal organ serviced by the autonomic nervous system has a separate set of connections with the sympathetic and the parasympathetic branches. These two distinct sets of connections operate quite differently, often having opposing effects on the organs they control, as shown in Figure 3-5. For example, the sympathetic system increases heart rate, dilates the pupils, and inhibits digestive activity; the parasympathetic system has the opposite effect in each case.

The sympathetic and parasympathetic systems do not operate in a counterproductive fashion, however. Instead, they work together to allow our bodies to function well when either relaxed or highly aroused. The balance between these two systems maintains our normal state, somewhere between extreme excitement and complete relaxation. However, there are times when we need an emergency source of energy, for example, when we are stressed or feeling strong emotion. At these times our sympathetic nervous systems come into play.

For instance, imagine that you are hiking in the wilderness when a bear suddenly confronts you. The result will probably be the classic response that prepares you (and probably the bear, too) for fight or flight. Your pupils dilate, your heart pumps like mad, and epinephrine (commonly called adrenalin) pours into your blood vessels. These effects produce distinct sensations in your body, but they also serve a critical function. Under the influence of the sympathetic nervous system, organs such as the heart operate at their upper limits.

This response serves us well in emergencies, whether we need to escape from a bear in the woods or rescue a child from a burning house. However our bodies cannot continue at this pace for very long. If they did, we would soon be exhausted. It is at this point that the parasympathetic nervous system comes into play, providing a braking mechanism for each of the organs activated by the sympathetic nervous system. This counter system helps us conserve energy and resources, and it is active in restoring our bodies to normal.

Sympathetic and parasympathetic responses take place in different ways. The parasympathetic nervous system tends to affect specific glands and organs independently of one another, often one at a time. In an emergency, however, there is no time to waste. As a result, the sympathetic nervous system acts as a unit, simultaneously mobilizing most or all of the various sympathetic effects outlined in Figure 3-5.

3.4 The Central Nervous System—The Brain and Spinal Cord

The average human brain weighs approximately 1,390 grams (or roughly 3 pounds). It can store more information than many great libraries combined, and its communication network has more potential interconnections between cells than the number of atoms in our solar system. How does the brain work? How do electrical impulses and chemical transmissions translate to memories, creating insights, intelligence, and feelings? The answers to these questions are still far from complete, but we are piecing together more and more clues. Much of what we know has to do with the brain's physical structure.

If the top of a person's skull were removed so that you could look straight down on the brain, you would see something like the image in Figure 3-6. In its natural state, the human brain looks much like a soft, wrinkled walnut, its outer surface filled with crevices and folds. The left and right sides appear to be separated by a long, deep cleft (called the longitudinal sulcus) that runs from the front to the back. The area of the brain visible

Sympathetic Nervous System A part of the autonomic nervous system that functions to produce emergency responses such as increased heart rate, pupil dilation, and inhibited digestive activity; works in tandem with the parasympathetic nervous system

Parasympathetic Nervous System A part of the autonomic nervous system that functions to conserve energy, returning the body to normal from emergency responses set in motion by the sympathetic nervous system

Figure 3-6 Bisected View of the Human Brain Showing the Locations of Major Structures and Areas

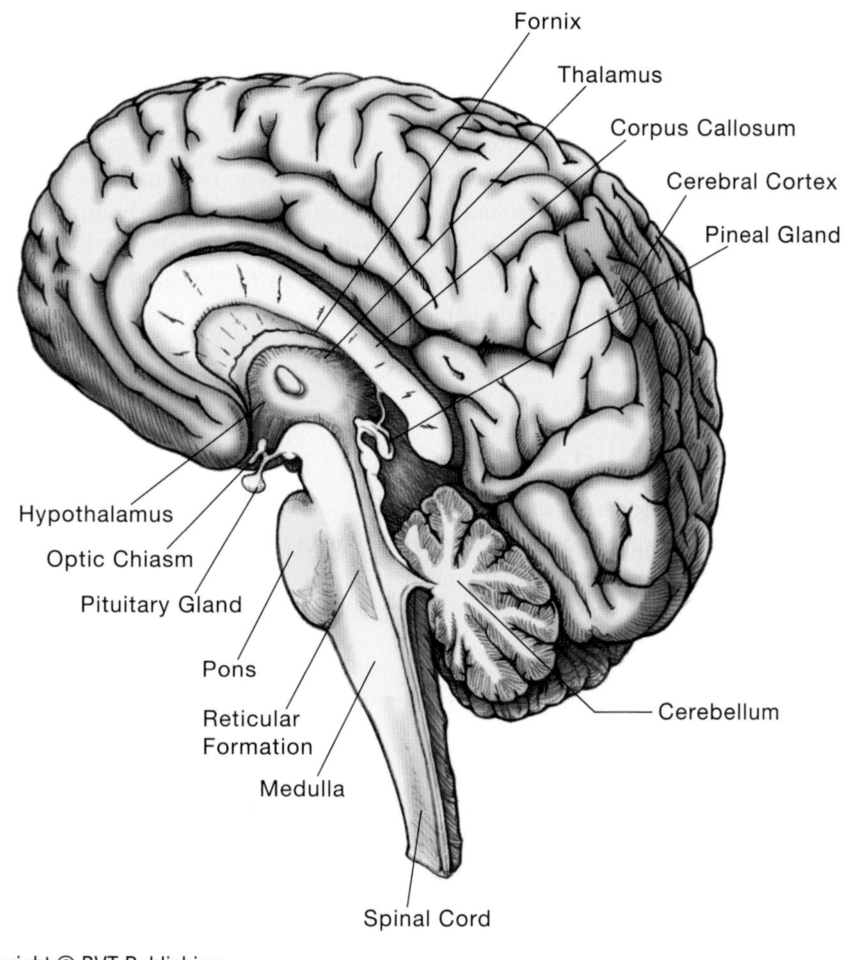

from the top is known as the cortex. The cortex is divided into two sides, or **cerebral hemispheres**; while not precisely identical, they are almost mirror images of each other.

Under the cortex are many other structures, as shown in Figure 3-6. Starting from the spinal cord and working roughly upward through the base of the brain, these include the medulla, the pons, the cerebellum, the reticular formation, and the structures of the limbic system, the hypothalamus, and the thalamus.

3.4a The Spinal Cord

Housed within a hollow tube-like structure composed of a series of bones called vertebrae, the spinal cord looks something like a long, white, smooth rope extending from the neck to the small of the back. Along the length of the spinal cord are spinal nerves that branch out between pairs of vertebrae. These nerves connect with various sensory organs, muscles, and glands served by the peripheral nervous system. The spinal nerves occur in thirty-one matched pairs, with one nerve of each pair connected to the right side

Cerebral Hemispheres The two sides (right and left) of the cerebrum

Medulla Structure found low in the brain that controls vital life support functions such as breathing, heartbeat, and blood pressure, as well as many reflexive functions, such as coughing and sneezing

of the spinal cord and its counterpart connected to the left side. Thus, the spinal cord can help coordinate the two sides of the body.

Because the brain occupies the commanding position in the CNS, the spinal cord is often overlooked in discussions of the biological bases of behavior. However, the spinal cord fills the very important function of conveying messages to and from the brain. In addition, the spinal cord controls reflexes, which are simple circuits of sensory and motor neurons that initiate responses to specific stimuli.

All complex behaviors require integration and coordination at the level of the brain. However, certain basic reflexive behaviors (such as a leg jerk in response to a tap on the kneecap or the quick withdrawal of a hand from a hot stove) do not require brain processing. Different parts of the spinal cord control different reflexes. For example, hand withdrawal is controlled by the upper spinal cord, whereas an area in the lower cord controls the knee-jerk response. The brain is not directly involved in controlling these simple reflexive responses, but it is clearly aware of what action has transpired (see Figure 3-7).

3.4b The Medulla

The **medulla** is the lowest part of the brain, located just above the spinal cord. This structure is in a well-protected location, deep and low within the brain. The placement is fortunate, since the medulla contains centers that control many vital life-support functions such as breathing, heart rate, and blood pressure. Even the slightest damage in a critical region of

Figure 3-7 Nerve Cell Body

A simple reflexive response involves the interaction of a sensory neuron, an interneuron, and a motor neuron. Interneurons function to both convey sensory information to the brain and to stimulate motor neurons to activate the withdrawal reflex.

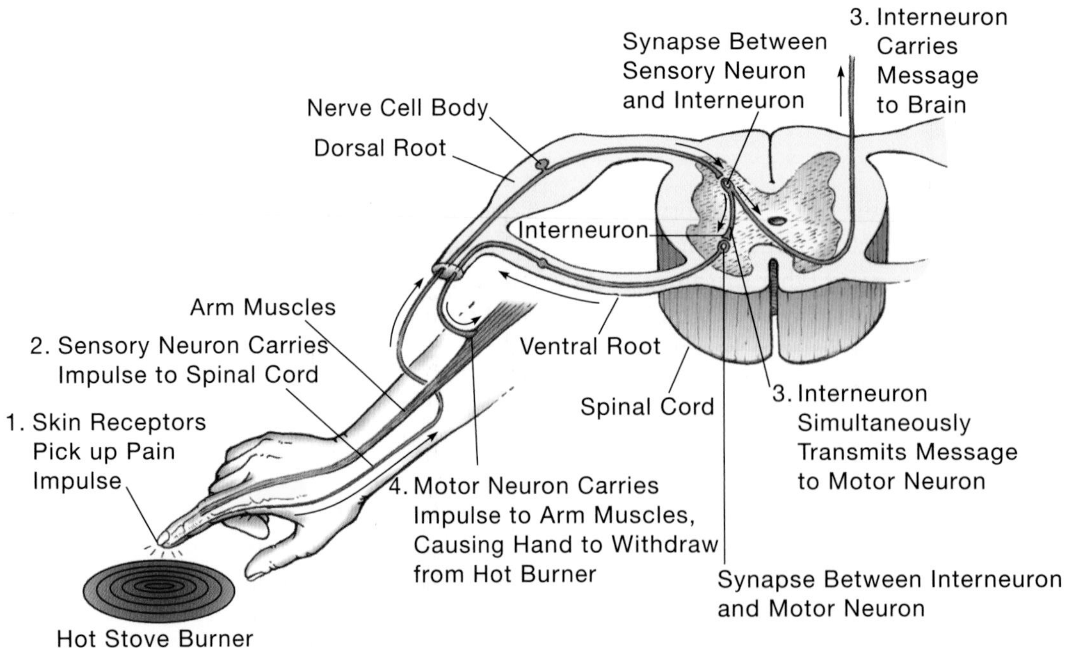

the medulla can cause death. The medulla also plays an important role in regulating other reflexive, automatic physiological functions such as sneezing, coughing, and vomiting.

Pons Brain structure located just above the medulla that functions in fine-tuning motor messages, programming species-typical behaviors, processing sensory information, and controlling respiration

Cerebellum Brain structure located beneath the overhanging back part of the cerebral hemispheres that functions to coordinate and regulate motor movements

3.4c The Pons

The **pons** is a large bulge in the lower brain core, just above the medulla. The pons plays an important role in fine-tuning motor messages as they travel from the motor area of the cerebral cortex down through the pons to the cerebellum. Species-typical behaviors (such as the feeding patterns of a particular species of animals) are mediated by the pons, which appears to program the patterns of muscle movement that produce these behaviors.

The pons also plays a role in processing some sensory information, particularly visual information. In addition, the pons contains specialized nuclei that help control respiration, mediate pain and analgesia, and influence facial expression.

3.4d The Cerebellum

The **cerebellum** is a distinctive structure, about the size of a fist, tucked beneath the back part of the cerebral hemispheres. It consists of two wrinkled hemispheres covered by an outer cortex. The cerebellum's primary function is to coordinate and regulate motor movements that are broadly controlled by higher brain centers. The cerebellum fine-tunes and smooths out movements, particularly those required for rapid changes in direction.

Figure 3-8 Medulla

Although it fills the very important function of conveying messages to and from the brain, the spinal cord is often overlooked in discussions of the biological bases of behavior.

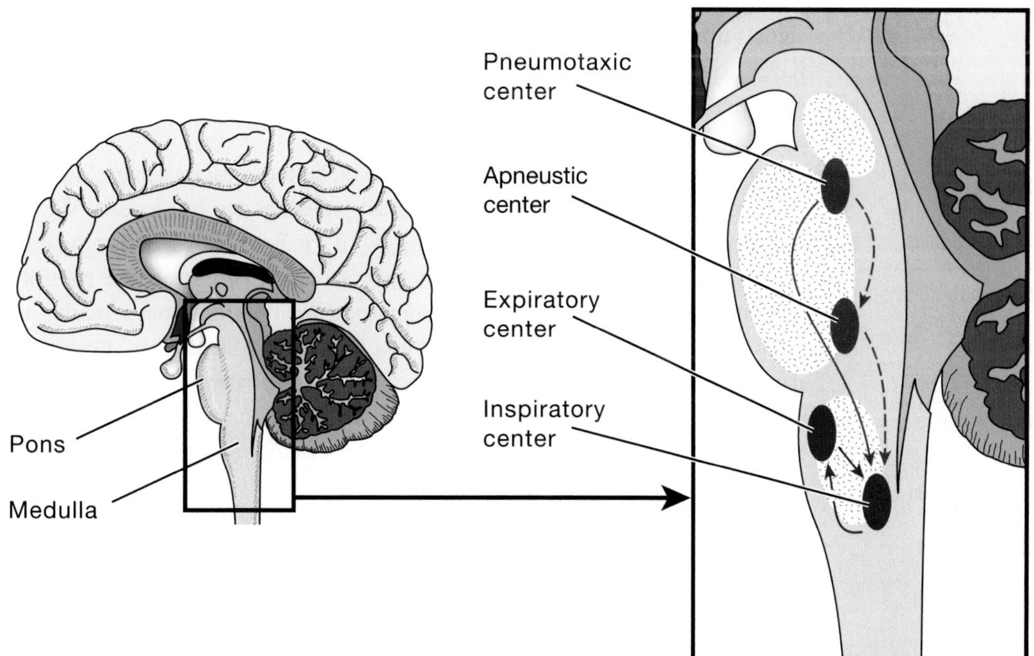

For example, when you reach out to catch a moving ball, your cerebellum is involved in the timing of your movements. This kind of timed movement clearly involves learning. Experiments with animals have shown that the activity of specific cells in the cerebellum changes during the course of learning and that blocking projections from cells within the cerebellum disrupts learned responses (Wikgren, Lavond, Ruusuvirta, & Korhonen, 2006).

Damage to the cerebellum results in awkward, jerky, uncoordinated movements and may even affect speech. Professional boxers are especially susceptible to slight damage to the cerebellum, which results in a condition called punch-drunk syndrome. Motor impairment following alcohol intoxication may also be related to cellular changes in the cerebellum. Researchers have demonstrated that alcohol facilitates inhibition in the cerebellum by activating GABA receptors.

3.4e The Reticular Formation

The **reticular formation** consists of a set of neural circuits that extend from the lower brain, where the spinal cord enters, up to the thalamus (refer back to Figure 3-6). Research has demonstrated that the reticular formation plays a critical role in consciousness and in controlling arousal or alertness. For this reason, it has become common to refer to this web-like collection of nerve cells and fibers as the **reticular activating system**, or **RAS**. These neurons are primarily noradrenergic; that is, they use the neurotransmitter norepinephrine. Stimulants such as amphetamine and Ritalin facilitate norepinephrine and increase alertness. Research suggests that attention deficit hyperactivity disorder (ADHD) results from insufficient, rather than excessive, arousal produced by the noradrenergic system, explaining why treatment with amphetamines is often successful (Pliszka, McCracken, & Maas, 1996; Halperin et al., 1997; Zikopoulos & Barbas, 2007; Hodgkins, Shaw, McCarthy, & Sallee, 2012).

Some of the neural circuits that carry sensory messages from the lower regions of the brain to the higher brain areas have ancillary or detouring fibers that connect with the reticular system. Impulses from these fibers prompt the reticular formation to send signals upward, making us more responsive and alert to our environment. Experiments have shown that mild electrical stimulation of certain areas within this network causes sleeping animals to awaken slowly, whereas stronger stimulation causes animals to awaken rapidly, with greater alertness.

The reticular formation also seems to be linked to sleep cycles. When we fall asleep, our reticular systems cease to send alerting messages to our brains. While sleeping, we may screen out our extraneous stimuli, with the possible exception of critical messages such as the sounds of thunder or a baby's cough. Although the role of the reticular formation in sleep is still not fully understood, we do know that reticular neurons inhibit sleep-active neurons during wakefulness (Osaka & Matsumura, 1994) and that serious damage to this structure may cause a person to be extremely lethargic or to enter into a prolonged coma. Recent evidence also suggests that patients in a severe coma may be aroused by electrical stimulation of the reticular system (J. Cooper, Jane, Alves, & E. Cooper, 1999; E. Cooper, Scherder, & J. Cooper, 2005). The role of the RAS on sleep and dreaming patterns is considered further in Chapter 5.

Reticular Formation Set of neural circuits extending from the lower brain up to the thalamus that plays a critical role in controlling arousal and alertness; also known as the *reticular activating system*

Reticular Activating System (RAS) See Reticular Formation

Limbic System Collection of structures located around the central core of the brain that play a critical role in emotional expression, as well as motivation, learning, and memory; key structures of the limbic system include the amygdala, the septal area, and parts of the hypothalamus

3.5 The Limbic System

The **limbic system** is the portion of the brain most closely associated with emotional expression; it also plays a role in motivation, learning, and memory. The limbic system

Figure 3-9 The Limbic System

Major limbic structures include the amygdala, the septum and septal nuclei, the fornix, the hypothalamus, and the cingulate gyrus.

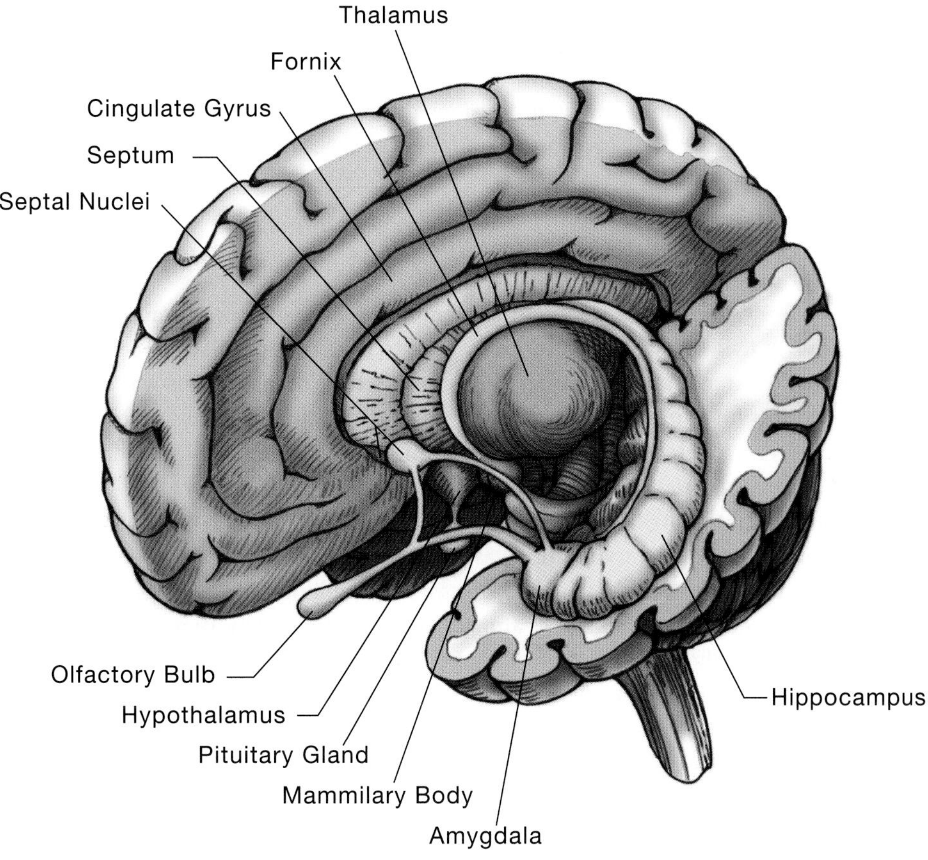

Adapted figure of "Primary Areas of the Motor Cortex and Somatosensory Cortex," article from "Specializations of the Human Brain" from *Scientific American,* September 1982, p. 182 by Norman Geschwind.

is a collection of structures located around the central core of the brain, along the innermost edge of the cerebral hemispheres. Figure 3-9 shows some key structures of the limbic system, including the amygdala, the hippocampus, the septal area, and parts of the hypothalamus. Damage to or stimulation of sites within this system may profoundly affect emotional expression, either by causing excessive reactions to situations or by greatly reducing emotional responses (Halpern & O'Connell, 2000).

3.5a The Amygdala

Amygdala A small limbic system structure located next to the hippocampus in the brain; plays an important role in the expression of anger, rage, fear, and aggressive behavior

The **amygdala**, a small structure next to the hippocampus, plays an important role in the expression of anger, rage, and aggressive and fear-motivated behavior. Electrical stimulation or surgical damage to some areas of the amygdala may cause an animal to go into a blind rage, attacking everything in sight, whereas on other parts of the amygdala the same procedures may produce extreme passivity, even in threatening situations. Researchers also believe that the amygdala plays significant roles in social cognition and in decision making. Amygdala damage in humans results in the inability of thoughts or memories to trigger emotional states. These emotional states are essential to normal social functioning and decision making. For example, when you see a snake, or even think of snakes, an aversive emotional state is produced motivating you to stay away. Likewise, when you make a decision to invest a large sum of money, an emotional state induced by the thought of either making more or losing it all guides your decision to invest, or not. People with amygdala damage lose these functions, making decisions difficult (Bechara & H. Damasio, 2002; Bechara, H. Damasio, & A. Damasio, 2003; Clark et al., 2008; Damasio, 1995).

3.5b The Hippocampus

Another limbic-system structure, the **hippocampus**, seems to be important for learning and memory. Individuals who experience damage to this structure have difficulty storing new information in memory. In one sad case, a man whose hippocampus was completely removed from both sides of his brain was unable to retain any new information in memory. He remembered skills and information learned prior to the surgery but was unable to store memories of anything that happened after the surgery. We discuss the implications of this finding in Chapter 7. Recent evidence suggests that the hippocampus may also undergo significant alterations as a result of stress during early development. For example, a study of women who had a history of childhood sexual abuse or posttraumatic stress disorder found that hippocampal size was decreased by 19 percent compared to control subjects who had no such history. Hippocampal function was also significantly reduced in these women (Bremner, et al., 2003; Nemeroff et al., 2006). Whether these deficits were significant enough to impair learning and memory is unknown.

3.5c The Septum

Still another area of the limbic system, the **septal area**, is associated with the experience of pleasure. James Olds demonstrated this in the 1950s in a series of experiments on brain stimulation in rats, which were mentioned in Chapters 1 and 2. Olds implanted electrodes in various regions of rats' limbic systems and wired the electrodes in a way that allowed the rats to stimulate their own brains by pressing a lever. When the electrodes were placed in sites within the hypothalamus and the septal area, the rats seemingly could not get enough stimulation. They would press the lever several thousand times per hour, often to the point of exhaustion. Because the animals labored so incessantly to produce this experience, such behavior was interpreted as meaning they liked the feeling. In fact, it seemed as though they were experiencing something akin to intense pleasure, which led to the label "pleasure center" (Olds, 1956).

Researchers have been more reluctant to study the effects of stimulating human limbic systems, although a similar procedure has been used in a few instances to achieve therapeutic effects. Robert Heath (1972), a Tulane University researcher, is one of the pioneers in this area. In the early 1970s he experimented with limbic system stimulation on two subjects, a female epileptic and a man troubled with emotional problems. Heath hypothesized that the pleasure associated with such stimulation would be of therapeutic value to these patients. When stimulation was delivered to the septal area, both individuals reported intense pleasure. The male patient, in fact, used a self-stimulating transistorized device to stimulate himself incessantly (up to 1,500 times per hour). According to Heath,

Hippocampus Structure in the brain's limbic system that seems to play an important role in memory

Septal Area Structure in the brain's limbic system that plays a role in the experiencing of pleasure

"He protested each time the unit was taken from him, pleading to self-stimulate just a few more times" (1972, p. 6).

In other kinds of motivated behavior, such as eating, drinking, and sexual behavior, organisms typically cease when they are satiated; however, this did not happen in experiments like those just described. Why? This question and related questions have led to the development of a separate area of study called intracranial self-stimulation (Olds & Forbes, 1981). Researchers are actively involved in seeking to understand the mechanisms that underlie the reinforcing effects of electrical and chemical stimulation of various brain sites. Research suggests that the dopamine system plays an important role in the mediation of reinforcement associated with *intracranial self-stimulation* as well as with drugs such as cocaine. When laboratory animals are administered drugs that temporarily block dopamine receptors in the brain, self-stimulation behavior is suppressed. The brain areas believed to be involved in pleasure and reward are referred to as the **mesolimbic-cortical system**, which includes the septum, the nucleus accumbens, and pathways leading to the frontal cortex.

3.5d The Hypothalamus

As its name **hypothalamus** indicates (*hypo* means below in Greek), this grape-sized structure lies below the thalamus. Although it is small, the hypothalamus has an important impact on several bodily functions and behaviors, and thus has been a major focus of many investigations (some of which are discussed in later chapters). The hypothalamus contains control mechanisms that detect changes in body systems and correct imbalances to restore *homeostasis*, the maintenance of a relatively constant internal environment. Shivering when we are cold and perspiring when we are hot are both homeostatic processes that act to restore normal body temperature, and both are controlled by the hypothalamus. The hypothalamus is also critical to motivation. It contains nuclei (densely packed concentrations of specialized cell bodies) that govern eating, drinking, and sexual behavior.

The hypothalamus is also the hub of the neuroendocrine system, which is discussed later in this chapter. This system—composed of the hypothalamus, pituitary gland, and various other hormone-secreting endocrine glands—is essential to a variety of behaviors, including sexual expression, reproduction, aggression, and reactions to stress. You may have heard the brain's pituitary gland described as the master gland since it secretes substances that control the activity of other glands throughout the body. However, the term *master* is somewhat a misnomer because the pituitary gland itself takes direction from the hypothalamus. The hypothalamus plays an integrative role in the expression of emotions, partly through interacting with the endocrine system and partly as a key member of the limbic system (Drevets, Price, & Furey, 2008).

3.5e The Thalamus

Located above the hypothalamus are two egg-shaped structures that lie side by side, one in each hemisphere. These are the left and right halves of the **thalamus**, a structure that has often been referred to as the brain's relay station because of the role it plays in routing incoming sensory information to appropriate areas within the cerebral cortex. Many of the cell nuclei in the thalamus also perform initial data processing before relaying information to the cortex.

Distinct regions in the thalamus are specialized for certain kinds of sensory information. For example, when you hear a sound, the message transmitted from your ears passes

Mesolimbic-Cortical System The system of dopamine-containing neurons that originate in the ventral pons, project through the nucleus accumbens and septum, and terminate in the frontal cortex; mediates the reinforcing effects of eating, sex, and addictive drugs

Hypothalamus Small structure located below the thalamus in the brain that plays an important role in motivation and emotional expression, as well as controlling the neuroendocrine system and maintaining the body's homeostasis; part of the limbic system

Thalamus Structure located beneath the cerebrum in the brain; functions as a relay station, routing incoming sensory information to appropriate areas in the cerebral cortex; seems to also play a role in regulating sleep cycles

through specialized neurons in an auditory area of the thalamus and is then relayed to the auditory cortex, an area in the cerebral cortex specialized for processing sound impulses. With the sole exception of the sense of smell, all sensory information is routed through specialized regions of the thalamus. In addition to this function, the thalamus also appears to work in conjunction with the reticular formation to help regulate attention and sleep cycles. Attention deficit hyperactivity disorder (ADHD) appears to be caused by disruptions in brain circuits between the thalamus and the frontal cortex (Dickstein, Bannon, Castellanos, & Milham, 2006; Qiu et al., 2011).

3.6 The Basal Ganglia

The **basal ganglia** consist of several subcortical brain structures, including the **caudate nucleus**, the **putamen**, and the **substantia nigra**. These structures receive messages from the cortex and the thalamus. The primary function of the basal ganglia is in the control and initiation of motor movement. People with damage to the basal ganglia have great difficulty in initiating movement. In addition, movement is often weak and poorly coordinated. One of the most common disorders of the basal ganglia is a condition referred to as Parkinson's disease. Parkinson's disease results from the destruction of the dopamine-containing neurons of the substantia nigra. This disease occurs most often in the elderly; however, it may occur in individuals in their late forties or fifties, such as actor Michael J. Fox. Parkinson's disease is characterized by difficulty in initiating movement, rigidity, and tremors, often in the hands. Parkinson's disease is commonly treated with drugs that increase dopamine neural transmission, but embryonic and stem cell transplants into the substantia nigra are perhaps the most promising treatments for the future (Correia, Anisimov, Li, & Brundin, 2006; Deierborg, Soulet, Roybon, Hall, & Brundin, 2008).

Basal Ganglia Neural structures involved in the initiation of motor movement and emotion; includes the caudate nucleus, putamen, and the substantia nigra

Caudate Nucleus A component of the basal ganglia located adjacent to the putamen; involved with the control and initiation of motor movement; an area of the brain affected by Huntington's disease

Putamen A component of the basal ganglia located adjacent to the caudate nucleus; involved with the control and initiation of motor movement; an area of the brain affected by Huntington's disease

Substantia Nigra A region of dark-colored neurons in the upper brainstem that sends axons to the caudate nucleus and to the putamen; an area of the brain affected by Parkinson's disease

Cerebral Cortex Thin outer layer of the brain's cerebrum (sometimes called the gray matter) that is responsible for movement, perception, thinking, and memory

3.7 The Cerebral Cortex

A major structure of the human brain is the **cerebral cortex**, the thin outer layer of the brain. The Latin word *cortex* means bark, and the cortex covers the brain in much the same way as bark covers a tree trunk. This portion of the brain is also called the neocortex, or new cortex, since it was the last part of the brain to develop during evolution (see Figure 3-10).

You may wonder why the cortex is wrinkled and convoluted. The answer has to do with the economics of space. The cortex's folds and wrinkles are nature's solution to the problem of cramming the huge neocortical area into a relatively small space within the skull. In the same way that crumpling a piece of paper allows it to fit into a smaller container than will a flat sheet, the cortex's folds permit it to fit into the fixed space of the skull. The size of the skull is essentially fixed because increases in skull size would require commensurate increases in the size of female pelvic structures to allow for full-term childbirth. As this example illustrates, evolutionary changes to one structure often require changes to others.

The body is represented in an upside-down fashion along the motor cortex and the somatosensory cortex. Larger cortical areas represent the hands and face, due to the fact that these areas require more motor control and sensation.

The cortex is gray in color, which is why it is often referred to as the gray matter of the brain. The gray color comes from the lack of the whitish myelinated coating that insulates the neural fibers of the inner part of the brain. The inner core of the brain is often called

Figure 3-10 Localization of Cortical Functions in the Four Lobes of the Left Cerebral Cortex

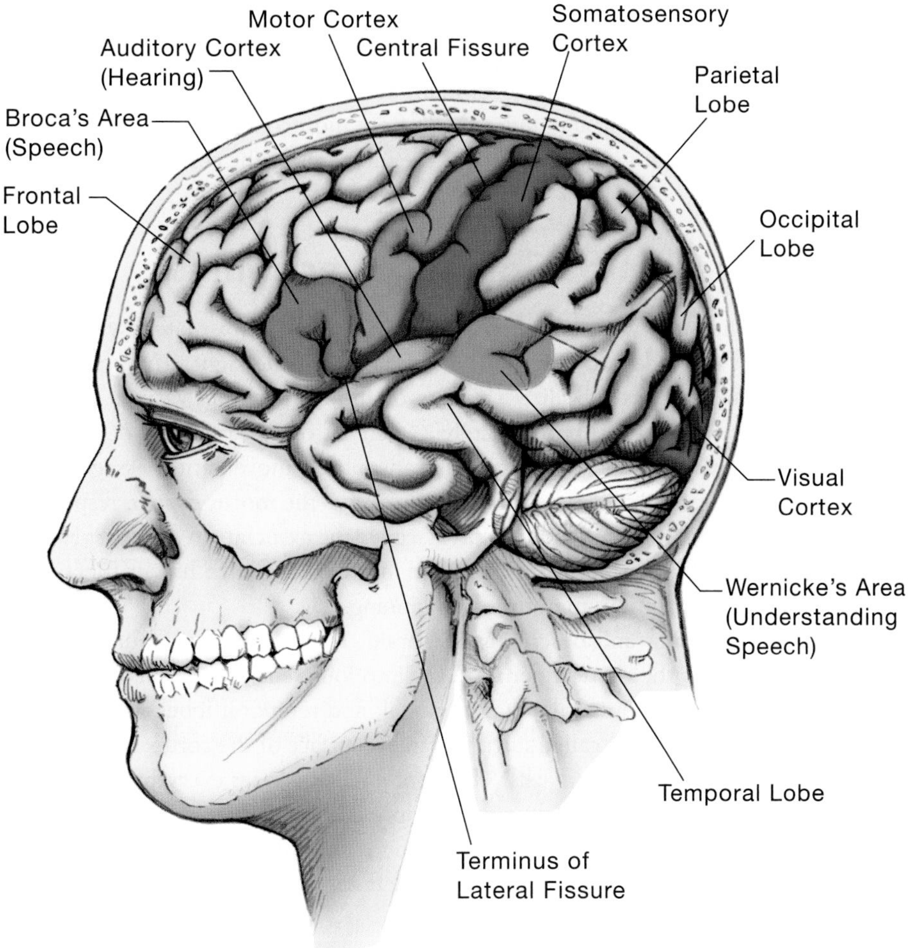

the white matter because it contains three kinds of myelinated neural fibers: *commissural fibers*, which pass from one hemisphere to another; *projection fibers*, which convey impulses to and from the cortex; and *association fibers*, which connect various parts of the cortex within one hemisphere. The cortex is mainly composed of the unmyelinated fibers (thus its grayish brown appearance) and cell bodies of billions of neurons. It is the part of the brain responsible for higher processes such as perceiving, thinking, and remembering.

The cortex is the part of the brain in which our memories are stored, we make decisions, we see a sunset or recognize and appreciate a melody, and we organize our worlds and plan for the future. Without a cortex, we would cease to exist as unique, functioning individuals. This is not to say that the cortex acts alone in running our lives. Instead, it functions as an executive, interpreting incoming information and making decisions about how to respond. As we go about our daily lives, our cerebral cortex constantly analyzes a vast array of incoming messages, evaluating them against stored information about past experiences and then making decisions that are translated into messages and sent to other neural structures, appropriate muscles, and glands.

Although we know the cortex functions in this manner, we are far from understanding precisely how it controls our lives. For example, while we know that memory is largely a cortical function, science has yet to explain exactly how the brain initiates a command to search for and retrieve a specific recollection. Nor are we even sure where specific memories are stored, or how the cortex can spontaneously generate new ideas and insights. Investigations of the higher mental processes of the cortex are likely to remain at the frontier of psychology and neuroscience for many years to come, and only time will tell if science is capable of unraveling and understanding the most complex of its functions. Let us examine, however, what we do know about the functions of the cortex.

3.7a Localization of Cortical Functioning

As mentioned earlier, the two hemispheres of the brain are approximately symmetrical, with areas on the left side roughly matched by areas on the right. To some degree, researchers have been able to localize a variety of functions within various regions of the two cortical hemispheres. Approximately 25 percent of the total area of the cortex is involved in receiving sensory messages or transmitting movement messages to our muscles. These regions are called the **sensory cortex** and the **motor cortex**, respectively. The remaining 75 percent of the cerebral cortex, called the **association cortex**, is involved in integrating sensory and motor messages, and in processing such higher functions as thinking, language, perception, memory, and planning.

To facilitate studying and describing the brain, researchers have found it convenient to divide each of the cortical hemispheres into four separate regions called lobes. These four regions—the frontal, parietal, occipital, and temporal lobes—are shown in Figure 3-10. Two long fissures, called sulci, within the surface of the cortex separate these four lobes, and also serve as landmarks. The frontal lobe includes everything in front of the *center sulcus*, except the forward tip of the temporal lobe. The parietal lobe lies behind the central sulcus and above the *lateral sulcus*. The temporal lobe lies under the lateral sulcus, and the occipital lobe lies at the back of the brain.

Sensory Cortex Region of the cerebral cortex involved in receiving sensory messages

Motor Cortex Region of the cerebral cortex that transmits messages to muscles and controls virtually all intentional body movements

Association Cortex The largest portion of the cerebral cortex (about 75 percent), involved in integrating sensory and motor messages as well as processing higher functions such as thinking, interpreting, and remembering

Frontal Lobe Largest, foremost lobe in the cerebral cortex; an important region for movement, emotion, and memory

Broca's Area Region of the left frontal lobe that is the primary brain center for controlling speech

The Frontal Lobe

The **frontal lobe** is the largest of the four lobes in each hemisphere and is an important center for both the motor and association cortexes. The motor cortex, a narrow strip just in front of the central sulcus along the back of the frontal lobe, contains neurons that contribute to the control, planning, and execution of motor movement. Virtually all body movement, from throwing a ball to wiggling a small toe, involves the motor cortex.

The body is represented in an upside-down fashion along the motor cortex; that is, neurons controlling facial muscles are at the bottom of the motor cortex, and those that control movement of the toes are at the top part. (Refer to Figure 3-11.) Larger areas of the motor cortex are devoted to the muscles involved in talking and moving the fingers, reflecting the critical role of speech and tool use in human behavior.

Nerve fibers that descend from the motor cortex on one side of the brain activate muscles on the opposite side of the body. That is, the right motor cortex controls movements of the opposite, or contralateral, side of the body.

In the nineteenth century, a French neurosurgeon, Pierre Paul Broca, reported that damage to another area of the left frontal lobe caused difficulty in speaking. Subsequent research has confirmed that this frontal lobe region, called **Broca's area** after its discoverer, is the primary brain center for controlling speech (refer back to Figure 3-10). People who

Figure 3-11 Primary Areas of the Motor Cortex and the Somatosensory Cortex

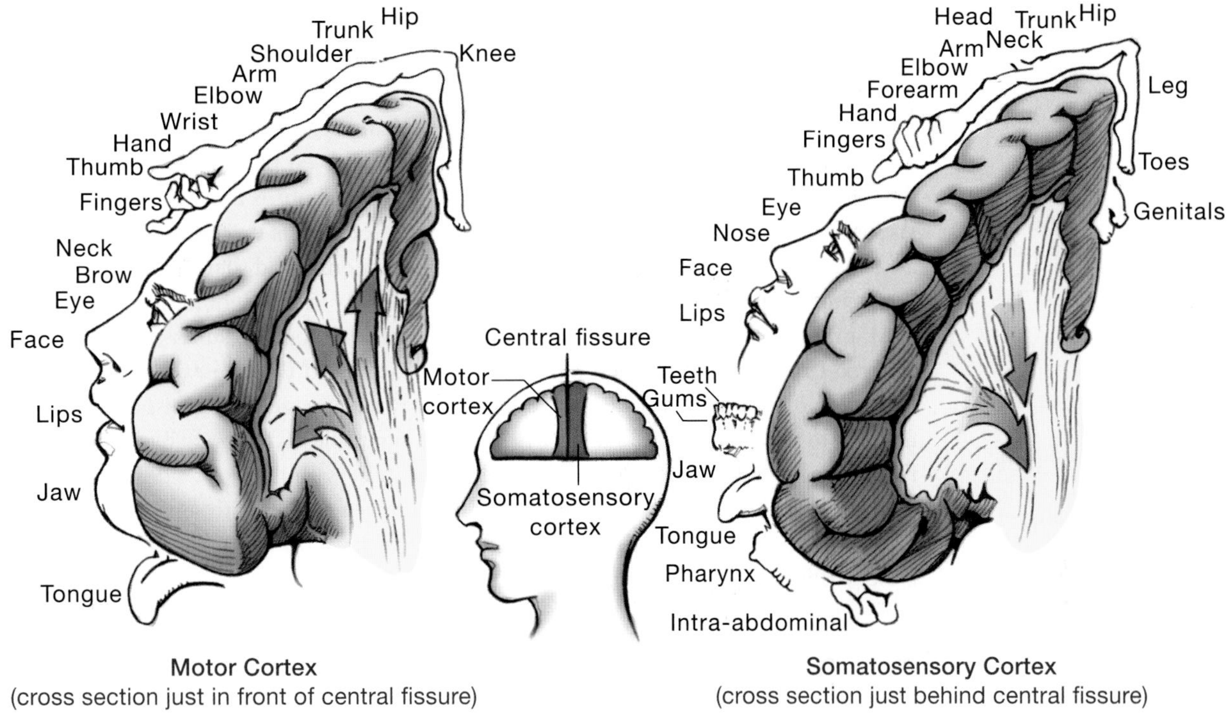

have been injured in this critical area typically have trouble articulating the right words to describe things, even though their comprehension of what they hear or read is unaffected. This condition is called *expressive aphasia* or **Broca's aphasia**.

The association areas of the frontal lobes seem to be important in making decisions, solving problems, planning and setting goals, memory, and adapting to new situations. If the association areas were damaged, we would probably have trouble understanding complex ideas and planning and carrying out purposeful behavior. A considerable amount of our emotional lives is influenced by our frontal lobes as well. Extensive, reciprocal connections exist between the inferior (lower) frontal lobes and limbic system structures known to be involved in emotional behavior.

Well into the 1960s, a fairly common surgical procedure was used to separate the most forward part (prefrontal) of the frontal lobe from the rest of the cortex. This procedure, known as a prefrontal lobotomy, was carried out on thousands of mental patients as a desperate attempt to minimize their dysfunction and calm their moods. This procedure, wrought with severe criticism, met with limited success (Valenstein, 1973).

Broca's Aphasia The loss of the ability to speak or understand spoken or written language; also known as *expressive aphasia*

Parietal Lobe Region of the cerebral cortex located just behind the central fissure and above the lateral fissure; contains the somatosensory cortex as well as association areas that process sensory information received by the somatosensory cortex

The Parietal Lobe

The **parietal lobe** lies just behind the central fissure and above the lateral fissure. At the front of the parietal lobe, directly across from the motor cortex in the frontal lobe, is an area called the **somatosensory cortex**. This portion of the parietal lobe receives sensory information about touch, pressure, pain, temperature, and body position. Like the motor

Somatosensory Cortex Area of the parietal lobe, directly across from the motor cortex in the frontal lobe, that receives sensory information about touch, pressure, pain, temperature, and body position

Occipital Lobe Region at the rear of the cerebral cortex that consists primarily of the visual cortex

Visual Cortex Portion of the occipital lobe that integrates sensory information received from the eyes into electrical patterns that the brain translates into vision

Temporal Lobe Region of the cerebral cortex located below the lateral fissure; contains the auditory cortex

Auditory Cortex Region of the temporal lobe located just below the lateral fissure; involved in responding to auditory signals, particularly the sound of human speech

Wernicke's Area Area of the left temporal lobe that is the brain's primary area for understanding speech

Wernicke's Aphasia A loss of the ability to comprehend spoken or written language; also referred to as *receptive aphasia*

Agnosia An inability to know or recognize objects through the senses, usually caused by brain injury or disease, resulting in the failure to recognize or identify objects visually even though they can be seen

Prosopagnosia An inability to visually recognize particular faces, usually caused by brain disease or injury (patients with prosopagnosia can see a face but may not be able to recognize it as familiar)

cortex, the somatosensory areas in each hemisphere receive sensory input from the opposite side of the body. Thus, when you stub your left toe, the message is sent to your right somatosensory cortex. As in the motor cortex, the body is represented in an upside-down fashion, with the largest portions receiving input from the face and hands, as shown in Figure 3-11. Each of the primary somatosensory areas in the parietal lobes lies directly across the central fissure from the corresponding area in the frontal lobe's motor cortex.

The parietal lobe is involved in relating visual and spatial information. For example, it allows you to know that an object is still the same even though you view it from a different angle and identify objects by touch. The parietal lobe is also involved in complex visuospatial tasks such as mental rotation. Mental rotation is the imaginary rotation of a familiar object in your mind. Researchers have demonstrated that mental rotation can be disrupted by magnetic interference of neural activity in the right parietal lobe (Harris & Miniussi, 2003). People with damage to their parietal lobe also suffer a peculiar deficit referred to as sensory neglect. Sensory neglect occurs to the contralateral side of the body (opposite from the side of the brain that was damaged). That is, a person with damage to the left parietal lobe may neglect the right side of the body by failing to dress it as neatly as his left side, or may draw a self-portrait with the right side either missing or drawn with a marked lack of detail. While reading, a person with sensory neglect may read only the left side of a page. Such people also have difficulty following directions, either from instructions or from a map.

The Occipital Lobe

At the rear of each hemisphere lies the **occipital lobe**. This lobe consists primarily of the **visual cortex**, a complex network of neurons devoted to vision. People think they see with their eyes, but it is the visual cortex that takes the sensory information received by the eyes and integrates it into vision. The visual cortex of each hemisphere receives sensory messages from both eyes. Nerve fibers from the right visual field of each eye go to the right hemisphere; fibers from the left visual field send impulses to the left hemisphere. In addition to receiving primary visual information, the visual cortex is also responsible for the processing of color, shape, three-dimensional form, and motion of objects. As you can imagine, damage to the occipital lobe results in varying degrees of visual impairment, ranging from the inability to perceive shapes, colors and motion, to complete blindness.

The Temporal Lobe

A primary function of the **temporal lobe** is hearing. The **auditory cortex**, located on the inner surface of the temporal lobe in a region below the lateral sulcus, receives information directly from the auditory system. These auditory signals are then transmitted to an adjacent structure, known as **Wernicke's area**, which is involved in interpreting sounds, particularly the sound of human speech (refer back to Figure 3-9). This area was named after Germany's Carl Wernicke, who reported that patients who were injured in the rear portion of the left temporal lobe, just below the lateral sulcus, often had trouble understanding the speech of others. This condition is known as **Wernicke's aphasia**. Another major function of the temporal lobe is for object recognition and identification. Damage to either temporal lobe can cause peculiar disorders referred to as **agnosias**, where patients cannot name or identify familiar objects. One of the most thoroughly studied agnosias is called **prosopagnosia**, which is the inability to recognize familiar faces, even though the person could be recognized by other nonfacial cues such as voice.

3.7b Sex Differences in the Brain

As you might expect, the brains of males and females are not identical. The differences are largely due to both the quantities and the distribution of sex hormones during early development. Females, on average, tend to be more proficient at language skills, arithmetic calculation, and recalling landmarks along a route. Males, on the other hand, outperform females on certain spatial tasks, mathematical reasoning, and orientation skills (Kimura, 1992). These differences may be partially explained by the differences in the thickness of the cerebral cortex. Females generally have thicker left hemispheres, while males have thicker right hemispheres. The sex hormone estradiol influences the development of the cerebral cortex by increasing the rate of cell loss in areas where estradiol is present. Females have more estradiol in their right hemispheres, and thus greater cell loss, and males have more in their left hemispheres during development (Sandhu, Cook, & Diamond, 1986). Overall, even though females tend to have thicker left hemispheres, the size of all cortical structures is smaller in females (Allen, Damasio, Grabowski, Bruss, & Zhang, 2003).

Other noncortical brain structures that show sexual dimorphism include the hypothalamus, which was described earlier. Several structures within the hypothalamus are larger in males than in females. Again, these differences appear to result from different levels of sex hormones during early development, and these anatomical differences appear to contribute to differences in sexual behavior.

While it is clear that sex differences occur in a number of regions throughout the brain, psychologists believe that cognitive differences between males and females are more influenced by environmental factors than neurological ones. For instance, there is currently much concern about the small number of qualified female applicants to advanced programs in science, computing, and mathematics at our major universities. While Lawrence Summers, a former president of Harvard University, recently suggested that this is attributable to a lack of cognitive abilities in female students (Bombardieri, 2005), others attribute this to environmental factors such as poor precollege preparation, socialization, and fewer role models (Spelke, 2005).

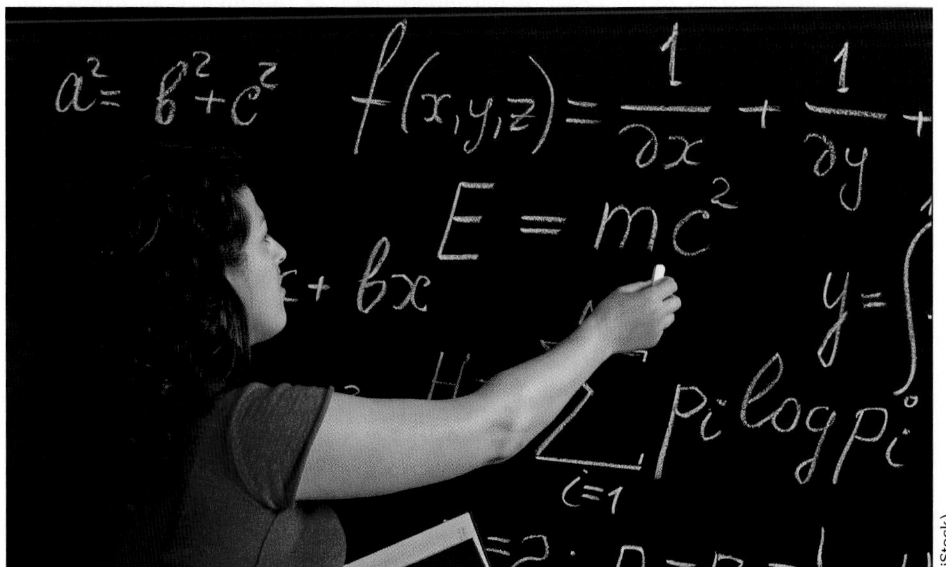

Psychologists believe that cognitive differences between the sexes are influenced more by environmental factors than by neurological factors. For example, poor socialization and a lack of role models may be why few qualified female applicants apply to advanced programs in math and science.

3.7c Lateralization of Function

You may have noticed in a preceding discussion that both Broca's area and Wernicke's area were identified in the left hemisphere. Indeed, in most people (approximately 96 percent of right-handed people and 70 percent of left-handers), verbal abilities such as the expression and understanding of speech are governed more by the left hemisphere than the right hemisphere; there are other differences as well. Furthermore, the right side of the brain seems to be more specialized for spatial orientation, including the ability to recognize objects and shapes and to perceive relationships among them.

The term **lateralization of function** is used to describe the degree to which a particular function is controlled by one hemisphere rather than both. If, for example, a person's ability to deal with spatial tasks is controlled exclusively by the right hemisphere, we would say that such an ability in this person is highly lateralized. In contrast, if both hemispheres contribute equally to this function, the person would be considered bilateral for spatial ability.

Studies have shown that the two hemispheres are asymmetrical, differing in anatomical, electrical, and chemical properties. Although each hemisphere is specialized to handle different functions, they are not entirely separate systems. Rather, our brains function mostly as an integrated whole. The two hemispheres constantly communicate with each other through a broad band of millions of connecting nerve fibers called the **corpus callosum**, shown earlier in Figure 3-6. While in most people a complex function such as language is controlled primarily by regions in the left hemisphere, interaction and communication with the right hemisphere also play a role. Furthermore, if a hemisphere that is primarily responsible for a particular function is damaged, the remaining intact hemisphere may take over the function. For example, if a person were to experience an injury to the language-processing area of the left hemisphere, the right hemisphere might develop a greater capacity to handle verbal functions. This is particularly true if the damage occurs early in life.

A vivid example of this phenomenon was provided in a report of an adolescent female who underwent surgical removal of her left hemisphere due to severe, progressive brain disease. Prior to the onset of her illness she was a normal, right-handed girl with above average language and reading capabilities. After surgery, her verbal skills were markedly diminished, a finding consistent with loss of the hemisphere that had governed most of her verbal skills prior to the hemispherectomy. However, her right hemisphere clearly was able to assume the direction and organization of at least some verbal abilities, as evidenced by her demonstrated ability to recognize and comprehend words and to engage in oral reading of familiar material (Patterson, Vargha-Khadem, & Polkey,, 1989). This capacity to switch cortical control from one hemisphere to another tends to diminish as we grow older.

Lateralization of Function Degree to which a particular function, such as the understanding of speech, is controlled by one rather than both, cerebral hemispheres

Corpus Callosum Broad band of nerve fibers that connects the left and right hemispheres of the cerebral cortex

Split-Brain Research

Many important discoveries about how each hemisphere influences behavior have come from split-brain research, which began in the 1950s with Roger Sperry's investigations of cats whose brains had been bisected. Initially, Sperry and his colleagues made the startling discovery that the left hemisphere of a split-brain cat could learn something while the right hemisphere remained ignorant of what had been learned, and vice versa (Sperry, 1968). In the decades since this landmark study, additional experiments with split-brain subjects have added greatly to our knowledge about hemispheric lateralization of function.

Some of these studies have involved split-brain research with human subjects. This radical surgery is not performed for experimental purposes but is occasionally performed to control very severe cases of epilepsy that have become incapacitating and even life threatening. During an epileptic seizure, neurons in the site of a damaged area begin to fire, and the abnormal activity can spread from one hemisphere to the other through the corpus callosum. Although drugs are often successful in decreasing the abnormal brain activity, the medication is not always effective; in these cases, the only recourse may be to sever the corpus callosum. This procedure is usually very effective in controlling the seizure; the patients appear to be essentially unchanged in intelligence, personality characteristics, and behavior. However, their brains do not function in entirely the same manner after the surgery. After being disconnected, the two hemispheres operate independently: Their motor mechanisms, sensory systems, and association areas can no longer exchange information.

This difference makes itself felt in a variety of ways. For instance, the right hand might arrange some flowers in a vase, only to have the left hand tear it apart. Occasionally, people with split brains may be embarrassed by the left hand making inappropriate gestures, or perhaps doing some bizarre thing like zipping down the fly on a pair of trousers after the right hand zipped it up. With time, such symptoms usually subside as the person learns to compensate for and adjust to the independent functioning of the two hemispheres.

Scientists have developed a number of procedures for detecting the effects of split-brain surgery. For instance, in one study a woman recently recovered from split-brain surgery sat in front of a screen while pictures were flashed to either the left or the right of her visual field. Information presented to her left visual field was transmitted only to her right hemisphere, and vice versa. Each stimulus appeared on the screen for only about one-tenth of a second, so that the subject did not have time to shift her eyes to get a better look. Her task was to identify verbally what she was shown and then to reach

Figure 3-12 Split-Brain Research

When the image of the orange enters the right visual field, it crosses to the left hemisphere where the subject can articulate what he saw. When the image enters the right hemisphere, the participant reports that he saw nothing.

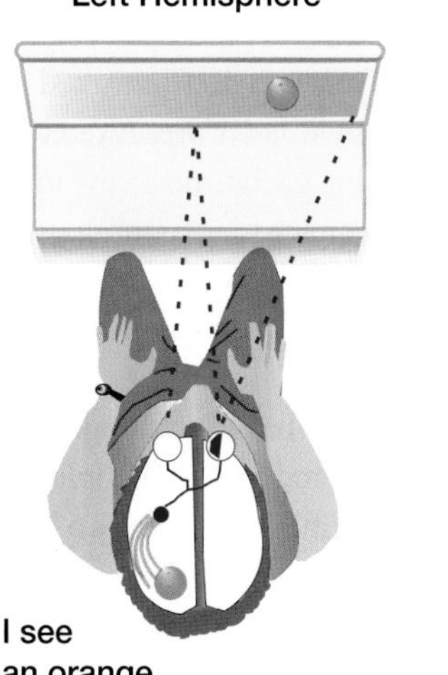

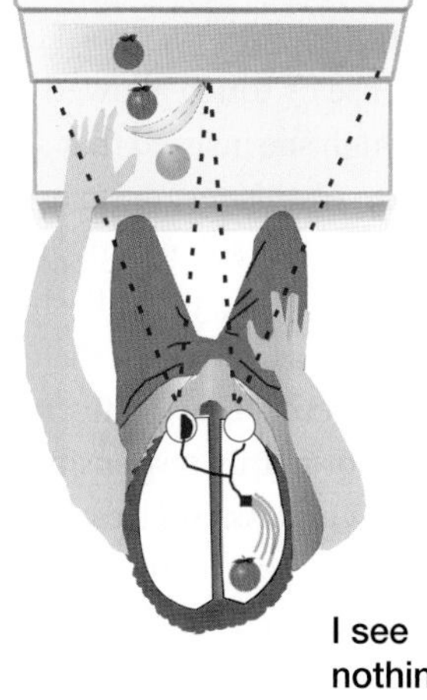

BVT*Lab*

Visit **www.BVTLab.com** to explore the student resources available for this chapter.

under the screen and select the object, solely by touch, from a collection of objects (LeDoux, Wilson, & Gazzaniga, 1977).

Images in the right visual field fall on the left side of each retina (the image-recording part of the eye), and images in the left visual field fall on the right side on each retina. Half of each retina sends information to the occipital cortex on the same side of the brain, while information from the other half of each retina crosses over to the cortex on the opposite side of the brain. Thus, if a person stares straight ahead, information from the entire left visual field will reach the right hemisphere and vice versa (see Figure 3-12).

Normally, this information is transferred between the two hemispheres through the corpus callosum, so that both hemispheres have information about both the left and right visual fields. In split-brain people, however, this is no longer possible (see Figure 3-13). In this particular experiment, researchers made sure that both fields did not receive the information by flashing the image for such a short period of time that each hemisphere received only the information in the opposite visual field. (In one-tenth of a second the subject would not have time to shift her eyes, an action that would have enabled her to perceive the image in both hemispheres.)

Testing the Effects of Split-Brain Surgery

In the experiment just described, do you think that the woman was able to identify correctly, both verbally and by touch, objects projected in the left and right visual fields? If yes, why? If no, why not? What differences, if any, do you think were noted between her responses to left versus right visual field images? Take some time to reason out the probable results of this experiment.

The results of the experiment showed a difference in the subject's responses to images presented in her left and right visual fields. When a picture of a cup was projected to the right of the dot (and thus projected to her left hemisphere), the subject was able to quickly name the object, and she had no trouble locating the cup by touch. (She could locate the object with her left hand since naming the object out loud conveyed information about its nature to her right hemisphere via auditory input from her ears.) Additional objects presented to her right visual field presented no problems.

When a picture of a spoon was flashed to the left side of the dot, however, the results were quite different. The subject reported seeing nothing. Despite this reply, the researchers pressed her into trying to pick out the object from the articles on the table. After feeling the various objects with her left hand, she held up the spoon, a result she dismissed as a lucky guess. When asked to identify it verbally, she called it a pencil. Time after time her sense of touch allowed her to identify objects presented to her right hemisphere, even though she insisted that she saw nothing each time a new image was flashed.

In a variation of this test, a sexually suggestive picture of a nude was flashed to the left side of the dot. The subject giggled and blushed, but when she was asked what she saw, she replied, "Nothing, just a flash of light." When the experimenter pressed further and asked why she was laughing, she exclaimed, "Oh, Doctor, you have some machine!"

These results reveal that in this individual (as well as in the majority of people) the left hemisphere is primarily responsible for language and speech. People with intact brains have no problem with tasks such as the one just described since the two hemispheres work together in perceiving and naming things. However, after a split-brain operation, each side of the bisected brain is cut off from the other side. Therefore, even though the subject of this study was able to identify the spoon with her hand, she could not name it. Her right hemisphere, with its undeveloped language and speech areas, was essentially mute. Her response to the picture of the nude was similar. Even though her left hemisphere did not

Figure 3-13 Passage of Visual Information in Brains with an Intact and a Severed Corpus Callosum

A. When the corpus callosum is intact, visual information in the right visual field is focused on the left half of each retina; it then passes through the optic nerve to the left hemisphere of the brain. Information from either hemisphere can pass through the corpus callosum to the opposite side.

B. When the corpus callosum is severed, information from the eyes is transmitted to the brain in the same way as described above. However, information from the left visual field (in the right hemisphere) cannot be processed by the left hemisphere (where language areas are located).

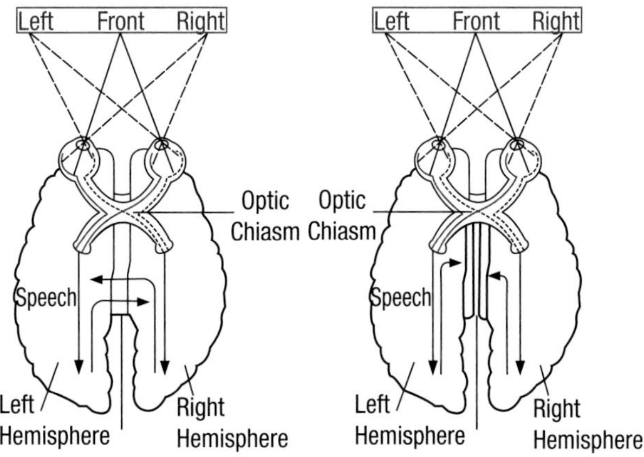

know what had happened, her blushing and giggling revealed that her right hemisphere had processed the information and produced an emotional response.

Would she have been able to identify the spoon with her right hand after its image had been projected to the right side of her brain? The answer is no. Since the left hemisphere governs her right hand, and her left hemisphere knew nothing about the object, she would have been unable to identify it with her right hand.

Investigating patients who have undergone split-brain surgery has also led to a better understanding of how the left and right hemispheres differ in respect to specific tasks. For example, the right hemisphere appears to specialize in our ability to recognize objects and familiar others. In an experiment with a split-brain patient, images of the self and other familiar people were presented to the left and right hemispheres independently using a special projection device as described above. The patient easily recognized images of self presented to either hemisphere but could only recognize familiar others when their images were presented to the right hemisphere (Uddin, Rayman, & Zaidel, 2005; Uddin et al., 2008).

The information presented in this chapter has only touched on what scientists know about the brain. Although there are still many unanswered questions, new methods developed in recent years have added greatly to our knowledge. In the next section we look at some techniques used to study the brain.

3.7d How the Brain Is Studied

Surgical Lesions

As investigators attempted to link specific behavioral deficits with specific locations of brain damage, some of the earliest clues about how the brain functions came from observations of people with head injuries. For example, if a blow to the back of the head impaired a person's vision, the natural conclusion was that the injured region of the brain was responsible for vision. This way of learning about the brain has provided some valuable insights, but it also has some serious limitations. One is the impracticality of waiting for the right kind of injury to occur so that the role of a specific brain site can be assessed. In addition, it is often difficult to determine the precise location and amount of damage inflicted by a given injury. Because of such limitations, researchers concluded that it might be more efficient to create the injuries with surgical techniques. The areas of brain damage created by such procedures are called lesions, and the technique is called **lesion production**.

For obvious ethical reasons, lesion production is used with nonhuman subjects (although in some cases, lesions have been produced in human brains for therapeutic purposes, for example, to destroy an area in the amygdala that is responsible for abnormal cellular activity associated with uncontrollable rage). Typically, an animal is anesthetized, a small hole is drilled in its skull, and a specific part of the brain is destroyed. A special device called a *stereotaxic apparatus* allows researchers to insert a fine wire into a specific brain area. Sufficient electric current is then passed through the wire to destroy a small amount of brain tissue at its tip. This refined lesion technique has allowed researchers to identify the relationship of specific behaviors to precise locations in the brain.

Brain Stimulation

A second technique, **brain stimulation**, involves stimulating precise regions with a weak electric current or specific chemicals that activate neurons. During electrical stimulation, a stereotaxic device is used to implant tiny wires called microelectrodes at specific brain sites. Stimulation of the targeted area often results in some kind of behavioral response (for instance, the pleasure response that results from stimulating the septal area).

During chemical stimulation a small syringe needle called a *microcanula* is inserted into a specific region of the brain. Once the microcanula is inserted, small amounts of chemical can be injected into surrounding cells, either stimulating or inhibiting specific receptors. The results provide researchers with valuable information about where certain behavioral functions are localized within the brain. Because brain stimulation is generally painless, and because measures can be taken to minimize tissue damage, this method may be used with human as well as nonhuman subjects. For example, chemical stimulation of dopamine neurons in the nucleus accumbens with drugs like cocaine may help us understand the process of addiction.

Lesion Production Technique for studying the brain that involves surgical damage to a precise region of the brain (most commonly done with experimental animals)

Brain Stimulation Technique for studying the brain that involves stimulating precise regions with a weak electric current

Electrical Recording Technique for studying the brain in which tiny wires implanted in the brain are used to record neural electrical activity

Electrical Recording

Another technique used for studying the brain is **electrical recording**. In this technique, tiny wires implanted in the brain are used to record the electrical activity of neurons. Scientists using this technique have been able to record the responses of a single brain neuron to a stimulus such as a beam of light. In some studies, electrical activity is transmitted through several implanted electrodes while the subject engages in various behaviors. The electrical messages are then fed into a computer, which analyzes the complex relationships between the behaviors and patterns of neuron activity.

Radioactive Labeling

At any given time, some areas of the brain are more active than others. While you are reading this text, your occipital lobes are more active than your frontal lobes. Likewise, when you smell perfume, your olfactory bulbs become more active. When cells—in this case neurons—become more active, they require more energy in the form of glucose, which is carried to cells via the blood supply. Researchers can take advantage of this fact and administer small amounts of radioactive chemical into the blood supply. One such chemical, called 2-deoxy-D-glucose (2-DG), is taken into active cells just like glucose. Several hours later, the brain can be sliced into thin sections and placed on photographic plates. The sections of the brain that were most active following the administration of 2-DG are enhanced on the film. This technique, which is obviously restricted to laboratory animals, has been very valuable in identifying areas of the brain that are involved in different sensory, motor, and cognitive tasks.

Electroencephalography

Lesion production, stimulation, electrical recording, and 2-DG studies are all *invasive,* in that they require surgery. Fortunately, technology has made possible a variety of brain study methods that do not require surgery and are noninvasive. One technique, **electroencephalography** (**EEG**), has been around for quite some time. Because the brain constantly generates electrical activity, electrodes placed on the scalp can be used to record the electrical activity of the cortex. The electroencephalograph amplifies these very small electrical potentials thousands of times and records them on paper in patterns called brain waves. The brain waves vary according to a person's state—whether they are alert and mentally active, relaxed and calm, sleeping, or dreaming. The EEG has also been used to diagnose such conditions as epilepsy, attention disorders, brain tumors, and a variety of other neurological conditions that generate abnormal brain-wave patterns.

The EEG is also used to investigate attention processes by examining brain-wave patterns produced during stimulus presentation. These wave patterns associated with specific stimuli are called *evoked potentials*. Some years ago, research psychologists (Donchin & Herning, 1975) reported an interesting application of evoked potentials. Donchan recorded EEG activity in his subjects as they were exposed to various familiar or expected stimuli and an occasional unexpected or rare event. Enhanced computer analysis of the resulting evoked potentials revealed that the perception of an unexpected event was consistently associated with a particular brain-wave component called P300. For example, a subject might be exposed to a series of visual stimuli, some familiar and others not. In this case, the unfamiliar stimuli are unexpected and result in the recording of a P300 wave or evoked potential (P300 because it is a positive wave occurring 300 milliseconds after the unexpected stimulus). This kind of research contributes to our understanding of the relationship between mental processes, such as attention, and brain activity.

Electroencephalography (EEG) Technique used to measure and record electrical activity of the cortex

Computerized Axial Tomography (CAT) A procedure used to locate brain abnormalities that involves rotating an X-ray scanner around the skull to produce an accurate image of a living brain

Computerized Axial Tomography

Neuroscientists have recently developed some effective techniques for observing living brains. The first of these, **computerized axial tomography** (CAT), was developed in the early 1970s. It is a refined X-ray technique that provides an accurate image of the brain. An X-ray scanner is rotated in a circular path around the skull, sending a thin beam of X-rays through the brain. A detector measures the amount of radiation that reaches the other side. Because different brain tissues absorb different amounts of radiation, the CAT scanners produce excellent pictures that can be used to locate tumors, lesions, and a variety of neurological abnormalities. In the past, this information could only be obtained by autopsy.

Positron Emission Tomography

A third noninvasive technique, the **positron emission tomography (PET)** scan, also takes advantage of the fact that glucose is utilized at higher rates in active cells. Each time a neuron fires, it expends tremendous energy; thus, active brain cells metabolize a great deal of glucose. The scientists who developed the PET scan reasoned that if they could find a way to measure glucose utilization, they could tell which parts of the brain are active at different times in response to different stimuli. The use of radioactive isotopes paved the way.

The technique works as follows: A patient receives an intravenous injection of a glucose-like sugar that has been tagged with a radioactive fluoride isotope. Active brain cells then metabolize the sugar, but they cannot metabolize the radioactive component. Thus, the isotope accumulates within the cells in direct proportion to their activity level. As it decays, it emits charged particles called positrons. Instruments scanning the brain detect the radioactivity and record its location, and a computer converts this information into colored biochemical maps of the brain.

The PET scan has proven to be a useful tool in mapping the brain, pinpointing locations involved in movement, sensation, thinking, and even memory. There is also some evidence suggesting that PET scans may be helpful in both the diagnosis and treatment of various behavioral disorders. Some researchers report that the brains of schizophrenics and severely depressed people reveal different patterns from those of healthy people (Dunn et al., 2005).

Magnetic Resonance Imaging

A fourth noninvasive technique is **magnetic resonance imaging (MRI)**. This procedure uses harmless radio waves to excite hydrogen protons in the brain tissue, creating a magnetic field change that is detected by a huge magnet that surrounds the patient. The information is fed into a computer, which compiles it into a highly detailed, three-dimensional colored picture of the brain. The images created are much sharper and more detailed than those provided by the CAT scan. The MRI can pinpoint tumors and locate even the slightest reduction in blood flow in an artery or vein. It can also provide biochemical information, distinguishing between cancerous and noncancerous cells. In addition, MRI has been shown to be particularly helpful in diagnosing various diseases associated with brain abnormalities, such as multiple sclerosis (a degenerative disease of the CNS characterized by tremors and impaired speech), spinal cord abnormalities in children, and brain lesions associated with epilepsy.

A version of magnetic resonance imaging called **functional magnetic resonance imaging (fMRI)** provides high-resolution three-dimensional images of the brain during specific tasks. Regional changes in cerebral blood flow can be measured during a visual task, for example, and mapped onto an image of the brain's visual cortex. Researchers using fMRI can actually watch the brain as a subject is engaged in specific cognitive or motor tasks to determine the relative contributions of various brain areas to these activities.

Positron Emission Tomography (PET) Technique for studying the brain that involves injecting a subject with a glucose-like sugar tagged with a radioactive isotope that accumulates in brain cells in direct proportion to their activity level

Magnetic Resonance Imaging (MRI) Procedure for studying the brain that uses radio waves to excite hydrogen protons in the brain tissue, creating a magnetic field change

Functional Magnetic Resonance Imaging (fMRI) A method of magnetic resonance imaging that measures energy released by brain cells that are active during a specific task

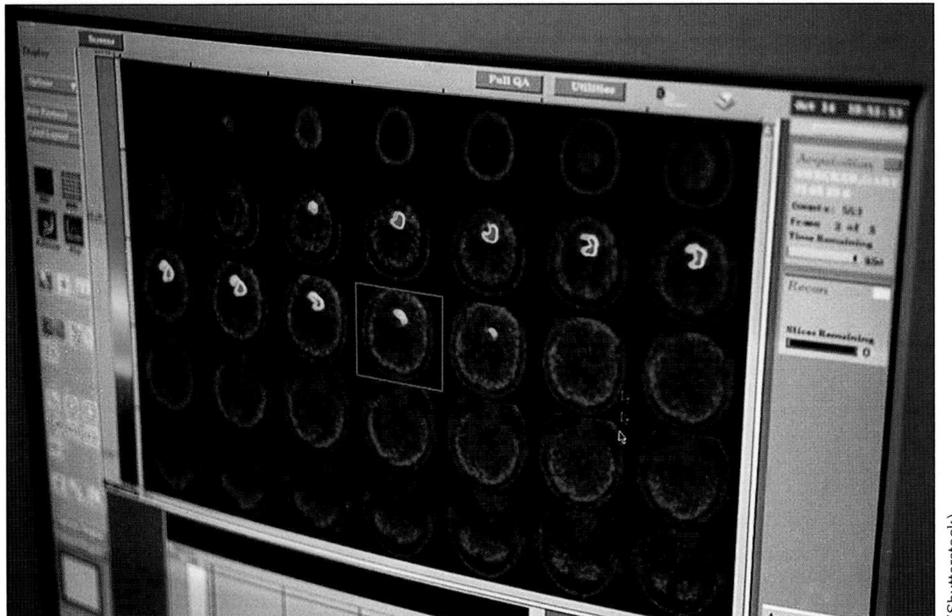
(Shutterstock)

Computer screen of a series of PET scans. PET stands for positron emission tomography. PET scans identify areas of the brain that are most active in response to a variety of tasks

3.8 The Endocrine System

Up to this point in this chapter, we have covered only the nervous system. However, the nervous system is not the only biological system that governs behavior. To be complete, a discussion of biological foundations of behavior should also consider the role of the endocrine system, which is illustrated in Figure 3-14.

The **endocrine system** consists of several glands located throughout the body. Glands in the endocrine system are *ductless*; that is, they have no external excretory ducts but rather secrete internally directly into the bloodstream or lymph fluid. (The lymph system is a system of vessels and organs that makes up your immune system.) The major endocrine glands include the pituitary, the thyroid, the parathyroids, the adrenals, the pancreas, and the gonads. The location of the various endocrine glands is shown in Figure 3-14. Each of these glands produces **hormones**, which are secreted directly into the bloodstream. A single gland may produce several different hormones.

Like neurotransmitters, hormones act as chemical messengers. In fact, some important chemicals within the body can function as both neurotransmitters and hormones. Norepinephrine, for example, acts as a hormone when released by the adrenal glands and as a neurotransmitter when released by a neuron. There is, however, a key difference in the way these two classes of chemicals act. Because neurotransmitters only need to travel across a synaptic gap (a fraction of the distance that most hormones travel through the bloodstream), they have a much more immediate effect on behavior than that of chemicals in the endocrine system.

The endocrine system often works in tandem with the nervous system. For example, when a person is suddenly exposed to a fear-inducing stimulus, such as the bear in the earlier example, heart rate increases instantly in response to sympathetic nervous system input. At the same time, the adrenal glands secrete epinephrine, which has a similar effect on heart rate. In this fashion, the two major regulating systems of the body often work together.

Endocrine System System of ductless glands, including the pituitary, thyroid, parathyroids, adrenals, pancreas, and gonads, that secrete hormones directly into the bloodstream or lymph fluids

Hormones Chemical messengers secreted by the endocrine glands that act to regulate the functioning of specific body organs

Figure 3-14 The Major Glands of the Endocrine System

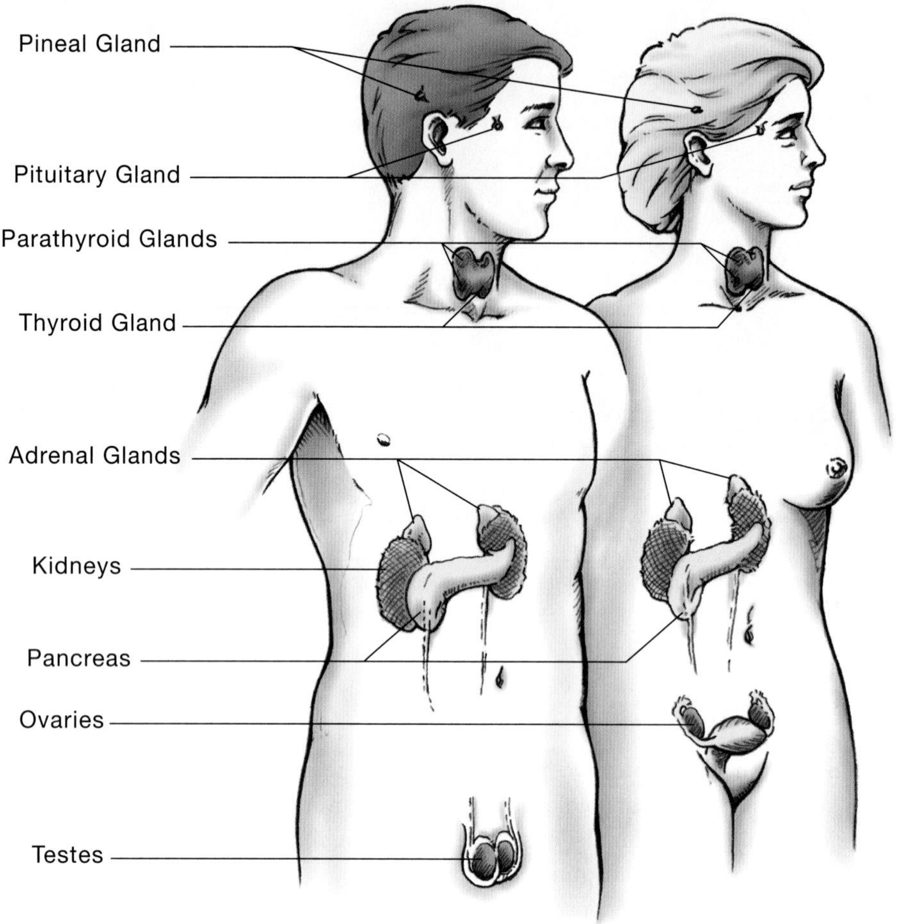

The hypothalamus is a key interface between the nervous system and the endocrine system. As noted earlier, this region of the brain controls the activity of the pituitary gland through production of a group of chemicals known as *hypothalamic-releasing factors*. These chemicals, in turn, stimulate the pituitary to produce hormones that stimulate other glands.

Once an endocrine gland releases a hormone into the bloodstream, the substance travels throughout the body. However, each hormone exerts its primary influence only on certain specific organs and cells, often referred to as *target organs*. Some hormones, called trophic hormones, affect only the activity of another endocrine gland. For example, hormones called gonadotropins stimulate only the gonads.

Endocrine glands do not produce a steady stream of hormones. Instead, target organs signal the secreting glands either to increase or decrease secretions. Hormones are secreted until the target organ is stimulated; at this point, the target organ releases another substance that circulates back through the system to regulate hormonal activity in the initiating gland. This *negative-feedback mechanism* provides an internal control that limits extremes of hormone production.

Through these general mechanisms, the endocrine system influences many important physiological functions including metabolism, emotional responses, and motivation. A number of these effects are of particular interest to psychologists.

3.8a The Pituitary Gland

Located in the brain below the hypothalamus, the **pituitary gland** produces the largest number of different hormones, some of which trigger other glands to release other hormones. For this reason, the pituitary gland is sometimes called the master gland, but, as we have seen, it is actually controlled by the hypothalamus.

The pituitary gland also produces a number of huge protein molecules called neuropeptides, mentioned in our earlier discussion of endogenous opioids. Each neuropeptide consists of a long chain of amino acids that is broken down by enzyme action into various lengths of small chains. These substances act as neurotransmitters, and they influence a number of functions such as eating and drinking, sexual behavior, sleep, temperature regulation, pain, and responses to stress.

3.8b The Thyroid Gland

The **thyroid gland**, located within the neck, responds to pituitary stimulation by releasing the hormone **thyroxine**. This substance affects a number of biological functions, the most important of which is the regulation of metabolism (the transformation of food into energy). Because metabolism is in turn closely linked to motivational and mood states, the thyroid has an important impact on behavior. For example, if too little thyroxine is produced (a condition known as *hypothyroidism*), a person behaves in a lethargic manner, demonstrates little motivation to accomplish tasks, and often manifests symptoms of depression. Excessive thyroxine output (*hyperthyroidism*) may have just the opposite effect, causing hyperactivity, weight loss, anxiety, and excessive tension (Samuels, 2008). An undersecretion of thyroxine early in life produces *cretinism*, a condition characterized by low intelligence and various body defects such as dwarfed stature and dry, wrinkled skin. Fortunately, all of these conditions can be prevented or remedied by medical treatments.

3.8c The Adrenal Glands

The **adrenals** are a pair of glands, located just above each kidney, that influence our emotional state, level of energy, and ability to cope with stress. They consist of two distinct parts: an inner core called the *adrenal medulla* and an outer layer called the *adrenal cortex*. The adrenal medulla produces epinephrine and norepinephrine, both of which prepare the body to respond to emergencies by making the heart beat faster, diverting blood from the stomach and intestines to the voluntary muscles, and enhancing energy resources by increasing blood sugar levels. The adrenal medulla is able to act quickly in threatening situations because it is stimulated directly by neural impulses.

As suggested earlier, in the discussion of the peripheral nervous system, epinephrine and norepinephrine act in a way that is similar to the sympathetic nervous system. In fact, these hormones and the nervous system perform basically the same work. The sympathetic nervous system works more quickly, producing its effects almost instantly; yet the effects of the adrenal hormones can persist much longer. It is the lingering effects of hormones that explain why it often takes time for strong emotional arousal to subside after the cause for anxiety has been removed.

Pituitary Gland Gland in the endocrine system located directly below and connected to the hypothalamus; produces a number of hormones, many of which trigger other endocrine glands to release hormones

Thyroid Gland Endocrine gland located in the neck; produces the hormone thyroxine, which influences metabolism, growth, and maturation

Thyroxine The major hormone produced by the thyroid gland; regulates metabolism

Adrenal Glands Glands within the endocrine system, located just above the kidneys, that influence emotional state, energy levels, and responses to stress by releasing hormones

At times of stress, the hypothalamus causes the pituitary to release ACTH, *adrenocorticotropic hormone*, which in turn stimulates the adrenal cortex to increase its secretion of a number of hormones that influence metabolism. The higher metabolic rate makes the stressed person more active, and therefore more able to cope with an emergency. Prolonged stress, however, can have a debilitating effect on the body, including the brain and the immune system. A chronic state of tension, nervousness, fear, or even panic can take a terrible toll on one's emotional and physical well-being. Furthermore, abnormally high metabolic rates deplete vital body resources, which over time can lead to exhaustion and increased susceptibility to illness. Stress-related problems and stress-management techniques are discussed in Chapter 9.

3.8d The Gonads

The **gonads**—ovaries in the female and testes in the male—produce several varieties of sex hormones. The ovaries produce two classes of hormones: the estrogens (the most important of which is estradiol), which influence development of female physical sex characteristics and regulation of the menstrual cycle; and the *progestational compounds* (the most important is progesterone), which help to regulate the menstrual cycle and prepare the uterus for pregnancy. As we mentioned earlier, estradiol also contributes to sex differences in the cerebral cortex and the hypothalamus.

The primary output of the testes is the *androgens*. The most important of these hormones is testosterone, the function of which is to influence the development of both male physical sex characteristics and sexual motivation. In both sexes, the adrenal glands also secrete sex hormones, including small amounts of estrogen and greater quantities of androgen (this is where females get testosterone).

Around the onset of puberty, the sex hormones play a critical role in initiating changes in the primary sexual systems (the growth of the uterus, vagina, penis, and so forth) and the secondary sex characteristics, including body hair, breast development, and voice changes. They also exert strong influences on the fertility cycle in women, and they seem to contribute to sexual motivation. Chapter 9 discusses the relationship of sex hormones to sexual motivation in more detail.

3.9 Drugs and Behavior

A wide variety of commonly used drugs have the effect of changing thought processes, emotional states, or behavior (Snyder, 1984). Solomon Snyder, an expert on neurotransmitters, stated, "Virtually every drug that alters mental function does so by interacting with a neurotransmitter system in the brain" (1984, p. 23). This interaction may happen in a variety of ways. Some drugs increase neural activity by releasing neurotransmitters from the presynaptic vesicles; some actually mimic certain excitatory transmitters. Other drugs may prevent transmission of neural impulses by binding or attaching themselves to receptors on the postsynaptic membrane, thus preventing the kind of contact between excitatory transmitters and postsynaptic receptors that is necessary to trigger EPSPs. Still other drugs interfere with the reuptake of intact chemicals or the recycling of their breakdown products. In this section we examine some of the more common drugs used to alter behavior.

Gonads Glands within the endocrine system (ovaries in females and testes in males) that produce sex hormones, which influence development of sexual systems and secondary sex characteristics as well as sexual motivation

It is not uncommon for people in our society to have a few glasses of wine at a party and then to follow through the next morning with a few cups of coffee or tea to help clear the cobwebs. Most of us regularly consume a variety of chemicals (such as alcohol and caffeine) that alter our perceptions and behavior. Such substances, as well as nicotine, marijuana, sleeping pills, cocaine, and narcotics, are called psychoactive drugs.

Continued use of many of the psychoactive drugs tends to lessen their effects, so that the user develops a **tolerance** to the drug. For example, repeated injections of opiates, such as heroin, result in the development of tolerance, which means that the user must continually increase the amount of drug taken to get euphoric effects. Along with tolerance, physiological **dependence** on the drug may also develop over time. If a person becomes drug *dependent*, withdrawal symptoms such as cramps, nausea, tremors, headaches, and sweating occur in the drug's absence. In some cases a severe form of dependence called **addiction** may occur. Addiction is a brain disease caused by repeated administration of drugs that rapidly increase dopamine activity. Excessive dopamine activity results in structural and functional changes to the mesolimbic system and the frontal cortex. For example, drugs such as alcohol, cocaine, amphetamines, and opiates are all powerfully addictive (Ettinger, 2017). One of the most ironic things about drug addiction is that the original reason for taking the drug (for example, to relieve pain) may be replaced by a desperate need to maintain adequate levels of the drug just to avoid withdrawal symptoms. We will see in Chapter 7 that tolerance to opiate drugs is a learned response and contexts surrounding drug use are important cues to its development.

The three major groups of drugs, classified by their effects, are depressants, stimulants, and hallucinogens. The remainder of this chapter looks at these types of drugs and their effects on people.

3.9a Depressants: Sedatives, Opiates, and Alcohol

Drugs that tend to slow or depress activity in the central nervous system are classified as **depressants**. Substances in this category include sedatives, opiates, and alcohol.

Sedatives

Sedatives are drugs that induce relaxation, calmness, and sleep. This group of drugs includes *barbiturates,* such as Phenobarbital and Seconal; and the *benzodiazepines*, including Valium and Xanax. Many of these drugs are widely prescribed by physicians as remedies for emotional and physical complaints such as anxiety, insomnia, gastrointestinal disorders, and respiratory problems. Chapter 16 discusses some of these drugs and their uses for treating psychological disorders.

All the sedative drugs, particularly barbiturates (also known as barbs or downers) are prime candidates for drug abuse. Tolerance for barbiturates develops quite rapidly, and abusers of these drugs often increase their consumption to the point at which respiratory function, memory, judgment, and other mental and physical processes are seriously impaired. Because barbiturates can be particularly lethal after an overdose, these drugs are becoming less frequently prescribed. The effects of sedative and depressant drugs such as alcohol, barbiturates, and benzodiazepines taken in combination can be lethal. For instance, combining a nonlethal dose of alcohol with a nonlethal dose of barbiturates can cause death (Gillett & Warburton, 1970).

Virtually every drug that alters behavior does so by interacting with a neurotransmitter system in the brain. The sedative drugs are no exception. The mechanisms whereby they accomplish their effects are well understood. For example, it is known that sedative drugs increase the sensitivity of postsynaptic receptors for *gamma-amino-butyric acid*,

Tolerance A decrease in the effectiveness of a drug observed after repeated administration

Dependence Physiological adaptation to repeated drug administration that can lead to withdrawal symptoms upon cessation of drug use

Addiction A brain disease caused by repeated administration of drugs that rapidly increase dopamine activity resulting in structural and functional changes to the mesolimbic system and frontal cortex (not all drugs that cause dependence necessarily cause addiction)

Depressants Psychoactive drugs, including opiates, sedatives, and alcohol, that have the effect of slowing down or depressing central nervous system activity

Sedatives Class of depressant drugs, including tranquilizers, barbiturates, and benzodiazepines, that induce relaxation, calmness, and sleep

an important neurotransmitter that acts to inhibit neural transmission (L. Richter et al., 2012). By increasing the inhibition generated by GABA, the sedative drugs reduce neural activity in the brain circuits, including the frontal cortex and the amygdala, involved with emotional arousal.

Opiates

Opiates or **narcotics** are another category of depressant drugs. *Opium* is derived from a sticky resin secreted by the opium poppy. Two of its natural ingredients, *morphine* and *codeine*, have been widely used as painkillers. A third derivative, *heroin*, is obtained by chemically modifying morphine.

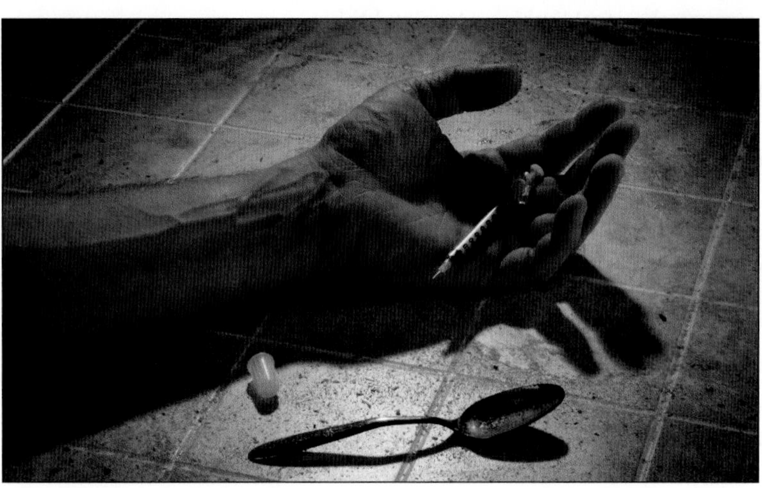

(iStock)

The mortality rate among narcotics addicts is about 7 times greater than among the general population.

Heroin is snorted (inhaled through the nostrils) or injected directly into the veins. When it is injected, the almost immediate effect is a rush, which users describe as an overwhelming sensation of pleasure akin to sexual orgasm. This rush may be the closest many heroin addicts come to sexual orgasm, however, as regular use of opiates often significantly decreases sexual interest and activity. Shortly after it is injected, heroin decomposes into morphine, which produces other effects commonly associated with opiate usage: a sense of well-being, contentment, and drowsiness.

However, increasingly larger doses of heroin are needed to produce these effects, and the user quickly acquires tolerance and dependence. The long-term effects of this dependence can be devastating. People addicted to heroin do almost anything to ensure their supply of the drug—cheat, steal, or prostitute themselves.

What happens when a heroin addict tries to break the habit? After a few hours without heroin, the user begins to experience withdrawal symptoms such as vomiting, runny nose, aching muscles, and abdominal pain. Intense drug cravings associated with abstinence often result in relapse to drug use again.

Opiates themselves produce little physical damage to the user. Chronic opiate use may damage the body's immune system, thus increasing the addict's susceptibility to disease. Research indicates that the mortality rate among narcotics addicts is approximately 7 times greater than that of the general population. There are a variety of reasons for this statistic. Addicts often cause harm to themselves through drug-related habits, such as using nonsterile needles, obtaining contaminated heroin, or not eating properly. Carelessness about using sterile drug paraphernalia increases the risk of potentially life-threatening infectious diseases such as AIDS, hepatitis (a liver infection), and endocarditis (inflammation of a membrane in the heart) (Wang, Zhang, & Ho, 2011). The incidence of opiate abuse has dramatically increased over the past ten years. In 2014, more than twenty-eight thousand people died from prescription opiates and heroin. This represents seventy-eight American deaths each day. The drastic increase in opiate deaths coincides with a significant increase in prescription sales. Enough opiates are produced each year to provide every U.S. citizen a dose every four hours (twenty-four hours a day) for a month (Chen, 2016).

Opiates (Narcotics) A class of depressant drugs that includes opium, morphine, codeine, and heroin

Alcohol

Like other depressants, alcohol retards the activity of neurons in the central nervous system, particularly in the cerebral cortex and the cerebellum, by increasing the sensitivity of postsynaptic GABA receptors (Wallner & Olsen, 2008). It is an extremely potent drug that affects behavior in a highly variable manner. Some people become more communicative and expressive under its influence, perhaps even boisterous and silly. Others become aggressive, abusive, and sometimes violent. People under the influence of alcohol may engage in behaviors they normally keep in check, probably because alcohol suppresses the inhibitory mechanisms of the cerebral cortex.

These behavioral effects may be evident at relatively low levels of alcohol consumption. As intake increases, it is accompanied by more pronounced impairments of coordination, reaction time, thinking, and judgment. When blood alcohol content reaches 0.10 percent (the equivalent of four to six beers or three to four 1.5-ounce shots of 80 proof alcohol), a person's chance of having a severe accident behind the wheel of a car or otherwise may be as much as 5 or 6 times greater than normal. In most states, the legal limit for blood alcohol levels when driving is 0.08.

Prolonged and excessive use of alcohol can lead to addiction and have disastrous physical effects. Liver and heart disease are commonly associated with alcohol abuse. Malnutrition is also a problem because excessive drinkers typically eat poorly since their daily consumption of liquor provides hundreds of calories. In addition, alcohol interferes with the proper absorption of B vitamins, so vitamin B deficiency is common. A prolonged deficiency of these essential vitamins can lead to brain damage, a complication that occurs in about 10 percent of alcoholics. Alcoholic brain damage, which can include cerebral and cortical atrophy and reduced brain weight, has been associated with a variety of cognitive and behavioral impairments. Alcoholics also tend to develop various kinds of infections at a rate higher than normal—due in part to alcohol's immune suppressing effects (Friedman, Newton, & Klein, 2003; Hote et al., 2008). The National Institute on Alcohol Abuse and Alcoholism (NIAAA) estimated that there are more than seventeen million (7.2 percent of the adult population) alcohol addicts in the United States, and many of them are not receiving adequate treatment (Alcohol Facts and Statistics, 2017). It is further estimated that alcohol abuse affects one in four households.

Heavy drinking during pregnancy causes further complications. Because alcohol passes from the mother's body to the fetus, the infant may be born with an alcohol addiction. Drug withdrawal in a baby can be fatal. Offspring of mothers who drink heavily while they are pregnant may suffer from *fetal alcohol syndrome*, which is characterized by retarded physical growth, intellectual development, and motor coordination as well as abnormalities in brain metabolic processes and liver functioning.

3.9b Stimulants: Caffeine, Nicotine, Amphetamines, and Cocaine

Drugs that stimulate the central nervous system by increasing neural transmission are called **stimulants**. The most widely consumed of these drugs are caffeine and nicotine, both of which are mild stimulants. Amphetamines and cocaine are the most frequently used of the stronger stimulants.

Stimulants Psychoactive drugs, including caffeine, nicotine, amphetamines, and cocaine, that stimulate the central nervous system by increasing the transmission of neural impulses

Caffeine

Found in a variety of products—including chocolate, coffee, tea, and many carbonated soft drinks such as colas—caffeine has long provided people with a quick lift. Caffeine acts quickly. Within a few minutes after caffeine is consumed, heart and respiration rates and blood pressure increase.

People experience these physical effects in a variety of ways. Most feel mentally stimulated; some experience a brief burst of energy. People who consume a large amount of caffeine (for example, six or more cups of coffee) may feel more pronounced effects: irritability, headaches, the jitters, difficulty concentrating, nausea, and sleep disturbances. People can become dependent on caffeine, as evidenced by the countless numbers of people who just cannot function without their daily quota of coffee, tea, or cola.

Caffeine exerts its effects on the nervous system by blocking adenosine receptors. Adenosine is an inhibitory neurotransmitter that produces behavioral sedation and regulates the dilation of blood vessels (Ettinger, 2017).

(Shutterstock)

Caffeine is a stimulant that works by blocking adenosine receptors in the nervous system.

Nicotine

Nicotine is second only to caffeine on the list of widely used stimulants. Found in tobacco, nicotine increases heart rate, blood pressure, and stomach activity, and constricts blood vessels. Paradoxically, it may have either a relaxing or a stimulating effect on the user, depending on the circumstances and the user's expectations. Nicotine is addictive, and people who stop smoking may experience a variety of withdrawal symptoms including craving for tobacco, increased appetite, stomach cramps, headaches, restlessness, irritability, insomnia, anxiety, and depression.

The long-term effects of smoking have been well publicized. Over five hundred thousand people die every year from coronary heart disease, cancer, respiratory diseases, and other diseases caused by smoking. There is also evidence that women who smoke while pregnant have a higher incidence of miscarriages, stillbirths, low birth-weight babies, and babies who die from sudden infant death syndrome (SIDS) than women who do not smoke (Shea & Steiner, 2008; Zotti, Replogle, & Sappenfield, 2003).

Amphetamines

Amphetamines are much more powerful stimulants, sold under such trade names as Adderall® and Dexedrine® and known on the street as methamphetamine, which is a slightly altered version of amphetamine. These drugs tend to dramatically increase alertness and activity, counteract fatigue, and promote feelings of euphoria and well-being. These effects are most likely caused by the influence of amphetamine on both norepinephrine- and dopamine-containing neurons. Amphetamines increase the activity of these neurotransmitters by increasing the amount released from the nerve terminal and by preventing their reuptake (Ettinger, 2017).

Amphetamines A group of powerful stimulants, including Benzedrine, Dexedrine, and Ritalin, that dramatically increase alertness and promote a feeling of euphoria

People use amphetamines for a variety of reasons: to stay awake, to feel good, to improve energy levels, to increase confidence, and to lose weight (amphetamines are short-term appetite suppressants). Most users take the drug orally, but some inject it directly into a vein. When amphetamines are used in excess, they can cause muscle and joint aches, tremors, and feelings of paranoia. In extreme cases amphetamines produce both punding, which is a repetitive motor response, and *amphetamine psychosis*, which combines paranoia with hallucinations and difficulty recognizing people. Methamphetamine addiction has become a major problem in many areas of the country.

Cocaine

Cocaine is a powerful central nervous system stimulant that is extracted from leaves of the coca shrub. It is often sniffed (snorted) through a straw into the mucous membranes of the nasal passages. A solution of the drug may also be injected into the vein. Crack is the street name given to cocaine that has been processed from cocaine hydrochloride (the crystalline derivative of the coca leaf that is sold on the street as coke) into freebase by using ammonia or baking soda and water, and heating the mixture. (The baking soda causes a crackling sound when the base is heated, thus giving rise to the street name.)

COCA-COLA
SYRUP ❖ AND ❖ EXTRACT.
For Soda Water and other Carbonated Beverages.
This "INTELLECTUAL BEVERAGE" and TEMPERANCE DRINK contains the valuable TONIC and NERVE STIMULANT properties of the Coca plant and Cola (or Kola) nuts, and makes not only a delicious, exhilarating, refreshing and invigorating Beverage, (dispensed from the soda water fountain or in other carbonated beverages), but a valuable Brain Tonic, and a cure for all nervous affections — SICK HEAD-ACHE, NEURALGIA, HYSTERIA, MELANCHOLY, &c.
The peculiar flavor of COCA-COLA delights every palate; it is dispensed from the soda fountain in same manner as any of the fruit syrups.
J. S. Pemberton;
Chemist,
Sole Proprietor, Atlanta, Ga.

(Wikimedia Commons/Public Domain)

When Coca-Cola® first appeared on the market in 1885, it contained cocaine. Cocaine was removed from soft drinks in 1903.

No matter which form is used, many of cocaine's effects are similar to those of amphetamines. They include increased alertness and abundance of energy, feelings of euphoria, and a sense of well-being. Cocaine increases heart and respiration rates, constricts blood vessels, and dilates the pupils. It is metabolized very quickly, so its effects often last only twenty to thirty minutes. Thus, to maintain a high, the user must take the drug frequently—one reason why a cocaine habit can become very costly.

Like other drugs, cocaine seems to derive its effects by altering normal patterns of dopamine activity, primarily in the mesolimbic cortical system (the brain's reward system). There is good evidence that cocaine blocks the reuptake of dopamine and norepinephrine, increasing the time these chemicals actively stimulate their receptors.

Cocaine is perhaps the most powerfully addictive substance we know. Its abuse can lead to severe problems including heart and lung damage, anemia, damage to the nasal tissues, immune system impairment, and, in rare cases, sudden death. Despite these facts, cocaine use continues to be problematic in America. In 2010, surveys revealed that over forty-two million Americans had used some form of cocaine, and about 2,700 people try it for the first time each day. About 8 percent of high school seniors report having tried cocaine at least one time (National Institute on Drug Abuse, 2016). Although there is no known cure for cocaine addiction, research in the author's laboratory has resulted in a cocaine vaccine. Rats vaccinated with the cocaine antibody preparation became resistant to cocaine's reinforcing and analgesic effects (Johnson & Ettinger, 2000; R. Ettinger, W. Ettinger, & Harless, 1997). Whether or not an anti-cocaine vaccine will become available to treat cocaine addicts remains to be seen.

3.9c Hallucinogens: LSD and Ecstasy

LSD

Derived from the ergot fungus that grows on rye grass, **LSD (lysergic acid diethylamide)** became recognized for its psychoactive properties in the 1940s. Throughout the 1950s and early 1960s, researchers experimented with it as a tool for treating behavioral and emotional disorders, as a pain reliever for people suffering from terminal disease, and as a drug that might have possible military applications. Eventually, LSD fell into disrepute, largely because of its unpredictable effects. However, this official disfavor did not curtail its growing popularity as a street drug used to alter and expand consciousness. In recent years, LSD's popularity has somewhat resurged, particularly among high school students. In 1997, 14 percent of high school seniors reported that they had experimented with LSD at least once. This number has steadily decreased to about 3 percent (National Institute on Drug Abuse, 2016).

LSD is one of the most powerful known **hallucinogens**. A tiny amount can produce profound distortions of sensations, feelings, perception of time, and thought. Some users describe an LSD trip as spiritual, mind expanding, and a source of ecstasy. Some claim that the drug adds to their creativity, but this assertion is unfounded. Others have painful, frightening experiences in which they may feel that they have lost control, that their bodies are undergoing change, or that they have left their body behind. Having a good LSD experience one time is no guarantee that the next LSD experience will not turn into a nightmare.

Brain researchers are still not sure how drugs such as LSD produce hallucinogenic effects, but they theorize that hallucinations result from the disruption of the neural circuits responsible for filtering sensory information. Normally, serotonin modulates awareness by filtering a large proportion of sensory and somatosensory information that is unnecessary for normal functioning. LSD appears to open these filters so an increased amount of sensory information is processed (González-Maeso et al., 2007).

Ecstasy

Ecstasy, or MDMA, is a much less powerful hallucinogenic drug than LSD, and some researchers do not even classify it as such. However, ecstasy is known to produce both bodily and visual distortions in some users. The most prominent effects of ecstasy are mood enhancement and a profound sense of well-being. Users may also experience a sense of depersonalization and thought disturbances. Ecstasy exerts these effects by causing the release of large amounts of serotonin. By releasing large amounts of serotonin, and also interfering with its synthesis, ecstasy leads to serotonin depletion. As a result, it takes the human brain a significant amount of time to rebuild the store of serotonin needed to perform important physiological and psychological functions. Not all of ecstasy's effects, however, are as desirable as these. Users commonly experience hyperthermia, rapid heart rate, high blood pressure, muscle rigidity, and convulsions. Of the recreational drugs discussed here, ecstasy is by far the most toxic to the nervous system and repeated use appears to irreversibly destroy serotonin-containing neurons (National Institute on Drug Abuse, 2016). Fortunately the use of ecstasy has declined over recent years from 8.3 percent of high school seniors in 2003 to about 3.6 percent in 2014 (2016).

LSD (Lysergic Acid Diethylamide) Hallucinogenic drug derived from a fungus that grows on rye grass that produces profound distortions of sensations, feelings, time, and thought

Hallucinogens Class of psychoactive drugs, including LSD and ecstasy, that alter sensory perceptions, thinking processes, and emotions, often causing delusions, hallucinations, and altered sense of time and space

3.9d Marijuana

As a recreational drug, **marijuana** is the most widely used of the illegal psychoactive drugs, second in popularity only to alcohol. Marijuana use appears to have leveled off since its all time high in 1997, when it was estimated that 50 percent of twelfth graders had used marijuana. In 2015, more than two million Americans had tried marijuana and 45 percent of twelfth graders had used it at least once (National Institute on Drug Abuse, 2016).

(Shutterstock)

Marijuana has been found to have medicinal qualities, although the controversy surrounding its legalization in the United States is likely to continue for some time.

Marijuana is derived from the flowering top of the *Cannabis sativa*, a hemp plant once known primarily as an excellent material for making ropes. The mind-altering component of marijuana is the chemical THC (delta 9-tetrahydrocannabinol).

Until recently, researchers did not know how marijuana altered the activity of the brain to produce its euphoric effects. However, William Devane and his coworkers have recently identified receptors for THC in the brain, as well as a natural substance that binds with these THC receptors. The brain's natural THC has been named **anandamide**, meaning bliss (Devane et al., 1992). It is now believed that anandamide plays an important role in regulating mood, pain, movement, and appetite.

Two physiological effects of marijuana use are increased heart rate and enhanced appetite. Small doses often produce euphoria and enhance some sensory experiences, such as listening to music. Marijuana impairs reaction time and the ability to concentrate on complex tasks; some people become confused, agitated, or extremely anxious under its influence. Marijuana impairs a person's perceptual skills and motor coordination, thus significantly increasing his or her risk of having an accident while driving an automobile. Recall may also be impaired while under the influence of marijuana. There are few if any long-term effects of marijuana use.

Medical practitioners have discovered that marijuana can be therapeutic in some situations. For example, it can be helpful in epilepsy and glaucoma (a disease that can cause blindness). It has been shown to reduce the nausea that often accompanies chemotherapy treatment for cancer patients, and it may now be used to prevent some of the weight loss associated with AIDS diseases. Because of these legitimate medical uses, marijuana is legally obtained for these purposes in many states. Controversy still surrounds the issue of marijuana legalization in the United States and is likely to continue for some time. Several states have legalized marijuana for recreational use, including Washington, Colorado, Alaska, and Oregon. Other states are considering legalization, and this trend is expected to continue.

Marijuana Drug derived from the hemp plant *Cannabis sativa*, containing the chemical THC (delta 9-tetrahydrocannabinol)

Anandamide A naturally occurring substance that binds to THC receptors in the brain; marijuana contains THC, which also binds to these receptors.

CHAPTER REVIEW

Overview of the Nervous System: Organization and Function

1. The nervous system of humans and other vertebrates consists of two major parts: the central nervous system (CNS) and the peripheral nervous system (PNS).
2. The CNS consists of the brain and the spinal cord. It occupies the commanding position in the nervous system, as it coordinates and integrates all bodily functions.
3. The PNS transmits messages to and from the CNS. It is subdivided into the somatic nervous system and the autonomic nervous system.

Neurons: Basic Units of the Nervous System

4. There are three major classes of neurons: sensory neurons that carry messages to the CNS; motor neurons that transmit messages from the CNS to muscles and glands; and interneurons that act as intermediaries between sensory and motor neurons.
5. Neurons have four common structures: The cell body, which handles metabolic functions; the dendrites, which receive neural messages; the axon, which conducts a message to the end of the neuron; and the terminal buttons at the end of the axon, which release transmitter substances.
6. The transmission of a neural message involves both electrical and chemical aspects. Electrical processes are activated when the dendrites (or cell body) of a neuron respond to an impulse from neighboring neurons by undergoing a change in permeability of the cell membrane. Voltage changes then occur due to an influx of positive sodium ions through the more permeable membrane. These voltage changes are called graded potentials. When the sum of graded potentials reaches a sufficient magnitude, an electrical signal or action potential is generated that flows along the length of the neuron.
7. Neural impulses are transmitted from one neuron to another, across the synaptic gap, via chemical messengers called neurotransmitters. These transmitter substances may act either to excite or inhibit action potentials in the receiving neuron.
8. Variations in neurotransmitter levels, or in responsiveness to these chemical messengers, have been linked with various psychological disorders and the action of numerous drugs.
9. Endogenous opioids, which are part of a family of neurotransmitters known as neuropeptides, have been linked to a range of behavioral and mental processes, including inducing euphoria, counteracting stress, modulating food and liquid intake, facilitating learning and memory, and reducing pain.

CHAPTER REVIEW

The Peripheral Nervous System

10. The PNS, which transfers information to and from the CNS, has two divisions: somatic and autonomic.
11. The somatic nervous system serves the major skeletal muscles that carry out intentional movements. It also contains nerves that transmit sensory information from the skin, muscles, and sensory organs of the body.
12. The autonomic nervous system controls the glands and smooth muscles of internal organs. The two subdivisions of the autonomic nervous system, the sympathetic and parasympathetic systems, operate in an integrative fashion to allow the body to function optimally when either relaxed or highly aroused. The sympathetic system is particularly active during emotional emergencies. The parasympathetic system, which provides a braking mechanism for organs activated by the sympathetic system, is more involved during relaxation and body restoration.

The Central Nervous System

13. The spinal cord conveys messages to and from the brain, helps coordinate the two sides of the body, and mediates certain basic reflexive behaviors (such as the quick withdrawal of a hand from a hot stove).
14. The medulla, the lowest part of the brain, contains centers that control many vital life-support functions such as breathing, heartbeat, and blood pressure.
15. The pons, a large bulge in the lower brain core, plays a role in fine-tuning motor messages and in processing some sensory information.
16. The cerebellum, tucked beneath the back part of the cerebral hemispheres, coordinates and regulates motor movements.
17. The reticular formation or reticular activating system, a set of neural circuits extending from the lower brain up to the thalamus, plays a role in controlling levels of arousal and alertness.
18. The limbic system, a collection of structures located around the central core of the brain, is closely associated with emotional expression. It also is active in motivation, learning, and memory.
19. The hypothalamus, located beneath the thalamus, helps to maintain homeostasis within the body's internal environment. In addition, it plays a key role in controlling emotional expression and serves as the hub of the neuroendocrine system.
20. The thalamus, located beneath the cerebral cortex, plays a role in routing incoming sensory information to appropriate areas within the cerebral cortex.
21. The basal ganglia consists of several structures involved in motor movement, including the caudate nucleus, putamen, and substantia nigra.

CHAPTER REVIEW

The Cerebral Cortex

22. The cerebral cortex, the thin outer layer of the cortex, is the part of the brain responsible for higher mental processes such as perceiving, thinking, and remembering.
23. To some degree, researchers have been able to localize a variety of functions within various regions or lobes of the cortex of the two hemispheres. The frontal lobe contains the motor cortex, a narrow strip of brain tissue that controls a wide range of intentional body movements. The primary brain center for controlling speech is also in the frontal lobe. The parietal lobe contains the somatosensory cortex, which receives sensory information about touch, pressure, pain, temperature, and body position from various areas of the body. The occipital lobe consists primarily of the visual cortex, devoted to the business of seeing. Hearing, a primary function of the temporal lobe is localized in the auditory cortex.
24. Split-brain research, in which the primary connection between the two hemispheres (the corpus callosum) is severed, has revealed important information about the degree to which a particular function is controlled by one rather than both hemispheres (lateralization of function). This research has supported the interpretation that in most people the left hemisphere is primarily responsible for language and speech, logic, and mathematics. In contrast, the right hemisphere appears to be more important in perceiving spatial relationships, manipulating objects, synthesizing (generalizing the whole from segments), and artistic functions.
25. A number of techniques are employed to study the brain: lesion production, brain stimulation and electrical recording via implanted wires, electroencephalography (EEG), computerized axial tomography (CAT), positron emission tomography (PET), and magnetic resonance imaging (MRI) and fMRI.

The Endocrine System

26. The endocrine system is composed of several ductless glands that secrete hormones directly into the bloodstream. The endocrine system often works in tandem with the nervous system to regulate a variety of bodily responses. The hypothalamus functions as a key interface between the nervous system and the endocrine system.
27. The endocrine system influences many important physiological functions, mental processes, and behavior patterns, including disease regulation, metabolism, emotional responses, and motivation.

CHAPTER REVIEW

28. The pituitary gland produces hormones that trigger other glands to action. Among other important products of the pituitary are growth hormones, which control a number of metabolic functions including the rate of growth, and neuropeptides, which act as neurotransmitters that influence such things as eating and drinking, sexual behavior, sleep, pain reduction, and responses to stress.
29. The thyroid gland produces thyroxine, which helps to regulate metabolism. Lethargy and hyperactivity are related to too little or too much thyroxine, respectively.
30. The paired adrenal glands produce a variety of hormones, including epinephrine and norepinephrine, which prepare the body to respond to emergencies and cope with stress.
31. The gonads secrete several varieties of sex hormones that influence development of physical sex characteristics, sexual reproduction, and sexual motivation.

Drugs and Behavior

32. Sedative drugs such as Librium, Valium, barbiturates, and Seconal induce relaxation and sleep. They are often prescribed for anxiety and sleep disorders.
33. Opiates or narcotics such as morphine and heroin induce a state of euphoria and are highly addictive. The opiates (Vicodin and Oxycodone) are often prescribed to control pain.
34. Alcohol acts as a central nervous system depressant in the cerebral cortex and cerebellum. Alcohol is the nation's number one drug problem.
35. The major stimulants include caffeine, nicotine, amphetamine, and cocaine.
36. Amphetamine and cocaine are powerful stimulants that are highly addictive.
37. The hallucinogens such as LSD and ecstasy produce changes in perception and emotions.
38. Marijuana has few, if any, long-term effects on cognition, but it does disrupt cognitive functioning (including memory) when a person is under its influence. A number of states have legalized marijuana for medical purposes.

TERMS AND CONCEPTS

Acetylcholine (ACh), pg. 73
Action Potential, pg. 69
Addiction, pg. 103
Adrenal Glands, pg. 101
Agnosias, pg. 91
All-or-None Law, pg. 69
Amphetamines, pg. 107
Amygdala, pg. 83
Anandamide, pg. 109
Association Cortex, pg. 88
Auditory Cortex, pg. 90
Autonomic Nervous System (ANS), pg. 76
Axon, pg. 66
Axon Hillock, pg. 69
Basal Ganglia, pg. 86
Brain Stimulation, pg. 96
Broca's Aphasia, pg. 89
Broca's Area, pg. 89
Caudate Nucleus, pg. 86
Cell Body, pg. 65
Central Nervous System (CNS), pg. 63
Cerebellum, pg. 81
Cerebral Cortex, pg. 86
Cerebral Hemispheres, pg. 77
Computerized Axial Tomography (CAT), pg. 98
Corpus Callosum, pg. 92
Dendrite, pg. 65
Dependence, pg. 103
Depressants, pg. 103
Dopamine, pg. 74
Electrical Recording, pg. 97
Electroencephalography (EEG), pg. 97
Endocrine System, pg. 99
Endorphins, pg. 74
Excitatory Postsynaptic Potentials (EPSPs), pg. 72
Frontal Lobe, pg. 88
Functional Magnetic Resonance Imaging (fMRI), pg. 98
Gamma-Amino-Butyric Acid (GABA), pg. 74
Glia, pg. 65
Glutamate (Glutamic Acid), pg. 74
Gonads, pg. 102
Graded Potential, pg. 69
Hallucinogens, pg. 108
Hippocampus, pg. 84
Hormones, pg. 99
Hypothalamus, pg. 85
Inhibitory Postsynaptic Potentials (IPSPs), pg. 72
Interneuron, pg. 65
Lateralization of Function, pg. 92
Lesion Production, pg. 96
Limbic System, pg. 82
LSD (Lysergic Acid Diethylamide), pg. 108
Magnetic Resonance Imaging (MRI), pg. 98
Marijuana, pg. 109
Medulla, pg. 80
Mesolimbic-Cortical System, pg. 85
Motor Cortex, pg. 88
Motor Neuron, pg. 65
Myelin Sheath, pg. 70
Nerve, pg. 76
Nervous System, pg. 63
Neuron, pg. 65
Neurotransmitter, pg. 71
Node of Ranvier, pg. 70
Norepinephrine , pg. 74

TERMS AND CONCEPTS

Occipital Lobe, pg. 90
Opiates (Narcotics), pg. 104
Parasympathetic Nervous System, pg. 77
Parietal Lobe, pg. 90
Peripheral Nervous System (PNS), pg. 63
Pituitary Gland, pg. 101
Pons, pg. 81
Positron Emission Tomography (PET), pg. 98
Prosopagnosia, pg. 91
Putamen, pg. 86
Resting Potential, pg. 67
Reticular Activating System (RAS), pg. 82
Reticular Formation, pg. 82
Sedatives, pg. 103
Sensory Cortex, pg. 88
Sensory Neuron, pg. 65
Septal Area, pg. 84
Serotonin, pg. 74
Somatic Nervous System, pg. 76
Somatosensory Cortex, pg. 90
Stimulants, pg. 105
Substantia Nigra, pg. 86
Sympathetic Nervous System, pg. 77
Synapse, pg. 70
Temporal Lobe, pg. 90
Terminal Button, pg. 66
Thalamus, pg. 85
Thyroid Gland, pg. 101
Thyroxine, pg. 101
Tolerance, pg. 103
Visual Cortex, pg. 90
Wernicke's Aphasia, pg. 90
Wernicke's Area, pg. 90

POP QUIZ

True or False

___ 1. The terminal buttons of one neuron secrete a neurotransmitter into the synapse where it stimulates the axon of a second neuron.

___ 2. Neurotransmitters may have either an excitatory or inhibitory effect on the postsynaptic membrane.

___ 3. Following the body's response to an emergency situation, the parasympathetic nervous system resumes control of bodily functions such as heart rate and digestion.

___ 4. The cerebellum is the brain structure responsible for higher mental processes such as perceiving, thinking, and remembering.

___ 5. Marijuana may have a sedative effect, stimulant effect, or an antidepressant effect.

Multiple Choice

6. Which is the last part of the neuron to be involved in the transmission of a neural impulse toward the next neuron?
   a. Axon hillock
   b. Cell body
   c. Dendrites
   d. Terminal button
7. Two factors that relate to the perceived intensity of a stimulus are how many neurons are firing action potentials and ______.
   a. if the axons have myelin sheaths
   b. the voltage associated with each action potential
   c. the rate at which these neurons are firing
   d. whether the supply of neurotransmitter is exhausted
8. The two major divisions of the peripheral nervous system are which of the following?
   a. Afferent and efferent
   b. Sympathetic and parasympathetic
   c. Somatic and parasympathetic
   d. Somatic and autonomic
9. A major difference between the sympathetic and parasympathetic nervous system is that the sympathetic nervous system provides which function?
   a. Increases the level of functioning in all the affected bodily systems
   b. Decreases the level of functioning in all the affected bodily systems
   c. Stimulates the different parts of the body independently of one another
   d. Simultaneously stimulates the different parts of the body

POP QUIZ

10. Which role does the reticular formation play?
    a. Life-supporting functions such as breathing and heartbeat
    b. The fine-tuning of motor messages
    c. Coordinating and regulating motor movements
    d. Controlling levels of arousal and alertness
11. If you were to electrically stimulate a person's occipital lobe, that person would most likely have which of the following reactions?
    a. Have difficulty recalling their phone number
    b. Report a visual experience
    c. Move a part of their body
    d. Report an auditory experience
12. If a split-brain operated patient sees "air x plane" briefly while focusing on the "x," the patient would say that he or she saw which of the following words?
    a. Plane
    b. Airplane
    c. Air
    d. That patient would report that he or she did not see a word.
13. The pituitary hormones do which of the following?
    a. Have a variety of target organs
    b. Have the thyroid as their only target organ
    c. Directly influence the hypothalamus to begin secreting hormones
    d. Become neuropeptides
14. What are the three major types of psychoactive drugs?
    a. Sedatives, opiates, and hallucinogens
    b. Depressants, amphetamines, and cocaine
    c. Depressants, stimulants, and hallucinogens
    d. Alcohol, opiates, and hallucinogens
15. A person admitted to a hospital following drug use is experiencing hyperthermia, rapid heart rate, high blood pressure, muscle rigidity, and convulsions. Most likely he took which one of the following drugs?
    a. Seconal
    b. Heroin
    c. Ecstasy
    d. Cocaine

Answer Key: 1.F 2.T 3.F 4.F 5.F 6.d 7.c 8.d 9.d 10.d 11.b 12.a 13.a 14.c 15.c

(Shutterstock)

Sensation *and* Perception

Did you ever wonder whether other animals perceive the world as we do? What is the world like from a bird's point of view, a bat's, or an insect's? Psychologists have known for a long time that the sensory worlds of different animals are very unlike our own. The world to an insect is defined in terms of odors and tastes that tell it what foods to eat and how to find a mate. The world of the bat is a complex multidimensional acoustical space that allows for precise navigation and the perception of prey. Neither of these species perceives the world as we do. Even though a bird's dominant sense is vision, like our own, their world is also quite different.

Consider the prairie falcon. The structure of its eye allows for high-resolution vision of the ground while in flight. In fact, it can keep its prey in sharp focus during a 150-mile-per-hour dive. At this speed our world becomes a blur. The prairie falcon's eye is not as well adapted to vision while perched, however. This bird often perches with its head tilted to one side to allow an image to fall on the top part of its inner eye (the retina) where it can bring the image into sharp focus. While the falcon is in flight, this is not a problem because images from the ground normally fall on the top part of the retina (Waldvogel, 1990).

This chapter is concerned with both the sensory processes that bring us information about our environments and the neural activity that gives this information meaning. Although many of the processes described in this chapter may seem to be physiological and not psychological, it is important to remember that our sensations and perceptions form the raw material on which much of our behavior is based. As our prairie falcon demonstrates, behavior is both limited by, and defines, an organism's perceptual abilities.

4.1 Principles of Sensation and Perception

All perceptions begin with a *stimulus*, some type of physical energy such as a sound or a flash of light, to which we can respond. The stimulus produces a physiological change in specific sensory receptor cells; and this information is then transmitted to the brain, where it is organized and interpreted. The direct effect of stimulation of receptor cells by a stimulus is referred to as **sensation**. Our organization and interpretation of sensory experience is referred to as **perception**.

Five major senses provide us with important information about the outside world. These senses are vision, hearing, smell, taste, and the skin senses (pressure, temperature, and pain). In addition, the so-called body sense (kinesthesis) allows us to detect movement and the position of our bodies. Although the messages differ, the process by which sensory information reaches our brains is the same. This process is called transduction.

Sensations Basic, immediate experiences that a stimulus, such as a sound, elicits in a sense organ, such as the ear

Perception Process of interpreting, organizing, and often elaborating on sensations

Transduction Process by which sensory organs transform mechanical, chemical, or light energy into the electrochemical energy that is generated by neurons firing

4.1a Transduction

In order for us to sense and perceive the surrounding world, information about external events must reach our brains. This information comes in many forms: mechanical energy for hearing and the skin senses, chemical energy for smelling and tasting, and light energy for seeing. However, as you recall from Chapter 3, the brain is able to respond only to the electrochemical events that are generated by neurons firing. Therefore, before we can perceive our environment, all sensory input must be transformed into neural activity that can be processed by the brain. The process by which sensory organs transform mechanical, chemical, or light energy into neural activity is called **transduction**.

Psychophysics Study of the relationship between the physical aspects of external stimuli and our own perceptions of these stimuli

Each sense receptor has specialized cells designed to respond to a particular kind of energy. For example, our eyes contain chemicals called photopigments that change their shape when they are hit by light. These shape changes initiate a series of events that ultimately culminate in the transmission of neuronal activity to the brain. Likewise, other kinds of receptors transduce other kinds of energy into electrical impulses.

Distinguishing Types of Sensory Impulses

We know that the brain cannot respond directly to physical energy such as pressure or light. This information must first be transduced into neuronal signals. If all sensory messages are converted to neuronal signals, how does the brain distinguish among them? How can it differentiate among the impulses that represent sight, sound, taste, and smell? Take a moment to consider this question before reading on.

Perhaps a useful clue to answer this question comes from some discoveries made in brain surgery, when various sites on the surface of an alert patient's cortex have been electrically stimulated. Such stimulation may produce vivid sensations. For example, stimulation of the occipital cortex at the back of the brain can create sensations of flashing lights, and stimulating the auditory region on the side of the brain can cause the patient to hear tones (Penfield & Perot, 1963).

As this evidence reveals, the ability to distinguish sensations does not depend on differences between the sense organs but rather on that part of the brain that is activated by the sensory messages. Chapter 3 pointed out that sensory nerves carry impulses to particular target sites within the brain. It is now widely believed that the distinctiveness of sights, sounds, smells, and tastes are related to unique properties of tissue in various parts of the brain. Later in this chapter we will examine remarkable evidence of this fact as we explore the world of individuals with synesthesia—the ability to hear flavors or see sounds, for example.

4.1b What Do We Perceive?

The fact that sensations result from the transduction of physical energy in the environment into neural impulses raises an interesting question: Since noises, smells, sights, and sounds surround us, why are we not equally aware of all these sensations? For instance, as you are reading, your nervous system is being bombarded with stimuli from numerous different sources. Beside the visual stimuli this book provides, there are other sounds, sights, smells, and tactile sensations. Your world is full of different kinds of physical energy.

Although many of these physical events are transformed into sensations and ultimately perceptions, many also go unheeded. What factors determine whether or not we perceive the things happening around us? There are several factors; the most important are sensory thresholds, attention, and adaptation. The investigation of these factors can be traced from the very beginnings of psychology to the present in a field of psychology called **psychophysics**. Psychophysics is the part of psychology that focuses on the relationship between physical aspects of external stimuli and our perceptions of them.

4.1c Psychophysics

Sensory Thresholds

The psychological world constructed by our brain is much simpler than the physical complexity of the world around us because our sense organs do not inform our brains about all of the events that take place. Our perception of various sensory inputs can occur only when the strength of a stimulus reaches a minimal or **threshold** level of intensity sufficient to activate a sensory process. For example, our sense of smell is activated only when an adequate number of chemical molecules are present in the air.

One of the most important reasons we do not respond to many stimuli, therefore, is simply the biological limitations of our senses. If our senses responded to all the sights, sounds, smells, and other stimuli around us, we would be overwhelmed by too much stimulation. Two kinds of sensory thresholds operate to limit our perception of sensation: Absolute thresholds and difference thresholds.

Threshold Minimum level of intensity or strength of a stimulus that is sufficient to activate a sensory process (for instance, the minimum number of molecules that must be present in the air for us to smell a substance)

Absolute Threshold Minimum physical intensity of a stimulus that can be perceived by an observer 50 percent of the time

Difference Threshold The minimum difference in intensity that we can distinguish between two stimuli 50 percent of the time; also known as the *just noticeable difference (jnd)*

Absolute and Difference Thresholds

Imagine yourself waiting at a restaurant for a special person with whom you will dine. When the person arrives and takes a seat at your table, you think you perceive a subtle scent of perfume or cologne but you're not quite sure. For several minutes, you wonder whether you are imagining the scent or if you really do smell it. As you begin talking, you move closer. Suddenly you recognize the scent. Although it is not strong, it is detectable enough to distinguish clearly. How intense did the scent need to be just to notice it, and how much more was necessary to recognize clearly its identity? Both of these questions are about sensory thresholds. The first question pertains to what psychologists call an absolute threshold, and the second question refers to a difference threshold.

Absolute Thresholds

When you first noticed the perfume or cologne but couldn't be sure what it was, its intensity was at your **absolute threshold**. An absolute threshold is defined as the minimum physical intensity of a stimulus that can be perceived by an observer 50 percent of the time. Figure 4-1 demonstrates some absolute thresholds for the five major senses. These values are average, and your sensory organs may be more or less sensitive than those of the sample. Absolute thresholds for various sensory modalities differ from person to person. In addition, these averages represent ideal conditions in a laboratory. Clearly, you could not hear a watch ticking 20 feet away under normal circumstances.

Difference Thresholds

As your friend moved closer and you could now distinguish the scent, this change in intensity was sufficient to reach your difference threshold. A **difference threshold** is the minimum increase in the intensity of a stimulus necessary to just notice a change 50 percent of the time. This increase in intensity is also referred to as a *just noticeable difference*, or *jnd*. You may wonder why thresholds are defined as stimulus intensities perceived 50 percent of the time. As you can see in Figure 4-2, our perception of a stimulus changes as stimulus intensity increases.

In an experiment to test your threshold for a particular stimulus, the experimenter might present you with a series of stimuli at different intensities, and you would report whether you perceived a stimulus or not after each trial. All of the stimuli would be presented several times to you in random order. A graph such as Figure 4-2 could then be constructed with your responses, either yes or no, as to whether or not you perceived a stimulus on each trial. The percentage of correct responses perceived at each stimulus intensity is then plotted on the figure. For example, if the stimulus intensity was very low, you might report perceiving it only 25 percent of the time when it was actually presented. Responding yes 50 percent or more of the time to particular stimulus intensity indicates better than chance. Below 50 percent is poorer than chance performance.

Weber's Law and the Just Noticeable Difference

Our perception of a particular stimulus is always relative to its background level or its context. Thus, the degree of

Figure 4-1 Absolute Sensory Thresholds

SIGHT

Candle flame seen from a distance of 27 km (17 miles)

TOUCH

The wing of a bee falling on your cheek from a distance of 1 cm (0.39 inch)

TASTE

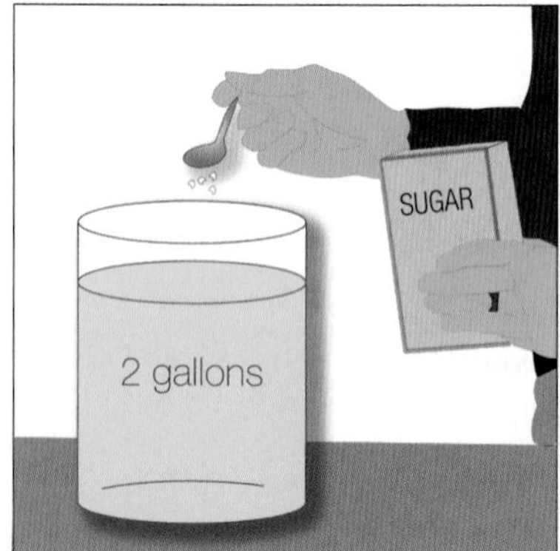

One teaspoon of sugar dissolved in 2 gallons of distilled water (1 part in 2,000)

SMELL

One drop of perfume in a three-room house (1 part in 500,000)

HEARING

Ticking of a watch in a room 6 meters (20 feet) away

increase or decrease in intensity that is necessary to produce a jnd depends on the original strength of the stimulus. In 1834, a German scientist, E. H. Weber (the W is pronounced as a V), conducted a classic experiment that revealed one of the first major principles of sensation. He discovered that the difference threshold for various stimulus intensities tends to be a constant fraction of the original stimulus intensity. Thus, as the strength of the original stimulus increases, the magnitude of the change must also increase in order for a jnd to be perceived. This relationship is known as **Weber's law**.

Weber's Law One of the major principles of sensation, based on the fact that for various stimulus intensities, the difference threshold tends to be a constant fraction of the stimulus—as the strength of the original stimulus increases, the magnitude of the change must also increase for a just noticeable difference to be perceived

In mathematical form, Weber's law is expressed as the following equation:

$$\Delta I = kI$$

where ΔI is the change in stimulus intensity necessary for a jnd, I is the initial stimulus intensity, and k is a value known as Weber's constant.

Although this sounds complicated, it is really quite simple to apply. In a psychophysics experiment you might be asked to judge the difference between two weights—say one 10 lb. weight and another 10.10 lb. weight. The difference of 0.10 lb. is not enough to tell

Figure 4-2 Measuring Stimulus Thresholds

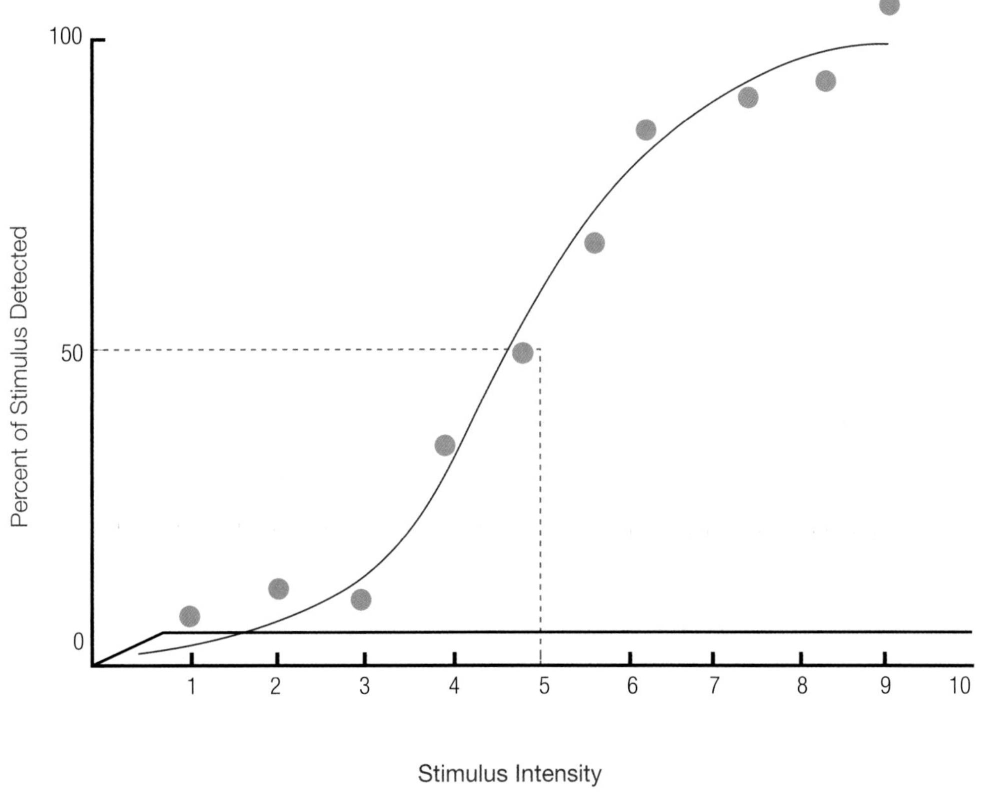

the difference (0.10 lb. is less than 1 jnd for 10 lb.). However, if the second weight were increased to 10.20 lb., you could now detect a noticeable difference. The ratio of stimulus intensity for a jnd of weight is 1/50, or 0.02 lb. Using this ratio and Weber's Law, how many pounds would have to be added to a 100 lb. weight for you to just notice a difference? If you answered 2 lb. (not 0.2 lb.), you would be correct, because $\Delta I = 0.02 \times 100$, or 2. The fraction, 0.02 or 1/50, is called a Weber's constant. Weber discovered that this constant remains the same for each dimension of sensation, but changes for different stimulus dimensions. For instance, Weber's constant for brightness of light is 1/60, and for the taste of salt, 1/3 (Goldstein, 2010).

$$\Delta I = kI \qquad \Delta I = 0.02 \times 100, \text{ or } 2$$

Attention

Another factor influencing how much of the outside world we perceive is attention. In most situations, it is impossible to be aware of all the stimuli around us, even if we are biologically capable of responding to them. Instead, we pay attention to some but not to others. For example, while talking to your dinner date you may not have been aware of the music in the background because you were listening to your friend. After it stops, however, your attention might shift so that you hear the next song.

Attention Psychological selection mechanism that determines which stimuli an organism responds to or perceives

Sensory Adaptation In perception, the decrease in the response of sensory receptors to stimuli when exposed to continual, unchanging stimulation

Signal Detection Theory Theory that says our ability to detect a sensory stimulus (signal) depends not only on the intensity of the signal but also on variables such as distractions and motivation

Attention is a selective psychological process in that we are aware of certain stimuli and not others at any given moment. Attention does not block the physical and biological response of our sense organs to these stimuli; it simply increases or decreases our psychological perception of these events. Of course, some stimuli are difficult to overlook—for example, someone mentioning your name in a conversation at the next table. At other times attention to one stimulus interferes with our perception of another. Later in this chapter, we consider several characteristics of stimuli that are particularly effective in capturing our attention.

Sensory Adaptation

Sensory adaptation describes the decrease in the response of sensory receptors when they are exposed to continual, unchanging stimulation. Sensory adaptation occurs in all of the sensory organs, but some adapt more quickly than others. In fact, perception is actually dependent on stimulus change. If stimuli remain constant, we adapt to them, and they are no longer perceivable.

Take a few moments to think about how your various senses adapt to continual, unchanging stimulation. Which of the senses seems to adapt the most quickly? Which sense modality is the slowest to adapt?

Our receptors for smell are the quickest to adapt, which is fortunate for people who live near industrial plants or have jobs requiring them to work in foul-smelling environments. Most of our other senses adapt fairly quickly to constant stimulation. For example, you are probably not aware of background noises in your room until they actually change. You may only notice that your refrigerator is quite noisy when it shuts off.

Sensory adaptation in the visual system also occurs when a stimulus remains constant. Visual adaptation is much more difficult to detect because our eyes continually move, rapidly changing the location of the stimulus within the eye. These rapid scanning movements of the eye are called saccadic movements. Experiments with special contact lenses can fix an image on the surface of the eye, allowing for visual adaptation. In such experiments, subjects report seeing an image quickly fade and disappear.

You can conduct a simple experiment to demonstrate sensory adaptation to yourself. Place ice-cold water in one container, lukewarm water in another, and water so hot you can barely stand it in a third. Put your right hand in the ice water and your left hand in the very hot water. After a couple of minutes, put both hands into the container of lukewarm water. Since your right hand was previously adapted to ice water, the lukewarm water feels very hot. Conversely, your left hand feels cold because it has adapted to the high temperature.

Unfortunately, the one sense modality that adapts very slowly (and usually only to a slight degree) is pain. People who are faced with chronic pain may learn to live with their discomfort, but seldom do they experience anything resembling acceptable adaptation. Research has demonstrated that although we often adapt somewhat to mild pain, we may not adapt to extremely painful stimuli (Coren & Ward, 1989). In one experiment, subjects rated the pain they felt from immersing their hands in hot water over a period of time. Figure 4-3 shows the results. Adaptation was complete for lower temperatures, but it diminished with increasing pain to the point where there was no adaptation to the most painful stimulus level (Hardy, Stolwijk, & Hoffman, 1968).

Signal Detection Theory

Other important variables that influence what we do or do not perceive are addressed by **signal detection theory**. According to this perspective, our ability to detect a sensory

Figure 4-3 Pain Adaptation

Average estimates of intensity of pain from different durations of hand immersions in hot water of different temperatures

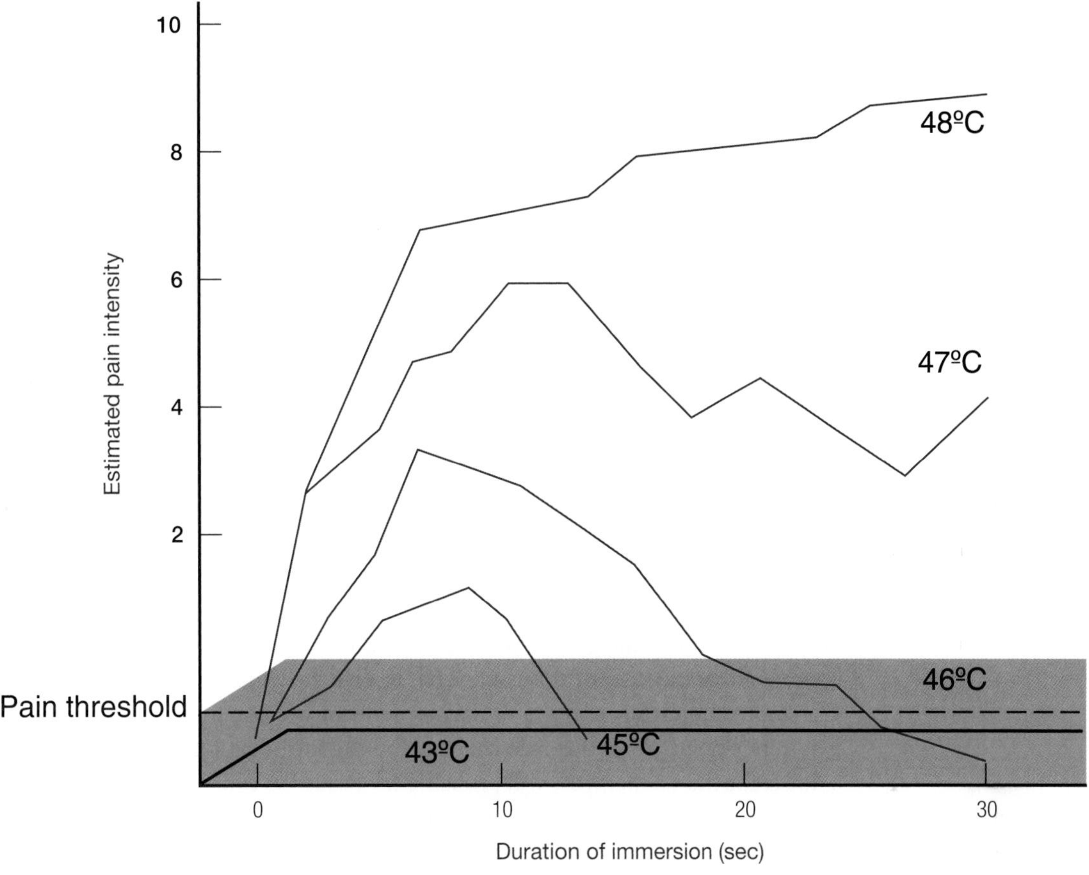

Data from D. Kenshalo editor, *The Skin Senses* © 1986. Courtesy of Charles C. Thompson, Publisher, Springfield, Illinois.

stimulus (signal) depends not only on the intensity of the signal but also on other variables such as distracting factors and our own internal psychological state (expectations, motivation, fatigue, and so forth).

The origins of signal detection theory may be traced to early efforts to understand how people are able to distinguish certain target stimuli against a background of random noise. *Noise* is the term employed by psychologists to describe any kind of distracting and irrelevant stimuli, and it is analogous to the background static you hear on the radio while cruising down the freeway and trying to tune in your favorite station. The stronger the static, the harder it is to detect the music. This example refers to *external noise* or other distracting factors in the outside environment.

Our signal detection performance may also be influenced by *internal noise* in our sensory systems caused by an ongoing, variable, random firing of neurons (the nervous system is never completely inactive). Thus, sensory inputs occur against a variable background of external and internal noise, the level of which affects our ability to detect signals.

BVT *Lab*

Flashcards are available for this chapter at **www.BVTLab.com.**

Background noise is not the only variable taken into account by signal detection theory. Other factors also play an important role, as is illustrated in the following example. Suppose that during a drive to a vacation destination you decide to pass the time by playing a game with your younger sibling. The game consists of seeing who can rack up the most spottings (detections) of a specific make of car—say a Volkswagen bug. How well you play the game will depend on a variety of factors, including such things as distracting noise (radio playing, conversations, etc.); your *expectations* about when or where these particular stimuli are likely to occur; and the particular criterion you set for how sure you must be before reporting a signal has been detected, in this case the spotting of a VW bug. Do you wait until all features of the car are clear before announcing a spot, or do you react to the first bug-like body style you see off in the distance? As we will see, response criterion plays a significant role in perception.

Response Criterion and Signal Detection

The setting of a response criterion involves going beyond the dimension of sensation. In our example, let's assume that there are no consequences for a *false alarm* (i.e., reporting a VW bug when none is present) and that winning the game is important to you. That is, you need all the correct spottings or "hits" (reporting a VW bug when it is present) you can get. Under these conditions, you would probably be inclined to report spottings for any distant vehicle that bore any resemblance, however vague, to a VW bug. Under these conditions your perception of bugs is going to be quite good. That is, every occurrence of a VW bug is spotted early. On the other hand, what happens to signal detection performance when the game plan is modified? For instance, suppose you agree with your opponent that the loser of this contest has to give the winner a dollar, and, to make things even more interesting, every false alarm (reporting a VW when none was present) results in a minus point. With this rule change, and the introduction of the added incentive of a dollar for the winner, you will probably try harder to avoid false alarms and thus raise your response criterion by requiring a stronger stimulus before reporting a sighting.

This can be illustrated in what is termed a receiver operating characteristic (ROC) curve, which is presented in Figure 4-4. This figure shows the probability of a hit (reporting a spotting when a VW bug was present) on the vertical axis and the probability of a *false alarm* (reporting a VW bug when none was present) on the horizontal axis.

Point A on the ROC curve represents "bug" perception in our first example when there were no penalties for false alarms. The probability of both hits and false alarms are high because there is no cost to saying "bug" often. When a false alarm results in subtracting a point from total hits, our perception changes and is reflected by Point B. We miss a few bugs, but we avoid costly mistakes. Points falling below the diagonal line indicate that the probability of a false alarm is greater than the probability of a hit. When this occurs (Point C), objects are considered below threshold (undetectable).

Our example demonstrates that potential positive and negative consequences associated with hits, misses, and false alarms create a response bias—an inclination or tendency to respond in a certain way. Let's consider a more serious example where response bias is quite important. Imagine your task is to monitor a radar screen for Scud missiles (a ballistic missile developed by Russia and recently used in the Iraq War). The detection of Scuds on the monitor is difficult because of the background noise on the monitor and other friendly air traffic. In this case, launching defensive missiles could result in destroying target Scuds (a hit) or destroying friendly air cover (a false alarm). On the other hand, a miss (failing to detect a Scud) could be fatal. Both of these considerations bias your perception of whether a blip on the radar screen represents a Scud missile. Where on the ROC curve would you

Figure 4-4 Receiver Operating Characteristic (ROC) Curve

Points falling above the diagonal line represent stimulus intensities above threshold. Points below the diagonal line represent stimulus intensities that are below threshold.

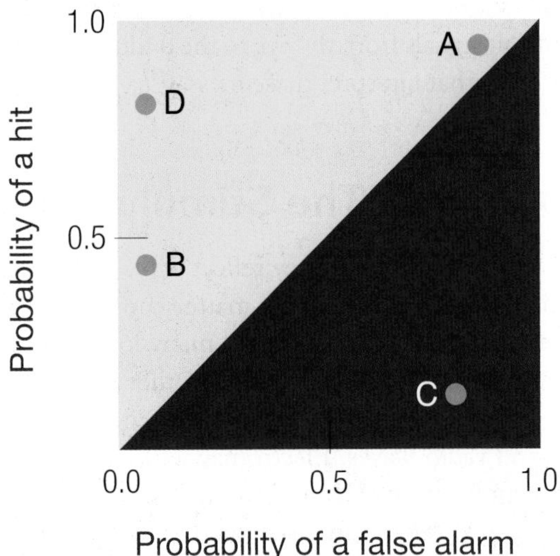

like to be in this case? If you answered position D, you are correct. Special training under simulated conditions can alter one's response bias in this case toward position D.

According to signal detection theory, there is no such thing as an absolute threshold for a given stimulus modality because detecting a signal depends not only on stimulus strength but also on background noise and such psychological variables as expectation and response bias.

Signal detection theory has helped us to understand that detecting and responding to stimuli in our world is often much more complex than a simple relationship between physical energy and sensory processes. Furthermore, signal detection theory has provided the impetus for developing techniques to improve people's vigilance in important signal detection tasks such as monitoring radar screens (air traffic controllers, military radar technicians), reviewing X-ray screens at airport security checkpoints, or evaluating data readouts from medical monitoring equipment in hospital intensive care units. Some of the recommendations for improving performance include frequent breaks to counteract boredom and fatigue; mild physical exercise; providing occasional "real targets" to detect; and providing information about signal detection performance in the form of feedback about the number of hits, misses, and false alarms.

The principles we have just discussed relate to all sensations, but each sense also has distinct properties to which we respond in unique ways. The following sections explore the major senses: vision, hearing, taste, smell, and the senses of touch and of body position.

4.2 Vision

In many ways, vision is our most important sense. It contributes enormously to our awareness of the surrounding environment, and it provides extremely valuable information that we can use to change our location or actions. Much of what we do depends on an adequately functioning visual system. When a person is deprived of his or her vision, as in an accident, the adjustment is often long and arduous. Vision's primary importance is reflected in the fact that a greater portion of our brains is devoted to vision than to any of the other senses.

Our visual systems are composed of three major parts: the eyes, which capture and respond to light energy; the neural circuits that transmit signals from the eye to the brain; and the visual centers within the brain that interpret these messages.

(Shutterstock)

Virtually all matter consists of oscillating, electrically charged particles that discharge many forms of electromagnetic radiation, only one of which is light. We see things because they reflect light.

4.2a Light: The Stimulus for Vision

We see things because they reflect light. Light is a form of electromagnetic radiation. Virtually all matter consists of oscillating, electrically charged particles that discharge many forms of electromagnetic radiation, only one of which is light. Other varieties include cosmic rays, gamma rays, X-rays, ultraviolet rays, infrared rays, microwaves, and TV and radio waves. Electromagnetic radiation travels in waves, and different forms of this energy have different wavelengths. A wavelength is precisely defined by how far the radiation travels between oscillations. Wavelength is measured in nanometers, (nm); a nanometer is equal to a billionth of a meter.

Figure 4-5 shows the full range of the electromagnetic spectrum. Note that light that is visible to the human eye ranges from roughly 400 to 750 nm, only a small portion of the electromagnetic spectrum. All living things do not share our own blindness to other segments of the full spectrum. For example, some insects can discern ultraviolet light, and some avian predators use infrared radiation to detect prey.

Properties of Light

Brightness, hue, and saturation are three properties of light that are particularly important in the psychological study of vision. **Brightness**, or the intensity of light, is measured by the number of *photons* (particles of electromagnetic radiation that we see as light). In general, the more intense the light source, the more photons are emitted, the brighter a light appears, and the higher the amplitude of the light wave.

Brightness Intensity of light, measured by the number of photons, or particles of electromagnetic radiation, emitted by a light source

Hue The color we perceive, determined partly by the wavelength of light and partly by the complex process by which an organism's visual system mixes wavelengths

Saturation Proportion of colored or chromatic light to noncolored or nonchromatic light, which determines how colorful light appears

Hue, or the color we perceive, is determined partly by the wavelength of light. In normal eyes, wavelengths of 400 nm are perceived as violet, 500 nm appear blue-green, 600 nm appear yellow-orange, and 700 nm look red. The perception of color is not just a matter of wavelength, however. Several colors, such as purple and white, are not even in the spectrum of visible light. These colors are produced when the visual system mixes various wavelengths in a complex process that creates a broad variety of hues.

Saturation, a third dimension of light, determines how colorful light appears. White corresponds to a completely colorless state; the more white is present in color, the less saturated it is. If you were to add white paint slowly to red paint, the color red would undergo a gradual transition from a saturated deep red to a shade of pink, which is unsaturated red. Saturation may, therefore, be viewed as the proportion of colored (*chromatic*) light to noncolored (*achromatic*) light.

Figure 4-5 The Electromagnetic Spectrum

This figure shows the full range of the electromagnetic spectrum. Visible light represents only a small part of the complete spectrum. The visible spectrum can be obtained by passing white light (such as sunlight) through a prism. Visible light ranges from about 400 nm to 750 nm.

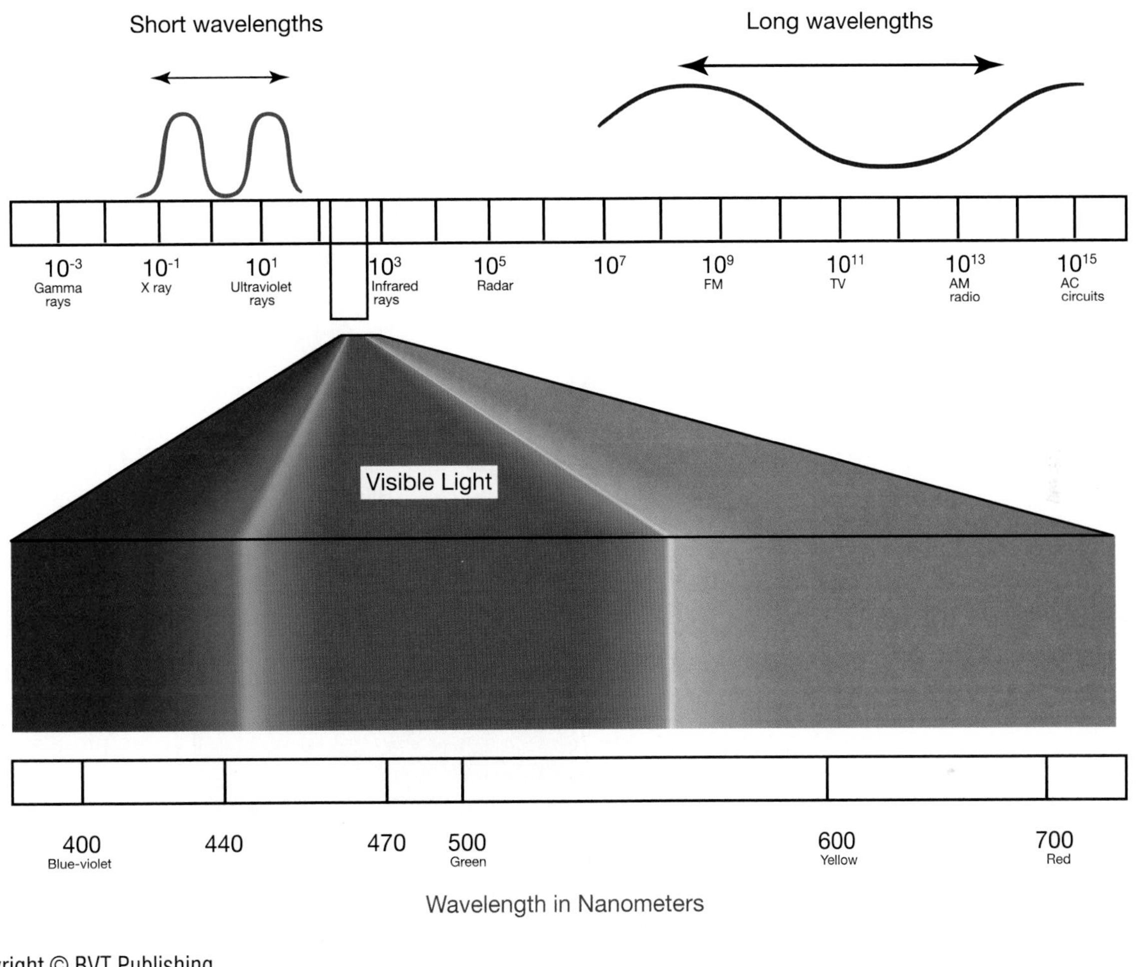

4.2b Structure and Function of the Eye

Brightness, hue, and intensity describe the stimulus of light; however, our primary concern is how we receive that stimulus. For that, we must have some understanding of how our eyes work.

Figure 4-6 illustrates several key structures of the human eye. Two components of the eye are most relevant to our discussion. One is the image-focusing part, roughly comparable to a camera. Major structures within this unit are the cornea, lens, iris, and pupil. The other primary component of the eye's visual system is the image-recording part, called the retina. The film in a camera is roughly analogous to the retina.

Visual sensations result when patterns of light that enter the eye are focused on the light-sensitive retina. When a light beam first enters the eye, it passes through the cornea, a thin, transparent membrane that bends or refracts light waves to bring them

Figure 4-6 The Structure of the Eye

This cross-sectional drawing of the eye illustrates several key structures, including the image-focusing structures—the cornea, lens, iris, and pupil—and the image-recording structure, the retina. The retina consists of several layers of cells, as shown in the magnified inset. Visual information leaves the retina through the optic nerve, which travels to several brain structures for vision.

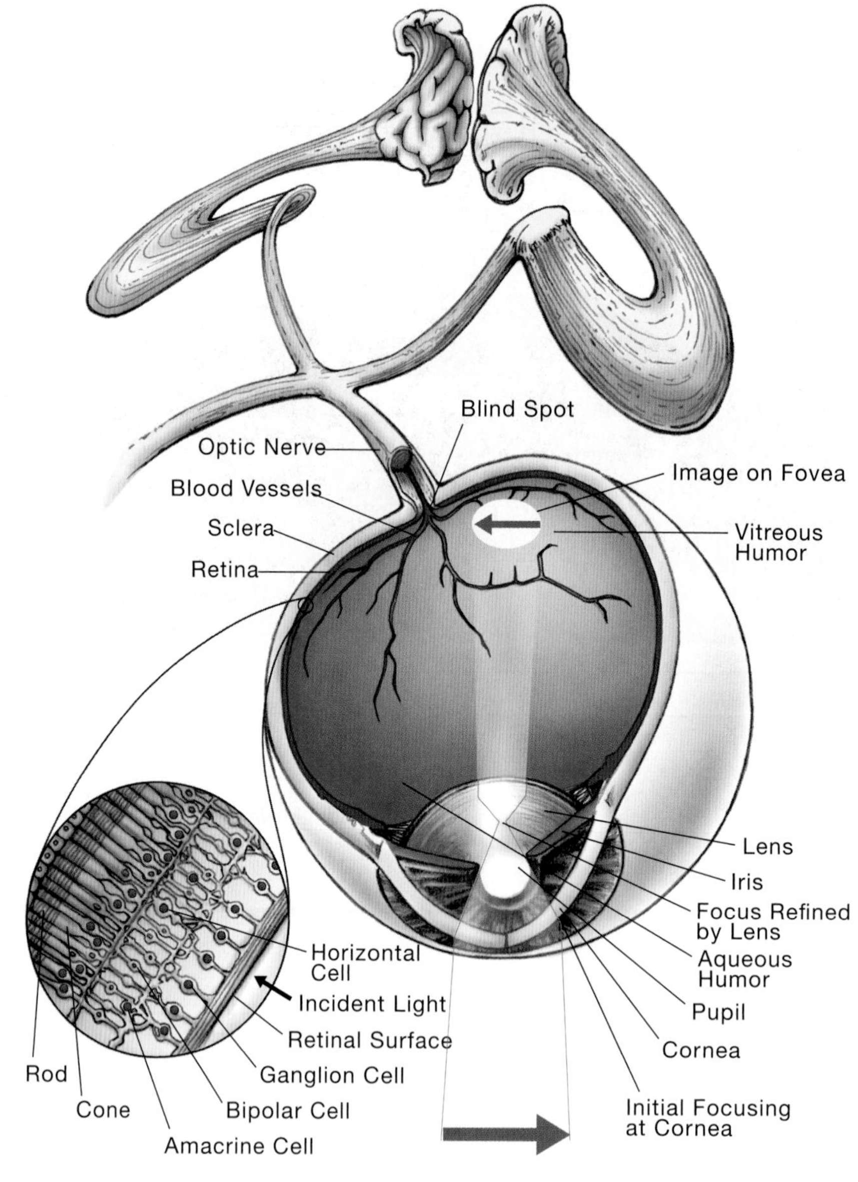

into sharper focus on the retina. Light then passes through the *aqueous humor*, a watery fluid that helps nourish the cornea.

Light next passes through a small opening in the *iris* called the *pupil*. The iris is a pigmented set of muscles that constrict or expand to control the amount of light that can enter. The pupil dilates (opens wide) to let more light in when illumination is low; it constricts (becomes smaller) in response to a bright light. Eye color is determined by the amount of pigmentation in the iris. Heavy pigmentation produces brown eyes; little pigmentation results in blue eyes.

After light passes through the pupil, it enters the *lens*, an oblong elastic structure that further refracts and focuses the light beam into an image that is projected through the *vitreous humor* (a clear fluid that supplies nutrients to the interior of the eye) onto the retina. The focusing power of the lens resides in its ability to adjust its shape from flat to more rounded, depending on the distance between the object viewed and the eye. This focusing process is called **accommodation**. If the lens is functioning properly, a clear image is projected onto the retina. However, abnormalities in eye shape often make it impossible for the lens to accommodate correctly. When this happens, a person may be either nearsighted or farsighted. (A nearsighted person is able to see distinctly for only a short distance; someone who is farsighted can see distant objects clearly but cannot see near objects in proper focus.)

(iStock)

Hue is the color we perceive and is determined in part by the wavelength of light.

The Retina

Most of the structures of the eye function to focus light onto the retina, a thin layer of tissue at the back of the eye that records images. The insert in Figure 4-6 shows the key parts of the **retina**: **rods**, **cones**, bipolar cells, and ganglion cells. Light focused on the retina passes through several layers of neurons en route to the primary *photoreceptor cells*, the rods and cones. Once light passes through the retina, excess light not absorbed by the receptor cells is absorbed by the backmost part of the eye called the pigment epithelium. In humans, the pigment epithelium is quite dark, allowing it to absorb most of the light not absorbed by photoreceptors. If this light were to be reflected back into the retina and not absorbed, vision would be distorted because of the scatter of light inside the retina.

Not all animals have dark-colored pigment epithelium, however. Animals that forage at night rely more on sensitivity (the ability to detect light) than on acuity (the ability to finely focus light), and their eyes reflect light off of the pigment epithelium rather than absorb it. This reflected light is absorbed by the photoreceptors on its second pass through the retina. Light reflected off of the pigment epithelium is what you see when your car headlights catch an animal at night. This kind of reflection occurs in human eyes when more light than can be absorbed enters the eye. For example, the "red eye" in flash photography is caused by red light being reflected off your pigment epithelium.

Rods and Cones

There are approximately 120 million rods and 6 million cones in each of our eyes. The rods and cones are distributed in an orderly fashion across the inner layer of the retina. The densest concentration of cones occurs in a region of the retina called the *fovea* (see Figure 4-6). Because our vision is sharpest when images are focused on the fovea, we move our eyes around until the image is projected to the fovea when we wish to focus clearly on an object. The prairie falcon discussed in the opening to this chapter does this by tipping its head.

Our perception of color depends largely on the cones. Different cones respond to different wavelengths of light. However, the cones are relatively poor light sensors as

Accommodation In vision, the focusing process in which the lens adjusts its shape, depending on the distance between the eye and the object viewed, in order to project a clear image consistently onto the retina

Retina Thin membrane at the back of the eye containing photoreceptors called rods and cones; functions to record images

Rods Photoreceptor cells distributed across the inner layer of the retina that are important in peripheral vision and seeing in dim light

Cones Photoreceptor cells distributed across the inner layer of the retina that play an important role in the perception of color

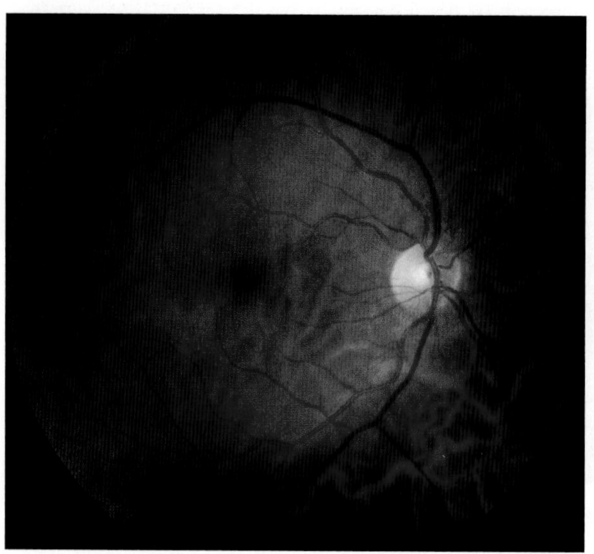

(iStock)

Most of the structures of the eye function to focus light onto the retina, shown here, which records images.

compared to the rods. A considerable amount of light must be projected onto a cone before it responds by converting this energy to neural signals. Thus, the cones are not much good at night, which is why your friend's colorful sweater is hard to see in a dark theater and why that great paint job on your car is hardly noticeable at night.

Rods are extremely sensitive photoreceptors, allowing us to see in dim light. Our peripheral vision (vision away from the center of focus) depends primarily on the rods, which are concentrated around the edges of the fovea and elsewhere on the surface of the retina. (No rods are in the fovea, and only a relatively few cones are located outside the fovea.)

You can demonstrate for yourself some of the distinguishing features between the rods and cones next time you are outside on a clear night. Pick out a distant object that is barely discernible, such as a faint star. If you look slightly to the side of the object, it is easier to detect because you have moved the image away from your fovea to the outer part of your retina, which is filled with light-sensitive rods.

Both the rods and the cones contain *photopigments* that respond to light. Their chemical response transduces light energy into neural signals. Neural signals are passed on from the rods and cones to the *bipolar cells*, which in turn pass information to the *ganglion cells*. The axons of the ganglion cells travel across the inner surface of the retina and converge to form the *optic nerve*, which carries visual messages to the brain.

The part of the retina where the optic nerve exits the eye is known as the *optic disk*. There are no photoreceptor cells at this point. Consequently, the optic disk region is a blind spot—an image that is projected there will not be recorded. We are usually unaware of our blind spot, for a number of reasons. For one, our eyes are constantly moving, allowing us to pick up the image in another part of the retina. Furthermore, an image that hits the blind spot in one eye is focused somewhere else in the other eye, thus

Figure 4-7 Finding Your Blind Spot

Because there are no photoreceptors when the optic nerve exits the eye, this leaves a blind spot on your retina. To find your blind spot, close your left eye and focus your right eye on the black cross. Then, move the book to about 12 inches directly in front of your face. The figure should disappear, but not the vertical lines.

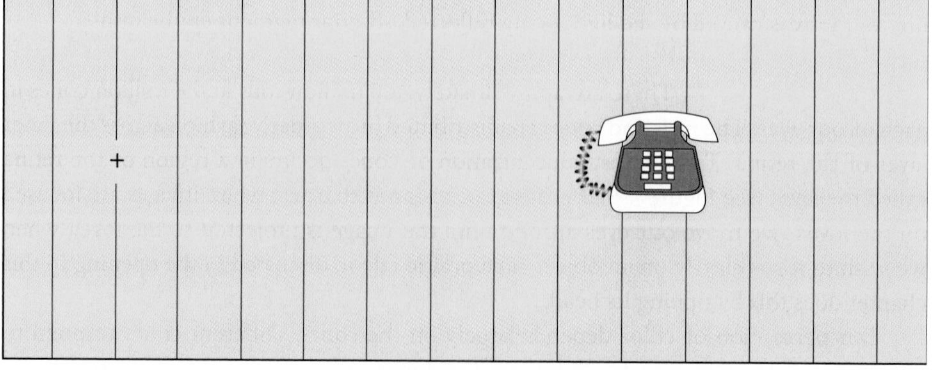

compensating for the momentary blindness. To see your blind spot in action, try the exercise in Figure 4-7. When the image in the figure falls on your blind spot, it will disappear.

In summary, visual information is passed through a three-cell chain, from rods and cones to bipolar cells to ganglion cells. Two other kinds of retinal cells—*horizontal cells* and *amacrine cells*—do not transmit visual signals toward the brain. Instead, they transmit signals laterally across the retina, allowing interaction between adjacent photoreceptor, bipolar, and ganglion cells. This interaction, termed lateral inhibition, functions to enhance our perception of images by "turning off" neighboring photoreceptors.

Dark Adaptation Process by which an organism's vision gradually becomes more sensitive to minimal levels of light due to a chemical change in the rods and cones of the retina

Dark and Light Adaptation

You have probably had the experience of walking out of the light of your home or apartment into the dark of night. At first, you may not be able to see anything. In a short time, however, dim outlines of objects begin to appear; soon you can find your way about fairly easily. This process is called **dark adaptation**, and it is due to a slow chemical change within the cones and the rods as they gradually become more sensitive to minimal levels of light. As Figure 4-8 shows, the rods reach full sensitivity about thirty minutes after you enter darkness, compared to ten minutes for the cones.

During World War II, American pilots in Europe applied this knowledge to their advantage by wearing goggles with red lenses when they were on alert for air raids. The red lenses prevented their rods from adapting to the indoor light. When a night raid occurred, these pilots were completely dark-adapted and ready for night flight. In poor lighting, our eyes are most responsive to light in the 550–655 nm range, which corresponds

Figure 4-8 Dark Adaptation

The amount of light necessary for detection is related to the amount of time spent in the dark. Dark adaptation mainly occurs within the rods, which reach their full sensitivity in about thirty minutes. The cones also adapt to the dark and reach their full sensitivity in about ten minutes.

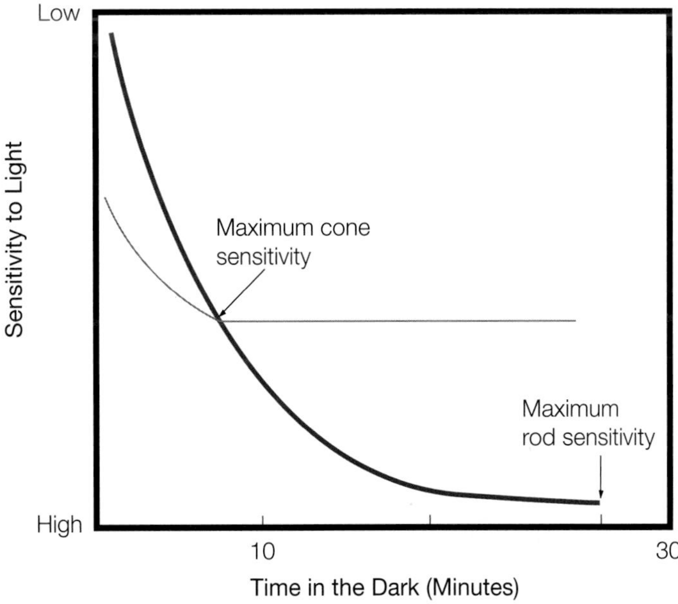

Adapted figure from OpenWetWare under a CC by SA 3.0 license at http://www.openwetware.org/wiki/Image:DarkAdaptation.jpg

Light Adaptation Process by which an organism's vision adjusts to bright lighting, due to a chemical change within the rods and cones of the retina

to yellow-green. This is why many emergency vehicles, such as fire engines, are now often painted a lime or yellow-green color.

When you return from the dark to your well-lit home, just the opposite process takes place. **Light adaptation** is a much faster process than dark adaptation. However, after your eyes have become completely dark-adapted, a brief exposure to bright light does not entirely reverse the process. For example, if you look into the bright lights of an approaching car for a few seconds, your dark adaptation is only slightly lessened for a brief moment or two.

A few specialized techniques can help you maintain your night vision if you must use a light for a short period of time. One suggestion is to avoid exposure to white light. If you must read a road map while driving at night, for example, use a flashlight with a red filter. Cockpits of airplanes use red light for this reason.

When better night vision is required, specialized night vision equipment can be used. These night goggles capture small amounts of light and intensify it with a special power supply that then transmits the light onto a photo cathode screen. The photo cathode screen emits electrons onto a phosphorescent screen, thereby illuminating it. The image on the phosphorescent screen appears in a monochrome green color to the viewer.

Figure 4-9 Neural Processing of Vision

Visual information from your right visual field from both eyes (blue) crosses to the left thalamus at the optic chiasm. Information from your left visual field from both eyes (red) crosses to the right thalamus and visual cortex.

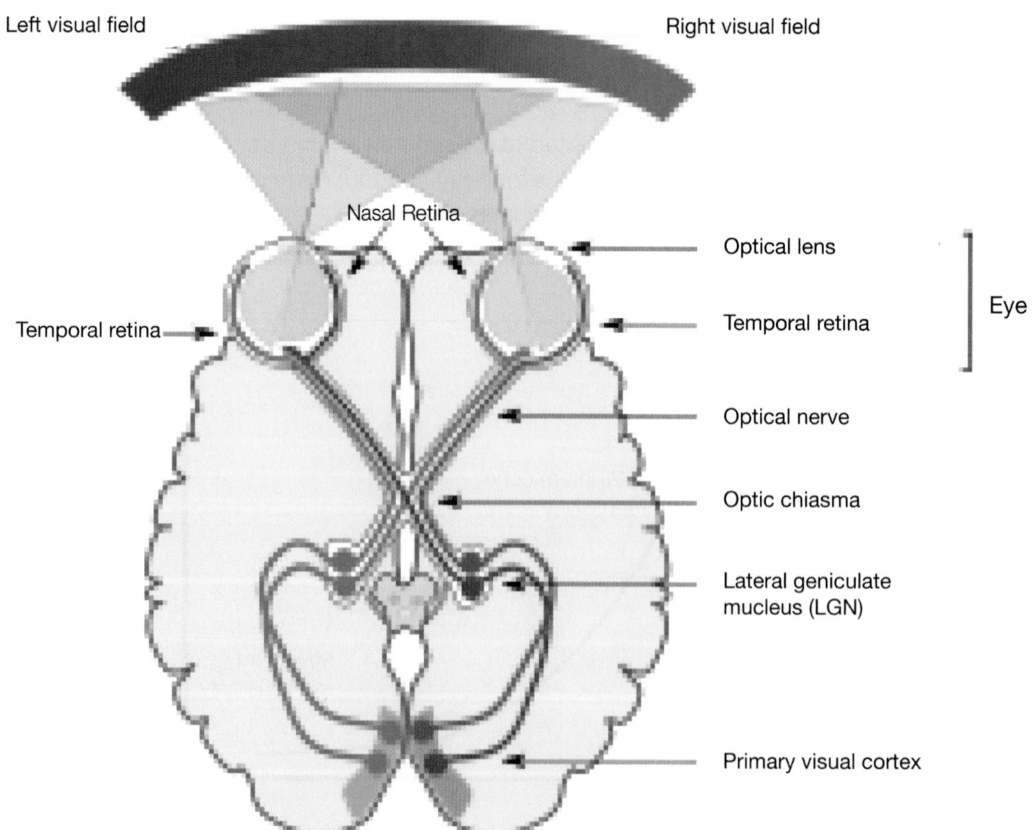

Adapted from Human Visual Pathway by Miquel Perello Nieto under a CC by SA 4.0 license at https://commons.wikimedia.org/wiki/File;Human_visual_pathway.svg

Neural Processing of Vision

Visual signals from the retina are projected to the brain along the optic nerve. Before reaching the visual cortex at the back of the brain, visual information from the two eyes converges in a region of the thalamus called the *lateral geniculate nucleus*. As discussed in Chapter 3, the thalamus acts as a relay station, directing incoming sensory information to appropriate areas within the cortex. The two lateral geniculate nuclei, located in the left and right hemispheres of the thalamus, combine information from both eyes before sending it on to the cortex. From the lateral geniculate nuclei, this information is then sent to the visual cortex in the right and left hemispheres of the occipital lobe.

Research has yet to determine exactly how these neural signals are translated into visions of the things that we see. Perhaps the most revealing research to date has been conducted by David Hubel and Thorsten Wiesel (1979), who received the Nobel Prize in 1981 in recognition of their work. Hubel and Wiesel inserted electrodes into the visual cortexes of cats in order to study the responses of single cells to a variety of visual stimuli. They discovered that many cortical cells respond only to specific stimuli, such as movement in one direction, or lines, or contours in particular orientations. From the responses of single cells, the visual cortex seems to be able to extract information about size, shape, and movement. How do all these individual signals yield the solid images that we see?

If you used a powerful magnifying glass to examine a photograph in this book, you would discover that the image is composed of dots, as Figure 4-10 illustrates. The dots are closely packed in dark areas and farther apart in light areas. When we look at only a small area of the dots, highly magnified, it is difficult or impossible to decipher the overall image. However, when we back off, the individual dots become indistinguishable.

Lateral Inhibition Our perception of particular patterns and shapes results from the inhibitory interaction between neighboring areas of the retina by a process called lateral inhibition. The effect of lateral inhibition is to enhance contours and edges by heightening the contrast between light and dark borders. An interesting demonstration of how lateral inhibition enhances contrast at borders is presented in Figure 4-11. This figure shows a series of uniformly shaded bands (called Mach bands) that appear to darken on their border with a lighter band. To prove to yourself that each band is indeed a uniform shade, cover the bands on each side of a selected band.

4.2c **Color Vision**

Among mammals, only primates (humans, apes, and monkeys) are able to perceive a full range of colors. Cattle have no color vision (the colorful cape of the matador is merely a prop for human observers). Most color vision experts think that dogs do not see color either, although some evidence suggests that they may have some limited capacity to discern colors (Jacobs, 1983). Surprisingly, simpler organisms such as fish, birds, reptiles, and insects have excellent color vision (Nathans, 1987). Before examining what is known about how we perceive colors, let us briefly consider how colors are mixed to produce all the various hues.

Figure 4-10 Pictures Composed of Dots

Pictures such as this one are often composed of small dots. The dots are not distinguishable unless a section of the picture is magnified. Visual information appears to enter the visual system as dots, edges, contours, movement, and shapes. This information may then be analyzed by a pattern, or "dot detection" system, in the brain.

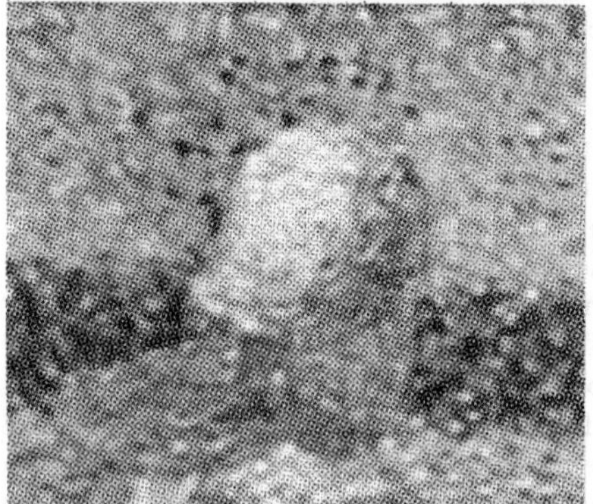

A Sunday on La Grande Jatte, Georges Seurat, 1884. Wikimedia Commons/Public Domain

Additive and Subtractive Color Mixing

Color is a psychological phenomenon in that our brains produce it as they perceive light reflected from objects. The potential for color perception is not inherent in the objects themselves; instead, the reflected beams of light determine it. Most light, including light from incandescent lamps and from sunlight, is called *white light*. We do not perceive it as being colored, yet it contains all the wavelengths for the various colors within the visible spectrum. The grass growing outside your front door appears green because it absorbs most of the wavelengths in the white light falling on it but reflects green light. Thus, the

Figure 4-11 Mach Bands

The bands in this figure are uniformly shaded, but they appear to either lighten or darken at the borders. This illustrates the contour-enhancing effects of lateral inhibition.

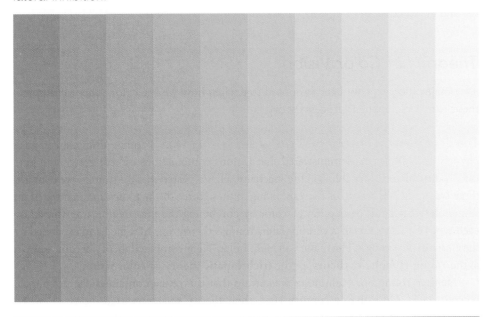

perception of different colors depends on different sets of wavelengths being absorbed and those reflected.

From working with pigment agents, such as paints or crayons, you probably know that different mixtures of the primary colors produce all the hues: red, blue, and yellow. Interestingly, when colored lights rather than pigments are mixed, the primary colors are red, green, and blue. Physicists who have experimented with mixing different colors of light report that all the various hues can be obtained by mixing red, green, and blue lights. Combining this information about primary pigments and light colors leads us to conclude that humans with normal color vision are able to distinguish a vast array of colors formed from various combinations of four basic hues—red, blue, yellow, and green—and two hueless colors, white and black.

You probably know that if you mix yellow and blue paints, the result is green. However, when yellow and blue light are combined, the result is almost white. Why is this so? Take a moment to formulate an answer before reading on.

Explaining the difference between subtractive and additive color mixing provides an answer to our question. Most, if not all, of your experience mixing colors has probably been of the subtractive variety. **Subtractive color mixing** occurs when paint or other pigments are mixed. When light falls on a colored object, some wavelengths are absorbed (subtracted) and others are reflected. The wavelength of the reflected light determines the hue we perceive. For example, when yellow and blue paint are mixed, these two pigments subtract or absorb nonyellow and nonblue wavelengths. The result is a pigment that reflects only those wavelengths that are between yellow and blue, which is green.

Additive color mixing occurs when lights with different wavelengths simultaneously stimulate the retina. Our resulting color perception is based on the adding or combining

Subtractive Color Mixing
Color mixing process that occurs when pigments are mixed, so that when light falls on the colored object, some wavelengths are absorbed (or subtracted) and others are reflected

Additive Color Mixing
Color mixing that occurs when lights of different wavelengths simultaneously stimulate the retina, so that color perception depends on the adding or combining of these wavelengths

Young-Helmholtz Theory (Trichromatic Theory of Color Vision) The postulation that the human eye contains three types of color receptors (for red, green, and blue), which form the basis for our perception of all colors

Opponent-Process Theory of Color Vision Theory that explains color vision based on six primary colors, which are grouped into three pairs: red-green, blue-yellow, black-white (Receptors in the eye are sensitive to specific pairs, and the presence of one member of a pair inhibits perception of the other.)

of these respective wavelengths. Unlike subtractive color mixing, which takes place in the object we are viewing, additive mixing is done by our visual systems. The colors you perceive on your television screen are products of additive color mixing. If you were able to magnify this picture many-fold, you would see that images are composed of tiny red, green, and blue dots. (That's why color monitors are called RGB—red, green, and blue—monitors.) A close examination of a yellow object would reveal that it consists of red and green dots.

Theories of Color Vision

Two major theories have been proposed to explain how we see colors: the trichromatic theory and the opponent-process theory.

The Trichromatic Theory of Color Vision

In 1802, Thomas Young, an English physicist and physician, demonstrated that various combinations of red, green, and blue can produce all the other colors in the spectrum. He suggested that the human eye contains three types of color receptors corresponding to these three distinct hues and that the brain somehow creates our perception of color by combining the information transmitted by each type of receptor. Half a century later, Young's theory was modified and expanded by the German physiologist Hermann von Helmholtz. Their combined theory became known as the **Young-Helmholtz theory**, or the **trichromatic theory of color vision**.

Neither Young nor Helmholtz was aware that the retina contained distinct photoreceptor cells. More than a century later, their theory was supported, however, when research revealed that there are three distinct kinds of cones in the human retina, each containing a different photopigment. These cones are maximally sensitive to light of three wavelengths: 435, 540, and 565 nm. Figure 4-5 reveals that these wavelengths correspond to blue, green, and yellow-green. However, to be consistent with earlier convention, researchers continue to refer to these receptors as blue (S cones), green (M cones), and red (L cones) for their respective wavelengths. Although the photopigments in each of these types of cones respond most effectively to light in the wavelengths we have listed, light of a particular wavelength stimulates more than one type of receptor.

The trichromatic theory explains the effects of mixing colors of different wavelengths. However, it does not explain some other phenomena, such as negative afterimages (discussed in the following section) and the fact that color-blind people almost always fail to distinguish pairs of colors rather than just one color. A second theory, the opponent-process theory, helps to explain these phenomena.

The Opponent-Process Theory of Color Vision

In the 1870s, a German physiologist, Ewald Hering, proposed a theory of color vision asserting that yellow is as basic a color as red, blue, and green; that is, that yellow is not a mixture of other colors. Hering believed we see six primary colors (red, green, blue, yellow, black, and white) rather than the three proposed by Young and Helmholtz. He further theorized that these six colors are grouped into three pairs, which form three types of receptors. One receptor, the black-white pair, contributes to our perception of brightness and saturation; the other two receptors, a red-green and a blue-yellow pair, are responsible for our perception of color.

Hering believed that the two members of each pair tend to work in opposition to each other, one inhibiting the other (hence the name **opponent-process theory of color vision**). According to this viewpoint, if our eyes are struck by light containing more red wavelengths than green, the red inhibits the green, and we perceive red. The blue-yellow system works similarly, which is why we never perceive such shades as greenish red or bluish yellow.

Hering's opponent-process theory is consistent with what we know about color blindness. Approximately 8 percent of males and 0.05 percent of females exhibit some form of color blindness, but only rarely are individuals totally blind to color. Most people with color-vision problems have difficulty detecting pairs of colors. Red-green color blindness is the most common. People with red-green color blindness cannot see either red or green, but they can see other colors. Yellow-blue color blindness is much less common.

Hering was also intrigued with the phenomenon of negative afterimages. Figure 4-12 provides a demonstration. If you stare for about a minute at the three colored dots on the woman's nose then quickly stare at a blank sheet of white paper or a wall, a realistic color image of the woman should appear. The three dots should no longer appear red, green, and blue, but green, red, and yellow respectively. Her hair will appear dark and her skin tones tan.

This phenomenon fits in nicely with the opponent-process theory. When you stare at the image, specific color receptors of each pair become fatigued. When you shift your eyes to the white surface, the light it reflects stimulates the color-pair components equally. However, since the overloaded component is fatigued, it responds only minimally. This imbalance in the opponent pair produces the faint afterimage in real color. Most contemporary vision experts believe that both the trichromatic theory and the opponent-process

Figure 4-12 Negative Afterimages

Stare at the three dots on the nose of the woman in the image for about a minute. Then shift your focus to a white sheet of paper or a wall. You should see a faint image in natural colors—the complements of the image. The red, green, and blue dots should appear as their complements green, red, and yellow respectively.

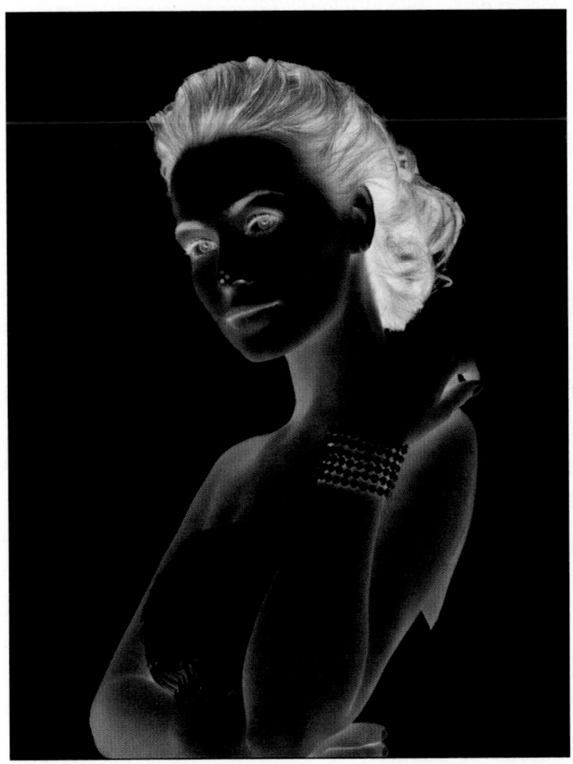

(Shutterstock, adapted by BVT Publishing)

Loudness In hearing, the intensity of a sound as measured by decibels, which is determined by the amplitude of a sound wave

theory are correct. In fact, our color perception may be a product of both mechanisms. The trichromatic system operates at the level of the photoreceptors with three kinds of light-sensitive pigments in the cones. At the same time, the on-and-off type of process described by Hering and later verified by Hurvich and Jameson (1957) has been identified in ganglion cells of the retina and in the lateral geniculate nuclei. Researchers using fMRI have found a large number of brain cells that respond in an opponent manner to red-green and blue-yellow stimuli in the visual cortex (Engel, Zhang, & Wandell, 1997; Schluppeck & Engel, 2002). These findings suggest that the opponent-process mechanism operates not at the level of the cones but rather along the neural path from the photoreceptor cells to the visual cortex. Thus, color vision results from interplay between a trichromatic system operating at the level of the photoreceptor cells and an opponent-process mechanism working in the visual cortex.

4.3 Audition

People who become deaf after years of normal hearing often report feeling a great deal of stress and a profound sense of isolation. Audition allows us to enjoy perhaps the richest form of communication. A deaf person cannot easily engage in conversation with others, whereas a blind person can converse with people either person-to-person or over the phone. Thus, while our ears may bring us less information than our eyes, they convey a special type of social communication that is exceedingly important to our appreciation of life.

4.3a Sound: The Stimulus for Audition

Most of the sounds we hear consist of physical energy in the form of rhythmic pressure changes in the air. When an object vibrates to produce sound, it sets air molecules in motion. The vibrating motion of the sound source alternately pushes air molecules together and pulls them apart. The forward thrust of the vibrating object as it moves toward you *compresses* the air, making it denser. As the vibrating object moves away from you, it pulls the molecules farther apart, thus *rarefying* the air, making it thinner. These changes in air pressure constitute sound waves, and they travel at a speed of approximately 1,100 feet per second.

When the compressed-air portion of the sound wave arrives at your ear, it bends the tympanic membrane (your eardrum) inward. The negative pressure of the following rarefied portion of the sound wave causes your eardrum to bend out. These movements or vibrations of the eardrum begin the complex process of transducing the energy of sound waves into the neural signals that carry auditory messages to the brain.

Sound waves most commonly travel through the medium of air. However, other media such as the ground, water, wood, or metal also convey sound waves. Perhaps you have listened to a conversation in the next room with your ear against the wall, have heard an approaching train by pressing your ear against a metal rail, or have heard sounds while swimming underwater.

Properties of Sound Waves

Two properties of sound waves influence our perception of sound: amplitude and frequency. The amplitude or intensity of a sound wave determines the **loudness** of a sound. Loudness is measured in *decibels* (dB). A decibel is not a linear unit like a pound or an inch; rather, it is a point on a sharply rising curve of intensity. For example, 10 dB is 10 times greater than 1 dB, but 30 dB is 1,000 times greater than 1 dB, and 100 dB is approximately 10 billion times greater than 1 dB. To most people, a sound at 10 dB is quite soft, whereas one as loud as 130 dB is painful. Figure 4-13 shows the decibel levels of a number of common sounds.

Pitch Dimension of hearing that determines how high or low a sound is, measured in hertz; determined by the frequency of a sound wave

A second important property of a sound wave is its frequency, which determines the **pitch** that we perceive. Sound wave frequency is measured in Hertz (Hz), or cycles per second. The higher the pitch, the shriller we perceive a sound to be. The average human ear can perceive sound waves within the range of 20 to 20,000 Hz. We are most sensitive to sound waves in the 100–3,500 Hz range, which is, conveniently, the range within which most human speech falls. The lowest-pitched note on a piano, at 27.5 Hz, is barely audible to us. The highest sound a piano can make has been recorded at 4,180 Hz.

Nonhuman animals can perceive sound wave frequencies well above the upper limits for humans. For example, dogs can hear up to 80,000 Hz, which is why you can use a special whistle to call your dog in the middle of the night without waking your entire household. The upper limits of the audible pitch range are even higher for dolphins, extending well beyond 100,000 Hz. Pigeons and other birds apparently rely on very low frequency sounds to aid in long distance navigation.

Distinguishing Different Sounds of the Same Pitch

You may have noticed that the same notes sound different when produced by different instruments. Middle C played on the piano sounds quite different from the same note played on the violin, in spite of the fact that both instruments produce sound waves with exactly the same frequency. What explains this distinction? Try to formulate an answer before reading on.

Neither the violin nor the piano produces a pure note of a single frequency. In fact, very few of the sounds we hear are pure tones. Most are a combination of a *fundamental frequency* and a unique set of additional frequency components called *overtones*. Combined

Figure 4-13 Decibel Levels of Several Common Sounds

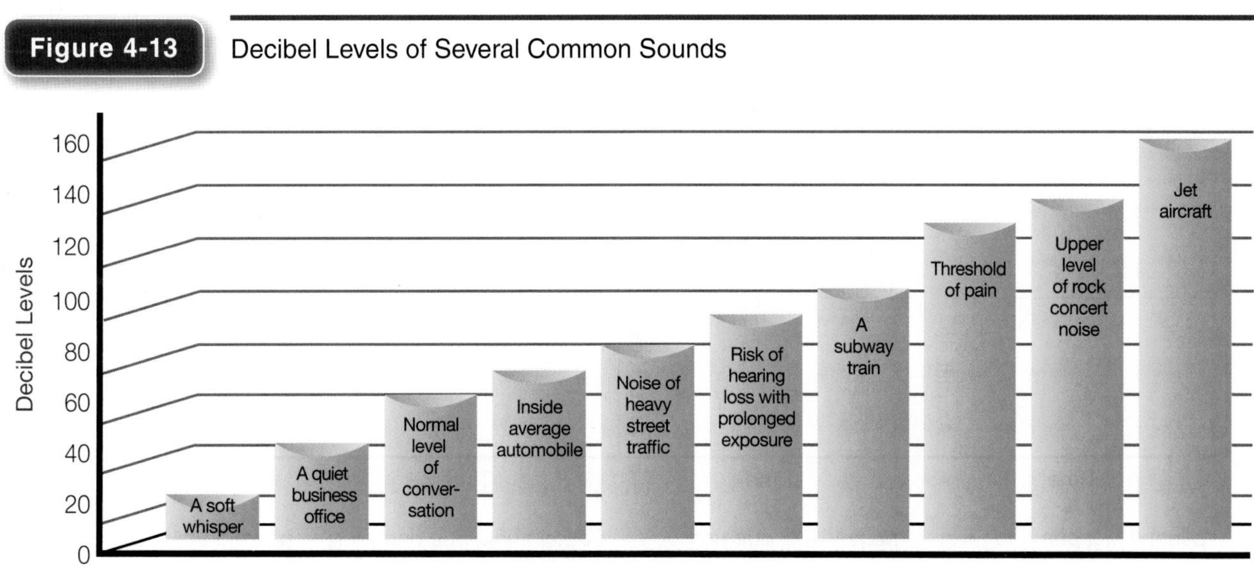

Timbre Quality of complex sound that is a product of the combination of fundamental frequency and additional frequency components called overtones

with the fundamental frequency, these overtones add a characteristic quality called **timbre** to complex sounds. Our ability to distinguish between the sounds of various musical instruments depends on differences in timbre. If sound filters were used to screen out all overtones, it would be impossible for a person to identify various instruments just by hearing them play.

Figure 4-14 summarizes the three properties of sound waves. Before reading on, see if you can tell how samples *A, B, C,* and *D* would be perceived.

4.3b Structure and Function of the Ear

The Outer Ear

The ear has three major parts: the outer ear, the middle ear, and the inner ear (see Figure 4-15). What most of us call our ears are merely the pinnas, the odd-shaped, flesh-covered cartilage that protrudes from the sides of our heads. The function of the

Physical Properties and Perceptual Dimensions of Sound Waves

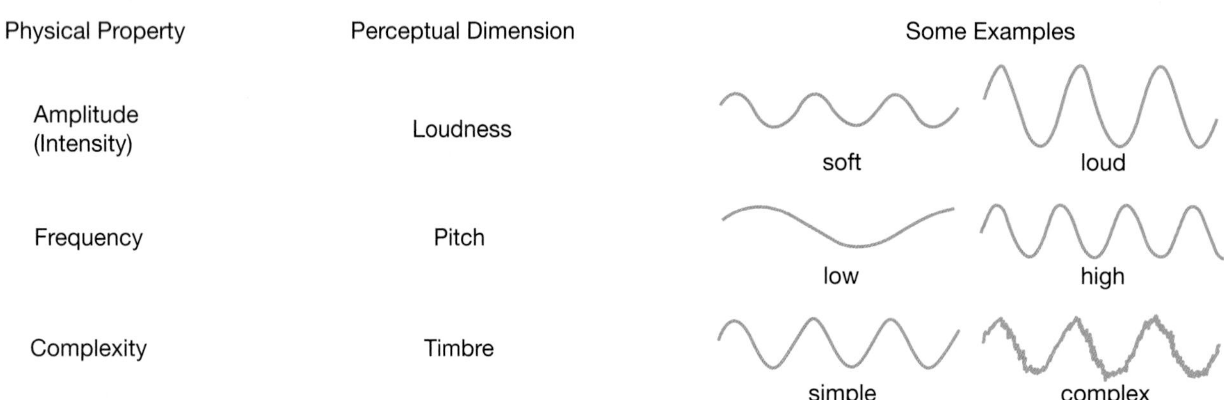

Physical Property
Perceptual Dimension
Some Examples
Amplitude (Intensity)
Loudness
soft
loud
Frequency
Pitch
low
high
Complexity
Timbre
simple
complex

Considering only the perceptual dimensions of loudness and pitch, how would the following sound waves be perceived? (See answers inverted below.)

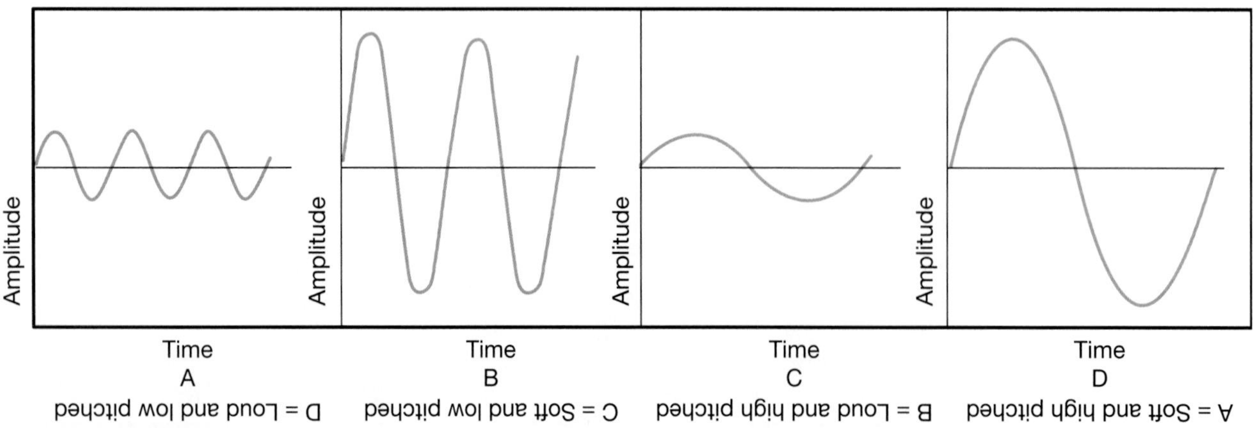

pinna is to collect and funnel sound waves down the *auditory canal*, which, along with the pinna, forms the outer ear.

Figure 4-15 Anatomy of the Human Ear

The outer ear, consisting of the pinna and auditory canal, collects and funnels sound waves to the eardrum. These sound waves cause the eardrum to vibrate. The eardrum, which serves as the opening to the middle ear, is connected to three small bones, called ossicles, that amplify the intensity of movement as it is transmitted to the inner ear. The last bone in the series, the stapes, pushes against a membrane called the oval window, which separates the middle ear from the inner ear. The movement of the oval window generates pressure waves within the fluid-filled cochlea, causing the flexible basilar membrane to bend. The bending of hair cells in the Organ of Corti causes neural messages to be transmitted along the auditory nerve to the brain.

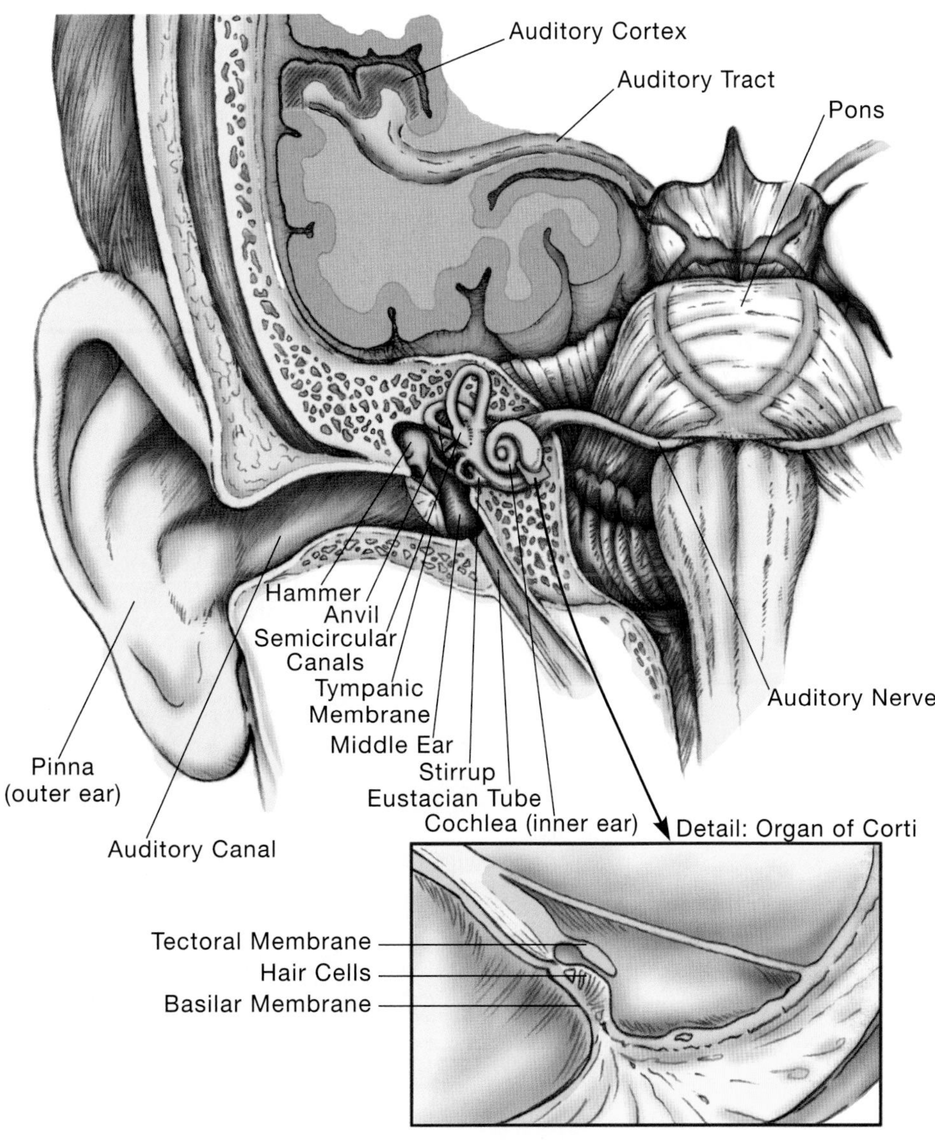

The Middle Ear

Tympanic Membrane Membrane stretched across the end of the auditory canal that vibrates in response to sound waves; also known as the *eardrum*

Ossicles Set of three tiny linked bones (the malleus, incus, and stapes) in the middle ear that receive a sound stimulus from the tympanic membrane and transfer it to the oval window of the inner ear

Cochlea Coiled, fluid-filled chamber in the inner ear with two flexible surfaces: the oval window and the round window

Basilar Membrane Membrane in the cochlea of the inner ear that vibrates in response to pressure waves, causing auditory hair cells on the adjoining organ of Corti to release neurotransmitters that activate neurons of the auditory nerve

At the end of the auditory canal, sound waves strike the eardrum, or **tympanic membrane**, causing it to start vibrating. The eardrum, which serves as the opening to the middle ear, is connected to a set of three tiny linked bones called **ossicles**. The ossicles act like a system of levers that transfer and amplify (or dampen) the intensity of a sound stimulus. When the eardrum vibrates, it nudges the first bone in the series, the malleus (hammer), which in turn moves the incus (anvil), which moves the stapes (stirrup).

The Inner Ear

When the ossicles vibrate in response to sound waves, the last bone in the series, the stapes, pounds against an opening to the inner ear called the oval window. The inner ear consists of a snail-shaped, coiled chamber called the cochlea, which is filled with fluid. The **cochlea** consists of three wedge-shaped chambers: the *vestibular canal*, the *cochlear duct*, and the *tympanic canal* (see Figure 4-16). The tympanic canal and cochlear duct are separated by the **basilar membrane**.

Except for two locations, where it is covered by flexible, elastic material, the cochlear wall consists of hard bone. The two flexible spots are the *oval window* and the *round window* at the base of the tympanic canal. These two flexible surfaces allow pressure waves to be generated within the fluid that fills the vestibular and tympanic canals.

Figure 4-16 The Cochlea of the Inner Ear

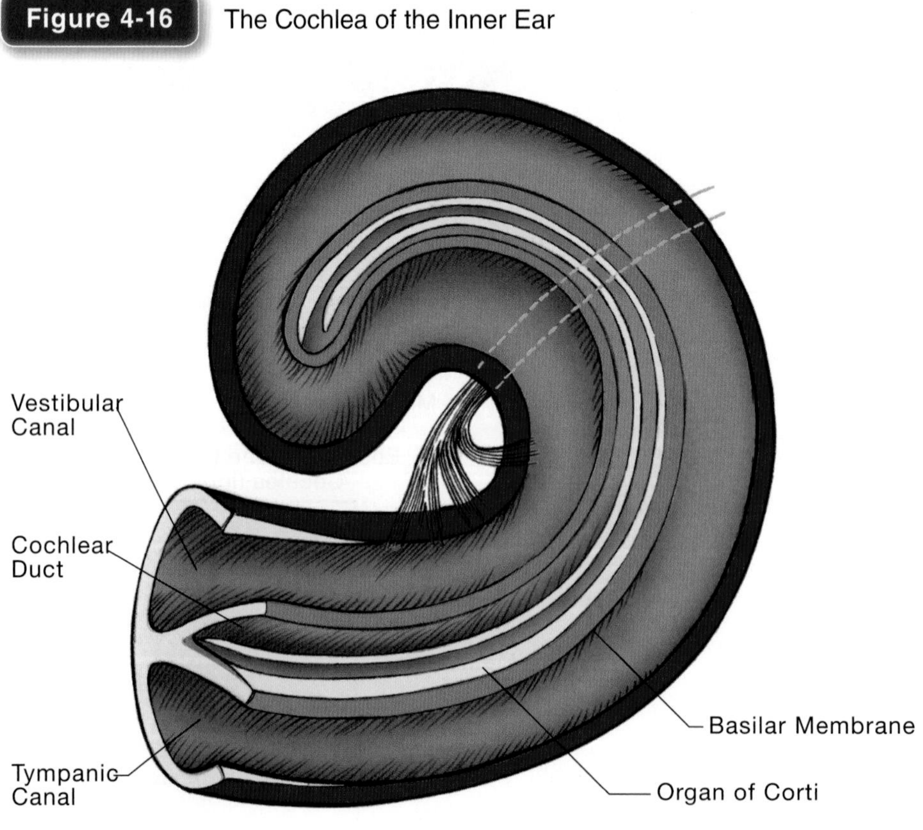

Auditory Receptors

When the oval window is pushed inward by the action of the stapes, the round window compensates by bulging outward. These mechanical displacements are translated into pressure waves that flow through the vestibular and tympanic canals, causing ripples in the flexible basilar membrane. Another structure, the **organ of Corti**, sits on top of the basilar membrane. It consists of the following: a layer of supporting cells resting on the basilar membrane, rows of specialized neurons known as auditory hair cells that project upward, and a *tectorial membrane* that hangs over the basilar membrane like an awning. The hair cells terminate in tiny hairlike protrusions called *cilia*. When the basilar membrane ripples in response to pressure waves, the cilia are moved against the relatively stationary tectorial membrane, bending like tiny clumps of seaweed swept back and forth by invisible underwater currents. This bending of the cilia causes the hair cells to release neurotransmitters that activate adjacent neurons of the *auditory nerve*, which carries messages to the auditory cortex in the brain.

Organ of Corti Structure in the inner ear located directly above the basilar membrane, consisting of auditory hair cells, a tectorial membrane, and cilia

Place Theory of Pitch Discrimination Theory that we discriminate different pitches because sound waves of different frequencies displace different regions on the cochlea's basilar membrane

In summary, sound waves are converted into mechanical movements of the ossicles in the middle ear, which in turn act on the inner ear to produce pressure waves that travel through the fluid of the cochlea, flexing the basilar membrane and activating hair cells of the organ of Corti, which in turn activate neurons of the auditory nerve. In this complex manner, the physical energy of sound waves is converted into neural impulses that our brain translates into sounds.

4.3c Theories of Audition

How can we distinguish between high- and low-pitched sounds, so that we can automatically tell a child's voice from an adult's or hear the differences between notes of a musical scale? There are two major theories explaining how we discriminate pitch: the place theory and the frequency theory.

The Place Theory

Primarily, Georg von Békésy, who was awarded the Nobel Prize in recognition of his monumental contributions to the science of hearing, developed the **place theory of pitch discrimination**. Békésy theorized that sound waves of different frequency displace different regions on the basilar membrane, allowing us to perceive varying pitches. He conducted experiments with guinea pigs to test this theory, using a microscope to observe the basilar membrane through tiny holes cut in various locations along the cochlea. When the guinea pigs were exposed to tones of varying frequencies, different regions of the basilar membrane showed the greatest response.

For example, Békésy noted that high-pitched tones caused the most displacement in the portion of the basilar membrane close to the oval window, whereas intermediate-range tones caused the greatest response farther along the basilar membrane. Unfortunately, Békésy's theory did not hold up as well for low-frequency tones, those below 4,000 Hz. The manner in which tones below this level displace the basilar membrane is largely indistinguishable (von Békésy & Wever, 1960). Subsequent research confirms that the place theory holds up well for all but tones in the lower frequency range (Lewis, Baird, Leverenz, & Koyama, 1982; Recanzone & Sutter, 2008).

Another problem with the place theory is that it does not explain how we can make very fine discriminations between tones that differ only slightly. The displacement in the basilar membrane is virtually identical for two tones whose frequencies differ by as little as 1 or 2 Hz, and yet many people can discriminate tonal differences this small.

Frequency Theory

The **frequency theory of pitch discrimination** helps account for our ability to distinguish tones in the 20–4,000 Hz range. According to this interpretation, first advanced by Ernest Rutherford in the nineteenth century, our perception of low tones depends on the frequency with which the hair cells trigger firing of fibers in the auditory nerve. Thus, our perception of pitch in the lower frequency range is determined by the frequency of impulses traveling up the auditory nerve. Research has demonstrated that fibers in the auditory nerve actually do fire in rhythm with tones in the low-frequency range. Thus, if we listen to middle C on a piano (262 Hz), our auditory nerve fibers fire at a rate of 262 times per second.

Perceiving Pitch in the 1,000 to 4,000 Hz Range

Single auditory neurons are capable of firing up to 1,000 times per second. How, then, can we account for pitch perception in the 1,000–4,000 Hz range? (Remember, place theory does not adequately explain our perception of tones below 4,000 Hz.) See if you can come up with a possible explanation before reading on.

Since one hair cell can fire no more than 1,000 times per second, researchers have theorized that groups of interrelated neurons fire in a staggered fashion to convey frequencies above 1,000 Hz. This conception of a group of neurons working together is a version of the frequency theory appropriately named **volley theory** (Wever, 1949). For example, three neurons working in concert, each firing at 1,000 impulses per second, could produce a perception of a 3,000 Hz tone if their respective messages were appropriately integrated.

The best available evidence suggests that pitch is determined by both the *place* of maximal excitation of the basilar membrane and the *frequency* with which auditory nerve fibers fire. Place theory seems to explain how we discriminate among higher pitched tones above 4,000 Hz, whereas the frequency theory, with the volley principle, seems to offer the best explanation of pitch discrimination in the lower frequencies (Plack, 2005).

Frequency Theory of Pitch Discrimination Theory that perception of low tones depends on the frequency with which auditory hair cells in the inner ear's organ of Corti trigger the firing of neurons in the auditory nerve

Volley Theory Related to the frequency theory of pitch discrimination, postulates that since single auditory neurons cannot fire rapidly enough to enable us to perceive tones in the 1,000–4,000 Hz range, pitch perception is made possible by groups of interrelated neurons firing in concert

Auditory Localization Ability to locate the origins of sounds by differences from ear to ear in variables such as intensity and the time the sound arrives at each ear

4.3d Auditory Localization

People are usually able to locate the origins of sounds rather well. Infants can identify which side a sound comes from very early, and within a few months localize sounds in their environments. This ability, called **auditory localization**, is the result of the difference in the sounds that arrive in each of our two ears (Goldstein, 2010). One key difference is in the intensity of loudness of the sounds. If someone sitting to the left of you blows a whistle, the sound wave reaching your left ear is more intense than the sound striking your right ear. This occurs because a large object like the human head does not transmit high-frequency sounds very well; your right ear is in a sound shadow. By the time the sound wave circumnavigates your head to reach your right ear, its intensity diminishes somewhat. Our brains use this information about differing intensities to determine the origin of a sound (Semple & Kitzes, 1987).

In addition to intensity difference, another important auditory localization cue has to do with the time a sound arrives. As we learned earlier, sound waves travel through the air at the relatively slow rate of approximately 1,100 feet per second. Thus, a sound originating from the left strikes the left eardrum fractions of a second before it completes the somewhat longer journey to our right ear. Here again, our brains utilize information about these minuscule time differences to help us localize sounds (Plack, 2005). Research has shown that the occipital and parietal lobes are involved in the spatial localization of sounds. Using magnetic stimulation to induce "virtual" lesions to different regions of the brain, researchers have determined that the right occipital cortex receives sound information prior to the parietal lobe. When the right occipital cortex is inhibited by magnetic stimulation 50 milliseconds (msec) after sounds are presented, auditory localization is disrupted. Similarly, but delayed by 50 msec, inhibition of the parietal cortex partially disrupts one's ability to localize sounds. The 50-msec delay in processing by the parietal lobe appears to be essential for normal sound localization (Collignon, Davare, DeVolder, & Poirier, 2008).

Sensorineural Hearing Loss Hearing loss caused by damage to either the hair cells of the inner ear or the auditory nerve; can be caused by loud noise

4.3e Hearing Loss

Roughly twenty million people in the United States suffer some hearing loss, making it the most common of all physical disabilities. Hearing loss can have a number of causes, including prolonged exposure to loud noises, infection, head injuries, prolonged use of certain drugs, and excessive wax buildup. Regardless of the cause, all hearing difficulties can be divided into two classes: sensorineural hearing loss and conduction hearing loss.

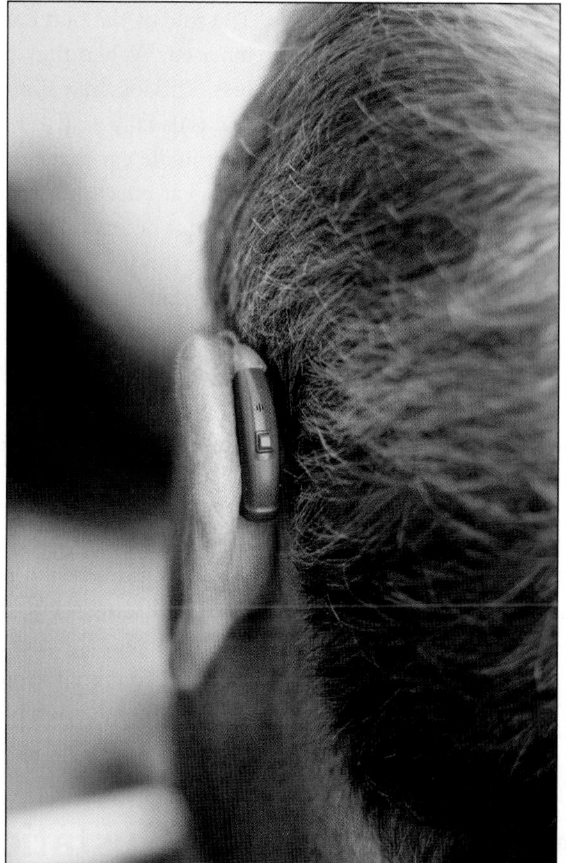

(Shutterstock)

The most common example of sensorineural hearing loss is presbycusis, the gradual loss of sensitivity to high frequencies that occurs with aging.

Sensorineural Hearing Loss

Damage to either the hair cells of the inner ear or the auditory nerve can cause **sensorineural hearing loss**. The most common example of this type of impairment is the gradual loss of sensitivity to high frequencies that occurs with aging, a condition called *presbycusis*.

Research has shown that high-frequency deafness begins at a surprisingly early age. Most thirty-year-olds are unable to hear tones above 15,000 Hz, and by ages fifty to seventy years, the upper limit of the average person's hearing range drops to 12,000 Hz and 6,000 Hz, respectively. Some medical researchers believe that presbycusis is due, at least in part, to a lessening of blood flow to the inner ear, which destroys some of the critical neural elements in this structure.

Exposure to excessively loud noises can also cause permanent damage to the sensitive structures of the inner ear. This type of hearing loss is often accompanied by an annoying condition called tinnitus, a continuous ringing in the ears. The effects of exposure to loud noises may accumulate over a person's life, thereby contributing to a steady loss of hearing with advancing age. Hearing loss is not just age related, however. Brief exposure to extremely loud noises can produce similar damage.

Most people do not willingly stand next to a jet as it takes off or expose themselves to some other equally intense sound that can cause permanent damage. However, many people go to rock concerts where noise levels are often measured in the 100–300 db range. The ringing in your ears you may have experienced after attending a rock concert may indicate damage to the hair cells of your inner ear. You may not notice any change in your hearing after one concert because the damage is often quite minimal. However, the effects are cumulative. In a few years, you may notice that you no longer hear the phone ringing in the back bedroom or that people complain that the volume on your TV is too loud. Young people who spend a great deal of time listening to loud music can suffer permanent damage to the hair cells. Rock guitarist for The Who, Pete Townshend, suffers a significant hearing loss most likely caused by loud music. Today, about one in five teenagers suffer from some degree of hearing loss caused by listening to loud music through headphones or earbuds. This rate is nearly 30 percent higher than it was in the 1980s and 1990s, before these devices became popular (American Osteopathic Association, 2017).

Conduction Hearing Loss

The role of the outer and middle ear is to conduct sound energy to the receptors of the inner ear. When they fail to function properly, the result is called **conductive hearing loss**. This loss may simply be due to a buildup of earwax in the auditory canal, a condition that is usually easy to remedy. Sometimes an ear infection can cause so much pressure in the middle ear that the eardrum ruptures, resulting in impaired hearing. In young children, ear infections frequently cause an increase in pressure because the Eustachian tube may not be fully developed. Inserting small tubes through the tympanic membrane can relieve this pressure.

A fairly common cause of conduction deafness is a disease called otosclerosis, in which a spongy substance around the base of the stapes hardens, cementing the bone in a locked position. Replacing the stapes with a plastic substitute can surgically repair this disease, which tends to occur in young adults.

Conduction hearing loss does not produce total deafness, as is often the case with severe forms of sensorineural impairment. One reason is that sounds can be transmitted directly through the bones of the skull to the inner ear. (This is why a tape recording of your voice probably sounds odd to you. When you talk, the sound of your voice is normally transmitted not only through the air to your outer ear receptacles but also directly through your skull to your inner ear. Since you are accustomed to hearing this blending, the tape-recorded sound of your voice sounds different.) Many hearing aids, designed to amplify sound transmission via bone conduction, can markedly reduce the effects of conduction hearing loss.

4.4 Gustation and Olfaction

The senses of taste, or **gustation**, and smell (**olfaction**) are classified as chemical senses because chemical substances in the environment activate both. Taste and smell are often called minor senses because, relatively speaking, humans utilize vision and audition more than these other senses. We may not rely as much on the senses of smell and taste as do many other animals. However, these minor senses contribute greatly to our experience. The taste of chocolate, smell of the air after a spring rain or of meat sizzling on the barbecue, the sensuous smell of perfume—all contribute immeasurably to our quality of life. Sometimes smells and flavors provide crucial information. Odors such as the smell of gas or smoke signal danger, for instance, and taste may have evolved as a signal for both bad and particularly nutritious foods. For instance, foods low in calories or that may be toxic are often bitter tasting, while foods high in caloric value are the most flavorful and desired.

Conductive Hearing Loss Hearing loss caused by the failure of the outer and middle ear to conduct sound energy to the inner ear's receptors, sometimes because of an infection or buildup of ear wax

Gustation The sense of taste, which, like olfaction, is activated by chemical senses in the environment

Olfaction The sense of smell, which, like taste, is activated by chemical substances in the environment

Figure 4-17 Distribution of Taste Qualities on the Tongue

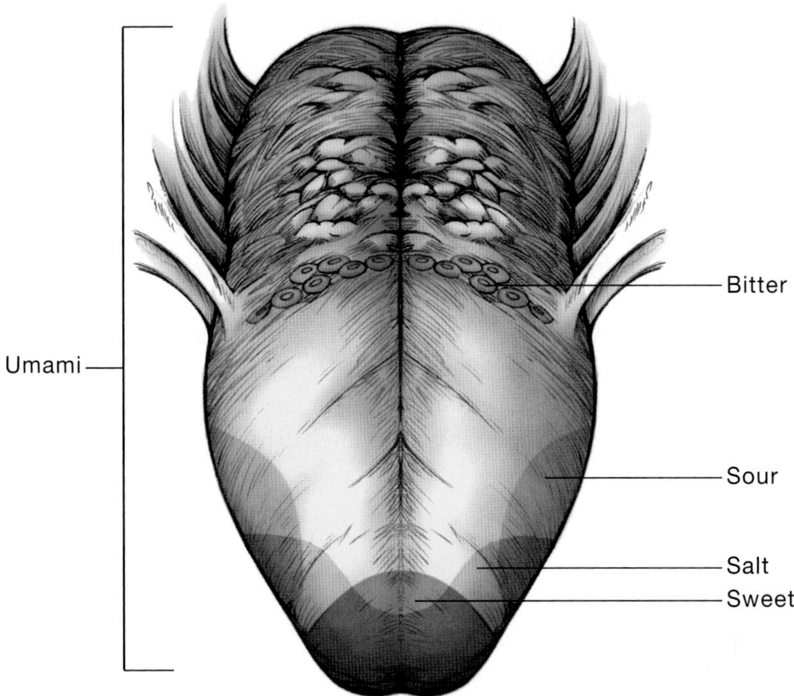

4.4a Gustation

As Figure 4-17 shows, different parts of the tongue are most sensitive to different taste qualities. The tip of the tongue is most responsive to sweet flavors, the tip and forward portion of each side respond to salty substances, the sides to sour substances, and the back or base to bitter flavors. The fifth basic taste quality is umami (Japanese for meaty or savory). The umami taste appears to be detected all over the tongue and palate. These regional differences only reflect zones of greatest sensitivity; taste receptors of each taste bud respond to some degree to a wide range of taste qualities. So, don't assume that these regions of the tongue have only flavor-specific taste receptors. How then is it possible to differentiate between literally thousands of tastes when it appears that there are only five different primary taste qualities? Historically, it has been presumed the perception of taste is coded by neurons that are dedicated to specific taste qualities (salty, bitter, sweet, etc.) and that contributions from these dedicated neurons, or labeled lines, gave rise to different taste experiences. This *labeled-line theory*, however, does not appear to account for recent electrophysiological data and the complexity and range of our taste experiences. According to an alternative, *across-fiber pattern theory*, individual neurons are not coded or labeled for a particular taste quality; rather, they appear to cooperate with other neurons to provide a unique pattern of firing, or "fingerprint," for each unique taste (McCaughey & Scott, 1998; Schiffman, 2000; Roper & Chaudhari, 2010).

The receptors for taste are located in the little bumps on the tongue called *papillae*. Each papilla contains as many as two hundred *taste buds*, which in turn contain a number

BVT Lab

Visit **www.BVTLab.com** to explore the student resources available for this chapter.

of receptor cells called *microvilli*. The microvilli are hairlike projections that extend into the saliva that coats the tongue. When we take food into our mouths, chemicals that are dissolved by saliva stimulate the receptor cells, which transduce this chemical energy into neural signals that are transmitted to regions of the brain including the medulla, the thalamus, and the gustatory cortex.

Taste is believed to play an important role in the survival of many species. For example, sweet and umami tastes signal energy-rich foods including carbohydrates, fats, and proteins. We find these energy-rich foods preferable because of their taste. Bitter tastes, on the other hand, signal potential toxins and low calorie foods. Our preference for calorie-rich foods is largely mediated by the release of dopamine in the mesolimbic system. Eating carbohydrates and fats result in an increase in dopamine release, which then makes these foods more valuable and memorable (Costa et al., 2007). We also know that when highly palatable (calorie rich) foods reach your stomach they signal the release of dopamine as a way of regulating food intake (de Araujo, Ferreira, Tellez, & Ren, 2012). Both of these neural mechanisms ensured that our ancestors selected the appropriate diets, but they can backfire on us now and are believed to be major contributors to obesity. We discuss this more in Chapter 8.

4.4b Olfaction

Unlike many other animals, humans do not depend on the sense of smell to identify friends, repel enemies, and attract mates. Nevertheless, odors do enhance our enjoyment of life, particularly those smells connected with the food we eat. Odors enter the nasal cavity as airborne molecules, either through the nostrils or through the back of the oral cavity. The receptor cells for odors lie in the *olfactory mucosa,* or the mucous membrane that lines the nasal cavity (see Figure 4-18). Tiny hairlike projections (cilia) extend outward from the receptor cells, catching the airborne molecules.

We do not know exactly how the chemical energy of various odors is converted to neural signals that carry differing smell messages to the brain. However, one widely held theory is that the cilia on the olfactory receptor cells are specialized to accommodate odor molecules with particular shapes. This viewpoint suggests that substances have different odors because they have different molecular shapes, an idea supported by the observation that molecules with similar shapes have similar odors. Presumably, odor molecules are transported and bound to the receptor cells by a specialized protein called *olfactory binding protein*. Once bound to receptors, a pattern of neural firing travels first to the olfactory bulb and then along the olfactory nerve to higher brain centers in the amygdala and the olfactory cortex, adjacent to the gustatory cortex. Olfactory signals reach the cortex without going through the thalamus as all other senses do.

Unlike taste, there doesn't appear to be a set of primary odors, even though researchers have attempted to classify odors by their similarity in chemical structure. So, how do we discriminate between the more than ten thousand complex odors humans can perceive? Although olfactory receptors do not fire to specific odor compounds, the patterns of neural activity generated by receptors with a broad range of sensitivities to different odors contributes to our ability to discriminate smells (Goldstein, 2010).

Odors have a powerful ability to stimulate recall of old memories and to elicit feelings connected with experiences well removed in time. Because of this effect, odors are often used to sell products. It is difficult to pass by the delectable odors emanating from the chocolate chip cookie franchise in a local shopping mall. Car dealerships often spray a "new car" scent into used vehicles. The outsides of bread wrappers may be infused with a fresh-baked smell, and inexpensive vinyl-covered furniture is sometimes treated with a leather scent.

Figure 4-18 The Olfactory System

When we smell something, molecules of its fragrance enter the nasal passage from the nose and/or throat. Receptor cells in the olfactory mucosa transduce these stimuli into neural messages that are transmitted along the olfactory tracts to the brain.

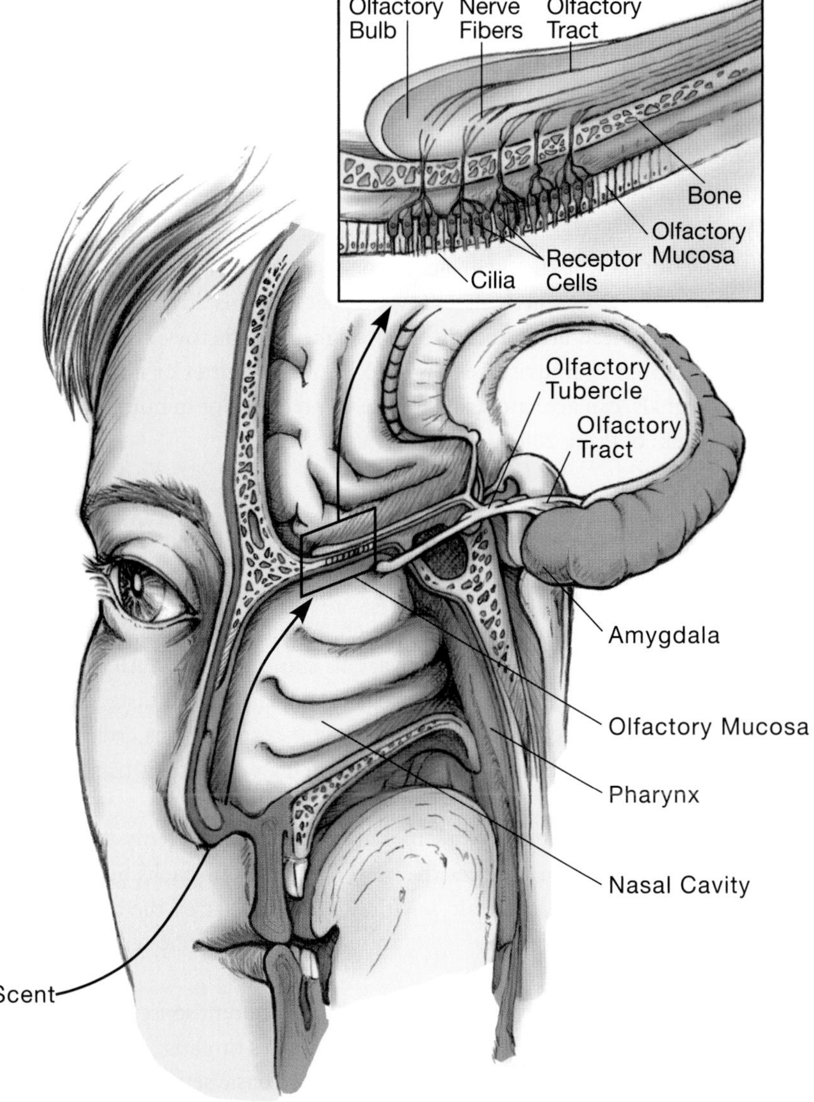

Adapted figure of "Schematic Diagram of Proposed Circuitry in the Analgesic Effects" from *Introduction to Biological Psychology* by Philip Grove and George Rebec. Copyright © 1992 by Philip Grove and George Rebec. Reprinted with permission of McGraw-Hill.

Chemical Communication: Pheromones

Some perfume manufacturers have implied, sometimes not so subtly, that their product contains an aphrodisiac-like product that will attract a potential mate. Other perfumes contain animal pheromones, presumably because if pheromones work for animals they must also work for people. These odors that attract sexual interest, called *pheromones*, do exist among a variety of animals; the females of many species secrete pheromones during their fertile periods. Pheromones serve many other functions in animals beside identifying receptive mates. They may also function to identify offspring, define territories, identify dominance, signal alarm, aid in the location of food sources, and aid in the aggregation of social animals. In mammals, pheromones are primarily detected by specialized receptors in the nasal cavity called vomeronasal organs (VNOs). While humans do have these nasal structures, they lack neuronal elements found in other species. Attempts to demonstrate pheromone effects in humans have been quite inconsistent. There is evidence, for example, that females living together may begin to exhibit synchronized menstrual cycles and that mothers may identify their infants by olfactory signals. Additionally, reports suggest that females respond to male steroids secreted by axillary hair cells when the hormone is applied directly to the female VNO. Researchers report that under these conditions, females responded with a significant reduction in nervousness and tension as well as with other autonomic changes (McClintock, 1998; Grosser, Monti-Bloch, Jennings-White, & Berliner, 2000). Research also suggests that humans do detect pheromone-like compounds and that these are transmitted through the olfactory system, not through the VNO (Savic, Hedén-Blomqvist, & Berglund, 2009). Whether or not pheromones, or other olfactory signals, can activate sexual interest and behavior in humans remains to be confirmed (Wysocki & Preti, 2004).

4.5 The Skin Senses

The fourth type of sensation is the sense of touch. As Figure 4-19 shows, our entire skin surface is embedded with receptors for the various skin sensations. All of these various receptors are the dendrites of neurons. Unlike vision, hearing, and taste, our skin senses use no specialized receptor cells other than neurons. These neurons do have specialized dendrite endings, however, that modify the manner in which they transduce physical energy into a neural firing.

Receptors for different kinds of skin senses are distributed unevenly over the body. For example, our faces are much more sensitive to touch than our backs because the receptors are more densely packed in the skin of the face than that of the back. Researchers have attempted to link particular kinds of skin receptors to specific sensory experiences, with only limited success.

The sense of touch is actually a composite of three different senses: pressure, temperature, and pain. More complex sensory experiences such as tingling, itching, tickling, and wetness are produced from combinations of these three basic sensations.

4.5a Pressure

We experience the sensation of pressure when a mechanical force causes a displacement of the skin. Sensory adaptation occurs very quickly, which is why we are soon unaware of the pressure of tight-fitting pants or snug shoes. (If you continue to be aware of your tight shoes, it is probably because you are feeling the sensation of pain rather than pressure.) Some parts of our bodies are much more sensitive to pressure than others. The most sensitive regions are the face and fingers; the least sensitive are the back and the legs.

Figure 4-19 A Cross-Sectional Drawing of the Skin

Different receptors in the skin are sensitive to specific kinds of stimuli.

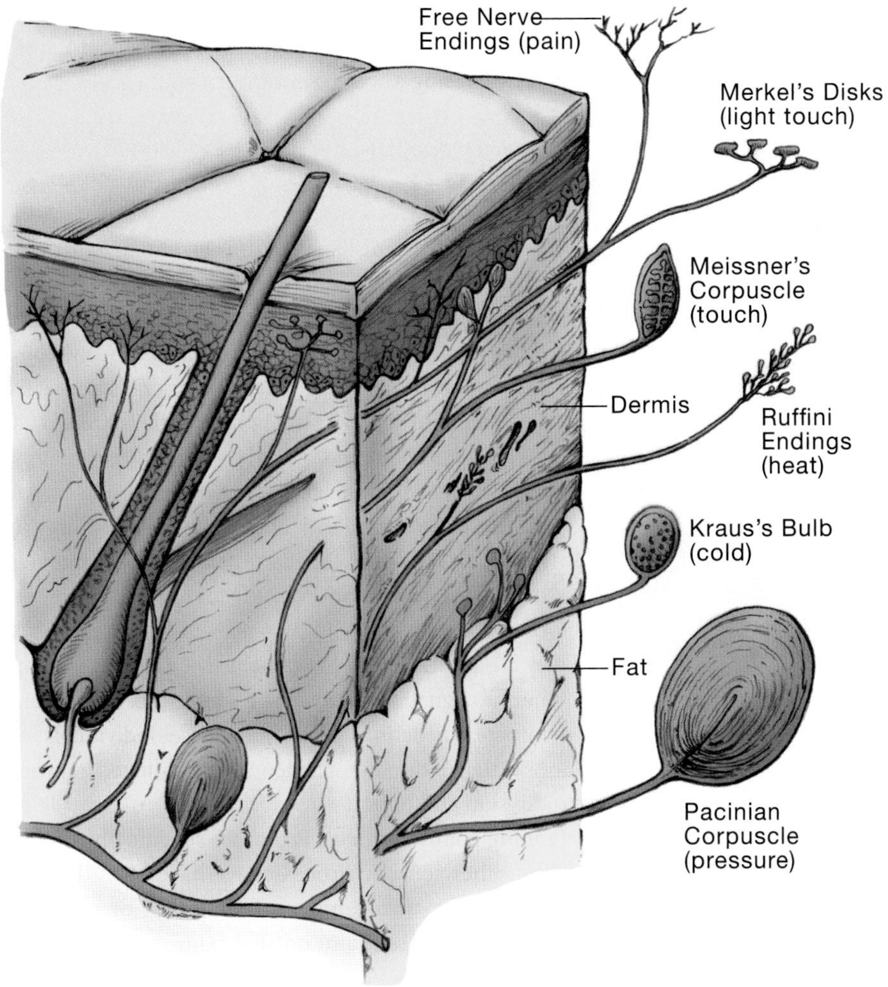

4.5b Temperature

The detection of changes in body temperature is of great importance because most animals cannot survive when body temperature either falls too low or rises too high. As body temperature decreases, organisms can adapt behaviorally by seeking warmth or insulation. As it rises, organisms may, for example, seek a cooler environment or water immersion.

Certain very localized areas of the skin seem to be sensitive to cold but not warmth; other spots show just the opposite sensitivity. This observation is consistent with general agreement among researchers that different specialized dendrite endings, called *free-nerve endings*, respond to cold and heat. Receptors for warm temperature respond more rapidly as temperature increases, while receptors for cold respond in an increasing manner as temperature decreases. Detectors for cold appear to be located closer to the skin's surface than are heat detectors. This may explain why you experience a brief sensation of cold when you place your hand in a stream of hot water to check the temperature of your morning shower. Under other conditions, spots sensitive to cold can be stimulated with a hot stimulus. The perception of cold in this case is called *paradoxical cold*. It is paradoxical because a hot temperature produces a cold sensation. Some chemicals produce the sensations of cold and warm. For example, menthol produces a cold sensation by stimulating cold receptors, while methyl salicylate (found in ointments like Ben-Gay) or capsaicin increase peripheral blood flow, thereby causing a warm sensation.

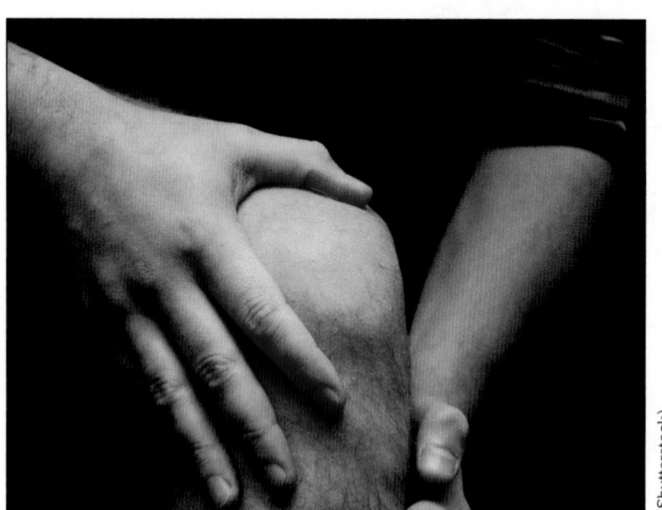

(Shutterstock)

The sensation of pain is necessary. Pain acts as a warning that something is harming us. Nearly one-third of the American adult population experiences persistent or recurrent chronic pain.

4.5c Pain

As much as we dislike pain, it is essential. Pain acts as a warning that something is harming us, and it drives us to seek necessary medical attention. Despite its importance (and regardless of the fact that nearly one-third of the American adult population experiences persistent or recurrent chronic pain), relatively little is known about what causes pain and how to relieve it. Fortunately, an even smaller number of people suffer from a condition known as *congenital pain insensitivity* where they do not have pain sensations at all. Apparently, these individuals have a genetic mutation that leads to the nonexpression of sodium channels in pain-transmitting neurons (Cox et al., 2006). As you recall from the previous chapter, neural signaling depends on the influx of sodium to initiate an action potential. These individuals often experience serious accidental self-inflicted injuries to the skin and bones.

One fact that makes understanding pain so difficult is that no specific physical stimulus exists for pain as it does for the other sensory processes we have been discussing. A sound that is too loud, a light too bright, or a temperature too hot or cold can all produce pain sensations. Some pain researchers maintain that pain results from overstimulation of any sensory receptors; others believe that pain results when damaged tissue releases chemicals that stimulate *free nerve endings* in the skin, which then transduce the chemical energy to neural signals that carry pain messages to our brains. Chemicals believed to be involved in this process include *prostaglandins*, *bradykinins*, and *substance P* (P for pain protein).

Pain researchers have identified nerve fibers that transmit pain signals from the point of injury to the spinal cord and then on to the brain. One set of rapidly transmitting, myelinated fibers conveys a message of localized, sharp, pricking pain, which is probably the only sensation we feel when the pain begins and ends quickly (as when our skin is pierced by a needle). However, if the pain stimulus is more severe, as might result from a burn or a damaging body blow, we perceive a second sensation within a second or two. This message, which is conveyed by unmyelinated slow nerve fibers, induces an awareness of a burning, searing, throbbing, or aching pain that is usually more diffuse.

Gate-Control Theory
Theory that neural gates in the spinal cord allow passage of pain signals to the brain (These gates may be closed by the simultaneous firing of nonpain nerve fibers, so that pain is not perceived.)

Gate-Control Theory of Pain

One widely discussed attempt to explain some of the phenomena associated with pain perception is called the **gate-control theory** proposed by Melzack and Wall (1965). This theory suggests that when nerve fibers conveying pain messages are activated, neural gates in the spinal cord are opened to allow passage of pain signals on their way to the brain. However, the firing of other nonpain nerve fibers can close these pain gates if they are activated simultaneously with the pain fibers. Thus, this theory suggests that competition from other sensations may block our perception of pain.

Research support for the gate-control theory has been inconsistent, and not all of its propositions have fared equally well under close scrutiny. Nevertheless, some of its major tenets, particularly its emphasis on pain as a perceptual as well as sensory phenomenon, have been widely supported by experimental evidence. A number of phenomena make this interpretation seem particularly plausible. For example, we know that pain relief can be induced in both humans and other animals by electrical stimulation of certain areas within the spinal cord. Presumably, such stimulation inhibits the spinal transmission of pain messages, perhaps by closing pain gates.

The gate-control theory also suggests an explanation for why people are often unaware of pain when they are injured under conditions of high stress and intense emotions. For instance, a woman who cuts herself while rescuing a child through a broken window may not notice her own injury until the crisis has passed. It seems plausible that intense emotions can create competing stimuli that overload the neural circuits, thereby blocking the pain pathways.

Substance P A peptide neurotransmitter that signals pain from peripheral nerve fibers to the spinal cord

Nociceptor A sensory receptor specialized in transmitting pain signals to the spinal cord

Endorphins A class of neurotransmitter substances that function to inhibit the transmission of pain information; morphine and other opiates act by facilitating endorphin transmission

Periaqueductal Gray Area (PAG) A region of the brain stem that controls pain signals sent to higher brain centers; receives signals from endorphin-containing neurons for pain analgesia

Neurotransmitters and Pain

In Chapter 3, we discussed several neuropeptides that served as neurotransmitters. Two neuropeptides play important roles in the transmission of pain signals from sensory neurons to the brain. The first, **Substance P**, is found throughout the midbrain, pons, and medulla, as well as in the spinal cord. In the spinal cord, Substance P appears to be the neurotransmitter released by incoming sensory neurons called **nociceptors**, that signal pain. Another group of neuropeptides, called **endorphins**, possess pain-killing (analgesic) properties similar to opiate drugs. The term *endorphin* means internal morphine. The parts of the brain where the endorphins are believed to inhibit pain include the **periaqueductal gray area (PAG)** of the brainstem, which is believed to be the center of the pain circuit. Endorphins also modulate pain signals in the thalamus and several cortical areas.

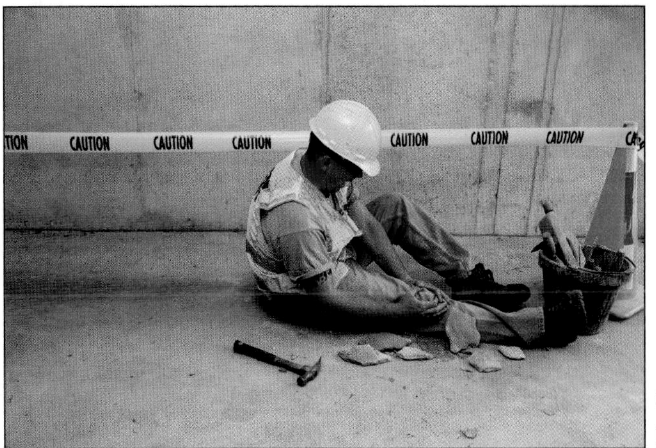

(iStock)

Substance P appears to be the neurotransmitter released by incoming sensory neurons that signal pain.

As sensory neurons transmit pain signals to the spinal cord, they excite afferent neurons that ascend to the brainstem and the thalamus in the brain (see Figure 4-20). In the PAG region, these afferent neurons cause the release of endorphins, which (through the involvement of several other neurons) results in the excitation of descending neurons. These descending neurons release serotonin at the original sensory neuron synapse in the spinal cord, inhibiting the afferent neurons signaling pain. Therefore, serotonin appears to be involved in the inhibition of pain signals to the brain. It is for this reason that physicians may prescribe certain SSRIs (antidepressants; selective serotonin reuptake inhibitors) for pain management.

Figure 4-20 The Periaqueductal Gray Region of the Brain Stem

Pain messages are transmitted through the spinal cord to the periaqueductal gray (PAG) region of the brain stem. Endorphin- and GABA-containing neurons interact to cause the release of serotonin in the spinal cord, inhibiting pain transmission. Pain messages are also transmitted to the thalamus and other brain areas in which pain is perceived.

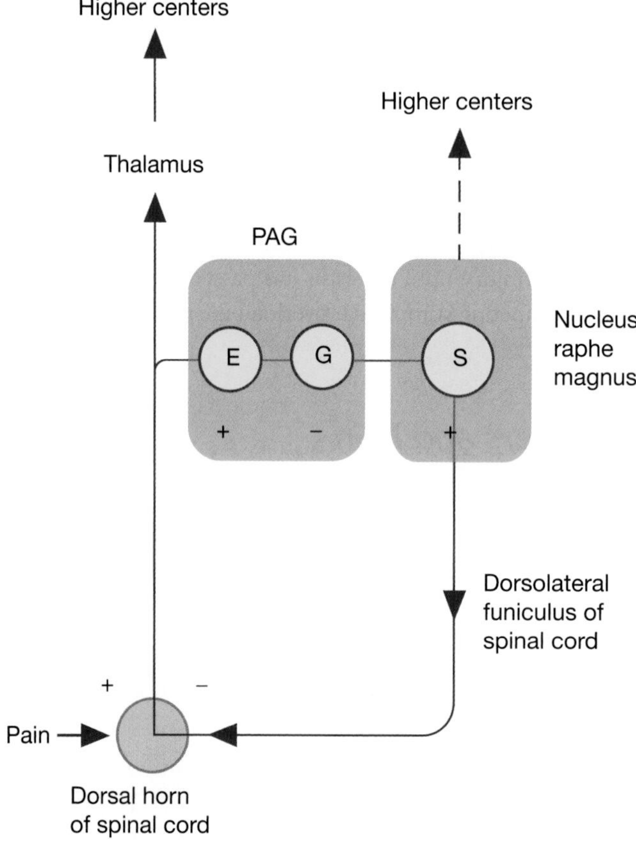

Source: Groves and Rebec, 1992 to Groves, P. U., & Rebec, G. V. (1992). *Introduction to Biological Psychology*, 4th ed. Dubuque, IA: Wm. C. Brown Publishers.

4.6 Kinesthesis and Equilibrium

Try closing your eyes and moving your hand to various positions. You will have no trouble keeping track of where your hand is. With your eyes still closed, try touching your nose. Again, you will have no problem. Finally, with eyes closed, try standing on one foot. This task is a little tougher, but you will probably find you can maintain your balance reasonably well.

All of these simple exercises are accomplished without the aid of the senses discussed so far in this chapter. Rather, these tasks are aided by two interrelated sensory systems called *kinesthesis* and *equilibrium*. These two **body senses**, working in concert, tell us the orientation of our bodies in space, the relative position of the various body parts, and the movement of any parts of the body.

Body Senses Term used to describe the two interrelated sensory systems of kinesthesis and equilibrium

Figure 4-21 The Semicircular Canals

These fluid-filled canals contain specialized receptor cells that are stimulated by head movement.

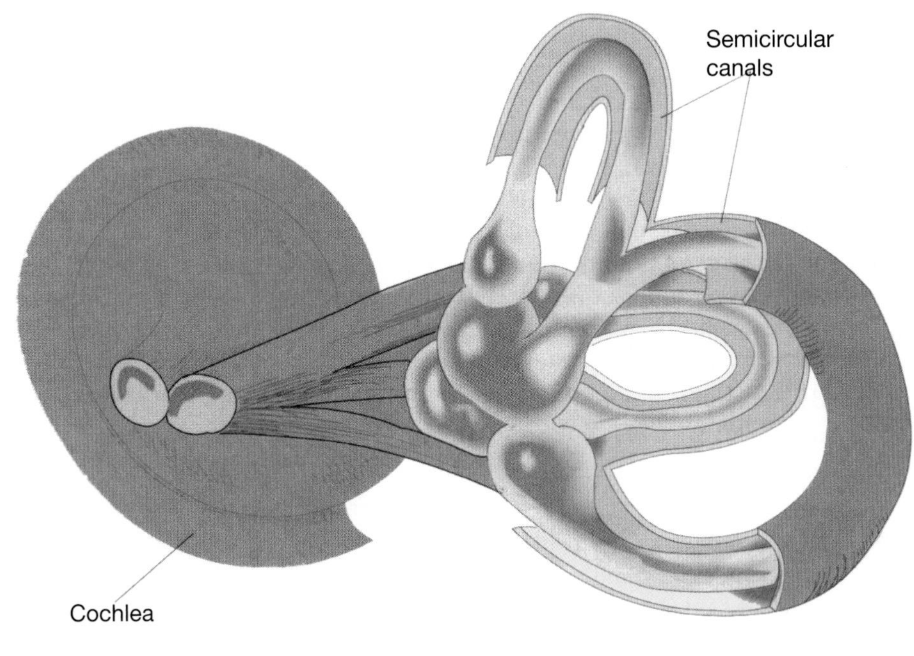

The sense of **kinesthesis** is diffused throughout the entire body. It consists of specialized nerve endings embedded in the muscles, tendons, and joints that tell the brain whether muscles and tendons are being stretched, contracted, or relaxed. The cortex translates this sensory information into perceptions about locations of various parts of the body in relation to other parts. Kinesthesis allows us to throw a ball without watching what our arms are doing, and it helps us take appropriate corrective action when we stumble or slip.

The sense of **equilibrium**, or balance, is localized within the inner ear. It comprises two sets of sensory receptors: the semicircular canals and the vestibular sacs. The **semicircular canals** are three ring-shaped structures, oriented at right angles to each other so that they lie roughly in each of the three dimensions of space (see Figure 4-21). Each is filled with a fluid (endolymph) that moves when the head is rotated. The lining of the semicircular canals contains hair cells that bend in the direction of the fluid flow. When you move your head, the fluid flows in the canal along the plane in which your head is moving. This movement is transduced to neural messages, which tell your brain that your head is either accelerating or decelerating. If velocity is kept at a constant rate (in an airplane or a subway, for example), motion is not usually detectable. The viscosity of endolymph fluid is apparently changed by alcohol consumption, which contributes to the "spins" when you've consumed too much.

Another source of information comes from the **vestibular sacs**, located at the junction of the semicircular canals and the cochlea. These sacs contain hair cells weighted with crystals of calcium carbonate. When the head is tilted, gravitational forces cause the weighted cilia to shift; this action in turn triggers neural activity in adjacent nerve fibers. This information, in conjunction with information received from the semicircular

Kinesthesis Bodily sense that provides information about perceptions of the location of various body parts in relation to other parts and about the position of the body in space

Equilibrium The sense of balance, localized within the inner ear and comprising two sensory receptors: the semicircular canals and the vestibular sacs

Semicircular Canals Three ring-shaped structures in the inner ear that provide information about the body's equilibrium or balance

Vestibular Sacs Structure at the junction of the semicircular canals and cochlea of the middle ear that provide information about the head's position in space

Synesthesia A condition in which one type of sensory stimulation evokes the sensation of another, as when the hearing of a sound produces the visualization of a color

canals (as occurs in a swaying car or a boat on a rough sea), sometimes produces motion sickness. Motion sickness occurs when motion information signaled by the visual system does not match unusual vestibular stimulation.

4.7 Synesthesia

Synesthesia is the bizarre, and quite rare, condition in which sensations from one modality cause perceptions in another. For example, an individual with synesthesia might experience a vivid green color while tasting lemonade, see black numbers in different colors, or even see distinct colors while listening to different musical notes. Scientists have long known about these experiences. Francis Galton, a cousin of Charles Darwin, even wrote about them in 1880. Although long thought to be a mere curiosity, fakery, or a strange memory, synesthesia may actually shed light on understanding normal brain organization and function. It is believed that synesthesia is the result of cross-wiring between cortical brain centers' sensory processing (Banissy et al., 2012). The processing of colors and numbers, for example, occurs in adjacent cortical regions where the temporal, parietal, and occipital lobes converge. In a series of brain-imaging experiments, this cross-wiring idea was supported. Upon presenting black numbers on a white background to a synesthete, both the number area and the color area showed increases in activity—something that does not occur with normal subjects (Nunn et al., 2002). Synesthesia appears to run in families, and there is high correlation of synesthesia between monozygotic twins (Bosley & Eagleman, 2015), suggesting a genetic disposition. It also occurs more frequently in women and creative people. It is estimated that there are about fifty distinct types of synesthesia, and it occurs in one in two hundred people (Ramachandran & Hubbard, 2003). In some synesthetes, stimuli with strong emotional content (e.g., love, hate, etc.) are more likely to elicit a synesthetic response (Ward, 2004).

4.8 Perceiving the World

Up to this point, we have been looking at the processes by which we receive sensations about the physical world through our various sense organs. How we interpret or perceive

Figure 4-22 Test for One Form of Synesthesia

A synesthete who links color with specific numbers has no difficulty quickly identifying the pattern of black 2's among the 5's. They may appear as they do in the figure on the right.

5 5 5 5 5 5 5 5
5 5 5 5 5 5 5
5 5 5 5 2 5 5
5 5 5 5 2 5 2
5 5 5 5 2 2 2 2
5 5 5 5 5 5

5 5 5 5 5 5 5 5
5 5 5 5 5 5 5
5 5 5 5 2 5 5
5 5 5 5 2 5 2
5 5 5 5 2 2 2 2
5 5 5 5 5 5

Figure 4-23 Perceptual Organization

Perceptual organization is the process whereby we organize structural elements into objects.

these sensations depends on other processes. Our perceptions are much more than what we see, hear, smell, taste, or sense with our skin and body senses. Our brains organize and give meaning to the constant input of sensory messages through an active process of selecting, ordering, synthesizing, and interpreting. In the rest of this chapter, we consider some of the basic principles that govern our perceptions.

4.8a Perceptual Organization

Look at the illustration in Figure 4-23. Rather than meaningless dots, lines, and colors, you no doubt perceive a familiar animal. Virtually everything we perceive with our eyes is made up of elementary sensations in the form of points, lines, edges, brightness, and varied hues. The process by which we structure these elementary sensations into the objects we perceive is called **perceptual organization**.

Gestalt psychologists identified the major principles of perceptual organization in the first half of the last century. This group of influential German psychologists included Max Wertheimer, Kurt Koffka, and Wolfgang Köhler. As mentioned in Chapter 1, they theorized that we perceive figures and forms as whole patterns that are different from the simple sum of individual sensations. They outlined several principles that influence how people organize sensations into whole patterns called *Gestalts*. These include figure and ground, perceptual grouping, and closure.

Figure and Ground

One feature of perceptual organization identified by the Gestalt psychologists is our tendency to differentiate between **figure** (the part of an image on which we focus our attention) and **ground** (the background against which the figure stands). For example, the black words on this page stand out as figure against the white background.

Figure 4-24 illustrates an ambiguous figure-ground relationship. At first glance, you may see either two light-faced profiles as a figure against a darker ground, or a dark vase as the figure against a lighter ground. This figure further demonstrates the distinction

Perceptual Organization Process by which we structure elementary sensations (such as the sight of lines, brightness, and points) into the objects we perceive

Figure In perception, the part of an image on which we focus our attention

Ground In perception, the background against which the figure that we focus on stands

Figure 4-24 The Rubin Vase

Used to illustrate the figure-ground principle of perceptual organization, this illustration is ambiguous because either the dark gray or the light gray can serve as figure or ground.

Source: Shutterstock

between sensation and perception. The pattern of sensory receptors activated in our retinas remains constant while our perceptions shift between the two figure-ground patterns. The manner in which our brains organize these constant sensory stimuli allows us to perceive either the faces or the vase, but not both at the same time.

The figure and ground organization principle also applies to senses other than vision. For example, when you listen to music, the melody may stand out as the figure against a background of chords that serve as ground. However, a sudden change in tempo, rhythm, or volume may suddenly bring a chord to the forefront, where it becomes the central figure. Perhaps you are listening to a friend describe some important political event when a voice on the TV set behind you mentions your favorite athletic team. Suddenly the TV announcement becomes the focal point of your attention, and your friend's voice becomes background noise. You cannot focus on your friend's voice and the TV announcer at the same time. One must be figure, and one must be ground.

Figure 4-25 Perceptual Grouping Principles

Part A illustrates the principle of proximity. The pattern on the left can be seen as either columns or rows because the dots are spaced equally. The patterns to the right are seen as columns because of the horizontal spacing. Parts B and C demonstrate the grouping principle of similarity (in B we see rows, and in C we see columns). Pattern D illustrates the principle of continuity, in which stimuli that flow smoothly into one another form a group.

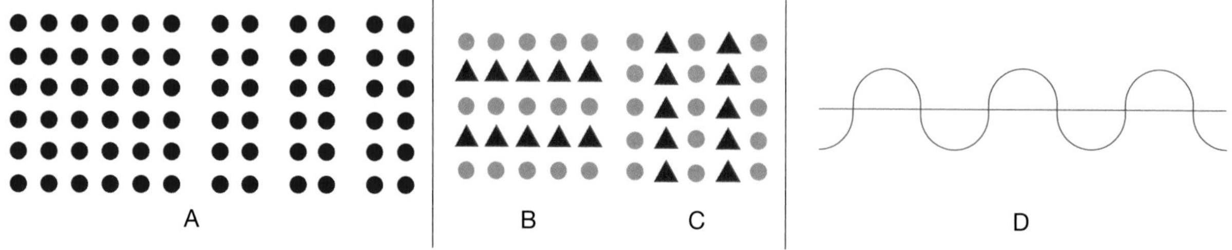

Perceptual Grouping

Gestalt psychologists also demonstrated the role of **perceptual grouping** to explain how we organize sensory input into meaningful wholes. Patterns of stimuli are grouped into larger units in three major ways: **proximity**, **similarity**, and **good continuation**.

Figure 4-25 illustrates these three perceptual grouping principles. The principle of proximity suggests that, all else being equal, we tend to organize our perceptions by grouping elements that are the nearest to each other. The principle of similarity suggests that we group elements that are similar to one another. A final grouping principle, good continuation, suggests that we are more likely to perceive stimuli as a whole or single group if they flow smoothly into one another, as opposed to being discontinuous.

Closure

Another powerful organizing principle is our inclination to perceive incomplete figures as complete. A careful examination of Figure 4-26 reveals that what appear to be two overlapping triangles are actually incomplete figures. Furthermore, the solid white triangle does not exist; it is merely an illusion. The perceptual process that allows us to see these as complete figures is referred to as **closure**.

Perceptual Grouping Tendency to organize patterns of stimuli into larger units according to proximity, similarity, and good continuation

Proximity Perceptual grouping principle whereby, all else being equal, we tend to organize perceptions by grouping elements that are the nearest to each other

Similarity In perception, the principle that we tend to group elements that are similar to each other (In social psychology, similarity of beliefs, interests, and values is recognized as a factor attracting people to one another.)

Good Continuation Perceptual grouping principle that we are more likely to perceive stimuli as a whole or single group if they flow smoothly into one another than if they are discontinuous

Closure Perceptual organizing principle that we tend to perceive incomplete figures as complete

Figure 4-26 The Principle of Closure

We can see two overlapping triangles in this illustration because of our tendency to fill in missing perceptual information. The solid white triangle is merely an illusion induced by closure.

Attention and Perception

Selective Attention and Inattentional Blindness Another basic principle of perceptual processing is **selective attention**, the process of focusing on one or a few stimuli of particular significance while ignoring others. As was shown earlier in the discussion of your dinner date, we never attend equally to all of the stimuli we receive at any given point in time. If we did, our nervous systems would become hopelessly overloaded. Instead, certain stimuli are focused on, and the other events fade into the background. Through this process of selective attention our perceptual ability is enhanced. A relatively recent and somewhat surprising demonstration of selective attention comes from an experiment conducted by Simons and Chabris (1999). In their experiment, 192 college students were asked to watch a seventy-five-second video in which three black-shirted players and three white-shirted players tossed a basketball back and forth. The students were instructed to count the number of tosses between like-shirted players. The six players are seen moving randomly around in a hallway tossing the ball between similar colored players. Midway through the video, a person dressed in a gorilla costume appeared among the players, faced the camera, thumped its chest, and then walked out of camera view. The surprising outcome of this experiment was that 50 percent of the subjects, when asked, reported that they never saw the gorilla! Upon reviewing the video, these subjects were amazed they had actually missed seeing it. Thus, selective attention to some aspect of a visual scene can cause **inattentional blindness** to other aspects. Inattentional blindness has been observed in many other experiments using highly salient stimuli (Most et al., 2001). This phenomenon has long been employed by magicians to distract viewers' attention.

(Image provided by Daniel Simons, www.theinvisiblegorilla.com)

Selective attention to some aspect of a visual scene can cause inattentional blindness to other aspects. (Simons, D. J. & Chabris, C. F. [1999]. Gorillas in our midst: Sustained inattentional blindness for dynamic events. Perception, *28, 1059–1074.)*

To some extent, we control our attention. For example, at this moment your attention is focused on the printed words of this book. Hopefully, your desire to understand the principles discussed here is sufficient inducement to allow you to screen out a variety of background stimuli. Psychologists have discovered that certain characteristics of stimuli tend to capture attention almost automatically. We next examine several important principles that affect our attention to stimuli.

Complex Stimuli There is evidence that stimuli that are difficult to process may command additional attention. For example, some of the complex illustrations in this chapter require a fair amount of effort to comprehend. Psychologists believe that the more we focus on one category of stimuli, the less we can respond to others. This phenomenon, called the *inverse hypothesis*, also relates to the concept of selective attention: The more complex the stimulus, the less attention we can focus on any particular aspect of it.

Sudden Change A sudden change in either the quality or quantity of a background stimulus generally causes a shift in attention. For example, you may notice the quiet as a fan or motor that you haven't noticed shuts off, or a sudden movement to your side can catch your attention while you're driving. As we mentioned earlier, a main characteristic of our sensory systems is to respond to stimulus change.

Selective Attention The process of focusing on one or a few stimuli of particular significance while ignoring others

Inattentional Blindness The failure to see one aspect of a visual scene due to selective attention to another aspect of the scene

Contrast and Novelty Contrast and novelty also tend to capture our attention. For example, a brightly lit neon sign along a dark stretch of highway often diverts our attention because it contrasts with its surroundings. The same sign among many neon signs downtown might not get our attention. Things that are novel or unusual also tend to attract our attention. For instance, wearing an unusual hairstyle or clothing is a good way to get noticed.

Stimulus Intensity Another way to get attention is to vary the intensity of a stimulus. This is why TV commercials may increase their volume slightly above the sound of normal TV programming and why they often use very bright and colorful images. Sudden reduction of stimulus intensity can also command attention. If your friends across the room suddenly begin whispering, you may prick up your ears in an effort to hear what they are saying.

Some professors may use this perceptual concept in their lectures. To cause their students to pay attention to a point, they may lower their voices to a level that is barely audible. As a result, students often lean forward in their seats while they concentrate on the ensuing words of wisdom.

Repetition Repetition is another way to attract attention. This is one reason why TV and radio ads often use jingles that are repeated again and again. Many popular tunes draw our attention because they have a catchy beat that repeats over and over again.

Sign Stimuli Finally, some stimuli appear to attract our attention by activating motivational mechanisms such as fear, hunger, or sexual arousal. When certain stimuli or features of a stimulus activate motivation they are referred to as **sign stimuli**. These stimulus features are believed to have played important roles in guiding and directing behavior throughout our evolution (Eibl-Eibesfeldt, 1989). While sign stimuli are probably more important in guiding the behavior of lower animals, they are also important in motivating and directing human behavior. The all too familiar use of an attractive, exposed body to catch our attention for advertising is an example of how sign stimuli attract our attention. Yawning in primates and humans often elicits a yawn in another. In this case, yawning is a sign stimulus.

4.8b Spatial Perception

The major function of vision is to represent the spatial arrangement of objects in our environment. Objects are seen at varying distances and from different perspectives, yet we recognize their form and size quite accurately. This poses two related problems for perception. First, how do we perceive depth or distance? Second, how do we recognize objects from different perspectives?

The Perception of Depth

Earlier in this chapter, we learned that visual images are focused on the retina, which is essentially an image-recording layer of neural tissue that lines the back of the eye. Since retinal images are two-dimensional, how can we perceive that objects in our environment are three-dimensional? How do we determine how close or far away they are? Clearly, these types of discrimination are essential for normal functioning. Can you imagine what it would be like to walk through a busy city if you could not accurately estimate how far away approaching cars happened to be? A variety of perceptual cues allow us to judge

Sign Stimuli Stimuli that naturally elicit a change in motivational state and behavior

Binocular Cues Visual cues for depth or distance, such as binocular disparity and convergence, that depend on both eyes working together

Monocular Cues Distance cues, such as linear perspective and height on a plane, that can be used with just one eye

accurately the distance of objects. Some of these cues, called **binocular cues**, depend on both eyes working together; others, called **monocular cues**, can be used with just one eye.

Binocular Cues Seeing with both our eyes provides important binocular cues for distance perception. Perhaps the most accurate of these is **binocular** or **retinal disparity**. Binocular disparity is based on the fact that since the eyes are a couple of inches apart, each has a slightly different view of the world. To demonstrate this phenomenon, stare at this page and alternately close one eye at a time. Note that the page appears to shift its position slightly. Normally our brains fuse these two images into a single three-dimensional image. At the same time, the brain analyzes the differences in the two images to obtain information about distance.

Figure 4-27 Binocular (Retinal) Disparity and Convergence

Part A illustrates that the closer an object is, the greater the retinal disparity. Part B illustrates the convergence of the eye that is necessary to view nearby objects. Both binocular (retinal) disparity and convergence are important depth cues for perception.

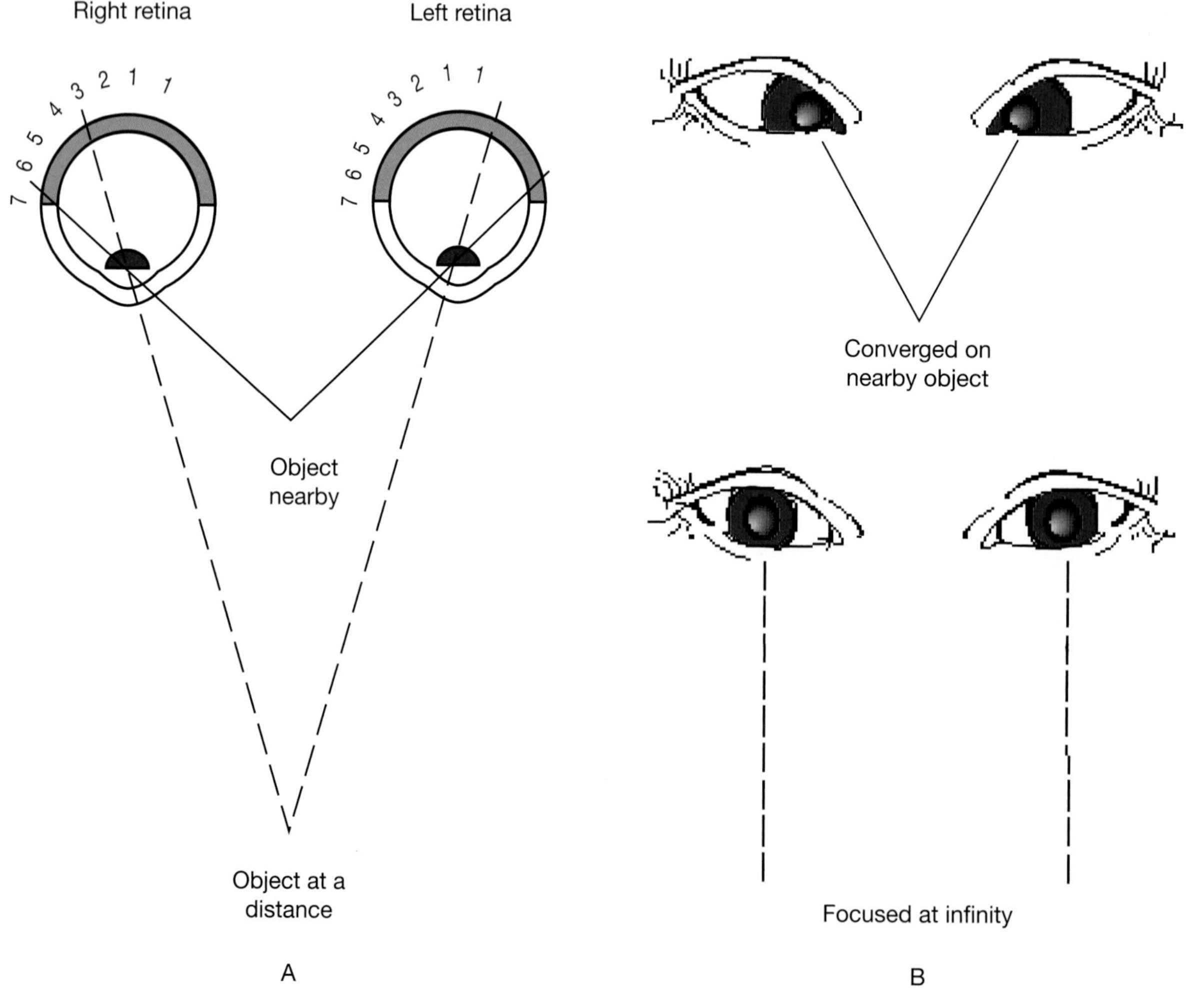

There is greater binocular disparity when objects are close to our eyes than when they are far away. Hold the index finger of one hand very close to your face and align it with the same finger of the other hand as far away as possible. Now alternately close each eye. Your closest finger seems to leap back and forth, while the far one shifts only slightly. Figure 4-27A shows why close objects create more significant disparity, whereas those that are far away create only minor disparity. The difference in the angle of the two eyes to the far object is much slighter than the difference for the close object. The ability of the visual system to utilize binocular disparity is quite impressive. The minimum disparity required to detect a depth difference is 1 micron (a millionth of a meter). This is less than the diameter of a photoreceptor!

Many of us are familiar with **stereograms**, which are two-dimensional images that upon viewing for a few moments convert into a three-dimensional image. These images are usually created by a computer repeating a pattern from left to right. When the viewer's eyes diverge, by looking beyond the poster, the brain is tricked into seeing a three-dimensional image. The slight difference in vertical repetitions of the pattern creates the illusion of depth just as one's eyes create depth perception when viewing a scene. Stereograms are discussed later on in this chapter under the section on visual illusions.

Another important binocular distance cue is called **convergence**. When we look at an object that is no more than 25 feet away, our two eyes must converge (rotate to the inside) in order to perceive it as a single, clearly focused image. This rotation of the eyes is necessary to allow them to focus on the same object, but it creates tension in the eye muscles. As Figure 4-27B shows, the closer the object, the greater the tension. Objects far away require no convergence for sharp focusing. Consequently, muscular feedback from converging eyes becomes an important cue for judging the distance of objects within roughly 25 feet of our eyes.

Binocular (Retinal) Disparity The difference in the retinal image of an object as seen from each eye, due to the difference in viewing angles, that provides an important binocular cue for depth; also known as *retinal disparity*

Stereogram An image that is able to convey the experience of depth perception using binocular cues

Convergence Binocular distance cue based on the fact that the two eyes must converge or rotate toward the inside to perceive objects closer than about 25 feet (The closer the object, the more rotation is necessary and the more muscle tension created.)

Figure 4-28 Monocular Cues for Depth Perception

Many monocular cues also contribute to depth perception. Objects far away tend to be higher on our plane of view. Objects closer to us block objects that are farther away. When you look at this stretch of road, the sides (lines) of the road converge. Objects that are closer tend to be larger than similar objects at a distance.

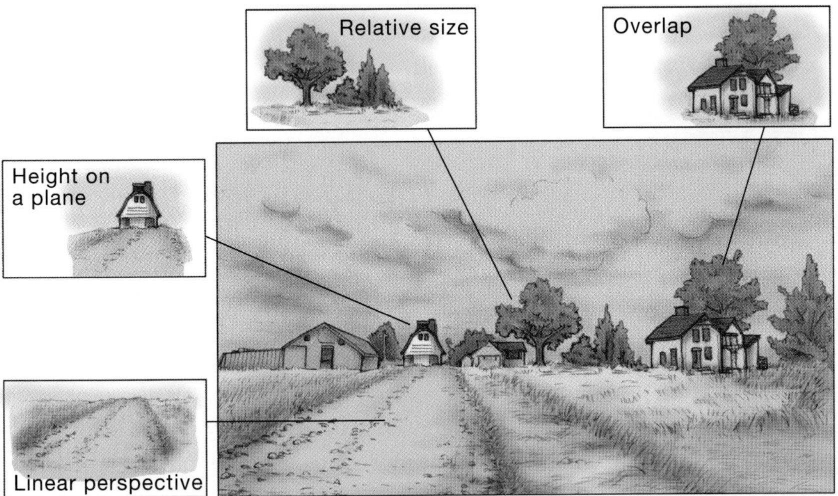

Height on a Plane Important monocular depth cue based on the fact that objects that are highest on one's plane of view appear to be farthest away

Overlap Important monocular distance cue based on the fact that objects close to us tend to block out parts of objects that are farther away; also known as *interposition*

Linear Perspective Important monocular distance cue based on the fact that parallel lines converge when stretched into the distance

Relative Size Monocular distance cue based on the fact that objects of the same size appear to be smaller the farther they are from the viewer

Texture Gradient Monocular distance cue based on the fact that textured surfaces (such as a grassy lawn) appear to be smoother, denser, and less textured when they are far from the viewer than when they are close

Aerial (Atmospheric) Perspective Monocular distance cue based on the fact that distant objects tend to appear fuzzier and less clear than those close to the viewer due to dust and haze

Relative Motion (Motion Parallax) Monocular distance cue based on the fact that moving objects appear to move a greater distance when they are close to the viewer than when they are far away

Monocular Cues

If objects that are far away create little retinal disparity and no convergence, how can we judge their distance? A number of one-eye, or monocular, cues provide that information.

Figure 4-28 illustrates several important monocular cues for distance perception. One of these is elevation, or **height on a plane**. Note that the objects in the photo that appear to be farther away are higher on your plane of view. This cue is always present. If you look around your room or gaze out the window, you will see that the farther away an object is, the higher it will be on your plane of view and the more you have to lift your gaze to perceive it.

Another distance cue, called **overlap** or *interposition*, describes the phenomenon in which objects close to us tend to block out parts of objects that are farther away from us. If you look around your room again, you will notice that your textbook blocks your view of the desk under it, that the desk in turn blocks your view of the floor, and so forth.

A third distance cue, called **linear perspective**, is based on the fact that parallel lines converge when stretched into the distance. For example, when you look at a long stretch of road or railroad tracks, it appears that the sides of the road or the parallel tracks converge on the horizon.

If we know how large objects are, we can judge their distance by their apparent size in relation to each other. If you look out your window and see two people, one 50 yards away and the other 200 yards away, you notice a great difference in their **relative size**. Instead of concluding that one person is a pygmy and the other a giant, you take this cue as evidence that the smaller person is a greater distance from you.

Another monocular cue, **texture gradient**, involves perceived change in the texture of surfaces as they extend farther from our eyes. For example, if you look at a textured surface such as an expanse of grassy lawn or a rock-strewn field, the elements close to you seem to be farther apart or less dense than those that are farther away. The close elements are also clearer. A striking illustration of this phenomenon is provided in Figure 4-29.

Objects that are far away appear fuzzier than those close by, because as distance increases, smog, dust, and haze reduce the clarity of the projected image. This depth cue, called **aerial** or **atmospheric perspective**, can sometimes cause us to judge distance inaccurately, especially if we are accustomed to the smoggy atmosphere of urban areas.

A final monocular cue for distance may be demonstrated if you gaze at the scene outside your window and move your head from side to side. You will notice that objects nearby seem to move a much greater distance than objects farther away. This cue, called **relative motion** or **motion parallax**, is particularly noticeable when you look out the window of a moving car and observe nearby objects moving much more rapidly than distant ones.

(iStock)

Consider texture gradients as a cue for depth. Texture is invariant in that it always appears finer or denser as distance increases and coarser as objects move closer.

Gibson's Theory of Direct Perception

Our preceding discussion of spatial perception assumes that perceptual processing is necessary; that is, the spatial cues we described draw upon both past experience (memory) and cognitive processing for spatial representation such as depth. An intriguing and quite different perspective proposed by James Gibson (1979, 2002) argues that all of the visual information necessary for spatial representation is available from the environment. That is, spatial representation is a process of **direct perception**, not a process of cognition. **Gibson's theory of direct perception** holds that certain information

Figure 4-29 Texture Gradients

The fine texture in the foreground of this picture fades away in the distance.

Source: iStockphoto

from the environment is invariant. These **invariants** are sufficient to represent depth or distance without additional cognitive processing. For instance, consider texture gradients as a cue for depth. Texture is invariant in that it always appears finer or denser as distance increases and coarser as objects move closer. Similarly, the apparent movement differences between near and faraway objects (motion parallax) remain invariant and directly reveal distance information (Goldstein, 2010).

Not all psychologists agree with Gibson, however. Considerable evidence suggests that we do not just "pick up" spatial information, but rather we construct it out of perceptual data. Further research on perceptual invariance and direct perception will either support or weaken Gibson's theory.

Direct Perception The interpretation of sensory information directly by the brain as opposed to perceptual interpretation resulting from cognitive processing

Gibson's Theory of Direct Perception A theory of perception that argues that all information necessary for perception is available to the sensory system and no cognitive processing is necessary to complete the perceptual process

Invariant Sensory information from the environment that is constant from one experience to the next (for example, texture is invariant because it is always finer at close distances than at further distances)

Visual Cliff Device that produces the illusion of a cliff, allowing researchers to test the ability of animals to perceive and respond to depth cues

Perceiving Depth: The Visual Cliff Experiment

There can be little doubt that many distance cues are enhanced by experience. In fact, before a classic experiment more than thirty years ago, many psychologists believed that distance or depth perception depended on learning. However, Eleanor Gibson and Richard Walk (1960) provided convincing evidence that some aspects of depth perception are inborn or innate, at least in some species.

The device created by Gibson and Walk is called the **visual cliff**. The visual cliff is an elevated glass surface. A checkerboard-patterned plane lies just under half of the glass surface. There is nothing under the other half except for the checkerboard painted on the floor, roughly 3.5 feet below. This design produces the illusion of a deep side and a shallow side.

Infants of many species that can walk immediately after birth were tested on the apparatus. All of these newborn animals, including kittens, puppies, lambs, chicks, piglets, and kids, refused to cross over to the deep side, suggesting that depth perception is innate in these species. Even chicks whose initial visual experience occurred on the visual cliff would not step over the deep side. Evidence also suggests that depth perception in this case is based on the monocular cue motion parallax, which is the dominant cue for depth perception in most animals.

Since human babies could not be tested until they were able to crawl (usually around the age of six months), their depth perception was more difficult to interpret. Obviously, a lot of learning can take place in the first six months of life. Most of the infants tested would not spontaneously crawl onto the deep side, something that infants of other species would never do. Yet some infants, especially those who began crawling at a very young age, can be enticed to crawl over the cliff.

Some researchers argue that by the time human infants can be tested on the visual cliff, they may have already learned to avoid drop-offs. Others have argued that the kind of depth perception required for the cliff is an innate capacity in humans that emerges at about six months after birth, the age at which most infants begin to need this capability (Richards & Rader, 1981). Which explanation is correct? At this point, we can say with confidence that depth perception is an innate ability in many species of animals. In humans it is either innate, or it is learned very early in life. Human infants are clearly not living in a visual world that is "one great blooming, buzzing confusion," as stated by William James in 1890. Rather, their world appears to be perceived much like our own.

Size, Color, and Shape Constancies

Size Constancy When you bid farewell to friends at the dock and see them sail off into the distance, you do not assume that their boat is shrinking. Instead, you realize

Figure 4-30 Size Constancy

The man who is walking in these pictures is the same size in each shot. As he moves closer he appears to shrink.

that the boat remains the same size even though the image projected onto your retinas gets smaller and smaller. Your perception of the boat adjusts automatically, taking into consideration changes in the distance between you and it. This perceptual phenomenon, known as **size constancy**, is but one of several forms of **perceptual constancy** that allow us to adjust for varying conditions and changing patterns as we perceive the world. Size constancy is illustrated in Figure 4-30. In this illustration, the man walking is the same size in both pictures. However, as he approaches the foreground, he appears to shrink.

In a classic study of size constancy, A. H. Holway and Edwin Boring (1941) found that subjects were able to make extremely accurate judgments of the size of a circle located at varying distances from their eyes under conditions that were rich with distance cues. As distance cues were progressively eliminated, however, subjects' judgments of circle size became increasingly dependent on the size of the retinal image. Thus, the subjects' perceptions of the size of the circle increased when it was moved closer and decreased as it was moved away, a complete breakdown in size constancy. Therefore, an important cue for size constancy is apparent retinal size.

Size Constancy One form of perceptual constancy, in which the retinal image of an object becomes smaller as the object recedes into the distance or larger as it approaches; the viewer adjusts for this change and perceives the object to be constant in size

Perceptual Constancy The fact that objects are normally perceived to be constant in size, color or brightness, and shape, even though their retinal images change according to different conditions

Brightness Constancy An element of perceptual constancy perceiving objects that we see at night or in poor lighting to be the same brightness as they appear during the day

Color Constancy An element of perceptual constancy perceiving objects that we see in the dark to be the same color as they appear during the day even though their retinal images change

Shape Constancy Element of perceptual constancy perceiving objects as maintaining the same shape even though their retinal images change when we view them from different angles

Brightness and Color Constancy

Brightness constancy and **color constancy** also help us perceive our world as constant. When you look out your window at night, the trees, grass, and bushes do not appear to be the same color or brightness as they are during the daytime. Since you already know that the leaves of the bushes are a dark green and the grass and trees are brighter green, however, you perceive these qualities to be constant even under conditions of different illumination.

Shape Constancy

Another element of perceptual constancy is **shape constancy**. When we look at objects from different angles, the shape of the image projected to our retinas is different in each instance. Nevertheless, we perceive the object as unchanged (see Figure 4-31). When we view a door from straight on, it appears rectangular in shape.

Figure 4-31 Shape Constancy

We perceive the opening door as being rectangular despite the image projected on our retinas.

Illusion False or inaccurate perception that differs from the actual physical state of the perceived object

When the door is opened, we still perceive it as rectangular despite the fact that the image projected on our retinas is trapezoidal.

In summary, we perceive our dynamic environment as essentially stable and containing constant stimulus properties. This occurs even though our visual system receives a varied array of stimulus properties including changes in size, brightness, color, and shape. These constancies are the result of several factors. One critical factor appears to be object familiarity. Experience may influence our perception of an object as its visual properties change, for example, as with relative size. However, as we noted for depth perception, perceptual constancies have been demonstrated very early on in human development and early on in the development of other animals, suggesting that some perceptual constancies may be innate.

Throughout this chapter we have emphasized that our perceptions of physical stimuli are not exactly the same as the properties of the physical stimulus. Some of this discrepancy is produced by our nervous system during the process of transducing the physical sensation. Other discrepancies are more related to the perceptual organization of stimuli. In the next section we will examine stimuli that produce considerable perceptual ambiguity because of these discrepancies.

4.8c Visual Illusions

Visual **illusions** are of interest to psychologists because they provide insights into normal perception, not because they are errors in perception. The illusions discussed here are important because of their relation to spatial perception.

The Ames Illusion

The *Ames room*, as shown in Figure 4-32, provides perhaps one of the most vivid illusions. A person standing on one side of the room appears to be a giant; someone on the other side appears to be a dwarf. It is even more amazing that when people cross the Ames room, they steadily appear to grow or shrink, depending on the direction in which they are walking. This illusion is produced by conflicting environmental cues.

The Ames room was designed to fool the observer into thinking it is shaped like a normal rectangular room. However, as you can see from the diagram in the figure, the room is definitely not rectangular. Both windows are trapezoidal, and one is much larger than the other. In addition, the floor is uneven so that one end of the Ames room is higher on the plane than the other. The relationships between the various objects in the room were altered in this manner to change relationships that we are accustomed to perceiving between people and their environments. Since we have not experienced this kind of arrangement before, however, our perceptual constancy processes cause us to perceive the room as rectangular and the windows as equal in size and rectangular in shape. Recent research has shown that the Ames room illusion persists (although in somewhat diminished form) even when subjects are allowed to leave the viewing point indicated in the figure and move about the room (Gehringer & Engel, 1986).

The Müller-Lyer Illusion

One of the most widely analyzed visual illusions is the *Müller-Lyer illusion*, illustrated in Figure 4-33. Ignoring the angled lines (arrowheads) at the ends of each vertical line, decide which line is longer. Most people see the line on the right as longer, but actually

Figure 4-32 The Ames Room

In the Ames room, people appear to change size as they move about. As you can see from the diagram, the person on the left is twice as far away as the person on the right. The illusion occurs because the depth cues are not apparent to the viewer.

(Mark McKenna)

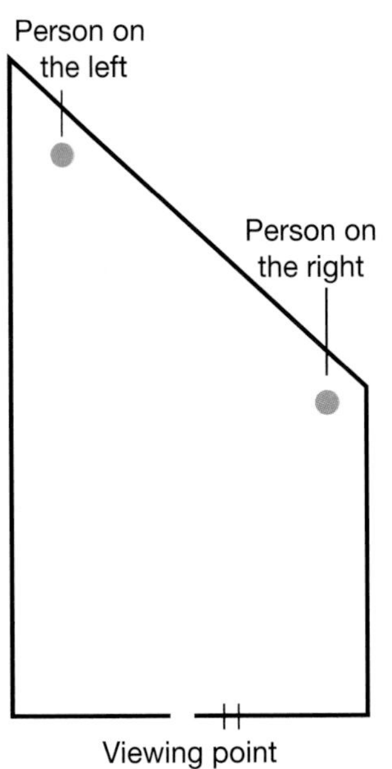

the two are of equal length. How can the Müller-Lyer illusion be explained? Think back to what you have learned about perceptual constancy in this chapter, and try to formulate an answer before reading on.

Actually, psychologists do not all agree about why the Müller-Lyer illusion fools us. According to one interpretation that enjoyed popularity for a period of time, the illusion

Figure 4-33 The Müller-Lyer Illusion

The two vertical lines are equal in length.

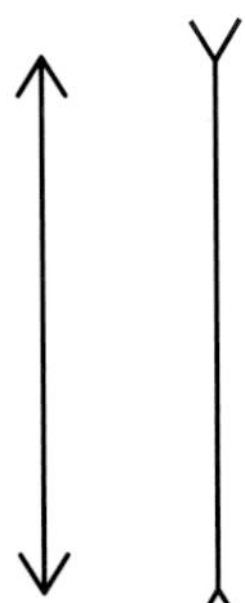

is created by the fact that the outward-turning angles draw the viewer's eyes farther out into space; the inward-turning angles draw the eyes back toward the center.

One study cast serious doubt on this interpretation, however. In this experiment an apparatus was designed to hold a subject's eyes and head very still while the lines of the Müller-Lyer illusion were flashed into one eye and the arrowheads into the other. When these sensations were combined in the subject's brain, the same illusion resulted (Gillam, 1980). This finding indicates that the illusion is created by something more than the movement of the eyes.

A British psychologist, Richard L. Gregory (1978), has proposed a more likely interpretation—that the Müller-Lyer illusion is the result of size constancy. According to Gregory, the angled lines provide linear perspective cues. As Figure 4-34 shows, the vertical line on the left, enclosed by the inward-turning angled lines, is perceived as being closer than the line with the outward-turning angled lines. We have already learned that if two objects appear to be the same size and we think one is closer, then size constancy causes us to assume that the farther one is bigger.

Gregory's theory is supported by research demonstrating that the Müller-Lyer illusion is either very weak or absent in cultures in which people have little exposure to angles (Segall, Campbell, & Herskovits, 1966). For example, the Zulus of southeast Africa, who live in circular huts with few straight lines and corners, do not judge distance from such linear cues as effectively as we do. These people respond only minimally to the Müller-Lyer illusion.

The Moon Illusion

An illusion you are probably familiar with is the *moon illusion*. Most people have had the experience of looking at a full moon on the horizon and thinking how huge it looks. When the moon is low on the horizon, it appears larger than when it is overhead. Yet the actual size of the moon's image on the retina is the same regardless of its position in the sky. Why does this illusion occur?

Figure 4-34 What Causes the Müller-Lyer Illusion?

This illustration suggests that the Müller-Lyer illusion results from depth cues and size constancy.

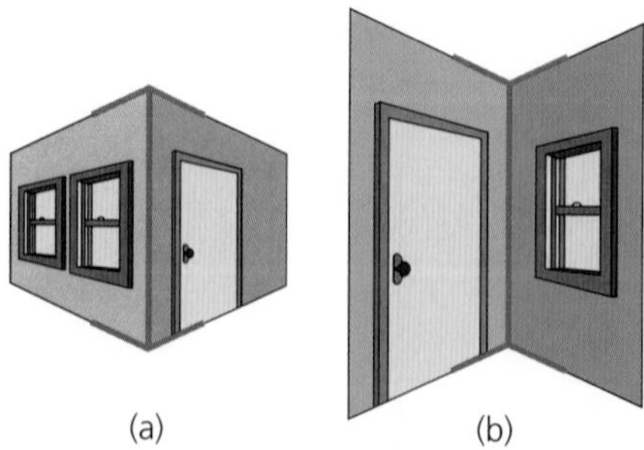

(a) (b)

The moon illusion also seems to result from size constancy. When the moon is low, it appears to be farther away than when it is overhead. This effect results from the presence of visual cues for distance, such as overlapping structures and relative size. Compared to the trees or buildings on the horizon, we perceive the moon to be very far away. In contrast, when we look at the moon overhead, we have no visual cues for distance. Consequently, we tend to underestimate its distance. As in the Müller-Lyer illusion, we assume that the moon on the horizon is larger because distance cues, specifically terrain, tell us it is farther from us than the identically sized moon overhead (Kaufman et al., 2007; Yantis, 2001).

The Ponzo Illusion

The *Ponzo illusion* is illustrated in Figure 4-35. The two horizontal lines are equal in length, although we perceive the "distant" line as longer. The Ponzo illusion is an illusion of perspective. The converging lines at the top of the figure are associated with distance, falsely suggesting that the top horizontal line is farther away. An object that is farther away and yet occupies the same visual angle as an object that is closer to us must then be longer.

The Poggendorff Illusion

One last illusion is the *Poggendorff illusion*, shown in Figure 4-36a. It appears that if the diagonal lines were continued toward each other, the one on the right would pass above

Figure 4-35 The Ponzo Illusion

The two horizontal lines are of equal length.

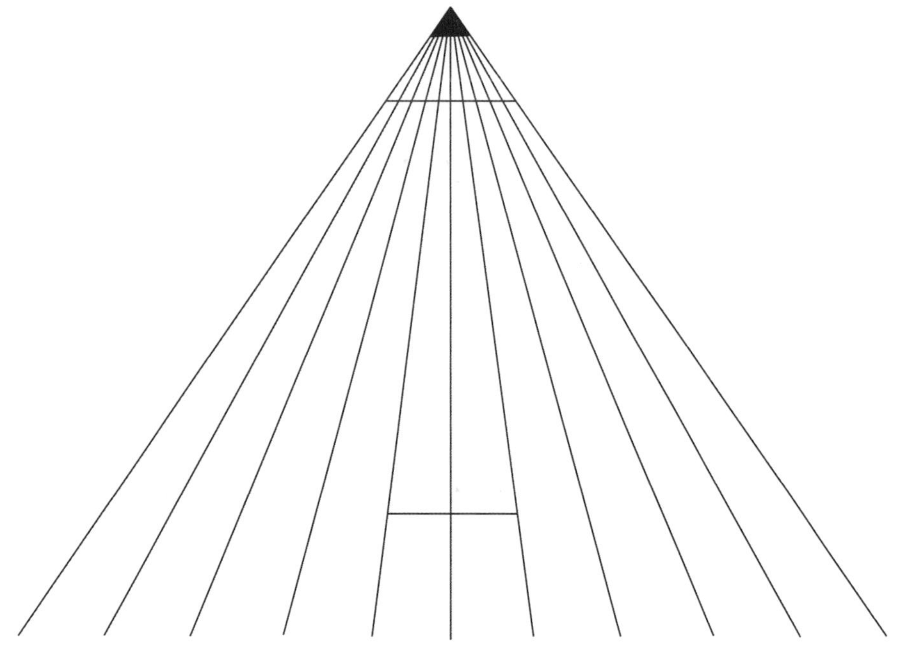

Figure 4-36 The Poggendorff Illusion

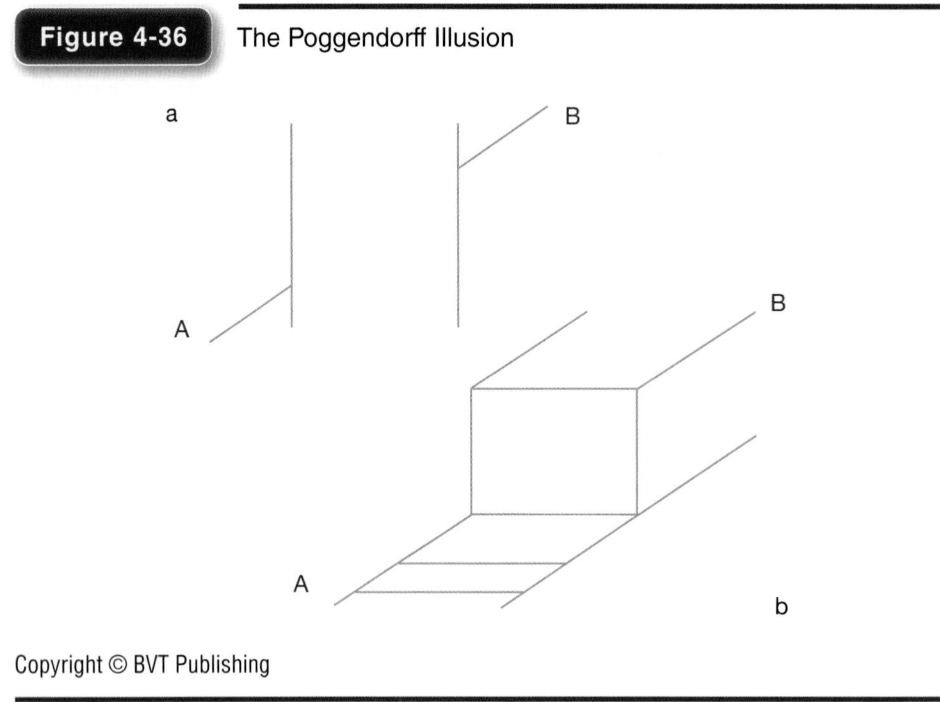

the left line. In reality, they would join, as you can determine by laying a straight edge along their projected paths. Many psychologists believe this illusion results from our inclination to maintain shape constancy. Figure 4-36b illustrates one possible example of something we have experienced that influences our perception of the Poggendorff illusion. Clearly, if lines *A* and *B* were the leg and back support, respectively, of an overturned chair, they could never meet.

Stereogram

Stereograms, discussed earlier, are optical illusions of depth created from flat two-dimensional (2-D) images. Typically these illusions are presented as wall posters, but many can now be found on the web and viewed on a computer screen. Upon examination, these illusions appear to be random dots or repeating patterns of small images. After viewing more carefully, however, a 3-D image emerges from the background. Stereograms depend on binocular vision and the inhibition of ocular convergence. When viewed with the proper convergence, which is typically produced by viewing behind the image, a hidden 3-D scene or image appears. Stereograms are similar to the 3-D illusions produced by a stereoscope. These visual devices present a 2-D image of the same object from slightly different perspectives to each eye. The brain interprets this retinal disparity as depth and thus creates a 3-D image. When viewing a stereogram while allowing your eyes to diverge and focus on a point farther away than the stereogram image, binocular disparity produces the illusory 3-D image.

Figure 4-37 Stereogram Constructed from a Single Repeating Image

In this stereogram, a three-dimensional image of a grasshopper should appear after several minutes of viewing while allowing your eyes to diverge and focus beyond the image.

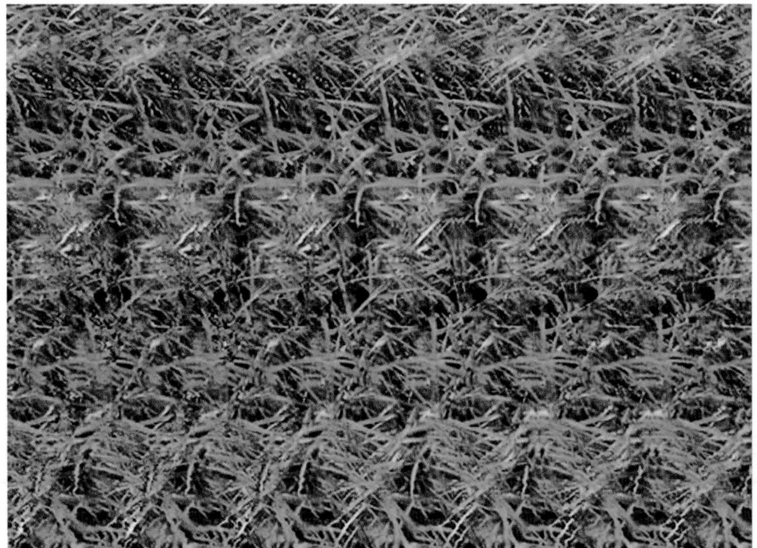

(Shutterstock)

4.8d Perceptual Sets

In addition to the cues we have been discussing, our perceptions are also influenced by many subjective factors. Such factors include our tendency to see (or hear, smell, feel, or taste) what we expect or what is consistent with our preconceived notions of what makes sense.

This phenomenon is known as **perceptual set**, and it is illustrated in Figure 4-38. You can try this demonstration out on two friends. Show one friend picture *A* (keep *B* and *C* covered), and ask what is seen. The response will probably be an old woman. Then show picture *C* while covering *A* and *B*. Again, an old woman is likely to be seen. Next, repeat the procedure with a different friend, but this time start with picture *B* followed by *C*. In this situation, your friend is likely to report seeing a young woman in both pictures. The difference is explained by the fact that the particular image seen in picture *C* depends on the viewer's previous experience. Since the first friend was initially exposed to the picture of the old lady, he or she developed a perceptual set to see an old lady in picture *C*. In contrast, the second friend's perceptual set was geared toward seeing the youthful image in picture *B*.

Motivational state can also have a strong impact on how we perceive our environments, presumably by the mechanism of establishing perceptual sets. For example, if you drive down a main thoroughfare while feeling hunger pangs, you probably notice almost every sign advertising food. You may even misread signs so that an ad in the window of the local garden store seems to say *steaks* instead of *stakes*.

Perceptual Set Tendency to see, hear, smell, feel, or taste what we expect or what is consistent with our preconceived notions

Figure 4-38 A Demonstration of Perceptual Set

A

B

C

Source: Adapted from W. E. Hill, 1915 and E. G. Boring, 1930.

Another form of perceptual set is the tendency to perceive stimuli that are consistent with our expectations and to ignore those that are inconsistent. This phenomenon is frequently referred to as **selective perception**. For example, if you believe that all neatly dressed elderly women are honest, you might not even think twice about the elderly woman at the next table when your wallet disappears in a restaurant—even if she is the most obvious suspect. Likewise, people who distrust groups of people because of their appearance, religion, or ethnic background are unlikely to recognize the good qualities of an individual who is a member of one of those groups. We're sure if you think about it for a while you can recognize instances where your behavior was influenced by a perceptual set of this sort.

Selective Perception A form of perceptual set; the tendency to perceive stimuli that are consistent with expectations and to ignore those that are inconsistent

In this chapter, we examined the process of sensation where some aspect of the physical environment is transduced into neural activity. This neural activity is interpreted by the nervous system as vision, audition, olfaction, gustation, or one of the skin senses. The way we organize this information into useful representations of our environment was described as perceptual organization. We discussed a number of these organizational processes and showed how conflicting processing cues can lead to illusions. Although experience can clearly influence these organization processes, much of perceptual organization appears to be either innate or defined very early in development.

CHAPTER REVIEW

Principles of Sensation and Perception

1. Sensations are basic, immediate experiences that a stimulus elicits in a sense organ. Perception refers to the process of interpreting, organizing, and elaborating on the raw materials of sensation.
2. The process by which sensory organs transform mechanical, chemical, or light energy into neural firing is called transduction.
3. The ability to distinguish sensations does not depend on differences between the sense organs, but rather on what part of the brain is activated by the sensory messages.
4. Many of the physical events surrounding us go unheeded. The most important variables determining whether or not we perceive things happening around us are sensory thresholds, attention, and adaptation.
5. Our perception of various sensory inputs can occur only when the strength of a stimulus reaches a minimal or threshold level of intensity sufficient to activate a sensory process. Weber's law describes the relationship between stimulus intensity and our perception of stimulus change.
6. Attention refers to the control of our behavior by specific stimuli or stimulus situations.
7. Adaptation refers to the decrease in the response of sensory receptors when they are exposed to continual, unchanging stimulation.
8. Signal detection theory maintains that our ability to detect a sensory stimulus (signal) depends not only on the intensity of the signal but also on other variables like distracting factors such as noise, expectations, motivation, and fatigue.

Vision

9. Our visual systems consist of three major parts: The eyes, which capture and respond to light energy; the neural circuits that transmit signals from the eye to the brain; and visual centers within the brain that interpret these messages.
10. Visible light, the stimulus for vision, has three particularly important properties: Brightness, or the intensity of light; hue, or the color we perceive; and saturation, which is the proportion of colored light to noncolored light.
11. Two key components of the eye are the image-focusing part, consisting of the cornea, lens, iris, and pupil, and the image-recording part, called the retina.

CHAPTER REVIEW

12. The primary photoreceptor cells in the retina, the rods and cones, contain photopigments that respond to light. Our perception of color is largely dependent on the cones. The rods are extremely sensitive photoreceptors that allow us to see in dim light.
13. Two major theories of color vision have been proposed: The trichromatic theory and the opponent-process theory. Most vision experts believe that color vision may result from interplay between a trichromatic system operating at the level of photoreceptor cells and an opponent-process mechanism working at later stages.

Audition

14. Most of the sounds we hear consist of physical energy in the form of rhythmic pressure changes in the air.
15. Three characteristics of sound waves that influence our perception of sound are loudness (amplitude), pitch (frequency), and timbre (a combination of a fundamental frequency and additional frequency components called overtones).
16. Auditory perception results when sound waves are converted into mechanical movement of the ossicles in the middle ear, which in turn act to produce pressure waves within the fluid of the inner ear that stimulate hair cells, which transduce the physical energy of sound waves into neural impulses that our brains translate into sounds.
17. The best available evidence suggests that our perception of pitch is determined by both the place of maximal excitation on the basilar membrane and the frequency with which auditory nerve fibers fire.
18. Auditory localization is the result of differences in both the loudness and the time of arrival of sounds reaching each of our ears.
19. Hearing loss may result from either damage to the neural structures that transmit auditory messages to the brain (sensory neural hearing loss) or inability of the outer and middle ear to conduct sound energy to the receptors in the inner ear (conductive hearing loss).

Gustation and Olfaction

20. Our taste receptors, located on little bumps on the tongue called papillae, can distinguish only four different sensations: sweetness, saltiness, sourness, and bitterness.
21. The receptors for odors lie in the mucous membrane that lines the nasal cavity.

CHAPTER REVIEW

The Skin Senses

22. The sense of touch is a composite of three different senses: pressure, temperature, and pain.
23. The sensation of pressure occurs when a mechanical force causes a displacement of the skin.
24. Different specialized dendrite endings respond to cold and heat.
25. Some pain researchers maintain that pain results from overstimulation of any sensory receptor; others believe that pain occurs when damaged tissue releases chemicals that stimulate specialized nerve endings in the skin.

Kinesthesis and Equilibrium

26. The two body senses of kinesthesis and equilibrium, working in concert, tell us the orientation of our bodies in space, the relative position of the various body parts, and the movement of any parts of the body.

Synesthesia

27. Synesthesia is the bizarre, and quite rare, condition where sensations from one modality cause perceptions in another.

Perceiving the World

28. The process by which we structure elementary sensations into the objects we perceive is called perceptual organization.
29. Three important principles that influence how people organize sensations into whole patterns, called Gestalts, are figure and ground, perceptual grouping, and closure.
30. Figure and ground refer to our tendency to differentiate between the part of an image we focus on (figure) and the background against which the figure stands (ground).
31. According to the principle of perceptual grouping, we tend to group patterns of stimuli into larger units in three major ways: proximity, similarity, and good continuation.
32. Another organizing principle is our inclination to perceive incomplete figures as complete, a process known as closure.
33. Selective attention refers to the process of focusing on one or a few stimuli of particular significance while ignoring others.

CHAPTER REVIEW

34. Characteristics of stimuli that tend to capture attention almost automatically include sudden change, contrast and novelty, intensity, repetition, and stimulus difficulty.
35. Key stimuli capture attention by activating motivational systems.
36. Binocular cues for perceiving distance include retinal disparity and convergence.
37. Important monocular cues for distance perception include height on a plane, interposition, linear perspective, relative size, texture gradients, aerial perspective, and relative motion.
38. According to Gibson's theory of direct perception, all of the information necessary for spatial representation is available to us from the environment in the form of environmental invariances. Other theories of perception argue that spatial representation requires complex cognitive processing of available stimuli.
39. Research has revealed that depth perception is clearly an innate ability in many species of animals, and that in humans it is either innate or is learned very early in life.
40. Perceptual constancy allows us to adjust for varying conditions and changing patterns as we perceive the world. When we look at objects at different distances and angles and under different levels of illumination, we are able to make the necessary adjustments to maintain a degree of constancy in our perception of size, shape, brightness, and color.
41. A perceptual illusion is a false perception in that it differs from the actual physical state of the perceived object.
42. A tendency to perceive what we expect or are inclined to see, a phenomenon known as perceptual set, may have a strong impact on how we perceive our environments.

TERMS AND CONCEPTS

Absolute Threshold, pg. 121
Accommodation, pg. 131
Additive Color Mixing, pg. 137
Aerial (Atmospheric) Perspective, pg. 166
Attention, pg. 124
Auditory Localization, pg. 146
Basilar Membrane, pg. 144
Binocular Cues, pg. 164
Binocular (Retinal) Disparity, pg. 165
Body Senses, pg. 156
Brightness Constancy, pg. 169
Brightness, pg. 128
Closure, pg. 161
Cochlea, pg. 144
Color Constancy, pg. 169
Conductive Hearing Loss, pg. 148
Cones, pg. 131
Convergence, pg. 165
Dark Adaptation, pg. 133
Difference Threshold, pg. 121
Direct Perception, pg. 167
Endorphins, pg. 155
Equilibrium, pg. 157
Figure, pg. 159
Frequency Theory of Pitch Discrimination, pg. 146
Gate-Control Theory, pg. 154
Gibson's Theory of Direct Perception, pg. 167
Good Continuation, pg. 161
Ground, pg. 159
Gustation, pg. 148
Height on a Plane, pg. 166
Hue, pg. 128
Illusion, pg. 170
Inattentional Blindness, pg. 162
Invariant, pg. 167
Kinesthesis, pg. 157
Light Adaptation, pg. 134
Linear Perspective, pg. 166
Loudness, pg. 140
Monocular Cues, pg. 164
Nociceptor, pg. 155
Olfaction, pg. 148
Opponent-Process Theory of Color Vision, pg. 138
Organ of Corti, pg. 145
Ossicles, pg. 144
Overlap, pg. 166
Perception, pg. 119
Perceptual Constancy, pg. 169
Perceptual Grouping, pg. 161
Perceptual Organization, pg. 159
Perceptual Set, pg. 175
Periaqueductal Gray Area (PAG), pg. 155
Pitch, pg. 141
Place Theory of Pitch Discrimination, pg. 145
Proximity, pg. 161
Psychophysics, pg. 120
Relative Motion (Motion Parallax), pg. 166
Relative Size, pg. 166
Retina, pg. 131
Rods, pg. 131
Saturation, pg. 128
Selective Attention, pg. 162
Selective Perception, pg. 176

TERMS AND CONCEPTS

Semicircular Canals, pg. 157
Sensations, pg. 119
Sensorineural Hearing Loss, pg. 147
Sensory Adaptation, pg. 124
Shape Constancy, pg. 169
Signal Detection Theory, pg. 124
Sign Stimuli, pg. 163
Similarity, pg. 161
Size Constancy, pg. 169
Stereogram, pg. 165
Substance P, pg. 155
Subtractive Color Mixing, pg. 137
Synesthesia, pg. 158
Texture Gradient, pg. 166
Threshold, pg. 121
Timbre, pg. 142
Transduction, pg. 119
Tympanic Membrane, pg. 144
Vestibular Sacs, pg. 157
Visual Cliff, pg. 167
Volley Theory, pg. 146
Weber's Law, pg. 122
Young-Helmholtz Theory (Trichromatic Theory of Color Vision), pg. 138

POP QUIZ

True or False

___ 1. The simplest explanation as to why we become accustomed to a foul-smelling environment and after a while do not even notice it is offered by signal detection theory.

___ 2. Light energy is transduced into electrochemical energy by the lens.

___ 3. The function of the pinna and auditory canal is to amplify the intensity of a sound stimulus.

___ 4. A person suffering from conduction hearing loss would still be able to hear through bone conduction.

___ 5. The psychological principle that states that we would tend to focus on a stimulus that is complex is known as selective attention.

Multiple Choice

6. What is the discovery that the difference threshold tends to be a constant fraction of the original stimulus intensity called?
   a. Weber's law
   b. Threshold consistency
   c. Adaptation
   d. The attention factor
7. Which of the following structures does light energy pass through first?
   a. Aqueous humor
   b. Retina
   c. Vitreous humor
   d. Pupil
8. A person whose lens cannot correctly focus an image on his or her retina has a problem associated with which of the following?
   a. Maintaining the proper pupil size
   b. Accommodation
   c. Convergence
   d. Adaptation
9. The one type of sight-destroying or sight-limiting problem that medical procedures cannot compensate for or overcome involves damage to which of the following?
   a. Optic nerve
   b. Visual cortex
   c. Cornea
   d. Lens

POP QUIZ

10. What are sound waves?
    a. Changes in the concentration of photons
    b. Changes in the complexity of air molecules
    c. Changes in air pressure caused by the vibration of an object
    d. A bending of the cilia of hair cells
11. What are the two factors that allow us to locate the place of origin of a sound stimulus?
    a. Frequency and complexity
    b. Arrival time and closure
    c. Intensity and kinesthesis
    d. Intensity and arrival time
12. Temperature receptors for cold ________while the receptors for heat ________.
    a. are closer to the skin's surface / are farther away from the skin's surface
    b. are farther away from the skin's surface / are closer to the skin's surface
    c. use myelinated fibers / use unmyelinated fibers
    d. are stimulated by increasing pressure to the skin / are stimulated by decreasing pressure to the skin
13. Astronauts experiencing weightlessness in space do not know when they are upside-down because the absence of gravity would disrupt their ________sense(s).
    a. vestibular
    b. kinesthesis
    c. equilibrium and kinesthesis
    d. olfactory
14. It is believed that synesthesia is the result of which of the following?
    a. Cross-wiring between cortical brain centers involved in sensory processing
    b. Damage to free nerve endings
    c. The inability of certain stimuli to reach a threshold
    d. Damage to the occipital lobe in the brain
15. When watching a travelogue video of the Grand Canyon, you perceive depth as a result of which of the following?
    a. Only monocular cues
    b. Only binocular cues
    c. Both monocular and binocular cues
    d. Relative size, aerial perspective, and motion parallax

Answer Key: 1.F 2.F 3.F 4.T 5.T 6.a 7.a 8.b 9.b 10.c 11.d 12.a 13.c 14.a 15.a

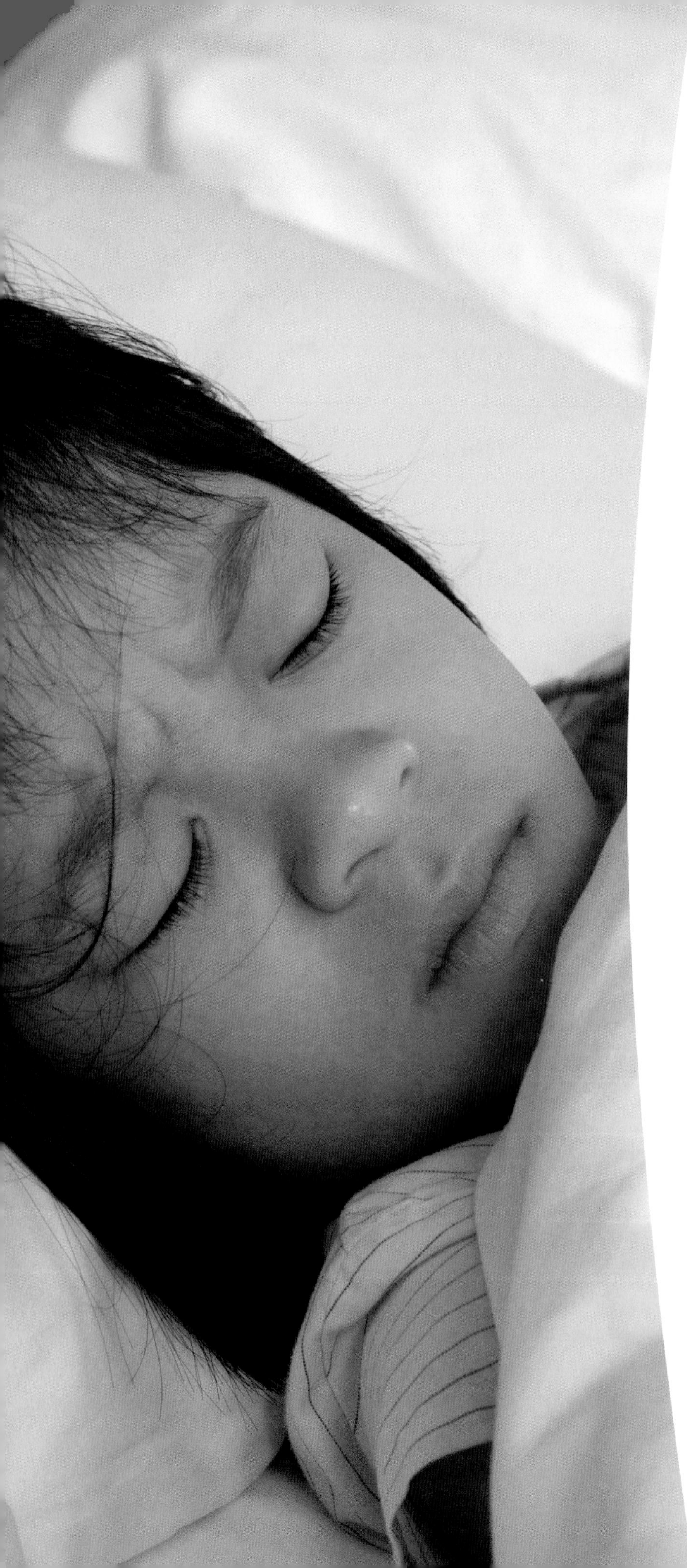

Chapter 5

(Shutterstock)

Sleep, Dreaming, *and* Consciousness

Just like everyone else, when you are trying to concentrate on your studies, your attention wanders off occasionally. You may find yourself fantasizing about another person, a special place, or a problem that doesn't seem to get resolved. When you realize that your attention has drifted away from studying, you again focus on your reading, but it is only a moment before your attention wanders once more—this time to consider whether you should have something to eat.

Sound familiar? If you are like most people, you spend a great deal of time making up fantasies and mulling over issues of similarly grandiose proportions. Such daydreams are mild shifts from a state of alertness, in which your thoughts move from external focal points to internal stimuli. When you daydream, you create pictures in the "mind's eye" that are akin to waking dreams. Most of us spend a significant portion of our waking hours daydreaming—according to research, about one-third of our time (Giambra, 2000). The vividness of daydreams waxes and wanes over a ninety-minute cycle, with peak vividness occurring roughly every ninety minutes.

Interestingly, this cycle is remarkably similar to the cycle of dreaming in our sleep. It is a natural variation in alertness that occurs without our attempting to regulate it and often without our even being aware that we are drifting in and out of daydreams. This chapter looks at variations in consciousness, both in natural states, such as sleeping and dreaming, and states that are induced by hypnosis. We will also explore what it means to be conscious, and review cases where consciousness has been affected by brain damage. Before we examine these states, we will first examine their cyclic nature.

5.1 Biological Rhythms

All biological systems (plants and animals) are influenced by cycles or **biological rhythms** of physiological activity. For instance, many plants are on annual rhythms of growth that are influenced by variations in the level of illumination. Behavior, body temperature, and other physiological processes of most animals vary on a twenty-four-hour cycle that is also influenced by available illumination. When a cycle is approximately annual, such as growth cycles in some plants, it is called a *circumannual cycle* (*circa* meaning "about" and *annual* meaning "year"). Cycles that vary around a twenty-four-hour period are referred to as circadian rhythms (*dia* meaning "day").

5.1a Circadian Rhythms

Circadian rhythms are typically examined under conditions in which illumination can be varied. For example, the activity of rats is on a circadian rhythm occurring primarily during the night. When maintained on a twelve-hour light-on and twelve-hour light-off cycle, the activity of rats nicely conforms to a circadian pattern. If the new twelve-hour light on-off periods are shifted, activity also shifts to conform to the new day-night schedule. This can be seen on the activity charts in Figure 5-1a and 5-1b.

Biological Rhythms Natural variations in biological functions, hormonal activity, temperature, and sleep that typically cycle every twenty-four to twenty-five hours, also called *circadian rhythms*

In this figure, each square across represents thirty minutes, and each square down represents another twenty-four-hour day. The dark marks represent activity. Note that

Suprachiasmatic Nucleus (SCN) An area of the hypothalamus that is located above the optic chiasm and that exerts the main control over biological rhythms; also referred to as a *biological clock* because damage to this area disrupts daily cycles in sleep and other biological functions

most of the wheel-running activity occurs during the dark phase of a twelve-hour light/dark cycle. In part *a*, the dark phase is from 7 P.M. to 7 A.M. In part *b*, the dark phase was shifted from 1 A.M. to 1 P.M. Note that the activity adjusts quickly to this new schedule. Under constant illumination in part *c*, you can see that the activity becomes free-running. In rats—and people—the free-running clock runs about one hour slow each day (that is, the free-running clock is set for a twenty-five-hour day). This is illustrated by the advancement of wheel running by about one hour (two 30-minute squares) each twenty-four hours.

When activity cycles are no longer under the control of the light schedule, they are based on the animal's biological clock. Interestingly, most biological clocks are not adjusted to twenty-four-hour cycles, as Figure 5-1c reveals. Regular variations in daily illumination normally keep biological clocks adjusted to twenty-four-hour cycles—much like a slow running watch that is reset each day.

People exhibit circadian rhythms of activity as well. We normally begin to feel less active several hours after the onset of the dark part of our day-night cycle and most alert several hours after light onset. As with other animals without a light-dark schedule, we adjust to a twenty-five-hour free-running clock. The implications of biological clocks for shift work and jet lag will be discussed later in this chapter.

Researchers have identified the **suprachiasmatic nucleus (SCN)** of the hypothalamus as an important neural structure that functions as a biological clock. The SCN is

Figure 5-1 Records of Wheel-Running Activity of Rats

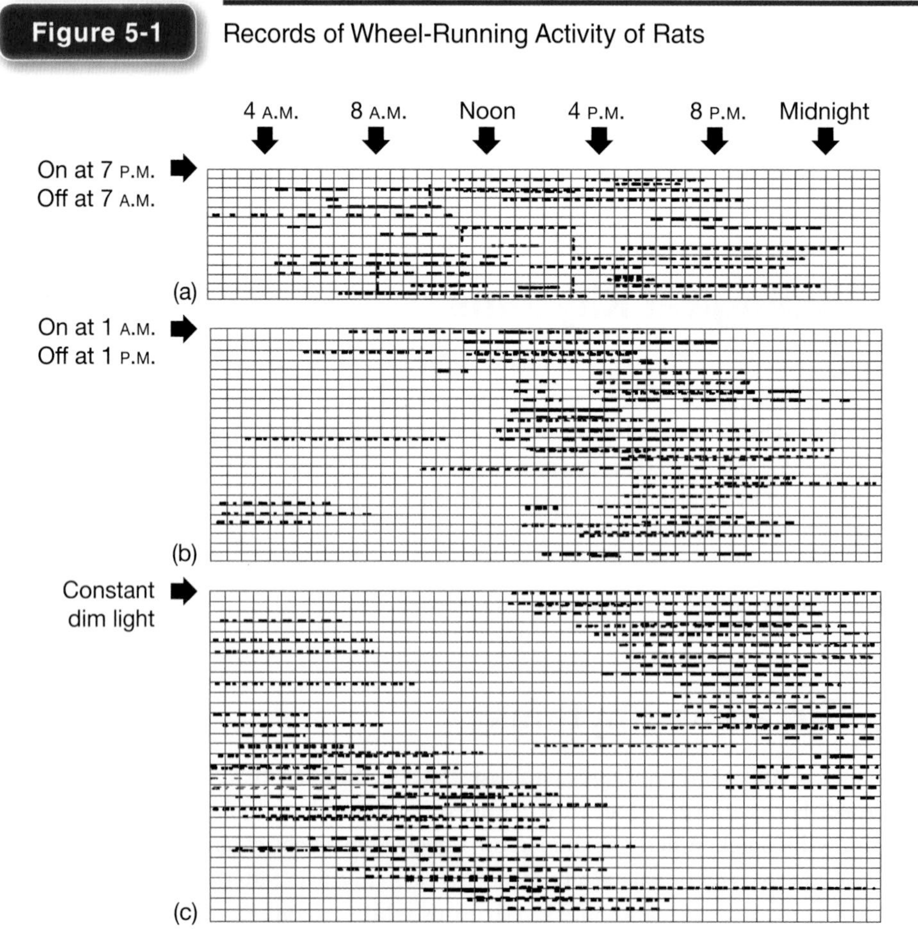

Source: Courtesy of Dr. Richard Ettinger

located on the floor of the hypothalamus just above the optic chiasm (the point at which the optic tracts from each eye intersect). This location easily allows the SCN to "monitor" the activity of the visual system. During periods of illumination the optic tracts will be more active than during dark periods. The SCN is vital for our daily well-being. It prepares us for our daily period of activity by anticipatory increases in heart rate, body temperature, and certain hormone levels, thereby synchronizing our endocrine and autonomic nervous systems with the time of day (Buijs, van Eden, Goncharuk, & Kalsbeek, 2003). Lesions of the SCN have been shown to disrupt circadian rhythms of activity and other physiological processes. These lesions also disrupt normal sleep-wake cycles, but not the total amount of sleep during a twenty-four-hour period. Numerous other "clocks" or pacemakers abound in cells throughout our bodies. These cellular pacemakers regulate important biological functions including the activity of hormones, neurons, and cellular metabolism. These pacemakers, or clocks, appear to be synchronized to each other and to illumination by cues from the SCN (Hastings, Maywood, & Reddy, 2008).

Sleep Natural, periodically occurring state of rest characterized by reduced activity, lessened responsiveness to stimuli, and distinctive patterns of brain activity

REM (Rapid Eye Movement) Sleep State of sleep characterized by rapid eye movements and often associated with dreaming

NREM (Non-Rapid Eye Movement) Sleep Stages of sleep during which rapid eye movements typically do not occur (Dreaming occurs far less frequently during NREM sleep than during REM sleep.)

5.2 The Science of Sleep and Dreaming

At least once every day, we experience a dramatic shift in consciousness when we go to sleep; we experience still another state of consciousness if we dream while sleeping. We spend roughly one-third of our lives sleeping, and the question of what happens when we sleep and dream has fascinated people for ages. As far back as four thousand years ago, Egyptians were interpreting dream symbols (a distant crowd, for example, was seen as a warning of death), and dream diaries existed long before the emergence of psychology as a science. Systematic sleep and dream research was not possible, however, until the technological breakthroughs of the past half-century.

Sleep is a natural, periodically recurring state of rest characterized by reduced activity, lessened responsiveness to stimuli, and distinctive patterns of brain activity. In 1937, Loomis, Harvey, and Hobart used the recently invented *electroencephalograph* (EEG) to demonstrate that brain waves change in form when a person shifts from a waking to a sleeping state. These researchers also observed further systematic changes in brain waves throughout the sleep period, a discovery that ultimately provided the basis for distinguishing between different stages of sleep.

(Shutterstock)

At least once every day, we experience a dramatic shift in consciousness when we go to sleep. We spend roughly one-third of our lives sleeping

5.2a Stages of Sleep

REM and NREM Sleep

In the early 1950s, Eugene Aserinsky, a graduate student working with sleep researcher Nathaniel Kleitman at the University of Chicago, observed systematic changes in the eye movements of sleeping infants. He noted periods of sleep during which the eyes moved rapidly, followed by intervals of little or no eye movement. This observation provided the distinction between **REM** (rapid eye movement) and **NREM** (non-rapid eye movement) **sleep**. These researchers found that when adult subjects were awakened during REM sleep,

BVT *Lab*

Flashcards are available for this chapter at **www.BVTLab.com**.

they almost invariably reported dreaming, but that they rarely reported dreams when awakened after NREM sleep (Aserinsky & Kleitman, 1953; Dement & Kleitman, 1957).

Research since the 1950s has confirmed the connection between REM sleep and dreaming. However, we have also learned that dreaming is not limited to REM sleep and that REM is not synonymous with dreaming. People awakened during REM sleep do not always report dreams. Likewise, people awakened from NREM sleep sometimes report having some kind of mental activity (such as a vague recall of some event), although they do not consistently label such activity dreaming. For this reason, it is difficult to estimate the exact proportion of NREM dreaming to REM dreaming. However, there is widespread agreement among sleep researchers that NREM sleep is considerably more dream-free than REM sleep, and that dreams reported during REM sleep are usually much more vivid, tend to last longer, and are more visual than the thought-like processes that occur during NREM sleep. These differences are perhaps due to different physiological processes mediating REM and NREM sleep and dreaming (Takeuchi, Ogilvie, Murphy, & Ferrelli, 2003).

Rapid eye movements have little, if anything, to do with dream content. For example, people who have been blind for more than fifty years and cats raised in the dark who have never seen anything still show rapid eye movements during sleep. Some researchers believe that the rapid eye movements may be comparable to the occasional muscle twitches that occur during dreaming, in that both of these processes reflect a kind of overflow from a nervous system activated by dream activity. During REM sleep, skeletal muscle activity is greatly suppressed, leaving us relatively paralyzed.

Of course, our eyes are not the only parts of our bodies to show activity as we sleep. During a night's sleep, body activity may vary from lying very still to thrashing and twisting in bed. In extreme cases, some people may talk in their sleep, sleepwalk, or have sleep terrors.

At what stage of sleep would you expect people to sleepwalk, talk, or have sleep terrors? You now know that dreams generally take place during REM sleep. Based on this information, can you predict during which phase of the sleep cycle the greatest amount of body movements occur? Do you think sleepwalking is most likely to occur during REM sleep or during one of the stages of NREM sleep?

It seems logical that sleepwalking and sleep terrors would take place when people dream, during REM sleep. When we are dreaming, our sympathetic nervous system causes an increase in breathing and heart rate, as well as an elevation of blood pressure. Certain hormones associated with emergency situations may be released, and genital tissues may become engorged with blood, resulting in penile erection or vaginal lubrication. All of these signs of activation and arousal, together with brain waves similar to those of the waking state, suggest that the greatest amount of body movement should take place during REM sleep.

However, the true state of affairs is just the reverse. Typically, the only parts of the body to move vigorously during dreams are the eyes. Muscular movement is inhibited during REM sleep by activity in a network of cells called the *pontine reticular formation*, located in the pons of the brain. When these cells become active, the body experiences a profound loss of muscle tone, making it almost impossible for a dreaming person to move. Thus, sleepwalking and sleep terrors almost invariably occur during NREM sleep. One study of cats demonstrated the link between the pons and the loss of muscle tone during dreaming. When researchers destroyed a small portion of the region of the pons that produces *atonia* (loss of muscle tone), cats became very active during REM sleep (Morrison, 1983). Sometimes the inhibitory processes of REM sleep lessen for a moment. When this occurs, the nerve fibers in our muscles fire sporadically, resulting in jerks and twitches (Chase & Morales, 1983, 1990).

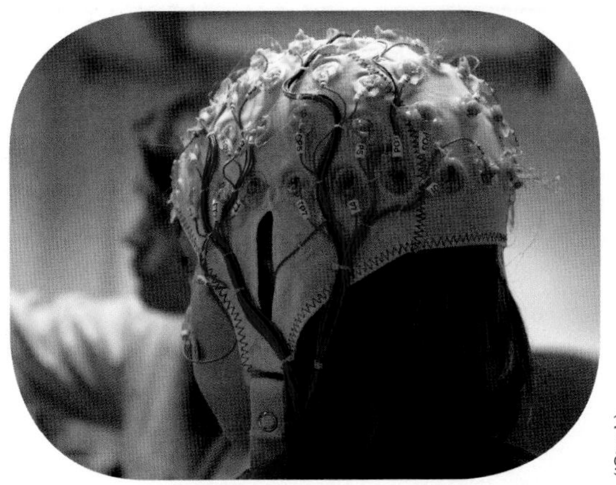

(iStock)

The electroencephalograph shows the changes in brain waves by using electrodes like these placed on the head.

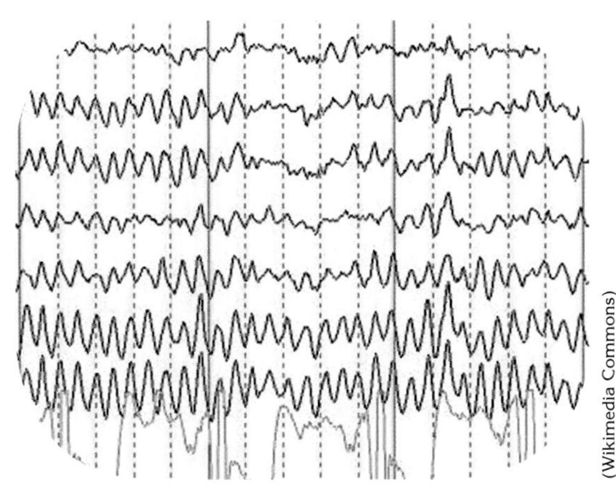

(Wikimedia Commons)

In these typical EEG recordings from several electrodes, each electrode contributes to one trace in the EEG record.

It seems puzzling that body movement is inhibited during periods of sleep when the eyes and brain are the most active. However, it is probably a good thing that our movements are inhibited when we dream. Can you imagine how battered and bruised we might be if we physically acted out all our dreams?

Sleep researchers have discovered that when some humans enter REM sleep, they thrash violently about, leap out of bed, and may even attack their bed partners. They are not paralyzed during REM as most people are, and they may actually act out their dreams (Chase & Morales, 1990). This recently recognized abnormality is called *REM behavior disorder* (Mahowald & Schenck, 1989; Ferini-Strambi et al., 2005). In an interesting court case, a husband awoke to find that he had attacked and killed his wife while they both slept. His only (but successful) defense was that he recalled dreaming that he was being attacked, and he fought back. Clearly more research on the relationship between dreaming, REM, and motor movement is needed. Interestingly, REM behavior disorder is quite prevalent in patients with Parkinson's disease. Progressive damage to structures within the pons as a result of Parkinson's disease may explain this prevalence (Lai, Hsieh, Nguyen, Peever, & Siegel, 2008). As you may recall from Chapter 3, the pons is involved in the control of motor movement.

Measuring Stages of Sleep

Further distinctions between various stages of sleep have been made possible by sophisticated measuring devices such as the EEG; the *electrooculogram* (EOG), which measures movements of the eye; and the *electromyograph* (EMG), which measures electrical activity in the muscles. Figure 5-2 shows the left and right eye movements of a person during REM sleep, as measured by an EOG. Research using these and other devices has revealed systematic changes in the brain-wave patterns, muscular activity, levels of breathing, and heart rate during the course of a night's sleep. These measures have not only clarified the differences between REM and NREM sleep, they have also allowed researchers to identify four distinct stages of sleep in addition to REM sleep. Figure 5-3 demonstrates characteristic brain-wave patterns of each of these stages, as well as REM sleep and wakefulness.

Figure 5-2 Electrooculogram Recording of Eye Movements During Sleep

This illustration shows the left and right eye movements of a person during REM sleep.

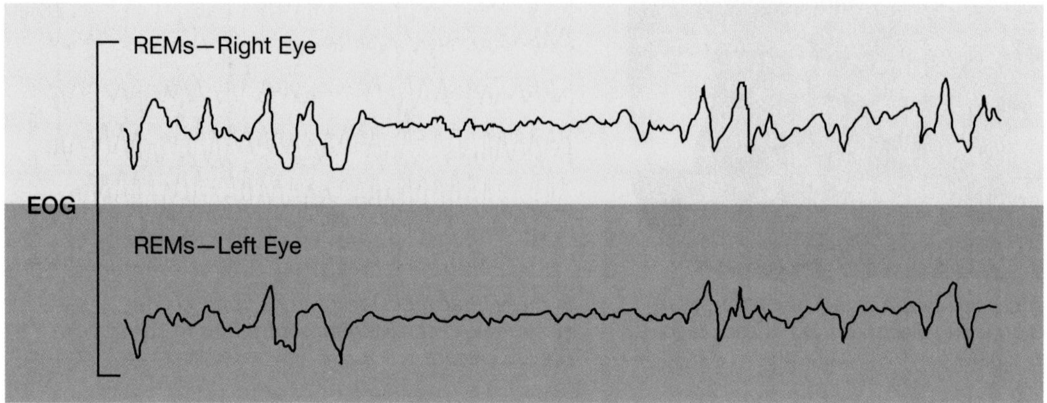

Data from: Figure of "Stages of Sleep and Characteristic Brain Wave Patterns" from *The Sleep Disorders* by Peter Hauri

Characteristics of Waking and Sleep States

When we are awake and alert, the EEG reveals low-amplitude, high-frequency waves called *beta waves*. (The two key characteristics of brain waves are their *amplitude*, or height, and their *frequency*, measured in cycles per second.) When we are relaxed and drowsy, just before falling asleep, our brain waves show an *alpha* rhythm of higher amplitude and slower frequency (8 to 12 cycles per second). In this drowsy state, breathing and heart rate also slow down, body temperature drops, and muscles relax. The different brain waves associated with different states of arousal are shown in Figure 5-3.

Stage 1 The light sleep that occurs just after dozing off is known as **Stage 1 sleep**. It is characterized by low-frequency (4 to 7 cycles per second), low-amplitude brain waves called *theta waves*. Some slow eye movements, irregular breathing, and muscle relaxation may accompany Stage 1 sleep. People are easily awakened during Stage 1 sleep, and often they do not realize they have been sleeping. This stage typically lasts from about one to ten minutes.

Stage 1 Sleep Light sleep that occurs just after dozing off, characterized by brain waves called theta waves

Stage 2 After a period of Stage 1 sleep, we gradually drift into the deeper **Stage 2 sleep**, characterized by brief bursts of brain activity called *sleep spindles* (12 to 14 cycles per second), as well as another brain-wave pattern called the *K complex*, a low-frequency, high-amplitude wave that occurs in response to either an external stimulus, such as the sound of a voice, or internal stimulus, such as stomach cramps. Eye movements are minimal during Stage 2, and muscular activity often decreases to an even lower level.

Stage 2 Sleep Stage of sleep that typically follows Stage 1 sleep characterized by brief bursts of brain activity called sleep spindles as well as K-complex responses to stimuli such as noises

Stage 3 About thirty to forty-five minutes after the person falls asleep, the cycle then progresses into an even deeper level of sleep, and there is a gradual increase in the incidence of low-frequency (0.5 to 2.0 cycles per second), high-amplitude *delta waves*. When these waves account for 20 percent to 50 percent of the EEG tracing, a person is in **Stage 3 sleep**.

Stage 3 Sleep Stage of sleep that typically follows Stage 2 sleep, characterized by an EEG tracing, 20 to 50 percent of which consists of delta waves and virtually no eye movements

Figure 5-3 Different Stages of Sleep and Characteristic Brain-Wave Patterns

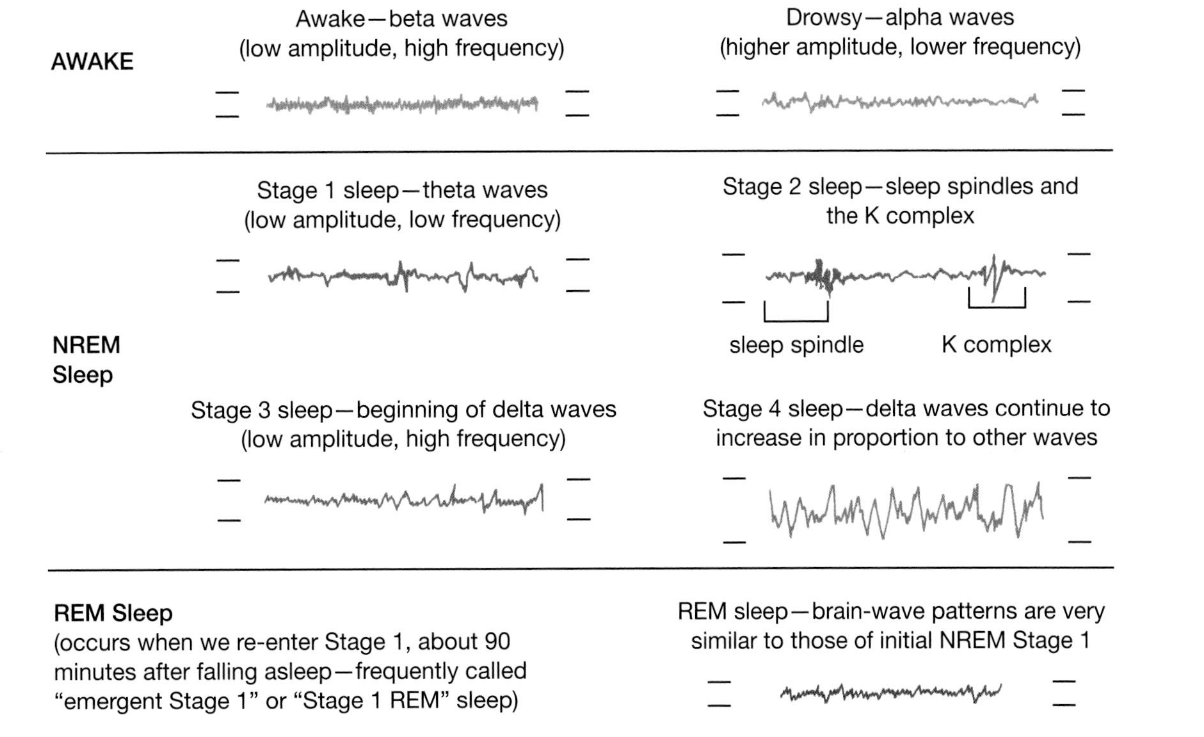

Stage 4 As sleep continues, delta waves continue to increase in proportion to other brain waves. When they exceed 50 percent, a person is said to be in **Stage 4 sleep**, the deepest level of sleep. It is difficult to arouse a person from Stage 4 sleep. If your alarm clock rings at this point, you will probably be disoriented and confused when you awaken. During Stages 3 and 4 there are virtually no eye movements, and the EEG patterns become much more synchronized.

5.2b The Sleep Cycle

It takes roughly forty-five minutes to reach Stage 4 sleep after first dozing off. People typically remain in Stage 4 for about thirty to forty minutes, then return gradually through Stages 3 and 2 to Stage 1 again. The first period of REM sleep occurs when we reenter Stage 1, about ninety minutes after falling asleep. During this period, which is frequently called emergent Stage 1 or Stage 1 REM sleep, brain-wave patterns are very similar to those of the initial NREM Stage 1, with the exception that "sawtooth-like" waves are present.

In a night's sleep, we move through successive cycles, drifting up and down between the various phases of REM and NREM sleep. These cycles last about ninety minutes, and we generally complete about five of them during the course of a night. The first episode of REM sleep may last only five to ten minutes. However, with each subsequent cycle, the REM periods become progressively longer and deep sleep stages become shorter. In later cycles, we may go only to Stage 2 and then back to REM. The final episodes of REM sleep before awakening may last forty-five minutes or more. Figure 5-4 demonstrates the typical sequence of sleep stages.

Stage 4 Sleep Deepest level of sleep, characterized by an EEG tracing exceeding 50 percent delta waves and virtually no eye movements

Figure 5-4 Typical Sequence of Sleep Stages

Sleep grows progressively less deep throughout the sleep cycle and REM periods tend to lengthen throughout the night. S1 refers to Stage 1.

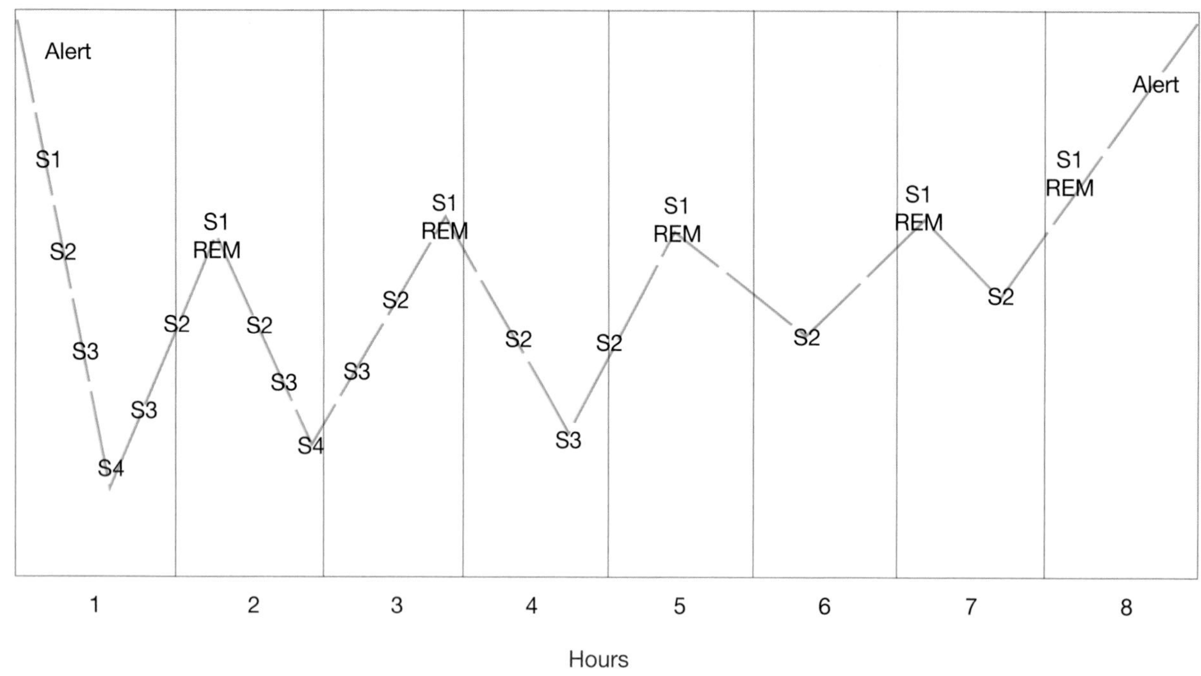

5.2c Change in Sleep Patterns with Age

Sleep patterns are not stable throughout our lives. The percentage of the night's sleep that is spent in an REM state decreases throughout the life cycle. Newborn babies may sleep an average of sixteen hours per day, with roughly 50 percent of that time spent in REM sleep. Adults in their twenties sleep about eight hours, of which about 20 percent is REM sleep. Throughout middle age, there is further decline in both the time spent sleeping and the proportion of sleep spent in the REM phase, until between the ages of sixty and seventy years, when a person is likely to sleep only about six hours and be in an REM phase only 15 percent (approximately one hour) of this time.

The amount of time spent in Stage 4 sleep also changes with age, so that by the time we are in our sixties, deep sleep (Stage 4) is likely to disappear altogether. As a consequence, older people are more easily awakened. It is not uncommon for people who were sound sleepers throughout most of their lives to find that in old age they awaken five or six times during a typical night.

Different animals also appear to require different amounts of sleep. Figure 5-5 compares the duration of sleep for several species of animals.

Reticular Activating System (RAS) Set of neural circuits extending from the lower brain up to the thalamus that plays a critical role in controlling arousal and alertness; also known as *reticular formation*

5.2d Brain Mechanisms of Sleep

Figure 5-6 shows the major brain areas involved in sleep and wakefulness. The **reticular activating system (RAS)** is a pathway of neurons that originates in the medulla and

Figure 5-5 Comparison of Sleep Duration for Different Animals

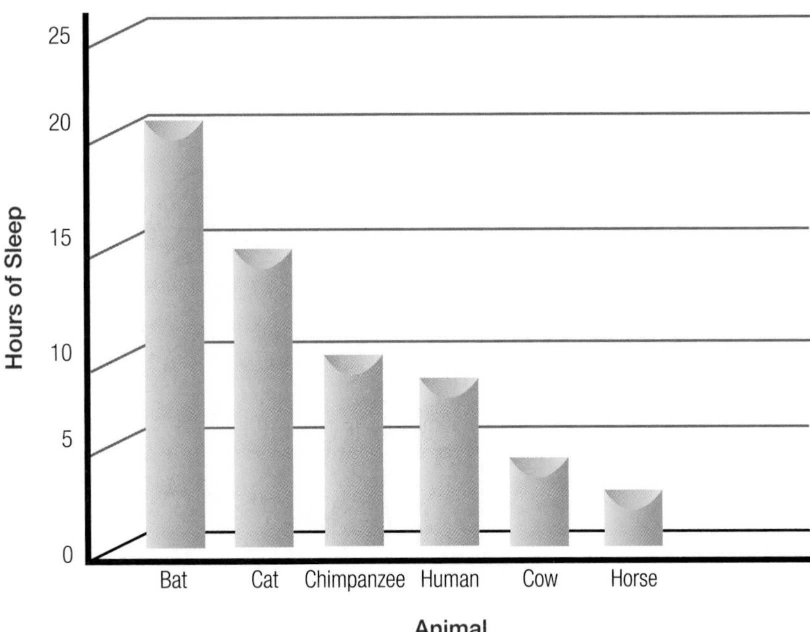

Data from "Clues to the function of mammalian sleep," by J. M. Siegel, *Nature*, 2005; 437, p. 1264–1271

extends to the thalamus. This system is primarily responsible for our awakened state. The RAS is activated by any sensory input, but it also generates its own activity. When the RAS is activated, it increases our alertness and level of arousal. Damage to the RAS can lead to a marked lack of activity and an increase in sleep. On the other hand, electrical stimulation of the RAS increases arousal and will awaken a sleeping animal.

Another brain area involved in sleep is the **raphe nucleus**. Serotonin neurons in this region originate below the RAS in the brainstem and ascend through the pons and the medulla to the midbrain. The raphe nucleus becomes most active at the time of sleep onset. This increase in raphe activity acts to inhibit the RAS, thus decreasing arousal and promoting sleep onset. In experimental animals, electrical stimulation of the raphe nucleus can induce sleep, while damage to this system greatly reduces sleep.

Neurotransmitters of Arousal and Sleep

The primary neurotransmitter of the RAS is norepinephrine. As you might expect, drugs that increase the activity of norepinephrine neurons, such as amphetamines, increase alertness and arousal. During the waking part of your day, your RAS is quite active filtering the constant array of stimuli entering your sensory systems and, thereby, allowing you to attend to specific events. Likewise, acetylcholine neurons, originating in the basal forebrain, activate cortical structures that are essential to ongoing behavior and thought processes. So, the essential neurotransmitters of arousal are norepinephrine and acetylcholine. On the other hand, serotonin and adenosine appear to be the neurotransmitters of sleep. Research has shown that destruction of the raphe nucleus, or disruption of serotonin synthesis, results in insomnia. Restoring serotonin can reverse both of these effects.

Raphe Nucleus A group of serotonin-containing neurons extending from the raphe nuclei, located in the pons and medulla throughout the limbic system and forebrain

Figure 5-6 Major Brain Areas Involved in Sleep and Arousal

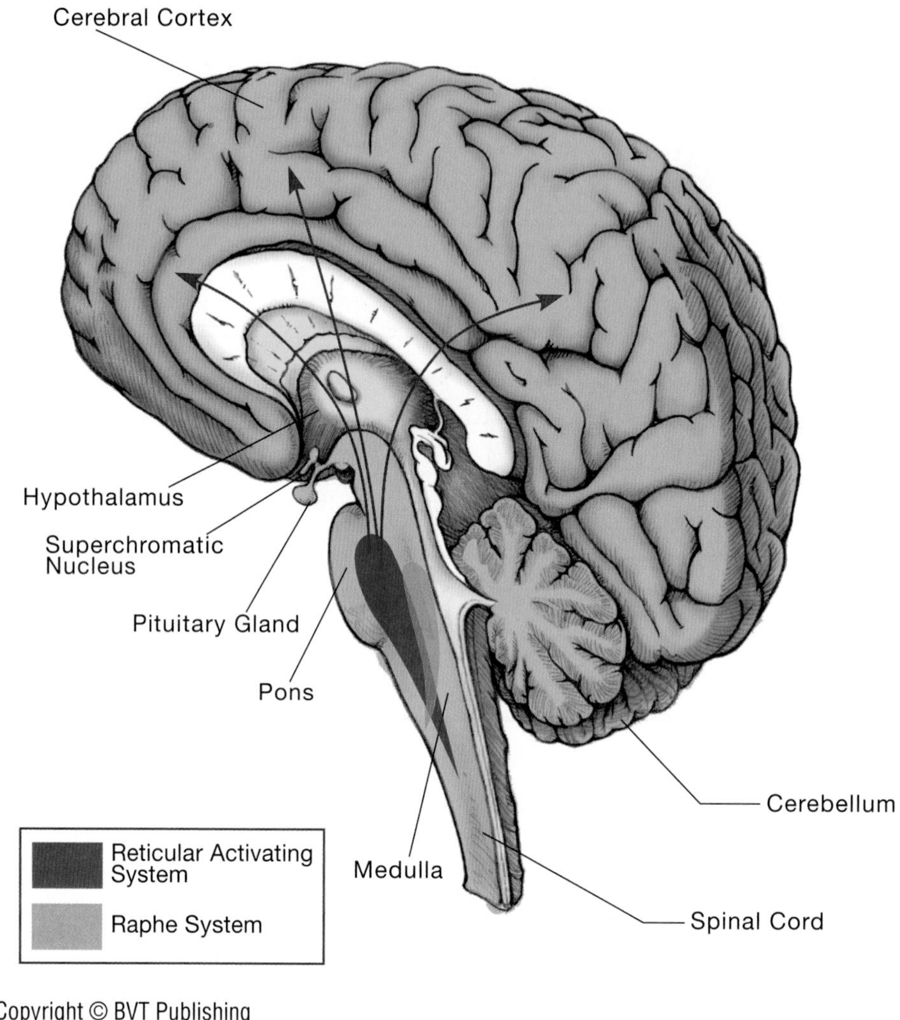

Although serotonin is believed to be involved in sleep onset, its role in maintaining sleep and dreaming is less certain. The serotonin system is virtually silent during REM sleep (Wilkinson & Jacobs, 1988). Another neurotransmitter that has more recently been implicated in sleep is adenosine, a byproduct of neural activity that seems to accumulate during wakefulness. Its accumulation begins to promote sleep by inhibiting cholinergic neurons that keep our cortex aroused (Gallopin et al., 2005; Szymusiak & McGinty, 2008). Interestingly, caffeine keeps you alert by blocking adenosine receptors and, thereby, their inhibiting effects on cholinergic neurons.

Other hormones and neurotransmitters are probably involved to a greater extent once sleep is initiated. In fact, the neurotransmitter acetylcholine in the brainstem is directly involved in dreaming and REM sleep. Injections of acetylcholine into the pons in animals can induce REM sleep. These facts led one researcher to remark, "acetylcholine is the stuff of which dreams are made" (Palca, 1989). Sleep-promoting medications like Ambien® and Lunesta® work by increasing the activity of GABA neurons, which in turn inhibit acetylcholine and norepinephrine throughout the brain.

Another hormone involved in the sleep-wake cycle is **melatonin**. In humans melatonin is produced by the pineal gland during the dark phase of the light-dark cycle. Its production is inhibited by light. Some research suggests that taking melatonin several hours before a desired sleep time can promote sleep onset. Melatonin appears to work by activating receptors in the suprachiasmatic nucleus and adjusting circadian rhythms (Srinivasan et al., 2009). Melatonin may also be effective in inducing sleep after traveling east, when sleep onset may be difficult because one has not adjusted to the advanced clock.

Melatonin A hormone produced by the pineal gland that regulates circadian rhythms (Melatonin may promote sleep onset in individuals with insomnia or those who have traveled east.)

5.2e The Function of Sleep

Is Sleep Necessary?

In a widely reported personal experiment in 1959, New York disc jockey Peter Tripp staged a wake-athon, remaining awake for 200 hours. It was not easy. Halfway through his wake-athon, he began to hallucinate. His ability to think and reason deteriorated dramatically, and by the end of his ordeal he was unable to distinguish between fact and fantasy. He also became increasingly paranoid. At one point, Tripp was convinced that a physician who had arrived to examine him was planning to haul him off to jail (Luce, 1965).

Sleep Deprivation Studies

Tripp's experience, though fascinating, is of limited scientific value because it took place in an uncontrolled environment. Several subsequent studies have been carefully controlled, and they provide more reliable findings. In one experiment, for instance, six volunteers were deprived of sleep for 205 consecutive hours (Kales et al., 1970). By the end of the third day, subjects were hallucinating and experiencing delusions (false or distorted beliefs). They also developed hand tremors, double vision, and reduced pain thresholds. Their reflexes were largely unimpaired, however; and physiological functions such as heart rate, respiration, blood pressure, and body temperature showed little change from normal throughout the course of the experiment. After the experiment was over, no long-term effects were evident. Subjects slept a few days, then awoke feeling fine.

In another experiment conducted by famed sleep researcher William Dement (1972), a seventeen-year-old subject stayed awake for 268 consecutive hours, after which he needed only 14 hours of sleep to recover to a normal state. In contrast to Peter Tripp, this young man remained lucid and coherent throughout his vigil.

Findings such as these caused some researchers to question the importance of sleeping in our lives. A few even speculated that people might learn to get by without any sleep, particularly if scientists could isolate the factor that makes us sleepy and find a way to counter it. With this idea in mind, a team of researchers at the University of Chicago Sleep Research Laboratory devised an ingenious device to study the effects of total sleep deprivation in rats.

Rats were studied in pairs. One was deprived of sleep, and the other acted as a control. Both rats were placed on a plastic disk located above a water pan as shown in Figure 5-7. If the disk rotated, the rats had to walk to avoid falling into the water. The rats were connected to an EEG that monitored their brain waves. Whenever the sleep-deprived rat fell asleep, the EEG registered the changes and opened a circuit, causing the disk to rotate. Both rats would have to walk to avoid falling into the water. The control rat could sleep when his counterpart was awake, but the sleep-deprived rat was jarred awake at each lapse of consciousness. The sleep-deprived rats lasted as long as thirty-three days, but they all eventually died. In contrast,

Figure 5-7 Experimental Apparatus for Producing Sleep Deprivation in Animals

Rats are placed on a platform located above a tub of water. As the platform rotates, the animals must keep moving to avoid being pushed into the water by the plastic divider. Brain waves of the animals are constantly recorded by an EEG to determine their sleep-wake state. Whenever a sleep-deprived rat falls asleep, the rotation of the platform forces them into the water.

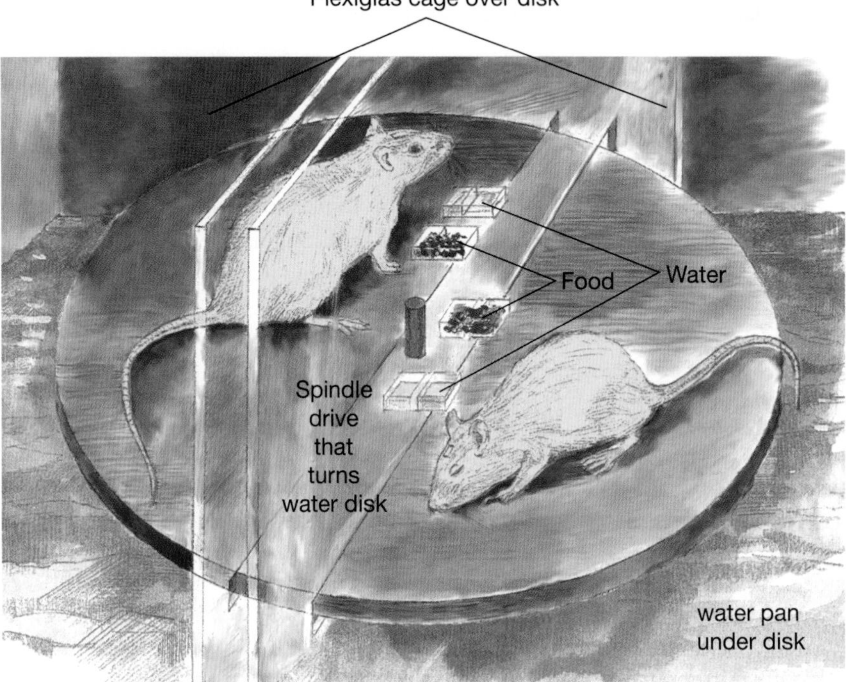

all the control animals survived, apparently no worse for the experience (Rechtschaffen, Gilliland, Bergmann, & Winter, 1983). A more recent experiment by researchers in the same laboratory, using the same research design and apparatus, reported similar results. All ten of the totally sleep-deprived rats in this study died within eleven to thirty-two days, whereas all paired controls survived (Everson, Bergmann, & Rechtschaffen, 1989).

In both of these experiments, the University of Chicago scientists were unable to determine the precise cause of death. A variety of sleep-deprivation effects were observed prior to death, including a progressively scrawny appearance, skin ulcers, increased food intake, weight loss, an increase in energy expenditure, a decrease in body temperature, and shifts in levels of the hormones norepinephrine (increase) and thyroxine (decrease). These physiological correlates of prolonged total sleep deprivation constitute a reliable syndrome indicative of the importance of sleep, at least for rats.

The few studies of sleep-deprived humans have not revealed the syndrome of severe physiological effects, including death, observed in studies of total sleep deprivation in rats. However, a rare neurological disorder called fatal familial insomnia, which results in damage to regions of the thalamus, suggests that severe sleep deprivation in humans is also fatal (Gistau, Pintor, Matrai, & Saiz, 2006).

5.2f Theories of Sleep Function

From the studies just described, it seems evident that sleep is necessary, but why it is necessary is not clear. A number of theories have been suggested to explain why we need sleep. However, none of them have become widely accepted by psychologists.

Sleeping to Conserve Energy

One explanation for why we sleep roughly one-third of every twenty-four-hour period is that sleep conserves energy, thus preventing exhaustion. We burn more calories while awake than asleep. Perhaps in our evolutionary history, when food resources were limited, sleeping eight hours a day may have been a helpful mechanism for limiting the use of scarce energy resources.

Sleeping to Avoid Predation

A related theory argues that sleeping enhances survival by prohibiting animals from interacting with their environment during times when they are not physiologically suited to function adaptively. For example, prehistoric man adapted to sleeping at night because his night vision was poor relative to his predators, such as the saber-toothed tiger. Grazing animals sleep only two to four hours per day, presumably because they need to spend considerably more time foraging.

Sleeping for Restoration

According to this theory, sleep restores resources that we deplete in our daily activities. This explanation is supported by studies showing that people often sleep longer after particularly tiring events. In one study, for example, the sleep of human subjects was monitored after no exercise, a 15-km run, a 42-km run, or after an ultra-triathlon. Sleep patterns were essentially the same after no exercise, the 15-km, and the 42-km runs. However, sleep was significantly disrupted following the ultra-triathlon, with increased wakefulness and decreased REM sleep time (Driver et al., 1994). Strenuous exercise does appear to increase slow-wave sleep time, however. An earlier study (Shapiro et al., 1981) found that the duration of total sleep and slow-wave sleep were significantly increased following a 92-km road race.

We still do not know exactly what restorative processes occur during sleep, or what (if any) kinds of physiological processes or energy sources are depleted when we are awake. There is tentative evidence that certain kinds of tissue restoration, such as cell repair, may occur during sleep. Growth hormone, which promotes tissue growth, is secreted at higher levels in Stage 4 sleep. Some researchers also believe that certain brain neurotransmitters are restored during sleep and that the amount of sleep we need is related to the levels of these chemicals that are present when we fall asleep. Recent research suggests that sleep is also essential for brain homeostasis. Metabolic waste that accumulates from neural activity cannot be excreted through the blood, as is other metabolic waste, because these chemicals cannot pass through the **blood-brain barrier**. Nedergaard and Goldman (2016) provide evidence that these waste products are eliminated through the brain's system of ventricles and cerebral spinal fluid, and this process occurs only during sleep. Approximately 2 kg (more than the weight of your brain) of waste is excreted each year through these systems.

Blood-Brain Barrier Glial cells tightly packed around capillaries in the brain to prevent substances from entering or leaving the blood

Sleeping for Memory

An alternative to this idea is the suggestion that sleep aids in memory consolidation. It is well known that information learned prior to sleep is better remembered than if sleep did not occur and, in addition, that performance is better if sleep follows a learning task. For example, animals demonstrate poorer performance when sleep deprivation occurred immediately following training when compared to performance if sleep deprivation was delayed by six hours after training (Palchykova, Winsky-Sommerer, Meerlo, Dürr, & Tobler, 2006). The brain is far from being in a quiescent state during sleep, and the patterns of activity during slow-wave sleep also appear to be necessary for memory consolidation (Gais, Lucas, & Born, 2006; Steriade & Timofeev, 2003). Memory performance in humans is also enhanced by post-training sleep. This memory-enhancing effect of sleep has been shown to be independent of total sleep time and a subject's level of arousal (Kuriyama, Mishima, Suzuki, Aritake, & Uchiyama, 2008). Taken together, these studies suggest that sleep may promote the storage of newly learned information. Perhaps you could use this to your advantage by studying psychology just before you sleep as opposed to just after waking!

While we have described the beneficial effects of sleep on memory performance, we also know that sleep deprivation causes impaired memory formation. Staying up all night after a long study session may actually hinder performance on your exam rather than be beneficial. Using the rotating platform procedure illustrated in Figure 5-7, researchers can evaluate the effects of sleep deprivation on behavior as well as on neural growth and functioning. In experiments with laboratory animals, ninety-six hours of sleep deprivation caused as much as a 50 percent reduction in new cell growth in the hippocampus compared to non-sleep-deprived controls (Mueller et al., 2008). As you recall from Chapter 3, the hippocampus is essential for the formation of new memories. Experiments such as this support a significant role for sleep in new cell growth in the hippocampus that is essential for memory formation.

5.2g **Dreaming**

What is the function of dreaming? How many times per night do we dream? Is the content of a dream significant? Do animals dream? What happens when people are permitted to sleep but not to dream? Answers to some of these questions have been sought by depriving people of REM sleep and observing changes in their well-being and behavior.

REM Deprivation Studies

Experiments designed by William Dement have attempted to answer these questions. In a study conducted in 1960, Dement used both an EEG and an EOG to register the beginning of REM sleep. For seven consecutive nights, human subjects were permitted to sleep during other stages but were awakened as soon as they entered REM sleep. The total amount of REM sleep they could experience was reduced by about 75 percent. In contrast, a control group was awakened the same number of times as the REM-deprived subjects, but only during NREM sleep. Both groups were monitored throughout the course of the experiment.

REM-deprived subjects demonstrated a number of effects not shown by the control group. They became increasingly irritable, anxious, hostile, and aggressive as the experiment progressed; they also had trouble concentrating on tasks. In addition, they showed signs of being REM-starved, entering REM sleep almost as soon as they dozed off, so that over the course of the one-week experiment, Dement found it more and more difficult to prevent REM sleep. On the first night, subjects had to be awakened an average of twelve times. By the seventh night, this figure had more than doubled to an average of twenty-six awakenings. When Dement's subjects were allowed to sleep without interruption on the eighth night, most (but not all) showed a REM rebound effect, spending about 50 percent more time in REM than they had prior to the onset of the experiment. This REM rebound effect has recently been shown to occur immediately after a period of forced wakefulness during a night's sleep. Subjects who were awakened and asked to sit quietly in an illuminated room for varying periods of time demonstrated a marked increase in the length of their first and second REM episodes after returning to sleep.

Such results have been interpreted as supporting the theory that we sleep to dream, and some psychologists have cited Dement's findings as evidence that REM deprivation can produce severe emotional consequences. To investigate this possibility further, researchers turned to animal studies, with mixed results.

In one study, rats were placed on tiny platforms over water where the only possible way to sleep was standing up (Morden, Mitchell, & Dement, 1967). The rats were able to experience NREM sleep because their muscle tone allowed them to sleep standing up. Recall, however, that muscle tone is lost when REM begins. Thus, whenever REM sleep began, the rat's legs would collapse, toppling it into the water. What happened to these rats? Contrary to what we might expect based on Dement's earlier findings, the REM-deprived rats did not show any significant behavioral or emotional difficulties.

Other research has reported quite different results. In one recent study at the University of Chicago Sleep Laboratory, twelve rats were deprived of REM sleep using a rotating platform apparatus similar to the one shown in Figure 5-7. In contrast, a paired control group of rats was permitted to sleep during any of the four stages. While the rats in the control group survived with no sign of debilitation, all twelve rats assigned to the REM-deprivation condition died (or were put down when death seemed imminent) within sixteen to fifty-four days. These physiological changes have been observed in other studies, and they include death, deteriorated appearance, skin lesions, weight loss, increased energy expenditure, and decreased body temperature (Rechtschaffen, Bergmann, & Everson, 2002).

Not surprisingly, this research model has not been used on humans. However, researchers believe that if humans experienced the duration of sleep deprivation used in animal studies, similar consequences would be observed.

BVT*Lab*

Visit **www.BVTLab.com** to explore the student resources available for this chapter.

Do Animals Dream?

Perhaps you've wondered whether your pet dog or cat was actually dreaming as it jerked about during its sleep. The fact is that REM sleep has been recorded in all mammals studied, as well as in several species of birds. In fact, there is good evidence that REM sleep in animals corresponds with dreaming. Recall the cats with lesions in the pons, which prevented the normal motor inhibition that occurs during REM sleep? These cats were observed to stalk and attack nonexistent objects during REM sleep. Perhaps we will never know for sure whether animals dream during REM sleep, but these and other observations make it seem quite possible. Keep these observations in mind as you consider the following proposed functions of dreaming.

Dreams as Expressions of the Unconscious

Manifest Content In psychoanalytic theory, the disguised version of the latent content, or true meaning, of dreams

Latent Content In psychoanalysis theory, the hidden content or true meaning of dreams

Sleep Disorders Class of disorders that interfere with sleep, including apnea, terrors, nightmares, and sleepwalking

Another theory was proposed almost a century ago by Sigmund Freud as to why we dream. In his classic book *The Interpretation of Dreams* (1900), Freud called dreams the royal road to the unconscious, and dream content and interpretation played a major role in the development of his theories. According to Freud, symbolic processes that represent wishes or desires that become fulfilled by the dream code are the contents of a dream. That is, dreams are disguised expressions of wishes that have been repressed. For example, a person who is sexually frustrated might dream repeatedly about sexual themes. Freud noted that these dreams might not seem to be sexual to the untrained observer, however. The reason for this discrepancy is that we recall only the **manifest content** of our dreams. The manifest content is a disguised version of the **latent** (hidden) **content**, which is the true meaning of our dreams. Thus, a train passing through a tunnel in a dream might be the manifest representation of a penis entering a vagina. If the person having this dream also reported other dreams in which umbrellas, rifles, or swords (all representing the male organ) and boxes, chests, and ovens (female representations) appeared, Freud would be convinced that the dreams expressed a sexual conflict.

Why do we dream about manifest representations instead of the real thing? Freud believed that if people expressed their true desires directly in dreams, the result would be such startling, upsetting dreams that they would awaken immediately. Thus, our unconscious mind expresses our deep-seated wishes symbolically to ensure a good night's sleep.

Freud saw dreams as a mechanism to discharge libidinous energy stored in the *id*. The id, according to Freud, was the biological component of personality consisting of life and death instincts. During wakefulness the expression of the id's wishes are constrained by the *superego*, an individual's conscience. During dreaming, however, the wishes of the id are left unrestrained and may be expressed symbolically. People often either forget their dreams, or they are remembered only incompletely because they are selectively forgotten as a protective cover-up by the *ego*. The ego, according to Freud, functions as a protective intermediary between the wishes of the id and the reality of the real world.

As we saw in Chapter 1, Freud's psychodynamic theory failed largely because it was not testable. The proposed interactions between unconscious processes, although interesting, provide little insight into the functions or meanings of dreams. We conclude, with the perhaps unsatisfactory conjecture, that although the brain states associated with dream sleep appear to be necessary, dreams themselves may not be. Dreaming may merely be the byproduct of otherwise important neural functioning.

5.3 Disorders of Sleep

It's now 2:00 A.M., and you haven't been able to fall asleep even though you're exhausted. By 3:00 A.M. you still haven't slept, and all you seem to be able to think about is your midterm exam in psychology at 9:00 A.M. At 4:00 A.M., you realize that you dozed off briefly, but now you're pondering your decision to trade in your old car for a newer one. Can you really afford the higher payments?

This occasional pattern of sleeplessness is quite common. However, a sizable minority (perhaps one in five adults) finds little comfort in the night. These children and adults suffer from a variety of **sleep disorders** including insomnia, sleep apnea, sleep terrors and nightmares, and sleepwalking.

5.3a Insomnia

(Shutterstock)

About 15 percent of the adult population suffers from chronic insomnia, and as much as 30 percent of the population suffers from occasional insomnia. Approximately twice as many women as men suffer from insomnia.

People with **insomnia** have difficulty going to sleep, experience frequent awakenings during the night, and typically experience earlier than normal awakenings. Figures released in 2008 by the U.S. Department of Health and Human Services suggest that approximately 15 percent of the adult population suffers from chronic insomnia, and as much as 30 percent of the population suffers from occasional insomnia. Approximately twice as many women as men seem to be affected (What is Insomnia?, 2011).

Insomnia may have a variety of causes, including stressful events, depression, emotional disturbances, and drug use. The most common form of insomnia, *temporary* or *situational insomnia*, is related to stress associated with a particular situation—loss of a job, death or illness of a loved one, a relationship that falls apart, and so on. Such events cause stress or worry that may produce heightened physical arousal, which inhibits sleep. Stress may be the most common cause of sleep loss among college students, who may experience insomnia prior to exams or class presentations.

People who suffer from long-lasting sleep loss, or *chronic insomnia*, are more likely to report a serious erosion of the quality of their lives. Although we are not sure exactly what causes chronic insomnia, this condition seems to be associated with anxiety or depression. Sleeping potions (benzodiazepines, barbiturates, or alcohol) may be prescribed to relieve insomnia. These drugs may be helpful in small doses for a brief period. However, they often have an effect that is just the opposite of that desired. Sleeping potions, including alcohol, erode the quality of sleep by reducing the amount of REM sleep and Stage 4 sleep. In addition, people quickly develop a tolerance to these drugs, requiring ever-increasing dosages to produce a sedative effect. The result is a kind of drug-dependence insomnia. Nonprescription, over-the-counter drugs are not the answer either, for they have little or no sleep-inducing capability.

Because drugs should only be used for relatively short durations and for the most severe cases of insomnia, psychologists have emphasized behavioral techniques as alternatives for the management of insomnia. For instance, stress reduction techniques may work to refocus attention away from stressful events or problems that are keeping one from falling asleep. Additionally, engaging in behaviors that decrease, as opposed to increase, neural arousal before attempting sleep may be effective. For instance, quietly listening to music or reading a novel as opposed to talking to friends, watching a horror movie, or even studying.

5.3b Sleep Apnea

A second sleep disorder is a disturbing condition known as **sleep apnea**. People with this disorder do not breathe regularly during sleep. In fact, their breathing actually stops for as long as a few seconds to a minute or two. As the need for oxygen becomes acute, the person briefly awakens, gulps in air, and then settles back to sleep, only to repeat the cycle when breathing stops again. A person with this disorder is unlikely to be aware that he or she wakes up to breathe as often as several hundred times a night. In one extreme case, a man monitored in the sleep laboratory could not sleep and breathe at the same time. Fortunately, most cases are not so severe. It has been estimated that about 6.6 percent of the general population and as many as one out of ten men over age forty have this

Insomnia Sleep disorder characterized by a consistent inability to get to sleep or by frequent awakening during sleep

Sleep Apnea Sleep disorder characterized by irregular breathing during sleep

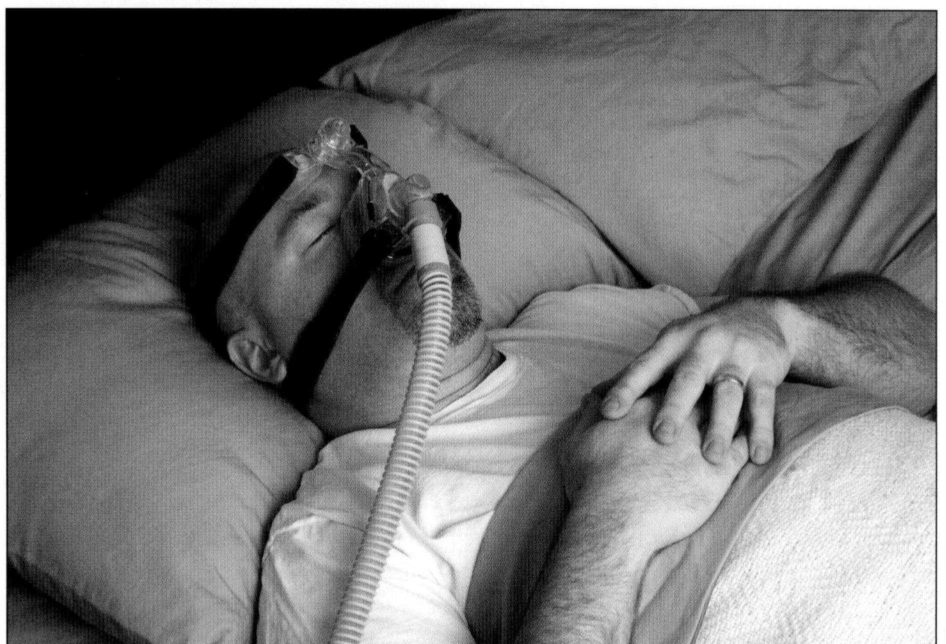
(Shutterstock)

The nasal continuous positive airway pressure (nCPAP) machine is used to treat severe sleep apnea by delivering a continuous flow of air to the nostrils through a nose mask.

disorder. Sleep apnea in old age may be even more common, perhaps occurring in as many as one-third of elderly people (What is Sleep Apnea?, 2012).

Sleep apnea seems to occur when the brain stops sending signals that trigger the breathing response. It may also be caused by a blockage in the upper air passage. (Some apnea victims are older, obese men whose airways may become blocked by their overly thick necks.) Some researchers believe that sleep apnea may be one cause of *sudden infant death syndrome (SIDS)*, commonly called crib death (Franco, Szliwowski, Dramaix, & Kahn, 1999). There is evidence that breathing centers in the medulla of the brain stem malfunction or die off, causing susceptible infants to stop breathing (Machaalani & Waters, 2008; Sawaguchi et al., 2002). Several risk factors appear to be implicated in these brain stem abnormalities, including sleep position and cigarette smoking in the infant's households.

Extreme cases of apnea may be relieved by a *tracheostomy*, an operation in which a valve is surgically inserted into the throat. In recent years, medical researchers have developed a nonsurgical approach to treating severe sleep apnea in which a continuous flow of air is applied to the nostrils through a nose mask. This technique, called *nasal continuous positive airway pressure (nCPAP)*, is now often the treatment of choice for this disorder (N. Mohsenin, Mostofi, & V. Mohsenin, 2003).

5.3c Narcolepsy

Narcolepsy Sleep disorder characterized by falling asleep suddenly and uncontrollably

A peculiar sleep disorder called **narcolepsy** manifests itself as uncontrollable sleep attacks in which a person falls asleep suddenly, perhaps while talking, standing, or driving. The attack may last only a few minutes, or it may last half an hour or more. EEG monitoring reveals that these sleep attacks involve the immediate onset of REM sleep. Since REM sleep produces a loss of muscle tone, most victims collapse the moment they lapse into sleep. For this reason, narcoleptic attacks can endanger a person's life, particularly if they occur while driving or operating dangerous machinery.

One of the authors knew a student who displayed narcoleptic attacks prior to or during examinations. This student would suddenly slump off to sleep while sitting, only to awaken after he hit the floor. Although we still don't know why narcolepsy occurs, the fact that many narcoleptics seem most likely to have sleep attacks during periods of high anxiety or tension suggests that narcolepsy may be some kind of reaction to stress. However, researchers have linked narcolepsy to a neurodegenerative disorder in the brain mechanisms that control sleep and waking. This disorder may involve inadequate production of the hypothalamic hormone orexin, which is believed to play a role in arousal and the inhibition of REM sleep (Scammell, 2003; Szymusiak & McGinty, 2008). Although physicians sometimes prescribe stimulant drugs to reduce the frequency of sleep attacks, there is no effective treatment yet.

5.3d Nightmares

A **nightmare** is a bad dream that occurs during REM sleep. Nightmares typically leave a strong impression on the dreamer; people often awaken after a nightmare with vivid recall of the dream. Sometimes nightmares are repetitive. Many dream theorists once believed that repetitive nightmares reflected areas of conflict or sources of emotional turmoil in a person's waking life. Recent research, however, suggests that there is a strong genetic contribution to the occurrence of nightmares, which tend to run in families, with a greater prevalence in females. In addition, nightmares tend to occur throughout one's life and are frequently associated with psychiatric disorders (Hublin, Kaprio, Partinen, & Koskenvuo, 1999, 2001).

People often confuse sleep terrors with nightmares. **Sleep terrors**, like nightmares but more common, are frightening experiences associated with sleep; however, sleep terrors occur during Stages 3 and 4 of NREM sleep, not during REM sleep. Sleep terrors may occur with a piercing scream or cry for help. Typically, the sleeper sits up, stares unseeingly, and perhaps gasps or hyperventilates. Occasionally, the sleeper jumps out of bed. Full awakening doesn't always occur following a sleep terror. In fact, it is more common for the individual to lie down and continue sleeping. People awakened by a sleep terror usually recall a sense of intense fear but do not recall the content of a dream. They go back to sleep easily and do not recall the experience when they awaken the next morning.

Sleep terrors, unlike nightmares, seem to be related to daytime stress and fatigue. For example, a child who moves to another city or school may be more prone to sleep terrors. Following the September 11, 2001, attacks in New York and Washington, D.C., the incidence of sleep terrors rose sharply in the United States. Although sleep terrors may be associated with some personality disorders, they are not themselves evidence of an underlying disorder or considered abnormal.

5.3e Sleepwalking

For many years it was believed that people who sleepwalk (called somnambulism) are acting out dream events. We now know that **sleepwalking** occurs during Stage 3 or 4 of NREM sleep, when the body is capable of movement. The duration of sleepwalking can vary from a few minutes to more than half an hour. During this time it is virtually impossible to awaken the person. If awakening occurs, the individual is typically disoriented

Nightmare Bad dream that occurs during REM sleep

Sleep Terror Sleep disorder in which a person suddenly awakens from Stage 4 sleep in panic, typically with no recollection of a bad dream

Sleepwalking Sleep disorder, characterized by walking in one's sleep during Stage 3 or 4 of NREM sleep; also known as *somnambulism*

(Shutterstock)

Sleepwalking occurs during Stage 3 or 4 of NREM sleep, when the body is capable of movement. During this time, it is virtually impossible to awaken the person.

but does not recall the episode. Contrary to popular belief, there is no danger involved in awakening a sleepwalker—it is just difficult. After awakening, the person typically returns to sleep. Approximately 20 percent of the population has experienced sleepwalking, with the majority of episodes occurring between six and twelve years of age.

Sleepwalkers can negotiate obstacles, although they move quite clumsily and often fall down or bump into things. Occasionally sleepwalking may subject a person to extreme danger. In one case reported in a news account, a man sleepwalked out the door of a travel trailer as it was being pulled along a highway. Parents can reduce the possibility of their child being injured during sleepwalking by adjusting the environment—for instance, putting gates across windows and at the tops of stairs. Frequent sleepwalking in adults, particularly elderly adults, is considered serious because of the consequences of falling.

5.3f Sleep Talking

Practically everyone talks during sleep on occasion, but it is much more prevalent in children than adults. Unlike sleepwalking, **sleep talking** (somniloquy) appears to occur equally across periods in the sleep cycle. Some people talk during NREM sleep, while others talk exclusively during REM sleep. In some individuals, however, sleep talking can occur during both NREM and REM sleep. When sleep talking occurs during REM sleep, it may reflect dream content. Contrary to myth, sleep talkers rarely reveal secrets.

In contrast to sleepwalking, talking while asleep is usually purposeless and unrelated to stress or other events that occur during the waking state. The typical duration of sleep talking is just a few seconds, but it may last several minutes. The talking may be either unintelligible or fully articulated speech. There is usually no recollection of sleep talking if the person is awakened during talking or when they awaken the following morning. Sleep talking is not considered a symptom of any underlying disorder, nor is it of any clinical significance.

Sleep Talking The production of speech or speech sounds associated with sleep without subjective awareness; also referred to as *somniloquy*

Problems Related to the Sleep-Wake Schedule

People who continually change their sleep-wake schedule because of rotating shifts, frequent travel, or other interruptions from a consistent schedule often have difficulty with sleep and alertness later during the day. No matter what the cause of the disturbance in the schedule, the severity of the sleep problem is proportional to the size of the disturbance. For example, we have no difficulty adjusting to a one-hour shift that occurs during changes from standard time to daylight savings time. However, an eight-hour shift that results from a changing work schedule or a long flight can cause difficulty.

Hypnosis State of altered consciousness characterized by a deep relaxation and detachment, as well as heightened suggestibility to the hypnotist's directives

Because the normal sleep-wake cycle is slightly longer than twenty-four hours (approximately twenty-five hours), it is generally less disruptive to travel from east to west than west to east; that is, it is easier to delay than to advance sleep-wake behavior. This explains why it is easier to adjust to forward rotations in shift work. For example, it is easier to adjust to schedules rotating clockwise (from an 8:00 A.M. to 4:00 P.M. schedule to a 4:00 P.M. to 12:00 P.M. schedule) than the reverse. Can you figure out how many days one should stay on a shift before rotating, given that our internal clocks governing sleep-wake cycles are on a twenty-five-hour schedule as opposed to a twenty-four-hour schedule?

5.4 Hypnosis

Hypnosis is a fascinating phenomenon that has aroused considerable controversy within the discipline of psychology. It is also an area that some psychologists consider worthy of research. Much of its credibility stems from the thoughtful research and writings of renowned psychologist Ernest Hilgard. According to Hilgard (1975), hypnosis represents a state of dissociated experience as opposed to a passive experience controlled by the hypnotist. A dissociated experience involves a deliberate cognitive effort to conform to the demands of the hypnotist. In addition, an amnesia-like process separates or dissociates this cognitive effort from awareness. For instance, in using hypnosis to treat pain, a subject dissociates pain and the cognitive effort to reduce it from immediate experience, perhaps by amnesia.

It has been suggested that hypnotized people are experiencing an altered level of arousal similar to a dreaming state. In fact, the word *hypnosis* was derived from Hypnos, the Greek god of sleep. However, hypnosis is not a state of sleep. Hypnotized people are very relaxed and calm, but EEG recordings demonstrate that they are not asleep. Efforts to differentiate between the brain waves, heart rates, and respiration of hypnotized and non-hypnotized people have been largely unsuccessful (Wallace & Fisher, 1991).

If hypnotized subjects are not in a different state of physiological arousal, in what way is a hypnotic state unique? Observations of countless hypnotized people indicate that hypnosis is characterized by total relaxation and a strong sense of detachment. Hypnotized people are alert and particularly attentive to the hypnotist's words, appearing to have few or no independent thoughts. Under hypnosis, a person may become largely oblivious to stimuli other than the hypnotist's voice.

Although psychologists have not agreed on a precise definition of hypnosis, a functional working definition is that hypnosis is a state of heightened suggestibility in which a person is unusually willing to comply with the hypnotist's directives, including those that alter perceptions of self and the environment.

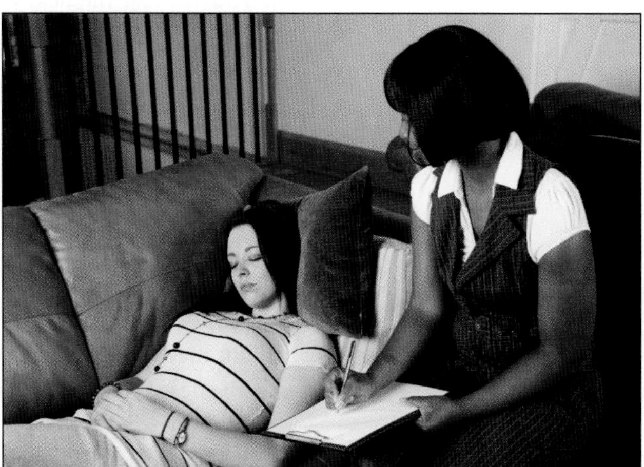

(iStock)

Psychologists have not agreed on a precise definition of hypnosis, but a functional working definition is that it is a state of heightened suggestibility in which a person is unusually willing to comply with the hypnotist's directives.

5.4a Phenomena Associated with Hypnosis

Hypnosis has been linked to a number of phenomena, sometimes accurately and sometimes with a fair amount of hyperbole. Its reputed effects include improved athletic performance, symptomatic relief of physical ailments, pain reduction, enhanced memory, age regression, imaginary sensory experiences (hallucinations), and posthypnotic suggestions subjects carry out as if they were their own ideas. The evidence for these effects is evaluated in the following paragraphs.

Hypnosis and Athletic Ability

You may have heard reports about people demonstrating amazing feats of strength or other outstanding athletic performances, allegedly as a direct result of hypnotic suggestion. Although many of the reports of performance are true, a caveat must be kept in mind: There is no evidence that hypnosis can increase a person's capacity to perform beyond natural limits. It may, however, act as a powerful motivator, providing the extra impetus to close the gap between potential and actual performance. In this sense, its effects may be similar to the emergency response that enables a 150 lb. man to lift a 500 lb. steel pipe off an injured child.

Hypnosis and Relief of Physical Ailments

Well-documented evidence shows that suggestions given to hypnotized people can help relieve the symptoms of a variety of stress-related illnesses, including asthma, ulcers, and colitis. Hypnosis, however, has not been very effective in treating addictive disorders such as alcoholism, drug abuse, smoking, and overeating (Barnes et al., 2010).

Hypnosis and Pain Relief

In the nineteenth century, before anesthesia was discovered, a few surgeons used hypnosis to block surgical pain. However, most of the medical community looked on this practice with suspicion, and it was even suggested that hypnotized patients were faking pain relief. Today, most medical practitioners acknowledge that hypnosis can be very effective in reducing the pain associated with childbirth, back problems, arthritis, dental procedures, burns, and even major surgery (Evans, 1989; James, Large, & Beale, 1989; Spanos, Perlini, & Robertson, 1989). One early study found that hypnosis was more effective than aspirin, acupuncture, or morphine in reducing pain (Stern, Brown, Ulett, & Sletten, 1977). Although this result has not been widely replicated, hypnosis is being used more frequently to manage chronic pain and is used in combination with drugs for minor surgery (Faymonville, Meurisse, & Fissette, 1999; Price & Bushnell, 2004). While it appears that hypnosis may be an effective alternative to chronic pain management, research in this area has been plagued with poorly designed experiments that often lack consistent methods to induce hypnosis and the necessary control conditions to compare its effectiveness (Elkins, Jensen, & Patterson, 2007; Patterson & Jensen, 2003).

Hypnosis and Memory Enhancement

For a time, claims about the memory enhancement capabilities of hypnosis led to its widespread use by police departments, often to help witnesses recall criminal acts. Certainly, some limited benefits are associated with its use in law enforcement—for example, as a way to calm a frightened, traumatized victim of an assault so that he or she can concentrate on the events surrounding the crime. However, there is little substance to claims that it can enhance a person's recall of a criminal act (Kebbell & Wagstaff, 1998). Furthermore, there may actually be danger to relying too heavily on hypnosis. Psychologists have also used hypnosis to investigate suspected cases of past child abuse. However, it may well be that hypnosis actually planted false memories of abuse in clients rather than uncovering repressed memories of real abuse (Loftus, 1994; Stocks, 1998). Similarly, hypnosis has occupied a central role in the so-called recovery of alien-abduction memories. A more careful analysis of these cases suggests that the suggestion of possible abduction during hypnosis may help to create these memories (Clancy, 2005). In summary, there is no reliable evidence that hypnosis enhances either distant or recent memories. Furthermore, evidence obtained during a hypnotic state is not admissible in court.

Posthypnotic Suggestion

Posthypnotic suggestions motivate people to perform a variety of actions after they return to a normal state of consciousness. Subjects typically carry out these suggestions without any recall of the instructions they received, and they often attempt to justify or rationalize the behavior in other ways. For example, in one classroom demonstration, a hypnotized student volunteer was given a posthypnotic suggestion to open a window when she observed her instructor loosen his tie. Right on cue, she raised her hand and asked if it would be okay to open a window, since the room seemed stuffy.

Can hypnosis be used to make you do something you would not ordinarily do? Could it be used to get you to commit a crime, disrobe in front of strangers, or engage in some type of act that you would normally consider unacceptable? Take a moment to evaluate this question based on what you have already learned about hypnosis before reading on.

A common misconception is that hypnosis cannot be used to motivate behavior in which a person would not ordinarily engage. It is true that most hypnotized people would not comply with direct suggestions to behave in an antisocial or inappropriate way. However, a hypnotist can alter the perceptions or awareness of a susceptible subject in such a way that such behaviors seem necessary or appropriate.

5.4b Explaining Hypnosis

A number of theories have been offered to explain hypnosis. One explanation that was briefly mentioned at the beginning of this section is Ernest Hilgard's **dissociation theory**. According to Hilgard, a hypnotized person operates on more than one level of awareness, which allows some behaviors to become divorced or dissociated from our experience by an amnesia-like process. According to this theory, a part of a hypnotized person's awareness (which Hilgard calls the hidden observer) is observing and remembering all that goes on, even though the person is not consciously aware of this process.

Hilgard formulated this hidden observer concept during a classroom demonstration in which he suggested that his subject would be unable to hear anything until Hilgard touched his shoulder. The suggestion worked, and the subject ceased responding to any verbal stimuli. A student then asked if the subject really could not hear. Hilgard asked his subject if some part of him could hear, and if so, he was to signal by raising a finger. The finger rose. Everybody in the room was surprised, including Hilgard (and the subject, who asked why he had raised his finger).

Posthypnotic Suggestion Suggestion or instruction to a hypnotized person that motivates that person to perform an action or actions after returning to a normal state of consciousness

Dissociation Theory A theory of hypnosis, proposed by Ernest Hilgard, in which our behaviors become separated from or dissociated from our awareness

Hilgard touched the subject's shoulder (so that he could hear again) and then asked him what he had experienced. The subject said that the room had suddenly grown very quiet and that he had let his mind wander when suddenly he felt his finger move. Hilgard asked the part of the subject that had made his finger rise to explain what had happened. This second part of the subject's "mind," the so-called hidden observer, accurately reported everything that had transpired (Hilgard, 1977).

This account suggests that two separate states of awareness may occur concurrently—which, incidentally, is how Hilgard defines the hypnotic state. There is nothing mystical about this. All of us have had experiences in which our awareness seems divided or dissociated. An example of this phenomenon is driving your car while thinking about a complex problem and then suddenly realizing that you have arrived at your destination without remembering your drive. The route you drove was dissociated from your awareness by amnesia.

A modified version of Hilgard's dissociation theory proposes that there are several levels of behavioral control: conscious, executive control (similar to Hilgard's cognitive effort) and lower levels of control that can be directly activated by hypnosis. For instance, when a subject undergoes hypnosis for pain analgesia, the hypnotic suggestions directly activate lower levels of control for pain reduction. That is, pain analgesia resulting from hypnosis is not mediated through a cognitive effort (consciously thinking about a reduction in pain). Thus, there is no need for amnesia to dissociate this cognitive effort from our experience as hypothesized by Hilgard.

As a test of this version of dissociation theory, researchers had subjects engage in cognitively demanding tasks while they underwent hypnosis for pain reduction. According to Hilgard's dissociation theory the cognitively demanding tasks should compete with the cognitive resources for analgesia, resulting in little reduction in pain. On the other hand, if cognitive processing is not necessary for analgesia, subjects under hypnosis should experience a reduction in pain. This is, in fact, what the researchers found (Miller & Bowers, 1993).

Not all psychologists agree that hypnosis involves dissociation of our awareness. As an alternative they argue that hypnosis is an example of compliance to the hypnotist's suggestions and does not involve an altered state of arousal. According to Barber (1975; Barber & Wilson, 1977), all of the phenomena associated with hypnosis can be demonstrated in people who are not hypnotized. Hypnosis works because the subject is willing to go along with the hypnotist's suggestions uncritically. Barber compares being hypnotized to becoming a vicarious participant in the story line of a good novel or movie. To support this viewpoint, Barber and others have demonstrated that many hypnotic phenomena can be shown by nonhypnotized subjects who are instructed to think along with the hypnotist or merely to pretend they are hypnotized.

In one experiment, sixty-six nurses were divided into three matched groups. Subjects in one group were hypnotized using traditional techniques. Subjects in a second group were encouraged to focus their imaginations uncritically on whatever suggestions were provided. The third group, acting as a control, received no special instructions. All subjects were then asked to perform the same tasks, such as watching an imaginary TV program, drinking imaginary water, and hearing nonexistent music; their performance on these tasks was rated using a scoring system.

If Barber's ideas about hypnosis are correct how should these groups compare in their hypnosis scores? Think about this before reading on.

Comparisons of the scores obtained by subjects in the different groups revealed that those in the pretend-hypnosis group actually obtained somewhat higher scores, on the average, than those in the hypnotized group—which is what Barber's theory predicted

(Barber & Wilson, 1977). That is, hypnosis may not represent a different state of alertness, but a predisposition to attend to the hypnotist's suggestions. Supports for this contention comes from the observation that most people cannot be hypnotized, and those who are tend to be highly suggestible. **Hypnotic suggestibility**, which can be measured by standardized tests, not only predicts which individuals can be hypnotized but also predicts how effective hypnosis may be in alleviating pain (Dufresne et al., 2010; Milling, Coursen, Shores, & Waszkiewicz, 2010).

At present there is no universally accepted theory of hypnosis. This is, in part, because of our inability to describe adequately and objectively a hypnotic state. Until we can define hypnosis in objective terms, such as a particular physiological state, different investigators will not know whether they are indeed studying the same phenomenon. As a result, several conflicting theories are bound to exist. On the positive side, there is evidence that there is an increasing interest in hypnosis research from several related disciplines including medicine, dentistry, and psychology (Price & Bushnell, 2004).

5.5 Consciousness

Consciousness is a difficult concept to define. We all know what it means to be conscious, but we have a difficult time explaining what it really is. Philosophers, psychologists, theologians, and more recently neuroscientists, have all attempted explanations of what it is to be conscious. The scientific study of consciousness can be traced to psychology's very roots. William James (1842–1910) even defined psychology as "the description and explanation of states of consciousness" (James, 1890).

Antonio Damasio, a neurologist and neuroscientist, has proposed a definition of consciousness as *"the special features that exist in the mind that permit us to know that we ourselves exist and that things around us exist."* In other words, having a sense of self and the world around us. Any definition of consciousness must contain both a reference to our awareness of self—our feelings and our memories—and a reference to our awareness that things outside of us exist (Damasio, 2000, 2001, 2010; Parvizi & Damasio, 2001).

Neuroscientists believe that consciousness evolved from more primitive states of awareness that allowed animals to more efficiently interact with their environments—for example, avoiding places and things that harmed them and to seeking those that promoted reproduction and survival. In humans, consciousness allows us to explore our past by rehearsing our memories and to anticipate the future and the consequences of our actions.

5.5a Neurobiology of Consciousness

Several brain structures are essential for consciousness, and individuals who have suffered damage to these areas demonstrate various disruptions to their consciousness. Individuals with damage to areas of the somatosensory cortex demonstrate **sensory neglect**. For example, a stroke affecting the right parietal lobe can lead to neglect of the left visual field. In serious cases, an individual may fail to eat food on the left side of his plate, shave and groom the left side of the face, or fail to react to stimuli on the left side. They may even fail to recognize the left half of the body.

The cingulate cortex seems critical for one's conscious awareness of self. Patients with damage to the cingulate can experience an emotion like anger, but they don't feel their emotions. In fact, these patients don't recognize their emotions in a mirror and they

Hypnotic Suggestibility The predisposition to attend to a hypnotist's suggestions

Consciousness A sense of self and the world around us

Sensory Neglect A lack of awareness of or attention to stimuli on one side of the body when damage has occurred to the opposite-side parietal lobe

Free Will The assertion that our choices and actions are not caused by antecedent events, but emerge spontaneously from the mind

cannot identify the emotional state of another's face. So, while the cingulate cortex is not involved in emotions per se, it is essential for our feelings of our emotions (Medford & Critchley, 2010). Numerous other brain structures contribute vitally to our consciousness, and neuroscientists are investigating their contributions. It is becoming increasingly clear that consciousness cannot be separated from the brain and body. Damage to various brain structures results in an array of disruptions to our conscious experiences.

Conscious Will

Does our conscious will cause our behavior? Most of us never question whether our conscious decisions to act actually affect, or cause, our actions. We assume that when we decide to act, that our conscious decision caused our behavior. Furthermore, we tend to assume that our actions are free or not caused by antecedent conditions. Philosophers refer to this idea as **free will**. Modern neuroimaging studies, however, may contradict this notion. In one experiment participants were asked to press one of two buttons while watching random sequences of letters appearing on a computer screen. They could press the buttons at any time, but they were to report which letter was on the screen at the moment they decided to press. The researchers found that several brain regions reliably predicted which button was going to be pressed 1,500 milliseconds before the decision was consciously made! Furthermore, a population of only 256 neurons was sufficient to predict the impending decision to press with over 80 percent accuracy, 700 milliseconds before the participant's awareness (Fried, Mukamel, & Kreiman, 2011; Haggard, 2011). These and other findings suggest that our notion of free will is merely an illusion (Harris, 2012; Wagner, 2002).

Suggested Remedies for Insomnia

Psychologists have developed a number of behaviorally based remedies for insomnia. Perhaps one or more of the following suggestions may be helpful to you or someone you know.

1. **Adopt a regular schedule.** Go to sleep and get up at about the same time every day, even on weekends. Many insomnia sufferers have erratic sleep patterns. A regular schedule can establish a predictable rhythm that will greatly improve sleep. Avoid spending excessive time in bed, since this behavior can perpetuate insomnia.
2. **Try to engage in a relaxing, calming activity before going to bed.** Some people find that a warm bath is helpful; others prefer listening to soothing music or reading. Avoid high-stress activities such as discussing money with your partner, watching an action movie, or trying to debug a computer program.
3. **A number of procedures are designed to relax your body.** These may be helpful before retiring. You can learn about relaxation techniques from several books that are easily found in bookstores.
4. **A daily exercise routine can also help promote a good night's sleep.** It is probably not a good idea to engage in this activity just before going to sleep, however, since exercise can be very energizing.
5. **Avoid drinking large quantities of beer, wine, or distilled spirits before retiring.** These substances may help you fall asleep, but they are likely to interfere with your ability to stay asleep once their sedative effect wears off. In addition, avoid all stimulants after midday. One of the most commonly consumed stimulants, caffeine, is found in chocolate, coffee, tea, and many carbonated soft drinks. Caffeine-free forms of these products are available.
6. **Avoid eating a large meal just before retiring to bed.** If you need a snack, choose something high in carbohydrates.
7. **Make your bedroom environment as sleep-compatible as possible.** Use curtains or shades that shut out external light. If you must sleep in a noisy area, try using earplugs or turning on a fan or air conditioner to mask the noise.
8. **Try not to get upset about not sleeping.** This suggestion is often easier said than done. However, remember that anger will only energize you more, thus adding to your problem. It would probably be much better to get up and read a book or engage in some form of relaxation until you feel sleepy enough to doze off.
9. **Finally, if these suggestions are not working, a physician may be able to prescribe a mild hypnotic** (e.g., Ambien). Such a drug, over the course of a short time, may be quite effective in alleviating insomnia. Other nonprescription pharmacological remedies include the histamine blocker Benadryl® or taking melatonin several hours before your desired sleep time.

CHAPTER REVIEW

Biological Rhythms

1. All biological systems are influenced by rhythms of physiological activity. When these rhythms are on a twenty-four-hour cycle, they are called circadian rhythms.
2. Circadian rhythms appear to be controlled by the suprachiasmatic nucleus of the hypothalamus.

The Science of Sleep and Dreaming

3. Sleep is a natural, periodically recurring state of rest, which is characterized by reduced activity, lessened responsiveness to stimuli, and distinctive brain-wave patterns.
4. Researchers distinguish between REM (rapid eye movement) and NREM (non-rapid eye movement) sleep. Dreaming is more likely to occur in REM than in NREM sleep. However, dreaming is not limited to REM sleep.
5. During a normal night's sleep we pass through four stages of sleep in naturally recurring, successive cycles. These stages range from very light sleep, characteristic of Stage 1, through Stage 4, the deepest level of sleep. Dreaming occurs most commonly during Stage 1 sleep.
6. During dreaming, muscular activity is inhibited. Sleepwalking almost invariably occurs during NREM sleep (Stage 3 or 4).
7. As people grow older, there is a decline in both the time spent sleeping and the proportion of sleep spent in the REM phase.
8. Different species of animals seem to require different amounts of sleep.
9. The major brain areas involved in sleep and waking are the ascending reticular activation system (RAS) and the raphe system.
10. Research suggests that sleep is necessary, but it is not clear why. A number of theories have been suggested: Sleeping conserves energy, restores depleted resources, helps clear the mind of useless information, facilitates memory, or allows us the opportunity to dream.
11. People deprived of dreaming tend to increase their time spent dreaming in subsequent uninterrupted sleep periods, a phenomenon known as REM rebound.
12. To date, research has not provided a definitive answer to why we dream. Some explanatory theories are that dreams are the brain's attempt to explain random bursts of neuronal activity: Dreams are a form of mental reprogramming in which the brain is reorganized to accommodate new information, dreaming provides a low-stress solution to dealing with problems, and dreams are disguised expressions of unconscious wishes.

CHAPTER REVIEW

Disorders of Sleep

13. Sleep disorders include insomnia, sleep apnea, narcolepsy, sleep terrors and nightmares, and sleepwalking.

Hypnosis

14. Hypnosis is a state of heightened suggestibility in which a person is unusually willing to comply with the hypnotist's directives.
15. Hypnosis can act as a powerful motivator, but it cannot increase a person's capacity to perform beyond natural limits.
16. Evidence suggests that hypnosis can help to alleviate pain and relieve the symptoms of a variety of stress-related illnesses. However, it has been shown to be only marginally beneficial in criminal investigations.
17. Explanations of hypnosis include dissociative theories.
18. A person's hypnotic suggestibility can be measured by standardized tests and accurately predicts which people (about one in five) can be hypnotized.

Consciousness

19. Consciousness is a sense of self and the world around us. Neuroscientists are now describing the brain structures that interact to bring about consciousness.
20. Free will is the assertion that our choices and actions are not caused by antecedent events, but emerge spontaneously from the mind.

TERMS AND CONCEPTS

Biological Rhythms, pg. 187
Blood-Brain Barrier, pg. 199
Consciousness, pg. 211
Dissociation Theory, pg. 209
Free Will, pg. 212
Hypnosis, pg. 207
Hypnotic Suggestibility, pg. 211
Insomnia, pg. 203
Latent Content, pg. 202
Manifest Content, pg. 202
Melatonin, pg. 197
Narcolepsy, pg. 204
Nightmare, pg. 205
NREM (Non-Rapid Eye Movement) Sleep, pg. 189
Posthypnotic Suggestion, pg. 209
Raphe Nucleus, pg. 195
REM (Rapid Eye Movement) Sleep, pg. 189
Reticular Activating System (RAS), pg. 194
Sensory Neglect, pg. 211
Sleep Apnea, pg. 203
Sleep Disorders, pg. 202
Sleep, pg. 189
Sleep Talking, pg. 206
Sleep Terror, pg. 205
Sleepwalking, pg. 205
Stage 1 Sleep, pg. 192
Stage 2 Sleep, pg. 192
Stage 3 Sleep, pg. 192
Stage 4 Sleep, pg. 193
Suprachiasmatic Nucleus (SCN), pg. 188

POP QUIZ

True or False

___ 1. In an environment that is lighted twenty-four hours a day, a person's biological clock would adjust to a twenty-five-hour free-running clock.

___ 2. After being deprived of REM sleep, people spend increased time in REM sleep, which is referred to as REM rebound.

___ 3. Freud believed that people dream in order to solve problems.

___ 4. Nightmares occur during REM sleep; sleep terrors occur during Stage 3 and 4 sleep.

___ 5. The "hidden observer" is associated with the dissociation theory of hypnosis.

Multiple Choice

6. What is a biological rhythm that is approximately one year in length called?
   a. Circumlunar rhythm
   b. Diurnal rhythm
   c. Circadian rhythm
   d. Circumannual rhythm
7. Which of the following bodily functions are reduced during REM sleep?
   a. Muscular activity
   b. Brain-wave activity
   c. Heart rate
   d. Breathing
8. Theta waves, slow eye movements, irregular breathing, and muscle relaxation characterize which sleep stage?
   a. Stage 1 sleep
   b. Stage 2 sleep
   c. Stage 3 sleep
   d. Stage 4 sleep
9. If you normally sleep eight hours each night, you probably experience ______complete sleep cycle(s) each night.
   a. one
   b. three
   c. five
   d. eight

POP QUIZ

10. Which of the following functions of sleep would be more applicable to a person barely surviving in a Third World country in the midst of a famine than to a typical American?
    a. To restore depleted resources
    b. To conserve energy
    c. To prevent boredom
    d. To consolidate memory
11. According to Freud, the ________is the "true" meaning of a dream.
    a. plot
    b. latent content
    c. manifest content
    d. analogy content
12. What is the sleep disorder whereby a person falls asleep suddenly and uncontrollably called?
    a. Sleep terrors
    b. Somnambulism
    c. Narcolepsy
    d. Apnea
13. A person who is sleepwalking is experiencing which of the following?
    a. Acting out a dream
    b. In REM sleep
    c. Experiencing sleep terrors
    d. In Stage 3 or Stage 4 sleep
14. Which of the following statements does ***not*** describe a hypnotized person?
    a. He or she is highly suggestible to the hypnotist's instructions.
    b. He or she is passive.
    c. He or she has few, if any, independent thoughts.
    d. He or she is not alert.
15. That people can selectively focus attention on one thing (the hypnotic suggestion) and still perceive other things "subconsciously" describes Hilgard's ________theory.
    a. psychoanalytic
    b. dissociation
    c. role-playing
    d. meditation

Answer Key: 1.T 2.T 3.F 4.T 5.T 6.d 7.a 8.a 9.c 10.b 11.b 12.c 13.d 14.d 15.b

(Shutterstock)

Learning *and* Behavior

In March 2007, the U.S. Fish and Wildlife Service announced that after thirty years of conservation efforts, grizzly bear populations were no longer considered endangered in the Yellowstone Park area. While the population of these bears has increased significantly so, too, has the threat of a grizzly bear attack. Each year several visitors to the park are attacked by bears (National Park Service, 2016). Trying to protect an endangered species that may pose a significant danger to humans has presented some special problems for conservationists.

These problems are particularly evident in the Yellowstone and Glacier National Parks regions of Montana and around the resort town of Whistler in British Columbia, Canada. After years of living close to civilization and foraging through garbage cans and campsites, both grizzly and black bears in these areas behave as if they have lost their fear of humans. In the past, before these regions were as heavily populated, the bears avoided human contact whenever they could. Now bears that have become accustomed to humans react differently, with the result that in recent years a number of people have been injured or killed. Bears that injure humans must be destroyed; thus rangers have been put in the position of bringing the grizzly bear even closer to extinction. Over one thousand black bears and more than 380 grizzlies were shot in British Columbia in 2011 because of conflicts with humans. These numbers have been rising steadily over the last decade as bears have learned to forage in neighborhoods and campgrounds (Pynn, 2016).

Most efforts to relocate bears to other areas have been remarkable for their lack of success. For instance, when bears are trapped and transported deep into the wild, they often return to human habitats where the living is easy. Recently, however, wildlife officials have begun a new program that looks far more promising. The goal of this program is to reestablish fear of humans in these animals, using aversive conditioning (Harden, 2002). Aversive conditioning has utilized rubber bullets, loud noises, dogs, and other forms of hazing; however, brief electric shocks have been the most effective in reestablishing fear of humans in these animals.

Protecting endangered species may seem to be far from the topic at hand; yet it illustrates some of the principles that are basic to learning processes, not just in bears, but also in humans and other animals. As we will see, much of our learning takes place by associating events, just as the bears learned to associate painful shocks with the presence of humans.

An understanding of learning is relevant to many other fields that seem to have little to do with psychology, from designing behavior treatment programs to understanding our immune system. The pages that follow present at least a portion of what psychologists have learned about learning, and they help to explain how we can apply this knowledge to our lives. Before we discuss the applications of learning, we begin by defining what we mean by learning.

6.1 Defining Learning

Learning may be defined as a relatively permanent change in potential behavior that results from experience. This definition contains three important elements. The first element is change. Most learning tends to produce lasting changes in the behavior of the learner. We hope that the bears in the opening example of this chapter will continue to associate humans with the discomfort they experienced during aversive conditioning.

Second, this definition excludes changes in behavior that result from anything other than experience. For example, behavior can be modified by nonexperiential events like diseases, injury, or maturation. A broken leg would result in numerous changes in your behavior, few of which are learned. We know that grizzly bears have learned to associate people with aversive consequences when we see that they now avoid humans and the places where humans are likely to be.

Learning Relatively enduring change in potential behavior that results from experience

The third element of this definition speaks of *potential* behavior. Although learning causes changes in behavior, it is not always reflected directly in performance. The absence of observable behavior change does not necessarily mean that no learning has taken place; however, a change in behavior under the appropriate conditions must be observable at some time to claim that learning has occurred. For example, suppose a young boy often sees his father strike his mother during arguments. For the time being, the father's actions may have no apparent effect on the boy's behavior. When the boy becomes an adult, however, he strikes his wife during an argument. During the boy's childhood, we would have had no reason to believe that he had learned to be physically violent when frustrated. However, the potential for this behavior clearly was acquired; it simply required the necessary circumstances for it to occur.

Rats in a maze demonstrate another example of learning that cannot be observed immediately. If there is no reinforcement (such as food) at the end of the maze, rats explore the alleys with no indication that learning is taking place. When food is placed at the end of the maze, however, they quickly negotiate the twists and turns to reach it. Some learning had taken place during the exploration, but it required a proper incentive to be reflected in actual performance.

6.1a How Learning Takes Place

You should now have an understanding of what learning is. But how does it take place? For instance, you go to a familiar restaurant and order something unique that you've never eaten before. Throughout the meal you comment on how distinctive and flavorful your dish is. Later in the evening, you become quite ill and nauseous. This illness may be completely unrelated to the meal you ate earlier. Perhaps it's a touch of the flu. However, the association of illness with the meal leads to an aversion to this unique dish that you found flavorful earlier. This aversion may last for years. Most of us can think of examples of food aversions we've acquired such as this. For patients undergoing radiation or chemotherapy, food aversions can be quite common, and they are acquired in the same fashion. A flavor or smell that is followed by treatment that makes the patient ill is less desirable than before. This is an example of a conditioned taste aversion, a subject to which we will return later (Garcia & Koelling, 1966).

This kind of learning is called **associative learning**. It describes the process by which we make a connection or an association between two events, such as the flavor of a particular food and illness—or how the bears, in the opening example, learn to associate pain with humans. Associative learning may take place in two primary ways: through Pavlovian conditioning and through operant conditioning. Both of these processes contribute continually to your ongoing behavior.

Associative Learning
Learning by making an association between two stimulus events (Pavlovian conditioning) or by learning an association between a response and its consequence (operant conditioning)

Pavlovian Conditioning
Learning that takes place when a neutral stimulus (CS) is paired with a stimulus that already produces a response (After conditioning, the organism responds to the CS in some way. The response to the CS is called a conditioned response.)

Operant Conditioning
Learning an association between one's behavior and its consequence (reinforcement or punishment)

Pavlovian conditioning (or *classical conditioning*) involves learning an association between two stimuli and results in a change in behavior. For example, the flavor of our unique dish at the restaurant becomes associated with illness, a small child learns to associate the sight of a physician's syringe with the discomfort of an injection, or bears learn to associate painful shocks with humans. We will see later that Pavlovian conditioning contributes to your emotional states, the functioning of your digestive and immune systems, and even to the development of tolerance to drugs.

In **operant conditioning** (or *instrumental conditioning*), people or other animals learn to associate their own behavior with its consequences, which results in a change in behavior. Thus a child learns that pressing a button brings an elevator, a college student learns that answering questions in a certain class produces praise, a porpoise learns that jumping through a hoop results in a tasty morsel of fish, and you learn that driving through a stop sign produces a ticket.

Psychologists believe that most kinds of learning can be described in terms of Pavlovian and operant conditioning. However, certain kinds of learning, such as learning language, may involve more complex processes. This kind of learning is labeled **template learning** because there appears to be a neural template that facilitates it. First, however, we turn our attention to Pavlovian and operant conditioning processes.

6.2 Pavlovian Conditioning

Some years ago, one of the author's psychology students came to him with a problem. She was enrolled in a biology class in which students spent much of their time in a laboratory. When she entered the lab early in the term, she suddenly felt an overwhelming state of anxiety bordering on terror. She was unable to remain in the laboratory; consequently, she could not complete her assignments. Perplexed and concerned, she tried a number of times to return to the lab, but she could not shake her feeling of terror.

Here are some of the facts in the case just described: The student had completed two previous terms of biology without experiencing any discomfort in the laboratory segments. Between her previous biology class and the present term was a one-year absence from college, during which she gave birth to her first child. Her problem in the biology laboratory commenced immediately after returning to resume her studies. Take a moment to consider the facts and try to explain the woman's fear response before reading on.

If you guessed that the student had some terrible experience during her year's absence from college that somehow became associated with the environment of the biology laboratory, you are correct. Because of complications during the delivery of her baby, her physician decided to perform a caesarean section (surgical removal of the baby through an incision in the abdomen and uterus). There was not time for her to be psychologically prepared, and she panicked. She found herself unable to breathe when she received an injection of anesthesia (a rare response during this type of medical procedure and probably related to stress). For a few terrible moments she was convinced she would die. Fortunately, the feeling subsided quickly, and the operation proceeded smoothly.

Let's see how Pavlovian conditioning may have contributed to her present anxiety in the biology laboratory. The trigger for this woman's original fear response was her experience on the operating table. Because this experience took place in an environment with medical smells, the woman associated these smells with her awful experience at the hospital. The odors of antiseptic and anesthetic agents in the biology laboratory were similar enough to the medical smells of the operating room to trigger the same fear response that the woman had developed while receiving anesthesia for her operation.

The connection was not a conscious one. In fact, Pavlovian conditioning rarely occurs at a conscious level. In this case the woman was not aware that she had been conditioned. Yet it followed a Pavlovian model that was first recognized around the turn of the last century by the Russian physiologist Ivan Pavlov (1849–1936). You will see in this section that most of your emotional responses are conditioned similarly.

6.2a Pavlov's Discovery

Pavlov's real interest was the physiological mechanisms involved in digestion. In fact, he never associated his own research with psychology and insisted that he was dealing only with physiological mechanisms. Toward this end, Pavlov was investigating the salivation responses of dogs by placing the animals in a harness-like apparatus, shown in Figure 6-1. A surgical procedure exposed each dog's salivary glands, which were connected directly

Template Learning Learning that depends on a particular type of perceptual experience during a critical time in development (for example, imprinting and language learning)

Figure 6-1 Pavlov's Conditioning Apparatus

During a typical conditioning session, an assistant, sitting behind the mirror, rang a bell (the conditioned stimulus) and then presented food (the unconditioned stimulus) to the hungry dog. Salivation was measured by collecting it via a tube attached to the dog's salivary gland. A revolving drum recorded the amount of saliva collected. Initially, salivation occurred only after food was presented (the unconditioned response). After several condition trials, however, salivation occurred (the conditioned response) after the presentation of the conditioned stimulus.

Adapted from An *Introduction to Psychology,* by R. N. Haber and A. H. Fried, 1975, New York, NY: Holt, Rinehart and Winston. Copyright © 1975 by Holt, Rinehart, and Winston.

to a device that measured the flow of saliva. Pavlov then presented a stimulus, meat powder. When the food entered the dog's mouth, the immediate result was the natural, reflexive response of salivation.

However, Pavlov soon noted an unexpected occurrence. His dogs began to salivate to stimuli other than food in their mouths. For example, an animal might start salivating at the mere sight of the experimenter. The sound of Pavlov's footsteps or the sight of the food dish also caused salivation.

This discovery changed the course of Pavlov's study, for Pavlov now began to investigate how other stimuli could cause dogs to salivate. His experiments are generally recognized as the first systematic study of learning, and the processes that he outlined came to be called primary (as in "the first") conditioning. (Pavlovian conditioning is also called classical conditioning because Pavlov described it as conditioning of the classical type.) A basic outline of this model of learning follows.

A hungry dog, secured in Pavlov's apparatus, hears a bell. A moment later, the dog is given meat powder; copious salivation results. This procedure is repeated several times, with one stimulus (the sound of the bell) followed consistently by another stimulus (food). Eventually, the dog salivates when it hears the bell, even when no food follows. The dog has associated the bell with food. However, what is learned is more than a mere association between two stimuli. Rather, Pavlovian conditioning may be best described as the learning of relations among events so as to allow the organism to represent its environment (Rescorla, 1988a). Put another way, Pavlov's dog learned something about important relationships existing in its environment, namely that the sounding of a bell signaled the availability of food. Consequently, when the bell rang, the dog salivated in *anticipation* of eating food. Many conditioned responses function to prepare the learner for a change in events.

The fact that a previously neutral stimulus (a stimulus, such as the sound of the bell, that does not elicit the to-be-learned response) eventually produces a response (salivation) ordinarily associated with another stimulus (food) is clear evidence that learning has taken place. Pavlov identified four key events or elements for Pavlovian conditioning:

1. **The unconditioned stimulus (UCS)** Meat causes dogs to salivate. This response occurs automatically, without learning or conditioning. A stimulus that elicits an unlearned response or reflex is called an unconditioned stimulus. In our opening example of aversive conditioning with bears, electric shock was a UCS.

2. **The unconditioned response (UCR)** Salivating at the presentation of meat is an automatic response that does not require learning. An unlearned response is called an unconditioned response. In our opening example of aversive conditioning, fear and anxiety following electric shocks were UCRs.

3. **The conditioned stimulus (CS)** The bell initially is a neutral stimulus in that it does not elicit the to-be-learned response by itself. It causes salivation only when the dogs learn the association between the bell and the unconditioned stimulus, the food. A stimulus to which an organism learns to respond is called a learned or conditioned stimulus. In our opening example of aversive conditioning, seeing humans or being in places where humans are likely to occur are examples of CSs.

4. **The conditioned response (CR)** Pavlov's dogs were conditioned to salivate when a bell sounded. Such a learned response is called a conditioned response. In our opening example of aversive conditioning, fear and the motivation to avoid humans are examples of CRs. Notice that Pavlovian CRs are changes in emotional or motivational states, not overt behaviors such as running away.

Figure 6-2 summarizes the steps by which conditioning took place in Pavlov's model. The conditioning in Pavlov's dogs was measured by collecting saliva secreted following the presentation of the CS. Other conditioned responses may take place and be measured at a physiological level. For instance, in the Health, Psychology, and Life segment at the end of this chapter, we discuss Pavlovian conditioning of the immune system, which could have far-reaching medical implications.

Unconditioned Stimulus (UCS) In Pavlovian conditioning, a stimulus that elicits an unlearned response or reflex

Unconditioned Response (UCR) In Pavlovian conditioning, an unlearned response or reflex caused by an unconditioned stimulus

Conditioned Stimulus (CS) In Pavlovian conditioning, a stimulus that elicits a response only after being associated with an unconditioned stimulus

Conditioned Response (CR) In Pavlovian conditioning, a learned response to a conditioned stimulus

Differentiating Between the UCR and the CR

At first glance, the unconditioned response and conditioned response often appear to be identical. The UCR in Pavlov's experiments occurred when the dogs salivated in response to meat, and the CR was also salivation. However, the UCR and the CR may be quite different depending on both the nature of the CS and the UCS. In our opening example of taste aversion conditioning, illness was the UCR and an aversion to food was the CR.

Figure 6-2 Pavlov's Conditioning Procedure

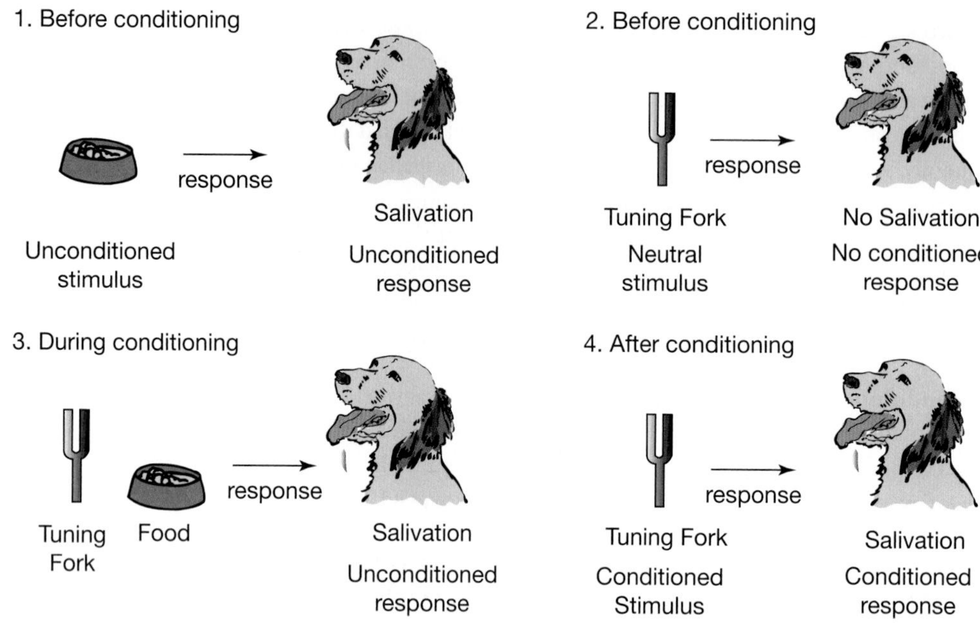

In some cases, the CR and the UCR can be opposites. In the author's laboratory, for example, the context of morphine or cocaine administration (CS) elicits tolerance to the drug (CR), while the UCRs to morphine and cocaine are analgesia and euphoria. This is demonstrated by testing the effectiveness of morphine on acute thermal pain. After repeated trials where morphine is administered in a certain context, animals become tolerant and morphine is no longer effective. If, however, these animals are tested in a novel context, morphine is once again an effective analgesic.

Unconditioned and conditioned responses also differ in their intensity. An unconditioned response is generally more intense than is a response that has been conditioned. For example, dogs salivate more copiously when meat is actually placed in their mouths than they do when they either hear a bell or see the person who feeds them.

What do dogs salivating to a sound have to do with our lives as humans? We can best put this question in perspective by returning to the case of the biology student. The same elements that Pavlov traced in his dogs can be found in this conditioning experience. The unconditioned response is fear, a natural response to the frightening event in the hospital room (the UCS). Fear or anxiety is the learned or conditioned response. Just as Pavlov's dogs learned to associate the bell with food, the young woman may have learned to associate medical smells (the CS) with the hospital event.

In this case, the woman needed to be exposed to only one conditioning event. One profoundly frightening event can establish a conditioned fear that may last a lifetime. In other cases, several conditioning trials or events may be necessary for learning. Fortunately, conditioned phobias (persistent, irrational fears) may be eliminated or extinguished using therapy techniques that are also based on Pavlovian conditioning principles (see Chapter 16). A few therapy sessions with the author's student were sufficient to extinguish her fear of the biology laboratory successfully.

The difference between the repeated pairing that Pavlov used on his dogs and the single experience of the young woman illustrates one way in which Pavlovian conditioning experiences may vary. The following discussions deal with other variations on the same theme, exploring both the ways in which learning is acquired and the ways in which it can be extinguished.

6.2b Acquisition of Pavlovian Conditioning

The period during which an organism learns to associate the conditioned stimulus with the unconditioned stimulus is known as the **acquisition** stage of conditioning. Each paired presentation of the two stimuli is called a trial. In cases such as Pavlov's conditioning experiments, these repeated trials strengthen, or reinforce, the association between the CS and the UCS.

Several factors influence how easily a Pavlovian conditioned response is acquired. For example, conditioning takes place more easily when the neutral or conditioned stimulus is clearly different from other stimuli. Had Pavlov signaled the arrival of food by quietly humming a Russian ballad, his dogs might never have perceived the connection, because such sounds are commonplace and might not have been noticed. In contrast, Pavlov's dogs could hardly overlook a ringing bell. This property of the CS is referred to as *stimulus salience*. The more salient the CS, the more readily conditioning is acquired.

The intensity of the UCS will also influence conditioning. Typically, the more intense the UCS, the more readily conditioning takes place.

Another factor influencing acquisition is the frequency with which the CS and UCS are paired. Frequent pairings generally facilitate conditioning. If bells were only occasionally accompanied by feeding, Pavlov's dogs would have been less likely to be conditioned.

Finally, and perhaps most important, is the degree to which the CS and UCS are related. By this we mean the contingency between the CS and the UCS (Bouton, 2016). This important issue demands extra attention.

6.2c Stimulus Contingency and Conditioning

Perhaps the best way to illustrate the concept of stimulus contingency is to review a classic experiment conducted by Robert Rescorla (1968). In Rescorla's experiment, rats were exposed to one of two conditioning procedures: A stimulus-contingent procedure or a noncontingent procedure. In the stimulus-contingent procedure, a series of CSs and UCSs (tones and shocks) were presented, but a UCS (shock) never occurred unless a CS (tone) preceded it. That is, the presentation of the UCS was contingent upon a CS preceding it. Occasionally, however, CSs were presented without being followed by a UCS. This procedure is illustrated in the top part of Figure 6-3.

In the noncontingent procedure, the same number of CS and UCS presentations occurred, however, the presentations of the CS and the UCS were independent. That is, the presentation of a UCS (shock) was not contingent upon the prior occurrence of a CS (tone). Occasionally in this procedure there were close pairings of the CS and the UCS, but these were random occurrences. This procedure is illustrated in the bottom part of Figure 6-3. When Rescorla tested both groups for conditioning, he found that conditioning only occurred for the rats in the stimulus-contingent procedure. No learning occurred with the noncontingent procedure. Rescorla's experiment is important because it demonstrates that more than occasional CS-UCS pairings are necessary for conditioning, as Pavlov and his followers had believed. For example, Pavlov believed

Acquisition In Pavlovian conditioning, the process of learning to associate a conditioned stimulus with an unconditioned stimulus; in operant conditioning, the process of learning to associate responses with a reinforcer or punisher

Figure 6-3 Stimulus Contingency in Pavlovian Conditioning

Stimulus contingency and temporal contiguity occur in the top figure. That is, the occurrence of a UCS is always preceded by the occurrence of a CS. In the bottom figure, there is no contingency. UCS presentations are occasionally paired with CS presentations, but they are not contingent (dependent) on the occurrence of a CS.

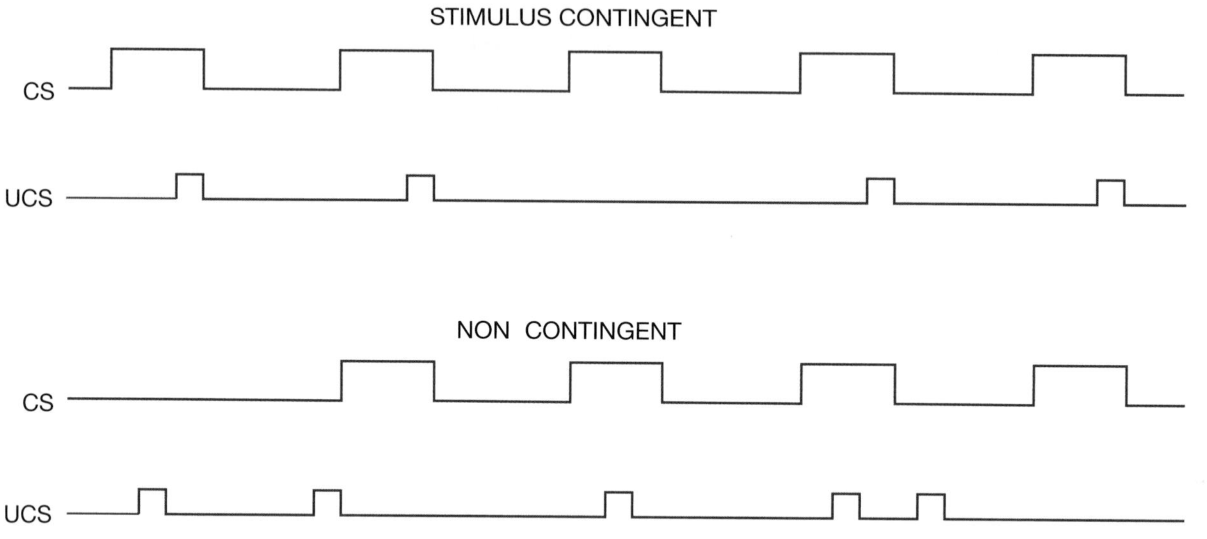

Data from: Figure of "Pairing of the CS with the USC: Four Temporal Relationships in Classical Conditioning" from *The Psychology of Learning* by S. H. Hulse, H. Egenth, and J. Deese, Copyright © 1980 by S. H. Hulce, H. Egeth, and J. Deese.

that occasional pairings of the CS and UCS were sufficient for conditioning, and therefore, some conditioning should have taken place during the noncontingent procedure. In summary, what is necessary for Pavlovian conditioning is that the UCS be contingent (depend) upon the prior occurrence of the CS (Rescorla, 1968).

The idea of stimulus contingency can perhaps be simplified by considering an example from weather forecasting. Imagine two forecasters—one proficient, the other not. Both predict rain on numerous occasions, but rain never occurs without a rain forecast from the proficient weather forcaster. On the other hand, rain is just as likely with or without a rain forecast from the nonproficient forcaster. The proficient forcaster demonstrates a stimulus contingency because rain is contingent upon a forecast for rain. That is, rain doesn't occur unless it is forecast, even though rain doesn't occur after *every* rain forecast. Thus, upon hearing a forecast for rain, you prepare for it. The nonproficient weatherman demonstrates the lack of stimulus contingency because rain is just as likely whether or not it is forecast. As you can guess, you can't depend on the forecast so you don't prepare for rain.

There are several ways in which stimulus contingency can be presented and the ease of conditioning also depends upon them. We next consider several important examples of conditioning trials where the timing of CS and UCS presentations vary.

6.2d CS-UCS Timing and Conditioning

Conditioning occurs most easily when the CS is presented just moments before the UCS appears, and it is continued until after the presentation of the UCS. For example, the bell rings before food is presented to Pavlov's dog, and it continues until the animal begins to salivate as food enters its mouth. This timing sequence is called **delayed conditioning**. The ideal CS-UCS interval in delayed conditioning depends somewhat on the associations to be learned. Typically, CS-UCS delays between 0.5 and 2 seconds are optimal.

Conditioning may still take place when timing is varied. For instance, **simultaneous conditioning** takes place when the conditioned stimulus is presented at the same time as the unconditioned stimulus. Another variation in timing is known as **trace conditioning**. Here, the conditioned stimulus begins and ends before the unconditioned stimulus is presented. Finally, in **backward conditioning** the UCS is presented prior to the CS. Figure 6-4 illustrates all four variations in timing.

Delayed conditioning with short CS-UCS intervals generally yields the most rapid rate of learning. In contrast, the least effective sequence, backward conditioning, usually results in little or no learning. An exception to the rule that the delay between CS and UCS onset must be short is conditioned taste aversions, which were briefly introduced earlier (Bouton, 2016).

Conditioned Taste Aversions

John Garcia was the first to study conditioned taste aversions (sometimes called the Garcia effect) (Garcia, Kimeldorf, & Hunt, 1961). In his experiments, rats were first exposed to a novel taste, in this case, saccharin. Several hours later, the rats were exposed to moderate doses of radiation, which made the rats ill. To test for conditioning, the rats were given access to two drinking spouts, one containing plain water and the other, saccharin solution. Normally rats would prefer the saccharin solution to water, but these conditioned rats did not. The lack of a saccharin preference is called a **conditioned taste aversion**. Conditioned taste aversions reliably occur with long CS-UCS intervals. In numerous experiments, the interval between the CS (the taste of saccharin) and the UCS (illness) has been as long as twenty-four hours (Etscorn & Stephens, 1973).

Conditioned taste aversions are quite common in individuals who have undergone chemo or radiation therapy for cancer. Most often, these aversions develop to novel or rare tastes or smells. The young child of a student in one of the author's classes developed a puzzling aversion to his mother soon after he began a series of radiation treatments. Merely picking up her child would result in his pushing and squirming to get away. On a few occasions, the child even vomited on his mother. It turns out this conditioned aversion was elicited by the smell of a new perfume his mother began wearing soon after his treatment began. After a few treatment sessions, the perfume (a CS) began to elicit nausea and anxiety (CRs) in her child. Because these aversions can last for many years, the perfume was discarded after this author suggested avoiding its use for a few days as an experiment.

Preparedness and Selective Associations

Not all associations are as readily learned as the association between a novel taste or smell and illness. In fact, most learned associations require numerous trials containing CS-UCS presentations. When associations are learned quickly, like conditioned taste aversions, they are considered to be prepared. That is, animals may be prepared biologically to learn certain associations more quickly than others. The survival advantage for animals to quickly learn to avoid foods that have made them ill is fairly clear.

In addition, not all CSs are as easily associated with a UCS as others. For instance, in a similar experiment, Garcia and Koelling (1966) used two types of CSs (taste and an audiovisual stimulus) and two types of UCSs (illness and mild shock) to test for selective associations. Before reading on, consider which associations were easily learned in this experiment.

Delayed Conditioning In Pavlovian conditioning, learning that takes place when the conditioned stimulus is presented just before the unconditioned stimulus is presented and continues until the organism begins responding to the unconditioned stimulus

Simultaneous Conditioning In Pavlovian conditioning, learning that takes place when the conditioned stimulus is presented at the same time as the unconditioned stimulus

Trace Conditioning In Pavlovian conditioning, learning that takes place when presentation of the conditioned stimulus begins and ends before the unconditioned stimulus is presented

Backward Conditioning In Pavlovian conditioning, presenting the unconditioned stimulus prior to the conditioned stimulus (backward conditioning results in little or no conditioning)

Conditioned Taste Aversion A learned aversion to a relatively novel taste or smell that occurs followed by illness or nausea

Figure 6-4 Variations in CS-UCS Presentations and Pavlovian Conditioning

Delayed conditioning generally yields the most rapid conditioning. Backward conditioning rarely results in conditioning.

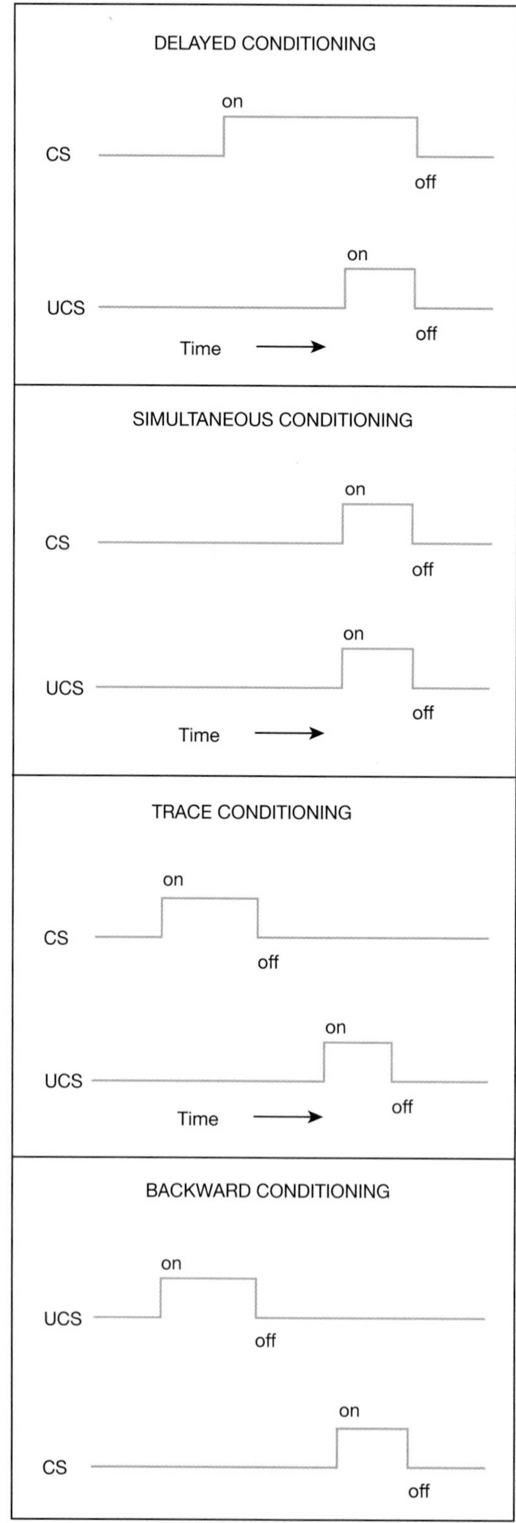

The results of the experiment clearly support the notion of selective associations. Rats easily learned the taste-illness and the audiovisual stimulus-shock associations, but they did not learn either the taste-shock or the audiovisual stimulus-illness associations. Other experiments have also demonstrated that certain CS-UCS associations are more easily learned than others. These learned associations are referred to as selective associations because certain CS-UCS combinations seem to belong together. Some psychologists have speculated that the concepts of preparedness and selective association may account for the relative ease with which people learn certain phobias (exaggerated fears of heights or insects, for example).

Extinction In Pavlovian conditioning, the process by which a conditioned response is eliminated through repeated presentation of the conditioned stimulus without the unconditioned stimulus; in operant conditioning, the process of eliminating a response by discontinuing reinforcement for it

Reinstatement In Pavlovian conditioning, the reappearance of a conditioned response after extinction has taken place

6.2e Extinction and Reinstatement

Would Pavlov's dogs have continued to salivate at the sound of the bell if it were no longer accompanied by food? The answer, of course, is no. They would salivate less and less at the sound until, without any additional presentations of the UCS, they eventually would cease salivating altogether.

This process is called **extinction**. Extinction occurs in Pavlovian conditioning when the CS is repeatedly presented alone, without the UCS. Extinction does not mean that a response is totally stamped out, however. Once extinguished, a conditioned response can undergo **reinstatement** in much less time than it took to acquire it in the first place. For instance, the Pavlovian conditioned response of salivating to a bell may have been established only after numerous pairings or trials. After extinction, however, the conditioned response might be reinstated after only one or two pairings of the bell and the food. In the author's laboratory, tolerance to morphine (a CR) can be extinguished by placing animals in a context (CS) where drugs have repeatedly been administered (UCS) without giving them an injection. Reinstatement of tolerance, and drug-seeking behaviors, can be

Figure 6-5 Acquisition, Extinction, and Reinstatement

This figure demonstrates rapid acquisition of the CR (salivation to the bell) after several trials in which the bell (CS) is paired with food (UCS). During extinction, the UCS no longer follows the CS, and the CR decreases. Later, salivation (CS) occurs following the presentation of a single CS-UCS paring. This is referred to as reinstatement.

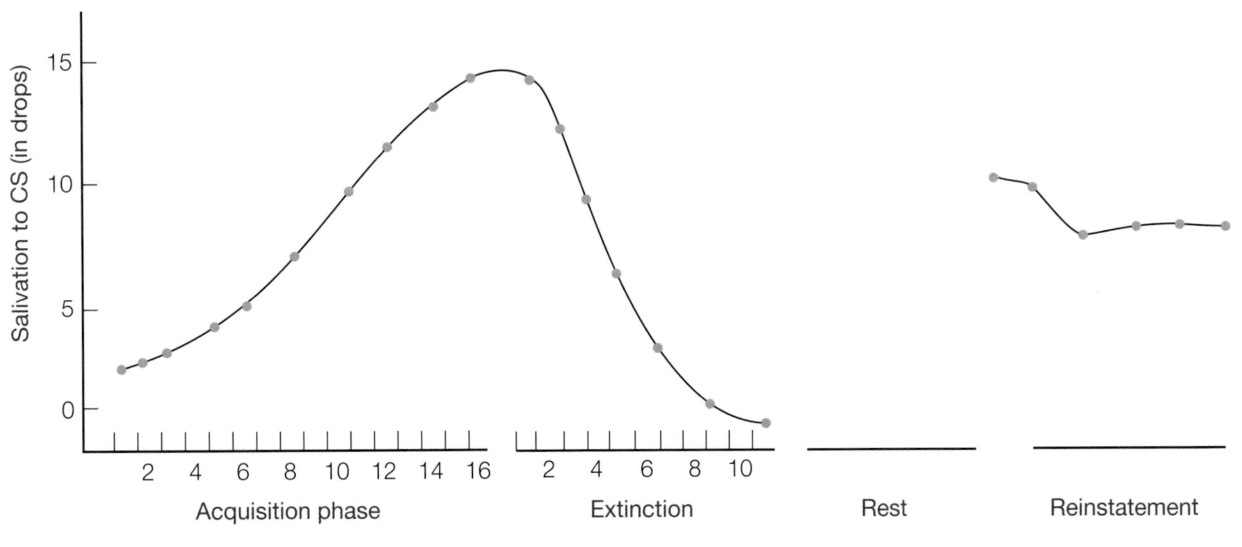

quickly reinstated after one drug injection. This may partially explain why it is so easy for drug addicts to return to drug use after treatment (Widholm, 2010).

As Figure 6-5 demonstrates, reinstatement may bring the conditioned response to a higher level than before extinction.

6.2f Stimulus Generalization and Discrimination

When a response has been conditioned to a particular stimulus, other stimuli may also produce the same response. For example, a war veteran who has been conditioned to dive for cover at the sound of gunfire may show the same response at the sound of a car backfiring. The more similar a new stimulus is to the original CS, the more likely it is to elicit the CR.

When people and other animals respond to similar stimuli without undergoing training for each specific stimulus, it is referred to as stimulus **generalization**. For example, Pavlov's dogs may have salivated to a variety of similar bell sounds, or our biology student may experience anxiety when confronted with other smells similar to the anesthetic used during her surgery—and we hope the bears associate pain with all humans, not just the rangers who administered the shocks.

Just as a learned response may generalize to similar situations, it may also be restricted through the process of **discrimination**. Early in the conditioning process, stimulus generalization may cause a learner to respond to a variety of similar stimuli. With time, however, she learns that only one of these stimuli, the CS, is consistently associated with the UCS. Once the learner discriminates between stimuli, she responds only to the CS. For example, if the war veteran experienced a variety of jarring loud noises without the accompaniment of bullets whizzing through the air, he would soon learn to discriminate between noises like a car backfiring and a gunshot.

6.2g Second-Order Conditioning

We have seen that through Pavlovian conditioning, an organism learns to respond to a previously neutral stimulus, the CS, in a similar way as to the UCS. You might wonder whether the process can be carried one step further. With its newly acquired level, can the CS now be used to condition a response to other stimuli?

The answer is yes. For example, if a salient tone (CS_1) is repeatedly paired with a mild shock (UCS), the tone will come to elicit fear (the CR). Now if a light (CS_2) is paired with the tone (CS_1) for several trials, it will elicit a fear response when presented alone. This process is called **second-order conditioning** (see Figure 6-6). In second-order conditioning, a conditioned stimulus (CS) serves as an unconditioned stimulus (UCS) for the conditioning of a second association.

Second-order conditioning can greatly extend the impact of Pavlovian conditioning on our lives. We have a virtually unlimited capacity to make associations between events. This ability is one reason why therapists treating such things as Pavlovian conditioned phobias often trace convoluted processes by which everyday stimuli come to produce an unreasonable fear in a person (Bouton, 2016).

We have seen that Pavlovian conditioning is a form of associative learning that accounts for certain types of behaviors. However, Pavlovian conditioning does not explain all forms of learning. It is clearly involved in the learning of emotional and motivational states, but it does not by itself account for why you are diligently (we hope) reading this textbook. What is the UCS that automatically causes you to study? Obviously, there is none. To learn why you study and why you engage in a host of other voluntary behaviors, we must examine the second kind of associative learning, operant conditioning.

Generalization Process by which an organism responds to stimuli that are similar to the conditioned stimulus, without undergoing conditioning for each similar stimulus

Discrimination In Pavlovian and operant conditioning, the process by which responses are restricted to specific stimuli; in social psychology, the behavioral consequence of prejudice in which one group is treated differently from another group

Second-Order Conditioning A learned association between two conditioned stimuli (CS_2–CS_1) that can occur following conditioning to CS_1 and an unconditioned stimulus

Figure 6-6 Second-Order Conditioning

In Stage 1, before conditioning, sounding the bell (CS) does not elicit salivation (CR). During conditioning, the CS_1 (bell) is paired with the UCS (food), which leads to conditioned salivation (CR). In Stage 2, before conditioning, a tone (CS_2) does not elicit a response. During conditioning, a tone (CS_2) is paired with the bell (CS_1). After conditioning, the tone (CS_2) will elicit a conditioned response.

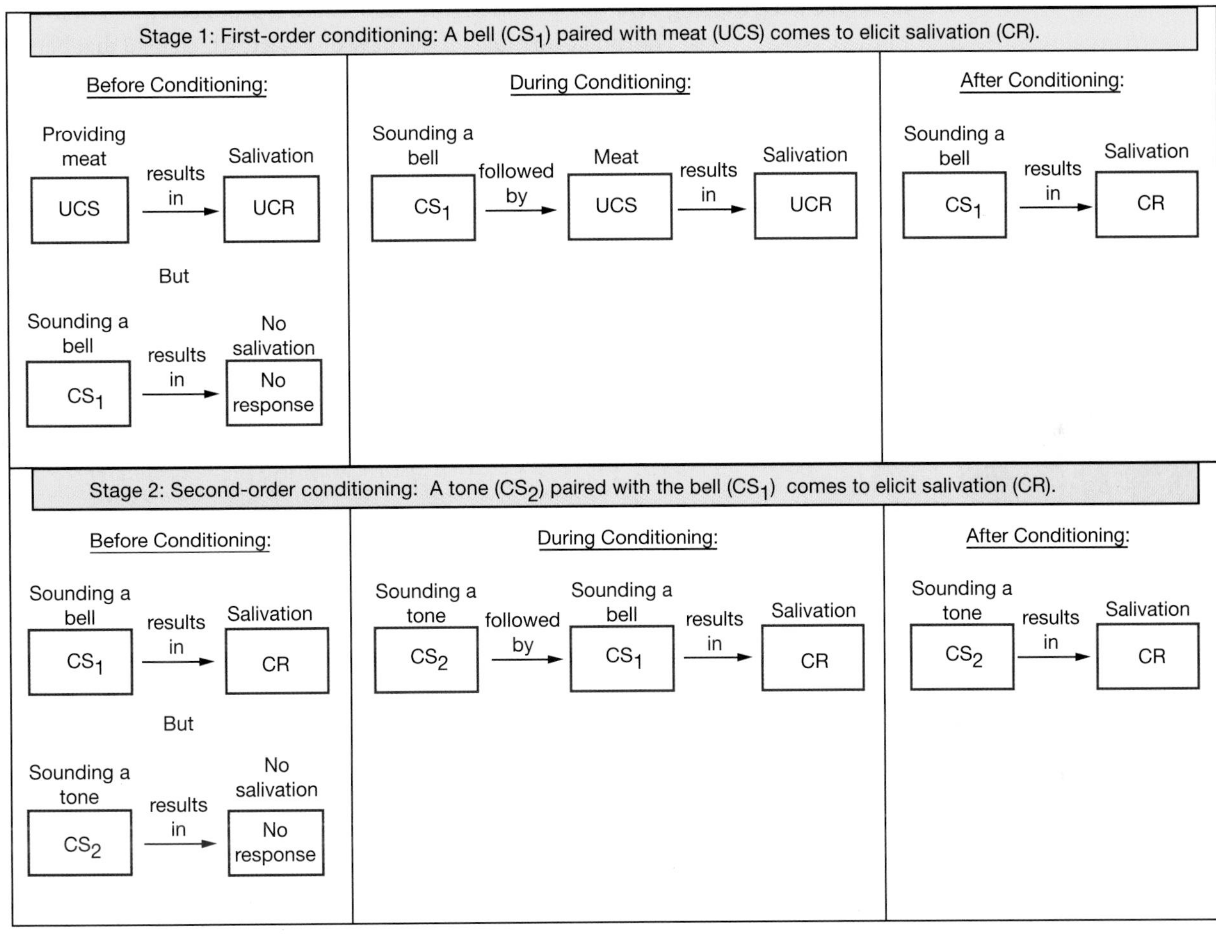

6.3 Operant Conditioning

Operant conditioning takes place when behavior is influenced by its consequences. We can trace the identification of operant conditioning to the American psychologist Edward Thorndike (1911). At about the same time that Pavlov was investigating involuntary, reflexive responses, Thorndike was analyzing the effects of stimuli on voluntary, operant behavior.

Thorndike believed that animals learn to make voluntary responses that help them adapt to their environments. To test his theory, he designed a device called a *puzzle box*. He placed hungry cats in wooden boxes latched from the inside. Outside, he dangled a piece of fish in full view. The cats howled, meowed, clawed, and frantically explored in their attempts to get out of the box. Eventually, they accidentally tripped the latch and gained access to the food. The next time the cats found themselves inside the box, they repeated some of the same trial-and-error behavior as before, but they generally took less time to escape from the box. With each additional trial, the cats' actions became less variable until they learned to trip the latch immediately (Thorndike, 1898).

Thorndike explained his results by suggesting that behavior will be strengthened if it is followed by a positive consequence. Alternatively, behavior that does not lead to a satisfying consequence will be eliminated. Thus some of the cats' behaviors, such as clawing at the walls and howling, ceased to occur because they did not produce food. On the other hand, the latch-tripping behavior was strengthened because it produced fish. On the basis of these observations, Thorndike formulated the **Law of Effect**, which held that behavior followed by a satisfying consequence (effect) would be strengthened. This law, although considerably modified over the years, is the underlying foundation of operant conditioning.

B. F. Skinner (1904–1990), founder of behavior analysis. At Harvard circa 1950 by Silly rabbit, available under a Creative Commons Attribution License CC BY 3.0 at https://commons.wikimedia.org/wiki/File:B.F._Skinner_at_Harvard_circa_1950.jpg

Thorndike's puzzle box illustrates why the term *operant* has been applied to this type of learning. His cats learned to *operate* on their environment in a manner that resulted in satisfaction. Another way of saying the same thing is that their behaviors were instrumental in achieving a positive outcome. Thus, this conditioning model is sometimes called *instrumental conditioning*.

Thorndike's pioneering efforts were followed by the monumental contributions of Harvard psychologist B. F. Skinner. Skinner's research spanned several decades, and it provided much of what we know about operant conditioning. Perhaps the best way to become acquainted with the principles governing operant conditioning is to take a close look at one of Skinner's basic demonstrations.

6.3a Operant Conditioning in a Skinner Box

A hungry rat is placed in a box similar to that shown in Figure 6-7. This chamber, called a *Skinner box*, is empty except for a bar protruding from one wall with a small food dish directly beneath it.

After a short time in a Skinner box, the rat begins to examine its surroundings. As it explores, it eventually approaches the bar. When the rat is near the bar, a food pellet is released into the dish. The next bar approach followed immediately by food delivery occurs after some additional exploration. Soon the rat spends most of its time around the bar. Next the rat must contact and exert some force on the bar before food is delivered. As with approaching the bar, this activity soon comes to predominate. The operant response of bar pressing is "selected" by the food it produces, and the rate of pressing steadily increases.

Response Strength or Response Selection?

The concept of selection needs more elaboration because it is a part of Thorndike's original Law of Effect that has been changed considerably. Thorndike thought that reinforcement strengthened bonds or associations between behavior and the reinforcer—thus the term *reinforcement*. Currently, psychologists view the reinforcement process as one of selection. That is, reinforcement acts to select or guide behavior (Skinner, 1981). The rat in Skinner's box spends most of its time pressing the lever not because the association between lever pressing and food was strengthened but because it is the effective response and the other ineffective responses have dropped out. A statement made by Michelangelo when asked how he produced such marvelous statues illustrates this idea: He stated that he simply removed that part of the stone that was not the statue. The concept of selection as used here shares many features with the term *natural selection*. While natural selection is viewed as operating over successive generations, response selection operates over the lifetime of the individual. Both result in adaptations to environmental changes.

Law of Effect Behavior followed by reinforcement will be strengthened, whereas behavior followed by punishment will be weakened (theory, originally proposed by Edward Thorndike, that is the foundation of the operant conditioning theory)

Figure 6-7 A Skinner Box Used for Operant Conditioning

Measuring Operant Behavior

Perhaps the most common measure of operant behavior is its rate of occurrence. Skinner designed a device called a cumulative recorder that is used to measure operant behavior in a laboratory environment. A recording pen rests on paper that moves slowly at a fixed rate. Each time an animal makes an operant response, such as pressing a bar, the pen moves up a fixed distance and then continues on its horizontal path. The more frequently an animal responds, the more rapidly the pen climbs up the chart. The result, called a **cumulative record**, is a reliable measure of operant behavior.

Discriminative Stimuli

You may have wondered about the light above the bar. Skinner used it to introduce a new variable, setting the dispenser to deliver food only when both the bar is pressed and the light is on. When the light is off, no food is delivered. Under these conditions of *differential reinforcement* (that is, reinforcement which takes place only under certain circumstances), the rat soon learns to make the appropriate discrimination: It presses the bar only when the light is on. In this circumstance, the light serves as a **discriminative stimulus**, that is, a stimulus that controls the response by signaling the availability of reinforcement.

Cumulative Record A chart recording of operant responses over time; the time increment is indicated along the horizontal axis (as response rate increases, the slope of the record increases)

Discriminative Stimulus In operant conditioning, a stimulus that controls a response by signaling the availability of reinforcement

Figure 6-8 A Cumulative Record

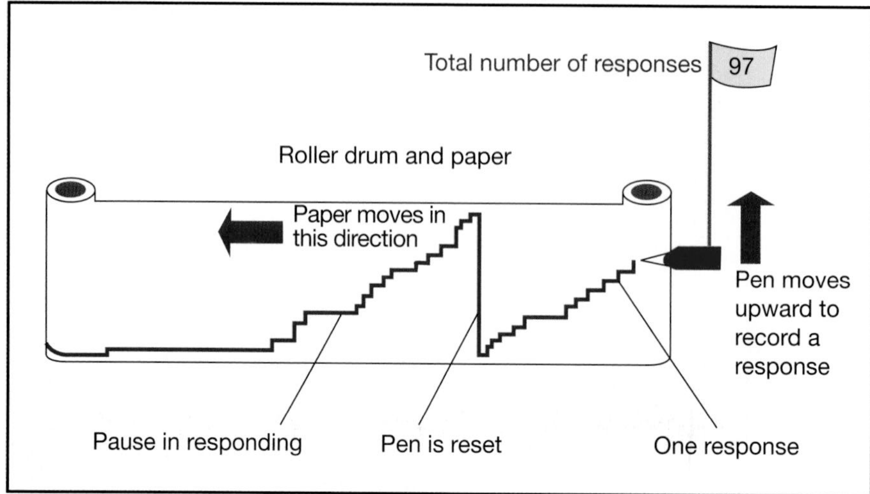

Skinner's experiments illustrate the primary features of operant conditioning. An animal's behavior is selected or controlled by the immediate consequences of that behavior. For Skinner's rats, bar pressing was controlled by the delivery of food. Unlike Pavlovian conditioning, in which the learner passively responds to a stimulus, operant conditioning occurs when the learner acts on the environment as a result of the consequences for that act. Sometimes response consequences are quite apparent as with Skinner's example. However, consequences may be much more subtle, such as an approving nod by a parent for acting politely or a change in facial expression by a friend for a compliment.

6.3b Reinforcement

Reinforcement In operant conditioning, any procedure in which an event following a specific response increases the probability that the response will occur

Positive Reinforcement In operant conditioning, any stimulus presented after a response that increases the probability of the response

Negative Reinforcement In operant conditioning, any stimulus that increases the probability of a response through its removal (For example, pounding on the wall [operant behavior] may be maintained by the termination of a loud noise [negative reinforcer] in an adjoining room.)

Operant conditioning stresses the effects of consequences on behavior. These consequences are described as reinforcement (or a reinforcer) and punishment (or a punisher). **Reinforcement** is defined as a stimulus whose delivery following a response leads to an increase in either the frequency or probability of that response. Punishment, on the other hand, is defined as a stimulus whose delivery following a response results in a decrease in the frequency or probability of that response. We shall first examine procedures used to study the effects of reinforcement, and then we will discuss punishment.

In studying operant conditioning, researchers have experimented with different types of reinforcers and different schedules for delivering reinforcement. Their findings help to explain how and why operant conditioning takes place.

Positive and Negative Reinforcement

Positive reinforcement is any stimulus presented following a response that increases the probability of the response. **Negative reinforcement** is a stimulus that increases the probability of a response through its removal when the desired response is made. Introductory psychology students frequently misunderstand negative reinforcement, often confusing it with punishment by assuming that it is used to stop a behavior. In fact, quite the opposite is true: Negative reinforcement, like positive reinforcement, increases the occurrence of a desired behavior. It is important to remember that the terms positive and negative refer only to whether a stimulus is presented (positive) or removed (negative), not its hedonic value. Since the previous examples in this chapter have illustrated positive reinforcement, we look here at some examples of negative reinforcement and the procedures used to study them (Bouton, 2016).

Escape and Avoidance Procedures

A rat is placed in a Skinner box, the floor of which consists of a metal grid that can be electrified. A mild current is activated. As the rat tries to escape, it bumps into a bar, and the shocking current immediately ceases. The pattern is repeated several times until the rat remains poised by the bar, ready to press it at the first jolt. This form of learning, called **escape conditioning**, clearly involves negative reinforcement. The shock, an unpleasant stimulus, may be terminated only by the appropriate operant response. The removal of, or the escape from, the shock thus acts as the reinforcer for the bar press response. Taking aspirin to alleviate headache pain is essentially escape behavior maintained by the termination of the headache.

(Shutterstock)

People who live in western Oregon are accustomed to carrying umbrellas. Out-of-staters learn to always have one on hand on a cloudy day (avoidance conditioning). Much of human behavior is maintained by avoidance conditioning.

The escape conditioning procedure can be modified slightly by introducing a warning signal that allows the rat to avoid the shock altogether. If the light goes on a few seconds prior to each shock, the rat soon learns to respond to this discriminative stimulus by pressing the bar in time to avoid the shock. This type of learning is called **avoidance conditioning**.

These examples bring to mind many parallels in our own lives. For instance, if you live in a dormitory or an apartment building, you may find that you pound on the wall of an adjoining room to get your noisy neighbor to quiet down. Your pounding behavior is thus maintained by negative reinforcement, the removal of the noise. People who live in western Oregon are accustomed to carrying umbrellas. Out-of-staters or optimistic natives have had to experience getting drenched while running back to fetch an umbrella (escape conditioning) before learning to have one always on hand on a cloudy day (avoidance conditioning). Much of human behavior is maintained by avoidance conditioning. In fact, our punitive legal system is a set of aversive consequences established to keep us in line. As long as we behave lawfully, we avoid these aversive consequences. You may attend your classes not because of positive reinforcement but to avoid the aversive consequences of failing exams. We pay taxes promptly to avoid the aversive consequences of not paying them on time, and we obtain a flu shot to avoid the consequences of getting the flu.

Escape Conditioning In operant conditioning, learning that takes place when an organism performs a response that will terminate an aversive stimulus

Avoidance Conditioning In operant conditioning, the learning of a response to a discriminative stimulus that allows an organism to avoid exposure to an aversive stimulus

Primary and Conditioned Reinforcers

Primary reinforcers usually satisfy a biologically based need, such as hunger, thirst, sex, or sleep. However, some social events like parental contact may be primary reinforcers. It is obvious why food, water, sex, or sleep reinforce. However, why do things like money reinforce? The answer lies in the concept of conditioned reinforcement. A variety of neutral stimuli associated with primary reinforcement can also become **conditioned reinforcers**.

Primary Reinforcer In operant conditioning, a stimulus that satisfies a biologically based drive or need, such as hunger, thirst, or sleep

Conditioned Reinforcer A stimulus that takes on reinforcing properties after being associated with a primary reinforcer

BVT Lab

Flashcards are available for this chapter at **www.BVTLab.com**.

Much of our behavior is influenced more by conditioned reinforcement than by biologically significant primary reinforcement. Words of praise, pats on the back, good grades, and money are some of the conditioned reinforcers that influence our lives.

We have seen that conditioned reinforcers acquire their reinforcing properties through association with a primary reinforcer, but what is the critical element that determines this association? For many years, psychologists believed that the strength of conditioned reinforcement depended simply on the frequency with which it had been paired with primary reinforcement (Bouton, 2016).

Research suggests otherwise. Instead of the frequency of pairings, the crucial factor seems to be the reliability with which the conditioned reinforcer predicts the availability of the primary reinforcer (Rose & Fantino, 1978). For example, a coin that always produces raisins when inserted in a "chimp-o-mat" quickly becomes a strong conditioned reinforcer; coins that are less predictive of raisins are much weaker conditioned reinforcers for the chimp, no matter how often they have been paired with raisins. Thus, conditioned reinforcers acquire their reinforcing properties just like Pavlovian conditioned stimuli: Through stimulus associations. Money is a powerful conditioned reinforcer for most of us because of its strong association with things we want.

Continuous Versus Partial Reinforcement

In addition to the type of reinforcer used, another factor that influences the effectiveness of reinforcement is the consistency with which a behavior is reinforced.

In laboratory demonstrations of operant conditioning, a behavior may be reinforced every time it occurs. This method is called a **continuous reinforcement schedule**. For instance, a rat receives a food pellet each time it presses a bar. Outside the laboratory, particularly in the everyday lives of humans, continuous reinforcement is unusual. For example, smiling at the food server in your college cafeteria does not always produce an extra-large helping of food, nor does getting out of the house twenty minutes early always ensure your favorite parking space on campus. These behaviors persist, however, because they are sometimes reinforced. A **partial reinforcement schedule** exists when behavior is reinforced only part of the time. There are striking differences between the effects of continuous and partial reinforcement schedules on behavior.

Continuous reinforcement schedules almost always produce the highest rate of acquisition of a new behavior. For example, a rat learns to bar-press most rapidly when it receives food each time it makes the appropriate response. However, what happens when reinforcement is withdrawn? Extinction begins, and the rat quickly ceases its bar-pressing behavior.

Behaviors that are acquired on partial instead of continuous schedules of reinforcement are slower to be established. However, these behaviors are remarkably more persistent when no reinforcement is provided. For example, a rat accustomed to only intermittent reinforcement for bar pressing continues to press long after the food dispenser has run dry. This is particularly true when the partial reinforcement is delivered in an unpredictable fashion. This phenomenon is known as the **partial reinforcement effect** (Bouton, 2016).

Continuous Reinforcement Schedule In operant conditioning, the presentation of a reinforcer for each occurrence of a specific behavior

Partial Reinforcement Schedule In operant conditioning, a schedule that reinforces behavior only part of the time—for example, a ratio or interval schedule

Partial Reinforcement Effect Behaviors that are acquired on partial instead of continuous reinforcement schedules tend to be established more slowly but are more persistent when no reinforcement is provided

Partial Reinforcement Schedules

Partial reinforcement is typically delivered in either of two basic ways—ratio or interval schedules. On a *ratio schedule*, a certain percentage of responses receives reinforcement. For instance, a slot machine in a casino might be programmed to provide some kind of payoff on 10 percent of all plays. An *interval schedule*, in contrast, is time-based: Subjects are reinforced for their first response after a certain amount of time has passed, regardless

Figure 6-9 Schedules of Reinforcement

Stylized cumulative records from several common schedules of reinforcement: Panel A shows a fixed ratio schedule with characteristic pauses in responding; panel B illustrates a variable ratio schedule with typical high response rates; panel C illustrates the scalloped pattern of responding observed on fixed interval schedules; and panel D shows the stable pattern of responding found on variable interval schedules.

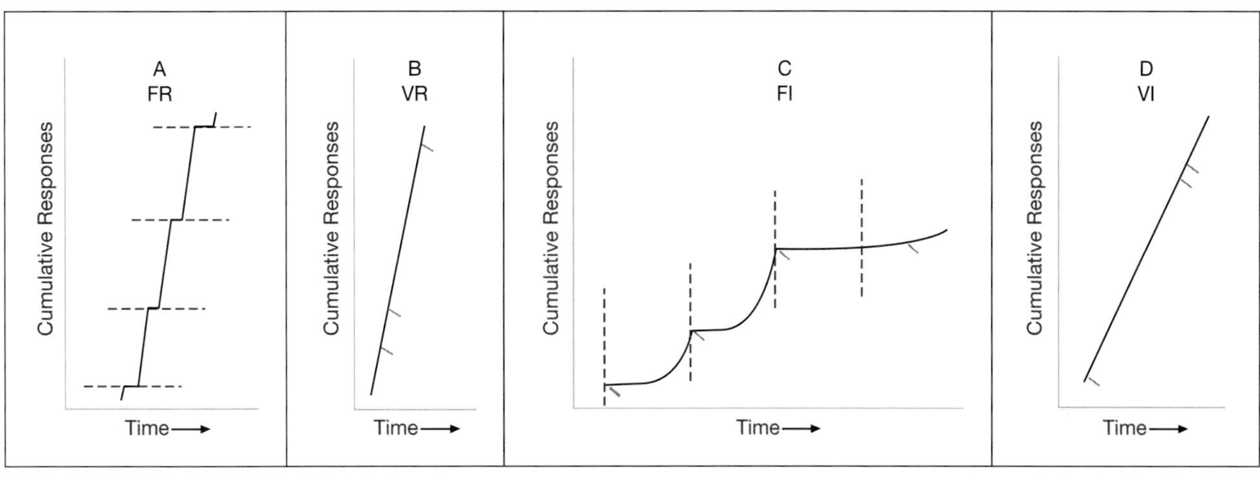

of how many responses might occur during that period. An example of an interval schedule is finally getting to speak to your friend after repeated dialing of her phone number resulted in busy signals, or cruising in a parking lot for a vacant space. In many natural environments, an animal's foraging is maintained by an interval schedule. Birds searching for food find it after the passage of variable amounts of time, not after a specific number of attempts.

Both ratio and interval schedules may be either variable or fixed. *Variable schedule* reinforcement is delivered unpredictably, with the amount of time or number of responses required varying randomly around an average. In contrast, *fixed schedule* reinforcement is always delivered after a constant number of responses or a fixed interval of time. These categories combine to form four basic partial reinforcement schedules: fixed ratio, variable ratio, fixed interval, and variable interval (see Figure 6-9).

Fixed Ratio Schedule On a **fixed ratio (FR) schedule**, reinforcement occurs after a fixed number of responses. For example, a rat receives a food pellet after twelve bar presses, and a strawberry picker receives a dollar after filling twelve small boxes with berries. Both are on an FR-12 schedule. This schedule tends to produce rather high rates of responding. The faster the rat bar-presses, the more pellets it gets; and the quicker the strawberry picker works, the more money she or he earns. Fixed ratio schedules are also used in programmed instruction where students proceed at their own pace and receive feedback after each section of work is completed. Programmed instruction is often quite successful in generating high rates of academic work (Lee & Belfiore, 1997). The fixed ratio schedule is illustrated in panel A of Figure 6-9.

Fixed Ratio (FR) Schedule
Partial reinforcement schedule in operant conditioning in which reinforcement occurs after a fixed number of responses

This fact explains why some factories and businesses pay workers (like the strawberry picker) on a piecework basis. However, there are some limitations to this practice. For example, if workers in an automobile assembly plant were paid only according to the

Variable Ratio (VR) Schedule Partial reinforcement schedule in operant conditioning in which reinforcement is provided after an average of a specific number of responses occur

Fixed Interval (FI) Schedule Partial reinforcement schedule in operant conditioning in which reinforcement is provided for the first response after a specified time has elapsed

Variable Interval (VI) Schedule Partial reinforcement schedule in operant conditioning in which opportunities for reinforcement occur at variable time intervals

number of cars they ran through the assembly line, the quality of their work might suffer. Another potential limitation of the fixed ratio schedule is that people and other animals often pause briefly after reinforcement is delivered, probably because they have learned that their next few responses will not be reinforced. The pause following reinforcement on a fixed ratio schedule is termed *postreinforcement pause*. Postreinforcement pause may be one reason payday typically occurs on Friday.

Variable Ratio Schedule A **variable ratio (VR) schedule** of reinforcement also requires the occurrence of a certain number of responses before reinforcement is delivered. Unlike a fixed ratio schedule, however, the number of responses required for each reinforcer varies. For example, a rat on a VR-6 schedule receives a food pellet on the average of every six bar presses, but any given reinforcer may require fewer or more than six responses. The pattern of behavior maintained by a VR schedule is illustrated in panel B of Figure 6.9.

Variable ratio schedules produce high response rates. Furthermore, because of the unpredictable nature of reinforcement, there is typically no postreinforcement pause; it is possible that reinforcement will occur on the very next response. Behavior that is maintained on this schedule is often very slow to extinguish.

Gamblers are very familiar with variable ratio schedules. For example, a person who always bets on 13 at the roulette wheel is on a VR-38 schedule (the wheel has thirty-six numbers plus 0 and 00). On average, 13 comes up every thirty-eight spins. However, during a hot streak, 13 might occur three times in twenty spins (of course, it also might not occur at all). Similarly, a slot machine may be rigged to pay off once every twenty times a coin is deposited, on the average (a VR-20 schedule). The gambler does not know when it will return a few of the coins it has swallowed. It is the unpredictable, highly variable nature of these payoffs that makes gambling so compelling to some people (Haw, 2008). In fact, gamblers often put in much more than they get back—a result that doesn't occur on interval schedules. Experimental animals also show the tendency to respond at very high rates on VR schedules, sometimes at the cost of forgoing the food they've earned on previous ratios.

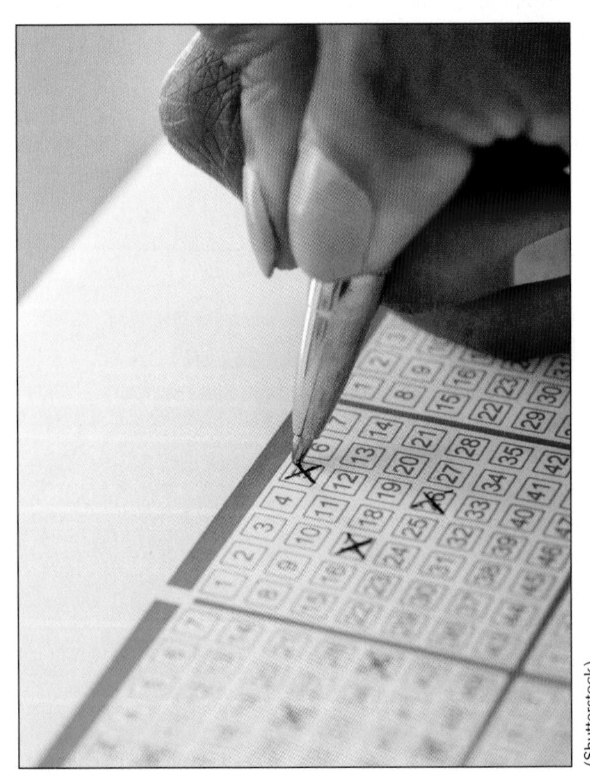
(Shutterstock)

A woman marks up lottery tickets. Gamblers do not know when the lottery tickets will pay off. Their gambling behavior is maintained by a variable ratio schedule of reinforcement.

Fixed Interval Schedule On a **fixed interval (FI) schedule**, reinforcement is provided for the first response after a specified period of time has elapsed. For example, a rat on an FI-30 schedule, whose bar press has just produced a food pellet, will receive its next reinforcer the first time it bar-presses after thirty seconds have elapsed.

The response rates of animals on FI schedules quickly adjust to this contingency. Because no reinforcements occur for a period of time, no matter how often an animal responds, it typically stops working after reinforcement is delivered and then begins to respond toward the end of the interval. Thus this pattern of reinforcement tends to produce regular, recurring episodes of inactivity followed by short bursts of responding. This is illustrated in panel C of Figure 6-9.

Variable Interval Schedule Finally, a **variable interval (VI) schedule** involves variable time intervals between opportunities for reinforcement. Thus an animal on a VI-45 schedule might receive reinforcement for a response after thirty seconds have elapsed, then after sixty seconds, and then after forty-five seconds. This schedule averages out to reinforcement every forty-five seconds. See panel D of Figure 6-9.

As you might guess, the random, unpredictable occurrence of reinforcement on this schedule tends to produce more steady rates of responding than fixed interval schedules. The steady, persistent pattern of behavior maintained by VI schedules makes them quite useful to researchers studying the effects of other variables on behavior. For example, a researcher interested in examining the effects of certain drugs on behavior might examine the pattern of responding on a VI schedule both before and after drug administration.

Applying Reinforcement Schedules

We have seen that partial reinforcement affects behavior differently from continuous reinforcement and that reinforcement schedules may further influence performance. What are the practical implications of these findings?

An Application of Reinforcement Schedules

Assume that you are the parent of a young boy who has not yet learned to clean his room each day. What type of reinforcement schedule(s) would be most effective in establishing room-cleaning behaviors? Would you use the same schedule throughout training? Think about these questions before reading on.

The best way to establish a daily room-cleaning routine would be to use a continuous reinforcement schedule. During the initial stages of training, you would reinforce your son each time he completed his task, perhaps with points that could either be turned in for little payoffs (like reading a story) or accumulated for more sizable prizes like a trip to the zoo. It would also be important to praise the boy for each good job and perhaps display a chart of the child's performance. Associating the chart and praise with other reinforcers allows them to become conditioned reinforcers.

You cannot monitor and reinforce this behavior indefinitely, however. Once the room-cleaning behavior is established, you could begin shifting to a partial reinforcement schedule, reinforcing the behavior only some of the time. A variable ratio schedule would be the logical choice since it is very resistant to extinction and it is response, not time, dependent. Gradually, you would make the schedule more demanding until just a few words of praise delivered now and then would be sufficient.

Partial reinforcement can be a good way to maintain a child's room cleaning, but it may contribute to less desirable behavior in some circumstances. Consider the case in which a father tells his young daughter that she cannot leave their yard unless accompanied by an adult. Since children typically test the limits, the little girl sneaks over to her friend's house at the first opportunity, a lapse that the father overlooks because he is too busy. In this manner, a pattern of inconsistency is established, with the child discovering she can get away with inappropriate behavior at least some of the time. These unpredictable victories over the system can be powerfully reinforcing. In essence, parents who inconsistently enforce rules are training their children to be gamblers. Like Atlantic City slot machine players, these children are conditioned to keep pushing the button until the inevitable payoff is provided.

The reinforcement schedules we have been discussing share a common assumption: The learner will produce the desired behavior so that it can be reinforced. In operant conditioning, however, it is sometimes difficult to get an animal (humans included) to make the initial correct response so that it can be reinforced. The next section discusses methods for increasing the probability that a desired response will occur.

6.3c Reinforcing the Initial Operant Response

In operant conditioning, many responses occur spontaneously. For example, rats placed in Skinner boxes invariably get around to pressing the bar during the course of their explorations. In other circumstances, however, the behavior may not occur without some additional help. For instance, no matter how many times you say "roll over" to your untrained dog, the odds are remote that it will perform the trick so that you can reinforce it. Some special techniques can be used to encourage the desired response, however.

Verbal Instruction

Sometimes desired behavior could be established by simply describing the appropriate response. Parents and educators often use this method. When you learned to drive, most of your instruction was probably verbal: Someone sat next to you and told you when to turn, brake, and accelerate. Verbal instruction is also provided in writing. Perhaps you first learned to operate a computer from a set of instruction manuals.

Shaping

You may have wondered how researchers trained rats to press levers in several of the experiments already discussed in this chapter. The procedure used is referred to as shaping. **Shaping** involves a systematic process whereby responses that are increasingly similar to the desired behavior are reinforced step by step until finally the desired behavior occurs. For example, hungry rats are first reinforced for being near the lever. Later they must touch it, and finally they are required to exert sufficient force on the lever to operate it.

Shaping is especially effective for establishing novel behaviors. For instance, the learning of speech by a young child is shaped from nonsensical babbling to closer and closer approximations of the appropriate sounds of words. The reinforcement during this process may be as subtle as a change in facial expression of the parent. Later, reinforcement may be the appropriate response of the listener to a command.

Many therapists use shaping to obtain desirable behavior in emotionally disturbed children and adults. An example of this is the case of a nine-year-old boy with autism, a profound emotional disability that blocks normal patterns of social interaction. His parents consulted a behavior therapist, who used shaping to establish social behavior. At first, the boy learned to obtain candy from a machine that was activated remotely. (Since no social pressures were imposed, this procedure was nonthreatening.) The next step was more complex. The boy was placed in a room that contained a variety of toys, the candy machine, and another boy about his age, a confederate of the therapist. The ensuing behavior was viewed through a one-way glass.

The disturbed youth made no overtures to the other boy. However, each time he looked at him, the therapist activated the candy dispenser. Once this behavior was established, the next step was to reinforce the boy when he took a step toward the other boy. In this fashion the autistic boy gradually learned to stand next to his would-be playmate and then to interact with him. (Even a normally undesirable act like grabbing a toy from him was acceptable at first because it represented an interaction.) Gradually, over a period of weeks, a number of social behaviors were shaped, and eventually the candy machine became a less important reinforcer than the other boy. Shaping is commonly used to teach autistic children a variety of new behaviors as well as to enhance their social skills (Noell, Call, & Ardoin, 2011).

Shaping In operant conditioning, a technique in which responses that are increasingly similar to the desired behavior are reinforced, step by step, until the desired behavior occurs

Modeling

Another technique for producing a new operant response is through modeling. **Modeling** involves demonstrating the desired behavior to the learner. Many athletic skills, such as diving, hitting a tennis ball, and riding a skateboard, are more easily learned by watching someone else or watching your own performance on video. Videotape has been successfully used with both adults and children to model a variety of skills including reading (Dowrick, 1999; Dowrick, Kim-Rupnow, & Power, 2006). Modeling can teach a wide range of behaviors, undesirable as well as desirable. For instance, a young child who observes a parent using physical punishment may behave more aggressively, even when punished for it.

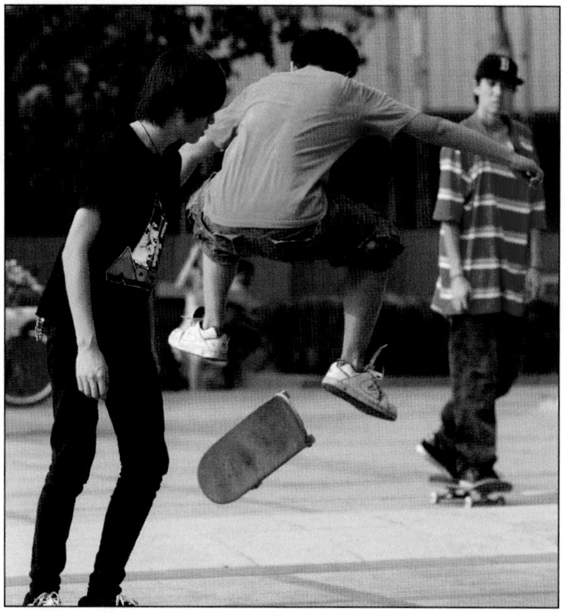

(Shutterstock)

Modeling involves demonstrating the desired behavior to the learner. Many athletic skills, such as diving, hitting a tennis ball, and skateboarding, are more easily learned by watching someone else.

Physical Guidance

The best strategy for training a dog to roll over is to guide compliance to the command by gently manipulating the animal. As the dog scrambles back onto its feet, you can then provide a reinforcer such as a piece of meat or a pat on the head. After several sequences of command, manipulation, and reinforcement, the animal should begin to roll over on command without any manipulation.

This same technique might be used to train a child to drink from a cup. A parent's hand over a child's hand holding a cup can guide the child through the appropriate sequence of lifting the cup to the mouth. Each response is then reinforced by both the parent's praise and the act of drinking (it is a good idea to offer an especially tasty liquid in this initial training).

So far we've discussed the application of reinforcement to shape and increase rates of behavior; now we turn our attention to the use of punishment. From the very earliest experimental studies, its use and effectiveness have been controversial; however, because punishment is so frequently applied as a learning procedure, it deserves our careful consideration here.

6.3d Punishment and Operant Behavior

Certainly punishment is widespread—from spanking misbehaving children to keeping students after school, meting out traffic fines, and incarcerating people in prisons. However, the fact that many people and institutions rely on punishment to control behavior does not necessarily mean that it is more effective than reinforcement. People have long debated the relative advantages and disadvantages of reinforcing desirable behavior versus punishing undesirable acts. There is no simple answer. Nevertheless, research has provided ample data that can help us make better informed choices as we confront this issue in our own lives. We begin by defining punishment.

Punishment (or a *punisher*) is defined as a stimulus whose delivery following a response results in a decrease in the frequency or probability of that response. We often think of punishment as an unpleasant or aversive stimulus, such as a spanking. However, punishment may also involve the withdrawal of positive reinforcers—such as playtime,

Modeling Learning process in which an individual acquires a behavior by observing someone else performing that behavior; also known as *observational learning*

Punishment A procedure in which the presentation of a stimulus following a response leads to a decrease in the strength or frequency of the response

watching TV, money, or the use of the family car. Students sometimes confuse this second form of punishment with the process of extinction discussed earlier. The two are quite different. For example, if we wished to stop a child's temper tantrums through extinction, we would simply withhold our attention (which presumably is the reinforcer of this behavior). In contrast, modifying this behavior through punishment might be accomplished by withdrawing TV-watching privileges each time a temper tantrum occurred.

6.3e Limitations of Punishment

Extinction of Punished Responses

One limitation of punishment is its long-term effectiveness. In some cases, punishment suppresses the unwanted behavior for a short time, but does not eliminate it. In fact, there is ample evidence that suppressed behavior may reemerge when the prospect of punishment is gone or sharply curtailed. To eliminate a response with punishment, the contingency between the response and punishment must be maintained. When punishment is discontinued, the response emerges. This is referred to as *extinction* of punishment. This is also true for reinforcement. When either reinforcement or punishment is discontinued, responding returns to its prereinforcement or pre-punishment level (Bouton, 2016). For example, a child who is punished by a parent each time she raids the cookie jar will probably learn to suppress this behavior. However, if punishment hasn't occurred for some time, she is likely to raid again.

Emotional Side Effects of Punishment

Another potential problem is that punishment may produce undesirable emotional side effects such as fear and aggression. This outcome is particularly true when punishment is severe. For example, a child who receives constant, severe punishment from a parent may learn to fear that parent. The process by which this fear response is learned is Pavlovian conditioning. In this case, a parent who consistently punishes may become a conditioned stimulus for fear. The subject will learn to withhold the punished behavior but also learns to fear the punishing situation. This could lead to problems interacting with the parent that may generalize to other relationships. In fact, punishment may induce aggression against the punisher (Gershoff & Bitensky, 2007).

The negative emotional effects of punishment are often generalized to related behaviors. Thus, a child who is singled out for harsh punishment in one class may begin to react negatively to school in general. In contrast, people who are reinforced for desirable behavior generally feel good about themselves, are motivated to perform well, and are optimistic about future endeavors that they anticipate will lead to additional positive consequences. Similarly, the child who is punished by being sent to his or her room, having to write repeatedly on the chalkboard, or having to run extra laps on the track may actually be learning to associate these events and places with punishment and react negatively to them on later occasions.

Physical Punishment and Modeling

Children are often punished by physical means, such as slapping or spanking. Considerable evidence suggests that youngsters who are punished physically learn to model or imitate these aggressive acts and often become more aggressive in their interactions with others

(Bandura & Walters, 1959; Kuppens, Grietens, Onghena, & Michiels, 2009). Thus, parents who spank or hit misbehaving children may be teaching them more than is intended, namely, that physical aggression is acceptable and that it typically gets the aggressor what they want.

BVT Lab

Visit www.BVTLab.com to explore the student resources available for this chapter.

6.3f Advantages of Punishment

While it is important to be aware of the limitations of punishment, most psychologists do not advocate total abolition of all punishment for controlling or modifying behavior. Although reinforcement is preferable in most cases, punishment is sometimes essential as a way to suppress undesirable actions so that a desirable alternative behavior may occur.

For instance, assume you are the parent of a young child who constantly strays out of your yard. To avoid establishing a pattern of partial reinforcement caused by inconsistent punishment, you might decide to wait until the day occurs when she stays home, so you can reinforce her. Theoretically, this idea is a good one. However, the behavior might not occur spontaneously, and in the meantime your child might get lost or hit by a car.

In other instances, punishment is desirable because reinforcement of an alternative behavior is impractical. For example, punishment may be the only practical method to train your dog to refrain from barking at night. The immediate and consistent application of punishment can be very effective here.

In such cases, it is necessary to apply sufficient punishment to suppress an unwanted behavior. At the same time, you would also reinforce the desired behavior with appropriate reinforcement.

Immediate Application of Punishment

Punishment, like reinforcement, works best when it immediately follows behavior. Perhaps one of the more common violators of this rule is the parent who says to a misbehaving child, "Wait until Dad (or Mom) comes home." This long delay dramatically reduces the effectiveness of punishment.

Sometimes, however, punishment cannot be delivered immediately. For instance, punishing a child who intentionally emits distracting noises during a church service would disrupt the service for everyone. In cases like this, it would be valuable to have established a verbal command such as "stop," as a conditioned punisher. Conditioned punishment is discussed below.

Consistent Application of Punishment

A second point that should be remembered in applying punishment is that it loses effectiveness if it is inconsistent. Inconsistencies may occur over time or from one person to another. In the first case, inappropriate behavior may be punished in one instance and ignored the next. As we noted earlier, such inconsistencies place the learner on a variable ratio schedule of reinforcement (not punishment), a practice that can produce remarkable persistence of undesirable behavior. The dog owner who only occasionally punishes his barking dog, or the parent who only punishes nagging inconsistently, may be doing just this.

Inconsistencies from person to person are quite common. Two parents often have differing concepts of discipline. Children in this type of home environment frequently learn to play one parent against the other, a situation that can teach the child to manipulate others for personal gain.

Intensity of Punishment

Punishment needs to be strong enough to accomplish the desired goal of suppressing undesirable behavior, but it should not be too severe. You probably know some people who believe that if a little bit of punishment works, a lot will work even better. Unfortunately, this philosophy often results in negative side effects such as fear and aggression. Moderate punishment, especially when it is designed to be informative, can redirect behavior so that new responses can be reinforced. When punishment is severe, however, the intent is more likely to be retribution than a redirection of behavior.

In most circumstances, physical punishment should be avoided. Instead of getting a spanking, a misbehaving child could be sent to a time-out room for five minutes. (A time-out room is a boring but safe place, such as a laundry room with nothing but a stool for the child to sit on.) Note that even this type of punishment can be overdone, however. Whereas five minutes is usually ample time for a young child to be alone in a time-out room, one or two hours is probably unreasonable.

Conditioned Punishment

As with reinforcement, stimuli associated with punishment can become powerful conditioned punishers when they reliably predict punishment. If the command "no" reliably predicts a slap on the rear of your barking dog, the command alone on later occasions may be sufficient to suppress barking. However, the effects of a conditioned punisher, like a conditioned reinforcer, will extinguish if they are no longer occasionally paired with a primary punisher. The author used an electric shock collar occasionally to punish his dog for running away. Can you use what you have learned so far to describe an effective method for establishing a verbal command such as "no" as a conditioned punisher?

Conditioned punishers are established in the same way as conditioned reinforcers, and they can more easily be delivered immediately. To condition the command "no," it needs to be reliably paired with a primary punisher. Saying the command "no" as the dog begins to escape and following this with a brief shock has conditioned the dog to associate the command "no" with an aversive event. After a few pairings, the command can be delivered immediately and quite effectively. However, the effects of a conditioned punisher, like a conditioned reinforcer, will extinguish if they are no longer occasionally paired with a primary punisher (Bouton, 2016).

In all, it seems that punishment can be useful for modifying behavior under certain circumstances. When punishment is used, however, it should be applied in moderation and in combination with incentives for desirable behavior.

6.4 Comparing Pavlovian and Operant Conditioning

As we have seen, both Pavlovian and operant conditioning involve learning relationships or associations between two events. Pavlovian conditioning involves learning associations between a conditioned stimulus (CS) and an unconditioned stimulus (UCS). Operant conditioning involves learning associations between behavior and its consequences, reinforcement or punishment. Each learning process produces a change in response, whether it is the conditioned response of anxiety to medicinal smells or an operant response such as playing a video game. However, Pavlovian and operant conditioning involve very different procedures and result in different kinds of responses. These two differences will be examined more closely.

First, the procedures for Pavlovian and operant conditioning differ. In Pavlovian conditioning experiments the researcher typically presents two stimuli: a novel CS immediately preceding the UCS, which naturally elicits some response. After several paired presentations of these stimuli, the researcher can test for a conditioned response by presenting the CS alone. If learning occurred, the CS will now elicit a conditioned response. In operant conditioning experiments, the researcher shapes a particular response by closely following approximations to that response with reinforcement. Learning has occurred when the new response is demonstrated.

Second, and perhaps more important, the kinds of responses for operant and Pavlovian conditioning are different. Pavlovian conditioned responses are typically reflexive responses or changes in emotional or motivational states, not voluntary behavior. Salivation is not a voluntary response by dogs but rather a reflexive response, which occurs during and prior to the ingestion of food. The anxiety you may experience while waiting at your dentist's office is also a change in behavior, but it is emotional behavior, not a voluntary response. Operant responses, on the other hand, are typically voluntary responses such as lever pressing, riding a bicycle, verbal behavior, and covert behavior like thinking.

Although it is possible to dissociate Pavlovian and operant conditioning in the laboratory, rarely in nature is there so clean a distinction between the two processes. In fact, both are typically involved in the adaptive behavior of most animals, including people. Consider a squirrel foraging for nuts among several species of deciduous trees, some dropping nuts, others not. At first the behavior of the squirrel might appear somewhat random as it scrambles among the leaves under the different trees. When nuts are located under a leaf of a certain color and size, this increases the likelihood that similar color and shaped leaves will be approached and turned. Finally, the squirrel attends primarily to the leaves with nuts among them and no longer forages near the others. In this example, both Pavlovian and operant conditioning lead to the adaptive behavior of the squirrel. Pavlovian conditioning was involved in learning the association between leaves of a certain color and shape, and the nuts found under them. Operant behavior was involved in learning the association between approaching and turning these particular leaves and finding nuts. This is referred to as the **two-factor theory of learning**. Without both types of learning, the squirrel's foraging behavior would be far less successful.

6.4a Two-Factor Theory of Avoidance Learning

Many learning situations, like the example above, involve both Pavlovian and operant conditioning. Let us return to the case of avoidance learning demonstrated by the biology student, discussed earlier in this chapter. This example was originally presented to illustrate Pavlovian conditioning, and Pavlovian conditioning was most likely the first learning process that took place. Through pairing with the frightening experience at the hospital, the medicinal odors became the CS that triggered a fear response.

Operant conditioning also occurred, however. Since fear is unpleasant, any responses that reduce or eliminate fear are strengthened through negative reinforcement. When the young woman avoided the biology lab, she was operating on her environment to alleviate her fear. The student's avoidance behavior kept her far from the biology lab; and since she was never exposed to the laboratory long enough to find out that the UCS would not occur, her conditioned fear was maintained. Thus her avoidance behavior involved two factors: the first being the acquisition of conditioned fear to the medicinal odors (Pavlovian conditioning), the second being the operant avoidance response that was maintained by negative reinforcement (Bouton, 2016).

Two-Factor Theory of Learning A theory of avoidance learning that involves both Pavlovian and operant conditioning

Many human phobias are products of two-factor learning. An understanding of the principles underlying this kind of conditioning provides a clue for treating such fear responses. In order to extinguish conditioned phobias, a person must be exposed to the CS in the absence of the UCS. To do this, the operant avoidance behavior must be prevented. One possible way to accomplish this would be initially to expose a relaxed subject to a very mild version of the feared stimulus (for example, a mildly medicinal odor in a nonthreatening situation). Gradually, more intense versions of the conditioned fear stimulus would be introduced. This technique, called systematic desensitization, is discussed in Chapter 16. Conditioned fear responses and anxiety are discussed in more detail in Chapter 15.

6.5 Cognitive Influences on Learning

To this point, we have focused on associative learning through either Pavlovian or operant conditioning. Many contemporary psychologists (including learning theorists) have argued that associative learning may provide too mechanistic an interpretation for all forms of learning. As conditioning was originally proposed by Pavlov, Thorndike, Skinner, and others, it did not take into account cognitive processes that cannot be observed. Another theoretical perspective, **cognitive learning theory**, attempts to identify the role that cognitive processes play in learning. Not all learning theorists agree that internal cognitive processes are necessary to account for learned behavior, however. As you read this final section, keep in mind that the examples discussed can also be explained without reference to cognitive processes.

As you might guess, cognitive theorists stress the individual's active participation in the learning process. They suggest that we learn by forming a cognitive structure in memory that preserves and organizes information pertaining to the key elements in a situation. Thus, in addition to forming conditioned associations between stimuli (Pavlovian conditioning) and behavior and reinforcement (operant conditioning), we form mental representations of our environments. These representations, along with external stimuli, guide behavior. Although learning is involved in the formation of these representations, the roles of Pavlovian and operant conditioning in the formation of internal representations are just beginning to be systematically explored (Fiser, 2009).

Cognitive learning theories did not become an important force in psychology until the late 1960s, but their roots go back many years. One important early influence was Edward Tolman's research on latent learning in rats.

6.5a Latent Learning

A fundamental principle of operant conditioning is that reinforcement is essential for learning new behavior. However, more than eighty years ago, psychologist Edward Tolman and his associates demonstrated that rats would learn a maze even when they were not reinforced. Tolman called this phenomenon **latent** (or hidden) **learning** because it is not demonstrated by an immediately observable change in behavior at the time of learning. Such learning typically occurs in the absence of a reinforcer, and it is not demonstrated until an appropriate reinforcement appears.

In a classic latent-learning experiment, three groups of rats were run for sixteen consecutive days in the complex maze shown in Figure 6-10. An error was recorded each time a rat entered a blind alley in the maze. Rats in one group, the reinforcement group, received food when they reached the goal box at the end of the maze on each of the sixteen days. A second group, the nonreinforcement group, also explored the maze each day; however, they did not receive food when they reached the end. Rats in a third group, the latent-learning group, received no reinforcement for the first ten days and then were reinforced for the remaining six days.

Cognitive Learning Theory Theoretical perspective that attempts to study the role of thinking and memory processes in learning

Latent Learning Learning that is not demonstrated by an immediately observable change in behavior

Figure 6-10 Classical Latent Learning Experiment

In Edward Tolman's experiment, three groups of rats were made to run for sixteen consecutive days in the maze shown in the top part of the figure. Results for the three groups are shown at the bottom of the figure. The rats in the latent learning group (solid black line) that received rewards beginning on Day 11 performed as well as rats that received rewards beginning on Day 1 (solid blue line).

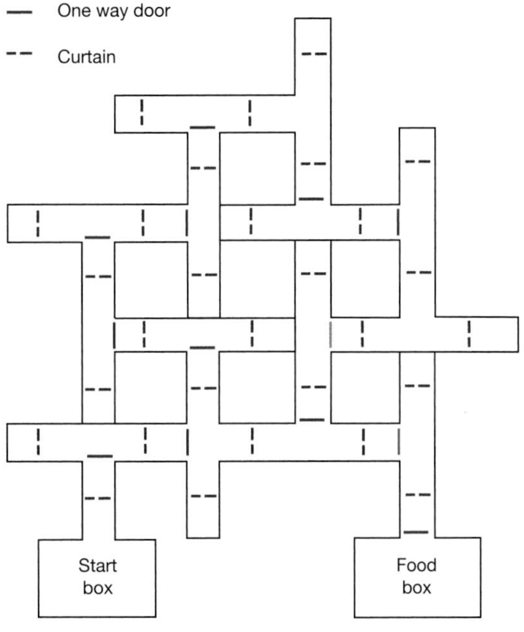

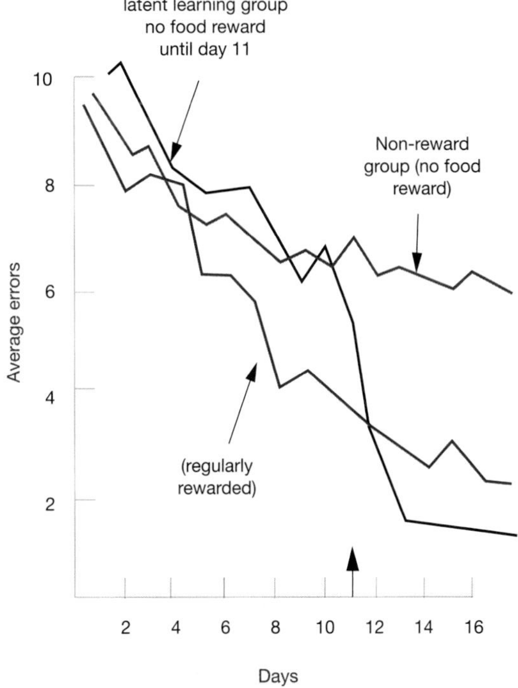

Adapted from "Introduction and Removal of Reward and Maze Performance in Rats," by E. Tolman and C. Honzik, 1930, University of California Publications in *Psychology*, 4, 257–275

Over the first ten days, rats in the reinforcement group showed considerably more improvement than animals in either of the other groups. In fact, the animals in the nonreinforcement group showed very little improvement in performance over the entire sixteen days. However, after food was introduced on Day 11 for rats in the latent-learning group, they immediately began to perform as well as animals in the reinforcement group. This occurrence clearly demonstrated that Tolman's rats were learning something about the maze even with no reinforcement (Tolman & Honzik, 1930).

This latent-learning experiment demonstrates the distinction between learning and performance, for learning can take place even when it is not demonstrated by performance. The experiment also poses a question: If no responses can be observed, what is being learned? Tolman answered this question by claiming that his rats were developing a **cognitive map**, or mental representation, of the maze in the absence of reinforcement. Later, when, reinforcement was introduced, the map allowed the animals to reach a high level of performance quickly.

Tolman and his associates conducted a number of additional experiments that demonstrated how cognitive maps work in problem solving. For example, once rats had learned how to get through a complex maze to reach food, obstructions were placed in their way and new routes introduced. Tolman suggested that these complications were quickly mastered because the rats were able to re-sort and rearrange the mental picture of the maze, and thereby find the new route with ease (Tolman, Ritchie, & Kalish, 1946).

Cognitive maps have become a very important concept in contemporary learning theory. Research suggests that a variety of organisms—including rats, chimpanzees, birds, and bees—use cognitive maps in adapting to their environments (Gould & Marler, 1987; Shettleworth, 1983). Humans also create mental representations of their environments that allow them to function more effectively. For instance, you can easily navigate your college campus and use shortcuts without ever having used them previously. To do this, you rely on a cognitive map—a mental representation—of your campus.

6.5b Cognitive Processes in Learning

We have presented cognitive learning as separate from the associative types of learning, which is the traditional way of viewing learning. Pavlov, for instance, stressed that *temporal contiguity* (that is, closeness in time) of the CS and the UCS is essential for Pavlovian conditioning. Indeed, most learning theorists after Pavlov continued to view Pavlovian conditioning as a relatively automatic form of learning that is strengthened through repeated pairings of the CS and the UCS.

Recent evidence has caused some psychologists to question this view, however. According to their interpretation, cognitive processes are involved even in Pavlovian conditioning (Rescorla, 1988a, 1988b, 1999; Turkkan, 1989).

According to this cognitive perspective, the learner during Pavlovian conditioning first observes that the CS and UCS typically occur together and stores this information in memory. Later, when the CS appears by itself, the learner retrieves the information from memory, and the conditioned response occurs in anticipation that the UCS will occur. In other words, it appears that the CS and UCS become associated not simply because they occur contiguously in time but rather because the CS provides information about the UCS (Rescorla, 1987). Indeed this view is supported by Rescorla's experiment described earlier where he demonstrated that mere contiguity between a CS and UCS is not sufficient. Rather, it was stimulus contingency that was essential. Recent interpretations of Rescorla's experiments stress the importance of how much information the CS conveys about the UCS. That is, the more informative or predictive the CS, the better conditioning will be.

Cognitive Map Internal representation of the relationship between events or spatial elements

Studies of a phenomenon known as *blocking* also support this interpretation. In such experiments, subjects are exposed to repeated CS-UCS pairings (for example, a light with a shock). Later, after conditioning is established, a second stimulus (such as a tone) is added to the original CS so that both stimuli now occur prior to the UCS. According to Pavlov, the second stimulus should quickly become conditioned since it is regularly paired with the UCS. However, this outcome does not occur (Halas & Eberhardt, 1987; Kamin, 1969). Apparently, the previous conditioning of the response to the light somehow interferes with or blocks the tone from becoming an effective CS.

Learning theorists refer to the information concept to explain these results. They argue that since the original stimulus already predicts the occurrence of the UCS, the new stimulus is irrelevant because it provides no new information about the occurrence of the UCS. If the UCS is now changed in some way, for example its intensity is increased, learning will occur to the second CS (the tone) because now tone predicts larger shocks than did the light alone. Learning theorists believe that the predictability of the relationship between the CS and UCS is probably more important than either the timing or the frequency of pairings. We now know that CS-UCS pairings, while necessary for Pavlovian conditioning, are not sufficient by themselves to ensure that learning will occur.

Cognitive factors may be important in operant as well as Pavlovian conditioning. Although the operant conditioning emphasizes the consequences of behavior, those consequences do not automatically strengthen or weaken responses. Rather, they provide the learner with important information about the probable consequences of a given behavior under certain circumstances. Cognitive theorists view individuals as information-processing systems that store this relevant information about consequences. Later, when confronted by similar circumstances, the learner retrieves this information from memory and acts accordingly. Thus, from the cognitive perspective, operant behavior is guided by expectations of probable outcomes (Colwill & Rescorla, 1986; Rescorla, 1987, 1999; Williams, Butler, & Overmier, 1990).

The cognitive theorists stress the argument that events occurring in Pavlovian and operant conditioning do not automatically stamp in behavior. Instead, they provide relevant information that helps to establish expectancies, and it is these expectancies that form the basis for subsequent behavior.

6.5c Observational Learning

Much of human as well as other animal learning occurs by watching or listening to others. This is referred to as **observational learning**, and it involves both the Pavlovian and operant processes already discussed.

One of the major findings of observational-learning research is that children tend to behave in a manner similar to their parents, both during their childhood and later on in life. Thus child abuse and other maladaptive behaviors are often passed on from one generation to the next just as are warm, nurturing behaviors.

There are strong cognitive components in learning by observation. People observe the behaviors of others and then store cognitive representations of these acts in memory, where they remain until the right influence triggers the individual to enact that behavior.

The role of observation and imitation in learning is explained in **social learning theory**, and Albert Bandura (1977, 1992) of Stanford University is probably its leading proponent. Bandura and his colleagues have performed a number of studies that demonstrate the importance of observational learning in our lives. In one widely cited experiment, children observed adults beating on a 5-foot inflated BoBo doll and were then placed in a similar situation. The researchers found that children who had observed this

Observational Learning
Learning process in which an individual acquires a behavior by observing someone else performing that behavior; also known as *modeling*

Social Learning Theory
Theory that emphasizes the role of observation in learning

aggressive behavior were more likely to act aggressively when placed in the same situation than did children in control conditions who had observed a quiet model (Bandura, D. Ross, & S. Ross, 1963).

Social learning theorists use the term *models* to describe the people whose behaviors we observe and often imitate. These models can range from parents (usually the most influential models in our lives) to people we see on television or in movies. Humans have a great capacity to store mental representations. In this fashion, we learn from the examples of others.

Some of the behaviors we observe become part of our own behavioral repertoire, but we also observe many responses that we never imitate. (Watching another diner chew gum at an elegant restaurant, for instance, may cause you to resolve never to do such a thing.) Our brains process all these stored memories of previously observed behaviors, selecting out those that seem appropriate in a given situation. Once an observed behavior becomes part of our own response system, it becomes subject to the rules of reinforcement discussed earlier. In this fashion, imitative behaviors become either strengthened or weakened.

Bandura has identified four key steps in observational learning. The first is simply having our attention drawn to a modeled behavior. (As you recall, modeling was already discussed as a procedure to produce an initial operant response.) Second, we store a mental representation of the behavior in our memories. Third, a specific type of situation triggers us to convert the remembered observation into actions. Finally, if our actions are reinforced, we add the behavior to our repertoire of responses.

Learning by observation, or modeling, can exert a powerful influence on our lives. Being able to learn by watching, listening, and even reading is extremely useful. Can you imagine how tedious it would be to acquire all our behaviors by trial and error or shaping? Modeling allows us to profit from the experiences of others. For example, in one study, researchers tried a variety of strategies to increase the sociability of nursery school children who normally kept to themselves. The most effective strategy turned out to be to have these youngsters watch a film showing sociable children. The film was even a faster agent of social change than a shaping procedure that involved praising and paying attention to children when they behaved sociably.

Observational learning and modeling also contribute significantly to the problem of bears foraging in neighborhoods and campgrounds as described in the chapter opening. Cub bears that are reared in wild foraging environments remain in wild habitats for much of their adult lives. On the other hand, cub bears that forage with their mothers in human habitats continue this pattern well into adulthood (Mazur & Seher, 2008)

6.6 Biological Bases of Learning

You now appreciate that learning involves relatively permanent changes in the behavior of the learner. You may wonder what kinds of changes actually occur to represent this learning. Searching for these changes has been a long and exciting endeavor. As you will see, even though these findings have important implications for human learning, we have yet to observe the neuronal changes that represent learning in people.

Investigating the biological mechanisms of learning in humans, or even rats, is not practical at present because of the extremely large number of neurons involved. As you recall from Chapter 3, the human brain contains more than one hundred billion neurons. Thus researchers interested in the cellular changes that represent learning have focused on another species with a relatively simple nervous system. The species that has proven to be most valuable for this research is the *Aplysia*, a shell-less marine snail. The *Aplysia* has about twenty thousand neurons, many connections (synapses) of which have been well studied.

Figure 6-11 Marine Animal *Aplysia* Used to Study the Biology of Learning

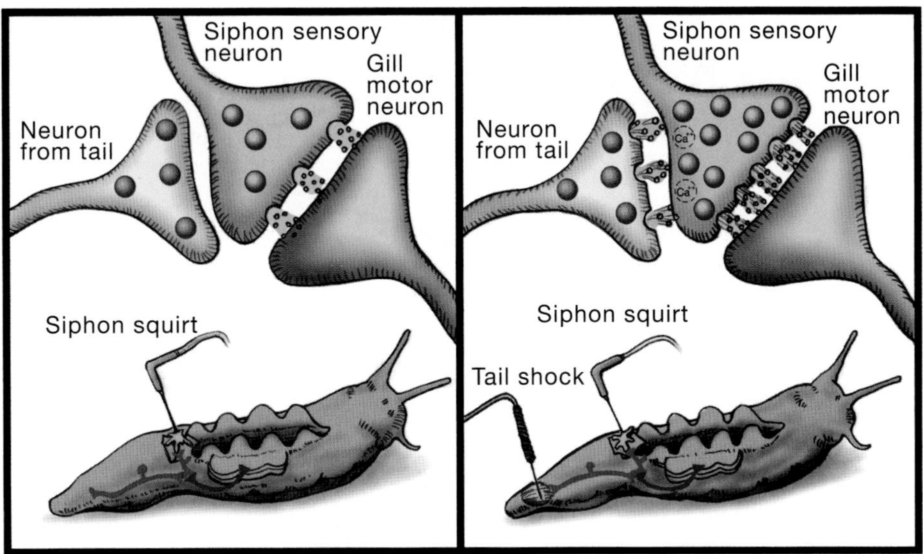

6.6a Pavlovian Conditioning of the Aplysia

Investigations by Eric Kandel (Hawkins, Abrams, Carew, & Kandel, 1983) of Pavlovian conditioning in *Aplysia* have focused on a protective reflex of the gill, which is the respiratory organ of the *Aplysia*. For instance, when the *Aplysia* is touched strongly on the tail or the siphon, the gill withdraws into the mantle. Refer to Figure 6-11 for a diagram of the *Aplysia*. Because this protective response is easily observed and occurs reliably, it is an ideal response for Pavlovian conditioning. To condition a gill withdrawal response, a mild touch (squirt of water) is applied to the siphon. This mild touch (the CS) by itself does not cause a gill withdrawal response. Immediately following the CS, a shock is applied to the tail (the UCS), and this does cause the gill to withdraw. After a number of paired CS-UCS (touch-shock) trials, the siphon squirt (CS) results in a conditioned gill withdrawal response (the CR).

What kinds of changes in the nervous system of the *Aplysia* mediate this conditioning? Kandel and others have recently identified several cellular changes that occur. The neurons involved are illustrated in Figures 6-11 and 6-12. When stimulated, the UCS neuron (the sensory neuron receiving shock) transmits a strong signal to the modulatory neuron, which in turn activates the motor neuron to cause the gill to withdraw.

In Figure 6-12, you can see that the modulatory neuron also has contact with the CS neuron (the sensory neuron receiving touch). Notice, however, that this synapse is at the end of the axon before its synapse with the motor neuron. If the CS neuron was recently active (because the CS was presented before the UCS), chemical events involving the neurotransmitter serotonin occur on both the presynaptic membrane of the CS neuron and on the postsynaptic motor neuron. After several conditioning trials, this chemical activity leaves the CS neuron facilitated and the postsynaptic motor neuron strengthened, or potentiated—that is, the CS nerve terminal is now more permeable to calcium ions (Ca++) and the postsynaptic motor neuron fires more easily. As you recall from Chapter 3, calcium is involved in the release of the neurotransmitter into the synapse. When more calcium flows

Model of Neuronal Connections in *Aplysia*

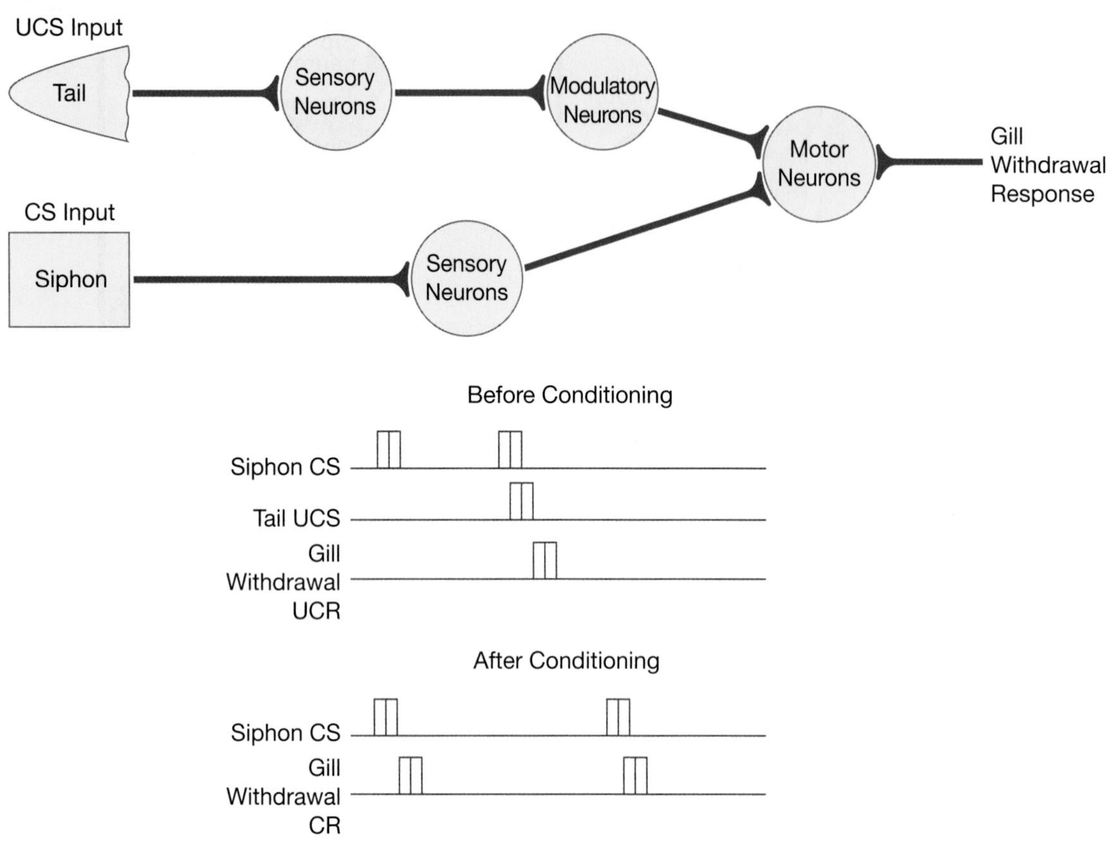

into the nerve terminal, more neurotransmitter is released. Therefore, the next time the CS occurs (without the UCS), the activity of the CS neuron results in more neurotransmitter being released at the motor neuron synapse. If sufficient neurotransmitter is released from the CS neuron, the motor neuron will now fire, causing the gill withdrawal response. The withdrawal response to the mild siphon touch is now a conditioned response.

In summary, paired presentations of the CS and the UCS leave the CS neuron facilitated and the postsynaptic neuron potentiated. **Synaptic facilitation** and **long-term potentiation** allow the CS to activate the motor neuron for the gill response. These synaptic changes are relatively permanent (thus the term *long-term potentiation*), and they will not occur if the delay between the CS and the UCS is much longer than 0.5 seconds. Likewise, they will not occur if the CS follows the UCS, as in backward conditioning (Hawkins et at., 1983; Kandel & Hawkins, 1992; Antonov, Antonova, Kandel, & Hawkins, 2003).

Synaptic Facilitation An increase in the size of a postsynaptic potential to a weak stimulus resulting from neuronal changes that underlie learning and memory

Long-Term Potentiation (LTP) An increase in a neuron's sensitivity to fire following a burst of signals to that neuron's dendrites

Chemical changes like this are believed to underlie all of the learning processes discussed in this chapter. In fact, as you read this text or perfect your tennis serve, similar changes are occurring throughout your brain. Without additional memory processes, however, learning would clearly be of little value. In the next chapter we discuss the processes of memory that allow our experiences, as represented, to influence our behavior. We conclude the next chapter with more discussion of these biological processes.

Pavlovian Conditioning

A few years ago, researchers Robert Ader and Nathan Cohen (Ader, Cohen, & Bovbjerg, 1982) observed a curious effect as they were studying Pavlovian conditioned taste aversion. In their experiment, rats were given drinks of a saccharin-flavored water (the CS), followed immediately by injections of a drug that made them nauseous (the UCS). As you might predict, the animals immediately acquired a taste aversion that caused them to avoid or reduce their consumption of the sweet solution. The rats were then exposed to several extinction trials in which they were presented with the sweet solution but no toxic drug. (Extinction is a process designed to reduce the strength of the association between the CS and UCS through repeated presentations of the CS alone without the UCS.)

During this stage of the study, something unexpected happened. For no apparent reason, some of the rats died. Ader and Cohen considered a variety of possibilities to explain what had happened. One of their primary clues was that the drug they used to induce nausea, cyclophosphamide, is also known to suppress the body's immune system.

Ader and Cohen reasoned that perhaps the saccharin water had become a conditioned signal that suppressed the rats' immune systems in the same way as the drug with which it had been paired. If this were the case, the repeated exposures to the sweetened water alone during the extinction trials may have suppressed their immune systems so much that they fell victim to disease-bearing microorganisms in the laboratory.

To test this possibility, they conditioned other rats, using the original design with one modification. Before the extinction trials in which rats received only the CS of sweet water, they were injected with red blood cells from sheep that would normally trigger the rats' immune systems to produce high levels of defensive antibodies. The researchers' hypothesis was supported: The conditioned animals produced significantly fewer antibodies than their control animals. Ader and Cohen also tested the immune-system responses of mice that had been classically conditioned to respond to the sweet water. They found that if these conditioned mice received only half the usual dosage of cyclophosphamide, together with exposure to the CS, their immune systems were suppressed as completely as if they had been given a full dosage of the toxic drug.

Other researchers have confirmed and extended Ader and Cohen's findings. For instance, Grochowicz et at. (1991) demonstrated that conditioned immunosuppression effectively prolonged the survival of transplanted heart tissue in rats. Immunosuppression in tissue transplant procedures is necessary to prevent the immune system from attacking the newly transplanted tissue. In experiments with humans, researchers recruited thirty-four healthy male volunteers to participate. Twenty-four of the subjects received five days of conditioning using strawberry milk as the CS and the immunosuppressive drug, cyclosporine, as the UCS. The control group consumed the strawberry milk, but was given a placebo. Neither the researchers nor the subjects were informed as to which group they were in. After five days of conditioning, both groups consumed strawberry milk (CS) before receiving identical-looking placebo tablets. The researchers then measured lymphocyte production in both groups. The conditioning group had significantly suppressed immune responses compared to the control group (Goebel et at., 2002). These results not only confirm earlier work by Ader but also demonstrate conditioned immune suppression in humans. It is anticipated that conditioning of the immune system will be applied to treat human lupus and arthritis, as well as other autoimmune disorders.

Health Implications

Certainly, these findings extend our knowledge of how the brain and body interact to reduce or increase our vulnerability to disease. Beyond this, they may lead to a practical medical application in the future. For instance, one major problem associated with many drugs used to combat disease is that they often produce serious side effects. Although cyclophosphamide is toxic enough to have been selected as the nausea-inducing UCS in Ader and Cohen's experiment, it has a legitimate and very valuable medical use as treatment for lupus, an immune-system disorder in which the body turns against itself. If Pavlovian conditioning could be used to condition the body of a lupus victim into responding to a significantly lowered dosage of the drug, a diseased person might be able to benefit from cyclophosphamide without having to experience its debilitating side effects. Experiments are currently being conducted with lupus patients to determine whether conditioned immunosuppression can effectively augment drug therapy.

The same kinds of benefits might also be obtained with drugs used to treat cancer and MDS. Hopefully, in the years to come, these conditioning principles can be applied to alleviate suffering and improve the treatment of many victims of disease.

CHAPTER REVIEW

Defining Learning

1. Learning may be defined as a relatively permanent change in potential behavior that results from experience.
2. Associative learning, the process by which connections or associations are made between two events, may take place in two primary ways: Pavlovian conditioning and operant conditioning. Pavlovian conditioning involves learned associations between two stimuli. In operant conditioning, people or other animals learn to associate their own behavior with its consequences.

Pavlovian Conditioning

3. The four key elements in Pavlovian conditioning are the unconditioned stimulus (UCS), the unconditioned response (UCR), the conditioned stimulus (CS), and the conditioned response (CR). After pairing a previously neutral stimulus (CS) with a stimulus (UCS) that automatically elicits an unlearned response (UCR), the CS will cause a response on its own.
4. Factors that facilitate the acquisition of a Pavlovian conditioned response include a CS that is clearly different from other stimuli, frequent pairings of the CS and the UCS, and the order and timing with which the CS is paired with the UCS.
5. The acquisition of Pavlovian conditioning depends on a predictive relation between the CS and the UCS called stimulus contingency.
6. When certain associations are acquired very quickly, they are called selective associations. Conditioned taste aversions are examples of selective associations.
7. Extinction, or cessation of the CR, occurs in Pavlovian conditioning when the CS is repeatedly presented alone, without the UCS.
8. A CR can be reinstated following extinction with one or two conditioning trials. In some cases, reinstated CRs are stronger than their preextinction levels.
9. When a response has been conditioned to a particular stimulus, other stimuli may also produce the same response. This principle is called generalization.
10. Early in the conditioning process, a learner may respond to a variety of similar stimuli (generalization). However, with time, he or she learns that only one of these stimuli, the CS, is consistently associated with the UCS. This process of learning to make distinctions between the CS and similar but not identical stimuli is called discrimination.
11. A Pavlovian conditioning variation in which a neutral stimulus becomes a CS through association with an already established CS is referred to as second order conditioning.

CHAPTER REVIEW

Operant Conditioning

12. In operant conditioning, humans and other animals learn to associate their behavior with either reinforcing or punishing consequences.
13. Reinforcement is defined as a procedure that increases the probability that a response will occur.
14. A positive reinforcer is any stimulus presented following a response that increases the probability of the response. A negative reinforcer is a stimulus that increases the probability of a response through its removal when the desired response is made.
15. In escape conditioning, an organism learns to produce a response that will allow termination or escape from an aversive stimulus (negative reinforcer). In avoidance conditioning, the individual learns to emit an appropriate avoidance response, thereby averting any exposure to the aversive stimulus.
16. A primary reinforcer is a stimulus that satisfies a biologically based drive or need. Secondary reinforcers are stimuli that acquire reinforcing properties through association with primary reinforcers.
17. A continuous reinforcement schedule exists when behavior is reinforced every time it occurs. A partial reinforcement schedule exists when behavior is reinforced only part of the time.
18. Behaviors that are acquired on partial instead of continuous schedules of reinforcement are slower to be established, but they are remarkably more persistent when no reinforcement is provided.
19. Four varieties of partial reinforcement schedules include those based on a percentage of responses that are reinforced (fixed ratio and variable ratio) or passage of a certain amount of time before a response is reinforced (fixed interval and variable interval).
20. Methods used to encourage the occurrence of an initial desired operant response include physical guidance, shaping, modeling, verbal instruction, and increasing motivation.
21. Punishment can be defined as a procedure that decreases the probability that a given behavior will occur.
22. The effectiveness of a punisher in producing a desired change in behavior depends upon its intensity, consistency, and the delay between a response and punishment.
23. Principles that may improve the effectiveness of punishment include immediacy, consistency, moderation, and combining it with positive reinforcement (always reinforcing acceptable alternatives to the punished behavior).

CHAPTER REVIEW

Comparing Pavlovian and Operant Conditioning

24. Pavlovian conditioning involves learning associations between a CS and a UCS. Operant conditioning involves learning associations between behavior and its consequence.
25. Most learning situations combine both Pavlovian and operant conditioning in what is called two-factor learning.
26. Many human phobias are a result of two-factor learning. First, an individual acquires a fear of a neutral stimulus (Pavlovian conditioning), and then the individual acts to reduce or eliminate this fear by learning to avoid the frightening stimulus (operant avoidance conditioning).

Cognitive Influences on Learning

27. Cognitive theorists suggest that we learn by forming a cognitive structure, or representation, in memory that preserves and organizes information relevant to a given situation.
28. The roots of cognitive learning theories go back many years to studies of latent learning in rats.
29. Cognitive theorists suggest that what is learned in Pavlovian conditioning is not a mere contiguity between the CS and UCS but rather an expectancy that the UCS will follow the CS.
30. From the cognitive perspective, operant behavior is also viewed as being guided by expectations of probable outcomes.
31. Cognitive theorists believe that there are strong cognitive components in learning by watching and imitating others, a process called observational learning.
32. The role of observation and imitation in learning is explained in social learning theory. In some circumstances, teaming by observation, or modeling, may be even more effective than operant conditioning in shaping our behavior.

Biological Bases of Learning

33. Learning involves structural and chemical changes at synapses within the brain.
34. Researchers have identified these changes in the marine snail, *Aplysia*.
35. In the *Aplysia*, learning involves both presynaptic facilitation and postsynaptic potentiation of motor neuron synapses.

TERMS AND CONCEPTS

Acquisition, pg. 227
Associative Learning, pg. 222
Avoidance Conditioning, pg. 237
Backward Conditioning, pg. 229
Cognitive Learning Theory, pg. 248
Cognitive Map, pg. 250
Conditioned Reinforcer, pg. 237
Conditioned Response (CR), pg. 225
Conditioned Stimulus (CS), pg. 225
Conditioned Taste Aversion, pg. 229
Continuous Reinforcement Schedule, pg. 238
Cumulative Record, pg. 235
Delayed Conditioning, pg. 228
Discrimination, pg. 232
Discriminative Stimulus, pg. 235
Escape Conditioning, pg. 237
Extinction, pg. 231
Fixed Interval (FI) Schedule, pg. 240
Fixed Ratio (FR) Schedule, pg. 239
Generalization, pg. 232
Latent Learning, pg. 248
Law of Effect, pg. 234
Learning, pg. 221
Long-Term Potentiation (LTP), pg. 254
Modeling, pg. 243
Negative Reinforcement, pg. 236
Observational Learning, pg. 251
Operant Conditioning, pg. 222
Partial Reinforcement Effect, pg. 238
Partial Reinforcement Schedule, pg. 238
Pavlovian Conditioning, pg. 222
Positive Reinforcement, pg. 236
Primary Reinforcer, pg. 237
Punishment, pg. 243
Reinforcement, pg. 236
Reinstatement, pg. 231
Second-Order Conditioning, pg. 232
Shaping, pg. 242
Simultaneous Conditioning, pg. 229
Social Learning Theory, pg. 251
Synaptic Facilitation, pg. 254
Template Learning, pg. 223
Trace Conditioning, pg. 229
Two-Factor Theory of Learning, pg. 247
Unconditioned Response (UCR), pg. 225
Unconditioned Stimulus (UCS), pg. 225
Variable Interval (VI) Schedule, pg. 240
Variable Ratio (VR) Schedule, pg. 240

POP QUIZ

True or False

___ 1. A new behavior that is acquired as a result of an individual's maturation is considered a learned behavior.

___ 2. When a CR that has been extinguished suddenly returns after an interval of rest, we say spontaneous recovery has occurred.

___ 3. Shaping involves the physical guidance of the subject to make the desired response.

___ 4. Bandura's study involving children and a Bobo doll demonstrated modeling.

___ 5. Research interested in the biological mechanisms of learning has focused on operant conditioning in the marine snail *Aplysia*.

Multiple Choice

6. Associative learning describes the process by which a connection or association is made between which of the following?
   a. Two stimuli
   b. A behavior and the consequences of that behavior
   c. A problem and the solution to that problem
   d. Both a and b are correct.

7. Young children frequently cry when their mothers leave them. Sometimes they start to cry as soon as the babysitter arrives. Why does this occur?
   a. Babysitter is a UCS associated with the mother leaving.
   b. Babysitter uses negative reinforcement.
   c. Babysitter is a CS associated with the mother leaving.
   d. Child dislikes the babysitter.

8. Which of the following is not an important factor in the initial acquisition of a CR?
   a. The motivation of the individual to perform the CR
   b. The timing of the presentation of the CS and UCS
   c. That the CS is clearly different from other stimuli
   d. How frequently the CS and UCS have been paired

9. What should one do to extinguish a CR?
   a. Pair the CS with a second-order stimulus
   b. Repeatedly present the CS while not presenting the UCS
   c. Withhold the UCR
   d. Not present the CS for a period of several days

POP QUIZ

10. What is teaching an organism to respond to only one of a series of similar stimuli called?
    a. Operant conditioning
    b. Generalization
    c. Extinction
    d. Discrimination training
11. What is the most commonly used measure of the strength of an operant response?
    a. The rate of response
    b. The calculation from the Law of Effect
    c. The variety of stimuli that elicit the response
    d. How much generalization is shown
12. Your child gets a gold star on her perfect spelling test. After accumulating several stars, the child may trade them for playtime. What does the gold star represent?
    a. A conditioned reinforcer
    b. A primary reinforcer
    c. A UCS
    d. A discriminative stimulus
13. Immediately after being reinforced, a rat on which schedule of reinforcement would show the longest pause before its next bar press?
    a. FR
    b. VR
    c. FI
    d. VI
14. Which of the following is ***not*** a limitation or undesirable side effect of punishment?
    a. It may induce counteraggression against the punisher.
    b. Fear or anxiety may develop.
    c. Positive reinforcers lose their reinforcing properties.
    d. The results are often temporary.
15. What is the basic premise of observational learning?
    a. Behavior learned through observational learning is never extinguished.
    b. Insight into the model's motivation is gained.
    c. Learning may occur without physical responses or reinforcement.
    d. All learning results from modeling.

Answer Key: 1. F 2. T 3. F 4. T 5. F 6. d 7. c 8. a 9. b 10. d 11. a 12. a 13. c 14. c 15. c

(Aldomurillo/iStock)

Chapter 7

Memory

The female digger wasp begins each day with an inspection tour of up to fifteen separate nesting sites where her larvae are kept in underground burrows. After this initial inspection tour, the female wasp begins hunting for caterpillars to replenish her nests. Quite remarkably, she returns to each burrow, in turn, with just enough food to replenish each nest. The female digger wasp not only remembers the condition of each nest as it was during her morning checkout visit, she must also remember where each burrow is located with respect to various landmarks. Her memory of nest condition and location serves to guide her behavior on return visits later in the day (Tinbergen, 1958).

John Kingsley came to our attention in a shocking news story about an eighty-three-year-old Alzheimer's patient who was found unattended in his wheelchair at a dog racetrack outside of Spokane, Washington. Attached to his chair was a note misidentifying him. John did not know who he was or how he got to the races. He couldn't help authorities find his family or his previous caregivers. John Kingsley, like many other patients during advanced stages of Alzheimer's disease, is alive, but without life. Without a memory of his past or the ability to remember anything new, John's life is nothing but the existing moment.

It has been said that memory is the most important function of our brains. Can you imagine what life might be like if you could not remember your experiences? Without memory, you, like John, would have no history and thus no identity. You would have no skills, for all knowledge is based on memory. All but the most primitive responses require memory. Our very consciousness—perceiving, thinking, and feeling—depends on our ability to store and use information about our past each day. In lower animals, like the digger wasp, primitive memories can lead to extremely complex patterns of intelligent behavior that would otherwise not be possible.

Psychologists have studied memory for years, but in many ways it is still a mystery. What changes take place in our brains that allow us to store memories, sometimes for a lifetime? By what process do we retrieve these memories from a brain cluttered with information? We explore such questions in this chapter. Although we do not have all the answers, we will see that there is much that we do understand about what we remember, how we remember, why we forget—and even what we can do to improve memory. We begin by defining memory.

7.1 What Is Memory?

Memory, like the term *learning* from the previous chapter, is not something we can observe. Rather, we infer from your behavior that you have memory. That is, if your performance on exams is better after studying the material than before studying, we infer that memory has occurred. We now know that memories reside inside of you as structural changes within your brain. As we will see, these structural changes occur passively without your attention, but they can be facilitated by actively participating in memory processes. We begin with a formal definition of memory that was offered by Estes (1972):

> Memory is some property or state of the organism that resulted from experience and that has the consequence of altering the organism's potentialities for future responses.

7.1a Information Processing and Memory

Psychologists once viewed humans and other animals as organisms that merely experience and respond to stimuli. They did not concern themselves with the internal events that govern complex processes such as learning and memory.

Memory (1) Process or processes of storing newly acquired information for later recall (2) recall for a specific experience, or the total collection of remembered experiences stored in our brains

Information-Processing Model of Memory A model of memory that proposes three stages in memory processing: sensory memories, working (short-term) memories, and long-term memories

Encoding In memory, the process of perceiving information and then categorizing or organizing it in a meaningful way so that it can be more easily stored and recalled

Storage Process by which encoded material is retained over time in memory

This outlook has changed over the last two decades. Most psychologists have come to view the human brain as an information-processing system. That is, information is not simply stored in the brain and then later retrieved; instead, it is shaped or modified in ways that allow organisms to adapt to their environments efficiently. In other words, people and other animals actively participate in the assimilation of their experiences. Learning and memory are not static or fixed processes, but dynamic processes that continue to change over the course of time.

The **information-processing model of memory** is particularly helpful in conceptualizing memory processes. In the following pages, we examine the various stages that appear to be part of the memory process.

7.1b Memory Processes

You are sitting quietly at your desk, studying for an exam. From somewhere in your apartment complex you hear a muffled scream. This is not particularly unusual; you live in a big housing unit, and you often hear strange noises, including an occasional scream or loud shouting. Nevertheless, your attention is diverted. A few moments later, you hear an engine start in the parking lot below. You hear the sound of an engine being revved, and then of a car speeding through the parking lot. You rush to the window and catch a fleeting glimpse of a red sports car. Could there be a connection between the scream and this vehicle? Maybe you will end up as a key witness in a murder trial. Your imagination runs rampant for a minute or two; then you return to your books.

Will you accurately remember what you have just seen and heard if a violent incident did occur on this day? The chances are very good that you will remember something. The accuracy of your recall will depend on three separate processes. First, you encode or translate incoming information into a neural code that your brain can process. Second, the encoded information is stored so that it can be retained over time. Finally, you must be able to find and recover this stored information when you need it later on, through the process of retrieval.

Encoding

Encoding involves first perceiving some particular stimulus event, such as the sound of a scream or a revving engine, and then translating or coding the information so that it can be more easily stored. This process involves categorizing or organizing information in some meaningful way, as described in Chapter 4. Is the information a sight, a sound, a smell, or some tactile sensation? The scream is processed as a sound, and we further categorize it as a signal of distress. When we encode material, it becomes associated or linked to what we already know. For instance, you encode the fact that the car has a manual transmission because you already know that glitches in the sound of acceleration indicate shift points. Memories that are connected to or associated with previous information are much easier to retain.

Storage

Storage is the process by which encoded material is retained over time in memory. Exactly how memories are stored is the topic of some of the most important current research in psychology. We know that memories do not just float around in our brains waiting to be retrieved. Some changes must take place in the brain to allow memories to be stored for later use. We investigate this topic in some detail later in the chapter.

The efficiency of the storage process is greatly influenced by the effort we put into encoding or organizing new memories. Suppose your roommate asks you to order a pizza by calling 234-4454. This number is easy to remember because it is organized in two clusters; after one or two rehearsals, you have it memorized at least for a few moments. If your roommate asks you to call and check on the order ten minutes later, however, you will probably need to ask her to repeat the number.

Now, assume that you meet someone interesting at a party. That person gives you a telephone number, 245-5565, and says, "Call me some time." Of course, nobody seems to have a pen at critical moments like this. Chances are you will choose a much more effective method for encoding and storing this number than the one for the local pizzeria. Perhaps you note the logical progression of ten units in the sequence 45, 55, 65, and use this method as a meaningful way to encode and store this information. You are likely to remember this number for a longer period after actively rehearsing and organizing it.

Retrieval

The final step in the process of remembering is **retrieval**. If you properly encoded and stored your new friend's telephone number, or information about the getaway car in the earlier example, you will be able to retrieve this information from memory at a later time. Generally speaking, the more effort we put into preparing information for storage, the more efficiently we can retrieve it.

Retrieval Process by which information stored in memory is accessed

Sensory Memory First system in the three-system model of memory, in which brief impressions from any of the senses are stored fleetingly, disappearing within a few seconds if they are not transferred to short-term memory

Short-Term (Working) Memory (STM) Immediate recollection of stimuli that have just been perceived (unless it is transferred to long-term memory, information in this memory system is usually retained only momentarily)

7.2 A Model of Memory

Psychologists distinguish between memories that stay with us, such as an important phone number, and those that are quickly lost. In fact, most psychologists today believe that there are several distinct memory systems that allow us to process, store, and recall information. Richard Atkinson and Richard Shiffrin (1968) first articulated the three-stage information processing model. Contemporary theories of memory still include several memory systems, but the distinctions between them may not always be clear. We first introduce these systems and then go into much more detail describing research that supports each system's role in memory.

7.2a Memory Systems

Sensory Memory

Research suggests that information that first comes to us through our senses is stored for a fleeting moment within **sensory memory**. Because of the highly transitory nature of this memory system, we usually are not consciously aware of sensory memory, nor do we actively organize or encode this information. The function of this memory system seems to be to hold or preserve impressions of sensory stimuli just long enough for important aspects of this information to be transferred to the next system, our short-term or working memory.

Short-Term Memory (STM)

Our **short-term memory** (STM; also referred to as **working memory**) comprises our immediate recollection of stimuli that we have just perceived. The amount of information this memory system can store is much more limited than that of sensory memory.

Long-Term Memory (LTM) Information transferred from short-term to long-term memory may be stored for periods of time from minutes to years—perhaps even indefinitely

Unless we repeatedly reinstate the information transferred to short-term memory, it will probably be retained only momentarily, perhaps for no more than about twenty seconds. For example, you have probably forgotten the number of the local pizzeria by now. Unless you repeatedly rehearse a phone number, it is likely to disappear from memory very quickly.

Long-Term Memory

Information that is transferred from short-term memory into **long-term memory (LTM)** may remain for minutes, hours, days, or perhaps even a lifetime. When we retrieve information from long-term memory, it passes through short-term memory. Figure 7-1

Figure 7-1 A Theoretical Model of Memory

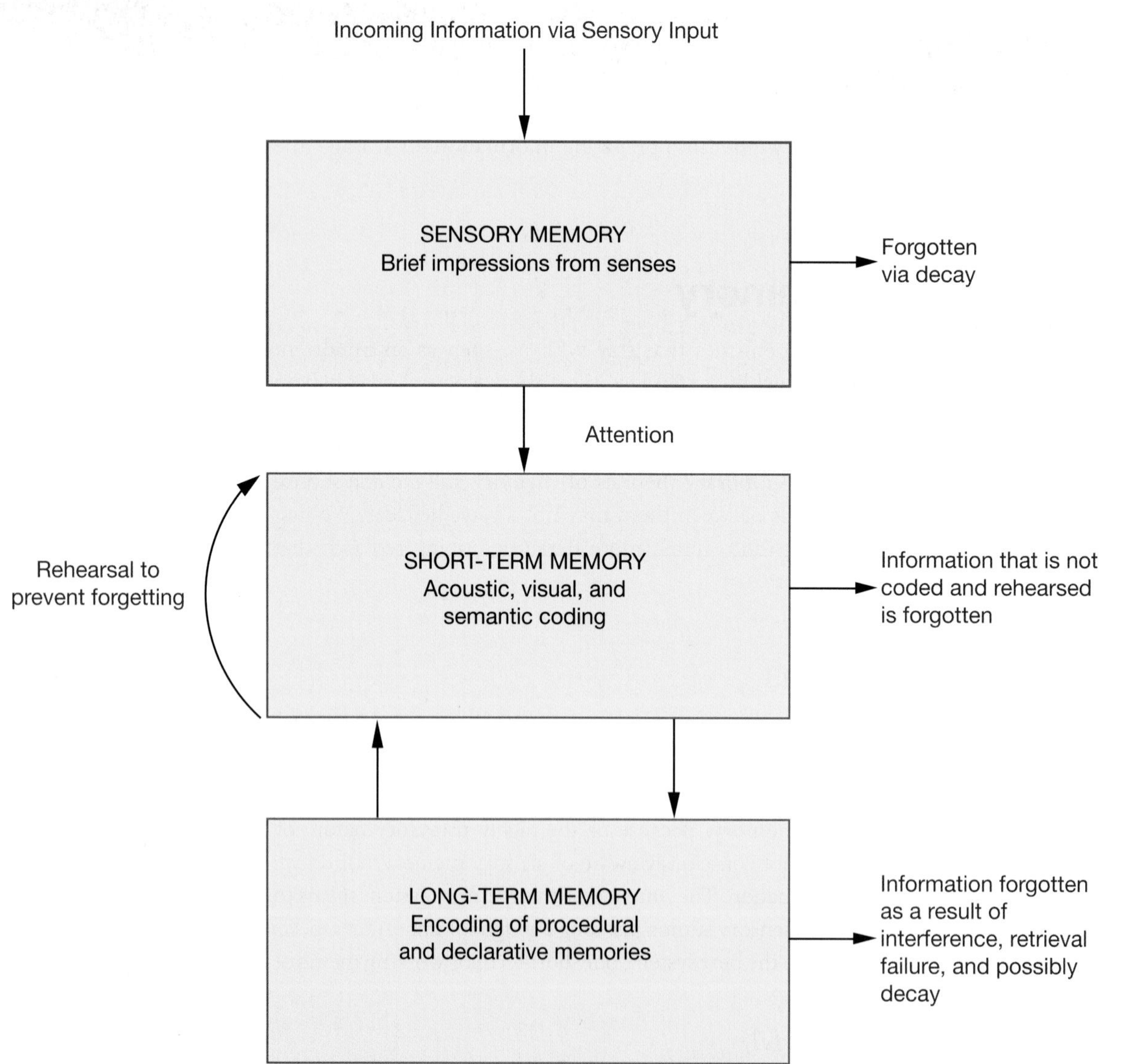

Adapted from figure of "A Theroretical Model of Human Memory System" from article "The Control of Short-Term" from *Scientific American,* Volume 225, August 1971, p. 82, by C. R. Akinson and R. M. Shiffrin.

presents a theoretical model of how information flows into and among these memory systems. Long-term memory is what most of us mean when we talk about memory.

Any time we can recall information, no matter how recently it passed through our sensory/perceptual systems, we are tapping memory. Let us look more closely at how these three memory systems work.

Iconic Memory Visual sensory memory, including fleeting impressions of what we see; also known as visual memory

7.2b Sensory Memory

Sensory memories, sometimes called sensory registers, are brief impressions from any of our senses. We are surrounded by sights, sounds, smells, tactile sensations, and countless other stimuli. When we first receive a particular stimulus, it is held momentarily in sensory memory. These fleeting impressions appear to be largely accurate reproductions of the original sensory inputs. For example, when you glance out the window, for a fraction of a second your brain absorbs the entire visual panorama of varied colors, shapes, and patterns. A similar process occurs when you walk into a cafeteria: Your nose captures a variety of odors and you hear a different set of noises from those you heard on the street.

Unless they are successfully transferred to short-term memory, these sensory impressions disappear within a second or two. That is because the only coding that takes place in sensory memory appears to be the physiological processes of our sensory systems—for instance, the transduction of sound and light waves to messages that are transmitted to our brains (see Chapter 4). Sensory memories are the most difficult memories to comprehend and investigate because of their limited duration.

Iconic (Visual) Memory

Visual sensory memory is called **iconic memory** (*icon* means "image"). It includes images of what we see. For many years, researchers thought that visual memory held only limited information. They based this assumption on evidence from research that had measured the storage capacity of visual sensory memory. Such studies would flash a grid of letters or numbers, such as those shown here, on a screen for a fraction of a second:

H C N M

P O X U

S J T B

Subjects would then be asked to recall as many of the items as possible. When this *whole report procedure* was used, most people could remember only four or five items, no matter how many were shown in the grid.

One researcher, George Sperling (1960), was convinced that subjects in these studies actually registered more than just four or five items; the problem was simply that they forgot the rest while they were reporting the first few items. To test his theory, he designed a new research strategy called the *partial report procedure*. Subjects were told that they would view a grid for one-twentieth of a second and then hear a tone. They would only have to report part of what they had seen. If they heard a high-pitched tone, they were to report only on the top row of four letters. A medium-pitched tone meant they were to report on the middle row, and a low tone meant the bottom row. The point at which a subject heard the tone varied from immediately after the letters disappeared to a maximum delay of one second.

Subliminal Perception The perception of and reaction to a brief or faint stimulus; occurs without conscious awareness

Echoic Memory Auditory sensory memory; fleeting impressions of what we hear; also known as *auditory memory*

Subjects' recall was best when the tone sounded immediately after the image disappeared—an average of 3.3 letters out of 4. Because subjects did not know what row they would be reporting until the image had disappeared, Sperling reasoned that they must have had nine or ten items available for immediate recall (three rows times 3.3 per row)—roughly twice the earlier estimates of what we can register in iconic memory. The later the tone sounded, the less subjects remembered.

Sperling concluded that his subjects were actually reading the letters from a brief afterimage, or iconic reproduction, of the original stimulus pattern. This image fades quite rapidly. From Sperling's research as well as other evidence, we know that an image stored in iconic memory generally fades within approximately 0.3 second as new information replaces it.

More recent research suggests that iconic (and perhaps other sensory) memories can actually aid in decision making. We know that decision making improves with increased amounts of memory information, but can iconic memories aid unconsciously in decisions? Vlassova and Pearson (2013) found that decisions about the movements of a brief iconic image were enhanced if subjects were required to wait 0.5 second before deciding, rather than deciding immediately as in Sperling's experiment. This effect was eliminated if a distracting stimulus was presented during the 0.5-second delay. These results suggest that information processing about an iconic stimulus continues briefly after its termination, even though subjects are not consciously aware of it. This phenomenon may be similar to the concept of **subliminal perception** in which we react to the presentation of a brief or faint stimulus without being consciously aware of it.

Echoic (Auditory) Memory

You may have noticed an auditory image or echo when you have turned off the radio and the voice of a commentator seems to linger momentarily. This auditory sensory memory is called **echoic memory**: After the physical sound stimulus ceases, an auditory image or echo persists for a second or two. Like iconic memory, echoic memories are held only briefly as they are replaced by new auditory stimuli.

We are constantly bombarded by sounds. Most of these go in one ear and out the other, which is to say that only a few selected sounds of importance are passed to our short- and long-term memory systems. It appears that echoic memory serves to filter incoming sounds quickly and to determine which (if any) are important enough to be transferred to short-term memory. For example, suppose you are sitting alone in a crowded airport. Every sound that is loud enough to be heard—talking voices, laughter, loudspeaker announcements, shuffling feet, background music—is temporarily stored in echoic memory. These unimportant auditory messages register fleetingly in your sensory memory system, but they are unlikely to be transferred into short-term memory. However, at some level you are aware of these sounds, and they are being processed. If you find something important among these inputs, for example, if you hear your name in a loudspeaker message, your attention is captured, and you transfer this information into short-term memory.

Are the auditory messages to which we do not attend actually lost, or is there an auditory image similar to the iconic image that remains for a moment? To find out, a number of researchers, most notably Anne Treisman (1960, 1964), have used a technique called shadowing. In this procedure, a subject wears headphones and is exposed simultaneously to two different recordings, one presented to each ear. To ensure that the subject pays attention to only one of the two messages, he or she is asked to shadow or repeat the message presented to one ear. This task is extremely demanding, so much so that subjects typically repeat the words in a dull monotone. When questioned at the end of a shadowing task, subjects are unable to provide any information about the message they did not repeat.

Do you think that subjects' inability to repeat material presented to the other ear means that the shadowing process blocks this channel of sensory input? Or do words that enter through the unattended ear register momentarily in echoic memory? If you were conducting an experiment that used shadowing, how would you answer these questions? See if you can devise a procedure before reading on.

To see if the information that subjects did not repeat was really lost, Treisman added one additional task to her experiment. Although subjects had been instructed to concentrate all their attention on the shadowing task, they were also told that when the recordings stopped and they heard a signal, they were to try to recall anything they could of the unattended messages. This additional task provided interesting results: If the subjects' attention was switched soon enough, it was possible for them to rehear some of the last words of the other message in the form of an echo.

Research indicates that auditory sensory memory for language stimuli can last up to 2.0 seconds. This is considerably longer than the estimated 0.3-second capacity of iconic memory. This difference makes sense, however, when we consider the nature of the sensory messages received by our eyes and ears. When we look around us, we can almost always look back if we fail to process something important through our iconic memories. In contrast, if we miss something in an auditory message, we cannot listen back. Therefore, there seems to be a good functional reason why auditory images should last longer than visual images.

BVT*Lab*

Flashcards are available for this chapter at **www.BVTLab.com**.

The Modality Effect

We also seem to recall information better if we hear it rather than see it. This phenomenon, known as the modality effect, probably reflects the fact that an echo lasts longer than a visual image in sensory memory. Have you ever noticed that you can remember a telephone number or items on a grocery list better if you read them aloud? Auditory afterimages give us more time to transfer this important information over into short-term memory for further organizing and processing.

7.2c **Short-Term or Working Memory**

Short-term memory (STM) is an intermediate memory process sandwiched between sensory memory and long-term memory. Short-term memory is often referred to as our working memory because it is the memory system within which we actively process information, both as we transfer it from sensory memory and as we retrieve it from long-term storage.

As its name suggests, short-term memory has a short duration. If you look up a term in this book's index and see that it is used on pages 342 and 563, you will probably find that after searching page 342, you must check again for the second page reference. Unless we make an active effort to remember information, it fades in about twenty seconds or less. However, we can retain information in our short-term memories for as long as we wish by active *rehearsal*—for example, by repeating a phone number over and over. Forgetting from short-term memory is believed to result from spontaneous fading of the memory trace over time or because information is replaced by new information. We are all familiar with how easily we can become distracted after looking up a new phone number, requiring us to look it up again. In cases like these, our short-term memories are replaced by distracting information.

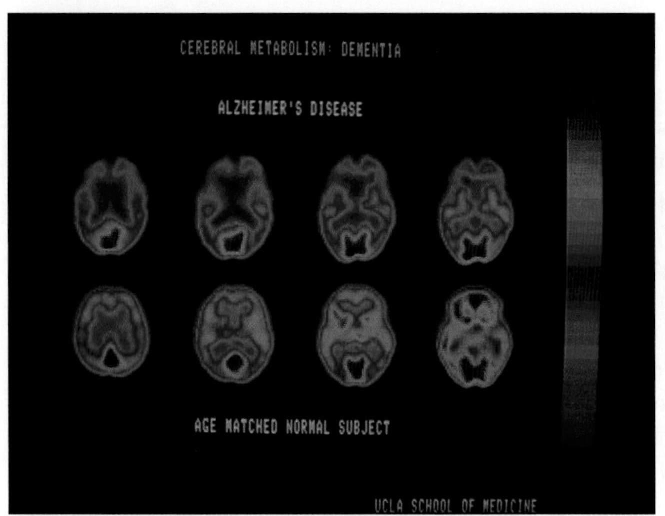

(© Roger Ressmeyer/Corbis/Getty Images)

A positron emission tomography (PET) scan of an Alzheimer's patient's brain reveals less neural activity compared to that of a healthy brain of the same age. A decline in working memory capacity may be a predictor of certain neurological disorders, including Alzheimer's disease.

Short-term memory also has a limited capacity. You can test your short-term memory capacity by reading the following list of numbers once, covering them, and writing down as many as you can in the order in which they appear.

9 2 5 7 6 1 3 7 8 4 5 6

If your short-term memory is like most people, you probably recalled about seven of these numbers. The capacity of this memory system is about seven items or chunks of unrelated information if the information has been encoded on the basis of how it sounds (acoustic coding), and about three chunks when items are encoded based on what they look like or what they mean (visual and semantic coding). Note that short-term capacity does not necessarily refer to seven numbers or letters. It refers to seven pieces of information that can be letters, words, or even meaningful sentences. The term *chunk* describes a meaningful unit of short-term memory. One important way that we can increase the limited capacity of our short-term memory is through chunking. Although short-term memory capacity is estimated to be approximately seven chunks or items, there is actually considerable variability in this number. Your short-term, or working memory capacity may even change during your lifetime. A decline in working memory capacity may also be a predictor of certain neurological disorders including Alzheimer's disease (Conway, Jarrold, Kane, Miyake, & Towse, 2007; Saunders & Summers, 2010).

Chunking

Chunking is the process of grouping items into longer, meaningful units to make them easier to remember. For example, the sequence 1, 9, 4, 1 consists of four numbers that could be treated as four chunks. This would leave room for about three more chunks in STM. However, we could combine these four digits into one meaningful chunk, 1941, the year America went to war with Japan. This method would leave space for at least five or six more chunks of information in STM.

You were probably unable to recall all twelve of the numbers in the previous short-term memory test. However, you might find it relatively easy to recall all twelve numbers by grouping or chunking them into four groups, a process that yields four individual numbers (925, 761, 378, 456). Many of us routinely chunk telephone numbers by grouping the first three digits together, and then treating the final four as separate chunks, thereby reducing the original seven numbers into five chunks. We may further improve our retention of the last four digits by chunking them by twos, for example, remembering 39 and 15 instead of 3-9-1-5.

We can also organize or chunk information held in STM according to its personal meaning, or we can match it with codes already stored in long-term memory. For instance, try reading once through the following list of letters and then recalling as many as possible from memory.

C P A N O W M A D D N B A

Chunking Process of grouping items into longer meaningful units to make them easier to remember

If you tried to recall these items as thirteen separate letters, you probably remembered no more than seven. However, if you coded them into four well-known chunks (CPA, NOW, MADD, NBA), you would have no trouble recalling them in proper sequence.

Coding in Short-Term Memory

Acoustic Coding Most of the information placed in STM is held there in acoustic form, according to how it sounds. This seems to be true even when the information comes through our visual rather than our auditory sense. For example, suppose you are walking along the edge of a wheat field with a friend, and suddenly a pheasant explodes out of the grass nearby. Your immediate recall of the name of the species of bird you just saw would probably be coded in your STM by the sound of the word *pheasant*, not by a visual image of the bird in flight.

(John Livzey/Getty)

A male Alzheimer's patient rests on his bed. Due to his loss of short-term memory, he relies on sticky notes on his dresser drawers to remind him how his clothes are organized.

Visual and Semantic Coding However, not all of the encoding we do in STM is acoustic. If it were, deaf people would be unable to store information in short-term memory. It appears that people with this handicap rely heavily on visual coding in which information is identified and stored as visual images of letters, words, shapes, and so on. For instance, the pheasant that flew out of the field a minute ago would be coded by its image or perhaps by the way its name appears in writing.

In some cases, auditory or semantic coding is not possible. For instance, briefly examine the two figures in Figure 7-2 and decide whether they are the same (but rotated) or different before reading on.

Figure 7-2 Typical Visual Stimuli Used by Shepard and Metzler

The objects are identical in this case, but rotated 90°. In other cases they may be mirror images of each other.

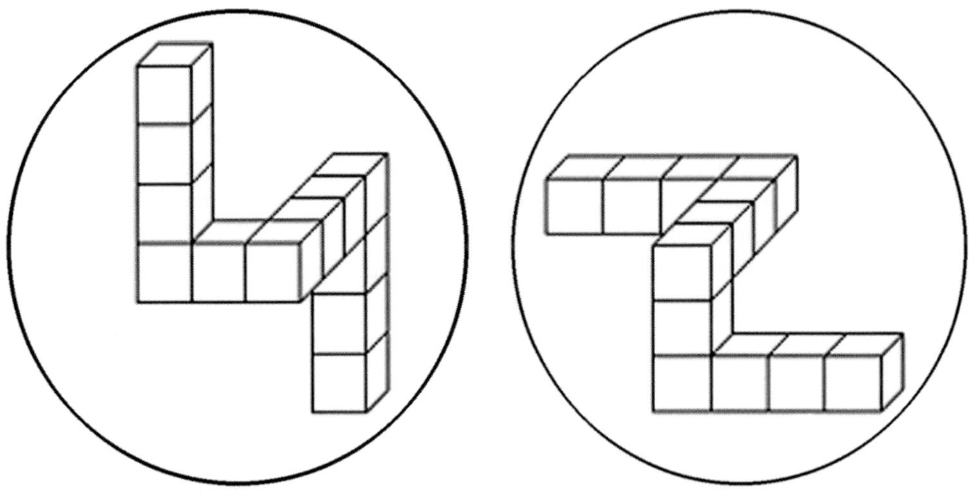

Jennifer Oneske/Wikimedia Commons/Public Domain

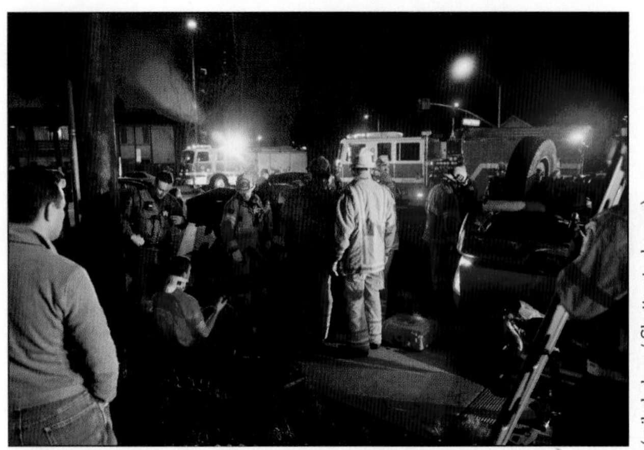
(mikeledray / Shutterstock.com)

Your long-term memory would help you react appropriately in emergency situations.

If you guessed that they were the same, but rotated, you were correct. The "mental" rotation to accomplish this was performed in short-term or working memory; the processing was clearly visual, not auditory. Experiments conducted by Shepard and Metzler (1971) have studied the processing of complex visual stimuli in short-term memory. In these experiments, subjects examined pairs of visual stimuli such as those in Figure 7-2 and were asked if they were the same or different. The dependent variable here was the amount of time it took subjects to decide. In some cases the stimuli were mirror images and therefore different; in other cases they were the same, but rotated. The degree of rotation could range from 0 to 180 degrees. Interestingly, subjects' response times were directly related to the amount of rotation difference between the two figures—that is, the larger the rotation difference, and the longer it took subjects to identify the figures as the same. This not only confirms that visual processing in short-term memory occurs, but also that it is an orderly process determined by the amount of processing required.

7.2d Long-Term Memory

Long-term, or reference, memory (LTM) is like a limitless storehouse that never quite fills up with the facts, feelings, images, skills, and other information that we keep accumulating. Long-term memory allows us to do more than simply store information from past experiences. Faced with new problems and situations, information in LTM is made available to our short-term (working) memory, thereby allowing us to deal with and process new information. We may "live" in our short-term memory, but it is our long-term memory that provides our historical perspective of just who we are; it allows us to understand and use the constant flow of new information we experience.

For example, suppose you are walking down the street and see a person lying prone next to a downed power line. In an instant, you would search your LTM to determine the significance of the scene. You have heard enough about the effects of high-voltage shock to guess that the person may be in cardiac arrest. Suppose this conjecture is confirmed by a pulse check. What next? If the person is lucky, your LTM also contains knowledge of cardiopulmonary resuscitation (CPR). You transfer this information into short-term memory and administer CPR. Then you search long-term memory for information you can use to keep the victim from going into post-trauma shock. This new information would displace the CPR information, which you no longer need, in short-term memory. It is this constant, ongoing interaction between short- and long-term memory that allows us to reason, solve problems, follow schedules, see relationships between events, ride a bike, and so forth.

Types of Long-Term Memory

The abilities just mentioned are diverse, including not only what we can do but also what we know. Most psychologists categorize long-term memories along these lines, as either procedural or declarative memories.

Procedural Memory Recall of how to perform skills such as bicycle riding or swimming

Declarative Memory Recall of specific facts, such as information read in a book

Episodic Memory Autobiographical memories about one's own experiences

Semantic Memory General, nonpersonal knowledge about the meaning of facts and concepts

Dual-Code Model of Memory Theory that memories may be stored either in sensory codes or in verbal codes

Procedural Memory

Procedural memories are memories of how to perform skills. These memories can be highly complex. Suppose you enter a local golf competition. Before teeing off, a friend provides you with some specific information about course conditions. As you play your round, you draw upon a storehouse of knowledge about how to adjust your strokes to accommodate all these factors: the proper follow-through on a sand shot, how much muscle to put behind a stroke on wet turf, how to adjust for wind at the third hole, and so forth. All of these actions are specific skills acquired through practice and reinforcement, and they constitute procedural memory.

Declarative Memory

Not all memory, of course, is based on recalling how to execute specific skills or procedures. For instance, your memory of what you have learned so far in your psychology class is based primarily on lecture notes and your readings in this book. Recall of specific facts such as these is made possible by **declarative memory**.

Procedural memories are often hard to acquire. It may have taken months to perfect your golf swing. Once established, however, these skill memories can be remarkably persistent. Facts stored in declarative memory are often established more quickly, but they are much more susceptible to forgetting.

Another difference between procedural and declarative memory seems to be the location of their storage areas in the brain. One especially interesting source of information comes from an unfortunate accident in which a fencing foil (narrow sword) was thrust through a young man's nostril into the left side of his thalamus. Since his injury, this person, known in the literature as N.A., appears to be unable to store virtually any new declarative knowledge in LTM. It is impossible for him to read a textbook and remember information on a previous page to which the author might refer. Even watching TV or carrying on a conversation is hopelessly confusing since words and plots don't appear to be registered in LTM. Interestingly, however, N.A. is still able to store procedural knowledge. He can learn how to do things like ride a horse, swing a golf club, or swim. These observations, as well as observations from many other patients with slight brain damage, seem to suggest that fact knowledge and skill knowledge are stored in different parts of the brain.

Episodic and Semantic Declarative Memories

Most psychologists now divide declarative memory into two distinct categories: episodic memory and semantic memory—a categorization that was originally proposed by Endel Tulving (1972, 1983, 2002). **Episodic memory** represents, essentially, autobiographical facts about a person's experiences, stored in roughly chronological order. This type of memory includes your memories of your first kiss, the day you graduated from high school, what you had for breakfast this morning, and the sequence in which you consumed these food items.

Semantic memory contains general, nonpersonal knowledge about the *meaning* of facts and concepts without reference to specific experiences. Knowledge about the principles of grammar, mathematical formulas, different kinds of food, and the distinction between afferent and efferent neurons are all examples of facts believed to be stored in semantic memory. Semantic memory is equivalent to an encyclopedic collection of facts about our world. In what form is this information stored in long-term memory? One widely discussed theory, the **dual-code model of memory** (Lacey & Campbell, 2006; Paivio, 1971, 1991), argues that memories may be stored either in *sensory codes* (for example, as visual images or sounds) or *verbal codes* (as words).

Eidetic Imagery The very rare ability to retain large amounts of visual material with great accuracy for several minutes; also known as *photographic memory*

Mnemonic Device Memory system, such as clustering or acrostics, that organizes material in a meaningful way to make it easier to remember

Clustering Mnemonic device that involves grouping items into categories

Some people appear to be able to use visual codes so efficiently that they can retain a vivid image of large amounts of visual material for several minutes. People with this ability, called **eidetic imagery** (or *photographic memory*), claim they can close their eyes and see an entire picture or printed page from a book as if they were looking directly at it rather than scanning their memory. Eidetic imagery is a very rare talent that appears to be more common among children than adults.

One of the most remarkable demonstrations of eidetic imagery comes from Stephen Wiltshire, an autistic artist who can re-create, in drawing, entire cityscapes accurately from memory. Some of the cities he has detailed from short helicopter rides include Tokyo, Rome, London, and New York. His detailed drawings of these cities from memory can be viewed at http://www.stephenwiltshire.co.uk/.

Which type of coding, verbal or sensory, is most common? Do we even use two codes to store declarative memories? These questions have been the subject of much debate in psychology. To complicate matters further, it appears that we store some memories in the form of abstract codes that are neither strictly verbal nor sensory. For example, if you describe a movie you have just seen to a friend, you will not repeat word for word what you heard the actors say. Instead, you will have abstracted your impressions of the movie into a commentary that is your own creation, including your views on the cinematography, the acting, the plot, and the mood.

Since most of us do not use eidetic imagery to remember everything we see, we often have trouble extracting information from long-term memory. Some bits of information can be maddeningly elusive. Our ability to access information depends largely on how it was encoded for storage—that is, the kinds of associations that were formed. Although encoding is largely a passive associative process outside of our attention, there are several strategies that seem to facilitate efficient encoding, which we examine in the following section.

Encoding Long-Term Memory

Many memory experts draw an analogy between long-term memory and a set of file cabinets or the card catalog in a library. Encoding information for storage is like numbering books or files and using index cards to provide cues or access codes. The better we organize our file systems, the more quickly we can access information and the longer we can remember it. Therefore, a key to efficient long-term memory is in the organization of material. A number of memory aids or **mnemonic devices** can help us to do this. The appropriateness or effectiveness of the various mnemonic devices outlined here varies from task to task. You may want to experiment with more than one approach for a given memory task.

Clustering

Clustering is a mnemonic device that involves grouping items into categories. For example, suppose you want to memorize the following shopping list:

toilet paper	green beans	matches
hamburger	bacon	milk
asparagus	chicken	sour cream
corn	broom	cheese

These twelve items, if treated separately, include about five too many chunks for your short-term memory. Thus, you can probably forget trying to hold them in STM by repeatedly rehearsing the list all the way to the grocery store. If you treat the items as separate, without trying to organize the list in some meaningful way, your LTM recall is also likely to prove inadequate for the task. A far easier method is to cluster or group the items under four subcategories: dairy items, meat, vegetables, and household products. Remembering four categories, each with three items, is a much more manageable task.

Acrostics Sentences whose first letters serve as cues for recalling specific information—a mnemonic device

Method of Loci The method of loci, developed by the early Greeks, involves forming pictorial associations between items you wish to recall and specific locations along a designated route you might travel (*loci* means "locations or places" in Latin).

The first step is to develop a route with which you are familiar. Imagine, for example that you are walking from the campus library to your apartment. Pick out specific locations along the way that are easy to remember—such as a bus stop bench, a flagpole, a large oak tree, a broken-down van parked on the street, the sidewalk leading to your apartment house, and so forth. Then create a series of images that associates each item on your list with a specific location along your route.

For example, to use the loci method to remember the grocery list in the clustering discussion, you might imagine toilet paper strewn on the bus stop bench, cornstalks leaning against the flagpole, a chicken sitting in the oak tree, and so forth. Picture these associations as vividly as possible. Later, when you need to remember the list, take a mental walk along your route.

Narrative Story Another way to remember information is to organize it into a narrative. The story does not need to be particularly logical or plausible; it simply has to place items within a meaningful framework. For example, suppose you want to remember the five explanations for why we forget: interference, organic amnesia, decay of the memory trace, retrieval failure, and motivated forgetting. (These explanations are discussed later in this chapter.) The following narrative provides one possible way to encode this information (the key words describing explanations for forgetting are italicized).

> The rotten odor emanating from his duffel bag was sufficient to run *interference* as Sam weaved his way through the crowded corridors. "Phew!" exclaimed his buddy Bill. "It smells like *something organic* is *decaying* in your duffel bag." "Oh, that is just the remnants of a crummy brown-bag lunch that my Mom *failed to retrieve* from my bag because she wants me to overcome my *motivation to forget* about the little details in my life," responded Sam.

An experiment by Gordon Bower and Michael Clark (1969) demonstrated how powerful a mnemonic device the narrative story could be. Subjects inexperienced in this technique were asked to try to memorize twelve lists, each containing ten nouns. Half the subjects were instructed to make up twelve brief stories, each containing one of the groups of nouns. The other half of the subjects merely spent an equivalent amount of time attempting to memorize the lists with whatever technique they chose. When tested later, subjects who had used the narrative story technique recalled an average of 94 percent of the words; those who had not, remembered only an average of 14 percent.

Acrostics **Acrostics** are sentences in which the first letter of each word serves as a cue for recalling specific information. If you took piano lessons at some point in your life, it is a good bet that you used another acrostic—the sentence "Every Good Boy Does Fine"—to help you memorize the notes on the lines of the treble staff. An example the author used to remember the Linnaean classification system in biology class was: "Kings Play Chess on Fine-Grained Sand." These stood for kingdom, phylum, class, order, family, genus, and species.

Acronym Meaningful arrangement of letters that provides a cue for recalling information—a mnemonic device

Maintenance Rehearsal System for remembering that involves repeatedly rehearsing information without attempting to find meaning in it

Elaborative Rehearsal System for remembering that involves using mnemonic devices (more effective than maintenance rehearsal)

Acronyms Another way to enhance memory is the use of **acronyms**, or meaningful arrangements of letters that provide cues for the recall of material. For example, many people have learned the colors on a color wheel in their order of appearance by remembering Roy G. Biv (red, orange, yellow, green, blue, indigo, and violet). To help students remember the notes in the spaces of the treble staff, piano teachers often use another acronym—FACE.

Do memory strategies really work? One experiment demonstrates not only that they do but also that we seem to learn memory systems at a fairly young age. Sixth grade children were shown to be much better at remembering lists than third graders (Ornstein & Naus, 1978). This difference reflected a difference in strategy. Whereas younger children used **maintenance rehearsal** to try to remember the list, the other subjects applied **elaborative rehearsal**. Maintenance rehearsal is simply repeating the words without any attempt to find meaning in them. In contrast, elaborative rehearsal involves organizing strategies such as clustering. When the younger children in this study were taught how to organize material, their recall improved to the level of the older subjects.

Retrieval from Long-Term Memory

The reason why the memory systems just described work so well is that they provide cues or handles that help us to access information. The more retrieval cues we can link to information, the more likely we are to recall it later on.

Retrieval Cues This phenomenon was demonstrated in an experiment conducted by Fergus Craik and Endel Tulving (1975). In the first phase of the study, subjects were given index cards containing single sentences with a word missing. After reading the sentence, they viewed a word flashed on a screen and pressed either a yes or no button to indicate whether or not the word fit the sentence. The sentence complexity varied from simple ("She cooked the ____________.") to complex ("The great bird swooped down and carried off the struggling ______________.").

Subjects saw a given word once. In some instances the word did not fit the sentence. In other cases it fit into a simple, medium, or complex sentence. For example, the word chicken would fit both of the sample sentences; house could fit neither. Subjects were told that the experiment was concerned with perceptions and speed of reaction time, so they made no special effort to store the words in their long-term memory.

After completing this phase of the experiment, subjects had a short rest period. They were then given the cards containing the sentences and asked to recall the word associated with each sentence.

Based on your understanding of memory processes described thus far, what kind of performance would you expect the subjects to exhibit on these retention tests? Would you predict that their ability to recall words was influenced by whether or not they matched with a sentence? Do you think that sentence complexity influenced recall, and if so, in what direction and why? Take a moment to formulate your answer before reading on.

Figure 7-3 demonstrates the results of this experiment. Subjects were much more likely to recall words that fit a sentence than words that did not. They were also considerably more likely to remember a word if it fit a complex sentence than if it fit a simple sentence.

It seems, then, that we remember things better if they are associated with specific cues. For example, we are more likely to remember the item "watch" if we can associate it with a visual cue, as suggested by the sentence, "He dropped the watch." We are even more likely to remember the item when it is used in a more complex sentence such as, "The old man hobbled across the room and picked up the valuable watch from the mahogany table." This complex sentence provides considerably more visual cues that can aid our retention.

Figure 7-3 Results of the Craik and Tulving Experiment

Subjects were more likely to recall words that fit into sentences than those that didn't. They were also more likely to recall words that fit complex sentences than those that didn't fit simple ones.

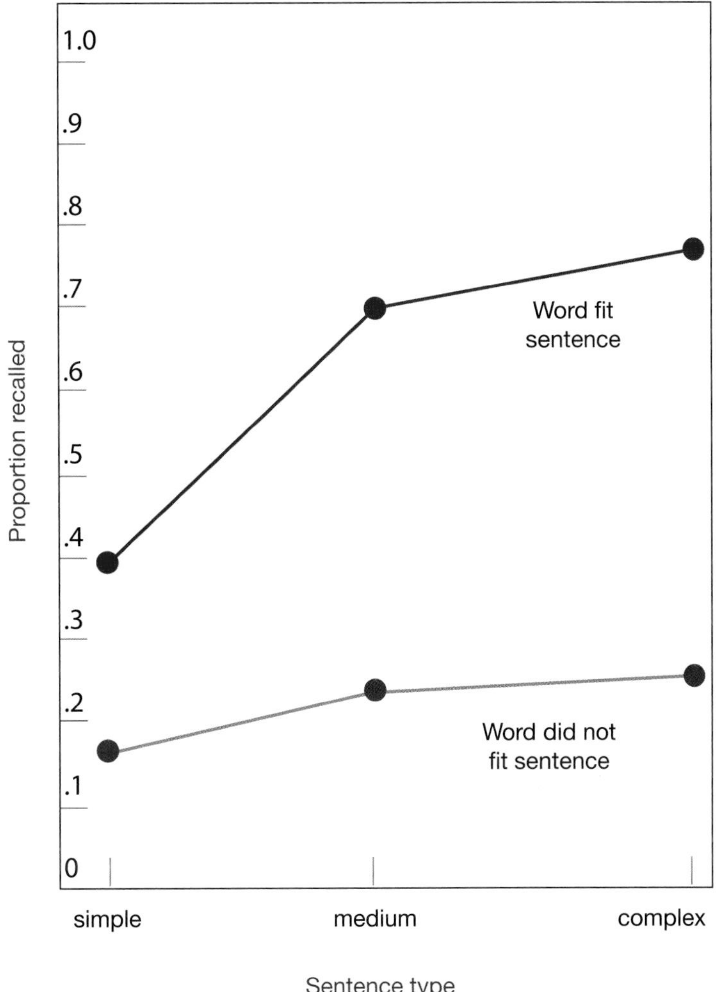

Data from "Results of the Craik and Tulving Experiment" from *The Journal of Experimental Psychology*, 104, p. 283, by F. I. M. Craik and E. Tulving. Copyright © 1975 by the American Psychological Association.

Testing Long-Term Memory

A number of methods have been used to measure our ability to store new material in long-term memory. The three most common techniques are recall tasks, recognition tasks, and relearning.

Recall In memory tests, a subject's ability to reproduce information to which he or she was previously exposed; fill-in-the-blank and essay questions test recall

Recognition In memory tests, a subject's ability to recognize whether he or she has been previously exposed to information; multiple-choice and true-false questions test recognition

Relearning Technique for testing memory that involves measuring how much more quickly a person can relearn material that was learned at some previous time

Recall

In a **recall** task, the subject is asked to reproduce information to which he or she was previously exposed. For example, a recall question designed to test your knowledge of the material in this chapter might ask you to name the three memory processes. Fill-in-the-blank or essay questions are other examples of recall tasks.

Recognition

A **recognition** task presents possible answers, from which the subject must pick the correct one. Instead of having to pull information from memory, a recognition test simply involves realizing whether you have been previously exposed to a particular bit of information. In a recognition test format, a question regarding three memory processes might read, "What are the three primary memory processes? (1) Encoding, networking, activation (2) Elaboration, storage, retrieval (3) Encoding, storage, retrieval (4) Association, networking, retrieval." This example is the familiar multiple-choice format often used in classrooms. However, not all multiple-choice questions are recognition tasks. Some cleverly worded questions may require respondents to synthesize information before an answer can be identified. True-false questions can be another example of recognition tasks.

Given the choice, most students prefer recognition tasks such as multiple-choice tests over recall tasks. This preference is not without justification, for research demonstrates that we can usually recognize much more than we can recall. Can you explain why recognition tests yield better performances than recall tasks? Try to answer this question by yourself before reading on.

A recognition test simply requires you to perform one memory task: You search through your memory to see if stored information matches the new information. The test stimulus is typically rich with retrieval cues that help you gain access to stored information. In contrast, a recall test requires you to perform two tasks, both of which are more difficult than the recognition task. First, you must search through your memory and reconstruct possible answers from information that is not presented to you in the test. Then, you must identify the correct answer from the varied possibilities and describe it well enough to demonstrate that you truly recall it.

Relearning

A third method of measuring memory, **relearning**, is perhaps the most sensitive measure of memory. Relearning is infrequently used today, primarily because it is so time consuming. Relearning involves measuring how much more quickly a person can relearn material that was learned at a previous time. For example, you might be asked to memorize a list of *nonsense syllables* (meaningless combinations of two consonants and a vowel, such as ZUD or XUT). The number of trials it took you to master the list would be recorded to measure your initial performance. The list would then be put aside for a period of time, and at a later point you would be asked to relearn it. If there is no memory trace of the nonsense syllables previously learned, it should take as much effort to relearn the list the second time as it did the first; that is, there would be no savings due to memory. However, if at least some recall for the nonsense syllables is prompted by your LTM, relearning should be faster than the original learning. For instance,

(Gdallimore/Wikimedia Commons/Public Domain)

Relearning involves measuring how much more quickly a person can relearn material that was learned at a previous time, such as a song from grade school. If your mind can recall the nonsense syllables, prompted by your long-term memory, relearning should be faster than the original learning.

if it takes ten trials for you to master the original list but only five to relearn it, there will be a savings of five trials thanks to memory. This would yield a savings score of 50 percent (five trials saved, ten original trials, or 50 percent).

Herman Ebbinghaus (1913) used the relearning method in the first systematic studies of human memory. He used the most reliable subject he could find, himself. He memorized countless lists of nonsense syllables, set them aside for varied periods of time, and then relearned the lists using savings scores as a measure of retention. Ebbinghaus invented the concept of nonsense syllables because he felt that people vary in their ability to make associations with real words like *dog*, *gun*, or *pit*.

Ebbinghaus's systematic studies of memory had a great impact on the then infant discipline of psychology. He is perhaps best remembered for *curves of forgetting*, which were derived from his accumulated data on savings scores. Figure 7-4 illustrates that forgetting is strongly influenced by the passage of time. It occurs very rapidly at first—within twenty minutes after mastering a list of nonsense syllables, Ebbinghaus had forgotten about 40 percent of it. However, after this initial rapid loss, the rate of forgetting declines significantly. Note that the savings score after twenty days was almost the same as the ten-day score. We will have more to say about this curve in the section on forgetting later in this chapter.

Ebbinghaus discovered that he could greatly improve his savings scores by rehearsing a list after he had already mastered it. This technique, called **overlearning**, is an extremely valuable approach to memorizing material that you wish to retain.

Overlearning Technique for memorizing material that involves rehearsing information after it has already been learned

Explicit Memory Memory that a person can recall through conscious effort

7.2e Explicit and Implicit Memory

Up to this point we have been discussing memories that are readily available to your consciousness. That is, through conscious effort you can recall a phone number, an answer to an exam question, or what you did on vacation last summer. These memories are referred to as **explicit memories,** and they play an important role in your construction of a meaningful past. However, by themselves, these explicit memories are not enough.

Figure 7-4 A Forgetting Curve

This curve illustrates the effects of time on retention.

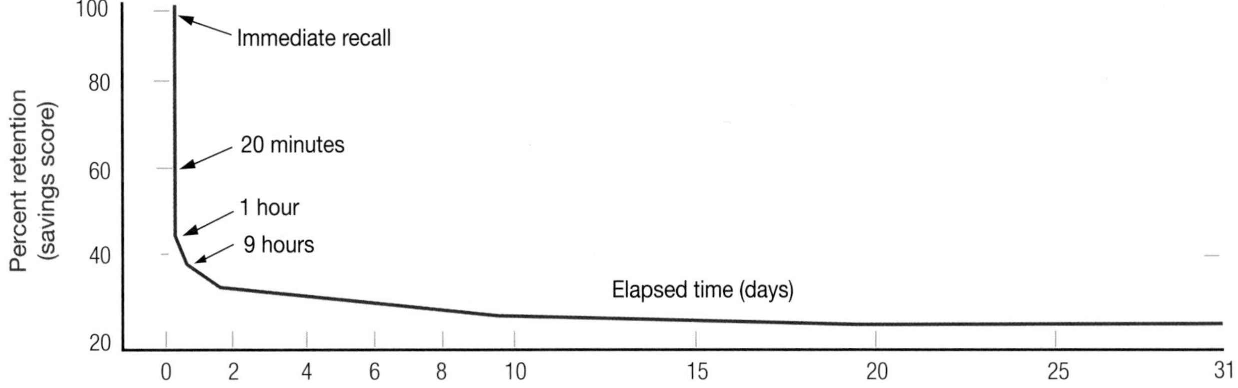

Data from Memory: *A Contribution to Experimental Psychology*, by H. Ebbinghaus, 1913, New York, NY: Dover

Implicit Memories
Memories that are unavailable to conscious awareness but contribute to explicit memories

Memories of your past that are unavailable to conscious awareness also contribute to this construction. You experience these unconscious, or **implicit memories**, when you have a sense of familiarity with objects or places. For instance, when you encounter an old acquaintance, you may at first sense that she is familiar and only later remember her name and the specific occasion when you met. In this case, the implicit memory served as a primer for the explicit memories of name and context. Implicit memories provide us with a sense of knowing and familiarity that are essential to everyday functioning.

How do psychologists investigate memories that are unconscious? Harvard psychologist Daniel Schacter demonstrated that implicit memories could be studied using word-completion tasks (Tulving & Schacter, 1990; Schacter, 1995; Schacter, Gallo, & Kensinger, 2007). In one such study, subjects were first shown a list of words, and then later they were asked to complete a series of word fragments. Subjects do much better completing fragments of words that were previously shown, even though they cannot remember those words before the completion task. An example of a word-completion task is shown in Figure 7-5. This research, and other research testing memory for nonverbal items, suggests that explicit and implicit memories are in fact distinct. More recent research using PET imaging to measure neural activity during explicit and implicit memory tasks has shown that these different memory systems rely on different neural structures (Uecker et al., 1997).

7.3 Memory as a Dynamic Process

We have seen that our ability to remember an event can be influenced by how that event was encoded or associated with earlier memories. What happens to those memories once stored? In this section, we will see that memory is a dynamic process in which our memories of events can change over time. For example, you may remember many details about

Figure 7-5 Example of Word-Completion Task

A typical word-completion task to demonstrate implicit memory: Subjects are first shown a list of words. Then, after a delay, they are asked to complete word fragments. Subjects are better at completing the words that were previously shown to them, even though they cannot remember seeing them.

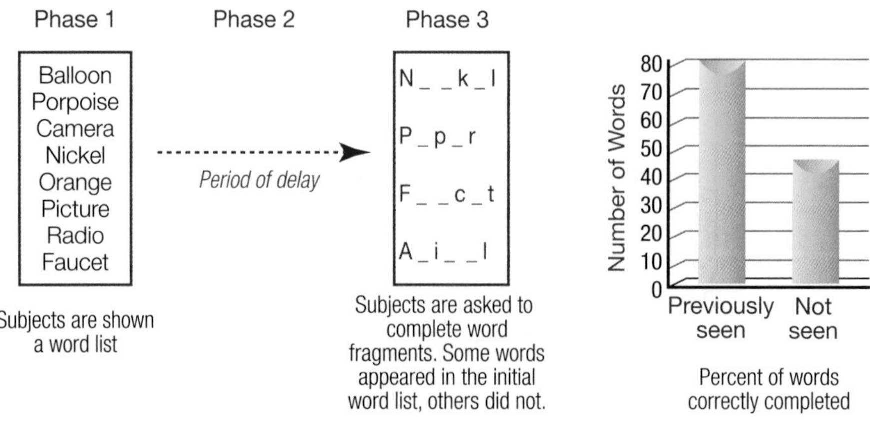

the moment when you first saw the World Trade Center explosion, but a good friend who was in the same room with you may have a different memory. Indeed, our memories often vary significantly from the actual facts. Why does this occur?

False Memory A memory of an event that never occurred; can be "planted" in a subject prior to recall by a variety of methods, including hypnosis

7.3a Constructive Memory

Psychologists believe that memory is a dynamic process, not merely the collection of facts that remain unaltered by further experiences. For instance, we frequently add or delete details to make new information more consistent with the way we already conceive our world. Thus, remembering is often a process of reconstructing an event rather than simply searching long-term memory for a perfect copy of it. As a result, our memories are not necessarily accurate representations of what actually occurred. Instead, they may be accounts of what we think happened, or perhaps what we believe should have happened.

Serious investigations of constructive processes in memory did not catch on in psychology until the last couple of decades. However, Sir Frederick Bartlett (1932), an English psychologist who tested college students' memories of simple stories set in unfamiliar cultures, pioneered this research more than fifty-five years ago. One story read by his subjects was an American Indian folktale titled "The War of the Ghosts." This story, along with a student's reproduction of the story from memory, is shown in Figure 7-6.

Bartlett found that his subjects never recalled the material exactly as it had been presented. Rather, they stored a few primary facts and organized the rest of the story around these central themes. Bartlett's subjects tended to modify their memories of the original stories in several ways: by shortening and simplifying the story; by focusing on and overemphasizing certain details; and by altering certain details to make the story fit their own views more closely. For example, in the student's rendition of "The War of the Ghosts," certain words have been changed, and the supernatural theme has been minimized.

7.3b False Memories

In the previous section, we saw how memories can change over time. Our biases, expectations, and even new learning can all contribute to reconstructions of our memories of the past. However, can memories of events that never occurred in our lives be planted and appear as real? Interest in these planted, or **false memories**, began to rise as reports from clinical settings suggested that under hypnosis, or the direction of a therapist, adult patients were able to recall instances of past child abuse. Were these reports accurate recollections of actual child abuse, or were they false memories unintentionally planted by the therapist? In an attempt to demonstrate the ease of planting false memories, psychologist Elizabeth Loftus designed the now famous "Lost in the Mall" experiment (Loftus 1997; Loftus & Bernstein, 2005; Loftus, Garry, & Hayne, 2008). Her work has led to significant changes in the ways patients are interviewed about their past. In one version of her experiment, with the assistance of a willing family member playing "Remember when _______," subjects were asked if they remembered being lost in a shopping mall as a young child. False details about the incident were mixed in with actual events that occurred during this time in the subject's past. Several days later, subjects reported elaborate memories of the incident that never occurred. These false memories contained details of clothing worn, feelings of fear, and descriptions of people who assisted the subject in being reunited with family.

Figure 7-6 The Original Version of "The War of the Ghosts" and a Subject's Reproduction of It

THE WAR OF THE GHOSTS

One night two young men from Egulac went down to the river to hunt seals, and while they were there it became foggy and calm. Then they heard war cries, and they thought: "Maybe this is a war party." They escaped to the shore, and hid behind a log. Now canoes came up, and they heard the noise of paddles, and saw one canoe coming up to them. There were five men in the canoe, and they said:

"What do you think? We wish to take you along. We are going up the river to make war on the people."

One of the young men said: "I have no arrows."

"Arrows are in the canoe," they said.

"I will not go along. I might be killed. My relatives do not know where I have gone. But you," he said, turning to the other, "may go with them."

So one of the young men went, but the other returned home.

And the warriors went on up the river to a town on the other side of Kalama. The people came down to the water, and they began to fight, and many were killed. But presently the young man heard one of the warriors say: "Quick, let us go home: that Indian has been hit." Now he thought, "Oh, they are ghosts." He did not feel sick, but they said he had been shot.

So the canoes went back to Egulac, and the young man went ashore to his house, and made a fire. And he told everybody and said: "Behold I accompanied the ghosts, and we went to fight. Many of our fellows were killed, and many of those who attacked us were killed. They said I was hit, and I did not feel sick."

He told it all, and then he became quiet. When the sun rose he fell down. Something black came out of his mouth. His face became contorted. The people jumped up and cried.

He was dead.

SAMPLE REPRODUCTION

Two youths were standing by a river about to start seal catching, when a boat appeared with five men in it. They were all armed for war.

The youths were at first frightened, but they were asked by the men to come and help them fight some enemies on the other bank. One youth said he could not come, as his relations would be anxious about him; the other said he would go, and entered the boat.

In the evening he returned to his hut, and told his friends that he had been in a battle. A great many had been slain, and he had been wounded by an arrow; he had not felt any pain, he said. They told him that he must have been fighting in a battle of ghosts. Then he remembered that it had been queer and he became very excited.

In the morning, however, he became ill, and his friends gathered round; he fell down and his face became very pale. Then he writhed and shrieked and his friends were filled with terror. At last he became calm. Something hard and black came out of his mouth, and he lay contorted and dead.

Source: Bartlett, F.C. (1932). *Remembering: A Study in Experimental and Social Psychology*. Cambridge University Press

You might be thinking that false memories such as this are only the products of gullible people with vivid imaginations. Recent research suggests otherwise. For example, Roediger and his colleagues have shown that memories for previously seen words or scenes can be planted in college students during a memory recall test. In these experiments, subjects were shown a list of words or pictures of familiar scenes and later asked to recall as many items as possible in collaboration with another subject. Unknown to the subject, the collaborator was really a confederate of the experimenter who deliberately recalled items that were not previously seen. Subjects typically reported with confidence that the planted items were seen earlier (Roediger, Meade, & Bergman, 2001; Roediger & McDermott, 1995; Roediger, Rajaram, & Geraci, 2007; Meade & Roediger, 2002). It is easy to see from these experiments how false memories could be passed from person to person.

Advertisements may also be designed to plant false memories and create feelings of nostalgia for their products. For instance, autobiographical ads suggest to consumers that they had certain pleasant experiences as children. Could referencing these planted experiences actually increase the likelihood that we create a false memory of an event? Loftus and her colleagues showed Disney ads to subjects that suggested they had actually shaken hands with Mickey Mouse (a remote possibility) or with Bugs Bunny (an impossibility) as a child. These ads successfully increased the confidence subjects had about their memories of these events (Braun, Ellis, & Loftus, 2001).

Is it possible to distinguish between true and false memories such as these? Memory researchers believe that true and false memories leave different sensory "signatures" that can be detected with brain imaging technologies such as the fMRI. These sensory signatures may occur in the visual or auditory cortices and reflect neural activation by implicit memories. False memories would not trigger implicit memories that could be detected by brain activation (Aminoff, Schacter, & Bar, 2008; Slotnick & Schacter, 2004).

Schemas In reference to memory, conceptual frameworks that individuals use to make sense out of stored information; in Jean Piaget's theory, the mental structures we form to assimilate and organize processed information

7.3c Schemas

The tendency to change details to fit our own cultural perspectives is consistent with recent findings on the impact of schemas on reconstructive memory processes. **Schemas** are conceptual frameworks we use to make sense out of our world. Because schemas provide us with preconceived expectations, they help make the world seem more predictable. However, they can also lead to significant distortions in our memory processes in that they often exert a strong impact on the manner in which memory for a particular event is encoded. Many memory distortions are consistent with our established schemas.

This idea was demonstrated in a classic study conducted more than forty years ago in which subjects were shown a picture of two men engaged in an argument. One man was black and the other was white, and the white man held a razor in his hand. After briefly viewing the picture, subjects were asked to describe the scene to someone who had not viewed the picture, who in turn passed the information on to someone else, and so on. As the information was passed from person to person, some of its features were altered. Most notably, the razor ended up in the hand of the black man (Allport & Postman, 1947). These findings suggest that the subjects' schemas (that is, their assumption that blacks were more prone to violence than whites) influenced the way they constructed and stored this information.

Some more recent studies have demonstrated another interesting point: When people remember information that is not consistent with their schemas, they are likely to distort the facts to make them fit better with their conceptual frameworks. For instance, in one study (Spiro, 1975) subjects read one of two different versions of a story about an engaged couple. In both versions, the male partner did not want to have children. The difference between the stories was that in one version the woman did not want children either, whereas in the other version she was upset because she wanted children. Subjects were asked to read the story; when they were finished, they performed some tasks involving paperwork. Then a postscript was added to the story: Some of the subjects were told that the couple married and lived together happily; others were told that they broke up and never saw each other again. Subjects were then asked to recall the story at a later date.

Can you predict the outcome of this experiment? Do you think that the relationship between the story version and the postscript influenced the way subjects remembered the story later on? Apply what you have learned about schemas and constructive memory processes to formulate a prediction before reading on.

If you predicted that subjects modified the story to fit their own views about roles of men and women in the family, you were right. Subjects who heard a postscripted ending that did not seem to fit the rest of the story tended to "remember" information that

BVT*Lab*

Visit **www.BVTLab.com** to explore the student resources available for this chapter.

resolved that contradiction. For example, those who read a version in which the couple disagreed about having children did not expect the couple to live together happily. When they remembered the story, they were likely to recall other facts that would make the ending fit the story, such as a compromise in which the couple had agreed to adopt a child instead of having one of their own.

Similarly, subjects who were told that the couple agreeing not to have children had broken up were likely to "remember" that this pair had other difficulties, such as parents who opposed the relationship. In contrast, subjects who read stories that matched the postscripted endings did not add new facts to the story. They had no reason to, because the stories were consistent with their schemas.

Although schemas can lead to memory distortions, they also provide important association cues that can aid recall. Consider an experiment in which subjects were asked to study a list of behaviors of a hypothetical person. Some participants were told that they were subjects in a memory experiment and that they should attempt to remember as many of the behaviors as possible. Others were told they were in an experiment designed to evaluate how people form impressions of others, and they were asked to try to form an impression (a schema) of the person. A later recall test revealed that subjects who attempted to fit the information into a schema demonstrated better recall than those who had merely attempted to memorize a list of behaviors (Hamilton, Katz, & Leirer, 1980).

We have seen that our memories may sometimes involve fiction as well as facts, a result of our tendency to fill gaps in our knowledge of previous events or to modify memories to match existing schemas. Such active constructive processes, which may occur in both the storage and retrieval stages of memory, may have a profound impact on a number of areas of human experience—for example, eyewitness testimony.

7.3d Eyewitness Testimony

The legal system places great value on the testimony of eyewitnesses. Police officers who file automobile accident reports, criminal investigators, and juries—all tend to give considerable credence to the accounts of people who were on the scene. In recent years, however, several findings have raised questions about the reliability of eyewitness testimony.

Psychologist Elizabeth Loftus has been the leading investigator in this area of research. The accumulating evidence of memory as a constructive process prompted Loftus to wonder to what degree eyewitness testimony might be influenced by people's tendency to reconstruct their memory of events to fit their schemas. She also wondered whether information received after the fact might be integrated into witnesses' memories of what they had seen. Is it possible that subtle differences in the way questions are worded might cause a witness to remember the event in a different light? Can witnesses be misled into "remembering" things that did not actually occur?

A number of studies by Loftus and other researchers have investigated such questions. In one study, subjects watched a film of a two-car accident and then filled out a questionnaire recalling what they had seen. There were four versions of the wording of one critical question. Some subjects were asked, "About how fast were the two cars going when they *contacted* each other?" In the three other versions, the words *hit, bumped,* or *smashed* were substituted for *contacted*. The word *contacted* yielded an average speed estimate of 32 mph, whereas the words *hit, bumped,* and *smashed* produced estimates of 34, 38, and 41 mph, respectively (Loftus & Palmer, 1974). The words used to describe the collision clearly influenced the way these subjects reconstructed their memories of the accident. It seems clear that the way witnesses remember an event can be influenced by the kinds of questions they are asked about the event.

Figure 7-7 Descriptive Language Can Influence What We Recall

Subjects viewed a film of an automobile accident. Later they were asked to judge the speed of the cars after hearing a description of the accident. If the words *smashed into each other* were used in the description, the estimates of speed were greater than if the words *contacted each other* were used.

After-the-fact information may do more than merely change our recollections. In some cases, it may cause people to incorporate completely false information into their memories. This idea was suggested in another study in which subjects watched a videotape of an automobile accident and then were asked questions designed to introduce false information (Loftus, 1975). Half the subjects were asked, "How fast was the white sports car going when it passed the barn while traveling along the country road?" The remaining subjects were asked the same question, but without the words "when it passed the barn."

In point of fact, there was no barn in the videotape. When subjects were questioned again about the accident a week later, however, 17 percent of those who heard "when it passed the barn" reported seeing a barn in the videotape. In contrast, only 3 percent of the subjects who had heard nothing about a barn remembered seeing the barn.

In another study, Loftus and her colleagues showed subjects a series of color slides depicting the sequence of events in an automobile accident. Each subject saw one of two possible versions of a critical slide in the series. In one version, a car was stopped at an intersection posted with a stop sign. In the other, a yield sign was substituted for the stop sign. Immediately after viewing the slide series, subjects were asked follow-up questions that presumed the existence of either a stop or yield sign. (Sometimes this information was consistent with what they had seen; in other cases it was not.) Then, twenty minutes after completing the questionnaire, they were shown several pairs of slides and asked to pick which one out of each pair they had seen before.

Misinformation Effect The presentation of misleading information that leads people to erroneous reports of that misinformation

State-Dependent Memory Phenomenon wherein recall of particular events, experiences, or information is aided by the subject being in the same context or physiological state in which the information was first encoded

When the follow-up questions presumed that subjects had seen the same sign as they had actually seen, subjects identified the correct slide in the retest 75 percent of the time. In contrast, when the questions had mentioned a sign not present in the original scene, the misled subjects identified the correct slide only 41 percent of the time (Loftus, Miller, & Burns, 1978). This same research team also demonstrated that the longer the time interval between observing an event and later exposure to inaccurate information, the less accurate recall is likely to be.

Such findings are alarming when we consider what often happens to eyewitnesses. First, a witness may be questioned repeatedly by police officers, some of whom may introduce erroneous information by asking leading questions. Friends and family members also ask questions and introduce new information. Later (probably much later), an attorney may question a witness on or off the stand. If intelligent college students can be misled into "remembering" erroneous information in controlled experiments such as those just described, how reliable are eyewitness accounts of real-world crimes and accidents?

Some controversy remains regarding the impact of misleading postevent information on memory. Some researchers maintain that the misleading information to which eyewitnesses are often exposed may not actually impair memory for an earlier event. However, regardless of whether or not misleading postevent information actually alters memory for the original event, there is extensive evidence for a **misinformation effect**—that is, that misleading information presented after an event can lead people to erroneous reports of that misinformation.

A number of studies indicate that people exposed to violent events are especially likely to incorporate misinformation into their memory. Shocking events may interfere with our ability to store details accurately, even though we have vivid flashbulb memories of what we were doing or feeling at the time. Since an eyewitness's recall of a violent event may lack many details, he or she may be inclined to fill in the gaps with subsequent misinformation (Loftus & Burns, 1982).

After the crash of TWA flight 800 in July 1996, several newspapers and television reports ran stories suggesting that a missile may have shot down the plane. In spite of evidence to the contrary, numerous witnesses claimed to have actually seen a missile. In this case, a few misleading reports actually changed the accounts of a number of witnesses (Davis & Loftus, 2007).

It is clear from these cases that memory is a constructive process, involving much more than merely placing bits of data in storage and then retrieving them later on. In the next section we look at several additional factors that may affect the way we remember an event.

7.3e State Dependency

Some research suggests that our internal state (for instance, emotions or physiological conditions) also forms a kind of context that influences recall. For example, research has demonstrated that recall of information learned while under the influence of a drug (such as alcohol, marijuana, or morphine) occurs more easily in the same drug state than in a nondrug state (Deutsch & Folle, 1973; Bruins Slot, & Colpaert, 2003).

This phenomenon, known as **state-dependent memory**, also appears to hold true for emotional states. People seem to remember things better when they are in the same mood or emotional state as they were when the information first entered their memories. In an experiment with college students, memory was significantly enhanced in the same state, either fear or relaxation, where learning took place (Lang, Craske, Brown, & Ghaneian, 2001).

7.3f Extreme Emotion

If you ask virtually any American who was an adolescent or older in 1963 what they were doing when they heard about John F. Kennedy's assassination, the odds are very good that they will be able to tell you an amazing number of details about where they were, what the weather was like, perhaps even what they were wearing. The same is true of those who remember the terrorist attacks of September 11, 2001.

This kind of vivid recall for earlier events associated with extreme emotion, surprise, or uniqueness has been called **flashbulb memory**. Such memories are so vivid that it is as if our brains had recorded them like a scene caught in the sudden glare of a camera's flashbulb. Our recall for such occurrences is not so precise for factual details surrounding the event itself, but rather for the specific setting and manner in which we first heard about the event.

Are flashbulb memories more permanent than our memories for ordinary events? While it appears that flashbulb memories are more vivid and accurate than normal memories, there is little evidence to support this perception. Flashbulb memories are prone to distortion and forgetting, just like normal memories. What appears to be different about flashbulb memories is not that they are more accurate, but rather that we are much more confident in their accuracy (Talarico & Rubin, 2007; Weaver, 1993).

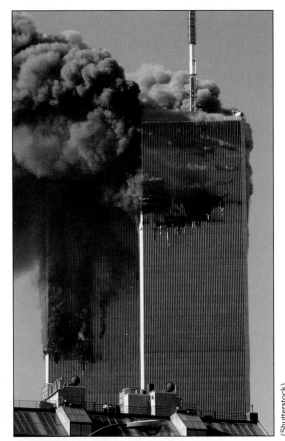

(Shutterstock)

A flashbulb memory is the vivid recall of an event associated with extreme emotion, surprise, or uniqueness, such as the September 11, 2001, attack on the World Trade Center.

Flashbulb memories may be triggered by any sudden, shocking event that has great personal significance to an individual. Researchers Talarico and Rubin at Duke University investigated the memories of the attacks of September 11, 2001, on the World Trade Center in New York (flashbulb memory) and compared them to memories of events that occurred on the previous weekend (ordinary memories). While both kinds of memories tended to decline in detail over a period of a year, subjects' beliefs in the detail and accuracy of flashbulb memories remained consistently high (Talarico & Rubin, 2007). Other researchers have confirmed this suspicion by also investigating memories surrounding the 9/11 attacks. They found that although participants typically remembered their location at the time, memories of other details were no longer accurate (Rimmele, Davachi, & Phelps, 2012). In summary, flashbulb memories appear to be no more accurate than everyday memories, but we do tend to believe that they are much more accurate than ordinary memories. Strong emotions tend to strengthen the subjective sense of remembering, but do not increase accuracy.

7.4 Forgetting

There is no single answer to the question "Why do we forget?" Forgetting seems to occur for many reasons. Among the explanations that psychologists have put forward to explain forgetting are the decay of the memory trace, problems with interfering material, a breakdown in the retrieval process, emotional and motivational conditions, and neurological disorders.

Flashbulb Memory An apparent vivid recall for an event associated with extreme emotion or uniqueness, such as the assassination of a president

7.4a Decay of the Memory Trace

Retroactive Interference
In memory, the phenomenon that occurs when a later event interferes with the recall of earlier information

One explanation of why we forget is that the memory trace (the neurochemical or anatomical changes in the brain that encode memories) for some information simply deteriorates, fading away with the passage of time. For example, Ebbinghaus may have forgotten many of his nonsense syllables because the memory trace grew gradually dimmer until they faded altogether. Figure 7-4 showing Ebbinghaus's data may actually be interpreted as a forgetting curve, with the most rapid decay occurring soon after initial learning. This suggests that decay is not a linear process and that a portion of Ebbinghaus's original list of nonsense syllables may be retained for a long time.

A number of psychologists believe that decay is at least partially responsible for forgetting. Some suggest that decay may cause us to lose material in short-term memory, but that any information in long-term memory is stored permanently, and failure to recall it is due to a retrieval difficulty (Shiffrin & Atkinson, 1969; Tulving, 1977). Other psychologists do not agree that long-term information storage is forever. They maintain that some memories may decay over time and become lost (E. Loftus & G. Loftus, 1980). Since long-term memories must be stored through some type of physical change in the brain, it seems possible that these physical codes can sometimes break down with the passage of time.

Exam 1

(Shutterstock)

Some explanations psychologists put forward as causes of forgetfulness are the decay of the memory trace, problems with interfering material, a breakdown in the retrieval process, emotional and motivational conditions, and neurological disorders.

The difficulty with proving that decay is ever the cause of forgetting lies in the need to rule out other possible explanations. We would have to ensure that no kind of activity occurs between initial learning and later recall that could interfere with establishing the memory trace. This task is not possible for both short- and long-term memory, since people's experiences cannot be held constant during such intervals. Consequently, it is virtually impossible either to prove or disprove the decay theory of forgetting.

7.4b Interference

There is evidence that forgetting is probably influenced more by what we do before or after learning than by the passage of time. According to the interference interpretation of forgetting, experiences that occur either before or after we learn something new interfere with our memory. There may be two types of interference: Retroactive and proactive.

Retroactive Interference

Retroactive (or backward) **interference** occurs when a later event interferes with recall of earlier information. Suppose, for instance, you look up a telephone number; as you pick up the phone and prepare to dial, your roommate distracts you by asking what time it is. When you return to making the call, you discover that the number has slipped from your memory. This situation is an example of retroactive inhibition of memory.

Proactive Interference

In **proactive** (forward-acting) **interference**, earlier learning disrupts memory for later learning. For example, if you learn a list of new vocabulary terms in your English class this afternoon, you may find that it is difficult to remember the psychology terms you review tonight. Figure 7-8 illustrates how psychologists study both types of interference effects.

Proactive Interference In memory, the phenomenon that occurs when earlier learning disrupts memory for later learning

Serial Position Effect Tendency to remember items at the beginning and end of a list more readily than those in the middle

You can put your knowledge of interference to practical use. For example, if you must study more than one subject in the same time period, you should choose subjects that are as dissimilar as possible, since similarity of information increases interference. Sleeping after you study material is the best way to reduce the possibility of retroactive interference. Even relatively brief naps (an hour or so after a study session) can help you remember new material.

The Serial Position Effect

Have you ever noticed that when you memorize a list of formulas, terms, or grocery items, you are more likely to remember those items at the beginning and end of the list than those in the middle? This phenomenon is called the **serial position effect.**

Why is it easier to remember items at the beginning and end of a long list? One possible explanation draws upon our knowledge of short- and long-term memory. Presumably, items at the beginning of a list move successfully into long-term memory because there is no competing information, that is, little proactive interference. As additional items move into memory, however, they may displace previously processed items because short-term memory can hold only a limited number of chunks. Items at the end of the list are remembered better than those in the middle because they have not been

Figure 7-8 Studying the Effects of Retroactive and Proactive Interference

When retroactive interference occurs, later learning (learning task B) interferes with the recall of information learned earlier (recall of task A). In proactive interference, earlier information (learning task A) disrupts memory for later learning (task B). If the control groups outperform the experimental groups in Step 3, interference has occurred.

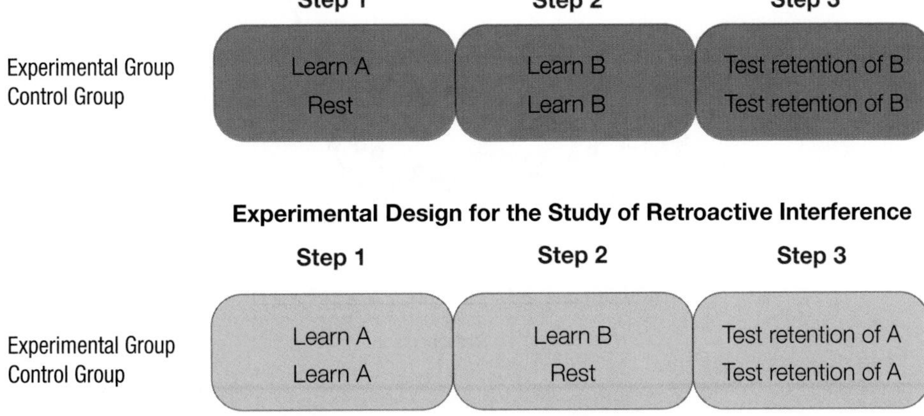

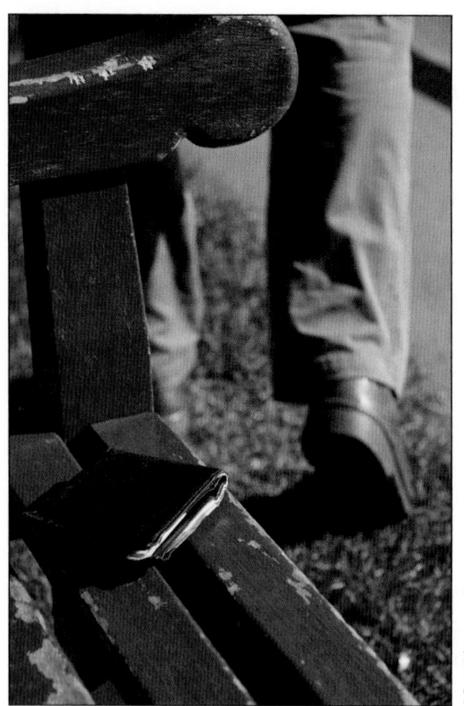
(iStock)

A number of psychologists believe that the decay of the memory trace is at least partially responsible for forgetting.

bumped or replaced by any additional material. In other words, retroactive interference is minimal at the end. In contrast, items in the middle of a list encounter interference from both preceding (proactive) and subsequent (retroactive) items. A typical serial position effect curve is shown in Figure 7-9.

The serial position effect shows up in a variety of situations. For example, when children learn the alphabet, letters in the middle are most difficult to remember. Similarly, students are more likely to miss test questions drawn from material in the middle of a lecture than information at the beginning or end.

7.4c Retrieval Failure

Suppose you are having trouble recalling the title of an old love song you heard last week. A friend drops by and announces that it is a splendid day today. Suddenly you remember the title, "Love Is a Many Splendored Thing." It is clear that your memory for the song title was intact, but it was just out of reach, waiting for the right retrieval cue.

Failure to recall information does not necessarily mean it is not there. It may simply be inaccessible because it was poorly encoded in the first place or because we have inadequate retrieval cues. Forgetting of long-term memories often reflects a failure of retrieval cues rather than decay or interference. Even memories that seem impossible to retrieve may pop into mind when the right cues are used.

Figure 7-9 The Serial Position

Subjects were shown a list of twenty words, one at a time, for either one or two seconds. They were asked to remember as many words as they could. Subjects in both conditions were more likely to remember words at the beginning and end of the list.

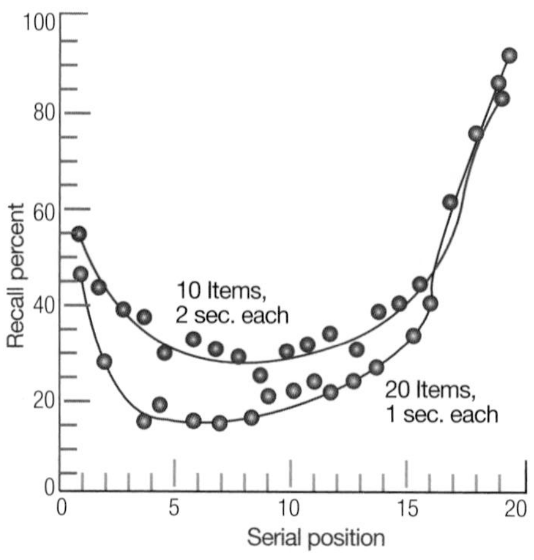

7.4d Motivated Forgetting

Sometimes we forget long-term memories because we do not want to remember them. Psychologists call this motivated forgetting: People often push certain kinds of memories out of conscious awareness because they are too embarrassing, frightening, painful, or degrading to recall.

Sigmund Freud's concept of repression is an example of motivated forgetting. Freud believed that we *repress* or forget certain ideas, feelings, and experiences because they are too painful to deal with on a conscious level. Repression thus lets us maintain a sense of self-esteem and avoid the anxiety that would result if this information were to surface in our awareness. As discussed in Chapter 14, there is some disagreement over the viability of Freud's concepts of repression and the unconscious mind as explanations of human behavior. However, psychologists do tend to agree that motivated forgetting does play a role in blocking at least some material stored in long-term memory. Suppressing unwanted memories from consciousness appears to be an active process involving both the prefrontal cortex and the inhibition of hippocampal activity. Both of these neural structures are critical for retrieving information into our working memory (C. Anderson et al., 2004; M. Anderson & Huddleston, 2012.

Organic Amnesia Memory deficits caused by altered physiology of the brain, which might result from an accident or certain physical illnesses

Retrograde Amnesia Memory loss for certain details or events that occurred prior to experiencing brain trauma; a form of organic amnesia

7.4e Diseases That Cause Forgetting

Forgetting is not normally caused by neurological disorders; however, certain diseases or accidents can alter the physiology of the brain. Memory deficits caused by the condition are referred to as **organic amnesia**. There are many types of organic amnesia; in this section, we look at three main types: amnesia caused by disease, retrograde amnesia, and anterograde amnesia (Schacter, 1999).

Amnesia Caused by Disease or Trauma

Some diseases produce actual physical deterioration of brain cells, impairing memory as well as a variety of other functions. For instance, cardiovascular disease is characterized by decreased blood circulation, which sometimes limits the oxygen supply to the brain to the point that some brain cells die. Strokes are another common physical cause of memory impairment. Here, a vessel in the brain ruptures, with resulting damage to cells. Alzheimer's disease is another illness that produces progressive, widespread degeneration of brain cells. This devastating disease produces severe memory deficits and other impairments of functioning. Alzheimer's disease is discussed in some detail in Chapter 12.

(Shutterstock)

Sometimes a blow to the head may cause loss of memory. American actress Drew Barrymore portrays a woman with amnesia from a trauma in the 2004 film 50 First Dates.

Retrograde Amnesia

Sometimes a blow to the head may cause loss of memory for certain details or events that occurred prior to the accident. This condition is called **retrograde amnesia**. In many of these cases, lost memories return gradually, with older memories tending to come back first. In almost all cases investigated, memories for recent events have been shown to be more susceptible to disruption than older memories. This suggests that the amnesia

Anterograde Amnesia
Memory loss for information processed after an individual experiences brain trauma caused by injury or chronic alcoholism

reflects a temporary loss of access to information rather than an actual destruction of the memory trace.

Retrograde amnesia is more likely to impair declarative memory, particularly the episodic type, than to interfere with procedural memory. For example, accident victims may not remember who they are or what they were doing prior to the accident, but they can remember old skills such as playing a musical instrument or speaking a foreign language.

Anterograde Amnesia

Amnesia can also work in the opposite direction. Some victims of brain damage may be able to recall old memories established before the damage, but cannot remember information processed after the damage occurred. This condition is called **anterograde amnesia**. It may be caused by injury to a specific area of the brain; it may also be associated with certain surgical procedures and chronic alcoholism. Unlike retrograde amnesia, anterograde amnesia is often irreversible. The following section provides some clues about why we forget.

7.4f **Daniel Schacter's Seven Sins of Memory**

The prominent memory researcher Daniel Schacter has summarized the main causes of memory failure as the *seven sins of memory*. Three of his seven sins—*transience*, *absent-mindedness*, and *blocking*—are all types of forgetting as described above. Three additional sins are types of memory distortion and include *misattribution*, *suggestibility*, and *bias*. The last sin, *persistence*, is the intrusion of unwanted memories that we would like to forget (Schacter, 1999). These sins of memory are presented in Table 7-1.

7.5 **The Biology of Memory**

We know that memories are not transitory events that float freely within our brains. When you learn the name of your psychology professor, your girlfriend's address, or how to play golf, some lasting changes take place within your brain. For decades, researchers have tried to understand the nature of these changes and to identify where they take place. A number of recent discoveries suggest that they are closing in on the answer.

7.5a **The Hebbian Rule**

Years ago, physiological psychologist Donald Hebb suggested that short- and long-term memory have different physical bases. Short-term memory, he proposed, is maintained by the firing of a collection of neurons arranged in a specific circuit labeled a cell assembly. Our recall of a telephone number when we put down a phone book and begin to dial is thus kept alive by neurons firing in a repeated pattern that forms a briefly held memory trace. Hebb maintained that this brief electrical activity does not bring about changes in the physical structure of the brain, which is why short-term memory is transitory.

Long-term memory is a different matter, however. Hebb suggested that information is transferred to LTM when physical changes take place in the form of new connections between neurons. These changes are thought to involve structural changes in the synapses between neurons, which occur when cell assemblies are simultaneously activated.

Table 7-1 Schacter's (1999) Seven Sins of Memory

Sin	Definition	Example
Transience	Lost memory over time	Forgetting the name of your first-grade teacher
Absentmindedness	Lost memory due to inattention	Forgetting an appointment or where you left your keys
Blocking	Lost memory due to interference	The tip-of-tongue syndrome where memories are temporarily unavailable
Misattribution	Memory distortion due to assigning it to the wrong source or context	Believing someone was at a crime scene when actually you saw them earlier that day
Suggestibility	Memory distortion caused by newer misleading information	Unreliable testimony in court brought about by leading questions or inaccurate information
Bias	Memory distortion caused by present information or beliefs	If your present romantic relationship is going badly, you may remember it being worse in the past than it really was
Persistence	The intrusion of unwanted memories	The continued recollection of an embarrassing or tragic moment

Hebb's conception of short- and long-term memory as distinct phenomena has been recently supported by research. So has the idea that memory is transferred from working electrical activation of neuronal circuits to a more lasting long-term memory coded by physical changes in neurons. Hebb's idea that experiences are recorded and memories stored via changes in neurons remained novel, and even controversial, for many years. However, most neuroscientists today support this hypothesis. Of particular interest is mounting evidence indicating that structural changes take place in the synapses of neurons providing the formation of long-term memories. Simultaneous firings of nerve circuits (Hebb's cell assemblies) appear to induce structural changes in specific neural connections. According to Hebb, "Neurons that fire together get wired together." In other words, the strength of the neural connections between two neurons strengthens if they are activated together. This prediction has become known as the **Hebbian rule**. The mechanism underlying the Hebbian rule is long-term potentiation.

Hebbian Rule Information is transferred to long-term memory when new connections between neurons are formed (These changes are thought to involve structural changes in the synapses between neurons, which occur when cell assemblies are simultaneously activated.)

7.5b Long-Term Potentiation

How do neurons change during encoding and the initial stages of memory? There appear to be at least two types of neuronal changes that underlie the initial formation of memories. These processes include synaptic facilitation (briefly discussed in Chapter 6) and the activations of specific genes, which code for protein synthesis and synaptic growth (Cavallaro, Schreurs, Zhao, D'Agata, & Alkon, 2001; Huang & Kandel, 2007; Kandel & Abel, 1995; Pittenger & Kandel, 2003). Both of these processes contribute to an altered neuronal state referred to as **long-term potentiation** (LTP), and they

Long-Term Potentiation (LTP) An increase in a neuron's sensitivity to fire following a burst of signals to that neuron's dendrites

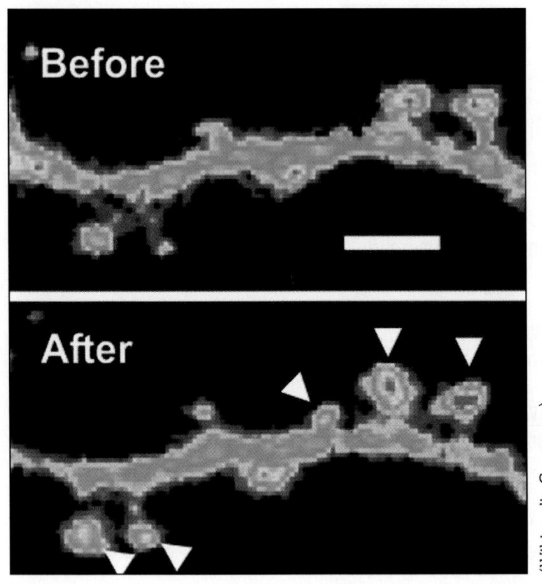

(Wikimedia Commons)

The high-magnification photographs depict the activity change of the dendrites of a neuron before and after LTP. Notice the increase in dendrite activity (red) after LTP.

provide support for Hebb's theory of how memories are formed. Long-term potentiation is defined as a change in the strength of a synapse resulting from simultaneous firing in both the presynaptic and postsynaptic neurons. Simultaneous firing will occur, for example, when a neuron activated by a CS is quickly followed by neuronal activation caused by the US (as in Pavlovian conditioning). The initial stages of encoding and memory appear to be associated with changes in the amount of neurotransmitter released as well as changes in sensitivity to neurotransmitters. Long-term storage involves changes in the expression of genes controlling protein synthesis and synaptic growth (Matsuzaki, Honkura, Graham, Ellis-Davis, & Kasai, 2004). Long-term potentiation has been observed in the sea slug *Aplysia* and in mammalian brain structures including the hippocampus, amygdala, and cortex (Monte-Silva et al., 2013). While considerable progress has been made in the understanding of the molecular changes underlying memory, much remains to be learned.

We see that the pioneering research of Hebb followed by the more contemporary research conducted by Alkon, Kandel, and many others has provided important insights into how long-term memories are formed. The next question: Where are these memories for specific experiences located?

7.5c Distributed Memory

Physiological psychologist Karl Lashley (1929, 1950) spent most of his research career searching for the **engram**, the place where memories are stored. His technique was to train rats in a variety of tasks, then surgically destroy selective regions of the cortex, and later test the rats' memories for the tasks. Lashley found that his rats could still perform learned tasks even after much of their brain was removed. He never did succeed in pinpointing specific brain sites of memory, a fact that led him to report humorously, "I sometimes feel, in reviewing the evidence on the localization of the memory trace, that the necessary conclusion is that learning is just not possible" (1950, p. 477).

In a more serious vein, Lashley concluded that memories do not reside in precise locations in the brain, but rather involve large areas of cortical tissue. This conclusion has been supported by extensive evidence collected over the last several decades, suggesting that memories are represented by large networks of neurons distributed over broad portions of the brain. However, some memory researchers have demonstrated that at least some simple memories may be localized within precisely defined brain regions.

For instance, more recent research by Richard Thompson (1985) has isolated the location of a memory trace for a specific experience. Rabbits were classically conditioned to blink one eye in response to a tone in the manner described earlier. After establishing this conditioned response, Thompson was able to obliterate it entirely by creating a lesion in the cerebellum. His finding: "Destruction of as little as one cubic millimeter of neuronal tissue in a region of the cerebellar deep nuclei on the left side permanently abolishes the learned eyelid response, and it can never be relearned" (Thompson, 1985, p. 300). While Thompson's research is noteworthy in its demonstration of a localized brain site for a specific memory, it should not be interpreted as evidence that the cerebellum is an important center for memory storage. Researchers continue to focus on the hippocampus and the cortex as the primary structures for memory.

Engram A neural representation of a specific memory

7.5d Neural Structures for Long-Term Memory

We know more about where long-term memories are processed than about the brain site where they are stored. Much of this information comes from studies of people who have experienced memory impairment through brain damage caused by stroke or injury. We examine some of this evidence here.

The Case of H.M.

In one famous case in the mid-1950s, a young man identified as H.M. suffered from a severely debilitating, epileptic condition. To ease his violent seizures, a neurosurgeon removed bilaterally (from both hemispheres) most of two limbic system structures, the hippocampus and amygdala (see Chapter 3). While the operation was successful in reducing the seizures, it had the unfortunate side effect of virtually eliminating the patient's ability to store newly acquired facts in long-term memory. H.M. remembered events that occurred up to three years before his surgery. Since he could learn new skills, it was also clear that his procedural memory was still intact. However, his declarative memory was virtually destroyed, and he was unable to consolidate new factual information (Damasio, 2001).

If you were introduced to H.M. and spent a few minutes with him, he would seem quite normal to you. However, if you left the room and returned a bit later, you would again be a total stranger to him. It is difficult to imagine what it would be like to have no sense of a past other than very old memories. H.M. expressed his frustration and confusion in an interview some years ago:

> Right now, I'm wondering, have I done or said anything amiss? You see, at this moment everything looks clear to me, but what happened just before? That's what worries me. It's like waking from a dream. I just don't remember. (Thompson, 1985, p. 305)

Since H.M. was able to recall his earlier life after his hippocampus and amygdala were removed, we can deduce that long-term memory is not stored in either of these two structures. It does appear, however, that these structures are involved in transferring information from short-term to long-term memory. H.M.'s experience also suggests that the process of **consolidation** may continue for several years. Since he lost much of his memory for events within the three years preceding his surgery, these memories were probably not completely consolidated when portions of his brain were removed. Finally, the fact that H.M. could acquire new skills, such as playing tennis, suggests that procedural memory and declarative memory are distinct memory systems that involves processing by different portions of the brain.

The Case of N.A.

Another famous case, mentioned earlier in this chapter, is that of N.A., the young man whose thalamus was damaged by a fencing foil. N.A.'s memory impairment was similar to that of H.M., although his retrograde amnesia affected only recent events dating back about one year. Like H.M., his ability to consolidate new information acquired after his injury is markedly impaired. The part of his thalamus affected was the left portion, and his impairment is most obvious when the material to be learned is verbal. (Recall from Chapter 3 that the left side of the brain is typically more involved in verbal tasks than the right side.) For example, he quickly forgets items on lists of words, but he is better at

Consolidation Process by which information is transferred from short-term electrical activation of neuronal circuits to a longer-term memory coded by physical cell changes in the brain

nonverbal tasks, such as remembering faces or learning how to negotiate mazes (Bloom, Lazerson, & Hofstader, 1985). From the evidence presented by this case, it seems likely that the thalamus plays an important role in consolidation.

In sum, memory researchers are beginning to identify specific areas of the brain that play a role in placing new memories in storage. What is the final resting place of memories for things more complex than a simple conditioned eye-blink? Although we still cannot answer this question, it seems likely that complex memories are distributed in the cerebral cortex in the form of networks of interrelated neurons.

7.5e Where Are Short-Term, Working Memories Processed?

We concluded from the previous section that long-term memories don't appear to be localized but rather are distributed in the cerebral cortex as vast networks of neurons. What about short-term, or working, memory? Where is it processed?

The neurons that function to retain a visual or auditory image in short-term memory appear to be localized in a relatively specific area of the frontal cortex called the prefrontal cortex. Figure 7-10 shows the prefrontal cortex and some of its connections to other brain regions. This area of the brain appears to play an intermediary role between memory and action. For example, in monkeys the neural activity of the prefrontal cortex corresponds to the short-term memory of a stimulus after the stimulus has been removed from view. In addition, damage to the prefrontal cortex does not affect long-term memory, but it does disrupt an organism's ability to bring this stored information to use (Goldman-Rakic, 1992; Goldman-Rakic, 1999; Wang et al., 2006). As we have seen, a major function of short-term memory is to bring long-term memories into action.

Further investigations of the prefrontal cortex have identified *dopamine* as the major neurotransmitter involved in short-term memory. Perhaps the decline in memory ability as we age is related to a decrease in the amount of dopamine in prefrontal cortex neurons. Evidence to support this idea has come from pharmacological manipulations that both increase dopamine activity and short-term memory (Söderqvist et al., 2012), as well as from studies of aged monkeys who perform poorly on tasks requiring short-term memory. These aged monkeys have depleted levels of dopamine, but the injections of dopamine appear to restore their memory to levels of healthy young monkeys (Goldman-Rakic, 1992).

7.6 Improving Memory

Although we cannot recommend dopamine injections for students with memory problems, there are some things we can recommend. This next section identifies several strategies that may help to improve academic memory.

Professors are accustomed to hearing a sad refrain from students dismayed by poor test scores. It goes something like this: "I can't believe I did so poorly on the exam. I spent a lot of time studying, but I just couldn't remember the facts when it came to test time." In such cases, chances are that the problem was more a function of inefficient study methods than a bad memory. Research on learning and memory suggests a number of practical strategies that you may apply to improve your efficiency and, therefore, your performance as you study material assigned in your courses.

Figure 7-10 The Prefrontal Cortex

The prefrontal cortex, along with connections to other brain areas, is important for short-term memory.

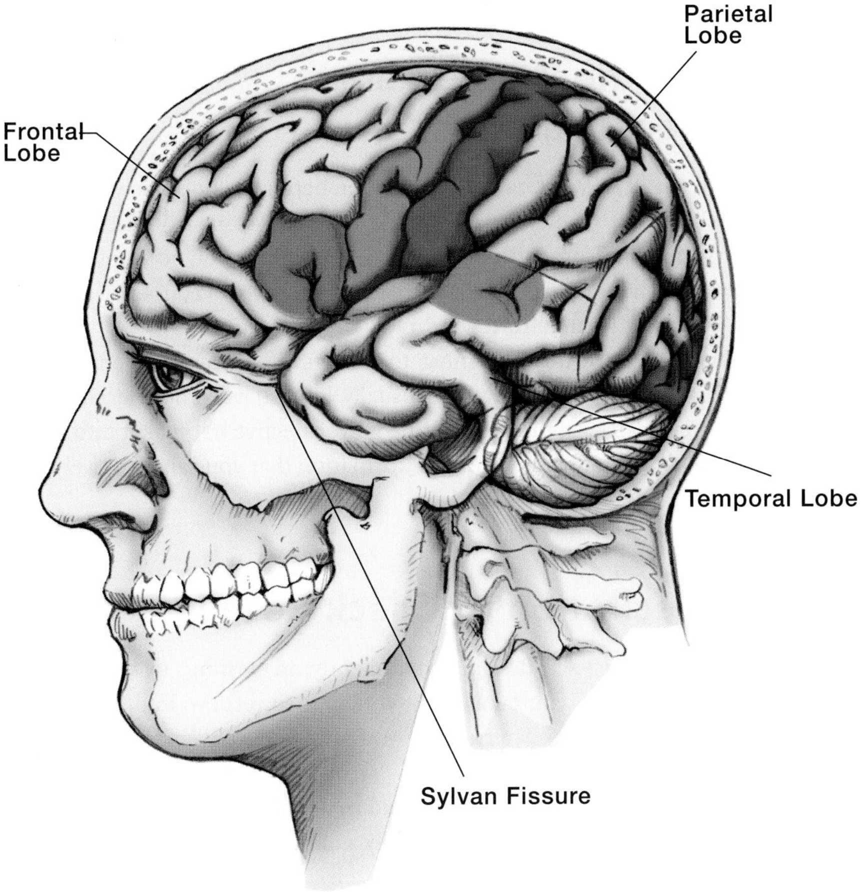

7.6a Reducing the Material to a Manageable Amount

Imagine that you have been assigned a few chapters to read for an exam. It is highly unlikely that you will be able to remember every single point made on every page of those chapters; it is also unlikely that every point is *important* to remember. Thus, part of the science of effective studying is to pick out and underline the important points, and then to focus on learning these key items.

The logic of this approach is evident if you ask yourself the following question: Who will do better on an exam, the person who tries to review everything in the assigned chapters once, or someone who reviews a fifth of that amount of material five times? Common sense suggests that most of us with normal memory capacities do better if we start by reducing a chapter to its key points, which might represent 20 percent of its total length, and then review this manageable amount of material a number of times.

Of course, there is some risk that in reducing material to its salient points you might overlook something that will later appear on the test. However, here again logic prevails. Whereas you might miss a few questions because of an error in judgment about what is important, you are likely to miss far more questions—and perhaps more important questions—if you attempt to remember everything in the assigned chapters.

7.6b Learning the Whole Versus Piecemeal Learning

In most cases, your recall of material will usually be better if you review it as a whole rather than breaking it into smaller parts. For example, assume you are reading this chapter for the first time, presumably underlining key points as you go along. When you review this information later on, you will be better off spending a couple of hours going over the entire chapter rather than reviewing a few pages at a time.

Reviewing material from the beginning to the end is particularly effective when the information is well organized and not unusually long. If you must learn extremely long, complicated material, it would probably be more effective to break it into segments containing the largest meaningful amount of information that you can effectively process at any one time.

7.6c Using Recitation to Check Recall

Recitation means repeating to yourself, either silently, in writing, or out loud, what you have just reviewed. When you take a test, you have to retrieve information; recitation while studying allows you to determine if you are effectively encoding material for easy retrieval.

Many students are content to read and reread material passively, without ever stopping to check their recall. This approach virtually guarantees that an exam is the first retrieval test they encounter, and the results are often disappointing. Information is not going to be processed and stored in an efficient manner when all we do is silently and passively read through it. It is far more effective to organize, meaningfully encode, and review and recite material actively.

Recitation accomplishes more than simply providing a check on how well we are remembering material. Rehearsing by actively retrieving information from memory is a powerful tool for firmly implanting memory for that information. Don't assume that everything you've underlined is firmly committed to memory.

As you review your underlining, stop frequently and try to recall what you have just read by reciting it in summary form. Reciting can be done either verbally or in writing. This technique is called reciting after the fact. If your recall is accurate, move on to the next section. If not, review the same material again and recite it once more. Do not continue until your recall is complete. As you become more familiar with the material, try reciting it at the beginning of a section, before you review your underlining (a process known as "reciting before the fact"). For example, when you get to the section in this chapter titled "Forgetting," try reciting all that you can recall about the five suggested causes of forgetting *before* checking the points you have highlighted. You will find that with each subsequent review of the material, accurate recitation before the fact gradually replaces recitation after the fact.

7.6d Overlearning

Many students have a tendency to stop reviewing material when they are finally able to recite it successfully. This tactic is a mistake. Recall that Ebbinghaus was able to improve his retention of nonsense syllables significantly by repeatedly reviewing them after he had reached 100 percent mastery. We encourage students to review material at least once or twice after they feel they have mastered it. The extra time spent in overlearning will pay handsome returns on test day.

7.6e Making Use of Study Breaks and Rewards

People are often able to function at peak efficiency only so long before their concentration begins to break down. Such attention lapses interfere with learning, but they can be minimized with a routine of frequent but short study breaks. We suggest working fifty minutes, then taking a ten-minute break. Although some individuals may be able to work at peak efficiency for longer than fifty minutes, a fifty-minute-on and ten-minute-off strategy seems to work well for many people.

To make the most of your ten-minute break, do something relaxing and enjoyable that provides a reward for fifty minutes of good effort: Call a friend, listen to a favorite piece of music, ask your roommate to give you a neck rub, take a walk, or play with your dog. The key is to do something rewarding while avoiding heavy "mental" work, so that you can return to your studies refreshed.

7.6f Spacing Study Sessions

Spreading your study sessions out over time is usually more effective than trying to learn a great deal of material all at once—that is, distributed practice is typically better than massed practice. For example, assume that you plan to spend six hours reviewing the material in this chapter after your initial reading. Your recall will probably be much better if you distribute your reviews over three two-hour sessions as opposed to cramming it all into one massed six-hour session. Considerable experimental evidence supports this advice.

7.6g Avoiding Interference

Try to eliminate as much interference from competing material as possible. Earlier in this chapter we discussed the value of avoiding studying similar material on the same day (the more similar the material, the greater the interference with recall). If you must work on two or more subjects in the same time frame, make them as dissimilar as possible to reduce the impact of proactive and retroactive interference.

By all means, do not study for more than one test on the same day. You may think this suggestion is impossible, particularly during final-exam season. However, if you plan in advance, and space your study sessions over time, you can probably avoid the need to double up your exam preparations on the same day. If you get in a bind and find that you must study for two tests on the same day, use the morning to study for one, followed by a nap, and then review the other subject before going to bed for your night's sleep. As we have seen, sleep helps us avoid interference while information is being consolidated into long-term memory.

7.6h Managing Your Time

Many of us tend to put tasks off until suddenly we find ourselves with too little time to do the job well. This human shortcoming is widely exhibited on college campuses.

One way to avoid the pitfalls of procrastination, while at the same time maintaining strong motivation in your college career, is to develop a formal schedule to manage your time. Although a schedule can be created in a number of ways, one method that we have found effective is to make multiple copies of a chart that lists all the hours of each day of the week. For a given week, first fill in all the slots of time that are already committed to time spent in class, at meals, sleeping, at your part-time job, and so forth. Next, designate several of the available slots as study time, keeping in mind the principles of spacing your study sessions as well as the value of sleep after study. For example, scheduling two to three hours of study followed by a nap is a good idea. If you have a good sense of how much study time each of your classes will demand, you may prefer to assign your study time slots to specific classes, leaving some flexibility in your schedule for day-to-day variations. The remaining empty slots on your chart may be designated as open or free time.

Time management works only when you treat your designated study times as serious commitments. Similarly, you should treat your free time as something you deserve, a time for renewal, and an opportunity to reward yourself for good effort. Sticking to a formal schedule can break the binds of procrastination while allowing you to enjoy your free time without worrying about your studies.

CHAPTER REVIEW

What Is Memory?

1. The term memory describes both the storage and retrieval of information.
2. The information-processing perspective on memory suggests that people actively participate in the assimilation of their experiences.
3. Memory consists of three separate processes: encoding or translating incoming information into a neural code that the brain can process; storage of information over time; and, finally, the process of retrieval whereby stored information is located and recovered.

A Model of Memory

4. One widely held perspective suggests that there are three distinct memory systems that allow us to process, store, and recall information: sensory memory, short-term memory (STM), and long-term memory (LTM).
5. Sensory memories are brief impressions from any of our senses. Visual sensory memory and auditory sensory memory are referred to as iconic memory and echoic memory, respectively.
6. STM, frequently referred to as our short-term memory, is an intermediate memory process, sandwiched between sensory memory and LTM, within which we actively process information.
7. STM has both a short duration and a limited capacity. Chunking—the process of grouping items into longer, meaningful units—is an effective way to increase the limited capacity of STM.
8. Most of the information placed in STM is held there in an acoustic form, according to how it sounds. Information is also sorted in STM based on what it looks like or what it means (visual and semantic coding).
9. Long-term memories are composed of both procedural memories and declarative memories. Procedural memories are memories for how to perform skills. Recall of specific facts is made possible by declarative memory.
10. Memories that are made available to consciousness are called explicit memories. Implicit memories are associated with feelings of knowing and familiarity, and not available to consciousness.
11. It has been suggested that declarative memory may be further subdivided into episodic memory (autobiographical facts about a person's experiences stored in roughly chronological order) and semantic memory (general, nonpersonal knowledge about the meaning of facts and concepts without reference to specific experiences). It has recently been suggested that episodic memory may be best conceptualized as a subsystem of semantic memory.
12. A number of memory systems, or mnemonic devices, can improve encoding of information in LTM. These include clustering, the method of loci, using narrative stories, acrostics, and acronyms.

CHAPTER REVIEW

13. The more retrieval cues that can be linked with information stored in LTM, the more likely we are to recall that information later on.
14. Many psychologists believe that much of the information in our declarative memories is stored in the form of networks of association between concepts or fragments of knowledge we have about things in our worlds.
15. The three most common techniques for testing LTM are recall tasks, recognition tasks, and relearning.
16. Research by Herman Ebbinghaus revealed that forgetting tends to occur very rapidly during the initial period after learning and that the rate of forgetting declines significantly thereafter.

Memory as a Dynamic Process

17. When we memorize a list of items, we are most likely to remember those items at the beginning and end of the list, a phenomenon known as the serial position effect.
18. It is often easier to recall a particular event or experience if we are in the same context in which the information was first encoded. Context includes external environment and internal state (physiological conditions, emotions, etc.). This phenomenon is referred to as state-dependent memory.
19. Flashbulb memory refers to an apparent vivid recall for earlier events associated with extreme emotion.
20. Memory is a dynamic and constructive process influenced by expectations and new information.
21. People may change details to reconstruct memories and make them consistent with their schemas, which are conceptual frameworks that they use to make sense out of their world.
22. Research has called into question the reliability of eyewitness testimony. Considerable evidence suggests that eyewitness testimony may be flawed by people's tendency to reconstruct their memory of events to fit their schemas.
23. Psychologists, and even advertisers, may easily plant false memories in people.
24. A number of studies indicate that people exposed to violent events are especially likely to incorporate misinformation into their memory.

Forgetting

25. Among the explanations put forth by psychologists to explain forgetting are the decay of the memory trace, interference, retrieval failure, motivated forgetting, and organic causes of forgetting.
26. Psychologists are not in agreement as to whether some memories may decay over time and become lost.

CHAPTER REVIEW

27. According to the interference interpretation of forgetting, experiences that occur either before or after we learn something new interfere with our memory. Retroactive interference occurs when a later event interferes with recall of earlier information. Proactive interference occurs when earlier learning disrupts memory for later learning.
28. Failure to retrieve memory may occur because it was poorly encoded in the first place or because we have inadequate retrieval cues.
29. Sometimes we forget long-term memories because we do not want to remember them, a process called motivated forgetting.
30. Memory deficits caused by organic factors may be of three kinds: amnesia caused by disease (impaired brain circulation, Alzheimer's disease, etc.); retrograde amnesia (loss of recall for events occurring just before a brain trauma); and anterograde amnesia (inability to recall information processed after brain damage).

The Biology of Memory

31. Memory results from structural changes that take place in the synapses between neurons. These changes are called long-term potentiation. These synapses are referred to as Hebbian synapses.
32. Changes in synaptic strength for long-term memories depend on the expression of genes for synaptic growth.
33. Extensive evidence suggests that memories may be represented by large networks of neurons distributed over broad portions of the cortex.
34. Evidence from a variety of sources strongly suggests that the hippocampus and amygdala are necessary for memory consolidation, particularly when it involves the transfer of declarative information from STM to LTM. The thalamus also appears to be involved in memory consolidation.
35. The prefrontal cortex and its connections to the parietal lobe are necessary for spatial short-term memory.
36. Dopamine appears to play an important role in the development of short-term memories.

Improving Memory

37. We can apply what we know about memory to improving study skills. Some of the most effective applications of the memory principles discussed in this chapter include reducing material to a manageable amount of important points, encoding material in a meaningful fashion, avoiding piecemeal studying, using active recitation in studying, overlearning by continuing to study material after mastery, taking study breaks, spacing study sessions over time, planning study sessions to minimize proactive and retroactive interference, and using time management techniques to balance study time with free time and other commitments in the most effective way.

TERMS AND CONCEPTS

Acronym, pg. 278
Acrostics, pg. 277
Anterograde Amnesia, pg. 294
Chunking, pg. 272
Clustering, pg. 276
Consolidation, pg. 297
Declarative Memory, pg. 275
Dual-Code Model of Memory, pg. 275
Echoic Memory, pg. 270
Eidetic Imagery, pg. 276
Elaborative Rehearsal, pg. 278
Encoding, pg. 266
Engram, pg. 296
Episodic Memory, pg. 275
Explicit Memory, pg. 281
False Memory, pg. 283
Flashbulb Memory, pg. 289
Hebbian Rule, pg. 295
Iconic Memory, pg. 269
Implicit Memories, pg. 282
Information-Processing Model of Memory, pg. 266
Long-Term Memory (LTM), pg. 268
Long-Term Potentiation (LTP), pg. 295
Maintenance Rehearsal, pg. 278
Memory, pg. 265
Misinformation Effect, pg. 288
Mnemonic Device, pg. 276
Organic Amnesia, pg. 293
Overlearning, pg. 281
Proactive Interference, pg. 291
Procedural Memory, pg. 275
Recall, pg. 280
Recognition, pg. 280
Relearning, pg. 280
Retrieval, pg. 267
Retroactive Interference, pg. 290
Retrograde Amnesia, pg. 293
Schemas, pg. 285
Semantic Memory, pg. 275
Sensory Memory, pg. 267
Serial Position Effect, pg. 291
Short-Term (Working) Memory (STM), pg. 267
State-Dependent Memory, pg. 288
Storage, pg. 266
Subliminal Perception, pg. 270

POP QUIZ

True or False

___ 1. The first step in the processing of a memory is the storage of the information in the nervous system.

___ 2. The peg-word mnemonic system involves pegging or hanging an item to be remembered onto a familiar location.

___ 3. The observation that people tend to remember events and facts that are inaccurate is evidence for memory being a constructive process.

___ 4. It is a well-established fact that LTM traces decay or fade with the passage of time.

___ 5. The mechanism underlying the Hebbian rule is long-term potentiation.

Multiple Choice

6. What is the process of locating and recovering an item from one's "memory bank" termed?
   a. Mnemonic
   b. Recall
   c. Retrieval
   d. A "hit"
7. Why do echoic memories last longer than iconic memories?
   a. Unlike light energy, sound waves produce echoes for us to refer to.
   b. We do not have a second chance to review auditory information, whereas it is usually possible to refer back to visual information.
   c. Visual information is continually being replaced, but auditory information is not.
   d. It is easier to concentrate on visual information.
8. Information is typically coded in working memory in ________form.
   a. acoustic
   b. semantic
   c. procedural
   d. visual
9. Where are the memories you have of your first day of psychology class this semester stored?
   a. Chronological memory
   b. LTM
   c. Sensory memory
   d. STM

POP QUIZ

10. Your ________ memory contains general, nonpersonal knowledge concerning the meaning of facts and concepts.
    a. episodic
    b. semantic
    c. procedural
    d. iconic
11. If it is necessary for you to remember a list of items in a specific order, which mnemonic device would probably be least appropriate to use?
    a. Narrative story
    b. Method of loci
    c. Clustering
    d. Peg-word
12. A student who is not doing well in psychology class would most likely hope that the professor would use which of the following techniques to measure memory of the material?
    a. Short answer
    b. Recall
    c. Relearning
    d. Recognition
13. To which of the following questions would people most likely estimate the "tallest" response?
    a. What is the height of your psychology professor?
    b. How short is your psychology professor?
    c. How tall is your psychology professor?
    d. People would give the same response to each question.
14. Which explanation of forgetting states that a "forgotten" memory is not really forgotten, but only inaccessible at the current time?
    a. Anterograde amnesia
    b. Decay
    c. Interference
    d. Retrieval failure
15. From the case of H.M. (discussed in the text), it seems likely that the hippocampus and amygdala are which of the following?
    a. Where LTMs are stored
    b. Only involved in the functioning of sensory memory
    c. Involved in the transferring of information from STM to LTM
    d. Involved in procedural memories

Answer Key: 1.F 2.F 3.T 4.F 5.T 6.c 7.b 8.a 9.b 10.b 11.c 12.d 13.c 14.d 15.c

Chapter 8

(Shutterstock)

Motivation

Each year, 198 professional bicycle racers (twenty-two teams of nine riders) from around the world participate in arguably the most arduous athletic event—the *Tour de France*. The Tour, as racers know it, consists of twenty-one daily races, or stages, covering up to 150 miles, often in mountainous terrain. Most of these racers will never win a stage, and most barely earn a livable wage racing as a professional. What keeps them going day after day suffering brutal climbs, frightening descents, and painful crashes?

On another continent in a darkened alley, a professional financier finds himself waiting for a seller who is over an hour late. He long ago lost his job with an international bank, his home in Pacific Heights, and his wife of fourteen years. Crack cocaine is his only reason to live, but he often wonders if it is worth living at all. How is it possible for someone with everything to live for to now be solely motivated by a drug?

These examples of highly motivated behavior reveal something about the role of motivation in determining our behavior. *Motivation* is a general term for the processes that influence and direct our actions. As we see in this chapter, these processes are considerably more complex than this brief definition implies; behavior is often influenced by a combination of several motivating processes, including emotions, which are the topic of the next chapter. Indeed, without emotions, motivated behavior would reflect an air of indifference. Can you imagine how boring dating would be if it were not colored by feelings of excitement, happiness, and possibly love? Similarly, think how hard it might be to become motivated to study for a test if one never experienced the angst of failure or the joy of success.

In this chapter, and Chapter 9, we examine the nature, sources, and manifestations of human motivation and emotion. We begin here by exploring motivation, some theories that try to explain motivation, and a few specific motivational processes that influence our behavior. In the following chapter, we discuss what emotions are, how they are aroused, and how they impact our lives.

8.1 The Nature of Motivation

A war veteran attracts national media attention by housing himself inside a cage and refusing to eat. A college graduate with great promise for an academic career gives up everything to work as a missionary under extremely impoverished conditions in a poor, undeveloped country. An athlete commits several hours a day to training even under adverse weather conditions. A distraught employee bursts into his employer's office firing a gun. You might ask the same question about each of these accounts: Why would someone do such a thing?

This question raises the issue of motivation, the *why* of behavior. In a sense, the entire study of psychology is concerned with the underlying causes of behavior, so you will see motivational concepts permeate every chapter in this text. Thus far, we have explored the biological foundations of behavior and the role that sensation, perception, and learning play in determining our actions. Here we will expand on how these factors contribute to motivational states. Often, changes in motivation explain the variations and inconsistencies in behavior when these variations cannot be attributed to differences in ability, training, or environmental conditions.

Beside explaining these variations, motivational concepts help to explain the distinction between learning and performance. Learning does not always lead directly to behavior. Recall from Chapter 6 the latent-learning experiment discussed, in which rats learned how to move through a complex maze but did not demonstrate this behavior until they were motivated by food. In a similar vein, if you learn to imitate the voice of

Motivation A condition or state that energizes and directs an organism's actions

Chris Rock, you probably will not use this voice to communicate with your dog, your professors, or your parents. You are likely to express this behavior only when you have an appreciative audience. Motivation is what often translates learning into overt behavior.

8.1a Defining Motivation

Motivation can include physiological factors, such as the body signals that tell us we are hungry, thirsty, or tired; however, there is more to motivation than the simple translation of body needs into action. Motivation may also include cognitive contributions such as a desire to achieve, the expected outcomes of our actions, or an urge to be with friends. In fact, **motivation** can be defined as any condition that energizes and directs our actions.

To illustrate, suppose you are reading this chapter late at night and are becoming increasingly aware of a familiar urge. Finally, you close your book and decide to do something about your intensifying hunger. It is time to get something to eat, but will any old food satisfy you? Not likely when the best pizzeria in town is only a few blocks away. So off you go into the night in mouth-watering anticipation of your favorite pizza.

This example of one of the most familiar motives, hunger, illustrates that motivation not only energizes or *activates* us to behave in a certain way but also *directs* or defines the direction of the resulting behavior. Motivation also has a direct impact on how *vigorous* or intense our behaviors are. If you had skipped dinner earlier in the evening, your trip to the pizzeria might be characterized by brisk walking rather than a leisurely stroll and you might consume all of it rather than saving one or two pieces for your roommate. Motivation is also a factor in your decision to eat pizza, not McDonald's, which was a block closer.

In all, we might say that motivation is the "why" of behavior, while physiology, learning, sensation, and perception help to explain how we behave. As we see in the following discussion, why people do what they do has not been easy to answer, and a complete answer will necessarily include several motivational influences.

8.2 Motivational Explanations of Behavior

Since its beginnings, psychology has attempted to conceptualize and explain behavior in terms of motivation. These explanations have not all been equally successful. Yet each of the approaches we consider here—instinct theory, cognitive motivation, biological motives, and sensation-seeking motivation—help contribute to our understanding of human and animal behavior.

Whether we attribute behavior to inherited behavior patterns, to the need to reduce drives, to learned expectations, or to biological states, it seems clear that no one theory explains all aspects of motivation. Certain behaviors, such as drinking a glass of water after exercising, might be explained predominantly by the reduction of a biological need. Other behaviors, such as continuing the habit of smoking despite the fact that it makes you cough or devoting four years to earning a college degree, have more complex explanations. It seems, then, that to understand behavior we must first determine what types of motivation are in question. In general, it is useful to classify motivation under several categories: innate or genetically determined motives, the reduction of drives, cognitive motives, biologically based motives, and sensation-seeking motives.

8.2a Instinct Theory

Instincts Innate patterns of behavior that occur in every normally functioning member of a species under certain set conditions

One of the earliest attempts to account for motivation was based on the notion of **instincts**, innate patterns of behavior that occur in every normally functioning member of a species under certain, set conditions. For example, a salmon may swim thousands of miles through ocean waters and up a river system to reach the exact spot in a gravel bed where it was spawned several years earlier. Likewise, an arctic tern, hatched in the northland, will depart for the southernmost portion of South America when the arctic days grow shorter. Such behaviors occur in virtually identical fashion among all members of a species, generation after generation.

The attempt to explain human behavior in terms of instincts was the dominant force in psychology in the late 1800s and the early 1900s, due in large part to Charles Darwin's emphasis on the similarity between humans and other animals. William James (1890), a highly influential early psychologist, argued that humans are even more influenced by instincts than are lower animals because they are motivated not only by biological instincts but also by a variety of psychosocial instincts such as jealousy, sympathy, and sociability. James proposed a list of fifteen instincts, which he suggested account for much of human behavior (Table 8-1). Other psychologists have suggested their own lists. Predictably, by the early 1920s, almost fifteen thousand instincts had been proposed to account for virtually every kind of human behavior imaginable.

Psychologists realized that there was a basic flaw to instinct theory. Instincts did not explain behavior—they simply provided another way of labeling it. Today, psychologists do not totally discount the idea that there are inborn or inherited factors in human behavior. In fact, the concept that genetic factors influence our behaviors is very much alive. Behaviors considered by some to be under the influence of genetics include your selection of a potential mate, personality traits, intelligence, and even your susceptibility to addiction and to severe behavioral disorders. However, since our behaviors are so profoundly influenced by learning, it is essentially impossible to find one example of human behavior that fits the literal definition of instincts as proposed by the early psychologists. At present, psychologists are interested in determining the extent to which our genes influence certain aspects of our behavior.

Table 8-1 Fifteen Instincts Proposed by William James That Account for Much of Human Behavior

Cleanliness	Jealousy	Rivalry
Constructiveness	Modesty	Secretiveness
Curiosity	Parental love	Shyness
Fearfulness	Playfulness	Sociability
Hunting	Pugnacity	Sympathy

Adapted from *The Principles of Psychology* by William James (1890).

8.2b Drive-Reduction Theory

Incentive Any external stimulus that can motivate behavior even when no internal drive state exists

Just as instinct theory reflected the late nineteenth century interest in Darwin's evolutionary theory, a second explanation of motivation fits well with early behavior theory. According to the *drive-reduction theory*, motivation originates with a need or drive (such as hunger or thirst) that is experienced as an unpleasant, aversive condition. This internal need motivates us to act in a way that will reduce the aversive condition. For instance, if we feel thirsty, we find something to drink; if we feel hungry, we seek food.

The drive-reduction theory explains motivation in these terms. According to this viewpoint, proposed by Clark Hull (1943), drives are any unpleasant internal conditions that motivate an organism to engage in behaviors that reduce this unpleasant state of tension. Hull postulated that there are two kinds of drives. *Primary drives* are induced by internal biological needs, such as water or food deprivation, and they do not depend on learning. In contrast, *secondary* or *acquired drives* are derived from experience.

The concept of acquired drives is directly linked with the ideas of Pavlovian conditioning, discussed in Chapter 6. Any neutral stimulus, for example, associated with a painful or frightening experience can come to elicit a similar emotional state. If you had a car accident while driving on icy roads, seeing ice may motivate you to avoid driving a particular stretch of road where the accident occurred. Avoidance of people, places, and activities may serve to reduce an aversive emotional state. While the drive-reduction theory seems to explain some motivation, it does not explain all motivation. A major problem with the drive-reduction approach is that many behaviors don't appear to reduce any primary or conditioned drive. For example, many people enjoy working out. Does this mean there is an exercise drive that is reduced by weightlifting, running, or cycling?

Another difficulty with the drive-reduction theory is that sometimes stimuli in our environments can energize or motivate us to behave in a certain way in the absence of an internal drive state. For instance, have you ever found yourself sampling home-baked cookies because they smell so good, even though you are not at all hungry? A number of studies have demonstrated that external stimuli, which psychologists call **incentives**, can motivate behavior even when no internal drive state exists. In one experiment, for instance, it was shown that a substance such as saccharin, which has no food value and does not satisfy hunger, reinforces behavior and motivates subsequent performance of animals just because it tastes good (Sheffield, 1966). In a related experiment Sheffield demonstrated that rats could learn a response that led to the initiation of copulatory behavior, even when copulation was interrupted before completion (Sheffield, Wulff, & Backer, 1951). These results suggest that behavior can be maintained by conditions that increase drive or arousal.

Still another problem with the drive-reduction theory has to do with the fact that many motivated behaviors do not decrease as they are expressed. According to the drive-reduction hypothesis, an internal need directs us to a goal, and reaching that goal reduces the tension of the drive. It follows, then, that when the drive is reduced, the motivated behavior should cease. However, sometimes a motivated behavior seems to be self-perpetuating. An example is the desire to explore our environments. When humans and other animals have the opportunity to explore their surroundings, these reinforcing experiences often motivate further exploration rather than less. Similarly, other motives, such as the need to achieve and the need for power, typically continue to grow and expand as they are expressed rather than diminish, as drive theory would predict.

For these and other reasons, the drive-reduction theory is inadequate to explain the wide range of human and animal behaviors we observe. Drive theories have, however, had an influence on our casual explanations of behavior. For instance, it is quite common to describe the emotion of anger as building up or for one to be filled with jealousy or with stress. Behaviors associated with these emotions are often explained in terms of a reduction in their corresponding drive state. Just because these are commonly accepted explanations for these actions, however, does not mean that drive theory is correct. In fact, drive theories have largely been replaced by more modern biological approaches.

Need for Achievement (nAch) Complex psychosocial motive to accomplish difficult goals, attain high standards, surpass the achievements of others, and increase self-regard by succeeding in exercising talent

8.2c Cognitive Theories of Motivation

The cognitive perspective offers an alternative explanation of motivation. According to this view, our cognitions, expectancies, beliefs, and other mental processes play an important role in motivating our actions. This view is exemplified by the role of expectations in both classical and operant conditioning. Recall from Chapter 6 that the cognitive viewpoint sees expectations as important in both Pavlovian conditioned responses and operant behavior. For example, when we study for an exam (an operant behavior), a consequence occurs (hopefully a good grade) that serves as a reinforcer. We form an association between the behavior and the reinforcement that follows. This association then generates an *expectation* that if the behavior is repeated, it will again produce positive consequences. These cognitive expectancies can also be learned by observation. For instance, if a child watches another behave aggressively with satisfactory consequences the child may come to expect positive consequences from aggressive behavior (Bandura, 1973).

During the 1930s and 1940s, Edward Tolman, and later Julian Rotter (1950s and 1960s), had championed the idea that expectations were important motivators. Both Tolman and Rotter maintained that our likelihood of engaging in a given behavior depends on two factors: that our expectations of a certain behavior will lead to a desired goal, and the value and location of that goal. According to Tolman, animals don't learn specific stimulus-response associations; they learn which behaviors lead to which goals. Thus, the likelihood that you will gather your courage and ask that alluring person you just met for a date is determined to some degree by your past experiences in asking people out. If your last several overtures have all resulted in rejection, you are less likely to try again because your cognitive expectation is rejection. However, you may overcome your expectations of failure if you try another approach. Rescorla (1999, 2007) has demonstrated how cognitive expectancies enter into our associations. What Rescorla proposes is that in addition to stimulus-stimulus (CS-UCS) associations, organisms also learn response-outcome associations during Pavlovian conditioning. These response-outcome associations are essentially learned expectancies that a certain behavior leads to a specific outcome.

Achievement Motivation

If you are the kind of person who is not content unless you make top grades, and who is committed to being highly successful in your chosen career, psychologists would say that you have a high **need for achievement (nAch)**. The concept of achievement motivation was first defined in 1938 by Henry Murray as the need to "accomplish something difficult, to overcome obstacles and attain a high standard, to rival and surpass others, to increase self-regard by the successful exercise of talent" (p. 164). Murray developed the *Thematic Apperception Test (TAT)* to measure the need for achievement and other human motives. Not until the 1950s, however, was the TAT refined (McClelland D., 1953) as a tool for assessing the need for achievement. The TAT asks people to make up stories about a series of ambiguous pictures. The idea is that people will project into the stories their own motives, interests, and values.

Cognitive Expectancy A learned expectancy of relationships between stimuli (in Pavlovian conditioning) and between responses and outcomes (in operant conditioning)

Cognitive Dissonance Theory Theory that people experience psychological discomfort or dissonance whenever two related cognitions or behaviors are in conflict

A number of studies show that people who score high in need for achievement differ notably from those with moderate or low nAch scores (Senko, Durik, & Harackiewicz, 2008). Table 8-2 summarizes some of the traits that characterize people who have a high need for achievement.

Since the achievement need is a cognitive motivation, it is highly influenced by learning and experience. Indeed, ample evidence demonstrates that the way in which we raise our children may significantly influence their need to achieve (McClelland & Pilon, 1983). One way to help instill a desire to achieve is to encourage children to set reasonable goals and to provide ample reinforcements for their successes. Being realistic about goals is especially important because reasonable goals are likely to be achieved, thus allowing children to experience success and develop cognitive expectancies for success in other situations.

Of equal importance is fostering independence. In one study, Marion Winterbottom (1958) found that children who demonstrated high achievement motivation usually had parents who expected them to master their own environments and to show independent behavior (by doing things such as earning their own spending money) well before their teenage years. Little things like expecting a child to pick out what he or she is going to wear to school or letting children have a vote in certain family decisions may encourage a sense of independence and motivate them to achieve success.

Cognitive Dissonance

What happens when our **cognitive expectancies** of a situation differ from the actual outcome? For example, what if we study hard for an exam expecting to earn an *A* and we actually receive a *C*? Does the discrepancy between expectancies and outcomes influence our behavior? In the next section we look at a theory of motivation that is based on these discrepancies.

Cognitive dissonance theory emphasizes the idea that we behave in ways to minimize inconsistencies in our beliefs, attitudes, opinions, and our behavior (Festinger, 1957). According to this theory, cognitions about one's self and the world around us can be either consistent or inconsistent. When cognitions are inconsistent, a negative motivational state results, which activates us to resolve the inconsistency. For example, suppose

Table 8-2 Characteristics of High Need-for-Achievement (nAch) Individuals

1. Optimistic about personal prospects for success; feel personally in control of their destinies and willing to delay gratification for the sake of achieving long-term goals (for example, willingness to extend education into postgraduate studies rather than going for the immediate economic rewards of a lesser job)
2. Tend to seek higher levels of socioeconomic success than parents and are more often successful in achieving this than people with low nAch scores
3. Inclined to set realistic career goals that are neither too easy nor too difficult for their skills, whereas low nAch scorers tend to select career goals that are either too easy or unrealistic in light of their abilities
4. Attain higher grades in academic courses related to career goals than do low-need achievers
5. Tend to be relatively independent and more concerned with succeeding on tasks than with how they affect other people

that you know you should continue studying this chapter for an exam tomorrow, but you also promised a friend you would go to the game. Because these two thoughts are inconsistent (because you can't do both), cognitive dissonance is generated. Cognitive dissonance motivates other thoughts or behaviors to resolve this inconsistency. For instance, you may resolve this either by generating a new belief that you already know the material well enough to pass the exam (so you might as well go to the game); or, dissonance could be resolved by changing your belief about the importance of keeping your promise (and calling off plans to go to the game). How could the dissonance that was created by getting a *C* on that exam be resolved? A common resolution would be to generate the belief that the exam wasn't a fair test of your knowledge. After all, if the exam were unfair, no amount of studying would have prepared you.

BVT*Lab*

Flashcards are available for this chapter at **www.BVTLab.com**.

Cognitive dissonance may also occur as a result of inconsistencies between your behavior and your beliefs, particularly when your behavior can be justified. Suppose you hold the belief that cheating on exams is wrong, but find yourself cheating. This inconsistency will generate considerable dissonance unless the cheating can be justified by a new belief that the professor's exams aren't really fair anyway. In both of these examples, dissonance is decreased by a change in beliefs.

Dissonance theory has generated considerable research over the years. In an early test of dissonance theory, Aronson and Mills (1959) asked for female volunteers to participate in a series of discussions about sex. Before participation, however, the subjects had to pass a "test" to determine whether they were indeed capable of handling the discussion material. At this point the subjects were divided into two groups. For the first group the "test" consisted of reading aloud sex-related words and descriptions of sexual behavior in the presence of a male experimenter. The "test" for the second group consisted of reading aloud only mildly descriptive sexual material. After completing the "test," the subjects from both groups were allowed to listen to a boring tape recording of discussions of sexual behavior in animals. As a test for cognitive dissonance, the subjects were then asked to rate the discussion and their willingness to participate again. Before reading on, consider which group of females had the greatest cognitive dissonance and how this might have influenced their rating of the discussion and their willingness to participate again.

Dissonance theory predicts that the subjects in the first group should have the greatest dissonance because of the discrepancy between their "test" (reading aloud sexually explicit material) and the boring nature of the discussions. To resolve this inconsistency, these subjects should rate the discussions as more interesting as well as be more willing to participate in future discussions than the second group. The results of this experiment confirmed these predictions.

More recently, researchers examined the role of cognitive dissonance in maintaining smoking in a group of 244 adolescent smokers. Smoking causes dissonance because smokers are aware that their habit is unhealthy and often leads to smoking-related disease and a shortened lifespan. One way to resolve this dissonance, according to the researchers, is to develop a compensatory health belief that engaging in other healthful behaviors can offset the risks of smoking. The researchers found that smokers who were not prepared to quit smoking engaged in more compensatory beliefs than those who were motivated to quit (Radtke, Scholz, Keller, Knäuper, & Hornung, 2011).

Dissonance theory has been supported in a wide range of experiments designed to create cognitive dissonance. Overall, experiments tend to support Festinger's assumption that subjects tend to reduce cognitive dissonance by either making a change in their behavior, or more likely, a change in their attitude to achieve consistency (E. Harmon-Jones & C. Harmon-Jones, 2008; Olsen & Stone, 2005).

Biologically Based Motives Motives such as hunger and thirst that are rooted primarily in body tissue needs; sometimes referred to as *drives*

Drive Commonly used to describe motives that are based on tissue needs, such as hunger and thirst

As we have seen, our behaviors may be energized and directed by a variety of complex cognitive motives that seem to demonstrate little or no relationship to biological needs. These motives are determined by learning, and they are aroused and satisfied by cognitive and social events rather than body tissue needs. Unlike the biological motives we discuss next, these motives do not need to be satisfied to ensure survival. However, much of human happiness and misery is associated with the satisfaction or thwarting of these important cognitive motives.

8.2d Biological Bases of Motivation

Biologically based motives are rooted primarily in body tissue needs, such as those for food, water, air, sex, sleep, temperature regulation, and the avoidance of pain. Psychologists generally use the term **drive** to refer to motives that are based on tissue needs. In both humans and other animals, basic biological drives such as hunger and thirst must be satisfied in order to ensure survival. (Recall that Clark Hull made a distinction between primary or biological drives and secondary or learned drives.)

While the underlying needs behind biological drives are inborn, the expression of these drives is often learned. For example, a hungry person is motivated by a state of physiological food deprivation. Consequently, that person learns how to search the environment effectively for food that will satisfy this basic need.

Hunger and Eating

What processes let us know we are hungry, and how do we know when we have eaten enough? Researchers have tried to answer these seemingly basic questions since the beginning of this century. In spite of extensive research, however, we are still a long way from a complete understanding of this extremely complicated biological drive. The following discussion examines what we have learned about many of the factors that influence hunger and eating; it also considers obesity and other eating disorders.

(Shutterstock)

Despite extensive research, the extremely complicated biological drive of hunger is not fully understood.

Hunger performs a critical biological function. It tells us when our bodies require more nutrition. What are the mechanisms that tell us we are hungry? Although the obvious answer to this question is that our empty stomachs tell us, the picture is actually much more complicated. Attempts to explain the possible biological bases of hunger have focused on a number of areas, including the stomach, monitoring mechanisms in the brain, and other body organs such as the liver. We consider the evidence in each of these areas of investigation.

The Stomach We have all experienced hunger pangs and growling stomachs when we have not eaten for some time. We are also familiar with the feeling of a full stomach when we have completed a meal. From our own experience, then, it seems logical that the contractions of an empty stomach are what make us hungry and that the pressure of food against the stomach walls tells us to stop eating. Do you believe that stomach contractions motivate you to eat and a sensation of fullness motivates you to stop? Think about this for a moment before reading on.

While people do associate hunger with an empty stomach, cancer patients who have had their stomachs removed still experience hunger, and experimental animals will stop eating a meal even when food is removed from the stomach as soon as it arrives. Despite this evidence, however, most hunger researchers believe that stomach sensations do contribute to our overall feelings of hunger and satiety (fullness). For example, strong evidence suggests that the stomach contains pressure detectors that are activated when the stomach is distended with food and/or fluids. These sensors seem to play a role in signaling satiety and thus inhibiting further eating. Nevertheless, research has made it clear that stomach contractions are not necessary for hunger and that we must look outside of the stomach for a complete explanation. One primary line of research has focused on the hypothalamus.

Figure 8-1 A Drawing of the Hypothalamus Showing the Location of the Ventromedial, Arcuate, and Lateral Nuclei

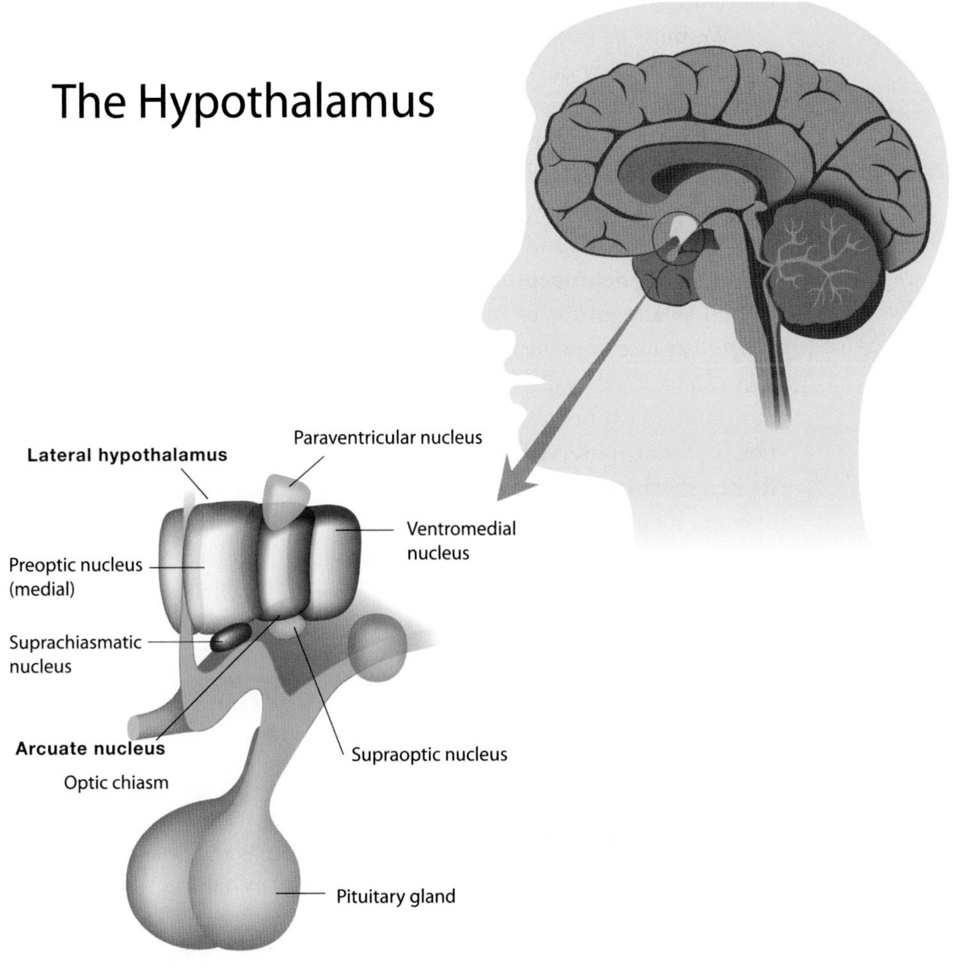

Source: Shutterstock

The Hypothalamus

Ventromedial Hypothalamus (VMH) A region of the hypothalamus in which damage results in faster gastric emptying and an increase in insulin production; also important for female sexual behavior

Lateral Hypothalamus (LH) An area of the hypothalamus that is important for taste sensation, mediating digestive processes, and salivation

Arcuate Nucleus An area of the hypothalamus, adjacent to the ventromedial nucleus, that regulates the secretion of neuropeptide Y and insulin

Neuropeptide Y (NPY) A potent stimulator of appetite and a regulator of insulin secretion

It has long been suspected that the hypothalamus is somehow involved in hunger motivation. A number of early studies identified two specific regions within the hypothalamus that appeared to serve as control centers for eating. One is the **ventromedial hypothalamus (VMH)**, located in the front center portion of this brain structure (see Figure 8-1). When the VMH is electrically or chemically stimulated, feeding behavior in animals is inhibited. Conversely, when the VMH is destroyed, the result in many species is extreme overeating and obesity, a condition called *hyperphagia*. These findings suggested that the VMH served as a satiety center that inhibited eating by somehow signaling an organism when it has had enough to eat.

Just as the VMH seemed to act as an "off switch" to inhibit eating, another structure in the hypothalamus seemed to act as an "on switch" or feeding center. Damage to the **lateral hypothalamus (LH)**, an area on the sides of the hypothalamus, produced just the opposite effect of lesioning the VMH. When the LH is destroyed, animals dramatically reduce food consumption or stop eating altogether, a condition known as *aphagia*. Conversely, electrical or chemical stimulation of the LH feeding center caused animals to eat—even if they are already satiated (Stellar, 1954). The experiments suggested that structures in the hypothalamus operate together to maintain a relatively constant state of satiety, much as a thermostat maintains a constant temperature in a house. The VMH and LH centers monitor the status of our bodies' energy resources.

We must be cautious, however, in interpreting these hypothalamic areas as simple feeding and satiety on/off centers. More recent research has revealed that these regions receive signals from several important hormones and neurotransmitters that appear to be critical for feeding motivation. Lesions to the VMH may actually lead to the secretion of large amounts of insulin, resulting in lowered blood glucose levels and thus an increase in hunger. Additionally, VMH lesions appeared to have impacted the nearby **arcuate nucleus** (Figure 8-1), which controls the secretion of several important neurotransmitters including **neuropeptide Y (NPY)**. Neuropeptide Y is a potent stimulator of appetite as well as a regulator of insulin secretion. Animals with VMH lesions appear to gain weight because of an increase in NPY and insulin secretion. An increase in insulin secretion results in all available fuel being converted into fat. These animals, therefore, are motivated to eat because they are chronically hungry. In addition, not all of the reduction in feeding observed after LH lesions can be attributed to a decrease in motivation. Rather, much of the decrease has to do with damage to nearby neural pathways involved in integrating the sensations of taste, smell, and the sight of food (Rolls & Baylis, 1994). In summary, while the hypothalamus is clearly involved in feeding motivation, specific neural centers do not function as simple on/off switches. Rather, the hypothalamus is responsible for regulating the secretion of neurotransmitters and hormones necessary for the initiation of feeding, glucose storage and release, and integration of sensory and metabolic information regarding the status of fuel reserves (Carlson, 2014).

Blood Glucose and Hunger

While research on the hypothalamus clearly reveals that it plays a vital role in feeding motivation, it still leaves questions unanswered. What internal bodily changes does the hypothalamus integrate to trigger hunger and to regulate how much we eat? What are the chemical and hormonal signals for hunger? To answer these questions, we need to know what internal biological conditions the hypothalamus monitors. One such variable that is affected by feeding and satiety is blood glucose. Because one of the most important body fuels is glucose, it seems logical that hunger might occur as time passes since our last meal and levels of glucose in our blood become lower.

The **glucostatic hypothesis** suggests that levels of glucose are monitored by *glucoreceptors* (cells sensitive to glucose in the bloodstream). Another substance, *insulin* (a hormone secreted by the pancreas), is also monitored, for insulin must be present in order for glucose to be used by cells. Hunger results whenever the glucoreceptors detect that glucose is unavailable, either because of low blood sugar levels or because there is not enough insulin present to enable cells to use the glucose in the bloodstream. Support for this theory was provided by evidence that insulin injections and other treatments that lower blood sugar levels have the effect of stimulating hunger, leading to eating (Epstein & Teitelbaum, 1967). We now know that detectors in both the liver and the brain monitor the rate of glucose utilization. The assumption is that while the decision to eat is made in the brain, signals from the liver convey essential information about glucose metabolism. This information about glucose is translated by the hypothalamus into increases in cell activity and the release of additional hormones and neurotransmitters (Melnick, Price, & Colmers, 2011).

Glucostatic Hypothesis Theory that hunger results when glucoreceptors detect a lack of glucose, either because blood levels of glucose are low or because insulin is not available in sufficient quantity

Cholecystokinin (CCK) A hormone that regulates the rate of food digestion and decreases appetite by affecting neurons in the hypothalamus

Leptin A hormone that is produced by fat cells and appears to signal satiety to neurons in the hypothalamus

8.2e Hormones Controlling Hunger

Research also suggests that there are several hormones involved in feeding regulation. There is especially strong evidence linking the hormone **cholecystokinin** (**CCK**) to appetite suppression (Dourish, Ruckert, Tattersall, & Iversen, 1989; Garlicki, P. Konturek, Majka, Kwiecien, & S. Konturek, 1990). CCK is released when food enters the duodenum; it then seems to travel through the bloodstream to the brain, where it acts to inhibit eating behavior. In one study, investigators found that brain levels of this hormone were significantly lower in obese rats than in normal rats, suggesting that the overweight rats consumed excessive food because their CCK levels were not sufficient to suppress their eating behavior (Straus & Yalow, 1979). Furthermore, animals that lack sensitivity to CCK (through a genetic manipulation) eat excessively and become obese (Zhu, Yan, Smith, Moran, & Bi, 2012). An alternative mechanism for CCK action that is consistent with other results may be that CCK disrupts the sensory signals for taste, thereby making food less palatable (Ettinger, Thompson, & Staddon, 1986). As you know from experience, taste changes as you eat a large meal. This is why meals often begin with bitter salads and finish with highly palatable and sweet desserts. As we eat, CCK is released and foods become less and less palatable.

Other neurotransmitters and hormones that have been implicated in feeding include neuropeptide Y, which was discussed above, and **leptin**. An injection of neuropeptide Y, which may be the most powerful stimulant to feeding we know of, into the hypothalamus of animals results in voracious eating, even if animals just completed a large meal. Another hormone, leptin appears to signal satiety. Leptin is secreted by fat cells and counters the effects of neuropeptide Y in the arcuate nucleus of the hypothalamus. Injections of leptin have been shown to inhibit eating and to increase metabolic rate (Baskin et al., 1999). Other hormones beside neuropeptide Y and leptin are certainly involved in eating, and some are presently under investigation for their potential in treating a variety of eating disorders. One thing, however, is very clear from several decades of research on feeding motivation: *There is no single physiological state or hormone that signals hunger or satiety*. Likewise, there will not be an easy cure for obesity in humans. It is becoming increasingly clear that leptin, neuropeptide Y, and several other hormones regulate energy balance and the motivation to eat through a system of neural circuits throughout the arcuate, lateral, and ventromedial nuclei of the hypothalamus (Leinninger, 2011; Cornier, 2011).

Obesity Condition in which an individual weighs 20 percent or more above the desirable weight for his or her height

So far, we have been exploring the control of hunger and eating and the mechanisms that motivate daily food intake. In addition, there must also be both short-term and long-term control mechanisms that allow most of us to maintain our weight at a relatively constant level over time. The integration of blood glucose levels, CCK, neuropeptide Y, and leptin activity all play a crucial role in eating motivation. The outcome of this integration is a decision to eat or not to eat (Toates, 2001). Although some people seem to be perpetually losing and regaining the same 10 or 20 pounds, most animals, including people, maintain a relatively constant weight that may fluctuate by only a few pounds over the long term. This is evidence that the integration of multiple chemical, behavioral, and environmental factors works remarkably well.

8.3 Eating Disorders: Obesity, Anorexia, and Bulimia

8.3a Obesity

We are a nation that seems obsessed both by food and losing weight. Television commercials besiege us with images of beautiful bodies and athletic-looking people engaging in energetic aerobic exercises. At the same time, we see ads for ice cream, doughnuts, double cheeseburgers, and pepperoni pizza. How many people do you know who are on a diet? Perhaps you are one. According to recent estimates, about 70 percent of adult Americans are overweight and 36 percent are **obese**, weighing 20 percent or more above the desirable weight for their height. In addition, over 30 percent of children are now overweight or obese (Centers for Disease Control and Prevention, 2016b). The economic impact of obesity in the United States is also staggering. It is estimated to cost well over $192 billion each year in direct and indirect medical expenses as well as in loss of productivity. Most health professionals agree that obesity places a person at greater risk of developing one or more health problems. Obesity greatly increases the risk of high blood pressure, stroke, heart disease, diabetes, cancer, gall bladder disease, respiratory problems, and arthritis (2016b).

People try to get rid of excess weight by starving or sweating it off, but the grim fact is that in most cases fat wins. This is not to say that people cannot lose weight. Quite the contrary, many people lose and regain the same 10 or 20 pounds over and over again. Studies demonstrate that of those people who go on fad diets, approximately 95 percent regain all of their lost weight within one year. Furthermore, as many as 75 percent of individuals placed on medically supervised diets regain most, if not all, of their lost weight.

Theories of Obesity

There are many theories about why people become overweight. Blame has been placed on genes, conditions of early development, metabolic factors, and learned responses to emotional stress. We briefly consider the evidence for each of these viewpoints.

Genetic Causes of Obesity

Several studies have demonstrated that a child whose parents are both of normal weight has less than one chance in ten of becoming obese. When one or both parents are overweight, however, the odds jump to approximately two out of five and four out of five, respectively. Of course, just because obesity runs in families is no proof that a genetic predisposition is involved. An equally logical explanation is that obese parents overfeed their children as well as themselves, thereby establishing a habit of excessive eating.

(iStock)

A number of studies link obesity with negative body image and depression.

To control for these environmental factors, researchers have compared the concordance rate of obesity in identical twins that have the same genes with that of fraternal twins who do not share the same genes. Specifically, *concordance* refers to the degree of agreement in the expression of a given trait in both members of a twin pair. Concordance is usually expressed as a correlation coefficient. Investigators have also compared the weight correlations between adopted individuals and their biological parents with correlations between the weights of adopted individuals and their nonbiological, adopting parents. Data from both of these kinds of studies have led obesity researchers to conclude that genetic influences have an important role in determining human obesity (Clément et al., 1998; Grilo & Pogue-Geile, 1991; Pérusse et al., 2005; Yeo, 2012). However, genetics is not the only factor contributing to obesity.

Early Childhood Experience

It has been found that the fat cells of obese people are as much as 50 to 100 percent larger than those of lean people. In addition, obese people often have a greater number of fat cells. Many researchers believe that eating patterns during childhood and adolescence strongly influence the size and number of fat cells in the body of an adult, and this theory has been supported by research. There is ample evidence that obesity among children is increasing at an alarming rate and that childhood obesity is associated with an increased risk of adult obesity (Ebbeling & Ludwig, 2008; Ferraro, Thorpe, & Wilkinson, 2003).

Metabolic Factors

Metabolic disturbances, also called *metabolic syndrome*, have often been blamed for obesity. Some people do seem to convert food into body tissue, primarily fat, at a faster rate than others, and they are likely to have trouble maintaining a desirable weight. Certainly variations in insulin secretion, as well as other hormones, can lead to obesity in humans.

Reactions to Emotional Stress

Many of us have a tendency to overeat when we are under stress. Campus cafeterias and local pizzerias seem to do a lot of business just before and during finals week. Some people who are chronically stressed, depressed, or anxiety-ridden tend to overeat as a matter of course. This tendency may be due to a number of factors.

One possible cause is experience. Unfortunately, some parents reinforce their children's good behavior with high-calorie goodies such as cookies or cake. This kind of experience helps a child learn to associate eating with feeling good, and food may also take on the symbolic meaning of love and acceptance. Again, parents often praise their children for eating lots of food—another experience that strengthens the association between food and feeling good. Later in life, these early experiences may show up as

BVT *Lab*

Visit **www.BVTLab.com** to explore the student resources available for this chapter.

craving food whenever a person feels rejected, depressed, disappointed, or unhappy. Certain foods, particularly those high in carbohydrates, produce a calming or sedative effect by altering levels of neurotransmitters. As we mentioned in Chapter 3, foods high in carbohydrates indirectly increase levels of serotonin in the brain, which may alleviate symptoms of depression. Thus, eating may be spurred by the desire to reduce unpleasant emotional states (that is, negative reinforcement).

Another factor that may contribute to overeating is the tendency to eat during emotional stress. A recent study examined the relationship between perceived stress and the drive to eat in 457 women. Those who reported greater stress had a significantly greater drive to eat. They also experienced an inability to inhibit eating, greater bouts of binge eating, increased hunger, and a decreased ability to restrain from eating (Groesz et al., 2012).

Obesity is clearly a significant problem for a large number of individuals. Each year in the United States alone, millions of dollars are spent annually by people trying to lose weight through diet and exercise programs. While the review of causes of obesity presented here is fairly complete, there is no simple explanation for why an individual becomes obese and how to treat it.

Dieting

Regardless of the cause, it is often very difficult for overweight people to take weight off and keep it off. Many dieters have had the experience of losing a great deal of weight and then discovering, much to their chagrin, that they regain the weight while eating much less than before they started their diet. Why does this happen?

When people go on a diet, especially a starvation diet, there is a pronounced reduction in their resting metabolic rate—the energy the body uses when in the resting state. This change in metabolic rate occurs because the body actually resists the weight loss. Ironically, the dieter and his or her body are working toward opposite goals. Although the dieter wants to take off extra pounds and inches, the body reacts to the sharp reduction in food intake as if it were protecting itself from starvation. It slows down its metabolic rate to conserve energy, thus ensuring that the brain, heart, and other vital organs will have sufficient fuel.

This change in metabolic rate produces highly inconvenient results for the dieter. For instance, assume that you normally consume 3,000 calories per day and you suddenly begin an 800-calorie diet. At first, you may experience weight loss. Then your body will eventually lower its resting metabolic rate to conserve its fat stores, resulting in the likelihood of hitting a plateau. If you tough it out, however, you will be able to reach your weight goal.

At this point, you will want to begin eating a more reasonable diet again—but beware. Your body is now likely to play one of its cruelest tricks. Used to conserving energy, your metabolism will continue running in low gear. Thus, even a modest increase in calorie consumption (often well below your pre-diet level) may result in gaining the pounds back. It may take weeks or months for your metabolism to readjust to a normal level, and by then you may have given up in disgust.

This scenario sounds discouraging; however, as with everything else, there are right ways and wrong ways of dieting. The "Health, Psychology, and Life" discussion toward the end of the chapter provides additional information to keep in mind if you are trying to lose weight. Remember, however, that no safe method will work quickly and easily. All weight-loss programs require considerable persistence.

8.3b Anorexia and Bulimia

Anorexia nervosa may affect as many as five in every one hundred teenage women. Within certain subgroups, particularly among athletes, the incidence increases to at least 35 percent. In recent years, there has been increasing recognition that this disorder often demonstrates early onset, occurring in prepubertal children age fourteen or younger. Anorexia is characterized by a prolonged refusal to eat adequate amounts of food. The result may be emaciation and even death, mostly caused by cardiac complications. Although most recorded cases of anorexia occur among women in their teens or early twenties, males, children, and older adults may also be afflicted.

While the causes of anorexia are still being investigated, clearly social influence, via the media and peers, probably plays a significant role in most cases. People with anorexia nervosa often have a distorted body image in which they perceive themselves as attractive only when dangerously thin (*DSM-5*).

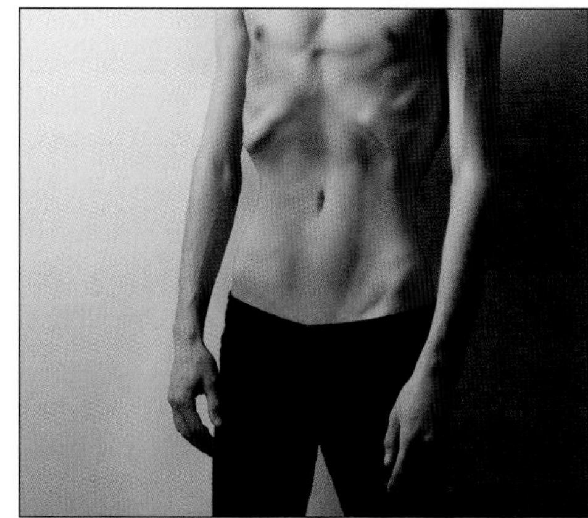
(Shutterstock)

Anorexia is a serious disorder that can result in emaciation and death.

Bulimia is a disorder in which a person, most commonly a young woman in her teens or twenties, engages in periodic episodes of binge eating and then uses either vomiting or a laxative to purge the body. Some bulimics maintain normal weight, and others are also anorexic. In one study, approximately half of the patients hospitalized for anorexia indicated that they periodically resorted to bulimic purges. Bulimia is especially common among college women; its incidence has been estimated to be as high as 20 percent.

Many people with bulimia frequently manifest depression, anxiety, sleep disturbances, poor body image, guilt, and substance abuse. In addition to these psychological problems, bulimia contributes to a variety of physical complications, including cardiac complications resulting from the loss of potassium, gastrointestinal difficulties, extensive tooth decay and enamel deterioration from vomiting, and hair loss.

Both anorexia and bulimia are serious disorders that may be fatal. As a result, many campus health and counseling centers, and a growing number of urban hospital centers, have added specialists to their staff who are experienced in treating eating disorders. A variety of therapeutic strategies have been shown to be effective in treating anorexia and bulimia, including the use of antidepressants and counseling. Although most patients recover from these disorders, as many as 30 percent may never respond to treatment and will prematurely die from the complications (Keel, Mitchell, Miller, Davis, & Crow, 1999; Wilfley, Kass, Kolko, & Stein, 2012).

8.4 Sensation-Seeking Motivation

Humans and other animals seem to require a certain amount of stimulation in order to feel good and function effectively. The need to manipulate and explore the environment and the need for sensory stimulation both fall under the category of **sensation-seeking motives**. These motives seem to be natural to a broad range of mammals. Observation of infants of many species, including humans, reveals a strong inclination to explore and manipulate the environment as soon as they are able. Animals have been shown to expose themselves willingly to various kinds of stimulation in the apparent effort to raise their level of physiological arousal. For example, young monkeys provided with mechanical puzzles, such as metal clasps used to seal a door, will tirelessly manipulate the object with no apparent reward beyond the opportunity to manipulate something.

Anorexia Nervosa Eating disorder characterized by prolonged refusal to eat adequate amounts of food; most common among young adults

Bulimia Eating disorder characterized by periodic episodes of binge eating followed by deliberate purging using either vomiting or laxatives

Sensation-Seeking Motive An explanation for the apparent need for certain levels of stimulation, including the need to explore the environment and the need for sensory stimulation

Arousal A physiological state in which an individual is able to process information effectively and to engage in motivated behavior

Optimum Level of Arousal Level of arousal at which an individual's performance on a specific task is most efficient

Yerkes-Dodson Law Principle that the optimum level of arousal for peak performance will vary somewhat depending on the nature of the task

We can observe this same drive in ourselves. Very few of us are content with constant, never-changing environments. Sometimes we seek quiet and solitude, but after a time we are likely to seek the sounds and sights of people and activity. We turn on the television, jog, play tennis, talk on the phone, and so forth. We may thrive on challenging games, complex puzzles, or the opportunity to explore new things.

Some psychologists believe that the motivation to seek stimulation evolved in many species because of its survival value. Organisms that explore and manipulate their environment become more aware of its parameters of safety and danger. But what about individuals who seek out stimulation by engaging in high-risk behaviors such as sky diving, bungee jumping, rock climbing, and even drug use? Do these individuals have a greater need for stimulation than others? Several lines of research suggest that the brains of individuals who seek stimulation and novelty differ in critical ways from those who do not. For example, research comparing low- and high-sensation-seeking individuals does reveal different patterns of physiology in reaction to aversive and fear-producing events. Low sensation seekers display greater startle responses to stimuli that precede aversive stimulation than do high sensation seekers (Lissek et al., 2007). In addition, the brains of sensation seekers have lower numbers of dopamine receptors in several midbrain regions. It is believed that sensation-seeking behaviors, like drug use, increase the activity of these otherwise depressed dopamine neurons, thereby giving these individuals a greater boost in rewarding effects of dopamine (Zald et al., 2008).

8.4a Optimum Level of Arousal

Arousal is a general concept referring to a behavioral state; we experience arousal as the ability to process information effectively and to engage in motivated behavior. A certain minimum level of arousal is essential in order to express goal-directed behavior. Conversely, too much arousal may leave us overstimulated, overloaded, and temporarily incapable of effective action. A number of researchers, most notably Donald Hebb (1955), have theorized that people have an optimum level of arousal, which is the level where their performance will be most efficient.

According to Hebb's **optimum level of arousal** theory, our performance on a task will improve as arousal increases up to an optimal level. Further increases will begin to interfere with our efficiency. This theory has been generally supported by research, but with some exceptions. For example, low levels of arousal have frequently been shown to hinder performance, but not under all experimental conditions (Orne & Scheibe, 1964).

The Yerkes-Dodson Law

The optimum level of arousal seems to vary according to the type of task a person is performing. For instance, the high arousal level you need to compete successfully in a 100-meter race would be inappropriate and even counterproductive for some other tasks, such as writing a book review.

According to the **Yerkes-Dodson law**, the optimum level of arousal for peak performance varies somewhat depending on the nature of the task (Yerkes & Dodson, 1908). If you are involved in a simple task, you probably perform best if your arousal level is relatively high. Conversely, you are likely to do better on a difficult task if your arousal level is somewhat lower. Figure 8-2 demonstrates the relationship between arousal and performance as predicted by the Yerkes-Dodson law. It is now generally recognized that the Yerkes-Dodson law somewhat oversimplifies the complex relationship between arousal

Figure 8-2 The Yerkes-Dodson Law Applied to the Concept of an Optimal Level of Arousal

The optimal level of arousal varies depending on task difficulty.

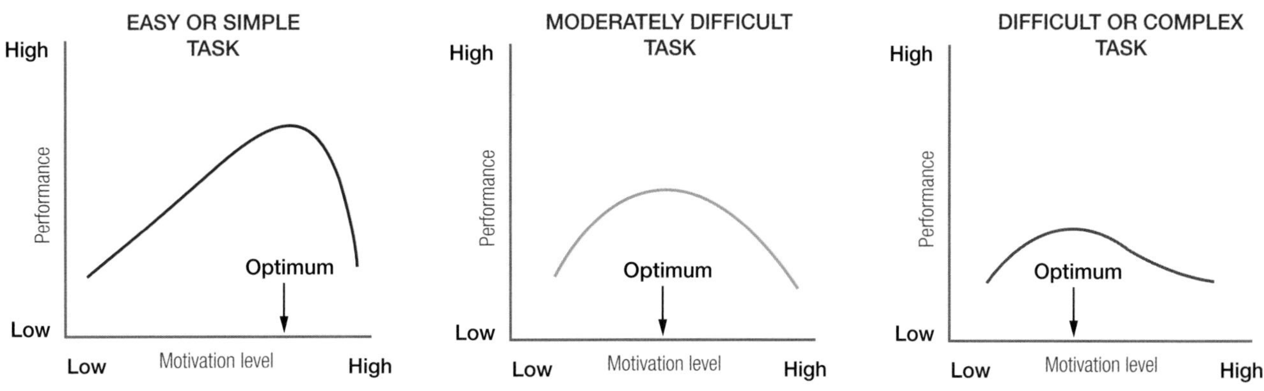

and performance. Nevertheless, data from diverse studies have generally supported these researchers' formulation (Watters, Martin, & Schreter, 1997).

8.5 Sexual Motivation and Behavior

Another important source of motivation is sexual motivation. Our sexuality is a richly varied, highly individualized, and potentially enriching aspect of our lives. We express our sexuality in many ways, and the feelings, thoughts, and attitudes we bring to this area of human experience also vary widely. In the remainder of this chapter, we present a brief overview of selected topics, which provide an introduction to certain behavioral, biological, psychosocial, and cultural aspects of sexuality. We will see how human sexual behavior can be motivated by all of these factors.

We begin by exploring the question of how biological and psychosocial factors influence human sexual behavior. It was once thought that sexual behaviors were motivated primarily by a physiological drive, mostly because of the dominant role of physiology in animal sexual behavior. In nonprimate mammals such as rats, for instance, hormones appear to be essential to sexual arousal and function. However, there is now general agreement that learning, emotions, and social norms become more important as the complexity of the organism increases. In humans, sexual interest and expression are controlled both by hormones and, even more, by the cerebral cortex—reflecting a combination of biological, psychological, and cultural factors.

All this is not to say that biology is irrelevant to human sexual motivation. In the following sections, we compare the effects of biological and psychosocial factors to see how they contribute to sexual motivation and arousal.

8.5a Biological Bases of Sexual Behavior

It is extremely difficult to distinguish between the effects of strictly physiological processes such as hormone production and those of psychosocial processes such as

Androgens Male sex hormones, the most common of which is testosterone

early socialization, peer group learning, and emotional needs. In recent years, however, a number of well-designed, carefully implemented studies have yielded information about the complex relationship between hormones and sexual activity. Which hormones are important in human sexuality? Have different hormones been linked with male versus female sexual functions? Take a few moments to consider these questions before reading on.

Hormone Levels and Male Sexual Behavior

The primary male sex hormones are **androgens**. The testes secrete about 95 percent of these androgens in the form of testosterone; the remaining 5 percent are produced by the adrenal glands. A number of lines of research have linked androgens with sexual activity. One source of information has been studies of men who have undergone castration (an operation involving removal of the testes, which is sometimes performed as medical treatment for such diseases as genital tuberculosis and testicular cancer). In one major investigation of a large group of castrated Norwegian males, most subjects reported significantly reduced sexual interest and activity within the first year after the operation (Bremer, 1959). However, other research suggests that castration has a highly variable effect on sexual desire and functioning. In one case, a forty-three-year-old man, castrated eighteen years previously, reported having intercourse one to four times weekly (Hamilton, 1943). Other writers have recorded incidences of continued sexual desire and function as long as thirty years following castration, without hormone treatment (Ford & Beach, 1951). Such findings, together with numerous other investigations, suggest that while sexual interest and activity generally diminish after castration, the amount of reduction is highly variable. The fact that this diminution occurs so frequently indicates that hormones are important in instigating sexual interest.

A second line of research investigating hormones and sexual functioning involves androgen-blocking drugs. Antiandrogens drastically reduce the amount of testosterone circulating in the bloodstream. One of these drugs, medroxyprogesterone acetate (MPA, also known by its trade name, Depo-Provera®), has been used effectively to treat sexual offenders (Emory, Cole, & Meyer III, 1995; Lehne & Money, 2000). However, altering sex hormone levels is far from a surefire treatment for sex offenders, especially in cases where sexual assaults have stemmed from nonsexual motives such as the need to express anger or to exert control over another person.

A third source of evidence linking androgens to sexual motivation is studies of hypogonadism, a state of androgen deprivation that results from certain diseases of the endocrine system or radiation to treat cancer. If this condition occurs before puberty, maturation of the primary and secondary sex characteristics is retarded, and the individual may never develop an active sexual interest. In adult males, the results have been more controversial. However, in a comprehensive review of more than thirty years of research on testosterone treatment, it was concluded that when hypogonadal men receive testosterone treatment they often experience a return of normal sexual interest and activity (Isidori et al., 2005).

Finally, there is evidence that males who take anabolic steroids (testosterone) to build muscle mass may experience increased levels of sexual motivation. Many professional and nonprofessional athletes take supplemental testosterone to increase hormone levels beyond their normal range. There is little doubt that supplemental testosterone is effective when used this way, and debates will rage for years about whether Mark McGwire's home run records would have been achieved without testosterone supplements.

Hormone Levels and Female Sexual Behavior

Many people assume that the female sex hormones, **estrogens**, play a major role in female sexual motivation and behavior. We do know that these hormones help maintain the elasticity of the vaginal lining and contribute to vaginal lubrication (Walling, Andersen, & Johnson, 1990). However, the role of estrogens in female sexual motivation is far from clear (Panjari & Davis, 2010).

Estrogens Hormones that influence female sexual development

Estrogens are not the only sex hormones present in females, however. Both the ovaries and the adrenal glands produce androgens in females, and the connection between androgens and female sexual motivation seems somewhat more substantial. Some of this evidence is anecdotal. For instance, the clinical literature on gynecology cites many cases in which women undergoing androgen therapy experience increased sexual interest and activity (Apperloo, Van Der Stege, Hoek, & Weijmar, 2003; Davis & Braunstein, 2012).

While androgens can be used to increase libido in both men and women, it is important to remember that interest in sexual behavior is dependent on many factors. Androgens by themselves are not sufficient to motivate sexual behavior in humans, even though they are often prescribed to treat sexual dysfunctions.

8.5b **Psychosocial Factors in Sexual Behavior**

Although hormones can, and do, influence human sexual motivation, our sexual behaviors are not strongly correlated with reproductive cycles and related biological events. Other animals stand in sharp contrast. Female sexual receptivity in other animals is governed by the reproductive cycle; biological cues (such as odors) are often necessary to instigate sexual activity, and hormone levels are closely tied to the ability to respond sexually.

In contrast, hormones are far from the only important factor influencing human sexuality. Indeed, it is likely that psychological and cultural conditions play a greater role in human sexual arousal and expression. Some evidence of the influence of psychosocial factors comes from our own experiences and observations. Ask yourself, for instance, what motivates your own sexual behavior, and what are the most important restrictions on your sexual behavior?

Most of us continue to express our sexuality throughout much of our lives because sexual activity is reinforcing. This reinforcement takes many forms, including a sense of self-esteem that comes from being loved, erotic pleasure and gratification, reduction of feelings of anxiety, and a sense of closeness to another person. Sexual expression can even serve the function of providing a way of relieving boredom and raising arousal levels. This diversity of reinforcers suggests that our incentives for sexual expression are largely psychosocial. It also underscores the basically social nature of humans, a propensity that greatly influences the manner in which we express our sexuality.

Societal Influences on Sexual Behavior

Social scientists have recorded in detail the tremendous variation that occurs in human sexual behavior in different societies (Crooks & Baur, 2014). Societies exist in which individuals in their sixties are more active sexually than the typical thirty-year-old American. In many societies, the marked gender differences in adolescent sexual behaviors that typify our own society are totally lacking. Such widespread fluctuations in sexual norms and behavior cannot be attributed to the influence of hormones.

Cultural Mores Established customs or beliefs in a particular culture

Nor can they be attributed to geographical factors. No other animal species has different sexual behaviors in different parts of the world. Rats in Ethiopia copulate the same way and are triggered by the same stimuli as rats in Oregon. The sexual patterns of dogs, cows, fowl, and higher primates are all highly similar, regardless of where they live. Thus, humans are unique in creating highly localized patterns of sexual behavior. This is perhaps the strongest evidence for the preeminence of psychosocial factors in human sexual motivation and expression.

Many of us have our own ideas about what is "normal" sexual behavior and what is not, but often the meaning of a given act (sexual or otherwise) cannot be fully understood without also understanding its cultural context. For example, in our own North American society, we may attribute sexual overtones to the act of two men embracing each other. In Italy, however (and in many other societies), it is completely normal (and nonsexual) for men to hug one another.

Such diversity exists among the cultures of the world that the very definition of what is sexually arousing may vary greatly. In one society, exposed female breasts may trigger sexual interest in men, whereas in a different society this sight may induce little or no erotic interest. Furthermore, the acceptability of certain sexual activities varies widely from culture to culture. In some societies, such as the Mangaians of Polynesia, sex is highly valued and almost all manifestations of it are considered beautiful and natural. Other societies, such as on the Irish island of Inis Beag, view any sexual act as undesirable and shameful (Crooks & Baur, 2014). Almost any sexual behavior is viewed in widely different ways in different societies. Masturbation by children may be overtly condemned in one society, covertly supported in another, openly encouraged in still another, and even occasionally initiated by parental example.

The diversity of sexual expression tends to mask a fundamental generalization that can be applied without exception to all social orders: Within the **cultural mores** (established customs and beliefs) of all societies, the conduct of sexual behavior is regulated in some way. The rules vary from one society to the next, but in no social order is sexuality completely unregulated.

The best way to understand the diversity of sexual expression is through examples. We look briefly at three societies with very different views of sexuality: the Polynesian society of the island Mangaia, the inhabitants of an island off the coast of Ireland known as Inis Beag, and the Dani of New Guinea. (These social groups have all been studied at some time during the last few decades. However, they may have undergone cultural change since they were observed.)

Mangaia

Mangaia is the southernmost of the Polynesian Cook Islands chain. In the 1950s, anthropologist Donald Marshall (1971) studied the inhabitants, and his accounts of Mangaian sexual practices have been widely quoted. When Marshall visited Mangaia, he observed a society in which sexual pleasure and activity is a principal concern, starting in childhood (Marshall, 1971). Children have extensive exposure to sexuality. They hear folktales containing detailed descriptions of sex acts and sexual anatomy, and they watch provocative ritual dances. At the onset of puberty, both sexes receive detailed instruction about sex. Once their instruction is completed, boys begin to seek out girls. Sex occurs in public privacy. Young males engage in a practice called *night-crawling*, in which boys enter their chosen lover's house at night and have sexual relations while other family members sleep nearby. (In the 1950s, when Marshall conducted his research, most Mangaian houses had only a single sleeping area.) If awakened, the other five to fifteen family members politely pretend to sleep. Parents approve of this practice and listen for sounds of laughter as a sign that their daughter is pleased with her partner. They also encourage their daughters to have a variety of lovers so that they may find a sexually compatible marriage partner. Young men gain social prestige through their ability to please their partners. These patterns persist on a daily basis throughout the adolescent years for unmarried men and women.

Sexual relations continue to occur frequently after marriage. A wide range of sexual activity is approved, including oral-genital sex and a considerable amount of touching before and during intercourse. Among the Mangaians, then, sexual activity is not only condoned but also actively encouraged.

Inis Beag In the community of the Irish island known as Inis Beag (a pseudonym), a sharp contrast to Mangaian practices is observed. When anthropologist John Messenger (1971) studied this society between 1958 and 1966, he observed that sexual expression is discouraged from infancy on. Mothers avoid breast-feeding their children, and after infancy parents seldom kiss or fondle them. Children learn to abhor nudity. They learn that elimination is dirty and that bathing must be done only in absolute privacy. Any kind of childhood sexual expression is punished.

As they grow older, children usually receive no information about sex from their parents. Young girls are often shocked by their first menstruation, and they are never given an adequate explanation of what has happened. Priests and other religious authorities teach that it is sinful to discuss premarital sexual activity, masturbation, or sex play. Religious leaders on the island have denounced even *Time* and *Life* magazines as pornographic.

Marriage partners generally know little or nothing about precoital sex play, such as oral or manual stimulation of the breasts and genitals. Beyond intercourse, sexual activity is usually limited to mouth kissing and rough fondling of the woman's lower body by the man. Men invariably initiate sex, using the man-on-top coital position, and both partners usually wear nightclothes during coitus. Female orgasm is unknown or considered a deviant response.

Sexual misconceptions continue through adulthood. For example, many women believe that menopause causes insanity, and some women confine themselves to bed from menopause to their death. During menstruation and also during the months following childbirth, men consider intercourse to be harmful to them. Many men also believe coitus to be debilitating, avoiding sex the night before a strenuous job. In general, sexual expression in Inis Beag is marked by anxiety-laden attitudes and rigid restrictions.

The Dani of New Guinea In both Mangaia and Inis Beag, sexuality receives a great amount of attention, albeit in different ways. In contrast, the Dani people of West New Guinea seem to be largely indifferent to sexuality (Heider, 1946). Sexual activity is infrequent among adults. Although courtship covers an extended period (marriages are held only during a certain feast that occurs every four to six years), there is almost no premarital sex. After marriage, a couple abstains from sex for at least two years and then has infrequent coitus. Following the birth of a child, husband and wife do not have sex for four to six years. During this time there is no reported masturbation, and extramarital sex is rare.

According to Karl Heider, who studied this society in the 1960s, the Dani culture does not overtly enforce these behavior patterns. Heider also observed no indications of hormonal or physiological deficiencies that could result in low sexual interest. In general, the Dani are relaxed, physically healthy people who live in a moderate climate and have an adequate food supply. They appear to be very calm, only rarely expressing anger. Heider believes that the apparent infrequency of sexual activity reflects the Dani's relaxed lifestyle and their low level of emotional intensity.

BVT Lab

Improve your test scores. Practice quizzes are available at www.BVTLab.com.

8.5c Sexual Orientation: Homosexuality

We have seen that the norms of sexual expression may vary considerably from society to society. Yet even within a single society, individuals express their sexuality in different ways. In this section we explore one variation in sexual behavior, homosexuality.

Different people have different views of what is sexually exciting, and sexuality can be expressed in a variety of ways. One way in which sexual expression varies from person to person is in **sexual orientation**—that is, the gender to which an individual is attracted. Attraction to partners of the same sex is called homosexual orientation, and attraction to partners of the other sex is called heterosexual orientation. Bisexuality refers to attraction to partners of both sexes.

Most people think of homosexuality as sexual contact between individuals of the same sex. However, this definition is limited in that it does not encompass all of the meanings of the term homosexual, which can refer to (1) sexual behavior, (2) emotional affiliation, and (3) one's own self-definition. The following definition incorporates a broader spectrum of elements: A **homosexual** person is an individual whose primary erotic, psychological, emotional, and social interest is in members of the same sex, even though that interest may not be overtly expressed. A homosexual person's gender identity agrees with his or her biological sex. That is, homosexual individuals perceive themselves as male or female, respectively, and are attracted to people of the same sex.

In our society, we tend to make clear-cut distinctions between homosexuality and heterosexuality. The delineation is not so clear-cut, however. At one end of a broad spectrum, a relatively small percentage of people consider themselves exclusively homosexual; at the other end, a greater number think of themselves as exclusively heterosexual. Between the two groups exist varying degrees of preference and experience.

The Incidence of Homosexuality

According to Alfred Kinsey and his colleagues (1948), the proportion of exclusively homosexual individuals in our society is approximately 2 percent of women and 4 percent of men (or roughly 3 percent of the total U.S. population). Some writers have speculated that the actual number of predominantly homosexual people is closer to 19 percent of the population (Luzer, 2013). This higher estimate was identified by using nondirect questionnaires as opposed to directly asking participants their sexual orientation, as it is believed that this method more accurately reflects the incidence.

Between the extremes on the continuum are many individuals who have experienced sexual contact with or been attracted to people of the same sex. Kinsey's estimate of this group's number was quite high. Some 37 percent of males and 13 percent of females in his research populations reported having had overt homosexual experiences at some point in their lives, and even more had been erotically attracted to members of the same sex. These statistics are quite close to the more recent estimate of 27 percent.

Attitudes Toward Homosexuality

Sexual Orientation Sex to which an individual is attracted

Homosexuality Primary erotic, psychological, and social interest in members of the same sex, even though that interest may not be expressed overtly

A monumental survey of 190 societies throughout the world, conducted by an anthropologist and a psychologist (Ford & Beach, 1951), found that homosexuality was accepted in approximately two-thirds of these societies. Homosexuality was also widely accepted in many earlier cultures. For example, more than half of 225 Native American tribes accepted male homosexuality, and 17 percent accepted female homosexuality (Pomeroy, 1965).

The Judeo-Christian tradition has had a far more negative view of homosexuality. Many religious scholars believe that the condemnation of homosexuality stems from a reformation movement beginning in the seventh century BCE, through which Jewish religious leaders wanted to develop a closed community distinct from others of the time. Homosexual activities had been a part of the religious services of many population groups, and one way of establishing the uniqueness of the Jewish religion was to reject religious rituals involving homosexual activities. Thus, homosexual behaviors were condemned as a form of pagan worship. Strong prohibitive biblical scriptures were written, for example, "You shall not lie with man as one lies with a female, it is an abomination" (Leviticus 18:22).

In recent years, there has been a shift in attitudes toward homosexuality, as evidenced by the 2015 Supreme Court ruling guaranteeing the right of same-sex marriage. This is not to say that anti-gay attitudes don't exist—quite the contrary. Anti-gay sentiment remains strong within certain segments of our society.

Theories of Homosexuality

Several theories have attempted to explain the development of homosexuality. There is still no single clear answer, but research conducted by Alan Bell, Martin Weinberg, and Sue Hammersmith (1981) helps shed some light on the question. Bell and his colleagues used a sample of 979 homosexual people matched to a control group of 477 heterosexual people. All subjects were questioned about their childhood, adolescence, and sexual practices; their responses were analyzed using sophisticated statistical techniques. Much of the information presented in this discussion is based on this study's findings, to which we refer in evaluating both psychosocial and biological explanations of homosexuality.

(Shutterstock)

One way in which sexual expression varies from person to person is in sexual orientation—the gender to which an individual is attracted.

Psychosocial Theories

Some theories seek to explain homosexuality as the result of learning, personal experiences, parenting patterns, or the individual's own psychological attributes. For instance, one explanation for homosexuality is that it may be the result of unhappy heterosexual experiences or the inability to attract partners of the other sex.

Is homosexuality a learned response? Does homosexuality result from unhappy heterosexual experiences? This view is commonly voiced in the effort to explain lesbianism, which people often assume is based in resentment, dislike, fear, or distrust of men rather than an attraction toward women.

Perhaps the best way to evaluate this explanation of homosexuality is to turn the argument around. Is female heterosexuality caused by dislike and fear of women? The answer is no—just as lesbianism is not caused by unhappy experiences with men. In fact, research indicates that up to 70 percent of lesbian women have had sexual experiences with men, and many report having enjoyed them. However, they prefer to be sexual with women (Klaich, 1974).

Bell and his colleagues report that lesbianism is not related either to unpleasant heterosexual experiences or to a lack of such experience (1981, p. 176). Their research found that homosexual and heterosexual people had dated about equally in high school,

Epigenetic Processes that alter gene expression without changing the DNA

a finding that contradicts the notion that homosexuality results from a lack of heterosexual opportunity. Both male and female homosexual subjects did tend, however, to feel differently about dating than did heterosexual subjects—few of them reported enjoying it. These feelings probably indicate that these subjects were less interested in heterosexual relationships. For example, although the homosexual males dated as much as the heterosexual males in the study, they tended to have fewer sexual encounters with females. The researchers concluded that "unless heterosexual encounters appeal to one's deepest sexual feeling, there is likely to be little about them that one would experience as positive reinforcement for sexual relationships with members of the opposite sex" (p. 108).

Another myth dispelled by the Bell research team is that young men and women become homosexual because older homosexuals have seduced them. In reality, not only did most subjects (both male and female) report that their first homosexual encounter had involved someone of about their own age, but homosexual subjects were less likely than heterosexual subjects to have had initial sexual encounters with a stranger or an adult.

Some people may believe that homosexuality can be "caught" from someone else—for instance, that a homosexual teacher, especially one who is well liked and respected, will become a role model for students. However, homosexual orientation appears to be established even before school age, and modeling is not a relevant factor (Marmor, 1980).

Another theory helps link homosexuality to certain patterns in family background. Sigmund Freud (1905) maintained that children's relationships with their fathers and mothers were a crucial factor. Although Freud viewed men and women as innately bisexual, he thought that individuals normally passed through a "homoerotic" phase in the course of heterosexual development. Certain people could become "fixated" at the homosexual phase if some kinds of life experiences occurred, especially if a boy had a poor relationship with his father and an overly close relationship with his mother. Although Freud's theory is frequently cited, it has received little support from research. In fact, Bell and his colleagues found that no particular phenomenon of family life could be singled out as especially consequential in the development of either heterosexual or homosexual orientations.

Biological Theories of Homosexuality

If psychosocial factors do not adequately account for homosexuality, is homosexuality determined by biology? This biological approach seems reasonable, because both sexual development and the expression of sexual behavior are determined by early hormonal influences on the developing body and brain.

One biological approach has focused on possible genetic contributions—that is, homosexuality may be determined by a "gay gene." Yet, considerable research occurring over sixty years has failed to identify genetic markers for homosexuality, even though there appears to be substantial heritability. The gay gene was first proposed in 1993, when researchers reported a correlation between a specific genetic marker and homosexuality. However, this research was never replicated, and its biological reality remains hypothetical or elusive at best. Investigators have now examined the entire human genome for evidence of a genetic determinant of homosexuality and have concluded that there is not sufficient evidence (Hyde, 2005). Researchers do believe, however, that **epigenetic** modifications to the way androgens masculinize the fetus and determine sexual preferences can and do occur (Rice et al., 2012). If epigenetics does contribute to sexual orientation, it most likely does so by altering developmental hormones, resulting in differences in brain structure that mediate sexual behavior.

Researchers speculate that prenatal hormone exposures can alter the masculine and feminine development of the fetal brain. There is a critical period during which the fetus is particularly sensitive to levels of testosterone. How could brain levels of testosterone be altered during gestation? Epigenetic alterations to androgen effects certainly can occur, as discussed above. In addition, evidence suggests that maternal stress during a critical period (perhaps between the second and the sixth months of pregnancy) results in decreased levels of fetal testosterone. The stress, which causes large amounts of adrenal hormones to enter the fetal bloodstream, inhibits the masculinization of the hypothalamus by testosterone. According to this theory, prenatal hormone imbalances during this period could contribute to homosexuality (Balthazart, 2012; Ellis & Ames, 1987; Roper, 1996; Swaab, Chung, Kruijver, Hofman, & Ishunina, 2002; Zuger, 1989). Laboratory research with animals has demonstrated that prenatal stress, which resulted in decreased levels of testosterone, also alters male sexual behavior. Prenatally stressed male rats responded to injections of testosterone with an increase in female sexual behavior (McLeod & Brown, 1988).

In conclusion, research seems to suggest that people may be biologically predisposed toward homosexuality as a consequence of epigenetics or abnormalities in testosterone exposure during prenatal development. The prenatal endocrine environment has a significant impact on sexual differentiation and behavior later in life. At this point, however, it seems most appropriate to think of sexual orientation as influenced by a variety of environmental and biological factors that are unique for each person, rather than trying to find a single cause.

Some Suggestions for Overcoming Obesity

Countless solutions have been proposed to deal with weight problems. Nevertheless, the great majority of obese people who try to reduce and maintain a lower weight ultimately fail. This discussion presents a few suggestions based on the clinical experiences and experimental findings of weight-loss specialists. Note: It is a good idea to consult a physician before embarking on a weight-loss program.

1. **Determine your calorie intake.** Many people are convinced they are overweight not because they eat too much, but rather because they have metabolic problems. Most adults of normal weight consume about 2,000 to 2,500 calories during each twenty-four-hour period, depending on their size, sex, and activity level. If you are overweight and convinced that you eat no more than your skinny friends, try keeping a record of everything you eat and drink for a period of a week or so. (There are a number of computer programs and cell phone apps that can help you track caloric intake.) Some people are shocked at the number of calories they consume without thinking about what they are doing.

2. **Reduce food intake, if necessary.** We add the disclaimer "if necessary" because for some obese people whose food consumption is in fact moderate, exercise without dieting may be more effective than eating less. However, if you are consuming more than a normal allotment of calories, it is helpful to reduce the amount you eat, particularly foods high in fat and sugar content. Consult a physician, dietician, or authoritative textbook to be sure your reduced food intake provides a healthy, balanced diet.

   Avoid crash diets that may reduce calories to only a few hundred a day. Your odds for success are much better if you cut back only moderately on daily calorie consumption. Research clearly demonstrates that a slow, steady weight loss, of perhaps only a pound or two per week, increases your chances of keeping excess pounds off once you reach your desired weight.

   Several tips may help you lower food consumption moderately. First, try stocking up on nutritious food that does not inspire lust in your taste buds. Get rid of cookies, candies, ice cream, porterhouse steaks marbled with fat, potato chips, cream cheese, soft drinks, and anything else you love to consume. It is a good idea to allow for some interesting variety in your diet so that you will not end up feeling so deprived that you lose all control and binge.

   Second, commit yourself to eating only at mealtime and always in the same place. This helps eliminate the urge to snack that often results from learned associations between certain activities and food (for example, raiding the refrigerator during TV commercials). It can also be helpful to reduce access to foods that require no preparation. It is all too easy to nibble from an open box of crackers or cookies without even thinking about what you are doing.

3. **Exercise.** When used in conjunction with reduced food intake, regular, moderate exercise is probably the best strategy for losing weight. Unfortunately, however, some people make the mistake of thinking they will drop all excess weight in a Herculean exercise program. Like crash diets, this strategy often fails due to physical burnout, injury, or boredom.

   Moderation is the key for most people. If you can burn off 200 to 300 calories each time you exercise, you will obtain noticeable results in a reasonable amount of time (assuming, of course, that your food intake is held to a moderate level). Most specialists recommend exercise sessions that last a minimum of twenty to thirty minutes and occur at least three times a week. The activities you choose should be strenuous enough to raise your heart rate appreciably and to allow you to burn 200 to 300 calories per session. All kinds of exercise possibilities exist. Choosing one that is relatively enjoyable, or at least not unpleasant, will pay dividends in greater perseverance. Studies indicate that thirty minutes of brisk walking burns off about 150 calories; bicycling on normal terrain burns off 200 calories; swimming, 275 calories; and jogging, 370. For many people, exercise actually seems to decrease the appetite.

   Recent research demonstrates that people who exercise either very intensively or for very long periods may experience an increase in their metabolic rate that can last for two or three days after cessation of exercise. In addition, the more muscle tissue a person has in relation to fat, the greater his or her metabolic rate. Muscle tissue consumes more calorie energy than fat. Such findings suggest that an exercise regimen that combines muscle building with extended periods of cardiovascular exercise (such as jogging, bicycling, or swimming for a couple of hours several times a week) may be the optimal strategy for weight control. However, such a rigorous exercise program poses the risk of burnout or perhaps injury for individuals who do not build slowly into a program in accordance with the rate of improvement in their physical fitness.

4. **Keep records and reward yourself.** Research indicates that people who keep records of how much they eat, when they eat, and what exercises they do before and during eating are more likely to benefit from a weight-loss program than those who do not record this information. These records may reveal certain patterns of which you were unaware, such as a tendency to eat more in the company of a certain friend or raiding the refrigerator when you are feeling depressed.

It may be helpful to include others in your efforts to lose weight. Sometimes the first 5 or 10 pounds are the toughest because nobody seems to notice. However, having someone around to praise you for the pound or two you have lost can be very reinforcing.

Setting up little rewards along the way can also be helpful. Perhaps you can treat yourself to a professional massage after you drop the first 5 pounds. Maybe after 10 or 15 pounds, you can take yourself to a beach resort where you can show off your gorgeous new body.

CHAPTER REVIEW

The Nature of Motivation

1. Motivation can be defined as any condition that energizes and directs behavior.
2. Motivation not only energizes or activates us to behave in a certain way; it also defines the direction of the resulting behavior. Motivation also has a direct impact on how vigorous or intense our behaviors are.

Motivational Explanations of Behavior

3. One of the earliest attempts to explain motivation was based on the notion of instincts, innate patterns of behavior that occur in every normally functioning member of a species under certain set conditions.
4. Because learning so profoundly influences our behaviors, it is essentially impossible to find one example of human behavior that fits the literal definition of instincts.
5. According to the drive-reduction theory, motivation originates with a need or drive, experienced as an unpleasant aversive condition, which motivates us to act in a way that will reduce the aversive condition. This theory, while limited in scope, does explain some aspects of motivation.
6. According to the cognitive perspective, our beliefs and expectations play an important role in motivating our actions.
7. One way to help instill a desire to achieve is to encourage children to set reasonable goals and to provide ample reinforcers for their successes.
8. It is useful to classify human motives under four categories: biologically based motives rooted primarily in body tissue needs; sensation-seeking motives expressed as a need for certain levels of stimulation; complex psychosocial motives that seem to demonstrate little or no relationship to biological needs; and multifactorial motives that are based on a combination of biological, psychological, and cultural factors.
9. According to the hypothalamic control theory, two regions within the hypothalamus may possibly serve as control centers for eating. One region, the ventromedial hypothalamus, seems to act as a satiety center that signals when an organism has had enough to eat. In contrast, the lateral hypothalamus seems to act as an "on switch" that instigates eating. New research suggests that although these areas of the hypothalamus are important, they do not act as mere on-off switches for eating. Rather, other hypothalamic structures, including the arcuate nucleus and the neurotransmitter neuropeptide Y, are also critical.
10. Blood glucose levels are monitored by cells within the hypothalamus which, in turn, stimulate either feeding or satiety mechanisms.

CHAPTER REVIEW

Eating Disorders: Obesity, Anorexia, and Bulimia

11. Obesity places a person at risk for developing one or more serious health problems, such as high blood pressure, heart disease, and depression.
12. Genetic factors, conditions of early development, emotional stress, and metabolic factors all have been suggested as possible causes of obesity.
13. Suggested causes for anorexia nervosa and bulimia include a disturbed body image, depression, anxiety, and possibly physical abnormalities involving neurotransmitters, the hypothalamus and/or the endocrine system.

Sensation-Seeking Motivation

14. The need to manipulate and explore the environment and the need for sensory stimulation both fall under the category of sensation-seeking motives.
15. Psychologists have theorized that people have an optimum level of arousal, which is the level where their performance will be most efficient. According to the Yerkes-Dodson law, the optimum level of arousal for peak performance varies, depending on the difficulty of the task.
16. In humans, sexual interest and expression are controlled less by hormones and more by the cerebral cortex, reflecting a complex combination of biological, psychological, and cultural factors.
17. While it is difficult to distinguish the effects of sex hormones and learning experiences on sexual arousal, research does indicate that androgens appear to facilitate sexual interest in both males and females.
18. Psychological and cultural conditions probably play a greater role than hormones in human sexual motivation. This tendency is reflected in the role of reinforcement and psychosocial conditioning, which maintain and constrain sexual expression, respectively.
19. Ideas about what is sexually arousing vary greatly across the cultures of the world. Sexual conduct is regulated in some way in all societies, but the rules vary from one society to the next.
20. A high rate of sexual activity and extensive sexual instruction of youths is the norm on the Polynesian island of Mangaia.
21. On the Irish island of Inis Beag, sexual expression is discouraged from infancy through old age. Sexual misinformation is common, and female orgasm is practically unknown.
22. The Dani people of New Guinea demonstrate little interest in sexual activity and abstain from sex for years at a time.

CHAPTER REVIEW

Sexual Motivation and Behavior

23. There are a number of psychosocial and biological theories that attempt to explain the development of homosexuality. Some of the psychosocial theories relate to parenting patterns, life experiences, or the psychological attributes of the person.
24. Theories of biological causation of homosexuality look to genetic and prenatal influences on hormone levels and sexual differentiation of the brain.
25. Evidence suggests that abnormalities in prenatal exposure to testosterone affect both sexual differentiation of the brain and sexual behavior later in life.

TERMS AND CONCEPTS

Androgens, pg. 328
Anorexia Nervosa, pg. 325
Arcuate Nucleus, pg. 320
Arousal, pg. 326
Biologically Based Motives, pg. 318
Bulimia, pg. 325
Cholecystokinin (CCK) , pg. 321
Cognitive Dissonance Theory, pg. 316
Cognitive Expectancy, pg. 316
Cultural Mores, pg. 330
Drive, pg. 318
Epigenetic, pg. 334
Estrogens, pg. 329
Glucostatic Hypothesis, pg. 321
Homosexuality, pg. 332
Incentive, pg. 314
Instincts, pg. 313
Lateral Hypothalamus (LH), pg. 320
Leptin, pg. 321
Motivation, pg. 312
Need for Achievement (nAch), pg. 315
Neuropeptide Y (NPY), pg. 320
Obesity, pg. 322
Optimum Level of Arousal, pg. 326
Sensation-Seeking Motive, pg. 325
Sexual Orientation, pg. 332
Ventromedial Hypothalamus (VMH), pg. 320
Yerkes-Dodson Law, pg. 326

POP QUIZ

True or False

___ 1. The concept of motivation incorporates both physiological and cognitive factors that influence behavior.

___ 2. The idea that your likelihood of being motivated to take an advanced course in math is determined in part by your success with difficult math courses in the past is known as cognitive advantage.

___ 3. Obese individuals have the same number of fat cells as normal-weight individuals, but these obese individuals' fat cells are 50–100 percent larger.

___ 4. Sensation-seeking motivations are based on our strong inclination to explore and manipulate the environment as soon as we are able.

___ 5. There is evidence to link androgens with sexual activity and motivation in both males and females.

Multiple Choice

6. Which of the following is ***not*** an effect motivation has on our actions?
   a. It directs or defines the direction of the resulting behavior.
   b. It has an impact on how vigorous or intense a behavior is.
   c. It controls instinctive behaviors.
   d. It energizes or activates one to behave in a certain way.
7. Which of the following behaviors illustrates the glucostatic theory of hunger?
   a. Some people prefer sweet foods over other tastes.
   b. People can easily detect changes on their blood glucose levels.
   c. People are only hungry when blood glucose levels drop.
   d. Drugs that deplete glucose cause immediate eating in animals.
8. Which of the following statements is ***not*** true about need for achievement (nAch)?
   a. People with a high level tend to be optimistic about chances of success.
   b. It can be measured using TAT.
   c. Studies have found that people with high levels of nAch tend to have stronger egos.
   d. Levels of nAch vary from individual to individual.
9. There is evidence that the stomach contains which of the following?
   a. Caloric receptors
   b. Glucoreceptors
   c. Liporeceptors
   d. Pressure detectors

POP QUIZ

10. A potent hormone that stimulates hunger and eating is which of the following?
    a. Leptin
    b. Neuropeptide Y
    c. Cholecystokinin
    d. Pancreatic hormone
11. Which one of the following does ***not*** stimulate hunger and eating behavior?
    a. Increased levels of the hormone neuropeptide Y
    b. Reduced blood sugar levels
    c. Increased levels of glycerol in the bloodstream
    d. Stimulation of the lateral hypothalamus
12. Following dramatic weight loss as a result of a very low calorie diet (a starvation diet), why do people frequently regain much of the "lost" weight?
    a. They "fall off the wagon" and engage in binge eating.
    b. Their bodies need to restock stored fat.
    c. Their resting metabolic rate had increased during the diet, and following the diet it is reduced.
    d. Their resting metabolic rate was reduced during the diet and stays at the lower level following the diet.
13. Which of the following statements is true?
    a. Androgen-blocking drugs such as Depo-Provera may be effective in reducing sexual interest and activity in human males.
    b. Following castration (removal of the testes), human males always report a dramatic decrease in sexual desire and behavior.
    c. Estrogens play a significant role in the sexual interest and activity of human females.
    d. There is no systematic relationship between blood androgen levels and strength of sexual motivation in young men.
14. Which society most actively encourages (encouraged) sexual activity?
    a. Colonial American
    b. Mangaia (in the Polynesian Islands)
    c. Dani (of New Guinea)
    d. Inis Beag (on an Irish island)
15. According to the text's definition of homosexuality, which of the following is true?
    a. Only men can be homosexual; women with a "homosexual orientation" are lesbians.
    b. Homosexuals have a gender identity disorder.
    c. A homosexual cannot engage in heterosexual activities.
    d. It is not necessary to overtly express homosexual behavior to be homosexual.

Answer Key: 1.T 2.F 3.T 4.F 5.T 6.c 7.d 8.c 9.d 10.b 11.c 12.d 13.a 14.b 15.d

(Getty/BraunS)

Emotion *and* Stress

As we saw in Chapter 8, the concepts of motivation and emotion are closely connected. In fact, most introductory texts include them in the same chapter. As we will see, they do this because, historically, emotions were seen as a source of motivation and as an explanation for human behavior. We are all familiar with accounting for our behavior as a result of an emotional state. For instance, we slammed the door because we were angry, we struck someone out of jealousy, or we ran because of fear. Our casual everyday explanations for the actions of ourselves and others are often in terms of an emotional state. As this chapter explains, this *commonsense* view has been challenged since the beginnings of psychology. Before we can examine the role emotions play in our behavior, we need to carefully define them.

In this chapter, we explore emotions in an effort to find out more about what they are, how they come about, what brain structures enable them, and how they influence our lives. We also explore a closely related topic—stress, including the effect of stress on our lives and the ways in which we can moderate some of the negative effects of stress.

9.1 The Components of Emotion

Although the terms **emotions** and *feelings* are often used interchangeably, feelings are only one component of an emotional response. In fact, lower animals clearly have emotional states, but little or no feeling at all. Perhaps you have seen the color changes of the panther chameleon as it expresses changes in emotion. Humans clearly have both, emotional responses and feelings, which are our sensory experience of the emotional state. In other words, emotions are specific changes in physiological responses, and our feelings are our sensory experiences of these changes. For example, when you experience fear, your body responds with an increase in epinephrine, which causes accelerated heart rate and respiration. We sense these changes and actually feel the emotion. Human emotions, therefore, include four integral components: physiological arousal, cognitive processes, behavioral responses, and affect or subjective feelings.

(Shutterstock)

The panther chameleon changes color as its emotional state changes.

9.1a Physiological Arousal

The first component of an emotion is *physiological arousal.* When someone describes their anger by saying, "The juices were flowing," this account is close to the mark. The "juices," in the form of epinephrine and other hormones associated with the arousal of anger, probably were flowing. As a result of this increased endocrine activity, we might guess that, for a few moments at least, heart rate increased dramatically, blood pressure probably increased significantly, and breathing may have become rapid and uneven.

Indeed, emotions are associated with mild to extreme changes in the physiological processes occurring within our bodies. In addition to the changes we just listed, these processes may include metabolic changes, altered muscle tension, changes in activity

Emotions Changes in physiological and behavioral states caused by a stimulus or stimulus context (Many of our emotions are experienced as feelings or moods.)

of the salivary and sweat glands, modified digestive processes, and changes in the levels of certain neurotransmitters in the brain. (Recall from Chapter 3 that the autonomic nervous system is involved in most of the physiological changes associated with emotional arousal.) In other species, these physiological processes can lead to changes in coloration, facial expression, piloerection, and other signals of emotion.

9.1b Cognitive Processes

A second component of emotion is cognitive process. Although psychologists differ in the extent to which they emphasize the role of cognition in emotional arousal and expression, there is a general consensus that perception, learning, and memory are all very much involved in experiencing emotions. Listening to music, or even just thinking about a favorite song, often elicits conditioned or learned emotions. In addition, we can easily generate physiological arousal associated with many different emotions by merely thinking about them. Professional actors are particularly good at this. For humans at least, cognitive processes are clearly involved in most emotional responses.

9.1c Behavioral Responses

Emotions also affect behavioral responses. They often motivate us to act out or express our feelings. These expressions may range from freezing, crying, or screaming in fear to smiling or laughing. Tone of voice, posture, and other kinds of body language are all common signals of emotion. In addition to expressing and communicating our emotion to others, behavioral reactions of emotions may also serve to either promote or reduce the emotion. For example, avoiding a situation that produces fear or going out of your way to meet a special person are examples of behavior maintained by a change in emotion (recall the two-factor theory in Chapter 6).

9.1d Feelings

All human emotions also include an affective component. Changes in physiology as well as behavior are detected by our senses and come to represent the feeling of an emotion. Feelings may be described as a general positive or negative state such as joy, anger, fear, or disgust, but many feelings of emotion don't easily fit these descriptions, as we all know well. When psychologists attempt to ascertain a person's emotional state, they typically ask the individual to describe the emotions he or she is experiencing. Most people respond by describing their feelings, as, "I am depressed," "I am extremely happy," or "I feel hurt."

Does one actually feel hurt or in pain during an emotion? We are all familiar with the pain associated with the loss of a significant other or the breaking up of a serious relationship, and many songs have been written about that pain. However, do we actually feel emotional pain in a way that is similar to physical bodily pain? According to modern brain imaging research, we do. The pain and suffering you experience with social loss is represented in the same brain regions as bodily

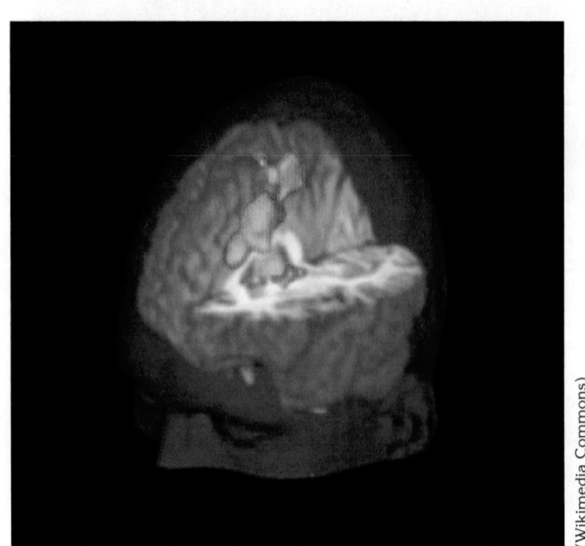

(Wikimedia Commons)

The feeling associated with physical pain is represented in the same brain structures as the feeling of emotional pain. The yellow region shown here is the cingulate cortex.

pain (Eisenberger, Lieberman, & Williams, 2003). We will discuss this in more detail in the section on the neurobiology of emotion. For most individuals, these subjective feelings come to constitute emotion even though they are only one aspect of them.

9.2 The Range of Human Emotion

Adoration, amazement, amusement, anger, anxiety, contempt, disgust, distress, ecstasy, embarrassment, envy, fear, guilt, humiliation, interest, jealousy, joy, loathing, rage, reverence, sadness, shame, sorrow, surprise, terror—these are just a few of the emotions we recognize. Some of these emotions overlap. Ecstasy and joy, for instance, clearly share certain elements. Thus, differences between emotions are often more a matter of degree than of kind. Furthermore, many emotional experiences may represent a blending of more basic emotions.

9.2a Plutchik's Emotional Wheel

According to Robert Plutchik (1980, 2001), there are eight primary or basic human emotions, which consist of four pairs of opposites: acceptance and disgust, fear and anger, surprise and anticipation, and sadness and joy. Plutchik adopted the unique approach of arranging these eight primary emotions on an emotion wheel (see Figure 9-1). He maintained that all human emotions are variations or derivations of these eight. The closer those emotions are to one another on the wheel, the more they have in common. For example, anticipation and joy both share an element of expectation, whereas fear and surprise share the quality of the unknown. According to Plutchik, adjacent emotions blend to form the more complex feelings listed on the outer rim of the emotion wheel. Many of us would probably agree that love involves at least some elements of joy and acceptance, and that contempt certainly involves components of both anger and disgust.

(iStock)

According to Robert Plutchik, there are eight primary or basic human emotions, and all human emotions are variations or derivations of these eight.

9.3 Theories of Emotion

We have learned that emotional expression is a complex process involving cognitions, subjective feelings, physiological arousal, and behavioral reactions. How do these processes interact to produce an emotional response? What is the usual sequence of events? Is it necessary to think before we feel, or do we feel an emotion and then later interpret it as fear or happiness? Psychologists have proposed contradictory answers to these questions, in a controversy that sometimes resembles the well-known debate about whether the chicken or the egg came first. We examine the evidence as we review several historical perspectives and several contemporary theories of emotion.

9.3a The James-Lange Theory

Imagine that after having trouble sleeping, you decide to take a midnight walk. It is dark and still; no one else is in sight. Suddenly, you hear a rustling in the bushes behind you, followed by rapidly approaching footsteps. Your response will probably be one of terror. You are likely to run for your life.

Figure 9-1 Plutchik's Emotional Wheel

According to Robert Plutchik, there are eight primary human emotions consisting of four opposite pairs. Adjacent emotions (such as joy and acceptance) blend to form more complex emotions (like love).

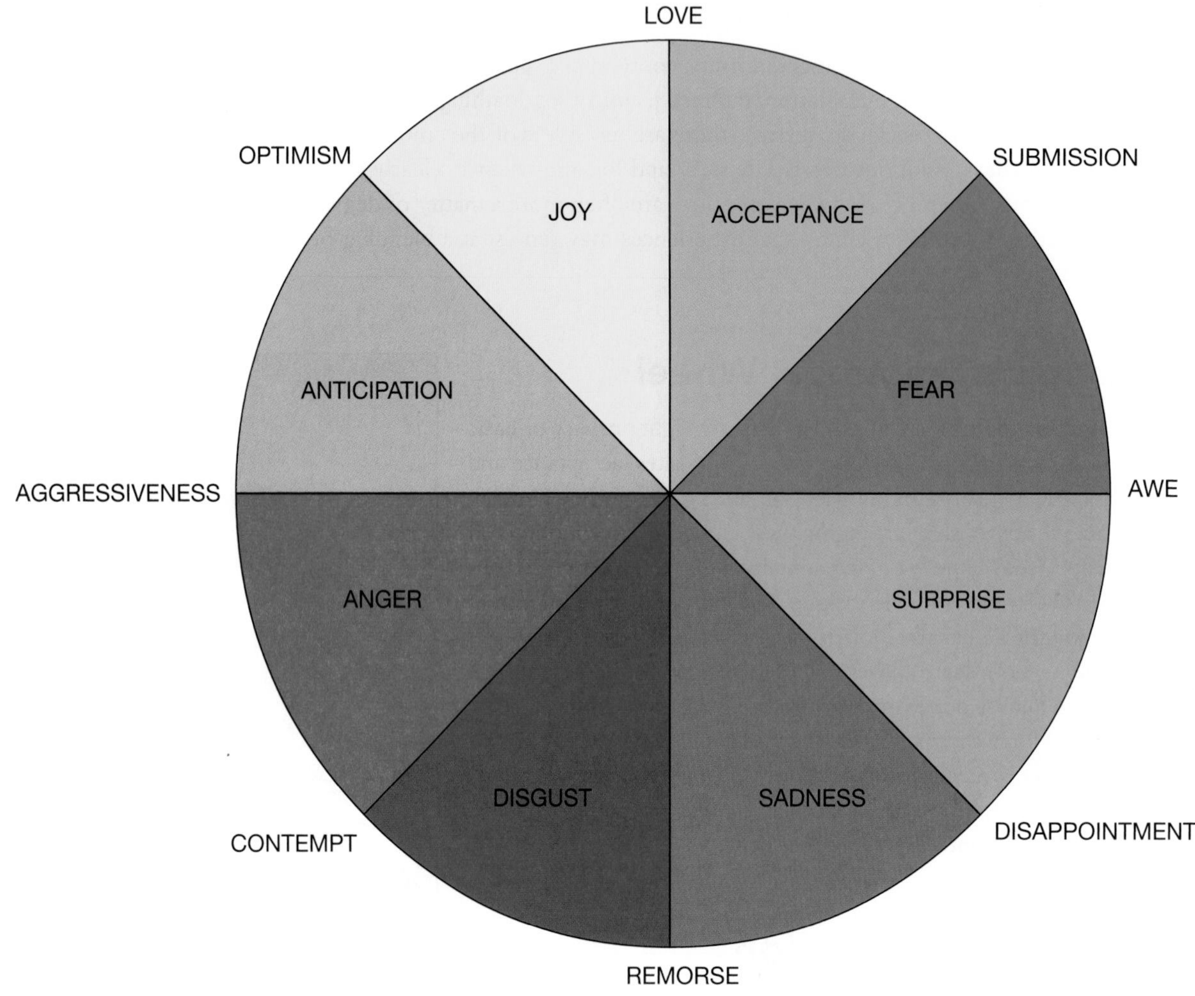

What would activate your feeling of fear in this situation? Is it triggered by the sounds you hear, which in turn induce you to run? Or is it more likely that your awareness of danger causes your heart to beat faster and your legs to carry you away, and that these physical responses trigger your emotional state, and you then feel fear? Decide which of these interpretations seems correct, and why, before reading on.

When such questions are put to students, the vast majority answer that hearing noises in the dark causes fear, which in turn triggers a flood of physical reactions. This common-sense interpretation of the activation of emotion seems quite logical (see Figure 9-2). We perceive and interpret a particular stimulus, in this case threatening noises; these cognitive processes give rise to an emotion (fear), which triggers certain physiological responses and body movements. Along these lines, we would also conclude that we cry

Figure 9-2 Theories of Emotions

The Commonsense View of Emotion. We perceive and interpret a particular stimulus, and these cognitive processes give rise to an emotion that triggers certain physiological reactions and body movements. "I see a bear, feel fear, experience a flood of physiological reactions, and run because I am afraid."

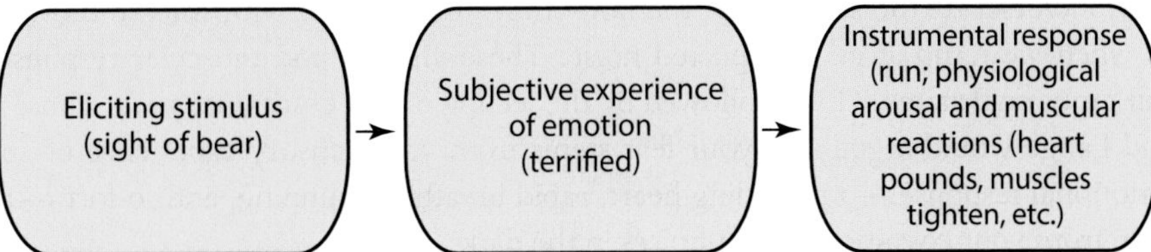

The James-Lange Theory. Environmental stimuli trigger physiological responses and bodily movements, and emotion occurs when the individual interprets his or her visceral and muscular responses. "I must be afraid because my heart is pounding and I am running like crazy."

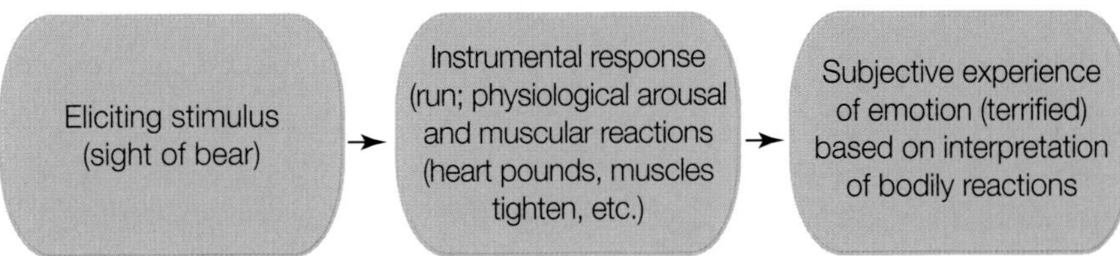

The Cannon-Bard Theory. Emotion is a cognitive event that is enhanced by bodily reactions. Bodily reactions do not cause emotion but rather occur simultaneously with the experience of emotion. "I am afraid because I know bears are dangerous."

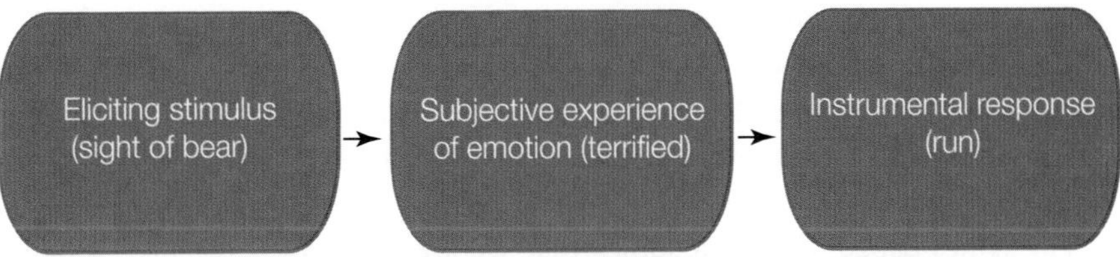

The Schachter-Singer Theory. Emotions depend upon a kind of double cognitive interpretation: We appraise the emotion-causing event while also evaluating what is happening with our bodies. "I am afraid because I know bears are dangerous and because my heart is pounding."

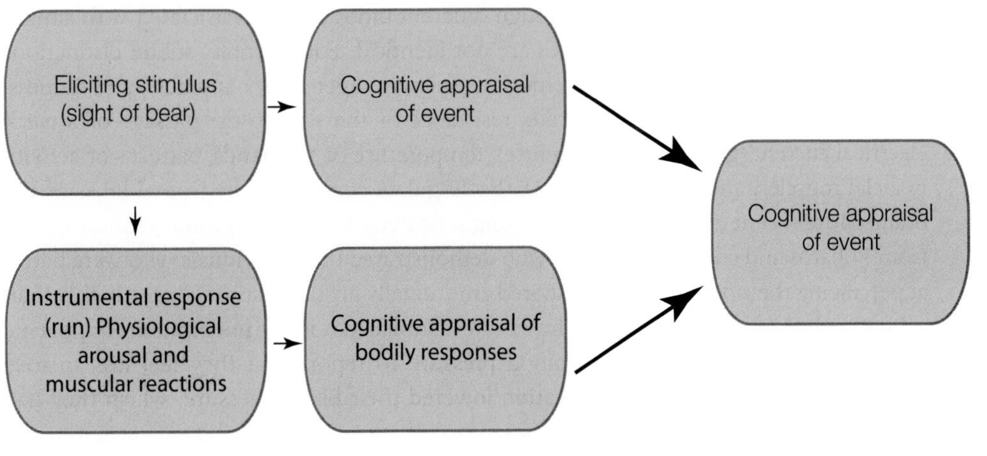

James-Lange Theory
Theory that explains emotional states (such as fear) resulting from an organism's awareness of bodily responses to a situation, rather than from cognitions about that situation

because we feel sad, rather than becoming sad because we cry, and that we laugh because we are happy, rather than being happy because we laugh.

However, the American psychologist William James (1884) and the Danish physiologist Carl Lange (Lange & James, 1922)—writing independently of each other—both questioned this commonsense view. Their interpretation, referred to as the **James-Lange theory**, suggests that environmental stimuli trigger physiological responses from viscera (the internal organs such as the heart and lungs). For instance, heart rate and respiration both increase. At the same time, the body may also respond with muscle movements, as when we jump at an unexpected noise. These visceral and muscular responses are our emotional states. This is followed by the feeling of the emotional state. Thus, James and Lange would argue that your fear stems from your sensory experience of specific emotional responses—a pounding heart, rapid breathing, running, and so forth—rather than from your cognitions about noises in the dark.

Although it might seem to contradict common sense, the James-Lange theory makes sense at some level. We have all encountered unexpected situations in which we seemed to respond automatically before we had a chance to experience emotion. For example, if a car suddenly veered onto the sidewalk and threatened to run you down, you would no doubt leap out of the way. You might not label your heightened arousal and reactive state as one of "fear" until a moment later, when the danger had passed, and you suddenly became aware that your knees were shaking and your heart was pounding. In such situations, the emotions seem to follow the bodily changes and behavioral reactions. James and Lange argued that we often encounter situations in which behavioral and physiological reactions occur too quickly to be triggered by emotions.

Some intriguing evidence collected from human subjects with spinal cord injuries provides support for the James-Lange theory. If feedback from the internal organs through the autonomic nervous system is important, we might expect that individuals with damage high on the spinal cord (quadriplegics) would experience emotional feelings of lower intensity than those with low injury (paraplegics), because a high injury would cut off feedback from a greater portion of the body. This conclusion is exactly what research has revealed. The higher the injury to the spinal cord, and consequently the less sensory feedback received, the less intense are the emotional feelings reported by an individual.

The James-Lange Theory assumes that we are able to discriminate subtle differences in physiological responses to distinguish among the wide variety of emotions we experience. While other theorists have challenged this assumption, psychologists today hesitate to reject the notion that people are able to discriminate between subtle differences in visceral and muscular patterns associated with specific emotions. Recent research has demonstrated that although different emotions are associated with similar physiological changes, these changes are not identical. For example, subtle distinctions have been demonstrated between emotions such as anger, fear, happiness, and sadness. These include variations in heart rate, resistance of the skin to the passage of a weak electrical current (galvanic skin response), temperature of the hands, patterns of activity in facial muscles, and neural activity in the cingulate cortex and the frontal lobes of the brain. More recent evidence demonstrating sensitivity to physiological responses comes from Pollatos and colleagues (2005), who demonstrated that individuals who were better at perceiving their own heart rates scored emotionally arousing stimuli more highly than subjects who were less sensitive to heart rates. Similarly, it is not uncommon for patients starting drug treatment for high blood pressure to report that they feel less anxious and stressed. Blood pressure medication lowered their blood pressure, which they had interpreted as stress and anxiety.

Certainly, these more recent findings do not prove the James-Lange theory, but it is possible that we are sensitive to a wide variety of these responses and that these changes serve as the basis for feelings of emotion (Damasio, 2005).

Cannon-Bard Theory
Theory that emotions occur simultaneously with physiological changes, rather than deriving from body changes, as the James-Lange theory suggests

Schachter-Singer Theory
Theory that a given body state can be linked to a variety of emotions depending on the context in which the body state occurs

9.3b The Cannon-Bard Theory

Walter Cannon not only criticized the James-Lange theory, he also proposed an alternate theory of emotion. Cannon argued that autonomic and muscular changes are not the cause of emotion. Instead, emotional experiences and physical changes occur simultaneously. This viewpoint, as modified by Philip Bard (1934), is known as the **Cannon-Bard theory**.

Cannon and Bard theorized that the thalamus (see Chapter 3) plays a key role in our emotional responses. It not only channels sensory input to the cerebral cortex, where it is interpreted but, at the same time, it also sends activation messages through the peripheral nervous system to the viscera and skeletal muscles. These activation messages trigger the physiological and behavioral responses that typically accompany emotions. Cannon and Bard would explain your emotional response to being approached in the dark in the following manner: The sensory input of the sounds you heard in the dark was relayed simultaneously to your cerebral cortex and your internal organs and muscles. This activity allowed you to perceive fear at the same time that your internal organs and muscles were reacting to the stimulus. Cannon and Bard would contend that when you feel fear, the emotion occurs at the same time as your pounding heart, rapid breathing, and flight from the source of the noise. James and Lange would suggest that your fear was caused by these physical changes. We will see that, while both theories are partially correct, both are incomplete.

More recent research has revealed that the hypothalamus, amygdala, and certain other structures in the limbic system (see Chapter 3) are the brain centers most directly involved in integrating emotional responses—not the thalamus. However, the Cannon-Bard theory should be credited with pointing out the important role of central brain processes in our emotional responses. The James-Lange theory, on the other hand, correctly identified the important role of peripheral, autonomic processes in emotion; and it proposed the distinction between feelings and emotions.

Both the James-Lange and Cannon-Bard theories correctly stress the importance of physiological processes in emotion. Neither theory, however, proposes a significant role for cognition. Another theory, known as the Schachter-Singer theory, presents an interesting assessment of the role of appraisal or judgment (cognitions) in our ability to correctly identify a variety of emotions from very few distinct physiological states.

9.3c The Schachter-Singer Theory

In the early 1960s, Stanley Schachter and Jerome Singer (1962) developed the **Schachter-Singer theory** of emotions, which combined elements from both the James-Lange and the Cannon-Bard theories. Schachter and Singer believed that emotion follows behavioral and physiological reactions and that, in addition, cognitive processes were central to emotional experience.

Schachter and Singer proposed that we appraise the emotion-causing event while evaluating what is happening with our bodies. The key process in emotional arousal is how we interpret physiological feedback in light of our present situation.

For example, suppose you have just run several blocks across campus to avoid being late to a class. You probably note that you are panting and sweating and that your heart is pounding, but you are unlikely to experience an emotional response to these heightened physical reactions. If you experience these same physical responses under different circumstances, however—for example, while running across a farmer's field to escape an enraged bull—you would probably interpret your arousal as fear.

The James-Lange view proposed that a given state of bodily reaction and arousal produces a specific emotion. Schachter and Singer suggested that a given physiological state could produce a variety of emotions, depending on the context within which it occurs. From this point of view, we might interpret highly similar patterns of arousal as reflecting distinctly different emotions in different contexts.

Schachter and Singer (1962) designed an ingenious experiment to test this theory. Male college student volunteers were told they would be participating in an experiment dealing with vision. All were given an injection of a substance the experimenters called Suproxin, which was described as a vitamin compound that would temporarily affect vision. In reality, some subjects were injected with the hormone epinephrine, which is known to increase heart and respiration rates and blood pressure, produce muscle tremors, and generally cause a jittery feeling. Other subjects, the control group, were merely injected with a placebo that produced no physical effects. The experimenters manipulated their subjects' cognitions about the cause of their arousal by providing accurate or inaccurate information about the connection between their symptoms and the earlier injection. Some of these subjects (the *informed group*) were told that some people react to Suproxin with the side effects just described. A second group of subjects (the *uninformed group*) received no information about side effects, and a third group (the *misinformed group*) received false information, for example that the drug might cause itching or facial numbness.

Next, all subjects experienced certain staged social cues during a twenty-minute "waiting period" before the vision test (which never actually took place). Subjects were placed, one at a time, in the waiting room with another person who was introduced as a fellow subject, but who was actually a confederate of the experimenters. Half of the waiting subjects were exposed to a *euphoria condition* in which the accomplice behaved in a happy manner, engaging in such playful activity as shooting baskets by throwing paper wads into a trashcan. These subjects were repeatedly asked to join in the good fun. In contrast, the other half of the subjects were assigned to an *anger condition*. They and the accomplice were asked to fill out a questionnaire, to which the accomplice reacted by grumbling loudly, tearing up the questionnaire, and eventually storming out of the room in a state of high anger. During these staged waiting periods, the subjects' behavior was observed through a one-way mirror; each subject was also questioned about his emotional state.

Assuming that Schachter and Singer's view of emotional arousal is correct, what pattern of results would you predict in this experiment? Were the subjects' assessments of their physiological state influenced by the confederates' antics? Were there differences between the informed, uninformed, and misinformed groups? Before reading on, take some time and attempt to predict the probable outcome of this experiment.

Schachter and Singer predicted that subjects in the informed group, who knew that the injected drug was the cause of their physical arousal, would not experience any strong emotion. It was assumed that they would observe their trembling hands and pounding heart and conclude that the drug was really doing its stuff. In contrast, subjects in the uninformed and misinformed groups would be aware of their arousal but have no obvious explanation for it. Therefore, it was assumed that they would cognitively appraise their environments for a logical explanation and a suitable label for the arousal they were experiencing (see Table 9-1).

The researchers' hypothesis is essentially what occurred. The subjects who had been uninformed or misinformed tended to use the confederate's behavior as a relevant cue for identifying and labeling their own unexplained arousal as either anger or euphoria.

Table 9-1 Result from the Schachter-Singer Experiment

Informed Group	Misinformed Group
Hmm—my hands are shaking, my heart is pounding, and I feel jittery all over. It must be the effects of the drug.	Euphoria condition: Boy, I feel great—on top of the world, just like that other guy over there.
	Anger condition: I don't blame the other guy for being mad. I'm ticked, too.

In contrast, subjects in the informed group or the control group, who were either not aroused or who had an appropriate explanation for their arousal, tended not to share the confederate's emotional state.

The Schachter-Singer theory has directed the attention of psychologists to the important role of cognitive interpretation in emotional experience. However, Schachter and Singer's theory and supporting research are not without their critics. Several researchers have criticized the design of the classic 1962 experiment, and some attempts to replicate its findings have produced somewhat inconsistent results (Leventhal & Tomarken, 1986; Marshall & Zimbardo, 1979). Furthermore, our own everyday experiences suggest that many emotions, particularly those that are triggered spontaneously and instantly by sudden stimuli, do not appear to result from interpreting and labeling unexplained arousal. For example, if you heard screeching tires as you were walking across a street, you would probably experience fear long before you had cognitively assessed why your heart was in your throat. In conclusion, the Schachter-Singer theory has lost favor among researchers investigating emotion over the last few decades. Modern neuroimaging studies, on the other hand, seem to provide more and more support for the James-Lange theory of emotion.

9.3d The Function of Emotional Expression

In the late nineteenth century, Charles Darwin (1872/1955) was one of the first to write extensively on the function of emotional expression. According to Darwin, each emotional "state of mind" was associated with a stereotyped set of reactions that were common within each species. In addition, emotional states that were essentially opposite were associated with an opposite set of reactions. For instance, in greeting its master, a dog displays a submissive posture like that shown in the top illustration in Figure 9-3a. This set of reactions is opposite from those displayed in the aggressive posture shown in the second image in Figure 9-3a.

Can you think of reasons why opposite emotional states are displayed with essentially opposite postures? What selective advantage might this have? Darwin believed that the behavioral expression of emotions allowed animals to communicate different emotional states and the advantage of opposite postures for opposite emotional states was that this minimized the possibility of emotional states being confused. Because there are few, if any, postural similarities between aggressive and submissive postures, they are unlikely to be treated similarly.

Darwin also believed that many human emotional expressions, particularly patterns of facial display, result from inherited traits that are universal in the human species. Enlisting the aid of missionaries and other people from all over the world, he conducted

Figure 9-3 Emotional Expressions in Animals

a. Emotional expression in dogs. Note that opposite postures represent opposing emotions.

b. Emotional expression in chimpanzees. These illustrations show the facial expressions of chimpanzees:

(a) glaring anger
(b) barking anger
(c) fear
(d) submission
(e) fear-affection
(f) affection
(g) frustration
(h) sadness
(i) crying
(j) excitement
(k) playfulness

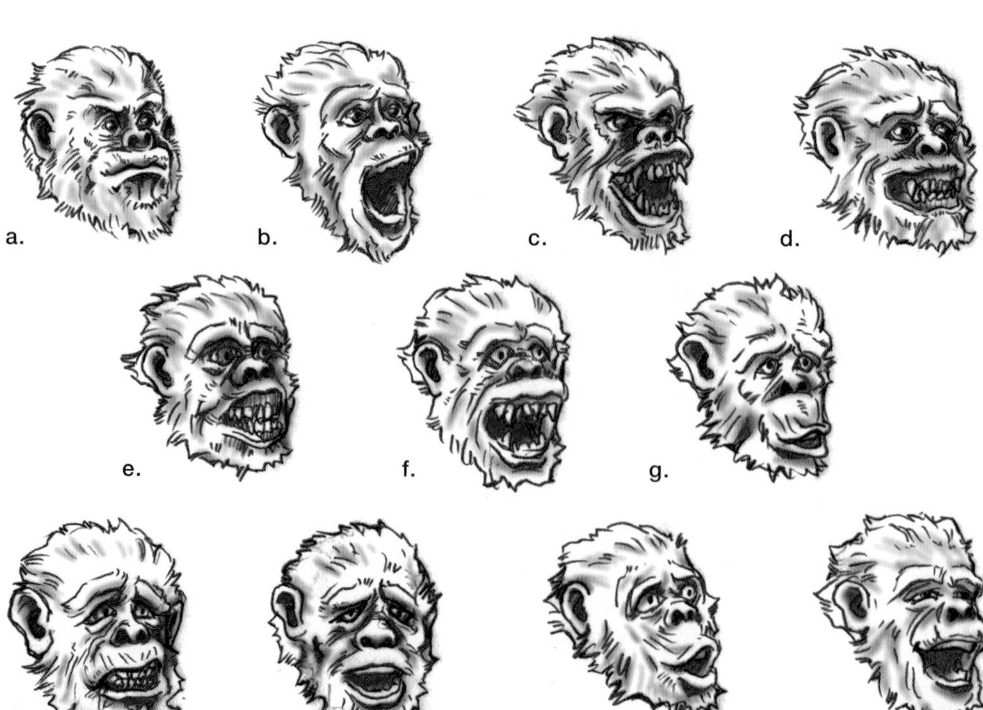

the first recorded study of facial expression of emotions. Darwin asked his recruits to observe and record the facial expressions of the local population in a variety of emotional contexts. Comparing their observations, he found a remarkable consistency in the facial expressions associated with such emotions as anger, fear, disgust, and sadness. Darwin interpreted this as evidence of the inheritance of emotional expression.

Facial Feedback Theory
Theory proposing that feedback from facial muscles intensifies the feeling of an emotion

9.3e Facial Feedback and Emotions

Darwin's findings were borne out a century later in studies by Paul Ekman and his associates (Ekman, 1982; Ekman & Friesen, 1984). These researchers demonstrated that people in various parts of the world not only show emotion with similar facial expressions, they also interpret these expressions in the same way. Ekman and his colleagues took photographs of American faces depicting happiness, anger, sadness, surprise, disgust, and fear. (Figure 9-4 shows examples of these six emotions.) They then asked people from several different cultures (including the United States, Japan, Brazil, Chile, Argentina, and the Fore and Dani tribes in remote regions of New Guinea) to identify the emotions shown in the photographs. People from all of these cultures were able to identify the emotion from the facial expression with better than 80 percent accuracy. Furthermore, American college students who viewed videotapes of emotions expressed facially by members of the Fore society were also able to identify these basic emotions, although they sometimes confused fear and surprise.

A number of researchers have argued that facial muscles respond very rapidly and with sufficient differentiation to account for a wide range of emotional experience; some have theorized that feedback from our own facial expressions determines our emotional experiences. This is now known as the **facial feedback theory** of emotion.

Figure 9-4 Facial Expressions Used by Paul Ekman

The faces, from left to right, were intended to represent happiness, anger, sadness, surprise, disgust, and fear.

The notion of universal facial expressions was supported by the cross-cultural research just discussed, and further support was provided by an intriguing two-part experiment conducted by Paul Ekman and his associates (1983). Here, professional actors were employed as subjects. In the first part of the experiment, each subject was coached, with the aid of a mirror, to assume a specific facial expression corresponding to each of the six emotions in Figure 9-4. They were told exactly which muscles to contract, but they were not asked to feel or express a particular emotion. As a control measure, some actors were coached to move muscles not involved in a particular emotional expression. As the subjects molded their facial expressions, several physiological responses were measured, including heart rate, galvanic skin response, temperature of the hands, and muscle tension in the arms. In the second phase of this experiment, subjects were simply asked to think of emotional experiences in their lives that produced each of the six emotions. For example, subjects might recall a recent encounter that made them angry.

Two major findings emerged from this study. First, the researchers noted that each of the four negative emotions of anger, fear, disgust, and sadness, whether induced by facial modeling or thinking of an emotional experience, was accompanied by a distinct physiological "fingerprint," or pattern, of physical responses. For example, heart rate was much greater in anger than in disgust, and the hands were colder in fear than in anger. Table 9-2 shows the increases or decreases in heart rate and skin temperature for each of the six acted emotions. Ekman's findings seem to support James and Lange's assertion that different emotions are associated with distinct patterns of physiological response.

Second, and perhaps most intriguing, is that when the subjects simply followed instructions to move their facial muscles to mirror a given emotion, they also experienced patterns of physiological arousal that were comparable to those recorded when they relived an actual emotional experience. In some instances, the physiological signs of emotion were more pronounced when the subjects merely moved their facial muscles than when they thought of an emotional experience.

Can you think of a possible application of the research findings of Paul Ekman and his colleagues? Might this information be applied to enhance our emotional lives? Think about this question for a moment or two before reading on.

Table 9-2 Heart Rate and Skin Temperature

Both heart rate and skin temperature were associated with different acted emotions in Ekman's experiment.

Specific Emotion	Change in Heart Rate (Beats/Minute)	Change in Skin Temperature (Degrees Celsius)
Anger	+8.0	+.16
Fear	+8.0	–.01
Distress	+6.5	+.01
Joy	+2.0	+.03
Surprise	+1.8	–.01
Disgust	–0.3	–.03

Data from "Changes in Heart Rate and Skin Temperature for Six Emotions" from *Science,* Volume 221 © 1983 by Paul Ekman et al.

Klüver-Bucy Syndrome A pattern of emotional deficit seen after damage to the amygdala

Ekman's findings do have some practical implications. We have all heard the sage advice to "keep our chins up" or to "put on a happy face" when we are feeling sad or depressed, and this research suggests that there may be some validity to this advice. Subjects felt happy just by contracting the facial muscles associated with happiness. Perhaps if we make the effort to act cheerful, smile, and laugh when we feel down in the dumps, we will in turn feel more cheerful and less sad.

Several studies have provided experimental support for this speculation (Izard, 1990). For example, in one study, subjects were instructed either to suppress or exaggerate the facial expression associated with the fear and discomfort of receiving electric shocks. The researchers monitored physiological arousal during the course of shock administration and also obtained written self-reports of the subjects' feelings. The results revealed that subjects who had been told to suppress their facial expression demonstrated lower physiological arousal and reported less negative feelings than the participants who were not instructed to conceal their facial reactions (Lanzetta, Cartwright-Smith, & Kleck, 1976).

In the preceding studies, subjects were instructed to alter facial expressions voluntarily while researchers attempted to measure their emotional experiences. Researchers are now beginning to utilize another approach. The widely used cosmetic drug Botox® reduces wrinkling by paralyzing facial muscles. If facial feedback contributes to our emotional experiences, wouldn't patients using Botox experience emotions differently? Several researchers have now begun to examine this, with surprising results. Research conducted by Davis et al. (2010) and Havas et al. (2010) suggests that patients do, in fact, experience emotions with less intensity after Botox injections than prior to treatment. Using functional imagery (fMRI), Hennenlotter and colleagues (2009) demonstrated that paralyzing facial muscles with Botox actually diminished brain activity in the emotional circuits of the brain. These results all tend to support the decades-old idea that feedback from facial muscles contributes to the intensity of our emotional experiences.

9.3f The Neurobiology of Emotions

In the preceding sections, we have seen that emotions and their corresponding feelings involve a number of physiological processes and brain structures. In this section we will examine several of the most important neural structures for emotion and clarify their roles in the different components of emotion described at the outset. Much of this research comes from animal studies of fear and aggression, but we are beginning to learn much more about more positive emotions such as happiness and love from human studies. Any discussion of fear and aggression must begin with the amygdala.

The Amygdala and Cingulate Cortex

The amygdala is located deep within the temporal lobes of both hemispheres of the brain. It is composed of several distinct regions that receive and transmit potentially harmful information about the environment to other brain structures to activate all components of fear and aggression. Early surgical studies demonstrated that damage to the amygdala and its surrounding regions severely disrupted all aspects of emotional responding (Klüver & Bucy, 1939). Animals with this damage demonstrated hyperreactivity, deficits in emotional expression, and hypersexuality. This pattern of emotional loss is known as the **Klüver-Bucy syndrome**. More recent studies have elaborated on the role of the amygdala in conditioned fear and found that anxiolytic drugs diminish anxiety through actions within the amygdala as well (M. Davis, 1992; LeDoux, 1992b).

Figure 9-5 The Amygdala and Cingulate Cortex

Locations of several neural structures essential for the expression and feeling of emotions

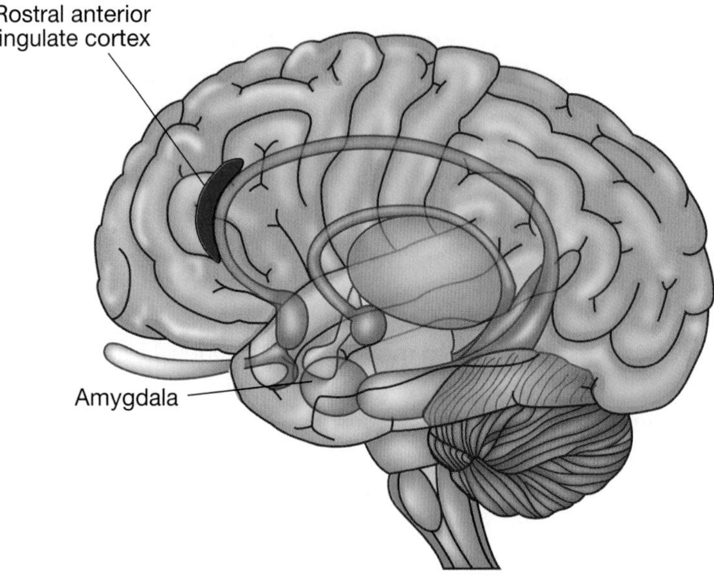

The **central nucleus of the amygdala** regulates all aspects of emotional behavior including sympathetic activation, increased respiration, behavioral arousal, facial expressions, and hormone release. It also sends signals to several cortical structures (Carlson, 2014). While the amygdala controls emotional behaviors, it is the cortex that interprets these emotional states as specific feelings and gives us our awareness of them. Several structures appear to interpret emotional states and their body sensations into feeling states (Damasio, 2004). Human patients with damage to the **cingulate cortex** express emotions, but they do not recognize feelings associated with them. That is, they can be provoked into anger, but do not feel angry, and they do not recognize emotion expressions in themselves or others.

Central Nucleus of the Amygdala Region within the amygdala that integrates sensory information related to fear and aggression and sends output to numerous parts of the body for emotional responses

Cingulate Cortex Area of the cortex deep in the midline that interprets emotional responses as a feeling state

In a surprising experiment conducted by Eisenberger, Lieberman, and Williams (2003), participants in an fMRI study were scanned as the researchers induced a sense of distress by deceiving the participants into believing they were being rejected by others during a computer game. When participants experienced distress, an area within the anterior cingulate cortex became activated (see Figure 9-6). Interestingly, this is the same area of the cingulate that becomes active when one experiences physical pain (e.g., burning by hot water). Activity in the prefrontal cortex (see Figure 9-6B) acts to suppress the feeling of pain. While poets and songwriters have long known that feelings can hurt, this was only recently confirmed by science. The feelings of physical and emotional pain are represented in the same cortical areas.

Figure 9-6 Eisenberger and Lieberman Experiment

Participants in an fMRI study revealed activity in the anterior cingulate (A) during emotional distress. Activity in the right ventral prefrontal cortex (B) is activated to mediate pain.

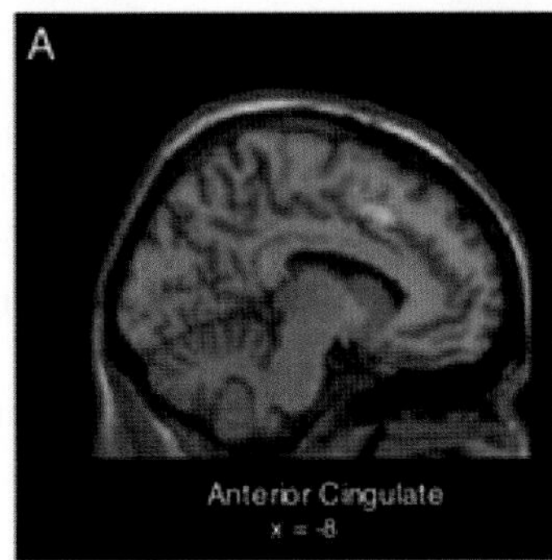

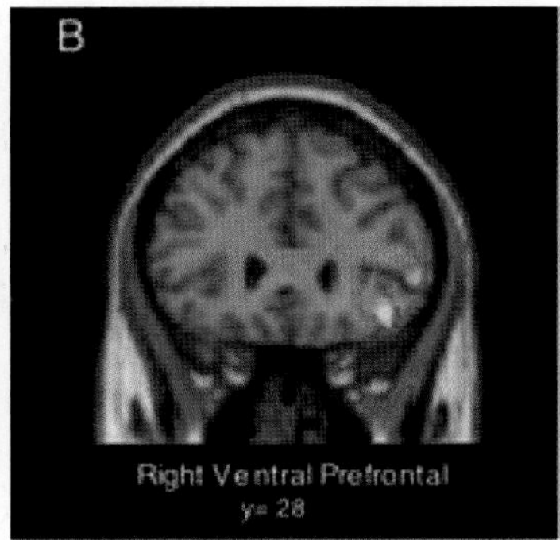

Source: "Does rejection hurt? An fMRI study of social exclusion," by Eisenberger, N., and Lieberman, M, *Science*, 302, 290–302. Copyright 2003 by The American Association for the Advancement of Science. Reprinted with permission.

9.3g Opponent Processes and Motivation

The author has a brother who is an avid rock climber. Some years ago, he experienced a climbing accident that almost ended his life. However, he is now back to rock climbing with just as much zest and enthusiasm as before, perhaps even more. What accounts for his continued participation in a sport that must arouse intense emotion at both ends of the scale—both high fear and ecstatic exhilaration? For that matter, why do people jump out of airplanes with a parachute strapped on their backs, shoot the rapids of wild rivers, ski off extremely steep mountain slopes, or return to a sport that almost killed them?

Some years ago psychologists Richard Solomon and J. D. Corbit (1974) proposed a theory of emotion that attempts to answer these questions. According to their **opponent-process theory of emotion**, people are inclined to maintain a relatively even keel or balance in their emotional lives. When a strong emotional response to a particular stimulus event disrupts this homeostatic balance, an *opponent process*, or opposite emotional response, is eventually activated to restore equilibrium in our emotional state. Thus, if our initial response to being confronted with class IV (whitewater) rapids is sudden terror, we will probably subsequently experience elation after successfully negotiating the rapids—a positive or opposite emotion that cancels out the original negative emotion, thus restoring us to a neutral or balanced emotional state.

From this perspective, emotions are viewed as possessing *hedonic value,* which is to say they vary from being extremely positive or pleasant to being very negative or unpleasant (Solomon, 1980, 1982). When an emotion of a particular hedonic value is aroused, it will be followed shortly by its hedonic opposite. Thus, when we are elated we can expect that this emotion may eventually give way to feeling somewhat down or depressed. Likewise, fear is replaced with elation (or at least relief), pain with pleasure, anxiety with calm, boredom with interest, and so forth.

Opponent-Process Theory of Emotion Theory that when a strong emotional response to a particular stimulus disrupts emotional balance, an opposite emotional response is eventually activated to restore emotional equilibrium

BVT *Lab*

Visit **www.BVTLab.com** to explore the student resources available for this chapter.

Solomon and Corbit theorized that under normal conditions, when we encounter a particular emotion-arousing stimulus only now and then, the opponent emotional states would be sufficiently equalized in intensity to balance each other out. Thus, if we go rock climbing only once each year, we can expect to continue experiencing the same relative intensities of high terror and elation that serve to balance our emotional equilibrium. However, what happens if we become avid climbers after our initial encounter with this exhilarating sport? Solomon and Corbit would argue that when we repeatedly expose ourselves to a situation that arouses the same intense emotion, our initial emotional reaction would gradually weaken over time while the opponent emotional reaction would grow stronger. Therefore, we can expect that our terror of heights will gradually diminish to a level of anxiety just sufficient to get the adrenaline pumping. In contrast, our euphoria after successfully negotiating a steep pitch could be expected to become more intense or powerful as time goes on.

This weakening of the initial emotional response together with the eventual dominance of the opponent-process emotion explains why river runners, rock climbers, skydivers, race car drivers, and other risk takers find that the more they engage in their thrilling sports, the more enjoyable these activities become. The opponent-process theory has also been used to explain addiction to certain drugs like nicotine, heroin and cocaine (Ettenberg, Raven, Danluck, & Necessary, 1999; Ettenberg, 2004; Knackstedt, Samimi, & Ettenberg, 2002; Koob & Le Moal, 2008; Watkins, 2000). Most people experience intense pleasure and an emotional high during their initial exposure to cocaine. However, as any addict can attest, the pleasure associated with using this drug typically decreases with repetitive use. Animals, for example, will initially seek the location where cocaine is administered, but later avoid that location. This is additional evidence that the motivation to seek the drug is eventually replaced by motivation to avoid withdrawal (see Figure 9-7).

This drug-related phenomenon stands as stark testimony to Solomon's observation that people who seek pleasure often pay for it later, and that with repeated pleasure seeking, the pleasure itself often loses much of its intensity. Of course, as previously noted, the reverse is also true: The fear component of risky, thrill-seeking activities often diminishes over time as exhilaration and euphoria intensify with each additional experience. It is in this way that the opponent-process theory accounts for the apparent shift in motivation for many activities. For instance, the motivation to use drugs the first few times may be the intense euphoria associated with those drugs. Later, the motivation shifts to the avoidance of the aversive nature of drug withdrawals.

In concluding our discussion of emotion, we must acknowledge that many questions remain to be answered. While there is renewed support for the James-Lange theory, no one theory of emotion will encompass all aspects of emotion and its expression. In the next section, we will examine in more detail one emotion, stress, and its relation to our well-being.

9.4 Stress

We have all learned that negative emotions such as fear, anxiety, anger, and depression often exact a price in our lives in the form of impaired functioning, fatigue, symptoms of physical discomfort, and even illness. Disruptive, unpleasant emotions play a major role both in contributing to stress and as key components in the manifestation of reactions to stress. Thus we end this chapter with a somewhat detailed discussion of the topic of stress, including comments about the nature of stress and stressors, physiological and psychological responses to stress, and the relationship between stress and illness.

Figure 9-7 Opponent Process

Part (a) demonstrates how, with repeated use of heroin, the pleasure decreases, while the displeasure associated with withdrawal increases. Part (b) portrays the likely response of a river runner as he repeatedly shoots the rapids. Each encounter with this sport may result in decreased fear and an increase in the pleasure associated with it.

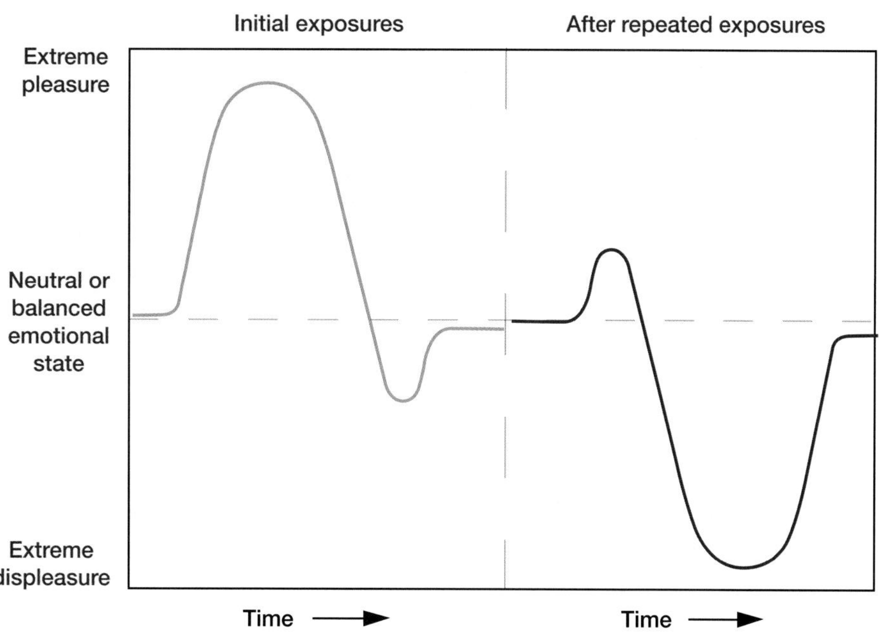

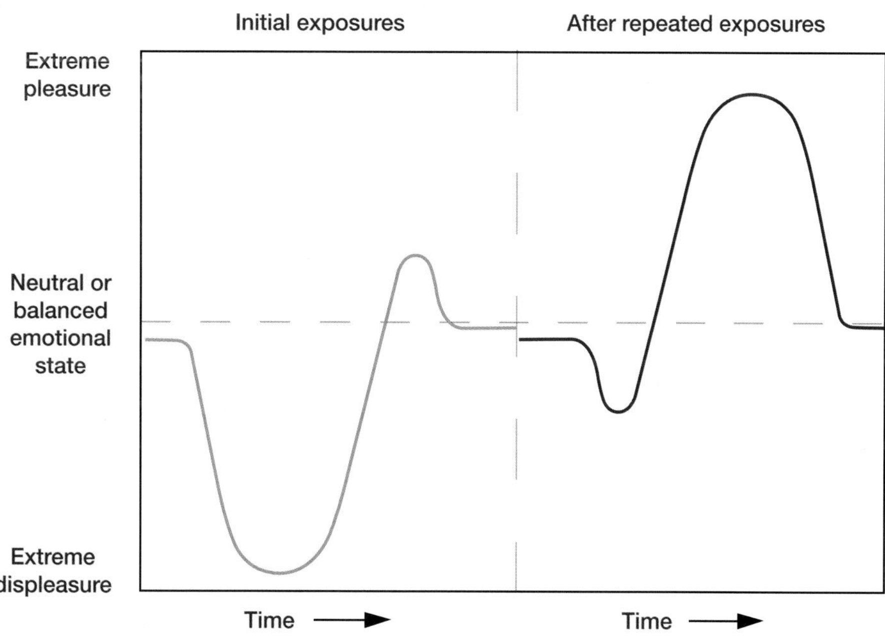

9.4a The Stress Response

Although we are all familiar with stress, it is an elusive concept to define. One reason for this is that stress means so many different things to different people—researchers and laypersons alike. Some of us think of stress as sweaty palms, a fast-beating heart, gritted teeth, and a churning stomach. Consistent with this impression, researchers have for many years focused on the physiological changes that accompany stress. More recently, however, the study of stress responses has been expanded to include emotional, cognitive, and behavioral changes as well as physical reactions. When we are feeling stressed, we may be more inclined to describe our condition as being unprepared for an exam, feeling crowded in our dorms, or being harassed by a supervisor on the job, rather than focusing on our bodily or psychological responses.

Most contemporary researchers believe that an adequate definition of stress must take into account the interplay between external stressors and our physical and psychological responses. This relationship is neither simple nor predictable because it varies from person to person and from day to day. As we see later in our discussion, this variation occurs because stress is inextricably connected to our cognitive appraisals of events (Lazarus & Folkman, 1984; Lazarus, 2001). According to Lazarus, **stress** is the process of appraising events (as harmful, threatening, or challenging), of assessing one's potential to control or cope with the event, and continuing reappraisal as new information becomes available. Appraisal and reappraisal do not always result in less stress; they may actually lead to an increase in stress if coping strategies are not effective or available. In the following section, we examine physiological and psychological responses to stress as well as the situations that produce stress. We then explore what we know about the role stress plays in some common illnesses.

9.4b Physiological Responses to Stress

In the 1930s, the Canadian researcher Hans Selye was conducting research that he hoped would lead to the discovery of a new sex hormone. The leads were promising. When he injected rats with extracts of ovary tissue, the results were consistent: Bleeding ulcers in the stomach and small intestine, enlargement of the adrenal cortex, and shrinkage of the thymus gland. Since no hormone was known to produce these effects, Selye was convinced that he was on the track of identifying a new one. His elation was quickly dampened, however, for when he injected extracts from other tissues, the effects were identical. Furthermore, the same thing occurred when he injected toxic fluids that were not derived from tissues.

Selye was devastated by this turn of events. However, instead of giving up, he tried to figure out what had happened. The answer occurred to him only when he stopped trying to relate his findings to the discovery of a new sex hormone. In his own words,

> It suddenly struck me that one could look at [my ill-fated experiments] from an entirely different angle. [Perhaps] there was such a thing as a single nonspecific reaction of the body to damage of any kind. (Selye, 1976, p. 26)

Selye went on to study how animals responded to a wide range of stressful events other than injections. He exposed rats to a variety of adverse conditions—such as extreme cold and fatigue, electric shock, immobilizing restraint, and surgical trauma—and noted the same physiological response pattern he had originally observed with injections of tissue extracts. As we see later in this chapter, Selye (1936, 1956, 1974, 1976) also learned that humans respond to stress with fairly consistent physiological patterns. The awareness

Stress A pattern of hormonal and physiological responses that accompany threatening events

that stress can have harmful effects on our bodies has led to many more studies, as well as techniques for reducing the impact of stress on our own lives.

Selye's observations of how his rats responded to stressors led him to formulate the concept of the **general adaptation syndrome** (**GAS**). According to this notion, when an organism is confronted with a stressor, its body mobilizes for action. This mobilization effort is mediated by the sympathetic nervous system as we saw in Chapter 3, and it works primarily through the action of specific stress hormones on the body's muscles and organ systems. The response to stress is *nonspecific*, for the same physiological reactions occur regardless of the stressor. Selye also noted that repeated or prolonged exposure to stress that is not adequately managed or reduced results in tissue damage (such as bleeding ulcers), increased susceptibility to disease, and even death in extreme cases.

Alarm, Resistance, and Exhaustion

Selye described three phases of the general adaptation syndrome: *alarm*, *resistance*, and *exhaustion* (see Figure 9-8). When an organism is exposed to a stressful event, it first experiences an alarm reaction in which it mobilizes to meet the threat. A sudden arousal of the sympathetic nervous system produces a flood of stress hormones—corticosteroids from the adrenal cortex, and epinephrine (often called adrenaline) and norepinephrine from the adrenal medulla.

These hormones prepare the body for "fight or flight" by producing a number of physiological reactions. First, our heart rate is likely to increase, as is blood pressure. This activity forces blood to parts of the body that may need it for strenuous physical activity such as flight away from danger. We experience this response as a pounding heart, like the rapid-fire thumping you may have felt after barely avoiding an accident on the freeway. Sugars and fats also flood the blood to provide fuel for quick energy. This emergency response provides extra reserves, with the result that people are often able to perform

General Adaptation Syndrome (GAS)
Progressive responses to prolonged exposure to stressful events during which an organism mobilizes for action and compensates for stress

Figure 9-8 Three Phases of Hans Selye's General Adaptation Syndrome

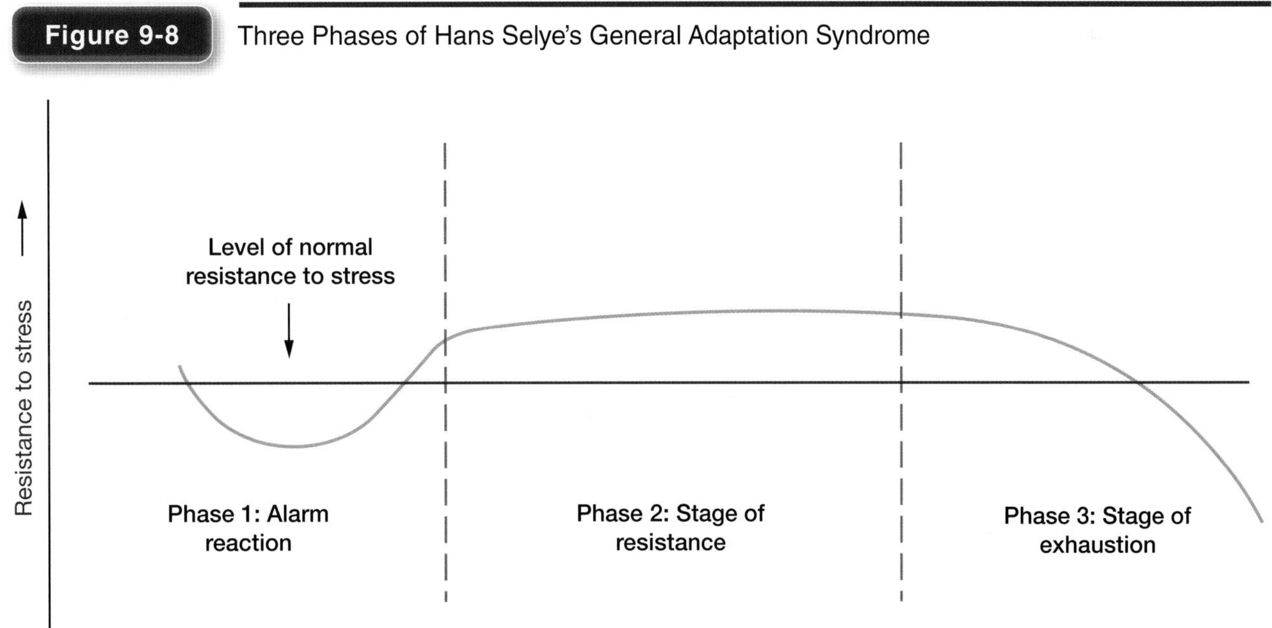

Adapted from *The Stress of Life*, by Hans Selye, M.D. New York, McGraw-Hill Book Company, Inc. 1956

BVT*Lab*

Improve your test scores. Practice quizzes are available at **www.BVTLab.com**.

seemingly superhuman feats (such as lifting a heavy beam off a person trapped in a mine cave-in) that they could not otherwise perform. Digestion slows or ceases during the alarm stage, making more blood available to the muscles and brain.

Our breathing rate also accelerates to supply increased oxygen to muscles poised for greater than normal output. Thus, people often have difficulty catching their breath after a severe fright. Still another response to stress is a tensing of the muscles in preparation for an adaptive response. This explains the stiff neck, sore back, and painful aching legs that many people experience after a long, hard exam or a rough day at work.

We also tend to perspire more when under stress—a response that acts as a kind of built-in air conditioner that cools our energized bodies. It also allows us to burn more energy (which produces heat) when we are faced with emergency situations. This is why many people find themselves drenched with perspiration after giving a speech or undergoing a stressful interview.

Finally, clotting agents are released into the blood when we are under stress, so that our blood will clot more rapidly if we are injured. One reason why we may not notice an injury we receive during an accident or fight is because the wound may have bled very little. Table 9-3 summarizes these responses to stress.

We are not able to maintain the alarm phase's high level of bodily response or sympathetic activity for very long. Eventually, the parasympathetic nervous system comes into play, providing a braking mechanism for the organs activated by the sympathetic system. At this point, the organism enters into the second stage of resistance. Now the body continues to draw upon resources at an above-normal rate, but it is less aroused than in the alarm state.

If the stress is prolonged or repeated, an organism is likely to enter the third stage, exhaustion. As a direct result of the continued drain on resources, the body tissues may begin to show signs of wear and tear during the exhaustion stage. Susceptibility to disease also increases, and continued exposure to the stressor is likely to deplete the organism's adaptive energy. The symptoms of the initial alarm reaction are likely to reappear, but resistance is now decreased, and the alarm reaction is likely to continue unabated. If the organism is unable to develop strategies to overcome or cope with stress, serious illness or even collapse and death may result.

Selye's model has had a profound impact on our understanding of stress and its links to illness. It not only provides a way of conceptualizing our physiological response to events in the environment, it also provides a plausible explanation for the relationship between stress and disease. Few medical experts today disagree with Selye's basic contention that prolonged stress will often produce bodily wear and tear and erode our ability

Table 9-3 Some Physiological Responses to Stress

- Heart rate and blood pressure increase, forcing blood to parts of the body that may need it for strenuous physical activity
- Digestion slows or ceases, so that more blood is available to other organs
- Breathing rate accelerates to provide increased oxygen to bloodstream
- Muscles tense in preparation for an emergency response
- Perspiration increases, acting to cool the body
- Clotting agents are released in the blood to prevent loss of blood in case of injury

to resist disease if it is not effectively coped with. However, Selye's theory has also been criticized on a few counts. One criticism is that Selye failed to acknowledge the important role of psychological factors in stress responses; for example, the significant role of cognitive appraisal in determining the extent to which we assess a particular environmental event as stressful. Furthermore, some newer evidence suggesting that particular stressors may be associated with distinctly different physiological responses calls into question Selye's assumption of nonspecificity in reaction to stress. For example, exercise stress produces a pattern of physiology quite different from emotional stress (Dinsdale & Moss, 1980).

(Shutterstock)

When we feel stressed, we may be more inclined to describe our condition in emotional terms rather than focusing on our bodily or psychological responses.

9.4c **Stressors**

We have been looking at the ways we respond to stress, but so far we have said relatively little about the situations or events that produce stress in our lives. Are some kinds of events more likely to cause stress than others? Are stressors always negative events? We explore these questions next.

Factors that Contribute to Stress

Our cognitive assessments have a lot to do with the degree of stress an event will produce in our lives, but it is not true to say that all events have the same potential for eliciting stress. What characteristics increase the likelihood that we will perceive an event as stressful?

Lack of Control One of the most important factors that contribute to the stressfulness of a situation is our lack of control over it. Thus, it is much less stressful for you to stick a needle into yourself (for example, when removing a splinter) than to have a physician stick a needle into your arm. Research reveals that uncontrollable or unpredictable events are generally more stressful than those we can control or predict. You might think that certain experiences, such as excessive noise, a nagging parent, or a series of painful rehabilitative exercises after a serious accident, would be stressful for anybody exposed to these events. This conclusion is not necessarily warranted, however. When people believe that they can predict, modify, or end an unpleasant event, they are likely to experience it as being less stressful (even if they take no action to modify it). The knowledge that something can be done may be sufficient to reduce the stress. Numerous experiments with laboratory animals support this argument.

Suddenness A second variable influencing how stressful we perceive an event to be is the suddenness with which it overtakes us. When people experience accidents, the sudden death of a loved one, or an unexpected pink slip at work, they may find it very difficult to mobilize adequate coping mechanisms. In general, it is easier to cope with challenges that we can foresee. Thus a person who loses a loved one after a protracted illness, or who loses a job after expecting to be terminated for months, may be much less stressed by these aversive events.

Ambiguity In general, a stressor that we perceive as ambiguous is likely to induce more stress than one that is clear-cut. In well-defined situations we may be able to determine an appropriate course of action (fight, flight, or adapt), but ambiguity forces us to spend resource-depleting energy trying to figure out the nature of the stressor and possible strategies to cope effectively with it. Research demonstrates that *role ambiguity* is a major cause of stress on the job. If you have a job in which your role is not clearly defined so that you do not know what is expected of you, you are likely to experience far more stress than if your employer's expectations are made clear.

9.4d Stress and Disease

Most of Selye's work focused on endocrine responses to stress in nonhuman animals, most notably rats. In recent years, however, increased attention has been directed to assessing the importance of psychological factors in stress reactions. It is now widely recognized that stress and the corresponding physiological changes that underlie it have profound effects on our health and well-being.

Stress is widely recognized as a major factor in a range of physical illnesses. It has been estimated that as many as three out of four visits to physicians are prompted by stress-related problems. Furthermore, stress and stress-related behaviors may be the leading contributors to early death.

Table 9-4 compares the leading causes of death in the United States in the early 1900s and in 2014. The major health problems of the early 1900s were infectious diseases (numbers 2, 3, and 4 in the table are all infectious diseases and total 539 per 100,000), followed by cardiovascular diseases. Today the leading health problems are no longer infectious diseases but cardiovascular diseases/strokes, cancers, respiratory diseases, and accidents. Although these diseases are not new, the proportion of people who die from them has increased dramatically since 1900. Most important, these are all diseases that,

Table 9-4 The Eight Leading Causes of Death in the United States, 1900 and 2014 (rates per 100,000 population)

1900	Rate	2014	Rate
1. Cardiovascular diseases (heart disease, stroke)	345	1. Cardiovascular disease	614
2. Influenza and pneumonia	202	2. Cancers	592
3. Tuberculosis	194	3. Respiratory diseases	147
4. Gastritis, duodenitis, and colitis	143	4. Accidents	135
5. Accidents	72	5. Stroke	133
6. Malignant neoplasms	64	6. Alzheimer's Disease	94
7. Diphtheria	40	7. Diabetes	76
8. Typhoid fever	31	8. Influenzas	55

Data for 1900 from Historical Statistics of the United State: Colonial Times to 1970, U.S. Bureau of the Census, 1975, Washington, D.C. U.S. Government Printing Office. Data for 2014 from National Vital Statistics Report.

in some part, can be attributed to individual behavior and lifestyle, and all of them have been linked to stress. This stress link may be direct through impaired immune function or indirect through cigarette smoking, excessive drinking, poor diet, and/or lack of exercise. In this section, we explore the evidence linking stress with several physical disorders: coronary heart disease, hypertension, infectious diseases, and cancer.

Heart Disease

Coronary heart disease (CHD) is a general label for illnesses that cause a narrowing of the coronary arteries, the vessels that supply the heart with blood. It remains a leading cause of death in developed countries. CHD accounts for nearly 40 percent of all deaths in the United States each year (Benjamin et al., 2017), many of which occur when people are still in the prime of life. About half of all middle-aged men and a third of middle-aged women will develop some form of CHD. Millions of Americans also experience reduced quality of life as a result of the ravages of CHD.

While factors such as smoking, obesity, diabetes, family history, diets high in fat, high serum cholesterol levels, physical inactivity, and high blood pressure are all linked to CHD, these risk factors considered together account for less than half of all diagnosed cases of CHD (Benjamin et al., 2017). Something else beside genetics, diet, exercise, and general health habits must be a factor in CHD; research over the past several decades has strongly implicated stress.

The story of how stress was first linked with heart disease begins with an unexpected discovery by cardiologists Meyer Friedman and Ray Rosenman (1974). In the late 1950s, Friedman and Rosenman were studying the relationship between eating behavior and disease among a sample of San Francisco couples. They found that although the women consumed amounts of cholesterol and animal fat equal to those consumed by their husbands, the women were dramatically less susceptible to heart disease than the men in the study. Since most of the men were employed and their wives were not, Friedman and Rosenman began to suspect that job-related stress might be implicated in the sex differences in CHD. Following up on this hunch, they mailed questionnaires to hundreds of physicians and business executives, asking them to speculate about what had caused the heart attacks of their patients, friends, and colleagues. Their responses overwhelmingly blamed job-related stress.

The next step was to conduct a field study. A sample of forty tax accountants was studied over several months, commencing at the first of the year. During the first three months, laboratory measures of two warning indicators, blood-clotting speed and serum cholesterol levels, were generally within the normal range. This changed, however, as the April 15 tax-filing deadline approached. During these few weeks, the accountants were under a great deal of pressure to finish their clients' tax returns, and both blood-clotting measures and serum cholesterol rose to dangerous levels. Once the tax-filing crunch passed, both measures returned to normal.

Convinced that responses to stress may be major contributors to coronary heart disease, Friedman and Rosenman embarked on a nine-year study of several thousand men, ages thirty-five to thirty-nine, who were physically healthy at the outset of their investigation. Each subject was asked specific questions about his work and eating habits and his usual ways of responding to stressful situations. Using subjects' responses, as well as observations of their behavior, the researchers divided participants into two groups roughly equal in size. Subjects in the **Type A** group tended to be hard driving, ambitious, very competitive, hostile, easily angered, very time conscious, and demanding of perfection in both themselves and others. In contrast, **Type B** subjects were relaxed, easygoing,

Coronary Heart Disease (CHD) Any illness that causes a narrowing of the coronary arteries

Type A Personality Individuals who are hard driving, competitive, hostile, time urgent, and demanding of both themselves and others, as described by Friedman and Rosenman in their study of coronary heart disease

Type B Personality Individuals who are relaxed, easygoing, not driven to achieve perfection, happy in their jobs, understanding, and not easily angered, as described by Friedman and Rosenman in their study of coronary heart disease

Hypertension Commonly referred to as high blood pressure: A condition of excessive blood flow through the vessels that can result in both hardening and general deterioration of the walls of the vessels

Type D Personality A personality type characterized by negativity, distress, and an inability to share emotions with others (a predictor of mortality in patients with cardiovascular disease or cancer)

not driven to achieve perfection, happy in their jobs, understanding and forgiving, and not easily angered (Friedman & Ulmer, 1984; Friedman & Rosenman, 1974).

By the end of the long-term study, it was clear that Type A subjects were far more prone to heart disease than their Type B counterparts. Over the nine-year period, 257 subjects in the total research population had suffered heart attacks, and approximately 70 percent of these were Type A. In other words, Type A subjects were more than twice as vulnerable as Type B. More recent research, however, has failed to consistently demonstrate a connection between Type A behaviors in general and CHD risk. Evidence now suggests that specific components of Type A behavior, like hostility and time urgency, may be as important risk factors as smoking and hypertension for CHD (Bunker et al., 2003; Welin, Lappas, & Wilhelmsen, 2000).

Hypertension

Hypertension, commonly referred to as high blood pressure, occurs when blood flow through the vessels is excessive, a condition that may cause both hardening and general deterioration of tissue in the vessel walls. It has been estimated that roughly seventy-three million Americans suffer from hypertension, and more than 360,000 Americans died in 2013 with hypertension being the main factor (American Heart Association, 2015).

A number of physical factors may contribute to hypertension, including such things as obesity and genetic predispositions. However, there is also substantial evidence linking stress and Type A personality factors to hypertension. In fact, a recent study involving 3,142 subjects over fifteen years revealed that subjects who scored high on time urgency and impatience (TUI), both subscales for Type A personality, were twice as likely to have high blood pressure than those scoring lower. The TUI component of Type A is characterized by a persistent preoccupation with time and pronounced impatience. If you find yourself annoyed following slower traffic or while standing in long lines, you may also be at greater risk for developing hypertension (Yan et al., 2003).

Since Friedman and Rosenman's description of Type A personality, other researchers have focused more carefully on which aspects of personality may actually predict coronary disease outcomes. As a result, the coronary-prone personality was further refined as Type D personality (Denollet, 2005). **Type D personality** is characterized by distress, negative emotions, and an inability to share emotions with others. The "D" in Type D personality refers to distressed. Research on Type D personality reveals that it is associated with higher mortality in patients with cardiovascular disease and cancer (Martin et al., 2011; Mols, Oerlemans, Denollet, Roukema, & Van-de Poll-Franse, 2012). While it is still difficult to predict which individuals will get and survive cardiovascular disease or cancer, we are getting closer to describing how personality contributes to disease processes and outcomes.

(Shutterstock)

A number of physical factors, including obesity and genetics, may contribute to hypertension.

Some people are genetically predisposed toward hypertension, and they may be more reactive to stress than those not genetically predisposed. Reactive people show a more pronounced blood pressure response to a range of stressors (such as exposure to cold water, public speaking, or participation in a challenging cognitive task) than do people without hypertension. It appears that reactive individuals display variants in genes coding for angiotensin receptors (Romano-Spica et al., 2003). Angiotensin is an important hormone involved in regulating fluid balance, and it is a primary target for drugs used to control hypertension.

Cancer A collection of many diseases, all of which result from genetic alterations in cells that produce runaway cell growth

Cortisol A stress hormone released by the adrenal glands that is known to decrease immune functioning and increase disease susceptibility

Infectious Diseases

Infectious diseases are caused by microorganisms such as bacteria and viruses. The most common of these diseases are common colds and influenza, but they also include diseases such as AIDS. Researchers have confirmed a strong correlation between stress and the onset and severity of infectious diseases. (One you may well know as the increase in the number of colds on campus associated with final exams.) The link between these diseases may, however, be more than a correlation. Evidence suggests that stress responses actually impair the ability of your immune system to fight off infections (Cohen & Williamson, 1991; Moynihan, 2003; Tausk, Elenkov, & Moynihan, 2008). Recent research even suggests that exposure to stressful events early in life may actually predispose individuals to disease by compromising how the immune system responds to an infection. This may in part explain why some individuals are more prone to infection throughout their lives than others (Avitsur, Hunzeker, & Sheridan, 2006).

Cancer

Evidence linking stress to cancer is certainly more controversial than that for CHD or hypertension. However, many specialists in the fields of oncology and behavioral medicine strongly suspect a connection. **Cancer** is a collection of many diseases, all of which result from genetic cell alterations that produce runaway cell growth. Although researchers do not completely understand all the mechanisms and agents involved in cancer, compelling evidence suggests a relationship between stress and cancer (Moynihan, 2003; Tausk et al., 2008). It has been estimated that 90 to 95 percent of all cancer cases can be attributed to environmental and lifestyle factors, including stress. The remaining 5 to 10 percent may be due to genetic defects (Anand et al., 2008). This suggests that cancer may be more preventable than previously believed and that its prevention will depend on major lifestyle changes.

Animal studies provide information not available in human research. For example, rats that are inoculated with cancerous cells and then exposed to inescapable electric shocks are less able to reject the cancerous cells than are rats that are subjected to escapable shocks (Visintainer, Seligman, & Volpicelli, 1983). This research suggests that the greater stress associated with an uncontrollable event may have reduced the animals' resistance to cancer. Other studies, in which animals have been exposed to stressors such as cold-water immersion, have also reported higher incidences of malignancies than among nonstressed animals (Ben-Eliyahu et al., 1991).

Researchers have also investigated the biological mechanisms linking stress to cancer, and they have implicated that specific stress hormones—primarily, **cortisol**—weaken the immune system (Lamkin et al., 2012). As we will see, the immune system guards against invaders and foreign tissue of all kinds, including cancerous cells. In fact, the immune system may produce tumor-specific chemicals that attack and destroy cancerous growth. Since we know that prolonged or severe stress can suppress immune response, it follows that stress may also allow cancer cells to proliferate more rapidly than might otherwise occur. In the past few years, we have witnessed a rapid expansion in research related

Psychoneuro-immunology The scientific study of the relationships between behavior and disease processes

Immune System A complex surveillance system that guards the body by recognizing and removing bacteria, cancer cells, and other hazardous foreign substances

to how psychological factors contribute to disease. The new field of **psychoneuro-immunology** and the establishment of new scientific journals, such as *Brain, Behavior, and Immunity,* are evidence that the medical community now takes seriously the influence of emotional states on disease processes.

Stress and the Immune System

The **immune system** is an exceedingly complex surveillance system that guards the body by recognizing and removing bacteria, viruses, cancer cells, and other hazardous foreign substances. When such substances are detected, our immune systems respond by stimulating lymphocytes (white blood cells) to attack and destroy these invaders. The actions of the *lymphocytes,* as well as other immune-system responses, are delicately regulated in an extremely complex process. If the immune system is suppressed, we become more vulnerable to a variety of infectious organisms and cancers. Conversely, a breakdown in the body's homeostasis may cause the immune system to become overactive, turning on itself to attack and destroy healthy body tissues. (This phenomenon occurs in autoimmune disorders such as rheumatoid arthritis.) While diet, age, heredity, and general health all affect the functioning of the immune system, stress also exerts a marked influence on *immunocompetence,* the immune system's ability to defend the body successfully (Moynihan, 2003; Tausk et al., 2008).

For instance, many studies of nonhuman animals have demonstrated that experimentally manipulated stressors—such as separation from mother, isolation from peers, exposure to loud noise, and electric shock—can reduce immunocompetence by suppressing the activity of the lymphocytes. Research with human subjects has revealed similar results. High-stress periods such as final exam week have been linked to reduced immunocompetence—a finding which helps explain why people may be more likely to become ill during finals (Jemmott et al., 1983). Research on adult subjects has also linked symptoms of a variety of infectious diseases, including colds, influenza, herpes, and mononucleosis, to stressful events (Cohen & Williamson, 1991; Jemmott & Locke, 1984).

In summary, there is considerable evidence linking stress with depressed immune function and the onset and progression of both infectious diseases and cancer. Studies with animals have demonstrated strong relationships between the stress of shock, isolation, and loud noise and the ability of the immune system to fight off infectious diseases as well as cancerous tumors. Interpreting data from humans is more difficult because of the difficulty in controlling for the amount and type of stress, but results are consistent with animal studies. Evidence suggests that the suppression in immune function that follows severe stress is mediated by the release of stress hormones and that stress can have lifelong consequences on the health of your immune system (Avitsur, Hunzeker, & Sheridan, 2006; Brannon et al., 2014; Tausk et al., 2008).

Managing Stress

Recent evidence linking stress with a variety of illnesses has prompted many health professionals to turn their attention to developing techniques for managing stress. These techniques take aim not only at our physiological, cognitive, and behavioral responses to stress but also at behaviors and thought patterns that may induce or increase stress. The following paragraphs summarize some strategies that have been successfully applied in various stress-management programs offered at hospitals, clinics, and corporations. For more information about these techniques or programs, check your library or bookstore for some of the many excellent self-help stress-management books currently available.

Managing Physiological Responses to Stress

Most of the physical damage associated with stress results from our bodies' physiological responses. These include the release of hormones and corticosteroids into the blood, resulting in increases in metabolism, heart rate, blood pressure, and muscle tension, and a decrease in the ability of our immune system to respond effectively to invasion. Many techniques have been developed to minimize these reactions; three of the most effective are *biofeedback*, *relaxation training*, and *exercise*.

Biofeedback We are seldom aware of the subtle physiological changes that take place when we are under stress, such as rising blood pressure or increased heart rate. The theory behind biofeedback is that if we learn to recognize these destructive changes, we can also learn to control them. Biofeedback provides individuals with information about their bodily processes that they can use to modify these processes. For instance, people who suffer from high blood pressure might be hooked up to a biofeedback apparatus that constantly monitors their blood pressure, sounding a tone that changes in pitch as their blood pressure rises or falls. Through this process, they may eventually learn to recognize symptoms of high blood pressure even when they do not hear a tone, so that they can apply techniques to control this response. Although biofeedback is not a panacea for all stress-related disorders, it has been helpful in treating migraine headaches, tension headaches, muscle tension, high blood pressure, and chronic pain.

Relaxation Training Virtually every formal stress-management program teaches some kind of relaxation technique. One of these is progressive relaxation, in which a person first tightens the muscles in a given area of the body (such as the legs), then relaxes them, and then progresses systematically to other body areas until the entire body is relaxed.

How effective is relaxation in controlling stress-induced effects such as muscle tension and high blood pressure? In one recent study, 378 subjects were assigned to one of three conditions. One group received meditation training, another received progressive relaxation, and the third group served as control. After exposure to a stressor, the meditation and progressive relaxation groups showed a greater reduction in anxiety than the control group (Rausch, Gramling, & Auerbach, 2006).

Relaxation training is also being used with some success in delaying the recurrence of some kinds of terminal cancer. It is believed that relaxation training may play a role in facilitating the body's immune system to fend off the rapid growth of cancer cells. While it is too early to critically evaluate this evidence, a number of treatment programs have begun to adopt relaxation training as part of cancer treatment (e.g., Cheung, Molassiotis, & Chang, 2003).

Exercise Have you ever noticed that some types of exercise, such as jogging a few miles or playing tennis, can help to relieve stress? Exercise helps to distract us from sources of stress, and it can also help to moderate some potentially damaging physical effects of stress by lowering blood pressure, improving circulation, and strengthening the heart muscle. In addition, people who regularly engage in some form of exercise are more likely to adopt a healthful diet and be nonsmokers. Of all the stress reduction techniques we know, exercise seems to provide the longest lasting benefits.

Cognitive Appraisal People involved in stress-management programs learn to pay attention to what they are thinking just before they experience stress. One of the benefits of this self-monitoring is the awareness of how frequently our own upsetting thoughts or negative self-talk trigger our feelings of stress. Negative self-talk such as, "I'll never be able to pass this exam" can make the difference between good performance and failure; it can also help to bring on the elevated physical reactions typical of stress responses.

To modify these common cognitive antecedents of stress, Canadian psychologist Donald Meichenbaum (1993) suggests a technique he calls stress inoculation, in which we learn to replace negative self-statements with positive coping statements. For example, when faced with the stress of an exam, we might use positive self-talk such as, "There's no point in imagining the worst; I've prepared as well as anyone, and I'll do the best I can." Although it may take some time to learn to alter negative self-talk successfully, the effect can be a reduction in anxiety and stress.

Many of us bring stress on ourselves by certain maladaptive behaviors. For instance, we may use our time poorly and then suddenly find ourselves under pressure, or we may habitually take on too many tasks to accomplish in the time we have. Stress management programs offer a variety of techniques for modifying such stress-producing behaviors. The following abbreviated list illustrates a number of these behaviors, as well as some strategies that are helpful in combating them.

- Procrastination: Time-management training can help people pace themselves to avoid leaving too much for the last minute. You may experience less academic stress if you learn to manage your study time more effectively and avoid last-minute cramming.
- The "superperson syndrome": For some people, an important part of stress management is learning to say "no" and to delegate tasks to others. Time-management training can also help people recognize their limits so that they do not commit to more work than they can complete.
- Disorganization: Stress-management programs often help people deal with disorganization by providing training in how to set goals for each day, establish priorities, avoid wasting time, and become task oriented.
- Lack of assertiveness: People who have difficulty standing up for their rights may be "boiling inside," generating tremendous amounts of stress. To combat this tendency, many stress-management programs incorporate assertiveness training, which teaches people to confront such situations rather than tiptoe around them.
- Going it alone: Facing stress alone is much more damaging than facing it with the support of people who care about us. Talking with others provides us with new perspectives; it may also boost our self-esteem and our sense that we are valued. Thus, an important tactic in managing stress is to talk things over with someone. If friends or family members are not able to provide support, a campus counseling center, community health center, or private clinic may be a valuable resource.

CHAPTER REVIEW

The Components of Emotions

1. Motivation and emotion are closely connected. Emotions often motivate our actions.
2. Emotions are composed of four integral components: cognitive processes, affect, physiological arousal, and behavioral reactions.

The Range of Human Emotion

3. According to Plutchik's emotion wheel, there are eight primary human emotions, which consist of four pairs of opposites: acceptance and disgust, fear and anger, surprise and anticipation, and sadness and joy.

Theories of Emotion

4. According to the James-Lange theory, environmental stimuli trigger physiological responses from the viscera and muscle movements. These visceral and muscular responses then activate emotional states.
5. Recent evidence has demonstrated that different emotions are associated with similar, but not identical, physiological changes. Support for the James-Lange theory is reemerged in recent years.
6. The Cannon-Bard theory suggests that internal physiological changes and muscular responses are not the cause of emotion but rather that emotional experiences and physical changes occur simultaneously.
7. The Schachter-Singer theory combines elements from both the James-Lange and Cannon-Bard theories. Schachter and Singer maintained that emotions depend on a kind of double cognitive interpretation: We appraise the emotion-causing event while also evaluating what is happening physiologically with our bodies.
8. New evidence from effects of the muscle-paralyzing cosmetic drug Botox supports the decades-old theory about the role of facial feedback in emotional experience.
9. Solomon and Corbit's opponent-process theory maintains that when a strong emotional response to a particular stimulus event disrupts emotional balance, an opponent-process is eventually activated to restore equilibrium in one's emotional state. Repeated exposures to stimuli that arouse intense emotions result in a gradual weakening of the initial emotional reaction as the opponent process becomes stronger.

CHAPTER REVIEW

Stress

10. There is a powerful relationship between emotion and stress. Stress may be defined as the process of appraising events (as harmful, threatening, or challenging), of assessing potential responses, and of responding to those events.
11. Hans Selye's observation of organisms' physiological responses to stress led him to formulate the concept of a general adaptation syndrome (GAS) composed of three phases: alarm, resistance, and exhaustion. A flood of stress hormones that prepare the body for fight or flight characterizes the alarm phase. In the resistance stage, the body returns to a less aroused state, but one in which it continues to draw upon resources at an above-normal rate. If the stress is not alleviated, an organism is likely to enter the third state of exhaustion in which its body tissues begin to show signs of wear and tear, and susceptibility to disease increases.
12. Factors that contribute to the stressfulness of a situation include our lack of control over it, its sudden onset, and a degree of ambiguity that forces us to spend resource-depleting energy trying to figure out the nature of the stressor.
13. Response to stress may be a major contributor to coronary heart disease.
14. Type A people, particularly those who display anger and hostility, are more prone to CHD than Type B people, who are more relaxed, easygoing, and not driven to achieve perfection.
15. People who deal with anger by suppressing it and those who exhibit Type A behavior may be particularly predisposed to develop hypertension.
16. Type D personality is characterized by distress, negative emotions, and an inability to share emotions with others.
17. Individuals with Type D personality are less likely to survive cardiovascular disease and cancer.
18. Stress hormones exert a pronounced effect on the immune system's ability to defend our bodies successfully against disease.

TERMS AND CONCEPTS

Cancer, pg. 369
Cannon-Bard Theory, pg. 351
Central Nucleus of the Amygdala, pg. 358
Cingulate Cortex, pg. 358
Coronary Heart Disease (CHD), pg. 367
Cortisol, pg. 369
Emotions, pg. 345
Facial Feedback Theory, pg. 355
General Adaptation Syndrome (GAS), pg. 363
Hypertension, pg. 368
Immune System, pg. 370
James-Lange Theory, pg. 350
Klüver-Bucy Syndrome, pg. 357
Opponent-Process Theory of Emotion, pg. 359
Psychoneuro-immunology, pg. 370
Schachter-Singer Theory, pg. 351
Stress, pg. 362
Type A Personality, pg. 367
Type B Personality, pg. 367
Type D Personality, pg. 368

POP QUIZ

True or False

___ 1. According to Plutchik's emotion wheel, there are only eight human emotions.

___ 2. Schachter and Singer's theory of emotion agrees with the James-Lange theory in that emotions follow physiological and behavioral changes.

___ 3. Psychological responses to stress include cognitive, emotional, and behavioral responses.

___ 4. Situations that an individual does not have control over and are sudden and ambiguous are likely to be perceived as stressful.

___ 5. Stressful events decrease the functioning of the body's immune system.

Multiple Choice

6. The physiological component of emotion is closely associated with which of the following?
   a. Autonomic nervous system
   b. Central nervous system
   c. Skeletal or somatic nervous system
   d. Brain stem functions
7. According to Plutchik's emotion wheel, emotions that are directly across from each other ______.
   a. are opponent processes
   b. have the most in common
   c. are opposites
   d. are secondary emotions
8. The James-Lange theory is supported by evidence that indicates which of the following?
   a. The hypothalamus is involved in emotional expression.
   b. Feelings of emotions are a consequence of physiological changes caused by emotional stimuli.
   c. Following a fear response, people experience elation.
   d. Individuals tend to look for an appropriate emotional label for physiological changes.
9. The facial feedback theory of emotion is partially supported by the observation that indicates which of the following?
   a. Emotions are always accompanied by changes in facial expression.
   b. Drugs that paralyze facial muscles (e.g., Botox) decrease the intensity of experienced emotions.
   c. We often experience the same emotion another is expressing.
   d. Forcing a smile can make people happy even when they are not.

POP QUIZ

10. Solomon and Corbit's opponent-process theory proposes that with repeated exposure to a situation that produces an intense emotion, the initial emotional reaction will ________ while the opponent emotional reaction will ________.
    a. weaken / remain constant
    b. remain constant / grow stronger
    c. weaken / grow stronger
    d. grow stronger / weaken
11. Which of the following is ***not*** a common cognitive response to a stressful situation?
    a. Disruptive thoughts
    b. Higher than normal levels of distraction
    c. Feelings of anxiety
    d. Impaired performance on cognitive tasks
12. Which of the following events should be least stressful?
    a. Having your parents tell you they are divorcing
    b. Having your roommate tell you to move out
    c. Having your partner initiate the breakup of a long-term relationship
    d. Initiating the breakup of a long-term relationship
13. What is the main reason why ambiguous situations may cause stress?
    a. One may not be able to determine an appropriate course of action.
    b. One needs time to mobilize a defense.
    c. One may feel out of control.
    d. One may not be able to plan ahead.
14. The evidence linking stress to ________ is less conclusive and more controversial than for the other illnesses listed.
    a. malfunctioning of the immune system
    b. coronary heart disease
    c. cancer
    d. hypertension
15. Stress affects the immune system by which of the following?
    a. Reducing immunocompetence
    c. Activating the immune system
    b. Enhancing immunocompetence
    d. Destroying the immune system

Answer Key: 1.F 2.T 3.T 4.T 5.T 6.a 7.c 8.b 9.b 10.c 11.c 12.d 13.a 14.c 15.a

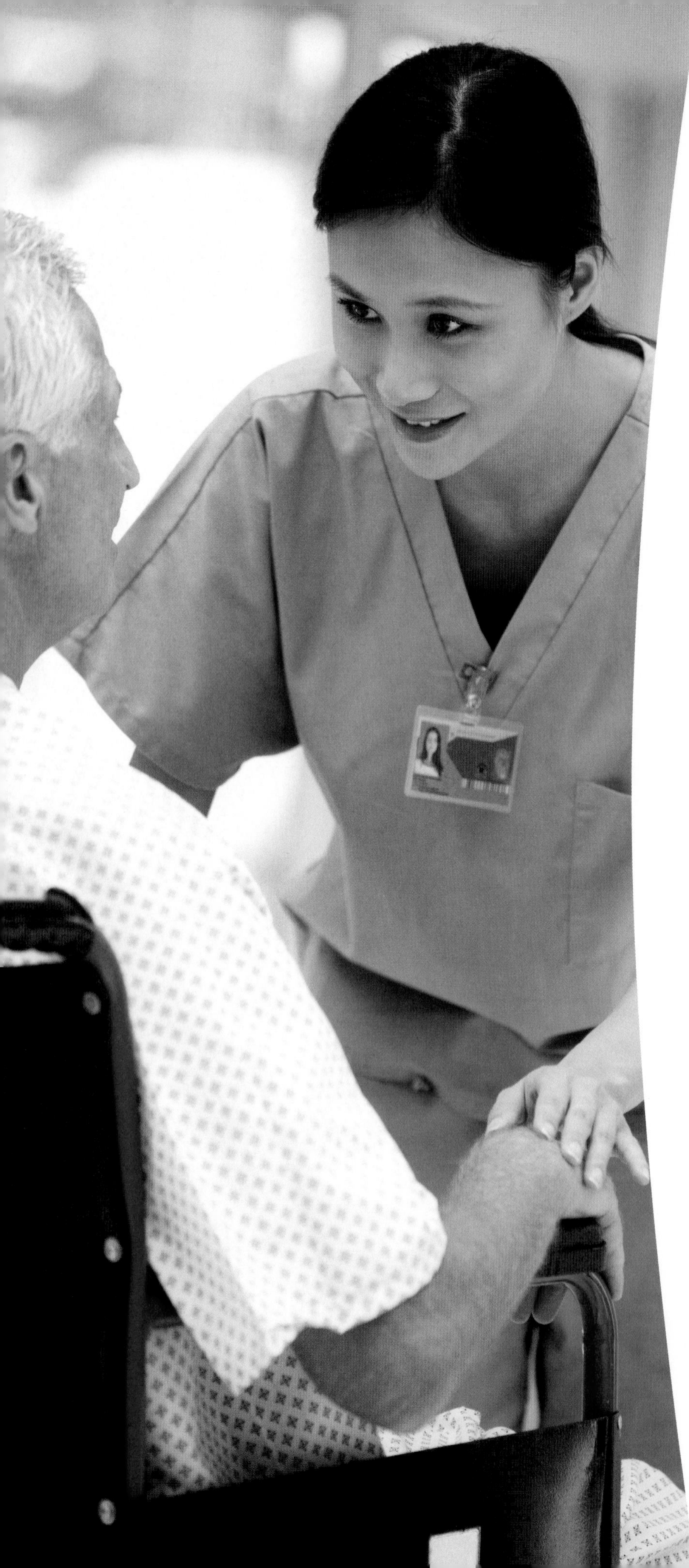

(Shutterstock)

Cognition: **Thinking** *and* **Language**

In Germany, around the turn of the century, there was a famous horse named Hans who performed amazing intellectual feats. When asked to solve spoken arithmetic problems, such as, "What is the sum of five plus one?" he consistently signed the correct answer by tapping his hoof the correct number of times. Some cynics declared that Hans was a hoax and that his trainer was somehow cueing the correct answer to the horse, but these assertions were dispelled when the horse provided the correct answer even when his trainer was not present.

Many people view abstract thought, problem solving, and language as qualities that set humans apart from other animals. Does Hans provide evidence disproving this belief? To answer this question, let us return to our narrative.

After the critics had seemingly been disproved, someone noticed an odd pattern. Hans had trouble solving math problems if the questioner either did not know the answer or was standing out of sight. What did this mean?

Hans was clever, but, as the saying goes, a horse is a horse. He did not understand either the words or the math problems; instead, he had learned to respond to subtle body language cues. Whenever his trainer or another questioner said something to him in an expectant tone of voice, then leaned forward and tensed up, Hans knew that he should start tapping his hoof on the ground. He would keep striking the ground until the trainer relaxed and stopped leaning forward. Hans knew that if he stopped tapping his hoof at this point, he would receive a carrot as reinforcement.

In the following pages, we explore thinking, problem solving, reasoning, and decision making, and the special qualities of human language. As discussed in Chapter 1, these processes constitute the core topics within the area of *cognitive psychology.* Hans' abilities demonstrate that cognitive processes can be misinterpreted, and oftentimes, complex behavior of humans and other animals can be reduced to simpler behavioral processes. The cognitive processes discussed in this chapter are not an exception.

10.1 Thinking

The term *think* has a variety of meanings in our everyday language. For example, we might remark to a friend, "I can't think of the name of that place," or "I think the president has done an excellent job so far." On the other hand, if your friend asks you to assist her with making a difficult decision, you may say, "Let me think about this for a while."

In the first two instances, the word think is synonymous with remembering and belief, respectively; in the third example, it implies a process of reasoning about a particular situation with the intent of solving a problem. Psychologists who study thought are interested primarily in this latter meaning. Thus, we may define **thought** or *thinking* as a collection of internal processes directed toward solving a problem. When we use symbols or concepts to imagine something internally, and to solve problems, we are said to be thinking.

Thinking is the process that lets us make sense out of our perceptions. Our ability to think also allows us to put what we have learned to use. Perhaps most important, thinking allows us to manipulate representations of objects, so that we can solve problems without actually going through any physical motions. For example, an architect working on a design for a new home on a hilltop does not have to draw several sets of plans to determine which will take best advantage of the view. Instead, he or she manipulates the various design features in order to arrive at a solution, even before getting out

Thought Any cognitive processes directed toward problem solving, understanding language, memory retrieval, and perceiving patterns in sensory inputs

BVT *Lab*

Flashcards are available for this chapter at **www.BVTLab.com**.

the drafting paper. Finally, thinking allows us to behave privately without committing ourselves. In a game of chess, we might think about the consequences of several moves before actually moving.

Cognitive psychologists who study thought are interested in determining how people transform and manipulate information to solve problems and make decisions. Before examining what research has revealed about how we accomplish these goals, we first consider a fundamental question: What are the basic components of thinking?

10.1a Components of Thinking

Thinking as Behavior

About half a century ago, many psychologists believed that thinking was essentially a matter of talking to ourselves. The leading proponent of this view was John Watson (1924), the founder of behaviorism. Like other behaviors, Watson argued, thinking involves specific motor actions; the only difference is that the muscular movements involved in thinking are usually much more difficult to observe than those of other kinds of behavior. Watson maintained that tiny movements of the tongue and throat, which he called *subvocal* or *implicit speech,* occur when we think. Watson further argued that there were many muscular combinations, including hand and arm gestures, which could become substitutes for words and therefore were involved in thinking.

Some early evidence supported Watson's view. For example, when researchers used sensitive recording devices, they were able to record very subtle movements of the tongue and throat muscles that occurred when subjects were silently thinking about various problems (Jacobson, 1932). One noteworthy study found that deaf people, who were accustomed to communicating with sign language rather than speech, exhibited muscular activity in their fingers when asked to solve problems (Max, 1937). Such findings certainly supported the notion that some relationship existed between thought and motor action—a relationship you may have noted yourself if you have ever observed people scratching their heads or furrowing their brows as they think. Watson, however, argued that there was more than just a relationship. He believed that subvocal speech and overt motor action were essential for thinking.

Watson's assertion was put to the test in an interesting experiment. The subject (a member of the research team) was injected with curare, a drug that temporarily paralyzes all of the skeletal muscles. Since the paralyzed subject could not move any muscles, he was unable to engage in subvocal speech, to breathe, or even to blink. His research associates provided artificial respiration and other vital support services while their colleague was temporarily immobilized. When the drug wore off, the subject reported that his mind had remained clear during the entire procedure. He also had been able to think not only about questions put to him during the experiment but also about the experimental procedure (Smith, Brown, Toman, & Goodman, 1947). These results were interpreted as evidence against Watson's theory and in support of the idea that thinking can be independent of motor action.

More recent versions of behaviorism continue to argue that thinking is behavior, but on a smaller scale that is usually verbal and unobservable to others. B. F. Skinner (1974) termed this kind of behavior **covert behavior**. According to Skinner, covert behavior, like thinking, had advantages in that we could act without committing ourselves. In other words, we could revoke the behavior if the private consequences were not reinforcing. In this way, a chess player might try a number of covert moves in order to test the consequences of each before committing to a move.

Covert Behavior Behavior that is unobservable in another person (e.g., thinking)

While it is too early to rule out the behavioral position completely, most psychologists agree that thinking is more than covert behavior. Even Skinner believed that covert behavior was not a complete explanation of thinking.

Mental Images

If thinking is not solely covert behavior, what else is there? One additional component is mental imagery, which may take the form of visual imagery, auditory imagery, smell imagery, or even tactile imagery. Most research, however, has focused on visual imagery.

For example, suppose you are trying to figure out how to assemble a new lawn mower after removing all the parts from the packing crate. You are likely to think about this task by manipulating visual pictures or mental images of the various parts. You might also use mental imagery to solve a mathematics problem, to picture the components of a perfect tennis swing, to compose or rehearse music, or if you recall from Chapter 7, identify the correct rotation of a three-dimensional object.

What are these mental images? Certainly they cannot be mere internal pictures, as this would require another "mind's eye" to interpret them, by perhaps another image. While some cognitive psychologists insist that mental images that represent the spatial properties of real objects exist, just as vision exists, other psychologists argue that the picture image analog is misleading even though visual imagery and vision share some of the same neural mechanisms (Pylyshyn, 1984, 2002). The difference between perceiving real objects and generating mental images appears to be the sequence of neural events, not the actual neural representation itself. For instance, when one visually or auditorily perceives a stimulus, perception begins in early visual and auditory cortical areas, respectively, before the frontal cortex is activated. This is referred to as **bottom-up processing**. However, when generating an auditory or visual mental image, the sequence is reversed. **Top-down processing** begins in the prefrontal cortex before activating the visual or auditory cortical areas (Navarro Cebrian & Janata, 2010; Mechelli, Price, Friston, & Ishai, 2004; Yomogida et al., 2004).

Although it appears that mental images are essential elements of thought, there is more to thought than representational images of sights, sounds, and touches. Most cognitive psychologists believe that there is another, more abstract or symbolic form of thinking that involves the use of *concepts*.

Concepts

Suppose you are the parent of a six-year-old who asks, "Where do babies come from?" You respond as well as you can by providing a simplified version of a very complex set of biological processes. This task may not be the easiest you have ever performed, but imagine how difficult it would be to answer this question if your child had not already acquired a representation or conception of the meaning of the terms you used to answer the question—terms such as *womb* and *fertilization*?

In order to think and communicate about the objects, living things, activities, physical properties, and relationships between things we encounter in our daily lives, we learn to simplify and provide order to our world by grouping events, objects, and so forth, into general categories that belong together. Our mental representations of these categories are referred to as **concepts**. For example, you have a concept of airplane, which refers to your representation of all cases of planes and excludes other flying objects like insects and birds. Concepts thus represent categories or kinds of things and their rules of combination, not just individual cases. Most of our knowledge is in the form of concepts rather than independent,

Bottom-Up Processing Perceptual processing that begins in peripheral sensory receptors and then activates higher cortical areas

Top-Down Processing A sequence of neural activation that begins in higher cortical areas, such as the prefrontal cortex, before activating brain areas involved in perception

Concepts Cognitive categories for grouping events, objects, or processes

(Shutterstock)

Mental imagery may take the form of visual imagery, auditory imagery, smell imagery, or even tactile imagery. You might also use mental imagery to solve a mathematics problem or to picture a perfect tennis swing.

specific items or instances. Furthermore, concept formation may be one of the most important cognitive functions that humans perform (Solso, O. MacLin, & M. MacLin, 2008).

A concept may represent a category to which all varieties of one kind of physical object belong. For example, our concept of *car* encompasses everything from a Model T to a BMW. Concepts also represent kinds of living things (*dogs, plants,* or *people*); types of activities (*reading* and *jogging*); physical properties (*little, pungent,* or *square*); and relationships between things (*taller than* or *prettier than*). Concepts may also represent more abstract ideas, such as *feeling good, love,* or *morality.*

Our ability to think and function efficiently would be greatly impaired if we were not able to form concepts. Without the general concept, *car,* we could never give our children simple instructions such as, "Watch out for cars when you cross the street." Instead, we would have to list every name of every automobile. Without concepts such as *happy* and *sad,* we could not describe someone's emotional behavior without an extended description of that person's facial expressions, vocal inflections, and the nature of communicated messages.

Concepts provide a sense of order to a world filled with unique objects and events. They allow us to group things that share certain features even though they are not identical. They also permit us to categorize most of the new objects or activities that we encounter, even though they may be quite novel. Since we can relate these new situations to objects or events with which we are already familiar, we can immediately understand something about them even though they are new.

Concepts range from broad to very specific. Examples of specific, narrow concepts are *sock, golden retriever,* and *red ball.* Examples of broader concepts are *footwear, dog,* and *ball.* We tend to organize concepts into hierarchies, with specific concepts grouped as subcategories within broader concepts. Thus, *airplane* represents a broad concept that may be subdivided into more specific lower-level categories, such as *propeller aircraft* and *jet aircraft*. Furthermore, *jet aircraft* may be subdivided into more specific concepts such as *jet fighters, commercial passenger jet,* and so forth.

There seems to be an optimal or basic level in each concept hierarchy that we naturally use when we think about objects or events. For example, look at the two objects pictured in Figure 10-1. What were the first labels for each of these objects that came to your mind? The odds are that you probably said, a *house* and a *car*. Certainly it would have been correct to classify them as a *white colonial-style house* and a *sports car*. However, these lower-level-category responses provide more detail than you need to think optimally about the objects. Likewise, you would have been correct if you had classified the objects as an *architectural structure* and a *motorized vehicle;* however, this concept level would not have been efficient either, because the categorizations are too imprecise.

Research has supported the idea that we rely on basic-level categories most of the time. When subjects are shown a picture of an object and are asked to verify (yes or no) that it illustrates a particular concept, they tend to react fastest at the basic level. For example, when shown a picture of a kitchen chair, subjects consistently classify it more quickly at the basic level (*chair*) than at either a subordinate level (*kitchen chair*) or a superordinate level (*piece of furniture*). As children develop and learn to think conceptually about their environments, basic-level categories are probably those they use first as they acquire the ability to name and classify events and objects. Many cognitive psychologists now believe that this dependence on basic levels of concepts continues to be a fundamental aspect of human thought throughout our lives.

How do we form these concepts that are so essential to our everyday thought and decision-making processes?

Association Theory

One theory as to how we form concepts was proposed by Clark Hull (1920), who described concept formation as the acquisition of stimulus-stimulus (S-S) associations. According to

Figure 10-1 How Do You Describe These Objects?

this view, we learn to associate a concept (such as *ball*) with a set of stimuli that share one or more common elements (e.g., roundness, small). Thus, we associate the concept *bird* with a pattern of stimuli (has wings, flies, lays eggs, etc.). We form a representation of a concept that is broad enough to allow us to generalize the response to many different instances of the concept. When we encounter a novel instance of the concept, such as an exotic bird we have never seen before, we respond correctly ("It is a bird.") on the basis of stimulus generalization (see Chapter 6). Clearly humans and other animals learn concepts by association, but other processes may also be involved. Eleanor Rosch (1978, 2002) proposed an alternative explanation as to how we form everyday concepts (Gabora, Rosch, & Aerts, 2008).

10.1b Prototypes and Exemplars

According to Rosch, the natural concepts that we learn in everyday life are represented in our memories by examples or **exemplars**. Thus, our concept of *fish* may be based on images of salmon, trout, or bass—all examples of fish that we have seen, rather than arbitrary rules such as "have fins," "breathe through gills," and "live in water." Rosch pointed out that most natural concepts—such as *furniture, fish, bird,* and *game*—are not easily described as some well-defined combination of discrete attributes; nor are all instances of a natural concept equally good examples of their respective categories. For any given concept category, some examples are more typical and some less typical. Rosch suggests that we often structure our concepts around best instances, or most typical representatives of the category, which she calls **prototypes**. The more closely objects or events match our prototypes for a concept, the more readily we include them in the category.

Suppose, for example, you were asked, "Is a robin a bird?" and "Is a penguin a bird?" You would respond yes to both questions, but you would probably be slower to respond to the second question. The reason is that robin is more typical of the concept of bird than is penguin. (It may, in fact, be the prototype around which you have organized your concept of bird.)

Rosch demonstrated this in an experiment in which she asked people to rank different instances of a given category according to the degree to which the instance typified the concept. For example, when subjects were asked to rank various examples of the concept *furniture, chair* and *sofa* received the highest ranks (most prototypical), *lamp* and *stool* received intermediate ranking, and *fan* and *telephone* were ranked as least typical of the concept (see Table 10-1). These rankings correlated with reaction time, with the most typical examples producing the fastest responses and the least typical examples resulting in the slowest responses (Rosch, 1975).

Exemplar Theory Theory that the natural concepts we form in everyday life are structured around prototypes or typical representatives of categories (such as robins and jays as prototypes of the concept *bird*)

Prototype Best or most typical representative of a category around which we often structure our concept of that category

10.2 Problem Solving

Imagine that you and a friend have just hiked the last leg of a weeklong backpacking trip. You arrive at your parked car hot, thirsty, and anxious to return to civilization—but when you try to start your car, the motor does not turn over. You quickly diagnose the problem: a dead battery. A few other vehicles are parked at the trailhead, but nobody is around to provide help. The nearest town is ten miles away on an absolutely flat country road. You have to be home in six hours for an important engagement, and it is a three-hour drive to your home. You have a problem.

Table 10-1 Furniture Items Ranked by Goodness of Example

Member	Goodness of Example Rank	Member	Goodness of Example Rank	Member	Goodness of Example Rank
Chair	1.5	Vanity	21	Mirror	41
Sofa	1.5	Bookcase	22	Television	42
Couch	3.5	Lounge	23	Bar	43
Table	3.5	Chaise lounge	24	Shelf	44
Easy chair	5	Ottoman	25	Rug	45
Dresser	6.5	Footstool	26	Pillow	46
Rocking chair	6.5	Cabinet	27	Wastebasket	47
Coffee table	8	China closet	28	Radio	48
Rocker	9	Bench	29	Sewing machine	49
Love seat	10	Buffet	30	Stove	50
Chest of drawers	11	Lamp	31	Counter	51
Desk	12	Stool	32	Clock	52
Bed	13	Hassock	33	Drapes	53
Bureau	14	Drawers	34	Refrigerator	54
Davenport	15.5	Piano	35	Picture	55
End table	15.5	Cushion	36	Closet	56
Divan	17	Magazine rack	37	Vase	57
Night table	18	Hi-fi	38	Ashtray	58
Chest	19	Cupboard	39	Fan	59
Cedar chest	20	Stereo	40	Telephone	60

Data from: "Furniture Items Ranked by Goodness of Example" from "Cognitive Representation of Semantic Categories," *Journal of Experimental Psychology*: General, Volume 104(3), © 1975, pages 192–253 by E. Rosch.

A problem exists when there is a discrepancy between your present status and some goal you wish to obtain, with no obvious way to bridge the gap. The essence of a problem is that you must figure out what can be done to resolve a predicament and to achieve some goal. In this example, your goal is to start your car so that you can get home on time, but the dead battery is preventing you from reaching that goal.

Problem solving is different from simply executing a well-learned response or series of behaviors, as a rat might do when it negotiates a maze to reach a food reward. It is also distinct from learning new information. For instance, you would not be problem solving if some hikers fortuitously returned to their car and told you they could take you to the nearest service station. The essence of all problems is that they require you to supply new knowledge or skills that allow you to achieve your goal.

Problems consist of three components: (1) the *original state* of the situation as it exists at the moment, as perceived by the individual; (2) the *goal state,* which is what the problem solver would like the situation to be; and (3) the *rules* or *restrictions* that govern the possible strategies for moving from the original state to the goal state. To return to the dead battery problem, your perception of the original state might be, "My car won't start because of a dead battery, and I am ten miles from the nearest garage." Your goal would be, "I want to be home in six hours." The rules or restrictions might include: "Walking to the nearest town is unacceptable because it would take too long" and "There are three other cars at the trail head but no people to provide help."

How would you go about solving such a problem? To treat this topic fairly, we have to admit there may be no ideal solution. Instead, there are a number of possibilities, ranging from hitchhiking to borrowing a battery from one of the parked cars so that you can drive your own battery to a service station for recharging. Each of these strategies, however, has its own risks. The solution to this problem (and other problems we discuss later) is not really the issue here. Instead, our concern is the way we approach problems—the strategies that can make problem solving easier and the potential stumbling blocks that get in the way of problem solving.

(Shutterstock)

Problem solving is different from simply executing a well-learned response or series of behaviors. The essence of all problems is that they require you to supply new knowledge or skills that allow you to achieve your goal.

10.2a Stages of Problem Solving

Problem-solving behavior generally involves three logical steps or stages: representing or defining the problem, generating possible solutions, and evaluating how well a given solution works.

Representing the Problem

Logically, the first step in problem solving is to determine what the problem is and to conceptualize it in familiar terms that will help us better understand and solve it. Consider the following problem:

> Two train stations are 50 miles apart. At 2:00 P.M. one Saturday afternoon, two trains start toward each other, one from each station. Just as the trains pull out of the stations, a bird springs into the air in front of the first train and flies ahead to the front of the second train. When the bird reaches the second train it turns back and flies toward the first train. The bird continues to do this until the trains meet. If both trains travel at the rate of 25 miles per hour and the bird flies at 100 miles per hour, how many miles will the bird have flown before the two trains meet?

The manner in which you represent this problem will significantly influence the ease with which you can generate solutions. Some problems can be represented visually. Thus, you might be tempted to draw a diagram showing the paths of the two trains and the zigzagging path of the bird as it goes back and forth between them. Unfortunately, this strategy will probably serve to complicate this problem rather than make it easier to solve.

A much more logical approach is to represent the problem mathematically. You know that the bird flies at 100 miles per hour and that it will keep flying until the trains

Figure 10-2 Connect the Dots Problem

Connect all nine dots using only four straight lines.

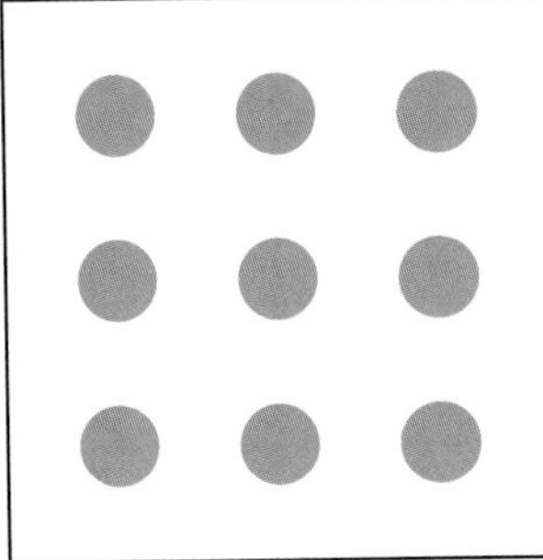

meet. All you have to do is figure out how long it will take the trains to meet and translate this figure into the bird's flying rate. Since the stations are 50 miles apart, and since each train travels at 25 miles per hour, they will meet at the halfway point between the stations in exactly one hour. Thus, the bird will have to fly for one hour, and since it flies at a rate of 100 miles per hour, it will fly exactly 100 miles.

Our understanding of a problem is influenced not only by how we represent it but also by how the problem is presented to us. Consider the problem illustrated in Figures 10-2 and 10-3. Your task is to connect all nine dots using no more than four straight-line segments. At first this seems impossible because we make the assumption that the lines cannot leave the square of the box. This assumption, or the failure to see novel strategies to problems, is referred to as **functional fixedness**.

Generating Possible Solutions

Once we have a clear idea of what the problem is, the next step is to generate possible solutions. Sometimes these solutions are easy. For example, if you sit down to begin studying and discover that your notes are missing, you might only need to search your long-term memory: Ah, yes, I remember lending the notes to my roommate, who missed yesterday's lecture. Assuming your roommate is nearby, your problem is solved. Other more complicated problems may require you to generate more complex strategies. Consider the following problem:

> Find a number such that if 3 more than 4 times the number is divided by 3, the result is the same as 5 less than 2 times the number.

One approach to this problem is to use a trial-and-error strategy, testing different numbers at random. However, this method is highly inefficient. A person who understands algebra might elect to apply an algebraic strategy. This procedure would lead to the formula $(3 + 4x)/3 = 2x - 5$. Solving for x yields the correct answer, 9. This example illustrates once again how representing a problem makes all the difference in the ease with which we can solve it. Subjects who represent the problem as a mathematical formula are able to solve it more readily than those who represent it as a word problem.

Functional Fixedness A failure to use familiar objects or strategies in novel or unfamiliar settings to solve problems

Figure 10-3 Solution to the Connect the Dots Problem

Functional fixedness may have prevented you from going outside the box boundary.

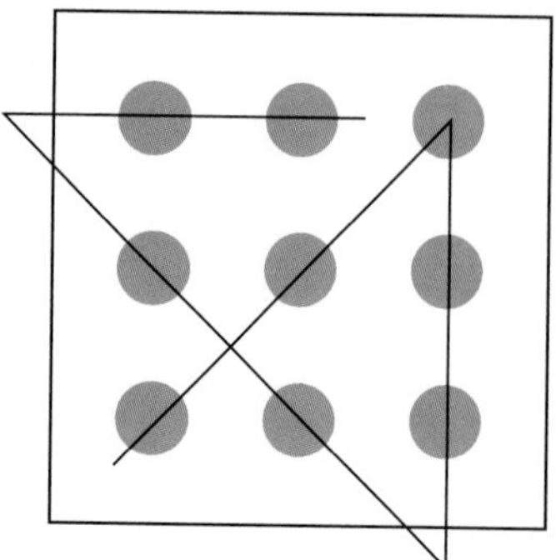

Evaluating the Solution

The final stage in problem solving is to evaluate your solution. In some cases, this is a simple matter. For example, solving for *x* in the previous problem and then plugging the obtained value into the original formula would quickly reveal whether or not the solution was correct. That is because the problem is clear-cut, with only one possible solution.

With some other types of problems, the solution may be much more difficult to evaluate. For example, college students often have trouble evaluating their answers to the problem, "What should I major in?" The reason for this difficulty has to do with the vague nature of the problem itself. Many students have not yet defined what their goals are and have only a hazy notion of their options. As a result, many students are not certain that they have made the best choice, even after they have selected a major. Problems that are unclear or poorly defined are almost always difficult to evaluate.

10.2b Strategies for Problem Solving

Whether a problem is clear-cut or vague, the way we approach it makes a critical difference in our ability to find a workable solution. A number of different strategies can be applied. We consider four common approaches: trial and error, testing hypotheses, algorithms, and heuristics.

Trial and Error

Some problems have such a narrow range of possible solutions that we decide to solve them through **trial and error**. For example, suppose you return to campus late Sunday after a weekend trip, and an acquaintance in your dorm tells you that you had a call from a woman who sounded distraught, insisting that you call immediately upon your return. Unfortunately, your dorm mate cannot find the slip of paper with her name and phone number, and has forgotten her name. The list of women who call you is somewhat limited, so you decide to call them one by one until you find out which one left the message. This trial-and-error process is not a bad strategy for solving the problem of the mystery caller, since the likely solutions are probably few in number.

Trial and Error Problem-solving strategy that involves trying possible solutions, one by one, to see which is correct

Testing Hypotheses

A somewhat more systematic approach to problem solving is provided by the strategy of **testing hypotheses**. Assume that the list of possible women callers is rather lengthy (you are a very social person) and that calling each one on a trial-and-error basis would be too time consuming. Instead, you may formulate specific hypotheses that generate a more efficient approach to solving your problem. For example, it sounds to you as though the person who called is going through a difficult emotional time. Based on this information, you may narrow your choices to those friends whom you know to have recently been distressed or agitated. Thus, your first calls would be to a friend whose father has been ill and another whose romance has been on shaky ground lately.

Algorithms

A third possible problem-solving strategy is the algorithm. **Algorithms** involve a systematic exploration of every possible solution until the correct one is found. This strategy originated in the field of mathematics, where its application can produce guaranteed solutions. Algorithms are especially well suited to computers, which can rapidly sort through hundreds, thousands, even millions of possible solutions without growing tired or suffering from boredom (both shortcomings of the human data processor).

Algorithms guarantee a correct solution if you are aware of all the possibilities—but in real life, that is a big "if." For instance, you could not apply an algorithm in solving the problem of the unknown caller, since the caller might have been someone you have never met or it might be a voice from the distant past that you would never think to include in your list of possibilities. In addition, people try to find shortcuts when faced with complicated problems, and often algorithms simply require too much effort. One type of short-cut strategy we commonly use is called a *heuristic*.

Testing Hypotheses Problem-solving strategy that involves formulating specific hypotheses that generate relatively efficient approaches to solving a problem and then testing the hypotheses in a systematic fashion

Algorithm A step-by-step problem-solving procedure often used in a systematic exploration of every possible solution (usually requiring the use of computers)

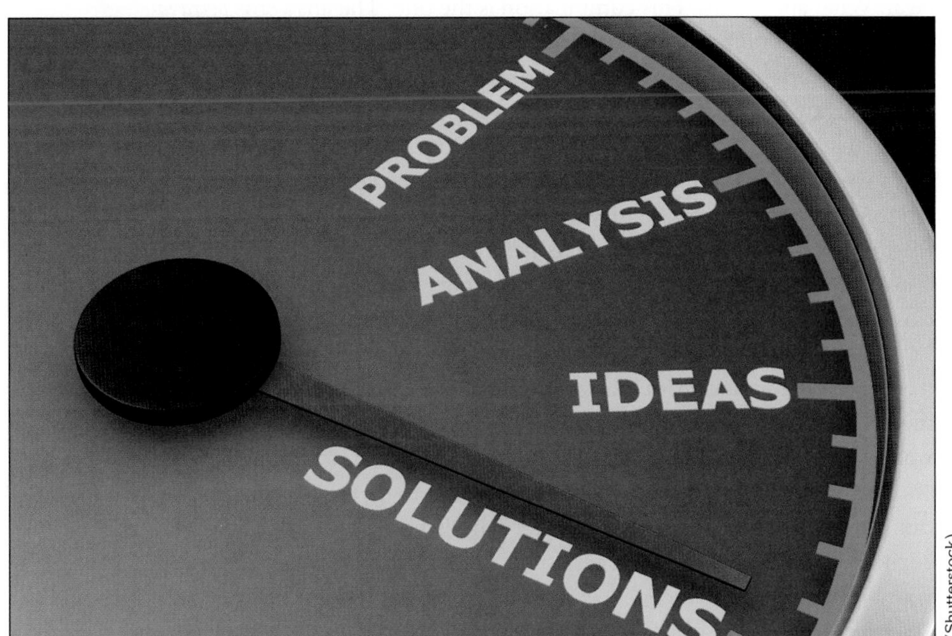

(Shutterstock)

The final stage in problem solving is to evaluate your solution. However, some types of problems, such as which major to pursue, are vague in nature and may be difficult to evaluate.

Heuristics

Heuristics refer to a variety of strategies or sets of empirical rules that may lead to solutions to problems. We all have a repertoire of "rule of thumb" methods for approaching problems, based on both experiences with strategies that have worked in the past and our own personal knowledge that can be applied to specific problems.

For example, in a game of chess there are an extremely large number of possible moves during the game. An algorithmic search that examines all alternatives at each point in the game would inevitably lead to a conclusion (win, lose, or draw). However, even the most sophisticated computer would find this strategy implausible. Alternatively, both humans and chess-playing computers use heuristic search methods. These heuristic strategies might include the following: Attack the opponent's queen, control the center of the board, or exchange pieces on the basis of position advantage. These heuristic strategies greatly reduce the number of alternative moves at any point in the game. Modern chess-playing software—for example, Houdini (Houdini, n.d.)—uses heuristics that were developed to utilize some of the same strategies that expert chess players use.

We use several kinds of heuristic strategies. One of the most common, **means-ends analysis**, involves first identifying the difference between the original state and the desired goal state, and then choosing a set of operations that will reduce this difference by progressing through a series of subgoals that systematically move you closer to the final solution. For instance, you would probably use means-ends analysis to solve the anagram *teralbay*, rather than using the algorithmic strategy to combine and recombine its eight letters 40,320 times.

To use means-ends analysis, you might begin by defining some subgoals that would help you move to a solution. Perhaps your accumulated knowledge about the English language would first prompt you to focus on certain common letter combinations (such as *ra, be, bay, able,* and *tray*) from the eight-letter anagram, and to exclude combinations that rarely or never occur (such as *aa, lbya, yblt, rtbl*). With these subgoals accomplished, you could then manipulate common letter combinations to seek a final solution. Do words with the combination *bay* in them work? No such luck. How about *able*? Again, no cigar. What about *tray*? This combination is the one: The answer is *betrayal*.

Another common heuristic strategy is **working backward** from a clearly defined goal to the original state. For example, suppose you decide to stay on campus over the Thanksgiving holiday to study for a major biology exam scheduled for the following week. On Thanksgiving Day, you discover that both your textbook and lecture notes are missing. After searching your memory, you remember leaving them in the biology laboratory, which is locked up for the holidays. You also recall that your lab partner is a good friend of the young man who is performing custodial duties in the science building. This young man is taking some time off from school to earn money to continue his education, and he lives close to campus. If you can find him, he can probably help you gain access to your books.

You have now defined your goal as getting into the biology lab. The best way to reach it is to work backward from that goal. The final step that will lead to this goal is phoning the janitor and asking if he would kindly take a few minutes to drive to campus and let you into the laboratory. What has to be done before this step? You must get the janitor's phone number from the telephone directory, but to do this you must have his name. You can get his name from your lab partner who is home for the holidays. Thus, you must begin by calling your lab partner at home. You now have a reasonable strategy for solving your problem.

Most of us are reasonably successful at solving the kinds of problems we encounter in our everyday lives. However, a number of relatively common situations can create obstacles to effective problem solving. Some of these obstacles have to do with the problem itself; others are the result of the way we approach the problem.

Heuristics Rule-of-thumb (quick-fix) problem-solving strategies such as means-ends analysis and working backward

Means-Ends Analysis Common heuristic problem-solving strategy that involves identifying the difference between an original state and a desired goal and then progressing through a series of subgoals to reach the solution

Working Backward Common heuristic problem-solving strategy that starts with describing the goal, then defines the step that directly precedes that goal, and works backward in this manner until the steps needed to reach the goal are defined

10.2c Characteristics of Difficult Problems

Problems come in many forms and vary greatly in difficulty. Two characteristics that can make a problem difficult to solve are lack of definition and complexity. We next examine each of these issues in turn.

Defining Problems

According to cognitive psychologists, problems exist on a continuum ranging from well defined to ill defined. *Well-defined problems* are those in which the original state and goal state are clearly specified, as are the rules for allowable problem-solving operations. Assembling a lawn mower from parts that arrive in a crate, putting together pieces of a jigsaw puzzle, and solving a mathematical problem are all examples of well-defined problems.

(Shutterstock)

In a game of chess, there are an extremely large number of possible moves. Heuristic strategies greatly reduce the number of alternative moves at any point in the game.

As we have already seen in our discussion of evaluating solutions, *ill-defined problems* are often more difficult. With these problems, we usually have a poor conception of our original state and only a vague notion of where we are going and how we can get there; we also have no obvious way of judging whether a solution we might select is correct. For example, it is not uncommon to reach the goal of graduating from college only to face a new problem of vast dimensions: what to do with the rest of our lives? Before we can work effectively toward solving such problems, we need to define our goals more clearly and have a better idea of what means are available to us.

Complex Problems

Try to solve the following two problems:

> Orcs are monsters that eat small humanlike creatures called hobbits (characters from Tolkien's *Lord of the Rings*). Three orcs and three hobbits are stranded on one side of a river. They have a small boat that holds a maximum of two creatures. The problem is to transport all six safely to the other side. If at any time orcs outnumber hobbits (on either side of the river), the orcs will dine on the outnumbered hobbit(s). How can all six get across in one piece?
>
> A man and his two sons want to use an available boat to get across a river. The boat has a maximum capacity of 200 pounds. The father weighs 200 pounds, and each son tips the scales at 100 pounds. How can all three safely cross the river?

The solutions to these problems are provided in Figure 10-4. If you were able to solve one of these problems successfully, you probably found it relatively easy to solve the other, since both require the same kind of strategy. However, observations of people who work on only one or the other of these problems, but not both, generally reveal that the "man and his sons" version is solved more quickly than the "orcs and hobbits" version. The reason for this difference is related to the number of steps required to solve each version. The father and his sons get across the river in only five steps, compared to eleven steps to get all of the orcs and hobbits across. In sum, complex problems with numerous steps are generally more difficult to solve than problems whose solutions involve fewer steps.

Cognitive Influences on Problem Solving

Mental Set In problem solving, a tendency to approach a problem or situation in a predetermined way, regardless of the requirement of the specific problem

Confirmation Bias In problem solving, the tendency to seek out evidence that confirms a hypothesis and to overlook contradictory evidence

Although complex and ill-defined problems tend to be inherently difficult, sometimes we have only ourselves to blame for the trouble we have solving problems. Three common obstacles that we often create for ourselves are mental set, functional fixedness, and confirmation bias.

Mental Set

Suppose you have three containers that have a maximum capacity of 21 ounces, 127 ounces, and 3 ounces, respectively, and a tap from which you can draw water. Your task is to use these three containers to obtain exactly 100 ounces of water. Attempt to solve this problem, as well as the other problems listed in Table 10-2.

How well did you do on these problems? Did you overlook a simpler solution on the sixth water container problem and perhaps get temporarily stymied on the seventh problem? If you answered "yes," you have just experienced firsthand how a mental set can inhibit or block effective problem solving. A **mental set** is a tendency to approach a problem in a set or predetermined way regardless of the requirements of the specific problem. When we operate under the influence of a mental set, we apply strategies that have previously helped us to solve similar problems, instead of taking the time to analyze the current problem carefully.

Mental sets often facilitate problem solving, but they can also get in the way. Consider how most people perform on the water container problems in the table. The chances are good that you figured out that the way to obtain 100 ounces is to fill the *B* container with 127 ounces and pour 21 ounces into the *A* container, and then fill *C* with 3 ounces twice. Once you solved this problem, you probably applied the same strategy (mathematically represented by the formula $B - A - 2C$) to the next several problems. Thus, this mental set helped you to solve these problems readily. But what about item six? If you are like most people, you probably applied the same formula to this problem as well. It worked, but problem six can also be solved by a simpler and more efficient method, expressed by the formula $A - C$.

It is interesting to note that when these problems are presented to students in a classroom demonstration, many dash along to item seven, at which point they often get stuck and sometimes even declare that it cannot be solved. Even though they are never told to solve all problems in the same way, the $B - A - 2C$ strategy has worked so well that the resulting strong mental set keeps them from considering another approach.

Mental sets can also impair even an expert's ability to solve problems. This is particularly true when considering alternative solutions requires broadening the search beyond their expertise (Wiley, 1998). This is similar to the adage "thinking outside the box."

Confirmation Bias

Another relatively common obstacle to problem solving is our inclination to seek out evidence that will confirm our hypothesis, while at the same time overlooking contradictory evidence. This phenomenon, known as **confirmation bias**, was demonstrated in investigations conducted by British researcher Peter Wason (1960). Wason asked his subjects to discover what rule applied to a three-number series. Initially the subjects were provided with one example of a positive instance of the rule to be discovered, such as 2, 4, 6. They were then told to propose additional series to the experimenter, who would indicate whether each did or did not conform to the rule.

Many of Wason's subjects tackled the problem we have just described by hypothesizing a specific rule, such as numbers increasing by two. They then proposed additional series, such as 4, 6, 8; 10, 12, 14; or 1, 3, 5, to verify their hypothesis. Wason responded that each of these series conformed to the rule. On this basis, many of Wason's subjects concluded that their hypothesis was correct, and they were visibly frustrated when told

Figure 10-4 Solutions to River-Crossing Problems

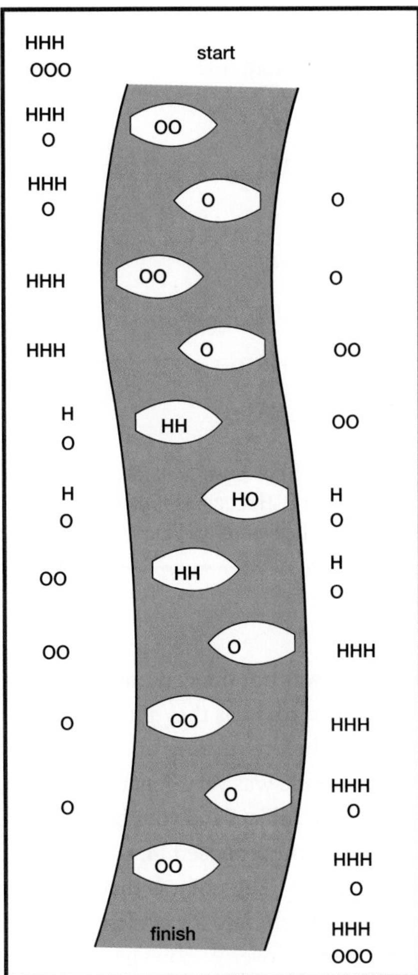

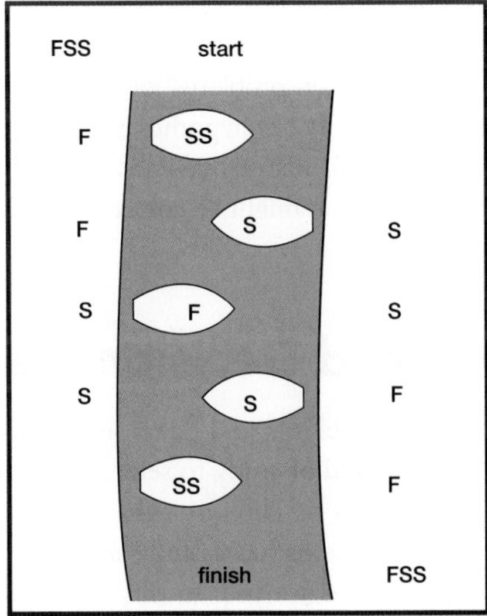

Data from: "Solutions to River Crossing Problems" from *Cognitive Psychology,* Volume 6, © 1974, pp. 270–292 by J. Grenno and J. C. Thomas.

Table 10-2 Water Container Problems

Problem No.	Container A	Container B	Container C	Obtain Exactly These Amounts of Water
1	21	127	3	100
2	14	163	25	99
3	18	43	10	5
4	9	42	6	21
5	20	59	4	31
6	23	49	3	20
7	10	36	7	3

Data from: "Water Containing Problems" from *Rigidity of Behavior: A Variational Approach to the Effect of Einstellung* by A. S. Luchins and E. H. Luchins. Copyright © 1959 by A. S. Luchins and E. H. Luchins. Available at https://en.wikipedia.org/wiki/Einstellung_effect.

that "numbers increasing by two" was not the general rule the experimenter had in mind. Can you figure out what they failed to do as they put their hypothesis to the test? Take a moment to consider this question before reading on.

The fact is, Wason's unknown rule was very general—"numbers in increasing order of magnitude." Thus, if you had been a subject and your initial hypothesis had been "numbers increasing by two," any series that you proposed (4, 6, 8; 10, 12, 14; or 1, 3, 5) would also have conformed to the unknown rule. The point is that you would never be able to solve this problem if you continued to search only for evidence that would confirm your initial hypothesis. The only way you could discover Wason's general rule would be to seek evidence that would *disprove* your hypothesis. For instance, you might have proposed 4, 6, 7 to disconfirm your "increasing by two" hypothesis. Discovering that this series also conformed to the rule would allow you to shift your thinking and quickly discover the correct solution.

People often have trouble with such problems for a simple reason: We are naturally more inclined to find instances that verify our hypotheses than those that disprove our theories. It is wise to keep in mind this confirmation bias and to remember that finding solutions may require us to look not only for what might be correct but also for what is incorrect.

10.3 Reasoning and Decision Making

Life constantly presents us with problems and decisions: How to get to class on time when the car does not start, what field of study to select as a major, what political candidate to support, how to get an A in psychology, what to do about an uncomfortable relationship. Our ability to solve problems successfully and make good decisions is greatly influenced by the reasoning processes we use. In this section we consider the ways in which people reason when they make a decision. We also examine some of the common thinking errors that can cloud our reasoning process. We end the section by examining certain aspects of decision making.

10.3a Logical Reasoning for Decisions

We often attribute a poor decision or failure to solve a problem to faulty reasoning, implying that there are normative standards for proper or correct reasoning. Such standards are available; in fact, they emerged ages ago from the discipline of formal logic, a branch of philosophy.

You may have already been exposed to the basic tenets of logic in your prior studies. If so, you know that there are two basic types of reasoning: inductive and deductive.

In **inductive reasoning**, we reach a general conclusion by generalizing from specific instances. For example, suppose that every male acquaintance expresses an interest in watching TV broadcasts of football games. This information might lead us to conclude that men in general enjoy this activity. With inductive reasoning, however, we can never be absolutely certain that we have reached a correct conclusion, because someday we might meet a man who hates watching TV football. As a result, our generalization about males is proven wrong.

When we engage in **deductive reasoning**, we begin with certain general assumptions or premises that we believe to be true, and we use these assumptions as the basis for drawing conclusions that apply to specific instances. For example, given the premise, or assumption, that all birds have feathers, we can conclude that if a specific animal is a bird, it will have feathers. As long as we begin with valid assumptions and follow certain rules of logic, we can be confident that our deductions are valid. On the other hand, if our premise is wrong, we can make faulty conclusions even though we follow the rules of deduction. For instance, if we assume that all birds fly, we might incorrectly conclude that a penguin is not a bird.

In real life, most of us tend to use both deductive and inductive reasoning. However, the discipline of formal logic has placed its emphasis primarily on deductive reasoning, providing a set of rules and systematic methods for reaching valid conclusions. A classical model for studying deductive reasoning is provided by the syllogism.

Inductive Reasoning Reasoning that draws broad conclusions by generalizing from specific instances

Deductive Reasoning Reasoning that begins with a general premise that is believed to be true, then draws conclusions about specific instances based on this premise

Syllogism Argument consisting of two or more premises, followed by a statement of conclusion that may or may not follow logically from the premises

(iStock)

When using deductive reasoning, it is important to begin with valid assumptions and to follow certain rules of logic in order to ensure that the deductions are valid.

Syllogisms

A **syllogism** is an argument consisting of two (or more) presumably true statements, called *premises,* and a statement of conclusion that may or may not follow logically from the premises. Once the form of a syllogism is established, a person is not asked to decide if the conclusion is factually true but, rather, is asked to decide whether the conclusion is valid. Consider the following examples:

All men are humans.

All humans are animals.

Therefore, all men are animals.

All women are child abusers.

All child abusers are highly intelligent.

Therefore, all women are highly intelligent.

The conclusion in the first example follows logically from the two premises; therefore, it is valid. Very few people have a problem with this kind of argument since its statements seem reasonable and consistent with our collective knowledge of the world. In contrast, the bizarre statements in the second example may have caused you to question the validity of the conclusion. If you rejected the second argument after accepting the first, however, you were not consistent in applying the principles of formal logic to your reasoning process.

As our example illustrates, the content of verbally expressed arguments can misdirect our reasoning processes and lead to faulty conclusions. Thus, logicians prefer to express syllogisms in a more abstract way by substituting letters for real words. If we abstract the previous two examples of syllogisms in this fashion, we see that both follow the same form.

All A's are B's.

All B's are C's.

Therefore, all A's are C's.

To apply the principles of formal syllogistic reasoning correctly, we must meet the following three requirements: (1) Each premise must be considered in terms of all its possible meanings. (Most premise statements are ambiguous in that they may refer to more than one possible relationship. (2) All of the varied meanings of the premises must be combined in every conceivable way. (3) A conclusion may be judged to be valid only if it applies to every conceivable combination of all possible meanings of the premises. If we can come up with at least one combination of the premise meanings that is inconsistent with the conclusion, we may judge the syllogism to be erroneous. Figure 10-5 illustrates how these principles may be applied to syllogisms.

10.3b Some Common Causes of Reasoning Errors

If we were able to apply the rules of formal logic consistently and systematically to our reasoning, we would often be successful in solving problems and making decisions. However, even students of logic probably find it difficult to apply these principles with total accuracy to every reasoning problem that occurs in everyday life. We often err because we are too quick to accept faulty premises or because our attitudes or experiences interfere with our ability to think logically.

Faulty Premises

Consider the following syllogisms:

The job applicant comes from a broken home.

People from broken homes are social misfits.

Therefore, the job applicant is a social misfit.

All women experience mood swings.

People with mood swings are not corporate presidents.

Therefore, women are not corporate presidents.

Figure 10-5 Logical Analysis of a Syllogism

Basic Form: All A's are B's.
All B's are C's.
Therefore, all A's are C's.

Note: The fact that all A's are B's does not necessarily mean that all B's are A's.

Premise	Diagram of the Possible Meanings	
All A's are B's.		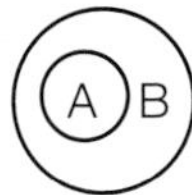
All B's are C's.	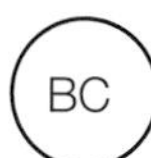	

Possible Combinations

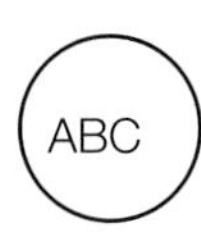

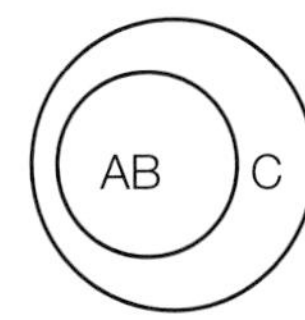

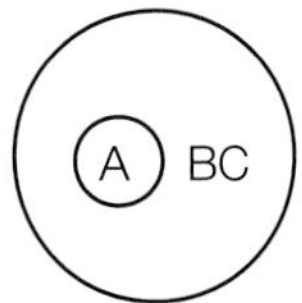

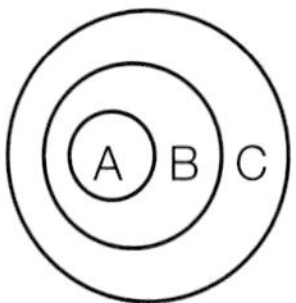

Conclusion: **The conclusion, "All A's are C's" is valid because it applies to every one of the possible premise combinations.**

In both of these examples, the conclusions are false even though the actual syllogisms are logically valid. The problem is that both arguments are based on faulty premises, since many people from broken homes are not social misfits, and not all women experience mood swings (in addition, some corporate presidents surely do experience mood swings). Unfortunately, we are often inclined to make bad judgments, not because we reason incorrectly, but rather because our initial assumptions or premises are false.

Belief-Bias Effect

Another possible source of trouble is the tendency to rely on cherished beliefs rather than logical analysis. This **belief-bias effect** may be stated as follows: People tend to accept conclusions that conform to their beliefs and reject conclusions that do not conform, regardless of how logical these conclusions are (Matlin, 2008).

A research study demonstrates this phenomenon. Subjects were asked to evaluate several syllogisms and to decide whether or not the conclusions followed from the premises. The conclusions were sometimes logically valid and sometimes not; in addition, their believability (the key variable in the experiment) varied greatly. Some conclusions were quite believable (for example, "Some good ice skaters are not professional hockey players"), and others were unbelievable ("Some professional hockey players are not good

Belief-Bias Effect Tendency to accept conclusions that conform to one's beliefs (and reject conclusions that do not conform), regardless of how logical or illogical these conclusions are

Subjective Probability The estimate of the likelihood of an outcome (often quite different from a mathematical probability)

ice skaters"). The results indicated that many subjects succumbed to the belief-bias effect, accepting believable but invalid conclusions and rejecting unbelievable but valid conclusions. We often face conflict between principles of logic and what we believe about the world. This research suggests that too much reliance on preexisting beliefs can impair our ability to think logically and make valid judgments.

10.3c Subjective Probability and Reasoning for Decisions

We have considered a number of situations in which the rules of formal logic have allowed us to decide whether a conclusion follows from the given facts; assuming that we have correctly applied the principles of logic, our true or false decisions have been relatively straightforward thus far. However, our lives are shaped by many everyday decisions in which the facts as we know them do not dictate a single, logical conclusion. For example, you know of several approaches to losing weight, and you have to select one option on the basis of the evidence at your disposal. *Decision making* is a process that occurs whenever we are faced with an array of alternative choices, and we choose one option while rejecting others.

Many of our everyday decisions are based on our *estimates of probabilities*, or **subjective probabilities**, of uncertain outcomes. Whether you decide to ask someone for a date, buy a lottery ticket, or plan a weekend camping trip, all depend on estimates of probabilities of success. In some cases our estimates may be based on mathematical probabilities, but in most cases our estimates are based on past experience. For instance, if the weatherman predicted an 80 percent chance of rain for the weekend, you may decide not to go camping. In this case, your estimate of success was influenced by a mathematical probability of rain. Your decision to ask a person for a date, on the other hand, will more likely be influenced by your estimate of success based on past experience. There are several heuristics that appear to influence our subjective probabilities. In this section, we will examine two: representativeness and availability. In addition to these heuristics, we will see how the context in which a problem is formulated or framed influences our decision-making process.

Representativeness Heuristic

Consider the following description of a friend of one of the authors and decide in which of the following two occupations she is most likely to be involved: police officer or host of a local radio talk show oriented to solving relationship problems.

> She is petite, soft-spoken, and very gentle. She almost never displays any aggressive or hostile behavior, although she is moderately assertive. She likes to read about psychology and enjoys dealing with people on a personal and emotional level. She is sensitive to others' needs and always willing to listen to viewpoints that may not be her own.

If you were not expecting to be tripped up, you probably guessed that the mystery person earns her living in radio because the description is more representative of your preconceived notion of a person who solves personal problems than of a police officer. The **representative heuristic** strategy entails judging the likelihood of something by intuitively comparing it to our preconceived notion of a few characteristics that represent a given category to us.

Representative Heuristic Strategy for categorizing an object based on one's preconceived notion of characteristics that are typical of that category

Gambler's Fallacy An incorrect assumption that randomness must result in an increase (or decrease) in the probability of an event in repeated trials when the event has only rarely or never occurred, even though the probability of the event remains the same

For example, most people probably have a stereotype image of a police officer. You might associate characteristics such as "tough," "aggressive," and "nonemotional" with this job. The extent to which our mystery person fits these stereotypes indicates how representative she is of this category. Clearly, the fit is quite poor. On this basis alone, many people would be unlikely to guess that she is indeed a police officer. On the other hand, traits such as "sensitive," "good listener," "likes psychology," and "assertive but not aggressive" do match many people's image of someone who hosts a talk show that focuses on solving relationship problems.

What useful piece of information is likely to be overlooked in the occupation decision problem you just considered? Think about this question before reading on.

Do you think you might have made a different choice if we had suggested that you consider the relative proportion of police officers and talk show hosts in the general population? In the greater metropolitan area of Portland, Oregon, there are more than one hundred police officers for every talk show host. This information might have influenced you to decide that the woman is probably a police officer (as indeed she is). On the other hand, it might have had no influence at all on your decision.

In one study, college student subjects were presented with a series of brief personality profiles allegedly drawn at random from a sample of one hundred attorneys and engineers (Kahneman & Tversky, 1973). They were asked to assign each profile to one job category or the other. Before the task began, they were told the relative proportions of attorneys to engineers in the sample—a proportion that the researchers varied with different groups of subjects, so that it might be 70 to 30 in some trials and 30 to 70 in others. Although you might expect this information about proportions to influence their decisions, it had virtually no impact. If a description stated that a person was politically active, argumentative, and articulate, subjects were likely to assign the profile to the attorney category no matter what the ratio. In this case, the subjects overlooked the information about probabilities, basing their decisions instead on how well the profiles matched their own stereotyped ideas.

Another common example of representativeness in estimating outcomes is our tendency to expect randomness in a short run of outcomes. For instance, suppose you observed four heads in four successive tosses of a fair coin. If you had to bet $10 on the fifth coin toss, how would you bet, heads or tails? Many people would bet on tails because "it's about time for tails." In other words, tails seems more representative of the random process than heads even though the outcome on the fifth toss is completely independent of the previous four. This bias in estimation of outcomes is referred to as the **gambler's fallacy**. Do you think that the gambler's fallacy applies to repeated purchases of lottery tickets?

(Shutterstock)

Estimating outcomes is our tendency to expect randomness in a short run of outcomes. This bias in estimation of outcomes is referred to as the gambler's fallacy.

Availability Heuristic

Another factor that influences our estimates is the degree to which we can access information relevant to a decision from our memories. This idea, called the **availability heuristic**, is based on two assumptions: first, that the probability of an event is directly related to the frequency with which it has occurred in the past; second, that events occurring more frequently are usually easier to remember than less common events.

For example, our decision to serve hamburgers rather than calamari (squid) to a group of teenagers at a Sunday picnic is no doubt a wise choice based on past experiences with teenagers who enjoy hamburgers but dislike exotic seafood. Similarly, we decide to carry an umbrella on a gray, overcast day because we remember that clouds often bring rain.

On the other hand, the easiest events to remember are not always the most common ones. For example, after the September 11th attacks in New York and Washington, D.C., air travel decreased significantly, resulting in severe financial problems for several major airlines despite the fact that the chances of similar attacks happening are statistically minute. Considering the extensive media attention following the attacks, it is understandable that many people might decide not to fly. We are not suggesting that this decision would necessarily be irrational. It does, however, illustrate decision making that is influenced by available vivid images rather than by the logical evaluation of probabilities.

This idea was tested in several experiments conducted by Tversky and Kahneman. In one experiment subjects were asked questions like the following:

> Are there more words in the English language that start with the letter "k" or that have the letter "k" as their third letter?
>
> Which is the more likely cause of death in women—breast cancer or heart attack?

Think about your own answers to these questions before reading on.

In both cases subjects' answers to the questions were generally wrong. When asked about the letter "k," subjects reported that it occurred more frequently when starting a word, not in the third position. Actually the letter "k" occurs much more frequently in the third position, but it is much more difficult to identify these words. Likewise, far more women die from heart attacks than from breast cancer, but breast cancer has received more attention in the media than heart attacks. This attention makes it more available to memory, thus influencing our estimate of true probability.

In a similar experiment conducted by Kahneman & Tversky (1973), subjects were asked to read lists of thirty-nine names of well-known people. (The list had nineteen names of familiar men and twenty names of familiar women). On one list the names of the women were more famous than the men, and on the other list the men were more famous. In both cases, subjects overestimated the number of males or females on the lists depending on how famous the names were, even though their frequencies were nearly identical. Why did they do this? According to the researchers, the famous names were more available to memory and therefore influenced subjects' estimates of gender proportions.

Availability Heuristic
Approach to decision making based on information assessed from memory (assumes that the probability of an event is related to how frequently it occurred in the past and that events occurring more frequently are easier to remember)

Framing

An additional factor that can influence subjective probabilities is the way in which a particular problem is formulated or framed. *Framing* entails manipulating the reasoning process by increasing the representativeness or the availability of an outcome. As we have demonstrated, both representativeness and availability greatly influence our subjective estimates of probability. How can problems be formulated to influence our estimates? Consider the now classic problems proposed by Kahneman and Tversky (Tversky & Kahneman, 1981).

BVT Lab

Visit **www.BVTLab.com** to explore the student resources available for this chapter.

> Imagine that the United States is preparing for the outbreak of an unusual Asian disease, which is expected to kill six hundred people. Two alternative programs to combat the disease have been proposed. Assume that the exact scientific estimates of the consequences of the programs are as follows:
>
> - If Program *A* is adopted, 200 people will be saved.
> - If Program *B* is adopted, there is a one-third probability that 600 people will be saved and a two-thirds probability that no people will be saved.

Which program would you select if the decision were yours to make? If you were like most (about 72 percent) of Kahneman and Tversky's subjects, you selected Program *A*. Within this frame (where lives are saved or gained), subjects are typically biased toward a sure thing, even though statistically the outcomes are the same ($200/600 = 1/3$ of 600). When decision alternatives are framed in terms of gains, people are more likely to be risk averse. What if the programs were framed as follows?

- If Program *A* is adopted, 400 people will die.
- If Program *B* is adopted, there is a one-third probability that nobody will die and a two-thirds probability that 600 people will die.

In this case the majority (about 78 percent) of the subjects chose Program *B*, which is the risky choice, even though statistically they are again the same. When decision alternatives are framed in terms of losses, people are more likely to be risk prone.

Suppose that you were given the following decision alternatives framed in terms of gains:

A. You can choose to have $200 immediately

or

B. You can choose to have a 40 percent chance of winning $500.

Which of the above alternatives is most attractive? Now consider similar alternatives framed in terms of losses:

A. You can choose to give me $200 immediately

or

B. You can choose a 40 percent chance of giving me $500.

If you were like most people, you would select *A* when it is framed in terms of gains (risk averse in terms of gains) and *B* when framed in terms of losses (risk prone in terms of losses). Although most of the research presented here is concerned with hypothetical gains and losses, people and other animals appear to behave as Kahneman and Tversky describe even when the gains and losses are real (Rachlin, Logue, Gibbon, & Frankel, 1986). The author has even demonstrated these framing effects with psychology students "gaining" or "losing" extra credit points!

In the previous section, we saw how probability estimates affect our decisions. In some instances our probability estimates can be inaccurate, leading us to undesirable decision outcomes. Perhaps now that you are aware of the potential shortcomings of your decision processes you will be less likely to be influenced by faulty judgments. On the positive side, representativeness and availability can facilitate decision making and thus serve as heuristics in decision-making processes. In many cases, they lead to quick and accurate decisions that serve us well most of the time.

10.3d The Role of Emotion in Decision Making

Up to this point, we have considered decision making to be a nonemotional, calculated process. In fact, you may believe that you make your best decisions when you try to eliminate emotion from the process. Can you make decisions, however, without the subjective feeling of emotion? If we could detach your emotional brain, would your decisions be made more quickly and with better judgment? These are certainly intriguing questions and ones we may only get partial answers to, but we do have evidence from individuals who suffered damage to parts of their brain that represent the feelings of emotion. These individuals do express emotions, but they are not aware of them. In many respects, people with damage to their frontal lobes can appear quite normal. They may move about normally and have normal perceptions, but they often had profound impairments in their emotional lives. They seem insensitive to others, act inappropriately in social settings, and don't recognize emotions of their own. What makes normal life impossible, however, is their inability to make and follow plans or decisions. According to Antonio Damasio (1995, 2005), people with frontal lobe damage are impaired because they lack the ability to experience the emotional consequences of the decision-making process. Damasio argues that one function of emotion, and its corresponding feeling, is to attach a **somatic marker** to possible outcomes of decisions. Decisions void of feeling cannot be acted upon. Consider the important decision about whether to make a large financial investment. You may use several of the strategies above to try and anticipate the probability of making a profit, while at the same time a somatic marker is generated by contemplating the consequences of either making money or losing it. If the fear and anxiety about losing money outweigh the positive hedonic affect associated with the possibility of making money, you are not likely to invest. The adage "listen to your gut" when you make a decision describes listening to Damasio's somatic marker.

10.4 Language

Our last topic, the ability to use **language**, is perhaps the most profound indicator of the power of human cognition. We can define language as a system of symbols and rules that enable us to communicate (Harley, 2008). Although other animals, such as bees, birds, dolphins, monkeys, and apes, demonstrate complex means of communication, the degree of abstraction in human language is far greater. Without language, our ability to communicate our thoughts would be limited to the basic kinds of meanings that we could indicate by nonverbal gestures. We would not be able to establish complex

Somatic Marker An emotion and its corresponding feeling attached to possible outcomes of a decision process

Language A system of symbols and rules that enable us to communicate

social structures and pass on knowledge from generation to generation. Our ability to remember, to reason, and to solve problems would also be severely curtailed, since so much of human information processing and thinking occurs at the abstract level of language symbols.

Language is the primary means by which we communicate with one another. This is not to say that language and communication are the same thing. An animal on the prairie that emits a cry of warning as a predator approaches, or a bee signaling the direction of a food source, is communicating messages. However, it is the ability to use abstract symbols to convey original messages that lifts human language to its heights.

(Shutterstock)

For a young child, crying is a rudimentary form of communication.

10.4a Psycholinguistics

Psycholinguistics is the study of how we translate sounds and symbols into meaning, and of what processes are involved in the acquisition and use of language. Psycholinguists have devoted considerable effort to studying the structure and rules of language. We begin our discussion at this level.

The Structure and Rules of Language

The people we talk to each day are able to make sense out of what we say to them because we all string sounds together according to a common set of rules. There are actually four levels of rules—phonemes, morphemes, syntax, and semantics—and psycholinguists analyze languages at each of these four levels.

Phonemes The basic structural elements of spoken language are called **phonemes**. All languages are made up of individual sounds that are recognized as distinct or different. The English language has about thirty-five phonemes; other languages may have as few as fifteen or as many as eighty-five (Eysenck & Keane, 2010). Most of the phonemes in the English language correspond to consonant and vowel sounds. For example, in the word *tap* we may identify three separate phonemes, corresponding to the consonant sounds *t* and *p* and the vowel sound *a*. (The letter *a* represents four different vowel sounds, as in *tap, pray, care,* and *water.*) Letter combinations, such as the *th* sound in *the* and the *sh* in *shout*, represent some phonemes. In some cases different letters represent the same sounds, such as the *a* in *bay* and the *ei* in *sleigh*. Thus, phonemes are not identical to the letters of the alphabet, even though individual letters correspond to many of the sounds unique to our language. Phonemes can be combined in numerous ways to create literally thousands of different words.

In order to represent ideas in our thought processes or to convey meaningful information, we must combine phonemes in ways that produce acceptable words. For instance, you quickly recognize that *dzashp* and *heeoiay* are not acceptable sound combinations in English, even though they are pronounceable.

Psycholinguistics Psychological study of how sounds and symbols are translated to meaning and of the cognitive processes that are involved in the acquisition and use of language

Phonemes Individual sounds (such as those represented by *s* and *sh* in the English spelling system) that are the basic structural elements of language

Morphemes A **morpheme** is the smallest unit of meaning in a given language. In the English language almost all morphemes consist of combinations of two or more phonemes (exceptions are the pronoun *I* and the article *a*). Many morphemes, like *book, learn,* and *read,* are words that can stand alone. Other morphemes must be attached as prefixes or suffixes to root words. For example, the word *replays* is a word that consists of three morphemes: *play*, which can stand alone; the prefix *re*, meaning "again" or "anew"; and the suffix *s*, which indicates "more than one."

The manner in which morphemes are formed and used also follows distinct rules. In the English language, for example, no more than three consonant sounds can be strung together in one morpheme. Rules also govern the manner in which suffixes can be added to form plurals. Thus, the plural forms of *hat* and *bus* are *hats* and *buses*. Morphemes also have fixed positions in the structure of language: A football broadcaster who repeats a critical play for home viewers is presenting a *replay*, not a *playre*.

Syntax Along with learning how to recognize phonemes and use morphemes, we also learn to use **syntax** (commonly known as grammar), the set of language rules that governs how words can be combined to form meaningful phrases and sentences. The sentence, "She purchased the dog small," is immediately recognizable as an improper sentence because one of the rules of English syntax is that adjectives generally precede the nouns they modify ("small dog"). If a Spanish-speaking person read this same sentence, translated word for word into Spanish, he or she would consider it to be grammatically correct since adjectives normally come after nouns according to Spanish rules of syntax.

Semantics Finally, language is characterized by a system of rules that helps us determine the meaning of words and sentences. The study of meaning in language is called **semantics**. For example, sentences may be syntactically correct but semantically incorrect. The grammatically correct sentence, "The dorm food is emotionally disturbed," is quite bizarre from the standpoint of semantics, for food cannot be emotionally disturbed (although some dorm food can lead to disturbed emotions!).

10.4b Theories of Language Acquisition

How do we learn all of these rules? A number of theories have been proposed to explain how we acquire language. Those explanations vary considerably in their emphasis on environment versus innate biological mechanisms.

The Learning Perspective

At one end of the continuum are theories of language acquisition that emphasize the role of learning. According to behaviorist B. F. Skinner (1957) and social learning theorist Albert Bandura (1971), children learn to shape sounds into words and words into sentences through processes of selective reinforcement and imitation.

This learning perspective is supported by research evidence. For example, babies whose parents reinforce their early attempts at meaningful sounds do tend to vocalize more than institutionalized children who receive less attention (Brodbeck & Irwin, 1946). Small children often imitate the words they hear their parents say, and this behavior is often reinforced.

Morpheme Smallest unit of meaning in a given language

Syntax Set of language rules that govern how words can be combined to form meaningful phrases and sentences; grammar

Semantics The study of meaning in language

Parents play a very important role in shaping language acquisition in their children. Jean Berko Gleason (2000), a Boston University psychologist, is an authority on language development. Her primary research has been focus on how social interaction between children and adults (especially parents) shapes the acquisition of language. Gleason believes that social relationships may be necessary to activate the process of children learning to communicate through language and that social interactions provide children with important information about the functions of language (Ely, Gleason, MacGibbon, & Zaretsky, 2001). Viewed from this perspective, learning language is much like learning any other complex behavior (Moerk, 2000).

Learning cannot account for all aspects of language development, however. During early language acquisition, children begin to utter unique wordlike sounds that are not imitations of others. Rather, they appear to be their own creations. Between eighteen and twenty-four months of age, infants begin to put several words together in what is called **telegraphic speech**, which is described in a later section. Again, telegraphic speech is not mimicked or instructed; rather, it appears spontaneously in syntactically correct ways—for example, *all gone, sit here, more milk*. Parents would rarely hear these word combinations in the reverse order (*gone all, here sit, milk more*). These universal observations suggest that some aspects of language acquisition are innate or genetically programmed.

The Genetic Perspective

Just as children are genetically programmed to follow the developmental sequence of sitting, crawling, and walking, Noam Chomsky (1965, 1968, 2011) maintains that the human brain is also programmed to learn speech according to a sequential pattern. This view of language acquisition, sometimes referred to as nativism, does not suggest that our brains are programmed to learn a specific language such as English or French. Instead, it argues that a newborn's brain is organized with the ability to recognize phonemes and morphemes and to learn the basic rules of grammar and semantics. Chomsky labeled this innate ability to learn language the **language acquisition device (LAD)**. He believes that without this innate mechanism we would be overwhelmed by the virtually unlimited number of possible variations in combinations of sounds and words, and thus would be unable to understand the rules of language. The more modern term for the LAD is **universal grammar** (UG), which is still believed to be the genetic component of the language faculty (Chomsky, 2011).

How can we possibly understand this limitless number of creative sentences? For instance, how do we know that the meanings of the following sentences are the same: "The young boy chased the girl," and "The girl was chased by the young boy"? According to Chomsky, our capacity to understand that these sentences have the same meaning is explained, not by learning or imitation, but by an innate capacity to grasp the rules that allow us to form sentences and transform them into other sentences with the same meaning. These rules are referred to as *transformational grammar*. Our understanding of the meaning of these two sentences prevails even though the arrangement of the words or morphemes is altered. Chomsky argues that meaning is contained in the *deep structure,* or underlying form, of a sentence, not its surface structure. *Surface structure* refers to the superficial appearance of the sentence. In our example above, the surface structure of the sentences was altered but the deep structure remained the same. This genetic position has been supported by a variety of data, and "there is strong evidence that the process of learning human speech is largely guided by innate abilities and tendencies" (Gould & Marler, 1987).

Telegraphic Speech An early stage of language development where sentences consist of two words in grammatically correct order

Language Acquisition Device (LAD) According to the genetic or nativist view, the prewiring that gives humans the innate ability to learn and understand language (the more modern term for LAD is *universal grammar*)

Universal Grammar (UG) The genetic component of the language faculty—similar to *language acquisition device*

Interactionist Approach An approach to language acquisition that assumes that both genes and the environment interact during development

Most contemporary psychologists believe that both learning and genetics interact for human language. Learning appears to contribute more to our rich vocabularies than our genes do, but our genes appear to account more for the enormous complexity of language rules or structures, and certainly to the brain regions that have developed for language (Ganger, 2000; Harley, 2008). As we will see, this **interactionist approach** has been useful not only for the study of human language, but also for the studies of personality and intelligence.

10.4c Stages of Language Acquisition

Language acquisition is one of the most impressive human accomplishments. The average six-year-old knows well over ten thousand words and can produce complex sentences that resemble adult speech (Gleitman & Gillette, 1999). To accomplish this, children must learn about seven new words each day from the time they start speaking to age 6. If you have studied a foreign language, you may appreciate the significance of this feat, since most second-year language students know fewer than one thousand foreign words. Language acquisition, however, is not merely the learning of a large vocabulary. Children must also learn to combine words into meaningful phrases and sentences using a vast set of complex rules. The sections that follow will briefly describe several stages in the acquisition of early language.

Early Vocalizations

Cooing and Babbling Sometime between four and six weeks, infants enter a stage of vocalization, called *cooing*, in which they emit sounds of pleasure when they are happy. At about six months, sometimes earlier, there is another significant stage referred to as *babbling*. The baby begins to utter repeatedly a variety of simple one-syllable consonant and vowel sounds like da-da-da, ba-ba-ba, or ma-ma-ma. In the first few months of babbling, the infant emits both sounds that are used in the adult language and those that are not.

At about nine or ten months, the babbling becomes intelligible as babies begin to imitate more purposefully the sounds of the speech of others, even though they may not yet understand them. At this point in language development, these vocalizations begin to approximate the phonemes of the language they hear every day. Thus, cooing and babbling provide babies with a basic repertoire of sounds, laying the foundation for real speech.

First Words

Children usually produce their first one-word utterances sometime around their first birthday, and they have learned a vocabulary consisting of about twelve words. They have already learned that sounds can be associated with meanings, and now they begin to use sounds to convey meaning. First words are usually very simple, and they often refer to concrete things like familiar people (*mama, dada*), toys (*ball*), consumables (*juice*), common implements (*cup*), animals (*da* or *dog*), words for greeting (*hi*), and a few action words (*eat, up, more*). These words may be oversimplifications of the actual words, but they nevertheless qualify as words if they are used consistently to refer to particular objects or events (thus "ba" for *bottle* or "nana" for *banana*).

A child may also use single words in a way that indicates much more. For example, a toddler who tugs on your leg and pleads "up" is probably conveying the meaning, "Pick me up," just as a child who points to a balloon and says "ba" with a rising inflection at the end is asking, "Is that a ball?" These single-word utterances designed to express a complete thought are called *holophrases*.

Condensed Speech

At approximately twenty months of age, children develop a vocabulary of about 179 words; sometime between eighteen and twenty-four months, they generally produce their first sentences, which usually consist of two-word utterances like "More milk," or "There ball." These early primitive sentences, called telegraphic speech, typically leave out articles (such as *a* and *the*), prepositions (*to*, *on*), conjunctions (*and*), and auxiliary verbs (*can*, *will*). This pattern of condensed speech is simply a reduction of complex speech, and it is typical of the first sentences spoken by children all over the world. Young children also have similar meaning in their short utterances, no matter what culture they belong to.

Harvard's Roger Brown (1973) extensively reviewed data from a number of diverse cultures to determine what early meanings are expressed in children's two-word sentences. He concluded that most two-word sentences are designed to express any of eight common semantic, or meaning, relations (see Table 10-3).

Expanded Language

From age two, language development progresses rapidly. Children expand their vocabulary at the rate of several hundred words for every six months of age. Children seem to be remarkably adept at determining the meaning of new words they hear from the context in which the word was spoken (McCathren, 2001; Markman, 1987). Two-word sentences give way to meaningful sentences that may lack absolutely correct grammatical structure but, nevertheless, display a syntax that approximates proper language structure (Valian, 1986). Children begin to make a shift from simple sentence grammar to a more complex syntax sometime between ages two and three. By age four or five, most children have learned most of the basic grammatical rules for combining nouns, adjectives, and verbs into meaningful sentences.

As they learn to combine morphemes into more complex words and into still more complex sentences, a number of errors typically occur, regardless of the language. For instance, when children first learn the basic rules of grammar (such as that plurals are

Table 10-3 Common Semantic Relations in First Sentences

Description	Example
They name an actor and an action.	"Daddy eat"
They modify a noun.	"Bad Doggy"
They indicate possession.	"Mommy shoe"
They specify a location.	"Dog outside"
They describe an action and a location.	"Go home"
They name an action and an object (leaving out the subject).	"Eat lunch"
They describe an actor and an object (leaving out the verb).	"Mommy lunch"

Adapted from Gleason, J. Berko & Ratner, N. Bernstein. (1998) *Psycholinguistics*, 2nd edition. Cengage Learning. Adapted with permission of the authors.

Broca's Area Region of the left frontal lobe that is the primary brain center for controlling speech

Wernicke's Area Area of the left temporal lobe that is the brain's primary area for understanding speech

formed by adding an "s" and the past tense of many verbs is formed by adding a "d" sound to the end), they may tend to overgeneralize these rules to instances where they do not apply. Thus, *oxes* may be used instead of *oxen; deers,* instead of *deer*; and "I sleeped in the bed," instead of "I slept in the bed." Children may also overgeneralize by applying concept words too broadly. For instance, a child who learns to recognize police officers by their uniforms may call every person in uniform "police."

Another common error in the early stages of sentence usage is oversimplification—using just enough words to convey a message, without being syntactically correct. For example, when a three-year-old child wants to play in the park, she might say to her mother, "Go park." Later on, the child learns to add the articles, prepositions, and other parts of speech that are necessary to form grammatically correct sentences such as, "I want to go to the park." Most children are quite successful at mastering these refinements. By the time they enter elementary school, they usually have a good comprehension not only of the general rules of their language but also of the exceptions.

10.4d Brain Mechanisms for Language

In the preceding sections, we have surmised that language exists at two levels: at the level of abstract language symbols in the external world, and at a level within the brain where these abstract symbols and their rules of combination are represented. In this section, we will examine several of the major brain structures where language appears to be represented and processed.

Most of what we know about the role of the brain on language processing comes from patients who have suffered from brain injuries or strokes. Sometimes these lesions produce disturbances in the comprehension and formulation of speech, referred to as *aphasias*. Aphasias can also occur in nonvocal sign languages. As you recall from Chapter 3, we described two major language areas that are involved in speech: Broca's area and Wernicke's area (see Figure 10-6).

Broca's Area

Damage to **Broca's area**, a small part of the frontal lobe in the left cortex, results in the inability to speak fluently and is referred to as *Broca's aphasia*. If the damage is more severe and also includes parts of the thalamus and basal ganglia, a more severe long-lasting speech impairment results. This suggests that fluent speech involves all of these areas.

Another common characteristic of Broca's aphasia is the inability to organize words so sentences follow proper grammatical rules. In addition, patients underuse or fail to use conjunctions (*and, or, if*), prepositions (*to* and *from*) and auxiliary verbs (*will* and *did*). For instance, a patient might say, "Go I home tomorrow," instead of, "I will go home tomorrow" (Damasio, 1992).

Wernicke's Area

Damage to **Wernicke's area**, on the other hand, does not disrupt the ability to produce speech, but it does disrupt the ability to comprehend both verbal and written speech. Wernicke's area is located in the left temporal cortex below the Sylvian fissure (see Figure 10-6). In many cases people with *Wernicke's aphasia* speak fluently and articulately, but they have difficulty finding appropriate words and understanding speech. A typical sentence produced by an individual with Wernicke's aphasia when asked to name a common object like an apron might sound like this: "Um … you see I can't, I can I can barely do; he would give me sort of umm …." In this case, language is unintelligible because of inappropriate word choice. Often Wernicke's aphasia includes the inability to comprehend language from others.

Other researchers have identified language disorders that appear to be much more specific. For instance, patients referred to as A.N. and L.R. have difficulty with some concepts. When shown pictures of objects like body parts, vehicles, animals, plants, tools, or human faces, these patients recognize what they are looking at but have difficulty retrieving names for these entities. They can even define the object's function, habitat, or value. If shown a picture of a raccoon, they might say, "Oh! I know what it is—it is a nasty animal. It will come and rummage in your backyard and get into the garbage. The eyes and the rings in the tail give it away. I know it, but I cannot say the name" (A. Damasio & H. Damasio, 1992). A.N. and L.R.'s, symptoms, as well as those of other patients with similar problems with proper nouns, have been attributed to damage in the anterior and middle regions of the left temporal lobe (see Figure 10-6).

Figure 10-6 The Left Hemisphere of the Brain

This illustration identifies several important language areas of the brain.

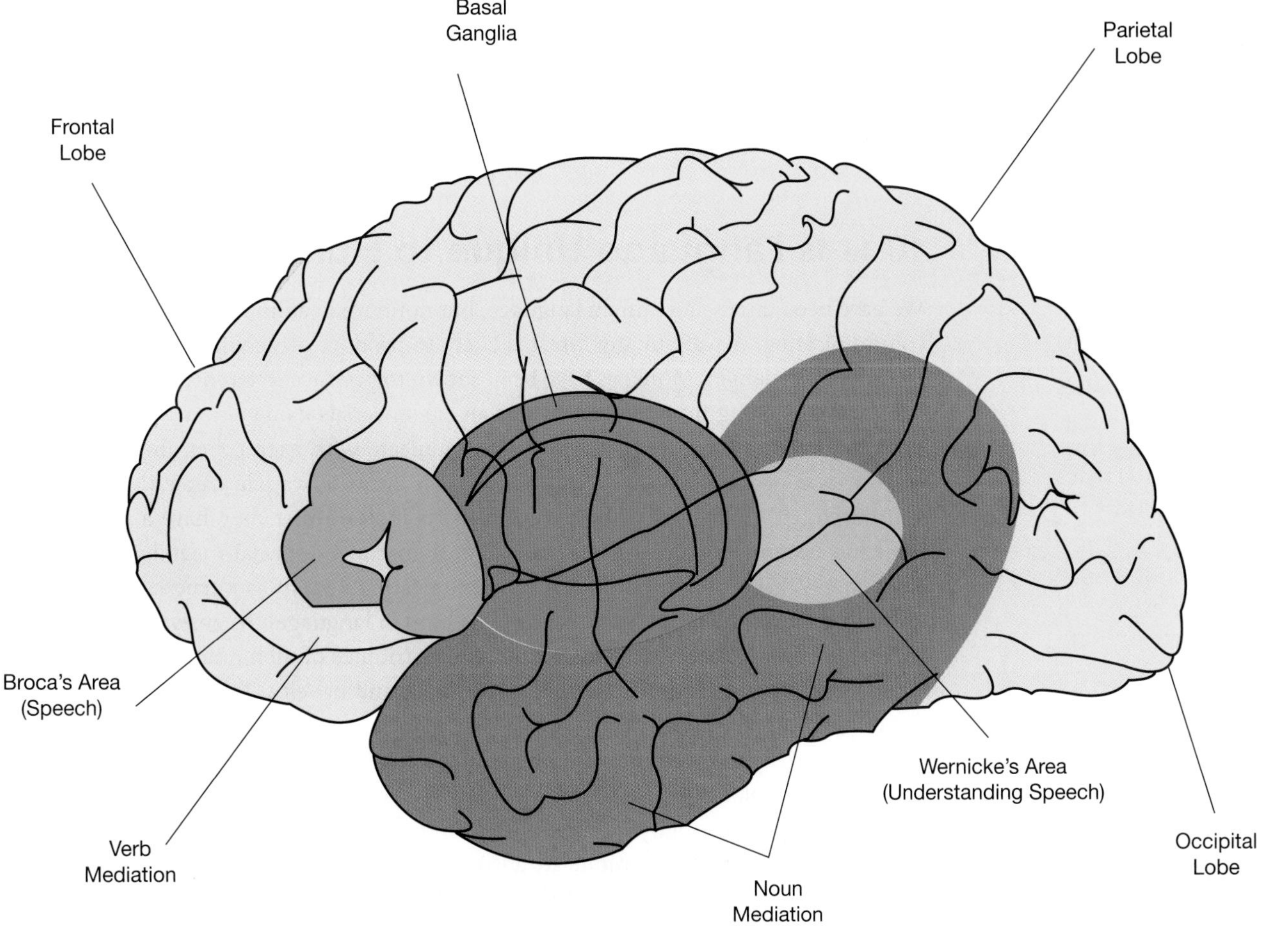

Although patients with temporal lobe damage often have difficulty using nouns to name people and other objects, they have little or no difficulty using verbs. Evidence from PET and fMRI studies (described in Chapter 3) and patients with brain damage suggest that verb use involves the left frontal lobe (Figure 10-6). People with left frontal lobe damage may have difficulty generating appropriate verbs. For instance, a patient may not be able to generate the verb *running* when shown a picture of a person running, even though they can say that they participated in the sport at school.

These studies suggest that the use and comprehension of language involve interconnections between areas within the left temporal lobe, the posterior frontal lobe, and the basal ganglia. Furthermore, different components of speech and grammar appear to be mediated by specific regions within the left hemisphere of the brain. For instance, the left prefrontal cortex is specifically involved in the syntactic processes of sentence comprehension, while Broca's area located in the inferior frontal gyrus is essential for the motor production of speech and the planning of speech articulation (Davis et al., 2008; Friederici, Rüschemeyer, Hahne, & Fiebach, 2003; Rogalsky, Matchin, & Hickok., 2008; Sakai, Homae, & Hashimoto, 2003).

In the past few years, tremendous progress has been made in understanding the brain mechanisms for language production and comprehension. However, much more research with both brain-damaged and normal people will be necessary before conclusions about how specific brain structures interact for language can be made.

We have briefly touched upon several important aspects of language processing, including its structure, its acquisition, and neural bases. However, a topic of such importance to human behavior deserves much more than we can provide in this context. The analysis of language at all levels continues to be both an active and a vital aspect of psychology and neuroscience. The final section of this chapter examines the topic of language in nonhuman animals. Do other animals possess language?

10.4e Is Language Unique to Humans?

We have been discussing human language, but nonhuman animals also have methods of communicating. A walk in any forest is likely to produce a cacophony of birdcalls that communicate danger. Monkeys have been shown to produce different sounds to indicate danger approaching from above, such as an eagle, versus danger from below, such as a prowling panther (Marler, 1967). Bees communicate with each other about the nature and location of food sources by engaging in an intricate waggle dance (Moffett, 1990; von Frisch, 1974). Studies with vervet monkeys indicate that they have a rudimentary semantic system in which specific calls appear to convey special meaning (Seyfarth & Cheney, 1992). Do these methods of communicating qualify as a true language in the sense that they contain the same features as human language? To answer this question, we first need to identify the primary criteria or attributes of all human languages: generativity, specialization, arbitrariness, displacement, and novelty. Table 10-4 defines these five criteria.

If we strictly interpret the criteria in the table, it is quite clear that birdcalls, monkey vocalizations, dolphin whistles, and bee dances do not qualify as language. This does not rule out the possibility, however, that nonhuman animals may have the ability to learn to use language to communicate abstract thoughts and ideas. Considerable research with apes, in fact, has challenged the view that only humans can communicate with abstract symbols.

Table 10-4 Attributes of Human Language

1. *Generativity:* The ability to provide for a huge variety of meanings in an unlimited number of utterances.
2. *Specialization:* The only purpose of the language is to communicate information to others.
3. *Arbitrariness:* The combination of sounds selected to refer to objects or events is purely arbitrary. Thus, our English *workbook* might just as well have been *zock.*
4. *Displacement:* Language can be generated in the absence of any eliciting stimulus. Thus humans can talk about dangerous dogs when no dogs are present, whereas a monkey vocalizes a sound indicating danger only when a predator is observed. Displacement also refers to the ability to communicate about things in the past and future, not just the present.
5. *Novelty:* Humans are able to express themselves with novel phrases and sentences that they have never heard before. Thus, human language is more than mere memorization and repetition of word strings.

Adapted from: "The Origin of Speech," by C. Hockett from *Scientific American* 1960, v. 203, pp. 89–96.

Some of the earliest language research attempted to teach chimpanzees to talk. These experiments were essentially failures, although one chimpanzee did learn to vocalize four words: *mama*, *papa*, *cup*, and *up* (Hayes, 1951; W. Kellogg & L. Kellogg, 1933). Later experiments used another strategy. Speculating that chimpanzees simply did not have the vocal apparatus to communicate verbally, Allen and Beatrice Gardner (1969, 1975) took another route; they taught American Sign Language (ASL) to a chimpanzee named Washoe.

The Gardners began training Washoe when she was eight months old. They used a variety of methods, including modeling and physical guidance (actually moving her hands) and applying operant conditioning methods. Washoe spent all of her waking hours with a trainer who communicated with her only through ASL. After four years of training, she could use 132 signs.

(Shutterstock)

It is quite clear that birdcalls, monkey vocalizations, dolphin whistles, and bee dances do not qualify as language. However, this does not mean animals don't have the ability to learn to use language to communicate abstract thoughts and ideas.

Not only was Washoe adept at imitating her trainer's signs, but she also seemed to create her own communications. For example, when an aggressive rhesus monkey menaced her, she signed "dirty monkey," and when she saw a swan for the first time, she signed "water bird." Since she already knew the signs for water and bird, her trainer speculated that she understood the meaning of the words and was thus able to combine them creatively. Washoe was never exposed to training in syntax, but she occasionally produced syntactically meaningful phrases like "gimme tickle" (chimpanzees enjoy being tickled). Washoe even seemed to be able to string words together in a creative and meaningful fashion, as evidenced by such requests as, "You me go out please." More recently the Gardners have trained several other chimpanzees to converse in signs. They present evidence that these chimpanzees initiate context-appropriate conversations with each other (Bodamar & Gardner, 2002; Jensvold & Gardner, 2000).

BVT Lab

Improve your test scores. Practice quizzes are available at **www.BVTLab.com.**

Other studies have used varying approaches, also with success. Psychologist David Premack (D. Premack, 1971; A. Premack & D. Premack, 1991) used operant conditioning to teach a chimpanzee named Sarah to associate pieces of plastic with different aspects of her environment. The plastic pieces, which differed in size, shape, and color, had magnetic backing so that they could be placed on a metal "language board" to form vertical sentences. Sarah learned a large number of symbols indicating names of trainers, objects, properties of objects (like "color of"), and prepositions; she also learned to combine words in an apparently meaningful fashion (such as "Mary give apple Sarah"). Premack and his associates believed that Sarah could also learn concepts. For example, when she was asked to compare a banana and a yellow ball, she arranged symbols on the magnetic board to indicate "the same." (This correct answer requires an appreciation of the concept of color.)

At the Yerkes Primate Research Center in Atlanta, Georgia, another study attempted to teach chimpanzees "Yerkish," a computer language. The star pupil of this study, Lana, was raised in a room with a computer that she learned to use to obtain food, drink, and so forth. Each key was labeled with a particular symbol that stood for an object or action. (For example, a circle with a dot inside signified juice.) Lana and other chimpanzees learned to use the computer to type requests, answer questions, and even to engage in a complex game with another chimpanzee that required them to use the computer symbols to make statements. Some of Lana's keyboard talk was quite amazing. For example, one day she observed that her trainer had an orange that she wanted, but Lana did not have a symbol for orange in her language repertoire. So Lana improvised and typed, "Tim give apple which is orange" (Rumbaugh, 1977; Savage-Rumbaugh, Rumbaugh, & Boysen, 1980; Savage-Rumbaugh, Pate, Lawson, Smith, & Rosenbaum, 1983).

The Rumbaughs trained another chimpanzee named Kanzi to communicate by using an elaborate board with 250 images, or lexicons, to create primitive sentences. The generated sentences appear to follow crude syntax and are often generated spontaneously (Savage-Rumbaugh, Shanker, & Taylor, 1998). While Kanzi's abilities have not satisfied all of the critics, this research has provided valuable insights in language acquisition as well as to helping us define exactly what language actually is.

The evidence we have just discussed, as well as findings from several other studies, seems to suggest that language (in at least some form) may not be unique to humans (Gillespie-Lynch, Greenfield, Lyn, & Savage-Rumbaugh, 2011). From your reading of the chimpanzee studies and a review of Table 10-4, what is your conclusion? Take a moment to consider this question before reading on.

Upon examination of Table 10-4, it appears that ape communication comes close to our criteria for language. For instance, the criteria of arbitrariness and, perhaps, novelty have been demonstrated in apes. However, the criterion of displacement, generating language in the absence of a stimulus, has not been adequately demonstrated. One criterion implied by displacement is that humans have a **theory of mind** and can attribute beliefs, desires, knowledge, and emotions to others (Seyfarth & Cheney, 1992). In other words, people can talk about an object in its absence, indicating we attribute knowledge of the object to another person. Our warning a child not to venture into the street until the light changes is prompted not by his or her behavior, but by a lack of knowledge about the street and the traffic. Likewise, children learn to attribute beliefs, desires, knowledge, and emotions to others and behave in ways to change or maintain them. To date there have been no convincing studies to indicate that communication by other animals meets this criterion (Call & Tomasello, 2008).

Theory of Mind The ability to attribute beliefs, desires, knowledge, and emotions to others

Other animals beside chimpanzees have demonstrated amazing vocabularies. Chaser, a border collie, has learned more than a thousand words. Psychologists John Pilley and Alliston Reid at Wofford College trained Chaser to associate more than a thousand objects with their respective names. In tests, where toys are randomly placed in a large room, Chaser will fetch the appropriate toy by name with astonishing accuracy (Pilley & Reid, 2011).

(Shutterstock)

Pigeons can learn to engage in sustained and natural conversation without human intervention, and one pigeon can transmit information to another entirely through the use of symbols.

In another series of experiments, psychologist Irene Pepperberg taught an African grey parrot named Alex a vocabulary of over 150 words. Alex could not only identify objects by name, he could describe some of their characteristics, such as their shape and color. Alex also appeared to be able to count the number of objects displayed on a tray (Pepperberg, 2002, 2006). It is important to note that although the cognitive capabilities of these animals is quite impressive, these researchers are not claiming that dogs or parrots are using language as we have defined it.

In all, much of the data obtained from nonhuman language studies can be explained by learning principles—none of which require us to assume that animals have true language capabilities. Certainly, if we confine our conception of true language ability to the criteria in Table 10-4, we must conclude that humans alone possess language. As the prominent linguist Noam Chomsky stated, "If animals had the capacity as biologically advantageous as language, but somehow hadn't used it until now, it would be an evolutionary miracle, like finding an island of humans who could be taught to fly" (Chomsky, 1993).

CHAPTER REVIEW

Thinking

1. We may define thought or thinking as a collection of internal processes or behaviors directed toward solving a problem.
2. Research has demonstrated the inaccuracy of John Watson's early contention that subvocal speech was essentially equivalent to thinking.
3. Modern behaviorists argue that thinking involves covert behavior maintained by private reinforcers.
4. Components of thought are mental images of visual scenes and sounds that we manipulate in some systematic or logical fashion.
5. Mental images activate the same cortical areas as perception, but in a reverse order. While perception involves bottom-up processing, imagery involves top-down processing.
6. A more abstract or symbolic form of thinking involves the use of concepts. Concepts represent general categories into which we mentally group things (objects, activities, kinds of animals, and so forth) that share certain features even though they are not identical.
7. We tend to organize concepts into hierarchies, ranging from very broad to very specific. There seems to be an optimal or basic level in each concept hierarchy that we naturally use when we think about objects or events.
8. Formal concepts, employed by laboratory researchers, are logical and well defined with clear, unambiguous rules specifying what features belong to that category.
9. In real life, most of the natural concepts that we use to think efficiently about past and present experiences tend to be more ambiguous than formal concepts.
10. A number of different theories have been proposed to explain how people form concepts. These include association theory, hypothesis-testing theory, and exemplar theory.

Problem Solving

11. A problem exists when there is a discrepancy between your present status and some goal you wish to obtain, with no obvious way to bridge the gap.
12. Problems consist of three components: The original state of the situation as it exists at the moment; the goal state, which is what the problem solver would like the situation to be; and the rules or restrictions that govern the possible strategies for moving from the original state to the goal state.
13. Problem-solving behavior generally involves three logical stages: representing or defining the problem, generating possible solutions, and evaluating how well a given solution works.

CHAPTER REVIEW

14. Algorithms involve a systematic exploration of every possible solution to a problem until a correct one is found.
15. Heuristics refer to a variety of rule-of-thumb strategies that may lead to quick solutions but are not guaranteed to produce results. Two commonly employed heuristic strategies are means-ends analysis and working backward.
16. Two characteristics that can make a problem difficult to solve are lack of definition and complexity.
17. Common obstacles we often create for ourselves when engaged in problem solving are mental set, functional fixedness, and confirmation bias.
18. Mental set is a tendency to approach a problem in a set or predetermined way, regardless of the requirements of the specific problem.
19. Confirmation bias refers to our inclination to seek evidence that will confirm our hypothesis at the same time that we overlook contradictory evidence.

Reasoning and Decision Making

20. There are two basic types of reasoning: deductive and inductive. Deductive reasoning involves beginning with certain assumptions we believe to be true and using these assumptions as the basis for drawing conclusions that apply to specific instances. In contrast, inductive reasoning reaches a general conclusion by generalizing from specific instances.
21. A model for studying deductive reasoning is provided by the syllogism, which is an argument consisting of two (or more) presumably true statements, called premises, and a statement of conclusion that may or may not follow logically from the premises.
22. We often err in our deductive reasoning processes because we are too quick to accept faulty premises, because we misinterpret a premise, or because our attitudes or experiences interfere with our ability to think logically.
23. Decision making is a process that occurs whenever we are faced with an array of alternative choices, and we choose one option while rejecting others.
24. Subjective probabilities of outcomes influence our decisions. While these estimates can facilitate decision making, they can also lead to undesirable decision outcomes.
25. Emotions enter into decision making by generating somatic markers to possible outcomes. Without emotion, decision making would not occur.

CHAPTER REVIEW

Language

26. The ability to use language is perhaps the most profound of all human behaviors.
27. Psycholinguistics is the psychological study of how we translate sounds and symbols into meaning, and of what processes are involved in the acquisition and use of language.
28. The basic structural elements of language are called phonemes.
29. A morpheme is the smallest unit of meaning in a given language.
30. Syntax refers to the set of language rules that govern how words can be combined to form meaningful phrases and sentences.
31. Language is also characterized by a system of rules that help us to determine the meanings of words and sentences. The study of meaning in language is called semantics.
32. Theories of language acquisition include the learning perspective, which emphasizes the role of experience in language acquisition, and the nativistic perspective, which maintains that the human brain is genetically programmed to learn speech. Most contemporary psychologists believe that genetics and environment interact in a complex fashion to provide us with the necessary foundations for learning language.
33. There appears to be a universal developmental sequence in which children learn language by progressing from babbling to one-word utterances to two-word utterances, and finally to expanded language using more complex sentences.
34. The major brain areas for language are located in the left hemisphere. These areas include Broca's area and Wernicke's area. Different components of speech and grammar appear to be mediated by specific regions within the brain.
35. Much of the data obtained from primate language studies can be explained by simpler principles, none of which requires us to assume apes have true language capabilities.
36. If we confine our conception of true language ability to the criteria of generativity, specialization, arbitrariness, displacement, and novelty, then we must conclude that humans alone possess language. However, if we define language as the ability to convey meaning through the use of symbols, it is clear that chimpanzees and other animals also have this ability.
37. There is no anatomical evidence that chimpanzees have the necessary cortical structures for language. The neural structures involved in human language do not appear to be present in other animals.

TERMS AND CONCEPTS

Algorithm, pg. 389
Availability Heuristic, pg. 400
Belief-Bias Effect, pg. 397
Bottom-Up Processing, pg. 381
Broca's Area, pg. 408
Concepts, pg. 381
Confirmation Bias, pg. 392
Covert Behavior, pg. 380
Deductive Reasoning, pg. 395
Exemplar Theory, pg. 384
Functional Fixedness, pg. 387
Gambler's Fallacy, pg. 399
Heuristics, pg. 390
Inductive Reasoning, pg. 395
Interactionist Approach, pg. 406
Language Acquisition Device (LAD), pg. 405
Language, pg. 402
Means-Ends Analysis, pg. 390
Mental Set, pg. 392
Morpheme, pg. 404
Phonemes, pg. 403
Prototype, pg. 384
Psycholinguistics, pg. 403
Representative Heuristic, pg. 399
Semantics, pg. 404
Somatic Marker, pg. 402
Subjective Probability, pg. 398
Syllogism, pg. 395
Syntax, pg. 404
Telegraphic Speech, pg. 405
Testing Hypotheses, pg. 389
Theory of Mind, pg. 412
Thought, pg. 379
Top-Down Processing, pg. 381
Trial and Error, pg. 388
Universal Grammar (UG), pg. 405
Wernicke's Area, pg. 408
Working Backward, pg. 390

RESEARCH PERSPECTIVES

Perspectives on Language

Perspective 1: Dr. Herbert S. Terrace

Herbert S. Terrace is a professor of psychology at Columbia University. He was B. F. Skinner's last doctoral student and has performed research projects on errorless discrimination in pigeons, autoshaping in pigeons and monkeys, and the linguistic competence of apes. He is currently investigating serial memory in pigeons and monkeys. The ability of these species to learn arbitrary lists shows that animals can think without language and that the serial competence needed to acquire a language is a cognitive skill that is phylogenetically quite old.

Perspective 2: Allen and Beatrix Gardner

R. Allen Gardner and Beatrix T. Gardner are professors in the Department of Psychology and Fellows of the Center for Advanced Study at the University of Nevada in Reno. In 1966, they began Project Washoe to study the nature of language and intelligence and the relation between human and nonhuman intelligence by cross-fostering an infant chimpanzee in a human environment. The results of their work, and follow-up studies by their colleague, Roger Fouts, are described in their 1989 book, *Teaching Sign Language to Chimpanzees* (SUNY Press).

PERSPECTIVE #1: *Language Competence of Apes*

Dr. Herbert S. Terrace

Q: *Dr. Terrace, do you feel that studying language acquisition in primates will help us understand human language acquisition, or do you think there are important differences in how we and other primates acquire and use language?*

A: Some psychologists, including myself, used to think that it would be valuable to study language learning in apes, but the results of various ape language projects suggest that language is uniquely human. There are at least two reasons to come to that conclusion: No evidence of spontaneity in combinations and what I would describe as lack of reference for the symbols various apes have been trained to use. The focus of the various ape language projects was, understandably, on grammatical competence. That is understandable, because Chomsky and other psycholinguists cited grammar as the crucial feature of language that distinguishes it from other forms of communication. I started my own project, centered on a chimpanzee named Nim, to try to obtain definitive evidence of grammatical competence. Nim was trained to use sign language because of the generally agreed upon limitations of the vocal apparatus of the ape. While looking for regularities in combinations of signs, I initially thought I found the evidence I was seeking. I examined more than 20,000 combinations of two or more signs and noticed that in combinations involving the word "more," "more" would occur in the first position of two sign combinations—"more eat," "more drink," "more play," and so on. Signs like "me" or "Nim" would usually occur in the second position of a two-sign combination. These regularities were the strongest evidence that would support the conclusion of the use of simple grammatical rules similar to those used by children. Somewhat unexpectedly, while I was looking at videotapes for other reasons, I noticed something I hadn't seen previously. Nim's signing seemed to occur almost exclusively in response to the teacher's signing. So after doing a discourse analysis of a dozen videotapes, I had quantitative data showing that his signing was not spontaneous. In fact, in most instances, it was imitative of what the teacher signed to Nim. This proved to be quite different from the results of a similar analysis that could be done of children first learning to use language. In fact, the discourse analysis I used was modeled after a classic study of language acquisition by children, which was performed by Lois Bloom of Teachers College at Columbia University. That's the first reason, I think, one has to say that apes lack the human ability to communicate with language.

The second reason is perhaps less obvious but even more fundamental. I think all the investigators studying ape language (including myself) make the mistake of assuming that the signs used in sign language or the symbols used by Rumbaugh and Premack function as words. However, looking at videotape records and films of other projects—for example, Washoe signing with the Gardners—I was struck by the fact that the signs seemed to be tricks that the chimpanzee used as a means to obtain particular kinds of reward, whether the reward was tickling, being chased, getting a banana, getting a drink, and so on. Children, unlike chimps, will use a word to tell you that they have noticed something about the environment. If a child says tree, he doesn't want you to bring the tree over to him, nor does he want a candy for saying tree, but those seem to be the only circumstances under which a chimp would sign. What is missing from apes is the ability to refer to features of the environment for their own sake, to share curiosity. If you don't have that, I can't see why one would even ask about grammatical competence, because I think in the evolution of language, the ability to refer to something undoubtedly preceded the appearance of grammatical competence. Once our ancestors began referring to features of the environment, there were too many things with which they had to keep track. In order to make sense of the various words, symbols, etc., there was pressure to organize them in grammatical rules. So, for the two reasons I have cited, I don't think the communication that has been observed between apes and teachers has very much to do with human language.

Q: *Would it then be your contention that apes and other nonhuman primates don't use language in a symbolic way?*

A: I think that apes can solve problems, which involve symbols that they have to think about or remember. That is, if you show an ape a triangle and, twenty seconds later, ask it to select that triangle from an array of stimuli including circles, squares, and so on, I'm certain the chimp can do it. However, that doesn't mean that they're using language. That means that they have the ability to represent features of the environment and remember those features in a nonlinguistic way. In fact, for the last ten years I have been studying how an animal thinks without language, and there is no question that animals do think. Descartes' contention that animals lack language and therefore can't think, notwithstanding. The intriguing question is how a nonlinguistic creature can solve problems without simply resorting to conditioned reflexes without language. Curiously, the same problem comes up in the study of human infants. Human infants are not born with language, and yet there is much evidence that they think. What, then, is the medium of their thought before language appears?

RESEARCH PERSPECTIVES

Q: *Has your research into this area provided you with any clues or any preliminary conclusions about the nature of that kind of thought?*

A: Yes. I have been studying how pigeons and, more recently, monkeys learn lists, which consist of photographs displayed on video monitors. My initial conclusions are that monkeys, in particular, use a spatial representation of the lists they have to produce in order to keep track of which is first, which is second, which is third, and so on. Animals have an obviously well developed sense of space that they use while foraging and hunting. Therefore, it is not unreasonable to assume that they could use their spatial abilities to represent things like the order of an item in a sequence. I suspect there are other ways that animals represent the world, and this is the subject of much current investigation.

Q: *What about studies in which chimps have been shown to converse among themselves or teach other chimpanzees sign language in the absence of human confederates? What do you think is operating in those circumstances, if it is not a form of language being used or passed on?*

A: Well, it's a question of the quality of that evidence. I have seen Nim sign "hug" to dogs and cats. I mean this is an overtrained, potentially conditioned, response. The reports of Washoe teaching signs to an adopted offspring don't make much sense to me because the most frequent sign the offspring learned was "George," the name of one of the trainers whom the offspring had never seen. Clearly, Washoe was using signs, and the offspring was in some interesting sense imitating Washoe, but I don't think that was communication. I think what we have is an interesting case of imitation, a phenomenon that is important in its own right. However, I don't see that it has anything to do with language.

Q: *Do you see any similarity at all between language acquisition in humans and the kinds of activities or actions you've seen among the chimpanzees?*

A: No. I think the crucial difference is, as I said earlier, that infants have an essentially innate ability to refer to features of the environment. You can actually see precursors of what I call the ability to refer before the first words are uttered, in shared eye movements. Infants will often look at an object, look at the parent to monitor whether the parent has seen the object, and when they sense that the parent has seen the object, they will smile, to say, "Ah, you see what I see." This is done without language. That kind of shared perception, as far as I can determine, is uniquely human. I believe it is from that kind of nonverbal communication that words occur in a very straightforward manner. It is very easy to build on that foundation. There are fundamental gaps in this kind of cognitive ability that separate human beings from their closest ape relatives.

Q: *Would you say, then, that the acquisition and the use of language would be based more upon some kind of prewired structure that humans possess and other animals don't, more than through learning?*

A: I don't think it's an either/or proposition. I think there is clearly evidence of prewired functions of the brain that are involved in language. One kind of evidence is essentially behavioral. There are generalizations that a child makes, having once begun to use language, which cannot be explained by simple learning or conditioning principles. I think Chomsky has very forcefully made that point. So, given the limited input that a child has, there must be some innate machinery that makes use of that input to produce novel constructions. The evidence of aphasia and lateralization is also consistent with the notion that there is hard-wiring for language. However, I don't think that makes language terribly different from other forms of hard-wired functions. We know that there are certain parts of the brain that are dedicated to detecting shapes, contours, colors, and so on, so it's not surprising that in the case of language we have evidence of biological constraints or innate determinants. Clearly, however, a large part of language is learned. That is demonstrated by the fact that children in Germany learn German, and children in the United States learn English. Therefore, there must be a learned component. That is why I stress that it shouldn't be viewed as an either / or dichotomy.

Q: *Can you tell us about the focus of your current research?*

A: My current focus really is how thinking occurs without language. I see that animals, particularly primates, are fascinating in the sense that they can illuminate how intelligence evolved. One of the strategies of science is always to simplify one's problem. Primates provide a simplification that allows one to study various forms of cognition without, if you will, the complication of language, which is inextricably an element of human thought, at least once a child is two or three years old. So I'm not studying language or communication in apes or other primates, but what I hope to accomplish is to see what intellectual and cognitive abilities had evolved upon which language can build.

Q: *Have you had any results in that area that you might be able to share with us?*

A: Well, the major one is the ability to produce and remember sequences, which is vital to the production of sentences, and is phylogenetically much older than the human species. You can get this in monkeys, and you can get it in a simple form even in pigeons. So my current concern is, how does the animal represent the sequence? These are the kinds of questions that don't require language, but certainly require some kind of thinking ability.

Q: *Do you think those studies have any implications for thinking and learning in humans?*

A: Yes, because even though in our conscious awareness we seem always to think in language, it is highly probable that much of our thinking is nonverbal. Much of it is unconscious, and if we had a good picture of what the nature of nonverbal thinking is in animals, I'm sure that it didn't stop with the human species. I suspect that ultimately we would find out about a component of human thinking that is very rarely considered.

Q: *Are there other implications of the research that you're doing now that you think might have some strong significance in the near future?*

A: Well, one point I just briefly touched upon is the study of thinking in human infants. That is unfortunately an area that's received very little attention. It's a very difficult area, and it poses the same problems as studying thinking in animals. How do you know what a baby is thinking, if the baby can't speak? There is a growing body of techniques available that will allow one to examine that problem. Another point that has to be made about an infant's ability to think is that anybody who doubts that an animal can't think because an animal lacks language, should ask themselves, "Well, what about human babies?" Do we want to reach the same conclusion about them? I think the answer is clearly no.

RESEARCH PERSPECTIVES

PERSPECTIVE #2: *Language Competence of Apes*

Allen and Beatrix Gardner

Q: *Do you feel that studying language acquisition in primates helps us to understand human language acquisition, or do you feel there are important differences in how we and other primates acquire and use language?*

A: Well, our notion is the modern notion that language is part of intellectual development. The old notion, almost medieval, is a brain separated into compartments—a language area, a social area, an emotional area, and so on. The modern notion is that the brain is integrated, and all aspects of intellectual development are inextricably intertwined. Our idea was to give the chimpanzees a rich intellectual environment like that of a human child, and let language develop within that.

Q: *So you see language development and acquisition as going hand-in-hand with the acquisition and development of the other skills, which we need for living?*

A: Yes. Just as with children, a young chimpanzee would have to be familiar with simple tools such as keys and light switches, articles of clothing like shoes, in order to learn the signs for keys, light, opening, or lacing. We kept our laboratory stocked with the objects and activities of a child's world. The chimps learned in that environment the way children learn. They learned to eat human style food, to use a cup and a spoon, clear the table, help wash the dishes. They learned to use the human toilet—including flushing and wiping themselves—and also to use signs to ask to go potty as a way to get out of lessons or postpone a bath. The primary objective was always to study the patterns of social and intellectual development with sign language as a strand in that development.

Q: *In the course of your studies, did you note similarities in the patterns of language acquisition and development between chimpanzees and human children?*

A: One of the most important similarities between chimps and children is that both take a long time to grow up. Wild chimpanzees in Africa are only weaned when they are four or five years old. They only start getting adult teeth at age six. They live with their mothers until they are seven to ten years old. Mothers have their first babies when they are between twelve and fifteen years old. In labs and zoos, chimpanzees live well over fifty years.

So, we can compare patterns of chimpanzee development with patterns of child development. There are some well documented steps in the development of language in human children. For instance, one of the things that has been described very well is the way children answer questions. They go from "what" and "where" to "who" and then on to "whose." The chimpanzees learned the American Sign Language version of these question words. The basic question types that are earlier for signing chimpanzees are also earlier for children. That similarity is very important. However, the object of our research went beyond the language. The object was to see how a chimpanzee would develop in a human intellectual environment. The purpose of the sign language was to complete that development. Other psychologists had tried to raise a chimp like a child, but they used English, and the chimpanzees couldn't make the sounds of English. You can't really say that you cross-fostered a chimp in a human environment if the chimp can't ask a question or carry on a conversation with you.

Our notion was that the sign language would complete the cross-fostering. Therefore, we had to have a naturally occurring language that human children learn, and not an artificial language used only to test some abstract theory. We were using sign language to support the cross-fostering rather than using cross-fostering to support the sign language. Of course, they interacted and supported each other. We assumed that if we used a suitable language, it would come in with the rest of the development. We and other comparative psychologists always understood this. The notion of a great divide between language and the rest of human behavior, and between human behavior and the rest of animal behavior is a throwback to scholasticism.

Q: *Have you noted similarities in all aspects of language acquisition and development—the acquisition of terms, syntax, usage, and so on?*

A: Oh, yes. In traditional Chomskyan linguistics, the child is born with language, and then, in three years you see all syntax. Back in the 1960s and 1970s, people said things like that, but most scientists understand now that there is a long period of linguistic development in young children. For that matter, high school students haven't quite mastered their native language, and even college students still have a lot to learn. This long period of development in human children gives us a scale for comparison. It shows that cross-fostered chimpanzees, up to five or six years old, were developing in a very parallel way. Not as fast—they are behind human children—but the patterns are very similar and, I would say, parallel.

Q: *Has the work that you've done recently differed qualitatively in any way from the work that you started doing, and if so, can you tell us a little bit about your most recent research efforts?*

A: Now, we're mainly working on the data from the first five years, but the chimpanzees are with Roger Fouts at Central Washington University. The work is going on into a second generation. Washoe's own baby died soon after birth, but Roger found a ten-month-old infant, Loulis, for Washoe to adopt. Roger then started a project in which the humans never spoke sign language when Loulis was around, which was practically all the time. So the only input Loulis got was from other chimpanzees, and he learned over fifty signs, which he could only have learned from the other chimps. During this period, which went on for five years, the other chimps went right on as a community of signers, even though there was practically no input from human beings. The cross-fostered chimpanzees went right on signing among themselves almost without any human influence.

In the second project with Moja, Pili, Tatu, and Dar, we had better human models of sign language than we had in the Washoe days. Everybody knew more signs, and there were some deaf people in the foster family who only spoke sign language. Not only did Loulis learn signs from Washoe and the other chimps, but Washoe also learned some new signs from the chimps of the second project.

In the Reno laboratory, we had several people for each chimp, but Roger had several chimps for each person, and there are many hours when the chimps were by themselves in a group. Video cameras are rolling to record conversations among the chimps when no human being is present. All sorts of chimp-to-chimp transmissions go on with no human support at all, if you don't count the video cameras. Roger and his students record conversations and topics of conversations and identify the chimps' favorite addressees in elaborate conversations among themselves. Loulis, for instance, switched from Washoe, his mother, his favorite addressee to Dar, his peer playmate, as the most common addressee. Although the chimpanzees haven't developed entirely new signs among themselves, certain variants of signs have become traditional within the group; for instance, making a quite noisy sign out of the *person* sign, by adding a slapping movement.

RESEARCH PERSPECTIVES

Q: *In the observations that were made of chimps who were conversing among themselves, did you see the kind of turn-taking and the other dynamics of the pragmatic uses of language in that situation as well as in interaction with the humans?*

A: Oh yes, that's one of the things that we saw starting in Reno. Things like tapping you to get your visual attention so they could sign to you, or making some noise to get you to turn around and at that point signing to you. That makes a lot of sense. You don't just put out signs, you want to converse with someone. One of the projects now is nailing down the observations of pragmatics, experimentally—What do signing chimpanzees do when a person or another chimp is facing the other way? What do they do to get a chimp to turn around—the sounds they make, like hand clapping, banging objects? Where in the sequence do they begin signing? They do things like touch each other to get attention and make kissing sounds, and they persist until the addressee responds.

In the formal experiment that is going on right now, one of our students, Mark Bodamer, has a setup to demonstrate this under experimental conditions. He is at a desk working, and the chimps are in another room, but they have a place where they can come and get his attention. They are behind a barrier, and he sits with his back to them. He has a video camera watching them. They come to the doorway, and they do various things to get his attention and distract him from his work, and only when he turns around do they start talking to him. They know enough not to sign to his back.

Q: *Does your research suggest to you that all primates have prewired structures in the brain, which direct language development? Would you say that there is a heavier learning component for language acquisition, a stronger biological component, or an interaction between the two?*

A: Well, that's a really good question—a question that shows the advancement of theory in the last twenty or thirty years. The notion of a compartmentalized brain for different functions is really phrenology. Yes, you have visual areas and hearing areas and motor areas but, the more advanced a function, the more generalized the brain. Just as you find that the more primitive the animal, the more prewired it is; the more advanced the animal, the more generalized its brain is; and the more different foods it can eat, the more different climates it can live in. The most generalized function of all, of course, is learning. The way human beings are different from other animals is not in having more specialized organs—that would be more primitive. The way human beings are more advanced than other animals is in being more general. We have the widest diet, the widest variety of climates in which we live and the widest number of things that we can learn. Therefore, in the modern view, the notion is that the most advanced functions are the most general ones. We see everything in modern development as part of the generalized, adaptive learning ability of our species. As primates, we are superb learners.

Q: *What do you feel are the more important implications of this research in the teaching and learning of humans? How would this kind of knowledge help people who are trying to find better ways to help human children learn?*

A: If you look at Skinnerian behaviorism, what you find is that the more reward and punishment, the stupider the animal gets. Even monkeys and rats, if given less drill, solve more advanced problems. The research in our area that has had negative results has been research in which chimpanzees or other animals have been given Skinnerian reinforcement in order to solve abstract problems, so that in the end all you get is sort of like tricks. We don't just want the chimps to take tests, we want to carry on conversations with them, have them tell us what they saw. This holds true for the education of children, also—the more you emphasize reward and punishment, the narrower, the stupider the behavior. Even in mentally challenged children that fact stands out.

POP QUIZ

True or False

___ 1. One component of thought is manipulation of concepts in a systematic or logical manner.

___ 2. The first step in problem-solving behavior involves generating possible solutions.

___ 3. When an individual incorrectly approaches a problem by applying strategies that have previously been successful with similar problems, that person is showing confirmation bias.

___ 4. The belief bias effect would cause an individual to accept believable but logically invalid conclusions.

___ 5. Careful evaluation of the research designed to teach language to chimpanzees leads to the conclusion that only humans possess all of the criteria for language.

Multiple Choice

6. The concept ________ is subordinate to the concept ________.
   a. dog / bulldog
   b. animal / dog
   c. teacher / person
   d. animal / bird

7. When is trial-and-error problem solving most effective?
   a. There is a wide range of solutions.
   b. There is a narrow range of solutions.
   c. Strategies are needed.
   d. There must be a "quick fix."

8. Which of the following makes it more difficult to solve a problem?
   a. The problem contains a syllogism.
   b. The problem is deceptively simple.
   c. The problem involves basic concepts
   d. The problem is ill defined

9. As a result of confirmation bias, why might people jump to a conclusion incorrectly in attempting to solve a problem?
   a. They tend to approach a problem in a predetermined way if the approach has been successful in the past.
   b. They stop an algorithm prematurely.
   c. They have a prototype of the correct solution.
   d. They do not look for evidence that will disprove their hypothesis.

POP QUIZ

10. When is a syllogism judged to be true?
    a. When both premises are true.
    b. When the logically obtained conclusion is also consistent with everyday beliefs.
    c. When the conclusion applies to every conceivable combination of all possible meanings of the premises.
    d. When the converse of each premise is also true (for example, if "all A's are B's" is the premise and "all B's are A's" is a true statement).
11. When making a decision, how easily you can recall a piece of information is an important component of which of the following?
    a. The framing heuristic
    b. The availability heuristic
    c. The representativeness heuristic
    d. Means-end analysis
12. Which language-acquisition perspective could best account for a young child (whose parents speak English grammatically) saying, "I goed to the zoo yesterday"?
    a. Syntactical
    b. Whorfian
    c. Genetic
    d. Learning
13. A basic question that chimpanzee research has ***not*** conclusively answered is which of the following?
    a. Can chimps talk?
    b. Can chimps convey meaning through the use of symbols?
    c. Can chimps communicate?
    d. Can chimps learn language?
14. The ability of humans, but not other animals, to attribute beliefs, knowledge, and emotions to others is referred to as
    a. Theory of Mind
    b. Linguistic relativity
    c. Thinking
    d. Mental representation
15. The observation that young children do not talk about objects that are not present in their immediate environment until they have mastered object permanence supports what position?
    a. Mental images are necessary for thought to occur.
    b. Children have a limited vocabulary.
    c. Thought has an impact on the structure of language.
    d. Language determines thought.

Answer Key: 1.F 2.F 3F 4.T 5.T 6.c 7.b 8.d 9.b 10.c 11.a 12.c 13.d 14.a 15.c

(Shutterstock)

Chapter 11

Development 1: **Conception** *Through* **Childhood**

We are constantly changing, growing, and developing throughout our lives, from conception to old age. During some periods, these changes take place very rapidly and are clear to anyone who is there to observe them; at other times, particularly later in life, they may not be so obvious. This chapter explores conception, prenatal (before birth) development, and childhood.

Chapter 12 continues where this chapter leaves off, exploring adolescence and the adult years. First, we outline some key issues that have been the center of debate among developmental psychologists and examine typical ways in which human development is studied.

11.1 Developmental Issues

A number of issues have influenced developmental theory and research; we explore three of the most important. The first is the ongoing nature versus nurture controversy: What are the relative influences of heredity and environment on development? A second question has to do with the way in which development proceeds: Do changes take place in a continuous fashion throughout our lives, or do they occur in stages, with qualitatively different changes taking place at different points in our lives? A third issue has to do with critical periods in development: Must certain experiences occur during a specific window of time in our lives in order for development to proceed normally, or can later experiences make up for earlier deficiencies? These three questions recur throughout the study of development; therefore, we will introduce each before proceeding with our discussion of human development.

11.1a Heredity and Environment

Some individuals are capable of prodigious intellectual feats; others have only average ability. Some of us are extroverted and outgoing; others are introverted and shy. A few of us are leaders; most are followers. Are such differences a consequence of inheritance, or are they learned?

The Nature-Nurture Argument

Nurture Argument One answer to this question is that we are products of the experiences that nurture our development from conception to death. The seventeenth-century English philosopher John Locke, who proposed that an infant's mind at birth is a *tabula rasa*, or blank slate upon which virtually anything can be written by experience, expressed this view. The behaviorist John Watson updated this view in the 1920s:

> Give me a dozen healthy infants, well-formed and my own specific world to bring them up in, and I'll guarantee to take any one at random and train him to become any type of specialist I might select—a doctor, lawyer, artist, merchant-chief and, yes, even beggar-man and thief, regardless of his talents, penchants, tendencies, abilities, vocations and race of his ancestors. (Watson, 1924)

Nature-Nurture Controversy Controversy over whether individual differences are the result of genetic endowment (nature) or the consequence of learning (nurture)

Epigenetics A field of genetics that investigates how gene expression is influenced by a number of environmental factors, including experiences, diet, and environmental toxins

Maturation Orderly unfolding of certain patterns of behavior, such as language acquisition or walking, in accordance with genetic blueprints

Nature Argument The opposing point of view in the **nature-nurture controversy** is that our genetic endowment, or nature, is what makes us who we are. The eighteenth-century French philosopher Jean-Jacques Rousseau saw human development as simply the unfolding of genetically determined attributes; in the twentieth century, developmental psychologist Arnold Gesell (1926) stated, "It is the hereditary ballast that conserves and stabilizes the growth of each individual infant" (p. 378).

Interaction Argument Neither the nature nor the nurture position is supported today in its extreme form. Instead, contemporary theorists are interested in how genetics and experience interact. Although heredity predisposes us to behave in certain ways (and also sets limits on what we can do), the environment is also critical. For example, although genetics determines whether your biological sex is male or female, gender-associated behaviors—from manner of dress, to enjoyment of activities, to your role in a relationship—are highly influenced, if not entirely determined, by social learning. Many of your behavioral traits, however, are influenced by an interaction between the environment and genetics. Recent advances in the science of **epigenetics** (*epi* meaning "above ") have renewed interest in how the environment influences gene expression. These environmental factors can include one's age, living environment, lifestyle, food choices, or drug and alcohol use. Scientists are now learning how epigenetics contributes to variations in individual behavior (Allis, Caparros, Jenuwein, & Reinberg, 2015). We explore the relative influence of heredity, the environment, and epigenetics on gender identity and gender roles later in this chapter.

Thus, human behavior develops within the context of our environments. While some behaviors or attributes are largely, if not exclusively, determined by experience, others seem to develop without any specific experience, as long as environmental conditions stay within a normative range. An example is the early stages of language acquisition, as we saw in Chapter 10. Another is the universal developmental sequence through which babies progress, from sitting without support to crawling and ultimately to walking. Virtually all babies crawl, commencing at around ten months, before they begin to walk at about thirteen or fourteen months. (Throughout this chapter, we quote average ages for different developmental milestones. Please note that there is a wide range of individual variation around these norms.) This biologically determined sequence occurs even if children are not encouraged to sit, crawl, or walk. Both language acquisition and walking are examples of **maturation**—the orderly unfolding of certain patterns of behavior in accordance with genetic blueprints.

11.1b Continuous Versus Stage Development

A second issue confronting developmental psychologists concerns the nature of changes that occur over the life span. We all know that adolescents are quite different from infants and that most elderly people are noticeably different from young adults. Are these differences created by a gradual, cumulative growth, with each new developmental change building upon earlier developments and experiences in a fashion characterized by continuity? Contrarily, do these changes exhibit *discontinuity*—that is, are the behaviors expressed at each new stage of development qualitatively different from those of the previous stage?

In general, psychologists who emphasize the role of learning have tended to view development as a gradual, continuous process. According to this view, the mechanisms that govern development are relatively constant throughout a person's life. Individuals accumulate experiences; therefore, development is seen as a *quantitative* change (change due to increases in the amount or quantity of experiences). Developmental psychologists who embrace this perspective believe that the only important difference between young people and those who are older is that the latter have experienced more in life and are likely to know more. In contrast, many psychologists who emphasize maturation, view development as a discontinuous process that occurs in a series of steps or stages. A stage is a concept used to describe how a person's manner of thinking and behavior are organized and directed during a particular period in their life.

Stage theorists are inclined to interpret the differences between children and adults as being *qualitative* in nature (differences due to distinctions in the kind and nature of experiences). For instance, adults are viewed as better problem solvers than children not just because they know more but also because they think differently, in a more logical and systematic fashion. Here and in Chapter 12 we discuss two influential stage theories: Jean Piaget's theory of cognitive development and Erik Erikson's theory of psychosocial development.

(Shutterstock)

Virtually all babies crawl, commencing at around ten months, before going on to walk at about thirteen or fourteen months.

An important aspect of the continuity-discontinuity issue is the question of whether development from infancy to old age is characterized more by stability or by change. For instance, will an introverted, withdrawn child grow up to be reclusive as an adult? How much can we rely on a person's present behavior to predict what that person will be like in the future? Many of us grow up to be older versions of our childhood selves. Stability is not inevitable, however; and at least some people develop into people quite different from their earlier selves.

11.1c Critical Periods in Development

A third developmental issue is the relative importance of different periods of development. Is the timing of training essential for optimal acquisition of certain skills, and is timing also necessary for the development of behavioral traits? Is it necessary to have certain experiences early in life to ensure normal development later on?

According to one point of view, there are **critical periods** during which an infant or child must experience certain kinds of social and sensory experiences. If the proper experiences are not provided at the right time, later experiences will not be able to make up for earlier deficiencies. Psychologists who argue for critical periods often cite animal research for support. One widely quoted source of evidence is the research of biologist Konrad Lorenz (1937), who was curious about why ducklings begin to follow their mothers shortly after they are hatched. In a series of experiments he demonstrated that newly hatched ducklings will begin to follow the first moving thing they see—their mother, a member of another species like a goose, or even Lorenz himself. Lorenz labeled this phenomenon **imprinting**.

Critical Period Periods in the developmental sequence during which an organism must experience certain kinds of social or sensory experiences in order for normal development to take place

Imprinting Process by which certain infant animals, such as ducklings, learn to follow or approach the first moving object they see

Psychologist Harry Harlow and his associates at the University of Wisconsin conducted another famous study. Harlow found that when baby monkeys are deprived of "contact comfort" with their mothers during early development, the result is emotional and social impairment. For instance, infant monkeys who were reared in isolation for the first six months or more showed severely disturbed behavior such as incessant rocking, timidity, and inappropriate displays of aggression. These traits persisted into adulthood, even after the imposed isolation was ended (Suomi, 1976). We discuss this research in more detail later in this chapter.

The evidence of critical periods in human development is inconsistent. For example, institutionalized infants who are deprived of loving, responsive care during their first six months are significantly more likely to be emotionally and socially maladjusted than infants who are institutionalized after they have experienced a period of close contact with responsive caregivers during the early months of their lives. Some psychologists view this as evidence that the first six months are a critical period for starting a child on the proper path toward healthy emotional and social adjustment.

However, not all research supports this view. In one study, for example, infants who had been subjected to a profoundly impoverished orphanage environment for most of their first two years were then transferred to another institution where they received one-on-one contact with loving caregivers. Despite the early lack of love and stimulation, these infants developed into well-adjusted adults without identifiable behavioral problems (Skeels, 1966). Numerous other investigations have shown that children adopted after infancy and raised by loving parents can often overcome early disadvantages associated with severely deprived environments.

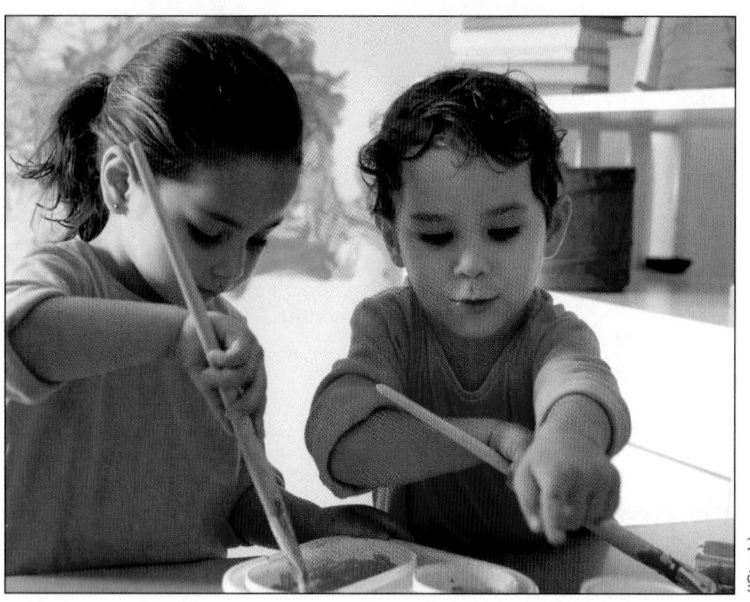
(iStock)

Research shows that later-life experiences can make up for social and sensory experiences that were lacking during early development.

Even Harlow's monkey studies cast doubt on the critical-period theory. If monkeys who had been deprived of contact comfort during infancy were later provided extensive contact with therapist monkeys, their behavioral deficits could be almost entirely overcome. Monkeys exposed to longer periods of isolation (twelve months instead of six months) also responded to this unusual therapy, but their recovery was not as complete (Novak & Harlow, 1975; Suomi & Harlow, 1972).

Another question related to the critical-period issue is whether bonding between parent and infant must take place at a certain point in early development. Most nonhuman mammals lick and groom their offspring during the first hours after birth, often rejecting their young if this early "getting acquainted" session is somehow prevented. Some child specialists have suggested that a similar critical period exists for humans in the first hours after birth, and that if contact is prevented, mother-infant bonding will not develop adequately; however, this notion has received little support from research. Instead, the parent-child relationship seems to be malleable, with plenty of opportunity to establish attachment throughout development.

In all, the evidence suggests that most effects of adverse early experience can be modified, if not overcome, by later experience. Certainly the kinds of experiences we have during our early development may strongly influence our feelings about ourselves and others, our styles of relating to people, our mode of expressing emotion, the degree to which we realize our intellectual potential, and countless other aspects of our adjustment. Most contemporary psychologists agree, however, that the concept of critical periods in infant development—at least when applied to emotional, intellectual, and behavioral traits—lacks supporting evidence.

11.2 Developmental Research

The task of developmental psychology is to describe and attempt to explain the nature of behavioral changes that occur throughout the life span. To realize this aim, researchers need to gather information about individuals at different points in their development. Three research designs have been developed for this purpose: the cross-sectional, longitudinal, and cross-sequential methods.

Cross-Sectional Design
Research design in which groups of subjects of different ages are assessed and compared at one point in time, so that conclusions may be drawn about behavior differences that may be related to age differences

Longitudinal Design
Research design that evaluates a group of subjects at several points in time, over a number of years, to assess how certain characteristics or behaviors change during the course of development

11.2a The Cross-Sectional Design

The most widely used research method in developmental psychology is the **cross-sectional design**. Groups of subjects of different ages are assessed and compared at one point in time, and the researcher draws conclusions about behavior differences that may be related to age differences. For example, suppose we want to determine whether there are age differences in television-viewing habits. Using the cross-sectional method, we might attach program-monitoring devices to the television sets of a sample population ranging from young adults to retirees and then analyze several months of viewing records. The result would be a profile of viewing habits of different age groups.

The cross-sectional study gives an accurate "snapshot" of one point in time, but it leaves an important question unanswered: Do its findings reflect developmental differences or changes in the environment? For instance, suppose we discover that young adults watch very few comedies, whereas older adults spend most of their television time viewing comedies. Does this mean that when the young people in our sample grow older, they will spend more time viewing comedies, or does it simply reflect the fact that the older subjects developed their viewing habits in an era when situation comedies were featured in television programming? One way to find out if a behavioral change is related to development is to conduct a longitudinal study.

11.2b The Longitudinal Design

The **longitudinal design** evaluates behavior in the same group of people at several points in time to assess what kinds of changes occur over the long term. To apply this method to the study of age-related television preferences, we might begin by monitoring the viewing habits of a group of young adults at age twenty. The same subjects might then be repeatedly observed at five-year intervals over the next fifty years. This method would allow us to assess reliably whether or not the television consumption habits of our subjects actually change with age, and if so, in what direction.

A famous example of a longitudinal investigation is Lewis Terman's long-term study of gifted children with IQs above 135. A Stanford University psychologist, Terman began his research in the early 1920s with a sample of 1,528 gifted boys and girls of grade-school age. These subjects were evaluated and tested at regular intervals, first to see if they would maintain their intellectual superiority, and later to see how well they adjusted to life. Although Terman died in 1956, Stanford psychologists Robert Sears and Pauline Sears continued his research.

This classic study has provided a wealth of information about the impact of superior intelligence on life satisfaction and on the course of development. Over time, Terman's gifted subjects have been shown to be healthier, happier, more socially adept, and more successful in their careers than are comparably aged people of average intelligence. They have also exhibited a much lower than average incidence of emotional disorders, substance abuse, suicide, and divorce (Terman, 1925, 1954). These findings have helped dispel the common myth that people of very high intelligence are more likely to exhibit severe behavior disorders than are people of average intelligence.

Unlike the cross-sectional design, the longitudinal approach allows researchers to track an individual's changes over time. However, the longitudinal approach does have some drawbacks. One is the large investment of time that it requires. Relatively few researchers are ready to embark on a Terman-like study whose results will not be evident for years. Another problem is the shrinking sample. Over time, subjects may drop out of the study as they move away, die, or simply lose interest.

Finally, environmental factors still play a role in longitudinal studies, and so researchers must be cautious in generalizing their findings. For example, suppose that as part of a longitudinal study you interview a group of college students in 1960 and then again survey the same group in 1990, asking them their opinions about abortion. You might find that as middle-aged adults these subjects expressed more support for a woman's right to choose abortion than they did as young adults. Does this mean that attitudes toward abortion become more liberalized in the period between early and

Figure 11-1 From Ovulation to Fertilization

The egg travels to the fallopian tube, where fertilization occurs. The fertilized ovum divides as it travels toward the uterus, where it becomes implanted.

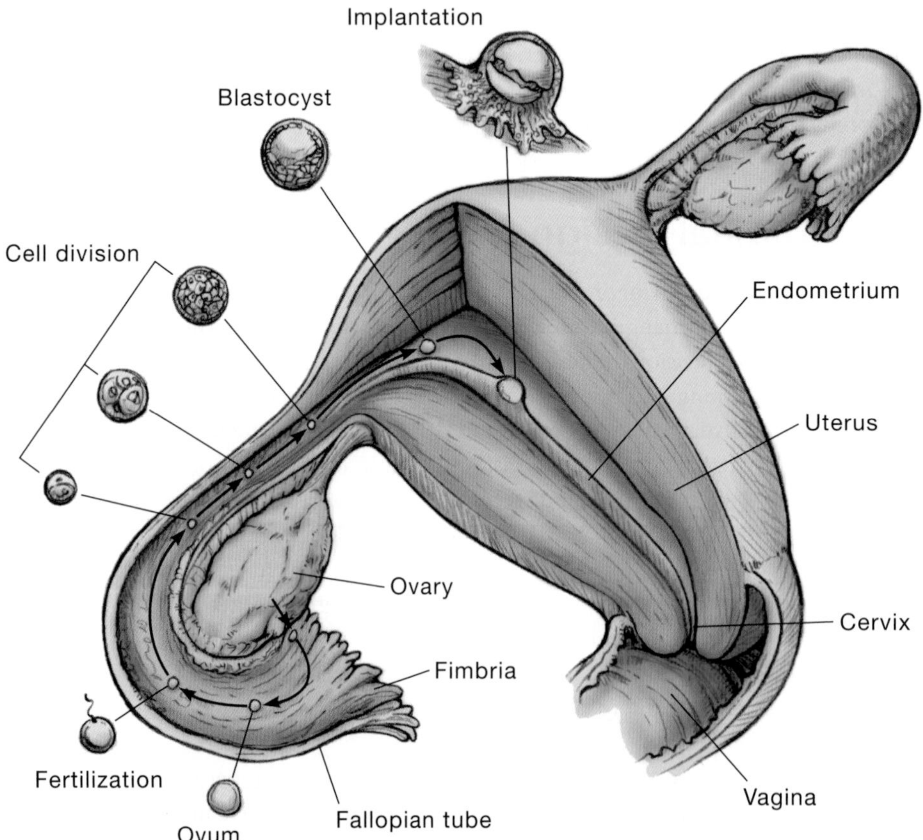

mature adulthood? Such a conclusion would overlook the dramatic social changes that have taken place in the past several decades. The attitudinal changes in our study group might well reflect social changes rather than a normal developmental pattern.

11.2c The Cross-Sequential Design

In an attempt to overcome some of the drawbacks of both the cross-sectional and longitudinal designs, researchers have combined the best features of each in a **cross-sequential design**. Subjects in a cross-sequential design are observed more than once, but over a shorter span of time than is typical of longitudinal studies. Subjects in cross-sequential studies with the same year of birth are said to belong to the same *birth* **cohort**. Developmental psychologists who use this research design generally choose cohorts whose ages will overlap during the course of the study. This method helps to avoid both the longitudinal shortcoming of limited generalization of findings and the potential cross-sectional problem of confusing the effects of growth with those of societal conditions.

Cross-Sequential Design Research design that combines elements of the cross-sectional and longitudinal designs by observing subjects more than once over a relatively short period

Cohort An experimental group of participants with similar characteristics or who share a particular experience

Gamete The reproductive cells, or sperm and ovum; also called *germ cells*

Chromosome A strand of DNA that contains the organism's genes

DNA (Deoxyribonucleic Acid) Chemical substance whose molecules, arranged in varying patterns, are the building blocks of genes

Identical Twins Twins who share the same genetic code; also known as *one-egg twins* or *monozygotic twins*

11.3 The Beginning of Life

For all of us, life begins in the same way. Shortly after a ripened ovum is released from one of our mother's ovaries, a sperm cell penetrates the ovum, fertilizing it. The sperm and ovum, collectively called **gametes** or **germ cells**, normally unite in the upper portion of the *fallopian tube*. The resulting new cell, called a *zygote*, then travels downward through the fallopian tube to the *uterus* or womb. (See Figure 11-1)

The nuclei of the sperm and ovum each contain twenty-three rod-like structures called **chromosomes**, twenty-two of which are autosomes (not sex-determining) and one of which is a sex chromosome. After fertilization, the zygote contains a complement of forty-six chromosomes arranged in twenty-three pairs, one chromosome in each pair from the sperm and one from the egg (see Figure 11-2).

11.3a Genes and Chromosomes

Chromosomes are composed of thousands of genes, the chemical blueprints of all living things. Genes determine physical traits such as eye color, blood type, and bone structure; they also have a significant impact on behavioral traits such as intelligence, temperament, and sociability.

Genes are made of **DNA** (**deoxyribonucleic acid**) molecules. Under high amplification, a DNA molecule looks like a long double strand arranged in a spiraling staircase fashion (Figure 11-3). Although DNA molecules are composed of the same chemical bases, the exact arrangement of chemicals varies, causing different DNA molecules to have different effects. A person's genetic code thus consists of a variety of patterns of DNA molecules arranged in gene groupings on specific chromosomes within a cell's nucleus. Each individual's genetic code is unique.

The exception, of course, is **identical twins** (also called **monozygotic** or **one-egg twins**), who share the same genetic code. Identical twins originate from a single fertilized ovum that divides into two separate entities with identical genetic codes. Identical twins are always same-sex individuals who physically appear to be carbon copies of each other. Since they have the same genes, any differences between them must be due to environmental influences.

Figure 11-2 Chromosome Complement of the Zygote After Fertilization

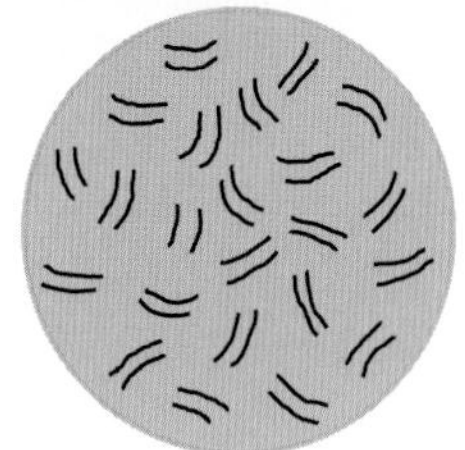
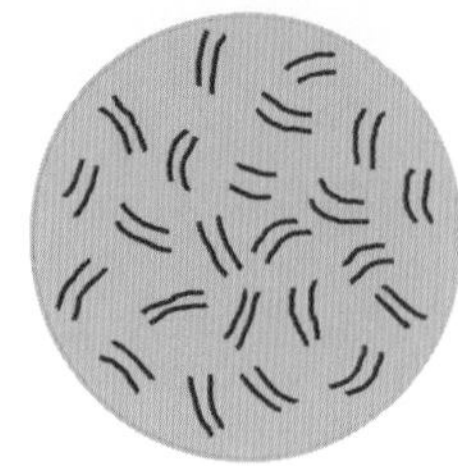

With the exception of the reproduction or germ cells, the body cells of women and men contain 23 pairs of chromosomes.

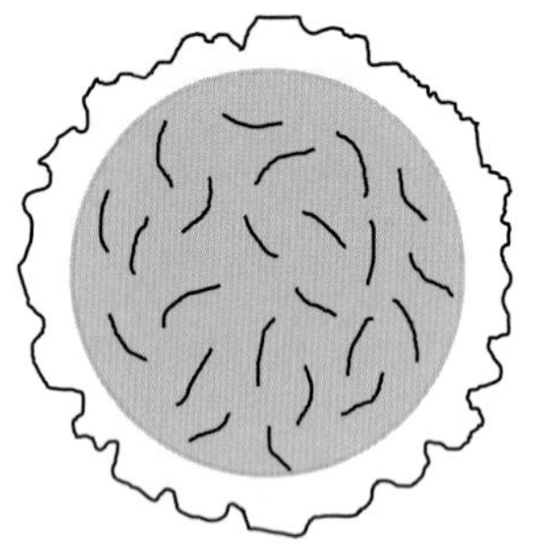
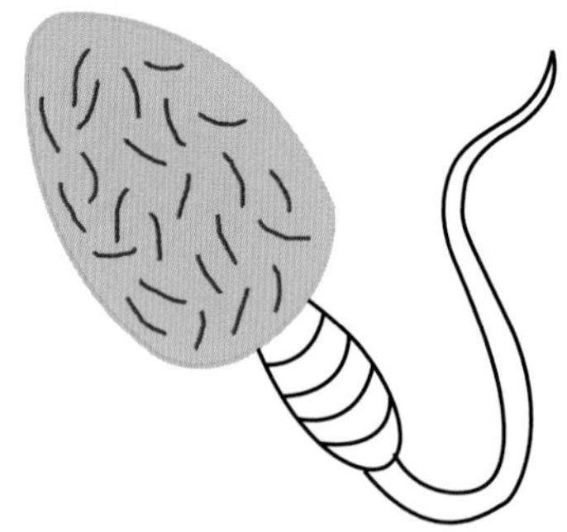

As a result of a biological process known as mitosis, mature germ cells contain only half the usual complement of chromosomes—one member of each pair.

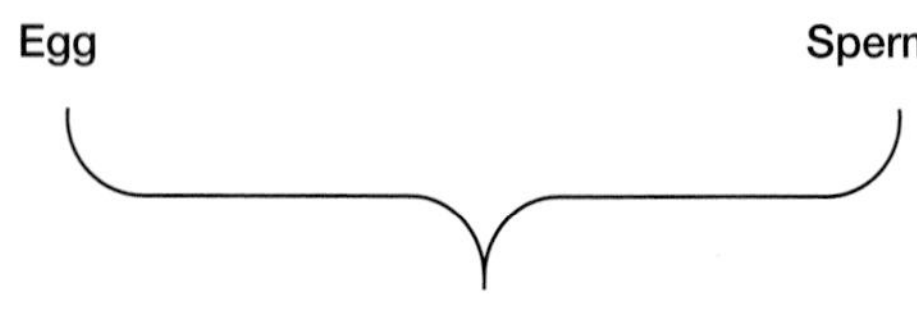

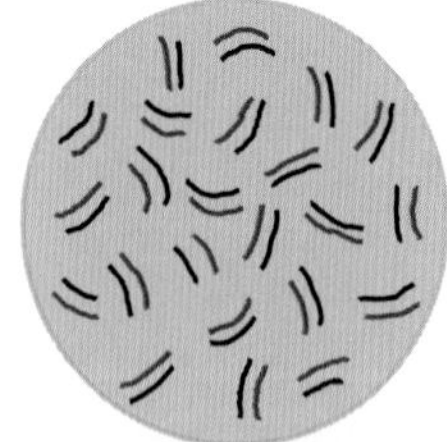

After fertilization, the zygote contains a complement of 46 chromosomes arranged in 23 pairs, one chromosome in each pair from the egg and one from the sperm.

Fraternal Twins Twins produced when two ova are fertilized by two different sperm cells, so that their genetic codes are no more similar than those of any other siblings; also known as *two-egg twins* or *dizygotic twins*

Identical twins may not be as identical as researchers assume, however. Recent genetics research suggests that identical twins may result from tiny genetic mutations that lead one part of the developing embryo to reject the other part, resulting in two nearly identical embryos (Hall, 1992). At present, we do not know the significance of these genetic differences on human development and behavior.

In contrast, **fraternal twins** (also known as **dizygotic** or **two-egg twins**) occur when the woman's ovaries release two ova, each of which is fertilized by a different sperm

Figure 11-3 Deoxyribonucleic Acid Molecule (DNA)

Arranged from two nucleotide strands that form the double helix structure connected by different arrangements of the base pairs adenine, cytosine, guanine, and thymine.

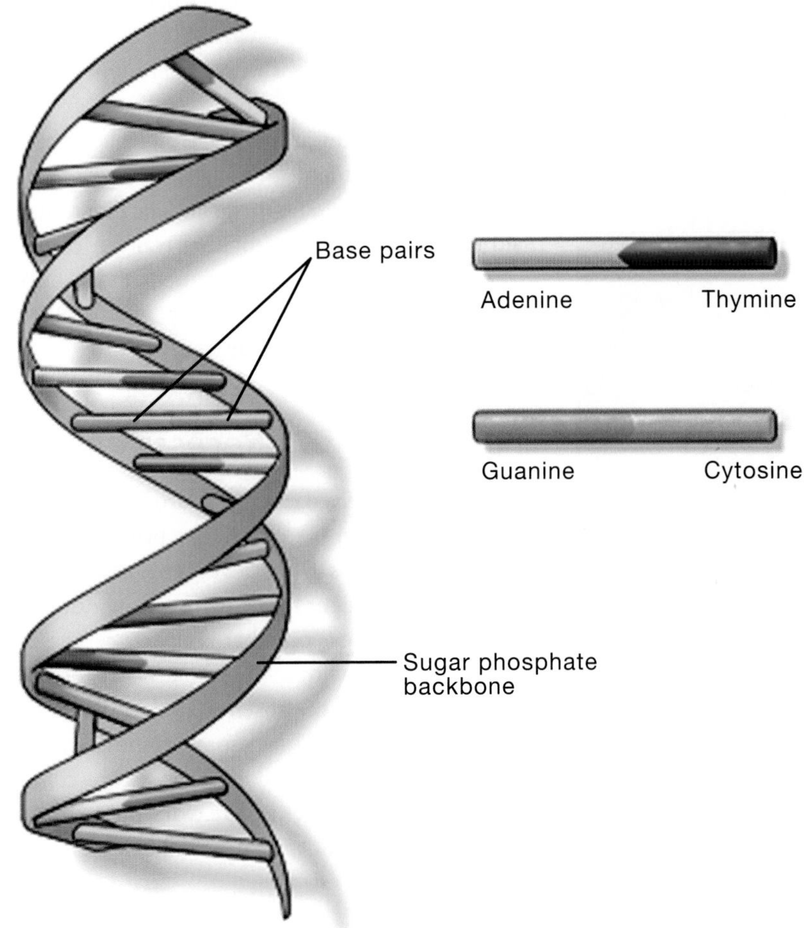

Source: U.S. National Library of Medicine

cell. Since fraternal twins result from the fusion of different germ cells, their genetic makeup is no more alike than that of any other siblings. Physical and behavioral differences between fraternal twins may be due to genetic factors, environmental influences, or a combination of the two.

Psychologists who seek to understand the relative roles of genetics and environment in determining behavioral traits often compare the degree to which both members of a twin pair express a particular trait. When identical twins are more alike (**concordant**) than fraternal twins in a particular trait, we can assume that the attribute has a strong genetic basis. Conversely, when a trait shows a comparable degree of concordance in both types of twins, we can reasonably assume that environment is exerting the greater influence. We will have more to say about twin studies throughout the remaining chapters of this text.

Concordance Degree to which twins share a trait—expressed as a correlation coefficient

(Featureflash Photo Agency/Shutterstock)

Identical twins, such as actors Matthew and Benjamin Royer, are always same-sex individuals who physically appear to be carbon copies of each other.

Genotypes and Phenotypes

The assortment of genes we inherit at conception is known as our **genotype**; the characteristics that result from the expression of various genotypes are known as **phenotypes**. Sometimes genotypes and phenotypes are consistent, as when a person with brown eyes (phenotype) carries only genes for brown eye color (genotype). However, a phenotype is often inconsistent with its genotype, so that a person with brown eyes may carry a blue-eye gene as well as a brown-eye gene. This happens because genes occur in pairs, one of which is contributed by the mother and one by the father.

If your genetic blueprint contains different genes for a trait, you are said to be **heterozygous** for that trait. In contrast, if you inherit identical genes from both your parents, you are **homozygous** for that trait. What determines how a phenotype will be expressed when a person is heterozygous for a particular trait?

Dominance and Recessiveness

Suppose you received a gene for brown eyes from one parent and a gene for blue eyes from the other. The principles of *dominance* and *recessiveness* would allow us to predict that the actual color of your eyes would be brown because genes for brown eyes are dominant over blue eye genes.

A **dominant gene** is one that is always expressed in the phenotype; it is the gene that prevails when paired with a subordinate or **recessive gene**. A recessive gene is one that may be expressed only in the absence of a dominant gene, or when it is paired with a similar recessive gene. Table 11-1 lists some dominant and recessive traits.

Not all human traits can be predicted as easily as eye color. Several traits, such as growth or metabolic rate, result from gene pairs working in consort with each other. This is a more complicated form of genetic transmission, in which several gene pairs interact.

Genotype Assortment of genes each individual inherits at conception

Phenotype The characteristics that result from the expression of an assortment of genes

Heterozygous Genotype that contains different genes for a trait (for instance, both brown-eye and blue-eye genes)

Homozygous Genotype that consists of the same gene for a trait (for instance, brown-eye genes inherited from both parents)

Dominant Gene Gene that prevails when paired with a recessive gene, so that it is always expressed in the phenotype

Recessive Gene Gene that is expressed in the phenotype only in the absence of a dominant gene or when it is paired with a similar recessive gene

Sex-Linked Inheritance Genetic transmission involving genes that are carried only on the X chromosome (females carry the XX chromosome pair; males carry the XY pair)

Sex-Linked Inheritance

You may be aware that certain undesirable traits, such as red-green color blindness and hemophilia (abnormal bleeding) are far more common among males than females. Have you ever wondered why males are more susceptible to these and other diseases that demonstrate **sex-linked inheritance**? The answer lies in the fact that the smaller Y chromosome carries fewer genes than the much larger X chromosome. (The sex chromosome pair in males is XY; in females it is XX.) The genes that determine whether or not a person develops these diseases are carried only on the X chromosome.

In the case of hemophilia, as long as a person has at least one dominant gene for normal blood clotting (which we designate as H, because geneticists use uppercase letters to denote dominant genes and lowercase letters for recessive genes), the disease will not be expressed (see Figure 11-4). Thus, a female can carry the recessive gene for hemophilia (h) on one of her X chromosomes but, nevertheless, have blood that clots normally due to the presence of a dominant H on the other member of her XX pair. A male, however, will be a bleeder if he inherits only one h gene from his mother, since the gene-deficient Y chromosome does not carry a gene that regulates blood clotting.

Table 11-1 Some Common Dominant and Recessive Traits

Dominant Traits	Recessive Traits
Dark hair	Light hair
Nonred hair (brunette or blond)	Red hair
Normal hair growth	Baldness
Curly hair	Straight hair
Brown eyes	Blue, green, hazel, or gray eyes
Normal color vision	Red-green color blindness
Normal visual acuity	Nearsightedness
Normal protein metabolism	Phenylketonuria (inability to convert phenylalanine into tyrosine)
Type A or type B blood	Type O blood
Normal blood clotting	Hemophilia
Normal blood cells	Sickle-cell anemia
Normal skin coloring	Albinism (lack of pigment)
Double-jointedness	Normal joints
Huntington's disease	Normal health
Abnormal digits in fingers or toes	Normal digits

Epigenetics

Epigenetics is a relatively new field of genetics investigating how the expression of genes is influenced by environmental factors such as individual experiences, diet, and other environmental factors (Allis, Caparros, Jenuwein, & Reinberg, 2015). Most psychologists no longer view development processes as influenced exclusively by either nature (genes) or nurture (an individual's experiences). Rather, development occurs as a continual interaction between the environment and an individual's genetic makeup. The expression of particular genes depends on environmental input, and this results in individual differences in behavior and personality.

One of the earliest discoveries in behavioral epigenetics demonstrates this by showing that the type of mothering an infant rat received early in life determined how it responded to stressful events later. Rats that received less nurturing were more sensitive to stress than those receiving adequate nurturing during early development (Meaney & Szyf, 2005). Other studies with animals have demonstrated how maternal behavior during early development alters genes that control for variations in sexual behaviors in adults (Cameron et al., 2008). An environmental event, such as the type of maternal care an infant receives, alters the way genes express for a variety of traits as well as for patterns of neuronal growth and development (McGowan et al., 2011). Clearly this emerging field will have a significant impact on how we understand the processes occurring during human development.

Epigenetics A field of genetics that investigates how gene expression is influenced by a number of environmental events including experiences, diet, and environmental toxins

Figure 11-4 Sex-Linked Inheritance of Hemophilia

A female can carry a recessive gene for hemophilia (h), a blood-clotting disorder, on one of her X chromosomes but not express the disease. A male, however, will express hemophilia if he inherits only one (h) gene from his mother, since the Y chromosome does not carry a gene that regulates blood clotting. The probability of a male inheriting this disease under these conditions is 0.50, or 50 percent.

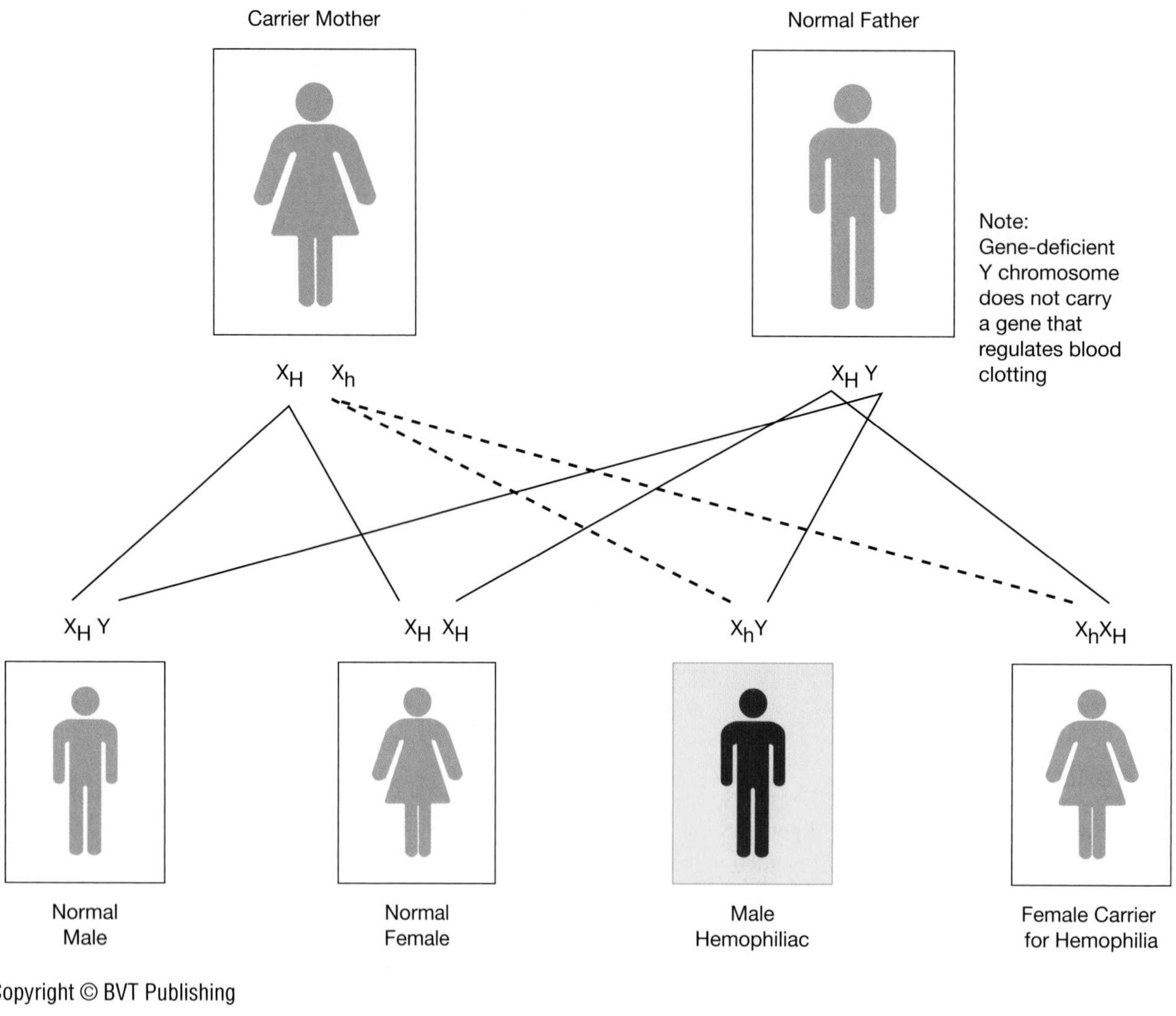

11.3b Genetic Abnormalities

Perhaps the greatest hope of most expectant parents is that their baby will be born healthy and normal. Thankfully, the odds are very high, about 99 percent, that this wish will be granted. This statistic means that about 1 percent of all babies born each year in the United States have some gene defect or chromosomal abnormality that produces a major physical and/or mental handicap. Some of these defects are apparent at birth or shortly thereafter; others do not show up until later in life. About half of all spontaneous abortions are due to chromosomal abnormalities. The following paragraphs describe some inherited abnormalities. These abnormalities range from harmless variations to severe clinical disorders.

Huntington's Disease

Huntington's disease, or *Huntington's chorea*, is one of the cruelest of all genetic diseases. Common symptoms include jerky, uncontrollable movements, loss of balance, intellectual impairment, and emotional disturbance (depression, irritability, etc.). Not uncommonly, the disease is confused with disorders such as Parkinson's disease, Alzheimer's disease, and schizophrenia.

Huntington's Disease A genetically transmitted disease that progressively destroys brain cells in adults; also known as *Huntington's chorea*

A dominant gene that does not produce symptoms until a person is thirty-five to forty-five years old causes Huntington's disease. Unfortunately, by that age a person is likely to have already had children, unaware that each child has a 50 percent chance of inheriting the illness. (Figure 11-5 illustrates the genetic transmission of Huntington's disease.)

The National Huntington's Disease Association (Huntington's Disease Information Page, 2016) has reported that at least 30,000 Americans have the illness and that an additional 50,000 to 100,000 people may have inherited the disease but do not yet know that they have it. Until recently there was no way to identify people who had inherited the gene until symptoms began to appear. However, in the early 1980s, Harvard molecular biologist and geneticist James Gusella and his colleagues (1983) announced that they had located a genetic marker for Huntington's disease on chromosome 4. Subsequent research has confirmed that a gene mutation on this chromosome is responsible for the

Figure 11-5 Genetic Transmission of Huntington's Disease

One parent who will eventually develop Huntington's disease (usually by age forty-five) has a single faulty gene (H) that dominates its normal counterpart (h). The probability that a child from this union will inherit Huntington's disease is 0.50, or 50 percent.

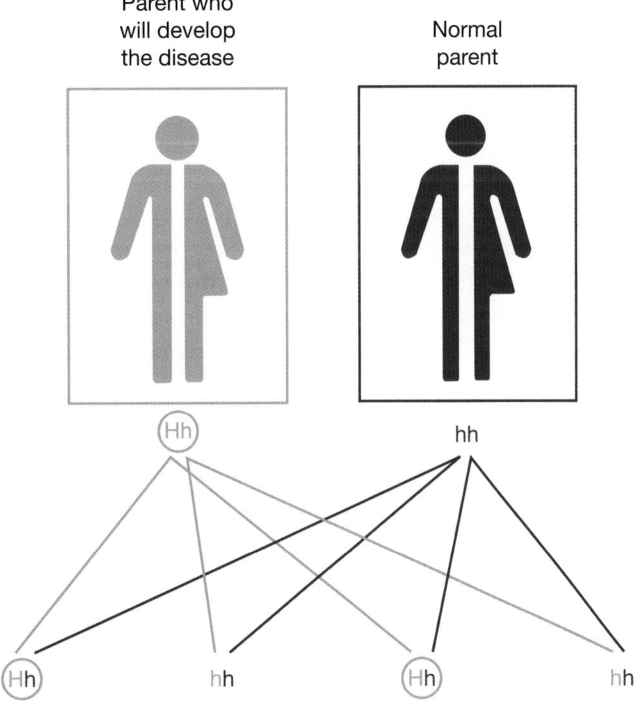

Phenylketonuria (PKU) Disease caused by a recessive gene that results in the absence of an enzyme necessary to metabolize the milk protein phenylalanine

disease (Lanska, 2000). Presently, markers for Huntington's disease can be identified in the blood before symptoms appear, making early medical intervention more successful (Borovecki et al., 2005).

The rapid emergence of genetic tests for a variety of serious diseases has also raised serious ethical dilemmas for health practitioners. If a genetic test indicates that a child will develop a deadly illness that will result in a painful and/or premature death, should that child be told his or her fate? Should such a test even be performed? Genetic counselors who struggle with these issues note that many people at risk for a serious genetic disease do not want to know if they carry a life-ending defective gene, for fear that such depressing news will be a blight on whatever healthy years remain. However, what if these at-risk individuals choose to have children while electing to remain ignorant about their chances of passing a defect on to their offspring? Does society have the responsibility or right to take steps to ensure against this eventuality? What kinds of legal and ethical issues might be encountered by people who, in spite of being aware of their genetic flaws and the associated risks, opt to become parents? Should insurance companies be allowed to withhold medical insurance from people whose medical records reveal they carry a gene that one day will be a cause of major medical expenses?

The ethical dilemmas just described are only a sample of issues that medical ethicists, genetic researchers and other concerned professionals discuss and debate as they seek to deal with the social, ethical, and moral issues that accompany the emergence of amazing new genetic technologies. Researchers work to understand what the genes can tell about predicting and someday curing inherited diseases as geneticists, lawyers, and counselors grapple with the many ethical questions in an effort to help people take advantage of the genetic revolution without falling prey to its pitfalls.

Phenylketonuria

Phenylketonuria (PKU) is another potentially devastating genetic disease. A recessive gene causes PKU that, when present in a double dose, results in the absence of an enzyme necessary to metabolize the protein phenylalanine found in milk. A newborn with phenylketonuria cannot metabolize milk to form phenylalanine. Unmetabolized phenylalanine converts to phenylpyruvic acid. The consequence is an excessive accumulation of phenylpyruvic acid, which damages the baby's developing nervous system and can lead to intellectual disability and a variety of other disruptive symptoms.

Fortunately, a routine screening process can be used to test levels of phenylpyruvic acid shortly after birth. Infants who show high levels of phenylpyruvic acid test positive for PKU, and they can be placed on milk substitutes. They must remain on the diet for several years until their brains have developed to the point when the acid can no longer damage them.

There are many other examples of diseases caused by genetic defects. These include such conditions as *muscular dystrophy, cystic fibrosis, sickle-cell anemia* (a blood disorder that primarily affects black people), and *Tay-Sachs disease* (a disorder characterized by progressive degeneration of the central nervous system that occurs primarily in Jewish people of Eastern European origin). However, many inherited diseases are caused not by the transmission of faulty genes but rather by chromosomal abnormalities. One of the best-known conditions caused by chromosomal abnormalities is Down syndrome (previously called Down's syndrome).

Down Syndrome

Down Syndrome
Chromosomal disorder characterized by marked intellectual disability as well as distinctive physical traits, including short stature, a flattened skull and nose, and an extra fold of skin over the eyelid; also known as trisomy 21 because it is caused by an extra (third) copy of the twenty-first chromosome

Down syndrome is the most common chromosomal disorder. It is characterized by a distinctive physical appearance—short stature, small round head, flattened skull and nose, oval-shaped eyes with an extra fold of skin over the eyelid, a short neck, a protruding tongue, and sometimes webbed fingers or toes. People with this syndrome also demonstrate marked mental retardation. Down syndrome children tend to be cheerful, affectionate, and sociable. Most are educable, and some acquire simple skills that allow them to earn an income and live independently in special environments.

Down syndrome is an autosomal chromosome disorder in which the twenty-first chromosome (the disorder is also known as *trisomy 21*) pair has an additional chromosome attached to it. A person with Down syndrome thus has forty-seven chromosomes rather than the normal forty-six. While there is inconclusive evidence that a small percentage of Down syndrome cases may have a genetic basis, most if not all instances of this disorder are caused by a chromosomal accident (Hamamy, al-Hakkak, & al-Taha, 1990. Older women are at greater risk of bearing Down syndrome children, a fact that has led many researchers to attribute this disorder primarily to deterioration of the mother's ova with age. However, evidence suggests that the syndrome may also be caused by a defect in the father's sperm (Abroms & Bennett, 1981; Malan et al., 2006; Martin, 1987).

(Shutterstock)

Down syndrome, the most common chromosomal disorder is characterized by a distinctive physical appearance and marked intellectual disability.

The development of several techniques for assessing fetal development and diagnosing birth defects like Down syndrome in utero have encouraged some couples with a history of genetic disease to conduct prenatal screening. If a woman and her physician have some reason to suspect that there may be fetal abnormalities, amniocentesis or another method of genetic analysis can help establish whether a problem exists. As Figure 11-6 illustrates, a needle is inserted through the woman's abdominal wall and into the uterus to draw a sample of the amniotic fluid (fluid surrounding the fetus). Fetal cells from the fluid are cultured for chromosome analysis, and the fluid is then tested. A variety of birth defects can be detected by this means. However, amniocentesis cannot detect all fetal abnormalities, and it is an invasive procedure requiring hospitalization. Other genetic screening tests are continually being developed and used.

11.4 Prenatal Development

The nine months, or approximately 266 days, of prenatal development take place in three stages: germinal, embryonic, and fetal. These stages of prenatal development are not to be confused with the customary convention of dividing pregnancy into three-month segments called *trimesters*.

Figure 11-6 Amniocentesis Procedure

This procedure consists of inserting a needle through the woman's abdominal wall into the uterine cavity to draw out a sample of amniotic fluid (fluid surrounding the fetus). Fetal cells from the fluid are cultured for chromosomal analysis.

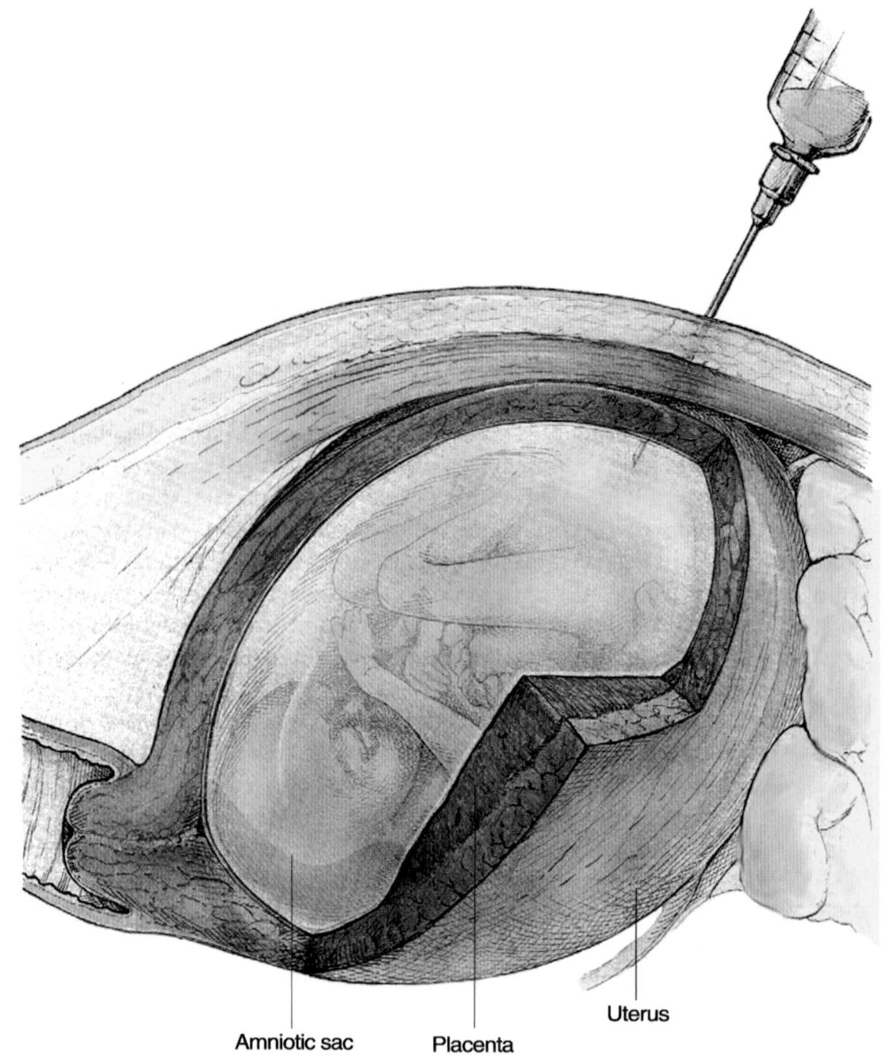

11.4a Germinal Stage

Germinal Stage First of three stages in prenatal development of a fetus that spans the first two weeks after fertilization; also known as the *zygote stage*

During the **germinal** or **zygote stage** (the first two weeks after fertilization), the zygote develops rapidly as it becomes attached to the walls of the uterus. By the end of the second week, various auxiliary structures—the amniotic sac, umbilical cord, and placenta—are well established, and the cell mass is called an embryo.

11.4b Embryonic Stage

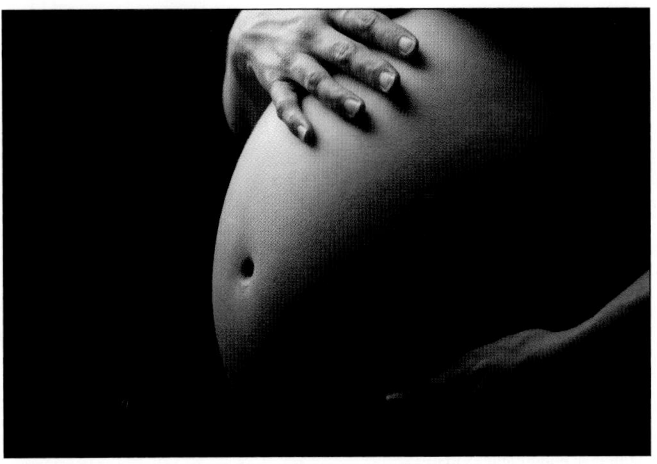
(iStock)

The three stages of prenatal development that occur during the nine months of pregnancy are germinal, embryonic, and fetal.

The second stage, the **embryonic stage**, lasts from the beginning of the third week to the end of the eighth. It is characterized by very fast growth and differentiation of the heart, lungs, pancreas, and other vital organs as well as the major body systems. During this stage, the embryo is extremely vulnerable to negative environmental influences such as faulty nutrition, drugs, and maternal disease. Because any of these environmental insults may have devastating, irreversible effects on the developing baby, the embryonic period is viewed as a critical stage of development. The vast majority of environmentally induced prenatal development defects, as well as most spontaneous abortions, occurs during this period. By the end of the embryonic stage almost all of the baby's structures and organs are formed; a few organs, like the heart, are already functioning. By the end of eight weeks the baby, now called a **fetus**, has clearly discernible features and a prominent head.

11.4c Fetal Stage

During the final **fetal stage**, which extends from the beginning of the third month to birth, bone and muscle tissue form, and the various organs and body systems continue to mature and develop. By the end of four months, external body parts—including fingernails, eyebrows, and eyelashes—are clearly formed. Fetal movement may be felt at this time. Future prenatal development consists primarily of growth in size and refinement of the features that already exist.

Throughout pregnancy, the fetus depends on the mother for nutrients, oxygen, and waste elimination as substances pass through the placenta and the umbilical cord to the fetus. Fetal and maternal bloods do not mix. Fetal blood circulates independently within the closed system of the fetus and inner part of the placenta; maternal blood flows in the uterine walls and outer part of the placenta. All exchanges between fetal and maternal blood systems take place as substances pass through the walls of the blood vessels.

11.4d The Effects of Alcohol and Drugs on Development

As we mentioned above, substances that can pass through the walls of the circulatory system can leave the mother's blood supply and enter the blood of the fetus. Many of the drugs discussed in Chapter 3 easily pass through capillary walls and other cell membranes, such as neurons. The reason some substances can pass through cell membranes and others cannot has to do with their ability to dissolve in cell membranes. This **lipid solubility** allows a substance to leave the blood supply and pass through other cell membranes. All drugs that affect the central nervous system are lipid soluble. That is, they can dissolve through capillary walls and enter other tissues, including neurons in the brain and tissues of a fetus. A number of lipid soluble substances can have catastrophic effects on a

Embryonic Stage Second stage of prenatal development, lasting from the beginning of the third week to the end of the eighth week after fertilization, characterized by fast growth and differentiation of the major body systems as well as vital organs

Fetus The developing infant after the embryonic stage up to the time of birth; see also *fetal stage*

Fetal Stage Third and final stage of prenatal development, extending from the beginning of the third month to birth, during which bone and muscle tissue form and the organs and body systems continue to develop

Lipid Solubility Lipid-soluble substances can dissolve in a cell's membrane, making it possible to leave the blood supply and enter other cells, including neurons in the brain or all fetal tissues

Critical Period A time during development when specific systems, structures, or abilities are most sensitive to external factors (such as specific stimuli and experiences, as well as the chemical environment surrounding tissues)

Teratogen Any substance (drug or toxin) that alters the course of normal development of a fetus; *teratogen* means "monster" in Greek

Fetal Alcohol Syndrome A pattern of physical, neurological, and cognitive abnormalities that result from fetal exposure to alcohol

developing fetus, particularly if they enter the fetal blood supply during **critical period**s of development. Because the brain of a fetus is undergoing rapid changes throughout pregnancy, it is particularly sensitive to chemical exposures. Any chemical that alters the course of normal development is considered to be a **teratogen**.

One of the most potent teratogens is alcohol. Alcohol consumed during pregnancy readily leaves the maternal blood supply and enters the blood, and ultimately all tissues of the developing fetus. Consequences of fetal exposure to alcohol depend on the phase of pregnancy and which systems and structures are in their critical periods of development during exposure. Some of the symptoms of fetal alcohol exposure include stunted growth, facial abnormalities, brain damage, and severe cognitive disabilities (NIAAA, 2016). This pattern of symptoms is called **fetal alcohol syndrome**. It is estimated that nearly 30 percent of pregnant women drink during pregnancy.

A number of other drugs can be teratogens as well, including nicotine, cocaine, methamphetamine, and even marijuana. All of these substances can cause developmental abnormalities and cognitive deficits. For example, low birth weight, premature birth, impaired movement, inattention, delayed language acquisition, and behavioral adjustment problems (Drinking and Your Pregnancy, 2006). Barry Lester at Brown University analyzed data from 1,618 mother-infant pairs, 84 of whom were exposed to methamphetamine. On average, the methamphetamine-exposed infants weighed about 10 percent less at birth than nonexposed infants. In addition, the meth-exposed infants showed greater lethargy, signs of physiological distress, and abnormal breathing. In general, the meth-exposed infants were significantly distressed and developmentally delayed (Smith et al., 2008).

Exposure to a wide range of drugs and toxins can alter the course of fetal development. Even prescription drugs used to treat anxiety, depression, and other psychological disorders can have profound effects on fetal development. It is critical that pregnant women restrain from alcohol and illicit drug use throughout their pregnancies as well as throughout the duration of breast feeding. Women taking prescription medications should notify their prescribing physician as soon as they suspect they may be pregnant.

11.5 Physical Development

The period from *infancy* (birth to roughly the toddler stage) through *childhood* (toddlerhood to the onset of adolescence) is marked by many important developmental changes. The remainder of this chapter deals with various aspects of physical, cognitive, and psychosocial development that occur during the first twelve or thirteen years. We begin by discussing physical development, including development of the brain, physical growth, and motor development.

11.5a Development of the Brain

A newborn's brain has most, if not all, the neurons it will ever have. However, it is still far from mature. At birth, the brain is only about 350 grams (25 percent of its adult weight), and the complex neural networks that form the basis for our skills and memories are just beginning to form. Growth occurs rapidly: By six months, the brain is 50 percent of its adult weight; at two years, 75 percent; and at five years, 90 percent of its adult weight. At age ten, the figure is 95 percent. These figures stand in sharp contrast to the weight of the entire body, which at birth is only about 5 percent of adult weight and at ten years is only about 50 percent. During this period of rapid growth (and to a lesser extent in the years that follow), neural networks become increasingly complex as changes take place in the size, shape, and density of interconnections among neurons.

The brain develops in an orderly fashion after birth. In the first few months the primary motor area of the cerebral cortex develops rapidly as the infant progresses from involuntary reflexive activity to voluntary control over motor movements. The cortical areas that control vision and hearing develop somewhat more slowly. By three months, however, these sensory areas, particularly those controlling visual perception, are more fully developed so that infants can reach out and touch objects they see. In the ensuing months, further development and refinement of sensory and motor capabilities are closely linked to changes in the brain and the rest of the nervous system.

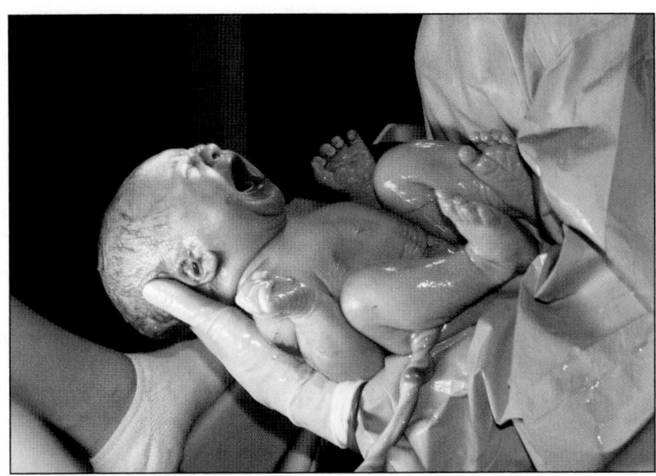
(Shutterstock)

A newborn's brain has most of, if not all, the neurons it will ever need.

Recall from Chapter 3 that certain cognitive functions tend to be localized in one of the cerebral hemispheres. At one time, it was believed that much of this hemispheric specialization, or localization of cortical functions, occurs gradually throughout childhood. Recent evidence suggests, however, that this specialization begins very early. One study demonstrated that most newborns are better able to process speech syllables in their left than right hemispheres. (Remember that verbal functions tend to be localized in the left hemispheres of most people.) By age three, nine out of ten children show this specialization for verbal processing. Left- or right-handedness also develops early, providing further evidence of hemispheric specialization during infancy.

Effects of Experiences on Brain Development

Do our early experiences influence the way our brains develop? Some experiments performed in the late 1960s indicate that they do. Mark Rosenzweig and his colleagues at the University of California, Berkeley conducted a series of experiments to compare how being raised in enriched as opposed to impoverished environments affected rats (Rosenzweig, 1966). Some of the rats were reared in sterile, dimly lit, individual cages with solid side walls that prevented them from seeing or touching other animals; others were raised in a large cage with ten to twelve other rats and plenty of toys such as ladders, wheels, and boxes (see Figure 11-7).

The researchers were not originally looking for significant brain differences. Most psychologists, at the time, had not considered that experience might alter brain anatomy. However, Rosenzweig and his associates routinely recorded brain weights as part of their research, and as a result they made an important discovery: The brains of the rats reared in the enriched environments were heavier than those of rats raised in solitary confinement. These variations were most pronounced in the cerebral cortex, where the average weight difference was 4 percent. Rats raised in the impoverished, sterile environments tended to develop a lighter and thinner cortex, with smaller-than-normal neurons (Rosenzweig, Bennett, & Diamond, 1972).

Other evidence provided by researchers at the University of Illinois has supported these findings, linking enriched early experiences with expanded networks of dendrites in the precise areas of the brain where the experiences are processed (Greenough & Green, 1981). The increased number of dendrites seems to preserve newly established neural networks. More branches mean more and larger synapses, suggesting that greater

Figure 11-7 The Environment Has a Profound Effect on the Development of the Brain

Mark Rosenzweig and his colleagues found that rats reared in enriched environments developed larger brains with thicker cerebral cortexes than rats reared in impoverished environments.

amounts of information can be transmitted more efficiently in these animals' brains. We now believe these environmental differences contribute to epigenetic changes to genes controlling neuronal growth and development (Kiefer, 2007).

Early experience seems to affect brain biochemistry as well as anatomy. In the enriched rats, Rosenzweig and his colleagues also found a significant increase in the activity of two enzymes, acetylcholinesterase and cholinesterase, both of which play an important role in the synaptic transmission of neural messages (Rosenzweig et al., 1972).

In both the Berkeley and University of Illinois studies, the anatomical and biochemical effects were not restricted to the earliest periods of development. Rats that were reared under normal laboratory conditions in their early days and then subjected to either impoverished or enriched environments showed similar weight and biochemical changes in their brains. Although the effects of environmental stimulation may be greater during early development, these findings indicate that the brains of rats, and possibly humans, are malleable throughout development.

Research during the past ten years has confirmed that some genetic blueprint waiting to be completed does not predetermine the development of the brain as development progresses. Rather, brain development, including the elaborate interconnections between neurons, depends upon neural stimulation. Even though infants are born with almost all of the 200 billion neurons they will ever have, the mass of their brain is only about one-fourth that of an adult. The brain becomes bigger not because more neurons develop but because the existing neurons get larger. Both the number of axons and dendrites, as well as the complexity of their connections, continue to increase. Contrary to popular belief, neuronal growth continues throughout adulthood and can be affected by both emotional stress and environmental enrichment. Stress, and the cascade of hormones associated with it, can reduce neuronal growth and turnover while environmental enrichment and exercise can increase it (Ekstrand, Hellsten, & Tingström, 2008). The term used to describe how modifiable the brain is, especially during early development, is **plasticity**. As we have seen, the brain is continually modified by developmental processes and environmental events.

How are neural connections increased? What is the mechanism that allows experience to rewire the brain? These questions are partially answered by the mechanism proposed by Donald Hebb more than forty years ago, now referred to as *Hebbian synapses*. Hebbian synapses were described in considerable detail in Chapter 7 as a neural mechanism for memory. As you may recall, Hebbian synapses refer to long-term changes in synaptic connections that are dependent upon particular patterns of neuronal activity. In a sense, cells that fire together get wired together.

Plasticity A term used to describe how modifiable the brain is, especially throughout development

Cephalocaudal Pattern of physical and motor development that is normal among humans, in which the head and upper portion of the body develop first and more rapidly

Proximodistal Pattern of development normal to humans in which infants gain control over areas that are closest to the center of their bodies (so that, for instance, control is gained over the upper arms before the fingers)

11.5b Physical Growth

Changes that take place in the brain are only part of the picture of what happens during development. Another significant change is physical growth. Children grow more rapidly during the first few years than at any other time. During the first six months, in fact, infants more than double their weight, and by their first birthday most infants have tripled their birth weight (the average newborn weighs 7 pounds) and increased their birth height by 50 percent. In the next two years they gain another 8 inches and 10 pounds, on the average. After their third birthday, this early growth levels off somewhat to about 2 or 3 inches per year, until the adolescent growth spurt.

Both physical growth and motor development follow two basic patterns. The first pattern is **cephalocaudal** (that is, from head to foot); the second pattern is **proximodistal** (inner to outer). The cephalocaudal pattern of development occurs first and most rapidly in the head and upper body, which is why newborns have large heads. It is also why a one-year-old's brain weighs approximately two-thirds of its eventual adult weight while the rest of the body is a much smaller proportion of its adult size. The cephalocaudal principle also explains why babies can track things with their eyes before they can effectively move their trunks, and why they can do many things with their hands before they can use their legs. Because development is also proximodistal, infants gain control over the upper portions of their arms and legs, which are closer to the center of the body, before they can control their forearms and forelegs. Control of the hands, feet, fingers, and toes comes last.

11.5c Motor Development

Another basic rule of development is that it proceeds from the simple to the more complex. This progression is particularly apparent in the acquisition of motor skills. The motor movements of young babies are dominated by a number of involuntary reflexes that offer either protection or help in securing nourishment. An example is the rooting reflex: When babies are stroked on the cheek, they turn their heads toward the sensation, vigorously "rooting" for a nipple. Other common reflexes are listed in Table 11-2. As development progresses, voluntary, cortically controlled movements begin to take over, and the primitive reflexes disappear according to the timetable shown. Some reflexes—such as coughing, sneezing, gagging, and the eye-blink—remain with us throughout our lives.

As the nervous system and muscles mature, more complicated motor movements and skills begin to emerge. There is wide variation in the ages at which babies are able to

Table 11-2 Primitive Reflexes in Human Infants

Name of Reflex	Stimulation	Behavior	Age of Dropping Out
Rooting	Cheek stroked with finger or nipple	Head turns, mouth opens, sucking movement begins	9 months
Moro (startle)	Sudden stimulus such as a loud noise or being dropped	Extends legs, arms, and fingers, arches back, draws back head	3 months
Darwinian (grasping)	Palm of hand stroked	Makes such a strong fist that the baby can be raised to standing position if both fists are closed around a stick	2 months
Swimming	Put in water facedown	Well-coordinated swimming movements	6 months
Tonic neck	Laid down on back	Turns head to one side, assumes "fencer" position, extends arms and legs on preferred side, flexes opposite limbs	6 months
Babinski	Sole of foot stroked	Toes fan out, foot twists in	6–9 months
Walking	Held under arm, with bare feet touching flat surface	Makes steplike motions that look like well-coordinated walking	2 months
Placing	Backs of feet drawn against edge of flat surface	Withdraws foot	1 month

roll over, sit without support, stand, and walk, but the sequence of these developments is universal.

Can different environmental experiences influence the rate at which we acquire motor skills? A number of studies have explored this question, and within a normal range of experiences, the answer seems to be no. As long as children are well fed, healthy, and free to initiate motor skills when they are ready, the role of environmental influences on motor development is quite limited. For example, regardless of the amount of training or encouragement children receive, they will not walk until the cerebellum has matured enough to create a readiness for walking, an event that occurs at about age one.

In certain Native American cultures, infants are wrapped in swaddling clothes and bound to cradleboards during most of their waking hours for the first twelve or more months of their lives. We have just seen that children will not walk until they reach a certain level of biological readiness. Is the converse true? Will children begin to walk when their biological clocks reach a certain point, even if they have not had earlier opportunities to crawl and otherwise move about on their own? Make a reasoned prediction before reading on.

If early training does not significantly accelerate the rate at which children master motor skills such as standing or walking, does the same rule apply to other physical skills such as bowel and bladder control? A classic early study assessed the effect of differential toilet training on twin boys. One was placed on a toilet once on the hour every day from two months of age, while the other did not begin training until age twenty-three months. The first twin did not demonstrate any control until twenty months, but by twenty-three months he had mastered bladder and bowel control. The other twin, with no prior training, caught up in short order as soon as training began (McGraw, 1940).

Later research has generally confirmed this finding, but at a later age. It is now widely recognized that no amount of encouragement, reinforcement, punishment, or pleading will induce successful toilet training until the necessary muscular and neurological maturation has occurred. Typically, girls learn this skill slightly before boys (thirty-two vs. thirty-five months). Unfortunately, toilet training is often begun long before an infant can voluntarily control the sphincter muscles in order to retain waste. While an early start does not hasten toilet training, it may result in emotional strain, particularly if parents put too much pressure on a child (Schum et al., 2002).

Most infants begin to walk, climb on furniture, and climb stairs between their fourteenth and eighteenth months. This is largely determined by the development of the cerebellum, which is involved in motor learning, maintaining posture, and muscle coordination.

Although the milestones are no longer so dramatic, motor development continues beyond infancy and early childhood. Parents are sometimes amazed to realize one day that the awkward child they observed banging around the house has been transformed into a coordinated athlete who performs with distinction.

BVT *Lab*

Flashcards are available for this chapter at **www.BVTLab.com.**

11.6 Cognitive Development

Cognitive development refers to the development of various behaviors such as perceiving, remembering, reasoning, and problem solving. When do children begin to remember? How do they categorize experiences? When can they see things from another's perspective, reason logically, and think symbolically? Most efforts to answer such questions lead inevitably to the writings of the late Swiss psychologist Jean Piaget.

11.6a Piaget's Theory of Cognitive Development

No one has provided more insights into cognitive development than Jean Piaget (1970, 1972). In the early 1920s, Piaget became interested in how children think while he was working with Alfred Binet in Paris on standardizing children's intelligence tests. At first, his goal was to find certain questions that the average child of a specific age could answer correctly. However, Piaget soon became intrigued with another finding: The mistakes made by many children of the same age were often strikingly similar (and strikingly different from those made by children of other ages). It occurred to Piaget that children's cognitive strategies are age-related and that the way children think about things changes with age regardless of the specific nature of what they are thinking about. These observations led Piaget to refocus his research. From this point until his death in 1980, he devoted his efforts to understanding how cognitive abilities develop. Piaget's theory gradually evolved from years of carefully observing and questioning individual children, including his own three offspring. The following paragraphs provide an overview of his major themes.

Schemas

Schemas In reference to memory, conceptual frameworks that individuals use to make sense out of stored information; in Piaget's theory, the mental structures we form to assimilate and organize processed information

Assimilation In Piaget's theory, the process by which individuals interpret new information in accordance with existing knowledge or schemas

Accommodation In vision, the focusing process in which the lens adjusts its shape, depending on the distance between the eye and the object viewed, in order to project a clear image consistently onto the retina; in Piaget's theory, the process of adjusting existing knowledge so that new information can fit more readily

Sensorimotor Stage In Piaget's theory, the period of development between birth and about age two years during which infants learn about their worlds primarily through their senses and actions

According to Piaget, the impetus behind human intellectual development is an urge to make sense out of our world. To accomplish this goal, he theorized, our maturing brains form "mental" structures or **schemas** that assimilate and organize processed information. These schemas guide future behavior while providing a framework for making sense out of new information.

Newborns are equipped with only primitive schemas that guide certain basic sensorimotor sequences such as sucking, looking, and grasping. According to Piaget, these early schemas become activated only when certain objects are present—for example, things that can be looked at, grasped, or sucked. However, as an infant evolves into a child and later an adult, these schemas become increasingly complex, often substituting symbolic representations for objects that are physically present (Piaget, 1977).

By the time we reach adulthood, our brains are filled with countless schemas, or ways of organizing information, that range from our knowledge of how to play a tune to the fantasies we concoct when we are bored. To Piaget, cognitive growth involves a constant process of modifying and adapting our schemas to account for new experiences. This adaptation takes place through two processes: assimilation and accommodation.

Assimilation and Accommodation

Assimilation is the process by which we interpret new information in accordance with our existing knowledge or schemas. In this ongoing process, we may find it necessary to modify the information we assimilate in order to fit it into our existing schemas. At the same time, however, we adjust or restructure what we already know so that new information can fit in better—a process Piaget called **accommodation**.

For instance, an infant who is accustomed to taking his nourishment from the breast uses a simple "suck and swallow" schema to guide this basic sensorimotor sequence. When switched from the breast to the bottle, the infant assimilates this new experience into the existing schema and continues to suck and swallow. What happens when the parents introduce a notable variation by filling the formula bottle with apple juice instead of milk? The baby's initial reaction may be to spit out the strange new substance. With time, the infant may come to like apple juice but dislike other types of juice. Basically, the infant has accommodated the new information by modifying the suck and swallow schema to one of "suck, taste, and swallow (maybe)."

Piaget believed that we learn to understand our world as we constantly adapt and modify our mental structures through assimilation and accommodation. As we develop, assimilation allows us to maintain important connections with the past while accommodation helps us to adapt and change as we gain new experiences.

Four Stages of Cognitive Development

Piaget viewed cognitive growth as a four-stage process with qualitatively different kinds of thinking occurring in each of these stages. Although all people progress through these stages in the same sequence, Piaget noted that the speed of this progression might vary from person to person. Table 11-3 outlines these four stages: sensorimotor, preoperational, concrete operations, and formal operations.

Sensorimotor Stage (Birth to About Twenty-Four Months)

During the **sensorimotor stage**, infants learn about their worlds primarily through their senses and actions. Instead of thinking about what is going on around them, infants discover by sensing (sensori-) and doing (motor). They learn by their actions, which gradually evolve from reflexes to more purposeful behaviors. For example, an infant might learn that shaking a rattle produces a sound or that crying at night produces parents. Thus, some of the schemas that develop during this stage are organized around the principle of causality, as the infant begins to perform cognitively organized goal-directed behaviors.

Object Permanence
Realization that objects continue to exist even when they are not in view; according to Piaget, a key achievement of the sensorimotor stage of development

Another key aspect of the sensorimotor stage is the gradual development of **object permanence**—the realization that objects (or people) continue to exist even when they are not immediately in view. Up to about the age of four months, an object ceases to exist for the infant when it is out of sight. After about four months, babies begin to look for objects they no longer see, and sometime between eight and twelve months they begin to retrieve objects they see being hidden manually. By age two, most children are able to incorporate into their schemas symbolic representation of objects that are clearly independent of their perception of these articles. At this point in development, toddlers gleefully and systematically search all kinds of possible hiding places for objects they have not seen hidden. Research by University of Illinois psychologist Rene Baillargeon (1987) revealed that object permanence in infants might occur as early as age two-and-a-half months (Aguiar & Baillargeon, 2002; Baillargeon, 2008; Wang, Baillargeon, & Paterson, 2005).

During this stage, infants are also capable of understanding numbers. In a series of experiments, psychologist Karen Wynn has demonstrated that children as young as nine months can understand both addition and subtraction of a large number of objects and areas (McCrink & Wynn, 2004). In addition, nine-month-old infants demonstrate *operational momentum*—a tendency to overestimate the outcome of addition and underestimate the outcome of subtraction. In a clever experiment, Wynn and her colleagues showed infants short videos of events involving either the addition or subtraction of objects. Each event type had several outcomes. The outcomes were numerically correct, too small, or too large. Infants gazed longer at the outcomes that violated operational momentum than either of the other outcomes, suggesting an early disposition to operational momentum (McCrink & Wynn, 2009).

Another important cognitive skill of the sensorimotor stage is imitation. Even a tiny baby may try to imitate the facial expression of an older person. Under controlled laboratory conditions, researchers have found that attempts at imitation are clearly present even among newborns seven- to seventy-two hours old (Meltzoff & Moore, 1983). For example, when an experimenter stuck his tongue out at a newborn, the infant responded in kind. This cognitive skill continues to be refined, and by the end of the sensorimotor period children imitate all kinds of behaviors (Anisfeld, 2005).

(Shutterstock)

As children reach age two years and beyond, they master object permanence and can think representatively, using symbols rather than depending on what they see or touch.

Preoperational Stage (Ages Two to Seven Years)

As children move beyond their second birthday, they increasingly use symbolic thought. Having mastered object permanence, they are now ready to think representatively, using symbols rather than depending on what they see or touch. The ability to use words to represent people, objects, and events allows children to make giant steps in cognitive development. Imagination

Preoperational Stage According to Piaget, the second major stage of cognitive development from ages two to seven years; preoperational children can develop only limited concepts and are unable to evaluate simultaneously more than one physical dimension

Centration Inability to take into account more than one perceptual factor at a time; in Piaget's theory of cognitive development, characteristic of the preoperational stage of development

Decentration Ability to evaluate two or more physical dimensions simultaneously

Conservation The understanding that changing the form of an object does not necessarily change its essential character; a key to achievement in Piaget's theory of cognitive development

Egocentrism The tendency of young children to view the world as being centered around themselves

becomes important as children's play activities become increasingly focused on make-believe. Three- and four-year-olds can now imitate another person's behavior after a lapse of time—a qualitative change from the immediate imitation that took place during the sensorimotor stage. The use of language, imaginative play, and delayed imitation all demonstrate an increasing sophistication.

Despite these advances, however, preoperational thought remains somewhat limited, for it depends largely on how things appear or seem to be. Children at this stage have yet to master logical reasoning processes based on rules and concepts, which is why Piaget used the term **preoperational stage**: Young children are able to develop only immature concepts, or *preconcepts*, in their effort to understand the world. For example, an adult has no problem distinguishing between a sports car and a sedan, or a new versus an old car. However, a small child has only an ill-defined, immature concept of a car—something that has wheels and doors and goes *"vroooom."*

Another limitation of preoperational thought is apparent in the phenomenon of **centration**—the inability to take into account more than one perceptual factor at the same time. (The ability to evaluate two or more physical dimensions simultaneously, a process called **decentration**, does not emerge until the end of the preoperational period.)

Piaget demonstrated centration and decentration in a simple experiment. When he poured equal amounts of liquid into two identical glasses, five-, six-, and seven-year-old children all reported that the glasses contained equal amounts. However, when the liquid from one glass was poured into a taller, narrower glass, the children had different opinions about which of the two glasses contained the most liquid. The five- and six-year-olds knew that it was the same liquid, but they were unable to generalize beyond the central perceptual factor of greater height, which normally indicates "more." Thus, they indicated that the tall glass had more juice. In contrast, the seven-year-olds generally reported there was no difference, a fact they knew to be true since they were able to decentrate, or simultaneously take into account the two physical dimensions of height and width.

The ability to decentrate enables children to master **conservation**, the understanding that changing something's form does not necessarily change its essential character. Research conducted by Piaget and others has demonstrated that children do not understand the principle of conservation until the concrete-operations stage of cognitive development.

Piaget also stressed the egocentric nature of preoperational thinking. **Egocentrism** does not imply selfishness, but rather the inability to perceive the world from any perspective other than one's own. In essence, Piaget said that preoperational children view life as though everyone else were looking at it from their perspective.

Piaget's conclusions about the degree of egocentric thinking in young children have not gone unchallenged. Did his young subjects perform poorly because their thinking was egocentric or because the problem was too difficult? Some later studies have shown that even three- and four-year-olds can successfully manipulate movable versions of simple scenes to show another's view (Borke, 1975). Researchers have also noted that four-year-olds seem to understand that two-year-olds perceive things differently, since they change their way of speaking when conversing with toddlers (Shatz & Gelman, 1973).

Although preoperational children are not necessarily incapable of viewing things from the perspectives of others, it is generally agreed that young children tend to be egocentric, as Piaget suggested. This explains why children, who see themselves as central to all events in their world, often view themselves as causing certain outcomes. For example, young children of divorcing parents may think that they are the cause of the estrangement. Needless to say, children in such highly vulnerable situations may require a great deal of assurance that they are not the cause of calamitous events such as divorce.

During the preoperational stage, infants begin to demonstrate an understanding that others have intentions, beliefs, and a mind of their own (Kovács, Téglás, & Endress, 2010; Senju, Southgate, Snape, Leonard, & Csibra, 2011; Scott, He, Baillargeon, & Cummins, 2012). Recall from the previous chapter that we referred to this as a *theory of mind*. This is demonstrated as a child begins to anticipate another's actions, show empathy, and understand what makes another happy or angry.

Concrete Operations Stage Third stage of cognitive development in Piaget's theory (ages seven through twelve years), during which children begin to use logical mental operations or rules, mastering the concept of conservation

Formal Operations Stage Fourth and final stage in Piaget's theory of cognitive development (ages twelve and up), during which individuals acquire the ability to make complex deductions and solve problems by systematically testing hypotheses

Concrete Operations Stage (Ages Seven to Twelve Years)

Between the ages seven and twelve, children again make a qualitative leap as they learn to engage in decentration and to shed their egocentrism. Whereas intuitive thinking and a dependence on imagination and the senses characterize the preoperational stage, children in the **concrete operations stage** begin to use *logical operations* or rules. This shift from a single-dimensional emphasis on perception to a greater reliance on logic is a major transition in cognitive development.

As we saw earlier, Piaget viewed mastery of the concept of conservation as a milestone of the concrete operations stage. Children master different aspects of conservation at various times during the concrete operations stage. For example, a child who understands conservation of substance will realize that a ball of clay rolled into the shape of a hot dog still has the same amount of clay. However, when the same child sees two identical clay balls weighed on a balance scale, and then watches as one of the balls is rolled into a hot dog shape, a strange thing may happen. Although the child understands conservation of substance, he or she may not yet understand the more abstract principle of conservation of weight—and thus does not realize the hot dog and ball will weigh the same. By the end of the concrete operations stage, children typically master all of the various dimensions of conservation: substance, length, number, weight, and volume.

Throughout this stage, thinking is still somewhat restricted by a tendency to limit the use of logical operations to concrete situations and objects in the visible world. For example, if you played the game Twenty Questions with an eight-year-old, the child would be likely to stick with concrete questions that, if correct, would solve the problem ("Is it a carrot?" "Is it a rabbit?"). In contrast, older children in the final stage of cognitive development might approach the problem more abstractly, asking general questions such as "Is it vegetable?" or "Is it animal?" before making specific guesses.

In the concrete operations stage, children are not yet able to deal with completely hypothetical problems of a "what if" nature in which they must compare what they know to be true with what may be true. For instance, if you ask concrete operational children what it would be like if people could fly, their answers would probably reflect what they have actually seen (in cartoons and movies as well as in real life) rather than total abstractions. Thus, you might be told that people would look funny with wings or that people cannot fly. In contrast, older children are more able to imagine things beyond their own experiences. Thus, a teenager might tell you that if people could fly, department stores would no longer need elevators, or that no one would need to take drugs to "get high."

Formal Operations Stage (Age Twelve and Older)

In the **formal operations stage**, individuals acquire the ability to make complex deductions and solve problems by systematically testing hypothetical solutions. Adolescents can now think about abstract problems. For example, younger children in the concrete operations stage would indignantly reject the syllogism, "People are faster than horses, and horses are faster than cars; therefore people are faster than cars," because it runs counter to concrete, observable facts: They know cars are faster than humans. In contrast, adolescents in the formal operations stage are able to evaluate the logic of this syllogism separately from its content.

Although Piaget originally believed that the formal operations stage almost always begins at about age twelve, he later revised this position to allow for a variety of situations that could either postpone or prevent the arrival of this stage. Piaget did maintain that once children enter the stage of formal operations, there are no longer any qualitative differences between their thought processes and those of older teenagers or adults. Any further advances in cognitive functions are merely refinements in the ability to think logically and reason abstractly.

This stage of cognitive development is marked by the emergence of the capacity to manipulate object representations, when they are not physically present, and by the ability to engage in deductive reasoning. Deductive reasoning requires manipulations of complex thoughts and concepts. Piaget devised the pendulum problem to illustrate deductive reasoning in the formal operations stage. A child is shown a pendulum consisting of an object suspended from a string. The child is then shown how to manipulate four variables: the length of the string, the weight of the suspended object, the height in the pendulum arc from which the object is released, and the force with which the object is pushed. Then the child is instructed to determine which of these factors, singly or in combination, influences how fast the object swings.

(Shutterstock)

The use of logical operations or rules can be demonstrated in a game of logic, such as chess.

Piaget discovered that typical seven- or eight-year-olds try to solve the problem by physically manipulating the four variables in a random fashion. For instance, they might release a light weight from high in the arc, and then release a heavy weight from a low point in the arc. Because they did not test each variable systematically, these younger children often arrived at erroneous conclusions (and then insisted that their answers were correct!). At age ten or eleven, children are more systematic in their approach, but they still lack the capacity to engage in careful hypothesis testing and deductive logic.

By adolescence, perhaps as early as age twelve, children's strategies change radically. Now they systematically keep one variable constant while manipulating the others. In this fashion, they can deduce that only one factor (the length of the string) determines how fast the pendulum swings. Adolescents also tend to work out a plan or strategy for approaching the pendulum problem before commencing their tests. The ability to think a problem through before actually performing any concrete physical manipulations represents a major qualitative change in cognitive functioning (see Table 11-3).

Evaluation of Piaget's Theory

Piaget's theory of cognitive development has been criticized for placing too much emphasis on the maturation of biologically based cognitive structures while understating the importance of an infant's social and cultural environment on their experience throughout development.

He has been criticized for ignoring individual differences in his attempt to portray developmental norms and for emphasizing more abrupt transitions through stages, versus a more continuous developmental process. Despite these criticisms, however, his theory has had a profound impact on developmental psychology and on educational procedures in the Western world. Its basic tenets have been repeatedly tested and largely

Table 11-3 Piaget's Four Stages of Cognitive Development

Cognitive Developmental Stage	Approximate Age	General Characteristics
Sensorimotor	Birth to about 24 months	Infants experience their world primarily by sensing and doing. They learn by their actions, which gradually evolve from reflexes to more purposeful behaviors. Cognitive growth marked by improving ability to imitate behavior and gradual development of object permanence.
Preoperational	2–7 years	The child begins to acquire the ability to use symbols to represent people, objects, and events. However, the child cannot reason logically, and thought tends to be limited by the inability to take into account more than one perceptual factor at the same time and to perceive the world from any perspective other than one's own.
Concrete operations	7–12 years	The child makes a major transition in cognitive development by shifting from a single-dimensional emphasis on perception to a greater reliance on logical thinking about concrete events. During this stage children master the principle of conservation.
Formal operations	12 years and older	Abstract reasoning emerges during this stage. Teenagers acquire the ability to make complex deductions and solve problems by systematically testing hypothetical solutions.

supported. Particularly noteworthy is recent research revealing that the occurrence of growth spurts in the development of the human brain tends to overlap with the timing of the major developmental stages described by Piaget. These findings add credibility to Piaget's assertion that biological maturation and cognitive development are closely associated. In conclusion, we can say that Piaget's theory has provided immense insights into understanding the development of thought, stimulating more research than any other developmental theory, and providing the impetus for many valuable changes in both education and in childcare.

11.6b Gender Differences in Cognitive Abilities

People have had questions pertaining to differences in the cognitive abilities of males and females for as long as human history has been recorded. Even today, after a century of research, many questions remain about the nature and origins of cognitive gender differences. In the following paragraphs we examine what research has revealed.

In the early 1970s, psychologists Eleanor Maccoby and Carol Jacklin (1974) conducted an exhaustive review of the psychological literature on gender differences, in which they analyzed, compared, and tabulated findings reported in more than two thousand journal articles. They concluded that cognitive gender differences were clearly demonstrable in only three areas: (1) females surpass males in verbal skills, (2) males have greater spatial skills, and (3) males excel in mathematical ability. Several years later, Janet Hyde (2007; Hyde & McKinley, 1997) reanalyzed the studies of verbal, mathematical, and spatial abilities included in Maccoby and Jacklin's original survey. Using a statistical technique called *meta-analysis* (a complex statistical procedure whereby data from many studies are combined and collectively analyzed), Hyde collectively analyzed data from several studies

BVT *Lab*

Visit **www.BVTLab.com** to explore the student resources available for this chapter.

and found that the cognitive gender differences reported by Maccoby and Jacklin were in fact quite small. Hyde and her associates speculated that this later finding may be due, at least in part, to the fact that high school and college years are when students are permitted to select their own courses and females tend to select fewer mathematics courses than do males. In recent years, psychologists have been increasingly cautious about assuming that these cognitive gender differences are significant. We examine each of these areas with particular attention to data that have emerged in recent years.

Verbal Skills

Verbal skills encompass such things as word knowledge and usage, grammar, spelling, and understanding analogies. Until recently, a preponderance of evidence suggested that females score higher than males on tests of verbal abilities. However, the difference may be so slight that it is insignificant. For example, in a recent large study in England, sex differences favored females for verbal ability. However, these differences were all less than 1 standard deviation (Calvin, Fernandes, Smith, Visscher, & Deary, 2010). Differences this small, although statistically significant, are rarely meaningful.

If females are slightly superior in verbal skills, it is possible that this difference may result from neurological factors. As we discuss later in this chapter, some evidence suggests that there may be differences between male and female brains that favor females in verbal skills. Modern imaging studies suggest that there are gender-specific differences in cortical regions responsible for different cognitive tasks. Additionally, these areas reveal gender-specific differences in activity favoring females during verbal tasks (Koles, Lind, & Flor Henry, 2010).

Spatial

Spatial aptitudes encompass the related abilities to perceive the position and configuration of objects in space and to manipulate these objects while maintaining a representation of their relationship. Spatial skills are used in such tasks as negotiating mazes, aiming at a target, arranging blocks to match geometric designs and visualizing how an object would look from a different perspective.

Evidence suggests that the spatial skills of males are superior to those of females. Why? Some theorists propose a biological explanation, noting that the portion of the brain most involved in spatial tasks (the right cerebral hemisphere) is more developed in males. Cortical activity in these regions was also greater in males than in females during these tasks (Koles et al., 2010).

As with verbal differences, however, we cannot rule out the impact of socialization. During the developmental years, boys are typically provided with more opportunities to develop spatial skills while girls are encouraged in verbal skills. It is quite likely therefore that gender differences, when they exist, can easily be accounted for by experience and socialization.

Mathematical Skills

Gender differences in mathematical abilities have also been both widely reported and controversial. Various explanations have included females' weaker analytic ability, poorer visual-spatial skills, the conditioning of more math-avoidance behavior in females, socialization processes that encourage people to view math interest or ability as inappropriate for females, and biological difference favoring males.

A recent meta-analysis of one hundred studies of gender differences in mathematics, conducted by Janet Hyde and her colleagues (Hyde, 2007; Hyde & Grabe, 2008), casts serious doubt on the widespread assumption that males perform better than females on mathematics tests. These researchers reported that the data derived from these combined studies revealed that during the elementary- and middle-school years there were no gender differences in problem solving and understanding mathematical concepts, and that females actually demonstrated a slight superiority in computation. However, small gender differences in problem solving that favored males were shown to emerge in high school and college. Hyde and her associates speculated that this latter finding may be due, at least in part, to the fact that high school and college "are precisely the years when students are permitted to select their own courses, and females elect somewhat fewer mathematics courses than do males" (Hyde & Grabe, 2008 p. 150). Other researchers argue that females tend to outperform males on mathematical computation tests (arithmetic problems), but males outperform females on mathematical reasoning tasks—story-type problems (Kimura, 1992). We discuss gender differences in academic abilities in Chapter 17 under the topic of *stereotype threat*. There we will see that conformity to negative stereotypes (e.g., the stereotype that females perform more poorly than males in mathematics) may also contribute to male-female differences in ability.

(iStock)

Researchers Doris Entwistle and David Baker have argued that differential socialization in early years may contribute to gender differences in math skills.

In conclusion, research on gender differences in cognitive ability has been controversial and somewhat inconsistent. Most psychologists agree that there is considerably more variability within each sex than there is between males and females for all abilities thus far examined. Any differences found are most likely attributable to socialization, to stereotype conformity or threat, and to opportunity more than to biology (Kurtz-Costes, Rowley, Harris-Britt, & Woods, 2008; Thoman, White, Yamawaki, & Koishi, 2008).

11.7 Psychosocial Development

Children's physical and cognitive growth is accompanied by psychosocial development—changes in the way they think, feel, and relate to their world and the people in it. This section first describes two areas of psychosocial development: the establishment of attachment and the impact of parenting styles. It then concludes with Erik Erikson's theory of psychosocial development.

11.7a Attachment

You may have observed babies at the age of seven or eight months and up to eighteen months who are content as long as a parent is nearby, but who cry virtually inconsolably if the parent leaves the room. Many a babysitter has spent frustrating hours cuddling, bouncing, and singing to a baby who refuses to take comfort from anyone but the real thing—Mom or Dad.

Attachment Intense emotional tie between two individuals, such as an infant and a parent

Indiscriminate Attachment Attachment typically displayed by human infants during the first few months, when social behaviors are directed to virtually anyone

Specific Attachment Highly selective attachment often displayed by human infants sometime between six and eighteen months, when increased responsiveness is displayed toward primary caregivers and distress may be displayed when separated from parents

Separate Attachment Attachment typically displayed by infants by about twelve to eighteen months, when fear of strangers diminishes and interest in people other than primary caregivers develops

Such experiences demonstrate one of the earliest and most profound aspects of early psychosocial development: **attachment**. Attachment is the term applied to the intense emotional tie that develops between two individuals, in this case an infant and a parent. Attachment has clear survival value in that it motivates infants to remain close to their parents or other caregivers who protect them from danger. Infants may establish intense, affectionate, reciprocal relationships with their parents, older siblings, grandparents, or any other consistent caregiver. However, the most intense attachment relationship that typically occurs in the early stages of development is between mother and child, and most of the available longitudinal research has focused on the development of this bond and its effects throughout one's lifespan.

Attachment develops according to a typical sequence (Ainsworth, 1963, 1979; Bowlby, 1980; Schachere, 1990). During the first few months, babies exhibit **indiscriminate attachment**. Social behaviors such as smiling, nestling, and gurgling are typically directed to just about anyone. This pattern continues for about six to seven months until babies begin to develop selective, **specific attachments**. At this time, they often show increased responsiveness to their parents or other regular caregivers by smiling more, holding out their arms to be picked up, and vocalizing more than to other people. This specific attachment is likely to become so strong that infants will show great distress when separated from their parents. When strangers attempt to offer solace, their overtures may be merely tolerated or perhaps overtly rejected.

Fortunately for the countless babysitters, grandparents, and friends who are distressed to be rejected, most infants progress to a third stage of **separate attachments** by about twelve to eighteen months. During this stage, infants take an active social interest in people other than their mothers or fathers. Fear of strangers also typically diminishes during this period.

How Attachment Develops

How do babies form attachments to primary caregivers? A number of early developmental theorists believed that feeding was the key ingredient in the development of attachment. Because the mother provides nourishment, so the reasoning went, the baby learns to associate mother with a sense of well-being and consequently wants her to remain close at hand. The popularity of this idea persisted until Harry Harlow and his associates released a series of landmark studies (Harlow & Zimmerman, 1958; H. Harlow & M. Harlow, 1966; H. Harlow, M. Harlow, & Suomi, 1971).

Harlow's research began as the study of learning abilities in rhesus monkeys. To eliminate the possible variable input of early experiences, he separated baby monkeys from their mothers shortly after birth and raised them in individual cages that were equipped with soft blankets. Unexpectedly, the monkeys became intensely attached to the blankets, showing extreme distress when they were removed for laundering. The behavior was comparable to that of baby monkeys when they are separated from their mothers.

Harlow and his colleagues were intrigued, for this finding contradicted the notion that attachment develops through feeding. The researchers decided to conduct some experiments to find out whether contact comfort is more important than food in developing attachment. They separated infant monkeys from their mothers, rearing them in cages containing two artificial "mothers." One was made of a wire mesh cylinder; the other was a similar wire cylinder wrapped with foam rubber and covered with terry cloth to which the infant could cling. A bottle could be attached to either artificial mother so that it could serve as the monkey's source of food.

If attachment were linked to feeding, we would expect the monkeys to form attachments consistently with the "mother" hooked up to the bottle. However, this anticipated outcome was not what happened. Monkeys who were reared with a nourishing wire mother and a non-nourishing cloth mother clearly preferred the latter, spending much more time clinging to their contact-comfort mother. Even while they were obtaining nourishment from the wire mother, the monkeys often maintained simultaneous contact with the cloth. The cloth mother also provided the baby monkeys with a secure base for exploring new situations. When novel stimuli were introduced, the babies would gradually venture away from their cloth mothers to explore, often returning to home base before exploring further. When a fear stimulus (such as a toy bear beating loudly on a drum) was introduced, the frightened infants would rush to their cloth mothers for security. If their cloth mothers were absent, the babies would freeze into immobility or cry and dash aimlessly around the cage.

The researchers concluded that the satisfaction of contact comfort was more important in establishing attachment than the gratification of being fed. When other qualities were added to the cloth mother, such as warmth, mechanical rocking, and feeding, the bonding was even more intense. Clearly, a strong parallel exists between this artificial situation and what often occurs when human infants have contact with the warm bodies of parents who cuddle, rock, and feed them. Harlow's demonstration that attachment does not depend on feeding should be reassuring to fathers of breast-fed babies.

(Courtesy of Harlow Primate Laboratory)

Harry Harlow raised monkeys with two mothers—one made of wire and the other of cloth. The infant monkeys preferred to be near the cloth figure over the wire figure, even though they received milk from the wire figure.

Effects of Attachment Deprivation

Although Harlow's experiments were aimed at determining whether or not food was the crucial element in forming attachments, they also provided some valuable information about emotional and social development. One particularly interesting finding has to do with the long-term effects of being raised without a real mother.

The young monkeys in Harlow's experiments seemed to develop normally at first. However, a different picture emerged when the females reached sexual maturity. Despite elaborate efforts to create ideal mating circumstances, most of them rejected the advances of male monkeys, and only four out of eighteen females conceived as a result of natural insemination (many more were artificially inseminated). Most of these unmothered mothers rejected their young; some were merely indifferent, while others pushed their babies away. In spite of this rejection, the babies persisted in their attempts to establish a bond with their mothers (and in some situations, they actually succeeded). In subsequent pregnancies, these deprived mothers became more adept at nurturing their offspring.

How does this finding relate to human behavior? Do human infants deprived of attachment with nurturing caregivers develop in a similar way, and if so, are the emotional scars permanent? Up until the 1970s, most developmental psychologists were inclined to answer "yes" to both of these questions, citing numerous studies of infants raised from birth in orphanages (Bowlby, 1965; Ribble, 1943; Spitz, 1945). These studies found that orphanage children who were provided adequate physical care and nutrition but were deprived of close nurturing relationships with adult caregivers often developed problems

(Getty)

The relationship between mother and child is the most intense attachment relationship that typically occurs in the early stages of development.

such as physical diseases of unknown origin, impaired physical and motor development, and impaired emotional and social development. In one study of ninety-one orphanage infants in the United States and Canada, over one-third died before reaching their first birthday, despite good nutrition and medical care (Spitz & Wolf, 1946).

These studies clearly demonstrate that an early lack of nurturance can have devastating effects. More recent evidence, however, adds some significant corollaries. Several studies conducted in the 1970s indicate that damage associated with emotional and social deprivation in early infancy can be overcome if the child later receives plenty of loving nurturance (Clarke & Clarke, 1976). Furthermore, as we saw earlier, Harlow found that he could reverse, or at least moderate, the effects of early environmental impoverishment by providing deprived monkeys with extensive contact with "therapist monkeys" (Novak & Harlow, 1975).

One of the most impressive indications that there is hope for babies deprived of early bonding was provided by evidence collected by Harvard University's Jerome Kagan and his associates. This research team studied a Guatemalan Indian society in which infants routinely spend the first year of their lives confined to small, windowless huts. (Their parents believe that sunlight and fresh air are harmful to babies.) Since the parents are occupied with subsistence tasks, they rarely cuddle, play with, or talk to their babies. The infants are listless, unresponsive, and intellectually delayed, as judged by standards of normal development. However, when they emerge from the dark huts shortly after their first birthdays, they rapidly evolve into youngsters who play, laugh, explore, and become attached just like youngsters who have not been similarly deprived (Kagan & Klein, 1973).

We do not mean to suggest that the effects of early deprivation are always transitory. There is a big difference between being raised from infancy to childhood in a sterile orphanage environment and receiving loving care at age six months, one year, or two years. It is also important to note that all infants who do establish early attachments do not necessarily express this bonding in the same manner. As the following discussion points out, some attachments are more secure than others.

Secure and Insecure Attachments

In the effort to find out more about infants' attachments, developmental psychologist Mary Ainsworth (1979) used a laboratory procedure that she labeled the "strange situation." In this procedure, a one-year-old infant's behavior in an unfamiliar environment is assessed under various circumstances—with the mother present, with the mother and a stranger present, with only a stranger present, and totally alone.

Ainsworth discovered that infants react differently to these strange situations. Some, whom she labeled *securely attached*, would use their mothers as a safe base for happily exploring the new environment and playing with the toys in the room. When separated from their mothers, they expressed moderate distress; and when reunited they would seek contact and subsequently stay closer to their mothers. *Insecurely attached* infants reacted differently. They showed more apprehension and fewer tendencies to leave their mothers' sides to explore. They were severely distressed when their mothers left, often crying loudly; when the mothers returned, the infants often seemed angry, behaving with hostility or indifference.

What accounts for these differences? The answer probably lies in a combination of two factors: parenting practices and the inborn differences among infants themselves. There is good evidence that some infants may be innately predisposed to form more secure attachments than others, just as some newborns seem to respond more positively to being held and cuddled (Thomas & Chess, 1977). A second factor in the babies' different reactions was the way in which their mothers responded to them at home. Mothers of the securely attached babies were inclined to be sensitive and responsive to their babies, noticing what they were doing and responding accordingly. For example, they would feed their infants when they were hungry, rather than following a set schedule. They also tended to cuddle their babies at times other than when feeding and diapering. In contrast, mothers of insecurely attached babies tended to be less sensitive and responsive. For example, they might feed their babies when they felt like it and perhaps ignore the child's cries of hunger at other times. These mothers also tended to avoid close physical contact with their babies. Research has also shown that mothers of anxious, insecurely attached children are less likely to become actively involved in the play of their offspring than are mothers of securely attached children (Roggman, Langlois, & Hubbs-Tait, 1987; Slade, 1987).

The establishment of a trusting, secure attachment between child and parent appears to have demonstrable effects on a child's later development. Several studies have indicated that children who are securely attached by eighteen months are likely to demonstrate much greater social competence as two- to five-year-olds than are insecurely attached babies. In general, securely attached children have been found to be more enthusiastic, persistent, cooperative, curious, outgoing, socially involved, competent, and appropriately independent.

Father-Child Attachment

We have seen that most investigations of attachment have focused on the mother-child bond. This tendency to overlook fathers probably reflects, at least in part, a general societal conception of fathers as less interested in or capable of providing quality childcare. In recent years, however, these notions have begun to change, and researchers have turned their attention to the role of fathers in their children's early lives (Ainsworth, 1989).

They have discovered that many fathers form close bonds with their offspring shortly after birth and that most infants form specific attachments to their fathers at about the same time as they establish these relationships with their mothers. Fathers tend to interact with their children somewhat differently than mothers. They often spend less time with their children, and that time is more likely to be devoted to play than to providing care. When fathers become the primary caregivers, however, they interact with their babies in a nurturing, gentle fashion no less effective than a mother's (Lamb, 2005; Roggman, 2004).

(Shutterstock)

A traditional societal conception of fathers maintains the idea that they are less interested in or capable of providing quality childcare. In recent years, however, these notions have begun to change, and researchers have turned their attention to the role of fathers in their children's early lives.

11.7b Parenting Styles and Social-Emotional Development

Permissive Parenting style in which parents adopt a hands-off policy, making few demands and showing reluctance to punish inappropriate behavior

Authoritarian Style of parenting in which parents rely on strictly enforced rules, leaving little room for children to discuss alternatives

Authoritative Style of parenting in which parents enforce clear rules and standards but also show respect for children's opinions

Most parents, naturally, want their children to grow up to be socially and emotionally competent. Certainly there is no shortage of "expert" child-rearing advice from talk shows, how-to books, parents and in-laws, and well-meaning friends. Unfortunately, much of this advice is based on armchair logic rather than solid empirical evidence. However, a good deal of psychological research provides important insights into how different parenting styles affect a child's social and emotional development. We briefly summarize the evidence here. Research has identified three specific styles of parenting: permissive, authoritarian, and authoritative.

Permissive Parents

Permissive parents are inclined not to control their children, preferring instead to adopt a hands-off policy. They make few demands and are reluctant to punish inappropriate behavior. Permissiveness sometimes stems at least in part from the parents' indifference or preoccupation with other functions. More commonly, however, permissive parents hope that providing their children with plenty of freedom will encourage the development of self-reliance and initiative.

Authoritarian Parents

In sharp contrast to the permissive style, **authoritarian** parents rely on strictly enforced rules as they try to make their children adhere to their standards. Authoritarian parents tend to be autocratic, leaving little room for discussion of alternative points of view and often using punishments to ensure compliance. Authoritarian parents generally direct minimal warmth, nurturance, or communication toward their children.

Authoritative Parents

The third type of parents, **authoritative** parents, also have definite standards or rules that children are expected to follow. Unlike authoritarian parents, however, they typically solicit their children's opinions during open discussions and rule-making sessions. Although children understand that certain standards of behavior are expected, they are also encouraged to think independently, and they acquire a sense that their viewpoints carry some weight. Both authoritarian and authoritative parenting styles seek to control children's behaviors. However, the former tries to achieve this goal through restrictive control without open communication, while the latter establishes reasonable rules in an atmosphere of warmth and open dialogue.

There is convincing evidence that neither the permissive nor the authoritarian parenting styles are conducive to developing social and emotional competence in children. Children of permissive parents tend to be immature, impulsive, dependent on others, and low in self-esteem. Since they have received so little guidance, they are often indecisive in new situations. Children from authoritarian homes may also have difficulty deciding how to behave because they are worried about their parents' reactions. Authoritarian-reared children are also less likely to express curiosity and positive emotions, and they tend to have few friends.

It is probably no surprise to you that well-adjusted children in these studies tended to be those of authoritative parents. This style of parenting provides a structure reflecting parents' reasonable expectations and realistic standards within an overall atmosphere of love and trust. Perhaps one of the primary advantages of this style is that it provides children the greatest sense of control over their lives. Their participation in family discussions means that the rules that ultimately emerge have been negotiated, rather than being arbitrarily imposed. Also, since authoritative parents tend to enforce rules with consistent, predictable discipline, children are more likely to acquire a sense of control over the consequences of their actions.

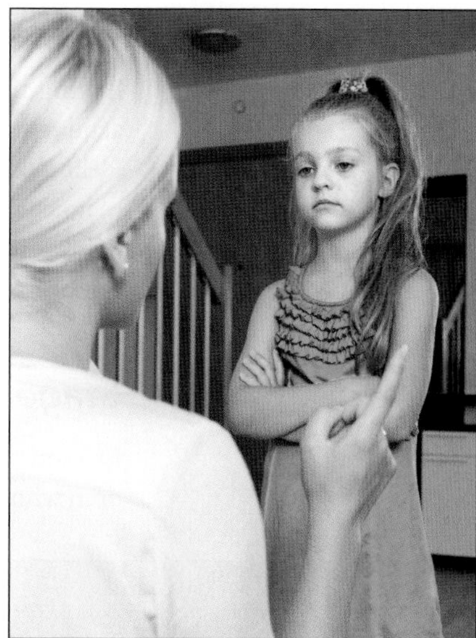

(Shutterstock)

In studies, well-adjusted children tended to be those of authoritative parents.

We have seen that parenting styles seem to influence the behaviors children express as they develop. However, the evidence is of a correlational nature, and as we learned in Chapter 2, correlation does not necessarily imply cause and effect. Perhaps authoritatively reared children are more socially and emotionally competent because of the manner in which they have been reared. However, it is also possible that some other characteristic coincidentally associated with authoritative parents may be the key factor. For example, parents who raise children in such a reasonable fashion may also have better relationships with one another; thus, their children's emotional and social development is likely to progress in a healthy fashion free of the stresses imposed by family conflicts. It may also be that children who are socially and emotionally well adjusted, for reasons other than parenting practices, may elicit more reasonable, democratic responses from their parents than do children who are less competent and more belligerent. Research conducted by Diana Baumrind tends to confirm that children reared by authoritative parents tend to be more competent and be better protected from substance abuse (Baumrind, 1991, 2012). The difference between authoritarian and authoritative parenting, which are equally demanding, is in how power is asserted. Authoritarian parents tend to be arbitrary, domineering, and concerned with status distinctions. Authoritative parents, on the other hand, tend to be reasonable, negotiable and outcome-oriented.

In all, we cannot conclude with absolute certainty that child-rearing practices influence all aspects of the social and emotional competence of children. Nevertheless, the evidence certainly indicates a high probability that this is the case.

11.7c Erikson's Theory of Psychosocial Development

Our discussion of psychosocial development would not be complete without a brief outline of Erik Erikson's *stage theory* (1963). Erikson has proposed the only theory of normal psychosocial development that covers the entire life span. He outlined eight stages, each of which involves specific personal and social tasks that must be accomplished if development is to proceed in a healthy fashion. Each of the eight stages is defined by a major crisis or conflict, suggesting that an individual's personality is greatly influenced by the success with which each of these sequential conflicts is resolved.

Only the first four stages in Erikson's theory apply strictly to the years of infancy and childhood. We briefly outline all eight stages here, however, providing a look ahead to Chapter 12, in which Erikson's thoughts regarding psychosocial development during adulthood are discussed.

Stage 1: Trust Versus Mistrust

During the first stage, which covers the first twelve to eighteen months of life, infants acquire either a sense of *basic trust* or a sense of *mistrust*. In this stage, infants acquire a feeling of whether the world is to be trusted, a conclusion that is shaped largely by the manner in which their needs are satisfied. If they are cuddled, comforted, talked to, and fed when hungry, infants are likely to learn to trust their world; if these interactions are not provided, they will probably become fearful and mistrusting.

Stage 2: Autonomy Versus Shame and Doubt

Erikson's next major stage occurs between eighteen months and three years, when children who have developed a basic trust become ready to assert some of their independence and individuality. How well this task is accomplished determines whether the child will achieve a sense of *autonomy* or a sense of *shame and doubt*.

During this stage, children learn to walk, talk, and do other things for themselves. Parents who encourage and reinforce these efforts can foster a sense of autonomy and independence. In contrast, when parents are overprotective, or when they disapprove of a child's initiative, the child is likely to become doubtful, hesitant, and perhaps ashamed.

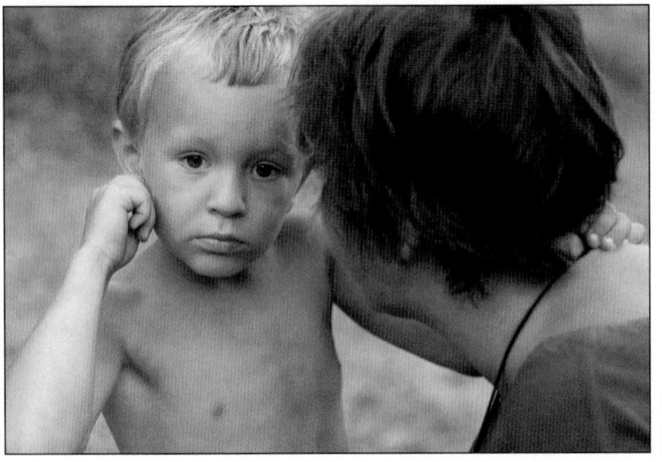

(iStock)

A child of overprotective parents or of parents who disapprove of the child's initiative is likely to become doubtful, hesitant, and perhaps ashamed.

Stage 3: Initiative Versus Guilt

Between about ages three and six, children broaden their horizons by exploring new situations and meeting new people. During this stage, a conflict exists between children's taking the *initiative* to strike out on their own, and the potential *guilt* they will feel if this behavior offends their parents. Parents who encourage inquisitiveness make it easier for a child to express such healthy behaviors, whereas those who actively discourage such actions may contribute to their children's ambivalence or even guilt about striking out on their own.

Stage 4: Industry Versus Inferiority

The next stage extends from about ages six to twelve. At this point, children are much more involved in learning to master intellectual, social, and physical skills. The peer group becomes much more important during this time as children constantly evaluate their abilities and compare them to those of their peers. If their assessments are positive, they may contribute to a sense of *industry* or achievement. In contrast, a poor self-assessment is likely to induce feelings of *inferiority*. Parents and other adult caregivers can help a child develop a sense of industry by encouraging participation in a variety of tasks that are challenging without being too difficult, and by reinforcing a child for completing such tasks.

Stage 5: Identity Versus Role Confusion

The next conflict occurs during adolescence, from approximately ages twelve to eighteen. Now an individual's major task is to secure a stable *identity*. According to Erikson, this stage is when we must integrate all of our experiences in order to develop a sense of "who I am." Young people who are unable to reconcile all of their various roles (as a dependent child, independent initiator of industrious actions, and so forth) into one enduring stable identity, experience *role confusion*.

Stage 6: Intimacy Versus Isolation

As adolescents emerge into young adulthood, they now face the task of achieving *intimacy*. According to Erikson, an adult who has previously achieved a stable identity is often able to form close, meaningful relationships in which intimacy can be shared with significant others. Failure to achieve intimacy is likely to result in a sense of *isolation*, in which the young adult may be reluctant to establish close ties with anyone else.

Stage 7: Generativity Versus Stagnation

The middle years of adulthood are characterized by still another conflict, this one between *generativity* and *stagnation*. Here, our central task is to determine our purpose or goal in life and to focus on achieving aims and contributing to the well-being of others, particularly children. People who successfully resolve this conflict establish clear guidelines for their lives and are generally productive and happy within this directive framework. In contrast, individuals who fail to accomplish these goals by the middle years of life are likely to become self-centered and stagnated in personal growth.

Table 11-4 Erik Erikson's Eight Stages of Psychosocial Development

Stage	Outcome	Description
Infancy: Birth to 18 months	Trust vs. Mistrust	If the child's world is safe, needs are met, and caregiver is consistent, the child will develop a sense of trust.
Toddler: 18 months to 3 years	Autonomy vs. Shame and Doubt	Child begins to assert independence. If successful and supported by parents, the child will develop autonomy. Otherwise, the child will develop a sense of insecurity and self-doubt.
Preschool: 3 to 6 years	Initiative vs. Guilt	Child learns to initiate tasks and follow through with plans. Otherwise, child will feel guilty about attempts if overprotected and punished
Elementary school: 6 to 12 years	Competence vs. Inferiority	If children are encouraged and supported for their initiative, they feel competent about their abilities. Otherwise, they begin to feel inferior.
Adolescence: 12 to 18 years	Identity vs. Role Confusion	As adolescents begin to transition into teenagers, they begin to test their sexual and occupational identities. Hindering these attempts can lead to confusion.
Early adulthood: 20 to 40 years	Intimacy vs. Isolation	Young adults begin to explore intimate relationships and develop a capacity for love. Avoiding intimacy can lead to isolation and loneliness.
Middle adulthood: 40 to 60 years	Generativity vs. Stagnation	During middle adulthood, careers and relationships are established. Adults contribute to society by raising families and being productive at work. Failing in these endeavors results in stagnation.
Older adulthood: 60 years and older	Ego Integrity vs. Despair	During this period, adults begin to reflect on their lives. Older adults feel a sense of satisfaction with their lives or despair from failure.

Stage 8: Ego Integrity Versus Despair

Gender Identity An individual's subjective sense of being male or female

Erikson's final stage extends into the older years of life. This phase of development is characterized by extensive reflection on our past accomplishments and failures. According to Erikson, individuals who can reflect on a lifetime of purpose, accomplishments, and warm, intimate relationships will find *ego integrity* in their final years. In contrast, people whose lives have been characterized by lack of purpose, disappointments, and failures are likely to develop a strong sense of *despair*.

Erikson's theory has been praised for recognizing the importance of sociocultural influences on development, and because it encompasses the entire life span. However, many of Erikson's assertions are so nebulous that they are virtually impossible to test.

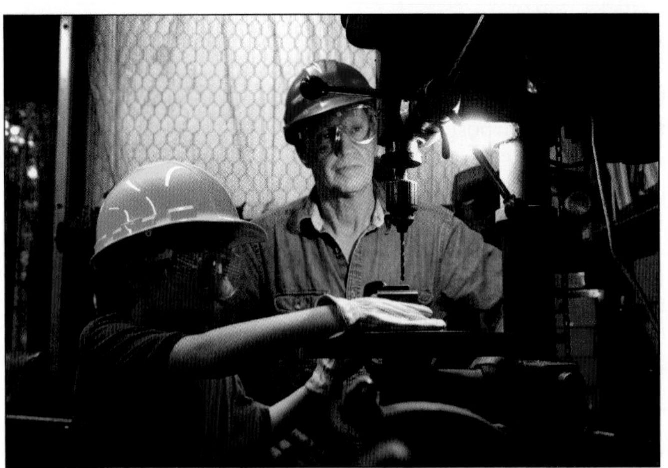

(iStock)

Gender roles are influenced by both biological and socialization factors.

11.8 Gender Identity

Gender identity refers to each person's subjective sense that "I am a male" or "I am a female," an identity that most of us form in the first few years of life. How do we come to think of ourselves as male or female? This question has at least two answers. The first centers on biological factors: The most obvious reason we think of ourselves as male or female is our biological sex. The second answer is based on social-learning theory, which says that our identification as either masculine or feminine results primarily from social and cultural influences during early development.

It seems clear that both biology and social learning help form our gender identity. Certainly there is a wealth of evidence implicating the important role of multiple biological factors in shaping our sense of maleness or femaleness. However, evidence also supports the role of social learning in shaping our gender identity and gender-specific roles. In this final section we attempt to unravel some of the mysteries surrounding gender identity formation. We begin our discussion by considering biological influences; then we look at social learning factors in gender identity and role formation.

11.8a Biological Influences on Gender Identity

Sexual Differentiation

Research efforts to isolate the biological factors that influence gender identity have resulted in the identification of several biological contributions to gender identity: sex determined by chromosomes, sexual differentiation of gonads, sex and sexual characteristics determined hormonal influences, and sexual differentiation of the brain.

Sex Chromosomes At the first level of differentiation, our biological sex is determined by the sex chromosomes present in the reproductive cells. We have seen that females have two similar chromosomes labeled XX, whereas males have dissimilar chromosomes labeled XY. Although science is far from a complete understanding of the role of sex chromosomes in determining biological sex, certain facts seem well established.

The Y chromosome must be present to ensure the complete development of internal and external male sex organs; in the absence of a Y chromosome, an individual will develop female external genitals. The presence of at least one Y chromosome (regardless of the number of X chromosomes) allows the development of male structures. Recent research has demonstrated that "only a small region of the Y, perhaps a single gene, is responsible for initiating the sequence of events that lead to testis formation and hence to male development. In the absence of this gene, called *TDF* (for *testis-determining factor*), female development ensues" (Hodgkin, 1988). However, two X chromosomes are needed for the complete development of both internal and external female structures.

Gonads Glands within the endocrine system (ovaries in females and testes in males) that produce sex hormones that influence development of sexual systems and secondary sex characteristics, as well as sexual motivation

H-Y Antigen Substance that appears to trigger the transformation of gonads into testes within the first few weeks of prenatal development

Sexual Differentiation of Gonads

During the first weeks of prenatal development, the **gonads**—the structures containing the future reproductive cells—have the capacity to become either testes or ovaries. Without specific masculinizing signals, the gonads develop as ovaries. Evidence implicates a substance called **H-Y antigen**, which appears to be under the control of male-determining genes on the Y chromosome. This substance triggers the transformation of the embryonic gonads into testes. In the absence of H-Y antigen, the undifferentiated gonadal tissue develops into ovaries. Thus, the presence of a Y chromosome causes the gonads to develop into testes.

Sex Hormones

As soon as the gonads differentiate into testes or ovaries, the control of biological sex determination passes to the sex hormones, and genetic influence ceases. Recall from Chapter 3 that the major gonadal sex hormones are the ovarian estrogens and the androgens produced by the testes, the most important of which is testosterone.

Considerable research has shown how sex hormones contribute to differentiation of the internal and external sex structures. If fetal gonads differentiate into testes, they soon begin to secrete androgens, which in turn stimulate the development of male structures. If, for some reason, a male fetus does not produce enough androgen, its sex organs will develop as female in form and appearance, despite the presence of the male chromosome. Thus, maleness depends on the secretion of the right amount of androgen at a crucial time. In contrast, a specific female hormone is not necessary for female structures to develop; in the absence of male hormones, the developmental pattern is female.

Under the influence of testosterone produced by the testes, the internal and external sex structures of chromosomal males differentiate in a male direction. In the absence of testosterone, female structures develop. Thus, the human form is biologically female until critical physiological events in the early stages of prenatal development begin the complex process of sex differentiation.

Sex Differentiation of the Brain

Evidence suggests that some important structural and functional differences exist in the brains of males and females. Like the development of sex structures, this sex differentiation process occurs largely, if not exclusively, during prenatal development. At least two major brain areas are involved: the hypothalamus and the left and right cerebral hemispheres. Most evidence for sex differentiation of the brain comes from studies of nonhuman animals, particularly rats. However, it seems likely that similar sex differences exist in the brains of all mammals.

In addition to other functions outlined in Chapter 3, the hypothalamus plays a major role in controlling the production of sex hormones and in mediating fertility and menstrual cycles through its interaction with the pituitary gland. The consequences of prenatal sex differentiation of the hypothalamus become most apparent at puberty.

Sexual Differentiation The process during development when male and female physical characteristics begin to take form

Hermaphrodite Individual with ambiguous or contradictory sex characteristics resulting from abnormal differentiation of internal and external sex structures

The female hypothalamus directs the pituitary to release sex hormones cyclically, creating the menstrual cycle, whereas the male hypothalamus directs a relatively steady hormone production. Thus, hypothalamic sex differences are the reason why female fertility is cyclic and male fertility is not.

Not only are there differences in hypothalamic function, the hypothalamus is structurally different in males and females. For instance, in males the preoptic area of the hypothalamus is about twice as large and contains far more neurons than the preoptic area in females. This increase in size is promoted by the presence of androgens in the brain (Gorski, 1985; Kimura, 1992).

Several researchers have reported sex differences in the structure of the two cerebral hemispheres, suggesting a possible biological basis for differences in the skills of males and females. This **sexual differentiation** is partially explained by the differences in the thickness of the cerebral cortex. Females generally have thicker left hemispheres, while males have thicker right hemispheres. The sex hormone *estradiol* influences the development of the cerebral cortex by increasing the rate of cell loss in areas where estradiol is present. Females have more estradiol in their right hemisphere, thus a greater cell loss, and males have more in their left hemisphere during development (Sandhu, Cook, & Diamond, 1986).

Abnormal Sexual Differentiation

We have seen that the differentiation of internal and external sex structures occurs under the influence of biological cues. When these signals deviate from normal patterns, the end result can be ambiguous biological sex. People with ambiguous or contradictory sex characteristics are sometimes called **hermaphrodites** (a term derived from the mythical Greek deity Hermaphroditus, who was thought to possess attributes of both sexes). This unusual situation can result from a variety of biological errors that produce markedly atypical patterns of hormonally induced prenatal sex differentiation.

We can distinguish between *true hermaphrodites* and *pseudohermaphrodites*. True hermaphrodites, who have both ovarian and testicular tissue in their bodies, are exceedingly rare. Their external genitals are often a mixture of male and female structures. Pseudohermaphrodites are much more common. They also possess ambiguous internal and external reproductive anatomy, but unlike true hermaphrodites, pseudohermaphrodites are born with gonads that match their chromosomal sex. Studies of pseudohermaphrodites have helped to clarify the relative roles of biology and social learning in the formation of gender identity. We consider evidence from several cases of pseudohermaphrodites: fetally androgenized females and androgen-insensitive males.

Fetally Androgenized Females

Occasionally, a chromosomally normal female (XX) is exposed to an excessive amount of androgens or androgenlike substances during the critical period of prenatal sex differentiation. These androgens may have two possible sources. First, the female fetus's own adrenal glands may malfunction, producing abnormally high levels of androgens. Alternately, drugs the mother takes during pregnancy may introduce androgens. (In the 1950s, for instance, some pregnant women were administered androgenlike synthetic hormones to reduce the risk of miscarriage.)

Regardless of the source, the effect of these prenatal androgens is similar. The internal reproductive structures of these chromosomal females do not appear to be affected, but the external genitals resemble those of male infants. The clitoris is often enlarged and may be mistaken for a penis, and the labia are frequently fused so they look like a scrotum. Physicians faced with such gender ambiguities typically obtain additional information about the composition of the chromosomes and the nature of the gonads.

Thus, most of these **fetally androgenized females** are correctly identified and reared as girls. Usually only a relatively minor amount of surgery and hormone therapy is necessary to make the appearance of their external genitals consistent with their internal sex structures and chromosomes.

Some years ago, John Money and Anke Ehrhardt (Money & Ehrhardt, 1972) provided some fascinating data from an extensive study of twenty-five fetally androgenized females. Their subjects, all of whom had received appropriate medical treatment and had been reared from infancy as girls, were matched with a group of nonandrogenized girls who shared similar characteristics of age, race, and socioeconomic status. Would you expect that differences were found in the behavior of the fetally androgenized females as compared to those in the nonandrogenized group? Why or why not? Take a few minutes to consider this question before reading on.

Money and Ehrhardt found marked differences in the behaviors of these two groups. Of the twenty-five fetally androgenized girls, twenty identified themselves as "tomboys"—a label with which their parents and friends concurred. These girls tended to be active and aggressive and to engage in traditionally male activities such as rough-and-tumble athletics and pushing trucks in dirt piles. They demonstrated little interest in bride and mother roles, disliked handling infants, and were uninterested in makeup, hairstyling, and jewelry. In contrast, only a few of the girls in the matched group of nonandrogenized girls claimed to be tomboys. In these cases, it appears, that hormones were more influential than socialization and rearing in determining gender identity.

Fetally Androgenized Female Chromosomally normal (XX) female who, as a result of excessive exposure to androgens during prenatal sex differentiation, develops external genitalia resembling those of a male

Androgen Insensitivity Syndrome (AIS) Condition in which the body cells of a chromosomally normal (XY) male fetus are insensitive to the action of androgens, with the result that internal reproductive structures do not develop, external genitals fail to differentiate into a penis and scrotum, and testes do not descend

Androgen Insensitivity Syndrome

A second pseudohermaphroditic condition is **androgen insensitivity syndrome (AIS)**. A chromosomally normal (XY) male fetus develops testes that produce normal levels of prenatal androgens. However, as a result of a genetic defect, his body cells are insensitive to the action of testosterone and other androgens, with the result that prenatal development is feminized. Internal reproductive structures of either sex do not develop, the external genitals fail to differentiate into a penis and a scrotum, and the testes do not descend. (Testes normally descend from their position inside the abdomen to the scrotum during the seventh month of prenatal development.) Instead, the newborn has normal-looking female external genitals and a shallow vagina. (Remember, in the absence of male hormones—or in this case, insensitivity to androgen—the developmental pattern is female.) Nothing unusual is suspected, and such babies are classified as girls and reared accordingly.

At puberty, breast development and other signs of normal sexual maturation appear as the result of estrogen production from the undescended testes. The error may not be discovered until adolescence or later, often as a result of medical consultation to determine why menstruation has not occurred.

Money and his colleagues (1966) reported an in-depth study of ten AIS individuals who had been reared as girls. Only one, a young girl with a very disturbed family background, showed any gender-identity confusion. The other nine were strongly identified as female by themselves and others, demonstrating strong preferences for the role of homemaker, fantasizing about becoming pregnant and raising a family, and engaging in typically female play with traditional girls' toys such as dolls. According to Money, there was nothing that could be viewed as traditionally masculine in the way these girls behaved, despite their XY chromosomes and male gonads. Later, in 1975, Money reported on a case where a young boy suffered traumatic penile loss during a routine circumcision operation. The parents of this child were encouraged to raise this child as a female, and the apparent success of this reassignment was widely publicized and may have led to many other controversial male-to-female gender assignments in males with phallic inadequacy.

Gender Role Set of behaviors that is considered normal and appropriate for each sex in a society

Socialization Process by which society conveys behavioral expectations to an individual through various agents, such as parents, peers, and school

Only many years later was it revealed that Money's subject had reassigned himself as male after many years of personal and familial conflict (Diamond & Sigmundson, 1999).

Other recent research also fails to confirm Money's conclusions. Males with androgen insensitivity seem to have fewer conflicts with gender identity later in life if they are raised as males (Reiner & Gearhart, 2004; Cohen-Kettenis, 2005). Socializing androgen insensitive males as females may only appear to affect gender identity early on; later in life, however, these individuals may develop severe gender conflicts, a condition known as gender dysphoria.

The results of the investigations into these biological accidents raise a fundamental question. Just what makes us male or female? Our chromosomes, our hormones, the appearance of our genitalia, or the sex we are socially assigned? Clearly, there is no simple answer. A complex process of the interaction of genetic, hormonal, and social factors determines gender identity. We look now at social influences on the development of gender roles.

11.8b The Socialization of Gender Roles

The issue of gender goes beyond the biological processes by which we acquire male or female characteristics. Society dictates a set of behaviors that are considered normal and appropriate for each sex. These standards are typically labeled **gender roles** or *sex roles*. How do gender roles arise? Are they biologically determined, or are they learned? It seems reasonable to assume from the previous section that the behavioral and identity differences between males and females are largely determined by biological factors. Nevertheless, most psychologists believe that gender roles are also strongly determined from the manner in which we are socialized as males and females. **Socialization** refers to the process whereby society conveys behavioral expectations to the individual. In the following paragraphs, we examine the influence of the most important agents of socialization: parents, peers, schools, and television.

The Influence of Parents on Gender Roles

Parents play a powerful role in the socialization of gender roles. Many parents have certain preconceived ideas about how boys and girls differ, and they communicate these views to their children from the very beginning. For example, in one study (Rubin, Provenzano, & Luria, 1974) parents were asked to describe their infants within twenty-four hours of birth. All babies included in this sample were of approximately the same height, weight, and muscle tone. Yet parents of girls tended to describe their daughters as soft, sweet, fine-featured, and delicate, whereas parents of boys used terms like strong, well-coordinated, active, and robust. Such perceptions may well influence the way children learn to think of themselves.

Parents often interact differently with boys and girls. Baby girls are often treated as if they were more fragile than boys, and they may receive more attention than boy babies. Parents often encourage boys to suppress emotion and to be independent, nonnurturant, and aggressive, while girls are expected to display the opposite characteristics.

Although increasing numbers of parents are becoming sensitive to the gender-role implications of a child's playthings, many others still encourage their children to play with toys and engage in activities that help prepare them for specific adult gender roles. Tea sets, miniature ovens, dolls, and dollhouses are still common girls' toys, while boys often receive trucks, toy guns, and footballs. Such parental influences may combine to produce men who are comfortable being assertive and competitive and women who are inclined to be nonassertive and nurturing.

The Influence of Peer Groups

The peer group is another agent of socialization, particularly during late childhood and adolescence. Most youths have fairly rigid views of what is gender appropriate and what is not. For girls, being popular and attractive may be very important. In contrast, boys may try to prove their worth on the athletic field. Individuals who do not conform to these traditional roles may be subjected to considerable pressure.

Psychologist Eleanor Maccoby (2002) has noted a pronounced segregation between the sexes that begins very early in life. This separation of the sexes is another aspect of the peer-group structure among American children that helps perpetuate traditional gender roles. Research conducted by Maccoby suggests that even preschool children select same-sex playmates about 80 percent of the time. By the time they enter the first grade, children voluntarily select other-sex playmates only about 5 percent of the time.

The Influence of Schools on Gender Roles

Still another influence in the development and perpetuation of gender roles is the school. Teachers' responses to their students are often guided by their own stereotypes about males and females (Colin Rogers, 1987). It is common for instructors to expect girls to excel in subjects like English and literature, whereas boys are often believed to be more proficient in math and science. Guided by such assumptions, teachers may differentially encourage and reward boys' and girls' performances in these particular subjects. Furthermore, girls often learn that hanging around their teachers and acting dependent is a good way to get their attention, whereas boys learn that independent or aggressive behavior works better. Research also shows that elementary school boys are much more likely to receive praise, criticism, and/or remedial help from their teachers than are elementary school girls (M. Sadker & D. Sadker, 1995).

The Influence of Television and Film on Gender Roles

Children regularly spend long hours in front of the television, and it would hardly be surprising to discover that television portrayals of men and women influence their learning of gender-role behaviors.

Recent years have witnessed a change in prime-time television and film, characterized by the portrayal of women in some lead roles as active, assertive, independent, and even sexually aggressive. At the time of this writing, women are being featured as professional and competent in the series *Law and Order* and *Grey's Anatomy* and as sexually assertive in shows such as *Desperate Housewives*. Market research also suggests that products advertised on television are more likely to be purchased by women than men and that women are making larger proportions of big financial decisions such as automobiles and homes. Hence, the presence of women in leading roles may have more to do with ratings and product marketing than with efforts to reverse the negative effects of traditional gender-role typecasting. Anyone who watches movies or television knows, however, that there are plenty of television shows and films that still portray females as seductive and as less competent than men.

Throughout this chapter, we have focused on the factors that influence human development and behavior from conception through childhood. We have seen that both genetics and the environment contribute to all aspects of development, including the developing brain. In the next chapter, we will focus on developmental changes that occur from adolescence through old age.

CHAPTER REVIEW

Developmental Issues

1. Contemporary developmental psychologists believe that humans are the products of both nature and nurture, and they are interested in how genetics and experience interact to shape development and the expression of human behavior.
2. Psychologists who emphasize the role of learning have tended to view development as a gradual, continuous process in which individuals undergo qualitative changes over the life span as they accumulate experiences. In contrast, psychologists who emphasize maturation (the orderly unfolding of certain genetically determined behaviors) view development as a discontinuous process that occurs in a series of stages.
3. Most contemporary psychologists agree that the concept of critical periods in infant development, at least when applied to emotional, intellectual, and behavioral traits, lacks supporting evidence.
4. Three research designs have been widely used in the study of development: the cross-sectional, longitudinal, and cross-sequential methods.

The Beginning of Life

5. Life begins when the germ cells (sperm and ovum) unite to produce a zygote. The zygote contains a complement of forty-six chromosomes arranged in twenty-three pairs, one chromosome in each pair from the sperm and one from the egg.
6. Chromosomes are composed of thousands of genes, the chemical blueprints that determine physical characteristics and influence behavioral traits.
7. The assortment of genes we inherit at conception is known as our genotype; the characteristics that result from expression of various genotypes are known as phenotypes.
8. A dominant gene is one that is always expressed in the phenotype; a recessive gene is one that may be expressed only in the absence of a dominant gene, or when it is paired with a similar recessive gene.
9. Many sex-linked diseases are more common in males than females because only a single dose of the defect-causing gene on the X chromosome is necessary to cause the disease. (The gene-deficient Y chromosome does not carry a gene that may counteract this adverse factor.)
10. About 3 percent of babies born each year in the United States have some gene defect or chromosomal abnormality that produces a physical and/or mental impairment.
11. Huntington's disease, carried by a dominant gene, does not cause symptoms until a person is thirty-five to forty-five years old.

CHAPTER REVIEW

12. Phenylketonuria (PKU) is a potentially devastating genetic disease, characterized by intellectual disability and other disruptive symptoms, that is caused by a recessive gene.
13. Down syndrome, the most common chromosomal disorder, is an autosomal chromosome disorder in which the twenty-first chromosome pair has an additional chromosome attached to it.

Prenatal Development

14. The approximately nine months of prenatal development takes place in three stages: germinal (the first two weeks after fertilization), embryonic (beginning of the third week to the end of the eighth), and fetal (from the beginning of the third month to birth).
15. Addictive drugs, alcohol, tobacco, and a multitude of medications can cross through the placenta and damage the developing fetus. No drugs should be used during pregnancy unless absolutely necessary and taken under close medical supervision.

Physical Development

16. Brain growth is very rapid in the early years of life. At age six months, the brain is 50 percent of its adult size; by age five, it has reached 90 percent of its adult size.
17. Research has revealed anatomical and biochemical brain changes associated with improved cortical functioning in animals exposed to environmental enrichment.
18. Both physical growth and motor development follow two basic patterns: cephalocaudal (from head to foot) and proximodistal (inner to outer).
19. Motor development follows a pattern of progression from the simple to the more complex.
20. Within a normal range of experiences, the role of environmental influences on motor development is quite limited.

Cognitive Development

21. Piaget formulated the concepts of schemas, assimilation, and accommodation to explain how we organize incoming information (schemas), interpret it in accordance with existing schemas (assimilation), and restructure it to fit better with already existing schemas (accommodation).
22. Piaget viewed cognitive growth as a four-stage process with qualitatively different kinds of thinking occurring in each of these four stages: sensorimotor, preoperational, concrete operations, and formal operations.

CHAPTER REVIEW

23. During the sensorimotor stage (birth to about twenty-four months), infants learn about their worlds primarily through their senses and actions.
24. The preoperational stage (ages two to seven) is characterized by an increasing use of symbolic thought, language, and imaginative play. However, children at this stage have yet to master logical reasoning processes based on rules and concepts and have difficulty taking into account more than one perceptual factor at the same time.
25. Between ages seven and twelve, children in the concrete operations stage again make a qualitative leap as they begin to use logical mental operations or rules. However, children in this stage are not yet able to deal with completely hypothetical problems.
26. In the formal operations stage (age twelve and older) individuals acquire the ability to think abstractly and to make complex deductions and solve problems by systematically testing hypothetical solutions.

Psychosocial Development

27. Attachment is the term applied to the intense emotional tie that develops between infants and their parents or other consistent caregivers. The most intense attachment relationship that typically occurs in the early stages of development is between mother and child.
28. Research suggests that satisfaction of contact comfort is more important in establishing attachment than is gratification of being fed.
29. Infants deprived of early attachment with nurturing caregivers may suffer serious development difficulties. However, there is evidence that damage associated with deprivation in early infancy can be overcome by ample loving nurturance during childhood.
30. In general, children who are securely attached to their mothers or other caregivers demonstrate a healthier picture of psychosocial adjustment than children who are insecurely attached.
31. Research has shown that most infants form specific attachments to their fathers at about the same time as they establish these relationships with their mothers.
32. The authoritative style of parenting is much more conducive to the development of social and emotional competence in children than either the permissive or authoritarian parenting style.
33. Erik Erikson's theory of psychosocial development outlines eight stages that people pass through during their journey through life: trust versus mistrust (birth to eighteen months); autonomy versus shame and doubt (eighteen months to three years); initiative versus guilt (ages three to six); industry versus inferiority (ages six to eleven); identity versus role confusion (ages twelve to eighteen); intimacy versus isolation (early adulthood); generativity versus stagnation (midlife); and ego integrity versus despair (older years).

CHAPTER REVIEW

Gender Identity

34. The formation of gender identity (a person's subjective sense of maleness or femaleness) occurs in the first few years of life as the result of a complex interplay of biological and social-learning factors.

35. Biological factors that influence a person's gender identity include the following: sex chromosome, gonads, sex hormones, external genitalia, and sexual differentiation of the brain.

36. Under normal conditions these biological variables interact harmoniously to determine our biological sex. However, errors may occur at any of the six levels. The resulting abnormalities in the development of a person's biological sex may seriously complicate acquisition of a gender identity.

37. Socialization refers to the process whereby society conveys its behavioral expectations to us. Parents, peers, schools, textbooks, and television all act as agents in the socialization of gender roles.

TERMS AND CONCEPTS

Accommodation, pg. 452
Androgen Insensitivity Syndrome (AIS), pg. 471
Assimilation, pg. 452
Attachment, pg. 460
Authoritarian, pg. 464
Authoritative, pg. 464
Centration, pg. 454
Cephalocaudal, pg. 449
Chromosome, pg. 435
Cohort, pg. 435
Concordance, pg. 437
Concrete Operations Stage, pg. 455
Conservation, pg. 454
Critical Period, pg. 446
Critical Period, pg. 431
Cross-Sectional Design, pg. 433
Cross-Sequential Design, pg. 435
Decentration, pg. 454
DNA (Deoxyribonucleic Acid), pg. 435
Dominant Gene, pg. 438
Down Syndrome , pg. 443
Egocentrism, pg. 454
Embryonic Stage, pg. 445
Epigenetics, pg. 439
Epigenetics, pg. 430
Fetal Alcohol Syndrome , pg. 446
Fetally Androgenized Female, pg. 471
Fetal Stage, pg. 445
Fetus pg. 445
Formal Operations Stage, pg. 455
Fraternal Twins, pg. 436
Gamete, pg. 435
Gender Identity, pg. 468
Gender Role, pg. 472
Genotype, pg. 438
Germinal Stage , pg. 444
Gonads, pg. 469
Hermaphrodite, pg. 470
Heterozygous, pg. 438
Homozygous, pg. 438
Huntington's Disease, pg. 441
H-Y Antigen, pg. 469
Identical Twins, pg. 435
Imprinting, pg. 431
Indiscriminate Attachment, pg. 460
Lipid Solubility, pg. 445
Longitudinal Design, pg. 433
Maturation, pg. 430
Nature-Nurture Controversy, pg. 430
Object Permanence, pg. 453
Permissive, pg. 464
Phenotype, pg. 438
Phenylketonuria (PKU), pg. 442
Plasticity, pg. 449
Preoperational Stage, pg. 454
Proximodistal, pg. 449
Recessive Gene, pg. 438
Schemas, pg. 452
Sensorimotor Stage , pg. 452
Separate Attachment, pg. 460
Sex-Linked Inheritance, pg. 438
Sexual Differentiation, pg. 470
Socialization, pg. 472
Specific Attachment, pg. 460
Teratogen, pg. 446

POP QUIZ

True or False

___ 1. A major drawback of the cross-sectional design is that it takes an extended period of time to collect all the necessary information.

___ 2. Huntington's disease is a genetic condition that newborn infants are routinely screened for; if the condition is present, dietary changes can prevent the symptoms of the disease.

___ 3. Results of experiments with rats suggest that early experience affects the development of the brain.

___ 4. Children are first able to understand the principle of conservation in the preoperational stage of cognitive development.

___ 5. Assimilation refers to the process whereby society conveys behavioral expectations to the individual.

Multiple Choice

6. Unlike psychologists who emphasize the role of learning, psychologists who emphasize maturation view development as a ________ process that results in ________ changes.
   a. continuous/qualitative
   b. continuous/quantitative
   c. discontinuous/qualitative
   d. discontinuous/quantitative

7. The research design used in developmental research that attempts to overcome some of the drawbacks associated with the other two designs is the ________ design.
   a. cross-longitudinal
   b. cross-sequential
   c. cross-sectional
   d. longitudinal

8. A person who is heterozygous for a sex-linked recessive trait (e.g., red-green color blindness) ______.
   a. will not exhibit the recessive trait in their phenotype
   b. is female
   c. may have offspring who exhibit the recessive trait regardless of the genetic makeup of the other parent
   d. All of the above are correct.

9. A newborn's brain has what percentage of neurons?
   a. Only 25 percent of the neurons of an adult
   b. 75 percent of all the neurons it will ever have
   c. 50 percent of all the neurons it will ever have
   d. Most—if not all—of the neurons it will ever have

POP QUIZ

10. What is a mental structure that guides future behavior while providing a framework for making sense out of new information called?
    a. An operation
    b. A schema
    c. Accommodation
    d. Assimilation
11. What is the correct order of Piaget's stages of cognitive development?
    a. Sensorimotor, concrete operations, preoperational, formal operations.
    b. Preoperational, sensorimotor, concrete operations, formal operations.
    c. Concrete operations, preoperational, sensorimotor, formal operations.
    d. Sensorimotor, preoperational, concrete operations, formal operations.
12. A child begins to use logic to solve problems during the ________ stage of cognitive development, and can first think abstractly in the ________ stage of cognitive development.
    a. formal operations/concrete operations
    b. preoperational/concrete operation
    c. concrete operations/formal operations
    d. preoperational/formal operations
13. The "strange situation" is used to evaluate which of the following?
    a. A child's stage of cognitive development
    b. Infant-mother attachment
    c. Mother-infant attachment
    d. A child's stage of psychosocial development
14. The stage of Erikson's theory of psychosocial development that is characterized by an extensive reflection concerning past accomplishments and failures concerns the ________ crisis.
    a. ego integrity versus despair
    b. initiative versus guilt
    c. generativity versus stagnation
    d. industry versus inferiority
15. If an adolescent developed breasts but, even after several years, did not begin menstruation, and all other causes had been ruled out, a medical doctor would most likely suspect which of the following?
    a. The presence of two Y chromosomes
    b. Androgen insensitivity syndrome
    c. DHT deficient male syndrome
    d. Fetally androgenized female syndrome

Answer Key: 1.F 2.F 3.T 4.F 5.F 6.c 7.b 8.d 9.d 10.b 11.d 12.c 13.b 14.a 15.b

(Shutterstock)

Chapter 12

Development 2: Adolescence *to the* End *of* Life

My teenage years were the worst years of my life. It seemed to me that my life just couldn't work out. I didn't feel very smart, I wasn't attractive, and there was really nothing that distinguished me from my peers. At this time, my parents were going through a messy divorce that left me feeling both guilty for their unhappiness and mad at them for mine. My emotions were always on a roller coaster. I was either so in love that I couldn't concentrate on anything else, or I was depressed and couldn't care less. Thoughts of suicide were not uncommon, especially after breaking up with my girlfriend my junior year of high school. At that time, I couldn't imagine life getting any worse, and at that time, perhaps, it couldn't have.

Although the experiences expressed above are not common to all adolescents in our society (we see in this chapter that there is no such thing as a typical adolescence), it is probably fair to say that most of us have some painful memories of our teenage years. It is also a fair prediction that most of us will experience a certain degree of conflict at other transitions in our lives, for the ages of thirty, forty, sixty, and so on, are all milestones that may seem to us to mark the closing of one phase of our lives or the entrance into another.

Whether the transition is to the entrance of adulthood, middle age, or the older years, much of the conflict we experience has to do with our images or expectations for the new era we are entering. How accurate are these images? Certainly not all adolescents go through a period of storm and stress, nor do all young adults embark on a career and start a family. For that matter, not all older adults fit our society's characterizations of old age. As we explore adolescent and adult development in this chapter, we note the diversity with which individuals experience various ages and stages of their lives. Perhaps the most striking diversity occurs during adolescence, and we begin by examining this transitional period.

12.1 Adolescence

Adolescence is a time of dramatic physiological change and social-role development. In Western societies, it is the transition between childhood and adulthood that typically spans ages twelve to twenty. Although most major physical changes take place during the first few years of adolescence, important and often profound changes in behavior and expectations occur throughout the period.

By cross-cultural standards, the prolonged period of adolescence in America and other modern Western societies is unusual. In many nonindustrial societies, adolescence is considered to be either nonexistent or nothing more than a period of rapid physical changes leading to sexual maturity. In such societies, some sort of "rite of passage" often marks the transition from childhood to adulthood (Dunham, Kidwell, & Wilson, 1986). Even in our own society, adolescence is a relatively recent phenomenon. Early in this century, before schooling requirements were extended through high school, children were often expected to join the work force when they became teenagers.

Our society has no single initiation rite that signals passage into adulthood. Instead, a variety of signposts may herald this transition, including graduation from high school or college, moving away from home, securing a full-time job, or establishing an intimate, monogamous relationship.

Puberty Approximately two-year period of rapid physical changes that occurs sometime between ages seven and sixteen in our society and that culminates in sexual maturity

Adolescence A period of transition from childhood to adulthood beginning around puberty and extending to adulthood (typically the teenage years, from thirteen to twenty years of age)

Adolescent Growth Spurt Period of accelerated growth that usually occurs within about two years after the onset of puberty

Gonadotropins Hormones released by the pituitary gland that stimulate production of testosterone in men and estrogen in women

Secondary Sex Characteristics Physical characteristics typical of mature males or females (such as facial, body, and pubic hair) that develop during puberty as a result of the release of testosterone or estrogen

Just as there is no one rite of passage into adulthood, in many ways there is no typical adolescence. Much has been written about the many conflicts and dilemmas faced by teenagers. However, the teenage years can also be a rewarding, relaxing, and exciting time of life, free from the stresses and responsibilities that come with adulthood. For most of us, adolescence probably varied between being a time of anxiety and stress and a time of freedom and optimism—depending on what day we were asked. Although we cannot describe a typical adolescence, we can describe some of the common physical, cognitive, and psychosocial changes that most teenagers experience.

12.1a Physical Development During Adolescence

Puberty (from the Latin *pubescere*, "to be covered with hair") describes the approximately two-year period of rapid physical changes that culminate in sexual maturity. In our society, the onset of puberty in girls generally occurs sometime between ages seven and fourteen, with the average about age ten. Boys typically enter puberty two years later at about age twelve, with a normal range of nine to sixteen years.

Physical Changes During Puberty

As we saw in Chapter 11, the first few years of life are marked by rapid growth. With **adolescence**, children enter a second period of accelerated growth, often called the **adolescent growth spurt**, which usually runs its course in the two years following the onset of puberty. Sexual maturity is reached soon after the growth spurt ends.

The physical changes that occur during puberty are quite dramatic and rapid. Suddenly, the body a person has inhabited for years undergoes a mysterious transformation. What causes these changes? One important factor is a genetically determined timetable that causes the pituitary gland to release a growth hormone that triggers the rapid growth that takes place at the start of adolescence (Romeo, Richardson, & Sisk, 2002). The hypothalamus also increases production of chemicals that stimulate the pituitary to release larger amounts of **gonadotropins**—hormones that stimulate production of testosterone in men and estrogen in women. The resulting developments (breasts; deepened voice; and facial, body, and pubic hair) are called **secondary sex characteristics**. The timetable that governs these processes may also be influenced by environmental factors as well as by an individual's health.

There is considerable variation in the rates of growth and development in different societies around the world. We cannot be certain about what causes these changes in human physical growth patterns (including height, weight, and rates of maturation) measured in sample populations throughout the world. However, the most likely cause is the improved standard of living in societies where these changes have been observed.

(Shutterstock)

During adolescence, children's bodies experience a growth spurt, which usually runs its course in two years. The onset of puberty can be dramatic; some may gain muscle tone or experience changes in metabolism and body type. Sometimes these changes can be desirable, but not always.

Effects of Early and Late Maturation

Adolescents are often very concerned with what other people think of them, and anything that sets them apart from the crowd is likely to have a notable impact on their psychosocial adjustment.

Thus, it is not surprising that being either the first or the last to go through puberty can cause a good deal of self-consciousness. The timing of physical and sexual maturity may also have an important influence on psychosocial adjustment, especially for males.

A number of studies have shown that early maturation often holds some advantages for boys. Males who mature early tend to be more poised, easygoing, and good-natured; they are also more likely to be school leaders, better at sports, more popular, and more successful academically (and later vocationally). However, those maturing early may find it difficult to live up to expectations that they should act mature just because they happen to have adult-like bodies. In addition, being thrust into adolescence at an early age shortens the period of transition from childhood. Early maturing boys tend to be more bound by rules and routines, more conventional in career and lifestyle choices, more cautious, and more inclined to worry about what other people think of them.

(Shutterstock)

For girls, the puberty process seems to be less advantageous than for boys, and they may feel terribly conspicuous at a time of life when they would most like to blend in. Early maturing girls tend to be at greater risk for a variety of behavioral problems, including smoking.

In general, late-maturing boys are more likely to be inappropriately aggressive and rebellious against adult authority; they may also lack self-confidence, feeling inadequate and insecure. On the other hand, late-maturing males tend to be more flexible during their youth and more insightful, independent, and less bound to conventional lifestyles and routines later on. A few of the differences between early and late maturing boys may persist into the adult years, but most disappear or are compensated for by the development of other traits.

For girls, early maturation generally seems to be less advantageous than for boys. Early maturing girls are bigger than practically all the boys their age; they also look more grown-up than most of the girls their age. As a consequence, they may feel terribly conspicuous at a time of life when they would most like to blend in with the crowd. Early maturing girls also tend to be at greater risk than their peers for a variety of behavioral problems, including smoking, risky sexual behaviors, alcohol and drug use, delinquency, and a sedentary lifestyle (Costello, Sung, Worthman, & Angold, 2007; Mendle, 2008; van Jaarsveld, 2007).

Early maturation, or precocious puberty, affects about one in five thousand children in the United States, and it is about ten times more common in girls than boys. In fact, over the past thirty years the number of girls diagnosed with precocious puberty has been rising (Cesario & Hughes, 2007). The causes of this increase aren't completely understood but may include a variety of environmental and genetic factors that affect endocrine functioning.

12.1b Cognitive Development During Adolescence

Although the most obvious changes of adolescence are physical, significant changes also take place in the way we think. With adolescence, individuals acquire the ability to think abstractly. Teenagers can engage in hypothetical reasoning, imagining all kinds of possibilities in a given situation. They also begin to approach problems more systematically and logically, rather than relying on trial-and-error strategies.

Piaget's Formal Operations Stage

As we saw in Chapter 11, Piaget maintained that most people enter the formal operations stage sometime around age twelve. This stage of cognitive development is marked by

BVT *Lab*

Flashcards are available for this chapter at **www.BVTLab.com.**

the emergence of the capacity to manipulate representations of objects, even when they are not physically present, and by the ability to engage in deductive reasoning. Advanced subjects such as mathematics and physics can be understood at this time. These cognitive abilities have important implications for the way adolescents perceive their world. With their increased ability to think logically and abstractly, teenagers often detect what they consider to be logical inconsistencies in other people's thinking, and they may be impatient with the thought processes and decisions of others. Adolescents also may question their own judgments, and the result is often confusion.

Adolescence is also a time when individuals begin to ponder and debate such complex issues as social justice, the meaning of life, the validity of religious dogma, and the value of material wealth. No longer constrained by personal experiences and concrete reality, teenagers can explore all kinds of "what if" possibilities. They may feel compelled to contribute to ending human misery, poverty, social injustice, and war. As adolescents grow older, however, much of their idealism is replaced with a more pragmatic or practical view.

Critique of Formal Operations Stage

In Chapter 11, we explored some criticisms of Piaget's theory, but we did not specifically discuss criticisms of his formal operations stage. A number of developmental psychologists have challenged Piaget's ideas about the timing of this stage. Researchers have found that the transition to formal operations does not necessarily occur abruptly at the onset of adolescence, for even relatively young children often demonstrate rudiments of logical thinking (Commons & Grotzer, 1990; Ennis, 1975; Keating, 1988). In addition, adolescents (and even adults) often revert to illogical thinking as they deal with issues and problems. Thus, unlike the sudden and dramatic physical changes of adolescence, the shift to formal operations is often gradual, spanning late childhood and adolescence and perhaps even extending into the adult years.

Some critics have also argued that many adolescents and adults never attain the level of formal operations logic. A number of studies in the United States have shown that only about 50 percent of college students attain the formal operations stage of cognitive development (Moshman, 2009). In addition, college students who had attained formal operations outperformed those who had not (Mwamwenda, 1993, 1999). Piaget noted that even though adolescents may attain the level of brain maturation necessary for abstract reasoning and logical thinking, they may never achieve the formal operations stage unless they are provided with adult models of formal reasoning and are schooled in the principles of logic. Thus, both neurological maturation and specific training may be necessary for higher cognitive development. As we see in the following section, whether we reach formal operations or not may have a profound influence on another area: moral development.

12.1c Moral Development During Adolescence

When we begin life, we are all *amoral*. We do not yet have even the rudiments of moral judgment. By the time we become adults, however, most of us possess a complex notion of *morality*. Morality is a system of personal values and judgments about the fundamental rightness or wrongness of acts, and of our obligations to behave in just ways that do not interfere with the rights of others. How do we evolve from amoral to moral, from a total lack of understanding our responsibilities to a complex perception of right and wrong?

Kohlberg's Theory of Moral Development

The question of how moral development occurs has occupied the attention of a number of developmental theorists, most notably Lawrence Kohlberg (1964, 1968, 1969; Puka, 1994). Kohlberg was more interested in the ways in which thinking about right and wrong change with age than the specific things that children might consider to be right or wrong. For example, whether we are eight, sixteen, or thirty-two, most of us would say that it is wrong to break our society's laws. However, our reasons for not breaking the law, as well as our views about whether we might be justified in breaking the law under some circumstances, might change drastically as we develop.

To learn how this change takes place, Kohlberg devised a series of moral dilemmas that typically involved a choice between two alternatives, both of which would be considered generally unacceptable by society's standards. "Heinz's dilemma" is an example.

> In Europe a woman was near death from a special kind of cancer. There was one drug that the doctors thought might save her. It was a form of radium that a druggist in the same town had recently discovered. The drug was expensive to make, but the druggist was charging ten times what the drug cost him to make. He paid $200 for the radium and charged $2,000 for a small dose of the drug. The sick woman's husband, Heinz, went to everyone he knew to borrow the money, but he could only get together $1,000, which is half of what it cost. He told the druggist that his wife was dying and asked him to sell it cheaper or let him pay later. But the druggist said, "No, I discovered the drug, and I am going to make money from it." So Heinz got desperate and broke into the man's store to steal the drug for his wife. (Kohlberg, 1969, p. 379)

What is your reaction to this story? Kohlberg would not be interested in whether you thought Heinz was right or wrong. (In fact, either answer could demonstrate the same level of moral development.) Instead, Kohlberg was interested in the process you used to reach your judgment, for your reasoning would indicate how advanced your moral thinking is.

Kohlberg asked his subjects a series of questions about each moral dilemma and then used a complex scoring system to assign a subject to a particular category or stage of moral reasoning. This approach led him to formulate a theory of moral development in which he proposed that we move through as many as six stages of moral reasoning that traverse three basic levels: preconventional, conventional, and postconventional.

According to Kohlberg, most children between ages four and ten have a **preconventional morality**, a kind of self-serving approach to right and wrong. In *Stage 1* of preconventional morality, children behave in certain ways in order to avoid being punished; during *Stage 2*, they behave in certain ways to obtain rewards. At this lowest level of moral development, children have not internalized a personal code of morality. Rather, they are molded by the standards of adult caregivers and the consequences of adhering to or rejecting these rules.

By late childhood or early adolescence, a person's sense of right and wrong typically matures to the level of **conventional morality**. Here, the motivating force behind behaving in a just or moral fashion is the desire either to help others and gain their approval *(Stage 3)* or to help maintain the social order *(Stage 4)*. As children and young adolescents progress through these stages, they begin to internalize the moral standards of valued adult role models.

A few individuals, particularly those who become adept at the abstract reasoning of formal operational thought, may progress to the final level of **postconventional morality**. *Stage 5* of postconventional morality affirms values agreed on by society

Preconventional Morality
Lowest level of moral development in Lawrence Kohlberg's theory, comprising Stage 1 and Stage 2, in which individuals have not internalized a personal code of morality

Conventional Morality
Second level in Lawrence Kohlberg's theory of moral development, consisting of Stages 3 and 4, in which the motivating force for moral behavior is the desire either to help others or to gain approval

Postconventional Morality
Third and highest level in Lawrence Kohlberg's theory of moral development, in which individuals are guided by values agreed upon by society (Stage 5) or by universal ethical principles (Stage 6)

Table 12-1 Lawrence Kohlberg's Levels and Stages of Moral Development with Stage-Graded Answers to the Story of Heinz

Stage Description	Examples of Moral Reasoning Favoring Heinz's Actions	Examples of Moral Reasoning Opposing Heinz's Actions
	Level One—Preconventional Morality	
Stage 1: Punishment and Obedience Orientation (The consequences of acts determine whether they are good or bad.)	He should steal the drug because he offered to pay for it and because it is only worth $200 and not the $2,000 the druggist was charging.	He shouldn't steal the drug because it is a big crime.
	He should steal it because if he lets his wife die, he would get in trouble.	He shouldn't steal the drug because he would get caught and sent to jail.
Stage 2: Instrumental Orientation (An act is moral if it satisfies one's needs.)	It is okay to steal the drug because his wife needs it to live and he needs her companionship.	He shouldn't steal the drug because he might get caught and his wife would probably die before he gets out of prison, so it wouldn't do much.
	He should steal the drug because his wife needs it and he isn't doing any harm to the druggist because he can pay him back later.	He shouldn't steal it because the druggist was not doing a bad thing by wanting to make a profit.
	Level Two—Conventional Morality	
Stage 3: Good Person Orientation (An action is moral if it pleases or helps others and leads to approval.)	He should steal the drug because society expects a loving husband to help his wife regardless of the consequences.	He shouldn't steal the drug because he will bring dishonor on his family, and they will be ashamed of him.
	He should steal the drug because if he didn't his family and others would think he was an inhuman, uncaring husband.	He shouldn't steal the drug because no one would blame him for doing everything that he could legally. The druggist, and not Heinz, will be considered to be the heartless one.
Stage 4: Maintaining the Social Order Orientation (Moral people are those who do their duty in order to maintain the social order.)	He should steal the drug because if he did nothing he would be responsible for his wife's death. He should take it with the idea of paying the druggist back.	He should not steal the drug because if people are allowed to take the law into their own hands, regardless of how justified such an act might be, the social order would soon break down.
	He should steal the drug because if people like the druggist are allowed to get away with being greedy and selfish, society would eventually break down.	He shouldn't steal the drug because it's still always wrong to steal, and his breaking the law would cause him to feel guilty.
	Level Three—Postconventional Morality	
Stage 5: Social Contract and Individual Rights Orientation (A moral person carefully weighs individual rights against society's needs for consensus rules.)	The theft is justified because the law is not set up to deal with circumstances in which obeying it would cost a human life.	You could not really blame him for stealing the drug, but even such extreme circumstances do not justify a person taking the law into his own hands. The ends do not always justify the means.
	It is not reasonable to say the stealing is wrong because the law should not allow the druggist to deny someone's access to a life-saving treatment. In this case, it is more reasonable for him to steal the drug than to obey the law	He shouldn't steal the drug because eventually he would pay the price of loss of self-respect for disregarding society's rules.

Table 12-1 *Continued*

	Level Three—Postconventional Morality	
Stage 6: Universal Ethical Principles Orientation (The ultimate judge of what is moral is a person's own conscience operating in accordance with certain universal principles. Society's rules are arbitrary, and they may be broken when they conflict with universal moral principles.)	He must steal the drug because when a choice must be made between disobeying a law and saving a life, one must act in accordance with the higher principle of preserving and respecting life.	Heinz must consider the other people who need the drug just as much as his wife. By stealing the drug he would be acting in accordance with his own particular feelings with utter disregard for the value of all the lives involved.
	Heinz is justified in stealing the drug because if he had failed to act in this fashion to save his wife, he would not have lived up to his own standards of conscience.	He should not steal the drug because, though he would probably not be blamed by others, he would have to deal with his own self-condemnation because he did not live up to his own conscience and standards.

including individual rights and the need for democratically determined rules; in *Stage 6* individuals are guided by universal ethical principles in which they do what they think is right as a matter of conscience, even if their acts conflict with society's rules. Table 12-1 summarizes Kohlberg's six stages of moral reasoning and illustrates how an individual at each stage might respond to Heinz's dilemma.

A person may progress from conventional to postconventional morality any time during adolescence. However, Kohlberg maintained that only about 25 percent of adults in our society progress beyond *Stage 4*, and that most of these individuals do so sometime during their adult years.

Evaluating Kohlberg's Theory

Kohlberg's theory is an impressive attempt to account systematically for the development of moral reasoning. His writings have also provided some guidelines for implementing moral education for children and adolescents. He suggests that people are often encouraged to advance to higher, more mature levels of moral reasoning through exposure to the more advanced moral reasoning of others. In addition, moral reasoning may develop at a faster rate and achieve a higher pinnacle if children have frequent opportunities to confront moral challenges. Parents and educators might take a cue from these suggestions by arranging for frequent moral consciousness-raising experiences during the developmental years of childhood and adolescence.

John Snarey (1985) reported his evaluation of data obtained from forty-five studies conducted in twenty-seven diverse world cultures that provide striking support for the universality of Kohlberg's first four stages. More recent reviews of seventy-five cross-cultural research studies conducted in twenty-three countries also supports Kohlberg's notion of universality of common moral values and moral judgment (Gibbs, Basinger, Grime, & Snarey, 2007).

Kohlberg's theory has been criticized for a number of reasons. Some critics argue that a high level of moral reasoning does not necessarily go hand-in-hand with moral actions, especially if a person is under strong social pressure.

Other critics take issue with Kohlberg's assertion that postconventional morality is somehow preferable to conventional morality. Since most adults in our society never reach these stages, critics argue that widespread moral education programs designed to take people to the sixth stage of moral development could have disastrous results. They ask where we would be if most people chose to act according to individual moral principles with little regard for society's rules. Finally, some argue that morality plays a relatively minor role in the judgments and decisions people make each day (Krebs & Denton, 2005, 2006).

Finally, we should mention that researcher Carol Gilligan argues that Kohlberg paid little attention to the significant difference between boys and girls, and men and women. Gilligan argues that Kohlberg's stage theory ignores critical differences between the sexes in social and moral understanding. For example, in a research study, she compared men and women's thinking about real-life dilemmas, such as abortion. Men tended to focus on issues about justice while women tended to focus on issues about care (Gilligan & Attanucci, 1988). Many psychologists agree that sex differences in moral reasoning should be considered in a complete theory of moral development (Levenson, 2009).

12.1d Psychological Development During Adolescence

In addition to the physical, cognitive, and moral development of adolescence, there are also significant social and behavioral changes. During this period, relationships with parents may be under stress, the peer group may become of paramount importance in influencing behavior, and there is an increased interest in sexual behavior. Perhaps the most important task an adolescent faces is to answer the question, "Who am I?"

Identity Formation

Considering the tremendous diversity of possible answers to questions such as, "Who am I?" and "Where am I headed?" it is understandable that a great deal of experimentation takes place during adolescence. This experimentation often takes the form of trying out different roles or "selves"—which explains the unpredictability of many teenagers who behave in different ways from one day to the next.

By experimenting with different roles, many adolescents eventually forge a functional and comfortable sense of self. For some, this process takes place with little conflict or confusion. Parents of these young people may wonder why such a fuss is made over the supposedly rebellious teenage years. Other parents may feel like tearing out their hair as their adolescent children blaze their own trails in unexpected directions.

The rapid social changes in contemporary society have greatly complicated the task of achieving a sense of identity. Not only traditional gender roles but also values associated with religion, marriage, and patriotism are being challenged in society today. Perhaps as a result, psychologists have found that contemporary adolescents continue to struggle with their identity crises well into their college years. In fact, as we see in this chapter, our sense of identity is likely to be modified and recast throughout our lives. However, it is during the glorious and confusing years of our adolescence that most of us first acquire a genuine appreciation of who we are and what we might become. (You might review Stage 5 of Erikson's theory of psychosocial development from the previous chapter.)

The Role of Parents and the Peer Group

An important part of establishing an identity is gaining independence from parents. Although this process begins long before adolescence, it is accelerated during the teenage years. As parental influence diminishes, the peer group's influence grows, but relationships between parents and their teenage children do not necessarily take a nosedive. The popular image of the teenage years as a time of rebellion and intergenerational warfare is more myth than fact, and most teenagers and parents resolve their conflicts with a minimum of fireworks.

The process of becoming a separate, unique individual is a natural part of the transition from child to adult. Certainly, most parents would be distressed if their grown children still depended on them for their sense of self and direction in life. However, the process of separation may give rise to difficulties. Parents may feel that their values are being rejected, and adolescents may be torn between the need to be dependent and the need to be independent.

(Shutterstock)

The process of establishing an identity by gaining independence from parents is accelerated during the teenage years. Teens pursue their interests and begin trying out new ideas and behaviors. This is all part of the process of becoming a separate, unique individual.

When conflicts increase, family tension often rises. Culturally defined adult behaviors—such as driving, drinking, and smoking—are sometimes used by adolescents as symbols of maturity or as a form of rebellion. Adolescents may reason that they are not children anymore as they seek to become increasingly independent of their parents' authority. However, they still need support from others. This need may be greater now than ever before, considering the profound physical and behavioral changes they are experiencing. In a sense it is paradoxical that adolescents' driving needs for independence force them to retreat from the very people who are likely to be the most supportive and nurturing. To satisfy their needs for both support and independence from their family, teenagers typically turn to other people who are in the same boat—namely, their peers.

Adolescent friendships are typically much closer and more intense than at any previous time in development. American teenagers spend over half their waking hours talking to and doing things with friends of the same age group. They tend to identify more with their peers than with adults, and most rate themselves as happiest when they are with their friends. Adolescents are also more inclined to share intimate information with peers than with parents or other adults (Berndt, 1982; Csikzentmihalyi & Larson, 1984). The important role of peers in adolescent development appears to be a worldwide phenomenon.

Young people may find it reassuring to be with friends who are experiencing the same kinds of awkward physical changes. Having friends the same age to go to for advice allows teenagers to get support and counsel without short-circuiting their independence from their parents. The peer group also provides a sounding board for trying out new ideas and behaviors. Finally, it is comforting for teenagers to feel they belong to a world of their own rather than being minor players in the adult world.

It is not surprising, then, that adolescents are strongly inclined to conform to the standards of their peer group in order to gain approval. This conformity may sometimes be taken to extremes in which they radically change their manner of dress, hairstyle, and behaviors—including risky sexual and drug-use behaviors. If they identify with a group whose values and behavioral styles are dramatically different from those of their parents, considerable strife and stress may result. Of course, teenagers often welcome parents' horrified responses as evidence that their rebellion has succeeded!

Despite the increased influence of peers and occasionally extreme acts of independence, however, the so-called generation gap between parents and teens is rather small. Parents continue to exert a strong influence on their teenagers' attitudes and values, and, in fact, adolescents are often more inclined to accept their parents' values and opinions than those of their peers. Peer influence is strong in matters of dress and hairstyles, problems related to school and dating, and drug and alcohol use, while teenagers appear to be more influenced by their parents in issues of politics, religion, and major decisions such as career choices (Abrahamson, Baker, & Caspi, 2002).

Sexual Development and Behavior

It is impossible to explore the psychosocial development of adolescents without taking notice of the changes that take place in sexual development and behavior. During adolescence, boys and girls go through rapid developmental changes and often begin engaging in sexual activities. Peer pressure, self-perceptions of popularity, and the emergence of powerful sexual motivation—all contribute to a variety of sexual behaviors that normally emerge in adolescence.

The Double Standard During Adolescence

Although children have been exposed to gender-role socialization since infancy, the emphasis on gender-role differentiation often increases during adolescence. Thus, in our society, teenagers receive the full brunt of the double standard. For males, the focus of sexuality may be sexual conquest, to the point that young men who are not exploitative or are inexperienced may be labeled with highly negative terms like "sissy." For females, the message and the expectations are often very different. Many girls learn to appear "sexy" to attract males, yet they often experience ambivalence about overt sexual behavior. If they do not have sexual relations, they worry that a boyfriend will lose interest. On the other hand, having sex might make a boy think they are too "easy."

Despite the double standard, contemporary adolescents are as likely to engage in sexual behavior with casual friends or acquaintances as with someone with whom they feel emotionally attached. Girls are also more inclined than boys to perceive themselves as more popular if they engage in sexual behaviors (Mayeux, Sandstrom, & Cillessen, 2008).

Peer Pressure and Sexual Behavior

While different social pressures may affect adolescent boys and girls, both males and females today are also affected by societal influence—the increasingly permissive attitudes toward sex.

A significant number of adolescents experience premarital sex by the age of fifteen. The results of numerous nationwide surveys of adolescent sexual behaviors reveal a strong upward trend beginning in the 1950s through the 1980s, a decreasing trend through the 1990s, and a steady trend of about 50 percent being sexually active from 2000 to 2015 (see Table 12-2). Sexual surveys conducted annually at the authors' institution between 1989 and 2016 show a much higher rate, with about 80 percent of students becoming sexually active by age nineteen. There is also accumulating evidence that young adolescents, under age fifteen, are engaging in intercourse and other sexual activities in increasing proportions. Results from several national surveys revealed that approximately 55 percent of boys and 54 percent of girls had engaged in noncoital (oral) sex by age fifteen (Lindberg, Jones, & Santelli, 2008). By the age of nineteen, this increased to more than 80 percent (Martinez & Abma, 2015).

Table 12-2 Percentage of Adolescents Who Reported Having Premarital Intercourse by Age Nineteen

	Females	Males
Kinsey et al. (1953)	20%	45%
Sorensen (1973)	45%	59%
Zelnik & Kantner (1977)	55%	No males in study
Zelnik & Kantner (1980)	69%	77%
Mott & Haurin (1988)	68%	78%
Ku et al. (1998)	43%	68%
Centers for Disease Control (2016c)	46%	47%

In broad terms, we can briefly summarize the major changes in adolescent sexual activities in the last five decades. First, there was a rapid increase in premarital sex through the 1980s, followed by a decline to about 50 percent, which has remained stable for the past decade. Second, the large differences in male and female sexual activity rates decades ago appear to have completely disappeared. Perhaps we should conclude with a warning when interpreting these numbers by saying that the data presented in Table 12-2 report premarital intercourse and do not include other sexual activities. There is some evidence that while sexual intercourse rates may be stable, the rates of other sexual activities are not (Martinez & Abma, 2015.

12.2 Adulthood

If you have recently entered adulthood or are presently making this important transition, you may be wondering what lies ahead in the remaining 70 percent of your life. Will you continue to grow and change, or has the die already been cast? Will you be the same person at age forty or age seventy that you are now at age nineteen or twenty?

It is now widely acknowledged that development continues throughout life and that this growth is not limited merely to physical changes. Contemporary developmental psychologists have been amazed at the extent of psychosocial change, and to a lesser degree cognitive development, that continues during the adult years. In all, we can say with some confidence that you will not be the same person at age forty that you are at nineteen or twenty.

Most psychologists divide the adult years into three periods: early adulthood (roughly twenty to forty), middle adulthood (forty to about sixty-five), and late adulthood (after sixty-five). Although these categories are convenient, they are somewhat arbitrary and carry the danger of promoting the notion of age-based expectations (the tendency to associate certain developmental tasks or appropriate behaviors with each phase of adult life). Young adults may be expected to marry and start families and careers, and people in the middle adult years are often expected to reach the top of their careers. However, as we noted at the beginning of this chapter, not all of us experience the phases of our lives in the same orderly fashion.

BVT*Lab*

Visit **www.BVTLab.com** to explore the student resources available for this chapter.

In fact, many age-based expectations in our society have begun to break. People often postpone marriage or decide not to marry at all; in addition, many people are becoming first-time parents in middle adulthood, and gray-haired retirees are now a common sight in many college classrooms. In all, we seem to be moving in the direction of what might be called an age-irrelevant society, and it can be argued that age, like race or sex, is diminishing in importance as a regulator of behavior.

One reason for this shift is that age, per se, is not the cause of changes in our lives. A thirty-year-old advertising executive is not more mature than she was as a college student simply because she is older. Rather, her increased maturity reflects the experiences she has encountered in her personal and professional life. Thus, instead of measuring development only by age categories, many of us find it useful to define our phase of adult development in terms of *perceived age*—how old we feel.

In keeping with this reduced emphasis on age, the following sections describe physical, cognitive, and social development in fairly general terms during the years between the twenties and the sixties. We begin with the physical changes that take place during adulthood.

12.2a Physical Development in Early and Middle Adulthood

During early adulthood—the twenties and thirties—people reach the peak of their biological efficiency. These are typically years of good health and high energy, which is fortunate considering that this is the time of life when most of us are busy establishing careers, adjusting to marriage, and perhaps responding to the boundless needs of small children.

Physical Capacities

A number of physical attributes are likely to reach their high point during early adulthood. During this period, most of us reach the peak of our reproductive capacities and enjoy the best health of any time of our lives. The speed with which we can react to complex stimuli is fastest at around age twenty and then gradually declines from the midtwenties on. However, simple reflex time (such as the knee jerk when tapped with a mallet) remains relatively constant from age twenty to eighty. Vision and hearing are at their best at around age twenty; as we move into our middle adult years, we can expect to become gradually more farsighted and to lose our ability to hear higher notes. Sensitivity to taste and smell also decline with age. Sweet and salty tastes decrease most rapidly, while the tastes of bitter and sour are actually heightened. There is about a tenfold increase in smell thresholds from age twenty to age eighty, with most of this increase occurring after age sixty (Wysocki & Preti, 2004).

Physical strength also tends to peak sometime in the mid- to late twenties. It then declines gradually, dropping about 10 percent between ages thirty and sixty (Bassey, 1998). Unless you happen to compete in swimming, cycling, running, or some other athletic endeavor requiring peak performance, you may hardly notice the barely perceptible decline in physical strength, stamina, and cardiac output over the third and fourth decades of your life. In fact, a number of world-class endurance athletes remain quite competitive throughout their forties and fifties. Among endurance athletes, the decrease in VO_2 max (a measure of oxygen utilization) between twenty-four and fifty years of age is only about 4 percent. In addition, individuals who maintain fitness can expect to have VO_2 max values far higher than younger, less athletic individuals. In fact, maintaining physical activity can slow the rate of decline in VO_2 max by as much as 50 percent (Fox, 2011). Maintaining a level of physical fitness may also contribute to fewer health problems and a reduction in the brain cell loss that normally occurs during aging. Numerous studies have revealed that physical fitness and continuing education protect against normal brain cell losses that occur during aging (Gordon et al., 2008).

Over time, however, middle adulthood brings a gradual decline in physical functioning and perhaps a corresponding increase in health problems. We may begin to notice that it is not so easy to rebound the morning after a late party, or that the body protests more after a hard workout on the tennis courts. Some of the most notable changes, particularly for women, have to do with changing hormonal patterns that, among other things, alter reproductive capacity.

Climacteric Physiological changes, including menopause, that occur during a woman's transition from fertility to infertility

Menopause Cessation of menstruation that takes place during the climacteric

Andropause A condition of low testosterone often attributed to the natural loss of testosterone production in older men; also referred to as *male menopause*

Hormonal Changes and the Climacteric

The term **climacteric** refers to the physiological changes that occur during a woman's transition from fertility to infertility. **Menopause**, one of the events of the female climacteric, refers to the cessation of menstruation. Menopause results from certain physiological changes, most notably a reduction in estrogen levels. It can take place anytime between forty and sixty, but most commonly occurs between forty-five and fifty (Crooks & Baur, 2011). Many women consider the cessation of menstruation and fertility to be the most significant biological change related to aging.

Do men also undergo a climacteric? Not in the same sense as women. For one thing, men often retain their reproductive capacity well into the older years (although with declining fertility). The hormonal changes, called **andropause**, men undergo are much more gradual. Male testosterone levels usually reach their peak sometime between the ages of seventeen and twenty, and then steadily, but slowly, decline at a rate of about 1 to 2 percent per year until around age sixty, when they level off. In recent years, there has been increasing interest in hormone replacement therapy for men. Evidence suggests that testosterone supplements in older men increase lean body mass, bone density, and libido. In addition, testosterone replacement may improve mood and cognitive functioning by altering neural activity essential for learning and memory (Janowsky, 2006; Lu et al., 2006)

The Double Standard of Aging

In a society that places a premium on youth, it can be difficult for both men and women to grow older. This process is usually more difficult for women than for men because of another double standard of our society—this one related to aging. Although a woman's erotic and orgasmic capabilities continue after menopause, it is not uncommon for her to be considered past her sexual prime relatively early in the aging process. The cultural image of an erotically appealing woman is commonly one of youth. As a woman grows away from this image, she is usually considered less and less attractive. Cosmetics, Botox® injections, and plastic surgery are often used to maintain a youthful appearance for as long as possible.

In contrast, men's physical and sexual attractiveness are often considered to be enhanced by age. Gray hairs and wrinkles may be thought to look "distinguished" on men, signs of accumulated life experience and wisdom. Likewise, while the professional achievements of women may be perceived as threatening to some males, a man's sexual attractiveness is often closely associated with his achievements and social status, both of which may increase with age (Buss, 1989; Shackelford, Schmitt, & Buss, 2005).

12.2b Cognitive Development in Early and Middle Adulthood

Intelligence

Crystallized Intelligence
Intelligence that results from accumulated knowledge, including knowledge of how to reason, language skills, and understanding of technology

Fluid Intelligence
Ability to perceive and draw inferences about relationships among patterns of stimuli, to conceptualize abstract information, and to solve problems

At one time, intellectual ability was believed to peak in young adulthood just as do most aspects of physical functioning. This view was supported by an early large-scale study that administered standardized intelligence tests to large samples of adults of varying ages. Young adults were found to score higher than middle-aged adults, who in turn outperformed older adults (Jones & Conrad, 1933). More recent longitudinal studies all suggest that there is an age-associated decline in intelligence, but all do not agree on just when this decline occurs and whether some aspects of intelligence are less susceptible to age-related change.

Crystallized Versus Fluid Intelligence

Some changes in specific kinds of intelligence do appear to be age-related, however. Psychologists distinguish between crystallized and fluid intelligence. **Crystallized intelligence** results from accumulated knowledge, including knowledge of how to reason, language skills, and understanding of technology; it is linked closely to education, experience, and cultural background. Crystallized intelligence is measured by tests of general information. Research indicates that crystallized intelligence increases with age and that people tend to continue improving their performance on tests of this form of intelligence until near the ends of their lives.

Fluid intelligence allows us to perceive and draw inferences about relationships among patterns of stimuli, to conceptualize abstract information, and to solve problems. It is measured by various kinds of test problems to which people are unlikely to have been exposed previously, such as grouping numbers and symbols according to some abstract principle. Fluid intelligence seems to be relatively independent of education and cultural influences. It peaks sometime between ages twenty and thirty and declines steadily thereafter (Kaufman, 2001).

It is possible that these age-related differences may somehow be an artifact of the research strategy used, since much of the basic research on crystallized and fluid intelligence has relied on the cross-sectional approach. However, since fluid intelligence depends more on optimal frontal lobe functioning than does crystallized intelligence, it seems likely that it is more adversely influenced by age-associated neurological declines. Recent research confirms that declines in fluid intelligence are strongly correlated with age-related decreases in functioning of the frontal lobes (Rabbitt et al., 2008).

A Fifth Stage of Cognitive Development

Recall that Piaget saw formal operations as the highest level of cognitive functioning. Some critics disagree, maintaining that many adults progress beyond formal operations to what might be called a fifth stage of intellectual development. One theorist, Patricia Arlin (1989), believes that adults develop cognitively to the level of *problem finding*. Someone at the problem-finding stage is concerned with posing new questions about the world and trying to discover novel solutions to old problems. Arlin believes that problem finding allows intellectually maturing adults to progress beyond Piaget's formal operations to the level of creative thinking.

12.2c Psychosocial Development in Early and Middle Adulthood

We saw in Chapter 11 that Erik Erikson described two primary developmental tasks in early and middle adulthood: first the establishment of intimacy, and then the achievement of generativity through commitments to family, work, and future generations. The two major topics in this section—"Single and Married Lifestyles" and "Commitments to Parenting and Work"—explore some of the ways in which people respond to these challenges.

Single and Married Lifestyles

As we make the transition from adolescent to young adult, the central focus of our psychosocial adjustment is likely to shift from wanting to be liked by people to needing a loving relationship with someone special. Establishing an intimate relationship requires courage, and a certain amount of self-abandon and willingness to compromise personal preferences. In Erikson's view, two people who achieve true intimacy are able to fuse their identities while at the same time retaining a sense of self. Too much independence may prevent the establishment of intimacy and result in a state of isolation.

Erikson emphasized traditional marriage as a vehicle for fulfilling intimacy needs, but there is plenty of statistical evidence that the commitment to marriage is changing in our society. Can the decision to remain single or cohabit also provide a satisfactory adjustment? The following discussions explore the evidence.

(Shutterstock)

According to Erik Erikson, two people who achieve true intimacy are able to fuse their identities while at the same time retaining a sense of self.

Single Living Increasing numbers of young and middle-aged adults in our society live alone, many out of choice. This increase is most pronounced among people in their twenties and early thirties. For example, a comparison of census figures between 1965 and 2015 reveals that the percentage of young adults who are married has decreased from about 80 percent in 1965 to about 50 percent in 2010 (Centers for Disease Control and Prevention, 2013). This is the lowest marriage rate in the past hundred years. In addition to fewer adults getting married, marriage is more often postponed into one's thirties, compared to the early twenties a few decades ago.

Although single life is still often seen as the period before, in between, or after marriage, these societal attitudes may be changing. Until recently in the United States, a stigma was often attached to remaining single, especially for women. Today it seems quite possible that more and more people will remain single, either as an option to marriage or following a divorce. There may also be a reduction in the number of people who marry primarily for convention's sake.

Various conditions contribute to the increasing numbers of single adults. These factors include people marrying at a later age, more women placing career objectives ahead of marriage, an increase in the number of cohabiting couples, high divorce rates, a greater emphasis on advanced education, and an increase in the number of women who need not depend on marriage to ensure economic stability.

Although single living is common in our society, most adults still choose to enter into a long-term relationship with a partner, even though it may not be a lifelong bond.

Cohabitate Living together in a sexual relationship without being married

There are several kinds of long-term intimate relationships. We will look at the most common: cohabitation and marriage.

Cohabitation The past few decades have seen a significant increase in the number of couples choosing to **cohabitate** (living together in a sexual relationship without being married). Between 1974 and 2010, the percentage of marriages preceded by cohabitation increased from 10 percent to about 57 percent—rates higher than marriage. This dramatic increase in cohabitation has been attributed to a growing inclination to question traditional mores, particularly those pertaining to marriage, as well as to our recessed economy. Today, many people believe that sexuality is an important part of life, and that marriage is not the only lifestyle that legitimizes sexual relations.

Does Cohabitation Lead to Better Marriages?

Does the experience of living together have a measurable effect on the longevity and happiness of a subsequent marriage? There are two opposing views, one arguing that living together has a positive effect on marriage and the other arguing just the opposite—cohabitation leads to less stable marriages. What do you think? Can you think of arguments to support each of these opposing viewpoints? Consider these questions before reading on.

The more popular point of view among college students is that living together will result in happier and more stable marriages. Over 80 percent of college seniors now believe that it is a good idea to cohabitate before marriage. In this view, cohabiting allows the couple to explore their compatibility before making a long-term commitment. Trial experiences with the struggles and joys of an everyday relationship allow individuals to identify their own needs and expectations.

Figure 12-1 Marriage Rates

The percentage of young adults (twenty-five to thirty-five years old) who are married has declined over the past forty-five years from approximately 80 percent to fewer than 50 percent.

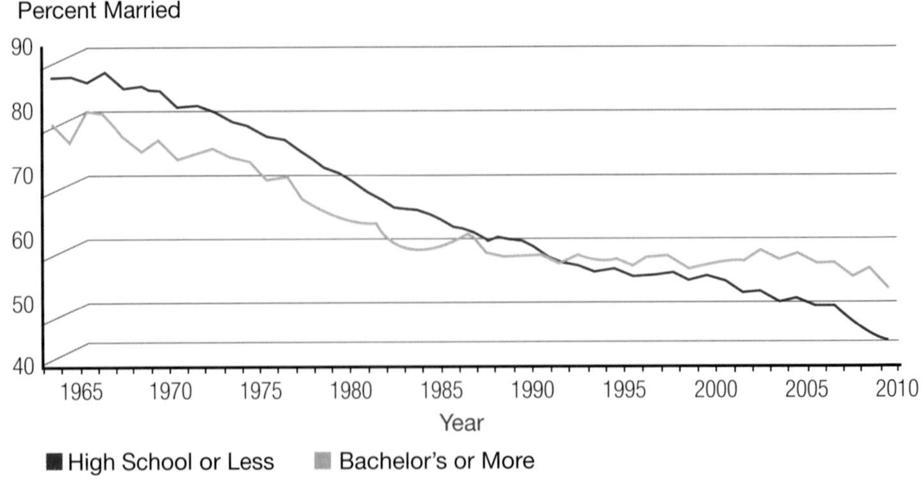

Data from Statistical Abstracts, 2012

Table 12-3 Number of Marriages and Divorces per 1,000 Resident Population

While both marriage and divorce rates appear to have declined over the past few decades, the percentage of marriages that end in divorce remains about 50 percent.

	1970	1975	1980	1985	1990	2004	2006	2012	2014
Marriages	10.6	10.0	10.6	10.1	9.8	7.4	7.3	6.8	6.9
Divorces	3.5	4.8	5.2	5.0	4.7	3.7	3.6	3.3	3.2

Centers for Disease Control, 2014

The opposing view suggests that living together will have an overall negative impact on the institution of marriage, particularly its long-term stability (Copen, Daniels, Vespa, & Mosher, 2012). Faced with conflict, a couple that is living together may find it easier to end the relationship than to make a grand effort to resolve their problems. Once the pattern of breaking up has been established, people may be more likely to respond to marital conflict in the same way.

U.S. Census data on the outcome of cohabitation reveals that about 50 percent enter marriage within five years of cohabitation and more than 40 percent of these cohabitations involve children. Most research suggests that couples that live together prior to marriage are at a greater risk of divorce than non-cohabitating couples. In summary, we can conclude that cohabitation is now occurring more frequently than marriage in young adults and that many of these relationships involve children. The reasons for declining marriage rates and increasing cohabitation rates are complex, but include both increases in acceptance of cohabitation and the economy.

Marriage

In spite of rapidly changing mores, people do not seem to be permanently substituting single living, cohabitation, or other alternative lifestyles for traditional marriage. As discussed above, statistics show that the percent of young people who are married has begun to decline over the forty-four-year period from 1970 to 2014 (see Table 12-3). Divorce rates during this period have also decreased, but they still represent about one in two marriages.

There are good reasons why the institution of marriage is found in virtually every society; it serves several personal and social functions. It provides societies with stable family units that help to perpetuate social norms, as children learn society's rules and expectations from parents or kinship groups. It also structures an economic partnership that ties child support and subsistence tasks into one family unit. Marriage regulates sexual behavior and also provides a framework for fulfilling people's needs for social and emotional support.

While people's expectations for marriage have increased, our society's supportive network for marriage has decreased. In a mobile, urban society in which a couple often settles down far from their extended families, many married couples are isolated from their families and neighbors. This geographical distance puts further demands on the marriage, for there is often no place else to turn for such things as childcare assistance, emotional support, and financial or household help.

Another development influencing marital patterns is increased longevity. "Till death do us part" now means many more years than it did in the past, raising the question of how long even the best marriage can be expected to fulfill so many functions.

The World of Work

If you were to pick at random any young or middle-aged adult today and ask, "Who are you?" the chances are good that most would reply, "I am a teacher" (or computer programmer, medical technologist, or some other profession). Adults are inclined to define or identify who they are by what they do. This tendency has probably always been true of men; now, it is also true of most women, since the majority of adult American women have occupations outside the home. Beyond the sense of competence that successful parenting can provide, much of what people do to fulfill generativity needs involves their work.

(iStock)

The virtually unlimited number of career possibilities can seem overwhelming to young adults and can lead to uncertainty and job dissatisfaction.

During late adolescence, many individuals struggle with developing a career track—one reason why so many college students change their majors one or more times. By young adulthood, most of us accomplish the crucial task of choosing a career. In some ways, careers have become more accessible to both sexes than at any previous time in history. Earlier in this century, advanced education was a privilege enjoyed mostly by the affluent, but today almost any motivated high school graduate can attend college. Traditional pressures for sons to follow in their fathers' footsteps and for women to become homemakers are diminishing, and new fields of specialization provide many more potential careers for both sexes.

However, this increased freedom has also been the source of new frustrations and anxieties. As we saw in the discussion of decision making in Chapter 10, virtually unlimited opportunities can seem overwhelming, and young adults are often unsure what to do about their careers. This uncertainty may carry over into the work situation and contribute to a tendency of young workers to be less satisfied with their jobs than middle-aged or older adults.

How many Americans are satisfied with their jobs? According to a government survey, only half of the respondents answered *yes*. This is down from about 90 percent reported in surveys conducted in 1980.

One of the most noteworthy recent trends is the dramatic increase in the number of women in the work force. Today, roughly two out of every three women age twenty-five to forty-four work outside the home, a figure that has doubled since the early 1950s (Fullerton Jr., 1999). More than 47 percent of the workforce is made up of women—a trend that is expected to rise above 50 percent by 2018.

There are important practical benefits to working. For one, a job provides a way to broaden social networks, as well as an escape from the sense of isolation that many nonworking women experience. Another benefit is the increased financial security provided by two incomes. Dual-career families are better able to afford the extras that add to enjoyment of life and are less likely to be confronted with the stress of financial crises. Finally, Erikson's assertion that a man's sense of identity and self-worth is strongly influenced by his work also now applies to women. A number of studies have shown that women who enjoy their work have higher self-esteem, a greater sense of pride and power, better emotional and physical health, and a greater sense of overall life satisfaction than women who do not work outside the home.

Dual-provider families also face some potential disadvantages, however. One of the biggest problems is finding enough time for everything. At the end of the workday, the couple must face mundane tasks such as paying the bills, doing housework, washing clothes, and preparing meals. If they have children, there are additional demands that may make it difficult to spend quality time together or to enjoy leisure activities. This schedule can exact a high price both in diminished energy levels and downgraded quality of a relationship. Unfortunately, women seem to bear the brunt of these increased pressures, and they often must contend with role overload if husbands neglect to share domestic duties equally.

12.3 The Older Years

What kinds of associations or images come to your mind when you hear the words *old people* or *old age*? If you are like most Americans, young and old alike, you are likely to think of old people as forgetful, cranky, touchy, depressed, frail, unhealthy, poorly coordinated, and not as smart as when they were younger. You are also likely to view the older years as a time when people become more dependent on others, less interested in sex, obsessed with physical complaints, more isolated from friends and family, unreliable, and likely to be institutionalized in nursing homes. Are these stereotypes more myth than fact? In the remaining pages of this chapter we explore the evidence about the physical, cognitive, and psychosocial developments that accompany older adulthood.

12.3a The Graying of America

People today are living longer and retaining their health and vigor longer than previous generations. In fact, the proportion of older people in the American population has increased quite dramatically in recent years. Whereas in 1900 the average life expectancy was slightly less than fifty years, by the 2000s it had increased to approximately seventy-seven years, and by 2015, eighty-one years for females and seventy-six years for males. Only 4 percent of the American populace was older than sixty-five in 1900, but in 2008, this figure had increased to 13 percent (more than 6.8 million people). Over the past few

Figure 12-2 Older Population by Age Group, 1900–2050

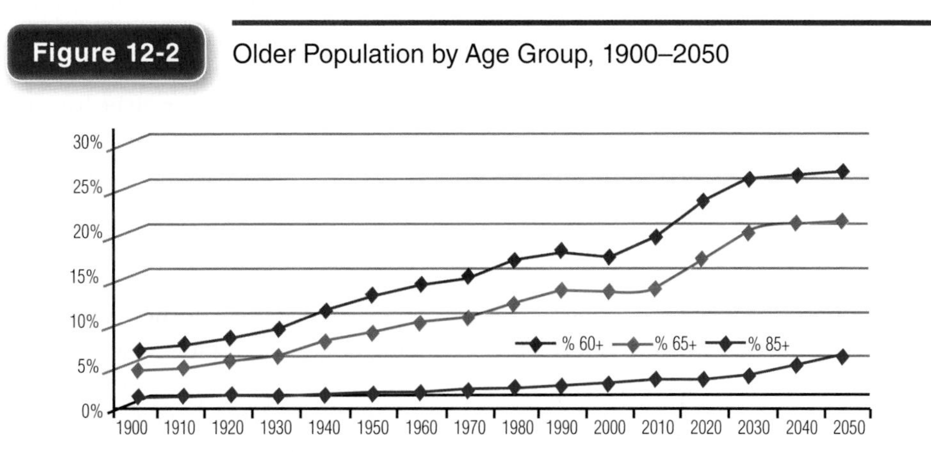

Data from Administration on Aging, 2012

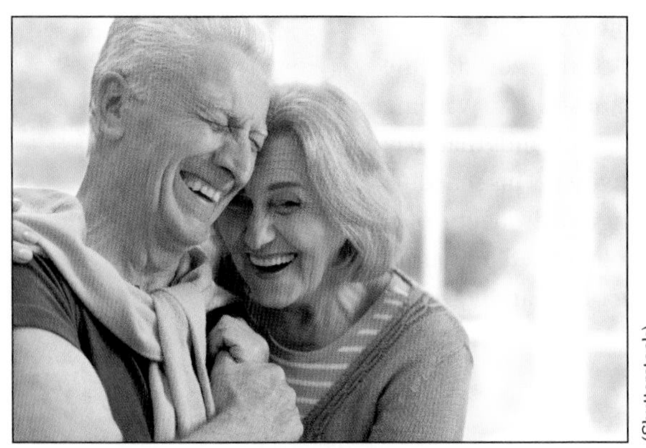

(Shutterstock)

As of the year 2000, the average life expectancy increased to approximately age seventy-seven.

decades, the proportion of American people sixty-five and older has grown at twice the rate of the rest of our population. By the year 2020, it is estimated that more than 16 percent of the American population will be sixty-five or older (Administration On Aging, 2014).

The so-called graying of America may be attributed to a number of factors. To some extent, it is a function of an increased birthrate that commenced around the turn of the twentieth century, combined with higher immigration rates early in that century. However, much of this trend is caused by technological changes since 1900 that have resulted in longer life spans and lower mortality rates for the elderly. Improved medications and medical procedures prolong the lives of many older people.

The graying of America has significant implications for changing family patterns, employment trends, social policies, and political trends, but our concern is with the individuals who are experiencing longer life spans. Does a longer life mean a welcome prolongation of life's so-called "golden years," or has technology merely expanded the pain and travail of life on a downward slide?

12.3b Physical Development in the Older Years

We noted earlier that physical decline in such things as muscle strength, vision, and hearing begins in early to middle adulthood. While many of these changes are barely noticeable in the middle years, they often are disturbingly obvious as we grow older. One area in which there are often sharp declines is vision. Older people may become more farsighted; they may also have trouble perceiving color and depth and adapting to changes in lighting. (Night vision commonly declines with age.) The changes in vision are largely caused by a reduction in the elasticity of the eyes' lenses. This makes it more difficult for the ciliary muscles to change the shape of the lens. As a result, older people often need to hold reading material farther away to keep it in focus.

Hearing loss is also common. Many older people have difficulty following a conversation, particularly when there is competing noise from the television, radio, or other background sound. This decline can increase a sense of isolation and perhaps even contribute to mild paranoia if older people assume that others are trying to hide something from them by whispering. Other frequent accompaniments to aging are reduction in taste and smell sensitivity (which explains why food often does not taste as good to older people). About 25 percent of people between sixty-five and sixty-eight have no sense of smell, and by age eighty, this increases to more than 50 percent. There is also a diminution of the body senses and equilibrium (see Chapter 4), which may be one reason why older people are more likely to lose their balance and fall.

The organ systems also show a decline in functional efficiency with age. When we are young, our hearts, lungs, kidneys, and other organs have the potential to increase their outputs to a level several times greater than normal under emergency conditions, a capacity that is known as **organ reserve**. For example, strenuous physical activity can cause a young heart to work six times harder than normal. As we grow older, organ reserve is reduced. The heart's ability to pump blood declines by about 1 percent per year from the early twenties on, and by age sixty, blood flow from the arms to the legs is slower than at age twenty-five. By age seventy-five, there has been an average decline in lung

Organ Reserve Potential ability of organs such as the heart, lungs, and kidneys to increase their output to a level several times greater than normal under emergency conditions

capacity of approximately 50 percent in men and 30 percent in women. Furthermore, muscle fibers decrease in number at an average rate of 3 to 5 percent per decade after age thirty (Fleg, Morrell, Bos, Brant, & Talbot, 2005).

Although the statistics we have just cited may seem to paint a rather depressing picture, there is a brighter side to the story. Glasses, hearing aids, and other medical procedures can adequately compensate for many of the visual and hearing difficulties of older people. There is also evidence that regular exercise can significantly reduce deterioration of many bodily functions that accompany aging. It has been estimated that disuse accounts for about half of the functional decline that occurs between ages thirty and seventy. It would appear that the advice "Use it or lose it" has some validity. Despite the declines associated with the older years, widespread evidence indicates that older people enjoy reasonably good health, some virtually to the ends of their lives.

Neuronal Changes During Aging

In the previous section we reviewed a number of sensory and structural changes that occur during later years. What about the brain? Does it change too? Normally, the effects of aging on the brain are not noticeable until we reach about fifty to sixty years of age. At this time, the brain begins to decrease in size as a result of both neuron and glial cell loss. Just how much neuronal degeneration occurs during normal aging is difficult to determine because of wide variations in cell numbers between individuals and the difficulty in diagnosing cognitive diseases such as Alzheimer's disease in some individuals. For instance, early research suggested that between the ages of eighteen and ninety-five years there might be a 50 percent loss in cell numbers in the frontal and temporal lobes. More recent estimates from healthy individuals suggest that it may be closer to only 10 percent (Ances, Ortega, Vaida, Heaps, & Paul, 2012)

As with other bodily functions, the normal deterioration in the brain can be significantly reduced by both physical exercise, which increases blood flow to the brain, and by using your brain. Experiments with aging rats have demonstrated new cell growth and synapse formation after exposure to a stimulating environment (Greenough, McDonald, Parnisari, & Camel, 1986). It is believed that people who continually engage in stimulating aerobic activities such as walking can greatly reduce the rate of normal cell deterioration by increasing the production of essential nerve growth hormones (Erickson, Miller, & Roecklein, 2012).

12.3c **Cognitive Changes in the Older Years**

It is often said that old people have poor memories, and that intelligence declines sharply in the later years. How accurate is this picture? For most people, the ability to learn and retain meaningful information declines only slightly in the later years. The characterization of old age as a time of cognitive decline may be related to a few conditions. One of these is a decline of fluid intelligence that usually does accompany aging; another is the highly visible condition of senility that affects a relatively small percentage of older people. Let us look at both of these factors.

Memory, Intelligence, and Aging

As we saw earlier in this chapter, there seem to be two types of intelligence. Crystallized intelligence tends to hold steady or perhaps even improve somewhat in the later

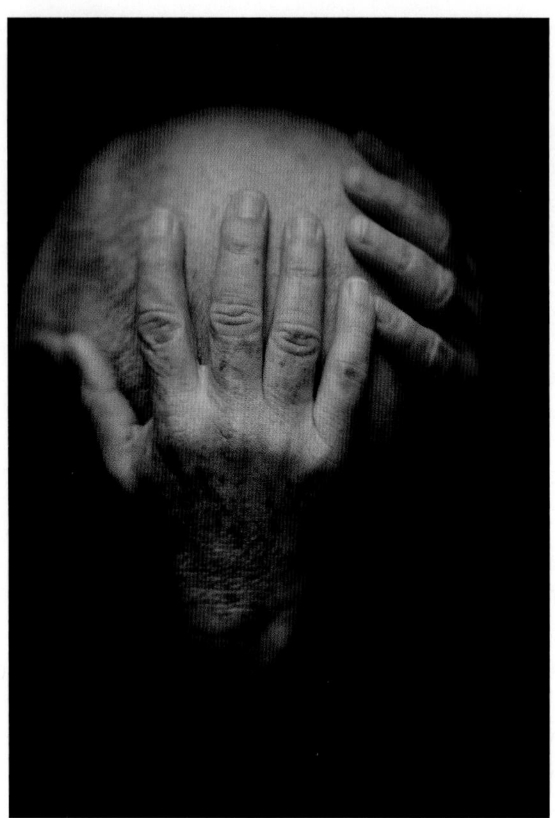

(iStock)

Dementia is most often associated with a series of small strokes, brain tumors, neurological disorders, or chronic alcoholism.

years—a finding that is consistent with our tendency to continue to add to our storehouse of knowledge as we grow older, often up to the end of our lives. In contrast, fluid intelligence declines with age, a process that may be related to a reduced efficiency of neurological functioning, particularly in the frontal lobes (Rabbitt, 2005; Aine, Sanfratello, Adair, Knoefel, Caprihan, & Stephen, 2011).

There is another possible explanation for the discrepancy between crystallized and fluid intelligence in the later years. People may be more likely to maintain crystallized abilities because they are exercised or used on a regular basis, whereas older people may be less frequently challenged to use their fluid abilities. This suggestion presents another version of the "Use it or lose it" concept mentioned earlier.

Memory—particularly short-term, or working, memory—does decline with aging. While diseases such as Alzheimer's disease contribute significantly to memory impairments in older individuals, a gradual decline in memory even occurs in healthy aging. There are several factors that contribute to this decline, including decreased blood flow to the brain as well as a normal decline in the production of several essential nerve growth hormones. Both of these declines can be delayed significantly by increasing both physical and cognitive activity (Miller et al., 2012).

Senile Dementia

For a small number of people, old age brings a nightmare of deteriorating cognitive functions known commonly as senility or more technically as **senile dementia** (a collective term that describes a variety of conditions characterized by memory deficits, forgetfulness, disorientation of time and place, decline in the ability to think, impaired attention, altered personality, and difficulties in relating to others). Approximately ten million Americans are afflicted with senile dementia, including 50 percent of people over seventy-five. Dementia has many causes, some treatable and some that cannot be remedied at the present time. Occasionally, the confusion characteristic of dementia can be attributed to improper use of medications, hormonal abnormalities, infectious diseases, or metabolic disorders. (Dementia resulting from these causes may often be remedied by medical treatment.) More commonly, it is associated with a series of small strokes, brain tumors, neurological disorders, or chronic alcoholism—all of which can result in irreversible loss of brain neurons.

Senile Dementia Collective term describing a variety of conditions sometimes associated with aging, including memory deficits, forgetfulness, disorientation of time and place, declining ability to think, and so forth

Alzheimer's Disease An incurable disease that destroys neural tissue, resulting in an impaired capacity to remember, think, relate to others, and care for oneself

The most common form of senile dementia is **Alzheimer's disease**, a currently incurable condition that robs individuals of the capacity to remember, think, relate to others, care for themselves, and even to be aware of their own existence. In the mid-1980s, the National Alzheimer's Disease and Related Disorders Association estimated that roughly 2.5 million Americans, most over sixty, had this dreadful illness. Current estimates suggest that approximately 11 percent of people over 65 have Alzheimer's disease and that this rate increases to about 50 percent of persons over eighty-five years old (Centers for Disease Control and Prevention, 2016a). Alzheimer's disease alone accounts for 60 percent of all cases of senile dementia in people over age sixty-five. This represents about 5.3 million people and is projected to increase to 14.0 million Americans by 2050.

A tremendous amount of research is currently underway to determine the cause(s) of this disease, and some clues have been uncovered. The most promising line of evidence suggests that victims of Alzheimer's disease produce an abnormal protein called beta-amyloid protein, which deposits amyloid plaques in the brain. Amyloid proteins duplicate themselves to such an excessive extent in people with Alzheimer's disease that they create tangled webs, known as neurofibrillary tangles, that produce massive neurological damage and ultimately choke the life out of affected brain cells (Blennow, de Leon, & Zetterberg, 2006; Pastorino & Lu, 2006). Promising new lines of research are aimed at developing drugs that target amyloid proteins and develop antibodies against it (Cardinale & Biocca, 2008; Lambracht-Washington & Rosenberg, 2013; Vasilevko & Cribbs, 2006).

12.3d Psychological Development in the Older Years

We have seen that the popular stereotype of old age as a time of rapidly deteriorating physical and cognitive functioning is much more myth than fact, but what about the mental health of older people? Is aging associated with depression, despair, dissatisfaction, unhappiness, and a breakdown of interpersonal relationships? Fortunately, this generalization is true of only a small proportion of aging people.

In reality, the older years do tend to be the golden years for a large number of individuals. Several major national surveys have found that satisfaction with life in general, feelings of well-being and marital satisfaction actually tend to be higher among the aged than among younger adults. Despite the common misconception that many older people end up in institutions for the aged, only about 5 percent of America's aged population live in institutions. For most, old age is a time of continued independence, with the additional freedom from the burdens of job and family obligations.

This situation is not always the case, however. Some older people—who are widowed, isolated from friends, in poor health, economically disadvantaged, or resentful of being forced to retire—may find the older years to be far from golden. Admittedly, some of these factors are beyond most individuals' control, but in many ways our satisfaction in old age is the product of our own attitudes and behaviors.

Successful Aging

Many Americans see continued active involvement in life as the best road to successful aging. Older people are encouraged to remain active and not to retire from their lives when they retire from their jobs. However, might there not also be advantages to cutting back, relaxing, and gracefully withdrawing from the bustle of life?

These descriptions summarize two popular theories of successful aging that have generated considerable discussion and research. It is clear that the more involved and active older people remain, the more happy and fulfilled they will be. Thus, older people should pursue hobbies, travel, do volunteer work, engage in active grandparenting, or involve themselves in other endeavors that help to sustain a relatively high level of activity. As people age, however, they may no longer find the consequences of these activities as rewarding as they once were. Aging not only makes many activities more difficult because of the changes in sensory abilities (like vision, audition, and taste), it makes the consequences more aversive. For instance, playing tennis or going on long walks may result in fatigue and sore muscles; engaging in intellectual activities may result in embarrassment from a failing memory. For these reasons, many people may abandon activities they enjoyed earlier. B. F. Skinner

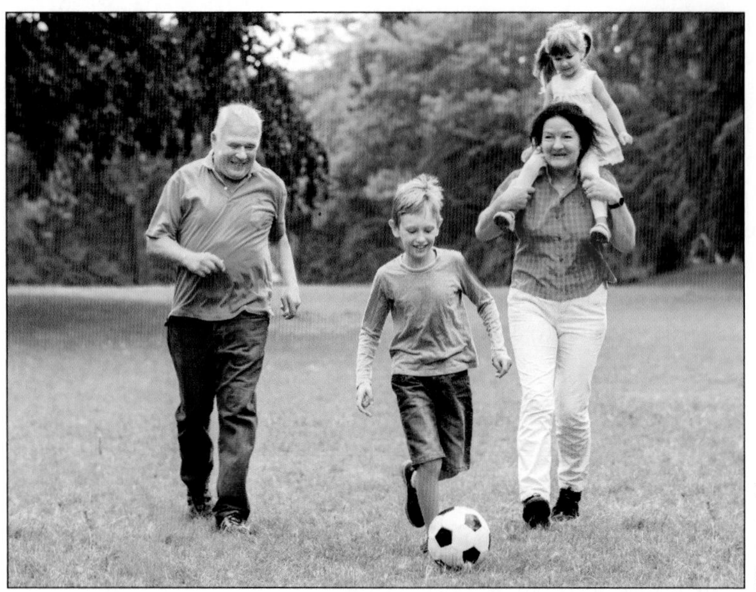

(Shutterstock)

Many Americans believe remaining active is the key to successful aging. Older people are encouraged to remain active and not to retire from their lives when they retire from their jobs.

offers some particularly useful advice on how the aging intellectual can compensate for some of these changes (Skinner, 1987). It is perhaps this advice that kept him intellectually active through the last months of his long and productive life. Recall that Erik Erikson viewed successful aging as conditional upon achieving integrity. He believed that people who are able to view their lives retrospectively with a sense of satisfaction and accomplishment are likely to achieve a sense of unity or integrity. In contrast, people who view their lives as a series of disappointments and failures are likely to experience unhappiness and despair. Recall Ebenezer Scrooge in Charles Dickens's *A Christmas Carol;* his forced life review produced a dramatically more optimistic focus to his life in his remaining years.

Maintaining close personal relationships has been shown to be especially important for maintaining health and recovering from illness in the elderly. A number of studies have demonstrated the health benefits of **social support** from family, friends, and health-care providers in reducing risks of disease and prolonging life. For instance, in a large longitudinal study of nearly 1,300 participants between the ages of sixty-five and ninety-five, morbidity increased from about 41 percent in those with close social ties to over 68 percent in those without social support (Mazzella et al., 2010).

How does social support facilitate recovery from surgery and disease as well as prolong life? How might **social isolation** increase an individual's risk of disease? Think about these questions before reading on.

There are several possible ways that social support might influence health. First, it has been suggested that people who live in isolation live in physically different circumstances, and it is these circumstances that influence health. These conditions might include the type and location of housing, diet, and opportunities for physical exercise. Another possibility is that social support acts as a buffer to life stressors. This buffering hypothesis argues that people with social contacts are protected (or buffered) from the harmful effects of stress. In addition, people with social contacts are more likely to receive advice about good health practices, receive encouragement, be physically active, and have a greater sense of personal control (Brannon et al., 2014).

Social Support An environment in which a person has close relatives or personal friends

Social Isolation An environment lacking social interaction, such as one in which an elderly person lives alone

In this chapter we reviewed the developmental changes that occur during adulthood. Physical, cognitive, and psychosocial changes continue throughout our lives. During these later years, there is considerable variability between individuals in how quickly these changes occur. It appears that maintaining a physically active and cognitively stimulating lifestyle can greatly reduce the rate of detrimental changes in late adulthood. In addition, maintaining close social contacts throughout our lives may contribute to health and longevity.

CHAPTER REVIEW

Adolescence

1. In America and other modern Western societies the period of adolescence is prolonged. Unlike many nonindustrial societies, our society has no single initiation rite that signals passage into adulthood.
2. Puberty is the approximately two-year period of rapid physical changes that culminates in sexual maturity. The adolescent growth spurt usually runs its course in the two years following the onset of puberty.
3. In general, research has shown that early maturation holds some advantages for boys and some disadvantages for girls.
4. The onset of adolescence is marked by the emergence of the capacity to manipulate objects mentally that are not physically present and by the ability to engage in deductive reasoning, both traits Piaget associated with the formal operations stage of cognitive development.
5. According to Lawrence Kohlberg's theory of moral development, most children between the ages of four and ten exhibit a preconventional morality in which they behave in certain ways to avoid being punished or to obtain rewards. By late childhood or early adolescence, we achieve the level of conventional morality exemplified by the desire either to help others or to help maintain the social order. Some adults progress to the final level of postconventional morality, in which they affirm individual rights and perhaps are guided by universal moral principles that may conflict with society's rules.
6. It is during our adolescence that most of us first acquire an identity or sense of self. An important part of establishing an identity is gaining independence from parents. As parental influence diminishes, the peer group's influence grows.
7. Adolescent sexuality in America is influenced by considerable pressure to be sexually active, perceived popularity, and increased sexual motivation.
8. Over the past four decades, there has been a strong upward trend in the numbers of adolescents who engage in sexual behaviors. The levels of sexual activity are now essentially the same for female and male adolescents.

Adulthood

9. Many age-based expectations (the tendency to associate certain developmental tasks or appropriate behaviors with each phase of adult life) have begun to break down in contemporary society. We appear to be moving in the direction of an age-irrelevant society in which such attributes as age, race, and sex are diminishing in importance as regulators of behavior.
10. During early adulthood (the twenties and thirties) people reach the peak of their biological efficiency. During this time, most of us enjoy the best health of any time in our lives.

CHAPTER REVIEW

11. Middle adulthood (the forties and fifties) brings a gradual decline in physical functioning and perhaps a corresponding increase in health problems.
12. Our society has a double standard of aging that tends to regard postmenopausal women as past their sexual prime, whereas men's physical and sexual attractiveness is often considered to be enhanced by the aging process.
13. Research has shown that people retain their intellectual abilities well into middle age and beyond. Some changes in specific kinds of intelligence do appear to be age related. Crystallized intelligence, which results from accumulated knowledge, tends to increase with age. In contrast, fluid intelligence, or the ability to conceptualize abstract information and to solve problems, tends to decline after age thirty.
14. Erik Erikson identified traditional marriage as the avenue for fulfilling intimacy needs. Today, however, an increasing number of people remain unmarried, and many are able to fulfill their intimacy needs through close friendships and/or cohabitation relationships.
15. Studies have linked marital happiness to positive communication, high levels of physical intimacy, mutual empathy, spending focused time together, sharing values, and flexibility.
16. Having children may be associated with both positive and negative consequences. On the positive side, parenthood may enhance a couple's love and intimacy and provide them with a sense of accomplishment and a chance to discover untapped personal dimensions and resources. On the debit side, children often sap energy, reduce time for each other, and place a drain on emotional and financial resources.
17. Young workers generally tend to be less satisfied with their jobs than middle-aged or older adults, but most Americans are now unsatisfied with their jobs.

The Older Years

18. Over the past few decades, the proportion of American people sixty-five and older has grown at twice the rate of the rest of our population.
19. In the older years, people experience a decline in all sensory functions together with a reduction in organ reserve (the capacity of organs like the heart and lungs to increase their outputs under emergency conditions).
20. There is ample evidence that regular exercise can significantly reduce the deterioration of both physical and cognitive functions that accompany aging.
21. For most people, the ability to learn and retain meaningful information declines only slightly in the later years.
22. Many older men are using testosterone replacement to preserve muscle mass, bone density, and cognitive functioning as they age.

CHAPTER REVIEW

23. The most common form of senile dementia is Alzheimer's disease, which has been linked with beta-amyloid protein that creates neurofibrillary tangles that destroy brain cells. Research is focusing on drugs and antibodies that target amyloid.
24. Studies have shown that satisfaction with life in general and feelings of well-being tend to be higher among the aged than among younger adults, particularly if they remain both physically and cognitively active.
25. Happiness in the later years does not appear to be correlated with a particular lifestyle. Some older people are happiest when they are busy and socially involved; others may enjoy indulging in plenty of relaxation. Older people tend to select a lifestyle that reflects their personality and the kinds of activities they engaged in while they were younger.
26. Maintaining a network of social support seems especially important for the health of older adults. Social isolation is associated with a greater risk of disease and prolonged recovery from illness.

TERMS AND CONCEPTS

Adolescence, pg. 484
Adolescent Growth Spurt, pg. 484
Alzheimer's Disease, pg. 504
Andropause, pg. 495
Climacteric, pg. 495
Cohabitate, pg. 498
Conventional Morality, pg. 487
Crystallized Intelligence, pg. 496
Fluid Intelligence, pg. 496
Gonadotropins, pg. 484
Menopause, pg. 495
Organ Reserve, pg. 502
Postconventional Morality, pg. 487
Preconventional Morality, pg. 487
Puberty, pg. 484
Secondary Sex Characteristics, pg. 484
Senile Dementia, pg. 504
Social Isolation, pg. 506
Social Support, pg. 506

POP QUIZ

True or False

___ 1. Adolescence refers to the approximately two-year period of rapid physical change that culminates in sexual maturity.

___ 2. Typically, by late childhood or early adolescence, an individual would be functioning at the level of conventional morality.

___ 3. The term *climacteric* refers to physiological changes associated with the transition from fertility to infertility for both men and women.

___ 4. The brain begins to decrease in size as a result of neuron loss by about age forty.

___ 5. The activity theory proposes that the aging process is a consequence of wear and tear on one's body.

Multiple Choice

6. What does the adolescent growth spurt indicate?
   a. It occurs at a younger age in boys than in girls.
   b. It refers to a four-year time span of rapid physical growth in early adolescence.
   c. It is completed before a child reaches sexual maturity.
   d. It occurs after a child reaches sexual maturity.
7. When people have cognitively matured to the point at which they can explore hypothetical or "what if" possibilities, Piaget would say that they are in the ________ stage.
   a. sensorimotor
   b. preoperational
   c. concrete-operations
   d. formal-operations
8. Kohlberg was more interested in a person's ________ rather than in his or her ________.
   a. moral behavior/moral reasoning
   b. yes or no answer to a moral dilemma/moral behavior
   c. yes or no answer to a moral dilemma/moral reasoning
   d. moral reasoning/yes or no answer to a moral dilemma
9. The popular image of the teenage years as a time of rebellion, storm, and stress is considered which of the following?
   a. Substantiated by studies
   b. Applicable only to early adolescent years
   c. More myth than fact
   d. True only in America

POP QUIZ

10. When do most people reach the peak of their reproductive capacities and enjoy the best health of any time in their lives?
    a. Middle adulthood
    b. Early adulthood
    c. Later adulthood
    d. Late adolescence
11. What is one problem with cross-sectional studies on intelligence?
    a. Older groups experienced less formal education.
    b. Older groups have less experience with standardized tests.
    c. Groups have experienced varied cultural conditions.
    d. All of the above reasons are valid.
12. Approximately what percentage of young adults (twenty-five to thirty-five) are married today?
    a. 60 percent
    b. 50 percent
    c. 80 percent
    d. 25 percent
13. Which of the following vision problems is ***not*** increasingly common in the older years?
    a. Night vision problems
    b. Perceiving color
    c. Farsightedness
    d. Nearsightedness
14. Current evidence links the cause of Alzheimer's disease to which of the following?
    a. An excess of the beta-amyloid protein
    b. A defective gene on chromosome 21
    c. Environmental factors
    d. Gene mutations on several chromosomes
15. Erikson's developmental task of the older years—ego integrity versus despair—is consistent with the idea that older people ______.
    a. select a lifestyle that reflects their personality
    b. are concerned with problem finding
    c. conduct a life review
    d. demonstrate postconventional thought

Answer Key: 1.F 2.T 3.F 4.F 5.F 6.c 7.d 8.d 9.c 10.b 11.d 12.b 13.d 14.a 15.c

Chapter 13

(Getty/Kali9)

Intelligence

People have always been aware of differences in intelligence between individuals, but not until the closing decades of the 1800s were any efforts made to quantify or measure people's intelligence. The story of how and why the intelligence testing movement began is an interesting one, and it is a good place to start this chapter.

The story centers on Sir Francis Galton, a British biologist who also happened to be the cousin of Charles Darwin. Galton was very much influenced by his cousin's theory of natural selection (see Chapter 1), and he saw the process of survival of the fittest at work in British society. He declared that among humans, the "most fit" were those with high intelligence. Although, how could we identify these superior people? Independently wealthy himself, Galton assumed that those individuals in the upper stratum of society must be the most intelligent. The very fact that they had risen to the top was evidence that they had adapted most successfully to their environment. (No matter that the upper classes were born with a head start denied to the rest of society! Since Galton believed that intelligence was inherited, this detail was of minor importance, for a son would inherit his father's intelligence as well as his hard-earned wealth.) Galton also believed that men were intellectually superior to women, and that Caucasians were superior to other races.

Galton was not satisfied merely to assume that the upper classes were intellectually superior to the rest of society. The late, renowned biologist Stephen Jay Gould noted, "quantification was Galton's god" (Gould, 1981), and Galton would not rest until he had proven his theory by measuring people's intelligence. Galton designed a number of procedures (including simple tests of sensory acuity and reaction time as well as some very precise skull measurements) to measure attributes that he thought were the basis of human intelligence. The 1884 International Exposition was taking place in London, and there, Galton set up a laboratory. For threepence, visitors could expose themselves to Galton's procedures and find out how they rated.

Thus, the first intelligence test was conducted on some ten thousand visitors to the exposition. The results may have disappointed Galton, for they documented neither the superiority of the upper classes nor even the superiority of the Caucasian male. However, this episode marked the beginning of scientific efforts to determine what intelligence is and how to measure it. Although our understanding of intelligence and our ability to measure it have come a long way since Galton's time, we see in this chapter that intelligence is still an elusive concept. (We also meet up with Francis Galton a few more times, for several of his observations about intelligence are still relevant today.)

We begin by trying to define intelligence, and then move on to explore some of the methods that are used to measure people's intelligence. Several theories of intelligence will be reviewed, and we also discuss one of psychology's most debated controversies: To what degree is intelligence a product of heredity, and to what degree is it a product of the environment?

13.1 Defining Intelligence

Virtually all of us have used the term *intelligent* to describe friends and acquaintances, but what is intelligence? What attributes must a person display to earn the label *intelligent*? Consider the personal traits ascribed to the following two hypothetical people and decide which person sounds more intelligent to you:

PERSON A

1. Speaks clearly and articulately
2. Sees all aspects of a problem
3. Is a good source of ideas
4. Deals effectively with people
5. Makes good decisions
6. Deals with problems resourcefully
7. Is sensitive to other people's needs and desires
8. Thinks before speaking and doing

Intelligence According to David Wechsler, the global capacity of a person to act purposefully, to think rationally, and to deal effectively with his or her environment

PERSON B

1. Displays a good vocabulary
2. Is intellectually curious
3. Learns rapidly
4. Thinks deeply
5. Solves problems well
6. Displays logical reasoning
7. Displays interest in the world at large
8. Is verbally fluent

Admittedly, making a judgment based on this limited information is not easy. Nevertheless, there is reason to believe that you may have found yourself favoring Person *A*. This prediction is based on research conducted by Yale psychologist Robert Sternberg and his colleagues (Sternberg, Conway, Ketron, & Bernstein, 1981; Sternberg, 1985). Sternberg surveyed several hundred laypeople who represented a broad spectrum of society, as well as more than one hundred psychologists with a special interest in intelligence. Both the nonpsychologists and the specialists were asked to list specific kinds of behavior that they thought were indicative of intelligence or the lack of intelligence. A list of 170 indicators emerged from this study.

According to Sternberg, most of these behaviors fall into one of three categories: *analytical intelligence* (the ability to write clearly, do mathematics, and read critically), *practical intelligence* (knowing how to do and fix things, skills, and street smarts), and *creative intelligence* (the ability to formulate and to solve problems). The nonpsychologists and the experts had remarkably similar views, with one major difference: Laypeople were much more inclined than the research psychologists to include dimensions of social competence as attributes of intelligence. Since social competence traits were ascribed only to Person *A* (items 4, 7, and 8), we predicted that you would be likely to consider Person *A* more intelligent than Person *B*.

We have mentioned a number of important attributes of intelligence, but how do these attributes relate to the concept of intelligence? Can we define it precisely? Several psychologists have risen to this challenge. Lewis Terman (1921), an influential pioneer in intelligence research and testing, defined **intelligence** as the ability to think abstractly. David Wechsler (1944), who developed tests that are used widely today to measure intelligence, considered intelligence to be the ability to act purposefully, to think rationally, and to deal effectively with the environment. Robert Sternberg (1982) reported that most experts view intelligence as a person's capacity for goal-directed adaptive behavior.

All of these definitions seem reasonable, and they are acceptable to many people, including many psychologists. However, they each pose additional problems. What does it mean to think abstractly, act purposefully, or engage in goal-directed, adaptive behavior? Because these descriptions are ambiguous, they may mean different things to different people.

Virtually all intelligence researchers agree that intelligence is not a precisely measurable commodity that we possess. Rather, it is a concept or label invented to describe differences in individual behavior. If you wanted to conduct research in which intelligence was one of your key variables (for example, a study of the relationship between birth order and intelligence), you would need to define intelligence operationally. How would you develop a precise operational definition of intelligence that would allow you to quantify and measure this variable? Can intelligence be defined operationally? Take a couple of minutes to consider this question before reading on. (You may wish to review the information about operational definitions in Chapter 2.)

Unfortunately, the only operational definition of intelligence that most psychologists have agreed on to date may be stated as follows: Intelligence is what intelligence tests measure. Virtually all intelligence research to date, whether it is based upon correlational or experimental studies, has used test scores to measure intelligence. To make a reasonable judgment about how sound this practice is, you need more information about how intelligence is measured.

BVT Lab

Flashcards are available for this chapter at **www.BVTLab.com**.

13.2 Measuring Intelligence

We saw at the beginning of this chapter that Sir Francis Galton's early intelligence-testing efforts had disappointing results because they failed to support his beliefs about the superiority of the upper-class Caucasian male. The story did not end there, however. Other researchers followed Galton, and they also sought to use science to justify class, racial, and gender biases. Over a period of many years, procedures for measuring intelligence evolved considerably, so that today there are a number of highly regarded devices for measuring intelligence. We'll see also that issues regarding the misuse and biases in intelligence testing are still with us. This section provides a brief overview of what has happened since Galton.

13.2a Binet and Intelligence Testing

The so-called modern intelligence testing movement was launched around the turn of the twentieth century by French psychologist Alfred Binet in response to an urgent need to ease problems of overcrowding in French schools. The French government had recently made education compulsory for all children, but it had not anticipated two outcomes of this edict. First, the classrooms were filled to overflowing, and second, teachers now had to cope with a much wider range of differences in students' abilities than ever before. It soon became apparent that a sizable number of children needed special classes.

What method would one use to identify children with special needs? Since Binet was the leading French psychologist at the time, he was asked to develop an objective test to identify such students. With a number of collaborators, most notably Theodore Simon, Binet set out to devise a measure for children's intellectual skills.

Binet and his collaborators reasoned that virtually all children follow essentially the same course of intellectual development, but that some progress more rapidly than others. Thus, children of subnormal intelligence were presumed to be merely "retarded" in their development. Taking this reasoning one step further, Binet theorized that a child of low intelligence should perform on tests of intellect like a normal child of a younger age—and conversely, that a precocious child should perform like an older child of average intelligence. Binet coined the term *mental level* to express a child's composite test score. This term, later referred to as **mental age**, corresponds to the chronological (calendar) age of children who, on the average, receive a similar test score. Thus, a six-year-old who scored as well as an average eight-year-old would be said to have a mental age of eight. Binet and his collaborators reasoned that it would be possible to obtain accurate estimates of children's ability to profit from the standard school curriculum by comparing their mental age to their chronological age (Binet & Simon, 1905).

Guided by this theoretical perspective, Binet and his associates developed a series of subtests covering a range of reasoning and problem-solving abilities. (Subtests are discrete groups of test items used to measure a particular skill or aptitude, which when evaluated together form an entire test.) The end result was a fairly elaborate test that first appeared in 1905, followed by a major revision three years later. Unlike Galton's attempt to differentiate between "superior" and "inferior" people, the Binet test was quite successful in evaluating the intellectual level of Parisian schoolchildren, and it was generally reliable as a predictor of children's success in regular schoolwork.

Mental Age In IQ testing, the chronological age of children who, on the average, receive a test score similar to that of the subject (e.g., a six-year-old whose composited score is equivalent to that of a nine-year-old has a mental age of nine)

The Intelligence Quotient

A few years after Binet's pioneering efforts, German psychologist L. Wilhelm Stern devised a simple formula to avoid the problem of dealing with fractions that arose when mental age was compared to chronological age. His formula,

MA *(mental age)*/CA *(chronological age)* $\times$ 100,

yielded an **intelligence quotient** or **IQ** score, which provided a rough index of how dull or bright a child was compared to her or his peers. For example, a child with a mental age of seven and a chronological age of five has an IQ of 140 ($7/5 \times 100 = 140$).

Do you think that this IQ formula (MA/CA $\times$ 100) is applicable to adults? Why or why not? Can you think of an alternative approach to calculating adult IQs? Give these questions some thought before reading on.

An average six-year-old can do certain things, like telling the difference between a slipper and a boot, which most four- and five-year-olds cannot do. Consequently, such items became six-year-level subtest items. In similar fashion, Binet and later Lewis Terman (whom we discuss in the next section) were able to select items that differentiated between average seven- and eight-year-olds, nine- and ten-year-olds, and so forth. However, as they moved up the chronological age scale, it became increasingly difficult to find items that would demonstrate proportionate age differences while maintaining the integrity of the IQ formula.

The credibility of the original formulation completely breaks down in the adult age range. Consider, for example, a twenty-year-old who performs on an IQ test as well as an average thirty-six-year-old. Would it be logical to conclude that the younger person has an IQ of 180 ($36/20 \times 100 = 180$)?

The fact that this conclusion is clearly not justifiable indicates why psychologists needed to devise an alternative method for computing adult IQs. As we see shortly, they resolved the problem by designing adult intelligence tests in which IQ is determined by comparing a subject's performance to the average performance of others in the same age bracket. This approach is now also utilized in the calculation of children's IQ scores, since the original IQ formulation is no longer considered to be applicable to any age group.

13.2b The Stanford-Binet Intelligence Scale

Stanford University psychologist Lewis Terman imported Binet's test to America shortly after Binet's death in 1911. Terman discovered that the age norms developed for French students did not work very well with American children. Consequently, he revised Binet's scale as he translated many of the original items, added some new questions, and established new age norms using Caucasian California students to evaluate how effective test items were for measuring age-related changes. Terman labeled the revised test the **Stanford-Binet test**—a name it still retains more than ninety years and five editions (SB5) later.

The concept of designing different test items or questions appropriate for different age levels reflects Binet's original conception that average children of different ages have different capabilities. Although the test was originally designed for children, the more recent editions are used with all ages.

The Stanford-Binet has been widely used for a longer period of time than any other test of intelligence, and it is still highly regarded by most specialists in the testing field. It possesses impressive predictive ability, providing reasonably good estimates of a child's ability to do well in school. A number of studies have shown substantial positive correlations between Stanford-Binet IQ scores and grade school, high school, and college grades.

Intelligence Quotient (IQ) Intelligence measurement derived by dividing an individual's mental age by the chronological age and then multiplying by 100

Stanford-Binet Test IQ test developed by Lewis Terman, who revised Binet's scale and adapted questions to U.S. students

The correlations are generally stronger at the lower grade levels. The current edition measures fluid reasoning, knowledge, quantitative reasoning, visual-spatial processing, and working memory.

13.2c The Wechsler Adult Intelligence Scale

Since the early days of its use, one of the most frequent criticisms of the Stanford-Binet test has been that it places too much emphasis on verbal abilities such as word knowledge, sentence interpretation, and so forth. In so doing, the test discriminates against people for whom English is a second language as well as members of American subcultures who have their own unique style of verbal communication. Another criticism of the Stanford-Binet test has been that it was originally designed for children and still remains far more applicable to children than adults.

In the late 1930s, psychologist David Wechsler developed a new kind of intelligence test to avoid these two problems. His initial product, published in 1939, was a test designed exclusively for people in late adolescence or adulthood. According to Wechsler, intelligence was defined as "the global capacity of a person to act purposefully, to think rationally, and to deal effectively with his or her environment." His original test, now called the **Wechsler Adult Intelligence Scale (WAIS)** included numerous subtests that were arranged according to the aptitude being tested rather than the subject's age level. These subtests were grouped into several categories such as verbal and performance skills. The modern version has kept this structure but has modified the test to include four major categories or scales: *verbal comprehension, perceptual reasoning, working memory*, and *cognitive processing speed.* (Table 13-1 provides examples of subtests from the most recent revision of the WAIS.) This structure allows for the calculation of separate subtest scores as well as an overall IQ. The WAIS-IV makes it possible to identify individuals with special strengths in these subtest areas and to detect superior intelligence even in people who might have had limited opportunities to develop verbal skills. The WAIS IV may also be used to diagnose cognitive impairment related to these subtest areas.

13.3 Evaluating Intelligence Tests

Earlier in this chapter, we asked whether intelligence could be defined operationally, and we had to settle for the operational definition that intelligence is "what intelligence tests measure." We now know something about intelligence tests, but we still do not have enough information about the dependability of these tests to evaluate our operational definition.

To be a good measure of intelligence, a test must be well designed, reliable, and a valid instrument for assessing the particular abilities that indicate intelligence. A look at the processes by which IQ tests are constructed and evaluated can help us determine how effective modern intelligence tests are.

13.3a How Intelligence Tests Are Developed

The process by which IQ tests (as well as other assessment methods) are developed can be simplified into four steps: developing test items, evaluating these test items, standardizing the test, and establishing norms. We take a brief look at this process.

Wechsler Adult Intelligence Scale (WAIS) Intelligence test developed by David Wechsler in the 1930s with subtests grouped by aptitude rather than age level (now in its fifth major revision—WAIS V)

Table 13-1 Examples of the Subtests of the Wechsler Adult Intelligence Scale IV (WAIS IV, 2008 Revision)

Verbal Comprehension Subtest: A Measure of Verbal Concept Formation	Perceptual Reasoning Subtests: A Measure of Nonverbal and Fluid Reasoning
1. *Information* Measures general information and knowledge about common events, objects, or people. "What is the capital of the United States?" "Who is Shakespeare?"	1. *Picture Completion* Measures attention to fine detail. Identifying the missing part of a picture from a set of possibilities.
2. *Comprehension* Focuses on issues of social rules and concepts or solutions to common problems. "Why do we have zip codes?" "What does 'A stitch in time saves nine' mean?"	2. *Block Design* Create geometric designs to match patterns using multicolored blocks.
3. *Similarities* Measures concept formation. State how seemingly dissimilar items may be similar. "How are good and bad alike?"	3. *Matrix Reasoning* Use logic to identify missing figures in a matrix of images (see Figure 13-1).
4. *Vocabulary* A measure of expressive knowledge. Definitions of common words such as "trek."	4. *Visual Puzzles* Identify pieces needed to complete a puzzle composed of geometric shapes.
	5. *Figure Weights* Identify arrangements of different symbols with different weights necessary to balance a scale.
Working Memory Subtests: A Measure of Working Memory and the Ability to Memorize New Information	**Processing Speed Subtests: A Measure of the Ability to Focus Attention and to Order Visual Information**
1. *Letter-Numbering Sequencing* Assesses working memory. A series of random letters and numbers must be remembered and repeated in their appropriate ascending orders.	1. *Symbol Search* Measures visual processing speed. Consists of a series of paired groups of symbols in either a search group or a target group. Requires rapid identification of whether a symbol appears in a target group.
2. *Arithmetic* Emphasizes assessing working memory rather than mathematical skill. Tasks may include computing simple addition and subtraction on a list of numbers or computing how many 45-cent stamps could be purchased for a dollar.	2. *Digit-Symbol Coding* Measures visual-motor coordination and mental processing speed. Requires a translation between symbols and numbers.
3. *Digit Span* Assesses working memory by requiring recall of a series of numbers or letters either forward or backward.	3. *Cancellation* Select items to be deleted from a set of geometric shapes according to instructions.

Developing a Pool of Test Items

Test constructors generally begin by developing a large pool of potential test items that seem to fit their particular testing needs. For example, the developers of the original Stanford-Binet scales started out with many items that seemed able to differentiate between the intellects of children of different ages. These items were based on such things as common sense and direct observation. Since children's abilities to construct things out of blocks were known to improve with age, for instance, several kinds of block-building tasks of varying complexity were included in the original test item pool. Furthermore, since the ability to repeat digits from memory also reflected age-graded differences in intellect, measures of these abilities were also included in the test item pool. Test constructors today may invent new test items, or they may modify existing ones from other tests.

Standardization Procedures Uniform and consistent procedures for administering and scoring tests, such as IQ or personality tests

Evaluating the Test Items

The next step in test construction is to separate the effective test items from those that are ineffective or misleading. To accomplish this task, all the items in the test pool are administered to large numbers of subjects who are representative of the intended test population. For example, since the developers of the Stanford-Binet were trying to differentiate between high, average, and low intelligence among a broad spectrum of children, they administered their pool of items to thousands of preschool children. They found that some items were effective in reliably differentiating between children of different age levels, and others were not. The test items that were ineffective were discarded.

Standardizing the Test

As test items are being evaluated and selected, test constructors must also develop **standardization procedures**—uniform and consistent procedures for both administering and scoring a test. Why are uniform procedures so crucial?

Figure 13-1 Example of a Matrix Reasoning Problem from the WAIS

Which set of shapes from the five alterations best replaces the "?" in the matrix?

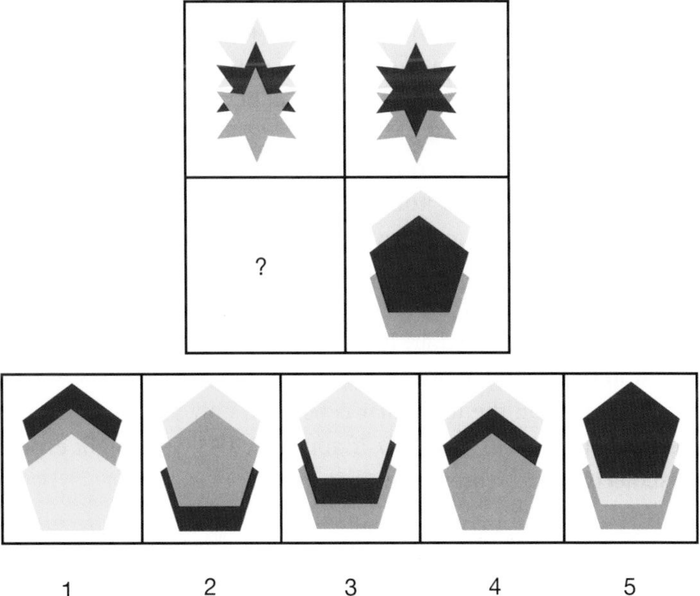

Norm Standard that reflects the normal or average performance of a particular group of people on a measure such as an IQ test

Suppose you are developing a Binet-type intelligence test and one of your subtests evaluates the ability of young children to build a bridge out of wooden blocks, guided only by a pictorial model. An average six-year-old can master this task, but it is too difficult for the average five-year-old unless the examiner provides some hints or directives. If testers administered this kind of item in an inconsistent fashion, providing additional hints to some subjects but not to others, two kinds of errors might result. First, during the development stage, the test designers might make errors in age-grading the difficulties of the item, assuming that younger children were able to perform the task. Later, after the test had already been developed, errors could be made in assessing the intellect of a child subject.

The purpose of standardization procedures is to avoid these kinds of errors. A standardized test includes instructions that spell out precisely how it should be administered and scored, so that the testing situations are as identical as possible for all subjects. Thus, all testers are required to use the same demonstrations, impose the same time limits, and provide the same directions (no random helpful hints). Testers who provide hints that other testers do not provide can give their subjects an edge over other testers' subjects.

Establishing Norms

Once the items for an intelligence test have been selected and standardization procedures implemented, the final step is to establish norms. A **norm** reflects the normal or average performance of a particular group of people. For example, if you developed an intelligence test for adults and found that the average score of twenty- to twenty-five-year-olds was 185 points, a score of 185 would become your basic norm or standard of performance for people in this age category. Similarly, if forty- to forty-five-year-olds scored 169 on the average, 169 would be the norm for this age group. The frequency and magnitude of scores that deviate from these norms are then analyzed to provide a basis for evaluating other levels of performance.

Most intelligence tests assign IQ scores of 85 and 115 to performances that fall one standard deviation below or above the norm for a particular age group. (See Chapter 2 and the Statistics Appendix for a discussion of *standard deviation*, a statistical measure that indicates the degree to which scores are dispersed around an average.) Approximately 68 percent of people who take an IQ test achieve scores within a narrow range of about 85 to 115. About 95 percent of IQ scores fall between 70 and 130, and almost all (99.7 percent) are within a range of 55 to 145.

This method of assigning IQ scores is based on the concept of a normal distribution. Recall from Chapter 2 that a normal distribution forms a bell-shaped or normal curve. Many human attributes, including intelligence, are distributed along a normal or bell-shaped curve. Figure 13-2 demonstrates a typical distribution curve of IQ scores. This curve provides the basis for determining where a particular score falls relative to other scores. Thus, if you achieved an IQ of 130 on the test that provided the basis for the curve shown in the figure, approximately 98 percent of subjects would achieve an IQ score lower than you on the test. That is because only a fraction over 2 percent of subjects scored higher than 130. Similarly, if you scored 85, you might expect that about 84 percent of subjects would score higher than you.

A Typical Normal Distribution of IQ Scores

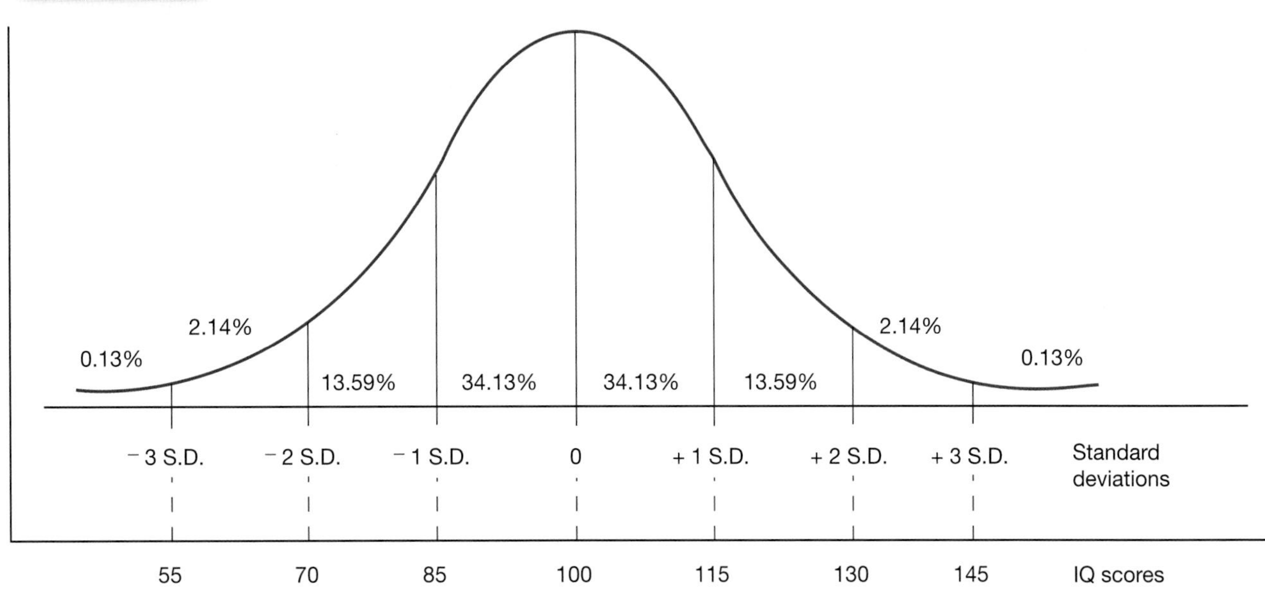

13.3b Test Reliability and Validity

The procedures we have just described are designed toward one end: developing a test that will provide a sound, accurate measure of intelligence for the intended subjects. A test that meets this criterion is said to possess two qualities, reliability and validity, and psychologists use a number of methods to check for these qualities.

Determining Test Reliability

A good test must measure, with dependable consistency, a quality called **reliability**. Since a person's intelligence does not fluctuate widely over time, developers of IQ tests hope to achieve a quantitative consistency in the scores people obtain on their tests. This consistency may be assessed in a variety of ways.

One common method for evaluating test reliability is to give the same person or group of people the same test more than once. This procedure yields a measure of **test-retest reliability**. However, this method may itself be unreliable: People often score better the second time they take a test simply because they are more familiar with the test items or the test routine. One way to minimize this problem is to use an **alternate-forms reliability** check. Subjects take two different forms of a test that are as similar as possible, but not identical, in content and level of difficulty. This approach eliminates the possibility that a subject will score higher because of familiarity with specific test items, but it does not avoid score improvements that might result from practice taking a particular kind of test. Even practice effects can be averted, however, by calculating **split-half reliability**. The reliability of a subject's performance on a single administration of a test is assessed by comparing performance on half of the test items with performance on the other half (most commonly, scores for the odd- and even-numbered questions are compared). If the two scores obtained by any of these three methods generally agree, a test is considered to be reliable.

Reliability In psychological testing, the dependable consistency of a test over time, or the consistency in responses among similar items on the same assessment

Test-Retest Reliability Method for evaluating test reliability by giving a subject (or subjects) the same test more than once

Alternate-Forms Reliability Method of assessing test reliability in which subjects take two different forms of a test that are very similar in content and level of difficulty

Split-Half Reliability Measure of test reliability in which a subject's performance on a single administration of a test is assessed by comparing performance on half of the test items with performance on the other half of the test items

Validity In psychological testing, the ability of a test to accurately measure what it is supposed to measure

Criterion-Related Validity Method of assessing test validity that involves comparing peoples' test scores with their scores on other measures already known to be good indicators of the skill or trait being assessed

Concurrent Validity Type of criterion-related validity that involves comparing test performance to other criteria that are currently available

Predictive Validity Type of criterion-related validity assessed by determining the accuracy with which tests predict performance in some future situation

Aptitude Test Test designed to predict an individual's ability to learn new information or skills

Achievement Test Test designed to measure an individual's learning (as opposed to the ability to learn new information)

Assessing Test Validity

Suppose that you construct a simple test of intelligence based on manual dexterity. You design a pegboard task in which subjects' scores are based on the speed with which they insert pegs of varied diameters into holes with comparable dimensions. Assume further that you design two alternate forms of this test that are comparable in format and level of difficulty. You administer both forms of the test to several hundred children and adults and determine that the alternate-forms reliability is very high. Does this outcome mean that you have made an important breakthrough in intelligence testing?

Not necessarily. Just because a test is reliable does not necessarily mean that it also has **validity**. A test is considered valid if it accurately measures what it is supposed to measure. All you have measured in your test is the speed with which people can fit pegs into holes—a skill that may be completely unrelated to their level of intelligence.

Measuring Test Validity

How would you go about finding out if fast peg fitters were more intelligent than slow peg fitters? In other words, how do you measure the validity of your test (or any other test for that matter)? Take a few moments to see what ideas you can come up with before reading on.

One of the simplest ways to assess whether a test measures what it is supposed to measure is to compare peoples' test scores with their scores on other measures or criteria that are known to be good indicators of the skill or trait being assessed. This technique is called **criterion-related validity**.

There are two types of criterion-related validity: concurrent and predictive. **Concurrent validity** involves comparing test performance to other criteria that are currently available. For example, you might compare subjects' scores on your peg task to their IQ scores as assessed by established intelligence tests whose validity is recognized. If you found that high, average, and low scores on your manual dexterity task were consistently associated with correspondingly high, average, or low IQ scores, you might reasonably conclude that your test is a valid measure of intelligence.

Predictive validity is assessed by determining the accuracy with which tests predict performance in some future situation—for example, how well the Stanford-Binet scores of grade school children predict their high school grades or how precisely Scholastic Aptitude Test (SAT) scores predict a student's scholastic standing after one year of college. In most cases, these tests do have predictive validity in that they do quite well in predicting academic success. In some colleges and universities, SAT scores are used to determine eligibility for admission; in other schools they are used for academic advising and placement in some courses.

13.3c Achievement and Aptitude Tests

We live in a society that places a good deal of emphasis on intelligence and aptitude testing. Whether or not you have taken any of the intelligence tests we have mentioned, the odds are that you have experienced plenty of tests, mostly in educational settings.

Many students are confused about the difference between aptitude tests and achievement tests. IQ tests and college entrance exams are generally classified as **aptitude tests**—tests designed to predict your ability to learn new information or a new skill. In contrast, **achievement tests** are intended to measure what you have already learned. Examples of achievement tests are final exams that test what you have learned in your various courses.

Although most psychologists distinguish between aptitude and achievement tests, they are quick to acknowledge that the differences are far from clear-cut. For example, it is reasonable to assume that your scores on the achievement exams given in this course will reflect not only your mastery of general psychology, but also your aptitude for learning. The reverse is also true. A test such as the WAIS contains many subtests that measure a range of specific skills or aptitudes, a composite of which presumably reflects overall intelligence. However, many of the items also measure what you have already learned or achieved. For example, your ability to define words (vocabulary) or figure out what is missing from a picture (picture completion) is related to how much you have learned by exposure to previous information. Unfortunately, most items on widely used IQ tests reflect, at least to some degree, what we have already learned. Furthermore, since intelligence test constructors are typically middle- and upper-middle-class white people, these items may also reflect cultural biases. As we see later, this drawback raises some fundamental questions about the tests' applicability for members of racial minorities and lower socioeconomic levels.

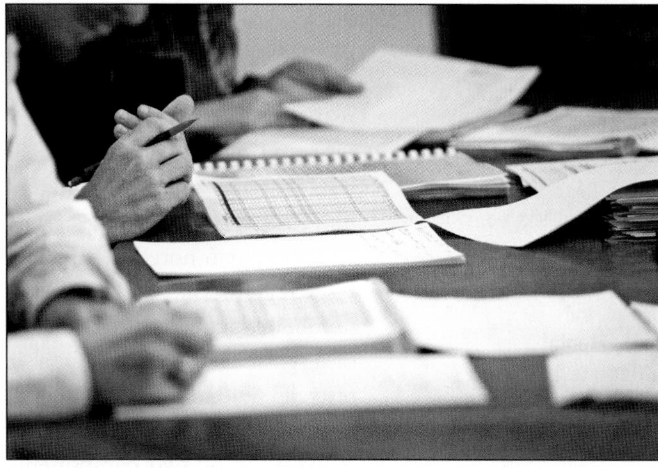
(iStock)

To be a good measure of intelligence, a test must be well designed, reliable, and a valid instrument for assessing the particular abilities that indicate intelligence.

There have been several attempts to design tests to measure a kind of pure intelligence, that is, a person's basic capacity to behave intelligently rather than a reflection of how much that person has learned from previous experiences. Unfortunately, these efforts have fallen short of expectations, and to date there is still no clear measure of people's aptitudes as distinct from what they have already learned.

13.4 Theories of Intelligence

A number of different theories of intelligence have emerged since Galton's original attempts to measure intelligence. The earliest theories were based on statistical similarities between varieties. These groups of similar abilities were referred to as factors. Different theorists proposed that different factors, or abilities, contributed to our intelligence. Later, theorists began to look at intelligence more as a process for approaching and solving problems. We will first examine some of the older structural theories that conceptualize intelligence as a combination of several abilities.

13.4a Factorial Theories

Many theorists have been concerned with the *structure* of intelligence—that is, the skills and abilities that it comprises. This focus is true of the first widely influential theory of intelligence, proposed in 1904 by Charles Spearman.

Spearman's Two-Factor Theory

Spearman's view of intelligence reflected his use of *factor analysis*, a statistical procedure that enables researchers to identify groupings of test items that seem to tap a common ability or factor. For example, people who are quickly able to assemble colored blocks

BVT Lab

Visit **www.BVTLab.com** to explore the student resources available for this chapter.

G-Factor One of the factors in Charles Spearman's conceptualization of intelligence; consists of general intelligence, which is largely genetically determined

S-Factor One of the factors in Charles Spearman's two-factor theory of the structure of intelligence; consists of specific abilities or skills

Primary Mental Abilities In L. L. Thurstone's theory of the structure of intelligence, the separate and measurable attributes (for instance, numerical ability) that make up intelligence

to match pictures of complex designs also tend to perform well when asked to assemble pieces of a puzzle. We could view these two behaviors, as well as other behaviors that reflect an ability to visualize and manipulate patterns and forms in space, as defining a spatial ability factor. Spearman developed his model of intelligence by applying a statistical procedure called factor analysis to the scores of a large number of subjects on diverse tests that assessed many different intellectual skills and abilities. Factor analysis allowed him to assess which of these skills were related to each other.

Spearman noted that some subjects consistently scored high on all of the various tests, regardless of what they were supposed to be measuring, and that a roughly equal number could be counted on to score low. People who scored high (or low) on one kind of test also tended to score at a similar level on other tests, but their scores on various skill tests did tend to differ somewhat.

These statistical observations prompted Spearman to propose that intelligence is made up of two components: a **g-factor**, or general intelligence, and a collection of specific intellectual abilities that he labeled **s-factors**. According to his view, we all have a certain level of general intelligence (g-factor), probably genetically determined, that underlies all of our intelligent behavior. We also have specific abilities (s-factors) that are more useful on some tasks than on others. This theoretical perspective leads to the prediction that a person with a high g-factor will score higher on most skill tests than a person with an average level of general intelligence. It would not be particularly surprising, however, for individuals with average general intelligence to score higher on some specific skills because of a particular strength in their s-factors.

Thurstone's Primary Mental Abilities

One of Spearman's strongest critics was Louis Leon Thurstone (1938). Thurstone used factor analysis on the scores of a large number of subjects on over fifty different ability tests, but he found no evidence for general intelligence ability as Spearman had proposed. Instead, he declared that human intelligence is a composite of seven **primary mental abilities**: verbal comprehension, numerical ability, spatial relations, perceptual speed, word fluency, memory, and inductive reasoning.

Thurstone considered each of the mental abilities to be independent, so that it could be measured separately from other abilities. Unlike Spearman, Thurstone did not believe that a person's intelligence could be expressed as a single score. Rather, assessing any person's intelligence would require measuring all seven of these primary abilities.

Guilford's Structure of Intellect

There have been many attempts, since Thurston's time, to isolate different kinds of intellectual attributes. One of the most ambitious efforts was that of J. P. Guilford (1967, 1977, 1982, 1998), who also bases his model of intelligence on factor analysis. Guilford proposed that intelligence consists of 150 separate abilities, with no overall general intelligence factor.

Guilford believed that any intellectual task can be analyzed in terms of three major intellectual functions: the mental *operations* that are used (how we think); the content upon which those operations are performed (what we think about); and the products of applying a particular operation to a particular content. Each of these three functions is divided into a number of subfunctions, and there are 150 possible interactions or combinations of these subfunctions. Guilford thus maintained that he had isolated 150 kinds of intelligence.

Table 13-2 L. L. Thurstone's Primary Mental Abilities

Ability	Brief Description
Verbal comprehension	The ability to understand the meaning of words, concepts, and ideas
Numerical ability	The ability to use numbers quickly to compute answers to problems
Spatial relations	The ability to visualize and manipulate patterns and forms in space
Perceptual speed	The ability to grasp perceptual details quickly and accurately and to determine similarities and differences between stimuli
Word fluency	The ability to use words quickly and fluently in performing such tasks as rhyming, solving anagrams, and doing crossword puzzles
Memory	The ability to recall information such as lists of words, mathematical formulas, definitions, etc.
Inductive reasoning	The ability to derive general rules and principles from presented information

The factorial approaches of Spearman, Thurstone, and Guilford served two important purposes. First, they provided logical models of the structure of human intellect. Second, they established that intelligence may be conceptualized as comprising many separate abilities that operate more or less independently. However, none of these approaches addressed the very important question of *how* people solve problems and interact effectively (i.e., intelligently) with their environments. More recently, two new theoretical models of intelligence have emerged, both of which seek to understand intelligence as a process. Robert Sternberg and Howard Gardner developed these two models.

13.4b Process Theories

Sternberg's Successful Intelligence

Robert Sternberg's initial approach to developing a theory of what he called "practical intelligence" (1979, 1981, 1982, 2005) focused on how people process information in order to solve problems and deal effectively with their environments. Sternberg conducted a number of experiments to study the steps people go through when solving the kinds of problems typically encountered in intelligence tests. He has identified the following six steps:

1. *Encoding:* Identifying the key terms or concepts in the problem and retrieving any relevant information from long-term memory
2. *Inferring:* Determining the nature of relationships that exist between these terms or concepts
3. *Mapping:* Clarifying the relationship between previous situations and the present one
4. *Application:* Deciding if the information about known relationships can be applied to the present problem
5. *Justification:* Deciding if the answer can be justified
6. *Response:* Providing the answer that seems best based on proper information processing at each of the previous stages

One of Sternberg's most interesting findings is that good problem solvers who score high on intelligence tests spend more time analyzing a question, particularly in the encoding stage, than those who score lower. He reached this conclusion by presenting a subject with a problem, such as "Washington is to one as Lincoln is to ______," and then measuring how long it took a person to indicate comprehension of the question. Then he showed the subject the answer choices—(*a*) 5; (*b*) 10; (*c*) 15; (*d*) 50—and recorded how long it took to obtain an answer. If you remembered that George Washington's picture is on a one-dollar bill and Abraham Lincoln's is on a five, you may have realized that the correct answer is (*a*). Sternberg discovered that his highly intelligent subjects spent longer than average analyzing a question before signaling that they understood it, but were able to recognize the correct answer more quickly than subjects with average intelligence.

(iStock)

In contrast to achievement tests, which measure what one has already learned, aptitude tests are designed to predict one's ability to learn new information or a new skill.

Perhaps you have noticed that students who earn top grades are often among the last to finish an exam. These slow finishers sometimes express embarrassment or concern that their slowness reflects some intellectual inadequacy. Now, thanks to Sternberg's model, we have evidence that intelligence does not necessarily equal speed, and that people who score highest on tests often take a sufficient amount of time to analyze problems carefully.

Sternberg's research has some practical implications. If we can analyze how people use the various steps to process information and solve problems, it may be possible to teach them strategies for improving their performances. For example, a common factor in low test scores is the tendency of some students to rush through a test without carefully analyzing each question and considering a range of options. Such people have a tendency merely to grab onto the first answer that seems halfway reasonable. We have found that the exam scores of these speedy test takers can sometimes be improved by suggesting that they take their finished exams back to their desks and spend the remainder of the test period carefully considering their answers.

By learning to think about how they approach problems and learning how to function more effectively, Sternberg believes people can be taught to construct their own problem-solving strategies. In this sense, teaching people to apply problem-solving strategies more effectively can increase their intelligence, at least as it is measured by intelligence tests. A good deal of formal education seems to focus on teaching people lots of facts rather than teaching them how to think. Perhaps with more emphasis on the latter, we might increase the intelligence scores of our students.

Sternberg (1980, 2003, 2005) has recently expanded his information-processing approach into what he calls the **triarchic theory of successful intelligence**. According to this theory, intelligence is a multidimensional trait comprised of three different abilities: analytical, practical, and creative. The *analytical* aspect of intelligence involves mastering a sequence of components or steps in the process of solving complex verbal, mathematical, or spatial reasoning problems. This analytical ability is heavily emphasized in most contemporary intelligence tests. People with highly developed analytical intelligence often do well in academic settings and score high on achievement tests and standard IQ tests. However, such individuals do not necessarily exhibit unusual creativity or insight.

Triarchic Theory of Successful Intelligence Theory that intelligence is a multidimensional trait comprising analytical, creative, and practical abilities

These latter characteristics are more likely to be manifested by individuals endowed with high levels of *creative* intelligence, which is the ability to combine experiences in insightful ways that lead to novel or creative solutions to complex problems. Sternberg believes that people with only average analytical intelligence may score very high on the creative aspect of intellect, and vice versa.

Sternberg has also observed that some people may be highly adept at manipulating and/or adapting to their environments. This component, labeled *practical* intelligence, is exemplified in people who seem to be "street smart" and have skills to accomplish a variety of tasks. Finally, Sternberg emphasizes that it is important to consider intelligence within a cultural context. Failing to do so may bias our definitions of intelligence to fit a particular world view. The range of successful skills and knowledge vary widely between cultures, and these differences must be taken into account in any theory of intelligence (Sternberg & Grigorenko, 2006).

Sternberg believes that while people vary in their capacity to use each of these three forms of intelligence, all are important in our daily functioning. Furthermore, all people, including those with high IQ scores on standard tests, can benefit from training designed to strengthen each of these three aspects of intelligence.

Gardner's Theory of Multiple Intelligences

Harvard University's Howard Gardner (1983, 1999, 2006, 2011) outlined a view of human intelligence that reflects both his dissatisfaction with the idea that intelligence is a single trait that can be measured with an IQ test and his belief that the factorial approach to describing the structure of human intellect fails to capture the complexity, diversity, and practicality of human intelligence. In this sense, Gardner is philosophically aligned with Sternberg.

However, Gardner's view of intelligence differs from Sternberg's in another important respect because he advocates the inclusion of certain kinds of mental abilities that fall well outside the realm of what has traditionally been labeled as intelligence. Gardner observes that in the world community, there are many different kinds of things people can do well that are assigned different values in different cultures. To reflect this diversity, Gardner has proposed that humans have seven kinds of intelligence that are independent of each other.

The first form of human intellect in Gardner's theory of multiple intelligences is *linguistic intelligence*. Linguistic intelligence includes the kind of verbal ability or skill with words that writers or orators display. A second form of intelligence, *logical-mathematic intelligence*, is typical of scientists, logicians, and mathematicians. A third type of intellect is *spatial intelligence*, the ability to think accurately about the spatial aspects of the surrounding environment.

These first three types of mental abilities probably fit your own notion of intelligence. Indeed, all three fall within the category of what has traditionally been viewed as intelligence, and they are the types of skills that are tested on most formal measures of intelligence. However, Gardner does not stop here. He proposes four additional types of intelligence, each of which he considers as important as the first three. Thus, *musical intelligence* is the type of intelligence manifested by musicians, composers, or other individuals who can think and express themselves musically. *Bodily kinesthetic intelligence*, another mental ability that is overlooked in traditional definitions of intelligence, involves using one's body or parts of the body to make something or solve a problem. Accomplished dancers, athletes, and craft persons would have a high degree of bodily kinesthetic intelligence. *Interpersonal intelligence* is the capacity to perceive and understand the needs, motives, and behaviors of other people. This kind of personal intelligence might be particularly noteworthy in accomplished therapists and teachers. People who can accurately assess and understand their own needs and abilities and who use this knowledge to function effectively manifest *intrapersonal intelligence*. *Naturalistic intelligence* is the ability to carefully observe the natural world. Finally, *existential intelligence* is an ability to address questions about one's own existence.

Gardner's conceptualization serves to humanize or democratize our view of human intelligence by broadening its definition. Instead of equating intelligence with IQ scores or special abilities, Gardner stresses the importance of certain other components of successful functioning that are overlooked in more traditional definitions. Yet over the course of human history, Gardner reminds us, skills such as bodily kinesthetic skill, interpersonal intelligence, and musical ability probably have had more value in human culture than the types of verbal, mathematical, or spatial abilities that are commonly equated with intelligence.

13.5 Hereditary and Environmental Influences on Intelligence

What determines intelligence? Although we may disagree with many of Sir Francis Galton's early ideas about intelligence, most of us would probably agree with one of his observations: Intelligence tends to run in families. You may have noticed that some of your brightest friends seem to have highly intelligent parents, while those with more average abilities often are offspring of parents who seem to be of average intelligence.

The degree of relationship or correlation between the IQs of parents and their children has been shown to be approximately 0.35 (see Table 13-3). Recall from Chapter 11 that a coefficient of correlation always falls between –1.00 and +1.00, and that the closer it is to +1.00, the stronger is the relationship between two variables). Researchers have found that parents with high IQs tend to have children with high IQs, and parents with low IQs are somewhat prone to having children with relatively low IQs. This finding lends credence to the widespread assumption that intelligence does indeed run in families.

Was Galton correct in saying that intelligence is largely inherited? From our previous discussions of the contributions of genes and the environment on behavior (see Chapter 11), you are probably aware that environment as well as heredity contributes to most individual traits. Indeed, nowhere does the nature versus nurture controversy rage more actively than in the question of intellect.

According to the hereditarian view, genetics determines the structural and functional efficiency of the brain, which in turn clearly influences intellectual functioning. In contrast, the environmentalist view says that environment plays a greater role than genes in shaping human intellect, and that the positive relationship in parent-child IQs reflects the fact that adults tend to create home environments that are similar to those they experienced in their own childhood. With comparable sources of intellectual stimulation, an environmentalist position would argue that it is not surprising that children develop a level of intelligence similar to that of their parents.

Which point of view is more accurate? Even after years of research, we still are not certain exactly what relative influences heredity and environment have on intelligence.

13.5a Isolating Contributions to Intelligence

How can we determine to what extent intelligence (or any other human attribute) is influenced by heredity or by environment? Take a moment to consider what research strategies might effectively be used to answer this question before reading on.

If ethics were not a consideration, an obvious choice might be to take people with clearly different genetic makeups (for example, unrelated children) and raise them in identical environments. If we could orchestrate this situation, and all our identically reared children developed similar IQs, we could then conclude with confidence that genetic differences have little or no influence on intelligence and that environment is the major determinant of intellect.

For obvious reasons, such an experiment has never been conducted. Most parents would not permit their children to be taken from them at an early age so that they might be raised in a controlled environment. Even if we were able to obtain a sample group and create a special environment for them, it is impossible to ensure that two people's experiences are identical. Even identical twins who grow up together do not have exactly the same environments, for each twin may relate differently to other family members and to individuals outside the home.

Since psychologists must work within both ethical and practical constraints, research into the relative impact of heredity and genetics has taken several forms other than the hypothetical method we just described. The following paragraphs highlight what researchers have been able to discover through a number of studies of twins, adopted children, orphanage and environmental enrichment programs, birth order studies, and even some animal research.

13.5b Twin Studies

The intellectual differences that exist among all of us are a product of only two factors: genes and environment. Identical twins are unique in that only one of these factors, environment, contributes to differences in intelligence between members of a twin pair. Thus, a considerable amount of attention has focused on twin studies.

A hereditarian who discounts the role of environment in determining intelligence would predict a very high positive correlation between the IQs of identical twins, whether they were raised together or in separate environments. Environmentalists, in contrast, would predict a much lower IQ correlation for separated identical twins than for twins reared together, since they place greater weight on environment in determining IQ scores.

What has the evidence shown? Table 13-3 presents the median IQ correlation coefficients for a variety of relationships as determined by a number of studies. You can see that identical twins reared together are highly similar in tested intelligence (.86), and that the second highest degree of correlation is demonstrated by identical twins reared separately (.72).

The slight decline in the degree of IQ correlation among sets of separated identical twins provides some evidence for the environmentalist prediction that IQ correlation will be reduced by differences in the environment. However, identical twins reared separately are still more similar in IQ than fraternal twins of the same sex who are reared together (.62). This finding seems to undermine the environmentalist view that fraternal twins reared together should have a higher degree of IQ correlation than identical twins reared apart. Indeed, research suggests that IQ correlations of same-sex fraternal twins reared together may be even less than the .62 figure shown in Table 13-3. These studies yielded correlations ranging from .38 to .61, with a median of .47.

For years, many psychologists viewed such findings as evidence that heredity plays a larger role than the environment in determining intelligence. The most widely quoted and best known of these studies was conducted by the late English psychologist Sir Cyril Burt (1966), who reported remarkable IQ similarities between fifty-three pairs of separated identical twins purportedly reared in totally different environments. In the early 1970s, however, American psychologist Leon Kamin (1974) became suspicious when he noticed several peculiarities in Burt's data and procedures. Shortly after, an investigative reporter for the *London Sunday Times* discovered that two of Burt's collaborators, who had supposedly collected much of his data, never existed (Gillie, 1976). By the end of the 1970s, even Burt's most staunch supporters conceded that his research was fraudulent and that he had

Table 13-3 Approximate Correlation Coefficients Between IQ Scores of Persons with Different Amounts of Genetic and Environment Similarity

Relationship	Media Correlation
Identical (monozygotic) twins	
Reared together	.86
Reared apart	.72
Fraternal (dizygotic) twins	
Reared together	
Same sex	.62
Opposite sex	.62
Reared apart	(no data available)
Sibling	
Reared together	.38
Reared apart	.24
Parent and child	
Live together	.35
Separated by adoption	.31
Genetically unrelated persons	
Unrelated children reared together	.25
Adoptive parent and adopted child	.15

These data were obtained from a variety of studies, most of which were relatively recent investigations. (Bartels et al., 2002; Nathan & Guttman, 1984; Segal, 1985; Stevenson et al., 1987; Tambs et al., 1984; Wilson, 1986). The correlations in the table reflect the median of a range of correlations obtained from several individual studies. Note that as the drgree of genetic similarity decreases, so does the magnitude of obtained correlations. It is also noteworthy that a shared environment increases the IQ correlations in all cases where applicable.

perpetrated a massive hoax on the world scientific community (Hearnshaw, 1979). The spurious data from Burt's research are not included in Table 13-3.

This unfortunate episode demonstrates that scientists engaged in research do not always maintain ethical standards. However, Burt's fraud did not seriously weaken the hereditarian case, since other studies of identical twins reared apart have reported similarly high IQ correlations.

Psychologists continue to study twins in the hope that such research will lead to a better understanding of the relative contributions of heredity. For instance, research conducted by Bouchard on several sets of identical and fraternal twins reared apart indicate a much greater degree of similarity in identical than fraternal twins in a wide range of intellectual, emotional, and behavioral attributes (Bouchard, 1984; Tellegen et al., 1988). This evidence suggests that genetic factors are important in producing differences in intelligence between people—but again, environmentalists can also find some support in these same data. For example, preliminary findings have revealed that when identical twins were reared in dramatically different environments, the spread between their respective IQs widened to as great as 20 points in one case. Thus, the debate rages on (Plomin & Bergeman, 1991; Plomin, Kennedy, & Craig, 2006; Plomin, 2003; Dudley, 1991). Hopefully, when enough reliable data are collected, psychologists may be able to reach some consensus on the implications of twin study findings.

13.5c Evaluating the Hereditary and Environmental Evidence

We have explored a considerable range of evidence in the previous discussions, some of which seems to support each side of the nature-nurture controversy. Many of the twin studies provide strong indications of the role of heredity in determining intelligence. We could continue exploring this controversy by examining still more evidence. Yet, no matter how much more research we study, most of us would still reach the same conclusion.

It is simply not possible, in light of our current state of knowledge, to determine precisely what percentage of our IQ is attributable to genes, and what percentage is the product of experience. Perhaps with newer molecular genetics techniques and a greater understanding of the human genome we will move beyond quantitative genetics to how specific genes contribute to cognitive ability (Plomin, 2003). As of this writing, however, there is no consensus among genetics researchers as to which genes might contribute to intelligence.

(iStock)

Identical twins are unique in that environment is the only factor that contributes to differences in intelligence between members of a twin pair.

A continuing debate within this highly controversial area focuses on the ongoing efforts to ascertain the relative contributions of nature and nurture in shaping human intelligence. In a recent survey of several hundred psychologists and educational specialists with expertise in areas related to intelligence testing, these experts believed the heritability of intelligence to be roughly 60 percent (Snyderman & Rothman, 1987). A more recent survey of teachers found that 94 percent of them believed genetics is at least as important as environmental factors in determining intelligence (Walker & Plomin, 2006).

13.6 Racial Differences in Intelligence

13.6a Within- and Between-Group Differences and Intelligence

While many psychologists agree that differences within groups (i.e., within the white population) can be partially attributed to hereditary factors, this does not lead to the conclusion that differences between groups (e.g., white people and African Americans) are attributable to hereditary factors, as Jensen assumed. A useful analogy has been proposed to illustrate this error. Imagine drawing two random samples of seeds from a bag containing several genetically different varieties (see Figure 13-3). One sample is planted in enriched soil, the other sample in regular soil. The plants within each planter will differ somewhat. This **within-group difference** is attributable to genetic differences within each random sample of seeds. The plants grown in the different soils (environmental conditions) will also differ.

Within-Group Differences Differences, or response variability, within treatment conditions

Figure 13-3 Within-Group and Between-Group Differences

The variability within groups (different sizes and shapes) results from the genetic variability within the seeds only because the soil was the same. The variability between groups (also different sizes and shapes) results from both genetic variability (within-group variability) and environmental conditions that differed between groups (the soil condition).

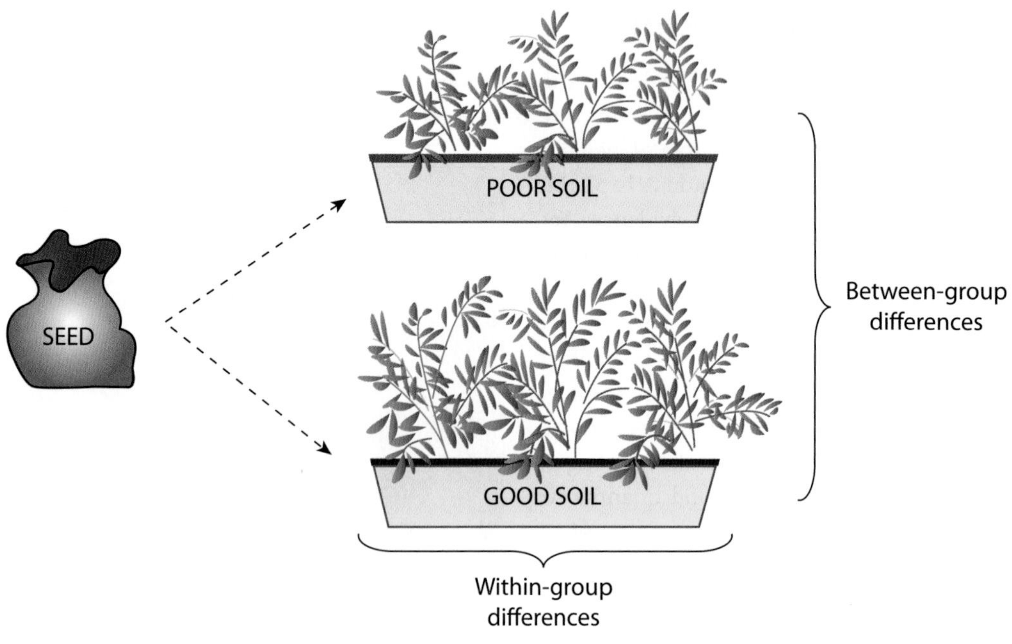

Most likely, the plants grown in the enriched soil will be much taller than the ones grown in regular soil. This difference is a **between-group difference**, and it is attributable to both random genetic differences and the different environmental (soil) conditions. It would be a mistake to claim the differences in height between the two groups of plants was attributable to the genetic differences in the samples alone.

Heritability is a statistical concept that estimates the relative contribution of genetic factors to variability in measures of a particular trait found among members of a sample population. Even if this estimate is accurate, we should not conclude that heredity accounts for 80 percent of our intelligence and environment the rest. Rather than estimates of the percentage of our intellects that is due to heredity, heritability percentages provide estimates of the amount of variation in intelligence that may be attributed to heredity among individuals within a population.

Between-Group Differences Differences, or response variability, between treatment conditions

Heritability An estimate ranging from 0 to 1.0 that indicates the proportion of variance in a trait that is accounted for by heredity

Some researchers have provided somewhat higher estimates of the heritability of intelligence. Arthur Jensen, an educational psychologist and hereditarian, was probably the most controversial advocate of the viewpoint that IQ differences are due primarily to heredity. For several decades, Jensen and his colleagues argued that heredity accounts for approximately 80 percent of the differences in IQ scores between African Americans and white people (Jensen, 1969; Rushton & Jensen, 2005), an extreme position that has not always been supported by research. Needless to say, members of both the scientific community and the general public have challenged this controversial view.

Figure 13-4 The Large Degree of Overlap Between the Distribution of IQ Scores for African Americans and Caucasian Americans

The difference between the mean IQ scores for African Americans and Caucasian Americans is about 15 points.

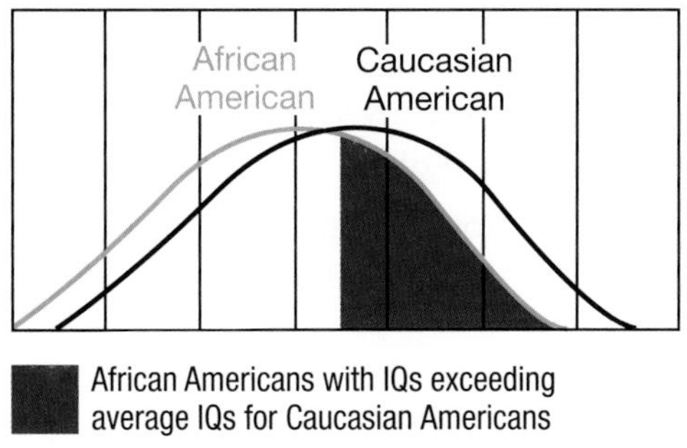

Numerous studies conducted over the last fifty to sixty years have found that African Americans score an average of about 15 IQ points (one standard deviation) below Caucasian Americans on standard tests of intelligence. For instance, on the Stanford-Binet test, the difference between African Americans and Caucasian Americans was 17.4 IQ points for the age group twelve to twenty-three years (Thorndike, Hagen, & Sattler, 1986). However, as Figure 13-4 reveals, the scores of significant numbers of both African American and Caucasian American individuals fall at all points in the distribution, and there is a great deal of overlap between the two races on IQ scores. Furthermore, the fact that the range of scores for both groups extends from very low to very high indicates that the IQ differences among individuals within one racial group are profoundly greater than differences between the average scores of the two groups. Finally, a substantial number of African Americans have IQs that far exceed the average IQ for Caucasian Americans.

In view of the comparably wide distribution of IQ scores in both populations and the great overlap between each, we must conclude that knowing if a person is Caucasian American or African American provides little basis for predicting his or her IQ. Even Arthur Jensen conceded that all levels of human intellect are present between both races. Still, we are left with the puzzling matter of a 15-point spread between the two races.

Today, opinion among many psychologists is that intelligence differences between racial groups are largely the result of environmental factors. The findings on which this conclusion is based come from a variety of research studies. In fact, researchers have argued recently that the difference between these scores has decreased by about a third since 1972, and the present difference is about 10 points (Dickens & Flynn, 2005). These researchers argue that there aren't any reasons that differences will not continue to drop as measures of social and economic factors continue to improve.

In concluding this discussion, the safest thing to say is that neither genetics nor environmental conditions alone account for the differences in intelligence observed either within or between groups of individuals. Experiments with animals and correlational studies with people seem to suggest that genetic differences can be overridden by environmental circumstances. Unfortunately, the history of intelligence testing has been largely motivated by attempts to justify racial attitudes. Given these suspicious beginnings, test biases and the role of heredity versus environment will continue to be actively discussed. In the next chapter we will confront some of these same issues as we examine the determinants and the assessment of personality.

CHAPTER REVIEW

Defining Intelligence

1. Both psychologists and laypersons have similar views about what constitutes intelligence, except that laypersons are more likely to include social competence in their list of attributes.
2. The only operational definition of intelligence that psychologists have agreed on is that intelligence is what intelligence tests measure.

Measuring Intelligence

3. Alfred Binet and his associates, who devised a test to measure French schoolchildren's intellectual skills, launched the modern intelligence-testing movement.
4. Lewis Terman revised the original Binet test to make it applicable to American children.
5. The Stanford-Binet is an individually administered IQ test comprised of a series of subtests that are graded by age level.
6. Studies have demonstrated substantial positive correlations between Stanford-Binet IQ scores and school grades.
7. The Wechsler Adult Intelligence Scale (WAIS) is an individually administered IQ test designed for people in late adolescence or adulthood and includes eleven subtests grouped into two major categories or scales—a verbal scale and a performance scale.
8. Group intelligence tests, which are widely used today, are cheaper, quicker, and easier to administer than individual tests like the Stanford-Binet or WAIS. However, group tests are limited by the inability of the tester to determine accurately each subject's level of comprehension of directions and motivation to perform well.
9. Aptitude tests are designed to predict the ability to learn new information or a new skill, whereas achievement tests are intended to measure what has already been learned. Intelligence tests tend to measure both aptitude and achievement.

CHAPTER REVIEW

Evaluating Intelligence Tests

10. The process used to develop IQ tests can be simplified into four steps: developing test items, evaluating these test items, standardizing the test, and establishing norms.
11. Good tests of IQ (or any other psychological assessment device) must possess both reliability and validity. Reliability refers to measuring a trait with dependable consistency. A test that possesses validity is able to measure accurately what it is supposed to measure.
12. Thus far, it has been impossible to eliminate cultural bias from IQ tests. Test questions often reflect the mainstream values and experiences of white middle-class city dwellers.

Theories of Intelligence

13. Factorial models of intelligence are concerned with the structure of intelligence. Spearman, Thurstone, and more recently, Guilford proposed factorial models.
14. Spearman proposed that intelligence is made up of two components: a g-factor, or general intelligence, and a collection of specific intellectual abilities that he labeled s-factors.
15. Thurstone proposed that human intelligence is a composite of seven primary mental abilities: verbal comprehension, numerical ability, spatial relations, perceptual speed, word fluency, memory, and inductive reasoning.
16. Guilford's structure of intellect model proposes that intelligence consists of 150 separate abilities, with no overall general intelligence factor.
17. Unlike the factorial models, Robert Sternberg's triarchic theory of successful intelligence maintains that intelligence is a multidimensional trait comprising three different abilities: analytic, practical, and creative.
18. Howard Gardner proposed a theory of multiple intelligences, suggesting that there are nine kinds of intelligence. In addition to the linguistic, logical-mathematical, and spatial intelligences that are included in traditional definitions, Gardner gave equal billing to musical intelligence, bodily kinesthetic intelligence, inter- and intrapersonal intelligence, naturalist intelligence, and existential intelligence.

CHAPTER REVIEW

Hereditary and Environmental Influences on Intelligence

19. Evidence from twin and adoption studies, and from selective-breeding studies of animals, has been used to support the role of heredity in determining intelligence. However, other experiments, together with evidence from orphanage and birth-order studies, suggest that environment is also important.
20. Heritability percentages provide estimates of the amount of variation in intelligence that may be attributed to heredity.

Evaluating the Hereditary and Environmental Evidence

21. Heritability studies may falsely assume that heredity and environment are additive in their contributions to intelligence. Some psychologists argue that heredity and the environment interact throughout development to determine intelligence.
22. It is argued that within-group differences in intelligence cannot be used to explain between-group (racial) differences.

Racial Differences in Intelligence

23. Significant numbers of scores of both African Americans and white people fall at all points in distributions of IQ scores, and there is considerable overlap between the two races on IQ scores.
24. The fact that African Americans score somewhat lower on IQ tests than Caucasian Americans, on the average, may be attributed to the higher incidence of socioeconomic and educational disadvantages in the African American versus Caucasian American population.
25. The differences between the IQ scores of Caucasians and African Americans have dramatically decreased over the past twenty-five years.

TERMS AND CONCEPTS

Achievement Test, pg. 524
Alternate-Forms Reliability, pg. 523
Aptitude Test, pg. 524
Between-Group Differences, pg. 534
Concurrent Validity, pg. 524
Criterion-Related Validity, pg. 524
G-Factor, pg. 526
Heritability, pg. 534
Intelligence, pg. 516
Intelligence Quotient (IQ), pg. 518
Mental Age, pg. 517
Norm, pg. 522
Predictive Validity, pg. 524
Primary Mental Abilities, pg. 526
Reliability, pg. 523
S-Factor, pg. 526
Split-Half Reliability, pg. 523
Standardization Procedures, pg. 521
Stanford-Binet Test, pg. 518
Test-Retest Reliability, pg. 523
Triarchic Theory of Successful Intelligence, pg. 528
Validity, pg. 524
Wechsler Adult Intelligence Scale (WAIS), pg. 519
Within-Group Differences, pg. 533

RESEARCH PERSPECTIVES

Perspectives on Intelligence

Perspective #1: Dr. Robert Sternberg

Dr. Robert Sternberg grew up in Maplewood, New Jersey, went to Yale University for an undergraduate degree in psychology, and then went to Stanford University where he received his PhD in experimental psychology in 1975. After graduating, he took a position at Yale and is now a professor of psychology. Dr. Sternberg developed an information-processing approach to intelligence and has been studying the limitations of traditional intelligence testing and creating measures for what he calls "practical intelligence"—the ability "to go into an environment and figure out what you need to know, and then work effectively within that environment."

Perspective #2: Dr. Howard Gardner

Howard Gardner is a professor of education and codirector of Project Zero at Harvard University. Trained in developmental psychology and neuropsychology, he has long been investigating the development and breakdown of symbol-using skills, with a special emphasis on artistic thinking. More recently, he has carried out investigations in the areas of creativity and intelligence, culminating in the books mentioned in the interview. At present, he is engaged in efforts for school reform in the United States. In 1981, he was awarded a MacArthur Prize Fellowship, and in 1990 he became the first American to win the University of Louisville Grawmeyer Award in Education.

PERSPECTIVE #1: *Are Intelligence Tests Intelligent?*

Dr. Robert Sternberg

Q: *Dr. Sternberg, do you view intelligence as a fixed ability or do you think that it changes considerably throughout our lifetime?*

A: I think it changes. It changes in two ways. One is—clearly, it develops. As children get older, they become more intelligent. Also it's possible to develop it through interventions, through having a better environment, or through programs that directly teach intellectual skills. So I see it as a flexible kind of ability.

RESEARCH PERSPECTIVES

Q: *Do you think that there is any genetic component that is at all significant?*

A: I think that there is a genetic component. Plus, there is also an environmental one and, as most people believe, I think they're interactive, but one of the goals of my own research is devising programs to help people develop their intelligence. I have a book called *Intelligence Applied*, which is a program for developing intellectual skills according to the triarchic model—analytic, creative, and practical skills. Right now we also have a program called "Developing Practical and Creative Intelligence for Schools." So, in general, I think it's something that can be developed, and I believe the data are consistent with that point of view.

Q: *Do you feel that the environmental component is the one that has the most impact on intellectual development?*

A: Well, I think that relates to questions about environment versus heritability. However, the genetic component you can't do a whole lot about. As I said, I believe there is a genetic component but that it's a given. What you can do is maximize the quality of the environment. This is something you can do something about. Height is frequently given as an example of how environment can influence a highly heritable trait. Height is partially genetic—it's largely genetic—but environmental intervention can certainly increase height.

Q: *This brings up the question of twin studies. Do you think that there is a great deal we can learn from investigating differences in twin intelligence?*

A: I think that twin studies are useful if your question is on specific cognitive tests such as psychometric intelligence tests. What is the proportion of individual difference variation that's heritable? The thing to remember is, first of all, intelligence is broader than what is measured by most of the tests, so you're only looking at a portion of intelligence through the tests that are used. The second thing is that heritability can vary with place, time, and group. In other words, there's not one heritability for intelligence. It's different in different countries; it's different in different periods; it's different for different ethnic groups. So it's not like there is a fixed n^2, contrary to what many people think. So I think that there is some usefulness in twin studies, but you have to understand what questions they answer.

Q: *Do you have any theories or hypotheses about why there might be differences in heritability and intelligence from one culture to another?*

A: I think that it depends on a lot of factors. It depends on the amount of variation in the population, in the gene pool. It depends on the amount of variation in the environment. It depends on how much difference there is in opportunities and in how much potential mobility there is in a society. So I think that there are a lot of factors that can affect heritability.

RESEARCH PERSPECTIVES

Q: *There has been a lot of recent interest in the area of crystallized versus fluid intelligence, especially in the elderly. Is there any evidence to suggest that there is more flexibility in fluid intelligence as we age than had previously been thought?*

A: Well, the going view is that crystallized ability tends to increase across the life span and that fluid abilities tend to level off and then to decline. I think that the evidence on that is in favor of this view. However, there are two factors that need to be taken into account. One is compensation. As you grow older and develop more crystallized skills, you can compensate for things you can't do in other ways. So less fluid ability doesn't necessarily imply that your total performance is any less. Even before you're older, there are some things you just stop liking to do—you no longer want to do them—and so you find ways of having other people do them or ways around them or ways to make them easier for yourself. Part of what life is about is working out compensatory mechanisms for the things that you either don't like or don't do well. At the same time, you capitalize on your strengths. So by a pattern of capitalizing on your strengths and compensating for your weaknesses—even though it's probably the case that fluid ability at some point starts to decline—performance doesn't necessarily decline.

The other thing I want to mention is that in a study we did on creativity, rated creativity of products started to decline roughly at about age forty. However, when we compared the ages of the people rating creativity with the ages of the people being rated, we found cohort matching, meaning that people tended to rate as more creative products of their own age cohort. That would mean that people who are older or younger than the raters would tend to be rated lower because of the age mismatch. In other words, what constitutes intelligence changes with age, and in our assessments we may be using a standard that doesn't apply as well to older people as it does to younger ones. Our life tasks change over time, and so what it means to be intelligent may change as well. As an adult, what I need to succeed is not the same as what a student needs to succeed in school. At the same time, the kid who can be a straight A student in school is not necessarily the best person in the world of work. So our developmental tasks change, and I think we need to recognize that what it means to be intelligent can also change with age.

Q: *That brings up an interesting point about the relationship between creativity and intelligence. How closely related do you think they are?*

A: Well, according to my own theories, intelligence is one component of creativity, and there's also a creative part of intelligence, so they're like overlapping circles.

Q: *Do you think creativity is an ability that can be increased or fostered through some type of intervention or training?*

A: Yes, absolutely! As I said, we have programs for teaching creative intelligence in school. I don't know if you know my investment model, but every element in that theory is trainable. Basically, the idea of the investment model is that creative people buy low and sell high. In other words, they come up with ideas that aren't very popular at the time. Then, once they have convinced people of the worth of those ideas, they move on to the next idea. They go against the crowd; they're contrarians. That's a style that can be taught. In other words, don't always follow others but follow your own beliefs and ideas.

RESEARCH PERSPECTIVES

Q: *Some researchers have used the results of intelligence tests to support such contentions. What is your view?*

A: Any technology is misused from time to time. So the biggest problem is not so much in the tests but in overinterpretation of them. In other words, making too much of differences or misconceiving differences. So the problem is not with the method; it's with what people do with the method. In terms of racial differences, there are differences in scores. The disagreement is as to why there are those differences. In my own research I emphasize socialization. When I say socialization, I mean that parents want to have smart kids. They try to socialize their kids to be smart. However, people are brought up in different ways and sometimes the concept of intelligence in a group does not correspond to the IQ test concept, or the school conception of intelligence. You may have kids who are smart, who are socialized to be smart in their home environment or community environment, but that doesn't match with what the school or the test is looking for. So you may see differences in test scores, but those tests are based on particular sets of skills. If, for example, I were to go into a hunting-and-gathering culture, I might not look very smart there. I don't expect that I would be terribly successful in what's required for adaptation in that kind of culture. Different cultures mean different things by "smart person."

Q: *Given that fact, do you think there is any validity in trying to develop so-called culture-free intelligence tests?*

A: No, I think it's impossible. Intelligence manifests itself in a culture. It exhibits itself, and you can't speak of intelligence outside of culture because we define what we mean by intelligence in terms of cultural acts. What we put on tests is not culture-free. Rather, the content reflects what we value. So to talk about intelligence outside of culture doesn't make sense. There are certain processes that are intelligent in any culture, but the way they're manifested differs from culture to culture. For example, take something like setting up a strategy to solve problems. This process is an important aspect of intelligence in any culture; it's universal. However, the strategies that are considered to be intelligent may vary from one culture to another. Use of time and being able to allocate resources well are aspects of intelligence in any culture. However, what's considered good time allocation may vary from one culture to another.

Q: *Are you doing any research right now that bears on the question of intelligence testing that you might be willing to share with us?*

A: Well, I used the pilot version of my own test in a program for selecting gifted high school kids for a program this summer. There was an analytical section that is more like an SAT, but there was also a creative section and a practical section. Therefore, rather than just selecting kids because they're good at one thing, we selected kids who are good at any one of those three. The interesting thing relevant to all these questions about group differences is that we had a very heterogeneous group with respect to ethnic diversity. I think part of the reason for that was precisely that we did look for a broader range of abilities and not just IQ. We're analyzing the data right now. We hope to issue a report in a couple of months.

RESEARCH PERSPECTIVES

PERSPECTIVE #2: *Are Intelligence Tests Intelligent?*

Dr. Howard Gardner

Q: *Dr. Gardner, do you view intelligence as a fixed ability or do you feel it changes considerably throughout our lifetime?*

A: Well, of course that question presupposes I believe there's a single thing called intelligence, and I don't. To be sure, in fact, both common language and scientific tradition defend the notion that there's such a thing as a single intelligence. People who believe there's a single intelligence can cite as evidence for the fixed nature of that intelligence the fact that there's a high degree of heritability, meaning that people who share all the genes in common are very likely to have similar intelligences, and people who share half their genes in common are more likely to have similar intelligences than people who are genetically unrelated. The whole thrust of my work has been to challenge the notion of there being a single kind of intelligence.

Q: *Could you kind of give us a brief overview of some of the components that you see as going into intelligence?*

A: Even using the word "components" assumes there's a single thing called intelligence. That's sort of what Robert Sternberg's position would be. He would say, Yes, there's intelligence, but it is composed of many different components." I say there are in fact at least seven different intelligences; and I claim that, as a species, human beings have evolved over thousands, maybe millions, of years and developed this set of intelligences. Everybody has all of them, but no two people have exactly the same blend or combination. The first two intelligences, linguistic and logical mathematical, are the ones that are usually valued in school and tested in standard tests. So when people on the street say "intelligence," they usually mean some kind of a blend of language and logic. I often say it needs to be a *superficial* blend of language and logic because the instruments test how quickly you can switch from one thing to the other, which is a test of superficiality, not necessarily of depth. I claim there are five other intelligences: musical, spatial, bodily kinesthetic, interpersonal (understanding of other people), and intrapersonal (understanding of yourself). Those aren't components of intelligence—those are seven separate intelligences.

I challenge the notion of a single thing called intelligence on the basis both of biology—what we understand about the brain and how it's evolved—and on the basis of what we know about human abilities as they play out in different cultures. I think many of the kinds of things we look at in standard intelligence tests in our culture don't even exist elsewhere. Conversely, survival in a sailing culture would depend on whether you could find your way around without tipping over or getting knocked out by storms, and we have no way of knowing from our intelligence tests whether people in our culture whom we call intelligent could do that at all. So I reject the notion that tests of intelligence do more than predict a certain kind of scholastic skill.

RESEARCH PERSPECTIVES

Q: *What, then, is your view of the practicality of developing culture-free intelligence tests as alternatives to some of the standard intelligence and IQ tests that are administered today?*

A: I think the most you could hope to do, given that you believe in testing at all, is to develop an instrument that is in no obvious way biased within a particular culture. So let's just say we might, over the long run, be able to produce in North America a test that does not seem to be skewed for or against any particular group within that culture. The notion that we could somehow produce something that would be usable around the world is, I think, preposterous. You have to be very naive to think that anything that we do around here just happens to be culture-free.

Q: *Have you conducted any research or are you in the process of conducting any research that bears upon some of the applications of your work, for instance, developing learning environments?*

A: I published my book *Frames of Mind* in 1983, and I saw that as basically a contribution to the field of psychology. In fact, it has had some influence in psychology, and it's been controversial. Overwhelmingly, its biggest impact has been in the educational arena. So I have really been devoting my efforts to exploring the educational implications of this theory. How do you assess intelligences? What kind of curricula do you set up? Which environments are productive for the enhancement of intelligences? I now have about fifty people working with me on those questions, and there are literally hundreds of schools in the country that are exploring educational implications of the theory; some of them are doing research. My 1993 book, *Multiple Intelligences in Theory and Practice* describes what people are actually doing with the theory. While I do talk about museums and apprenticeships and things like that, most of it is about the implications in the school. To give you one specific example, we have a project called Spectrum, which was started about in an effort to figure out whether, as young as the age of three or four, kids already have different intellectual profiles from one another. We find that some kids will be strong in one intelligence and others in another, and there's no question that as young as three or four, kids have very different profiles of intelligence. It's not the case that we're all alike until five and then we begin to differentiate.

We created a very rich environment that we call a Spectrum classroom, which is as much like a children's museum as like a classroom. Over the course of a year, we watched how kids interact with the materials in that classroom: musical instruments, all kinds of games, stuff to take apart and put together again, different learning centers. We even have a miniature version of the classroom that kids take apart and put together so that it will look like the regular class. We have little photographs of all the kids and teachers on pieces of wood, and we look at the kids' personal intelligences by the way that they can identify and reconstruct the habits of kids in the classroom.

So there's two points. One is, you can do research in intelligences, and you can find evidence for them very early. The second is, you don't have to do standard tests. You can create environments that themselves allow you to look at people's profiles of intelligence.

RESEARCH PERSPECTIVES

Q: *You mentioned that your research has shown that there are noticeable differences in intelligence profiles between one individual and another at an early age. Have you made any recommendations based upon that in terms of educational environments or tracking people into certain educational areas?*

A: That's a very interesting question, because when I wrote *Frames of Mind,* I did not particularly have special educational interventions in mind. What happened was, many people read the book, and it became like a Rorschach inkblot test. You had some people reading the book that said what we need to do is to find people's talents as early as possible and to stream them and track them as much as possible. Other people said you need to find a kid's weaknesses as early as possible and really try to shore them up. While still other people, like the Key School in Indianapolis, said that we ought to give every kid exactly the same amount of time each day in each area of intelligence. So it's quite clear the theory itself doesn't contain within it a particular recipe.

What we've done in Spectrum is to write a little essay for parents on the kids' particular strengths and weaknesses and actually suggest what might be done either if you, as a parent, wanted to play for strength or if you want to shore up weaknesses. Initially, we just told what to do to build on strengths. However, many parents said they wanted to know about the weaknesses, so we felt we should tell them. I then came to the conclusion that whether to build strengths or shore up weaknesses is really a value judgment. Therefore, I don't think it's appropriate for psychologists to say you should do one or the other.

Let me give you a concrete example why: If you're a recent immigrant from Southeast Asia and you have a kid who's very strong in an area, you're probably going to want to push that as far as you can because that's going to be his or her meal ticket to being successful in America. If, however, you are very comfortably middle class and there's no question that your kid is ever going to be able to make a living, you might want to have a much more rounded child or even work on areas of weakness. You can see why, if I as a psychologist recommended only one of those, I would not be doing a service to somebody whose set of needs and priorities are very different.

Q: *Another topic that comes to mind when discussing intelligence is the topic of creativity. How would you describe the relationship between different intelligences and a person's creative ability? Are they linked in any way?*

A: That's an area that I'm totally involved in at the present time, so this is very close to the center of my work. Just as I don't believe there's a general intelligence, I don't believe there's a general creativity. People are creative or not creative in particular domains within a society. Those domains map roughly into the intelligences. Some people are creative in music; some are creative in math, and so on. Second of all, and more complexly, creativity is not something that's in somebody's head. It's always an interaction between whatever abilities you have, whatever domains exist in the culture, and judgments made of the quality and originality of your work. So we can't talk about X or Y being creative in an area alone. We have to say, "How do people assess that person's work?" Although that judgment may be faulty in the short run, over the long run we hope it will be less faulty. There are people like Emily Dickinson or Gregor Mendel whose work was not appreciated during their lifetime. We don't, therefore, conclude they weren't creative. We conclude they needed to have an audience that was receptive to what they did.

My general belief about the relationship between intelligence and creativities is as follows: In order to be creative, you have to have a certain kind of personality. You have to have a sense of what kinds of ideas or products might possibly find a future audience, though it may not necessarily find an audience now. This is important, because you can have a terrific brain and a terrific set of intelligences, but if you want to be accepted and you want to do what people are going to like, you'll never be creative. You've got to have the kind of personality that's willing to take risks, to be knocked down, to be criticized, and keep on going. This doesn't mean that you pay no attention to the criticism, but you can't be floored by it. So there are many people who are highly intelligent in any definition, who never do anything creative because they don't want to take a chance. There are some people who are highly intelligent and who are willing to take a chance, but their work is never appreciated so we have to assume it's not creative. So this is a quite different way of thinking about creativity. I have another 1993 book, *Creating Minds: The Anatomy of Creativity as Seen Through the Lives of Freud, Einstein, Picasso, Stravinsky, Eliot, Graham, and Gandhi*, where I lay out that argument in some detail. I'm sure it's going to cause hackles to rise.

Q: *Do you think that creativity can be fostered or increased in any way through intervention?*

A: Definitely, but it's even easier to abolish. I mean if you chastise people or kill them if they do original kinds of things, you simply destroy creativity. Most cultures throughout history have wanted to get rid of creativity because it's a destabilizing kind of influence. The most creative societies have exploded pretty quickly because there wasn't enough stability: Florence in the Renaissance, Greece in classical times, and so on.

After twenty-five years in education I've boiled down my educational recipe to three points: model and practice with feedback. If you want kids to be creative, you've got to model what it's like to pursue new questions, to make mistakes, to take a chance. You've got to give kids plenty of practice in doing that, and you've got to let them know how they're doing. So creativity is very much a sociological issue as well as a psychological and biological issue. You could look at a person's brain and know where every single wiring was, and it wouldn't tell you the faintest thing about whether they were creative or not. You'd have to see what they do living in a certain culture and how it's valued by people in that culture.

POP QUIZ

True or False

___ 1. A good operational definition of intelligence is "the ability to think abstractly."

___ 2. The Stanford-Binet test allows for the calculation of overall IQ and also of the verbal and performance IQ.

___ 3. If a person took the same IQ test three times and received a similar score each time, it could be said that this test is reliable.

___ 4. Sternberg's and Gardner's models of intelligence seek to understand intelligence as a process.

___ 5. Most psychologists believe that differences in intelligence between racial groups are largely—if not exclusively—the result of environmental factors.

Multiple Choice

6. In developing his intelligence test, Binet reasoned that a child with high intelligence would perform on the intelligence test similar to which of the following?
   a. A child of the same chronological age
   b. An older child of average intelligence
   c. An older child of below-average intelligence
   d. A child of the same age and of average intelligence
7. Which of the following is ***not*** an advantage of group-administered intelligence tests compared to individual intelligence tests?
   a. Can be given to a number of people at the same time
   b. Are quicker to administer
   c. Encourage the best possible performance from individuals
   d. Are more easily scored
8. Because intelligence tests ________, one should receive the same IQ score regardless of who administers and scores the test.
   a. are standardized
   b. have established norms
   c. are valid
   d. are reliable
9. If a test measures what it is supposed to measure, it has ________.
   a. validity
   b. norms
   c. reliability
   d. consistency

POP QUIZ

10. Which of the following are designed to measure a type of ability that is different from the type of ability measured by the other three tests?
    a. Aptitude tests
    b. Otis-Lennon school ability test (OLSAT)
    c. Achievement tests
    d. Wechsler Adult Intelligence Scale (WAIS)
11. Guilford used the term content to describe which of the following?
    a. How we think
    b. What we think about
    c. How we apply our thinking
    d. Primary ability
12. Good problem solvers who score high on intelligence tests ________ than people who score low on intelligence tests.
    a. take a longer time to encode information
    b. take a shorter time to encode information
    c. arrive at the correct solution faster
    d. make more careless mistakes
13. Which two people would you expect to have IQs that are most similar?
    a. A parent and child
    b. Fraternal twins reared together
    c. Two same-sex siblings
    d. Identical twins reared apart
14. ________ is the psychologist who proposed that the difference in average IQ scores between black people and white people is due primarily to genetic factors.
    a. Jensen
    b. Skeels
    c. Sternberg
    d. Gardner
15. Current opinion among psychologists is that differences in intelligence test scores between racial groups are ________.
    a. nonexistent
    b. larger than they were fifty years ago
    c. a result of the environment as opposed to genes
    d. a result of genetic differences between races

Answer Key: 1.F 2.F 3.T 4.T 5.T 6.b 7.c 8.a 9.a 10.c 11.b 12.a 13.d 14.a 15.c

(iStock)

Chapter 14

Personality: Theories *and* Assessment

What makes people different from one another? The ancient Greeks thought the answer had something to do with the four basic body fluids or *humors*: blood, phlegm, black bile, and yellow bile. According to the Greek physician Hippocrates (460–371 BCE), there were four possible personality types. *Sanguine* individuals had an abundance of blood; they tended to be cheerful, optimistic, and active. *Phlegmatic* people were listless, sluggish, and tired because they had too much phlegm. Sad, brooding, *melancholic* temperaments resulted from too much black bile; and *choleric* (excitable, easy to anger) personalities resulted from an excess of yellow bile.

Although Hippocrates's terminology still survives in descriptive adjectives that we use today, both the typologies psychologists use to distinguish personalities and the explanations of what causes personality differences have changed considerably in the last 2,300 years. In this chapter, we look at some more contemporary conceptions of personality, including both theories that describe personality traits and the psychoanalytic, behavioral, and humanistic explanations of what makes each of us unique. Like Chapter 13, this chapter also describes assessment techniques, although here our interest is in assessing people's personalities instead of their intelligence.

14.1 Defining Personality

You have often heard statements like, "Mary has a great personality" or "John has no personality at all." Do these statements reflect logical observations about human personality? Consider this question and formulate a response before reading on.

The notion of personality as an attribute that people possess in varying amounts is a common one. However, personality is not something we possess in large or small quantities, nor is it a concrete trait that is easily observable, such as blue eyes or blond hair. Rather, personality is what we are, a collection of many traits and attributes, the sum total of which constitutes a unique person unlike anyone else. We begin this chapter by trying to define personality.

Although personality psychologists have not reached a general consensus on a formal definition of **personality**, a common theme can be found in most definitions. A leading personality theorist of our time, Columbia University's Walter Mischel (1986, 2004, 2007), defines personality as the "psychological invariance that distinctively characterizes an individual and that underlies the variations in the thoughts, feelings, and actions that occur across contexts and over time." We use Mischel's formulation as a working definition in this chapter.

A key aspect of virtually all definitions of personality is their emphasis on the individual. We may best describe *personality psychology* as the study of individuals—their distinctive characteristics and traits and the manner in which they integrate all aspects of their functioning as they adapt to their environments.

Since for most personality theorists the focus of personality research is nothing less than the total person, it is not surprising that personality psychology's domain is very broad. You will find that many of the discussions in the following pages relate closely to other chapters in this book, particularly discussions of development, learning, behavioral disorders, and assessment techniques.

Personality Distinctive patterns of behavior, emotions, and thoughts that characterize an individual's adaptations to his or her life

14.2 Theories of Personality

In view of the far-reaching nature of personality psychology, it is common for personality theorists to attempt to integrate most or all aspects of human behavior into a single theoretical framework. A number of theories have been developed based on this attempt. Virtually all of these theoretical perspectives share a focus on the whole person, although they take different approaches. The *trait theories* are primarily descriptive theories in that they attempt to identify specific dimensions or characteristics that are associated with different personalities. It is important to remember that identifying and describing personality characteristics is not the same as explaining them. As with other branches of science, classification and description often precede explanation.

Other theories make an attempt to explain personality differences in terms of unconscious motivation, learning, self-actualization, or the heritability of personality. Predictably, the major viewpoints are the *psychoanalytic theory* of Sigmund Freud and his followers, with the emphasis on the role of unconscious motivation in personality; the attempts of *behavioral* and *social-learning theories* to explain how our personalities are shaped by interacting with our environments; the *humanistic* view of personality as molded by our capacities for personal growth and self-actualization; and biological approaches that attribute personality to inherited dispositions. Because the trait theories help to describe and characterize personality, we begin with them.

14.2a Trait Theories

A number of theorists have tried to identify the behavioral traits that are the building blocks of personality. How do these trait theorists determine what traits are relevant in describing personality? A few different approaches have been used. One approach, known as the *idiographic approach*, defines traits by studying individuals in depth and focusing on the distinctive qualities of their personalities. A second approach, known as the *nomothetic approach*, studies groups of people in the attempt to identify personality traits that tend to appear in clusters. This approach uses the factor analysis technique we learned about in Chapter 13. We look at one representative of each method.

First, we'll examine the idiographic approach of Gordon Allport, followed by the nomothetic approach of Raymond Cattell.

Allport's Cardinal, Central, and Secondary Traits

Gordon Allport (1897–1967) considered patterns of traits to be unique attributes of individuals. Thus, Allport conducted thorough and detailed studies of individuals in depth, often through long-term case studies. His research led him to conclude that all people have certain *traits*, or personal dispositions, that are the building blocks of personality (1937, 1961, 1965, 1966). He described these traits as "predispositions to respond" or "generalized action tendencies." He further maintained, "It is these bona fide mental structures in each personality that account for the consistency of its behavior" (1937).

Why do traits produce consistencies in behavior? According to Allport, traits are both enduring and broad in scope, and so they act to unify a person's responses to a variety of stimulus situations. For example, a person with the trait of friendliness might be expected to be pleasant and sociable when meeting strangers, helpful and supportive on the job, and warm and sensitive when relating to family members. Allport believed that our personality traits determine our unique patterns of response to environmental events. Thus, the same stimuli might be expected to produce quite a different response in different people. For example, a person with the trait of shyness might react to meeting strangers by acting in a withdrawn, noncommunicative manner—a very different reaction from that of the person with the friendliness trait.

Allport described three types of traits that operate to provide each person's unique personality structure. A **cardinal trait** is a powerful, dominating behavioral predisposition that seems to provide the pivot point in a person's entire life. For example, if you are the kind of individual who organizes your life around competitiveness—beating classmates on exams, being the fastest down the ski slope, and so forth—we might say that competitiveness is your cardinal trait. Allport recognized that only a very small number of people have cardinal traits. Some famous and infamous examples that come to mind are Adolf Hitler (hatred), the Marquis de Sade (cruelty), Don Juan (lust), and Albert Schweitzer (reverence for life).

All of us possess Allport's second type of trait, the **central trait**. Central traits—such as sensitivity, honesty, and generosity—are major characteristics of our personalities. While less pervasive than cardinal traits, central traits are quite generalized and enduring; it is these traits that form the building blocks of our personalities. Allport found that most people could be characterized by a fairly small number of central traits (usually five to ten).

Finally, we also have a number of less generalized and far less enduring **secondary traits** that affect our behaviors in specific circumstances. Examples of secondary traits might include our dress style preferences or patterns of exercise, both of which are quite changeable and thus not central or enduring aspects of personality.

Cardinal Trait In Gordon Allport's trait theory of personality, a powerful, dominating behavioral predisposition that is an organizing principle in the lives of a small number of people

Central Trait In Gordon Allport's trait theory of personality, a major characteristic such as honesty or sensitivity

Secondary Trait In Gordon Allport's trait theory of personality, any of a variety of less-generalized and often short-term traits that affect people's behavior in specific circumstances

Surface Traits In Raymond Cattell's trait theory of personality, dimensions or traits that are usually obvious (such as integrity or tidiness) and that tend to be grouped in clusters that are related to source traits

Source Traits In Raymond Cattell's trait theory of personality, basic, underlying traits that are the center or core of an individual's personality

Five-Factor Model of Personality Defines personality by five basic dimensions: neuroticism, extraversion, openness to experience, agreeableness, and conscientiousness

Cattell's Sixteen Personality Factors

Raymond Cattell (1950) took just the opposite approach from Allport, studying groups of people rather than individuals. He began his work by identifying certain obvious personality traits, such as integrity, friendliness, and tidiness. He called these dimensions of personality **surface traits**. He then used both direct observations of behavior in everyday situations (what he called "life records") and a variety of questionnaires to obtain extensive data about surface traits from a large number of people. Statistical analysis of these data revealed that certain surface traits seemed to occur in clusters, and Cattell theorized that these clusters probably indicated the operation of a single underlying trait. Cattell applied factor analysis (a complex statistical procedure) to determine what the surface trait clusters had in common. This analysis yielded a list of sixteen primary or **source traits** that he considered to be at the center or core of personality. He listed each of these traits as a pair of polar opposites, such as "trusting" versus "suspicious."

Cattell and his colleagues developed a questionnaire called the 16 Personality Factor Questionnaire (16PF) to measure these source traits. Table 14-1 shows Cattell's sixteen personality profiles from its fifth edition (Cattell & Cattell, 1995).

Five-Factor Model of Personality

Perhaps the most widely adopted trait theory of personality is known as the **Five-Factor Model of Personality** originally proposed by Norman (1963). According to this model, five basic dimensions can define personality: neuroticism, extraversion, openness to experience, agreeableness, and conscientiousness (McCrae & Costa, 2008). While all personality researchers do not agree on the names of these dimensions or on how to measure them, most agree that all versions of the five-factor model are useful in predicting behavior and in assisting with the diagnosis of certain psychological disorders (Miller et al., 2010; Kotov, Gámez, Schmidt, & Watson, 2010). These five factors or dimensions are described below. Note the similarity between Cattell's 16PF traits and the five-factor traits.

Table 14-1 Cattell's Personality Factor Profiles from the 5th Edition, 1993

Abstractedness	Imaginative and abstract versus practical-solution oriented
Apprehension	Insecure and self-doubting versus complacent and confident
Dominance	Aggressive and assertive versus passive and submissive
Emotional Stability	Calm and stable versus high-strung and emotional
Liveliness	Enthusiastic and happy go lucky versus serious and introspective
Openness to Change	Liberal and free thinking versus traditional and conservative
Perfectionism	Compulsive and controlled versus indifferent and impulsive
Privateness	Pretentious and discreet versus unpretentious
Reasoning	Abstract and intelligent versus concrete and less intelligent
Rule Consciousness	Moralistic and rule bound versus free-thinking and nonconforming
Self-Reliance	Leader and self-sufficient versus group oriented and follower
Sensitivity	Sensitive and sentimental versus tough-minded and objective
Social Boldness	Uninhibited and socially bold versus timid and shy
Tension	Driven and tense versus relaxed and easy-going
Vigilance	Suspicious and distrustful versus trusting and accepting
Warmth	Open and warmhearted versus aloof and critical

Neuroticism Negative emotionality characterized by the ease with and extent to which people experience negative emotions

Extraversion (alternate spelling of Extroversion used in the Five-Factor Model) An outgoing personality trait characterized by an energetic, gregarious, and positive outlook (In Jung's definition: Extroversion, a personality trait manifested by sociability, friendliness, and interest in people and events in the external world)

Openness to Experiences A personality trait characterized by the enjoyment of adventure and new ideas

Agreeableness A personality trait characterized by compassion, cooperation, and good-naturedness

1. **Neuroticism** (negative emotionality versus positive emotional stability) is characterized by the ease and extent to which people experience negative emotions such as anger, anxiety, sadness, resentment, and shame. Neurotic people are often depressed, anxious, and irritable even when there is nothing in particular to be sad or irritable about. They tend to see the down side of life rather than its positive aspects.

2. **Extraversion** (outgoing and confident versus introverted, shy, and insecure): Extraverted people tend to be energetic, gregarious, and positive as opposed to introverted individuals, who tend to be shy and socially isolated. In addition, extroverts tend to be outgoing and interested in new and stimulating activities.

3. **Openness to experiences** versus reserved and resistant: People who are open to new experiences tend to enjoy adventure and new ideas. They are curious, imaginative, and creative.

4. **Agreeableness** versus antagonism: Agreeable individuals are compassionate, cooperative, and good-natured as opposed to those who tend to be irritable, abrasive, and uncooperative. Agreeable people tend to have friendly, secure, and fulfilling relationships.

Table 14-2 Ten Personality Traits Used to Assess the Five-Factor Model of Personality

For each of the ten characteristics that follow, rate the tendencies, from 1 to 7, that best characterize you. A 1 indicates that you disagree strongly and a 7 indicates that you agree strongly. Use a 3 or 4 when you neither agree nor disagree with the trait.

1. Extroverted and enthusiastic
2. Critical and quarrelsome
3. Dependable and self-disciplined
4. Anxious and easily upset
5. Open to new experiences and adventurous
6. Reserved and quiet
7. Sympathetic and warm
8. Disorganized and careless
9. Calm and positive
10. Conventional and conforming

To assess your tendencies toward these five factors, compare ratings on the following characteristics:

Neuroticism: High score on item 4 and low score on item 9 (for example, a 6 and 2 would indicate a fairly high neuroticism score)

Extraversion: High score on item 1 and low score on item 6

Openness: High score on item 5 and low score on item 10

Agreeableness: High score on item 7 and low score on item 2

Conscientiousness: High score on item 3 and low score on item 8

Source: Adapted from Gosling, S. D., Rentfrow, P. J., and Swann, W. B. (2003). A very brief measure of the Big-Five personality domains. *Journal of Research in Personality,* 37(6), 504–528.

5. **Conscientious** versus careless and impulsive: Conscientious individuals tend to show self-discipline, and they are responsible and dependable. Their behavior tends to be planned rather than spontaneous and irresponsible.

The five factors of personality are typically assessed using multi-item inventories much like Cattell's 16PF or the Minnesota Multiphasic Personality Inventory (discussed later in this chapter). Gosling, Rentfrow, and Swann (2003) proposed a shortened version consisting of ten traits that seem to be about as useful as the longer multi-item versions. This is summarized in Table 14-2.

Research on the five-factor model indicates that personality traits tend to mature and stabilize around the age of thirty and persist well into adulthood (see Figure 14-1). There are a few exceptions to this stability, however. People do tend to become more conscientious as they get older, and they also tend to become a bit less neurotic (Costa & McCrae, 1992, 1994).

14.2b Evaluating the Trait Theories

Trait theories offer the distinct advantage of providing specific methods for measuring or assessing basic characteristics that can be used in comparing individuals. While they often disagree about which basic traits are needed to describe personality, these theories share a common assumption that traits may be used to explain consistencies in behavior and to explain why different people tend to react differently to the same situations.

Conscientiousness A personality trait characterized by self-discipline, responsibility, and dependability

Figure 14-1 Scores for Neuroticism and Conscientiousness by Age in Years

Scores for neuroticism and conscientiousness tend to change in one's late twenties and then appear to stabilize after age thirty.

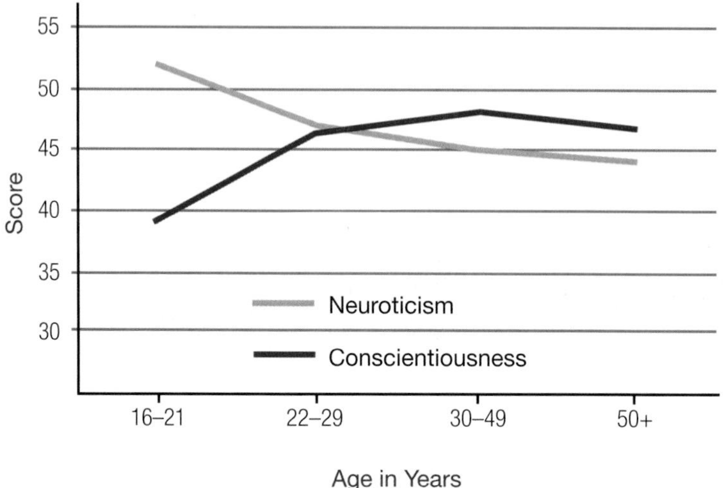

Data from: Costa et al., 1999. Donnellan, B. M., & Lucas, R. E. (2008). Age differences in the big five across the life span: Evidence from two national samples. *Psychology of Aging, Sept. 23*(3), 558–566.

Descriptions Versus Explanations of Behavior

A trait theorist such as Allport might observe that a woman who returns excess change to a cashier, admits to damaging a fixture in a motel, and refuses to accept help from a classmate during an exam behaves in these ways because she has the trait of honesty. What is the problem with this kind of reasoning? Think about this question before reading on.

How do we know that the woman just described has the trait of honesty, and that this trait is the cause of her behavior? The only answer Allport or other trait theorists might provide is "because she is honest in much of her behavior." If you have taken any logic courses, you may recognize this response as an example of circular reasoning, in which we first deduce the existence of a trait from observing a behavior, then use our deduction to explain the behavior. For instance, if we observe the woman returning extra money to a cashier we might conclude she is honest. *Honest* is a description of her behavior; it cannot be used to explain why she returned the money. For this reason, most psychologists insist that traits are only descriptions, not explanations.

Related to this point are criticisms of the view that traits produce consistent behavior from one situation to the next. Cattell went so far as to contend that a person's 16PF scores could be used to predict such diverse things as success in school, accident-proneness, or marital happiness.

A number of psychologists, most notably Walter Mischel, have argued that while people may possess certain enduring behavioral predispositions, they do not act with consistency from one situation to the next. You may have noticed that you are shy in some kinds of situations and more assertive in others. Such inconsistencies are common to many of us, and a considerable body of research indicates that many personality "traits" may be situational, or state dependent.

One early study observed more than ten thousand children who were given opportunities to steal, cheat, or lie in a variety of contrived situations at home, in the classroom, and on the playground (Hartshorne & May, 1928). It found very little consistency in the behavior of subjects. Most of the children would lie, steal, or cheat in some circumstances, but not in others. The researchers thus concluded that the so-called trait of honesty was actually a collection of *situation-specific habits*.

Later studies have reported similar inconsistencies in behavior. For example, a study of punctuality among several hundred college students revealed virtually no consistency in their time of arrival at a variety of college-related events. Walter Mischel's (1968) investigation of college students' conscientiousness (turning in assignments on time, arriving before a lecture begins, and so forth) revealed a similar lack of situational consistency. Mischel went on to examine the research literature on this topic and found very little evidence that behavior is consistent across diverse circumstances.

More recently, Mischel has argued that an individual's thoughts and behaviors are not solely a function of one's personality system, but of a system of situation-behavior (if … then) relationships. For example, one does X when in situation A, but does Y when in situation B. It is these if … then profiles that define an individual's personality dynamics (Mischel, 2004).

Despite situational variance in behavior, however, our tendency to be honest (or happy, shy, outgoing, or any other quality) over a variety of situations is somewhat predictable. If we average out our behaviors across a range of situations, at least some of our most distinctive profiles contribute to a consistency that tends to be enduring over the life span. For example, a child who is gregarious during her early developmental years is likely to remain friendly and outgoing throughout her life.

Where do these traits, or situation-behavior profiles, come from in the first place? This question leads to a final criticism of trait theories; they offer essentially no understanding of how personality develops. Instead of telling us about the origin of traits, how they are learned, how they may be changed, and how they interact to shape behavior, these theories offer little more than a rather static view of personality as a collection of characteristics or behaviors. For answers to the question of where traits come from, we turn to the psychoanalytic, behavioral, humanistic, and biological theories of personality.

BVT *Lab*

Flashcards are available for this chapter at www.BVTLab.com.

14.3 Psychoanalytic Theory

The most influential, most comprehensive and systematic, and most widely studied personality theory of all time is the psychoanalytic theory of the Viennese physician Sigmund Freud (1856–1939). It is impossible to do justice in a few pages to Freud's theoretical interpretations, originally published in twenty-four volumes between 1888 and 1939. However, we attempt to acquaint you with some of the most important features of his theory.

14.3a The Historical Context of Freud's Theory

Although Freud presented the Western world with a bold new vision of human nature, his views also reflected his own upbringing in the Victorian climate of nineteenth-century Austria. Freud was the firstborn child in a large, middle-class Jewish family. Almost his entire life was spent in Vienna where, as a young man, he received a medical degree and entered private practice as a neurologist. The Victorian climate strongly influenced attitudes toward sexual behavior, particularly among women. Women were not encouraged to behave sexually or enjoy sexual relations. In addition, women were relatively oppressed

Free Association Psychoanalytic technique developed by Sigmund Freud in which patients relax and say whatever comes to their minds

Unconscious Mind According to Freud's theory, the vast reservoir of the mind that holds countless memories and feelings that are repressed or submerged because they produce anxiety

Psychoanalysis Technique developed by Freud in which an individual's revelations of normally unconscious cognitions are interpreted

compared to women today in most of the Western world. Men held most of the powerful positions, had money and prestige, and were envied by aspiring women. These times and his female patients influenced the development of Freud's theory. As you read this section on Freud's ideas, keep these things in mind.

Freud's interest was in nervous disorders, but early in his medical career he noticed that many of his patients showed no evidence of nervous system pathology. A patient might be unable to walk, see, or hear, and yet no neurological impairment could be found. Freud suspected that such symptoms might be psychological rather than physical. After observing neurologists such as Jean Charcot and Freud's colleague Joseph Breuer, both of whom were using hypnosis to treat cases similar to his own, Freud incorporated Breuer's *cathartic* method into his treatment regimen. This approach involved hypnotizing patients and then encouraging them to recall the first time their symptoms were experienced, and to talk freely about the circumstances surrounding this occurrence. When such experiences could be relived, the effect was often a release of bottled-up emotions in a kind of cathartic experience, followed by a marked reduction of the symptoms. Eventually, Freud dispensed with hypnosis, expanding the cathartic technique into a method known as **free association**. Freud encouraged patients to relax and to say whatever came to their minds, no matter how embarrassing, painful, or trivial.

14.3b Personality and the Unconscious

Through listening to his patients free-associate about their early experiences, fears, and concerns, Freud gradually began to formulate a concept of the **unconscious mind**, which ultimately became central to his personality theory. He envisioned the mind as being like an iceberg, with most of it hidden beneath the surface in the vast reservoir of the unconscious. He theorized that memories and feelings are repressed or submerged in the unconscious because they are too painful or anxiety producing to be tolerated in conscious thoughts. Free association could open a door to the unconscious, allowing a person to release or express its contents.

Freud used the term **psychoanalysis** to describe his interpretation of a patient's revelations of normally unconscious cognitions. The psychoanalytic theory of personality gradually evolved from his attempts to explain certain recurrent themes that emerged from his use of psychoanalysis. Thus, the psychoanalytic perspective provides both a theory of personality and a method for treating behavioral disorders. (We discuss the therapy side of psychoanalysis in Chapter 16.)

The more Freud listened to his patients, the more convinced he became that unconscious thoughts and feelings are powerful molders of personality. He believed that these ever-present forces emerge into consciousness in disguised form—influencing our relationships with others, the kind of work we do, the beliefs we hold, and the symptoms of emotional disorders. Freud believed that the workings of the unconscious could be seen in the kinds of dreams we have. As you may recall from Chapter 5, Freud was particularly fond of analyzing dreams, which he considered to be a major outlet for unconscious wishes. Freud also believed that slips of the tongue or pen can provide insights into the unconscious. For example, the woman who describes her father as "kind, generous, and insensitive" (instead of "sensitive") might be expressing thinly disguised, repressed hostility.

Freud's training in physiology and medicine led him to conclude that we are biological organisms dominated by biological needs, especially sexual needs, which must be controlled if we are to become civilized human beings. In his view, our perpetual struggle to tame these impulses leads to the emotional conflicts that so profoundly shape our personalities. Considering the extreme sexual repression of the Victorian period, it is not surprising that Freud's initial theories of personality placed such an emphasis on conflicts surrounding sexual urges. Many years later, the deaths of millions of people in World War I also had a profound impact on Freud, and he modified his theory to include an equally strong emphasis on aggressive urges in molding personality. Thus, the **psychoanalytic theory** depicts personality as shaped by an ongoing conflict between people's primary drives, particularly sex and aggression, and the social pressures of civilized society.

Freud also theorized that early childhood experiences play a major role in molding personality. After listening to countless revelations of what he considered to be profoundly significant events in his patients' early years, he concluded that such experiences place an indelible stamp on personality and behavior. In the next several paragraphs, we explore Freud's view of the structure, dynamics, and development of personality.

Psychoanalytic Theory Theory of personality that views people as being shaped by ongoing conflicts between primary drives and the social pressures of civilized society

Id In Freud's psychoanalytic theory, the biological component of personality consisting of life instincts and death instincts

Libido In Freud's psychoanalytic theory, the energy that fuels the id and motivates all behavior

Pleasure Principle According to Freud, the principle guiding the id that seeks immediate gratification of all instinctive drives regardless of reason, logic, or the possible impact of behaviors

14.3c The Structure of Personality

One of the best known aspects of Freud's theory is his conceptualization of human personality as composed of three interacting systems or structures: the id, ego, and superego. These structures are not physically present in the brain; they are psychological concepts or constructs that Freud developed to help explain certain aspects of human behavior. These three systems are interrelated and interactive, but each has its own characteristics, as Table 14-3 illustrates.

The Id

According to Freud, the **id** is basically the biological component of personality. It consists of a vast reservoir of instinctual drives that Freud called the *life instincts* (such as hunger, thirst, and sex); it also includes the *death instinct*, which is responsible for aggressiveness and destruction. The id is fueled primarily by a form of energy called **libido**, which motivates all behavior. It operates according to the **pleasure principle**, seeking immediate gratification of all instinctive drives—regardless of reason, logic, or the probable impact of the behaviors it motivates. Freud believed that only the id is present at birth; thus a newborn's behaviors are dominated by the id. This viewpoint has a ring of truth for

Table 14-3 Mental Structure According to Freud

Structure	Consciousness	Contents and Function
Id	Unconscious	Basic impulses (sex and aggression); seeks immediate gratification regardless of consequences; impervious to reason and logic; immediate, irrational, impulsive
Ego	Predominantly conscious	Executive mediating between id impulses and superego inhibitions; tests reality; seeks safety and survival; rationally and logically taking account of space and time
Superego	Both conscious and unconscious	Ideals and morals; strives for perfection; observes, dictates, criticizes, and prohibits; imposes limitations on satisfactions; becomes the conscience of the individual

Primary Process Thinking According to Freud, wish-fulfilling mental imagery used by the id to discharge tension

Ego In Freud's psychoanalytic theory, the component of personality that acts as an intermediary between the instinctual demands of the id and the reality of the real world

Reality Principle According to Freud, the tendency to behave in ways that are consistent with reality: governs the ego

Superego According to Freud, the third system of personality that consists of an individual's conscience as well as the ego-ideal (the "shoulds" of behavior)

anyone who has observed a hungry infant's demanding cry for attention regardless of any important tasks in which Mom or Dad are engaged.

The id cannot tolerate any tension, and so it seeks immediate gratification. However, since it operates at an essentially unconscious level, it is not able to interact effectively with external reality to achieve gratification. The newborn is largely helpless, driven by basic instincts but dependent on others for fulfilling these needs. Freud believed that the id seeks to discharge tension by conjuring up mental images of the object it desires. Thus, a hungry baby might form an internal image of the mother's breast, or we might have dreams about sex. Freud called this wish-fulfilling mental imagery **primary process thinking**.

In sum, the id is the storehouse of largely unconscious, biologically based, instinctive drives that provide the basic energy source for the entire personality system. It is also the foundation from which the ego and superego later evolve.

The Ego

A newborn's world is not designed to serve his or her every need. No matter how much a baby cries or carries on, a mother's breast or a bottle does not always appear magically. Thus, infants soon come to realize that immediate gratification is not always possible. According to Freud, such discoveries prompt the development of the **ego** as an outgrowth of the id. The ego develops gradually, as the infant learns to cope with the real world. It functions as an intermediary between the instinctual demands of the id and the reality of the world. Freud's concept of the ego explained how the id-dominated infant who might lie helplessly, crying for food, gradually evolves into a toddler who is able to reach into the cookie jar or say the word "milk."

The ego operates according to the **reality principle**. That is, it seeks to satisfy the id's wants and needs in ways that are consistent with reality. To accomplish this goal, the ego must be largely conscious and in direct contact with the external world. Furthermore, to carry out its executive functions of screening the id's impulses, the ego system must include our abilities to perceive, think, learn, and remember. Thus, what psychologists now call cognitive processes were considered by Freud to be functions of the ego.

The Superego

In the early years of life, the ego only needs to check external reality to determine whether a particular id impulse may be expressed. Morality has no influence at all. Thus, if a toddler is hungry and a freshly baked cake that Mom baked for the school fund-raiser is within reach, the outcome is predictable even though such behavior is "wrong."

As the toddler becomes an older child, however, Freud theorized that a third system of personality emerges. The **superego** is a composite of the moral values and standards of parents and society that we incorporate into our personalities as we develop. While the id is driven to seek pleasure and the ego to test reality, the superego is concerned with striving for perfection. The superego makes the task of the ego much harder by forcing it to consider not just what is real, but also what is right.

According to Freud, the superego includes two distinct subsystems. The first, the conscience, consists of the moral inhibitions or "should nots" of behavior that stem from punishment (either parental punishment or punishing ourselves through guilt). The second subsystem, the *ego-ideal*, is the "shoulds" of behavior for which we receive approval and/or reinforcement and to which we aspire. Freud believed that emotions such as guilt and pride are essential in the functioning of our superegos. He particularly emphasized the role of guilt both in inhibiting id impulses and in contributing to many personality disorders.

Figure 14-2 Sigmund Freud's Personality Structures

An "iceberg" is the representation of Freud's personality structures. According to Freud, the mind operates mostly beneath the surface of conscious awareness. The id operates completely below conscious awareness, while the ego and superego operate both above and below conscious awareness, like an iceberg.

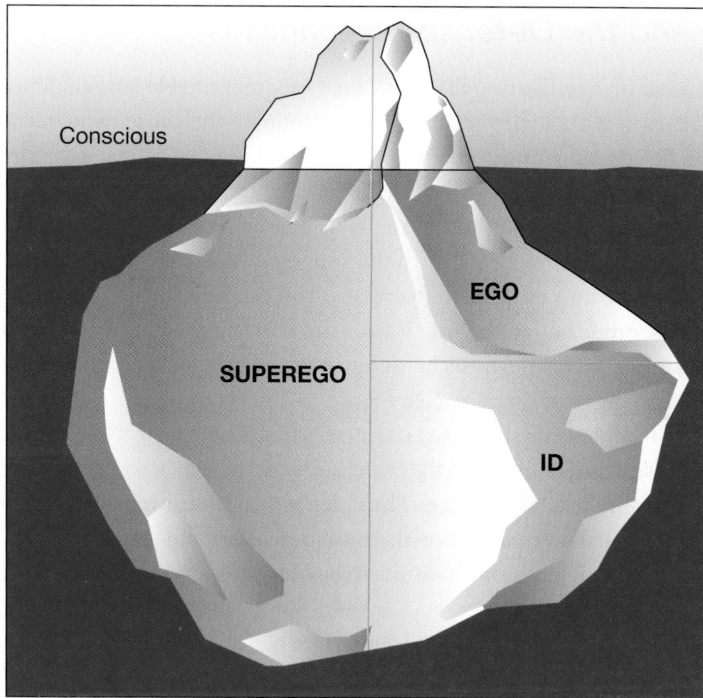

The superego, then, is the moral arm of personality that tries to prevent the id from expressing its primitive impulses. Even though the superego shares some characteristics with the id (for instance, it is irrational) and the ego (it is controlling), it nevertheless stands in opposition to both of them. Unlike the ego, which merely suppresses the id long enough to find a rational way to satisfy its needs, the superego tries to block id impulses totally. In this sense, it is the original "spoilsport." If the superego is too successful in its task, the end result is a rigid, guilt-ridden, inhibited personality. If the superego consistently plays a weak hand, however, the result is a self-centered, self-indulgent, antisocial personality.

14.3d Personality Dynamics

Personality theorists use the term *dynamics* to refer to the forces that shape personality. According to Freud, the dynamics of personality reside in the continuous interaction and clash between the impulse-driven id, the guilt-inducing superego, and the ego, which acts as mediator by reconciling reality with the demands of both the id and the superego. The interplay among these personality forces requires a delicate balance that is difficult to achieve. No matter how well we have adjusted to external reality and integrated a system of morality into our daily lives, Freud maintained that the id's primitive urges inevitably

Anxiety Free-floating fear or apprehension that may occur with or without an easily identifiable source

Defense Mechanism In Freud's psychoanalytic theory, an unconscious maneuver that shields the ego from anxiety by denying or distorting reality

create conflicts that upset this balance. A severe breakdown of this balance may result in various forms of behavioral disorders, such as amnesia, paralysis, or blindness—just the kinds of symptoms that aroused Freud's interest in the first place.

When the ego is faced with conflicts that threaten to disrupt the balance among the systems of personality, it sounds an alarm in the form of anxiety that, in turn, induces it to fall back on a variety of mechanisms designed to control this anxiety.

Anxiety and the Defense Mechanisms

Anxiety is a kind of free-floating fear with no easily identifiable source. Since its source is abstract, a person with anxiety cannot act to eliminate the cause, which is why anxiety can be such a devastating emotion. Freud maintained that anxiety stems primarily from an unconscious fear that our id will cause us to do something that will result in punishment or guilt. (In terms of the three systems of personality, the ego experiences anxiety when an impulse that is unacceptable to the superego threatens to be expressed in overt behavior.) When the ego is not able to relieve this anxiety through rational, problem-solving methods, Freud suggested that it resorts to certain less rational maneuvers called defense mechanisms. The purpose of **defense mechanisms** is to shield the ego from some of the harsh aspects of reality (see Figure 14-3).

All defense mechanisms share two characteristics: They protect the ego from anxiety by denying or distorting reality, and they operate unconsciously so that we are not aware a distortion of reality has taken place. Thus, defense mechanisms are not subject to the normal checks and balances of rational, conscious reasoning—a limitation that causes people who are using defense mechanisms to be absolutely convinced of the correctness of their viewpoint.

People often assume that using a defense mechanism is a sign of weakness, or of a disturbed personality. According to Freud, all of us, well-adjusted and otherwise, use the

Figure 14-3 The Purpose of Defense Mechanisms

Defense mechanisms serve to shield the ego from the harsh aspects of reality.

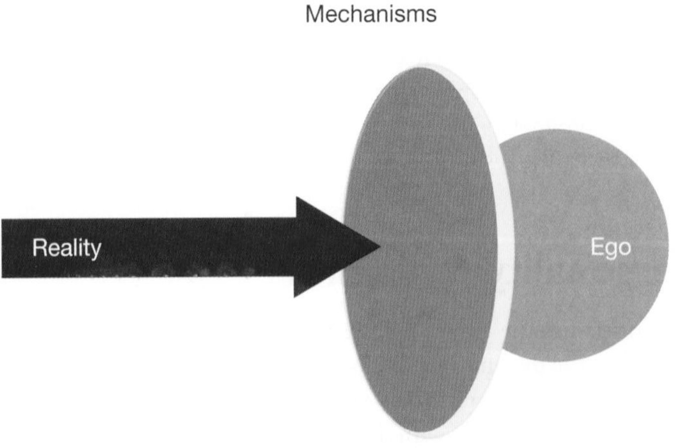

(iStock)

Sigmund Freud maintained that anxiety stems from an unconscious fear that our id will cause us to do something resulting in punishment or guilt.

common defense mechanisms in our everyday lives. Therefore, if you recognize yourself in some of the examples of defense mechanisms in the following paragraphs, do not conclude that you are "weak." Most of us resort to such defensive maneuvers on occasion. In fact, in some situations, the ability to defend ourselves by using repression or some other defense mechanism may actually be helpful. We look here at a number of defense mechanisms: repression, rationalization, projection, displacement, regression, and reaction formation.

Repression The ego's first line of defense against anxiety is often **repression**. This defense mechanism involves holding back or banishing from consciousness a variety of unacceptable impulses and disturbing memories. For example, you might repress the aggressive impulses you feel toward a teacher or employer because these feelings are unacceptable and, therefore, anxiety provoking.

Freud believed that all defensive reactions to anxiety first begin with a massive inhibition or repression of id urges. We first attempt to fend off anxiety-arousing thoughts and feelings by blocking them out. Repression is the most basic and pervasive of the defenses against anxiety, and it underlies all other defense mechanisms. Since the id has such an overwhelming number of disruptive urges, however, this primary defense mechanism is unable to contain them all. Thus, we use other secondary defense mechanisms.

When we repress an impulse or feeling, such as hostility toward a parent, we block it from our conscious awareness because it is too painful or threatening to face directly. This mechanism is involuntary, and we are unaware of the process. In contrast, when we *suppress* something, such as an urge to hit back after being slapped, we are fully aware of our impulse, and we voluntarily hold it in check. Although the end result of each process may be the same—namely, blockage of a particular behavior—there is a considerable difference between the two.

Repression In psychoanalytic theory, the defense mechanism by which ideas, feelings, or memories that are too painful to deal with on a conscious level are banished to the unconscious

Rationalization Defense mechanism in which an individual substitutes self-justifying excuses or explanations for the real reasons for behaviors

Projection Defense mechanism in which an individual reduces anxiety created by unacceptable impulses by attributing those impulses to someone else

Displacement Defense mechanism in which a person diverts his or her impulse-driven behavior from a primary target to secondary targets that will arouse less anxiety

Sublimation Form of the defense mechanism *displacement,* in which impulse-driven behaviors are channeled toward producing a socially valued accomplishment

Regression Defense mechanism in which an individual attempts to cope with an anxiety-producing situation by retreating to an earlier stage of development (In statistics, this is a procedure for predicting the size of one variable based on a knowledge of the size of a correlated variable and the coefficient of correlation between the two variables.)

Rationalization

Another widely used defense mechanism is **rationalization**, in which we substitute self-justifying excuses or explanations for the real reasons for our behaviors. For example, the parent who severely disciplines a child with physical punishment may rationalize this behavior by invoking the old saying, "Spare the rod; spoil the child." The real motive, however, may be to vent repressed aggression and hostility.

College students often rationalize their poor performance on an exam by stating that they had too many distractions to study adequately, that they had worked hard all semester and deserved a chance to have a little fun, or that they just could not get into the subject matter. What is the harm in these excuses? Not much, probably—as long as the excuses do not become a habit. After all, it would be a grim world if we came away from every unsuccessful event with a deep sense of failure. However, an overdependence on rationalization, or any other defense mechanism for that matter, may lead to serious problems.

Consider the case of a student who began and dropped an introductory psychology class four times. Each time, he had a supposedly legitimate excuse. During one term, he had to drop out because his sick mother needed extra attention; another time financial problems caused him to lighten his class load so he could work longer hours. A look into his background revealed that quitting classes was a common occurrence when his grades were getting low. When this pattern was called to his attention, he denied that he was a dropout by choice; instead, he was a victim of circumstances, and it is likely that he truly believed in his own excuses. It appears more likely that this individual was avoiding the consequences of poor grades or the necessary increase in study time to correct his situation.

Projection

A third defense mechanism, **projection**, occurs when we reduce the anxiety created by our own unacceptable impulses by attributing these impulses to someone else. An example is the married woman who blames an extramarital sexual affair on the man who "led me on." In addition to allowing us to project our unacceptable impulses onto another, projection provides a mechanism for blaming others for our own shortcomings. For example, a student might project the blame for a poor exam performance onto a "devious professor who purposely writes ambiguous questions just to make students squirm."

Displacement

In the defense mechanism known as **displacement**, individuals divert their impulse-driven behavior from primary targets to secondary ones that will arouse less anxiety. Thus, a student who does not want to risk expressing anger toward a professor may come home and pick a fight with his roommate instead.

Displacement can sometimes produce a socially valued accomplishment. When it does, it is called **sublimation**. Freud believed sublimation is a mechanism that provides a major impetus for the development of culture and the production of artistic endeavors. He suggested that Leonardo da Vinci's paintings of the Madonna resulted from a displacement or redirection of da Vinci's impulse to achieve intimacy with his mother, from whom he had been separated in early childhood. Freud also maintained that many repressed sexual urges of youth, particularly those centered on masturbation, are transformed or sublimated into such socially acceptable activities as athletics, music, art, or horseback riding.

Regression

Sometimes people may attempt to cope with anxiety-producing situations by retreating to an earlier stage of development in an effort to recapture the security they remember. This defense mechanism of **regression** may be expressed in such familiar behavior as a child returning to the infantile pattern of thumb sucking on the first day of school or a newlywed running home to Mom and Dad after the first serious argument with the new spouse.

Reaction Formation In **reaction formation**, the ego unconsciously replaces unacceptable impulses with their opposites. Thus, a person with a barely controllable fascination with obscene literature and films may become involved in an obscenity-fighting group that actively reviews and censors sexually explicit literature and movies. In this fashion, the id impulses may be expressed, but in a disguised form that is acceptable to the ego.

Reaction Formation Defense mechanism in which the ego unconsciously replaces unacceptable impulses with their opposites

Psychosexual Development Stages of development, in Freud's perspective, in which the focus of sexual gratification shifts from one body site to another

Oral Stage According to Freud, the first stage of psychosexual development, spanning birth through twelve to eighteen months, during which the lips and mouth are the primary erogenous zone

Anal Stage In Freud's theory of psychosexual development, the period between about twelve months and three years of age, during which the erogenous zone shifts from the mouth to the anal area

14.3e Freud's View of Personality Development

Freud's experiences in conducting psychotherapy convinced him that personality is essentially formed within the first few years of life. He believed that most of his patients' symptoms stemmed from unresolved conflicts, particularly conflicts involving sexual themes that emerged in the early years.

Psychosexual Development

At the time Freud formulated his theory, it was traditional to view childhood as a period when sexuality remains unexpressed. Freud challenged this thinking, asserting that a child is very aware of the sexual pleasure inherent in body stimulation. His concept of this sexual urge was quite broad, dealing with several different parts of the body (called *erogenous zones*) that play key roles in the arousal and gratification of the sexual drive. Freud theorized that a child progresses through a series of stages of **psychosexual development** in which the focus of sexual gratification shifts from one body site to another. The manner in which a child goes through these stages, said Freud, is a major determinant of the personality that emerges as development progresses. Table 14-4 summarizes these stages.

The first phase of psychosexual development is the **oral stage**, spanning the first twelve to eighteen months of life. During this stage, the lips and mouth are the erogenous zone, and the id's pleasure-seeking energies find an outlet in sucking, chewing, and biting. Thus, babies suck not just because they are hungry but also because they find such activity to be sensually pleasurable.

At some point during the second year of development, the erogenous zone shifts from the mouth to the anal area; this is the start of the **anal stage**. This shift coincides with the neurological development of the anal sphincter muscles, and it marks the beginning of the anal stage (twelve to eighteen months to age three). Freud believed that the nature of toilet training during this stage could have serious ramifications for later adult personality. (We elaborate on this point later.)

Table 14-4 Sigmund Freud's Stages of Psychosexual Development

Stage	Time Span	Focus of Sexual Gratification
Oral	Birth through first 12–18 months	Lips and mouth
Anal	12–18 months to age 3 years	Anal area
Phallic	Age 3 to age 5 or 6	Genitals
Latency	Age 5 or 6 to puberty	No focus—sexual drives unexpressed
Genital	From puberty on	Sexual relations with people outside the family

Phallic Stage According to Freud, the third phase of psychosexual development, spanning age three through age five or six, during which the focus of sexual gratification is genital stimulation

Oedipus Complex In Freud's theory of psychosexual development, the attraction a male child feels toward his mother (and jealousy toward his father) during the phallic stage

Electra Complex The female counterpart to the Oedipus complex

Latency Period Fourth stage of psychosexual development in Freud's theory, extending from about age five to puberty, during which sexual drives remain unexpressed or latent

Genital Stage Fifth and final stage in Freud's theory of psychosexual development, beginning with puberty, during which sexual feelings that were dormant during the latency stage reemerge

Fixation In Freud's theory of psychosexual development, arrested development that results from exposure to either too little or too much gratification

The third phase of psychosexual development, the **phallic stage**, occurs from the age of three to age five or six. During this time, the focus of sexual gratification shifts to genital stimulation. At the same time, the so-called family romance may emerge in which a child feels sexual attraction to the parent of the other sex and experiences jealousy of the same-sex parent. Freud coined the term **Oedipus complex** to describe this reaction. He believed that most children find this situation stressful, so they resolve it by repressing their feelings of sexual attraction and identifying with the same-sex parent. The **Electra complex** is the female counterpart to the Oedipus complex.

The fourth stage of psychosexual development, the **latency period**, extends from age five or six to puberty. Freud believed that sexual drives remain unexpressed, or latent, during this period. Finally, during the last phase of sexual development, the **genital stage** (from puberty on), sexual feelings that were dormant during the latency period reemerge in full force. Adolescents and adults seek to gratify these drives through sexual relations with people outside the family.

Fixation

Freud believed that a child might experience an arrest in development at one of the early stages of psychosexual development as a result of exposure to too little or too much gratification. This phenomenon is called **fixation**, and it can influence adult personality.

Fixation at the Oral Stage

According to Freud, children thwarted from experiencing oral stimulation (sucking, biting, eating) may be inclined to eat excessively or smoke as adults. Frustration during the oral stage might also lead to a later lack of trust of others, or to certain aggressive oral behaviors such as verbal hostility. Excessive gratification can also affect personality, so that infants who are always given a bottle or pacifier may be overly dependent as adults; toddlers who are subjected to very early and stressful toilet training (before adequate anal sphincter muscle development) may, as adults, be obsessively concerned with cleanliness and orderliness.

Freud never explained clearly the precise mechanism whereby fixation occurs, and few of the predictions stemming from this concept have been supported by research.

14.3f Evaluating Freud's Psychoanalytic Theory

Freud based his theory on his own analysis of his patients' free associations and dreams. Therefore, it is not surprising that perhaps the most serious shortcoming of Freud's theory is the difficulty in testing it empirically. As we saw in Chapter 2, a good scientific theory contains terms that may be defined operationally and is constructed in such a way that it generates hypotheses or predictions about behavior that can be confirmed or disproved by empirical tests. Freud's vague pronouncements about personality meet neither of these requirements, and terms such as "primary process thinking" and "oral dependent personality" are virtually impossible to define operationally. Although many experiments have attempted to prove or disprove Freud's basic ideas, the collective results have been discouraging at best (Fisher & Greenberg, 1977).

Another difficulty broached by critics has to do with predicting behavior. Psychoanalytic theory provides no clear predictions about how a particular collection of experiences will affect personality and behavior. For example, punitive toilet training might produce a compulsively neat personality, but then again it could also result in an excessively sloppy individual. Freud did recognize this limitation of his theory, particularly as it related to predicting adult personality from childhood experiences. He admitted, "We never know beforehand which of the determining factors will prove the weaker or the stronger. We can only say at the end that those which succeeded must have been the stronger" (1933, p. 227).

BVT*Lab*

Visit www.BVTLab.com to explore the student resources available for this chapter.

Freud has also been criticized regarding the sample of individuals who served as the basis for much of his theory. Freud based virtually his entire theory on his observations of a relatively small number of troubled patients, primarily middle- and upper-class Austrian women. How might such a limited sample have influenced his theorizing? Think about this question for a moment before reading on.

Perhaps Freud's failure to appreciate the strengths of healthy personalities resulted in a theory that tended to emphasize the negative and irrational components of human behavior. Freud's patients were also the products of a sexually repressed Victorian society. Thus, it seems likely that this group of people collectively experienced a far greater number of sexual conflicts than we might expect to find in a sample of contemporary Austrian or American people. Today, there is widespread agreement among Freud's supporters as well as his detractors that his theory placed far too much emphasis on sex as a dominant motivating force throughout life.

Another area of criticism is Freud's emphasis on the importance of early experience. As we saw in earlier in Chapters 11 and 12, behavior and personality are shaped throughout the life cycle. Freud did teach us, however, to recognize the importance of childhood experiences in molding personality and influencing our thoughts, feelings, and behaviors at later points in our development.

Freud also incorrectly assumed that women are inferior to men in a number of ways: sexually (because they do not have a penis and because they often lack the "maturity" to transfer their erotic sensitivity from the clitoris to the vagina); morally (because they do not experience the same degree of castration anxiety, and therefore a women's emergence from the Electra complex is more mild and incomplete); and culturally (because women's weaker superegos result in less sublimation of primitive urges into creative endeavors).

All these criticisms are valid, and from a contemporary perspective it is relatively easy to recognize Freud's shortcomings. We must keep in mind, however, that Freud developed his theory in a virtual vacuum of data about human development, thinking, emotions, and social behavior. From this perspective, it is remarkable that several of his theoretical perspectives continue to be supported by mainstream psychology today. We have Freud to thank for the concept of the unconscious. (However, most modern theorists do not believe that the unconscious plays a much greater role than the conscious mind in shaping behavior.) We also must credit Freud for the understanding that unresolved conflicts are central to many behavioral problems, for making sexuality from childhood through adulthood a legitimate topic for psychological research, and for introducing the concept of defense mechanisms.

In all, Freud created a theory of momentous proportions that has irrevocably influenced our view of human nature. While few people today agree with Freud's basic premises, or even his structure of the unconscious mind, no one suggests that his ideas were anything less than bold, creative, and highly courageous, considering the cultural context within which he worked. We can expect that Freud's personality theory will continue to influence the views of future generations, primarily because psychology has emerged from years of storm and controversy over Freudian doctrine. Freud's legacy to the science of behavior will always be his rigorous deterministic philosophy. He argued that human behavior had causes that were firmly rooted in the physical world.

14.3g Other Psychodynamic Theorists: The Neo-Freudians

Neo-Freudian Psychologists who were in general agreement with Freud's basic interpretation of the structure of personality, his focus on the unconscious, and his emphasis on childhood experience, but dissented regarding other aspects of Freud's theory, such as his emphasis on aggressive impulses and unconscious sexual conflicts

Personal Unconscious In Carl Jung's theory, the part of the unconscious that is akin to Freud's concept of a reservoir of all repressed thoughts and feelings

Collective Unconscious In Carl Jung's theory, a kind of universal memory bank that contains all the ancestral memories, images, symbols, and ideas that humans have accumulated throughout their evolution

Archetypes Powerful, emotionally charged universal images or concepts in Carl Jung's theory of the collective unconscious

Introversion Personality trait expressed as shyness, reclusiveness, and preoccupation with the inner world of thoughts, memories, and feelings

Freud was a very dynamic and influential theorist who attracted many students who were strongly affected by his psychoanalytic theory of personality. Some of these followers were highly creative, thoughtful individuals who, because of disagreement with some of Freud's pronouncements, eventually developed new interpretations of the psychodynamic forces that help to shape human personality. Freud's disciples and dissenters, or **neo-Freudians** as they were called, were in general agreement with Freud's basic interpretation of the structure of personality, his focus on the key role of unconscious forces in personality formation, and the importance of childhood experiences. As a group, however, the neo-Freudians agreed that Freud's theory placed too much emphasis on aggressive impulses and unconscious sexual conflicts, overstated the impact of biological determinants of personality, and failed to recognize the importance of social influences such as significant interpersonal relationships. Among the most influential of the neo-Freudians were Carl Jung, Alfred Adler, and Karen Horney. We briefly consider what each of these theorists added to the psychoanalytic perspective on human personality.

Carl Jung

Carl Jung (1875–1961) was once one of Freud's most avid students as well as his good friend. However, over the course of a seven-year relationship, he gradually evolved from a staunch supporter to an outspoken critic of certain aspects of Freud's brand of psychoanalytic theory. Jung (1916, 1933, 1953) objected to what he considered to be Freud's overemphasis on sexual motivation. He also came to believe that the unconscious contains much more than repressed thoughts, feelings, and impulses. Jung distinguished between what he called the **personal unconscious**—which is akin to Freud's concept of a reservoir of all repressed thoughts and feelings—and the **collective unconscious**, a kind of universal memory bank that contains all the ancestral memories, images, symbols, and ideas that humankind has accumulated. Jung used the term *collective* to stress that the content of this part of the unconscious mind is the same for all humans. He placed particular emphasis on one key component of the collective unconscious called **archetypes**, which consist of powerful, emotionally charged, universal images or concepts of such things as *mother* (a nurturing figure) and *shadow* (similar to Freud's notion of the id, which Jung later equated with the universal notion of sin).

(Getty Images)

Although an avid student and good friend of Sigmund Freud, Carl Jung came to disagree with certain aspects of Freud's theories.

One other important contribution of Jung that has endured and been incorporated into mainstream psychology, as well as popular language, was his description of two opposite personality traits: **introversion** and extroversion. Introversion is expressed as shyness, reclusiveness, and inner-directedness (or preoccupation with the inner world of our own thoughts, memories, and feelings), whereas extroversion is manifested by friendliness, sociability, and interest in people and events in the external world. Jung maintained that all of us contain the underpinnings of tendencies to be both introverted as well as extroverted. A healthy person, Jung argued, could strike a balance between these polar opposite traits by maintaining an interest in things and people in the surrounding environment while not losing touch with his or her own unique individuality.

Alfred Adler

Alfred Adler (1870–1937), like Jung, also felt that Freud was mistaken in centering his theory on the concept of repressed sexual and aggression conflicts. From his perspective, the single most important driving force in shaping human personality is not striving for ways to satisfy sexual and aggressive urges, as suggested by Freud, but rather striving for perfection or superiority (Adler, 1917, 1924, 1930). This quest for superiority did not necessarily mean achieving social distinction or professional eminence. Instead, Adler conceptualized **striving for superiority** as a universal urge to achieve self-perfection through successful adaptation to life's circumstances, meeting and mastering challenges, and personal growth. Adler theorized that all people acquire feelings of inferiority early in childhood as a result of their small stature, limited knowledge, dependency on adults, and lack of physical and social power. He suggested that we learn to compensate for or overcome this perceived inferiority by striving to bolster our self-sufficiency and to develop our abilities as quickly and successfully as possible.

(Wikimedia Commons/Public Domain)

Alfred Adler (1870–1937) was a medical doctor and psychotherapist. He emphasized the importance of feelings of inferiority in personality development. Adler collaborated with Freud and others to form the Vienna Psychoanalytic Society. Later, Freud discounted Adler's ideas as "honorable errors" and eventually shunned him from the Society.

A pitfall encountered by some individuals in the course of personality development is the inability to compensate successfully for early feelings of inferiority, an occurrence that can result in the formation of an *inferiority complex*—an exaggerated sense of personal incompetence and weakness. Adler considered inadequate parenting, particularly in the early formative years, to be the primary culprit in the development of an inferiority complex. In this sense he agreed with Freud's emphasis on the importance of early childhood experiences. However, instead of focusing on such troublesome points as arrested psychosexual development, Adler noted the adverse impact of overindulgent or neglectful parents. He believed that the manner in which parents interact with their children has a profound impact on how successful children are in overcoming their feelings of inferiority by becoming competent human beings. Thus, Adler anticipated a strong focus in contemporary psychology on the role of early social relationships as important shapers of human personality.

Adler asserted that people are inclined to behave in a neurotic or maladaptive manner because they have not been successful in overcoming feelings of inferiority. Personality disturbances arise when an inferiority complex erodes or blocks healthy striving for superiority. For example, Adler wrote about people who tend to engage in a kind of unconscious self-deception, or *overcompensation*, by acquiring power, financial status, impressive houses, and other superficial indicators of success as a way to cover up or conceal (even from themselves) their powerful feelings of inferiority.

Karen Horney

Karen Horney (1885–1952) was a German psychoanalyst and a contemporary of Freud. Her views differed somewhat from more traditional Freudian views, especially with respect to Freud's theory of sexuality. Horney did not believe that sex and aggression were the primary determinants of personality. She also disagreed with Freud's concept of **penis envy**, and that this was not the source of a woman's jealousy of power later in life. Perhaps one of her greatest contributions at the time was her Theory of Neurosis. Horney believed that neurosis was a continuous process occurring sporadically throughout one's lifetime. Her theory held that there were ten neurotic needs that must be balanced for a successful life (Horney, 1950). A neurotic person would overemphasize several of these needs and become consumed by their fulfillment.

Striving for Superiority In Alfred Adler's neo-Freudian theory, a universal urge to achieve self-perfection through successful adaptation to life's circumstances, mastering challenges, and personal growth

Penis Envy A reaction to the realization that a young girl did not have a penis (also, later in life, the source of a woman's jealousy of the power men held)

Table 14-5 Karen Horney's Ten Neurotic Needs

Neurosis is caused by an overemphasis of several of these basic needs.

Neurotic Need	Description in Neurosis
Need for Affection	An excessive desire to be liked and to please others
Need for a Partner	An exaggerated importance of love and for a partner to resolve one's problems or troubles in life
Need to Restrict One's Life	Restricting one's life within very narrow borders, avoiding material things, and making one's own needs secondary
Need for Power	A pattern of controlling others
Need to Exploit Others	An excessive need to manipulate and use others
Need for Prestige	A excessive need for material possessions, admiration, or public recognition
Need for Admiration	An exaggerated self-perception or personal admiration
Need for Achievement	Persistently pushing for greater and greater achievement
Need for Self-Sufficiency	A strong avoidance of dependence on others, overly independent
Need for Perfection	A desire for complete infallibility and perfection

14.4 Humanistic Theories of Personality

The humanistic personality theorists—so-called because of their emphasis on the unique characteristics of humanity and their rejection of animal models of behavior—emerged in the late 1950s and early 1960s as a third force in personality theorizing. This movement grew in part out of the humanists' dissatisfaction with the idea that either unconscious drives or the environment mold personality.

Although the humanistic perspective encompasses a range of viewpoints, its theorists agree on several points. First, virtually all humanistic theorists agree that a primary motivation for behavior comes from each person's strivings to develop, change, and grow in pursuit of full realization of human potential. Second, humanists collectively reject the notion that personalities are significantly influenced by the kinds of basic impulses postulated by Freud and his followers. Third, humanistic theories also tend to be *phenomenological*, emphasizing a subjective view of reality as seen from the individual's own frame of reference. We can learn more about personality from understanding what it is like to be "in the other person's shoes," argue the humanists, than from objectively observing and analyzing what people say and do. For humanists, the "stuff" of personality consists of our own subjective, personal view of the world, including our attitudes, beliefs, and feelings. The theories of the two most influential humanists, Carl Rogers and Abraham Maslow, both illustrate these features.

14.4a Rogers: The Concept of Self

Carl Rogers (1902–1987) began his professional career as a practicing psychotherapist in the late 1920s. Like Freud, his eventual emergence as a personality theorist was stimulated by what he observed in his patients' revelations. However, Rogers's reading was quite different from that of Freud. Instead of seeing people as driven by sexual and aggressive impulses, Rogers saw the inherent potential for good in each of us (1961, 1977, 1980). Through listening to his clients, he became convinced that the most enduring, driving force in people's lives is their constant striving toward self-fulfillment and the realization of their own unique potential. He considered this striving to be a positive, constructive force motivating us to engage in healthy behaviors that enhance our sense of self.

Central to Rogers's complex theory of personality was the concept of self, the basic core of our beings that glues the elements of our personalities together. The self was the central organizing, all-encompassing structure that accounts for the coherence and stability of our personalities. Rogers did not claim to have invented the concept of self—it was the Greeks who first provided us with the mandate "Know thyself." What Rogers did was to sensitize psychology to the role of this ancient maxim in the evolution and expression of human personality. "At bottom, each person is asking, Who am I, really? How can I get in touch with this real self, underlying all my surface behavior? How can I become myself? " (1961, p. 108).

In response to the question, "Who am I?" Rogers maintained that we derive a self-concept, or image of ourselves, that determines how we perceive and respond to the world. If we see ourselves as being likeable and attractive, we are likely to approach the intriguing person we see at a party. If, on the other hand, we see ourselves as boring and unattractive, we are less likely to make overtures.

Rogers believed that the key to healthy adjustment and happiness was a consistency or *congruence* between our self-concepts and our experiences. Thus, if you consider yourself to be likeable and easy to get along with, this image will be bolstered by your good relationships with your friends. The opposite is true when your experiences are not congruent with your self-concept. For instance, if you find that you cannot seem to get along with either your roommate or neighbors, you will probably feel anxious and troubled. In Rogers's view, such incongruence between self-concept and experiences is often an important factor in maladjustment. To regain a sense of congruence, you must change either your behaviors or your self-concept.

In addition to the interrelationship between the self and the outside world, Rogers suggested that all of us possess of a sense of the *ideal self*, what we would like to be. Just as maladjustment can be caused by experiences that contradict our self-concept, it can also be caused by discordance between the ideal self and the *real self* (our perception of ourselves as we really are).

Since Rogers's primary endeavor was as a psychotherapist, he was involved in treating the maladjustment that results from a poor fit between either the self and external reality or the ideal self and the real self. His therapy strategy was to help people initiate behavior changes where necessary, and ultimately to come to know, accept, and be true to themselves.

14.4b Maslow: Self-Actualization

Abraham Maslow's (1908–1970) initial training as a psychologist was in the behaviorist tradition. However, early in his career he began to question the idea that human actions can be explained solely in terms of biological determinants or in terms of reinforcing and punishing contingencies.

Most of Maslow's life was spent developing and expanding a theory of motivation and personality that emphasized people's positive strivings toward intimacy, joy, love, a sense of belonging, self-esteem, and fulfillment of their highest potential. Maslow proposed that a hierarchy of needs motivates us (see Figure 14-4). When our basic needs for such things as food, warmth, and security are met, we are then motivated toward higher needs—first for love and self-esteem, and then, for some people, for self-actualization (the need to reach our own highest potential and to do the things we do best in our own unique way).

Maslow derived his ideas about human motivation and personality from the study of healthy people, rather than from disturbed people observed in clinical settings. Perhaps it was his intense interest in creative, vibrant, well-adjusted people that led him to place a strong emphasis on such positive human qualities as joy, love, enthusiasm, creativity, and humor while largely ignoring other forces like guilt, anger, shame, conflict, and hostility. Maslow was influenced and inspired by his study of a number of historical and contemporary public figures whom he believed exemplified his concept of self-actualization. In 1950, he identified 38 people he assessed as having reached their fullest potential. This select group included a number of lesser known people Maslow knew personally, as well as many historical luminaries such as Ludwig van Beethoven, William James, Abraham Lincoln, Jane Addams, Albert Schweitzer, Albert Einstein, and Eleanor Roosevelt.

Maslow identified sixteen individual characteristics of the self-actualized person. If you would like to see how closely you fit his conception of a completely fulfilled person, take a look at his characteristics as listed here. These are the characteristics of the self-actualized person, according to Maslow:

Figure 14-4 Abraham Maslow's Hierarchy of Need

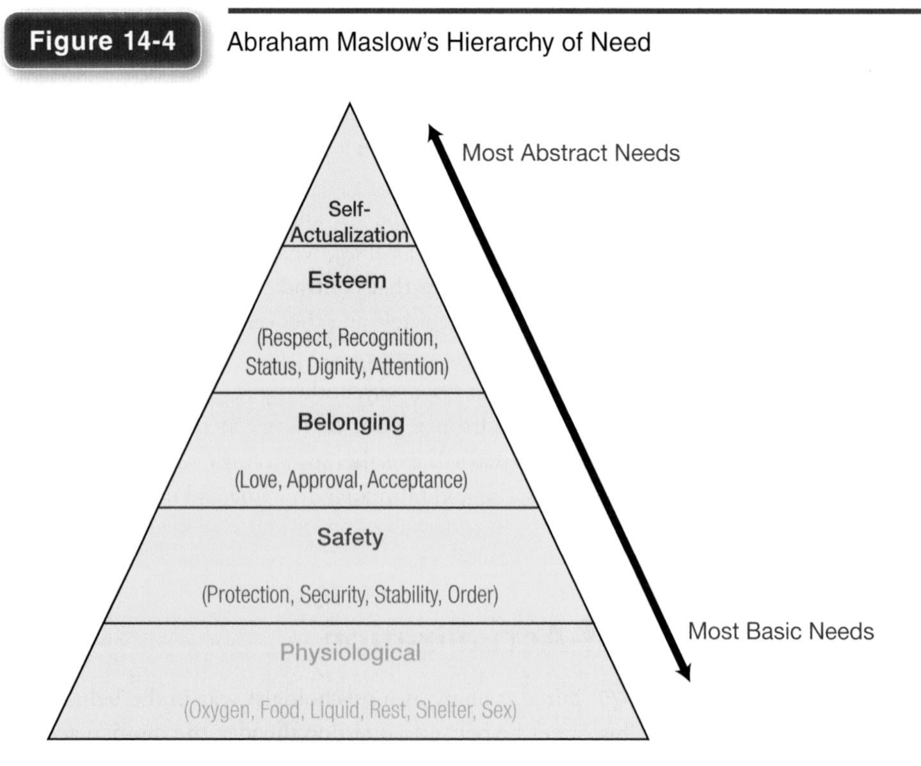

- Is accepting of self and others
- Takes a realistic, nonfanciful view of life
- Is inclined to appreciate people and new ideas, and is not inclined to view them in a stereotypical fashion
- Enjoys intimate and loving relationships with a few people
- Has a lively sense of humor
- Is disinclined to go along with tradition just for the sake of conformity
- Shows the ability to expand and improve the environment rather than merely adjust to it
- Is creative
- Has democratic values
- Is problem-centered rather than self-centered
- Is independent and able to function without being hindered by the opinions of others
- Is open and spontaneous
- Is inclined to seek privacy and is content spending time alone
- Feels a strong identification with the plight of all human beings
- Has the ability to separate means from ends
- Has a history of peak experiences (moments of profound intellectual insight or intense appreciation of music or art)

(Abraham Lincoln, by George Peter Alexander Healy (1869), oil on canvas. Wikimedia Commons/Public Domain)

Abraham Maslow identified thirty-eight people he assessed as having reached their fullest potential, one of whom was Abraham Lincoln.

14.4c Evaluating Humanistic Theories

Humanistic theories of personality have inspired psychologists and laypersons alike to consider the positive dimensions of human personality (The field of positive psychology described in Chapter 1 is an example). This approach provides a welcome focus on the healthy personality that has helped to broaden our perspectives on human nature. A number of valid criticisms have challenged the humanistic perspective, however.

One key objection has to do with the vague, subjective nature of many humanistic concepts. The humanists have been criticized for basing their theories on subjective, nonverifiable observations of people in clinical or natural settings. Rogers's concept of self and Maslow's principle of *self-actualization* are both terms that defy objective, operational descriptions. If you cannot describe something operationally, how can you conduct empirical research to test its validity? The fact that many humanists are demonstrably unconcerned about putting their ideas to empirical tests does not add to their credibility among psychologists who value verifiable evidence. Critics also claim that a theoretical perspective centered on such nebulous concepts as self-perception, the individual's subjective assessment of the world, and the meaning of his or her experiences does not add to our ability to explain behavior.

Humanistic theories have also been criticized for focusing so closely on the individual and the role of the self that they have largely ignored the impact of environmental and biological factors in shaping behavior.

Finally, the humanistic perspective evolved out of dissatisfaction with scientific approaches to animal and human behavior (see Chapter 1). As a result, humanistic theories were not intended to be evaluated by experimental verification. Humanistic theories are inherently untestable because of the vagueness of concepts and the lack of detail about how behavior results from specific situations or needs.

14.5 Behavioral and Social-Learning Theories of Personality

Whereas the psychoanalytic perspective looks to internal mechanisms to explain personality, and humanistic theories look to the satisfaction of inner needs, behavioral and social-learning theories take a distinctly different approach. These theories emphasize the role of external events in determining personality. We look first at the behavioral position, then at the perspective of social-learning theory.

14.5a The Behavioral Perspective

(Wikimedia Commons)

B. F. Skinner (1904–1990), founder of behavior analysis.

We have discussed the views of B. F. Skinner (1904–1990) and other behaviorists in previous chapters, so it should come as no surprise that these theorists reject the psychoanalytic notion that internal forces are the primary instigators of behaviors. To the extent that an individual has identifiable characteristics, behaviorists maintain that they are merely products of external environmental forces in the form of reinforcement contingencies.

According to Skinner, we do not need to assume that a man is a nonstop smoker because he was fed irregularly during infancy. His behavior can be explained, says Skinner, by noting the contingencies of reinforcement that have been associated with it. Not only is it a waste of time to search for personality structures in the form of internal forces, argues Skinner, it may also impede our efforts to understand the true causes of personality.

> The practice of looking inside the organism for an explanation of behavior has tended to obscure the variables that are immediately available for a scientific analysis. These variables lie outside the organism, in its immediate environment and in its environmental history. (1953, p. 31)

To Skinner, our personalities are the sum total of our overt and covert responses to the world around us. Furthermore, our patterns of responding to the environment are a direct outgrowth of the contingencies of reinforcement we have experienced in the past. We are unique individuals because no two people share identical reinforcement histories. Thus, from the perspective of behaviorism, conditioning (defined in Chapter 6) is responsible for the development of personality. The reason why two people act differently in the same situation is not because they have different traits, as trait theorists would argue, or because they have stronger or weaker superegos, as Freud would argue, but rather because of their unique histories of operant and Pavlovian conditioning. The behavioral position argues that explanations of behavior in terms of inner traits are not explanations at all, since the traits themselves are descriptions of the behavior. Essentially, any trait theory of personality will be circular.

Skinner and other behaviorists challenge the notion that enduring traits are evidence of some underlying behavioral predisposition, as trait theorists would claim. Instead, they suggest that the reason some so-called traits appear to be stable is because the environment is itself relatively stable. People are often subjected to a consistent pattern of reinforcement contingencies. As we saw in Chapter 6, relatively simple schedules of reinforcement can produce remarkably stable behavior patterns.

On the other hand, if sufficient changes are made in the environment (either the contingencies of reinforcement are changed or eliminated), the behaviorists note that certain enduring aspects of personality may undergo dramatic change. For example, suppose you become the new foster parent of an eleven-year-old boy who is submissive and introverted (socially withdrawn and emotionally reserved). You check with the child welfare agency that placed the child with you and find that these behavioral patterns were first noted in his case file record several years ago. Does this history mean you should expect these qualities to endure?

The behavioral view says no. If you change the boy's environment by reinforcing even the slightest indications of sociability (for instance, smiling at you) and assertiveness (such as his meekly saying he likes his eggs scrambled rather than fried), you will probably be able to increase the frequency of these behaviors gradually, using the operant principle of shaping (see Chapter 6). These environmental modifications are likely to change his personality by replacing his introversion and submissiveness with more sociable and assertive behavior patterns. As we shall see later in Chapter 16, some of the most effective methods for changing the behaviors of unhealthy personalities and behavior patterns have evolved out of the behavioral approach.

14.5b The Social-Learning Perspective

Like the behaviorists, social-learning theorists believe that external events are important determiners of personality. However, they part company with Skinner and other behaviorists on the issue of cognitive processes. Whereas Skinner asserts that internal cognitive processes such as thinking, perceiving, and feeling are not causes of behavior and personality, social-learning theorists emphasize our cognitive interpretations of external events to fit our memories, beliefs, and expectations.

A basic tenet of the social-learning approach is that cognitive processes greatly influence the molding of personality by mediating between external environmental events and behavior. Thus, unlike the more traditional behavioral approach, the social-learning perspective stresses the role of our thoughts, perceptions, and feelings in acquiring and maintaining our behavior patterns (which in the final analysis represent our personalities). Thus, instead of emphasizing how our environments control us, social-learning theory focuses on the interaction between cognition and environment in shaping personality.

Because of its emphasis on cognitive processes, the social-learning approach is sometimes referred to as the *social-cognitive perspective.* The following paragraphs outline the key tenets of Albert Bandura, the most influential representative of this perspective.

Bandura's Social-Cognitive Perspective

Albert Bandura (b. 1925) is perhaps the most eloquent spokesman for the viewpoint that observational learning strongly influences our behaviors (1982, 1983). Recall from Chapter 6 that observational learning is the process whereby we learn patterns of behavior simply by observing people *(models).* This process allows us to acquire cognitive representations of the behaviors of others, which may then serve as models for our own actions. Bandura maintains that throughout both childhood and adulthood, our

Reciprocal Determinism According to Albert Bandura, the principle that individual behaviors, and thus personalities, are shaped by the interaction between cognitive factors and environmental factors

Self-Efficacy Individual's belief that he or she can perform adequately and deal effectively with a particular situation

observations of which behaviors are rewarded and which are punished or ignored provide us with many such cognitive representations. Accordingly, our own consistent patterns of responding to various situations—in other words, our personality styles—reflect our observational learning.

Bandura has conducted numerous experiments that he believes demonstrate that children may learn "personality traits" through observation. In Chapter 6, we discussed his famous BoBo doll study, which demonstrated that children displayed increased aggression after observing an aggressive model. Another of Bandura's more interesting experiments concerned the ability to delay gratification—a propensity that many people would consider a basic personality trait.

Bandura and Walter Mischel (1965) conducted an experiment with nine- and ten-year-olds to find out whether this trait can be manipulated by observational learning. The experimenters wanted to see if they could modify children's inclinations to prefer immediate or delayed gratification by exposing them to adult models. Their first step was to determine the subjects' preference for high or low delay of reinforcement. They provided each child with a series of test situations in which they could choose between small, immediate reinforcers or larger payoffs for which they had to wait. The next step was to assign a child to one of three conditions: a live adult who modeled behavior opposite to the child's demonstrated preference, a symbolic model (written information) supporting a contrary position, or no model at all. After this phase was completed, the children's preferences were again evaluated by a second series of test situations. Finally, one month later, their preferences were again evaluated to see if any effects of the modeling persisted.

Another keystone of Bandura's social-cognitive perspective is his concept of **reciprocal determinism**. According to this principle, our behaviors, and thus our personalities, are shaped by the interaction between cognitive factors (such as thoughts, feelings, and perceptions) and environmental factors. For example, our response to first meeting our sweetheart's family is likely to be influenced not only by environmental factors (such as whether we meet at their home or in an environment with which we are familiar, such as the campus) but also by personal-cognitive factors such as our past experiences meeting strangers, our degree of anxiety about making a good impression, and our sense of self-worth.

Each of these two sets of factors—cognitive and environmental—can influence and change the other, and the direction of change is typically reciprocal rather than one-way. If we have a history of reinforcing experiences of meeting people for the first time, we are likely to perceive our present situation in a positive way and thus act in a sociable manner. Our actions might also have a decided effect on the environment—for instance, if our sweetheart's parents are so charmed by our friendliness that they quickly shift from aloofness to warm sociability. Thus, environmental stimuli, internal cognitive factors, and behavior all operate as reciprocal determinants of each other.

One final element of the social-cognitive perspective deserves mention. In recent years, Bandura has made the concept of self-efficacy a central component of his theory. **Self-efficacy** is described as our belief that we can perform adequately and deal effectively with a particular situation. Bandura believes that our sense of self-efficacy greatly influences personality development by affecting whether or not we will even try to behave in a certain way. For example, if we think that we are socially inept and boring, we are inclined to avoid social interactions with people. This behavior may cause others to view us as aloof or withdrawn, even further reducing our sense of social self-efficacy.

The concept of self-efficacy is sometimes confused with self-esteem, but Bandura does not equate the two. He views self-efficacy as a collection of specific evaluations that we make about our sense of adequacy in a variety of situations. Thus, a person who feels socially inept may at the same time have a strong sense of artistic self-efficacy.

Self-efficacy arises from a variety of experiences, including our past successes or failures, our observations of the performances of others ("Gee, I think I can do that" or "That looks too hard for me"), and our own particular feelings as we contemplate a task. (Anxiety or depression lower self-efficacy; excitement and anticipation tend to elevate expectations of good performances.)

Beside influencing what activities or situations we become involved in our self-efficacy judgments are likely to influence the amount of effort we exert. For instance, if you perceive yourself as a good student, you will probably be more likely to persist in your efforts to understand a difficult intellectual concept than a student with a lower sense of self-efficacy.

In summary, Bandura's social-cognitive perspective stresses the reciprocal interaction between environmental conditions and our beliefs and expectations. Bandura views people not as slaves to environmental contingencies but rather as individuals capable of assessing situations based on previous experiences, judging their own capability to deal effectively with these situations, and choosing their behavior accordingly.

14.5c Evaluating Behavioral and Social-Learning Theories

Both the behavioral and social-learning approaches focus on the important role of external events in shaping and molding our personalities. Bandura's social-cognitive theory extends this focus to include the reciprocal influence of cognitive behavior and external events.

An important contribution of behavioral and social-learning theories to the field of personality research is their emphasis on rigorous experimental research in testing personality theory. These two perspectives have helped foster a climate of empirical science that is sorely lacking in many other areas of personality theory.

Behavioral and social-learning theories have also provided important insights into why behavior may change from situation to situation, and why certain presumably enduring aspects of personality may not be so enduring after all. As we see in Chapter 16, the behavioral perspective has been the basis of some of our most effective models for altering dysfunctional behavior.

Behavioral theories have also received considerable criticism. As you might expect, much of this criticism comes from psychoanalytic and humanistic psychologists who emphasize the role of inner drives and needs in determining behavior. Other criticism comes from those who argue that personality is largely determined by genetics. Although Skinner and other behavioral theorists don't discount the role of genetic factors in personality, they consider genetic factors to be less important in determining individual differences in personality than environmental influences.

14.6 The Assessment of Personality

In our overview of trait theories and the psychoanalytic, humanistic, and behavioral perspectives, we have seen a variety of descriptions and explanations of human personality. Thus, it should come as no surprise that *personality assessment*, the measurement or assessment of personality, has been approached in a variety of ways.

Indeed, personality assessment is far from an exact science, and the reason has to do with the difficulty in pinpointing the subject matter. If psychologists limited their interests in human personality only to those overt behaviors that can be directly observed, the task of personality assessment would be relatively straightforward. However, as we have learned, personality theorists are also interested in the unconscious mechanisms, behavioral predispositions, and traits that presumably underlie our actions. How can abstractions like repression, anxiety, introversion, dominance, the self, and self-actualization be measured? Psychologists have devised a variety of methods for at least obtaining glimpses of these seemingly intangible dimensions. We comment on how well they have succeeded as we outline four of the most important methods: behavioral observation, interviews, paper-and-pencil questionnaires, and projective tests.

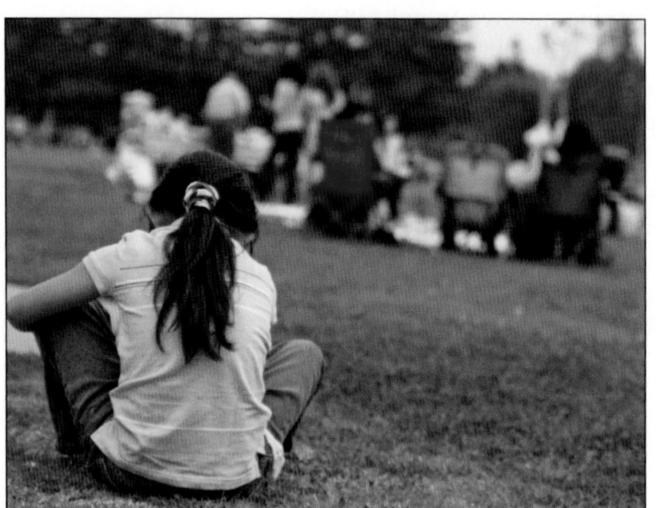
(iStock)

If a person is observed always sitting alone, the behavioral observation may be made that the person is shy and withdrawn.

14.6a Behavioral Observation

If you notice that a classmate always sits alone and appears flustered when a question is directed his way, you probably infer that he is shy and withdrawn. Similarly, if a roommate always remembers to deliver phone messages and cleans up after herself, you may conclude that she is a responsible person. Virtually all of us develop impressions of people by observing how they act. This process is the essence of one personality assessment method, **behavioral observation**. The assumption underlying this technique is that personality is best assessed within the environment in which behavior occurs. Behavioral and social-learning theorists who emphasize people's interactions with their environments favor this method. In their view, this technique is the best and most logical procedure for identifying the environmental events associated with particular types of behavior.

Clinical psychologists, clinical social workers, and psychiatrists also use this method to gain insight into their clients' personalities. For example, a client's gestures, manner of speaking, facial expressions, and reactions to the clinician's questions can all provide important information.

As logical and practical as this technique may seem, however, it also can be misleading. Certainly, all of us have discovered from time to time that our initial conclusions about people do not always hold up over time. For example, you might be surprised to observe your shy, introverted classmate talking animatedly and dancing up a storm at a party. Our observations of people can be misleading because they typically provide an opportunity to observe behavior in only a limited range of circumstances. The behavior we happen to observe in any given situation may not be at all typical of an individual's personality.

Can you think of any techniques that could make the behavioral observation method a more reliable tool for assessing personality? Take a moment to consider this question before reading on.

Behavioral Observation
Behavior assessment method that involves observing individuals' behavior as they interact with the environment

Psychologists sometimes go to considerable lengths to engage in more structured observations of behavior in a variety of situations. For example, a child psychologist interested in studying personality development in small children might observe a child's behavior in the natural setting of the classroom, playground, and at home with family.

By carefully recording the times and places certain behaviors occur (such as sharing things with others, engaging in aggressive behavior, acting in a submissive manner, or displaying dependency behaviors), important information might be obtained about the role of the environment in shaping certain personality traits.

Interview Method used in psychological studies in which an individual is asked questions that may be informal and unstructured or highly structured

This more structured approach to behavioral observation improves the reliability and precision of measurement. As we saw in Chapter 2, however, it is also limited because an observer's presence may influence the subject's behavior; any one observer's interpretation of behavior may reflect his or her own biases. Furthermore, as a matter of practicality, any observer is generally able to sample only a relatively limited range of a subject's behaviors in only a few situations.

14.6b Interviews

Another valuable method of learning about an individual's personality is to ask that person questions. Freud relied heavily on the **interview** approach; today advocates of all the theoretical perspectives we have considered, including the behaviorists, use interviews. Interviews range from informal, unstructured exchanges in which an interviewer asks a few broad questions and encourages the subject to talk extensively, to much more structured procedures in which very specific questions are asked in a prescribed sequence.

An important advantage of the interview technique is its flexibility. If some questions are confusing, the interviewer can clarify them; their sequence can also be varied to meet the subject's needs. A competent interviewer can establish a sense of rapport that may encourage more candor than that produced by less personal assessment methods, such as questionnaires. This technique also allows interviewers to delve into whatever areas of personality interest them. Unstructured interviews also provide the option of pursuing or dropping a particular line of questioning, depending on the amount of useful information that is being produced. Furthermore, an interview allows an interviewer to assess not only what a subject says, but also how it is said.

The interview method also has its limitations. The basic data of interviews—what people say about themselves—is virtually impossible to quantify. As a result, what gets recorded are largely the interviewer's impressions and inferences, and these are subject to observer bias. Secondly, since there is no standard way of conducting an interview, an interviewer's personal style may significantly influence the subject's responses. The same subject may respond gregariously to a warm, affable interviewer but hold back information when interviewed by someone with a less approachable style. Extensive clinical evidence suggests that an interviewer's approach may also influence the subject. It is noteworthy that interviewers who have a strong theoretical perspective on personality may influence subjects to respond in ways that are supportive of the interviewer's position.

(iStock)

An important advantage of the interview method is its flexibility.

While the observational and interview methods have strengths, neither method is as standardized or objective as personality psychologists would like them to be.

Paper-and-Pencil Questionnaire In personality testing, an objective, self-reporting inventory designed to scientifically measure the variety of characteristics or traits that make up personality

While both techniques allow psychologists to observe what people do or say, there is always the concern that knowing how people behave may not reveal what they are thinking or feeling. To compensate for these shortcomings, psychologists have developed a number of **paper-and-pencil questionnaires**: objective, self-report inventories designed to measure scientifically the variety of characteristics or traits that make up personality.

14.6c Questionnaires

Most paper-and-pencil questionnaires ask subjects to rate as true or false a collection of statements about their thoughts, feelings, and behaviors. Some of these questionnaires are designed to measure a very limited range of traits (Cattell's 16PF and the Five-Factor Model) or only a single personality characteristic such as anxiety, self-concept, or introversion-extroversion. Others are designed to provide more global measures of personality. Two noteworthy examples of questionnaires are the Minnesota Multiphasic Personality Inventory and the California Psychological Inventory.

Minnesota Multiphasic Personality Inventory

The best-known and most widely used objective personality inventory is the *Minnesota Multiphasic Personality Inventory*, or *MMPI* (Hathaway & McKinley, 1942). Originally designed to help diagnose and classify people with behavioral disorders, its developers started with a pool of one thousand possible test-item statements describing mood states, attitudes, and overt behavior. These statements were drawn from such sources as existing tests and psychiatry and psychology textbooks. Following a test development procedure similar to that described in Chapter 13 (see "How Intelligence Tests Are Developed"), the researchers administered these items to a standardization group of approximately two hundred psychiatric patients with a variety of diagnosed disorders and to 724 so-called normal individuals recruited from university applicants, hospital visitors, and residents of Minneapolis.

This procedure resulted in an early version of the MMPI that consisted of 566 statements about behavior, thoughts, or emotional reactions that the subjects rate as "true" of themselves, "false," or "cannot say" (undecided about the truth of the statement). Examples of the kinds of items found on the MMPI include "I am basically a happy person"; "I believe people are plotting against me"; "Sometimes I disobey laws"; and "I worry a lot about sex." (These examples are not exact replicas of MMPI items.)

The current revision of the MMPI (MMPI-2-RF) still contains 10 clinical scales designed to measure such conditions as depression, social introversion, schizophrenia, paranoia, and psychopathic personality. It also includes four validity scales designed to assess whether subjects have falsified or faked their answers. Table 14-6 lists all fourteen clinical and validity scales on the MMPI-2.

The MMPI is widely used for its original purpose of diagnosing behavioral disorders. Many clinical psychologists today find it helpful as an aid to the diagnostic process, and personality psychologists have also found it a useful source of information about the personalities of normal people. In fact, the MMPI has been translated and used in over one hundred different languages.

14.6d Projective Tests

Paper-and-pencil questionnaires such as the MMPI are relatively easy to standardize, administer, and score because they are highly structured and empirically constructed.

Table 14-6 MMPI-2 Scales and Descriptions

Scale	Abbreviation	Definition
		Validity Scales
Question	?	Corresponds to number of items left unanswered
Lie	L	Lies or is highly conventional
Frequency	F	Exaggerates complaints, answers haphazardly
Correction	K	Denies problems
		Clinical Scales
Hypochondriasis	Hs	Expresses bodily concerns and complaints
Depression	D	Is depressed, pessimistic, guilty
Hysteria	Hy	Reacts to stress with physical symptoms, lacks insight
Psychopathic deviant	Pd	Is immoral, in conflict with the law, involved in stormy relationships
Masculinity, femininity	Mf	Has interests characteristic of stereotypical sex roles
Paranoia	Pa	Is suspicious, resentful
Psychasthenia	Pt	Is anxious, worried, high-strung
Schizophrenia	Sc	Is confused, disorganized, disoriented
Hypomania	Ma	Is energetic, active, easily bored, restless
Social introversion	Si	Is introverted, timid, shy, lacking self-confidence

Their tight structure, however, can also be a liability, particularly because subjects must limit responses to "true," "false," or "cannot say." Partly in response to this limitation and partly out of a desire to tap unconscious thoughts and feelings, psychologists have developed projective tests.

Projective tests are collectively distinguished by a loose structure and unclear or ambiguous stimuli that allow respondents a wide latitude of response. Because the tests do not have obviously correct or socially more or less desirable responses, it is assumed that subjects "project" their own thoughts or feelings into their responses—hence the name projective tests or techniques. The underlying rationale, manner of development, and application of projective techniques is based primarily on psychoanalytic theory, which predicts that people will resort to hidden or inner processes to project structure onto ambiguous stimuli. A trained examiner then applies subjective clinical judgment to draw inferences about such dimensions of personality as unconscious conflicts, repressed impulses, hidden fears, and ego defenses. The two most commonly used projective techniques are the Rorschach inkblot test and the Thematic Apperception Test.

Projective Tests Personality tests that consist of loosely structured, ambiguous stimuli that require the subject's interpretation

Figure 14-5 A Sample Rorschach Inkblot

What does this image make you think of?

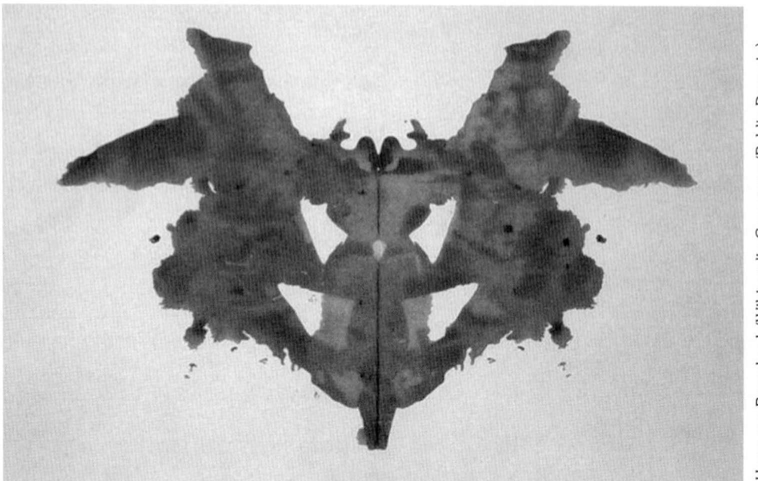

(Hermann Rorschach/Wikimedia Commons/Public Domain)

"A Sample of Rorschach Inkblot," by Hermann Rorschach.

The Rorschach Inkblot Test

The **Rorschach inkblot test**, developed in 1921 by Swiss psychiatrist Hermann Rorschach, consists of ten cards showing inkblots, such as the one in Figure 14-5. Blots are presented to a subject one at a time in an order prescribed by Rorschach. The subject is asked to examine each of the blots and say what it looks like or brings to mind.

Scoring of the Rorschach is highly complex, involving extensive training in one of several systems by which the responses are coded, scored, and interpreted. However, all of the various systems agree that the major scoring categories for each response include its *location* (where the subject focuses attention), its *determinants* (color, implied movement, shading, particular form, etc.), and its *content* (human, nonhuman animal, or object). Various interpretations may be assigned to a subject's responses. For example, if a person focuses on only a small portion of a blot, this tendency might indicate that this person pays attention to the little details and likes things to be neat and orderly. A person who gives very unusual or unique responses might be considered to be overly concerned with asserting independence and individuality, whereas someone who gives many obvious and common responses might be considered to be conventional and anxious to blend in with the crowd. These interpretations are very subjective, however; even the experts who work with the Rorschach all the time do not always agree on how various responses should be interpreted.

Rorschach Inkblot Test
Commonly used projective test in which the subject is asked to examine inkblots and say what they look like or bring to mind

The fact that clinicians who regularly use the Rorschach often disagree in their interpretations raises serious doubts about its validity as a diagnostic instrument. One of the problems in assessing the validity of the Rorschach test is that most clinicians use it along with several other diagnostic procedures. Thus, they typically interpret a person's Rorschach responses in the context of information obtained from such sources as interviews, family members, and other kinds of tests. As a result, it is very difficult to assess the capacity of this instrument by itself to provide valid personality assessments and accurate predictions of behavior. When researchers have attempted to study the diagnostic and predictive accuracy of Rorschach scores in isolation from other sources of information, they have found them to have little or no predictive validity.

Despite this liability, the Rorschach continues to be a widely used instrument for clinical diagnosis and personality assessment. Many clinical practitioners point out that the validity studies are not a fair representation of the manner in which they use the Rorschach in their practices. They claim that the Rorschach is just one of many assessment devices they use to evaluate their clients, and, as such, it continues to be a valuable diagnostic resource.

Thematic Apperception Test (TAT) Projective test for personality assessment in which the subject is shown cards depicting various scenes and is asked to describe what is happening in each scene

The Thematic Apperception Test

You may recall being introduced to the **Thematic Apperception Test (TAT)**, in Chapter 8, where we discussed its application in assessing achievement needs. The TAT consists of thirty cards that depict various scenes and one blank card (a redrawn example is shown in Figure 14-6). While recognizable, all the pictures are vague and ambiguous. In the standard administration of the TAT, the tester selects twenty cards on the basis of the sex and age of the subject, who is then shown the cards one at a time and asked to describe what is going on in each scene, what the characters are thinking and feeling, what led up to the portrayed situation, and what its outcome will be.

Like the Rorschach inkblot test, the TAT is based on the assumption that when people are asked to respond to unstructured stimuli, they will reveal certain aspects of their inner selves that they normally keep to themselves. As one of the developers of the TAT observed, "The test is based on the well-recognized fact that when a person interprets an ambiguous social situation, he is apt to expose his own personality as much as the phenomenon to which he is attending" (Murray, 1938, p. 530).

Formal systems for scoring and interpreting TAT responses are available. However, most clinicians tend to disregard these systems, relying instead on their own impressionistic, subjective assessments. Typically clinicians look for common themes that run through the stories (hence the term *thematic*). For example, if a person told several stories with themes of loneliness or isolation, an examiner might interpret this response as a sign of depression or alienation.

How valid is the TAT for clinical diagnosis? Many examiners use only a few cards that they think will be most productive in revealing aspects of a particular client's personality. This preselection compromises efforts to assess the test's validity because the clinician is likely to draw upon other sources of information in making the initial judgment about which cards to use. Furthermore, scoring tends to be highly subjective, based on an examiner's experience and clinical judgment that has already been influenced by knowledge of the subject. However, when the TAT has been used as a research tool in controlled experiments, it has demonstrated adequate levels of validity. An example is the research discussed in Chapter 8 that measured the relationship between need to achieve and various behaviors, in which the TAT was used to measure achievement motivation.

In all, although a wide range of methods are used to assess personality, none are without limitations. Most psychologists agree, however, that it is important to continue our efforts to understand the distinctive needs, values, and patterns of behavior that characterize individuals' adaptations to the situations of their lives. Therefore we can expect that personality assessment devices will continue to evolve.

Figure 14-6 A Sample Redrawn from One Card in the Thematic Apperception Test

After examining the drawing, write a brief description of the scene.

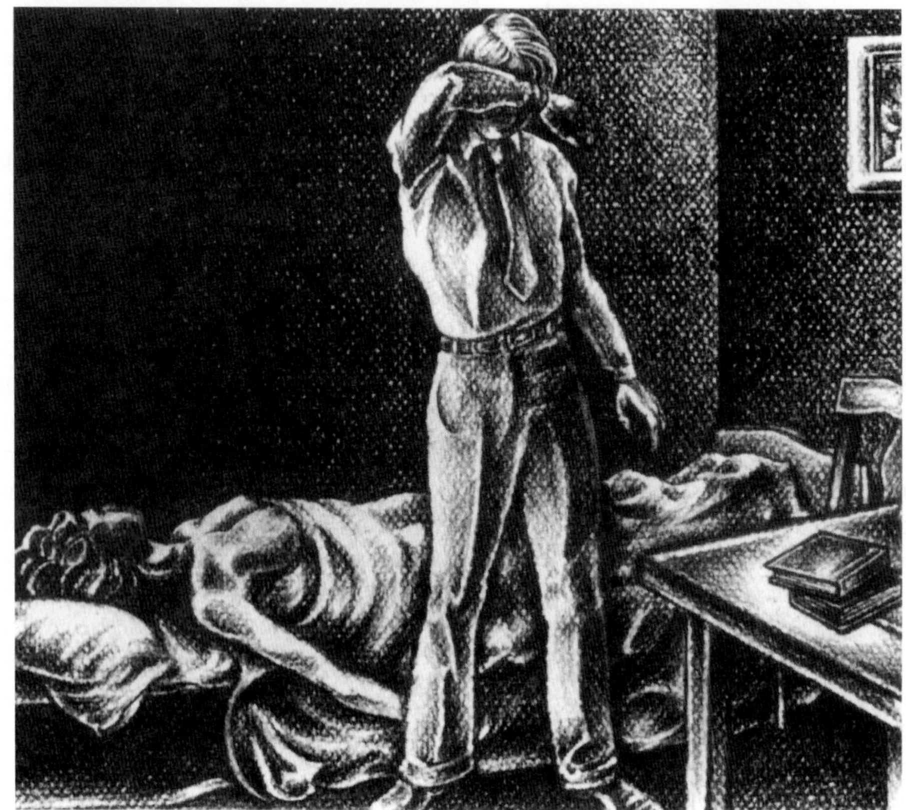

In the next chapter, we will continue with the topic of personality as we examine some of the most common personality and behavioral disorders. As we will see, the issues of definition, assessment, and genetic versus environmental determination that we discussed in this chapter will resurface.

CHAPTER REVIEW

Defining Personality

1. Personality is not an attribute that people possess in varying amounts. Rather, personality refers to the distinctive patterns of behavior that characterize each individual's adaptation to life situations.
2. We may best describe personality psychology as the study of individuals, their distinctive characteristics and traits, and the manner in which they integrate all aspects of their psychological functioning as they adapt to their environments.

Theories of Personality

3. Trait theorists attempt to identify the behavioral traits that are the building blocks of personality.
4. Gordon Allport's application of the idiographic approach led to a description of three types of traits that operate to produce an individual's unique personality structure. A cardinal trait is a dominating behavioral predisposition that provides the pivotal point in a person's life. Central traits are major characteristics of someone's personality, such as honesty or generosity. Finally, secondary traits are less enduring behavioral tendencies, such as dress style preference.
5. Raymond Cattell's nomothetic approach has yielded a list of sixteen primary or source traits that he considers to be the center or core of personality. He lists each of these traits as a pair of polar opposites, such as trusting versus suspicious. Cattell developed the 16 PF Personality Test.
6. The Five-Factor Model of personality has been widely adopted by personality psychologists. It includes the traits neuroticism, extroversion, agreeableness, openness to new experiences, and conscientiousness.
7. According to the Five-Factor Model, personality tends to stabilize around the time of one's thirties.
8. Critics of trait theories maintain that traits are only descriptions, not explanations, which so-called personality traits may be situational-dependent, and that trait theories offer essentially no understanding of how personality develops.

Psychoanalytic Theory

9. Sigmund Freud's psychoanalytic theory of personality evolved from his attempts to explain certain recurrent themes that emerged from his psychoanalysis of patients.
10. The psychoanalytic theory of personality depicts people as shaped by ongoing conflict between their primary drives, particularly sex and aggression, and the social pressures of civilized society. Freud also theorized that early childhood experiences play a major role in molding personality.

CHAPTER REVIEW

11. According to Freud, the dynamics of personality reside in the continuous interactions of the impulse-driven id, the guilt-inducing superego, and the ego, which acts as mediator by reconciling reality with the demands of both the id and the superego.

12. Freud maintained that the ego experiences anxiety when an impulse that is unacceptable to the superego threatens to be expressed in overt behavior. When the ego is not able to relieve this anxiety through rational methods, it resorts to certain less rational maneuvers called defense mechanisms that include repression, rationalization, projection, displacement, sublimation, regression, and reaction formation.

13. Freud theorized that a child progresses through a series of stages of psychosexual development in which the focus of sexual gratification shifts from one body site (erogenous zone) to another. During the first phase, the oral stage (from birth to twelve to eighteen months), the lips and the mouth are the erogenous zone. During the second or anal stage (twelve to eighteen months to age three), the erogenous zone shifts from the mouth to the anal area. During the third, phallic, stage (ages three to five or six), the focus of sexual gratification shifts to genital stimulation. The latency period (age five or six to puberty) is characterized by unexpressed or latent sexual drives. Finally, during the genital stage (from puberty on), sexual feelings are expressed in sexual relations with people outside the family.

14. Too much or too little gratification can result in a child becoming arrested or fixated at an early stage of psychosexual development.

15. Criticisms of psychoanalytic theory include concern about the inability to define operationally and test some of its basic tenets, its lack of clear-cut predictions about how specific experiences will affect personality and behavior, its failure to appreciate the strengths of healthy personalities, its overemphasis on the importance of early experiences, and the inherent assumption that women are inferior to men in a number of ways.

16. The neo-Freudians were a group of individuals, originally disciples of Freud, whose disagreement with some of Freud's basic tenets led them to develop their own psychoanalytic perspectives on human personality.

17. Carl Jung's major contribution was his concept of the collective unconscious, a storehouse of universal images or thoughts possessed by all humans. Jung also provided psychology with the concept of two opposite personality traits, introversion and extroversion.

18. Alfred Adler conceptualized striving for superiority as a universal urge to achieve self-perfection that emerges from childhood feelings of inferiority.

19. Karen Horney disagreed with Freud's emphasis on sexuality and aggression as determinants of personality. She developed a theory of neurosis based on ten neurotic needs.

CHAPTER REVIEW

Humanistic Theories of Personality

20. The humanistic personality theorists agree that a primary motivation for behavior comes from each person's strivings to develop, change, and grow in pursuit of the full realization of human potential.
21. Central to Carl Rogers's theory of personality was the concept of the self, the basic core of our being that is the central organizing, all-encompassing structure that accounts for the coherence and stability of our personalities.
22. Rogers believed that the key to healthy adjustment and happiness is a consistency or congruence between our self-concept and our experiences.
23. Abraham Maslow's theory of motivation and personality emphasizes people's positive strivings for intimacy, joy, love, a sense of belonging, self-esteem, and fulfillment of their highest potential.
24. Critics have objected to the vague, subjective nature of many humanistic concepts; the humanists have been criticized for basing theories on subjective, unverifiable observations of people in clinical or natural settings. The humanists have also been criticized for focusing so closely on the individual and the role of the self that they have largely ignored the impact of biological and environmental factors in shaping behavior.

Behavioral and Social-Learning Theories of Personality

25. According to the behavioral position, our personalities are determined by interactions with our environment and maintained by contingencies of reinforcement and punishment.
26. From the perspective of behaviorism, each person's own unique history of conditioning is the major contributor to the development of his or her unique personality. Personalities vary in different contexts because the contingencies for maintaining our personalities change in these different contexts.
27. Social-learning theorists also believe that external events are important determiners of personality. However, unlike traditional behaviorists, social-learning theorists emphasize our cognitive interpretations of external events to fit our memories, beliefs, and expectations.
28. According to Albert Bandura, our own consistent patterns of responding to various situations—in other words, our personality styles—reflect our observational learning (the process whereby we learn patterns of behavior simply by observing people).
29. Another keystone of Bandura's social-cognitive perspective is his concept of reciprocal determinism, which suggests that our personalities are shaped by the interaction between cognitive factors and environmental factors.

CHAPTER REVIEW

30. Bandura also believes that self-efficacy, or our belief that we can perform adequately and deal effectively with situations, greatly influences personality development by affecting whether or not we will even try to behave in a certain way.

The Assessment of Personality

31. Four of the most important methods for assessing personality include behavioral observations, interviews, paper-and-pencil questionnaires, and projective tests.
32. The assumption underlying behavioral observation is that personality is best assessed within the environment in which behaviors occur. Limitations of this method include the fact that an observer's presence may influence the subject's behavior and that any one observer's interpretations of behavior may reflect his or her own biases. To remedy these shortcomings, psychologists engage in more structured observations of behavior in a variety of situations.
33. Interviews, which range from informal, unstructured exchanges to much more structured procedures, have the important advantage of flexibility (questions can be clarified, sequence varied, etc.). However, it is virtually impossible to quantify the basic data of the interviewer's impressions and inferences, both of which are subject to observer bias.
34. Paper-and-pencil questionnaires are objective self-report inventories that typically ask subjects to rate a collection of statements about their thoughts, feelings, and behaviors. Examples include Cattell's 16PF and the Five-Factor Model.
35. The best-known and most widely used objective personality inventory is the Minnesota Multiphasic Personality Inventory (MMPI, MMPI-2-RF), which is designed to measure a variety of clinical conditions such as depression and paranoia. The MMPI is widely used for diagnosing psychological disorders. Criticisms of the MMPI concern its original standardization group, its reliability and validity, and its tendency to invade the privacy of the test taker. MMPI-2, the first revision of the original MMPI, employs restandardized norms that are more representative of the present population than the original norms.
36. Projective tests are collectively distinguished by a loose structure and ambiguous stimuli that allow respondents to project their own thoughts or feelings into their responses.
37. The Rorschach inkblot test, which consists of ten cards showing inkblots, has little or no predictive validity when considered in isolation from other sources of information.
38. The Thematic Apperception Test (TAT), which consists of a series of cards that depict various scenes, allows clinicians to look for common themes that run through the stories subjects tell about each scene. When the TAT has been used as a research tool in controlled experiments, it has demonstrated adequate validity.

TERMS AND CONCEPTS

Agreeableness, pg. 554
Anal Stage, pg. 565
Anxiety, pg. 562
Archetypes, pg. 568
Behavioral Observationt, pg. 578
Cardinal Trait, pg. 553
Central Trait, pg. 553
Collective Unconscious, pg. 568
Conscientiousness, pg. 555
Defense Mechanism, pg. 562
Displacement, pg. 564
Ego, pg. 560
Electra Complex, pg. 566
Extraversion, pg. 554
Five-Factor Model of Personality, pg. 553
Fixation, pg. 566
Free Association, pg. 558
Genital Stage, pg. 566
Id, pg. 559
Interview, pg. 579
Introversion , pg. 568
Latency Period, pg. 566
Libido, pg. 559
Neo-Freudian, pg. 568
Neuroticism, pg. 554
Oedipus Complex, pg. 566
Openness to Experiences, pg. 554
Oral Stage, pg. 565
Paper-and-Pencil Questionnaire, pg. 580
Penis Envy, pg. 569
Personality, pg. 551
Personal Unconscious, pg. 568
Phallic Stage, pg. 566
Pleasure Principle, pg. 559
Primary Process Thinking, pg. 560
Projection, pg. 564
Projective Tests, pg. 581
Psychoanalysis, pg. 558
Psychoanalytic Theory, pg. 559
Psychosexual Development, pg. 565
Rationalization, pg. 564
Reaction Formation, pg. 565
Reality Principle, pg. 560
Reciprocal Determinism, pg. 576
Regression, pg. 564
Repression, pg. 563
Rorschach Inkblot Test, pg. 582
Secondary Trait, pg. 553
Self-Efficacy, pg. 576
Source Traits, pg. 553
Striving for Superiority, pg. 569
Sublimation, pg. 564
Superego, pg. 560
Surface Traits, pg. 553
Thematic Apperception Test (TAT), pg. 583
Unconscious Mind, pg. 558

POP QUIZ

True or False

___ 1. Trait theories are descriptive theories that attempt to identify specific dimensions or characteristics of personality.

___ 2. One main criticism of trait theories is that people do not behave as consistently from one situation to another as trait theories would tend to predict.

___ 3. To Sigmund Freud, the dynamics of personality centered around conflict between the impulse-driven id, the guilt-inducing superego, and the ego or mediator.

___ 4. According to Abraham Maslow, self-actualized individuals tend to be conformists.

___ 5. Both behavioral observation and interviews might be influenced by observer bias.

Multiple Choice

6. Personality psychology may best be described as the study of which of the following?
   a. How much personality an individual has
   b. Individuals
   c. The development of personality traits
   d. The consistency of personality traits
7. Which of the following is ***not*** a common criticism of trait theories?
   a. These do not explain behavior but only label behavior as being the result of a personality trait.
   b. People's behavior is not as consistent from situation to situation as trait theories would have us believe.
   c. They do not attempt to describe behavior.
   d. They do not explain how personality develops.
8. Which concept does ***not*** belong with the other three?
   a. Reality principle
   b. Ego-ideal
   c. Superego
   d. Conscience
9. Which of the following pairs of terms do ***not*** belong together?
   a. Anal stage/toilet training
   b. Latency stage/Oedipus complex
   c. Oral stage/sucking
   d. Phallic stage/genital stimulation

POP QUIZ

10. ________ suggested that all people acquire a feeling of inferiority early in childhood.
    a. Adler
    b. Rogers
    c. Jung
    d. Allport
11. According to Carl Rogers, the person that you would like to become is your ________ self.
    a. goal
    b. ideal
    c. real
    d. future
12. What is one main criticism of humanistic theories?
    a. They emphasize the unconscious id more than the conscious superego.
    b. It is difficult to conduct experiments examining the concepts of humanistic theories.
    c. They do not emphasize negative influences on personality development.
    d. They completely ignore cognitive factors.
13. What principle is involved in the following situation? You find the students at your college to be friendly because most of them smile and say "Hi" when you greet them, whereas your roommate finds the students to be unfriendly and says no one ever smiles or says "Hi" to her.
    a. Rationalization
    b. Self-efficacy
    c. Reciprocal determinism
    d. Basic anxiety
14. Which of the following is ***not*** an important method used to assess an individual's personality?
    a. Psychoanalysis
    b. Paper-and-pencil questionnaires
    c. Projective tests
    d. Behavioral observation
15. If a psychologist asks you to tell a story concerning a scene on a card he or she shows you, that psychologist is giving you the ____________________:
    a. MMPI
    b. TAT
    c. 16PF
    d. Rorschach inkblot test

Answer Key: 1.T 2.T 3.T 4.F 5.T 6.b 7.c 8.a 9.b 10.a 11.b 12.b 13.c 14.a 15.b

(iStock)

Chapter 15

Behavioral Disorders

The letter in Figure 15-1 was written to the director of a state hospital by a patient who was being treated for a severe mood disorder (bipolar disorder). This patient made repeated attempts for release as well as numerous claims that his psychologist was a communist who beat and starved patients. Notice that although there is evidence of distorted thought, the writing is mostly coherent and organized. The style of writing here is also characteristic of severe mood disorder in that it is forceful and directed off the page.

Figure 15-2 represents a sample of doodling made by a patient at the same hospital diagnosed with schizophrenia. Notice here that the writing is not very coherent and that there are numerous references to Christianity and sex. These kinds of references are not uncommon with schizophrenic disorders.

Although these samples of behavior are not sufficient for a diagnosis, it is not difficult to see that these patients are severely disturbed. In fact, when someone's behavior deviates extremely from the way people customarily behave or speak, no one would question labeling their behavior abnormal.

What about the schoolteacher who functions well in his everyday life but confides in a friend that sometimes he hears the voice of his deceased child? Or the woman who becomes so melancholic in the winter she spends most of her day sleeping? Or the person who seems normal but refuses to ride in elevators? Are these also examples of abnormal behavior? Defining abnormality is not always an easy task. There are shades of gray on the continuum from normal to abnormal, and it is often difficult to know where to draw the line.

Psychology and psychiatry have a long history of debate in the interrelated areas of defining abnormality and classifying behavioral disorders. However, after extensive discussions and many changes, clinicians are beginning to reach some consensus about what constitutes disordered behavior. In this chapter, we first look at the criteria for defining abnormality and the classification of behavioral disorders; then we look more closely at some specific behavioral disorders.

15.1 Defining Abnormal Behavior

There is no universally accepted definition of mental illness or abnormality. However, psychologists who specialize in studying abnormal behavior tend to emphasize a common core of four criteria that may be used to distinguish between normal and **abnormal behavior**: *atypicality, dysfunctional, distressful*, and *dangerous*.

The behavior of the people described in the opening account is certainly *atypical*, and indeed all of the behavioral disorders that we consider in this chapter are atypical in a statistical sense. However, rarity alone is not a sufficient criterion for determining that a behavior is abnormal or disordered. If it were, we would have to conclude that people like Albert Einstein and Leonardo da Vinci were behaviorally disordered. More important from a psychological perspective is that the behaviors associated with behavioral disorders are often *dysfunctional*. That is, the individual's ability to function adequately in everyday social and occupational roles is impaired. The degree of dysfunction in behavioral disorders varies from relatively minor to so severe that a person may need to be hospitalized. Some psychologists believe that dysfunction may be the most important criterion for distinguishing behavioral disorders.

Despite the myth that severely disordered people are in their own little worlds that may be more comforting than the real world, people with behavioral disorders often experience a great deal of *emotional distress*. This third criterion may take the form of anxiety, depression, or agitation. People afflicted with some mental disorders are in considerable emotional pain. Finally, the behaviors of behaviorally disordered people are

Abnormal Behavior
Behavior that is atypical, maladaptive, or socially unacceptable, or that produces emotional discomfort

Figure 15-1 Letter from a Mental Patient to the Director of the State Hospital Where the Patient Was Being Treated for a Severe Mood Disorder

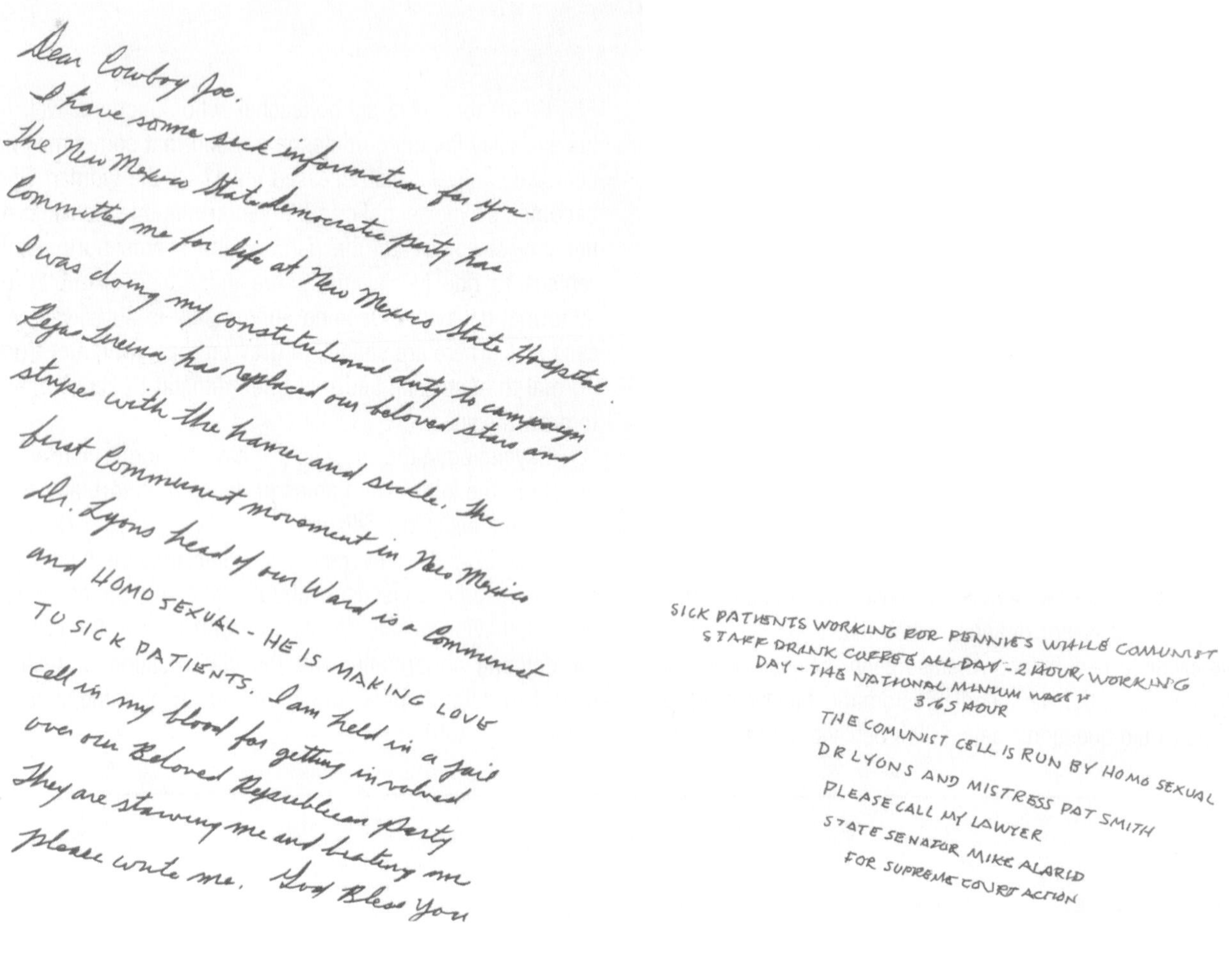

Dear Cowboy Joe.
I have some sick information for you.
The New Mexico State democratic party has
Committed me for life at New Mexico State Hospital.
I was doing my constitutional duty to campaign
Reya Lorena has replaced our beloved stars and
stripes with the hammer and sickle. The
first Communist movement in New Mexico
Dr. Lyons head of our Ward is a Communist
and HOMO SEXUAL - HE IS MAKING LOVE
TO SICK PATIENTS. I am held in a jail
cell in my blood for getting involved
over our Beloved Republican Party
They are starving me and beating me
Please write me. God Bless You

SICK PATIENTS WORKING FOR PENNIES WHILE COMUNIST
STAFF DRANK COFFEE ALL DAY - 2 HOUR WORKING
DAY - THE NATIONAL MINIUM WAGE IS
3.65 HOUR
THE COMUNIST CELL IS RUN BY HOMO SEXUAL
DR LYONS AND MISTRESS PAT SMITH
PLEASE CALL MY LAWYER
STATE SENATOR MIKE ALARID
FOR SUPREME COURT ACTION

Courtesy of Dr. Charles Lyons.

often judged to be *dangerous* to themselves or to others. Behaviors that reflect poor judgment, hostility, or injury to self or others may be signs of abnormality. However, contrary to popular assumptions, people with behavioral disorders such as anxiety, depression, or even schizophrenia are rarely in danger of inflicting injury to themselves or to others.

It is important to note that, to a certain extent, definitions of what is normal are both culturally based and era dependent. For example, while we may consider talking to oneself or hallucinating imaginary voices to be clear signs of a serious behavioral disorder, these same behaviors are viewed by people in certain Polynesian and South American societies as indications of a great gift or special status among deities.

All four characteristics of abnormality are not necessarily evident in all behavioral disorders. Aside from the fact that they are all atypical or uncommon, any given disorder may reflect only one or a combination of the characteristics of being atypical, dysfunctional, or in emotional distress. Specific symptoms also vary according to the disorder,

Figure 15-2 Doodling Produced by a Patient Diagnosed with Schizophrenia

Note references to Christianity and sex.

Courtesy of Dr. Charles Lyons.

BVT Lab

Flashcards are available for this chapter at www.BVTLab.com.

and these symptoms form the basis for classifying disorders. Although we will find that it is often hard to define abnormal behavior, practitioners are often in agreement on diagnosing and classifying them.

15.2 Classifying Behavioral Disorders

The first widely accepted system for classifying behavioral disorders was published in 1952 by the American Psychiatric Association in the *Diagnostic and Statistical Manual of Mental Disorders*, conveniently shortened to *DSM-I*. This scheme, which listed the symptoms of sixty disorders, was poorly organized and widely criticized. An improved version, *DSM-II*, was published in 1968. In 1987, the American Psychiatric Association published a revision of *DSM-III (DSM-III-R)* that provided even more precise behavioral criteria for diagnosing a broad array of behavioral disorders. *DSM-III-R* was the most widely used scheme for diagnosing and classifying behavioral disorders throughout the world. In 1994, the American Psychiatric Association released *DSM-IV,* and in 2000, it released *DSM-IV-TR* (text revision), which, like its predecessor, relied extensively on empirical research on the diagnosis of behavioral disorders. In 2013, the American Psychiatric Association released *DSM-5*, which again reclassified several of the major psychological disorders and refined diagnostic criteria for many of them. The behavioral disorders presented here include anxiety disorders, post-traumatic stress disorder, obsessive-compulsive disorder, depressive disorders, bipolar disorder, dissociative disorders, schizophrenia, and personality disorders. These disorders were selected because they are among the most common of the behavioral disorders or because they are unusual and interesting.

It is possible that some of the behaviors described in this chapter may not be all that different from those of your friends, loved ones, or even yourself. Does this similarity mean that people you know who share some of these symptoms are disordered? Although we all have times when we are depressed, anxious, or somewhat disorganized in our thinking, the key to diagnosis of a behavioral disorder is the possession of a cluster of symptoms that are persistent rather than transitory. Therefore, do not be too hard on yourself (or your friends). It has been estimated, however, that as many as 50 percent of the U.S. population will experience a diagnosable behavioral disorder at some point in their lives (Centers for Disease Control and Prevention, 2017; Kessler et al., 2005).

We end our discussion of each major category of disorder with an overview of theoretical explanations. Space limitations prevent us from considering them all. Therefore, each discussion includes a brief summary of the three best known *etiological* (explanatory) perspectives: psychoanalytic theory, behavioral explanations, and biological explanations. Chapter 16 discusses the treatment options for these behavioral disorders.

15.3 Attention-Deficit/Hyperactivity Disorder

Attention-Deficit/Hyperactivity Disorder (ADHD) A neurodevelopmental disorder characterized by inattention, lack of impulse control, and hyperactivity.

Attention-deficit/hyperactivity disorder (ADHD) is defined as a pattern of inattention and hyperactivity that interferes with educational, social, or occupational functioning (American Psychiatric Association, 2013). Typically, ADHD is first recognized in elementary school-aged children when they have difficulty sustaining their attention sufficiently to organize and manage tasks and activities. Children with ADHD not only lack in their ability to maintain attention but also commonly have difficulties in impulse control. They may speak out of turn, interrupt others, and fidget, causing distraction to others. The incidence of ADHD has been increasing at an alarming rate over the past few decades.

In 2000, the prevalence of U.S. children between the ages of four and seventeen being diagnosed with ADHD was about 7.5 percent. In 2015, this had increased to more than 13 percent, or seven million children (Centers for Disease Control and Prevention, 2015). Most often the symptoms of ADHD begin to dissipate in early adulthood, perhaps because of neural development that continues into one's midtwenties. The prevalence in adulthood decreases to about 2.5 percent.

15.4 Anxiety Disorders

Anxiety may be described as a generalized feeling of dread or apprehension typically accompanied by a variety of physiological reactions including increased heart rate, rapid shallow breathing, sweating, muscle tension, and drying of the mouth. Anxiety differs from fear in one important respect. Fear has an obvious cause, and once that cause is eliminated, the fear will subside. In contrast, anxiety is less clearly linked to specific events or stimuli. Therefore, it tends to be more pervasive and less responsive to changes in the environment.

We all experience occasional episodes of anxiety. For approximately forty million Americans, however, anxiety is such a pervasive condition that they are said to suffer from an **anxiety disorder**. Anxiety is also present in many of the other behavioral disorders we discuss in this chapter, but it is typically most pronounced in the various anxiety disorders.

The *DSM-5* describes a wide range of anxiety disorders. In this chapter we discuss the most common of these, including panic disorder, agoraphobia, social anxiety, specific phobias, and generalized anxiety disorder.

15.4a Panic Disorder

> Susan began her day as she always had. She rose early before her husband, started the coffee, and headed to the shower. She was rehearsing how she would conduct her sales meeting later in the morning when she began to feel as if someone, or something, had taken control of her body. Her heart rate jumped from a normal 65 to more than 150 beats per minute in an instant. Her respiration was strained, and she could not get air into her lungs. She grabbed the bathroom counter as she began to lose balance in a spinning room. Her skin felt cold and clammy, but at the same time she felt as if she were burning alive. A terror like she had never experienced overwhelmed her as she realized she must have had a heart attack and was now dying. She tried to scream out to her husband, but could not even make a sound. She was paralyzed with fear knowing she was going to die in her bathroom. Susan felt as though an hour had passed when she realized that her breathing was now under her control. She took long, deep breaths as her racing heart slowed back toward normal. Susan got up from the floor not even remembering the fall. At that moment her husband walked in carrying her morning coffee. She then realized this had all occurred within just a few minutes. What she didn't yet know was that this was only the first of many episodes to follow.

Susan just experienced a panic attack. She was quickly overcome by a debilitating state of fear that was not caused by a specific event. Almost as quickly as the attack came on, it dissipated, and she was relatively normal afterward. Her experience was not unlike those experienced by others who have suffered through a panic attack. The National Institute of Mental Health (2016) estimates that approximately 3 percent of the population, or about five million Americans, suffer from panic attacks each year.

Anxiety Disorder Any of a number of disorders that produce pervasive feelings of anxiety

Panic Disorder Anxiety disorder in which an individual experiences numerous panic attacks (four or more in a four-week period) that are characterized by overwhelming terror and often a feeling of unreality or depersonalization

Agoraphobia An anxiety disorder characterized by an intense fear of being in places or situations from which escape might be difficult or in which help might not be available, such as stores, theaters, and trains; often accompanies panic disorder

Phobia Any of a number of anxiety disorders characterized by a persistent fear of and consequent avoidance of a specific object or situation

Social Anxiety Anxiety disorder characterized by a persistent, irrational fear of performing some specific behavior (such as talking or eating) in the presence of other people

Having an occasional panic attack does not necessarily mean that you suffer from a **panic disorder**. *DSM-5* stipulates that a person experience recurrent, unexpected panic attacks and that at least one of the attacks be followed by a month or more of persistent concern about having additional attacks before being diagnosed with panic disorder.

Panic attacks sometimes occur during sleep and thus may be confused with sleep terrors (see Chapter 5), which also induce intense emotional responses. However, nocturnal panic attacks differ from sleep terrors in that the latter are typically followed by a quick return to peaceful sleep, with no later recall, whereas panic attacks are usually vividly recalled and are rarely followed by a quick return to sleep.

The panic attacks associated with a panic disorder can be so overwhelmingly terrifying that a person may feel driven to attempt suicide. During an attack, people may think they are going crazy or that death from a heart attack is likely. Sometimes an individual may have a sense of *derealization* (the feeling that the world is not real), or *depersonalization* (loss of a sense of personal identity manifested as feeling detached from one's body). Physical symptoms include erratic or pounding heartbeats, labored breathing, dizziness, chest pain, sweating and trembling, and feelings of choking and suffocating.

15.4b Agoraphobia

In the majority of panic disorder cases seen by clinicians, the subject also exhibits symptoms of **agoraphobia** (National Institute of Mental Health, 2016). Agoraphobia is characterized by intense fear of being in places or situations from which escape might be difficult or in which help might not be available in the event of a panic attack. Common focal points for agoraphobic fear are being outside the home alone or being in open, public places such as stores, theaters, buses, and trains. To avoid these situations, individuals with this disorder may stay away from all public places and, in extreme cases, become virtual prisoners in their own homes.

Less commonly, individuals may suffer a panic disorder without related symptoms of agoraphobia. Conversely, in some cases agoraphobia exists without any symptoms or prior history of panic disorder. The available data do not adequately explain why some people develop agoraphobia manifested as phobic avoidance behaviors while others do not. Agoraphobia is but one of several kinds of **phobia**, or disorders characterized by a persistent fear of and consequent avoidance of a specific object or situation. Individuals with phobic disorders may be terrified of spiders, snakes, heights, open spaces, being alone, or numerous other objects or situations. Although they usually realize that their fear is far out of proportion to any actual danger, this understanding does little to reduce the fear.

Phobias are among the most common behavioral disorders; approximately 10 percent of the general population each year has a specific phobia. A person who is afraid of heights may be more inclined simply to avoid climbing ladders or hiking along high mountain trails than to seek professional help. In addition to agoraphobia, *DSM-5* provides diagnostic categories for social phobias (social anxiety disorder) and specific phobias.

15.4c Social Anxiety Disorder

A **social anxiety** is a persistent, irrational fear of performing some specific behavior, such as talking, writing, eating, drinking, or using public lavatories, in the presence of other people. People with social anxiety (also termed *social phobia*) are compelled to avoid situations in which they may be observed behaving in an ineffective or embarrassing manner.

Many social phobics are particularly fearful of interaction with authority figures such as teachers, employers, or police officers. Some social phobics have a poor self-image with regard to their physical appearance; they may seek to correct what they perceive to be defects in their anatomy, even to the extent of undergoing elective plastic surgery. Approximately 7 percent of the adult population will suffer from social anxiety each year (National Institute of Mental Health, 2016).

A distinction is sometimes made between two forms of social anxiety. One kind, called *performance anxiety*, reflects fear of specific situations—such as speaking, acting, or sports—in which the individual must perform before an audience. This kind of social anxiety is manageable in that the individual can lead a relatively normal social life by simply avoiding such situations. However, a performance anxiety can limit career options or professional growth. The second type of social phobia, *social anxiety*, may impose more serious limitations by causing individuals to avoid all kinds of social situations in both professional and personal activities. Individuals with this anxiety have difficulty making new acquaintances, interacting with peers and supervisors on the job, enjoying recreational pursuits with others, attending social functions, and so forth. In extreme cases, victims can fear contact with anyone outside of their immediate family.

Specific Phobia Anxiety disorder characterized by an irrational fear of specific situations or objects, such as heights, small closed places, strangers or animals

15.4d Specific Phobia

In **specific phobia**, the source of the irrational fear is a specific situation or object, such as heights, small closed places, various living things (particularly dogs, cats, snakes, mice, and spiders), transportation (flying, cars, trains), thunder, and darkness (see Table 15-1). Although the specific phobias are the most common phobic disorders, they are also the least disruptive. Therefore, they are seen infrequently in clinical settings.

Table 15-1 Some Variations of Specific Phobias

Name	Object(s) Feared	Name	Object(s) Feared
Acrophobia	High places	Monophobia	Being alone
Agoraphobia	Open places	Mysophobia	Contamination
Ailurophobia	Cats	Nyctophobia	Darkness
Algophobia	Pain	Ocholophobia	Crowds
Anthropophobia	Men	Pathophobia	Disease
Aquaphobia	Water	Pyrophobia	Fire
Arachnophobia	Spiders	Syphilophobia	Syphilis
Astraphobia	Storms, thunder, lightning	Thanatophobia	Death
Claustrophobia	Closed places	Xenophobia	Strangers
Cynophobia	Dogs	Zoophobia	Animals or a single animal
Hematophobia	Blood		

15.4e Generalized Anxiety Disorder

Generalized Anxiety Disorder (GAD) A chronic state of free-floating anxiety or worry that has persisted for at least six months

Obsessive-Compulsive Disorder (OCD) Anxiety disorder characterized by persistent, unwanted, and unshakable thoughts or irresistible, habitual repeated actions

Generalized anxiety disorder (GAD) is characterized by excessive anxiety or worry about events or domains of life. For example, individuals with GAD may exhibit excessive worry about finances, their health, or school or work. While it is quite common for us to worry about life events, individuals with GAD exhibit exaggerated anxiety or worry about them. Their anxiety is far out of proportion to the real threat these events or concerns pose. During the course of generalized anxiety disorder the focus of anxiety may shift from one concern to another, or there may be no specific focus to one's anxiety at all. Symptoms of GAD include restlessness or feeling on edge, being easily fatigued, difficulty with concentration, irritability, muscle tension, and sleep disturbances. These symptoms typically begin during the teen years and may persist throughout one's life. The symptoms may dissipate for periods of time and reemerge during times of stress. About 3 percent of the population suffers from GAD at any given time (National Institute of Mental Health, 2016).

15.5 Obsessive-Compulsive and Related Disorders

15.5a Obsessive-Compulsive Disorder

If you have ever had the experience of not being able to get a catchy, repetitious jingle out of your mind, or of needing to go back and make sure you have locked all the doors even though you are sure you have, you should have a sense of what it is like to have an **obsessive-compulsive disorder (OCD)**. Here, a person's profound sense of anxiety is reflected in persistent, unwanted, and unshakable thoughts and/or irresistible, habitual repeated actions. Although the approximately 2.5 percent of Americans who have this disorder usually know that their obsessive thoughts or compulsive actions are irrational, they still cannot block out their thoughts or keep themselves from performing the repetitious act, often an extreme number of times (National Institute of Mental Health, 2016). There is one report of a woman who washed her hands more than five hundred times per day. (The hand-washing compulsion that Lady Macbeth acquired after helping her husband murder the king of Scotland is one of the most common compulsions reported.) The senseless, repetitious behavior seems to ward off a flood of overwhelming anxiety that would result if the compulsive acts were terminated.

In the classic manifestation of this disorder, obsessive thoughts lead to compulsive actions. The following case illustrates this connection:

> Carl, a twenty-four-year-old college student, began seeing a psychologist at his girlfriend's request because of his persistent checking behavior. Once they began living together she was shocked by his inability to sit through a television show, a complete dinner, or even a conversation without getting up to check to be sure the kitchen stove was off or to lock the door to their apartment. During the night Carl, would often get up to verify that everything was off and secure. Carl even insisted that they leave the theater in the middle of a movie because he was certain that the door to their apartment was left open. Reassuring him that she had checked was of little use once he began obsessing about it.
>
> Carl's obsessions appear to have begun in high school when he became obsessed with arranging and rearranging things in his room. At first his parents encouraged

his cleanliness and the order of his personal things. When he went off to college, they assumed his behavior would change in the presence of roommates who would likely be much messier than he. While Carl wasn't obsessed with the disorder of their shared dorm room, his obsessions about his own possessions persisted. Carl was meticulous about the folding and the order of clothes in his small closet and drawers. He also became concerned about the shared sink in their room. He spent hours washing and disinfecting the shared area where his roommate shaved and brushed his teeth. Any amount of hair or toothbrush splatter in the sink or on the counter repulsed him.

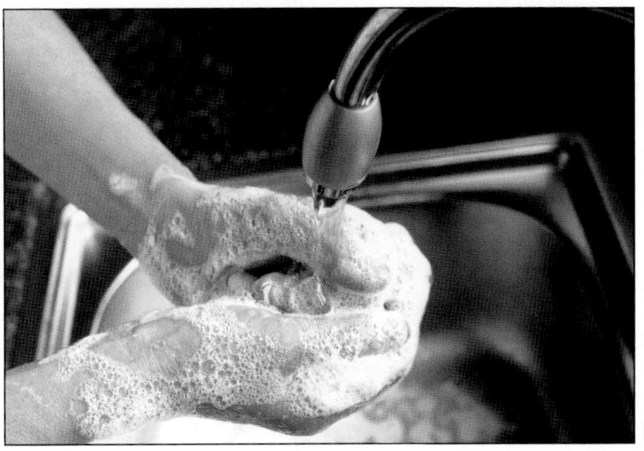
(Shutterstock)

Obsessive-compulsive disorder is characterized by persistent, unwanted, and unshakable thoughts or irresistible, habitual repeated actions.

After several months, Carl was granted a request to move into a single dorm room. In his single room, Carl was aware that his excessive concern about order was unusual. He was even embarrassed when others commented about how clean and orderly everything was. At one point prior to friends coming to visit, he actually disorganized everything to make his room look "normal." Carl found this to be so distressing that he spent their entire visit rearranging again rather than playing cards. Living in the shared space of dormitories was getting more and more difficult for Carl. His obsessions over the sanitary conditions of the showers, the many door knobs, and the shared kitchen space distracted him much of the time. He was also concerned about leaving his dorm room door unlocked and needed to check it frequently throughout the day. By his senior year, Carl had moved into a small but new apartment. Within a few months his girlfriend joined him, only to be stunned by his unusual behavior.

After two visits to the university psychologist, Carl was referred to a psychiatrist at the university hospital for medication. Following a brief visit, Carl was prescribed Zoloft, which he continues to take today. His obsessive symptoms of anxiety have improved, but his ritualistic checking has not. Carl's symptoms seem to come and go over time and are most severe when he is under stress.

In the case just described, Carl's obsessions about door locks and cleanliness lead to his compulsive checking and cleaning. Like Carl, most people who manifest this disorder demonstrate the components of both obsessions and compulsions. However, about 15 percent of cases experience only obsessive thoughts that are not accompanied by compulsive acts (American Psychiatric Association, 2013).

15.6 Trauma- and Stressor-Related Disorders

15.6a Post-Traumatic Stress Disorder

People who experience a profoundly traumatic event, such as an assault, an accident, or wartime combat, often exhibit a range of severely distressing symptoms as an aftermath of the occurrence. For example, a rape survivor may have vivid flashbacks of the attack in which she re-experiences all the terror of the assault. Many war veterans also have flashbacks of traumatic war experiences as an aftermath of their participation in the conflict.

Many of the survivors of and first responders to the attacks on the World Trade Center and the Pentagon on September 11, 2001, continue to experience flashbacks.

These symptoms are typical of **post-traumatic stress disorder (PTSD)**. According to *DSM-5R*, PTSD develops after a person has experienced, witnessed, or been confronted with an event that involved actual or threatened sexual violence, death, or serious injury. In response to this traumatic event, the person must have also experienced intense fear, helplessness, or horror. Characteristic symptoms of PTSD include recurrent distressing recollections or dreams of the traumatic event, acting or feeling as if the traumatic event were recurring, and intense distress associated with exposure to cues related to the traumatic event.

Post-traumatic stress disorder differs from other anxiety disorders in that it can be explained largely, if not solely, on environmental grounds. An examination of the life histories of people who have conditions such as phobias or obsessive-compulsive disorders does not reveal a consistent pattern of background factors. In contrast, all victims of PTSD, while certainly different from one another in many ways, share the experience of a profoundly traumatizing event(s). The lifetime prevalence of PTSD is about 7 percent of the U.S. population (National Institute of Mental Health, 2016).

15.6b Theoretical Perspectives on Anxiety, Post-Traumatic Stress, and Obsessive-Compulsive Disorders

How can anxiety disorders be explained? Psychoanalytic theory, the behavioral (learning) perspective, and biological explanations all provide some insight into these disorders. We look briefly at each perspective.

The Psychoanalytic Perspective

Freud (1936) explained the anxiety disorders as a result of internal conflicts, particularly those involving sexual or aggressive impulses. Recall, from Chapter 14, that Freud saw the ego's primary function as protecting a person from severe anxiety. It does this by mediating among the id's impulses, the superego's demands, and reality—often relying on the ego's defense mechanisms. According to psychoanalytic theory, anxiety and the symptoms of anxiety disorders appear when these defenses are overused or rigidly applied, or when they fail.

This perspective explains generalized anxiety disorders as the result of unacceptable impulses that the ego has blocked. These impulses are powerful enough to produce a constant state of tension and apprehension, but since they are unconscious, the person is unaware of the source of the anxiety.

Phobias may occur if the individual *displaces* this anxiety to some object, situation, or social function that can be avoided. Consider one of Freud's most famous cases, that of a five-year-old boy known as Little Hans, whose phobic fear of horses kept him from going outside his house. Freud concluded that Hans's fear of horses was an expression of anxieties related to an Oedipal complex. He unconsciously feared and hated his father (whom he perceived as a rival for his mother's affections), and he displaced this fear onto horses, which he could avoid more easily than his father.

Psychoanalytic theory has a different explanation for panic disorders and agoraphobia. According to this perspective, these disorders may both be rooted in an unresolved separation anxiety (a fear of being separated from parents) early in life. People who have

Post-Traumatic Stress Disorder (PTSD) Anxiety disorder that typically follows a traumatic event or events; characterized by a reliving of that event, avoidance of stimuli associated with the event or numbing of general responsiveness, and increased arousal

learned during childhood to protest intensely when they are threatened with separation from a parental figure may experience panic attacks later in life when they either perceive a threat of separation or actually experience removal of a significant other.

Still another explanation is suggested for obsessive-compulsive disorder, which is seen as the result of a fixation at the anal stage of psychosexual development. Freud believed that when children are subjected to harsh toilet-training experiences, they react with anger and aggressive urges that must be controlled if punishment is to be avoided. The persistent thoughts or repetitive behavioral rituals associated with this disorder serve to dissipate angry feelings before they can be translated into aggressive acts. The fact that compulsive behavior rituals often involve cleanliness themes lends support to Freud's contention that such neurotic acts reflect fixation during the anal period, a time focused on mastering "unclean" bowel and bladder functions.

(Francoise De Mulder/Getty)

This Ethiopian boy soldier suffers from post-traumatic stress disorder (PTSD).

The Behavioral Perspective

During the 1960s, several behavioral theorists (Bandura, 1969; Wolpe & Rachman, 1960) carefully analyzed Freud's published account of Little Hans and noted that his phobic response occurred only in the presence of a large horse pulling a heavily loaded cart at high speed. They further noted that Hans's phobia originally appeared after he had witnessed a terrible accident involving a horse pulling a cart at high speed. Not surprisingly, these observations led behaviorists to a different explanation than Freud's. Hans's phobia was a classically conditioned fear that had nothing to do with Oedipal complexes or displacement. Behavioral psychologists see conditioning, discussed in Chapter 6, as the source of anxiety disorders.

Pavlovian conditioning seems to provide a reasonable explanation. Phobias are the result of learned associations between previously neutral stimuli and frightening events. Thus, we might argue that a person develops a fear of strangers after being assaulted, or a fear of riding in cars after being in a bad automobile accident, or fears elevators after an aversive experience in a confined space. Once fear or anxiety is conditioned to certain stimuli, people may then learn to reduce this conditioned fear by avoiding the fear stimulus. This kind of conditioning was referred to as *avoidance learning* in Chapter 6. For instance, a person with a strong fear of elevators may avoid them by using stairs instead. The avoidance behavior here is maintained by negative reinforcement (fear reduction). Through the process of *stimulus generalization* (also discussed in Chapter 6) a variety of situations may serve to elicit fear and anxiety.

Why don't all people with fearful experiences develop phobias or severe anxiety? The answer to this question may be that certain brain structures involved in mediating conditioned fear, including the amygdala and the prefrontal cortex, don't turn off normally in some people. Recent experimental work with animals supports this idea. For instance, work with animals has demonstrated that the *amygdala* (see Chapter 3) is essential for the development of conditioned fear responses. In addition, during the course of fear conditioning, cells in the amygdala begin to fire with the onset of a conditioned stimulus (CS) that precedes shock. On the other hand, damage to the amygdala prevents fear conditioning in animals (Davis, 1992).

BVT*Lab*

Visit **www.BVTLab.com** to explore the student resources available for this chapter.

While the amygdala appears to be important in the acquisition of conditioned fear, the *prefrontal cortex* seems to be responsible for the extinction of conditioned fear. Animals with prefrontal cortex damage fail to extinguish conditioned fear when the unconditioned stimulus (shock) is no longer presented. People with post-traumatic stress syndrome also show a failure to extinguish conditioned fear responses. Perhaps anxiety disorders result when people can no longer turn off or inhibit conditioned fear responses (Charney, 2003; Davis, 1992; Davis, Walker, & Myers, 2003; LeDoux, 1992a; Debiec, Bush, & LeDoux, 2011).

Although both Pavlovian conditioning and operant conditioning account for many kinds of anxiety disorders, some questions may remain unanswered. How can we explain the fact that many people who have phobias have had no frightening experiences with the object or situation that they fear so greatly? Furthermore, although there are quite a few different kinds of phobias, the objects of these phobias tend to be limited to a fairly narrow range of stimuli. By far the most common phobias are *zoophobias* (fear of particular animals, such as snakes or mice). Yet in our own society today, we are exposed far more to motor vehicles and machines than we are to snakes. Why don't we develop proportionately more phobias to these objects?

Different theorists have approached our question about phobias in different ways; two answers are particularly interesting. The first argument is that evolution has built into humans a biological predisposition to react fearfully to certain classes of potentially dangerous stimuli, such as snakes and spiders. It is not difficult to believe that a natural wariness can have some adaptive advantage to humans, but is there any objective evidence to support this notion? The answer is a tentative yes. One series of experiments attempted to classically condition fear responses to both "evolutionally prepared stimuli" such as spiders and snakes, and to innocuous stimuli such as mushrooms. It found not only that fear responses to evolutionally prepared stimuli were much more easily established (often in only one trial) but also that these responses were very difficult to extinguish.

Not all theorists agree that biological predispositions explain why some phobias occur more readily than others. Bandura (1969) believes that modeling, or imitating the behavior of others, provides a more likely explanation for the acquisition of some anxiety disorders. For example, a child who observes a parent reacting anxiously to dogs or thunderstorms may also acquire a phobic fear of dogs or thunder. In this manner, phobias may be transmitted from one generation to the next. This is supported by evidence that animal phobias typically occur in children who are about age five and whose parents or other family members have the same phobia. Thus, the fact that relatively narrow ranges of stimuli become phobic objects may be due to social-learning mechanisms rather than biological predispositions.

How do behavioral theorists explain other anxiety disorders? Post-traumatic stress disorders, as we have seen, are clearly linked to traumatizing experiences and possibly the failure to inhibit conditioned fear responses. The behavioral explanation of obsessive-compulsive disorders is more complex. Some argue that compulsive, repetitious acts such as hand washing occur repeatedly because they provide a temporary reduction in anxiety. According to this argument compulsive behaviors are maintained by negative reinforcement.

Finally, in the case of panic attacks with accompanying agoraphobia, it has been suggested that individuals who experience sudden panic attacks develop a kind of anticipatory anxiety attached to situations in which they have previously experienced attacks. Indeed, they may become so fearful of future attacks that they subsequently avoid what they perceive as dangerous situations. Such phobic avoidance behaviors are then reinforced by a reduction in fear. However, this perspective does not provide an explanation of what causes the initial panic reactions. One possible explanation is that certain underlying physiological and biochemical anomalies affect the autonomic nervous system in such a way as to predispose certain individuals to experience panic attacks (for example, an amygdala that is overactive). These unanticipated attacks may lead to fearful attitudes that help to maintain the disorder via phobic avoidance behaviors. In this sense, we might view panic disorder with agoraphobia as resulting from an interaction of biological and psychological causes. The following discussion explores some of the suggested biological causes of obsessive-compulsive disorder and the other anxiety disorders.

Zoophobias are fears of particular animals, such as snakes or mice.

The Biological Perspective

Perhaps the best place to start is with a notion that has been suggested by several researchers—that some individuals with unusually responsive nervous systems may be biologically predisposed to develop certain anxiety disorders, particularly panic, phobic, and generalized anxiety disorders. Some evidence suggests that the autonomic nervous systems of individuals with anxiety disorders are more easily aroused by environmental stimuli.

The research program of Judith Rapoport and her colleagues (1990, 1991; Rapoport & Fiske, 1998), who have investigated the biology of obsessive-compulsive disorder, presents one of the most interesting perspectives on these disorders. Data from a number of studies have led Rapoport to postulate that certain behavioral subroutines related to such things as grooming, cleanliness, and checking key elements within one's territory have been programmed or hard-wired into the human brain over the course of evolution. Such behavioral packages are believed to have served crucial functions during the evolution of the human species. The repository of these hard-wired behavioral packages is presumed to be located within the **basal ganglia**, a group of brain structures that lie under the cerebral cortex and function as "way stations" between the input of sensory messages and resulting cortically initiated motor or cognitive outputs (refer to Chapter 3). Rapoport theorizes that in obsessive-compulsive patients, disturbances in these way stations have somehow short-circuited the loop that normally connects sensory input with behavioral output, thereby releasing stored, hard-wired behavioral packages.

For most of us, evidence provided by our senses and interpreted by higher brain centers (that we are clean or that the windows are locked, for instance) is sufficient to keep us from engaging in compulsive routines related to these concerns. According to Rapoport's model, however, people with the short-circuited loops feel compelled to engage in such things as hand washing (cleanliness subroutine) and repetitively checking the windows (territory subroutine). Rapoport and her colleagues have gathered an impressive array of evidence to support this intriguing biological theory, and evidence is rapidly accumulating from other laboratories also suggesting dopamine dysfunction in the basal ganglia underlies this serious disorder (Bhattacharyya et al. 2009; Denys, van der Wee, Janssen, De Geus, & Westenberg, 2004; Rotge et al., 2010).

Obsessive-compulsive disorder is believed to also involve the cingulate cortex, which lies deep in the central fissure of the brain. In the most severe cases of OCD, the risk of suicide dramatically increases, and drug and behavioral therapies are usually unsuccessful. An increasing number of these patients are receiving surgery to sever the connections between the cingulate cortex and the frontal lobes—a procedure referred to as a **cingulotomy**. About 70 percent of patients undergoing cingulotomy show signs of improvement (Keller, 2012).

Basal Ganglia A group of brain structures that lie under the cerebral cortex and function as "way stations" between the input of sensory messages and resulting cortically initiated motor or cognitive outputs

Cingulotomy A surgical procedure partially separating the cingulate cortex from the frontal lobes that is performed to treat severe obsessive-compulsive disorder

Somatic Symptom Disorder Type of somatic disorder characterized by multiple and recurrent physical symptoms that have no physical cause

Illness Anxiety Disorder A somatic disorder in which the individual is excessively fearful of contracting a serious illness or of dying; previously referred to as *hypochondria*

Other evidence for the biological perspective of psychological disorders comes from biologically based treatments. Currently drug therapies for most psychological disorders are the most commonly employed treatments. In many of these cases, drug therapies not only relieve symptoms but also reverse the pathology underlying these disorders. For example, ADHD is characterized by abnormal frontal lobe activity. Patients with ADHD may demonstrate EEG activity that resembles stages of early sleep (theta activity), as opposed to normal EEG rhythms seen during wakefulness (Gunkelman, 2014). Treatment with medication returns ADHD patients to normal cortical activity. Furthermore, the most successful treatments for panic and generalized anxiety disorders are drugs that increase the effectiveness of GABA, an inhibitory neurotransmitter that is abundant in the prefrontal cortex as well as the amygdala. Both are brain areas known to be involved in anxiety and fear. Recent evidence suggests that a GABA dysfunction in these regions may predispose individuals for anxiety disorders. Drugs that increase GABA activity are typically used to treat these disorders (Ettinger, 2017; Kalueff & Nutt, 2007; Roy-Byrne, 2005). In addition, drugs that inhibit the synthesis of GABA or block GABA receptors and its ability to inhibit target neurons produce anxiety in both animals and humans (Depino, Tsetsenis, & Gross, 2008; Richter et al., 2012). Taken together, this evidence suggests that anxiety disorders may result from GABA dysfunction in the frontal cortices and the amygdala. Additional evidence for the biological perspective will come from the treatment of depression and schizophrenia discussed later.

15.7 Somatic Symptom Disorders

Whereas the primary symptom of anxiety disorders is psychological distress, the somatic symptom disorders are expressed through *somatic,* or physical, symptoms. Dizziness, stomach pain, vomiting, breathing difficulties, difficulty in swallowing, impaired vision, inability to move the legs, numbness of the hands, and sexual dysfunctions are common symptoms of somatic symptom disorders. In all cases, however, the symptoms have no physiological basis.

The somatic symptom disorders affect a much smaller portion of the population than anxiety disorders—less than 1 percent. *DSM-5* classifies several types of somatic symptom disorders. We look at three: *somatic symptom disorder, illness anxiety disorder,* and *conversion disorder*.

15.7a Somatic Symptom Disorder

A person with **somatic symptom disorder** typically has multiple and recurrent physical symptoms that have no physical cause, but for which medical attention is repeatedly sought. People who have this disorder commonly complain about chest, stomach, and back pain; headaches; heart palpitations; vomiting; dizziness and fainting; and genitourinary symptoms.

15.7b Illness Anxiety Disorder

Like somatic symptom disordered individuals, people with **illness anxiety disorder** (previously termed *hypochondria*) also complain about a variety of physical difficulties (most commonly stomach and heart problems). The primary difference between the two conditions is that individuals with hypochondriasis are fearful that their symptoms indicate a serious disease, whereas those with somatization disorder typically do not progress beyond a concern with the symptoms themselves. A hypochondriac who notices a minor heart palpitation may be convinced it is a sign of severe cardiac disease, or may interpret a cough as a sign of lung cancer. Hypochondriacs have also been shown to be excessively fearful about death and often spend an inordinate amount of time consulting with physicians about imaginary symptoms of physical illness.

Conversion Disorder
Somatic symptom disorder that is manifested as a sensory or motor system disorder for which there is no known organic cause

15.7c Conversion Disorder

A third somatic symptom disorder, **conversion disorder**, typically manifests as a sensory or motor-system disturbance for which there is no known organic cause. Unlike the two previous categories of somatic symptom disorders, conversion disorders are seldom confused with genuine physical disease because their symptom patterns make no anatomical sense. In the condition known as *sensory conversion*, for example, individuals may lose sensitivity in specific parts of their bodies in which the loss-of-feeling pattern is neurologically impossible. Other forms of sensory conversion may be reflected in loss of sensitivity to pain, impaired vision or hearing, and in some cases, heightened sensitivity to touch. In another related condition, *motor conversion*, an individual may experience paralysis in some part of the body, usually a limb, or experience uncontrollable tremors or twitches.

Conversion disorders typically surface after a person has experienced serious stress or conflict, and the symptoms appear to allow the person to escape from or avoid that stress or conflict. This situation is apparent in the following case, in which a man developed a sensory conversion to escape from a nagging wife and mother-in-law:

> Phil, forty years of age, had a history of marginal work adjustment since his discharge from the Army at age twenty-five. In the fifteen years since discharge, he had depended on public assistance and financial aid from relatives to get by. He painted a very dismal picture of his married life, as one of almost constant harassment from his wife and mother-in-law. He had a history of minor illnesses involving his eyes, none of which had grossly affected his visual acuity.
>
> During the Christmas season, his wife and mother-in-law were being more demanding than usual, requiring him to work nights and weekends at various chores under their foremanship. Three days before Christmas, while shopping with his wife and mother-in-law, Phil suddenly became blind in both eyes.
>
> Neurological and ophthalmological exams were essentially negative in accounting for his blindness, and a diagnosis of conversion disorder was made. At this time, Phil did not seem greatly alarmed by his loss of sight, but instead displayed an attitude of patient forbearance. Observers in the hospital noticed that Phil could get about in the ward better than expected for a totally blind man. He was not concerned with this, but felt hurt and unjustly accused when other patients pointed out the discrepancy to him.

Phil's apparent lack of concern about his condition is fairly common among people with conversion disorders. The French psychiatrist Pierre Janet (1920) labeled this blasé attitude *la belle indifference*, or the noble lack of concern. Observers may incorrectly assume that a person with a conversion disorder is malingering, or deliberately faking symptoms. However, unlike malingerers, who tend to be cautious about discussing their symptoms for fear that their pretense will be discovered, individuals with a conversion disorder appear eager to talk at great length about their symptoms.

15.7d Theoretical Perspectives on Somatic Symptom Disorders

Recall, from Chapter 14, that Freud was profoundly influenced by experiences with patients whose physically manifested symptoms had no neurological basis. Freud thought such problems stemmed from unresolved sexual impulses, particularly Oedipal complexes. These unresolved incestuous yearnings, said Freud, produce intense anxiety, which the individual may then convert into physical symptoms. This conversion reduces the anxiety associated with repressed id impulses, a process Freud called *primary gain*. Freud noted that such disorders might also produce some *secondary gain*, allowing the person to avoid or escape from some currently stressful life situation.

Freud's concept of secondary gain is similar to the interpretation of somatic symptom disorders offered by some behavioral theorists. According to their viewpoint, the symptoms of a somatic symptom disorder are reinforced if they allow a person to escape from or avoid the negative reinforcer of anxiety. Reinforcement in the form of sickness benefit or disability insurance has also been noted to play a role in somatic symptom disorder. There is some evidence that biological predispositions or genetic factors may also play a noteworthy role in these disorders (Kellner, 1990).

15.8 Dissociative Disorders

In the **dissociative disorders**, the thoughts and feelings that generate anxiety are separated, or *dissociated*, from conscious awareness by memory loss or a change in identity. These uncommon disorders usually take the form of *dissociative amnesia*, *depersonalization-derealization*, or *dissociative identity*.

15.8a Dissociative Amnesia

The most common dissociative disorder is **dissociative amnesia**. Here, a person experiences sudden loss of memory, usually after a particularly stressful or traumatic event. The most typical manifestation is loss of memory for all events for a specified period of time. For example, a person involved in a terrible accident might block out all memory of the accident, as well as everything that happened just before or after it. Less commonly, a person may develop total amnesia for all prior experiences and will be unable to recognize relatives, friends, and familiar places. (In these cases, the individual usually retains reasoning and verbal abilities, talents such as the ability to play a musical instrument, and general knowledge.) Episodes of dissociative amnesia may last from several hours to many years. They typically disappear as suddenly as they appeared, and they rarely recur.

Memory loss may also result from organic brain disease associated with such illnesses as chronic alcoholism and Alzheimer's disease, as we read in Chapters 7 and 12. However, *dissociative amnesia* is easily distinguished from organic amnesia, in that memory loss due to organic causes (diseases, injury, or aging) is generally a gradual process that is not connected with traumatic events.

Dissociative Disorders
Group of disorders, including psychogenic amnesia, depersonalization-derealization disorder, and dissociative identity disorder, in which the thoughts and feelings that generate anxiety are separated or dissociated from conscious awareness

Dissociative Amnesia
An inability to recall important autobiographical information after a traumatic or stressful episode

15.8b Depersonalization-Derealization Disorder

Whereas a person with dissociative amnesia escapes from a stressful situation by blocking it out of awareness, a person with **depersonalization-derealization disorder** experiences a detachment or depersonalization of his or her thoughts and feelings. The individual may have the feeling of being outside of the body, as if watching from a detached perspective. The person may also experience a detachment from immediate surroundings, as if in a dreamlike state. To be considered a disorder, these symptoms must be persistent or recurrent.

15.8c Dissociative Identity Disorder

Dissociative identity disorder (previously termed *multiple personality disorder*) is a very uncommon form of dissociative disorder in which the individual alternates between an original or primary personality and one or more secondary or subordinate personality states. Usually the subordinate personality is aware of the primary personality but not vice versa.

In a sense, we all have multiple personalities in that we have conflicting behavioral tendencies—for instance, between the part of us that is socially conforming and the part that likes to cut loose. Most of us are able to find appropriate outlets for expressing different aspects of our personalities. However, not everyone is able to achieve a satisfactory synthesis. Dissociative identity disorder seems to provide an outlet for these different selves, by separating the conflicting parts and elaborating each into an essentially autonomous personality. Frequently, the separated personalities represent two extremes, from responsible and conforming to irresponsible and "naughty."

An interesting case of dissociative identity disorder that appears to have followed a long history of sexual abuse is the case of Truddi Chase who supposedly displayed ninety-two separate personalities. Apparently, these personalities began to emerge at the age of two years, and they replaced Truddi (the original personality) who was "asleep." Truddi's alternate personalities were referred to as her "troops" in the book *When Rabbit Howls* (Chase, 1990). The main personality of Truddi is a divorced mother of one child. Before treatment, Truddi supposedly knew nothing of the other personalities (troops), which were drawn out and actually participated in her treatment. Some of these other personalities included Rabbit—a character who only communicated through howls of pain; Miss Wonderful—a character who played the perfect woman; Sewer Mouth—a character who played a vulgar woman; Mean Joe—an 11-foot protector of the troops; Elvira—an irresponsible, carefree character; Twelve—an artistic, sensitive child; and The Front Runner—a character who kept track of all the other troops.

Dissociative identity disorder seems to occur more frequently in women than men, with nine times more women affected than men. Although childhood trauma, particularly sexual trauma, appears to be associated with multiple personality disorder, not all psychologists agree that this is a causal relation (Boysen, 2011).

Depersonalization-Derealization Disorder A persistent detachment from one's thoughts, feelings, or body sensations

Dissociative Identity Disorder A condition of separation in personality, or multiple personality, not attributable to disease or brain injury; previously called multiple personality disorder

15.8d Theoretical Perspectives on Dissociative Disorders

Dissociative disorders are among the least understood of all behavioral disorders. Thus, explanations are highly speculative. In some ways, all three of the dissociative disorders we have discussed—amnesia, depersonalization-derealization, and dissociative identity—seem to provide strong support for Freud's view that excessive application of the defense mechanisms can lead to serious disorders.

Psychoanalytic theory sees all of these conditions as resulting from massive reliance on repression to ward off unacceptable impulses, particularly those of a sexual nature. These yearnings increase during adolescence and adulthood, until they are finally expressed, often in a guilt-inducing sexual act. Normal forms of repression are not effective in blocking out this guilt, and so the person blocks the acts and related thoughts entirely from consciousness by developing amnesia or acquiring a new identity for the dissociated "bad" part of the self.

Behavioral theory does not offer a well-developed and cohesive explanation for dissociative disorders. A number of theorists within this perspective suggest, however, that the dissociative reactions may involve operant avoidance responses that are reinforced because they allow an individual to avoid anxiety associated with highly stressful events, such as early childhood abuse. There is no evidence that genetic factors or biological predispositions play a significant role in the development of dissociative disorders.

15.9 Depressive Disorders

> I do not care for anything. I do not care to ride, for the exercise is too violent. I do not care to walk, walking is too strenuous. I do not care to lie down, for I should either have to remain lying, and I do not care to do that, or I should have to get up again, and I do not care to do that either. I do not care at all. (Kierkegaard, 1844, p. 19)

The nineteenth-century Danish philosopher Søren Kierkegaard, who was subject to recurring bouts of severe depression, wrote this account in 1844. It provides a firsthand description of some of the characteristics of depression, the primary symptom of the **depressive disorders**.

We have all experienced depression on occasion, as a natural response to setbacks such as failing an exam, ending a relationship, or being rejected by a potential employer. Fortunately for most of us, depression is a transitory state that generally lifts in short order as life goes on. However, when feelings of sadness, dejection, and hopelessness persist longer than a few weeks and when these feelings are severe enough to disrupt everyday functioning, the depression is considered to be an abnormal behavioral state.

The common symptoms or signs of depression include a variety of psychological, psychomotor, and physical manifestations: severe and prolonged feelings of sadness, hopelessness, and despair; low self-esteem; a sense of worthlessness; eating disturbances (either undereating or overeating); sleep disturbances (either insomnia or excessive sleep); psychomotor disturbances characterized by a marked shift in activity level; a variety of somatic or bodily complaints; lack of energy with accompanying fatigue; loss of interest in and enjoyment of everyday activities; indecisiveness; difficulty in concentrating; and persistent thoughts of suicide and death.

Like anxiety, depression is associated with many varieties of behavioral disorders, including the anxiety and somatic disorders, substance-related disorders such as alcoholism (discussed in Chapter 3), and schizophrenia, which we discuss later in this chapter. In these and related conditions, depression is secondary to other symptoms. The *DSM-5* characterizes a number of depressive disorders, including major depressive disorder, disruptive mood dysregulation disorder, premenstrual dysphoric disorder, and substance-induced depressive disorders. In this chapter we focus on major depressive disorder.

Depressive Disorders Class of disorders, including major depression, dysthymic disorders, and substance induced depression, characterized by persistent depression

15.9a Major Depressive Disorder

People diagnosed as having **major depressive disorder** typically manifest their symptoms over an extended period, from several months to a year or longer. Their ability to function effectively may be so impaired that hospitalization is warranted. The following brief case study illustrates some of the common symptoms of severe depression:

(Shutterstock)

Depression is the primary symptom of the depressive disorders.

> Jamie is a twenty-eight-year-old woman who was recently divorced after a six-year marriage. She remembers feeling depressed during most of her high school years, especially during her senior year when she sought help following a suicide attempt. Jamie had an unremarkable childhood; her parents both worked, but she was rarely alone during her pre-high school years. She has two younger brothers (both appear without symptoms of depression), and she has always had several close friends. After graduating from college with a degree in interior design, Jamie has held several jobs and is now employed with an architectural firm. She enjoys her job but feels it is getting more stressful and contributing to her overwhelming fatigue.
>
> After Jamie's suicide attempt, she was prescribed medication, which she took regularly for about a year. The medication appeared to work somewhat, but she still felt depressed, and the drug made her drowsy and interfered with her concentration at work. Since her diagnosis Jamie has gained more than fifty pounds; she no longer swims or runs—activities she enjoyed throughout college. She now reports that she doesn't look forward to evenings with friends, travel, or even visiting her parents or brothers—all things she did when she was married. She spends her hours after work watching television and talking with girlfriends on the phone. She gets little pleasure from reading and finds she is often distracted by extreme loneliness and sadness. Although Jamie has had no other suicide attempts, she has contemplated it frequently since her divorce as the only solution to her pain. During these periods she finds herself soothed by chocolate, which she blames for her weight problem.

Jamie's case is not untypical. She has done well in her job, has a number of close friends, and is relatively healthy. In fact, most of her coworkers and friends would not consider her to be depressed. She is seeking help again now because she wants more from her life. She is tired of being alone and would like to begin dating, and hopefully, find another romantic partner. She doesn't like being with herself and feels no one else would like to be with her either. She also hopes that treatment will help her lose weight, since attempts at dieting have failed.

Earlier we mentioned that the depression in major depressive disorder is more likely to be accompanied by agitation than it is in bipolar disorder. This state may cause people to pace, wring their hands, or cry out and moan loudly. Depressed people who express this heightened motor activity continue to feel worthless and without hope.

Not surprisingly, people with major depressive disorder almost inevitably experience a breakdown in interpersonal relationships. Most of us do not enjoy being around irritable people; since many depressed people are irritable, it is understandable that friends, associates, and even family members may eventually gravitate away from them. In addition, depressed people often seek guidance and support from others, and it can be very frustrating for friends to observe that their efforts to provide help often seem to have

Major Depressive Disorder The persistent feeling of intense sadness, loss, and worthlessness, often accompanied by thoughts of suicide

no effect. Sometimes people may avoid depressed individuals because such interactions often make them feel gloomy or depressed.

Although often incapacitating and sometimes even life threatening (individuals who contemplate suicide are often deeply depressed), episodes of major depression are generally transitory in nature. In most cases the depression lifts over a period of months, regardless of whether or not it is treated. However, most people with diagnosed major depressive disorder experience one or more recurrence(s) of major depression later on in their lives. Research has linked certain key variables with the recurrences of major depression. Factors predictive of relapse include (1) early onset (before age twenty) of initial episode of major depression, (2) marital distress, and (3) relatives who express critical or hostile attitudes toward the recovered depressive.

15.9b Bipolar Disorder

In contrast to major depressive disorder, **bipolar disorder** (previously referred to as *manic-depressive disorder*) is characterized by extreme mood swings from immobilizing depression to euphoria and frantic activity. In some cases, periods of **mania** recycle, while in other cases episodes of depression and elation may alternate regularly, with months or years of symptom-free normal functioning between the disordered mood states. Other cases may be characterized by a series of intermittent manic episodes followed by a period of depression. Unlike the normal highs and lows most of us experience in response to life events, the depression and mania associated with bipolar disorder do not seem to be triggered by identifiable events. In some manic-depressives, depressive symptoms may occur concurrently with classic manic features, a condition referred to as *mixed mania*. The *DSM-5* further classifies bipolar disorder into two subcategories: bipolar I and bipolar II disorders. Bipolar I is characterized by at least one manic episode that occurs with major depression. Bipolar II disorder requires at least one episode of **hypomania** and major depression. The main difference between bipolar I and bipolar II disorders is the severity of the manic mood that cycles with major depression (*DSM-5*, 2013).

The lifetime prevalence of bipolar disorder is about 6 percent, a rate comparable to that of schizophrenia but far lower than the incidence of major depression (National Institute of Mental Health, 2016). Men and women are equally likely to develop bipolar disorder. Since the depression experienced in bipolar disorder is quite similar to what we already described as experienced in major depression (with noteworthy differences in sleep and activity level), we focus here on the manic symptoms of the disorder.

Bipolar Disorder A psychiatric disorder characterized by extreme mood swings from immobilizing depression to euphoria and frantic activity; previously referred to as *manic-depressive disorder*

Mania A mood state characterized by expanded self-esteem, reduced need for sleep, excessive talking about extravagant ideas, and delusions

Hypomania A mood characterized by persistent and pervasive elevated mood (a mood state less severe than mania)

According to *DSM-5*, manic episodes are characterized by "inflated self-esteem or grandiosity (which may be delusional), decreased need for sleep, pressure of speech, flight of ideas, distractibility, increased involvement in goal-directed activity, psychomotor agitation, and excessive involvement in pleasurable activities that have a high potential for painful consequences that the person often does not recognize" (American Psychiatric Association, 2013). Manic episodes often begin suddenly and escalate rapidly, as revealed in the following case:

> Rick was a completely normal high school kid. He was class president during his senior year and a member of the basketball team. He graduated as the only male valedictorian that year and was looking forward to attending a small, prestigious liberal arts college in the fall. Like most other kids his age, Rick experienced a full range of emotions, including a bout of depression after a yearlong

relationship with his girlfriend ended. This depression disappeared quickly, and he was seeing someone else within a few months. During the summer following graduation, Rick experienced his first significant symptoms. While working for his father in a family owned business, Rick made frequent out-of-town trips for business purchases. On one particular trip, he failed to return from his three-hour drive and ended up staying in an out-of-town hotel. For the next few days, he went on spending sprees, charging clothing and sports equipment with his father's business card. He returned a few days later after spending over $10,000. This first manic episode lasted a little over two weeks. During that time he slept very little, demonstrated bouts of anger and hostility, and talked enthusiastically about his new plans to open a clothing store of his own. This episode revealed behavior that was so uncharacteristic of Rick that his parents made arrangements for a psychiatric evaluation. He was not diagnosed with acute mania at that time, however. Rather, his psychiatrist reasoned that his behavior was completely normal—he was simply displaying some anxiety about attending college in a few months.

(iStock)

The depression experienced in bipolar disorder is similar to that in major depression, with differences in sleep and activity levels.

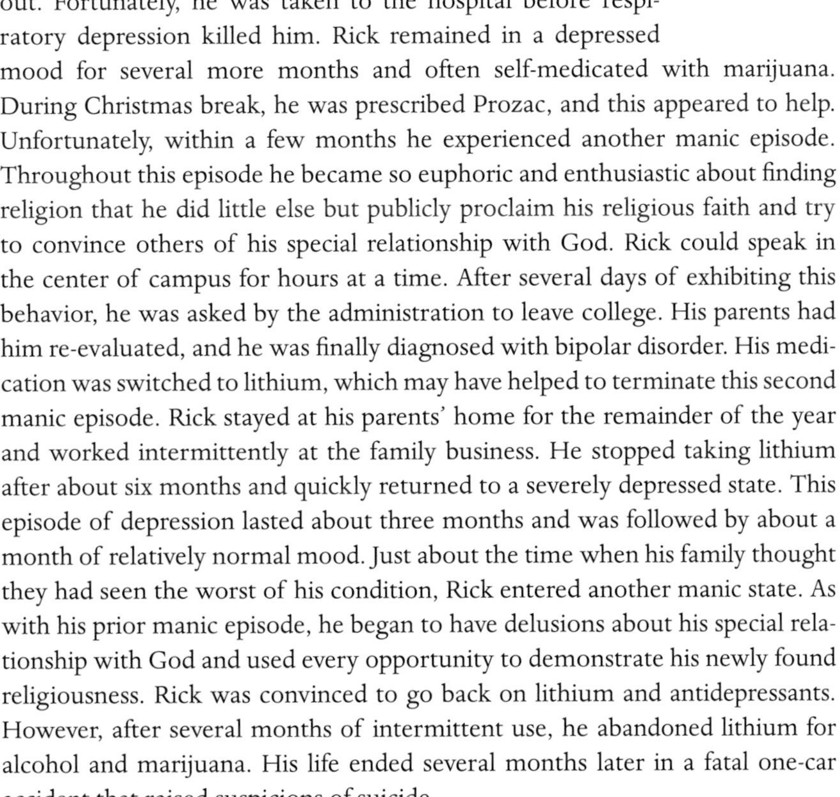

Midway through his first semester at college, Rick experienced his first severe depression. He stopped attending classes, slept for much of each day, rarely showered or changed clothes, and even attempted suicide by alcohol ingestion. On that occasion he consumed nearly a fifth of vodka before blacking out. Fortunately, he was taken to the hospital before respiratory depression killed him. Rick remained in a depressed mood for several more months and often self-medicated with marijuana. During Christmas break, he was prescribed Prozac, and this appeared to help. Unfortunately, within a few months he experienced another manic episode. Throughout this episode he became so euphoric and enthusiastic about finding religion that he did little else but publicly proclaim his religious faith and try to convince others of his special relationship with God. Rick could speak in the center of campus for hours at a time. After several days of exhibiting this behavior, he was asked by the administration to leave college. His parents had him re-evaluated, and he was finally diagnosed with bipolar disorder. His medication was switched to lithium, which may have helped to terminate this second manic episode. Rick stayed at his parents' home for the remainder of the year and worked intermittently at the family business. He stopped taking lithium after about six months and quickly returned to a severely depressed state. This episode of depression lasted about three months and was followed by about a month of relatively normal mood. Just about the time when his family thought they had seen the worst of his condition, Rick entered another manic state. As with his prior manic episode, he began to have delusions about his special relationship with God and used every opportunity to demonstrate his newly found religiousness. Rick was convinced to go back on lithium and antidepressants. However, after several months of intermittent use, he abandoned lithium for alcohol and marijuana. His life ended several months later in a fatal one-car accident that raised suspicions of suicide.

Rick's case is not untypical. His first symptoms came as acute mania when he was eighteen years old. This episode was followed within a few months by an episode of depression. The diagnosis of depression and its treatment with Prozac may have actually hastened his second manic episode where he exhibited some psychosis. Noncompliance with lithium is also quite common and can lead to an even more severe depression with an increased risk of suicide.

A manic episode often follows a three-stage course of accelerating intensity. In the first stage, *hypomania*, individuals typically retain their capacity to function in their daily lives and may even exhibit high levels of productivity. However, as they progress through the second and third stages of *mania* and *severe mania*, their thinking becomes more disorganized; their behavior often takes on a bizarre psychotic-like quality. These advanced stages may be accompanied by both **delusions** (exaggerated and rigidly held beliefs that have little or no basis in fact) and **hallucinations** (false perceptions that lack a sensory basis, such as hearing imaginary voices). Bizarre symptoms such as those described in this chapter's opening case are not often manifested, since modern drugs are quite effective in controlling such behaviors.

A number of studies have shown a disproportionately high incidence of bipolar disorder among creative individuals. One of the first studies to demonstrate this apparent connection found almost five times the incidence of mood disorder in a sample of American creative writers as in a matched control group. One study of forty-seven award-winning British writers and artists revealed that 38 percent had been treated for mood disorders.

Episodes of either mania or depression tend to last only a few weeks or months. When they lift, the person recovers and returns to a symptom-free life. Unfortunately, however, the symptoms tend to recur, and many people require periodic treatment and sometimes maintenance medication throughout their lives. This pattern takes its toll in the form of alienated friends and loved ones, financial problems, and careers that remain on hold due to the unpredictable nature of symptoms. One of the most devastating aspects of this disorder is the high risk of suicide associated with it (see Table 15-2). Available evidence indicates that people with bipolar disorders are more likely to kill themselves than any other group of people with a behavioral disorder.

15.9c Theoretical Perspectives on Depressive Disorders

Psychoanalytic theory, the behavioral-learning perspective, and biological explanations provide different insights into the causes of mood disorders. We look at each in turn.

The Psychoanalytic Perspective

Karl Abraham (1877–1925), a German psychoanalyst who was once a student of Freud, offered the first detailed interpretation of depression. Abraham suggested that mood disorders are rooted in an oral fixation. Frustrated in their efforts to achieve gratification at the oral stage of psychosexual development, individuals develop ambivalent feelings toward their mothers, which eventually transfer to other loved ones so that they are unable to relate successfully to people they love. The consequence is a regression back to the oral level, where these individuals can direct their original love/hate ambivalence toward the self. At times they excessively love themselves (mania), whereas at other times they experience exaggerated self-hatred (depression).

Delusion An exaggerated and rigidly held belief that has little or no basis in fact

Hallucination False perception that lacks a sensory basis; can be produced by hallucinogenic drugs, fatigue, or sensory deprivation (Auditory hallucinations can be associated with severe psychotic disorders.)

Table 15-2 Suicide Facts—United States—2014

1. Approximately 44,000 people in the United States take their own lives each year (probably an underestimation, since many suicides are not officially recorded).
2. For every successful suicide there are at least eight attempts. This translates to approximately 1.4 million suicide attempts each year in this country.
3. There are more than twice as many suicicdes as there are homicides.
4. Suicide rates in males are 3.5 times higher than females, although both have similar rates of suicide attempts.
5. Suicide rates rise steadily throughout a person's age, peaking for males in the 75 and older range.
6. Suicide was the third leading cause of death for ages 10–14 and the second leading cause of death for ages 15–34.
7. Single people are more likely to commit suicide than married or cohabiting people.
8. Suicide rates are similar across ethnicity groups, but is much higher in those reporting multiple ethnicities.

Source: The National Institute of Mental Health (NIMH), 2015.

In addition to emphasizing the love/hate ambivalence suggested by Abraham, Freud theorized that the fixation also causes a person to depend too heavily on others for gratification of basic needs and for maintaining self-esteem. Freud thought mood disorders were rooted in relationships involving overdependence and ambivalent feelings of love and hate. When a person experiences loss (or even the threat of loss) of such a relationship, the unconscious hostility toward the lost person surfaces as anger that is turned back against oneself. This anger takes the form of despair that may be so intense as to motivate suicide, the ultimate form of aggression turned inward.

Many critics ask why only the hate component of a person's love/hate ambivalence is turned inward. Presumably, if positive feelings were turned inward, a person would emerge from mourning with happy memories. Psychoanalytic theorists explain this paradox by arguing that loss of a loved one through death or separation is likely to be interpreted as rejection by a person who already feels ambivalent and emotionally dependent. Accordingly, an intense negative emotional state is a more likely consequence than happy memories.

What little research there is does not support Freud's speculations. Researchers have analyzed the dreams of depressed people and found that they reflect themes of disappointment, failure, and loss rather than anger, hostility, and aggression (Beck & Ward, 1961). Furthermore, if depressed people do turn their anger inward, we should not expect to find much evidence of overt hostility to others. In fact, studies have revealed that depressed people often direct excessive amounts of hostility toward people who are close to them. Finally, there is a lack of direct evidence that depressed people interpret the death of a loved one as rejection of themselves.

The Behavioral Perspective

Behavioral and learning theorists tend to view depression in a different light. They note that death of, or separation from, a loved one means the loss of a primary source of positive reinforcement (Ferster, 1965). Thus, a person whose spouse has recently died or one who has just divorced may sit at home alone. With no one there to provide ongoing positive reinforcement, he or she may fall into a rut, participating in fewer social and leisure activities that would normally function as primary sources of reinforcement.

Behavior theory suggests that depression can have other sources beside the loss of a loved one. Loss of a job, a move to a different geographic area that cuts us off from a primary circle of friends (for example, going away to college), or a prolonged illness can all substantially reduce opportunities for positive reinforcement; thus, all may be linked to depression. For instance, Swann et al. (1992) have conducted experiments demonstrating that depressed people prefer to interact with someone giving them unfavorable feedback, even when it makes them feel unhappy, rather than someone who gives them positive feedback. This evidence, however, does not rule out the possibility that depressed behavior precedes rather than follows a reduction in reinforcing experiences. It certainly seems plausible that people who become depressed may curtail their participation in reinforcing events. Thus, we are left with a chicken-and-egg question: Which comes first, the depression or the avoidance of reinforcing experiences?

Another behavioral perspective on depression is Seligman's theory of **learned helplessness** (Peterson, Maier, & Seligman, 1993; Seligman, 1975; Forgeard et al., 2011). This theory, which suggests that people become depressed when they believe they have no control over the reinforcers and punishers in their lives, evolved out of a series of experiments with animals. For example, in one study Seligman and Maier (1967) used dogs as subjects, assigning the dogs to one of three groups. Subjects in one group, the *escape group*, quickly learned to escape from repeated electric shocks by using their noses to press a panel. In contrast, animals in the *inescapable group* were exposed to the same pattern of shocks but were not provided with an escape response. Termination of the shock was independent of any actions taken by these dogs. Dogs in a third control group were placed in the same apparatus but not shocked. Animals in the inescapable group appeared to acquire a sense of passive resignation to the unavoidable shock.

In a later phase of the experiment, dogs from all three groups were placed in another experimental situation in which they could avoid a shock merely by jumping over a hurdle to a safe compartment after hearing a warning signal. This avoidance task was easily mastered by dogs previously assigned to either the escape or control conditions. Animals in the inescapable group, however, merely sat passively, making no effort to escape the shocks. Seligman and his colleagues labeled this phenomenon "learned helplessness."

What does this experiment have to do with human depression? Seligman argues that humans, like the dogs in the inescapable group, learn from past situations that their actions will be fruitless in producing desirable change in their environments. When individuals feel helpless to influence their encounters with reinforcers and punishers, the result is depression. According to Seligman, people are most inclined to become depressed if they attribute their helplessness and failure to internal inadequacies (such as a lack of ability, social incompetence, etc.) that are unlikely to change in the future instead of external environmental conditions that are changeable.

Support for Seligman's perspective on depression has been somewhat inconsistent. Some studies have demonstrated that mildly depressed people do tend to express defeatist, helpless behaviors. However, other studies of people hospitalized with severe depression demonstrate that although helplessness often accompanies depressive episodes, this pattern changes once patients' depressive episodes end. Such research has found that these formerly depressed subjects are no different from never-depressed control subjects in their tendency to view negative events with an attitude of helpless resignation. These findings suggest that an attitude of helplessness may be a symptom rather than a cause of depression.

Learned Helplessness A diminished ability to learn an avoidance response following exposure to unavoidable aversive stimulation may contribute to some forms of depression and nonresponsiveness in humans and other animals

The Biological Perspective

Considerable evidence points toward the role of biological factors in depressive disorders. Most of these findings are concentrated in two areas: genetics and brain biochemistry. We first look at the evidence suggesting the role of genetics.

Genetics

Some of the most compelling evidence linking genetics to mood disorders comes from twin studies. The average concordance rate for identical twins (65 percent) is almost five times that for fraternal twins (14 percent). If the data are further broken down according to the type of depressive disorder, the concordance rates for identical twins are much higher for bipolar than unipolar depression—72 percent versus 40 percent. Concordance rates for fraternal twins are approximately equal for the two disorders. It has also been demonstrated that concordance rates among identical twins are higher in severe than in milder forms of mood disorders. The higher concordance rates for identical twins than for fraternal twins are taken as evidence for a genetic contribution to these disorders.

Brain Biochemistry

If mood disorders can be genetically transmitted, this trait must be expressed through some physiological mechanism that makes a person vulnerable to mood disorders. Present evidence strongly suggests that this physiological expression takes the form of altered levels of neurotransmitters or their receptors in the brain. Recall from Chapter 3 that neurotransmitters are chemical messengers that enable nerve impulses to be transmitted from one neuron to another. The activity of several neurotransmitters is strongly linked to mood disorders.

(Shutterstock)

The search for a link between neurotransmitters and mood disorders began in the 1950s.

The search for a link between neurotransmitters and mood disorders began in the 1950s, when it was learned that two classes of drugs, the *monoamine oxidase inhibitors (MAOIs)* and the *tricyclics*, often alleviated the symptoms of depression. Subsequent studies of nonhuman subjects revealed that both of these drugs act to increase the brain levels of two neurotransmitters, norepinephrine and serotonin. Thus, it seemed that low levels of these neurotransmitters might contribute to depression. This and other research led to the first formal biochemical theory of mood disorders, known as the **monoamine theory**. This theory proposes that depression is related to reduction in activity of the monoamine neurotransmitters norepinephrine and/or serotonin in specific regions of the brain (the term monoamine refers to the molecular structure of these neurotransmitters). The Monoamine Theory has been supported by a number of studies and has gone through considerable revision since it was proposed more than forty years ago. As we will see in the next chapter, drugs that are effectively used to treat mood disorders increase the activity of norepinephrine and/or serotonin.

Evidence also suggests that the winter form of seasonal affective disorder (SAD) may be caused by biochemical disturbances. Evidence suggests that the winter form of SAD involves the hormone melatonin, a substance secreted by the brain's pineal gland that affects mood and subjective energy levels. Research suggests that winter SAD may be induced by too much melatonin or by excessively prolonged secretions of melatonin (Levitan, 2007; Lewy et al., 2007). Both serotonin and melatonin systems are influenced by photoperiodism, the earth's daily dark-light cycle. To the extent that SAD is related to disturbances in the earth's dark-light cycle, it seems logical to speculate that phototherapy

Monoamine Theory The first formal biochemical theory of mood disorders; proposes that depression is related to reduction in activity of the monoamine neurotransmitters norepinephrine and/or serotonin in specific regions of the brain may be effective in treating winter depression by acting to correct abnormalities in one or both of these two distinct biological systems. We will examine this in the next chapter.

As persuasive as the biological evidence is, we cannot at this time state that depression is simply caused by altered biochemistry. As we will see in the next section, severe behavioral disorders are most likely the result of genetic predispositions, altered brain biochemistry, and environmental factors.

15.10 Schizophrenia

David was first diagnosed with schizophrenia when he was twenty-six years old. At that time he was in his fourth year as an architecture student at the University of Oregon. David's life prior to attending the university was not unusual. He had many high school friends, he was outgoing, and he was exceptionally bright. Any eccentricities in his behavior during these years were attributed to deep passion for everything he did, but particularly for drawing. While in college, David began to withdraw socially during his freshman year. He started college as an art major, and he spent most of his time immersed in his drawings. At first, his artwork earned him praise because of his obsession with detail; later, however, this fixation began to take over, and he could never complete his assignments. He preferred spending time alone and would often be observed wandering aimlessly on campus, failing to recognize or respond to those who knew him. During his third year, David's advisor suggested he might do well in architecture since he seemed more intrigued with drawings of buildings. David's sketches were becoming increasingly complex and not well suited to his assignments. Discussions with his mentors were getting more and more frustrating as his elaborations began to reveal his psychosis. David would talk enthusiastically about his design concepts only to be met with an outright rejection of his increasingly bizarre ideas. At this point, David was becoming convinced that his professors were concealing their real interest in plagiarizing his work by their rejection of it. Rather than continuing to work in the student lab in the architecture building, David found it necessary to do his work in secret because his professors were spying on him. Within a few months David was convinced that co-conspirators of the plagiarism scheme were tapping his phone and following him everywhere. By now he was having great difficulty sleeping and was spending his time altering his drawings to conceal the innovations he had made.

After seeing and discussing his recent work, David's parents realized that their son needed professional help. After several appointments, he was diagnosed with paranoid schizophrenia and given a prescription for clozapine. David's psychiatrist encouraged him to schedule monthly appointments and to return to school to finish his architecture degree. David remained on the medication for several months and was showing signs of improvement, but he felt the medication dampened his creativity and made it difficult to draw. His paranoia quickly returned when he discontinued medication, forcing him to leave school altogether. During our initial visit, David's enthusiasm for architecture was easy to draw out—so too was his paranoia of members of the department at the university who were conspiring to steal his creations. It wasn't at all unusual for David to hear voices threatening him if he didn't reveal his work. On numerous occasions, one familiar voice threatened, "We know where you live, David."

While David could respond sensibly to questions about his past, he would lapse into incoherent speech, where sentences were only loosely connected, when we discussed his plans about his future. His thoughts also seemed to shift unpredictably, making it difficult to follow. If one didn't know of his medical condition, one might be easily convinced of his architectural genius during a rant about building design.

Of all the psychological disorders, **schizophrenia** is perhaps the most serious and debilitating. It typically emerges in early adulthood; although there may be periods of remission, schizophrenia is a chronic lifelong illness for most patients. It is characterized by extreme disruptions of perceptions, thoughts, emotions, and behavior. At any point, it affects about 1 percent of people throughout the world, and it is estimated that as many as three out of every one hundred people may experience this disorder at some time during their lives. Approximately six hundred thousand people receive treatment for schizophrenia annually in the United States. This disorder occurs with equal frequency in both sexes. The *DSM-5* characterizes a number of schizophrenic-related disorders; we will focus on schizophrenia.

Schizophrenia was once called *dementia praecox* (Kraepelin, 1918) because the disorder typically has an early (*praecox*) onset in the teenage or young adult years and is characterized by a progressive intellectual deterioration, or *dementia*. The term *schizophrenia* was later coined by Eugene Bleuler (1950) to describe what he saw as the primary symptom of this disorder: a dissociation of thoughts from appropriate emotions caused by a splitting off (the Greek *schizo*, or "split") of parts of the mind (the Greek *phrenum*, or "mind"). Laypersons often confuse schizophrenia with multiple personality, an entirely different disorder. Whereas the split in multiple personality disorder is between different personalities, all of which are capable of maintaining contact with reality, the split in schizophrenia is between thoughts and feelings. The result is often bizarre behavior that is highly dysfunctional.

Schizophrenia is distinguished from other behavioral disorders primarily by the characteristically extreme disturbances in thinking that cause people to behave in maladaptive ways. In addition to these thought disturbances, a constellation of other symptoms is used to diagnose this disorder. People diagnosed as schizophrenic may show considerable diversity of symptoms. They typically exhibit most, but not necessarily all, of a primary core of symptoms as well as one or more *secondary* symptoms that are used to assign the individual to a particular subtype of schizophrenia. We look at the primary symptoms that typify all forms of schizophrenia and then at the secondary symptoms of each subtype.

15.10a Primary Symptoms of Schizophrenia

The primary or core symptoms that are characteristic forms of schizophrenia include disturbances or abnormalities in at least one of the following domains: delusions, hallucinations, thinking and speech, motor behavior, and motivation and emotional expression (American Psychiatric Association, 2013).

Delusions and Disturbances of Thought

Delusions are rigid, fixed beliefs that are inconsistent with reality. These delusions seem to vary around several consistent themes: persecution, reference, grandiosity, influence, or nihilism. Table 15-3 describes several examples of delusional thoughts that may be associated with schizophrenia. In each case, the delusions are firmly held, despite conflicting evidence.

Schizophrenia Class of severe and disabling mental disorders characterized by extreme disruptions of perceptions, thoughts, emotions, and behavior

Hallucinations and Disturbances of Perception

A second primary symptom, disturbed perception, may include changes in how the body feels (including numbness, tingling, or burning sensations, or the feeling that organs are deteriorating or that parts of the body are too large or small), or a feeling of depersonalization that makes a person feel separated from his or her body. Many schizophrenics report changed perceptions of their external environment. For some, everything may appear two-dimensional and colorless; others report that they are hypersensitive to light, sound, or touch. Research also demonstrates that schizophrenics have considerable difficulty properly focusing their attention as they process sensory stimulation and that they are often unable to filter out irrelevant information.

The most common altered perceptions in schizophrenia are hallucinations. These may occur in any of the sense modalities, but most often a schizophrenic person hears voices that seem to be coming from outside the person's head. It has been suggested that at least some of the auditory hallucinations experienced by schizophrenics may be projections of their own thoughts. Most common are imagined voices that make critical or insulting comments about the schizophrenic person's character or behavior. For instance, a patient may hear, upon passing a woman on the sidewalk, "You raped that woman." Rarely do schizophrenics hear voices requesting them to do harmful things to themselves or to others.

Disturbances in Emotional Expression and Motivation

A third common symptom of schizophrenia is a disturbance in emotional expression. This symptom may take the form of a *blunted* or *flat affect,* characterized by a dramatic

Table 15-3 Several Varieties of Delusional Thoughts That May Be Associated with Schizophrenia

Delusion of influence	A belief that others are influencing one by means of wires, TV, and so on, making one do things against one's will
Delusion of grandeur	The belief that one is in actuality some great world or historical figure, such as Napoleon, Queen Victoria, or the president of the United States
Delusion of persecution	The belief that one is being persecuted, hunted, or interfered with by certain individuals or organized groups
Delusion of reference	The belief that others are talking about one, that one is being included in TV shows or plays or referred to in news articles, and so on.
Delusion of bodily changes	The belief that one's body is changing in some unusual way—for example, that the blood is turning to snakes or the flesh to concrete
Delusion of nihilism	The belief that nothing really exists, that all things are simply shadows; also common in the idea that one has really been dead for many years and is observing the world from afar

Source: "Functional and anatomical brain imaging: impact on schizophrenia research" by M. S. Buchsbaum, 1987, Schizophr Bull 13[1]:115–132. Copyright 1987 by Oxford University Press. Reprinted with permission.

lack of emotional expression. The person may stare vacantly with listless eyes, speak in a monotone, and show no facial expression. Differing theories have been offered to explain this lack of affect, including the possibility that schizophrenic people may be so absorbed in responding to internal stimuli that they are unresponsive to outside stimuli. It has also been suggested that by turning themselves off, schizophrenics are able to protect themselves from stimuli with which they feel incapable of coping.

Perhaps even more common than flat affect are inappropriate emotional responses, in which the emotional expression is incongruous with its context. For example, a schizophrenic person may laugh upon hearing of the death of a loved one, or may fly into a rage when asked an innocuous question such as, "Did you enjoy your dinner?" Mood states may shift rapidly for no discernible reason.

Schizophrenics may also have diminished volition to engage in purposeful behavior. They may sit for extended periods and show little interest in work or social activities.

Disturbances in Speech

In addition to abnormal speech patterns (such as incoherence and loose associations) that result from thought disturbances, two verbal dysfunctions may be viewed as primary examples of speech disturbances linked with schizophrenia. In **mutism**, the person may not utter a sound for hours or days, regardless of how much encouragement or prodding is provided. In the other disturbance, **echolalia**, a person might answer a question by repeating it verbatim or might repeat virtually every statement he or she hears uttered.

Disorganized or Catatonic Behavior

A fifth symptom of schizophrenia is grossly disorganized or catatonic behavior. Disorganized or abnormal behavior might include inappropriate, childlike behavior or unpredictable agitation. Catatonic behavior is characterized by a severe rigidness of posture that may be maintained for hours. In addition, catatonic postures can be molded into new and unusual positions. Throughout an episode of catatonia, an individual may be completely unresponsive even though they are often fully aware of what is going on around them.

For a diagnosis of schizophrenia, at least two of the above five symptoms must have been present during the preceding month. In addition, these symptoms must have been severe enough to disrupt social or occupational functioning (American Psychiatric Association, 2013). As mentioned, the prevalence of schizophrenia worldwide is about 1 percent of the population (National Institute of Mental Health, 2016). In some regions around the world, this incidence is much greater. For example, African Caribbean people living in England seem to have the highest incidence.

15.10b The Development of Schizophrenia

The first diagnosable features of schizophrenia typically emerge in a person's late teens or early twenties. The onset of symptoms may be either gradual or abrupt, but most schizophrenics develop their disease gradually over several years. Because there is no treatment for this disease, schizophrenia persists and gradually worsens over one's lifetime. There may be periods where symptoms appear to improve or go into remission, but it almost always returns.

Mutism Speech disturbance characteristic of schizophrenia in which an individual may not utter a sound for hours or days at a time

Echolalia Speech disturbance characteristic of some forms of schizophrenia in which people repeat virtually every statement they hear uttered

15.10c Positive and Negative Symptoms of Schizophrenia

Positive Symptoms
Represent an excess or distortion of normal behavior of schizophrenia; may include hallucinations, delusions, and excessive verbal behavior

Negative Symptoms
Represent diminished or absent behavior of schizophrenia; may include flattened emotions, diminished social behavior, apathy, anhedonia, and catatonic motor behavior

Schizophrenia is described as occurring with predominantly **positive symptoms** or **negative symptoms**. Positive symptoms are the expression of excessive or distorted behaviors such as delusions or hallucinations. Negative symptoms are expressed as diminished or absent behavior. For example, negative symptoms may include flattened emotions, apathy, catatonic motor behavior, or anhedonia (a lack of the ability to experience pleasure). Often patients first display positive symptoms; however, as their disease progresses in both duration and severity, more negative symptoms begin to appear. It is believed that negative symptoms begin to emerge as the disease causes more and more damage to the frontal lobes of the brain. We see evidence for this in the brain images depicted in Figure 15-3.

15.10d Theoretical Perspectives on Schizophrenia

Schizophrenia has spawned more research into causes and treatments than any other behavioral disorder. We shall look at the psychoanalytic, behavioral, and biological perspectives and then present a model that accounts for both biological and psychological factors.

The Psychoanalytic Perspective

Freud believed that schizophrenia occurs when a person's ego either becomes overwhelmed with id demands or is besieged by unbearable guilt. In both cases, the ego elects

Figure 15-3 PET Scans Comparing a Patient Diagnosed with Schizophrenia (right) with a Normal Subject (left). The color red indicates more frontal lobe activity than blue or yellow.

Note the difference in activity in the frontal cortex. Some studies suggest that schizophrenics have lower levels of frontal cortex activity than normal subjects.

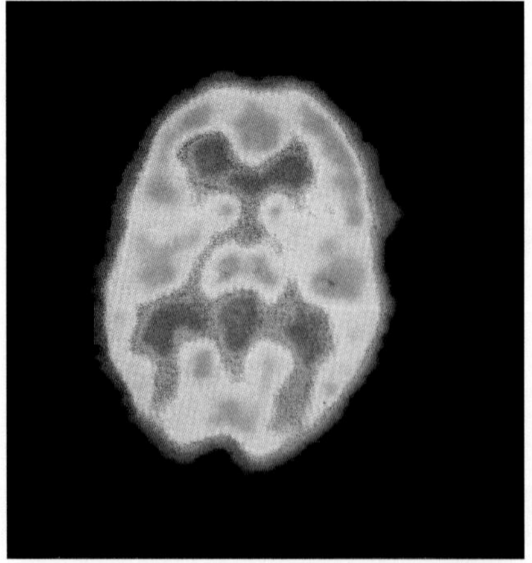

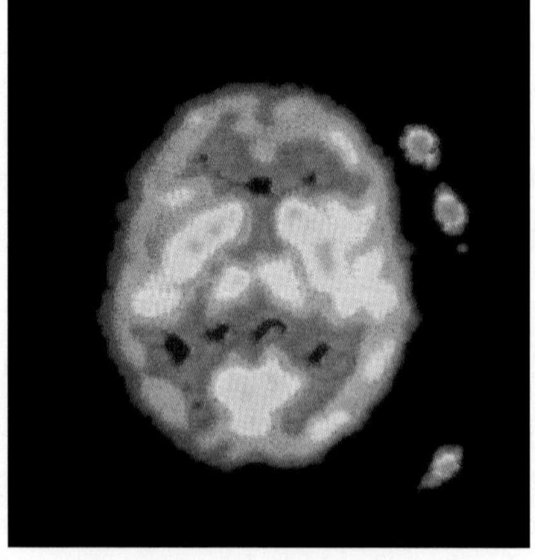

Source: "Functional and anatomical brain imaging: impact on schizophrenia research" by M.S. Buchsbaum, 1987, *Schizophr Bull 13*[1]:115–132. Copyright 1987 by Oxford University Press. Reprinted with permission.

to retreat rather than attempt to set things straight, and the person undergoes a massive regression back to the oral stage of psychosexual development. In the first phase of this retreat, *regressive symptoms* demonstrate a return to the infantile. A person may return to primary process thinking (see Chapter 14) and experience delusions of self-importance. Eventually, the regression becomes so extensive that all contact with reality is lost. At this point, the schizophrenic begins a struggle to regain reality. *Restitutional symptoms* appear, such as hallucinations, delusions, and bizarre speech patterns, which reflect an effort to reestablish verbal communication with other people. Today, only a very few psychoanalytic theorists place much credibility in Freud's explanation of schizophrenia.

The Behavioral Perspective

It is difficult to see how behavioral principles such as reinforcement and modeling contribute to the symptoms of people who are as out of touch with reality as schizophrenics. However, learning theorists propose that schizophrenics either have not been reinforced adequately for responding to normal social stimuli or, perhaps, have even been punished for such responses. As a consequence, normal patterns of attending to or reacting to appropriate social cues are extinguished or suppressed. To fill the resulting void, they begin to respond to inappropriate stimuli, such as imaginary voices emanating from the coffeepot. Other people's responses to these bizarre behaviors may then further reinforce these patterns. In fact, the worsening of schizophrenic symptoms can often be attributed to the consequences of these behaviors. While behavioral theory may have some difficulty explaining why some people become schizophrenic, as you will see in the next chapter, it may account for the persistence of some abnormal behaviors and it has been a useful approach in the treatment of schizophrenic behavior.

The Biological Perspective

The biological perspective provides a stronger explanation for schizophrenia. As with depressive disorders, substantial clues point toward both genetic and biochemical abnormalities.

Genetics

An extensive body of research indicates that certain people are genetically predisposed to develop schizophrenia (Gottesman & Shields, 1976; Gottesman, McGuffin, & Farmer, 1987; Pardes, Kaufman, Pincus, & West, 1989). Table 15-4 summarizes some of these data from a number of twin studies. Note that the concordance rate for identical twins appears to be between two to four times higher than that reported for fraternal twins. These data may be misleading, however, because the researchers did not indicate whether the identical twins in the studies developed within the same placenta or in two separate placentas. When identical twins develop within the same placenta and share the same blood supply, they are called *monochorionic twins*. Twins that develop in separate placentas and blood supplies are called *dichorionic twins* (see Figure 15-4). A more careful analysis of the concordance rate data suggests that concordance rates for dichorionic twins may be closer to 10 percent than the nearly 50 percent reported in some studies. Researchers speculate that this difference is due to environmental, not genetic, conditions (Phelps, Davis, & Schartz, 1997).

Family studies have shown a substantially higher incidence of schizophrenia among relatives of schizophrenics than among the general population. Adoption studies have provided further evidence. Several investigators have found that adoptees whose biological parent or parents were diagnosed as schizophrenic were considerably more likely to develop the disorder than adoptees whose biological parents were free of the illness.

Table 15-4 Concordance Rates of Schizophrenia Between Identical and Fraternal Twins

		Identical Twins		Fraternal Twins	
Investigator	**Country**	**Number of Pairs in Sample**	**Percentage Concordance Rate**	**Number of Pairs in Sample**	**Percentage Concordance Rate**
Gottesman & Shields	England	22	40–50*	33	9–19
Pollin et al.	USA	95	14–27	125	4–8
Fischer	Denmark	21	24–48	41	10–19
Kringlen	Norway	55	23–38	90	4–10
Tienari	Finland	17	0–36	20	5–14

Data from: "Concordance Rates of Schizophrenia Among Identical and Fraternal Twins" from *Schizophrenia: The Epigenetic Puzzle* by Irving I. Gottesman and James Shields. Copyright © 1982 by Irving I. Gottesman and James Shields.

*The range in the concordance rate figures reflects different estimates of what would constitute a concordant pair, which vary depending on how narrowly or broadly schizophrenia is defined. The lower figure is for the narrower definition, which requires a majority of the major symptoms of schizophrenia to be present.

Because much of the heritability of schizophrenia still remains unexplained, researchers are now focusing on epigenetic factors that contribute to its expression. Scientists hope to discover how environmental factors contribute to gene expression for schizophrenia (Gebicke-Haerter, 2012).

In all, while there is abundant evidence that genetics is an important factor in the development of schizophrenia, it seems unlikely that genes alone cause this disorder. If that were the case, the concordance rate between twins would be virtually 100 percent. Furthermore, even when both parents have schizophrenia, the odds are better than 50–50 that their offspring will not develop the disorder. Several schizophrenia researchers explain this discrepancy by theorizing that a genetic predisposition toward schizophrenia is by no means a sufficient condition to produce this disorder—certain environmental stressors must also be present. We return to this interaction hypothesis after considering some additional evidence of biological factors.

Brain Biochemistry As with the mood disorders, researchers studying schizophrenia have focused considerable attention on biochemical abnormalities and mechanisms of drug action to explain schizophrenia. Although several different biochemical hypotheses have been proposed over the years, the dopamine hypothesis appears to be the most promising. The *dopamine hypothesis* suggests that schizophrenia is caused either by abnormally high levels of the neurotransmitter dopamine or by above-normal activity of this neurotransmitter due to an increased number of receptors for dopamine.

This hypothesis is supported by research. For example, it is known that the *phenothiazines* (drugs that alleviate some of the symptoms of schizophrenia) reduce the activity of dopamine by blocking postsynaptic dopamine receptors. In addition, postmortem brain analyses have found an abnormal number of dopamine receptors in the brains of some schizophrenics, as well as abnormally high levels of dopamine activity in certain areas of schizophrenic brains. Considered together, these findings provide strong evidence linking dopamine to schizophrenia. The exact mechanism for dopamine

Figure 15-4 Identical Twins in (a) Separate Placentas (Dichorionic) and (b) Same Placenta (Monochorionic)

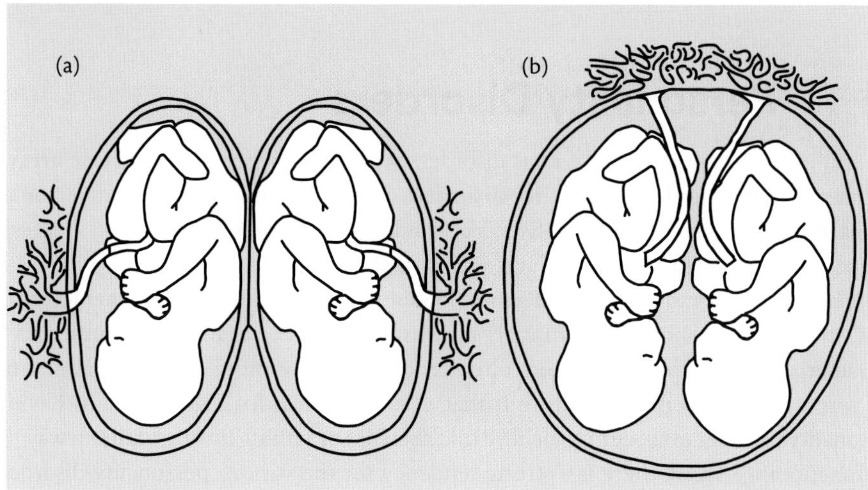

involvement, however, is still unknown (Carlsson, 1977; A. Carlsson & M. Carlsson, 2006; Murray, Lappin, & Di Forti, 2008; Takahashi, Higuchi, & Suhara, 2006).

Brain Structural Abnormalities There is also extensive evidence of structural abnormalities in the brains of schizophrenics. These findings, considered in tandem with data concerning biochemical irregularities, provide powerful evidence that schizophrenia is a progressive brain disease. Several of the new techniques for observing living brains, such as CAT and PET scans and magnetic resonance imaging (see Chapter 3), have provided evidence of various kinds of physical abnormalities in the brains of individuals diagnosed as having schizophrenia. These structural abnormalities include unusually large ventricles (hollow spaces within the brain filled with cerebrospinal fluid), reduced volume of temporal lobe gray matter, reduced volume of the hippocampus, and an unusually small corpus callosum (Andreasen et al., 1990; Kaplan, Lazoff, Kelly, Lukin, & Garver, 1990; Rossi et al., 1990; Steen, Mull, McClure, Hamer, & Lieberman, 2006; Woods et al., 1990). The PET scans in Figure 15-3 show some of these abnormalities.

At the present time, researchers are uncertain about both the causes of these varied brain abnormalities and their relationship to various types of schizophrenia. It remains to be seen whether one complex pattern of structural brain irregularities characterizes all schizophrenics, or whether a distinct pattern is associated with each subtype. Furthermore, additional research is necessary to reveal whether brain structural abnormalities are characteristic of all forms of schizophrenia.

Throughout this text, we have emphasized the role of genetic (biological) and environmental interactions in determining behavioral dispositions. Our discussion of schizophrenia is no exception. As strong as the biological evidence is, the fact remains that not everyone who is genetically predisposed toward schizophrenia becomes schizophrenic. On the other hand, we cannot simply ignore the strong evidence for some degree of heritability for schizophrenia. For further discussion of the biological determinants of schizophrenia, refer to the Research Perspectives segment at the end of this chapter.

BVT*Lab*

Improve your test scores. Practice quizzes are available at www.BVTLab.com.

We hope that continued research will eventually provide a clearer explanation of the causes of schizophrenia. Until that time, theorists will continue their attempts to explain schizophrenia in terms of both biological dispositions and environmental factors.

15.11 Personality Disorders

We end our discussion of behavioral disorders with a brief look at the diverse array of disorders grouped under **personality disorders**. *DSM-5* identifies ten related personality disorders: paranoid, schizoid, antisocial, avoidant, borderline, narcissistic, obsessive-compulsive, dependent, histrionic, and schizotypal.

The various personality disorders are linked by a number of shared characteristics. First, most tend to show up at an early age, usually no later than adolescence, and the characteristic maladaptive behaviors often tend to become more deeply ingrained over the years. Another common feature is that very few individuals diagnosed as having a personality disorder ever seem to believe that there is something wrong with the way they are functioning. Third, there is a strong tendency for the various personality-disordered behaviors to be rigidly ingrained, highly repetitive, and ultimately self-defeating. Finally, the prognosis for overcoming any of the personality disorders is rather poor, perhaps because individuals with personality disorders are generally more inclined to refuse therapy than are people with the other behavioral disorders outlined in this chapter. The antisocial personality disorder has been the subject of more research and theorizing than any of the other ten personality disorders, and it is among the most prevalent—therefore, it is the focus of our discussion.

15.11a Antisocial Personality Disorder

From the point of view of society at large, the most disruptive of the personality disorders is the **antisocial personality disorder**, also referred to as *psychopathic* or *sociopathic personality disorder*. Recent estimates indicate that almost 3.5 percent of the population has antisocial personalities, with six times as many men as women included in this diagnostic category. The following list summarizes some of the most prominent characteristics of an antisocial personality as outlined by *DSM-5* and by Hare (Neumann, Hare, & Newman, 2007) who has recently developed a psychopathology checklist to assist in diagnosing this devastating condition at an early age:

1. The person's history dating back to before age fifteen demonstrates a repetitive and persistent pattern of behavior in which either the basic rights of others or major age-appropriate societal norms or rules are violated. Commonly occurring behavior includes intimidation of others, physical fights, use of weapons, thievery or robbery, physical cruelty to people and animals, rape, persistent lying, arson, vandalism, and/or truancy.
2. There is a pervasive pattern of disregard for and violation of the rights of others occurring since age fifteen. Behaviors consistent with a diagnosis of antisocial personality disorder include unlawful behavior; aggressiveness and physical fighting; consistent irresponsibility, impulsivity, or failure to plan; deceitfulness; disregard for the safety of self and others; and a lack of remorse for the mistreatment of others (American Psychiatric Association, 2013).

Personality Disorders Diverse class of disorders that is collectively characterized by inflexible and maladaptive personality traits that cause either functional impairment or subjective distress

Antisocial Personality Disorder Personality disorder characterized by disregard for rights of others, lack of remorse or guilt for antisocial acts, irresponsibility in job or marital roles, failure to learn from experience, and a profound poverty of deep and lasting emotions

Unfortunately, our television newscasts are constantly reporting horrific crimes committed in our schools and workplaces. These acts of violence leave many innocent victims either dead or seriously wounded. Predicting these actions from the personalities of those who commit them is difficult, but their pathology does not just suddenly emerge in adulthood at the time of an act of violence. Psychologists now believe that psychopathic traits and behaviors emerge early in life and may be identifiable as early as five or six years of age (Hare & Neumann, 2006).

15.11b Theoretical Perspectives on Antisocial Personality Disorder

Despite several decades of extensive research, we still do not have a clear understanding of the origins of the antisocial personality disorder. The following paragraphs briefly consider the psychoanalytic, behavioral, and biological perspectives on the etiology of this condition.

(iStock)

From the point of view of society at large, the most disruptive of the personality disorders is the antisocial personality disorder.

The psychoanalytic perspective looks to the childhood development of personality dynamics. Recall that Freud and his followers maintained that our sense of right and wrong emerges with the development of the superego sometime during the childhood years. It is the superego that places moral and ethical restraints on one's actions. Theorists with a psychoanalytic orientation suggest that because of some aberration in the normal course of early personality development, a person with an antisocial personality disorder fails to acquire a superego. Consequently, he or she acts to satisfy id instincts without regard for social mores and unhindered by guilt or shame.

Behavioral theorists propose the view that people with antisocial personality disorder act impulsively and repeatedly manifest antisocial misbehavior because they have not learned to avoid punishment. Such inappropriate behaviors persist despite repeated social and/or legal sanctions.

What is the source of this apparent indifference to punishment? Psychologist David Lykken (1957) reasoned that people with antisocial personality disorder might have far less anxiety about the possible consequences of punishment than most people. To test this hypothesis, Lykken devised a complex learning task in which three groups of male subjects (imprisoned sociopaths, nonsociopathic inmates, and college students) were told that electric shocks would be randomly administered for incorrect responses as a stimulant for good performance. Successful mastery of the task was not made contingent on avoiding shocks, and subjects were not told that avoiding shock was desirable or even possible. (In actuality, it was possible to learn to avoid shocks while mastering the task.) Although all three groups performed equally well on the learning task, there were considerable differences in the way they responded to the shocks. The college men eventually figured out how to respond in such a way as to decrease their chance of receiving a shock, but individuals with antisocial personality disorder demonstrated little or no such learning. (The nonsociopathic inmates exhibited shock-avoidance behavior that fell between these two extremes.) Lykken's findings have been supported by other research showing that antisocial personalities demonstrate considerably less emotional responsiveness to threatened pain than nondisordered individuals (Hare, 1975; Hare, Frazelle, & Cox, 1978). Considered collectively, such findings suggest that punishments may have little meaning for people with antisocial personality disorder. Perhaps because of their lower degree of emotional responsiveness, such people seem to express the attitude, "You can't hurt me because nothing you do matters to me." Where does this lack of emotional responsiveness to aversive consequences come from? Is it learned or do psychopaths have disordered brains? To answer this, we briefly examine the biological evidence.

Several investigations have shown that 50 to 60 percent of people with antisocial personality disorder exhibit abnormal brain waves, compared to 10 to 15 percent of nondisordered people (Hare, 1970). More recently, EEG analysis of criminal psychopaths revealed that they produced different brain waves during image processing tasks when compared to nonpsychopathic individuals (Kiehl, Bates, Laurens, Hare, & Liddle, 2006). Although the meaning of these differences in brain activity is not known, they suggest that psychopaths may have dysfunctions of their limbic system and their frontal lobes, making them less sensitive to behavioral consequences and less able to control impulsive behaviors.

In this chapter we have defined, characterized, and discussed possible causes of the major behavioral disorders. Although considerable progress has been made in identifying causal factors in these disorders, this continues to be an active area of research from several theoretical perspectives. We can continue to expect that our understanding of these disorders will increase as this research progresses. In the next chapter, we will see how psychologists and other professionals treat behavioral disorders.

CHAPTER REVIEW

Defining Abnormal Behavior

1. While there is no universally accepted definition of abnormality, psychologists emphasize a common core of four criteria that distinguish between normal and abnormal behavior: atypicality, maladaptivity, emotional discomfort, and social unacceptability.
2. Any given behavioral disorder may reflect only one or a combination of these four criteria.

Classifying Behavioral Disorders

3. *DSM* is the most widely used scheme today for classifying and diagnosing behavioral disorders throughout the world. The current version is *DSM-5*.

Anxiety Disorders

4. A panic disorder is characterized by episodes of intense apprehension and overwhelming terror that occur as often as four or more times in a four-week period.
5. Most people who have a panic disorder also exhibit symptoms of agoraphobia. Agoraphobia is characterized by intense fear of being in places or situations from which escape might be difficult, or in which help might not be available in the event of a panic attack.
6. Less commonly, people may suffer a panic disorder without symptoms of agoraphobia. In some cases, agoraphobia exists without any symptoms or prior history of panic disorder.
7. Phobias, characterized by a persistent fear of and consequent avoidance of a specific object or situation, are among the most common behavioral disorders.
8. A social phobia is a persistent, irrational fear of performing some specific behavior in the presence of other people. A distinction is made between discrete performance anxiety and generalized social anxiety.
9. A specific phobia is an irrational fear of a specific situation or object, such as closed places or spiders.
10. Generalized anxiety disorder is characterized by a chronic state of anxiety that is omnipresent across a wide range of situations.

CHAPTER REVIEW

Trauma-Related Disorders

11. Post-traumatic stress disorder occurs after a person experiences a psychologically traumatic event (or events) outside the normal range of human experience. PTSD is characterized by vivid flashbacks and avoidance of stimuli associated with the traumatic event or numbing of general responsiveness.

Obsessive-Compulsive Disorder

12. An obsessive-compulsive disorder is characterized by a profound sense of anxiety that is reflected in persistent, unwanted, and unshakable thoughts and/or irresistible habitual actions in which the individual repeatedly engages in some ritualistic act.
13. Freud explained the anxiety disorders as a result of internal conflicts, particularly those involving sexual or aggressive impulses.
14. Behavioral theorists see Pavlovian conditioning as the source of the anxiety disorders.
15. The biological perspective on anxiety disorders presents evidence that genetic factors play a role in these disorders, which some people with unusually responsive nervous systems may be biologically predisposed to develop. Short-circuiting of hard-wired behavioral subroutines stored in the basal ganglia may be a cause of obsessive-compulsive disorder.

Somatic Symptom Disorders

16. A person with somatic symptom disorder typically has multiple and recurrent physical symptoms, for which medical attention is repeatedly sought, but which have no physical cause.
17. People with illness anxiety disorder also complain about a variety of physical difficulties. The primary difference between illness anxiety disorder and somatic symptom disorder is that people manifesting the former are fearful that their symptoms indicate serious disease(s), whereas those with somatization disorder typically do not progress beyond a concern with the symptoms themselves.
18. Conversion disorder typically manifests as a sensory or motor system disturbance for which there is no known organic cause.
19. Freud believed that somatic symptom disorders stem from unresolved sexual impulses. According to the behavioral/learning perspective, a somatic symptom disorder allows a person to escape from or avoid the negative reinforcer of anxiety. There is little evidence of biological factors in somatic symptom disorders.

CHAPTER REVIEW

Dissociative Disorders

20. A person with dissociative amnesia experiences sudden loss of memory, usually after a particularly stressful or traumatic event.
21. A person with a dissociative identity disorder alternates between an original or primary personality and one or more secondary or subordinate personalities.
22. Personality disorders are associated with some individuals who have experienced extreme physical and emotional abuse during childhood.
23. Psychoanalytic theory considers all dissociative disorders to be the result of massive reliance on repression to ward off unacceptable impulses, particularly those of a sexual nature. Behavioral/learning theory suggests that dissociative reactions may involve operant avoidance responses that are reinforced because they allow an individual to avoid anxiety associated with stressful events. There is no evidence linking biological factors to development of these disorders.

Depressive Disorders

24. Major depressive disorder is distinguished by deep depression.
25. People with major depressive disorder typically manifest their symptoms over an extended period (from months to a year or longer), are unable to function effectively, and experience a breakdown in interpersonal relationships.
26. Bipolar disorder is characterized by intermittent episodes of both depression and mania (highly energized, euphoric behavior and excessive activity).
27. In some cases of bipolar disorder, episodes of depression and mania may alternate regularly, with months or years of symptom-free normal functioning between the disordered mood states.
28. A manic episode often follows a three-stage course of accelerating intensity (mania, hypomania, and severe mania) in which the individual's thinking and behavior become progressively more disorganized and psychotic-like.
29. According to the psychoanalytic perspective, depressive disorders are rooted in relationships involving overdependence and ambivalent feelings of love and hate. When a person experiences actual (or threatened) loss of such a relationship, the unconscious hostility toward the lost person surfaces as anger that is turned back against oneself in the form of depression.
30. Behavioral and learning theorists see depression as emerging from the loss of a primary source of positive reinforcement through such things as separation from or death of a loved one or loss of a job.
31. Seligman's cognitive learning perspective suggests a theory of learned helplessness, which links depression to people's belief that they have no control over the reinforcers and punishers in their lives.

CHAPTER REVIEW

32. There is compelling evidence linking altered brain chemistry to severe depressive disorders.
33. The monoamine theory of mood disorders suggests that abnormalities in serotonin and/or norepinephrine activity result in depression.

Schizophrenia

34. A collection of primary or core symptoms that characterize many forms of schizophrenia includes disturbances in thought, perception, emotional expression, and speech, together with social withdrawal and diminished motivation.
35. Disorganized schizophrenia is indicated by marked disorganization and regression in thinking and behavioral patterns. A person with this disorder often behaves in an infantile manner and expresses wild swings in mood from fits of crying to episodes of uncontrollable giggling.
36. The distinguishing symptoms of catatonic schizophrenia are extreme psychomotor disturbances, which may range from stuporous immobility to wild excitement and agitation.
37. The dominant symptom of paranoid schizophrenia is the presence of well-organized delusional thoughts.
38. Freud believed that schizophrenia occurs when a person's ego either becomes overwhelmed with id demands or is besieged by unbearable guilt. In both cases, the person undergoes a massive regression back to the oral stage of psychosexual development.
39. One behavioral-learning view suggests that schizophrenics either have not been reinforced adequately for responding to normal social stimuli, or perhaps have even been punished for such responses. As a consequence, normal patterns of responding are extinguished or suppressed, and the schizophrenic instead begins to respond to inappropriate stimuli, such as imaginary voices.
40. An extensive body of research indicates that certain people are genetically predisposed to develop schizophrenia.
41. There is biochemical evidence that schizophrenia may be caused by abnormal dopamine activity.
42. There is also substantial evidence of structural abnormalities in the brains of schizophrenics.
43. According to the interactional model, two factors are necessary for schizophrenia to develop. The first is a biological vulnerability to schizophrenia; the second is severe life stress.

CHAPTER REVIEW

Personality Disorders

44. Personality disorders are grouped into six separate disorders: antisocial, avoidant, borderline, narcissistic, obsessive-compulsive, and schizotypal.
45. Common characteristics of antisocial personality disorder include a history dating back to or before age fifteen; lack of remorse or guilt over antisocial acts; repeated academic, vocational, and relationship failures; lack of insight; superficial charm; manipulative behavior; and extreme egocentricity.
46. Psychoanalytic theorists associate antisocial personality disorder with the failure to acquire a superego during early childhood development. Learning theorists suggest that antisocial personalities have not learned to avoid punishment. The biological perspective speculates that abnormalities in both the limbic and frontal lobes may underlie the disorder.

TERMS AND CONCEPTS

Abnormal Behavior, pg. 593
Agoraphobia, pg. 598
Antisocial Personality Disorder, pg. 626
Anxiety Disorder, pg. 597
Attention-Deficit/Hyperactivity Disorder (ADHD), pg. 596
Basal Ganglia, pg. 605
Bipolar Disorder, pg. 612
Cingulotomy, pg. 605
Conversion Disorder, pg. 607
Delusion, pg. 614
Depersonalization-Derealization Disorder, pg. 609
Depressive Disorders, pg. 610
Dissociative Amnesia, pg. 608
Dissociative Disorders, pg. 608
Dissociative Identity Disorder, pg. 609
Echolalia, pg. 621
Generalized Anxiety Disorder (GAD), pg. 600
Hallucination, pg. 614
Hypomania, pg. 612
Illness Anxiety Disorder, pg. 606
Learned Helplessness, pg. 616
Major Depressive Disorder, pg. 611
Mania, pg. 612
Monoamine Theory, pg. 617
Mutism, pg. 621
Negative Symptoms, pg. 622
Obsessive-Compulsive Disorder (OCD), pg. 600
Panic Disorder, pg. 598
Personality Disorders, pg. 626
Phobia, pg. 598
Positive Symptoms, pg. 622
Post-Traumatic Stress Disorder (PTSD), pg. 602
Schizophrenia, pg. 619
Social Anxiety, pg. 598
Somatic Symptom Disorder, pg. 606
Specific Phobia, pg. 599

RESEARCH PERSPECTIVES

Perspectives on Behavioral Disorders

Perspective #1: Dr. Irving I. Gottesman

Irving I. Gottesman was a professor of psychiatry and psychology at the University Minnesota. He received his PhD in clinical and developmental psychology from the University of Minnesota in 1960. His many awards and honors included the American Psychological Association's Hofheimer Prize for Research for his work with the late James Shields on the genetics of schizophrenia in twins. Dr. Gottesman was past president of the Behavior Genetics Association and the Society for Research in Psychopathology. His most recent publications on the genetic contributions to schizophrenia include "Theories of Schizophrenia: A Genetic-Inflammatory-vascular Synthesis" (2005) and "Deconstructing Schizophrenia: An Overview of the Use of Endophenotypes in Order to Understand a Complex Disease" (2007).

Perspective #2: Dr. Kurt Salzinger

Kurt Salzinger, PhD, professor of psychology and director of the combined PhD program in clinical and school psychology at Hofstra University, recently wrote an article ("Connections: A Search for Bridges Between Behavior and the Nervous System," *Annals of the New York Academy of Sciences* 658 (1992), 276–286) dealing with the question of how to relate body to behavior. He is the author of *Schizophrenia* (1973) and *Schizophrenia and the Immediacy Mechanism* (2006). Salzinger was past president of the New York Academy of Sciences and a winner of the Stratton Award from the American Psychopathological Association for his work in schizophrenia.

PERSPECTIVE #1: *Views on the Biological Bases of Behavioral Disorders*

Dr. Irving I. Gottesman

Q: *Dr. Gottesman, is there evidence that severe mental disorders such as schizophrenia and chronic depression are caused by abnormalities in brain structure and functions?*

A: Some of the evidence for that is direct and involves looking at the brain and looking at the way human beings with these disorders respond to biological intervention. In other words, they take medication or are the recipients of particular kinds of somatic treatments, such as electroconvulsive therapy in the case of depression. The other reason why we are so fond of biological and genetic explanations for the major mental disorders is that alternative explanations—sociological, anthropological, the "soft side" of psychology, including psychodynamic or Freudian explanations—have been found so wanting. So we have another large group of studies that provide indirect evidence of the importance of genetic and biological factors.

RESEARCH PERSPECTIVES

Q: *Can you describe some of the research that you've done along those lines?*

A: I have been involved for many years, going back to the late 1950s and continuing up to the present, with studies using twins as a main strategy. I have also been involved in family studies of major mental disorders, including an important strategy of adoption studies. I think that the twin studies and adoption studies have really had a major impact on the way psychologists, psychiatrists, and students in those areas have come to think about the causes of these major disorders.

Q: *Can you describe some of the results that you've seen?*

A: Yes. I would go back to one study that has stood the test of time and involves research that I did in London in the early 1960s. I had been invited over by one of the major figures in psychiatric genetics to the Maudsley Hospital in London where Eliot Slater had maintained a register of all twins who had been admitted to the outpatient or the inpatient departments. We only looked at same-sex pairs, that is, brothers and brothers, and sisters and sisters. So we were able to conduct the first modern postwar studies of the genetics of schizophrenia, using the twin method. We ended up with twenty-four pairs of identical twins where at least one of the members of the pair had schizophrenia, and thirty-three pairs of fraternal twins where at least one of the members of each pair had a diagnosis of schizophrenia. What we found at the end of our first period of investigation was that there was overwhelming but indirect evidence for the strong role of specific genetic factors in causing the differences that we observed between the rates of schizophrenia in the identical co-twins compared to the rates observed in the fraternal co-twins. It turned out that if one identical twin was schizophrenic, then 58 percent of their co-twins were also schizophrenic. In the fraternal sample, when the first twin was schizophrenic, then 12 percent of the fraternal co-twins were also schizophrenic. These numbers are to be compared with the expectation of developing schizophrenia in the general population, which is 1 percent. So you have this really striking finding that if you are the identical twin of a schizophrenic, then your chance of developing schizophrenia is fifty-eight times what it would be if you were a member of the general population. It's this contrast between the rates in identical co-twins and fraternal co-twins compared to the general population rate that puts you on a firm footing with regard to inferring the importance of genetics and therefore biological factors in causing schizophrenia. The same strategies, I might add here, have been applied to the affective disorders—bipolar disorders where you have both depression and mania at different times, and affective disorder where you have recurring depressions. For both of those disorders, similar findings have been generated in different centers throughout the world.

RESEARCH PERSPECTIVES

Q: *In any of your follow-up research since those early studies, have you been successful in identifying any of the specific genetic factors that might be responsible for them?*

A: That's where the difficulty comes in: making that leap from the indirect evidence using what are called population genetic approaches to the molecular genetic level where you would actually get at the genes involved or the biochemistry that must necessarily be involved. In order to do that, I began a new twin study in the middle 1980s with a colleague at St. Elizabeth's Hospital in Washington, D.C., Dr. E. Fuller Torrey. We have collected a nationwide sample of identical twins where one twin has schizophrenia and the other twin apparently does not. We also collected control pairs of identical twins where both have schizophrenia, a small sample where both are normal, and then another small sample where one has bipolar disorder and the twin is normal. These results that I mention are still preliminary. However, in one of the first published papers by the group at St. Elizabeth's Hospital, they were able to show, using the technique of magnetic resonance imaging, at least for the first fourteen pairs or so in the discordant twin series, that in all but one pair, the twin who was schizophrenic had enlarged ventricles in the brain compared to the normal co-twin. Now the difference was often very, very small and subtle; the only way you could see it was by looking at the images of both brains simultaneously, so that an outsider coming in and looking at the twin who has schizophrenia might not reach the conclusion that this twin had anything unusual in regard to the size of his or her ventricles. It's therefore a subtle difference, but it was so consistent that the statistical tests were something to knock your socks off. This is just the beginning on what will be done with these discordant twins using modern techniques. Another group connected to the project is using PET scans—positron emission tomography—and this will give us a view of the way the brain metabolizes glucose in order to see whether or not the energy consumption in the brain is different in the twin who is schizophrenic compared to the twin who is well.

Q: *Does your research or research of others suggest ways of trying to make any earlier determination of whether a person may have a hereditary disposition to schizophrenia or any of the major affective disorders?*

A: It's most definitely part of the research, and we go about that in two ways. One way is to collect careful retrospective accounts of the lives of these individuals who are adults at the time we encounter them. We do that not only by taking their word for what happened to them while they were growing up but by trying to collect information from their parents, especially the mothers, who would tell us such things as how much the person weighed when he or she was a baby, were there any complications that you were aware of in the delivery of this child, and so forth. The other strategy that is very important, and one with which I'm also connected, is what's called the high-risk strategy using a prospective longitudinal design. You start out with mothers and you can have fathers—who are schizophrenic and who then happen to have children—and you study their children from early in life and observe them over a long period of time, waiting, so to speak, for the other shoe to drop. We know that approximately 12 to 15 percent of the children of schizophrenic parents will eventually develop schizophrenia themselves. So you're in the position of observing infants who are apparently normal and watching them over time, knowing that if you have one hundred such infants born to a schizophrenic mother or father that by the time this group of one hundred reaches the age of, say, fifty-five years old, fifteen of them or so will develop overt schizophrenia, and others will develop what has come to be called schizophrenia spectrum disorders—that is, not the full blown manifestation of schizophrenia but certain abnormalities or aberrations in personality that still allow you to attach a description as schizotypal personality, paranoid personality, or schizoid personality.

RESEARCH PERSPECTIVES

Q: *Do you think that we are progressing to a point where, in the near future, we might be able to identify those people who are most at risk for developing schizophrenia and have some type of program of intervention?*

A: That's one of the major goals. Now you run into an ethical bind here, because when you start to notice the beginning of significant symptoms that may be related to the development of schizophrenia, you can't just sit idly by and watch the person develop into a full-blown case. So you inevitably get involved in recommending intervention, not by the project itself but by referring these people for care. So you have this ethical obligation to refer individuals who start to show the symptoms. You know already that they're at high risk based on earlier work,but now when you are actually meeting these children and having to continually talk to their parents about what you may be finding, there's no way out other than to try to prevent the further development of the disorder. I do think that we're not too far off from being able to identify children who are at much higher risk than others. This is not the same as saying that they will develop schizophrenia, but it's the same as saying we know something about these individuals, and therefore we ought to educate them at least in regard to the avoidance of certain environmental stressors that may be triggers for developing schizophrenia. Among these, my favorite candidates would be street drugs, especially PCP, LSD, cocaine, and things that have amphetamines. Those things are known to irritate, so to speak, the dopaminergic system of the brain. We know dopamine is somehow involved in the neurochemistry of schizophrenia, because all the medications that work to alleviate the symptoms of schizophrenia involve blocking of dopaminergic transmission in the brain.

Q: *What, in your opinion, is the role, if any, of psychotherapy in treating any of these disorders, especially disorders like depression, which people would feel are treatable by a psychotherapeutic approach?*

A: Well, once you give up a strict analogy between major mental disorder and an infectious disease, which I'm quite willing to do, then you're talking about disorders that are multifactorially determined. In other words, we're dealing with some kind of combination of genetic predisposing factors, together with unknown environmental factors that may be in the physical environment as well as in the psychological environment that combine to trigger episodes of major mental disorders such as schizophrenia and the affective disorders. This means you would be naive and foolish to omit from consideration the effects of psychotherapeutic intervention for individuals who have already developed the disorder. This is not the same as saying that psychotherapeutic intervention alone would very often be an efficient way of treatment, but in conjunction with the medication that has been found so useful for schizophrenia and for the major affective disorders, it's also quite clear that by adding to the therapeutic regimen some form of psychotherapy, you add tremendously to the ability of these medications to maintain a remission and to prevent recurrence of the episodes. There are whole series of studies coming out of centers in England, in California, and in Pittsburgh that show that even when schizophrenics are maintained on antipsychotic medication that, if you have that as your only way of intervening, those individuals still have a very high rate of relapse. Now the highest relapse rate of all, of course, comes from those individuals who stop taking their medication. If they are further exposed to psychological stressors of fairly specific kinds, those individuals have almost a 100 percent rate of relapse. So when it comes to talking about helpful intervention, we're looking for a combination of antipsychotic medication plus—I'll call it commonsense intervention—in order to get the best effect. Psychotherapy for schizophrenia is not the same as psychotherapy that is so familiar with regard to such things as neurosis. We're looking here at many studies—between a half dozen and a dozen—which say that the kind of intervention to use psychotherapeutically *does not* involve the psychodynamic approach made popular by Freud and his followers. Instead, it makes relevant an approach that has been called family therapy combined with education.

RESEARCH PERSPECTIVES

PERSPECTIVE #2: *Views on the Biological Bases of Behavioral Disorders*

Dr. Kurt Salzinger

Q: *Dr. Salzinger, is there evidence that severe mental disorders such as schizophrenia or chronic depression are caused by abnormalities in brain structure and function?*

A: The answer is yes, in the sense that for many years people have been looking at such facts as the first and most important aspect of the genetic findings. Twin studies originally and, more recently, adoption studies, have shown that there is some genetic component that makes it more likely that individuals who come from families that have schizophrenia will develop schizophrenia, and individuals who come from families that have depression will have a greater likelihood of depression. The next question, then, is why it doesn't occur more consistently in people, like transmission of eye color. As far as actual neural structure is concerned, there the evidence is perhaps less balanced, but in schizophrenia for example, there is evidence that suggests that the ventricles—open spaces in the brain—are larger. The question is, larger than what percent of the population? And in fact, if you find that if you examine discordant identical twins, people who have exactly the same genetic makeup, but one has schizophrenia and the other one does not, you find that the twin with schizophrenia has a larger ventricle than the individual who is normal. However, if you just look at the general population, normal individuals who have larger ventricles appear similar to schizophrenic patients, so you can't find any difference. The real problem as I see it is not merely to look for some kind of physiological factor or biochemical factor or anatomical factor. The real problem is trying to relate those differences to behavioral differences and then find which came first, so-called biological factors or behavioral factors.

Q: *Are you now, or have you been, involved in research to explore that question?*

A: Well, I'm not a physiological psychologist. On the other hand, I have been putting forth a theory of schizophrenia called the immediacy theory, which is based on the notion that, put most simply, schizophrenic patients differ from normal individuals in terms of responding to stimuli that are close in time. This means that a remote stimulus has less control over the behavior of a schizophrenic patient—it's less likely to influence his behavior than the behavior of a normal individual. Those stimuli that are around at the time will have the greatest effects on behavior. This factor I have been able to relate to the difference in the neurotransmitter dopamine. There is a dopamine theory in schizophrenia that says that schizophrenic patients have more dopamine in the synaptic gap than do normal individuals. What would the effect of that be? Well, if there's more dopamine there, that suggests that impulses go from neuron to neuron more quickly, and that suggests that in such a person the responses to immediate stimuli will come much more quickly than in an individual who doesn't have all that dopamine waiting for the slightest kind of stimulation to go on and do something. So here is a case where you can talk about relating behavioral effects to physiology. The immediacy hypothesis also says that if an individual has a tendency to respond quickly to stimuli that are close in time, that means that such an individual will be more likely to speak in ways that are puzzling because words that follow one another closely will, in fact, relate to one another, but words that follow one another over a longer period of time will not. What I'm talking about here is going off on tangents. To give you one example in a sentence, the word "mine" can be a possessive pronoun or it can also, of course, refer to the places where miners go and extract ore. Now if you look at the word mine out of context, that is, just as the word *mine*, you can use it either way. You can then see why schizophrenic patients may speak in ways that make other individuals say, "What? What? How did you get to that?"

Q: *Does this theory provide any clues to identifying people who might have a predisposition for schizophrenia before the onset of the more severe symptoms, or determining the chance that a person would develop schizophrenia at a later time in life?*

A: Well, the fact of the matter is that the best predictor at this point is, in fact, genetics. That is to say, if the individual is a child of a schizophrenic mother, then there is a higher probability that the child will become a schizophrenic than someone from the population at large. Now that probability isn't very great—the general predictability of schizophrenia in the population is about 1 percent—but it is several times larger than that. I haven't had a chance to study it, but it would be very interesting to look at children who are high risk and then see whether they do have a tendency to respond to stimuli closer in time to them. If they did respond to such stimuli, the reason that nobody says anything, for most people don't look at it being peculiar, is that we make allowances for children—we laugh about it, you know, because with a child you can take into account that something else is involved. Because it takes a while to notice a pattern and because one makes allowances for younger people, if there is a tendency to respond in this manner, it will not be noticed until there comes a time when obviously it makes a difference in the child's ability to plan. If a child has difficulty planning tasks and begins to respond to stimuli in ways that are peculiar, well here's a good tip-off for that. However, the important thing always, in my way of thinking, is to say, just to take my theory for the moment as if the immediacy is important, you then have to say, "How does this interact with the conditions surrounding the individual?" Well, while other things have happened to make you learn, how do you learn? You learn through reinforcement. You do things, and the consequences are rewarding to the individual. Well if the only items that are going to be rewarding are predominantly items that have to be close in time, then you can see that this individual can be conditioned in a peculiar way. In other words, if I do something and a week later something wonderful happens, I don't associate the two, and I will not be conditioned as a function of that event. To me, the important thing will be what happens in the next fifteen minutes. If nothing happens, my behavior will be affected because if I can't distinguish a relationship between the two events, I will be conditioned to do things that require immediate response or reinforcement.

Q: *Given the fact that the primary treatments for schizophrenia are pharmacological, do you see any possible efficacy for earlier pharmacological interventions along with behavioral interventions?*

A: There's a possibility. There's always a danger, of course, because any biochemical intervention has side effects. It might be useful, but I would be very much concerned that we have good evidence that the children were truly showing some of the symptoms of schizophrenic behavior. We still have to be concerned about the question of the reliability of the diagnosis. The *DSM-III-R* and *DSM-IV-TR* have made the diagnosis of schizophrenia narrower and narrower, and that, in essence, is a good thing. At the same time, the follow-up of high risk populations, and genetic studies following up children and others who have been diagnosed as having schizophrenia, have given rise to a new diagnosis called "spectrum." This, in fact, is just another way of saying that some of these children do not have schizophrenia; what they have is an increase in criminal activity; what they have is schizoid behavior; what they have is other manifestations of psychological dysfunction. Thus, it's almost forcing a result to say, "Oh yes, genetic effects are very powerful, look at this, what we have is a spectrum of schizophrenics, and we also have schizophrenia." However, it's a good example of another change of course about what we are to call schizophrenic behavior. That's what makes me uneasy about the intervention, and that's where we have to be careful.

Q: *What does evidence about the biological bases for these disorders suggest about the efficacy of psychotherapy in treating them?*

A: Well, that's an interesting question because there are two recent developments in the field of medicine. In all fields of medicine, aside from psychiatry, there has been an increased interest in, and use of, behavioral intervention. Prevention has become the word in medicine. A few years ago, the National Academy of Medicine said the one thing that we can do to prevent or have any effect on disease is changing behavior. Whether you're talking about running or whether you're talking about slowing down Type A kinds of behavior, these are profound effects, and we continue this in medicine. People are now doing experiments in which they are taking wings of hospitals and changing the environment of the rooms that were really terrible and making them like home and finding that these people respond much faster to drugs, require fewer drugs, respond better to operations, and on and on and on. In psychiatry, on the other hand, everybody is going to neurosciences, which means primarily studying the cell structure of the brain, so there's an interesting contradiction here. If medical illnesses, including cancer, AIDS, pneumonia, etc., are affected by behavioral intervention, then it makes sense to believe that behavioral disturbances will be affected by behavioral interventions. So, I think, we must go away from the notion of quick fix, which is typically the drug—the notion that, "Something's wrong; give me this thing so tomorrow I'll be better." Behavioral intervention takes a little longer. Even if the drug helps, you need behavioral intervention. For example, when you talk about schizophrenia, it certainly is useful not to have somebody who is terrified of voices continue in that state, because you can't work with such a person in a behavioral intervention. At the same time, somebody who is given a diagnosis of schizophrenia has had a very strange kind of life, and no matter what the drugs do, this person has to be conditioned in some way. Since one of the aspects of schizophrenia is that the individual has no friends, you have to teach that person such things as social skills: How do you make friends? How do you call up a member of the opposite sex and get a date? What do you say to them? So no matter what the drugs do, they don't provide behavioral repertoires, and those have to be provided to facilitate prevention. So I think it is not only that behavioral intervention is needed as a substitute for pharmacology—in some cases it's used that way—but also in the cases where pharmacology is in fact successful, there's even a greater call for behavioral intervention to really have it succeed.

POP QUIZ

True or False

___ 1. *DSM-5* is the most recent edition of the diagnostic manual.

___ 2. A person who does not leave his or her house because of fear associated with being in open public places suffers from social phobia.

___ 3. Anxiety disorders include agoraphobia, social anxiety, generalized anxiety, and phobias.

___ 4. Agoraphobia is an intense fear of being in places where escape may be difficult such as a theater, bus, or airplane.

___ 5. Disregard for the rights of others and impulsivity are two characteristics associated with antisocial personality disorder.

Multiple Choice

6. Which of the following statements is true?
   a. Most psychological disorders are chronic and untreatable.
   b. All psychological disorders result from brain abnormalities of some kind.
   c. Anxiety disorders occur when unacceptable impulses are blocked by the ego.
   d. The most successful treatment for anxiety disorders are drugs that increase GABA activity in the brain.
7. What does "recurring episodes of intense anxiety that have a sudden onset for no apparent reason" describe?
   a. Generalized anxiety disorder
   b. Panic disorder
   c. Obsessive-compulsive disorder
   d. Agoraphobia
8. Kimberly constantly thinks her immaculate house is dirty and spends most of her time cleaning, scrubbing, and straightening up. She could be diagnosed as suffering from which disorder?
   a. Thought disorder
   b. Specific dirt phobia
   c. Obsessive-compulsive disorder
   d. Generalized anxiety disorder
9. Which type of somatic symptom disorder typically develops soon after a specific serious stress or conflict?
   a. Multiple personality
   b. Conversion disorder
   c. Somatization disorder
   d. Hypochondriasis

POP QUIZ

10. Your careless smoking caused your family's home to burn down. You are most likely to develop which disorder?
    a. Panic disorder
    b. Dissociative identity disorders
    c. Dissociative amnesia
    d. Dissociative fugue disorder
11. A history of significant childhood trauma—primarily sexual abuse—is frequently associated with which of the following?
    a. Generalized anxiety disorder
    b. Dissociative identity disorder
    c. Dissociative amnesia
    d. Schizophrenia
12. Jeff alternates periods of euphoria and frantic activity with periods of deep depression and is suffering from which disorder?
    a. Seasonal affective disorder
    b. Obsessive-compulsive disorder
    c. Major depression
    d. Bipolar disorder
13. According to the cognitive-behavioral perspective, what is the cause of mood disorders?
    a. Repressed love-hate relationships
    b. Results of the loss of a primary source of reinforcement, such as the loss of a loved one or of a loss of any kind
    c. Results of Pavlovian conditioning
    d. Deficiency of brain chemicals
14. The disturbances in emotional expression associated with schizophrenia are characterized ______.
    a. by a blunted or flat affect
    b. as inappropriate
    c. neither of the above apply
    d. either of the above apply
15. Which of the following statements concerning schizophrenia is true?
    a. Manifestations of (symptoms) appear during middle and old age.
    b. The prognosis for overcoming schizophrenia is good.
    c. Schizophrenia may go in and out of remission early in the disease.
    d. Schizophrenic patients are typically dangerous to others.

Answer Key: 1.T 2.F 3.T 4.T 5.T 6.d 7.b 8.c 9.b 10.c 11.b 12.d 13.b 14.d 15.c

(Getty/monkeybusiness images)

Chapter 16

Treatment *of* Behavioral Disorders

Chapter 15 discussed a variety of behavioral disorders. The treatment of these disorders is the topic of this chapter, which describes the kinds of therapeutic interventions used to help people overcome or at least better cope with psychological disorders. This chapter begins by examining psychological therapies, or **psychotherapy**—any nonbiological, noninvasive technique or procedure designed to improve a person's adjustment to life. *Noninvasive* means that no attempt is made to alter body physiology or function, as occurs with biomedical therapies. The final section of this chapter explores biological treatments such as surgery, shock therapy, and drug therapies. We will discover that therapy may take many different forms; we will also see that these varied approaches share many common themes. Today, treatment for behavioral disorders is provided by a variety of clinicians, including clinical psychologists, clinical social workers, psychiatrists, medical doctors, and counselors.

16.1 Psychological Therapies

In the following pages, we discuss several different forms of noninvasive therapy, including psychoanalysis, cognitive therapy, and behavioral therapy. We begin this section with an overview of psychoanalysis, which is presented more for its historical value than for its present popularity and clinical value.

16.1a Psychoanalysis

Sigmund Freud developed the first formal model of psychotherapy at the end of the nineteenth century. Freud's technique, which became known as **psychoanalysis**, spawned a vast collection of observations and insights into the human condition that were eventually organized in the psychoanalytic theory of personality discussed in some detail in Chapter 14.

Psychoanalysis is based on a number of assumptions; the most fundamental is that disordered behavior results from unconscious conflicts and repressed urges, most of which are rooted in childhood experiences. A primary theme in many of these conflicts is the struggle between the id's sexual and aggressive impulses and the superego's moralistic commands. These conflicts generate anxiety, which the ego's defense mechanisms may not be able to ward off. As the individual tries more desperate strategies for coping with anxiety, symptoms of behavioral disturbances, such as phobias and conversion disorders, begin to appear. At this point, the person is likely to seek psychotherapy.

Freud believed that the only way to help people gain true relief from severe anxiety was to enter their unconscious, search out the anxiety-causing conflict(s), and help them gain insight or conscious awareness of the repressed conflict. Only then could the conflict be resolved. Put another way, the aim of psychoanalysis is to make the unconscious conscious. To accomplish this goal, Freud developed a number of therapeutic techniques.

Psychotherapy Any nonbiological, noninvasive psychological technique or procedure designed to improve a person's adjustment to life

Psychoanalysis Technique developed by Freud in which an individual's revelations of normally unconscious cognitions are interpreted

16.1b Techniques of Psychoanalysis

Classical Freudian psychoanalysis was organized around several major techniques. Probably the most important of these methods are free association, dream analysis, and interpretations of resistance and transference.

Free Association

If you visited Freud as a patient, you would be asked to lie down on a comfortable couch. Freud would sit behind you, out of your line of vision—a practice Freud believed helped to reduce distractions that might interfere with his patients' concentration. He would encourage you to say whatever came into your mind, no matter how silly or frivolous it might seem. As we saw in Chapter 14, Freud believed that through the process of **free association**, he could obtain glimpses of the unconscious conflicts and desires boiling below the surface of conscious awareness. He also believed that the actual process of venting repressed feelings (*catharsis*) could result in at least a temporary reduction in tension. Freud realized that free association is not an easy process, and that it often takes several sessions before a person begins to open up.

Dream Analysis

Freud placed great emphasis on **dream analysis**, or interpretation of dreams. He believed that dreams are the "royal road to the unconscious" and thus a rich source of information about the hidden aspects of personality. Freud provided his patients with suggestions on how to remember their dreams. During a session of analysis, patients were encouraged to report the apparent or *manifest content* of their dreams and then to work with Freud to uncover the hidden or *latent content* that often revealed the workings of the unconscious mind.

Resistance

Freud believed that what a patient does not say is as important as what is verbalized. He noted that his patients often exhibited **resistance**, or an unwillingness to discuss freely some aspects of their lives. Resistance can take many forms, including disrupting a session or changing the subject whenever a certain topic comes up, consistently joking about something as though it were unimportant (or avoiding the topic altogether), or missing appointments or arriving late. Freud believed that it was only natural to resist delving into certain areas because it is often very painful to bring unconscious conflicts into conscious awareness. Resistance was thus viewed as a sign that the therapist was getting close to the problem, and the unconscious was struggling to avoid giving up its secrets. One of the major goals of Freudian psychoanalysis was to detect and break through these resistances.

Transference

People who undergo long-term psychotherapy often begin to relate to their therapists in much the same way as they do to a parent, lover, or some other important person in their lives. Thus, feelings such as anger, love, hostility, and dependency that characterize a person's relationships with other important people might be transferred to the therapist.

Free Association Psychoanalytic technique developed by Sigmund Freud in which patients relax and say whatever comes to their minds

Dream Analysis Psychoanalytic technique involving the interpretation of dreams to learn about hidden aspects of personality

Resistance In psychoanalysis, a patient's unwillingness to describe freely some aspects of his or her life

("Tom Paine's Nightly Pest," by James Gilray (1782), etching. Wikimedia Commons/Public Domain.)

Sigmund Freud believed that dreams are the "royal road to the unconscious," and through interpretation, hidden aspects of personality can surface.

Freud believed that this process of **transference** exposes long-repressed feelings, which the patient can then work through with the help of the analyst.

Freud used transference as a model to gain insight into the significant relationships of his patients. He wrote extensively about the benefits of transference as a way of making a patient's strong feelings more accessible and thus easier to interpret and work through. (He also wrote about the potential dangers of therapists doing the same thing—of letting their relationships with their patients become complicated by their own past experiences and emotional histories, a process he called *countertransference*.)

Interpretation

To Freud it was important for analysts to interpret for patients the underlying meaning of their experiences, resistances, transferences, and dreams. He believed that such interpretations would help break through patients' defenses, providing them with insight into the causes of their neurotic behavior. This insight was also viewed as an excellent motivator to encourage a patient's active and willing participation in the therapeutic process. An example of psychoanalytic interpretation is provided in the following excerpt from a psychoanalytic therapy session:

> The patient is a middle-aged businessman whose marriage had been marked by repeated strife and quarrels. His sexual potency has become tenuous. At times he has suffered from premature ejaculation. At the beginning of one session, he began to complain about having to return to treatment after a long

Transference In psychotherapy, a process in which a patient begins to relate to the therapist in much the same way as to other important people in his or her life (such as a parent)

holiday weekend. He said, "I'm not so sure I'm glad to be back in treatment even though I didn't enjoy my visit to my parents. I feel I just have to be free." He then continued with a description of his home visit, which he said had been depressing. His mother was bossy, aggressive, and manipulative, as always. He feels sorry for his father. She has a sharp tongue and a cruel mouth. "Each time I see my father, he seems to be getting smaller; pretty soon he will disappear and there will be nothing left of him. She does that to people. I always feel that she is hovering over me ready to swoop down on me. She has me intimidated just like my wife."

"I was furious this morning. When I came to get my car, I found that someone had parked in such a way that it was hemmed in. I feel restrained by the city. I hate the feeling of being stuck in an office from nine until five."

At this point, the therapist called to the patient's attention the fact that throughout the material, in many different ways, the patient was describing how he feared confinement, that he had a sense of being trapped.

The patient continued, "You know I have the same feeling about starting an affair with Mrs. X. She wants to, and I guess I want to also. Getting involved is easy. It's getting uninvolved that concerns me."

In this material, the patient associates being trapped in a confined space with being trapped in the analysis and with being trapped in an affair with a woman.

At this point, the analyst is able to tell the patient that his fear of being trapped in an enclosed space is the conscious derivative of an unconscious fantasy in which he imagines that if he enters the woman's body with his penis, it will get stuck; he will not be able to extricate it; he may lose it.

The analyst goes on to say that one important goal of therapy would consist of making the patient aware of childhood sexual strivings towards his mother of a wish to have relations with her and of a concomitant fear growing out of the threatening nature of her personality, and that, like a hawk, she would swoop down upon him and devour him. These interpretations would give him insight into the causes of his impotence and his stormy relations with women, particularly his wife.

(Reproduced by permission of the publisher, F. E. Peacock Publishers, Inc., Itasca, Illinois. From Raymond J. Corsini, *Current Contents in Psychotherapies*, 3rd Edition, copyright 1984, pp. 37–39.)

(Wikimedia Commons/Public Domain)

Sigmund Freud was an Austrian neurologist who is best known for his theories of the unconscious mind and the defense mechanism of repression, as well as for creating the clinical practice of psychoanalysis through dialogue between a patient and trained therapist.

16.1c The Present Status of Psychoanalysis

Early in the twentieth century, psychoanalysis was the only form of psychotherapy available, and it remained the dominant force in psychotherapy until the early 1950s. Since that time, however, its popularity and influence have steadily declined; today very few psychotherapists practice classical psychoanalysis as developed by Freud. Instead, psychoanalytically oriented therapists are likely to practice a modified version in which patients sit in a chair and face the therapist rather than lie on a couch. In addition, treatment tends to be briefer in duration, with less emphasis on restructuring a person's entire personality and more attention directed to the patient's current life and relationships. Contemporary psychoanalysts still attempt to help people gain insights into the unconscious roots of their problems, but early childhood conflicts are not emphasized as much. One aspect of psychoanalysis that has not changed from the time of Freud is that the treatment simply does not work with severely disturbed or noncommunicative people. The best candidates for this type of therapy seem to be relatively young, intelligent, successful, and highly verbal individuals. As you might guess, the same observation might be made for the other forms of psychotherapy.

Cognitive Therapies Approaches to therapy that are based on the premise that most behavioral disorders result from distortions in cognitions or thoughts

Rational-Emotive Therapy (RET) Approach to therapy based on the premise that psychological problems result when people interpret their experiences based on self-defeating, irrational beliefs

16.1d Cognitive Therapies

The **cognitive therapies** (often called *cognitive-behavioral therapies*) are based on the premise that most behavioral disorders result from distortions in a person's cognitions or thoughts. A psychotherapist who operates within the cognitive framework attempts to demonstrate to clients how their distorted or irrational thoughts have contributed to their difficulties. The cognitive therapist uses a variety of techniques to help clients change these cognitions to more appropriate ones. Thus, while the goal of therapy may be to change people's maladaptive behavior, the method is to change what they think.

Over the last two decades, many psychotherapists have incorporated a cognitive orientation into their therapy practices. The primary models for the cognitive focus are provided by Albert Ellis's rational-emotive therapy and Aaron Beck's cognitive restructuring therapy.

(Shutterstock)

Psychoanalytically oriented therapists are likely to practice a modified version in which patients sit in a chair and face the therapist rather than lie on a couch.

Rational-Emotive Therapy

Albert Ellis (A. Ellis, 1962; A. Ellis & D. Ellis, 1984; Ellis & Dryden, 2007), who was originally trained as a psychoanalyst, developed **rational-emotive therapy** (RET) in the 1950s. After years of "being allergic to the passivity of psychoanalysis" and frustrated in his efforts to reform the Freudian approach to therapy, Ellis began experimenting with new methods. His efforts eventually culminated in his highly influential RET approach.

RET is based on the premise that behavioral problems result when people interpret their experiences on the basis of certain self-defeating, irrational beliefs. The therapist's approach is to help people find the flaws in their thinking, to challenge or dispute these maladaptive cognitions (in Ellis's words, to "make mincemeat" of them), and then to guide clients to substitute more logical or realistic thoughts. Ellis provides a brief summation of this model in the following quote:

> Rational-emotive therapy holds that when a highly charged emotional consequence (C) follows a significant activating event (A), A may seem to, but actually does not, cause C. Instead, emotional consequences are largely created by B—the individual's belief system. When an undesirable emotional consequence occurs, such as severe anxiety, this can usually be traced to the person's irrational beliefs, and when these beliefs are effectively disputed (at point D), by challenging them rationally, the disturbed consequences disappear and eventually cease to recur.

Cognitive Restructuring Therapy Cognitive therapy aimed at restructuring irrational thinking patterns such as the tendency to use negative self-labels

A number of self-defeating, irrational beliefs that Ellis has found to be particularly disruptive are listed in Table 16-1.

Ellis and other RET therapists take a much more active or directive role than either the psychoanalytic or humanistic therapists. To minimize a client's self-defeating outlook, RET therapists employ an eclectic, or highly varied, collection of therapeutic techniques, including such things as confrontation, persuasion, role-playing, interpretation, behavior modification, and reflection of feelings. The focus of therapy is on the here-and-now, rather than on the client's history. In Ellis's words, "rational-emotive therapists do not spend a great deal of time ... encouraging long tales of woes, sympathetically getting in tune with emotionalizing, or carefully and incisively reflecting feelings." All of these methods may be used occasionally and briefly, but RET therapists shy away from what Ellis calls "long-winded dialogues," viewing them as indulgent. Rather than helping the client *get better* during a therapy session, Ellis is more interested in helping clients get better by increasing their feeling of self-worth and by removing stumbling blocks to their personal growth.

Cognitive Restructuring Therapy

Like the rational-emotive approach, **cognitive restructuring therapy** approaches therapy with the premise that behavioral problems stem primarily from a few irrational beliefs that cause people to behave and emote in maladaptive ways. Aaron Beck, who developed cognitive restructuring therapy, believes that disturbed people typically have very negative self-images based on highly negative self-labels (Beck, 1976, 2005; Beck, Freeman, & Davis, 2004).

For example, a recent college graduate may be depressed and plagued with a defeatist, "What's the use?" attitude based on the belief that he is a mediocre person who is boring and unattractive to the other sex. Beck believes that people who do not value themselves have a tendency to overgeneralize from their experiences, and unconsciously seek out other experiences that will confirm their poor self-image. Thus, if our

Table 16-1 Some Self-Defeating Beliefs (According to Albert Ellis's Rational-Emotive Perspective)

1. The idea that you can give yourself a global rating as a human and that your general worth and self-acceptance depend on the goodness of your performance and the degree that people approve of you
2. The idea that you must have sincere love and approval almost all of the time from all the people you find significant
3. The idea that emotional misery comes from external pressures and that you have little ability to control your feelings or rid yourself of depression and hostility
4. The idea that people and things should turn out better than they do and that you have to view it as awful and horrible if you do not quickly find good solutions to life's hassles
5. The idea that life proves awful, terrible, horrible, or catastrophic when things do not go the way you would like them to go
6. The idea that your past remains all-important and that because something once strongly influenced your life, it has to keep determining your feelings and behavior today

hypothetical graduate were turned down on his first job interview and rebuffed by the attractive woman he met at a recent party, he may go on to apply for jobs for which he is clearly not qualified and perhaps to approach women that he senses are not interested in him—efforts that will validate his poor self-image because they will result in rejection. Such people are likely to continue to be victimized by their own self-defeating behaviors unless salvaged through therapeutic intervention.

Behavior Therapy Therapy based on the assumption that maladaptive behavior has been learned and can therefore be unlearned

Like Ellis, Beck's aim is to get his clients to restructure their thinking, particularly their negative self-labels. His methods, however, tend to be less confrontational and more experiential. A common strategy is for the therapist and client to make a list of the client's misguided self-impressions (although, at this point, the client is not likely to consider them to be misguided), and then to agree on some experiments to test these assumptions. For example, a therapist working with our college graduate might suggest that he obtain several job interviews for positions well within his level of expertise. Since the therapist is interested in setting up experiments that will disprove rather than confirm the client's negative self-image, some time might be spent providing guidance on how the client can conduct himself effectively in an interview session. Some efforts might also be made to change the client's thoughts about unsuccessful interviews from such negative statements as, "I'll never get a good job," or "This rejection proves I am a mediocre person" to "Looks like I may have some difficulty getting the job I want" or "How annoying to be turned down."

Evaluating Cognitive Therapies

Research on the outcomes of cognitive therapies suggests that, at least for some behavioral disorders, these methods can be quite effective. For instance, several studies evaluating therapy outcomes suggest that cognitive approaches are very effective in the treatment of depression (Beck, 2005; Hollon & Garber, 1990; Robinson, Berman, & Neimeyer, 1990). When cognitive behavior therapy is combined with antidepressant medication (discussed later in this chapter), treatment outcomes increase significantly (Craighead & Dunlop, 2014). Interestingly, there is some debate as to whether these positive outcomes can be attributed to "cognitive" or "behavioral" change. Merely because people label themselves, or their therapeutic approach, as cognitive does not necessarily imply that behavior change can be solely attributable to cognitive restructuring. We next examine behavioral therapies.

16.1e **Behavioral Therapies**

Traditional models of psychotherapy have emphasized the underlying causes of behavioral disorders, which are viewed as distinct from those that mold so-called normal behavior. For example, disordered behavior is viewed as the result of either unresolved conflicts or disordered thought processes. **Behavior therapy** departs from this traditional conception. Its central thesis is that maladaptive behavior has been learned and maintained by a history of reinforcement and/or punishment, and therefore it can be unlearned. The same principles that govern the learning and maintenance of normal behavior also determine the acquisition and maintenance of abnormal behaviors. Behavior therapy draws heavily upon the extensive body of laboratory research on human and animal learning to devise strategies for helping people to unlearn maladaptive behavior patterns at the same time that they learn more adaptive behavior patterns.

Pavlovian (or Classical) Conditioning Therapy Any behavior therapy that involves Pavlovian conditioning such as systematic desensitization therapy

Systematic Desensitization Behavior therapy using a Pavlovian conditioning technique that pairs the slow, systematic exposure to anxiety-inducing situations with relaxation training

Behavior therapy focuses on a person's behavior as being the source of the problem rather than attempting to identify underlying personalities, repressed conflicts, or unconscious motives that are causing maladaptive behavior. To change these disruptive behaviors, they enact appropriate changes in the interaction between the client and his or her environment.

For example, a person with a disabling fear of hospitals and medical personnel might be helped to gain exposure gradually to these feared situations until the anxiety is reduced to manageable levels. Parents of children who fight or squabble incessantly might be shown how to extinguish these inappropriate behaviors by no longer providing the inadvertent reinforcer of paying attention to them. A person who responds sexually to inappropriate stimuli, such as small children, might be treated through repeated exposures to an aversive stimulus paired with the stimuli that elicit the deviant arousal pattern. The following paragraphs outline some of the more commonly employed behavior therapies.

Pavlovian Conditioning Therapies

You may recall the account in Chapter 6 of the woman who was afraid of the biology laboratory. Her fear had been conditioned. Fears may often be acquired as a result of a traumatic experience. It follows, then, that Pavlovian conditioning principles should also be able to help people unlearn fears—and this is the basic premise of **Pavlovian (or classical) conditioning therapy**.

For example, suppose you are afraid of the dark as a result of a particularly frightening experience in a darkened room that occurred some years ago. Before this experience, darkness (the conditioned stimulus [CS]) was a neutral or a nonfrightening stimulus; but because of the pairing of the CS with the frightening event (an unconditioned stimulus [UCS]), fear has been learned as a conditioned response.

We know that repeated exposures to darkness without the association of a frightening experience would eventually cause a conditioned fear response to extinguish. However, you would probably be unwilling to expose yourself to solitary darkness long enough to extinguish your fear response. In view of this limitation, behavior therapists have devised a number of *counter-conditioning* strategies in which a client learns a new response (one that is incompatible with fear) to the threatening stimulus.

Systematic Desensitization

Perhaps the most widely used behavioral therapy technique is **systematic desensitization**, a strategy developed in the late 1950s by Joseph Wolpe (1958, 1985) to treat people who respond to specific stimulus situations with excessive anxiety or phobic fear. Wolpe's therapy method is based on the premise that people cannot be both relaxed and anxious at the same time. Therefore, he reasoned, if individuals can be trained to relax when confronted with fear-inducing stimuli, they will be able to overcome their anxiety. The key is to proceed slowly and systematically.

For instance, in one case known to the authors, a young woman in her midtwenties sought treatment at the urging of her husband, who was tired of sleeping "with a searchlight on every night." The woman had a deeply rooted fear of darkness that had generalized to situations other than just being in bed with the lights off. She was afraid to go anywhere if it was likely to be dark, particularly if she had to go alone.

The first step in treatment was to analyze her problem carefully, step by step. The goal of treatment was for the client to be unafraid of the dark no matter where she might encounter it—at home in bed, outside at night walking to a friend's house, and so forth. The next step was to construct a hierarchy of situations that triggered her fear of darkness, with the most intense fear-inducing situation at the top of the list and the least at the bottom. As Table 16-2 shows, this woman's fear hierarchy ranged from a mildly anxiety-provoking situation of walking in a commercial area at dusk with a companion to the intensely frightening situation of being in bed alone with no lights on.

The next phase of treatment was to teach her how to relax by training her first to recognize muscle tension in various parts of her body and then to relax all of the various muscle groups in a progressive fashion until she was in a state of complete, tranquil relaxation. Finally, when the client was fully relaxed, she was told to imagine as vividly as possible the scene at the bottom of her anxiety hierarchy. If at any time she found herself becoming anxious, she was instructed to signal, by raising a finger, her desire to switch off the image immediately, and to concentrate again on becoming deeply relaxed. When she was able to imagine this mildly threatening situation repeatedly without experiencing any anxiety, her attention was directed to the next image in the hierarchy. In this fashion, she was able to move up the hierarchy gradually and systematically until, after several sessions, she could imagine any of the scenes on her list with no discomfort.

The final phase of treatment was to instruct her to confront the anxiety-producing stimuli in the real world. Here again, she was encouraged to move slowly, starting with situations at the bottom of her anxiety hierarchy. As she received firsthand evidence that she was able to apply her newly acquired ability to relax in real life, she was encouraged to expose herself gradually to even the most fearful situation listed in the hierarchy. The treatment was successful. Several months after therapy was terminated, there was still no "searchlight" in the couple's bedroom at night.

Research has shown that systematic desensitization is often effective in dealing with specific fears and anxieties, such as those that occur in many phobic disorders. It is less effective in treating the diffuse fear that accompanies conditions such as generalized anxiety disorder. This may be because individuals with generalized anxiety or post-traumatic stress syndrome do not undergo extinction of conditioned fear as normal subjects do (see Chapter 15 for more discussion of this idea). Compared with other therapeutic approaches to dealing with specific fears and phobias, systematic desensitization often fares best.

Table 16-2 An Anxiety Hierarchy in Descending Order of Intensity

1. At home at night, alone in bed, no light
2. Outside at night, alone, walking in a poorly lighted residential area
3. At home, at night, alone, not in bed, power failure
4. At home, at night, in bed with husband, no light
5. Outside at night, with a friend or husband, walking in a poorly lighted residential area
6. At home at night, husband present, not in bed, power failure
7. Outside at night, alone, walking in a well-lighted commercial area
8. Outside at night, with a friend or husband, walking in a well-lighted commercial area
9. Outside at dusk, walking alone in a residential area
10. Outside at dusk, with a friend or husband, walking in a residential area
11. Outside at dusk, with a friend or husband, walking in a commercial area

Virtual Reality Therapy Use of virtual reality simulations to generate a variety of stimuli for systematic desensitization

Virtual Reality Therapy One difficulty that therapists encounter when applying systematic desensitization therapy is that patients find it difficult to imagine frightening or anxiety-provoking scenes. Using virtual reality simulations to generate a variety of stimuli for systematic desensitization therapy may be an effective method to overcome this difficulty (North et al., 2002). In a recent experiment, thirty patients with a flying phobia were randomly assigned to one of three treatment conditions. Group 1 received virtual reality exposure with physiological feedback (heart rate, etc.); Group 2 received virtual reality exposure without physiological feedback; and Group 3 received traditional systematic desensitization therapy with imagined stimulus exposure. During a three-month period, following eight weeks of therapy, eighteen of the twenty subjects receiving virtual reality exposure to flying (Groups 1 and 2) reported that they could fly in commercial airplanes without medication or alcohol. None of the ten subjects in the traditional systematic desensitization therapy with imagined flying scenes reported the ability to fly commercially (Wiederhold & Wiederhold, 2005; Wiederhold, et al., 2003). Over the past ten years, **virtual reality therapy** has been used successfully to treat a range of disorders including substance abuse, depression, phobias, PTSD, and anxiety (Hoffman, 2004; Opris et al., 2012; Rothbaum et al., 2001).

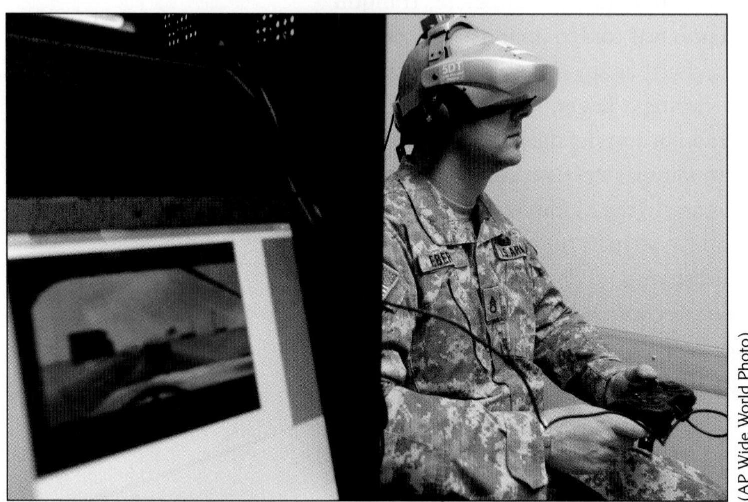
(AP Wide World Photo)

Virtual reality therapy provides systematic desensitization by generating a variety of stimuli to help a patient overcome fears and phobias.

Aversive Conditioning Aversive conditioning is another method of behavior therapy that is quite different from systematic desensitization. In aversion therapy, the goal is to condition an aversion to some specific stimulus such as inappropriate sexual stimuli, alcohol, or cigarettes.

For example, an alcoholic's behavior is normally characterized by excessive attraction to alcoholic drinks. However, suppose a chronic drinker is given a drug that induces nausea and vomiting when combined with alcohol (e.g., disulfiram, or Antabuse®). The drug alone will not make the person sick; however, immediately after alcohol enters the system, the person experiences violent nausea and vomiting. It does not take many pairings of the CS, alcohol, and the UCS, sickness, before the alcohol begins to elicit an aversion response (CR). This conditioned aversion may generalize to a variety of alcohol-related stimuli, including the taste and smell of alcohol and visual displays of containers of alcohol. Effective therapeutic intervention using this strategy actually combines both Pavlovian and operant conditioning. Once the Pavlovian conditioned aversion to alcohol is established, an alcoholic is inclined to actively avoid future contact with alcohol.

Aversive conditioning for alcohol addiction is not a pleasant experience, and you may wonder why anyone would undergo it voluntarily. The answer is that people who are desperate to overcome their alcohol dependency, or highly motivated to stop smoking, may consider continuation of the undesired behavior to be more aversive than the treatment. Clearly, aversive conditioning is not an appropriate treatment strategy unless the client consents to it.

Is aversion therapy effective? To answer this question, let us consider a hypothetical example. If you ever have overindulged in a favorite food and then become violently ill, the odds are good that you acquired an aversion for the food even though you knew that you got sick only because you ate too much. Such a conditioned aversion is often highly resistant to extinction, and that is one reason why this treatment should be effective. Conditioned aversions to novel flavors using laboratory animals can be long lasting. Nevertheless, when the motivation to drink is very strong, the addict may discontinue using the nausea-producing drug before the treatment has time to become effective. A number of studies have provided rather discouraging statistics about the effectiveness of aversion therapy in treating alcohol addiction for this reason (Garbutt, West, Carey, Lohr, & Crews, 1999). However, when patients continue using the nausea-producing drug, treatment is very effective.

Aversion therapy has also been used successfully to treat sexual offenders and deviant sexual behaviors. The goal of treatment is to condition an aversion to inappropriate sexual images (e.g., underage children) and promote normal sexual arousal to appropriate sexual stimuli. In a recent experiment, Weinrott et al. (1997) exposed juvenile sex offenders to an audiotaped crime scenario designed to elicit sexual arousal to prepubescent children. Immediately after listening to the audiotape the subjects watched an aversive video portraying sex offenders with negative social, physical, and legal consequences. After twenty sessions of aversion therapy, these subjects demonstrated significantly decreased sexual arousal to the deviant sexual scenario than control subjects who did not receive aversion therapy. The effects of this treatment were still evident even after three months.

Operant Conditioning Therapies Behavior modification techniques that attempt to influence behavior by manipulating reinforcers

Operant Conditioning Therapies

We learned in Chapter 6 that our behaviors are strongly influenced by their consequences. Reinforcers and punishers are powerful determinants of behavior, and by manipulating contingencies of reinforcement and punishment, behavior therapists are often able to exert a strong influence on behavior. Three versions of **operant conditioning therapies** (sometimes called *behavior modification* techniques) include attempting to induce desired behavior through *positive reinforcement*, or striving to eliminate undesirable or maladaptive behavior through either *extinction* or *punishment*.

Positive Reinforcement

The positive reinforcement therapy technique is based on the fact that people behave in ways that produce positive consequences or reinforcers. This approach to behavior therapy involves identifying the desired behavior, determining one or more reinforcers that will be effective in maintaining it, and then providing reinforcers contingent upon the client's voluntarily manifesting the desired behavior.

For instance, in one case reported by Arthur Bachrach and his associates (1965), a young anorexic woman had so drastically curtailed her eating that she was hospitalized, in danger of dying. When all else had failed, behavior therapy was applied to the woman, who by then weighed only 47 pounds.

How would you apply positive reinforcement to ensure proper eating behavior in this severely emaciated person? What steps would you follow? Consider this question for a few moments before reading on.

In the first step of treatment, the therapist determined an appropriate reinforcer that could be made contingent upon eating. A social reinforcer was chosen. The therapist sat with her when a meal was delivered; each time she swallowed a bite of food, the therapist reinforced her by talking to her and generally being attentive. If she refused to eat, the therapist left the room, and she remained alone until the next meal was served. In this manner, her eating behavior was gradually increased, and other reinforcers were introduced contingent upon her continuing to eat and gain weight. For example, other people joined her at mealtime, or having her hair done after an appropriate gain in weight reinforced her. This positive reinforcement method succeeded in inducing a dramatic gain in weight, and she was eventually discharged from the hospital. Her parents were instructed in ways to continue reinforcing her for appropriate eating behaviors, and a follow-up almost three years later revealed that she was maintaining an adequate weight.

Positive reinforcement is also a powerful tool for shaping desirable behaviors in everyday life. For example, a parent who wishes a child to use better table manners, or to be more responsible about room-cleaning chores, will probably find that reinforcing appropriate efforts in this direction will be a more effective agent of behavior change than punishment. As we saw in Chapter 6, the most effective approach is often *shaping*, which involves systematically reinforcing closer and closer approximations to the final desired behavior. For example, a child who picks up only a few toys might first be provided praise, then later the reinforcer might be made contingent upon picking up more and more toys, until eventually only a complete room cleaning is reinforced.

Another way that reinforcement can be applied to maintain adaptive behavior patterns is through the use of tokens that can later be exchanged for desired objects or privileges. The goal of token economies is to bring the desired pattern of behavior to a level where more natural contingencies maintain it indefinitely. *Token economies* have proven very successful in the treatment of a variety of severe behavioral disorders, including behaviors of those with intellectual disability, autism, chronic schizophrenia, eating disorders, and severe mood disorders. In a token economy, patients are reinforced with tokens for demonstrating appropriate behavior. For instance, a patient may be reinforced with tokens for dressing appropriately and interacting with other patients and staff. These tokens can later be exchanged for the privilege of seeing a movie or having visitors. The major advantage of token economies is that appropriate behaviors can be immediately reinforced, and there is less satiation to the reinforcer than there is with other primary reinforcers.

Punishment

In Chapter 6, we discussed how the use of an aversive stimulus such as an electric shock could be used in aversion therapy to condition an aversion response to an attractive but harmful stimulus. Aversive stimuli can also be used to punish disordered or self-injurious behaviors.

An early case involved a nine-month-old infant whose life was endangered by a chronic pattern of vomiting and regurgitating food (Lang & Melamed, 1969). From a six-month weight of 17 pounds, the infant had dropped to an emaciated 12 pounds. Attempts to feed him through a tube inserted through his nasal passage were a losing cause since he continued to regurgitate his food within minutes. The behavior therapists assigned to this case carefully evaluated the vomiting behavior. Using electrical recordings of muscular activity, they found they could detect when the infant was about to vomit. On this basis they designed a treatment strategy. Each time electrical recordings signaled that the infant was about to vomit, the therapists delivered a brief shock to his leg. This electrical shock was immediately effective in reducing the vomiting, and after a few short training sessions the undesirable behavior had completely ceased. Within a relatively short period, the child had gained considerable weight and was well enough to be discharged from the hospital. A follow-up one year later revealed continued healthy development, with no recurrences of the vomiting behavior.

Electric shock has also been effectively applied to eliminate head banging, biting, and severe scratching in young children. In these cases verbal signals are often issued prior to the delivery of a brief shock to establish them as effective conditioned punishers.

Numerous studies have reported long-lasting suppression of self-injurious behaviors using this technique (Foxx, 2003; Salvy, Mulick, & Butter, 2004).

Students are often disturbed by this case, on two counts. The first disturbing aspect is ethical. Many people cringe at the prospect of a helpless infant or a young child receiving electric shocks. It is true that there are ethical implications of using punishment to modify behavior, and such an approach should only be given consideration as a last resort. Nevertheless, in view of the fact that these behaviors can be life threatening if they persist, this approach to treatment seems justified.

The second reservation expressed by many students is a practical one. We have learned that punishment generally produces only a temporary suppression of undesirable behavior unless punishment is continued or another behavior pattern is reinforced in its place. Establishing verbal signals as conditioned punishers can prolong the effectiveness of these punishment procedures.

Modeling As we saw in Chapter 6, learning theorists have demonstrated that some kinds of learning appear to be taught through modeling. Modeling can be a helpful therapy technique for extinguishing irrational fears or for establishing new, more adaptive behaviors.

For example, suppose you are deathly afraid of the dark. Although this phobia might be treated by systematic desensitization as we described earlier, modeling might also be effective: You might observe others entering the dark with no visible adverse effects. Modeling may be live, or it may take place through films or videotapes. The beneficial, antiphobia effects of modeling techniques may be enhanced even further if relaxation training is also used to ensure the client is in a calm, tranquil state while observing the models.

Modeling may also be helpful in establishing new, more appropriate responses. For example, people who are shy or nonassertive may observe live or filmed vignettes of models acting out scenes in which people effectively initiate social contacts or behave in an appropriately assertive way. Ideally, these behaviors are shown to produce reinforcers, so that the observers may achieve a kind of vicarious reinforcement by identifying with the model (this is also how advertising works). Clients are often asked to participate actively in the desired behavior after viewing the models. Modeling and active role playing have been found to be considerably more effective than cognitive therapy alone in establishing appropriate assertive behaviors.

Evaluating Behavioral Therapies

Of all the psychological therapies, behavioral therapies appear to be the most effective for a wide range of behavioral disorders, especially those with definable symptoms such as phobias, eating disorders, self-injurious behaviors, addictions, and deviant sexual behaviors. There are several reasons for this success. First, because behavioral therapies focus on specific disordered behaviors, it is very easy to monitor outcomes throughout therapy. If appropriate changes are not occurring immediately, the approach can be modified to bring about desired changes. Second, behavior therapies are based upon well-defined and understood principles of human and animal learning and behavior (Bouton, 2016). No other therapeutic approach is based upon such an extensive research base. As we will see in the next section, however, psychological therapies by themselves may not be sufficient to treat some of the most serious behavior disorders. In these cases, drug therapy, often in combination with psychological therapies, is needed.

16.2 Biologically Based Therapies

We have been dealing exclusively with psychological approaches to treating behavioral disorders. There are also, however, a number of biological or medical therapies. Biomedical approaches to treatment are based on one or both of two assumptions: (1) Many behavioral disorders result from biological abnormalities including altered brain structure and/or altered brain chemistry, and (2) physiological intervention through surgery, electric shock, or drugs will alleviate or treat significantly the symptoms of behavioral disorders.

Only clinicians with medical degrees may use biomedical treatments. However, psychologists often refer clients to a psychiatrist or other medical practitioner when they feel that biomedical treatment might be helpful. In many cases, the treatment of behavioral disorders involves both psychological and biological therapy. This was strongly emphasized by Kurt Salzinger in the "Research Perspectives" segment at the end of Chapter 15. In this section we examine three types of biomedical treatment: psychosurgery, electroconvulsive (shock) therapy, and psychoactive drugs.

16.2a Psychosurgery

In the early decades of the twentieth century, mental hospitals throughout the Western world overflowed with severely disturbed patients, and there was a shortage of both professional staff and effective treatment strategies. During this time many mental health professionals became frustrated with what they perceived to be a general practice of using mental hospitals as little more than warehouses for severely disordered patients. In the effort to alleviate patient suffering and reduce problems of overcrowding, a number of psychiatrists were motivated to experiment with a variety of often-radical biological interventions.

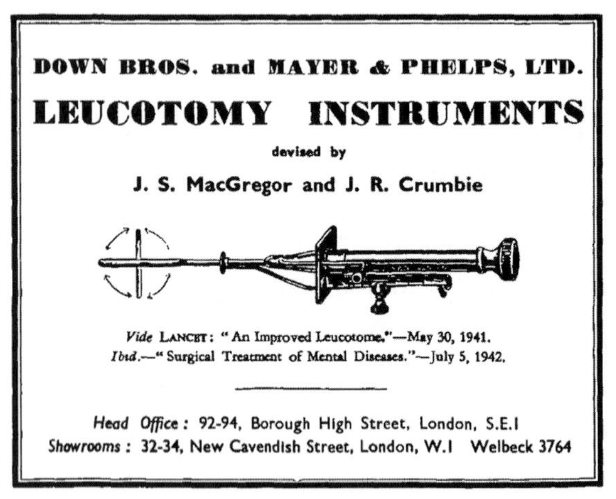

(Wikimedia Commons/Public Domain)

The leucotome was used to perform lobotomies.

One such person was a Portuguese neuropsychiatrist, António Egas Moniz. In 1935, Moniz attended a professional conference in London and was impressed by a report describing brain surgery on two chimpanzees in which the prefrontal areas (forwardmost portion of the frontal lobes) of their cerebral cortexes were removed. The effect of this surgery was to abolish the violent outbursts that both animals had been prone to prior to surgery. On the basis of this single instance of chimpanzee brain surgery, Moniz persuaded a colleague, Almeida Lima, to experiment with surgery on the frontal lobes of schizophrenics and other severely disturbed patients. The surgical procedure was to sever the nerve tracts connecting the frontal cortex to lower regions in the brain that mediate emotional responses, most notably the thalamus and hypothalamus. Essentially, the idea was to disconnect thought (mediated by the cortex) from emotion (mediated by lower brain centers). Such a procedure was expected to have a calming effect on patients troubled by severely disruptive emotional patterns.

This operation, known as a **lobotomy**, was originally performed by a very crude surgical procedure in which a hole was drilled through the skull on each side of the head, and a blunt instrument was then inserted and rotated in a vertical arc. The procedure was later refined as the *transorbital lobotomy* technique, in which an ice pick-like instrument called a leucotome was inserted into the brain through an eye socket and rotated back and forth.

Lobotomy Surgical procedure that severs the nerve tracts connecting the prefrontal cortex to lower brain areas that mediate emotional responses

Table 16-3 Comparisons of Common Treatment Approaches for Psychological Disorders

Type of Psychotherapy	Primary Founder(s)	Interpretation of Causes(s) of Disorders	Focus/Goal of Therapy	Methods of Therapy
Psychoanalysis	Sigmund Freud	Disordered behavior results from unconscious conflicts and repressed urges, which are rooted in childhood experiences	To enter the unconscious of disturbed people, search out the anxiety-causing conflict(s), and help these individuals gain insight or conscious awareness of the repressed conflicts	Techniques include free association, dream analysis, and interpretation of resistance and transference
Rational-Emotive	Albert Ellis	Psychological problems result when people interpret their experiences on the basis of certain self-defeating, irrational beliefs	To help people find the flaws in their thinking, to challenge or dispute these maladaptive cognitions, and then guide clients to substitute more logical realistic thoughts	Confrontation, persuasion, role-playing, interpretation, behavior modification, and reflection of feelings
Cognitive Restructuring	Aaron Beck	Psychological problems stem primarily from a few irrational beliefs that cause people to behave and emote in maladaptive ways	To help clients restructure their thinking, particularly their negative self-labels	Structure certain "experiments" or experiences to disprove a client's misguided self-impressions
Behavior	Joseph Wolpe, Albert Bandura, and others	Disordered or maladaptive behaviors can be modified by conditioning	To focus on people's current behaviors that are creating problems and help them unlearn maladaptive behavior patterns while learning more adaptive behavior	Systematic desensitization, aversive conditioning, positive reinforcement, extinction, and punishment
Biomedical	Antonio de Egas Moniz, James Watts, Ugo Cerletti, Lucio Bini, and others	Many psychological problems result from biological abnormalities	To eliminate symptoms of psychological disorders through biological intervention	Psychosurgery, electroconvulsive therapy, and psychoactive drugs

The lobotomy rapidly became popular in Europe as a treatment for a wide variety of disorders, including schizophrenia, severe depression, and occasionally anxiety disorders. Moniz claimed enthusiastically that the procedure was very effective in calming severely disturbed psychotics and that many lobotomized patients were able to leave the hospital. (Strangely, his claims about the effectiveness of the procedure were not modified even after he was partially paralyzed by a gunshot wound inflicted by one of his lobotomized patients.) Neurosurgeons Walter Freeman and James Watts (1950) introduced lobotomy to the United States, where it flourished until the late 1950s. By the time the popularity of lobotomies had begun to wane, more than forty thousand people were thought to have been recipients of this surgical intervention.

Lobotomized patients seemed more tranquil or calm after the operation and, thus, more manageable. However, some observant clinicians began to raise questions. They suggested that the so-called calming effect was actually more a conversion of emotionally labile patients into lethargic, vegetative patients. In addition, it was noted that very little research evidence had substantiated the effects of this treatment.

Once researchers began to investigate seriously the effects of lobotomies, they found that the claims of pronounced improvements in behavior had been greatly exaggerated. True, lobotomized patients had slightly higher rates of discharge from hospitals than matched controls, but this statistic was counterbalanced by higher rates of recidivism or return to hospitals. Furthermore, these studies provided some profoundly disturbing evidence—that some lobotomized patients had been transformed into lethargic, unmotivated, robot-like personalities that were hollow remnants of the individuals they had once been. This effect was dramatized in Ken Kesey's novel *One Flew Over the Cuckoo's Nest* (1962). Other irreversible side effects were uncovered, including memory loss, inability to plan ahead, seizures, and even death. Furthermore, lobotomies were found to produce no changes in the major manifestations of severe mental illness other than reduction of emotional agitation.

Such findings prompted several critics to call for a ban on all forms of psychosurgery. Although no formal prohibition was enforced, medical practitioners drastically curtailed their use of this method. (This movement away from psychosurgery gained momentum with the emergence of calming psychoactive drugs, with effects, unlike those of lobotomy, that were temporary rather than permanent.)

Psychosurgery did not die out completely. In fact, in the early 1970s there was a renewed interest in using surgical techniques to alter behavior when all other reversible treatment methods have failed. Newer surgical techniques produced only a small fraction of the brain damage associated with older procedures. For example, brain lesions created with radio waves (Cecconi et al., 2008; Rück et al., 2008) and cingulotomy (Keller, 2012) are being used to successfully treat patients with severe obsessive-compulsive disorder when other treatment methods have failed. These refined procedures may also be effective in alleviating symptoms of severe depression, uncontrollable rage attacks, extreme anxiety, schizophrenia, uncontrollable seizures, and severe pain.

16.2b Electroconvulsive Therapy and Magnetic Seizure Therapy

Electroconvulsive therapy (**ECT**) is a procedure in which electrical current is applied to the surface of the head, resulting in a convulsive seizure. Students often wonder how such a procedure could have come about to treat behavioral disorders. The story here is an interesting one.

In the early 1930s, a Hungarian physician, Laszlo Von Meduna, noticed that hospitalized psychiatric patients often seemed to experience a remission or lessening of their psychotic symptoms after undergoing a spontaneous seizure of the type that occurs in epilepsy. Excited by this discovery, Von Meduna began to experiment with different techniques for artificially inducing convulsions. He first used intramuscular injections of camphor oil to elicit seizures. Although several patients were made physically ill by the injections, a number showed remarkable improvement. Von Meduna soon substituted synthetic camphor, metrazol, which seemed to lessen the side effect of physical illness. The use of *pharmacoconvulsive* therapy (drug-induced seizures) quickly gained a foothold worldwide among psychiatrists desperate for a way to combat severe behavioral disorders.

Electroconvulsive Therapy (ECT) A method to induce seizures by strong electrical current applied to the brain; used to treat depression

Unfortunately, pharmacoconvulsive therapy was not without problems. Although the symptoms of behavioral disorders were often reduced, the procedure had other severe side effects, including painful preseizure spasms and uncontrollable convulsions that sometimes resulted in fractures and even death. In 1938, two Italian neuropsychiatrists, Ugo Cerletti and Lucio Bini introduced a safer, better-controlled method for inducing seizures using electric shock. By 1940, electroconvulsive therapy had become a major component of psychiatric treatment strategies worldwide.

Early ECT sessions resembled a scene from a horror movie. A wide awake and often terrified patient was strapped to a table, electrodes were attached to each side of the forehead, and a current of roughly 100 volts was then passed between the electrodes for a fraction of a second, producing severe convulsions and a temporary loss of consciousness. Upon regaining consciousness, the patient often seemed confused, distressed, and unable to remember events that happened both before and immediately after the procedure. In addition, the seizures induced by the electric current often produced such a rapid and intense contraction of skeletal muscles that bone fractures, bruises, and other injuries sometimes resulted. Altogether, this was not a pretty picture—but one that was repeated countless thousands of times due to compelling evidence that ECT was often amazingly effective in reducing symptoms of severe emotional distress, particularly depression.

Since the early days of the development of ECT, several modifications have been introduced to make this treatment safer and more humane. Today, patients are first put to sleep and administered a powerful muscle relaxant before the shock is delivered. General anesthesia circumvents the terror many patients experienced in the early years of shock therapy. The patient typically wakes up in a half hour or so, with no recollection of the treatment. ECT is now often applied to only one of the cerebral hemispheres, usually the one that is not dominant. This unilateral treatment has significantly reduced the confusion and memory loss associated with ECT.

Because of the cognitive effects of ECT, some clinicians now prefer to use **magnetic seizure therapy** (MST) as opposed to ECT. Magnetic seizure therapy uses strong magnetic fields to induce seizures rather than the strong electrical current. Seizures induced with magnetic fields do not appear to disrupt memory and cognitive functioning, as does ECT.

The most common applications of ECT and MST today are for severely depressed patients who have not responded to antidepressant drugs, who may not want to use medication because of pregnancy, or who cannot tolerate waiting for the slower acting drugs to take effect (Kayser et al., 2011). These therapies are also being used successfully for the treatment of bipolar disorder and some cases of schizophrenia (Baghai & Möller, 2008; Allan & Ebmeier, 2011).

One of the most perplexing aspects of these therapies is that no one is sure how the treatment works. We know that ECT and MST alter the electrochemical processes in many central nervous system structures, but we still have not been able to determine which of these changes, if any, are linked with their antidepressant effects. One popular theory is that seizure therapies increase the availability of the neurotransmitters norepinephrine and serotonin at the synapses in certain brain sites in a fashion similar to the chemical antidepressants. A similar explanation for how they work suggests that brain neurotransmitters are somehow normalized by this procedure, resulting in therapeutic benefit. Another intriguing possibility is that seizure therapies increase the synthesis of brain-derived neurotropic factor (BDNF), which is known to be linked to severe depression (Hu et al., 2010; Taylor, 2008). BDNF is a neuronal growth factor that is necessary for normal neuron functioning and survival. Low levels of BDNF are correlated with severe depression as well as cell loss in the hippocampus and the frontal cortex (Ettinger, 2017).

BVT *Lab*

Visit **www.BVTLab.com** to explore the student resources available for this chapter.

Magnetic Seizure Therapy (MST) A method of inducing seizures using strong magnetic fields as opposed to electrical current; used to treat depression, bipolar disorder, and schizophrenia

Deep Brain Stimulation (DBS) An invasive procedure in which an electrode is implanted deep in the brain and electrical current can be applied periodically

Psychoactive Drugs Drugs that have the effect of altering mood and behavior by changing neuronal functioning

The questions and concerns raised by ECT and MST will no doubt continue to be debated, and we can expect that they will continue to be used to treat approximately thirty thousand Americans per year.

16.2c Deep Brain Stimulation

A more recent alternative to ECT is to implant electrodes deep into brain structures and apply constant weak electrical stimulation to specific regions deep in the brain. The electrodes are left in the brain and attached to a stimulator that is implanted under the skin of the patient's chest. The current delivered to the electrodes can be adjusted by remote control. **Deep brain stimulation (DBS)** has been used to treat movement disorders such as Parkinson's disease as well as several psychological disorders including depression, bipolar disorder, and obsessive-compulsive disorder. Although its mechanisms of action remain elusive, it is suspected that DBS works in a manner similar to ECT and MST by increasing neurotransmitter release and increasing the production of BDNF (Holtzheimer & Mayberg, 2011). Dr. Helen Mayberg at the University of Toronto reported that four of her six patients with treatment-resistant depression were in remission following electrical stimulation to an area adjacent to the cingulate cortex. This stimulation dramatically reduces neural activity of this region as well as other limbic structures associated with depression (Mayberg et al., 2005).

16.2d Psychoactive Drugs

The use of drugs to control symptoms of behavioral disorders became a primary strategy of psychiatric practice during the 1950s. Since then, therapy with **psychoactive drugs** has become by far the most common form of treatment for all psychological disorders. The use of psychoactive drugs has contributed both to a decline in the number of people hospitalized for behavioral disorders and to a significant reduction in the average duration of hospitalization. Now, hospitalization of the mentally ill is seldom measured in terms of years, but is more often a matter of months or even weeks. Drugs are often so effective in controlling disruptive symptoms that many patients who might previously have required restraints or close observation in locked wards are now able to function reasonably effectively outside of a hospital setting. Even patients who still require hospitalization typically need less supervision than did their counterparts in the days before drugs were introduced. In other cases, drug therapy has been successfully used to calm patients so that psychological therapies can be applied. It is estimated that about 60 percent of the U.S. population will take some form psychoactive medication during their lifetime (Kessler et al., 2005).

The five major categories of psychoactive drugs that are used to control or alleviate symptoms of behavioral disorders are *antipsychotics, antidepressants, antimanics, anxiolytics*, and *stimulants.* Table 16-4 lists several commonly used drugs in these categories. The various widely used psychoactive drugs differ considerably in their effects. Some calm, some energize, some sedate, and some provide an emotional lift. However, they all share one common feature: Generally speaking, all psychoactive drugs merely help to control or manage symptoms rather than cure the disorder. When people cease taking these medications, symptoms usually recur.

Beside dramatically enhancing the ability of psychiatrists to treat patients, pharmacological therapy has stimulated an abundance of research, resulting in some important new hypotheses linking many behavioral disorders to neurobiological factors.

Antipsychotics

The **antipsychotic drugs**, sometimes called *neuroleptics* or *major tranquilizers*, were first used in the early 1950s to treat schizophrenia. As Table 16-4 shows, there are several varieties of these drugs. The most commonly employed are the *phenothiazines*. The most widely used drug in this group is chlorpromazine, sold under the name Thorazine®. Chlorpromazine has been the number one medication for treating schizophrenia since it was introduced to American psychiatry in 1952. One effect of this drug and other antipsychotic drugs is to calm and quiet patients, reducing their responsiveness to irrelevant stimuli. However, the antipsychotic effects of these drugs are not merely heavy sedation. In other cases where patients are severely withdrawn or immobile, antipsychotic drugs tend to increase activity and responsiveness. The therapeutic effects of antipsychotics are believed to result from the fact that antipsychotic drugs block dopamine receptor

Antipsychotic Drugs Drugs used to treat psychotic disorders such as schizophrenia

Table 16-4 Major Categories of Psychoactive Drugs

Category	Used To Treat	Chemical Group	Generic Name	Trade Name
Antipsychotics	Schizophrenic disorders, severe aggressive behavior	Phenothiazines Butyrophenones Thioxanthenes Dihydroindolones Dibenzodiazepine	Chlorpromazine Haloperidol Clozapine Aripiprazole	Thorazine® Haldol® Clozaril® Abilify®
Antidepressants	Major depressive disorders, obsessive-compulsive behaviors	Tricyclics Monoamine oxidase inhibitors Serotonin specific reuptake inhibitors Serotonin-norepinephrine reuptake inhibitor Dopamine agonists	Amitriptyline Imipramine Nortriptyline Fluoxetine Paroxetine Duloxetine Desvenlafaxine Bupropin	Elavil® Trofranil® Aventyl® Prozac® Paxil® Cymbalta® Pristiq® Wellbutrin®
Antimanics	Bipolar disorder, mania	Inorganic salts Dopamine agonist	Lithium carbonate Carbamazepine Quetiapine Aripiprazole	Lithane® Lithonate® Tegretol® Seroquel® Abilify®
Anxiolytic	Generalized anxiety, phobic anxieties, tension, sleep disorders	Propanediols Benzodiazepines	Meprobamate Chlordiazepoxide Diazepam Alprazolam Chlorazepate Halazepam Lorazepam Oxazepam Parzepam	Miltown® Equanil® Librium® Valium® Xanax® Tranxene® Paxipam® Ativan® Serax® Centrax®
Stimulants	Attention disorders, narcolepsy	Amphetamines	Amphetamine Methylphenadate	Dexadrine® Adderall® Ritalin® Concerta®

Antidepressant Drugs Drugs used to treat major depressive disorder; include the tricyclics, MAOIs, SNRIs, and SSRIs

sites in the brain, thus decreasing dopamine activity in both mesolimbic and motor areas of the brain. As we discussed in the previous chapter, schizophrenic symptoms appear to result from abnormal dopamine activity or sensitivity in certain regions of the brain (M. Carlsson & A. Carlsson, 1990; Takahashi et al., 2006).

Unfortunately, sizable percentages (perhaps as many as 40 percent) of patients who take phenothiazine drugs develop a serious side effect called *tardive dyskinesia (TD)*. This neurological disorder, which may occur months to years after drug therapy has commenced or has stopped, is typically manifested as uncontrollable muscular movements of the jaw, lips, and tongue. The severity of the symptoms may range from barely noticeable chewing movements to involuntary biting of the tongue. The antipsychotics' effects on motor structures within the brain cause these severe motor disturbances. Until recently, the antipsychotic and motor effects of these drugs were not separable. Antipsychotic drugs, however, are being used today that dramatically reduce the risks of TD and other movement disorders. These antipsychotics, Clozapine and Abilify, differ from the earlier antipsychotic drugs in that they do not affect dopamine in the motor areas of the brain as significantly as the phenothiazines did. Presently these newer generation antipsychotics are the most commonly prescribed drugs for treating schizophrenia (Ettinger, 2017; Seeman, 2002, 2011).

Even newer drugs are being developed that target specific genes associated with neurotransmitter receptor expression. It is hoped that by altering gene expression in specific regions of the brain, some behavioral disorders, like schizophrenia, may eventually be treatable rather than merely masked by drug therapy.

Antidepressants

The **antidepressant drugs**, also introduced in the 1950s, consist of four main groups: the *tricyclics*, the *monoamine oxidase inhibitors (MAOIs)*, the *selective serotonin reuptake inhibitors (SSRIs)*, and the *serotonin-norepinephrine reuptake inhibitors (SNRIs)* (see Table 16-4). As we saw in Chapter 15, these drugs are used to treat major depressive disorders and anxiety, and they are often very effective in elevating the mood of severely depressed patients. While it has been widely believed that these drugs act to increase levels of the neurotransmitters norepinephrine and/or serotonin in certain areas of the brain, it is more likely that their antidepressant effects may be related to increased expression of essential neuronal growth proteins. In other words, SSRIs and SNRIs appear to work by disengaging the breaks on serotonin neurons and elevating the activity of specific proteins that are essential for normal neuron functioning and survival. Recent evidence demonstrates that both SSRIs and SNRIs reverse the cell losses in both the hippocampus and the frontal cortex that are associated with depression (Neto, Borges, Torres-Sanchez, Mico, & Berrocosco, 2011).

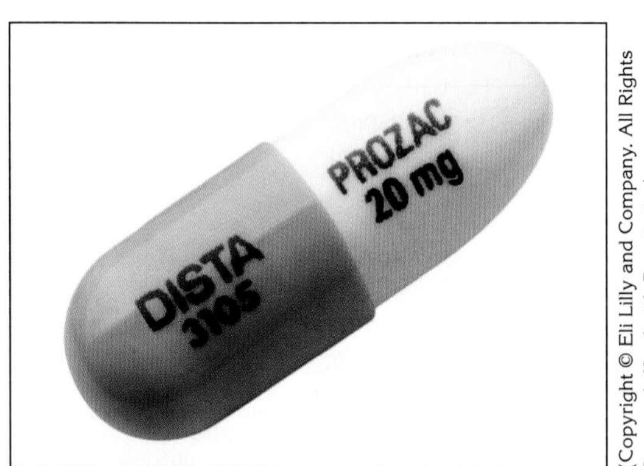

Selective serotonin reuptake inhibitors, such as Prozac, appear to be the most effective and most widely prescribed drugs to treat depression.

Of the major drugs listed in Table 16-4 to treat depression, the serotonin-norepinephrine reuptake inhibitors (Cymbalta and Pristiq) are presently the most widely prescribed drugs, with more than fifteen million people worldwide taking them every month. The MAOIs and the tricyclics have both undergone a marked reduction in use because of their adverse side effects. This is not to say that SSRIs and SNRIs have no side effects—to the contrary. These drugs are associated with sexual dysfunction, sedation, and weight gain. New antidepressant drugs are continually being developed for an ever-increasing market. In the future it may be possible to target specific genes in a neuron's DNA so it renews production of these essential proteins for neuron functioning.

Antimanics

The most widely prescribed drug used to treat symptoms of both mania and hypomania is the simple chemical compound, lithium carbonate. Lithium was the first **antimanic drug** used successfully to treat mania. This medication, a simple inorganic salt, has been found to be the most effective drug for controlling the manic symptoms of bipolar disorder and has even been shown to help reduce depression associated with it. Its greatest benefit, however, seems to be as a prophylactic, reducing the frequency and severity of manic episodes or perhaps preventing them altogether. Lithium is believed to accomplish its antimanic and antidepressant effects by increasing the activity of serotonin in the cortex as well as increasing the production of the essential neuronal growth proteins discussed above. Even though the drug is remarkably simple in chemical structure, the ways it works to alleviate mania are still poorly understood (Berk et al., 2007). There are a number of newer drugs, such as Tegretol and Valproate®, used to treat bipolar disorder, but they are no more effective than lithium.

When the manic phases of bipolar disorder are particularly severe and include psychotic symptoms, therapists may prescribe antipsychotic medication either alone or with lithium. Several antipsychotics are typically prescribed for mania, including Seroquel and Abilify.

Anxiolytics

The **anxiolytic drugs**, sometimes called minor tranquilizers, are used to reduce symptoms of anxiety and tension in people whose behavioral disturbances are not severe enough to warrant hospitalization. These medications are particularly helpful in reducing the symptoms of generalized anxiety disorders, panic disorders, and some sleep disorders. Like most of the drugs we have discussed in this section, the anxiolytic medications were introduced in the 1950s and widely used before their mechanisms of action were understood.

There are two major categories of anxiolytic drugs: *barbiturates* and *benzodiazepines*. The first to be introduced were the barbiturates, the most common of which is phenobarbital. The barbiturates work by increasing the effectiveness of the inhibitory neurotransmitter GABA. Overdose with barbiturates is often lethal, especially if they are used with alcohol. For this reason they are rarely prescribed today. When people stop taking barbiturates, severe withdrawal can occur, producing such effects as tremors, convulsions, and severe anxiety.

The benzodiazepine drugs work much like the barbiturates, but they are far less toxic. The most common benzodiazepines include Valium, Librium, and Xanax. All of these drugs, as well as some of the newer sleep medications (Ambien® and Lunesta®), increase the ability of the inhibitory neurotransmitter GABA to bind to its receptor. GABA receptors are located throughout the frontal cortex and the amygdala structures essential for anxiety and fear.

Some students are aware of several sleep and anxiolytic remedies available at health food stores. One of the most common is the extract from the root of the valerian plant, *Valeriana officinalis*. Valerian has been touted for many years as an effective anxiolytic and sedative. However, until recently, its mechanisms of action have not been known. In the author's laboratory, we discovered that valerian root extracts were as effective as Valium in reducing anxiety and that the anxiolytic ingredient was valerenic acid. Valerenic acid appears to work much like the benzodiazepines, by increasing the ability of GABA to bind to its receptor (Murphy, Kubin, Shepherd, & Ettinger, 2010).

Antimanic Drugs Drugs used to control the manic symptoms of bipolar disorder and hypomania

Anxiolytic Drugs Drugs used to reduce symptoms of anxiety and promote sleep; sometimes called minor tranquilizers

Stimulants

Stimulants Drugs that increase arousal and the activity of the central nervous system; used to treat attention disorders and narcolepsy

Stimulants are a class of drugs with arousing effects on the central nervous system. Typically, these drugs increase both norepinephrine and dopamine activity and are used to treat attention disorders and narcolepsy. Attention deficit/hyperactivity disorder (ADHD) is believed to be caused by both decreased dopamine and norepinephrine activity in the cortex and decreased norepinephrine activity in the reticular activating system. The combination of these deficits results in an underaroused cortex and a decrease in one's ability to regulate attention. Stimulant drugs are very effective in alleviating the symptoms of ADHD.

Drugs in this class include the amphetamines (e.g., Adderall) and methylphenidates (e.g., Ritalin), both commonly used to treat ADHD. Other stimulants include cocaine and methamphetamine. Neither of these drugs is currently used in the United States to treat psychological disorders.

16.2e Summary of Psychoactive Drugs

Presently, most psychological disorders are treated with both medication and some form of cognitive/behavior therapy. Over the past few decades much has been learned about the underlying pathology of the major psychological disorders and their pharmacological treatment. As neuroscientists learn more about the specific pathologies of these disorders, pharmacologists are quick to develop drugs to treat them. Several states have—and others are presently considering—legislation that allows clinical psychologists with appropriate training to prescribe medication to their patients. This privilege is presently reserved for psychiatrists and nurse practitioners with psychiatric training. This trend clearly demonstrates that professional psychologists view many psychological disorders as manifestations of underlying disease processes.

Over the years, the barbiturates have become gradually less popular, and they have been essentially replaced by the more recently developed benzodiazepines. The most widely used of these medications include Librium, Valium, and Xanax.

Like the barbiturates, the benzodiazepines also seem to have sedative and muscle-relaxing effects and work by facilitating the binding of GABA to its receptor sites. The anxiolytic effects of the benzodiazepines are believed to be mediated by the facilitation of GABA in the frontal cortex and in the amygdala.

Throughout this chapter, we have reviewed the major psychological and biological approaches to the treatment of behavioral disorders. It is important to remember that there is still considerable disagreement among professionals about causes and appropriate types of treatment for most of the disorders that we have discussed. While the fields of neuroscience and pharmacology have contributed considerably to our understanding and treatment of behavioral disorders, many professionals continue to apply therapy from an eclectic approach rather than focus on a single theoretical perspective. For instance, while drug therapy may be quite effective in alleviating symptoms of a disorder, a practitioner may augment drug therapy with cognitive or behavioral therapy so medication may be discontinued and a more functional behavior pattern maintained. Even in cases where medication may not be discontinued (e.g., schizophrenia, major depression, and bipolar disorder), patients may need psychological therapies to learn how to adapt to life with a long-term illness.

Guidelines for Seeking Professional Help

Many people are reluctant to seek professional help because they incorrectly believe that taking this step is an admission that they are weak and incapable of helping themselves. Quite the contrary, people who seek professional help demonstrate a high level of self-awareness and emotional maturity by recognizing that there are limitations to their ability to help themselves when faced with seriously disruptive psychological problems. If some day you find yourself seeking professional help, give yourself credit for having the wisdom to recognize that a skilled therapist can offer emotional support, a perspective other than your own, and perhaps recommend medication—all of which may help you make the desired changes in your life.

As we have seen in this text, however, not all therapists are equally effective in providing successful treatment. How do you go about selecting a therapist? Assuming your symptoms are not so acute that they demand immediate attention, we suggest that you shop carefully for a therapist. Most people, however, do not know where to start in making this kind of decision.

A good first step in locating a psychotherapist is to seek referrals from people you know who are likely to be familiar with your community's mental-health resources—your psychology instructor; your health-care practitioner; or perhaps your minister, rabbi, or priest. (The clergy often deal with people who have psychological problems, and they are quite familiar with community mental-health resources.) Do not hesitate to talk with friends who have used psychotherapy in the past. Sometimes firsthand recommendations can be especially helpful. You may also want to see if your college or university has a counseling center or clinic for students. Such a service may be free or relatively inexpensive. In addition, city, county, and state psychological associations can provide names of licensed clinical psychologists and psychiatrists in your area.

We recommend that you contact several sources and then pool the information. This process may leave you with several options. To narrow down your choices, consider the professional backgrounds of your prospective therapists. Remember that many so-called professional counselors have little or no professional training. States license practicing clinical psychologists, and you may inquire whether or not a therapist is licensed. If a prospective therapist is reluctant to provide this information, go elsewhere.

Cost may also be an issue as you seek to narrow your choices. Fees vary considerably, from no charge to $200 or more per forty-five- to fifty-minute session. Psychiatrists are usually on the upper end of the fee scale, psychologists are in the middle, and social workers and counselors are usually on the lower end. A higher fee does not necessarily indicate better therapy skills. Some mental-health agencies and private practitioners offer sliding fee schedules based on the client's income. Most health insurance companies now provide partial to full coverage for psychotherapy services, but note that they may require that you see a licensed psychotherapist.

To help determine if a specific therapist will meet your needs, you may wish to establish the following points at your first meeting:

1. **What do you want from therapy?** You and your therapist should reach an agreement on goals. This agreement is sometimes referred to as the therapy contract.

2. **What is the therapist's approach and what kind of participation is expected of you?** You can ask about the general process (what the therapist will do) during therapy sessions. You may also ask how long therapy is expected to last. Behavioral therapists typically recommend fewer sessions than psychoanalytic therapists because their perspectives differ considerably.

3. **How do you feel about talking with the therapist?** Therapy is not intended to be a light social interaction. It can be difficult. At times it may be quite uncomfortable for you to discuss personal concerns. However, for therapy to be useful, you want to have the sense that the therapist is open and willing to understand you.

4. **Is medication an option for you?** Some individuals are reluctant to take medication because of its side effects. Be sure to discuss these with your practitioner before commencing pharmacotherapy. Also discuss what kinds of improvements are typical and how long medication may be necessary.

5. **Research your condition using the resources you have learned about in this course.** What are the most effective treatment options for your particular condition? Be sure to discuss your research with your therapist.

While these suggestions may not ensure that you find a therapist who is a perfect fit for your needs, it is likely they will increase the odds that you will select a qualified therapist. If therapy doesn't appear to be progressing, discuss this with your therapist. If you feel at all uncomfortable with your sessions or your therapist, it may be time to select another.

CHAPTER REVIEW

Psychoanalysis

1. Psychoanalysis is based on a number of assumptions; the most fundamental is that disordered behavior results from unconscious conflicts and repressed urges, most of which are rooted in childhood experiences.
2. Major techniques of psychoanalysis include free association, dream analysis, and interpretations of resistance and transference.
3. Freud believed that it is important to break through patients' defenses and to provide them with insight by interpreting the underlying meaning of their experiences, resistances, transferences, and dreams.
4. Psychoanalysis as practiced today tends to be briefer in duration and less focused on restructuring a person's entire personality than was the case in Sigmund Freud's time.

Cognitive Therapies

5. Cognitive therapies are based on the premise that most behavioral disorders result from distortions in a person's cognitions or thoughts.
6. Rational-emotive therapy (RET) is based on the belief that behavioral problems result when people interpret their experiences based on certain self-defeating, irrational beliefs. The goal of therapy is to eliminate these maladaptive cognitions.
7. Like RET, cognitive therapy also aims to get clients to restructure their thinking, particularly negative self-labels, by arranging certain experiences that will disprove rather than confirm the client's negative self-image.

CHAPTER REVIEW

Behavioral Therapies

8. The central thesis of behavior therapy is that maladaptive behavior has been learned and that it can be unlearned; furthermore, the same principles that govern the learning of normal behavior also determine the acquisition of abnormal behavior.
9. Behavioral therapies, which include systematic desensitization, aversive conditioning, punishment, and reinforcement, apply conditioning principles to help people to overcome maladaptive behavior.
10. Systematic desensitization and virtual reality therapy involve training people to relax when confronted with fear-inducing stimuli.
11. In aversive therapy, the goal is to associate an aversive consequence with an inappropriate or harmful stimulus such as nicotine, alcohol, or sexually inappropriate stimuli.
12. The operant conditioning therapies, which include positive reinforcement and punishment, focus on manipulating consequences of behavior as a way to overcome behavioral problems.
13. In positive reinforcement therapy, the therapist first identifies desirable behavior and then provides appropriate reinforcers contingent upon the client voluntarily manifesting the desired behavior.
14. A token economy is the application of operant conditioning principles to earn points or tokens that can later be exchanged for primary (real) reinforcers. An example may be a child earning points that can be exchanged for money for small purchases.
15. In the punishment technique, aversive stimuli are used to punish maladaptive or self-injurious behaviors.
16. Virtual reality therapy is becoming increasingly more popular as computer-based scenarios can be more easily produced. It has been successfully used to treat phobias, anxiety, and substance abuse.
17. Behavior change through modeling or observing others can be a helpful therapy technique for extinguishing irrational fears or for establishing new, more adaptive behaviors.

CHAPTER REVIEW

Biologically Based Therapies

18. Lobotomy was originally performed as a very crude surgical procedure designed to improve a patient's mental state by severing the nerve tracts connecting the prefrontal cortex to lower regions in the brain that mediate emotional responses.
19. Lobotomies eventually fell into disrepute when research revealed that they produced no changes in the major manifestations of severe mental illness other than reduction of emotional agitation, and that many lobotomized patients had been transformed into lethargic, unmotivated, robot-like personalities.
20. Newer psychosurgery techniques, including radio wave lesions, produce only a small fraction of the brain damage associated with the older and more crude lobotomies and have been shown to have some value in alleviating symptoms of severe disorders that have resisted more conventional forms of therapy.
21. There is extensive evidence that electroconvulsive therapy (ECT) and magnetic seizure therapy (MST) often rapidly alleviate the symptoms of major depression. ECT and MST may work by increasing the activity of several neurotransmitters including norepinephrine and serotonin. They may also increase the synthesis of brain-derived neurotrophic factor, an essential growth factor for neuron survival.
22. Deep brain electrical stimulation involves implanting an electrode into a specific brain structure and applying electrical current directly.
23. Therapy with psychoactive drugs, by far the most common biomedical treatment, has contributed to both a decline in the number of people hospitalized for behavioral disorders and a significant reduction in the average duration of hospitalization.
24. The five major categories of psychoactive drugs that are used to control or alleviate symptoms of behavioral disorders are antipsychotics, antidepressants, antimanics, anxiolytic drugs, and stimulants.
25. The use of drugs to treat behavioral disorders has provided considerable insight into the biological bases of many severe behavioral disorders.

TERMS AND CONCEPTS

Antidepressant Drugs, pg. 664
Antimanic Drugs, pg. 665
Antipsychotic Drugs, pg. 663
Anxiolytic Drugs, pg. 665
Behavior Therapy, pg. 651
Cognitive Restructuring Therapy, pg. 650
Cognitive Therapies, pg. 649
Deep Brain Stimulation (DBS), pg. 662
Dream Analysis, pg. 646
Electroconvulsive Therapy (ECT), pg. 660
Free Association, pg. 646
Lobotomy, pg. 658
Magnetic Seizure Therapy (MST), pg. 661
Operant Conditioning Therapies, pg. 655
Pavlovian (or Classical) Conditioning Therapy, pg. 652
Psychoactive Drugs, pg. 662
Psychoanalysis, pg. 645
Psychotherapy, pg. 645
Rational-Emotive Therapy (RET), pg. 649
Resistance, pg. 646
Stimulants, pg. 666
Systematic Desensitization, pg. 652
Transference, pg. 647
Virtual Reality Therapy, pg. 654

POP QUIZ

True or False

___ 1. Resistance occurs when an individual undergoing psychoanalysis begins to respond to the therapist in much the same manner as he or she responds to other important people in his or her life.

___ 2. Systematic desensitization is useful in stopping people from continuing to engage in compulsive behaviors such as smoking, gambling, and alcohol abuse.

___ 3. Psychoanalysis assumes that behavioral disorders are rooted in unconscious conflicts and repressed urges rooted in early childhood.

___ 4. Research examining the success rate of different types of psychotherapy has shown that no particular type of psychotherapy is significantly superior to the others.

___ 5. Like lobotomies, electroconvulsive therapy and magnetic seizure therapy are mostly "historical" in nature, because these treatments are no longer in use.

Multiple Choice

6. Which of the following is *not* one of the therapeutic techniques of Freud's psychoanalysis?
   a. Interpretation of transference
   b. Emotive therapy
   c. Interpretation of resistance
   d. Free association
7. Contemporary psychoanalytically oriented therapists do which of the following?
   a. Pay more attention to a patient's current life and relationships
   b. Tend to desire a longer duration of therapy
   c. Sit out of view of a patient
   d. Attempt to gain insight into the unconscious roots of a patient's problems
8. Rational-emotive therapy tends to focus on _______. Cognitive behavior therapy focuses on ______.
   a. thoughts / behavior
   b. behavior / thoughts
   c. irrational beliefs / negative self-images
   d. negative self-images / irrational beliefs
9. Of what is developing a hierarchy of fears a component?
   a. Aversive conditioning
   b. Cognitive behavior therapy
   c. Extinction technique
   d. Systematic desensitization

POP QUIZ

10. What is the type of therapy in which a chronic drinker is given a drug that induces nausea when combined with alcohol called?
    a. Systematic desensitization
    b. Aversive conditioning
    c. Chemotherapy
    d. Counterconditioning
11. Cognitive restructuring therapy involves attempting to do which of the following?
    a. Instruct family members in how to accept the disturbed family member "as he or she is"
    b. Train patients to restructure their negative thinking into more positive thoughts which lead to a more positive self-image
    c. Change maladaptive patterns of interaction among family and friends
    d. All of the above
12. What is one reason researchers have found little difference in the effectiveness of various psychotherapy approaches?
    a. All therapists are well trained.
    b. All therapists must take the same licensing exam.
    c. Most approaches began as one approach anyway.
    d Almost all styles of therapy share certain common features.
13. What is the behavioral therapy that involves Pavlovian conditioning principles to unlearn fears called?
    a. Systematic desensitization
    b. Aversion therapy
    c. Cognitive restructuring
    d. Punishment
14. Electroconvulsive therapy is most effective for the treatment of which disorder?
    a. Schizophrenia
    b. Major depression
    c. Bipolar disorder
    d. Generalized anxiety disorder
15. The most effective treatments for severe psychological disorders all involve the use of which of the following?
    a. Psychoanalysis
    b. Cognitive-behavioral therapy
    c. Rational emotive therapy
    d. Psychoactive drugs

Answer Key: 1.F 2.F 3.T 4.T 5.F 6.b 7.a 8.c 9.d 10.b 11.b 12.d 13.a 14.b 15.d

(Getty/monkeybusiness images)

Chapter 17

Social Psychology

Imagine that you have volunteered to participate in a study in which you and several other students will discuss personal problems caused by the pressures of university life. You are told that to avoid embarrassment, you and five other participants (or perhaps two or one, depending on the group in which you are placed) will not see one another; instead, you will sit in individual cubicles and talk over an intercom system. Participants' microphones will be activated only when it is their turn to speak, and to preserve anonymity, the experimenters will not listen.

The experiment begins and the first voice you hear is that of a young man. Haltingly, he explains that he is having a great deal of difficulty adjusting to the pressures he is experiencing. He also states, with obvious embarrassment, that he is prone to epileptic-like seizures when he is under stress. You and the other participants talk, in turn, about your own reactions to stress. Now it is the first young man's turn to speak again. After a very short time, it is apparent that he is in trouble. He seems to fumble for words, then begins choking and pleading for help. He is clearly experiencing a seizure. What do you do?

We have just described an experiment conducted by two social psychologists, John Darley and Bibb Latané (1968). In the actual experimental design, the researchers had prerecorded all participants' voices so that only one subject actually took part in each group discussion, and that subject's reactions were the focus of the study. The results might surprise you. When subjects thought that they were the only ones aware of the emergency, Darley and Latané found that 85 percent offered help. In contrast, only 62 percent of subjects sought help when they thought there were two other bystanders, compared to a mere 31 percent of subjects who thought there were five others in the group.

Social psychologists use the term **diffusion of responsibility**, or **bystander apathy**, to explain Darley and Latané's findings. Our own sense of responsibility is diminished by the presence of other bystanders. Because we assume that they have as much responsibility to act as we have, we are less likely to intervene to give aid. Diffusion of responsibility helps to explain some other disturbing incidents. One is the widely reported 1964 stabbing murder of a woman named Kitty Genovese as at least thirty-eight residents of a Queens, New York, apartment complex looked on, making no move to intervene or call for help. These bystanders showed signs of extreme anxiety as a result of their experience (as did the subjects of Darley and Latané's experiment); they still did nothing to help, counting instead on the probability that someone else would intervene.

The wide publicity of the Kitty Genovese incident and the reenactment of a multiple rape in the 1988 film *The Accused,* which also took place in the presence of numerous onlookers, as well as other publicized cases, do not appear to decrease the tendency for bystander apathy. On October 5, 1992, hundreds of Oregon motorists witnessed the brutal attack of a university student who was assaulted while she waited at a bus stop. After hitting her repeatedly with a tire iron and banging her against parked cars, the assailant threw her into the trunk of his car, from which she later escaped. All of this took place in daylight at the edge of a crowded bus stop with motorists continually passing by—no one intervened or called for help. Even more recently, in 2009, at least twenty high school students watched or took part in a gang rape of a fifteen-year-old California girl outside of the school gym where hundreds of students were gathered to celebrate homecoming. Throughout the two-hour ordeal, more people came out to watch and even participate as word of the rape spread inside. Again, none of the witnesses attempted to stop the violence or call police.

Such incidents illustrate an important fact that we have not yet fully explored in this text—our actions are greatly influenced by social processes and our perception of our social environments. *Social psychology* is the field of psychology concerned with how social influences affect our behaviors, and it asks a number of questions that we attempt to answer in this chapter. How, for instance, do we form impressions of people, and how do these impressions influence our behavior? How important is physical attractiveness in selecting a potential mate? How likely are we to resist pressures to change our behaviors so that they conform to those of other people, even when we disagree with their actions or opinions? Is aggressive behavior inevitable for humans and other animals? What factors contribute to aggressive behavior?

Diffusion of Responsibility or **Bystander Apathy** Tendency for an individual to feel a diminished sense of responsibility to assist in an emergency when other bystanders are present

The scope of social psychology is far too broad to cover comprehensively in one chapter. Instead of taking a shotgun approach that touches on many topics with little depth, we have limited our discussion to the broadly researched areas of social perceptions, attribution, attitudes, prejudice, social influence, interpersonal attraction, and aggression. We begin with social perception.

17.1 Social Perception

We encounter many people each day, from the clerk at the grocery store to the classmate sitting behind us to the mechanic who is servicing our car. Even if our interactions with these people are very brief, we form impressions or perceptions of them. The term **social perception** describes the ways we perceive, evaluate, categorize, and form judgments about the qualities of people we encounter.

(Getty/peopleimages)

We form impressions or perceptions of the many people we encounter each day, even if the interactions are brief.

These social perceptions have a critical influence on our interactions. In fact, they are more important in guiding our behaviors than the attitudes and behaviors of the people around us. Thus, the subjects in Darley and Latané's diffusion of responsibility experiment did not intervene because they *perceived* that others would probably seek help, not because they observed others helping. Likewise, you may withdraw from a friend because you perceive that she is annoyed with you. Whether she actually is annoyed is not as significant in determining your response as your own perceptions.

Since these readings of other people are so important, it is worthwhile knowing how we form them. Three factors that influence our social perceptions are first impressions, schemas, and implicit personality theories.

17.1a First Impressions

First impressions are the initial judgments we make about people, and they play an important role in social perceptions. We are more likely to form opinions of others quickly, based on first impressions, than to refrain from forming opinions until we have more information. These first impressions may change as we get to know a person better, but we often tend to hang onto them even in the face of contradictory evidence. Thus, initial opinions may have a strong impact on our future interactions with people.

For example, if you first meet a new tenant in your apartment building at a party where he behaves in a loud and egotistical manner, it will probably be hard for you to perceive him as a sensitive, caring person when you later see him comforting a small child who has scraped his knee. The first information we receive about a person often seems to count the most, a phenomenon referred to as the **primacy effect**. Sometimes we refer to this as a *first impression*.

This effect was demonstrated in an experiment in which two lists of traits describing a person were read to two separate groups of subjects (Asch, 1946). In one group, subjects heard a description that began with positive characteristics (such as intelligent and industrious) followed by negative ones (impulsive, stubborn, and so forth). Their overall assessments of this person were positive. Subjects in the other group heard the same list, but in reverse order. The result? Their assessments were far more negative.

Research indicates that negative first impressions are often quickly formed and hard to overcome. In contrast, the opposite tends to be true of positive first impressions, which are often hard to earn but easily lost. For example, your reticence to conclude that your new dating companion is reliable (positive first impression) may subside only after several encounters in which he or she exhibits this trait. However, one incident of unreliable

Social Perception The way in which we perceive, evaluate, categorize, and form judgments about the qualities of other people

Primacy Effect The phenomenon that the first information we receive about a person often has the greatest influence on our perceptions of that person

behavior may cause you to quickly revise your social perception of this person. In contrast, if your companion is a few minutes late for your first date, you may quickly decide that he or she is flaky and unreliable (negative first impression), a characterization that may change only after numerous encounters in which your partner exhibits the trait of reliability.

17.1b Person Schemas

Recall from Chapter 7 that schemas are the conceptual frameworks we use to make sense out of our world. The concept of schemas helps explain how we perceive the people we meet. For example, you might have schemas of lawyers as aggressive and verbal, and of professors as studious and somewhat distracted. Social psychologists refer to these generalized assumptions about certain groups or classes of people as **person schemas**.

Person schemas provide a structure for evaluating the people we meet, allowing us to take shortcuts by concentrating on some facts and ignoring others. When we assess a person for the first time, we tend to pick up only the information that fits our existing schemas, ignoring the rest. This process is efficient, but unfortunately, it is not always the most accurate way of forming impressions.

Once we fit a person into a schema, we tend to use that schema as a general organizing principle for interpreting further information about the person. For example, if our first impression of a new neighbor is that she is unfriendly, we are likely to evaluate her failure to comment on our shiny new car as further evidence of her unfriendliness. If she then acts in a way that does not fit the schema (for example, picking up our garbage after it has been scattered by the wind), we may dismiss that act by concluding that she picked up the mess only because she was worried that it would blow onto her lawn.

17.1c Implicit Personality Theories

Just as person schemas guide us in fitting people into preexisting categories, we also make implicit assumptions about personality traits that usually go together. For instance, if we meet a person whom we perceive as intelligent, we may expect that person also to be skillful and imaginative. These assumptions about how traits are related to each other in people's personalities are called **implicit personality theories** (Cantor & Mischel, 1979). We may not be aware of many of our implicit assumptions. However, since these associations may be firmly rooted, they are likely to be activated when we meet people for the first time.

Our implicit personality theories are often organized around **central traits**—traits that we tend to associate with many other characteristics. For example, many people associate the trait of coldness with unsociability, humorlessness, and lack of popularity. Even a single central trait may play an important role in organizing our implicit personality theories about others. In an early study, Solomon Asch (1946) presented two groups of subjects with a list of seven traits, describing a hypothetical person. The list for each group differed on only one central trait dimension—*warm* versus *cold*—yet this difference influenced significantly the subjects' predictions about other traits of the hypothetical person. Thus, subjects who had been provided a trait list that included *warm* were more likely to predict that the hypothetical person was generous or had a good sense of humor than subjects whose list contained the word *cold*.

Psychologists use the term **halo effect** to describe our tendency to infer other positive (or negative) traits from our initial impressions or inferences. For example, in a recent study examining the halo effect, researchers found that thinner men were rated as more

Person Schemas Generalized assumptions about certain groups or classes of people

Implicit Personality Theories Assumptions people make about how traits usually occur together in other people's personalities

Central Trait In Gordon Allport's trait theory of personality, a major characteristic, such as honesty or sensitivity

Halo Effect Tendency to infer other positive or negative traits from our perception of one trait in another person

attractive, enthusiastic, and more likely to be successful than heavier men. Heavier men, on the other hand, were rated as more friendly and trustworthy than thinner men (Wade, Fuller, Bresnan, Schaefer, & Mlynarski, 2007).

17.2 Attribution Theories

An important part of social perceptions are the judgments we make about why people behave as they do. Our responses to other people are strongly influenced by these attributions, and we are constantly attempting to understand the reasons for other people's behavior. Attributions allow us to make sense out of other people's actions, figure out their attitudes and personality traits, and, ultimately, gain some control over subsequent interactions with them through our increased ability to predict their behavior.

According to **attribution theory** (Heider, 1946), we tend to attribute people's behavior either to *dispositional* (internal) *causes*, such as motivational states or personality traits, or to *situational causes*, such as environmental or external factors. This distinction can have important effects on our relationships with people. For example, suppose you have recently begun dating someone you like very much, and the two of you spend a weekend visiting your date's parents. Much to your dismay, your friend acts like a different person—restrained, impersonal, and physically unresponsive. What has caused the change? If you attribute it to external factors (that your date is ill at ease around his or her parents) you are unlikely to feel that the relationship is seriously threatened. However, if you attribute the change to an internal cause (that your partner no longer feels responsive to you), you may seriously reevaluate the relationship.

Whether we tend to attribute causes of our own behavior or that of others to dispositions or to situations may depend on gender. In a study to investigate gender differences in attribution style, researchers at Wellesley College measured the attributions of 176 male and 116 female freshman students. They found that females tended to attribute academic successes to their efforts (external), whereas males tended to attribute their successes to their ability (internal) attribution (Erkut, 1983). The reverse attribution style is often observed when males and females make attributions about their failures. Males often attribute failure to situations (e.g., bad luck or the exam wasn't fair), while females attribute failure to a disposition (e.g., their ability or their intelligence).

Clearly, our attributions for the causes of people's behaviors have an important impact on our own behaviors. How do we make these attributions? Two theories that attempt to explain this process are the correspondent inference theory and the covariation principle.

Attribution Theory Theory that we attempt to make sense out of other people's behavior by attributing it to either dispositional (internal) causes or situational (external) causes

Correspondent Inference Theory Theory that the attributions we make about other people's behavior are influenced by a variety of conditions, such as the social desirability of that behavior or whether the behavior results from free choice

17.2a The Correspondent Inference Theory

The **correspondent inference theory** attempts to explain the attributions we make about people's behaviors by looking at the conditions under which we make those attributions. Theorists Edward E. Jones (Jones et al., 1989) and his colleagues use the term *correspondent inference* to describe cases in which we attribute a person's behavior to an underlying disposition. For instance, in the earlier example of the new neighbor who behaved raucously at a party, you may have inferred that the person had a loud and unpleasant disposition. However, we do not always make dispositional attributions based on the behaviors we observe. If you watch a television game show emcee behaving in a solicitous and charming manner to guest participants, you are unlikely to infer that the host is a genuinely warm and caring person. Why do we make correspondent inferences about people's dispositions in some cases but not in others? Jones and his associates suggest several factors.

One important variable is the *social desirability* or "expectedness" of behaviors we observe. Some common behaviors are so socially acceptable that they reveal virtually nothing about a person. For example, we expect politicians running for office to smile and shake hands with strangers. This expected behavior fits in nicely with our schema of a politician, but it does not tell us very much about the politician's disposition. True, the candidate might actually be a warm and friendly person, but it is equally possible that the smiles, handshakes, and baby kissing are due instead to the influence of social norms. Thus, we are unlikely to draw correspondent inferences about the politician.

Attributions and Socially Undesirable Behavior

Do socially undesirable actions have the same impact on our attribution processes as socially acceptable behaviors? For instance, if you observe a tennis pro slam his racket on the court after a bad call, are you more likely to make a correspondent inference about his or her disposition than if you observed polite and controlled behavior? If so, can you explain why unacceptable behavior would be more telling than desirable behavior? Consider this question before reading on.

Several experiments have demonstrated that we are more likely to make correspondent inferences from socially undesirable or norm-deviant behaviors than from socially desirable behaviors. For example, in one study subjects listened to various versions of tapes of a man being interviewed for a job in which the interviewer opened the interaction by specifying the personality traits required for the job—traits such as independence and self-reliance. In one version, the applicant described himself in a way that closely matched the desired attributes, while in another version he described his traits as entirely different from those the interviewer was seeking. Most subjects indicated they were able to make confident judgments about the applicant's true character only when he had described himself as being the opposite of what the job demanded.

(Shutterstock)

Personality traits are a large part of a job interview.

Such findings are consistent with the correspondent inference theory. Apparently, when a person's behavior fits external social expectations, we tend to discount it as a clue to a person's true nature. It is the unexpected behavior, which deviates from socially desirable norms, that influences us to attribute actions to internal dispositions.

A second variable that determines whether we make correspondent inferences about a person's disposition is the degree to which his or her behavior is focused on achieving unique outcomes (or *noncommon effects*) that would be unlikely to occur as a result of some other behavior. For example, suppose a friend of yours, a physics major, signs up for a course in quantum mechanics. Will you be impressed? If you find out that the course is required for a degree in physics, you are likely to attribute your friend's action to external causes since it accomplishes the unique or noncommon outcome of obtaining a degree, a goal that could not have been achieved in any other way. If, on the other hand, you discover this course is an obscure offering that is neither required nor recommended for a physics major, you are more likely to make a dispositional attribution about your friend's great intellectual curiosity.

A third variable that influences correspondent inferences is whether or not we perceive a person's behavior as resulting from *free choice*. If we know that a person freely chose to behave in a particular manner, we probably assume that these actions reflect underlying dispositions. On the other hand, if that person was pressed to act in a certain way by situational forces, we are more inclined to attribute the behavior to external than internal causes. For example, if one of your friends told you while you were lunching together that she strongly supported a conservative political group, you would probably be more inclined to attribute a conservative political attitude to her than if she were to make the same comments during an event hosted by a politically conservative organization at your college.

17.2b Covariation Principle

A second theory of how people make attributions builds on the notion that when we try to figure out the causes and effects of particular events, we generally begin with the premise that cause and effect go together. Thus, if a cause is altered, the effect will also be changed, so that causes and effects can be said to *covary*. According to Howard Kelley (1987), when we make attributions about people's behavior (the effect), we tend to look at three potential causes: the *situation* or context in which the behavior occurs, the *persons involved*, and the *stimuli* or objects toward which the behavior is directed. Kelley's theory is known as the **covariation principle**.

Consider the following illustration of the covariation principle. Suppose you enroll in an art appreciation class. On your first visit to a gallery, you observe one member of the class, an intense-looking young man, lingering at each oil painting, staring with apparent rapture. Observing this behavior, you might wonder about this person. Your attribution of causes for this young man's behavior depends on factors inherent in the situation: the *context* in which the behavior occurred (the art gallery), the *persons involved* (the intense young man and other classmates), and the *stimuli* or objects toward which the observed behavior is directed (the oil paintings).

Kelley suggests that as we seek additional information to aid our interpretation of the causes of a person's behavior we act like social scientists, carefully analyzing the data, paying particular attention to variations in situation, persons, and stimuli on each of the three following separate dimensions:

1. *Distinctiveness* is the degree to which other stimuli are capable of eliciting the same behavior from the young man. Does he behave in the same way at other art galleries or museums that your class visits, or does the behavior occur only at this gallery? If it only occurs at this gallery, it is highly distinctive. We tend to attribute highly distinctive actions to situational causes.

2. *Consistency* is the degree to which the young man exhibits the same behavior in response to the same stimulus on other occasions. There is high consistency if the person behaves in essentially the same way on other visits to this art gallery. Consistency is important for both dispositional and situational attribution.

Covariation Principle
Theory that our attributions about people's behavior are influenced by the situations in which the behavior occurs, the persons involved, and the stimuli or objects toward which the behavior is directed

3. *Consensus* is the degree to which other people exhibit the same response to the stimulus as the actor. If other people react to the art in this gallery in the same or similar fashion, there is a high consensus. We tend to attribute low consensus responses to dispositional causes.

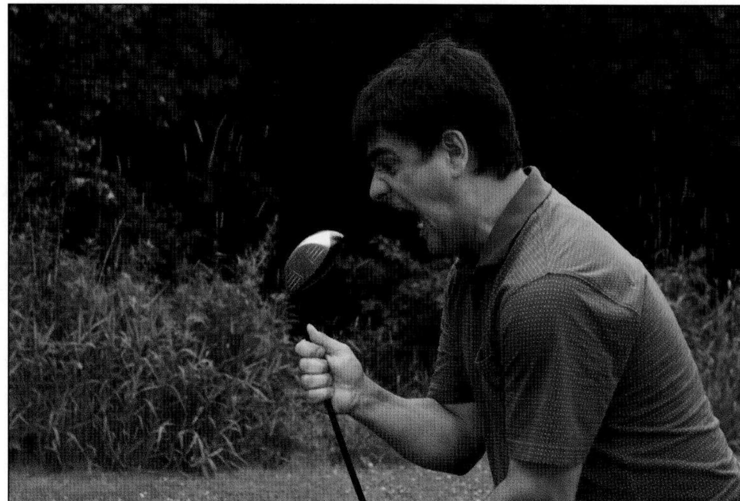
(iStock)

A person's unexpected behavior, which deviates from socially desirable norms, influences us to attribute his actions to internal dispositions.

According to Kelley, we take in information about all of these dimensions and use it to determine whether the behavior we have observed is caused by an internal disposition or by the situation. Thus, you might create the following checklist concerning the young man:

1. *Distinctiveness:* Low. The young man behaves the same way at other galleries.
2. *Consistency:* High. When you return to the same gallery on another occasion, the young man still displays high interest.
3. *Consensus:* Low. Other visitors do not show the same remarkable interest.

Based on this assessment, you will probably attribute the young man's behavior to the disposition of a genuine interest in art. Had you noted a pattern of high consistency, high consensus, and high distinctiveness, you would probably have attributed the young man's behavior to a situational cause, such as a curiosity about the particular artist displayed at the first gallery.

17.2c Attribution Errors

Both the correspondent inference theory and the covariation principle suggest that we make attributions in a rational, methodical way. Unfortunately, our judgments are not always accurate. We often make errors in the inferences we draw from other people's behavior, and these errors can usually be traced to a few common attribution errors. We look at a few of these errors, including the fundamental attribution error, false consensus error, and the illusion of control.

Fundamental Attribution Error

One of the most common attribution errors is a tendency to overestimate dispositional causes and to underestimate situational causes when accounting for the behavior of others. (Interestingly, we tend to do exactly the opposite when accounting for our own behaviors.) This inclination is so pervasive that it has been labeled the **fundamental attribution error**. For example, when a casual acquaintance complains that she has just failed a history exam, do you attribute her poor performance to a tricky test or a lack of adequate preparation time (both situational causes), or are you more inclined to assume

Fundamental Attribution Error Tendency to overestimate dispositional (internal) causes of behavior and to underestimate situational (external) causes of behavior

BVT Lab

Flashcards are available for this chapter at **www.BVTLab.com.**

she is not very bright (dispositional cause)? If you are like most people, you probably tend to overestimate the latter cause and discount the former. Had you failed the same exam, however, the odds are good that you would look for situational causes if you were a male, and for dispositional causes if you were female.

Some researchers have found that attribution biases depend upon whether one is male or female. For instance, males tend to attribute their failures to situations ("I prepared poorly" or "It was a tricky exam") and their successes to dispositions ("I'm talented" or "smart"). On the other hand, many females do just the opposite: They attribute success to situations ("I studied hard" or "I was lucky") and failure to dispositions ("I'm not very smart").

Consider another example: To what do you attribute the high degree of athletic ability we see in a professional athlete like Tiger Woods? If you are like most people, you attribute his ability to a disposition—his innate talent, not years of hard work. In fact, television commentators and sports writers continually comment about innate talent and instinct of athletes (dispositions), when, in reality, it is years of hard work and training (situations) that determine performance.

Research provides evidence of our tendency to make fundamental attribution errors. In one study, for instance, male college students were asked why they had chosen their majors and why they liked their current girlfriend; they were also asked the same questions about their best male friend (Nisbett, Caputo, Legant, & Marecek, 1973). Their answers indicated a strong tendency to attribute their best friends' choices to dispositional qualities ("He is the kind of person who likes …"), whereas they described their own choices in terms of environmental conditions, such as characteristics of their majors or their girlfriends ("Chemistry is a high-paying field;" "She is attractive and intelligent").

Why are we so quick to attribute other people's behavior to their inner dispositions? At least part of the answer lies in the fact that while we know what situational factors affect our own behavior, we have far less information about how such factors affect other people. Thus, we take the easiest path and assume that they acted in a particular way because "that is the kind of people they are." It is easier to draw conclusions from the behaviors we can observe than to look for hidden reasons. This conclusion is partially supported by recent research, which shows that our tendency to attribute other's behavior to dispositional factors tends to dissipate in favor of situational factors over time (Truchot, Maure, & Patte, 2003). As we get to know another person, we begin to see how their behavior is influenced by situational variables.

Psychologists have investigated a possible link between the fundamental attribution error and the quality of intimate relationships. Couples who share their lives either through marriage or cohabitation routinely make judgments or attributions to explain each other's behavior. For instance, if a man fails to notice that his partner is in need of some affection and nurturance, she might conclude that he is preoccupied with a problem at work (situation) or that he is insensitive and non-nurturing (disposition). These two kinds of attributions can be expected to have profoundly different implications for the quality of their relationship.

Do you think couples who experience a considerable amount of relationship conflict would be inclined to explain each other's behavior in ways different from couples who are happy with their relationship? Do distressed couples rely more on internal versus external attributions than happy couples, or is the pattern just the opposite? Think about these questions for a couple of minutes before reading on.

Research suggests that individual partners in distressed relationships are inclined to overestimate the role of internal, dispositional causes when trying to explain what they perceive as their partner's negative behavior and to attribute positive actions to situational causes. Thus, in such a relationship if one member fails to behave in a nurturing and affectionate manner, the other would likely conclude that he or she is an insensitive and non-nurturing person. In contrast, a kindly act exhibited in a distressed relationship might be attributed to such situational causes, as "He wants to give the impression that he is a good guy" or "She must want me to do something for her." Patterns among individuals who are happily paired tend to be just the reverse. Thus, individual members within a happy marriage tend to attribute their partner's positive behavior to internal, dispositional traits, whereas they are inclined to attribute negative actions to external situations (Graham & Connolly, 2006; Durtschi, Fincham, Cui, Lorenz, & Conger, 2011).

It is probably not surprising to hear that people who are experiencing unhappy, distressed intimate relationships are inclined to place the blame on each other. What is unclear at this time is whether the attribution biases typical of unhappy partners are the cause or an effect of marital distress. Hopefully, future research will clarify the nature of this relationship.

False Consensus Bias Attribution bias caused by the assumption that most people share our own attitudes and behaviors

Illusion of Control Attributional bias caused by the belief that we control events in our own lives that are really beyond our control

False Consensus

Another common attributional error is the assumption that most people share our own attitudes and behaviors. This assumption is known as **false consensus bias**, and it influences us to judge any noteworthy deviations from our own standards as unusual or abnormal.

For example, suppose you note that someone living in your apartment complex never laughs or even cracks a smile while listening to a certain television comedian you find hilarious. Consequently, you make a dispositional attribution: You assume that the other person has no sense of humor. This bias may be so strong that you do not stop to think that there are probably a number of people with good senses of humor who do not enjoy this comedian.

Illusion of Control

Have you ever had a bad experience, such as being in an auto accident, and then later lamented that if only you had left at a different time you could have avoided the situation? People often blame themselves or others for events that are beyond their control. This attribution error, called the **illusion of control**, is the belief that we control events in our lives, even those that are actually influenced primarily or solely by external causes. The illusion of control is reflected in the behavior of many gamblers, such as the slot player who thinks he can tell when a machine is ready to get hot by observing its patterns of payoff to other players.

Why do we hold on to the illusion that we are in control of such events? Most of us want to be in control of our own lives, and the feeling of being out of control can be very distressing, even when the uncontrollable event is highly negative. Thus, it may actually be less stressful to blame ourselves for losing a job in a round of company layoffs ("I should have seen it coming") than to acknowledge there was nothing we could do about it.

We have been talking about social perceptions and the inferences we make about other people's behavior. These perceptions all contribute to our attitudes about people, groups, and situations. Attitudes have been the subject of more research than any other topic in social psychology in attempts to both predict and explain human behavior. In the following section we explore this topic.

17.3 Attitudes

Attitude Any learned, relatively enduring predisposition to respond in consistently favorable or unfavorable ways to certain people, groups, ideas, or situations

The term *attitude* is so commonly used in everyday language that we all have some idea what it means. If you were asked to define what an attitude is, you might reply, "a person's feelings about something." This definition is not far off the mark. One of the pioneers in attitude measurement, L. L. Thurstone, defined an attitude as "the intensity of acquired positive or negative affect for or against a psychological object" (1946). Thurstone's interpretation allows us to define people's **attitudes** as learned, relatively enduring dispositions to respond in consistently favorable or unfavorable ways to certain people, groups, ideas, or situations. We use this definition because it points out that attitudes are learned, that they may change, and that they may predict behavior.

17.3a Acquiring Attitudes

How do we develop attitudes? As you might guess, attitudes are shaped by experiences, including our observations of behavior (both other people's and our own); Pavlovian and operant conditioning; and direct experiences with the *attitude object* (the people, ideas, or things about which we hold attitudes).

Behavioral Observation

Observing Others As we saw in Chapter 6, we learn some behaviors by observing and imitating influential role models (Bandura, 1986). By the same process, attitudes can be learned. Parents and peers have an especially strong influence on our attitudes. Thus, young people whose friends view adult authority figures with mistrust are likely to acquire this attitude, particularly if it serves a social adjustment function for them. In addition, it is quite common for children to possess attitudes about religion and politics that are similar to their parents.

Observing Ourselves Although it is commonly believed that attitudes cause behavior, the reverse may actually be more accurate. That is, our behaviors may determine our attitudes. Social psychologists Leon Festinger and Daryl Bem (Festinger, Carlsmith, & Bem, 2007) have proposed that when we are not sure how we feel toward a particular attitude object, we sometimes infer our attitudes from our own behavior (Nier, 2007). If you are a smoker, your attitudes about smoking may be more favorable than those of people who do not smoke. This idea will be discussed in more detail later, under the topic of cognitive dissonance.

Learning Attitudes

Pavlovian Conditioning Some of our attitudes are acquired through the associative process of Pavlovian conditioning described in Chapter 6. Whenever positive or negative experiences (elicited by an unconditioned stimulus, or [US]) are paired with an attitude object (the conditioned stimulus, [CS]), new attitudes are likely to be formed. For example, you may have a fairly positive opinion about dogs: They are often cute, soft, and cuddly; and they can keep you company when you're alone. However, if you have a frightening experience with a dog, your attitude (behavior) toward dogs may change. You may find yourself avoiding them or being anxious in their presence.

Advertisers employ Pavlovian conditioning techniques in their efforts to sway our attitudes toward a particular product. For example, not too many years ago, a manufacturer of a popular brand of men's shirts ran television commercials in which a presumably neutral object (a dress shirt, the CS) was worn by an attractive woman, with the implied suggestion that the shirt was all she was wearing. The expectation was that the women would serve as a US, eliciting favorable sexual feelings when men viewed or thought about the shirt. Although the average male viewer may have realized logically that the shirt had nothing to do with attractive women, the association may, nevertheless, be strong enough to influence his buying habits. (This author remembered it!)

(Shutterstock)

Advertisers use Pavlovian conditioning to influence our attitudes about their products.

Operant Conditioning We also acquire attitudes by receiving praise, approval, or acceptance for expressing them, and we may be punished for expressing other attitudes. When attitudes produce punishment (or when they fail to elicit social approval), they tend to decrease; when they are reinforced, they tend to increase. For instance, a child who discovers that making derogatory comments about a different racial group will earn approval from his parents is more likely to develop a strong racial prejudice than one whose derogatory comments are met with disapproval. Similarly, groups of friends tend to share similar attitudes because these behaviors are mutually reinforced within the group. We will return to this again when we discuss prejudice.

Direct Experience Finally, we learn many of our attitudes through direct contact with the attitude object. For instance, you may test-drive a car with a revolutionary new suspension system, and as a result of this experience develop a very favorable attitude toward the new design. Attitudes acquired through direct experience are likely to be more deeply ingrained and held more confidently than those learned through observation. Thus, trying the car yourself is likely to influence your attitude much more strongly than watching a television commercial or even hearing about the design from friends who have tried it. Automobile salespersons encourage you to drive a car early in their sales pitch. Here, directly receiving reinforcement (driving the car) is more powerful than the influence of modeling (seeing others drive it in a commercial).

17.3b The Function of Attitudes

Whether we learn them from our own experiences or from observing others, attitudes serve a number of important functions in our lives (Tesser, 1990). One is an *understanding function*. Attitudes provide a frame of reference that helps us structure and make sense out of the world and our experiences. For example, your attitudes about what personal attributes you favor in a date provide you with a frame of reference for evaluating prospective romantic interests. If a person possesses behavioral dispositions you evaluate positively, you are likely to respond favorably to that individual.

Just as we rely on our own attitudes to evaluate unfamiliar situations or objects, we also rely on the attitudes of others. For instance, suppose a friend has just attended the first lecture in a class you are thinking about taking. Your first question to her will probably be something like, "Well, how did you like the class and the instructor?" If her attitude is positive, you will be more likely to sign up as well.

A second function of attitudes is a *social identification function*. The attitudes of others provide us with important information about what they are like, just as the attitudes we express tell others about us. That is why, when you date a person for the first time, you

Figure 17-1 A Cognitive Model of Attitude

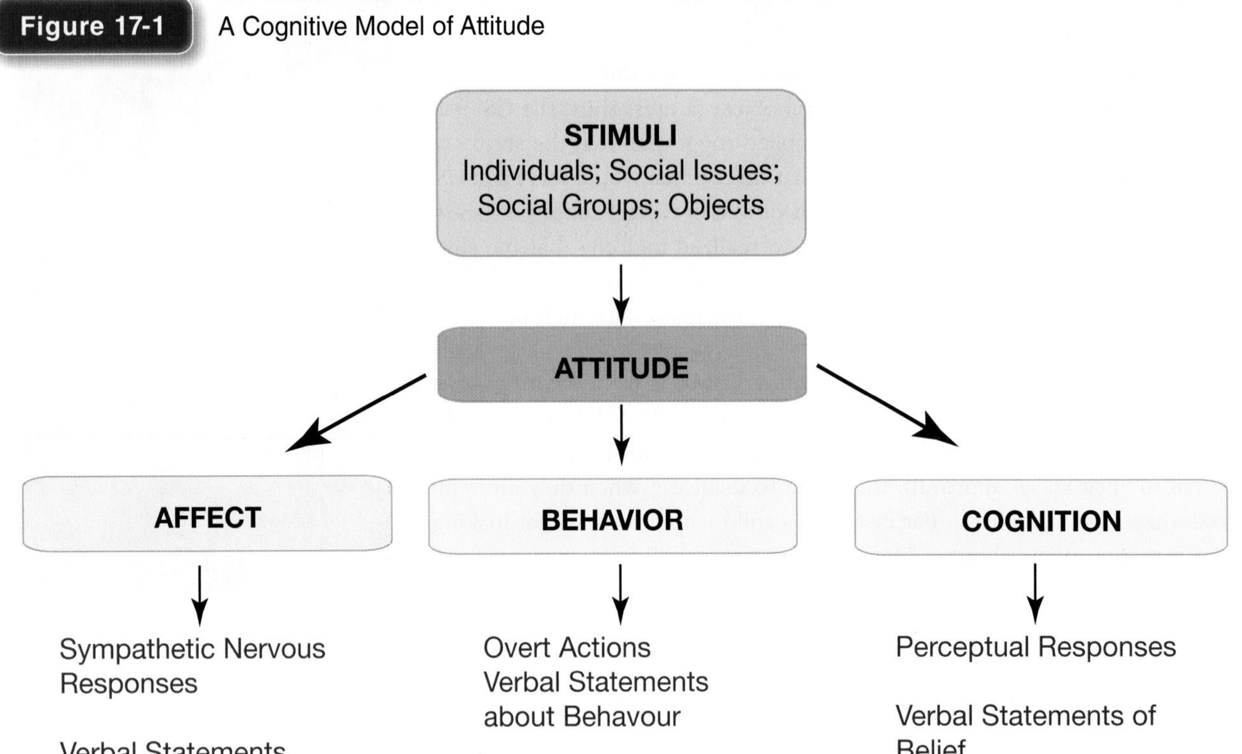

Source: Adapted figure of "The Three-Component (Tripartite) Model of Attitudes" from article "Empirical Validation of Affect, Behavior, and Cognition as Distinct as Components of Attitude" from *Journal of Personality and Social Psychology,* Volume 47, Number 6 © 1984, pp. 1191–1205, by S. Beckler.

usually exchange information about favorite activities, food preferences, music interests, and so forth. Our overall assessment of other people is often strongly influenced by what we perceive to be their likes and dislikes.

A third function of attitudes is a *social adjustment function*. The attitudes we express sometimes allow us to identify with or gain approval from our peers. For instance, if your attractive date expresses a deep enthusiasm for Russian literature, you may also immerse yourself in Tolstoy, Dostoevsky, and Turgenev. Of course, attitudes that serve a social adjustment function in one setting may have quite a different effect in a different environment. For example, if you begin describing your favorite passage from *Crime and Punishment* to some acquaintances during the next Saturday night dance, you might soon find yourself standing alone. This example brings up the concept of **impression management**, which describes our tendency to select carefully what information we reveal about our attitudes, depending on how we think such information will affect the responses of others. Figure 17-2 provides a classic example of impression management in action. In this case, Governor Mitt Romney switched his opinion on gay marriage during his 2012 presidential campaign. Back in 1994, when he ran for the U.S. Senate, he promised to be a "champion for full equality for gays and lesbians." Later, as governor of Massachusetts with his eyes on the White House, he flipped his position. "My view is that marriage itself is a relationship between a man and a woman" (Smith, 2012). Many political pundits believe this switch was to make his position clearly different from President Obama's.

Impression Management
Tendency of individuals to carefully select what information they reveal about their attitudes, depending on how they think such information will affect their image in the eyes of others

Figure 17-2 Impression Management in Politics

SOCIAL ADJUSTMENT AND EXPRESSED ATTITUDES

In 1994 Mitt Romney voiced his support for gay marriage in his statement while running for the U.S. Senate, "I promise to be a champion for full equality for gays and lesbians". His campaign distributed flyers during a Gay Pride gathering claiming he would be a strong advocate for gay rights.

During his 2012 run for president Romney had completely switched his position apparently to distance himself from President Obama. During his campaign he states "My view is that marriage itself is a relationship between a man and a woman. And that's my own preference."

Political candidates often change their expressed attitudes to manage the impression of voters.

Source: T. Smith on NPR, May 10, 2012

17.3c Do Attitudes Predict Behavior?

Whether attitudes serve a positive or negative function, it seems natural to assume that they influence our behavior. If you like jazz, you will be likely to attend a local concert where good jazz is being played; if you believe strongly that formal religion is important, you will probably participate actively in your church or temple. Do our attitudes, however, always guide our actions? Consider the student who is strongly opposed to cheating but finds at exam time that she is doing so poorly in one course that her chances of acceptance into a graduate program are jeopardized. In this situation, her motive to succeed coupled with her perceived failure may well have a stronger influence on her behavior than her attitude toward cheating.

To what extent do attitudes determine behavior? Social psychologists began investigating the relationship between attitudes and behavior more than seventy years ago, with surprising results. Sociologist Richard LaPiere (1934) conducted a widely known study in the early 1930s, a time when there was considerable prejudice against Chinese people in the United States. LaPiere traveled extensively throughout the West and Midwest with a Chinese couple he described as personable and charming. Considering the prejudices of the time, LaPiere expected to be turned away at many hotels and restaurants. However, his traveling companions were served at all of the 184 restaurants they visited and were rejected at only one of 67 lodging places. Approximately six months later, LaPiere wrote to each of the places he and the Chinese couple had patronized and asked whether they would accept Chinese people as guests at their establishment. Of those restaurants and hotel proprietors who responded (51 percent of the total), over 90 percent said they would not. Many social scientists interpreted these results as indicating that there is little or no relationship between attitudes and behavior.

In the years following publication of LaPiere's findings, dozens of other studies tested further the relationship between attitudes and actions, with similar results. These studies asked people to express their attitudes about a variety of subjects, such as racial minorities, church attendance, and cheating, and then compared their actual behavior in a measurable situation related to those attitudes. The measured relationship between

(Shutterstock)

Whether attitudes serve a positive or negative function, it seems natural to assume that they influence our behavior.

attitudes and behavior in such areas, and many others, was shown to be so small that attitudes were either unrelated or only slightly related to behavior.

Intuitively, it seems obvious that attitudes influence behavior, yet the findings of LaPiere and other early researchers point toward just the opposite conclusion. Can you explain this discrepancy? Try to answer this question before reading on, considering how LaPiere obtained support for his conclusions.

LaPiere and other early researchers employed a single instance of behavior (such as the yes or no responses to LaPiere's letter) as an indication of the relationship between attitudes and behavior. In contrast, more recent studies have measured a variety of behaviors relevant to attitudes. The results of these studies have been quite different.

For example, in one study, researchers measured people's attitudes toward environmental issues such as pollution control and conservation, and then observed subjects' behaviors over the next two months. Fourteen environmentally relevant behaviors were recorded, including recycling paper, picking up litter, and circulating petitions pertaining to clean environment issues. Considered individually, any one of these behaviors showed only a relatively small or moderate correlation with the subjects' environmental attitudes, but when these actions were treated collectively, attitudes and behaviors were strongly correlated (Weigel & Newman, 1976). A clear implication of this finding is that in order to make an accurate judgment about someone's attitude toward a particular object, issue, or situation, we should observe as many attitude-reflective behaviors as possible.

As we suspected from the start, studies using multiple behavior indices have suggested that attitudes are strong predictors of behavior. As the earlier example of attitudes toward cheating illustrated, however, our attitudes do not always predict our behaviors. What determines how influential our attitudes will be?

Social Expectations and Behavior

One important variable is the degree to which other social factors influence our behavior. As long as other influences are minimized, our attitudes are likely to guide our behaviors. An influence that is particularly likely to mask the predictive relationship between attitudes and behavior is social expectation. For example, a teenager who has a negative attitude toward drinking alcoholic beverages will usually say no when offered a drink. What if he attends a party at the college he plans to attend in the fall, however, and several college students encourage him to join the party and drink up? In this situation, the need to conform to social expectations is particularly strong, and he may well have a beer, despite his attitude toward alcohol consumption.

Another way that social expectations may influence our behavior is by our tendency to adopt, as self-characteristic, stereotypes about groups to which we belong. Could the stereotypes that black students perform more poorly on standardized academic tests or that girls underperform boys in math skills actually contribute to poor individual performance? Claude Steele of Stanford University has demonstrated that subjects do conform to negative group stereotypes by demonstrating poorer performance even when those before subjects are matched for ability. In several of his experiments, black college students underperformed when compared to matched-ability white students on difficult verbal tests when racial intellectual stereotypes were made salient. This vulnerability of subjects to conform to negative stereotypes has been termed **stereotype threat** (Steele & Aronson, 1995; Steele, Spencer, & Aronson, 2002; Nussbaum & Steele, 2007). Steele and others have observed a similar pattern of underperformance on math exams when testing similar-ability male and female students (Carr & Steele, 2009; Steele, 2012). Stereotype threat has been observed to contribute to underperformance in math in girls as young as six years of age (Galdi, Cadinu, & Tomasetto 2014). Stereotype threat appears to emerge before children are even aware of a math-gender stereotype.

Stereotype Threat The tendency to conform to negative stereotypes

Cognitive Dissonance Theory The theory that people experience psychological discomfort or dissonance whenever cognitions and behaviors are in conflict

Attitude Specificity

Another variable that influences how closely our behaviors reflect our attitude is the relevance of an attitude to the behavior being considered. People may be less inclined to behave consistently with broad attitudes. For example, you may know people who say they support equality of the sexes but refuse to share equally in household chores. In contrast, when there is a close association between an expressed attitude and a particular situation, the picture is often quite different. For instance, our attitudes about the relative skills of several friends who play tennis is probably a good predictor of whom we would ask to team with us in a doubles tournament.

Does Our Behavior Affect Our Attitudes?

We have seen that our attitudes are often consistent with our behavior, but could this relationship exist because our attitudes are affected by our behavior? Social psychologists have suggested that our behavior may shape our attitudes (Tesser, 1990). For instance, many a college student has looked with amusement or perhaps mild disdain upon young executives who dress up in their natty business suits and tuck a *Wall Street Journal* under their arms as they commute to impressive high-rise office buildings. These attitudes often change quickly, however, after the students graduate and join the ranks of the employed.

17.3d Changing Attitudes

We have just seen that experiences such as taking a job can produce a change in attitude, but how and why does this attitude change take place? Part of the answer lies in our need for consistency. Just as we attempt to fit new acquaintances into preexisting person schemas in order to minimize the differences between the familiar and the unfamiliar, we also are most secure when our attitudes are consistent both with other attitudes we hold and with our behavior. This is the basic idea behind *cognitive dissonance theory*, which sees attitude change as an attempt to maintain cognitive consistency.

Cognitive Dissonance Theory

Cognitive dissonance theory is concerned with the ways in which beliefs and attitudes are consistent or inconsistent with one another (Festinger, 1957). The cognitive dissonance model, however, focuses more closely on the internal psychological comfort or discomfort of the individual. According to this theory, a person experiences a state of discomfort, or *dissonance*, whenever two related cognitions (thoughts or perceptions) are in conflict. For example, imagine that you have always considered yourself a supporter of

BVT Lab

Visit www.BVTLab.com to explore the student resources available for this chapter.

a woman's right to choose abortion, but you find yourself protesting when you discover a close friend is considering an abortion. There is a discrepancy between what you believe and the way you perceive yourself acting, and if you become aware of it (it is quite possible that you will not), you will experience cognitive dissonance.

Like hunger, dissonance is an unpleasant state that motivates its own reduction. However, while hunger requires a person to interact with the environment to achieve its reduction, merely realigning the key cognitive elements to restore a state of consonance, or psychological comfort, may reduce dissonance. Thus, you may reduce your dissonance over the abortion issue by changing your attitude to oppose abortion, so that it will be consistent with your behavior. You might also restore consonance by philosophically aligning yourself with the notion that if you believe in something, you should support it with your actions even at the risk of personal hardship.

The cognitive dissonance theory has been supported by numerous studies. An example is a study of Princeton University men who had all indicated that they were opposed to banning alcohol from campus (Croyle & Cooper, 1983). These subjects were all asked to write a letter that forcefully argued *in favor of* banning alcohol from campus. Half of these writers were reminded that their participation in this effort was purely voluntary; the other half was authoritatively ordered to register their arguments. At a later point, after the letter-writing process was completed, the researchers again assessed the subjects' attitudes toward the proposed ban.

Based on cognitive dissonance theory, would you predict that subjects in either of these groups demonstrated noteworthy changes in their attitudes toward banning alcohol on campus? Only one group or both? Why? Think about these questions and make your predictions before reading on.

As predicted by the cognitive dissonance theory, writing a letter in favor of a policy they opposed created cognitive dissonance in the Princeton subjects, most of whom reduced this dissonance by changing their attitudes. This shift in attitudes was more pronounced for those subjects who saw their participation as voluntary in nature. Apparently, if we act contrary to our prevailing attitudes, and if we cannot attribute our actions to coercion, we are more likely to see the rationale for what we are doing and to come to believe in it.

This phenomenon is believed to have accounted, at least in part, for the success of certain brainwashing tactics on some American prisoners during the Iraq conflict. The captors begin by persuading prisoners to make some minor statement, such as, "America is certainly not perfect." Next, prisoners might be asked to write down some flaws in the U.S. system of government. Eventually, they might be encouraged to develop a speech denouncing America. The inducement to take these actions is typically something quite minor, such as a few extra privileges or more food. In the end, the prisoner's awareness that his actions were not induced by coercion and that others were aware of his unpatriotic statements might actually cause him to change his attitude toward his homeland to be consistent with his behavior, thus reducing dissonance.

Students may also experience cognitive dissonance after cheating on an exam or assignment. The attitude that cheating is wrong is inconsistent with their action of cheating. Typically, students resolve this dissonance by claiming that "cheating is OK because others do it" or because "the professor's exams are unfair anyway"—both are changes in attitude about cheating.

Persuasion

Cognitive dissonance theory helps explain why we change our attitudes. It does not explain how a speaker can persuade members of an audience to change their attitudes, or why a talk with someone we respect can be enough to convert us to supporters of a particular cause. We'll look at several characteristics of effective persuasion: the credibility, the power, and the attractiveness of the persuader.

If a close friend you respect and trust becomes involved in a fringe religious movement and tries to persuade you to join, you are more likely to reevaluate your attitude toward such movements than if you did not like the person who approached you. Research demonstrates that the source or origin of a persuasive communication is a very important determinant of whether or not we change our attitude. The probability that persuasion will succeed is highest when the source of persuasion is seen as possessing the qualities of credibility, power, and attractiveness.

A communicator with the quality of *credibility* is more likely to succeed in changing our attitude. Two important elements of credibility are perceived expertise and trustworthiness. Our perception of expertise involves our assessment of the communicator's knowledge about a topic and of his or her experience, education, and competence to speak authoritatively about it. For instance, when you watch the Super Bowl on television, you are less likely to dispute the views of a commentator who was once a football pro than those of your roommate, who has no athletic experience.

Another factor that influences how persuasive a communicator will be is *power*. Attitude change is particularly likely to occur when the communicator has the power to administer reinforcers or punishers to the subject. It is not surprising, therefore, that children often express attitudes similar to those of their parents, and that low-level management people may mirror the attitudes of higher-level executives.

A third strong influence on a communicator's effectiveness is *attractiveness*. A physically attractive communicator is often more effective than one whose appearance is either average or unattractive. Attractiveness is influenced not only by physical looks but also by likability, pleasantness, and perceived similarity to the audience. A communicator who does not have these qualities is usually less effective in changing people's attitudes than one who does.

17.4 **Prejudice**

Consider the following conversation overheard recently by the authors. The speakers are a third-year medical student and a college psychology professor.

> STUDENT: Homosexuals may not be the only people who get AIDS, but they are certainly the major reason why all of us now have to live in fear of this disease.
>
> PROFESSOR: The vast majority of AIDS cases in Central Africa have occurred among heterosexuals.
>
> STUDENT: Well, if that is true, then it probably just indicates that the Africans will not tolerate promiscuous relationships among homosexuals like what occurs in places like New York and San Francisco.

Prejudice Negative, unjustifiable, and inflexible attitude toward a group and its members

Stereotypes Preconceived and oversimplified beliefs and expectations about the traits of members of a particular group that do not account for individual differences

Discrimination In social psychology, the behavioral consequence of prejudice in which one group is treated differently from another group

Ingroup In social psychology, the group in which people include themselves when they divide the world into "us" and "them"

Ingroup Bias Tendency to see one's own group in a favorable light

Outgroup The "them" group when individuals divide the world into "us" and "them"

PROFESSOR: Many epidemiologists are now predicting that in a few years America will be just like Central Africa, with the majority of AIDS cases reported among heterosexuals.

STUDENT: Well, if this occurs it will be further evidence of what is already clearly obvious, homosexuals are so indiscriminate and promiscuous in their sexual practices that they don't care who they put at risk.

The medical student's point of view is an excellent example of **prejudice**—a negative, unjustifiable, and inflexible attitude toward a group and its members that is based on erroneous information. This definition contains three important elements. First, prejudice is usually characterized by very negative or hostile feelings toward all members of a group, often a minority, without any attention to individual differences among members of that group. Second, prejudice is based on inaccurate or incomplete information. For instance, the medical student in our example assumed incorrectly that AIDS is a disease of homosexuals and that heterosexuals who get AIDS are victims of the promiscuity of homosexual people. Finally, prejudice demonstrates great resistance to change even in the face of compelling contradictory evidence. The medical student was not about to revise his opinion that AIDS is inextricably linked to homosexuality, despite contradictory evidence.

Prejudice is built on **stereotypes**, preconceived and oversimplified beliefs and expectations about the traits of members of a particular group that do not account for individual differences. These stereotyped beliefs, coupled with hostile feelings, often predispose people to act in an abusive and discriminatory fashion toward members of a disliked or hated minority. The widespread incidence of **discrimination** (the behavioral consequence of prejudice in which victims of prejudice are treated differently from other people) throughout the world reveals what a profoundly adverse impact prejudice has on human society. In most every daily newspaper and every evening on the news there are reports of violence between groups fueled by prejudice. The conflicts between Protestants and Catholics in Ireland, between the Arabs and the Jews in the Middle East, and the tension between blacks and whites in South Africa are just a few.

To believe that Mexicans are lazy, that young blacks are gang members, that men are insensitive to women, that overweight people lack self-control, or that homosexuals are deviant is to stereotype all members of a group. To devalue or feel contempt for Mexicans, blacks, women, overweight people, or homosexuals is to be prejudiced. To avoid hiring, associating with, renting to, or acknowledging the contributions of such people is to discriminate. How can prejudice be explained? We turn next to that question.

17.4a Outgroups, Ingroups, and the Causes of Prejudice

Central to any explanation of prejudice is our inclination to define ourselves, at least partly, according to the particular group to which we belong. We all tend to categorize ourselves according to race, age, education, economic level, and so forth—a process that inevitably leads us to categorize people who do not share the same characteristics as "different." The result is that we divide our world into two groups: them and us. The very process of being in the **ingroup** category tends to create an **ingroup bias** (a tendency to see one's own group in a favorable light), while at the same time inducing a negative attitude or prejudice against the **outgroup**.

A number of studies have demonstrated that ingroup bias and prejudice toward the outgroup often occur when experimental subjects are separated into we / they groups based on trivial factors that bear no relationship to real-life social categories. By perceiving their ingroup as superior to an outgroup, people seem to be attempting to enhance their self-esteem. We all may remember the demonstration conducted with third-grade school children who were separated by their teacher into "privileged" (blue eyes) and "impoverished" (brown eyes) groups. The blue-eyed group members quickly developed strong prejudices against the outgroup members who only moments before were friends and peers.

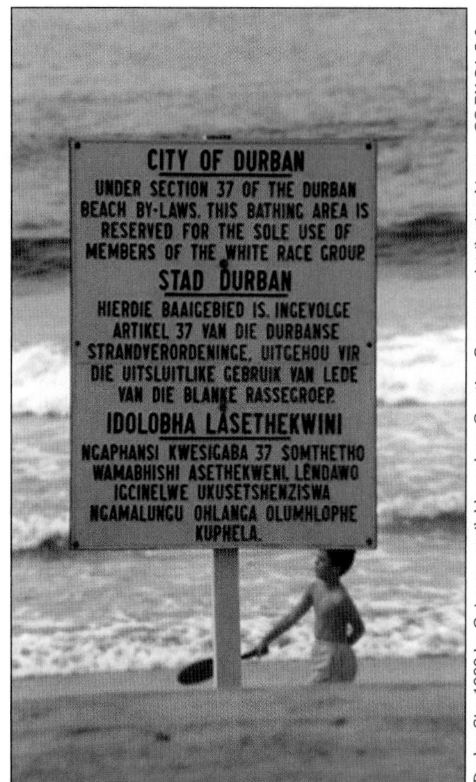

We all tend to categorize ourselves according to race, age, education, and economic level.

Competition Between Groups

If we already tend to view the world in terms of them and us, the addition of another ingredient—competition for jobs, power, or other limited resources—adds to the likelihood that hostility and prejudice will develop. In such circumstances, the more dominant group may exploit and discriminate against a less powerful group. This tendency was demonstrated during the development of the United States, when competition for land between European settlers and Native Americans led to prejudice, mistreatment, and extreme acts of discrimination against the minority Native Americans. Today in the United States, competition for jobs contributes to prejudice between whites and Hispanics, Native Americans and German immigrants, Chinese people and whites, Cuban immigrants and white Floridians, and whites and blacks. These tensions tend to increase during poor economic times and lessen as the economy improves.

Frustration, Scapegoating, and Prejudice

Just as competition can lead to hostility and prejudice under certain conditions, so can frustration. People who are frustrated by their lack of accomplishments or by adverse living conditions often vent their frustration on scapegoats who they perceive as being less powerful than themselves, such as members of a minority group. An example of how frustration may be tied to prejudice is provided by data relating economic conditions in the South from 1882 to 1930 to violence of white people toward black people. Research has shown whenever the price of cotton decreased during this period, the lynching of black people by white people increased (Hovland & Sears, 1940).

Can you think about cases of prejudice that may be attributed to frustration or scapegoating that are more current? Perhaps recent racial tension in the United States is a result of economic frustration.

17.5 Implicit Attitudes

In the last few pages we have seen that our attitudes can influence our behaviors, that our behaviors may result in attitude change, especially when they are dissonant, and a number of social phenomena such as compliance and persuasion can change our attitudes and our behaviors. So far, however, we have been assuming that our attitudes are

Implicit Attitude Unconscious attitude that may be socially undesirable and may influence one's behavior without one's knowledge

Implicit Association Test (IAT) Test that attempts to measure the strength of a person's implicit attitudes

explicit and that we are aware of the attitudes we have. However, are all of your attitudes explicit and available to your conscious awareness? Can some attitudes, because they may be socially undesirable, be influencing your behavior without you knowing? If you are asked to describe your attitudes to others, are you being accurate in your descriptions? Consider how one might respond to questions concerning their attitude about a university's affirmative action policy for admissions. Do you think that everyone would respond honestly and accurately to this question? Might, instead an answer depend on who's asking? Psychologists have long been concerned about the validity of subjects' verbal (and written) responses, especially on topics where subjects may be inclined to respond with socially desirable answers, not necessarily their own. Because of these problems, psychologists have devised research methods to assess people's **implicit attitudes** indirectly (Greenwald, McGhee, & Schwartz, 1998; Fazio & Olson, 2003; Kihlstrom, 2004).

17.5a The Implicit Association Test

The **implicit association test** (IAT) attempts to measure the strength of associations between groups of people; specific individuals, policies, and even products we might purchase; and the concepts of "good" and "bad." The stronger the association between images of the concept or group and negative or positive terms, the stronger one's implicit attitude toward the group or policy. During an IAT, to assess a subject's implicit attitude toward a religious group, for example, subjects would begin by assigning religious icons to appropriate religious groups. Next, the subject would assign a list of terms—such as horrible, friendly, awful, happy—as either "good" or "bad." Finally, religious icons and terms would appear and subjects assign them as "good" or "bad." The icons from a specific religious group (e.g., Judaism) might appear with terms assigned to "good," while terms associated with "bad" are paired with other religions. Subjects use a computer

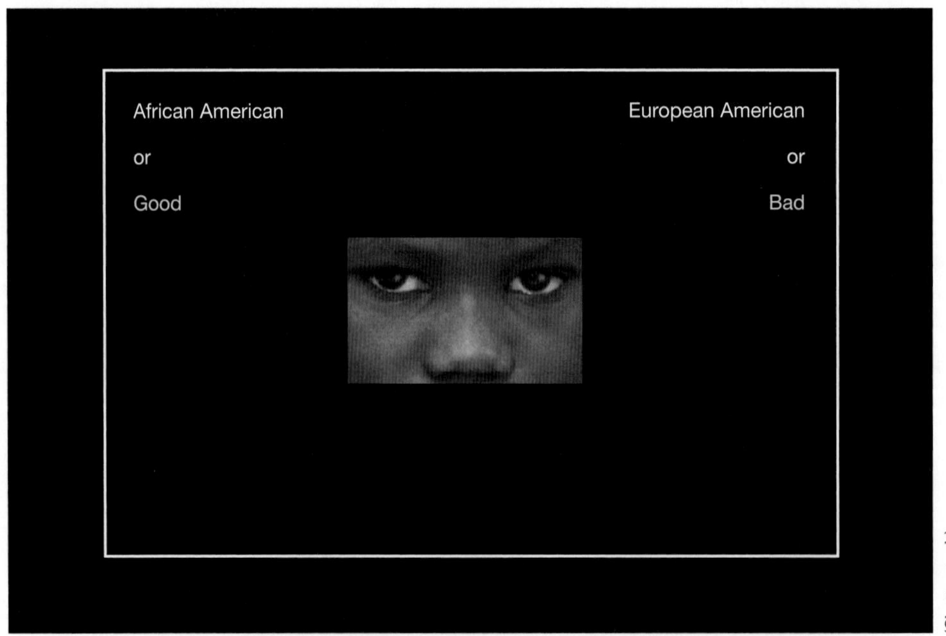

(Shutterstock)

The Implicit Association Test (IAT) records reaction time as subjects assign images and words to "good" or "bad" categories. In this illustration, a researcher is interested in measuring implicit attitudes toward racial groups.

keyboard to assign icons and terms into "good" and "bad" groups. The IAT measures a subject's reaction times to make these group assignments.

Research has revealed some interesting relationships between implicit and explicit attitudes on a range of issues. As you might expect, when the topic is quite sensitive, either personally or socially, explicit and implicit attitudes do not always agree. Disagreement between implicit and explicit attitudes also appears when attitudes are particularly strong. In these cases it appears that behavior is best predicted by implicit, not explicit attitudes (Mingzheng, 2005). Whether or not the IAT is an appropriate measure of our attitudes and whether implicit attitudes are any better predictors of our behaviors remain questions for future research. We next explore how our behaviors can be influenced by social contexts. Students can participate in IAT research by logging into the Harvard website.

Social Influence Efforts by others to alter our feelings, beliefs, and behavior

Conformity Tendency to change or modify behaviors so that they are consistent with those of other people

Informational Social Influence One basis of conformity in which we accept a group's beliefs or behaviors as providing accurate information about reality

Normative Social Influence Social influence in which we conform not because of an actual change in our beliefs, but because we think we will benefit in some way (such as gaining approval)

17.6 Social Influences on Behavior

We have seen how the people around us may change our feelings about certain people, groups, ideas, or situations. However, **social influence**—the efforts by others to alter our feelings, beliefs, and behavior—extends beyond merely changing how we feel about something. In this section we examine conformity, compliance, and obedience—all of which are forms of social influence that affect our behavior.

17.6a Conformity

Conformity refers to a tendency to change or modify our own behaviors so that they are consistent with those of other people. Often these shifts in opinion or actions are accompanied, at least to some degree, by a perceived social pressure to conform.

Our outward conformity to group standards may or may not mean that we have accepted the group's position. Morton Deutsch and Harold Gerard (1955) suggest that we should make a distinction between **informational social influence**, in which we accept a group's beliefs or behaviors as providing accurate information about reality, and **normative social influence**, in which we conform not because of an actual change in our beliefs but because we think that we will benefit in some way, such as gaining approval or avoiding rejection. It is helpful to keep in mind this distinction between informational and normative social influence as we explore what we have learned about conformity.

One of the first investigations of social influence explored how norms develop in small groups (Sherif, 1937). During an initial session, each subject was seated alone in a dark room and asked to stare at a tiny pinpoint of light about 15 feet away. The subject was then asked to estimate how far the light moved from its original position. (Actually, the light was stationary, but it appeared to move due to a perceptual illusion.) There was considerable variation in these initial estimates. During a second session, two other participants joined the subject; all three repeated the procedure of the first session, voicing their estimates in the presence of each other. This procedure was repeated in two more group sessions. Figure 17-3 shows what happened in the second, third, and fourth sessions. As you can see, the estimates of the three participants progressively converged, until by the fourth session they were essentially identical.

In the study just discussed, do you think that the subjects' final estimates reflected a genuine belief that theirs was the correct estimate (informational social influence), or do you think they felt pressured to conform even though they privately disagreed with the consensus group estimate (normative social influence)? How would you find out which

Figure 17-3 Results of Muzafer Sherif's (1937) Conformity Study Judging the Movement of a Light

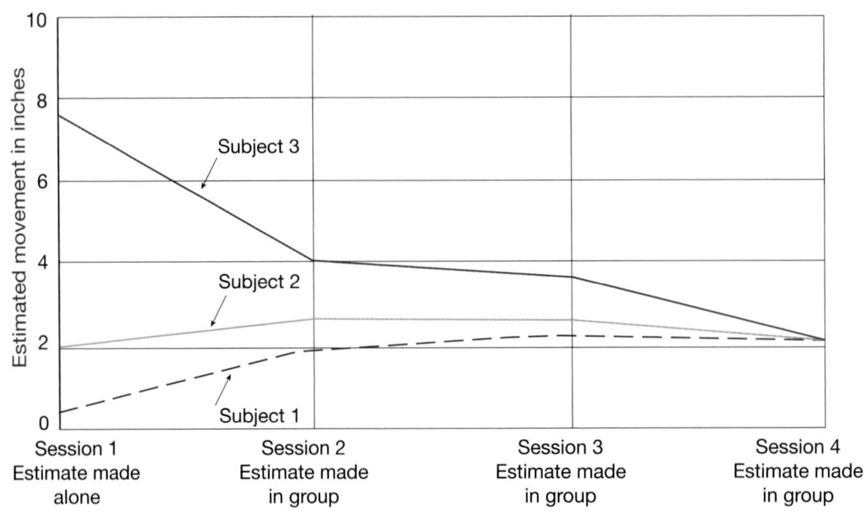

form of social influence was operative in this case? Give these questions some thought before reading on.

The researchers provided an answer to the question by conducting additional solo sessions after the group norms had been established. In these sessions, subjects' solo estimates continued to reflect the group norm rather than corresponding to their initial estimates in the first individual sessions. The fact that subjects continued to express group estimates clearly demonstrates that they were responding to informational and not normative social influence.

In the study we have been discussing, subjects were faced with an ambiguous situation in which it was difficult to distinguish between reality and imagination. In such a circumstance, it is understandable that they relied on others as sources of information. What about situations, however, in which people clearly know what is correct but still experience pressure to conform to group norms that deviate from the truth? For instance, what if you were asked which of the three comparison lines in Figure 17-4 was equal to the standard one—and although you knew that the answer was B, everyone else answered C? This was the experimental design used by Solomon Asch (1955) in a classic experiment.

The Asch Experiments

In Asch's experiment, seven men sat around a table and were asked to make a series of eighteen line-comparison judgments such as the one just described. Six of the men were confederates of the experimenter; the remaining subject was unaware that he was being set up. None of the eighteen tasks were ambiguous; the correct answer was always readily apparent. The experimental design called for each group member to provide his response in turn as Asch solicited answers sequentially from each man, moving from his left to right around the table. The naive subject was always located so that he was the sixth of the seven subjects to make his judgment. In the first two trials, all seven chose the correct line. In twelve of the remaining sixteen trials, however, the confederates unanimously chose the wrong comparison line.

Figure 17-4 Line Comparison Task from Solomon Asch's Experiment

Which comparison line(s) is (are) equal to the standard line?

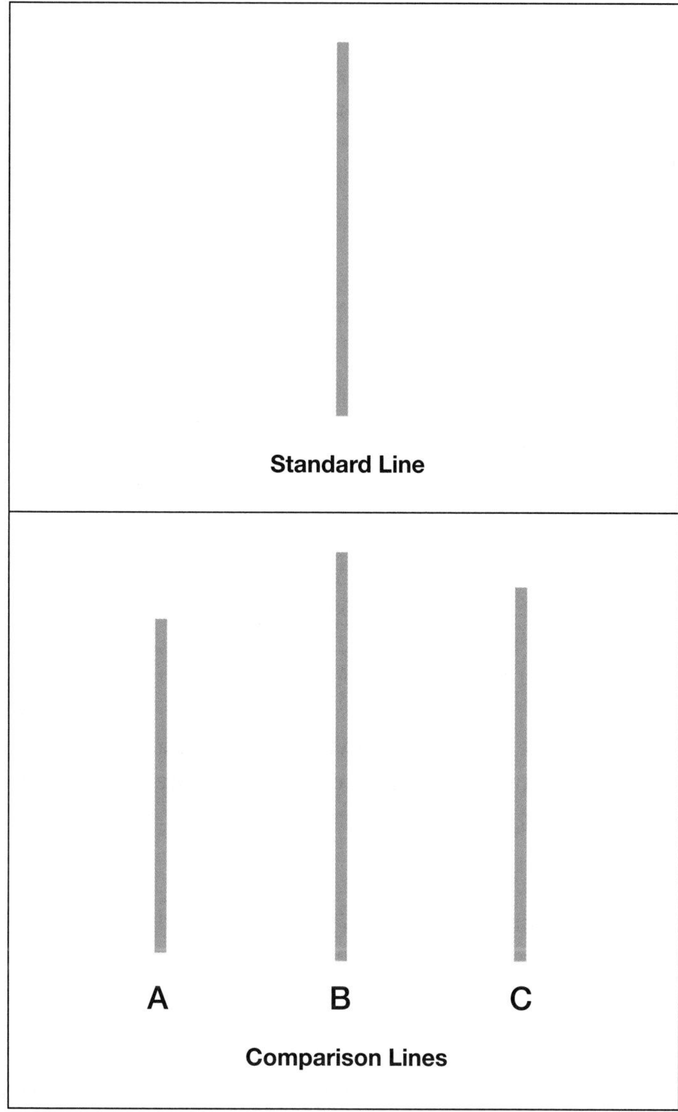

Source: Adapted from "Asch's Line-Comparison Talk" from article "Opinions and Social Pressure" from *Scientific American,* November 1955, p. 32, by Solomon Asch.

How did the subjects respond? Many showed signs of strain, leaning forward, straining, double-checking, and glancing around at the other group members. Nevertheless, about one in every three subjects adjusted his responses to match the incorrect judgments of the confederates in half or more of the twelve conformity trials. Only 25 percent of the subjects completely resisted group pressure by making the correct response on all twelve trials.

Since the correct answers were so obvious, Asch's experiment seems to clearly illustrate normative social influence. Just to make sure, Asch interviewed the subjects after the experiment was completed. He found that in some cases the answers had been the result of normative social influence; these subjects had gone along with the group consensus against their better judgment because they did not want to appear different from the others. However, some of the conforming subjects stated that they had thought that the majority opinion was probably correct and that their own perceptions were inaccurate. If this explanation is taken at face value, we must conclude that informational social influence occurs even in unambiguous situations where conformity goes clearly contrary to reality. (Of course, it is also possible that subjects who claimed they thought the majority was right might only have been attempting to justify their submission to the influence of the group.)

When Are We Most Likely to Conform?

In the years since Asch's study, numerous additional experiments have studied conformity. In general, this research has found that our tendency to conform will be increased in situations in which some conditions are met. We list these conditions briefly as a conclusion to our discussion of conformity.

1. Unanimity of the majority group: We are much more likely to conform if the majority group is unanimous; even one dissenter greatly reduces our inclination to conform. Asch found that if one dissident agreed with the subject, the subject was almost 18 percent less likely to conform.

2. Perception that the majority of group members are acting independently: If we perceive that the other members of a group are acting independently of one another, we are more likely to conform than if we sense some collusion among them.

3. Majority group size: The size of the group makes a difference. If there are at least three or four other people in the group, we are more likely to conform. Further increases in the group size generally do not increase the likelihood of conformity, and may even decrease it.

4. Familiarity with the attitude object: If we have no preconceived notions about the attitude object, we are more likely to act in a conforming manner than if this is not the case.

5. Low self-esteem: People whose sense of personal self-worth is low or who are especially concerned about social relationships are more likely to conform than people with higher self-esteem or less regard for social relationships.

6. Perceptions about other group members: We are more likely to conform if we consider the other group members to be of higher status than ourselves, or if we have high regard for the other group members. We are also more likely to conform if we perceive other group members as having power over us (in the sense of being able to administer reinforcers or punishers), or if we know that other group members will be able to observe our actions.

17.6b Compliance

Although both conformity and compliance involve yielding to some pressure exerted by others, **compliance** involves an element of coercion as well, in that it takes place in situations where we alter our behavior in response to direct requests from others. Compliance is a very common form of social influence. We all experience a barrage of requests daily—ranging from friends, lovers, or family members asking us to change certain aspects of our behavior to requests by politicians for votes. Social psychologists have noted a number of techniques or forms of pressure that people use to increase the likelihood of compliance with their requests. Two of these methods are the **foot-in-the-door technique** and the **door-in-the-face technique**.

Compliance Form of social influence in which people alter their behavior in response to direct requests from others; usually involves a degree of coercion

Foot-in-the-Door Technique Technique for encouraging compliance in which a person is first asked to agree to a relatively minor request that serves as a setup for a more major request

Door-in-the-Face Technique Method for encouraging compliance in which an unreasonable request is followed by a more minor, reasonable request that is the requester's goal in the first place

Obedience Social influence in which we alter our behavior in response to commands or orders from people perceived as having power or authority

Foot-in-the-Door Technique

Researchers have demonstrated that sometimes the best road to compliance is to begin by getting a person to agree to a relatively minor or trivial request that serves as a setup for a second, more major request (which is the actual goal). This so-called foot-in-the-door technique is widely used by salespeople who attempt to produce a favorable attitude toward their product. For example, if a car salesperson can get you to comply with an initial request to "come into the office, and we will run some numbers," you are more likely to develop the attitude that "I need that car." It has been suggested that the success of the foot-in-the-door technique is related to the fact that when people comply with a request, they begin to perceive themselves as "the kind of person who does this sort of thing" and thus are inclined to make even greater commitments to a particular line of requests in order to be consistent with their perceived self-image.

Door-in-the-Face Technique

Suppose you are moving to another apartment and you want your husky neighbor to help you move your piano. Anticipating a likely negative response to your request, you first ask if he would mind spending the afternoon helping you move all your stuff. As expected, he begs off, claiming a heavy study load. Next, you ask if he would have just a few minutes to help with the piano. How can he say "no" to such a reasonable request after he has already "slammed the door in your face" in response to the larger request? While some people might say no to both requests, research demonstrates that we are often more inclined to comply with a moderate request if we have already refused a larger one than if the smaller request is presented alone.

17.6c Obedience

All of us succumb routinely to social influence by conforming to behavioral standards established by others or by complying with the requests of associates. Less commonly, social influence takes the form of **obedience**, in which we alter our behavior in response to commands or orders from people we may perceive as having power or authority.

Milgram's Experiments on Obedience to Authority

The most dramatic study of obedience was conducted by social psychologist Stanley Milgram (1963). As you may recall from Chapter 2, Milgram sought to determine if subjects would inflict considerable pain on others merely because an authority figure instructed them to do so. His all-male subjects thought they were participating in a study of the effects of punishment on learning. They were told to use an intercom system to present problems to another person (a total stranger who was actually an accomplice of the experimenter) who was strapped in a chair in another room, and to administer a shock each time the "learner" gave the wrong answer to a problem. Labeled switches on the "shock apparatus" ranged from a low of 15 volts to a high of 450 volts; subjects were instructed to increase the voltage with each successive error the learner made.

According to design, the learner made many errors. The result was a progressive escalation of shock intensity that posed a serious dilemma for the subjects, virtually all of whom exhibited high levels of stress and discomfort as they administered the shocks. Should they continue subjecting the learner to pain, or should they refuse to go on? Whenever they hesitated or protested, the experimenter pressured them to continue, using such commands as, "It is absolutely essential that you continue" or "You have no other choice; you must go on."

Despite the fact that all subjects were volunteers, paid in advance, and obviously distressed, only a minority failed to exhibit total obedience. In fact, fully 65 percent proceeded to the final 450-volt level!

Why do people succumb to such destructive instances of obedience? This question has been explored and debated by both social scientists and laypersons. First, many people seem to believe that their personal accountability for their actions is somehow diminished or relieved by those authority figures who issue the commands. In Milgram's research, subjects were told at the outset that the experimenter, rather than the participants, was responsible for the learner's well-being. Thus, we can see how they may have felt less responsible for their own actions. It is disheartening, however, that this same logic has been employed by such people as Nazi war criminal Adolf Eichmann, who committed unimaginable atrocities against the Jewish people during Hitler's reign of terror, and more recently, U.S. military guards who tortured prisoners at the Abu Ghraib prison in Iraq, justifying their acts by claiming, "I was only following orders."

(AP Wide World Photo)

Nazi war criminal Adolf Eichmann used the logic that he was only obeying Hitler's orders when he committed unimaginable atrocities against the Jewish people during World War II.

A second factor contributing to obedience is that authority figures often possess highly visible symbols of their power or status that make it difficult to resist their dictates (symbols such as the white coat and title of a researcher, or the uniform and rank of a military officer). The impact of these external trappings of power was demonstrated in one experiment in which people were randomly stopped on the street and ordered to give a dime to a person in need of parking meter change. Subjects were decidedly more inclined to obey this order if it was issued by someone wearing a firefighter's uniform than if the source of the command was dressed in a business suit or laborer's clothes.

Finally, people often comply with orders, even orders that are potentially destructive in nature, because they are sucked in by a series of graduated demands that begin with seemingly innocuous or harmless orders and gradually escalate to orders of a more serious or potentially destructive nature. For example, a corporate executive might request that a supposedly loyal employee, who has a friend who works at a competitor company, ask the friend if his or her employer plans to introduce a new product line. Later, such requests might escalate to orders to ask specific questions about the nature of the products on the drawing board, followed by commands to conduct outright industrial espionage. In a sense, this escalation is what occurred with Milgram's subjects, who were first required to deliver only mild shocks followed by progressively more intense punishment. The problem with such a gradual escalation of demand intensity is that a person is often unable to distinguish a definite point at which disobedience is clearly a more appropriate course of action than obedience.

Groupthink A psychological drive for consensus at any cost that suppresses dissent and consideration of alternatives in group decision making

17.6d Groupthink

The term **groupthink** was proposed in 1972 by Irving Janis to explain how well intended groups can make poor, and often disastrous, decisions. He defined groupthink as "a psychological drive for consensus at any cost that suppresses dissent and consideration of alternatives in group decision making" (Janis, 1972, 2007). Anyone who has been involved in group decision making can attest to the pressures to conform when reaching a decision. We have also seen the hostile suppression of alternatives as a decision was being reached. Groupthink, therefore, involves the previously described social influence, conformity.

A number of recent political fiascoes have been attributed to groupthink, including the failure to anticipate the Japanese attacks on Pearl Harbor in 1941 and the invasion of Iraq based on the assumption they had developed weapons of mass destruction. Groupthink has also been used to account for the 1996 climbing tragedy that occurred on Mount Everest that resulted in eight deaths (Burnette, Pollack, & Forsyth, 2011). In all of these cases, knowledgeable and conscientious group members arrived at disastrous decisions even though they had the time and resources to explore alternatives.

According to Janis, not all groups are prone to groupthink, and there are ways to prevent it. Figure 17-5 summarizes Janis's recommendations. When these strategies are applied, group decisions can and often will be better than an individual decision.

Figure 17-5 Groupthink

Seven Strategies to Avoid Groupthink in Group Decision Making

1. Group leader should assign all members the role of critical evaluator.
2. Supervisors should avoid expressing opinions when assigning a group a task.
3. Several independent groups should work on the same problem if possible.
4. All effective alternatives should be examined.
5. Members should discuss the group's ideas outside the group.
6. The group should invite outside experts to share ideas.
7. At least one group member should be assigned the role of devil's advocate.

Source: Janis, 1972

17.7 Interpersonal Behavior: Attraction and Aggression

In this section we first analyze why we feel attracted to certain people as friends and lovers, and then we explore some of the causes of aggression.

17.7a Attraction

We have been exploring how we form perceptions of people, how we develop attitudes, and how other people influence our behavior. The most influential people in our adult lives are often the people to whom we are closest—our good friends and our partners in long-term, intimate relationships.

Factors that Contribute to Interpersonal Attraction

Have you ever had the experience of meeting a total stranger—at a party, on the first day of school, or in a bookstore—and feeling immediately that you liked one another? If so, you may have wondered what it was that made you feel close to the other person. This question has been the topic of research for over five decades, and the answers that social psychologists have found center on four primary variables: proximity, similarity, reciprocity, and physical attractiveness.

Proximity Although most people overlook **proximity**, or geographical nearness, in listing factors that attracted them to a particular person, it is one of the most important variables. We often develop close relationships with people whom we see frequently in our neighborhoods, in school, at work, or at church or synagogue.

Leon Festinger and his colleagues (1950), who evaluated friendship patterns among married Massachusetts Institute of Technology students living in a housing development consisting of seventeen two-story buildings with five apartments per floor, conducted the classic study of the effect of proximity on attraction. All of the residents were asked to name their three best friends among residents of the housing development. These friends almost invariably lived in the same building, with next-door neighbors being the most likely to be named as a friend and the next most likely living two doors away. When the friendship ratings of all participants were pooled, certain people emerged as being widely liked (that is, included in the lists of many of the residents). The people who were most often listed as friends lived in apartments close to heavily trafficked areas such as mailboxes, stairway entries, and exits. Not coincidentally, people with the fewest friends lived in more out-of-the-way apartments.

Proximity Perceptual grouping principle whereby, all else being equal, we tend to organize perceptions by grouping elements that are the nearest to each other (in social psychology, the geographical nearness of one person to another, which is an important factor in interpersonal attraction)

Mere Exposure Effect Phenomenon by which repeated exposure to novel stimuli tends to increase an individual's preference for such stimuli

The profound impact of proximity on interpersonal attraction has been confirmed by other research. Why is it such a powerful factor? Social psychologists have offered a number of plausible explanations. One is simply that familiarity breeds liking. Research has shown that when we are repeatedly exposed to novel stimuli—whether they are unfamiliar musical selections, nonsense syllables, works of art, or human faces—our liking for such stimuli increases (Burger, Soroka, Gonzago, Murphy, & Somervell, 2001; Brooks & Watkins, 1989). This phenomenon, called the **mere exposure effect**, explains in part why we are attracted to people in close proximity to us.

The mere exposure effect even seems to influence our view of ourselves. Many of us are seldom satisfied with photographs of ourselves; our faces do not look quite right. One possible reason may be that the face we see in the photo is not the one we see staring back at us in the mirror. Since left and right are reversed in mirror images, the face we see looking back at us is always slightly different from what others see. Thus, we prefer the mirror image of our faces, whereas others will prefer the natural version.

Another likely reason why proximity influences attraction is the fact that the more we see of others, the more familiar we become with their ways and thus the better able we are to predict their behavior. If you have a good idea of how someone is likely to behave in any given situation, you will probably be more comfortable with this person. It is also possible that when we know we will be seeing a lot of a person, we may be more motivated to see his or her good traits and to keep our interactions as positive as possible.

(Shutterstock)

Social psychologists have found that four factors contribute to interpersonal attraction: proximity, similarity, reciprocity, and physical attractiveness.

Similarity

A second factor attracting people to one another is **similarity**. Contrary to the old adage that opposites attract, people who are attracted to one another often share common beliefs, values, attitudes, interests, and intellectual ability. This tendency was demonstrated in one study in which thirteen men expressed their attitudes independently on forty-four separate issues prior to being housed together for ten days in the close quarters of a fallout shelter. At intervals of one, five, and nine days of confinement, each subject was asked to list the three men in the group he would like to remain and the three he would most like to see removed from the shelter. The results provided consistent and clear indications that the participants wanted to keep the men who were most like them (judged by the earlier attitude assessments) and to get rid of those who were least like them (Griffitt & Veitch, 1974). Those who have watched the television show *Survivor* have seen similar outcomes.

Why do we feel drawn to people who are like us? For one thing, people with similar attitudes and interests are often inclined to enjoy participating in the same kinds of leisure activities. Even more important, however, we are more likely to communicate well with people whose ideas and opinions are similar to ours, and communication is a very important aspect of enduring relationships. It is also reassuring to be with similar people, for they confirm our view of the world, validate our own experiences, and support our opinions and beliefs. Thus, the mutual reinforcement of behavior is important in maintaining close relations with others.

Reciprocity

No doubt all of us have had personal experience (on both the delivery and recipient ends) with the old adage, "Flattery will get you everywhere." People tend to react positively to flattery, compliments, and other expressions of liking and affection. In the study of interpersonal attraction, this concept is reflected in the principle of **reciprocity**, which holds that when we are the recipients of expressions of liking and loving, we tend to respond in kind, particularly if our own self-esteem is low. Furthermore, when we are provided with indications that someone likes us, we tend to have warm feelings about these people and to respond positively to them—a reaction that often influences them to like us even more.

The key words in these descriptions of reciprocity are *tend to.* We don't *always* like people who appear to like us. In some cases, some of us have experienced the

Similarity In perception, the principle that we tend to group elements that are similar to each other (In social psychology, similarity of beliefs, interests, and values is recognized as a factor attracting people to one another.)

Reciprocity The tendency to respond to others in a way similar to how they respond to or treat us

Physical Attractiveness
Physical features that persons of the opposite sex find appealing

often-unsettling realization that we are the love object of someone who engenders only mildly positive feelings in us. Furthermore, when people perceive that expressions of liking directed toward them are merely part of a phony ingratiation strategy rather than genuine reflections of affection, reciprocity of liking and affection is unlikely to occur. These exceptions notwithstanding, undisguised, genuine expressions of liking or loving often serve as important stimulants to interpersonal attraction.

Physical Attractiveness **Physical attractiveness** may profoundly influence our impressions of the people we meet. In general, research reveals that physically attractive people are more likely to be sought as friends, to impress potential employers favorably, to be treated better, and to be perceived as more likable, interesting, sensitive, poised, happy, sexy, competent, and socially skilled than people of average or unattractive appearance.

But what determines physical attractiveness? Do you think that both sexes are equally influenced by physical attractiveness in forming impressions of people they meet and in selecting a mate?

Cross-cultural research on sex differences in human mate preferences provide strong evidence that men worldwide place greater value than women on mates who are both young and physically attractive. In studies conducted by University of Michigan psychologist David Buss (1989; Buss et al., 1990), more than ten thousand subjects from thirty-seven samples drawn from thirty-three countries on six continents and five islands (African, Asian, European, North and South American, and Oceanic cultures) were asked to rate the importance of a wide range of personal attributes in potential mates. These personal characteristics included such qualities as dependable character, good looks, good financial prospects, intelligence, sociability, and chastity.

(Getty)

Evolution may have biased our perceptions of attractiveness toward mates with the best potential for successful reproduction.

In contrast to the apparent widespread male emphasis on youth and beauty, women in these cultures are more inclined to place greater value on potential mates who are somewhat older, have good financial prospects, and are dependable and industrious. This is not to say that physical attractiveness was unimportant in influencing mate selection among the women of these varied cultures. In fact, many of these women rated physical attractiveness as important, albeit less significant than earning potential.

What accounts for the apparent consistency across so many cultures in what males and females find attractive in a potential mate? Why do males rate physical attractiveness and youth as most important while females rate earning potential and dependability most important? According to Buss (1989; Buss et al., 1990; Buss & Shackelford, 2008) evolution has biased mate preferences in humans as it has other animals. Males are attracted to younger, physically attractive females because these characteristics are good predictors of reproductive value. That is, a younger female has more reproductive years remaining than an older female. Physical attractiveness is important because characteristics such as smooth unblemished skin, good muscle tone, lustrous hair, and full lips are strong cues to reproductive value. On the other hand, females tend to find older, established males more attractive because these characteristics are the best predictors of successful rearing of offspring. That is, females prefer a mate with wealth, a better territory, or a higher rank. Youth and physical attractiveness are less important to females because male fertility is less age-related than it is for females. Consider for a moment the marriages of celebrities you can remember. I would offer that there are far more older men married to young women than vice versa. While these observations don't necessarily support Buss's theory, they are certainly consistent with it.

Additional evidence that evolution may have biased our perceptions of attractiveness comes from studies of young infants. A fascinating study conducted by Judith Langlois and her colleagues (Langlois & Roggman, 1990; Langlois et al., 1987, 2000; Ramsey et al., 2004 at the University of Texas at Austin revealed that infants from two to eight months old demonstrated marked preferences for attractive faces. When they were shown pairs of color slides of the faces of adult women previously rated by other adults for attractiveness, the infants demonstrated a marked inclination to look longer at the most attractive face in the pair. These findings challenge the commonly held assumption that standards of attractiveness are learned through gradual exposure to the current cultural standard of beauty and are merely "in the eye of the beholder" (p. 363).

Research by Langlois and her associates (Ramsey, Langlois, Hoss, Rubenstein, & Griffin, 2004) provides additional evidence that infants prefer attractive faces. In one study, sixty twelve-month-old infants demonstrated positive emotional and play responses when interacting with an adult stranger who wore a professionally constructed, lifelike, and very attractive latex theater mask. In contrast, when the stranger wore a mask portraying an unattractive face, the infants demonstrated more negative emotions and less play involvement. In a second experiment, forty-three twelve-month-old infants played significantly longer with attractive dolls than with unattractive dolls. According to the researchers, these results extend and amplify earlier findings showing that young infants exhibit visual preferences for attractive over unattractive faces.

In a related study with college students, Langlois and colleagues (Ramsey et al., 2004) used computer-generated face composites that averaged the features of individual faces. In most cases, subjects rated the average composites more attractive than the individual faces. In addition, as the faces became more and more average, by adding additional composites, they were perceived as more attractive. That is, face composites that represent the average characteristics of a population are perceived as more attractive than

Figure 17-6 Most raters prefer the (a) the symmetrical version over (b) the nonsymmetrical version of the same face.

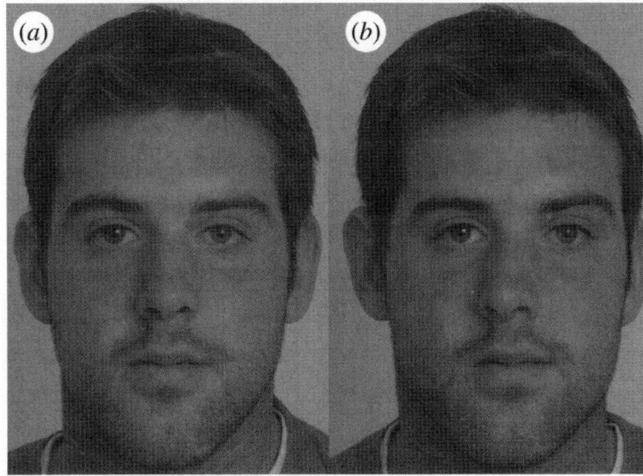

Source: Little, Jones, & DeBruine, 2011. Reprinted with permission.

Interpersonal Aggression Any physical or verbal behavior intended to hurt another person

Ethology The scientific study of the evolution of the behavior of animals, including humans

Sociobiology A specialization within biology that seeks to understand the biological factors that underlie social behaviors in all animal species, including humans

distinctive characteristics. Langlois interprets this as additional support for an evolutionary bias in what we perceive as attractive (Hoss & Langlois, 2003; Langlois et al., 2000; Rubenstein, Langlois, & Roggman, 2002).

Facial symmetry also contributes to our perception of attractiveness. Numerous experiments have shown that people across a wide range of cultures prefer symmetrical faces over nonsymmetrical ones. Again, this research suggests that we all tend to use the same features in what we find attractive (Little, Jones, & DeBruine, 2011). These attractiveness features do not appear to be learned or cultural, since young infants and several species of monkeys show similar preferences for symmetry and averageness.

17.7b Aggression

All of us have been victimized by the aggressive behavior of others, whether it is by someone who knowingly initiates a false rumor about us, a parent who strikes us in a fit of anger, or a teammate who ridicules our athletic ability. Sometime during our lives, more than a few of us may become victims of violent crimes such as rape, mugging, or assault—a grim prediction substantiated by evidence that roughly nineteen million Americans are victimized annually by violent crimes. Following nearly a decade of decreases in violent crime, crime rates began to increase in 2015 (Truman & Morgan, 2016). Whether this represents a change in trend will not be known for several years.

Criminal violence is an extreme form of **interpersonal aggression**—that is, any physical or verbal behavior intended to hurt another person. Many instances of interpersonal aggression may not qualify as criminal acts, but they can nevertheless be very hurtful. Why do people behave aggressively? Explanations have focused on both biological and psychological processes. We look briefly at the evidence for each.

Biological Bases of Aggression

The biological perspective has been approached by a number of researchers and theorists who seek to understand the biological factors that underlie social behaviors in all animal species, including humans. Many of these scientists believe that aggressive behavior, as well as other social behaviors, may be at least partly determined by biological mechanisms. The most intriguing biological approaches to social behavior are the fields of human **ethology** and **sociobiology**. While ethology is defined broadly as the study of the biology of behavior, sociobiology is considered the biology of social behavior. For instance, many ethologists and sociobiologists are interested in how certain behaviors enhanced survival and reproductive fitness of animals, including humans. These adaptive behaviors would then be more likely to be retained in the population through successive generations. Among the prominent spokespersons for this viewpoint are Harvard biologists Edward O. Wilson (1975, 1978), Nobel prizewinner Konrad Lorenz (1974), and the German ethologist Irenaus Eibl-Eibesfeldt (1989).

Lorenz's interpretation is particularly intriguing. He maintained that all animals, humans included, have an "aggressive instinct" directed toward their own kind. Lorenz believed that this aggressive inclination has great survival value and evolutionary significance for the species. For example, when the males of many species fight for mates, the strongest prevail, ensuring that the more fit will reproduce. An innate inhibition prevents most animals from killing members of their own species; however, Lorenz believed that humans never developed this inhibition, probably because with neither lethal claws nor sharp teeth, they were unlikely to inflict serious damage on one another. Today, however, our guns and bombs make us the most dangerous of all living creatures. Lorenz suggested that the situation is worsened by social norms that suppress our fighting instincts, thus causing our aggressive urges to build up to the point that they are sometimes released explosively in acts of extreme violence.

Fortunately for us, there is no evidence to support Lorenz's argument that aggressive urges build up within us until they reach this critical point. In addition, most contemporary psychologists are not very receptive to the idea that aggression is an instinct, but they do not reject the possibility that biology may contribute to aggression. In fact, there is considerable evidence that aggressive tendencies may be influenced by hormonal factors. One study demonstrated that boys and girls who were exposed to high levels of androgens before birth were found to be significantly more aggressive than their same-sexed siblings who had normal hormonal exposure (Reinisch, 1981).

Many studies have revealed strong correlations between testosterone levels and aggression in both animals and in humans (Birger et al., 2003; Hermans & Ramsey, 2008). Do higher testosterone levels lead to increases in aggression as this correlation implies? Does behaving aggressively increase testosterone? In an interesting twist on this relationship, researchers assigned male college students into one of two groups after collecting saliva for a testosterone assay. For fifteen minutes, one group of subjects played with a child's toy, while the other subjects handled a real gun. After providing saliva for the second test, the subjects were then offered water and a hot pepper sauce to mix with it until they found the concentration most preferred. Males who handled the gun had significantly elevated testosterone levels as well as hot pepper concentrations when compared to those subjects playing with a toy (Klinesmith, Kasser, & McAndrew, 2006). Clearly, the interaction between aggression and testosterone is more complex than assumed by previous research.

Other research has provided convincing evidence that aggressive behavior often results when certain regions within the limbic systems of the brains of humans and other animals are stimulated through implanted electrodes, lesions, or other abnormal physiological processes. For instance, electrical stimulation of certain regions within the hypothalamus and the amygdala can elicit aggressive behavior in animals, and surgical procedures to remove part of the amygdala in humans have been shown to greatly reduce aggressive behavior.

Research has also linked depressed serotonin activity to aggression in humans, including antisocial behavior, assault, arson, murder, and child molestation (Carlson, 2010; Wrase, Reimold, Puls, Kienast, & Heinz, 2006). In support of these observations, treatments with drugs that increase serotonin activity (SSRIs discussed in Chapter 16) seem to decrease aggressive tendencies in treated patients (Bond, 2005).

Can we conclude from this research that biological factors contribute to aggressive behavior in humans? The answer here is clearly yes. There is considerable evidence for biological dispositions to aggressive behavior in numerous animal species, including humans. However, aggressive behavior is also heavily influenced by environmental factors. We remind you of the problems addressed in Chapters 13 and 14 regarding parsing out hereditary and environmental influences on behavior. Behavior is the result of continuing interactions between the environment and genes, not additive contributions of each. In the next section, we look at some important psychological factors that contribute to aggressive behavior.

Psychological Bases of Aggression

Research on psychological contributions to aggression has focused on three major areas: the frustration-aggression hypothesis, social-learning theory, and the influence of media and film on violence.

Frustration-Aggression Hypothesis Theory that aggression is always a consequence of frustration and that frustration leads to aggression

The Frustration-Aggression Hypothesis More than seventy years ago, John Dollard and his colleagues (1939) proposed that there is a consistent link between frustration, the emotional state that results when something interferes with obtaining a goal, and aggression. In their widely influential **frustration-aggression hypothesis**, Dollard and his associates asserted that "Aggression is *always* a consequence of frustration" and that "Frustration *always* leads to aggression" (p. 1). According to this theory, we might expect that anytime we are thwarted in our efforts to finish a job, find the proper ingredients for a midnight sandwich, or win in a game of basketball, we become aggressive. This hypothesis does not mean that we always vent our frustration on the object of our frustration (such as our opponents on the basketball court). Rather, Dollard suggested that aggression may be delayed, disguised, or even displaced from its most obvious source to a more acceptable outlet. For instance, we may go home and yell at the dog after losing our basketball game. Despite these possible modifications in the mode of expression, the frustration-aggression hypothesis maintained that when we are frustrated, some kind of aggressive reaction is inevitable.

This theory is intuitively appealing, and certainly all of us have had the experience of lashing out against something or someone when we are frustrated. Does it seem reasonable to assume, however, that every time we are frustrated we respond with aggressive actions? A number of critics of the frustration-aggression hypothesis did not think so, and psychologist Neal Miller (1941) proposed a revision of the original hypothesis. Miller suggested that frustration could produce a number of possible responses, only one of which is aggression. Other responses to a frustrating situation may include withdrawal, apathy, hopelessness, and even increased efforts to achieve a goal. The response to a frustrating situation may be any behavior acquired through operant conditioning that eliminates or removes one from the aversive situation.

If aggression is only one of several responses to frustrating situations, then what circumstances will cause frustration to produce aggression? Social psychologist Leonard Berkowitz (1978) suggested that two conditions act together to instigate aggression. One is a *readiness* to act aggressively, which is often associated with the emotion of anger. That is, frustration may induce a readiness or inclination to act aggressively because sources of frustration are often aversive, arousing negative emotions such as anger (Berkowitz, 1986, 1989, 1993). Thus, any behavior that reduces the aversive emotion will be maintained by negative reinforcement, as described by the two-factor theory in Chapter 6.

The second factor influencing aggression is the presence of environmental cues, such as the presence of others who are perceived as accepting aggressive behavior, the availability of weapons, and the presence of an acceptable target for aggression. Thus, Berkowitz suggests that while we may respond to frustrating situations with anger, our anger is not likely to lead to aggressive behavior unless suitable environmental cues are present. A number of studies in which subjects experience frustration in either the presence or absence of suitable aggression cues has supported Berkowitz's prediction.

The frustration-aggression hypothesis, as first modified by Miller and later by Berkowitz, provides one important theoretical perspective on the psychological contributions to aggression. That is, aggressive behaviors are learned and maintained by their reinforcing consequences. However, frustration is not the only cause of aggression. What about the grade school student who hits the schoolyard weakling because he has seen another admired classmate do the same thing? What about the influence of violence in TV and in video games? Learning theory also helps to explain some other instances of aggressive behavior where frustration may not occur.

Social-Learning Perspectives on Aggression Social psychologists generally agree that human aggressive behavior is learned. We have discussed Albert Bandura's (1986) social-learning theory in several chapters, and this approach also helps us understand aggression. As you recall, Bandura emphasizes the processes of reinforcement and imitation of models. Anyone who has observed a child behaving aggressively to take a desired toy away from another has seen the power of reinforcement in shaping and maintaining aggression. If we learn that aggression will produce reinforcers, it is only natural that such behavior will become part of our repertoire. Even nontangible reinforcers, such as praise for "being tough" or "not taking guff from anybody," may increase the inclination to repeat such behaviors.

People may also learn to be aggressive by observing the behavior of others. A child who sees an adult or friend act aggressively may imitate this behavior. It is not only children who model aggressive behavior. Research has shown that adults are just as likely to model aggression as children (Mummendey, 1978).

There is now extensive evidence that children raised by parents who behave aggressively are strongly inclined to be aggressive themselves and that children who are victimized by physically abusive parents often tend to behave in the same fashion toward their own children. This evidence suggests that each generation learns to be violent by being a participant in a violent family (Kalmuss, 1984).

Parents and other significant role models can help to counteract the social roots of aggression by avoiding modeling aggressive actions, such as physically punishing or verbally abusing children or engaging in aggressive or violent encounters with other adults, including their spouses. From very early in life, children can be encouraged to develop socially positive traits such as nurturance, tenderness, sensitivity, cooperation, and empathy. Parents and other adult socializing agents can employ the power of positive reinforcement to strengthen such prosocial qualities in children, while at the same time discouraging inappropriate aggression and punishing aggressive behavior consistently but nonphysically.

The Effects of Violence in the Media and on Film Perhaps one of the most controversial subjects in psychology regards the effects of exposure to violence in media on children and young adults. If children learn to behave aggressively by observing their parents, other adults, and their peers, what effect does viewing violence on film have on their behavior? Most children in our society observe thousands upon thousands of murders and other acts of violence on television, and they actively participate in simulations of violence in sophisticated video games. The question of whether viewing violence actually increases a person's inclination to act aggressively has been the center of a long and lively debate. On one side of the issue, some psychologists (particularly psychodynamic psychologists) have argued that observing violence may be cathartic; for when we watch other people behaving violently, we vent some of our own frustration and anger vicariously, so that we are less likely to behave aggressively. Research evidence has not been very supportive of the catharsis hypothesis (D. Singer & J. Singer, 2005; Flannery, Vazsonyi, & Waldman, 2007). Most psychologists who are familiar with the extensive research are convinced that exposure to media violence increases the odds that the viewer will behave aggressively (Berkowitz, 1986; Anderson et al., 2003a).

Yale University's Dorothy Singer (D. Singer & J. Singer, 2005), a recognized authority on the behavioral consequences of television viewing, observed that longitudinal studies effectively establish the link between television violence and aggressive behavior in children and adolescents. One longitudinal study completed by Rowell Huesmann and his colleagues at the University of Michigan followed nearly eight hundred children between

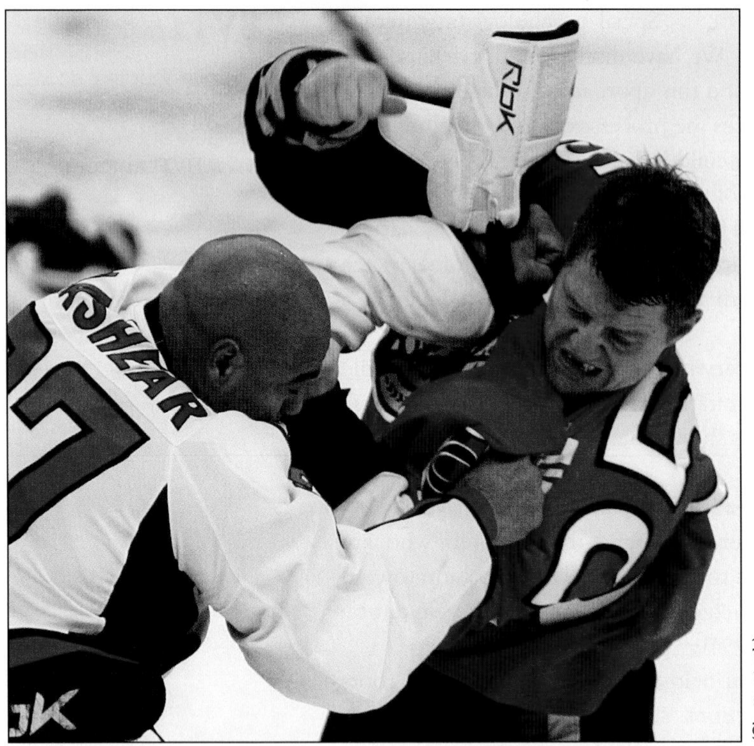

(Shutterstock)

The frustration-aggression hypothesis proposes that aggression results when the achievement of a goal is met with interference.

the ages of six and ten for fifteen years. Their study revealed that exposure to media violence at a young age predicted aggressive behavior as an adult nearly fifteen years later (Huesmann, Moise-Titus, Podolski, & Eron, 2003). Other studies have found that listening to music with violent lyrical content leads listeners to feel a greater sense of hostility and have more hostile thoughts than those who listened to less hostile music (Anderson et al., 2003a).

However, not all psychologists support these interpretations of the effects of media violence. One dissenter, Jonathan Freedman (1984, 2002), has argued that even those studies that have demonstrated a positive relationship between viewing violence and aggressive behavior in a natural setting do not necessarily demonstrate a cause-and-effect relationship. He suggests an alternate explanation: Aggressive persons are inclined to select television programs with high violence content.

Freedman's critique should not be dismissed lightly. We must note, however, that while his criticisms of media violence studies may be at least partially accurate, the fact still remains that virtually all of these studies reach the same general conclusion—viewing violence spawns aggressive behavior. It seems reasonable to conclude that the effect of viewing filmed aggression must be fairly substantial to show consistently across so many diverse research designs. Even if there were a paucity of research supporting a causal relationship between TV violence and aggressive behavior, some experts caution that violence on television may have other adverse effects, such as increasing one's acceptance of aggressive behavior in others and blunting one's sensitivity to violence; perhaps, most important, it may prime aggressive behavior (Huesmann, 2007).

For another perspective on the effects of media violence, Harold Schechter (2005) has written an extensive history on the portrayal of violent images and acts and argues that we are not exposed to more violent content today than we have been historically. In fact, modern entertainment with all of its sophisticated technology may not be as violent or brutal as the entertainment of previous generations. The author of this text was reminded of this again by his father, who grew up in Chicago during the 1920s and 1930s. At that time, youth gangs viciously ruled schools and neighborhoods, while adult gangs and the mob ruled downtown.

Throughout this chapter we have examined the powerful influence of social conditions on our behavior. We have seen that our impressions of others, our tendency to conform, our prejudices, and human aggression are all greatly influenced by social circumstances. Social psychologists, ethologists, and sociobiologists have all had a profound influence on our understanding of social behaviors. While some of their theories are still controversial and incomplete, they have changed the way we view human social interactions. We do have much to learn, however. Our world is now influenced by the diverse cultures of many nations, not just our own. Our ability to survive will depend on how well we learn to adapt and to celebrate these social influences, not merely reject them.

CHAPTER REVIEW

Social Perception

1. The term *social perception* describes the ways in which we perceive, evaluate, categorize, and form judgments about the characteristics of people we encounter. Three factors that influence our social perceptions are first impressions, schemas, and implicit personality theories.
2. Our first impressions about a person often seem to count the most, a phenomenon referred to as the primacy effect. First impressions are more difficult to modify if they are negative.
3. Person schemas, which are generalized assumptions about certain classes of people, provide a structure for evaluating the people we meet.
4. Implicit personality theories allow us to draw conclusions about what people are like, based on certain implicit assumptions about personality traits that usually go together. Implicit personality theories are often organized around central traits that we tend to associate with other characteristics.

Attribution Theories

5. Attributions are the judgments we make about why people behave as they do. We tend to attribute people's behavior either to dispositional (internal) causes, such as motivational states or personality traits, or to situations, such as environmental factors.
6. Biases in attribution processes include the fundamental attribution error (a tendency to overestimate dispositional causes and to underestimate situational causes when accounting for the behavior of others), false consensus bias (the assumption that most people share our own attitudes and behaviors), and the illusion of control (the belief that we control events in our lives).

Attitudes

7. Attitudes are learned, relatively enduring predispositions to respond in consistent ways to certain people, groups, ideas, or situations.
8. Attitudes are shaped by experiences, which include our observations of behavior (both other people's and our own), Pavlovian and operant conditioning, and direct experiences with the attitude object (the people, ideas, or things we hold attitudes about).

CHAPTER REVIEW

9. Studies that have measured a variety of behaviors relevant to a given attitude have revealed a strong correlation between attitudes and behavior.
10. Attitudes are particularly strong predictors of behavior when other factors influencing behavior are minimized, when an attitude is highly relevant to the behavior being considered, and when we are quite conscious of our attitudes when we act.
11. Consistency theories suggest that we sometimes change our attitudes in an effort to maintain consistency both among attitudes we hold as well as between our attitudes and behaviors.
12. According to cognitive dissonance theory, people experience an unpleasant state of dissonance whenever they perceive a discrepancy between their actions and their attitudes. In such a situation, attitudes may be changed to be more consistent with behavior, thus resulting in a state of consonance or psychological comfort.
13. The probability that persuasion will succeed is highest when the source of persuasion is seen as possessing any or all of the qualities of credibility, power, and attractiveness.

Prejudice

14. Prejudice is a negative, unjustifiable, and inflexible attitude toward a group and its members that is based on erroneous information, often in the form of stereotypes (preconceived and oversimplified beliefs and expectations about the traits of members of a particular group that do not account for individual differences).
15. Prejudice often stems from a marked tendency of people to categorize themselves as belonging to an ingroup (based on race, age, education, creed, economic level, etc.) and to have a negative attitude against people in outgroups who do not possess the same characteristics. By perceiving their ingroup as superior, people seem to be attempting to enhance their self-esteem.
16. People who are frustrated by their lack of accomplishments or by adverse living conditions often vent their frustration in the form of prejudice against members of a minority group that they perceive as being less powerful than themselves.
17. Racism, sexism, and other prejudicial attitudes are often passed directly from parents to children through the social learning mechanisms of observation and emulation.

CHAPTER REVIEW

Implicit Attitudes

18. Not all of our attitudes are explicitly known. Implicit attitudes may be better predictors of our behavior than explicit attitudes, particularly when they are strong.
19. The Implicit Association Test (IAT) measures implicit attitudes.

Social Influences on Behavior

20. The realm of social influence (the effects of others on our behavior) encompasses the related phenomena of conformity, compliance, and obedience.
21. Conformity refers to a tendency to change or modify our own behaviors so that they are consistent with those of other people.
22. Social psychologists make a distinction between conformity that results from informational social influence, in which we accept a group's beliefs or behaviors as providing accurate information about reality, and conformity via normative social influence, in which we conform not because of an actual change in our beliefs but because we think that we will benefit in some way, such as gaining approval or avoiding rejection.
23. A form of compliance called stereotype threat occurs when individuals adopt, as a self-characteristic, negative stereotypes about groups to which they belong.
24. Whereas both compliance and conformity involve yielding to pressure exerted by others, compliance involves an element of coercion as well, in that it takes place in situations where we alter our behavior in response to direct requests from others.
25. Groupthink is a psychological drive for consensus at any cost that suppresses dissent and consideration of alternatives in group decision making. Two methods employed by people who wish to increase the probability of compliance in others are the foot-in-the-door technique and the door-in-the-face technique.
26. Obedience occurs in situations in which people alter their behavior in response to commands or orders leveled by people they may perceive as having power or authority.
27. Psychologists have suggested three reasons why people may respond to social influence in the form of destructive obedience. First, people may believe that their personal accountability for actions is somehow diminished or relieved by those authority figures who issue the commands. Second, authority figures often possess highly visible symbols of power or status that make it difficult to resist their dictates. Finally, people often comply because they have first been "sucked in" by seemingly harmless commands.

CHAPTER REVIEW

Interpersonal Behavior: Attraction and Aggression

28. Factors known to contribute strongly to interpersonal attraction include proximity, similarity, reciprocity, and physical attractiveness. We often develop close relationships with people who we see frequently, who share similar beliefs, who seem to like us, and who we perceive as being physically attractive.
29. Cross-cultural studies suggest that physical attractiveness and youth are more important for males selecting a potential mate than for females, who seek characteristics of wealth, status, and industriousness in potential mates.
30. The biological perspective, championed by sociobiologists and ethologists, maintains that aggression between members of a species serves to ensure that strong, dominant individuals survive and reproduce.
31. The hormone testosterone has been linked to aggression in many species, including humans.
32. Engaging in aggressive behaviors can increase testosterone levels in males.
33. Low serotonin activity is associated with aggression, and SSRIs may be used to treat some forms of aggressive behavior.
34. Research has revealed that frustration often precedes aggressive behavior, particularly if suitable cues are present in the environment.
35. Social-learning theorists suggest that aggressive behavior is often learned by receiving reinforcement for aggressive acts and by observing and imitating the aggressive behavior of others.
36. The effects of television and media violence on aggressive behavior have been debated for decades. Most research indicates that viewing violence primes individuals for violent behavior.

TERMS AND CONCEPTS

Attitude, pg. 686
Attribution Theory, pg. 680
Central Trait, pg. 679
Cognitive Dissonance Theory, pg. 691
Compliance, pg. 701
Conformity, pg. 697
Correspondent Inference Theory, pg. 680
Covariation Principle, pg. 682
Diffusion of Responsibility or Bystander Apathy, pg. 677
Discrimination, pg. 694
Door-in-the-Face Technique, pg. 701
Ethology, pg. 708
False Consensus Bias, pg. 685
Foot-in-the-Door Technique, pg. 701
Frustration-Aggression Hypothesis, pg. 710
Fundamental Attribution Error, pg. 683
Groupthink, pg. 703
Halo Effect , pg. 679
Illusion of Control, pg. 685
Implicit Association Test (IAT), pg. 696
Implicit Attitude, pg. 696
Implicit Personality Theories, pg. 679
Impression Management, pg. 688
Informational Social Influence, pg. 697
Ingroup Bias, pg. 695
Ingroup, pg. 695
Interpersonal Aggression, pg. 708
Mere Exposure Effect, pg. 704
Normative Social Influence, pg. 697
Obedience, pg. 701
Outgroup, pg. 695
Person Schemas, pg. 679
Physical Attractiveness, pg. 706
Prejudice, pg. 694
Primacy Effect, pg. 678
Proximity, pg. 704
Reciprocity, pg. 705
Similarity, pg. 705
Social Influence, pg. 697
Social Perception, pg. 678
Sociobiology, pg. 708
Stereotypes, pg. 694
Stereotype Threat, pg. 691

POP QUIZ

True or False

___ 1. The tendency to feel a diminished sense of responsibility in an emergency when others are present is referred to as bystander apathy.

___ 2. The halo effect would predict that you perceive a well-mannered child as more attractive than his less-polite identical twin.

___ 3. Providing accurate information that contradicts a prejudiced individual's viewpoint is an effective way to alter that person's negative attitude.

___ 4. Conformity involves simply modifying behaviors so that they are consistent with those of others; compliance involves modifying behavior in response to direct requests from others.

___ 5. Leonard Berkowitz suggests that frustration will not result in aggression unless suitable environmental cues are present.

Multiple Choice

6. A person believes that elementary schoolteachers are nurturing people. This is an example of __________.
   a. a person schema
   b. an attribution
   c. prejudice
   d. an implicit personality theory

7. An assumption that behavior is determined by internal causes, such as personal attitudes or goals, is referred as __________.
   a. consensus
   b. fundamental attribution
   c. situational attribution
   d. dispositional attribution

8. Which of the following is included in the definition of attitudes?
   a. Attitudes involve predispositions to respond in a consistent way.
   b. Attitudes are learned.
   c. Attitudes are enduring.
   d. All of the above are included in the definition.

9. We probably will be in a state of _______ when people we like do not agree with us.
   a. nonbalance
   b. imbalance
   c. balance
   d. dissonance

POP QUIZ

10. A used car salesman tells you, "That's a fine car at an outstanding price." This salesman is not effective in persuading you to buy the car, in large part for what reason?
    a. There is little prestige associated with being a used car salesman.
    b. The salesman is unattractive.
    c. You doubt that the salesman is trustworthy.
    d. You doubt that the salesman has any expertise concerning cars.
11. We divide our world into two groups of people, "us" and "them." You and I belong to which group?
    a. Outgroup
    b. Ingroup
    c. Minority group
    d. Known group
12. During what periods do overt acts of prejudice tend to increase?
    a. Isolation between the groups
    b. Voluntary cooperation
    c. Forced cooperation
    d. Frustration
13. Who would be *least* likely to exhibit conforming behavior in Asch's experiment involving line-comparison judgments?
    a. An individual with low self-esteem
    b. An architectural drafts person
    c. A college freshman in a group of college seniors
    d. The last individual to answer in a group of seven subjects
14. What did Stanley Milgram's study examine?
    a. Obedience
    b. The authoritarian personality
    c. Conformity
    d. Compliance
15. A cross-cultural study of sex differences in mate selection found which of the following to be true?
    a. Men and women both place very high values on physical attractiveness.
    b. Women place greater value on physical attractiveness than men.
    c. Men place greater value on physical attractiveness than women.
    d. Men and women in industrial societies place less value on physical attractiveness than men and women in more primitive societies.

Answer Key: 1.T 2.F 3.F 4.T 5.T 6.a 7.d 8.d 9.d 10.c 11.b 12.d 13.b 14.a 15.c

Appendix

Statistics is one of the most commonly used mathematical tools in science. Without statistics, it would be virtually impossible to present and interpret the results of scientific experiments. Two particularly useful types of statistics frequently used in psychology are descriptive statistics and inferential statistics. *Descriptive statistics,* as the name implies, are used to describe and summarize the results of research. *Inferential statistics* are used in making decisions about hypotheses and to make generalizations from research samples to larger populations.

A.1 Descriptive Statistics

A.1a Measures of Central Tendency

Suppose your psychology instructor gives a sample test to 10 students who attended a study session. How would the instructor describe the test results? One way would be to name all students and list their test scores—10 names and 10 scores. That would probably work nicely in a small class, but it would certainly be inefficient and confusing with a class of 500. Moreover, a listing of numbers does not indicate much of anything about the study group as a whole. It also would be helpful to know the average, typical, or most representative score. What is needed is a measure of *central tendency* for the group of scores, a number that represents the average. We shall describe three commonly used measures.

The Mean

The **mean** (short for *arithmetic mean*) is computed by adding up all the scores and dividing by the number of scores. We can express this in mathematical form in the following:

$$\overline{X} = \frac{\Sigma X}{N}$$

This formula introduces some elementary statistical symbols. The letter X refers to the independent variable, which can take on many different values. It could be anything—IQ, anxiety, or learning errors. The researcher measures the variable for each subject and assigns a score to each subject to represent the level of the variable for that subject. The capital Greek letter sigma (Σ) in the formula is a shorthand symbol for "add up these scores." We then divide this sum by the number of scores (symbolized by N) to arrive at the mean, which is symbolized by $\overline{X}$ (read "X bar").

We have made up a list of 10 test scores from students attending our hypothetical study session and computed their mean in Table A-1. To compute the mean, we add up the 10 scores and divide by 10 ($\overline{X} = 83$). Table A-1 also gives the number of hours each student in our study session studied during the previous week. To keep the variable of study time distinct from test score, we signify study times by Y. So ΣY tells us to add up the study times, which is also done in Table A-1. Dividing this total by the number of scores gives us the mean study time of the students ($\overline{Y} = 8.35$ hours). We can express these steps in a shorthand formula.

Mean In descriptive statistics, the arithmetic average obtained by adding scores and dividing by the number of scores

Table A-1 Computation of Mean Test Score and Study Time for 10 Students Enrolled in a Study Session

Student's Name	X (Test Score)	Y (Study Time)
Rita	85	9.2
Charles	78	8.1
Dawn	82	8.4
Bruce	74	7.2
Lauri	89	9.6
Marie	91	9.5
John	87	8.9
Randy	79	6.3
Jeff	81	7.7
Suzan	84	8.6
	$\Sigma X = 830$ $N = 10$	$\Sigma Y = 83.5$ $N = 10$

The mean of the test scores (X) is

$$\overline{X} = \frac{\Sigma X}{N} = \frac{830}{10} = 83.0$$

The mean of study times (Y) is

$$\overline{Y} = \frac{\Sigma Y}{N} = \frac{83.5}{10} = 8.35$$

$$\overline{Y} = \frac{\Sigma Y}{N}$$

Now if we ask the teacher how the class performed on the test, the teacher could simply report the mean value of 83 points; if we ask how many hours these students studied, the teacher could report the mean from our group, which was 8.35 hours. This method is obviously much simpler than listing all the X and Y scores, and it gives a better idea of the students' general performance as well as the hours of study time per week that are typical of these students.

The Median

Median In descriptive statistics, the score that falls in the middle of a distribution of numbers arranged from the lowest to the highest

The **median** is the *middle score* in a list of scores that have been arranged in increasing order. If there is an odd number of scores, then there will be one score exactly in the middle. Thus, if the class had 11 students, the score of the sixth student in order would be the median—there would be five scores higher and five scores lower. With an even number of scores, there is no single middle score; instead, there are two scores that determine the middle (one is above and one is below the theoretical midpoint). In our example of 10 test scores, the middle two scores are the fifth and sixth scores. Table A-2 shows the 10 test scores from Table A-1, but this time we have arranged them in order. The middle point is between the fifth and sixth scores (83). We average these two scores to obtain the median.

Table A-2 Computation of the Median Test Scores for 10 Students Enrolled in a Study Session

Name	X (Test Score)
Marie	91
Lauri	89
John	87
Rita	85
Suzan	84
Dawn	82
Jeff	81
Randy	79
Charles	78
Bruce	74

(The *median* is the average of the two middle scores)

The median in this case is the average of the two middle scores (84 and 82).

$$\frac{84 + 82}{2} = 83$$

Note that if we had an odd number of scores, the median would be the middle score.

The mean and the median are typically close, but they are not usually the same, as they are in this case. They will be very close when the distribution of scores is symmetrical or equally balanced around the mean.

Now consider the set of test scores in Table A-3. Here we note that most of the 10 students from a study session didn't do very well—with the exception of two students who scored very high. This distribution of scores is asymmetrical and unbalanced. Technically, we call it skewed. The distribution of Table A-3 is skewed to the high end (positively skewed). The mean score is 76 and the median is 72.

Table A-3 Comparison of the Mean and the Median for a Set of Test Scores for 10 Students Enrolled in a Study Session

Name	X (Test Score)	
Mike	99	
Julie	98	
Lynn	76	
Ryan	74	
Bill	72	(The *median* is the average of the two middle scores)
Lauri	72	
Kathy	69	
John	68	
Sue	68	
Bob	64	

The median test score is $\frac{72 + 72}{2} = 72$

The mean test score is $\overline{X} = \frac{\Sigma X}{N} = \frac{760}{10} = 76$

The Mode

The **mode** is the most frequently occurring score. In a small set of scores as in Tables A-1, A-2, and A-3, there is the possibility that no score will occur more than once and, thus, there is no mode. However, suppose a psychologist gives an anxiety test to a group of 200 patients. With such a large group, it is convenient to set up a frequency distribution showing the various possible scores on the test and, for each possible score, how many people actually got that score. We have set up in Table A-4 such a frequency distribution for the anxiety scores from the 200 psychiatric patients. Looking down the frequency column in Table A-4, we see that 27 is the highest frequency. That is, 27 people obtained a score of 15. Therefore, 15 is the mode or the modal score. Note that the sum of all the frequencies is equal to *N*, the number of people taking the test—in this case, 200.

Frequency distributions can also be represented graphically. Figure A-1 shows a frequency distribution from Table A-4. The horizontal axis of the graph represents the values of the variable *X* (the anxiety score) and the vertical axis represents the frequency of each score.

A.1b Measures of Variability

Mode In descriptive statistics, the score that occurs most frequently in a distribution of numbers

There are differences among people: Not everyone gets the same score on a test or is the same height. These *individual differences* among people are a fact of life. The variability among people may be large when it comes to anxiety or test scores, but small when it

Table A-4 A Frequency Distribution of the Anxiety Scores of 200 Patients

Score (*X*)	Frequency (*f*)
20	10
19	10
18	12
17	15
16	20
15	**27**
14	15
13	21
12	22
11	12
10	10
9	8
8	7
7	5
6	3
5	0
4	2
3	1
2	0
1	0
	$\sum f = 200 = N$

The *mode*, the score that occurs most frequently, is equal to 15

comes to the number of fingers they have. How do we quantify the degree of variability in the scores?

The quickest and least informative measure of the variability in a set of scores is the range. The **range** is defined as the *highest score minus the lowest score*. In Table A-4, we see that the patients' anxiety scores range from a high of 20 to a low of 3, and so the range would be 20 – 3 = 17. Although the range as a measure of variability is easy to compute, it is based on only two scores (the highest and the lowest) and, therefore, tells us little about the variability in the entire distribution. Better measures of variability are the variance and standard deviation, both of which reflect the degree of spread or fluctuation of scores around the mean.

Range In descriptive statistics, a measure of variability that indicates the difference between the highest and lowest scores

Figure A-1 A Frequency Distribution Based on the Data in Table A-4

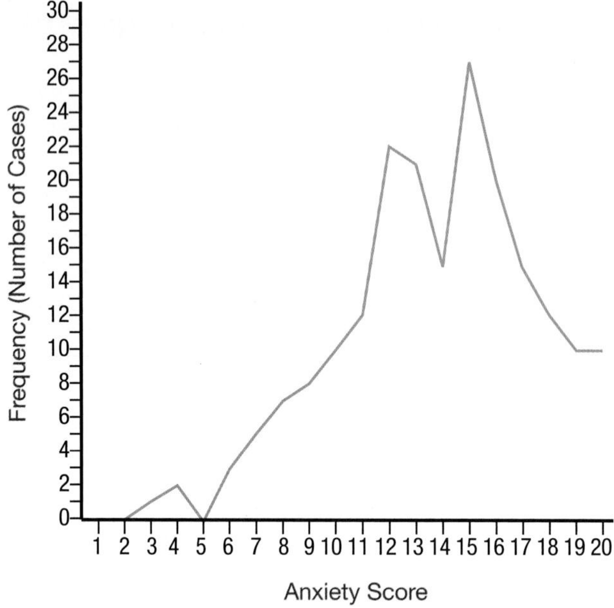

Table A-5 Comparison of the Mean and the Median for a Set of Test Scores for 10 Students in a Study Group.

Set A	Set B
36	36
22	32
21	28
21	24
20	20
20	20
19	16
19	12
18	8
4	4
$\Sigma X = 200$ $N = 10$ $\bar{X} = \frac{200}{10} = 20$ Range = 36 − 4 = 32	$\Sigma X = 200$ $N = 10$ $\bar{X} = \frac{200}{10} = 20$ Range = 36 − 4 = 32

Let's suppose we have a set of 10 scores with a mean of 20. Two such sets are shown in Table A-5. All but two of the scores in Set A cluster close to the mean. In Set B, we have the same mean, but the variability is higher, with several scores a long way from the mean. If we described both sets with a central tendency measure (such as the mean), the two sets would appear to be similar. If we described the variability of each set using the range, again, the two sets would appear to be similar. To reflect the differences between the sets more accurately, we need a measure of variability that takes into account all the scores (not just the highest and lowest).

Variance In descriptive statistics, a measure of variability that is the average of the squared distances of the scores from the mean

The variance and the standard deviation are both measures of variability that are based on all of the scores in the sample. The **variance** is essentially the *average of the squared distances of the scores from the mean*. It is symbolized by this sign: s^2.

To compute the variance, we first subtract the mean from each score as we have done in Table A-6. These differences are measures of each score's distance from the mean. Why not just calculate the mean of these distance scores? The reason is that the mean of these distance scores will always be equal to zero, regardless of how variable the scores are.

Table A-6 Computation of the Variance and Standard Deviation for Two Sets of Scores

Set A			Set B		
X	$(X-\bar{X})$	$(X-\bar{X})^2$	X	$(X-\bar{X})$	$(X-\bar{X})^2$
36	15	256	36	16	256
22	2	4	32	12	144
21	1	1	28	8	64
21	1	1	24	4	16
20	0	0	20	0	0
20	0	0	20	0	0
19	21	1	16	24	16
19	21	1	12	28	64
18	22	4	8	212	144
4	216	256	4	216	256
Sums	0	524		0	960

Set A

$$X^2 = \text{variance} = \frac{\Sigma(X-\bar{X})^2}{N} = \frac{524}{10} = 52.4$$

$$s = \text{standard deviation} = \sqrt{s^2} = \sqrt{52.4} = 7.24$$

Range = 36 – 4 = 32

Set B

$$s^2 = \text{variance} = \frac{\Sigma(X-\bar{X})^2}{N} = \frac{960}{10} = 96.0$$

$$s = \text{standard deviation} = \sqrt{s^2} = \sqrt{96.0} = 9.80$$

Range = 36 – 4 = 32

Standard Deviation In descriptive statistics, a measure of variability that indicates the average extent to which all the scores in a distribution vary from the mean

Normal Distribution In descriptive statistics, a distribution in which scores are distributed similarly on both sides of the middle value, so that they have the appearance of a bell-shaped curve when graphed

Instead, we square each score before adding them. These squared distance scores are also shown in Table A-6. Now we can add these scores up and divide by the number of scores. These steps are expressed in the following notational form:

$$s^2 = \frac{\Sigma(X - \overline{X})^2}{N} = 52.4$$

The **standard deviation** is simply the *square root of the variance*. This measure is somewhat easier to interpret because it is expressed in the same units as our independent variable, not a squared value like the variance. For this reason, the standard deviation is a more preferable measure of variability.

$$s = \sqrt{\frac{\Sigma(X - \overline{X})^2}{N}} = 7.24$$

The standard deviation and the variance are better measures of variability than the range because they take all of the scores into account, not just the highest score and lowest score. If we compare the two data sets in Table A-6, we see that, even though the range is the same in the two sets, both the variance and the standard deviation reflect the smaller average spread of scores in Set A relative to Set B. Unlike Set B, most of the scores in Set A cluster close to the mean of 20. The variance in Set A is 52.4 and in Set B is 96.0. The standard deviation in Set A is 7.24 and in Set B is 9.80. The range is 32 (36 – 4) in both data sets.

A.1c Normal Frequency Distributions

Earlier in this appendix, we introduced the frequency distribution and showed how it could be represented graphically. Figure A-2 presents the graph of what is called the **normal distribution** (or *normal curve*). This figure is not a graph of an actual data set (as in Figure A-1). Instead, this is a theoretical distribution defined by a mathematical equation. A normal distribution is symmetrical; if you fold it over at the mean, the two halves

Figure A-2 The Normal Distribution of IQ Scores

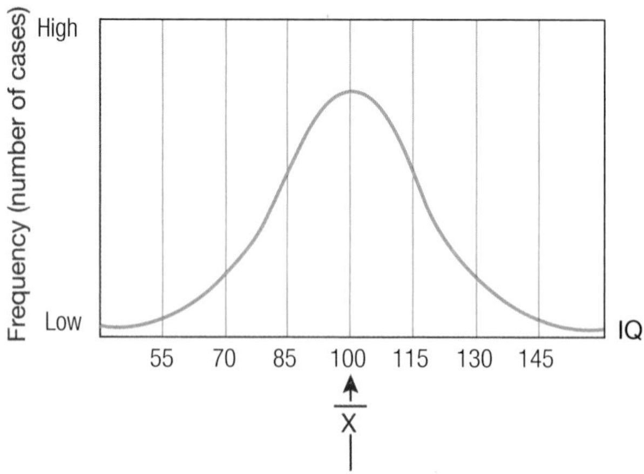

will match each other. Moreover, it is a bell-shaped curve; scores near the mean are most common, and the frequency drops off smoothly as we move to the extremes. The normal distribution is very useful because many variables are "normally distributed;" that is, the graph of the distribution of the variable would be very similar in shape to the graph in Figure A-2. The variable of IQ is a good example. IQ is normally distributed with a mean of 100 and a standard deviation of 15; therefore, if we obtained IQ scores for everybody, the mean IQ would be 100 and the standard deviation would be 15. Furthermore, if we drew a graph representing the frequency of each of the possible IQ scores, it would show the characteristic bell shape of a normal distribution.

If we know that a variable such as IQ is normally distributed and if we know the mean and the standard deviation, we can use the mathematical properties of the normal distribution to deduce more information about the variable. We can do this because, in any normal distribution, the standard deviation can be used to divide the distribution into sections containing fixed percentages of the scores. Figure A-3 shows a normal distribution divided up in this way for the variable of IQ. The fixed percentages are printed in the various sections of the curve. For example, about 34 percent of the IQ scores lie between the mean and a score of 115; that is, 34 percent of the people have IQs between the mean and one standard deviation above the mean. The standard deviation is a distance measure, and the "distance" from 115 to the mean of 100 is one standard deviation unit. An IQ of 130 would be two standard deviation units above the mean; an IQ of 145 would be three standard deviations above the mean. One standard deviation below the mean would be an IQ of 85; two standard deviations below the mean would be an IQ of 70; three standard deviations below the mean would be an IQ of 55. Regardless of the variable being measured, almost all of the scores will fall between three standard deviation units below the mean and three standard deviation units above the mean (for IQ scores, from 55 up to 145). Although it is theoretically possible to

Figure A-3 The Normal Distribution Divided into Standard Deviation Units

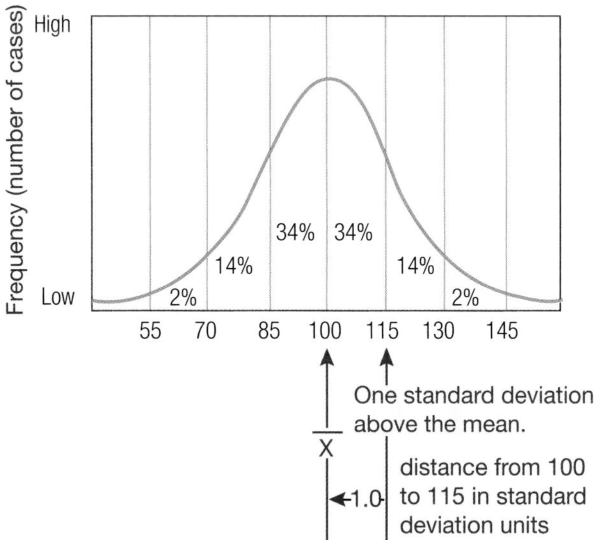

obtain scores outside of this range, scores more than three standard deviations from the mean are very rare. It is often convenient to convert the scores into standard deviation scores, called *z* scores, using the following formula:

$$z = \frac{X - \overline{X}}{s}$$

A major advantage of the *z* score is that it can be used as a common yardstick for all tests, allowing us to compare scores on different tests. For example, suppose you receive 80 on your history test, which has a class mean of 70 with a standard deviation of 10. On your psychology test, you got a 90, and the class mean was 85 with a standard deviation of 5. We also know that the distribution of test scores was approximately normal in each class. On which test did you do better? These test scores are not immediately comparable, but if you change each score into a *z* score using the mean and standard deviation for each test, you will discover that you did equally well on both tests in terms of where you stood in the class distribution (obtaining a *z* score of +1.00 on each test). Using the information in Figure A-3, we can infer that your score on each test puts you at approximately the 84th percentile—34 percent of the class scored between your score and the mean and another 50 percent of the class scored below the mean.

Figure A-4 again shows the IQ normal distribution, but this time we have two horizontal axes displayed. The upper one shows IQ scores, and the lower one shows the equivalent *z* scores. This figure shows that an IQ score of 115 is one standard deviation above the mean, and so the *z* score corresponding to 115 is +1.0. If your friend tells you that his *z* score in IQ is +2.0, you can see that he has an IQ of 130. If he tells you that his *z* score is +3.0 (145), he is either very brilliant or he is pulling your leg.

From Figure A-4, suppose we ask you to figure out what percentage of the people have IQs between 85 and 115, which is the same as asking how many people have *z* scores between –1.0 and +1.0. The answer is 68 percent: 34 percent between 85 and 100, and another 34 percent between 100 and 115. If we know that the scores are distributed normally, and we know the mean and standard deviation of the distribution, we

Figure A-4 The Normal Distribution and *z* Scores

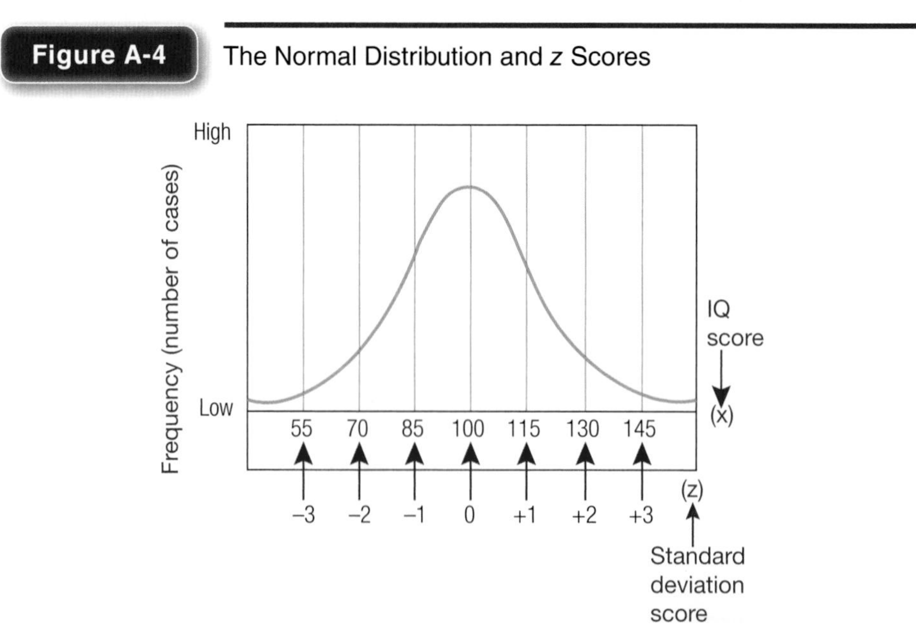

Figure A-5 The Normal Distribution of Waist Size in U.S. Men (Hypothetical)

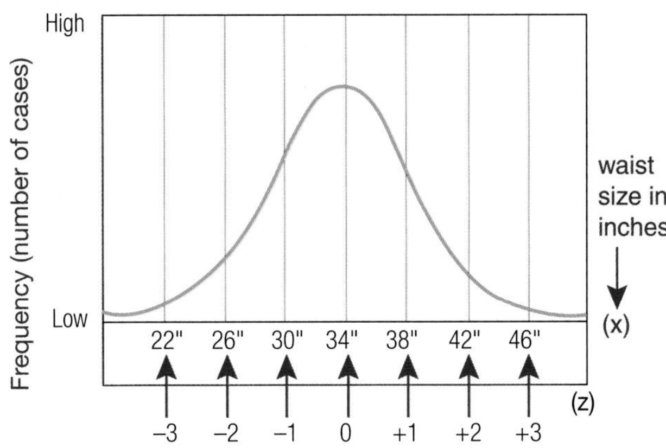

can find the percentage of scores between any two points by using a simple table (the *Standard Normal*) that can be found in almost any statistics textbook. An important thing to remember is that these percentages and the *z* score procedure apply to any normal distribution, not just the IQ distribution. The only difference between the IQ distribution and any other normal distribution of scores is that the other distributions probably have different means and different standard deviations. However, if you know that something has a normal distribution and if you know the mean and standard deviation of it, you can set up a figure like Figure A-4.

Suppose, for example, that we told you that waist size in U.S. men is normally distributed with a mean of 34 inches and a standard deviation of 4 inches. You could now set up a normal frequency distribution, as in Figure A-5. Almost all U.S. men have a waist size within the range of 22 inches (*z* score of −3; 22 is 3 standard deviation units below the mean) to 46 inches (*z* score of +3; 3 units above the mean). Now can you fill in the percentages and answer the following questions?

1. What percentage of men have waist sizes less than 30 inches?

2. What percentage of men have waist sizes greater than 38?

3. If Joe's waist size is 47, is he unusual?

4. If we randomly selected one man from the U.S. population, what is the probability (how likely is it) that his waist size will be equal to or greater than 38?

This last question brings us to the notion of probability. **Probability** refers to the *proportion of cases that fit a certain description*. In general, the probability of *A* (the likelihood that a randomly drawn object will be an *A* object) is equal to the number of *A* objects divided by the total number of all possible objects. The number of *A* objects divided by the total number of objects is the *proportion* of objects that are *A*, and so the probability is just a proportion.

Probability In statistics, the proportion of cases that fit a certain description

Correlation Coefficient
Statistics used to describe the degree of relationship between two or more variables. Positive correlations indicate that variables vary together in the same direction; negative correlations indicate the opposite

Suppose, as in question 4, we wanted to know the probability that a randomly selected U.S. man will have a waist size equal to or greater than 38. To find the probability of selecting at random such an individual, we have to know what proportion of all men have waist sizes of 38 or greater. In Figure A-5, we can see that 14 percent of the men have waist sizes between 38 and 42 inches and an additional 2 percent are greater than 42; so we add 14 percent and 2 percent and find that 16 percent of U.S. men have waist sizes of 38 or greater. In proportion terms, this becomes .16 (we move the decimal point two places to the left to translate a percentage into a proportion). In summary, the probability of selecting a man with a waist size equal to or greater than 38 is .16. This means that 16 out of every 100 random selections would yield a man who fits this description.

Suppose that scores on an anxiety scale are normally distributed in the population of all people in the U.S. with a mean of 50 and a standard deviation of 10. Calculate the probability that a randomly drawn person has an anxiety score that is equal to or less than 40. If you computed it correctly, you should have obtained a probability of .16.

A.1d Correlation

The **correlation coefficient** was introduced in Chapter 2. The correlation coefficient does not describe a single variable as the mean or standard deviation does. Instead, it describes the degree of relationship between two variables. It is basically a measure of the degree to which the two variables vary together, or *covary*. Scores can vary together in one of two ways: (1) A *positive covariation*, in which high scores in one variable tend to go with high scores in the other variable (and low scores go with low scores), or (2) *negative covariation*, in which high scores in one variable tend to go with low scores in the other variable (and low scores go with high scores). When there is a positive covariation, we say that the two variables are positively correlated, and when there is a negative covariation, we say they are negatively correlated. A common example of positive correlation

Table A-7 The Correlation Between Anxiety and Happiness

Name	Anxiety (X)*	Happiness (Y)
Joan	1	10
Larry	2	9
Ralph	3	8
Clint	4	7
Sue	5	6
Sharon	6	5
Sam	7	4
Bonnie	8	3
Marsha	9	2
Harry	10	1

*Here we have arranged the anxiety scores in order. Note that the happiness scores are in reverse order. When these data are graphed in a scatter plot (see Figure A-6), all the points fall on a straight line, which indicates that the correlation IS perfect (in this case, −1.0).

Figure A-6 A Scatter Plot of the Data from Table A-7 Relating Anxiety to Happiness

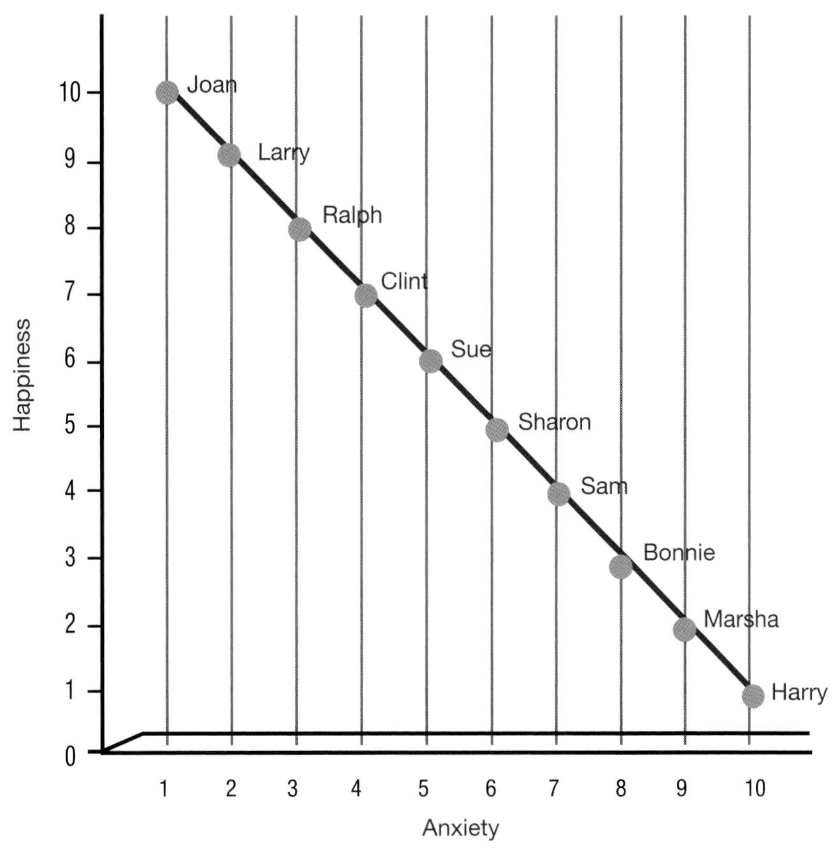

is the relationship between height and weight—the taller you are, the more you tend to weigh. A common example of negative correlation might be the relationship between the amount of alcohol a person drank in an evening and his or her ability to drive an automobile—the more the person drank, the lower his or her ability to drive.

Note that we used "tend to go with." Correlations are almost never perfect—not all tall people are particularly heavy, and not all short people are lightweights. In some cases, there may be a *zero correlation* between two variables—that is, no relationship between the variables. We might expect there to be a zero correlation, for example, between your height and your ability to learn psychology. So two variables can be *positively* or *negatively correlated* or *not correlated at all*, and the degree of correlation can be great or small. What we need is a statistic that conveniently measures the degree and the direction (positive or negative) of the correlation between two variables, and this is what the correlation coefficient does.

Table A-7 shows the scores of 10 people on two tests: a test of anxiety and a test of happiness. The possible scores on each test ranged from 1 to 10. Larger scores represent more of the variable being measured. Hence, a high score on the anxiety measure represents a high level of anxiety; a low score represents a low level of anxiety. Intuitively, we would expect a negative correlation between the two variables of anxiety and happiness—the less anxious you are, the more happy you will be, and vice versa.

Figure A-7 Scatter Plots Showing Four Possible Relationships

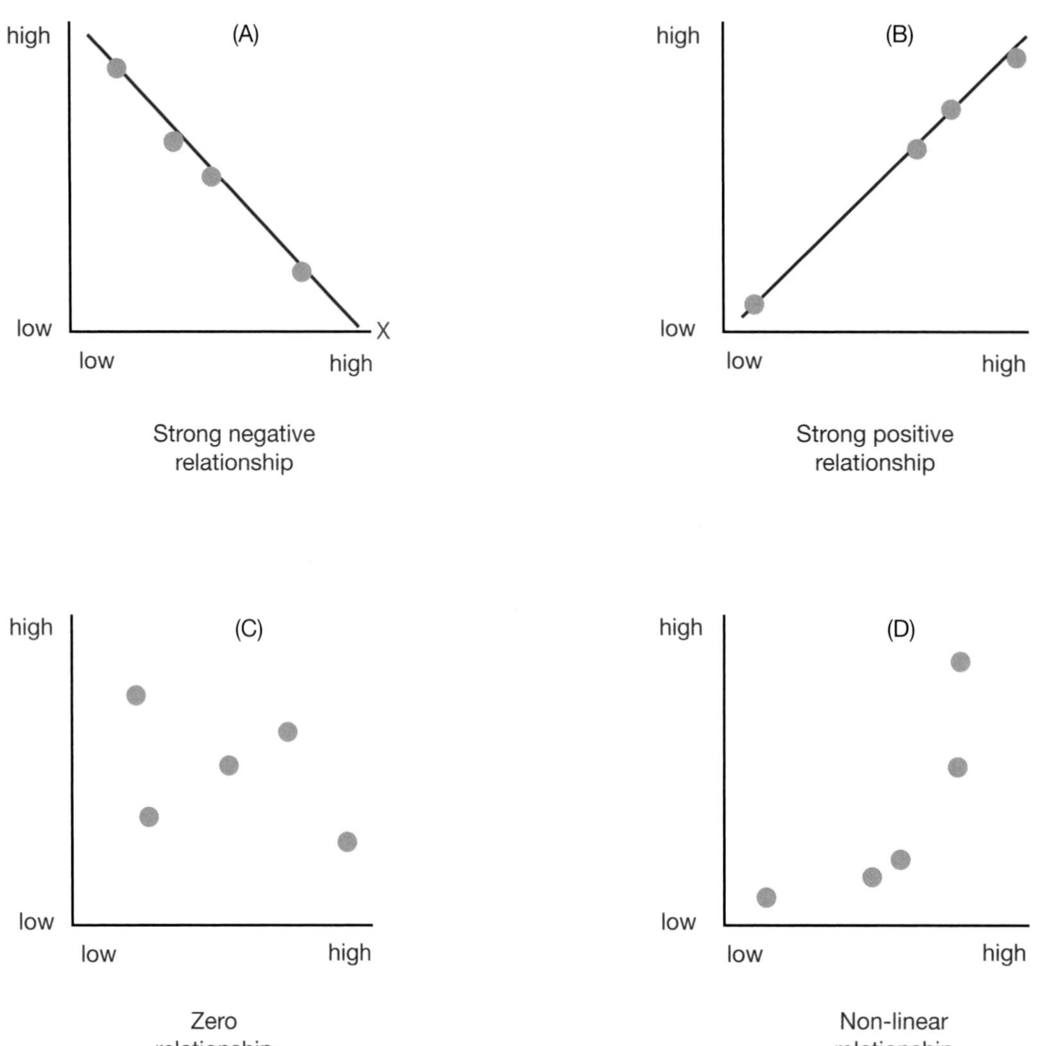

Table A-7 presents the anxiety and happiness scores for each of the 10 subjects. These data can be more easily visualized in a *scatter plot*, which we have set up in Figure A-6. In this scatter plot, the horizontal axis indicates the anxiety score, and the vertical axis indicates the happiness score. Each person is represented by a point on the graph that locates him or her on the two tests. For example, Clint had an anxiety score of 4 and a happiness score of 7. So we go over (to the right) to 4 on the anxiety scale and then up to 7 on the happiness scale, and we place a dot at that point to represent Clint's scores. The scores from all 10 people are represented in the graph. In this case, the 10 points all fall on a straight line, which means that the correlation is perfect. Further, the line slopes down to the right, which means that the correlation is negative in direction—high anxiety scores go with low happiness scores, and vice versa.

As we have said, however, correlations are almost never perfect. More often, the points are likely to be scattered all over the graph, hence the term "scatter plot." The closer the points are positioned on a straight line, the higher the degree of correlation. If

Table A-8 Calculating the Pearson Product-Moment Correlation Coefficient

Name	Anxiety (X)	X^2	Happiness (Y)	Y^2	XY (X times Y)
John	2	4	9	81	18
Ralph	5	25	6	36	30
Mary	9	91	4	16	36
Sue	1	1	3	9	3
Jan	3	9	2	4	6
Harvey	7	49	2	4	14
Jane	8	64	4	16	32
Joanne	6	36	5	25	30
$N = 8$ people	$\Sigma X = 41$	$\Sigma X^2 = 269$	$\Sigma Y = 35$	$\Sigma Y^2 = 191$	$\Sigma XY = 169$

$$r_{xy} \text{ (the correlation between } X \text{ and } Y) = \frac{N\Sigma XY - (\Sigma X)(\Sigma Y)}{\sqrt{[N\Sigma X^2 - (\Sigma X)^2][N\Sigma Y^2 - (\Sigma Y)^2]}}$$

$$\text{For these data: } r_{ANXIETY \cdot HAPPINESS} = \frac{(8)(169) - (41)(35)}{\sqrt{[(8)(269) - (41)^2][(8)(191) - (35)^2]}}$$

$$\frac{1352 - 1453}{\sqrt{(2152 - 1681)(1528 - 1225)}} = \frac{-83}{\sqrt{(471) - (303)}} = \frac{-83}{\sqrt{(142713)}} = \frac{-83}{377.77} = -.219$$

the points seem to cluster about a line that slopes downward to the right, then the correlation will be negative, as in Figure A-6. If the points seem to cluster about a line that slopes upward to the right, the correlation will be positive. Figure A-7 shows four scatter plots. In Panel A, the two variables in question are negatively correlated; the points all seem to cluster about a straight line that slopes downward to the right. In Panel B, there is a positive correlation; the points again all seem to cluster about a line, but this time the line slopes upward to the right. In Panel C, there is no correlation—the points are scattered all over, and there is no line that fits them very well. Panel D presents an interesting case. The points do seem to cluster about a line, but it is a curved rather than a straight line. The scatter plot does suggest that there is a relationship between the variables, but it is not a simple relationship. Most correlation coefficients are designed to quantify a simple straight-line relationship and will give misleading results when applied to a complex relationship such as the one in Panel D.

The **Pearson Product-Moment Correlation Coefficient** (symbolized *r*) is the most often used of several measures of correlation. It can take on any numerical value from −1.0 through 0.0 up to +1.0. A perfect negative product-moment correlation, as shown in Figure A-6, is equal to −1.0, and a perfect positive correlation is equal to +1.0. Correlations close to zero mean there is little or no relationship between the two variables *X* and *Y*. The size of the correlation (ignoring the sign) represents the degree of relationship. The sign of the correlation (positive or negative) tells us the direction of the relationship between the variables, but not the degree of the relationship. Thus, a correlation of −.77 is just as strong as a correlation of +.77, the only difference is the direction. Table A-8 shows the steps for calculating the Pearson product-moment correlation coefficient, in case you want to see exactly how it is done.

Pearson Product-Moment Correlation Coefficient
The most frequently used measure of correlation, ranging from −1.0 to +1.0. Correlations close to zero indicate little or no relationship between two variables; correlations close to + 1.0 or −1.0 indicate more significant positive or negative relationships

Linear Regression
A mathematical method to determine the slope and y-intercept of a straight line through a scatter plot using the general linear model $y = m(x) + b$, where m is the slope and b is the y-intercept of the regression line

In all the examples so far, we have been correlating the scores of a person on two different tests, but we can use correlations in other ways. We might correlate the scores of a person on the same test taken at two different times. If the test measures a variable that should be stable, then the correlation between two administrations of the test would indicate an aspect of the reliability of the test—that is, how consistent are a person's scores on the same test given on two different occasions? A good test should be reliable. Another common use of correlation is to determine the test's validity—does the test measure what it is supposed to measure? For example, a test of intelligence should correlate positively with performance in school. If it did, it would help us argue that the test really did measure intelligence. (See Chapter 13 for a discussion of validity.)

A.1e Linear Regression

One important use of correlational statistics is in a procedure called **linear regression**. A correlation coefficient tells us the degree to which a person's scores on two tests are related. Suppose, for example, that we try to predict your weight. We have no idea what to guess because all we know about you is that you are reading this book. If we knew that the average person reading this book weighs 142 pounds, then that would be our best guess, and we would make the same guess for every reader. However, if we knew your height, and we also knew the correlation between weight and height, then we could make a much more accurate guess of your weight. For example, if we knew that you were 6 feet, 6 inches tall, we would hardly guess 142 pounds. Someone that tall would almost certainly weigh more than 142 pounds. Likewise, if we knew you were 4 feet, 2 inches, 142 pounds would also be an inappropriate guess. We would adjust our prediction of your weight according to what we knew about your height. Linear regression is an accurate way of making this adjustment and allowing us to make as accurate a prediction as possible.

The higher the correlation between weight and height, the better we can predict a person's weight from knowing his or her height. If the correlation between the two variables is perfect (either +1.0 or –1.0), we can predict perfectly the value of one of the variables if we know the value of the other. But, because correlations are almost never perfect, our predictions are normally close, but usually not exactly correct. The lower the correlation is, the greater will be the average error in prediction.

Linear regression is used in many different settings. Many of you probably took the Scholastic Aptitude Test (SAT). From past research, we know there is a positive correlation between scores on the SAT and success in college. Therefore, the SAT can now be given to college applicants, and, on the basis of their scores, we can predict approximately how people will do in college. These predictions are used to help decide whom to admit. Similar procedures are used to process applications for law school, medical school, graduate school, or a job. Using linear regression techniques, the psychologist predicts the applicant's success on the job or in school, and these predictions are used to determine whether or not to hire or admit the applicant. It is a serious business, and the decisions made on this basis are extremely important to the people involved.

Linear regression is based on a mathematical equation for a straight line (hence the term *linear*). What we are looking for is the straight line that comes closest to the most points on a scatter diagram. Figure A-8 shows two different hypothetical scatter plots relating scores on the SAT to grade point average (GPA) in college. Each point in the diagram represents the SAT score and college GPA for one student. With data on SAT scores and college GPAs, we can proceed to use regression to make predictions for future students. First, we solve the equation for the best-fitting straight line (known as the *regression line*), a complex procedure we need not describe here. Then we draw the line on the scatter plot. Now we

Figure A-8 Scatter Plots Showing High (A) and Low (B) Correlations Between SAT Scores and College GPA

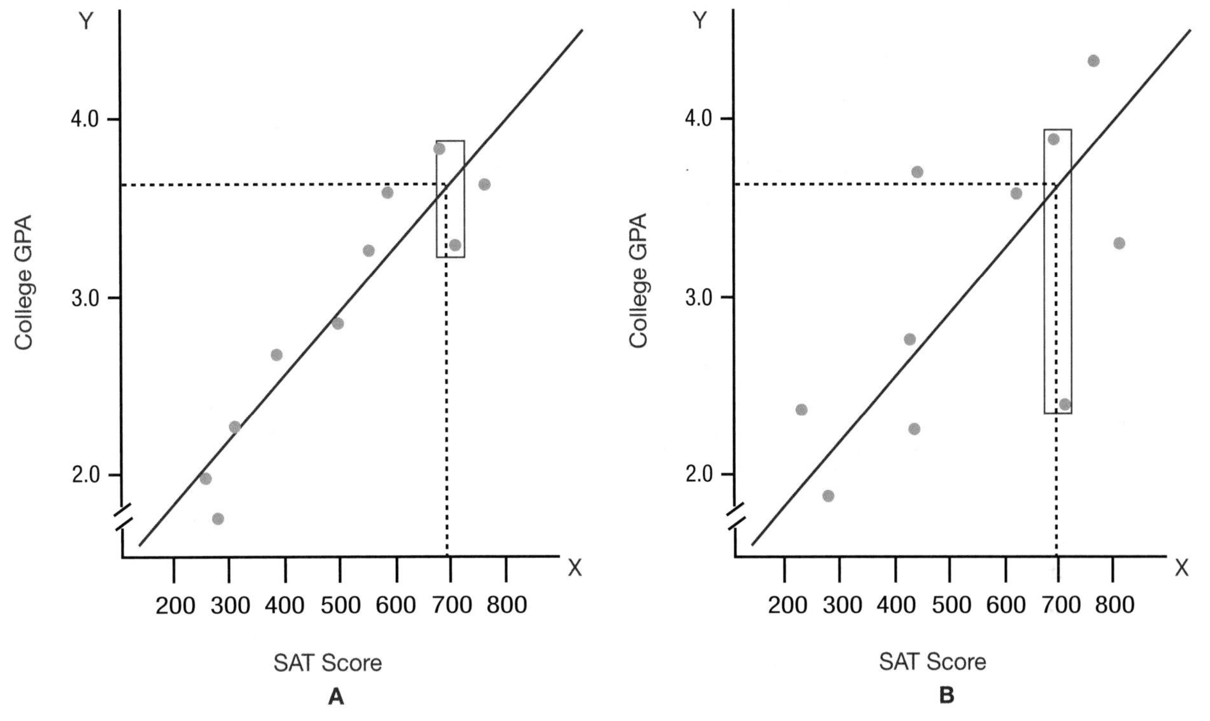

can use the line as a way to predict the GPA given a student's SAT score. For example, consider a student who scores 700 on the SAT; we draw a vertical line up from 700 until it intersects the regression line, and then we draw a horizontal line from this point to the Y axis and read off the predicted GPA. In this case, we come up with a prediction of 3.6 for the student's GPA.

This procedure will not give us perfect predictions. Not all students scoring 700 on their SAT had 3.6 averages in college; some were higher than 3.6 and some lower. As we have said, the main factor in determining the accuracy of the predictions is the degree of correlation between the two variables. If the variables are highly correlated, as depicted in Panel A, all the points will cluster closer to the regression line, and none of the predictions are likely to be far off. In fact, if the correlation were perfect, all the points would be right on the line, and there would be no error. (All students with 700 SATs would get 3.6 GPAs.) On the other hand, with low correlations, the points will be widely scattered, and many of them will be a long way from the regression line, as depicted in Panel B of Figure A-8. In such a case, the predictions can sometimes be way off. Take a look at the GPAs of the students who scored around 700 on the SAT in the two panels; these points are boxed in on the graphs. In the left panel, which depicts a high correlation, you can see that all the students ended up with high college GPAs, and all were fairly close to 3.6, the average we would predict using the regression line. In contrast, in the right panel, the students with 700 on the SAT varied widely in their GPAs, with some as low as 2.2 and others as high as 3.95. Regression would have predicted 3.6 for all of them, but this prediction would have been way off for some students. *The lower the correlation is between the two variables, the less precise will be our predictions*. In fact, if the correlation drops to

Multiple Regression Using more than one predictor variable to predict a response variable

Random Sample Sample group of a larger population that is selected by randomization procedures (a random sample differs from a representative sample)

zero, a regression equation will not improve our prediction at all—once again, our best guess would be the mean. Given some degree of correlation, however, we can do better using regression than by simply guessing the mean, and the higher the correlation is, the better our predictions will be.

Often, there is more than one variable that is correlated with the criterion (the number we are trying to predict). In such cases, a procedure called **multiple regression** can be used to improve and maximize the accuracy of our predictions. For example, in addition to SAT scores, we might also know each student's high school GPA and rank in his or her high school class. Rank, GPA, and SAT scores all could then be combined by using multiple regression to predict college GPA. Multiple regression techniques are also used by stockbrokers to predict the direction and amount of change in the price of a particular stock. As you can imagine, knowledge of an accurate set of predictor variables in this case could be quite valuable.

A.2 Inferential Statistics

Inferential statistics are used to make inferences from data, to draw conclusions, and to test hypotheses. Two of the basic concepts in inferential statistics are *estimation* and *hypothesis testing.*

A.2a Estimation

One use of inferential statistics is to estimate the actual value of some population characteristic. Suppose, for example, we wanted to know how knowledgeable, on average, U.S. adults are about current events. We could construct a test of current events with carefully worded questions covering as many areas of current news as possible. Since we are interested in the population of all adults in the U.S., we could test every American age 18 and older (the entire population) and compute a mean score on our test. However, it would be handy to have a short-cut method that did not require testing the entire population.

In order to estimate the mean and standard deviation of a variable in a population, we take a *sample* of the population and measure the variable in each member of the sample. We then compute the statistics from the sample scores and use these statistics to estimate what the mean and standard deviation would be if we could test every member of the population. For example, we might sample 200 U.S. adults and use their scores on our current events test to estimate what the whole population of adults is like. Public opinion polls and the TV rating services use this sampling approach and estimation procedure.

It is important that the sample be *representative* of the population, which is usually done by making the sample a random selection from all possible members of the population. A **random sample** is one in which everyone in the specified population has the same chance of being in the sample. For example, it would not be a fair sample for estimating Americans' knowledge of current events if we included only white female citizens of La Mirada, California. The second factor in sampling is sample size. A general rule is the larger the sample, the more accurate the estimates. If you randomly chose one person from the phone book, scheduled him or her for our test of current events, got a score, and then estimated that this score was the mean for all U.S. adults, you would almost certainly be off the mark. A sample larger than a single person is needed. How many should there be in the sample? The amazing thing about sampling is that the size of the sample necessary to get a fairly accurate idea of the population is much smaller than you might guess. A sample of 200 U.S. adults out of 150 million, if properly drawn, should provide a very accurate estimate of the entire population. There are ways of estimating how big a sample you need for a given level of accuracy. Of course, if the sample is not properly drawn and is not representative, then increasing the sample size will not improve the accuracy of estimation.

t-test A statistical test used to compare two sample means

A.2b Hypothesis Testing

When we set out to do an experiment in psychology, we always begin with a hypothesis. For our brief discussion, we use the example of a psychologist who wants to know if breathing pure oxygen after strenuous exertion facilitates recovery. The psychologist carefully devises a test of recovery time that gives a consistent score (i.e., it is a reliable measure) and accurately predicts recovery in real-life situations (i.e., it is a valid measure). The experimental hypothesis in the study is that athletes who breathe pure oxygen after exercise will recover more quickly than athletes who breathe normal air. The psychologist gets 30 athletes to volunteer for the experiment and randomly assigns them to one of two groups, 15 per group. The random assignment is designed to create two groups that are approximately equal in average recovery time at the start of the experiment. All of the subjects are then instructed to run 800 meters as quickly as they can. Immediately following each subject's run, they are seated and fitted with a breathing mask that delivers either pure oxygen or normal air. Heart rate and respiration rates are measured to determine recovery time.

After all of the subjects are tested, the psychologist finds that the mean recovery time for the athletes breathing pure oxygen was 118 seconds, and the mean recovery time for athletes breathing normal air was 126 seconds. Can the researcher conclude that breathing pure oxygen facilitates recovery? Think about your answer before reading on.

If the differences between the recovery times for the two groups were quite large (118 vs. 156 seconds) our psychologist could be confident that breathing pure oxygen does in fact facilitate recovery. Likewise, if the difference in recovery times was very small (118 vs. 119 seconds), we would be fairly confident that breathing pure oxygen had no effect. What do we conclude about results that fall between these extremes?

There has to be an objective way to decide whether or not the psychologist's hypothesis can be accepted. We cannot leave it up to intuition. Here we can turn to inferential statistics. There are many different kinds of inferential statistics; in this case a **t-test** for comparing two sample means is appropriate.

We want to decide whether the difference between 118 (the mean recovery time for athletes breathing pure oxygen) and 126 seconds (the mean recovery time for the athletes breathing normal air) is a real difference or whether it can be attributed to chance or measurement error. In other words, is it a *statistically significant difference*? A difference is said to be statistically significant if it is very unlikely that it would happen by chance alone. The difference in mean recovery times for the two groups is 8 seconds ($126 - 118 = 8$).

For a moment, let's assume that oxygen has no effect on recovery times. This assumption is called the *null hypothesis*. Note that the null hypothesis predicts no difference, whereas our experimental hypothesis (that breathing pure oxygen facilitates recovery) does predict a difference. Specifically, the null hypothesis predicts that the variable being manipulated (the independent variable) will have no effect on the behavior being measured (the dependent variable). It is the null hypothesis that is actually tested with inferential statistics. We then draw conclusions about our experimental hypothesis on the basis of our findings regarding the null hypothesis.

Figure A-9 Comparisons of Three Outcomes in Variability

Each figure shows the same mean (118 vs. 126) with different amounts of variability.

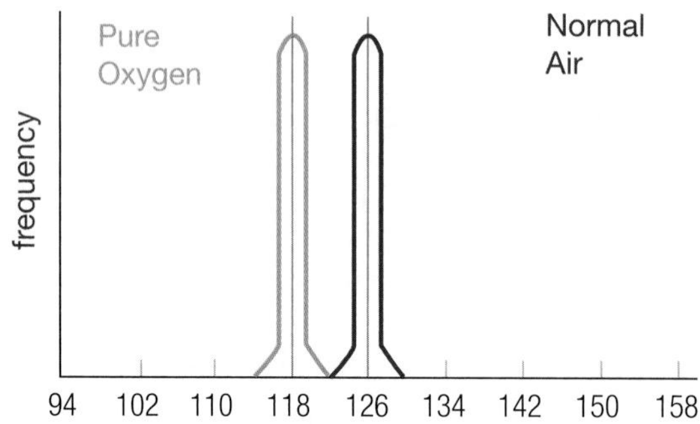

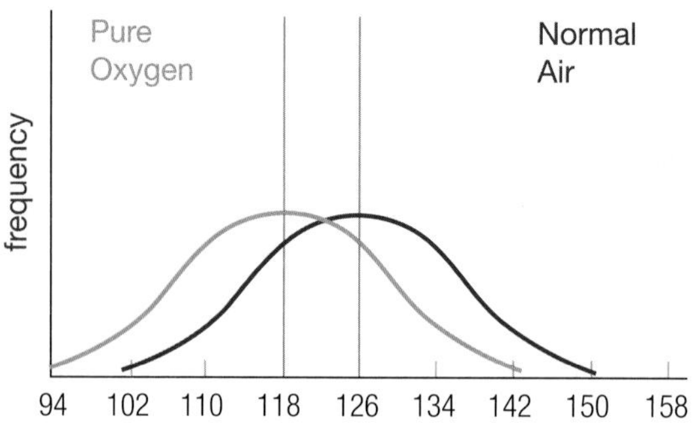

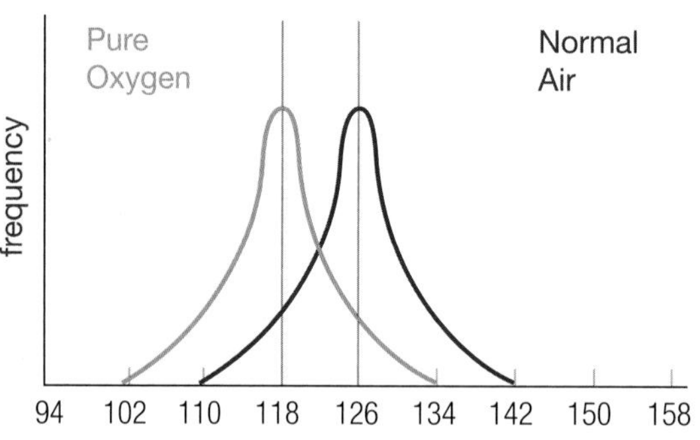

What we need to know is if the null hypothesis is true (that breathing pure oxygen does not affect recovery time), what is the probability that the two samples will differ by 8 seconds? If oxygen does not facilitate recovery, then any difference we find between our two groups will be just a chance difference. After all, we would not expect two random groups of 15 people to have exactly the same recovery times. Sample means will differ, and every once in a while there will be a difference of 8 seconds by chance alone, with no help from oxygen. The question remains, how often will we get a difference this large? Or, what is the probability of this difference occurring by chance alone?

In order to answer this question, we must know not only the mean values, but also the standard deviations in the two samples. We have to know how much variability between people there is in recovery times. Look at the three panels in Figure A-9. Each panel shows two frequency distributions, one for the oxygen group and one for the normal air group. Note that in each panel, the mean of the oxygen group is 118, and the mean of the normal air group is 126, but the three panels display quite different pictures in terms of variability in recovery times among people within each group. In the top panel, the variability within each group is very small (all of the recovery times are close to their respective means). In this case it looks as though the 8-second difference is a significant one.

In the middle panel, there is a great deal of variability in recovery times between people within each group. There is a lot of overlap in the two distributions. Many of the subjects breathing normal air recovered more quickly than the mean for the oxygen group. In fact, there is so much overlap in the two distributions that we would probably question whether the difference between 118 and 126 (the two means), which is very small compared to the variability, is just a chance difference. The two distributions look almost identical.

Situations like those depicted in the top panel are very rare indeed. Unfortunately, the middle panel is a more common outcome of an experiment—the means are so close together and there is so much overlap of scores that the groups appear to be indistinguishable on the dependent variable. The bottom panel represents the most common outcome of all. Here, the conclusion is less clear. The two distributions overlap somewhat, much more than in the top panel, but much less than in the middle panel. There is a moderate amount of variability among subjects within each group. Can we conclude whether the 118- to 126-second mean difference is a real one? Stated differently, is there a statistically significant difference between the means?

The *t*-test is designed to answer this question. The *t*-test is a ratio, the ratio of mean difference to an error term. A primary factor in the error term is the variability of scores within each group. In the top panel, the difference is 8 seconds, but the variability of scores within each group is very small. Therefore, the error term will be small. So if we divide the mean difference by this very small error term, we shall get a large number for the *t* statistic, and we then declare the difference to be significant. In the middle panel, the same 8-second difference will be divided by a very large error term, giving us a very small *t* value. We declare the difference nonsignificant. In the bottom panel, we have the borderline case. We divide the mean difference by a moderate-sized error term, and the *t* value obtained will be moderately large. What do we conclude? Fortunately for us, statisticians have prepared tables of the probability of various values of *t* occurring by chance. We compute the *t* statistic and then look it up in the statistical tables to find the chance probability of a *t* as large as the one we found. If the table tells us that the observed *t* statistic is unlikely to happen by chance, we conclude that what we have is not a chance effect but a real difference. Alternatively, most computer solutions to *t*-tests give the exact probability for each computed value of *t*. By convention, we use a cutoff probability of .05. That is, if the probability of obtaining a given *t* value is less than or equal to .05 we conclude that there is a significant difference between the two groups.

The null hypothesis says, "There is no difference in recovery times between groups breathing pure oxygen and those breathing normal air." If we obtain a significant *t* statistic, we conclude that the null hypothesis is wrong. Statistical inference is basically a procedure for drawing conclusions about the null hypothesis. Of course, our inference about the null hypothesis has implications for our experimental hypothesis. If we reject the null hypothesis and conclude that the observed difference between the groups is significant,

BVT*Lab*

Visit **www.BVTLab.com** to explore the student resources available for this chapter.

Table A-9 Type I and Type II Errors in Decisions Based on Experimental Data

Research Hypotheses	
Experimental Hypothesis	**Null Hypothesis**
Oxygen Facilitates Recovery	Oxygen Does Not Facilitate Recovery

Decision Errors
Type I Error: Rejecting the Null Hypothesis When It Is True
Example: Claiming oxygen facilitates recovery when in fact oxygen does not facilitate recovery
Type II Error: Accepting the Null Hypothesis When It Is False
Example: Concluding that oxygen does not facilitate recovery when in fact oxygen facilitates recovery

then we can further conclude that breathing pure oxygen does facilitate recovery because the athletes in our study who used pure oxygen recovered more quickly than athletes who did not breathe pure oxygen.

We do not discuss the details of actually calculating a t statistic. You can find that information in any elementary statistics book. Simply remember that when an experiment is done, the results will usually indicate some differences between the conditions in the study. The t-test, as well as many other types of inferential statistics, is used to help the experimenter decide whether the differences are large enough, relative to the variability, to allow rejection of the null hypothesis and support for the experimental hypothesis.

It is important to realize that statistical decisions are not always perfect; sometimes we make an incorrect decision on the basis of the data even though we have done everything correctly. There is always the chance, for example, that the samples are not truly representative of the populations from which they were drawn. There are two types of errors that can occur when we draw conclusions from experimental data, and these are depicted in Table A-9. A *Type I Error* is made when we conclude that the independent variable has an effect on the dependent variable, when the truth of the matter is that it has no effect. A *Type II Error* is made when we conclude that the independent variable has no effect on the dependent variable when, in fact, it does. Each type of error has a certain probability of occurring in any given experiment. By tradition, we require strong evidence for an effect of the independent variable on the dependent variable before we accept that such an effect exists. What this means is that we try to minimize the level of Type I Errors. However, you should note that Type I Errors and Type II Errors have an inverse relationship to one another—as one increases, the other decreases. Therefore, minimizing Type I Errors will normally result in an increase in Type II Errors. The task for the researcher is to balance these two types of errors, which requires a thorough understanding of research design and statistical procedures.

A.3 Advanced Statistical Techniques

A.3a Analysis of Variance

The *t*-test is used when testing the difference between the means of two groups. However, experiments may have more than two groups, and so the *t*-test is not used in such cases. Instead, a statistical procedure called **analysis of variance** is used. Analysis of variance is conceptually very similar to the *t*-test. The size of the mean difference between groups is compared to an error term that is, in part, a function of the variability within each group. In fact, the analysis of variance procedure and the *t*-test will lead to the same decision in the special case where there are just two groups. The test in analysis of variance is known as the *F*-test, named after the famous English statistician R. A. Fisher. Analysis of variance allows the experimenter to make inferences or draw conclusions about the differences among a set of means. It is a very common statistical procedure, and you are likely to encounter the *F*-test if you read psychology journals.

Analysis of Variance A statistical test used to compare more than two sample means

A.3b Factor Analysis

Factor analysis is a highly sophisticated correlational procedure that is used to identify the basic factors underlying a psychological phenomenon. The technique boils down to finding clusters of tests that correlate with one another. Suppose we administer the following six tests to 100 college students: (1) vocabulary, (2) ability to shoot baskets, (3) ability to write an essay on philosophy, (4) speed at running the 100-yard dash, (5) ability to understand statistics, and (6) speed at swimming 100 meters. Each person takes all six tests, and then we intercorrelate the tests. We correlate test 1 with 2, 1 with 3, 1 with 4, and so on. Suppose we find that tests 1, 3, and 5 correlate highly with one another and that 2, 4, and 6 correlate highly with one another, but that 1, 3, and 5 show little or no correlation with 2, 4, and 6. Why would this result be the case? Look at the tests: Tests 1, 3, and 5 all involve thinking or knowledge—they all require "academic ability." On the other hand, tests 2, 4, and 6 all require "physical ability." So probably 1, 3, and 5 all are measuring something in common, which we might call Factor A. Would you guess that Factor A has something to do with intelligence? Tests 2, 4, and 6 also seem to be measuring something in common. We will call it Factor B. Because tests 1, 3, and 5 do not correlate with tests 2, 4, and 6, we conclude that Factor A, which we now have decided to call *intelligence*, is not the same thing as Factor B, which we might label *athletic ability*.

In short, we have isolated two factors that are involved in performance on our six tests; one we call intelligence, and the other we call athletic ability. Factor analysis is basically a correlational technique that allows us to separate performance on a large number of tests into factors, by isolating clusters of tests (even when the clustering is not as obvious as it is in the foregoing example). Correlations between tests are high within a cluster but low among clusters. We assume that the clusters then "represent" and measure psychological factors.

This technique has been used extensively in two areas of psychology—intelligence testing and personality assessment. Intelligence consists of many factors, as does personality. With factor analysis, we can identify these factors and hope to learn more about intelligence and personality.

TERMS AND CONCEPTS

Analysis of Variance, pg. 743
Correlation Coefficient, pg. 732
Linear Regression, pg. 736
Mean, pg. 721
Median, pg. 722
Mode, pg. 724
Multiple Regression , pg. 738
Normal Distribution, pg. 728
Pearson Product-Moment Correlation Coefficient, pg. 735
Probability, pg. 731
Random Sample, pg. 738
Range, pg. 725
Standard Deviation, pg. 728
t-test, pg. 739
Variance, pg. 727

POP QUIZ

True or False

___ 1. A distribution of scores that is asymmetrical and unbalanced is said to be a normal distribution.

___ 2. A *z* score of +2.0 corresponds to a score two standard deviations above the mean.

___ 3. A scatter plot is used to visualize a frequency distribution.

___ 4. If tests of statistical significance indicate that the null hypothesis would only happen 5 percent of the time or less by chance, then psychologists would conclude that it was not a chance event but a real effect.

___ 5. Factor analysis is a highly sophisticated correlational procedure.

Multiple Choice

6. Descriptive statistics include all of the following concepts except which one?
   a. Measures of variability
   b. Correlation
   c. Hypothesis testing
   d. Measures of central tendency
7. In the distribution of scores 1, 1, 2, 3, 5, 6, which is the median?
   a. 1.0
   b. 2.0
   c. 2.5
   d. 3.0
8. The standard deviation is a better estimate of the variability of a distribution than the range because the standard deviation ______.
   a. is easier to compute
   b. is about the same as the mean, anyway
   c. relies on the median
   d. is less influenced by extreme scores
9. In a normal distribution of scores, more individuals would fall between *z*-scores from ________ than in the other three choices.
   a. 0 to +1.0
   b. +1.0 to +2.0
   c. +2.0 to +3.0
   d. +1.0 to +3.0

POP QUIZ

10. What does the correlation coefficient describe?
    a. Probability that scores vary together
    b. Pearson Product-Moment score
    c. Relationship between individual scores
    d. Degree of relationship between variables
11. The Pearson Product-Moment Correlation Coefficient measure of correlation can take on any numerical value from –1.0 to +1.0. The size of the correlation represents the ________ of the relationship, and the sign of the correlation represents the ________ of the relationship between two variables.
    a. degree/direction
    b. direction/range
    c. range/degree
    d. direction/degree
12. If you know an individual's score on one variable (e.g., height), you would use ________ to predict his or her score on a second variable (e.g., weight).
    a. estimation
    b. regression
    c. the median
    d. the correlation coefficient
13. Inferential statistics, such as the *t*-test, actually test which of the following?
    a. Experimental hypothesis
    b. Alternative hypothesis
    c. Null hypothesis
    d. Probability that the experiment worked out
14. What is a statistic commonly used to decide if there is a statistically significant difference between the means of two groups?
    a. *z*-score
    b. Pearson Product-Moment Correlation Coefficient
    c. *t*-test
    d. *F*-test
15. You conduct an experiment on the effects of caffeine on resting heart rate. You have four groups of subjects who receive different dosages of caffeine (no caffeine, low dose, medium dose, and high dose). You should use a(n) ________ to analyze the results of your study.
    a. factor analysis
    b. analysis of variance
    c. *t*-test
    d. correlation

Answer Key: 1.F 2.T 3.F 4.T 5.T 6.c 7.c 8.d 9.a 10.d 11.a 12.b 13.c 14.c 15.b

Glossary

A

Abnormal Behavior Behavior that is atypical, maladaptive, or socially unacceptable, or that produces emotional discomfort

Absolute Threshold Minimum physical intensity of a stimulus that can be perceived by an observer 50 percent of the time

Accommodation In vision, the focusing process in which the lens adjusts its shape, depending on the distance between the eye and the object viewed, in order to project a clear image consistently onto the retina; in Piaget's theory, the process of adjusting existing knowledge so that new information can fit more readily

Acetylcholine (ACh) The neurotransmitter that is released from motor neurons onto muscle fibers to make them contract; also involved in learning, memory, and cognition

Achievement Test Test designed to measure an individual's learning (as opposed to the ability to learn new information)

Acquisition In Pavlovian conditioning, the process of learning to associate a conditioned stimulus with an unconditioned stimulus; in operant conditioning, the process of learning to associate responses with a reinforcer or punisher

Acronym Meaningful arrangement of letters that provides a cue for recalling information—a mnemonic device

Acrostics Sentences whose first letters serve as cues for recalling specific information—a mnemonic device

Action Potential Electrical signal that flows along the surface of the axon to the terminal buttons, initiating the release of neurotransmitters

Addiction A brain disease caused by repeated administration of drugs that rapidly increase dopamine activity resulting in structural and functional changes to the mesolimbic system and frontal cortex (not all drugs that cause dependence necessarily cause addiction)

Additive Color Mixing Color mixing that occurs when lights of different wavelengths simultaneously stimulate the retina, so that color perception depends on the adding or combining of these wavelengths

Adolescence A period of transition from childhood to adulthood beginning around puberty and extending to adulthood (typically the teenage years, from thirteen to twenty years of age)

Adolescent Growth Spurt Period of accelerated growth that usually occurs within about two years after the onset of puberty

Adrenal Glands Glands within the endocrine system, located just above the kidneys, that influence emotional state, energy levels, and responses to stress by releasing hormones

Aerial (Atmospheric) Perspective Monocular distance cue based on the fact that distant objects tend to appear fuzzier and less clear than those close to the viewer due to dust and haze

Agnosia An inability to know or recognize objects through the senses, usually caused by brain injury or disease, resulting in the failure to recognize or identify objects visually even though they can be seen

Agoraphobia An anxiety disorder characterized by an intense fear of being in places or situations from which escape might be difficult or in which help might not be available, such as stores, theaters, and trains; often accompanies panic disorder

Agreeableness A personality trait characterized by compassion, cooperation, and good-naturedness

Algorithm A step-by-step problem-solving procedure often used in a systematic exploration of every possible solution (usually requiring the use of computers)

All-or-None Law An action potential will be passed through a neuron's axon as long as the sum of the graded potentials reaches a threshold (The strength of an action potential does not vary according to the degree of stimulation.)

Alternate-Forms Reliability Method of assessing test reliability in which subjects take two different forms of a test that are very similar in content and level of difficulty

Alzheimer's Disease An incurable disease that destroys neural tissue, resulting in an impaired capacity to remember, think, relate to others, and care for oneself

American Psychological Association (**APA**) The major professional organization of psychologists in the United States

Amphetamines A group of powerful stimulants, including Benzedrine, Dexedrine, and Ritalin, that dramatically increase alertness and promote a feeling of euphoria

Amygdala A small limbic system structure located next to the hippocampus in the brain; plays an important role in the expression of anger, rage, fear, and aggressive behavior

Anal Stage In Freud's theory of psychosexual development, the period between about twelve months and three years of age, during which the erogenous zone shifts from the mouth to the anal area

Analysis of Variance A statistical test used to compare more than two sample means

Anandamide A naturally occurring substance that binds to THC receptors in the brain; marijuana contains THC, which also binds to these receptors.

Androgen Insensitivity Syndrome (**AIS**) Condition in which the body cells of a chromosomally normal (XY) male fetus are insensitive to the action of androgens, with the result that internal reproductive structures do not develop, external genitals fail to differentiate into a penis and scrotum, and testes do not descend

Androgens Male sex hormones, the most common of which is testosterone

Andropause A condition of low testosterone often attributed to the natural loss of testosterone production in older men; also referred to as *male menopause*

Anorexia Nervosa Eating disorder characterized by prolonged refusal to eat adequate amounts of food; most common among young adults

Anterograde Amnesia Memory loss for information processed after an individual experiences brain trauma caused by injury or chronic alcoholism

Antidepressant Drugs Drugs used to treat major depressive disorder; include the tricyclics, MAOIs, SNRIs, and SSRIs

Antimanic Drugs Drugs used to control the manic symptoms of bipolar disorder and hypomania

Antipsychotic Drugs Drugs used to treat psychotic disorders such as schizophrenia

Antisocial Personality Disorder Personality disorder characterized by disregard for rights of others, lack of remorse or guilt for antisocial acts, irresponsibility in job or marital roles, failure to learn from experience, and a profound poverty of deep and lasting emotions

Anxiety Free-floating fear or apprehension that may occur with or without an easily identifiable source

Anxiety Disorder Any of a number of disorders that produce pervasive feelings of anxiety

Anxiolytic Drugs Drugs used to reduce symptoms of anxiety and promote sleep; sometimes called minor tranquilizers

Aptitude Test Test designed to predict an individual's ability to learn new information or skills

Archetypes Powerful, emotionally charged universal images or concepts in Carl Jung's theory of the collective unconscious

Arcuate Nucleus An area of the hypothalamus, adjacent to the ventromedial nucleus, that regulates the secretion of neuropeptide Y and insulin

Arousal A physiological state in which an individual is able to process information effectively and to engage in motivated behavior

Artificial Intelligence (**AI**) Field of specialization in which researchers develop computer models to simulate human cognitive processes and to solve problems

Assimilation In Piaget's theory, the process by which individuals interpret new information in accordance with existing knowledge or schemas

Association Cortex The largest portion of the cerebral cortex (about 75 percent), involved in integrating sensory and motor messages as well as processing higher functions such as thinking, interpreting, and remembering

Association for Psychological Science (**APS**) Professional group of academic and research psychologists founded in 1988

Associative Learning Learning by making an association between two stimulus events (Pavlovian conditioning) or by learning an association between a response and its consequence (operant conditioning)

Attachment Intense emotional tie between two individuals, such as an infant and a parent

Attention-Deficit/Hyperactivity Disorder (ADHD) A neurodevelopmental disorder characterized by inattention, lack of impulse control, and hyperactivity.

Attention Psychological selection mechanism that determines which stimuli an organism responds to or perceives

Attitude Any learned, relatively enduring predisposition to respond in consistently favorable or unfavorable ways to certain people, groups, ideas, or situations

Attribution Theory Theory that we attempt to make sense out of other people's behavior by attributing it to either dispositional (internal) causes or situational (external) causes

Auditory Cortex Region of the temporal lobe located just below the lateral fissure; involved in responding to auditory signals, particularly the sound of human speech

Auditory Localization Ability to locate the origins of sounds by differences from ear to ear in variables such as intensity and the time the sound arrives at each ear

Authoritarian Style of parenting in which parents rely on strictly enforced rules, leaving little room for children to discuss alternatives

Authoritative Style of parenting in which parents enforce clear rules and standards but also show respect for children's opinions

Autonomic Nervous System (ANS) A part of the peripheral nervous system that transmits messages between the central nervous system and the endocrine system, as well as to the smooth muscles of the heart, lungs, stomach, and other internal organs that operate without intentional control

Availability Heuristic Approach to decision making based on information assessed from memory (assumes that the probability of an event is related to how frequently it occurred in the past and that events occurring more frequently are easier to remember)

Avoidance Conditioning In operant conditioning, the learning of a response to a discriminative stimulus that allows an organism to avoid exposure to an aversive stimulus

Axon Extension of a neuron that transmits an impulse from the cell body to the terminal buttons on the tip of the axon

Axon Hillock A specialized region of the cell body near the base of the axon

B

Backward Conditioning In Pavlovian conditioning, presenting the unconditioned stimulus prior to the conditioned stimulus (backward conditioning results in little or no conditioning)

Basal Ganglia A group of brain structures that lie under the cerebral cortex and function as "way stations" between the input of sensory messages and resulting cortically initiated motor or cognitive outputs

Basal Ganglia Neural structures involved in the initiation of motor movement and emotion; includes the caudate nucleus, putamen, and the substantia nigra

Basilar Membrane Membrane in the cochlea of the inner ear that vibrates in response to pressure waves, causing auditory hair cells on the adjoining organ of Corti to release neurotransmitters that activate neurons of the auditory nerve

Behavioral Observation Behavior assessment method that involves observing individuals' behavior as they interact with the environment

Behaviorism Scientific approach to the study of behavior that emphasizes the relationship between environmental events and an organism's behavior

Behavior Therapy Therapy based on the assumption that maladaptive behavior has been learned and can therefore be unlearned

Belief-Bias Effect Tendency to accept conclusions that conform to one's beliefs (and reject conclusions that do not conform), regardless of how logical or illogical these conclusions are

Between-Group Differences Differences, or response variability, between treatment conditions

Binocular Cues Visual cues for depth or distance, such as binocular disparity and convergence, that depend on both eyes working together

Binocular (Retinal) Disparity The difference in the retinal image of an object as seen from each eye, due to the difference in viewing angles, that provides an important binocular cue for depth; also known as *retinal disparity*

Biologically Based Motives Motives such as hunger and thirst that are rooted primarily in body tissue needs; sometimes referred to as *drives*

Biological Psychology Branch of neuroscience, also known as *physiological psychology*, that focuses on the relationship between behavior and physiological events within the brain and the rest of the nervous system

Biological Rhythms Natural variations in biological functions, hormonal activity, temperature, and sleep that typically cycle every twenty-four to twenty-five hours, also called *circadian rhythms*

Bipolar Disorder A psychiatric disorder characterized by extreme mood swings from immobilizing depression to euphoria and frantic activity; previously referred to as *manic-depressive disorder*

Blood-Brain Barrier Glial cells tightly packed around capillaries in the brain to prevent substances from entering or leaving the blood

Body Senses Term used to describe the two interrelated sensory systems of kinesthesis and equilibrium

Bottom-Up Processing Perceptual processing that begins in peripheral sensory receptors and then activates higher cortical areas

Brain Stimulation Technique for studying the brain that involves stimulating precise regions with a weak electric current

Brightness Constancy An element of perceptual constancy perceiving objects that we see at night or in poor lighting to be the same brightness as they appear during the day

Brightness Intensity of light, measured by the number of photons, or particles of electromagnetic radiation, emitted by a light source

Broca's Aphasia The loss of the ability to speak or understand spoken or written language; also known as *expressive aphasia*

Broca's Area Region of the left frontal lobe that is the primary brain center for controlling speech

Bulimia Eating disorder characterized by periodic episodes of binge eating followed by deliberate purging using either vomiting or laxatives

C

Cancer A collection of many diseases, all of which result from genetic alterations in cells that produce runaway cell growth

Cannon-Bard Theory Theory that emotions occur simultaneously with physiological changes, rather than deriving from body changes, as the James-Lange theory suggests

Cardinal Trait In Gordon Allport's trait theory of personality, a powerful, dominating behavioral predisposition that is an organizing principle in the lives of a small number of people

Case Study Method of research that involves in-depth study of one or more participants who are examined individually using direct observation, testing, experimentation, and other methods

Caudate Nucleus A component of the basal ganglia located adjacent to the putamen; involved with the control and initiation of motor movement; an area of the brain affected by Huntington's disease

Cell Body The largest part of a neuron, containing the nucleus as well as structures that handle metabolic functions

Central Nervous System (CNS) The part of the nervous system that consists of the brain and the spinal cord

Central Nucleus of the Amygdala Region within the amygdala that integrates sensory information related to fear and aggression and sends output to numerous parts of the body for emotional responses

Central Trait In Gordon Allport's trait theory of personality, a major characteristic, such as honesty or sensitivity

Centration Inability to take into account more than one perceptual factor at a time; in Piaget's theory of cognitive development, characteristic of the preoperational stage of development

Cephalocaudal Pattern of physical and motor development that is normal among humans, in which the head and upper portion of the body develop first and more rapidly

Cerebellum Brain structure located beneath the overhanging back part of the cerebral hemispheres that functions to coordinate and regulate motor movements

Cerebral Cortex Thin outer layer of the brain's cerebrum (sometimes called the gray matter) that is responsible for movement, perception, thinking, and memory

Cerebral Hemispheres The two sides (right and left) of the cerebrum

Cholecystokinin (CCK) A hormone that regulates the rate of food digestion and decreases appetite by affecting neurons in the hypothalamus

Chromosome A strand of DNA that contains the organism's genes

Chunking Process of grouping items into longer meaningful units to make them easier to remember

Cingulate Cortex Area of the cortex deep in the midline that interprets emotional responses as a feeling state

Cingulotomy A surgical procedure partially separating the cingulate cortex from the frontal lobes that is performed to treat severe obsessive-compulsive disorder

Climacteric Physiological changes, including menopause, that occur during a woman's transition from fertility to infertility

Clinical Psychology Area of specialization involved in the diagnosis and treatment of behavioral problems

Closure Perceptual organizing principle that we tend to perceive incomplete figures as complete

Clustering Mnemonic device that involves grouping items into categories

Cochlea Coiled, fluid-filled chamber in the inner ear with two flexible surfaces: the oval window and the round window

Coefficient of Correlation Statistic used to describe the degree of relationship between two or more variables in which positive correlations indicate that variables vary together in the same direction and negative correlations indicate the opposite

Cognitive Dissonance Theory The theory that people experience psychological discomfort or dissonance whenever cognitions and behaviors are in conflict

Cognitive Expectancy A learned expectancy of relationships between stimuli (in Pavlovian conditioning) and between responses and outcomes (in operant conditioning)

Cognitive Learning Theory Theoretical perspective that attempts to study the role of thinking and memory processes in learning

Cognitive Map Internal representation of the relationship between events or spatial elements

Cognitive Psychology Approach to psychology that focuses on the ways in which organisms process information and investigates processes such as thinking, memory, language, problem solving, and creativity

Cognitive Restructuring Therapy Cognitive therapy aimed at restructuring irrational thinking patterns such as the tendency to use negative self-labels

Cognitive Therapies Approaches to therapy that are based on the premise that most behavioral disorders result from distortions in cognitions or thoughts

Cohabitate Living together in a sexual relationship without being married

Cohort An experimental group of participants with similar characteristics or who share a particular experience

Collective Unconscious In Carl Jung's theory, a kind of universal memory bank that contains all the ancestral memories, images, symbols, and ideas that humans have accumulated throughout their evolution

Color Constancy An element of perceptual constancy perceiving objects that we see in the dark to be the same color as they appear during the day even though their retinal images change

Compliance Form of social influence in which people alter their behavior in response to direct requests from others; usually involves a degree of coercion

Computerized Axial Tomography (CAT) A procedure used to locate brain abnormalities that involves rotating an X-ray scanner around the skull to produce an accurate image of a living brain

Concepts Cognitive categories for grouping events, objects, or processes

Concordance Degree to which twins share a trait—expressed as a correlation coefficient

Concrete Operations Stage Third stage of cognitive development in Piaget's theory (ages seven through twelve years), during which children begin to use logical mental operations or rules, mastering the concept of conservation

Concurrent Validity Type of criterion-related validity that involves comparing test performance to other criteria that are currently available

Conditioned Reinforcer A stimulus that takes on reinforcing properties after being associated with a primary reinforcer

Conditioned Response (CR) In Pavlovian conditioning, a learned response to a conditioned stimulus

Conditioned Stimulus (CS) In Pavlovian conditioning, a stimulus that elicits a response only after being associated with an unconditioned stimulus

Conditioned Taste Aversion A learned aversion to a relatively novel taste or smell that occurs followed by illness or nausea

Conductive Hearing Loss Hearing loss caused by the failure of the outer and middle ear to conduct sound energy to the inner ear's receptors, sometimes because of an infection or buildup of ear wax

Cones Photoreceptor cells distributed across the inner layer of the retina that play an important role in the perception of color

Confirmation Bias In problem solving, the tendency to seek out evidence that confirms a hypothesis and to overlook contradictory evidence

Conformity Tendency to change or modify behaviors so that they are consistent with those of other people

Connectionism The learning theory that says learning is the result of forming associations or connections between stimuli and responses (Modern connectionism is focused on discovering the neurobiological mechanisms underlying learned associations.)

Conscientiousness A personality trait characterized by self-discipline, responsibility, and dependability

Consciousness A sense of self and the world around us

Conservation The understanding that changing the form of an object does not necessarily change its essential character; a key to achievement in Piaget's theory of cognitive development

Consolidation Process by which information is transferred from short-term electrical activation of neuronal circuits to a longer-term memory coded by physical cell changes in the brain

Continuous Reinforcement Schedule In operant conditioning, the presentation of a reinforcer for each occurrence of a specific behavior

Control Group In experimental psychology, a group of participants who experience all the same conditions as participants in the experimental group except for the key factor (independent variable) the researcher is evaluating

Conventional Morality Second level in Lawrence Kohlberg's theory of moral development, consisting of Stages 3 and 4, in which the motivating force for moral behavior is the desire either to help others or to gain approval

Convergence Binocular distance cue based on the fact that the two eyes must converge or rotate toward the inside to perceive objects closer than about 25 feet (The closer the object, the more rotation is necessary and the more muscle tension created.)

Conversion Disorder
Somatic symptom disorder that is manifested as a sensory or motor system disorder for which there is no known organic cause

Coronary Heart Disease (CHD) Any illness that causes a narrowing of the coronary arteries

Corpus Callosum Broad band of nerve fibers that connects the left and right hemispheres of the cerebral cortex

Correlational Method Research method that uses statistical techniques to determine the degree of relationship between variables

Correlation Coefficient Statistics used to describe the degree of relationship between two or more variables. Positive correlations indicate that variables vary together in the same direction; negative correlations indicate the opposite

Correspondent Inference Theory Theory that the attributions we make about other people's behavior are influenced by a variety of conditions, such as the social desirability of that behavior or whether the behavior results from free choice

Cortisol A stress hormone released by the adrenal glands that is known to decrease immune functioning and increase disease susceptibility

Counseling Psychology Area of specialization involved in the diagnosis and treatment of problems of adjustment (Counseling psychologists tend to focus on less serious problems than do clinical psychologists; they often work in settings such as schools.)

Covariation Principle Theory that our attributions about people's behavior are influenced by the situations in which the behavior occurs, the persons involved, and the stimuli or objects toward which the behavior is directed

Covert Behavior Behavior that is unobservable in another person (e.g., thinking)

Criterion-Related Validity Method of assessing test validity that involves comparing peoples' test scores with their scores on other measures already known to be good indicators of the skill or trait being assessed

Critical Period A time during development when specific systems, structures, or abilities are most sensitive to external factors (such as specific stimuli and experiences, as well as the chemical environment surrounding tissues)

Critical Period Periods in the developmental sequence during which an organism must experience certain kinds of social or sensory experiences in order for normal development to take place

Cross-Sectional Design Research design in which groups of subjects of different ages are assessed and compared at one point in time, so that conclusions may be drawn about behavior differences that may be related to age differences

Cross-Sequential Design Research design that combines elements of the cross-sectional and longitudinal designs by observing subjects more than once over a relatively short period

Crystallized Intelligence Intelligence that results from accumulated knowledge, including knowledge of how to reason, language skills, and understanding of technology

Cultural Mores Established customs or beliefs in a particular culture

Cultural Psychology A field that investigates how cultural and religious traditions and practices shape and contribute to differences in human behavior

Cumulative Record A chart recording of operant responses over time; the time increment is indicated along the horizontal axis (as response rate increases, the slope of the record increases)

D

Dark Adaptation Process by which an organism's vision gradually becomes more sensitive to minimal levels of light due to a chemical change in the rods and cones of the retina

Decentration Ability to evaluate two or more physical dimensions simultaneously

Declarative Memory Recall of specific facts, such as information read in a book

Deductive Reasoning Reasoning that begins with a general premise that is believed to be true, then draws conclusions about specific instances based on this premise

Deep Brain Stimulation (DBS) An invasive procedure in which an electrode is implanted deep in the brain and electrical current can be applied periodically

Defense Mechanism In Freud's psychoanalytic theory, an unconscious maneuver that shields the ego from anxiety by denying or distorting reality

Delayed Conditioning In Pavlovian conditioning, learning that takes place when the conditioned stimulus is presented just before the unconditioned stimulus is presented and continues until the organism begins responding to the unconditioned stimulus

Delusion An exaggerated and rigidly held belief that has little or no basis in fact

Dendrite Branch-like extensions from a neuron with the specialized function of receiving messages from surrounding neurons

Dependence Physiological adaptation to repeated drug administration that can lead to withdrawal symptoms upon cessation of drug use

Dependent Variable In experimental research, the behavior that results from manipulation of an independent variable

Depersonalization-Derealization Disorder A persistent detachment from one's thoughts, feelings, or body sensations

Depressants Psychoactive drugs, including opiates, sedatives, and alcohol, that have the effect of slowing down or depressing central nervous system activity

Depressive Disorders Class of disorders, including major depression, dysthymic disorders, and substance induced depression, characterized by persistent depression

Descriptive Statistics Mathematical and graphical methods for reducing data to a form that can be readily understood

Developmental Psychology Field of specialization in psychology concerned with factors that influence development and shape behavior throughout the life cycle, from conception through old age

Difference Threshold The minimum difference in intensity that we can distinguish between two stimuli 50 percent of the time; also known as the *just noticeable difference (jnd)*

Diffusion of Responsibility or **Bystander Apathy** Tendency for an individual to feel a diminished sense of responsibility to assist in an emergency when other bystanders are present

Direct Perception The interpretation of sensory information directly by the brain as opposed to perceptual interpretation resulting from cognitive processing

Discrimination In Pavlovian and operant conditioning, the process by which responses are restricted to specific stimuli; in social psychology, the behavioral consequence of prejudice in which one group is treated differently from another group

Discriminative Stimulus In operant conditioning, a stimulus that controls a response by signaling the availability of reinforcement

Displacement Defense mechanism in which a person diverts his or her impulse-driven behavior from a primary target to secondary targets that will arouse less anxiety

Dissociation Theory A theory of hypnosis, proposed by Ernest Hilgard, in which our behaviors become separated from or dissociated from our awareness

Dissociative Amnesia An inability to recall important autobiographical information after a traumatic or stressful episode

Dissociative Disorders Group of disorders, including psychogenic amnesia, depersonalization-derealization disorder, and dissociative identity disorder, in which the thoughts and feelings that generate anxiety are separated or dissociated from conscious awareness

Dissociative Identity Disorder A condition of separation in personality, or multiple personality, not attributable to disease or brain injury; previously called multiple personality disorder

DNA (Deoxyribonucleic Acid) Chemical substance whose molecules, arranged in varying patterns, are the building blocks of genes

Dominant Gene Gene that prevails when paired with a recessive gene, so that it is always expressed in the phenotype

Door-in-the-Face Technique Method for encouraging compliance in which an unreasonable request is followed by a more minor, reasonable request that is the requester's goal in the first place

Dopamine A neurotransmitter involved with the initiation of motor movement, attention, and learning and memory; the dopamine system mediates reward and pleasure and is the substance of addiction

Down Syndrome Chromosomal disorder characterized by marked intellectual disability as well as distinctive physical traits, including short stature, a flattened skull and nose, and an extra fold of skin over the eyelid; also known as trisomy 21 because it is caused by an extra (third) copy of the twenty-first chromosome

Dream Analysis Psychoanalytic technique involving the interpretation of dreams to learn about hidden aspects of personality

Drive Commonly used to describe motives that are based on tissue needs, such as hunger and thirst

Dual-Code Model of Memory Theory that memories may be stored either in sensory codes or in verbal codes

E

Echoic Memory Auditory sensory memory; fleeting impressions of what we hear; also known as *auditory memory*

Echolalia Speech disturbance characteristic of some forms of schizophrenia in which people repeat virtually every statement they hear uttered

Educational Psychology Field of specialization in psychology concerned with the study and application of learning and teaching methods, focusing on areas such as improving educational curricula and training teachers

Egocentrism The tendency of young children to view the world as being centered around themselves

Ego In Freud's psychoanalytic theory, the component of personality that acts as an intermediary between the instinctual demands of the id and the reality of the real world

Eidetic Imagery The very rare ability to retain large amounts of visual material with great accuracy for several minutes; also known as *photographic memory*

Elaborative Rehearsal System for remembering that involves using mnemonic devices (more effective than maintenance rehearsal)

Electra Complex The female counterpart to the Oedipus complex

Electrical Recording Technique for studying the brain in which tiny wires implanted in the brain are used to record neural electrical activity

Electroconvulsive Therapy (ECT) A method to induce seizures by strong electrical current applied to the brain; used to treat depression

Electroencephalography (EEG) Technique used to measure and record electrical activity of the cortex

Embryonic Stage Second stage of prenatal development, lasting from the beginning of the third week to the end of the eighth week after fertilization, characterized by fast growth and differentiation of the major body systems as well as vital organs

Emotions Changes in physiological and behavioral states caused by a stimulus or stimulus context (Many of our emotions are experienced as feelings or moods.)

Encoding In memory, the process of perceiving information and then categorizing or organizing it in a meaningful way so that it can be more easily stored and recalled

Endocrine System System of ductless glands, including the pituitary, thyroid, parathyroids, adrenals, pancreas, and gonads, that secrete hormones directly into the bloodstream or lymph fluids

Endorphins A class of neurotransmitter substances that function to inhibit the transmission of pain information; morphine and other opiates act by facilitating endorphin transmission

Engram A neural representation of a specific memory

Epigenetic Processes that alter gene expression without changing the DNA

Epigenetics A field of genetics that investigates how gene expression is influenced by a number of environmental events including experiences, diet, and environmental toxins

Episodic Memory Autobiographical memories about one's own experiences

Equilibrium The sense of balance, localized within the inner ear and comprising two sensory receptors: the semicircular canals and the vestibular sacs

Escape Conditioning In operant conditioning, learning that takes place when an organism performs a response that will terminate an aversive stimulus

Estrogens Hormones that influence female sexual development

Ethology The scientific study of the evolution of the behavior of animals, including humans

Evolutionary Psychology A recent approach to both investigating and explaining human behavior in terms of natural selection

Excitatory Postsynaptic Potentials (EPSPs) Effects that result from excitatory neurotransmitters causing a depolarizing graded potential to occur on the dendrite or cell body of a receiving neuron, making the receiving neuron more likely to fire

Exemplar Theory Theory that the natural concepts we form in everyday life are structured around prototypes or typical representatives of categories (such as robins and jays as prototypes of the concept *bird*)

Experimental Group In experimental research, a group of participants who are exposed to different varieties of independent variables, so that resulting behaviors can be compared

Experimental Psychology Field of specialization in which the primary activity is conducting research

Experimental Research Research conducted in precisely controlled laboratory conditions in which participants are confronted with specific stimuli and their reactions are carefully measured to discover relationships among variables

Explicit Memory Memory that a person can recall through conscious effort

Extinction In Pavlovian conditioning, the process by which a conditioned response is eliminated through repeated presentation of the conditioned stimulus without the unconditioned stimulus; in operant conditioning, the process of eliminating a response by discontinuing reinforcement for it

Extraversion (alternate spelling of Extroversion used in the Five-Factor Model) An outgoing personality trait characterized by an energetic, gregarious, and positive outlook (In Jung's definition: Extroversion, a personality trait manifested by sociability, friendliness, and interest in people and events in the external world)

F

Facial Feedback Theory Theory proposing that feedback from facial muscles intensifies the feeling of an emotion

False Consensus Bias Attribution bias caused by the assumption that most people share our own attitudes and behaviors

False Memory A memory of an event that never occurred; can be "planted" in a subject prior to recall by a variety of methods, including hypnosis

Fetal Alcohol Syndrome A pattern of physical, neurological, and cognitive abnormalities that result from fetal exposure to alcohol

Fetally Androgenized Female Chromosomally normal (XX) female who, as a result of excessive exposure to androgens during prenatal sex differentiation, develops external genitalia resembling those of a male

Fetal Stage Third and final stage of prenatal development, extending from the beginning of the third month to birth, during which bone and muscle tissue form and the organs and body systems continue to develop

Fetus The developing infant after the embryonic stage up to the time of birth; see also *fetal stage*

Figure In perception, the part of an image on which we focus our attention

Five-Factor Model of Personality Defines personality by five basic dimensions: neuroticism, extraversion, openness to experience, agreeableness, and conscientiousness

Fixation In Freud's theory of psychosexual development, arrested development that results from exposure to either too little or too much gratification

Fixed Interval (FI) Schedule Partial reinforcement schedule in operant conditioning in which reinforcement is provided for the first response after a specified time has elapsed

Fixed Ratio (FR) Schedule Partial reinforcement schedule in operant conditioning in which reinforcement occurs after a fixed number of responses

Flashbulb Memory An apparent vivid recall for an event associated with extreme emotion or uniqueness, such as the assassination of a president

Fluid Intelligence Ability to perceive and draw inferences about relationships among patterns of stimuli, to conceptualize abstract information, and to solve problems

Foot-in-the-Door Technique Technique for encouraging compliance in which a person is first asked to agree to a relatively minor request that serves as a setup for a more major request

Forensic Psychology Field of specialization that works with the legal, court, and correctional systems to develop personality profiles of criminals, make decisions about disposition of convicted offenders, and help law enforcers understand behavioral problems

Formal Operations Stage Fourth and final stage in Piaget's theory of cognitive development (ages twelve and up), during which individuals acquire the ability to make complex deductions and solve problems by systematically testing hypotheses

Fraternal Twins Twins produced when two ova are fertilized by two different sperm cells, so that their genetic codes are no more similar than those of any other siblings; also known as *two-egg twins* or *dizygotic twins*

Free Association Psychoanalytic technique developed by Sigmund Freud in which patients relax and say whatever comes to their minds

Free Will The assertion that our choices and actions are not caused by antecedent events, but emerge spontaneously from the mind

Frequency Theory of Pitch Discrimination Theory that perception of low tones depends on the frequency with which auditory hair cells in the inner ear's organ of Corti trigger the firing of neurons in the auditory nerve

Frontal Lobe Largest, foremost lobe in the cerebral cortex; an important region for movement, emotion, and memory

Frustration-Aggression Hypothesis Theory that aggression is always a consequence of frustration and that frustration leads to aggression

Functional Fixedness A failure to use familiar objects or strategies in novel or unfamiliar settings to solve problems

Functionalism Approach to psychology that emphasized the functional, practical nature of the mind; influenced by Darwin's theory of natural selection, functionalists attempted to learn how mental processes—such as learning, thinking, and perceiving—helped people adapt

Functional Magnetic Resonance Imaging (fMRI) A method of magnetic resonance imaging that measures energy released by brain cells that are active during a specific task

Fundamental Attribution Error Tendency to overestimate dispositional (internal) causes of behavior and to underestimate situational (external) causes of behavior

G

Gambler's Fallacy An incorrect assumption that randomness must result in an increase (or decrease) in the probability of an event in repeated trials when the event has only rarely or never occurred, even though the probability of the event remains the same

Gamete The reproductive cells, or sperm and ovum; also called *germ cells*

Gamma-Amino-Butyric Acid (GABA) The major inhibitory neurotransmitter in the brain and spinal cord that plays an important role in regulating arousal and anxiety

Gate-Control Theory Theory that neural gates in the spinal cord allow passage of pain signals to the brain (These gates may be closed by the simultaneous firing of nonpain nerve fibers, so that pain is not perceived.)

Gender Identity An individual's subjective sense of being male or female

Gender Role Set of behaviors that is considered normal and appropriate for each sex in a society

General Adaptation Syndrome (GAS) Progressive responses to prolonged exposure to stressful events during which an organism mobilizes for action and compensates for stress

Generalization Process by which an organism responds to stimuli that are similar to the conditioned stimulus, without undergoing conditioning for each similar stimulus

Generalized Anxiety Disorder (GAD) A chronic state of free-floating anxiety or worry that has persisted for at least six months

Genital Stage Fifth and final stage in Freud's theory of psychosexual development, beginning with puberty, during which sexual feelings that were dormant during the latency stage reemerge

Genotype Assortment of genes each individual inherits at conception

Germinal Stage First of three stages in prenatal development of a fetus that spans the first two weeks after fertilization; also known as the *zygote stage*

Gestalt Psychology Approach to psychology that argues that the whole of an experience is different from the sum of its parts; an active force in current investigations of perceptual processes and learning, as well as therapy, where it emphasizes the whole person

G-Factor One of the factors in Charles Spearman's conceptualization of intelligence; consists of general intelligence, which is largely genetically determined

Gibson's Theory of Direct Perception A theory of perception that argues that all information necessary for perception is available to the sensory system and no cognitive processing is necessary to complete the perceptual process

Glia Non-neuronal cells that provide support and protection for neurons throughout the nervous system (The name glia comes from the Greek term for glue.)

Glucostatic Hypothesis Theory that hunger results when glucoreceptors detect a lack of glucose, either because blood levels of glucose are low or because insulin is not available in sufficient quantity

Glutamate (Glutamic Acid) An amino acid derived from glucose that plays an important excitatory function (found in MSG)

Gonadotropins Hormones released by the pituitary gland that stimulate production of testosterone in men and estrogen in women

Gonads Glands within the endocrine system (ovaries in females and testes in males) that produce sex hormones, which influence development of sexual systems and secondary sex characteristics as well as sexual motivation

Good Continuation Perceptual grouping principle that we are more likely to perceive stimuli as a whole or single group if they flow smoothly into one another than if they are discontinuous

Graded Potential Voltage change in a neuron's dendrites that is produced by receiving a signal from another neuron or neurons

Ground In perception, the background against which the figure that we focus on stands

Groupthink A psychological drive for consensus at any cost that suppresses dissent and consideration of alternatives in group decision making

Gustation The sense of taste, which, like olfaction, is activated by chemical senses in the environment

H

Hallucination False perception that lacks a sensory basis; can be produced by hallucinogenic drugs, fatigue, or sensory deprivation (Auditory hallucinations can be associated with severe psychotic disorders.)

Hallucinogens Class of psychoactive drugs, including LSD and ecstasy, that alter sensory perceptions, thinking processes, and emotions, often causing delusions, hallucinations, and altered sense of time and space

Halo Effect Tendency to infer other positive or negative traits from our perception of one trait in another person

Health Psychology Area of specialization concerned with the interaction between behavioral factors and physical health

Hebbian Rule Information is transferred to long-term memory when new connections between neurons are formed (These changes are thought to involve structural changes in the synapses between neurons, which occur when cell assemblies are simultaneously activated.)

Height on a Plane Important monocular depth cue based on the fact that objects that are highest on one's plane of view appear to be farthest away

Heritability An estimate ranging from 0 to 1.0 that indicates the proportion of variance in a trait that is accounted for by heredity

Hermaphrodite Individual with ambiguous or contradictory sex characteristics resulting from abnormal differentiation of internal and external sex structures

Heterozygous Genotype that contains different genes for a trait (for instance, both brown-eye and blue-eye genes)

Heuristics Rule-of-thumb (quick-fix) problem-solving strategies such as means-ends analysis and working backward

Hindsight Bias The tendency to believe we could have foreseen an event after it has occurred

Hippocampus Structure in the brain's limbic system that seems to play an important role in memory

Homosexuality Primary erotic, psychological, and social interest in members of the same sex, even though that interest may not be expressed overtly

Homozygous Genotype that consists of the same gene for a trait (for instance, brown-eye genes inherited from both parents)

Hormones Chemical messengers secreted by the endocrine glands that act to regulate the functioning of specific body organs

Hue The color we perceive, determined partly by the wavelength of light and partly by the complex process by which an organism's visual system mixes wavelengths

Humanistic Psychology Approach to psychology that emphasizes the role of free choice and our ability to make conscious rational decisions about how we live our lives

Huntington's Disease A genetically transmitted disease that progressively destroys brain cells in adults; also known as *Huntington's chorea*

H-Y Antigen Substance that appears to trigger the transformation of gonads into testes within the first few weeks of prenatal development

Hypertension Commonly referred to as high blood pressure: A condition of excessive blood flow through the vessels that can result in both hardening and general deterioration of the walls of the vessels

Hypnosis State of altered consciousness characterized by a deep relaxation and detachment, as well as heightened suggestibility to the hypnotist's directives

Hypnotic Suggestibility The predisposition to attend to a hypnotist's suggestions

Hypomania A mood characterized by persistent and pervasive elevated mood (a mood state less severe than mania)

Hypothalamus Small structure located below the thalamus in the brain that plays an important role in motivation and emotional expression, as well as controlling the neuroendocrine system and maintaining the body's homeostasis; part of the limbic system

Hypothesis Statement proposing the existence of a relationship between variables, typically as a tentative explanation for cause and effect; often designed to be tested by research

I

Iconic Memory Visual sensory memory, including fleeting impressions of what we see; also known as visual memory

Identical Twins Twins who share the same genetic code; also known as *one-egg twins* or *monozygotic twins*

Id In Freud's psychoanalytic theory, the biological component of personality consisting of life instincts and death instincts

Illness Anxiety Disorder A somatic disorder in which the individual is excessively fearful of contracting a serious illness or of dying; previously referred to as *hypochondria*

Illusion False or inaccurate perception that differs from the actual physical state of the perceived object

Illusion of Control Attributional bias caused by the belief that we control events in our own lives that are really beyond our control

Immune System A complex surveillance system that guards the body by recognizing and removing bacteria, cancer cells, and other hazardous foreign substances

Implicit Association Test (IAT) Test that attempts to measure the strength of a person's implicit attitudes

Implicit Attitude
Unconscious attitude that may be socially undesirable and may influence one's behavior without one's knowledge

Implicit Memories Memories that are unavailable to conscious awareness but contribute to explicit memories

Implicit Personality Theories Assumptions people make about how traits usually occur together in other people's personalities

Impression Management Tendency of individuals to carefully select what information they reveal about their attitudes, depending on how they think such information will affect their image in the eyes of others

Imprinting Process by which certain infant animals, such as ducklings, learn to follow or approach the first moving object they see

Inattentional Blindness The failure to see one aspect of a visual scene due to selective attention to another aspect of the scene

Incentive Any external stimulus that can motivate behavior even when no internal drive state exists

Independent Variable Condition or factor that the experimenter manipulates in order to determine whether changes in behavior (the dependent variable) result

Indiscriminate Attachment Attachment typically displayed by human infants during the first few months, when social behaviors are directed to virtually anyone

Inductive Reasoning Reasoning that draws broad conclusions by generalizing from specific instances

Industrial/Organizational (I/O) Psychology Field of specialization concerned with using psychological concepts to make the workplace a more satisfying environment for employees and management

Inferential Statistics Process of using mathematical procedures to draw conclusions about the meaning of research data

Informational Social Influence One basis of conformity in which we accept a group's beliefs or behaviors as providing accurate information about reality

Information-Processing Model of Memory A model of memory that proposes three stages in memory processing: sensory memories, working (short-term) memories, and long-term memories

Ingroup In social psychology, the group in which people include themselves when they divide the world into "us" and "them"

Ingroup Bias Tendency to see one's own group in a favorable light

Inhibitory Postsynaptic Potentials (IPSPs) Effects that occur when inhibitory neurotransmitters cause a hyperpolarizing graded postsynaptic potential on a receiving neuron, making the receiving neuron less likely to fire

Insomnia Sleep disorder characterized by a consistent inability to get to sleep or by frequent awakening during sleep

Instincts Innate patterns of behavior that occur in every normally functioning member of a species under certain set conditions

Intelligence According to David Wechsler, the global capacity of a person to act purposefully, to think rationally, and to deal effectively with his or her environment

Intelligence Quotient (IQ) Intelligence measurement derived by dividing an individual's mental age by the chronological age and then multiplying by 100

Interactionist Approach An approach to language acquisition that assumes that both genes and the environment interact during development

Interneuron Neuron of the central nervous system that functions as an intermediary between sensory and motor neurons

Interpersonal Aggression Any physical or verbal behavior intended to hurt another person

Interview Method used in psychological studies in which an individual is asked questions that may be informal and unstructured or highly structured

Introversion Personality trait expressed as shyness, reclusiveness, and preoccupation with the inner world of thoughts, memories, and feelings

Invariant Sensory information from the environment that is constant from one experience to the next (for example, texture is invariant because it is always finer at close distances than at further distances)

J

James-Lange Theory Theory that explains emotional states (such as fear) resulting from an organism's awareness of bodily responses to a situation, rather than from cognitions about that situation

K

Kinesthesis Bodily sense that provides information about perceptions of the location of various body parts in relation to other parts and about the position of the body in space

Klüver-Bucy Syndrome A pattern of emotional deficit seen after damage to the amygdala

L

Language Acquisition Device (LAD) According to the genetic or nativist view, the prewiring that gives humans the innate ability to learn and understand language (the more modern term for LAD is *universal grammar*)

Language A system of symbols and rules that enable us to communicate

Latency Period Fourth stage of psychosexual development in Freud's theory, extending from about age five to puberty, during which sexual drives remain unexpressed or latent

Latent Content In psychoanalysis theory, the hidden content or true meaning of dreams

Latent Learning Learning that is not demonstrated by an immediately observable change in behavior

Lateral Hypothalamus (LH) An area of the hypothalamus that is important for taste sensation, mediating digestive processes, and salivation

Lateralization of Function Degree to which a particular function, such as the understanding of speech, is controlled by one rather than both, cerebral hemispheres

Law of Effect Behavior followed by reinforcement will be strengthened, whereas behavior followed by punishment will be weakened (theory, originally proposed by Edward Thorndike, that is the foundation of the operant conditioning theory)

Learned Helplessness A diminished ability to learn an avoidance response following exposure to unavoidable aversive stimulation may contribute to some forms of depression and nonresponsiveness in humans and other animals

Learning Relatively enduring change in potential behavior that results from experience

Leptin A hormone that is produced by fat cells and appears to signal satiety to neurons in the hypothalamus

Lesion Production Technique for studying the brain that involves surgical damage to a precise region of the brain (most commonly done with experimental animals)

Libido In Freud's psychoanalytic theory, the energy that fuels the id and motivates all behavior

Light Adaptation Process by which an organism's vision adjusts to bright lighting, due to a chemical change within the rods and cones of the retina

Limbic System Collection of structures located around the central core of the brain that play a critical role in emotional expression, as well as motivation, learning, and memory; key structures of the limbic system include the amygdala, the septal area, and parts of the hypothalamus

Linear Perspective Important monocular distance cue based on the fact that parallel lines converge when stretched into the distance

Linear Regression A mathematical method to determine the slope and *y*-intercept of a straight line through a scatter plot using the general linear model $y = m(x) + b$, where m is the slope and b is the *y*-intercept of the regression line

Lipid Solubility Lipid-soluble substances can dissolve in a cell's membrane, making it possible to leave the blood supply and enter other cells, including neurons in the brain or all fetal tissues

Lobotomy Surgical procedure that severs the nerve tracts connecting the prefrontal cortex to lower brain areas that mediate emotional responses

Longitudinal Design Research design that evaluates a group of subjects at several points in time, over a number of years, to assess how certain characteristics or behaviors change during the course of development

Long-Term Memory (LTM) Information transferred from short-term to long-term memory may be stored for periods of time from minutes to years—perhaps even indefinitely

Long-Term Potentiation (LTP) An increase in a neuron's sensitivity to fire following a burst of signals to that neuron's dendrites

Loudness In hearing, the intensity of a sound as measured by decibels, which is determined by the amplitude of a sound wave

LSD (Lysergic Acid Diethylamide) Hallucinogenic drug derived from a fungus that grows on rye grass that produces profound distortions of sensations, feelings, time, and thought

M

Magnetic Resonance Imaging (MRI) Procedure for studying the brain that uses radio waves to excite hydrogen protons in the brain tissue, creating a magnetic field change

Magnetic Seizure Therapy (MST) A method of inducing seizures using strong magnetic fields as opposed to electrical current; used to treat depression, bipolar disorder, and schizophrenia

Maintenance Rehearsal System for remembering that involves repeatedly rehearsing information without attempting to find meaning in it

Major Depressive Disorder The persistent feeling of intense sadness, loss, and worthlessness, often accompanied by thoughts of suicide

Mania A mood state characterized by expanded self-esteem, reduced need for sleep, excessive talking about extravagant ideas, and delusions

Manifest Content In psychoanalytic theory, the disguised version of the latent content, or true meaning, of dreams

Marijuana Drug derived from the hemp plant *Cannabis sativa*, containing the chemical THC (delta 9-tetrahydrocannabinol)

Maturation Orderly unfolding of certain patterns of behavior, such as language acquisition or walking, in accordance with genetic blueprints

Mean In descriptive statistics, the arithmetic average obtained by adding scores and dividing by the number of scores

Means-Ends Analysis Common heuristic problem-solving strategy that involves identifying the difference between an original state and a desired goal and then progressing through a series of subgoals to reach the solution

Measure of Central Tendency In descriptive statistics, a value that reflects the middle or central point of a distribution of scores; the three measures of central tendency are the mean, the median, and the mode

Measure of Variability In descriptive statistics, a measure that indicates whether distribution scores are clustered closely around their average or widely spread out; two measures of variability are the range and the standard deviation

Median In descriptive statistics, the score that falls in the middle of a distribution of numbers arranged from the lowest to the highest

Medulla Structure found low in the brain that controls vital life support functions such as breathing, heartbeat, and blood pressure, as well as many reflexive functions, such as coughing and sneezing

Melatonin A hormone produced by the pineal gland that regulates circadian rhythms (Melatonin may promote sleep onset in individuals with insomnia or those who have traveled east.)

Memory (1) Process or processes of storing newly acquired information for later recall (2) recall for a specific experience, or the total collection of remembered experiences stored in our brains

Menopause Cessation of menstruation that takes place during the climacteric

Mental Age In IQ testing, the chronological age of children who, on the average, receive a test score similar to that of the subject (e.g., a six-year-old whose composited score is equivalent to that of a nine-year-old has a mental age of nine)

Mental Set In problem solving, a tendency to approach a problem or situation in a predetermined way, regardless of the requirement of the specific problem

Mere Exposure Effect Phenomenon by which repeated exposure to novel stimuli tends to increase an individual's preference for such stimuli

Mesolimbic-Cortical System The system of dopamine-containing neurons that originate in the ventral pons, project through the nucleus accumbens and septum, and terminate in the frontal cortex; mediates the reinforcing effects of eating, sex, and addictive drugs

Misinformation Effect The presentation of misleading information that leads people to erroneous reports of that misinformation

Mnemonic Device Memory system, such as clustering or acrostics, that organizes material in a meaningful way to make it easier to remember

Mode In descriptive statistics, the score that occurs most frequently in a distribution of numbers

Modeling Learning process in which an individual acquires a behavior by observing someone else performing that behavior; also known as *observational learning*

Monoamine Theory The first formal biochemical theory of mood disorders; proposes that depression is related to reduction in activity of the monoamine neurotransmitters norepinephrine and/or serotonin in specific regions of the brain

Monocular Cues Distance cues, such as linear perspective and height on a plane, that can be used with just one eye

Morpheme Smallest unit of meaning in a given language

Motivation A condition or state that energizes and directs an organism's actions

Motor Cortex Region of the cerebral cortex that transmits messages to muscles and controls virtually all intentional body movements

Motor Neuron Neuron that transmits messages from the central nervous system to muscles or glands—also known as efferent neuron

Multiple Regression Using more than one predictor variable to predict a response variable

Mutism Speech disturbance characteristic of schizophrenia in which an individual may not utter a sound for hours or days at a time

Myelin Sheath Insulating cover around some axons that increases a neuron's ability to transmit impulses quickly; made of specialized cells called glial cells

N

Narcolepsy Sleep disorder characterized by falling asleep suddenly and uncontrollably

Naturalistic Observation Psychological research using the observational method that takes place in a natural setting, such as a participant's home or school environment

Nature-Nurture Controversy Controversy over whether individual differences are the result of genetic endowment (nature) or the consequence of learning (nurture)

Need for Achievement (nAch) Complex psychosocial motive to accomplish difficult goals, attain high standards, surpass the achievements of others, and increase self-regard by succeeding in exercising talent

Negative Reinforcement In operant conditioning, any stimulus that increases the probability of a response through its removal (For example, pounding on the wall [operant behavior] may be maintained by the termination of a loud noise [negative reinforcer] in an adjoining room.)

Negative Symptoms Represent diminished or absent behavior of schizophrenia; may include flattened emotions, diminished social behavior, apathy, anhedonia, and catatonic motor behavior

Neo-Freudian Psychologists who were in general agreement with Freud's basic interpretation of the structure of personality, his focus on the unconscious, and his emphasis on childhood experience, but dissented regarding other aspects of Freud's theory, such as his emphasis on aggressive impulses and unconscious sexual conflicts

Nerve A cable-like bundle of myelinated axons that transmits signals from various structures of the body to the spinal cord and the brain

Nervous System A network of specialized cells called neurons and glia that coordinate action and transmit signals between different parts of the body; consists of the central nervous system and the peripheral nervous system

Neuron Type of cell that is the basic unit of the nervous system (A neuron typically consists of a cell body, dendrites, and an axon. Neurons transmit messages to other neurons and to glands and muscles throughout the body.)

Neuropeptide Y (NPY) A potent stimulator of appetite and a regulator of insulin secretion

Neuroticism Negative emotionality characterized by the ease with and extent to which people experience negative emotions

Neurotransmitter Chemical substance produced and secreted by neurons that causes a change in the receiving neuron's resting potential

Nightmare Bad dream that occurs during REM sleep

Nociceptor A sensory receptor specialized in transmitting pain signals to the spinal cord

Node of Ranvier Small gap or exposed portion of the axon of a neuron between the glial cells that form the myelin sheath

Norepinephrine A major excitatory neurotransmitter in the brain that is distributed throughout the central and peripheral nervous systems and is important in emotional arousal and stress

Normal Distribution In descriptive statistics, a distribution in which scores are distributed similarly on both sides of the middle value, so that they have the appearance of a bell-shaped curve when graphed

Normative Social Influence Social influence in which we conform not because of an actual change in our beliefs, but because we think we will benefit in some way (such as gaining approval)

Norm Standard that reflects the normal or average performance of a particular group of people on a measure such as an IQ test

NREM (Non-Rapid Eye Movement) Sleep Stages of sleep during which rapid eye movements typically do not occur (Dreaming occurs far less frequently during NREM sleep than during REM sleep.)

O

Obedience Social influence in which we alter our behavior in response to commands or orders from people perceived as having power or authority

Obesity Condition in which an individual weighs 20 percent or more above the desirable weight for his or her height

Object Permanence Realization that objects continue to exist even when they are not in view; according to Piaget, a key achievement of the sensorimotor stage of development

Observational Learning Learning process in which an individual acquires a behavior by observing someone else performing that behavior; also known as *modeling*

Observational Method Method of psychological research, providing descriptive information, in which participants are observed as they go about their usual activities

Observer Bias Tendency of an observer to read more into a situation than is actually there or to see; what he or she expects to see a potential limitation of the observational method

Observer Effect Tendency of participants to modify behavior because they are aware of being observed

Obsessive-Compulsive Disorder (OCD) Anxiety disorder characterized by persistent, unwanted, and unshakable thoughts or irresistible, habitual repeated actions

Occipital Lobe Region at the rear of the cerebral cortex that consists primarily of the visual cortex

Oedipus Complex In Freud's theory of psychosexual development, the attraction a male child feels toward his mother (and jealousy toward his father) during the phallic stage

Olfaction The sense of smell, which, like taste, is activated by chemical substances in the environment

Openness to Experiences A personality trait characterized by the enjoyment of adventure and new ideas

Operant Conditioning Learning an association between one's behavior and its consequence (reinforcement or punishment)

Operant Conditioning Therapies Behavior modification techniques that attempt to influence behavior by manipulating reinforcers

Operational Definition Definition specifying the operations that are used to measure or observe a variable, such as a definition of obesity specifying a certain weight-height relationship

Opiates (Narcotics) A class of depressant drugs that includes opium, morphine, codeine, and heroin

Opponent-Process Theory of Color Vision Theory that explains color vision based on six primary colors, which are grouped into three pairs: red-green, blue-yellow, black-white (Receptors in the eye are sensitive to specific pairs, and the presence of one member of a pair inhibits perception of the other.)

Opponent-Process Theory of Emotion Theory that when a strong emotional response to a particular stimulus disrupts emotional balance, an opposite emotional response is eventually activated to restore emotional equilibrium

Optimum Level of Arousal Level of arousal at which an individual's performance on a specific task is most efficient

Oral Stage According to Freud, the first stage of psychosexual development, spanning birth through twelve to eighteen months, during which the lips and mouth are the primary erogenous zone

Organic Amnesia Memory deficits caused by altered physiology of the brain, which might result from an accident or certain physical illnesses

Organ of Corti Structure in the inner ear located directly above the basilar membrane, consisting of auditory hair cells, a tectorial membrane, and cilia

Organ Reserve Potential ability of organs such as the heart, lungs, and kidneys to increase their output to a level several times greater than normal under emergency conditions

Ossicles Set of three tiny linked bones (the malleus, incus, and stapes) in the middle ear that receive a sound stimulus from the tympanic membrane and transfer it to the oval window of the inner ear

Outgroup The "them" group when individuals divide the world into "us" and "them"

Overlap Important monocular distance cue based on the fact that objects close to us tend to block out parts of objects that are farther away; also known as *interposition*

Overlearning Technique for memorizing material that involves rehearsing information after it has already been learned

P

Panic Disorder Anxiety disorder in which an individual experiences numerous panic attacks (four or more in a four-week period) that are characterized by overwhelming terror and often a feeling of unreality or depersonalization

Paper-and-Pencil Questionnaire In personality testing, an objective, self-reporting inventory designed to scientifically measure the variety of characteristics or traits that make up personality

Parasympathetic Nervous System A part of the autonomic nervous system that functions to conserve energy, returning the body to normal from emergency responses set in motion by the sympathetic nervous system

Parietal Lobe Region of the cerebral cortex located just behind the central fissure and above the lateral fissure; contains the somatosensory cortex as well as association areas that process sensory information received by the somatosensory cortex

Partial Reinforcement Effect Behaviors that are acquired on partial instead of continuous reinforcement schedules tend to be established more slowly but are more persistent when no reinforcement is provided

Partial Reinforcement Schedule In operant conditioning, a schedule that reinforces behavior only part of the time—for example, a ratio or interval schedule

Pavlovian Conditioning Learning that takes place when a neutral stimulus (CS) is paired with a stimulus that already produces a response (After conditioning, the organism responds to the CS in some way. The response to the CS is called a conditioned response.)

Pavlovian (or Classical) Conditioning Therapy Any behavior therapy that involves Pavlovian conditioning such as systematic desensitization therapy

Pearson Product-Moment Correlation Coefficient The most frequently used measure of correlation, ranging from –1.0 to +1.0. Correlations close to zero indicate little or no relationship between two variables; correlations close to + 1.0 or –1.0 indicate more significant positive or negative relationships

Penis Envy A reaction to the realization that a young girl did not have a penis (also, later in life, the source of a woman's jealousy of the power men held)

Percentile Numbers from a range of data indicating percentages of scores that lie below them

Perception Process of interpreting, organizing, and often elaborating on sensations

Perceptual Constancy The fact that objects are normally perceived to be constant in size, color or brightness, and shape, even though their retinal images change according to different conditions

Perceptual Grouping Tendency to organize patterns of stimuli into larger units according to proximity, similarity, and good continuation

Perceptual Organization Process by which we structure elementary sensations (such as the sight of lines, brightness, and points) into the objects we perceive

Perceptual Set Tendency to see, hear, smell, feel, or taste what we expect or what is consistent with our preconceived notions

Periaqueductal Gray Area (PAG) A region of the brain stem that controls pain signals sent to higher brain centers; receives signals from endorphin-containing neurons for pain analgesia

Peripheral Nervous System (PNS) Portion of the nervous system that transmits messages to and from the central nervous system that consists of the somatic nervous system and the autonomic nervous system

Permissive Parenting style in which parents adopt a hands-off policy, making few demands and showing reluctance to punish inappropriate behavior

Personality Distinctive patterns of behavior, emotions, and thoughts that characterize an individual's adaptations to his or her life

Personality Disorders Diverse class of disorders that is collectively characterized by inflexible and maladaptive personality traits that cause either functional impairment or subjective distress

Personality Psychology Field of specialization that focuses on exploring the uniqueness of the individual, describing the elements that make up human personality, and investigating how personality develops and how it influences people's activities

Personal Unconscious In Carl Jung's theory, the part of the unconscious that is akin to Freud's concept of a reservoir of all repressed thoughts and feelings

Person Schemas Generalized assumptions about certain groups or classes of people

Phallic Stage According to Freud, the third phase of psychosexual development, spanning age three through age five or six, during which the focus of sexual gratification is genital stimulation

Phenotype The characteristics that result from the expression of an assortment of genes

Phenylketonuria (PKU) Disease caused by a recessive gene that results in the absence of an enzyme necessary to metabolize the milk protein phenylalanine

Phobia Any of a number of anxiety disorders characterized by a persistent fear of and consequent avoidance of a specific object or situation

Phonemes Individual sounds (such as those represented by *s* and *sh* in the English spelling system) that are the basic structural elements of language

Physical Attractiveness Physical features that persons of the opposite sex find appealing

Pitch Dimension of hearing that determines how high or low a sound is, measured in hertz; determined by the frequency of a sound wave

Pituitary Gland Gland in the endocrine system located directly below and connected to the hypothalamus; produces a number of hormones, many of which trigger other endocrine glands to release hormones

Place Theory of Pitch Discrimination Theory that we discriminate different pitches because sound waves of different frequencies displace different regions on the cochlea's basilar membrane

Plasticity A term used to describe how modifiable the brain is, especially throughout development

Pleasure Principle According to Freud, the principle guiding the id that seeks immediate gratification of all instinctive drives regardless of reason, logic, or the possible impact of behaviors

Pons Brain structure located just above the medulla that functions in fine-tuning motor messages, programming species-typical behaviors, processing sensory information, and controlling respiration

Positive Psychology The study of human behavior aimed at discovering and promoting the positive strengths and attributes that enable individuals to thrive and succeed

Positive Reinforcement In operant conditioning, any stimulus presented after a response that increases the probability of the response

Positive Symptoms
Represent an excess or distortion of normal behavior of schizophrenia; may include hallucinations, delusions, and excessive verbal behavior

Positron Emission Tomography (PET) Technique for studying the brain that involves injecting a subject with a glucose-like sugar tagged with a radioactive isotope that accumulates in brain cells in direct proportion to their activity level

Postconventional Morality Third and highest level in Lawrence Kohlberg's theory of moral development, in which individuals are guided by values agreed upon by society (Stage 5) or by universal ethical principles (Stage 6)

Posthypnotic Suggestion Suggestion or instruction to a hypnotized person that motivates that person to perform an action or actions after returning to a normal state of consciousness

Post-Traumatic Stress Disorder (PTSD) Anxiety disorder that typically follows a traumatic event or events; characterized by a reliving of that event, avoidance of stimuli associated with the event or numbing of general responsiveness, and increased arousal

Preconventional Morality Lowest level of moral development in Lawrence Kohlberg's theory, comprising Stage 1 and Stage 2, in which individuals have not internalized a personal code of morality

Predictive Validity Type of criterion-related validity assessed by determining the accuracy with which tests predict performance in some future situation

Prejudice Negative, unjustifiable, and inflexible attitude toward a group and its members

Preoperational Stage According to Piaget, the second major stage of cognitive development from ages two to seven years; preoperational children can develop only limited concepts and are unable to evaluate simultaneously more than one physical dimension

Primacy Effect The phenomenon that the first information we receive about a person often has the greatest influence on our perceptions of that person

Primary Mental Abilities In L. L. Thurstone's theory of the structure of intelligence, the separate and measurable attributes (for instance, numerical ability) that make up intelligence

Primary Process Thinking According to Freud, wish-fulfilling mental imagery used by the id to discharge tension

Primary Reinforcer In operant conditioning, a stimulus that satisfies a biologically based drive or need, such as hunger, thirst, or sleep

Proactive Interference In memory, the phenomenon that occurs when earlier learning disrupts memory for later learning

Probability In statistics, the proportion of cases that fit a certain description

Procedural Memory Recall of how to perform skills such as bicycle riding or swimming

Projection Defense mechanism in which an individual reduces anxiety created by unacceptable impulses by attributing those impulses to someone else

Projective Tests Personality tests that consist of loosely structured, ambiguous stimuli that require the subject's interpretation

Prosopagnosia An inability to visually recognize particular faces, usually caused by brain disease or injury (patients with prosopagnosia can see a face but may not be able to recognize it as familiar)

Prototype Best or most typical representative of a category around which we often structure our concept of that category

Proximity Perceptual grouping principle whereby, all else being equal, we tend to organize perceptions by grouping elements that are the nearest to each other (in social psychology, the geographical nearness of one person to another, which is an important factor in interpersonal attraction)

Proximodistal Pattern of development normal to humans in which infants gain control over areas that are closest to the center of their bodies (so that, for instance, control is gained over the upper arms before the fingers)

Psychoactive Drugs Drugs that have the effect of altering mood and behavior by changing neuronal functioning

Psychoanalysis Technique developed by Freud in which an individual's revelations of normally unconscious cognitions are interpreted

Psychoanalytic Theory Theory of personality that views people as being shaped by ongoing conflicts between primary drives and the social pressures of civilized society

Psycholinguistics Psychological study of how sounds and symbols are translated to meaning and of the cognitive processes that are involved in the acquisition and use of language

Psychology Scientific study of the behavior of humans and other animals

Psychoneuro-immunology The scientific study of the relationships between behavior and disease processes

Psychophysics Study of the relationship between the physical aspects of external stimuli and our own perceptions of these stimuli

Psychosexual Development Stages of development, in Freud's perspective, in which the focus of sexual gratification shifts from one body site to another

Psychotherapy Any nonbiological, noninvasive psychological technique or procedure designed to improve a person's adjustment to life

Puberty Approximately two-year period of rapid physical changes that occurs sometime between ages seven and sixteen in our society and that culminates in sexual maturity

Punishment A procedure in which the presentation of a stimulus following a response leads to a decrease in the strength or frequency of the response

Putamen A component of the basal ganglia located adjacent to the caudate nucleus; involved with the control and initiation of motor movement; an area of the brain affected by Huntington's disease

R

Random Sample Sample group of a larger population that is selected by randomization procedures (a random sample differs from a representative sample)

Range In descriptive statistics, a measure of variability that indicates the difference between the highest and lowest scores

Raphe Nucleus A group of serotonin-containing neurons extending from the raphe nuclei, located in the pons and medulla throughout the limbic system and forebrain

Rational-Emotive Therapy (RET) Approach to therapy based on the premise that psychological problems result when people interpret their experiences based on self-defeating, irrational beliefs

Rationalization Defense mechanism in which an individual substitutes self-justifying excuses or explanations for the real reasons for behaviors

Reaction Formation Defense mechanism in which the ego unconsciously replaces unacceptable impulses with their opposites

Reality Principle According to Freud, the tendency to behave in ways that are consistent with reality: governs the ego

Recall In memory tests, a subject's ability to reproduce information to which he or she was previously exposed; fill-in-the-blank and essay questions test recall

Recessive Gene Gene that is expressed in the phenotype only in the absence of a dominant gene or when it is paired with a similar recessive gene

Reciprocal Determinism According to Albert Bandura, the principle that individual behaviors, and thus personalities, are shaped by the interaction between cognitive factors and environmental factors

Reciprocity The tendency to respond to others in a way similar to how they respond to or treat us

Recognition In memory tests, a subject's ability to recognize whether he or she has been previously exposed to information; multiple-choice and true-false questions test recognition

Regression Defense mechanism in which an individual attempts to cope with an anxiety-producing situation by retreating to an earlier stage of development (In statistics, this is a procedure for predicting the size of one variable based on a knowledge of the size of a correlated variable and the coefficient of correlation between the two variables.)

Reinforcement In operant conditioning, any procedure in which an event following a specific response increases the probability that the response will occur

Reinstatement In Pavlovian conditioning, the reappearance of a conditioned response after extinction has taken place

Relative Motion (Motion Parallax) Monocular distance cue based on the fact that moving objects appear to move a greater distance when they are close to the viewer than when they are far away

Relative Size Monocular distance cue based on the fact that objects of the same size appear to be smaller the farther they are from the viewer

Relearning Technique for testing memory that involves measuring how much more quickly a person can relearn material that was learned at some previous time

Reliability In psychological testing, the dependable consistency of a test over time, or the consistency in responses among similar items on the same assessment

REM (Rapid Eye Movement) Sleep State of sleep characterized by rapid eye movements and often associated with dreaming

Replication Studies Research conducted for the purpose of verifying previous findings

Representative Heuristic Strategy for categorizing an object based on one's preconceived notion of characteristics that are typical of that category

Representative Sample Sample in which critical subgroups are represented according to their incidence in the larger population that the researcher is studying

Repression In psychoanalytic theory, the defense mechanism by which ideas, feelings, or memories that are too painful to deal with on a conscious level are banished to the unconscious

Resistance In psychoanalysis, a patient's unwillingness to describe freely some aspects of his or her life

Resting Potential State in which a neuron is not transmitting a nerve impulse; a neuron in this state has a net negative charge relative to its outside environment, and this state of potential energy prepares it to be activated by a signal from an adjacent neuron

Reticular Activating System (RAS) Set of neural circuits extending from the lower brain up to the thalamus that plays a critical role in controlling arousal and alertness; also known as *reticular formation*

Reticular Formation Set of neural circuits extending from the lower brain up to the thalamus that plays a critical role in controlling arousal and alertness; also known as the *reticular activating system*

Retina Thin membrane at the back of the eye containing photoreceptors called rods and cones; functions to record images

Retrieval Process by which information stored in memory is accessed

Retroactive Interference In memory, the phenomenon that occurs when a later event interferes with the recall of earlier information

Retrograde Amnesia Memory loss for certain details or events that occurred prior to experiencing brain trauma; a form of organic amnesia

Rods Photoreceptor cells distributed across the inner layer of the retina that are important in peripheral vision and seeing in dim light

Rorschach Inkblot Test Commonly used projective test in which the subject is asked to examine inkblots and say what they look like or bring to mind

S

S-Factor One of the factors in Charles Spearman's two-factor theory of the structure of intelligence; consists of specific abilities or skills

Sample Selected segment of a larger population that is being studied in psychological research; two kinds of samples are the representative sample and the random sample

Saturation Proportion of colored or chromatic light to noncolored or nonchromatic light, which determines how colorful light appears

Schachter-Singer Theory Theory that a given body state can be linked to a variety of emotions depending on the context in which the body state occurs

Schemas In reference to memory, conceptual frameworks that individuals use to make sense out of stored information; in Jean Piaget's theory, the mental structures we form to assimilate and organize processed information

Schizophrenia Class of severe and disabling mental disorders characterized by extreme disruptions of perceptions, thoughts, emotions, and behavior

School Psychology Field of specialization concerned with evaluating students' interests and abilities and resolving learning and emotional problems

Scientific Method Careful observation of events in the world, the formation of predictions based on these observations, and the testing of these predictions by manipulation of variables and systematic observation

Secondary Sex Characteristics Physical characteristics typical of mature males or females (such as facial, body, and pubic hair) that develop during puberty as a result of the release of testosterone or estrogen

Secondary Trait In Gordon Allport's trait theory of personality, any of a variety of less-generalized and often short-term traits that affect people's behavior in specific circumstances

Second-Order Conditioning A learned association between two conditioned stimuli (CS_2–CS_1) that can occur following conditioning to CS_1 and an unconditioned stimulus

Sedatives Class of depressant drugs, including tranquilizers, barbiturates, and benzodiazepines, that induce relaxation, calmness, and sleep

Selective Attention The process of focusing on one or a few stimuli of particular significance while ignoring others

Selective Perception A form of perceptual set; the tendency to perceive stimuli that are consistent with expectations and to ignore those that are inconsistent

Self-Efficacy Individual's belief that he or she can perform adequately and deal effectively with a particular situation

Semantic Memory General, nonpersonal knowledge about the meaning of facts and concepts

Semantics The study of meaning in language

Semicircular Canals Three ring-shaped structures in the inner ear that provide information about the body's equilibrium or balance

Senile Dementia Collective term describing a variety of conditions sometimes associated with aging, including memory deficits, forgetfulness, disorientation of time and place, declining ability to think, and so forth

Sensations Basic, immediate experiences that a stimulus, such as a sound, elicits in a sense organ, such as the ear

Sensation-Seeking Motive An explanation for the apparent need for certain levels of stimulation, including the need to explore the environment and the need for sensory stimulation

Sensorimotor Stage In Piaget's theory, the period of development between birth and about age two years during which infants learn about their worlds primarily through their senses and actions

Sensorineural Hearing Loss Hearing loss caused by damage to either the hair cells of the inner ear or the auditory nerve; can be caused by loud noise

Sensory Adaptation In perception, the decrease in the response of sensory receptors to stimuli when exposed to continual, unchanging stimulation

Sensory Cortex Region of the cerebral cortex involved in receiving sensory messages

Sensory Memory First system in the three-system model of memory, in which brief impressions from any of the senses are stored fleetingly, disappearing within a few seconds if they are not transferred to short-term memory

Sensory Neglect A lack of awareness of or attention to stimuli on one side of the body when damage has occurred to the opposite-side parietal lobe

Sensory Neuron Neuron or nerve cell that carries messages to the CNS from receptors in the skin, ears, nose, eyes, and other receptor organs—also known as afferent neuron

Separate Attachment Attachment typically displayed by infants by about twelve to eighteen months, when fear of strangers diminishes and interest in people other than primary caregivers develops

Septal Area Structure in the brain's limbic system that plays a role in the experiencing of pleasure

Serial Position Effect Tendency to remember items at the beginning and end of a list more readily than those in the middle

Serotonin A neurotransmitter involved in the control of the sleep/wake cycle, mood, and appetite; deficiencies in serotonin are associated with sleep disorders, aggression, and depression

Sex-Linked Inheritance Genetic transmission involving genes that are carried only on the X chromosome (females carry the XX chromosome pair; males carry the XY pair)

Sexual Differentiation The process during development when male and female physical characteristics begin to take form

Sexual Orientation Sex to which an individual is attracted

Shape Constancy Element of perceptual constancy perceiving objects as maintaining the same shape even though their retinal images change when we view them from different angles

Shaping In operant conditioning, a technique in which responses that are increasingly similar to the desired behavior are reinforced, step by step, until the desired behavior occurs

Short-Term (Working) Memory (STM) Immediate recollection of stimuli that have just been perceived (unless it is transferred to long-term memory, information in this memory system is usually retained only momentarily)

Sign Stimuli Stimuli that naturally elicit a change in motivational state and behavior

Signal Detection Theory Theory that says our ability to detect a sensory stimulus (signal) depends not only on the intensity of the signal but also on variables such as distractions and motivation

Similarity In perception, the principle that we tend to group elements that are similar to each other (In social psychology, similarity of beliefs, interests, and values is recognized as a factor attracting people to one another.)

Simultaneous Conditioning In Pavlovian conditioning, learning that takes place when the conditioned stimulus is presented at the same time as the unconditioned stimulus

Size Constancy One form of perceptual constancy, in which the retinal image of an object becomes smaller as the object recedes into the distance or larger as it approaches; the viewer adjusts for this change and perceives the object to be constant in size

Skewed In descriptive statistics, an unbalanced distribution of scores

Sleep Natural, periodically occurring state of rest characterized by reduced activity, lessened responsiveness to stimuli, and distinctive patterns of brain activity

Sleep Apnea Sleep disorder characterized by irregular breathing during sleep

Sleep Disorders Class of disorders that interfere with sleep, including apnea, terrors, nightmares, and sleepwalking

Sleep Talking The production of speech or speech sounds associated with sleep without subjective awareness; also referred to as *somniloquy*

Sleep Terror Sleep disorder in which a person suddenly awakens from Stage 4 sleep in panic, typically with no recollection of a bad dream

Sleepwalking Sleep disorder, characterized by walking in one's sleep during Stage 3 or 4 of NREM sleep; also known as *somnambulism*

Social Anxiety Anxiety disorder characterized by a persistent, irrational fear of performing some specific behavior (such as talking or eating) in the presence of other people

Social Influence Efforts by others to alter our feelings, beliefs, and behavior

Social Isolation An environment lacking social interaction, such as one in which an elderly person lives alone

Socialization Process by which society conveys behavioral expectations to an individual through various agents, such as parents, peers, and school

Social Learning Theory Theory that emphasizes the role of observation in learning

Social Perception The way in which we perceive, evaluate, categorize, and form judgments about the qualities of other people

Social Psychology Field of specialization concerned with understanding the impact of social environments and social processes on individuals

Social Support An environment in which a person has close relatives or personal friends

Sociobiology A specialization within biology that seeks to understand the biological factors that underlie social behaviors in all animal species, including humans

Somatic Marker An emotion and its corresponding feeling attached to possible outcomes of a decision process

Somatic Nervous System A part of the peripheral nervous system that transmits messages to and from major skeletal muscles and from sensory organs to the central nervous system

Somatic Symptom Disorder Type of somatic disorder characterized by multiple and recurrent physical symptoms that have no physical cause

Somatosensory Cortex Area of the parietal lobe, directly across from the motor cortex in the frontal lobe, that receives sensory information about touch, pressure, pain, temperature, and body position

Source Traits In Raymond Cattell's trait theory of personality, basic, underlying traits that are the center or core of an individual's personality

Specific Attachment Highly selective attachment often displayed by human infants sometime between six and eighteen months, when increased responsiveness is displayed toward primary caregivers and distress may be displayed when separated from parents

Specific Phobia Anxiety disorder characterized by an irrational fear of specific situations or objects, such as heights, small closed places, strangers or animals

Split-Half Reliability Measure of test reliability in which a subject's performance on a single administration of a test is assessed by comparing performance on half of the test items with performance on the other half of the test items

Sport Psychology Field of specialization concerned with enhancing sport and exercise performance; focuses on helping people overcome psychological barriers that can impede performance and success in competition or performance

Stage 1 Sleep Light sleep that occurs just after dozing off, characterized by brain waves called theta waves

Stage 2 Sleep Stage of sleep that typically follows Stage 1 sleep characterized by brief bursts of brain activity called sleep spindles as well as K-complex responses to stimuli such as noises

Stage 3 Sleep Stage of sleep that typically follows Stage 2 sleep, characterized by an EEG tracing, 20 to 50 percent of which consists of delta waves and virtually no eye movements

Stage 4 Sleep Deepest level of sleep, characterized by an EEG tracing exceeding 50 percent delta waves and virtually no eye movements

Standard Deviation In descriptive statistics, a measure of variability that indicates the average extent to which all the scores in a distribution vary from the mean

Standardization Procedures Uniform and consistent procedures for administering and scoring tests, such as IQ or personality tests

Standard Score In descriptive statistics, a measure that indicates how far a score deviates from the average in standard units

Stanford-Binet Test IQ test developed by Lewis Terman, who revised Binet's scale and adapted questions to U.S. students

State-Dependent Memory Phenomenon wherein recall of particular events, experiences, or information is aided by the subject being in the same context or physiological state in which the information was first encoded

Statistical Significance Term used to describe research result in which changes in the dependent variable can be attributed with a high level of confidence to the experimental condition (or independent variable) being manipulated by the researcher

Statistics Mathematical methods for describing and interpreting data; two kinds of statistics are descriptive and inferential statistics

Stereogram An image that is able to convey the experience of depth perception using binocular cues

Stereotypes Preconceived and oversimplified beliefs and expectations about the traits of members of a particular group that do not account for individual differences

Stereotype Threat The tendency to conform to negative stereotypes

Stimulants Drugs that increase arousal and the activity of the central nervous system; used to treat attention disorders and narcolepsy; psychoactive drugs, including caffeine, nicotine, amphetamines, and cocaine, that stimulate the central nervous system by increasing the transmission of neural impulses

Storage Process by which encoded material is retained over time in memory

Stress A pattern of hormonal and physiological responses that accompany threatening events

Striving for Superiority In Alfred Adler's neo-Freudian theory, a universal urge to achieve self-perfection through successful adaptation to life's circumstances, mastering challenges, and personal growth

Structuralism Approach to psychology that attempted to break down experience into its basic elements, or structures, using a technique called introspection, in which subjects provided scientific reports of perceptual experiences

Subjective Probability The estimate of the likelihood of an outcome (often quite different from a mathematical probability)

Sublimation Form of the defense mechanism *displacement*, in which impulse-driven behaviors are channeled toward producing a socially valued accomplishment

Subliminal Perception The perception of and reaction to a brief or faint stimulus; occurs without conscious awareness

Substance P A peptide neurotransmitter that signals pain from peripheral nerve fibers to the spinal cord

Substantia Nigra A region of dark-colored neurons in the upper brainstem that sends axons to the caudate nucleus and to the putamen; an area of the brain affected by Parkinson's disease

Subtractive Color Mixing Color mixing process that occurs when pigments are mixed, so that when light falls on the colored object, some wavelengths are absorbed (or subtracted) and others are reflected

Superego According to Freud, the third system of personality that consists of an individual's conscience as well as the ego-ideal (the "shoulds" of behavior)

Suprachiasmatic Nucleus (SCN) An area of the hypothalamus that is located above the optic chiasm and that exerts the main control over biological rhythms; also referred to as a *biological clock* because damage to this area disrupts daily cycles in sleep and other biological functions

Surface Traits In Raymond Cattell's trait theory of personality, dimensions or traits that are usually obvious (such as integrity or tidiness) and that tend to be grouped in clusters that are related to source traits

Survey Research method that provides descriptive information in which a representative sample of people is questioned about their behaviors or attitudes

Syllogism Argument consisting of two or more premises, followed by a statement of conclusion that may or may not follow logically from the premises

Sympathetic Nervous System A part of the autonomic nervous system that functions to produce emergency responses such as increased heart rate, pupil dilation, and inhibited digestive activity; works in tandem with the parasympathetic nervous system

Synapse Includes the synaptic gap and a portion of the presynaptic and postsynaptic membranes that are involved in transmitting a signal between neurons

Synaptic Facilitation An increase in the size of a postsynaptic potential to a weak stimulus resulting from neuronal changes that underlie learning and memory

Synesthesia A condition in which one type of sensory stimulation evokes the sensation of another, as when the hearing of a sound produces the visualization of a color

Syntax Set of language rules that govern how words can be combined to form meaningful phrases and sentences; grammar

Systematic Desensitization Behavior therapy using a Pavlovian conditioning technique that pairs the slow, systematic exposure to anxiety-inducing situations with relaxation training

T

Telegraphic Speech An early stage of language development where sentences consist of two words in grammatically correct order

Template Learning Learning that depends on a particular type of perceptual experience during a critical time in development (for example, imprinting and language learning)

Temporal Lobe Region of the cerebral cortex located below the lateral fissure; contains the auditory cortex

Teratogen Any substance (drug or toxin) that alters the course of normal development of a fetus; *teratogen* means "monster" in Greek

Terminal Button Swollen bulb-like structure on the end of a neuron's axon that releases chemical substances known as neurotransmitters

Testing Hypotheses Problem-solving strategy that involves formulating specific hypotheses that generate relatively efficient approaches to solving a problem and then testing the hypotheses in a systematic fashion

Test-Retest Reliability Method for evaluating test reliability by giving a subject (or subjects) the same test more than once

Texture Gradient Monocular distance cue based on the fact that textured surfaces (such as a grassy lawn) appear to be smoother, denser, and less textured when they are far from the viewer than when they are close

Thalamus Structure located beneath the cerebrum in the brain; functions as a relay station, routing incoming sensory information to appropriate areas in the cerebral cortex; seems to also play a role in regulating sleep cycles

Thematic Apperception Test (TAT) Projective test for personality assessment in which the subject is shown cards depicting various scenes and is asked to describe what is happening in each scene

Theory A scientific theory is a logical explanation for all the relevant data or facts scientists have observed regarding certain natural phenomena. An essential aspect of scientific theories is that they must be both testable and refutable, not to be confused with the common usage of the term used to signify a hunch, a speculation, or an opinion.

Theory of Mind The ability to attribute beliefs, desires, knowledge, and emotions to others

Thought Any cognitive processes directed toward problem solving, understanding language, memory retrieval, and perceiving patterns in sensory inputs

Threshold Minimum level of intensity or strength of a stimulus that is sufficient to activate a sensory process (for instance, the minimum number of molecules that must be present in the air for us to smell a substance)

Thyroid Gland Endocrine gland located in the neck; produces the hormone thyroxine, which influences metabolism, growth, and maturation

Thyroxine The major hormone produced by the thyroid gland; regulates metabolism

Timbre Quality of complex sound that is a product of the combination of fundamental frequency and additional frequency components called overtones

Tolerance A decrease in the effectiveness of a drug observed after repeated administration

Top-Down Processing A sequence of neural activation that begins in higher cortical areas, such as the prefrontal cortex, before activating brain areas involved in perception

Trace Conditioning In Pavlovian conditioning, learning that takes place when presentation of the conditioned stimulus begins and ends before the unconditioned stimulus is presented

Transduction Process by which sensory organs transform mechanical, chemical, or light energy into the electrochemical energy that is generated by neurons firing

Transference In psychotherapy, a process in which a patient begins to relate to the therapist in much the same way as to other important people in his or her life (such as a parent)

Trial and Error Problem-solving strategy that involves trying possible solutions, one by one, to see which is correct

Triarchic Theory of Successful Intelligence Theory that intelligence is a multidimensional trait comprising analytical, creative, and practical abilities

***t*-test** A statistical test used to compare two sample means

Two-Factor Theory of Learning A theory of avoidance learning that involves both Pavlovian and operant conditioning

Tympanic Membrane Membrane stretched across the end of the auditory canal that vibrates in response to sound waves; also known as the *eardrum*

Type A Personality Individuals who are hard driving, competitive, hostile, time urgent, and demanding of both themselves and others, as described by Friedman and Rosenman in their study of coronary heart disease

Type B Personality Individuals who are relaxed, easygoing, not driven to achieve perfection, happy in their jobs, understanding, and not easily angered, as described by Friedman and Rosenman in their study of coronary heart disease

Type D Personality A personality type characterized by negativity, distress, and an inability to share emotions with others (a predictor of mortality in patients with cardiovascular disease or cancer)

U

Unconditioned Response (UCR) In Pavlovian conditioning, an unlearned response or reflex caused by an unconditioned stimulus

Unconditioned Stimulus (UCS) In Pavlovian conditioning, a stimulus that elicits an unlearned response or reflex

Unconscious Mind According to Freud's theory, the vast reservoir of the mind that holds countless memories and feelings that are repressed or submerged because they produce anxiety

Universal Grammar (UG) The genetic component of the language faculty—similar to *language acquisition device*

V

Validity In psychological testing, the ability of a test to accurately measure what it is supposed to measure

Variable Interval (VI) Schedule Partial reinforcement schedule in operant conditioning in which opportunities for reinforcement occur at variable time intervals

Variable Ratio (VR) Schedule Partial reinforcement schedule in operant conditioning in which reinforcement is provided after an average of a specific number of responses occur

Variance In descriptive statistics, a measure of variability that is the average of the squared distances of the scores from the mean

Ventromedial Hypothalamus (VMH) A region of the hypothalamus in which damage results in faster gastric emptying and an increase in insulin production; also important for female sexual behavior

Vestibular Sacs Structure at the junction of the semicircular canals and cochlea of the middle ear that provide information about the head's position in space

Virtual Reality Therapy Use of virtual reality simulations to generate a variety of stimuli for systematic desensitization

Visual Cliff Device that produces the illusion of a cliff, allowing researchers to test the ability of animals to perceive and respond to depth cues

Visual Cortex Portion of the occipital lobe that integrates sensory information received from the eyes into electrical patterns that the brain translates into vision

Volley Theory Related to the frequency theory of pitch discrimination, postulates that since single auditory neurons cannot fire rapidly enough to enable us to perceive tones in the 1,000–4,000 Hz range, pitch perception is made possible by groups of interrelated neurons firing in concert

W

Weber's Law One of the major principles of sensation, based on the fact that for various stimulus intensities, the difference threshold tends to be a constant fraction of the stimulus—as the strength of the original stimulus increases, the magnitude of the change must also increase for a just noticeable difference to be perceived

Wechsler Adult Intelligence Scale (WAIS) Intelligence test developed by David Wechsler in the 1930s with subtests grouped by aptitude rather than age level (now in its fifth major revision—WAIS V)

Wernicke's Aphasia A loss of the ability to comprehend spoken or written language; also referred to as *receptive aphasia*

Wernicke's Area Area of the left temporal lobe that is the brain's primary area for understanding speech

Within-Group Differences Differences, or response variability, within treatment conditions

Working Backward Common heuristic problem-solving strategy that starts with describing the goal, then defines the step that directly precedes that goal, and works backward in this manner until the steps needed to reach the goal are defined

Y

Yerkes-Dodson Law Principle that the optimum level of arousal for peak performance will vary somewhat depending on the nature of the task

Young-Helmholtz Theory (Trichromatic Theory of Color Vision) The postulation that the human eye contains three types of color receptors (for red, green, and blue), which form the basis for our perception of all colors

References

A

Abbey, A., Buck, P. O., Zawacki, T., & Saenz, C. (2003). Alcohol's effects on perceptions of a potential date rape. *Journal of Studies on Alcohol and Drugs, 64*(5), 669–677. http://dx.doi.org/10.15288/jsa.2003.64.669

Abrahamson, A. C., Baker, L. A., & Caspi, A. (2002). Rebellious teens? Genetic and environmental influences on the social attitudes of adolescents. *Journal of Personality & Social Psychology, 83*(6), 1392–1408.

Abroms, K. I., & Bennett, J. (1981). Changing etiologic perspectives in Down's syndrome. *Journal of the Division for Early Childhood, 2*, 109–112.

Ader, R., Cohen, N., & Bovbjerg, D. (1982). Conditioned suppression of humoral immunity in the rat. *Journal of Comparative and Physiological Psychology, 96*(3), 517–521. http://psycnet.apa.org/doi/10.1037/h0077887

Adler, A. (1917). *Study of organ inferiority and its physical compensation: A contribution to clinical medicine* [S. E. Jelliffe, Trans.] [Monograph]. New York, NY: The Nervous and Mental Diseases.

Adler, A. (1924). *Practice and theory of individual psychology.* New York, NY: Routledge, Trench, Trubner & Co., Ltd.

Adler, A. (1930). Individual Psychology. In C. A. Murchison (Ed.), *Psychologies of 1930* (pp. 395–408). Worcester, MA: Clark University Press.

Administration on Aging. (2014). Projected future growth of the older population [XLS file]. *Administration on Aging*. Retrieved from https://aoa.acl.gov/Aging_Statistics/future_growth/future_growth.aspx

Aguiar, A., & Baillargeon, R. (2002). Developments in young infants' reasoning about occluded objects. *Cognitive Psychology, 45*(2), 267–336. doi:10.1016/S0010-0285(02)00005-1

Aine, C. J., Sanfratello, L., Adair, J., Knoefel, J. E., Caprihan, A., & Stephen, J. M. (2011). Developmental and decline of memory functions in normal, pathological and healthy successful aging. *Brain Topography, 24*(3–4), 323–339. doi:10.1007/s10548-011-0178-x

Ainsworth, M. D. (1963). The development of infant-mother interaction among the Ganda. In B. M. Foss (Ed.), *Determinants of infant behavior* (pp. 67–104). New York, NY: Wiley.

Ainsworth, M. D. (1979). Infant-mother attachment. *American Psychologist, 34*(10), 932–937.

Ainsworth, M. D. (1989). Attachments beyond infancy. *American Psychologist, 44*(4), 709–716.

Alcohol Facts and Statistics. (2017, February). *National Institute on Alcohol Abuse and Alcoholism.* Retrieved from https://niaaa.nih.gov/alcohol-health/overview-alcohol-consumption/alcohol-facts-and-statistics

Allan, C. L., & Ebmeier, K. P. (2011). The use of ECT and MST in treating depression. *International Review of Psychiatry, 23*(5), 400–412. doi:10.3109/09540261.2011.614223

Allen, J. S., Damasio, H., Grabowski, T. J., Bruss, J., & Zhang, W. (2003). Sexual dimorphism and asymmetries in the gray-white composition of the human cerebrum. *NeuroImage, 18*(4), 880–894.

Allis, C. D., Caparros, M.-L., Jenuwein, T., & Reinberg, D. (Eds.) (2015). *Epigenetics* (2nd ed.). Woodbury, NY: Cold Spring Harbor Laboratory Press.

Allport, G. W. (1937). *Personality: A Psychological Interpretation.* New York, NY: Holt, Rinehart and Winston.

Allport, G. W. (1961). *Pattern and growth in personality.* New York, NY: Holt, Rinehart and Winston.

Allport, G. W. (1965). *Letters from Jenny.* New York, NY: Harcourt, Brace & World.

Allport, G. W. (1966). Traits revisited. *American Psychologist, 21*(1), 1–10. http://psycnet.apa.org/doi/10.1037/h0023295

Allport, G. W., & Postman, L. J. (1947). *The psychology of rumor.* New York, NY: H. Holt.

American Heart Association News. (2015, November 9). More aggressive treatment of high blood pressure saves lives in study. Retrieved from http://news.heart.org/more-aggressive-treatment-of-high-blood-pressure-saves-lives-in-study/

American Osteopathic Association. (2017). Hearing loss and headphones—is anyone listening? Retrieved from http://www.osteopathic.org/osteopathic-health/about-your-health/health-conditions-library/general-health/Pages/headphone-safety.aspx

American Psychiatric Association. (2013). *Diagnostic and statistical manual of mental disorders* (5th ed.). Arlington, VA: Author.

American Psychological Association. (2017). Boards and committees. Retrieved from http://www.apa.org/about/governance/bdcmte/index.aspx

Aminoff, E., Schacter, D. L., & Bar, M. (2008). The cortical underpinnings of context-based memory distortion. *Journal of Cognitive Neuroscience, 20*(12), 2226–2237. https://dx.doi.org/10.1162%2Fjocn.2008.20156

Anand, P., Kunnumakara, A. B., Sundaram, C., Harikumar, K. B., Tharakan, S. T., Lai, O. S.,... Aggarwal, B. B. (2008). Cancer is a preventable disease that requires major lifestyle changes. *Pharmaceutical Research, 25*(9), 2079–2116. https://dx.doi.org/10.1007%2Fs11095-008-9661-9

Ances, B., Ortega, M., Vaida, F., Heaps, J., & Paul, R. (2012). Independent effects of HIV, aging, and HAART on brain volumetric measures. *Journal of Acquired Immune Deficiency Syndromes, 59*(5), 469–477. https://dx.doi.org/10.1097%2FQAI.0b013e318249db17

Anderson, C. A., Berkowitz, L., Donnerstein, E., Huesmann, L. R., Johnson, J. D., Linz, D., ...Wartella, E. (2003a). The influence of media violence on youth. *Psychology Science in the Public Interest, 4*(3), 81–110. doi:10.1111/j.1529-1006.2003.pspi_1433.x

Anderson, C. A., Carnagey, N. L., & Eubanks, J. (2003b). Exposure to violent media: The effects of songs with violent lyrics on aggressive thoughts and feelings. *Journal of Personality and Social Psychology, 84*(5), 960–971. doi:10.1037/0022-3514.84.5.960

Anderson, C. M., Ochsner, K. N., Kuhl, B., Cooper, J., Robertson, E., Gabrieli, S. W.,... Gabrieli, J. D. (2004). Neural systems underlying the suppression of unwanted memories. *Science, 303*(5655), 232–235.

Anderson, M. C., & Huddleston, E. (2012). Toward a cognitive neurobiological model of motivated forgetting. In R. Belli (Ed.), *True and false recovered memories* (pp. 53–120). New York, NY: Springer.

Andreasen, N. C., Ehrhardt, J. C., Swayze, V. W., II, Alliger, R. J., Yuh, W. T., Cohen, G., & Ziebell, S. (1990). Magnetic resonance imaging of the brain in schizophrenia. The pathophysiologic significance of structural abnormalities. *Archives of General Psychiatry, 47*(1), 35–44.

Anisfeld, M. (2005). No compelling evidence to dispute Piaget's timetable of the development of representational imitation in infancy. In S. Hurley, & N. Chater, *Perspectives on imitation* (pp. 107–131). Cambridge, MA: The MIT Press.

Antonov, I., Antonova, I., Kandel, E. R., & Hawkins, R. D. (2003). Activity-dependent presynaptic facilitation and Hebbian LTP are both required and interact during classical conditioning in Aplysia. *Neuron, Jan 9; 37*(1), 135–147.

Antrop, I., Roeyers, H., Oosterlaan, J., & Van Oost, P. (2002). Agreement between parent and teacher ratings of disruptive behavior disorders in children with clinically diagnosed ADHD. *Journal of Psychology & Behavioral Assessment, 24*(1), 67–73. doi:10.1023/A:1014057325752

Apperloo, M. J., Van Der Stege, J. G., Hoek, A., & Weijmar Schultz, W. C. (2003). In the mood for sex: The value of androgens. *Journal of Sex and Marital Therapy, 29*(2), 87–102.

Arlin, P. K. (1989). Problem solving and problem finding in young artists and young scientists. In M. L. Commons et al. (Eds.), *Adult development: Vol 1. Comparisons and applications of developmental models* (197–216). Westport, CT: Praeger.

Arnsten, A. F., & Pliszka, S. R. (2011). Catecholamine influences on prefrontal cortical function: Relevance to treatment of attention deficit/hyperactivity disorder. *Pharmacology, Biochemistry, and Behavior, 99*(2), 211–216. doi:10.1016/j.pbb.2011.01.020

Aronson, E., & Mills, J. (1959). The effect of severity of initiation on liking for a group. *Journal of Abnormal Psychology and Social Psychology, 59*(2), 177–181. http://psycnet.apa.org/doi/10.1037/h0047195

Asch, S. E. (1946). Forming impressions of personality. *Journal of Abnormal Psychology and Social Psychology, 41*(3), 258–290. http://psycnet.apa.org/doi/10.1037/h0055756

Asch, S. E. (1955). Opinions and social pressure. *Scientific American, 193*(5), 31–35.

Aserinsky, E., & Kleitman, N. (1953). Regularly occurring periods of eye motility, and concomitant phenomena, during sleep. *Science, 118*(3062), 273–274. doi:10.1126/science.118.3062.273

Association for Psychological Science. (2017). Members. Retrieved from http://www.psychologicalscience.org/members

Athanasiou, R., Shaver, P., & Tavris, C. (1970, July). Sex. *Psychology Today, 4*, 37–52.

Atkinson, R. C., & Shiffrin, R. M. (1968). Human memory: A proposed system and its control processes. In K. W. Spence & J. T. Spence (Eds.), *The psychology of learning and motivation: Vol. 2. Advances in research and theory* (pp. 90–197). New York, NY: Academic Press.

Avitsur, R., Hunzeker, J., & Sheridan, J. F. (2006). Role of early stress in the individual differences in host response to viral infection. *Brain, Behavior, and Immunity, 20*(4), 339–348. http://dx.doi.org/10.1016/j.bbi.2005.09.006

B

Bachrach, A., Erwin, W., & Mohn, J. (1965). The control of eating behavior in an anorexic by operant conditioning techniques. In L. P. Ullmann, & L. Krasner (Eds.), *Case studies in behavior modification.* New York, NY: Holt, Rinehart and Winston.

Baghai, T. C., & Möller, H.-J. (2008). Electroconvulsive therapy and its different indications. *Dialogues in Clinical Neuroscience, 10*(1), 105–117.

Baillargeon, R. (1987). Object permanence in 3 1/2 and 4 1/2-month-old infants. *Developmental Psychology, 23*(5), 655–664.

Baillargeon, R. (2008). Innate ideas revisited: For a principle of persistence in infants' physical reasoning. *Perspectives on Psychological Science, 3*(1), 2–13. doi:10.1111/j.1745-6916.2008.00056.x

Balthazart, J. (2012). Oxford series in behavioral neuroendocrinology: *The biology of homosexuality.* New York, NY: Oxford University Press.

Bandura, A. (1969). *Principles of behavior modification.* New York, NY: Holt, Rinehart and Winston.

Bandura, A. (1971). *Social learning theory.* New York, NY: General Learning Press.

Bandura, A. (1973). *Aggression: A social learning analysis.* Englewood Cliffs, NJ: Prentice Hall.

Bandura, A. (1977). *Social learning theory.* Englewood Cliffs, NJ: Prentice-Hall.

Bandura, A. (1982). Self-efficacy mechanism in human agency. *American Psychologist, 37*(2), 122–147. http://psycnet.apa.org/doi/10.1037/0003-066X.37.2.122

Bandura, A. (1983). Temporal dynamics and decomposition of reciprocal determinism: A reply to Phillips and Orton. *Psychological Review, 90*(2), 166–170. doi:10.1037/0033-295X.90.2.166

Bandura, A. (1986). *Social foundations of thought and action: A social cognitive theory.* Englewood Cliffs, NJ: Prentice Hall.

Bandura, A. (1992). Social cognitive theory of social referencing. In S. Feinman (Ed.), *Social referencing and the social construction of reality in infancy* (pp. 175–208). New York, NY: Plenum Press.

Bandura, A., & Mischel, W. (1965). Modification of self-imposed delay of reward through exposure to live and symbolic models. *Journal of Personality and Social Psychology, 2*(5), 698–705. http://psycnet.apa.org/doi/10.1037/h0022655

Bandura, A., & Walters, R. H. (1959). *Adolescent aggression.* New York, NY: Ronald Press.

Bandura, A., Ross, D., & Ross, S. (1963). Imitation of film-mediated aggressive models. *Journal of Abnormal and Social Psychology, 66*(1), 3–11. http://psycnet.apa.org/doi/10.1037/h0048687

Banissy, M. J., Stewart, L., Muggleton, N. G., Griffiths, T. D., Walsh, V. Y., Ward, J., & Kanai, R. (2012). Grapheme-color and tone-color synesthesia is associated with structural brain changes in visual regions implicated in color, form, and motion. *Cognitive Neuroscience, 3*(1), 29–35. doi:10.1080/17588928.2011.594499

Barber, T. X. (1975). Responding to "hypnotic" suggestions: An introspective report. *American Journal of Clinical Hypnosis, 18*(1), 6–22. http://dx.doi.org/10.1080/00029157.1975.10403765

Barber, T. X., & Wilson, S. C. (1977). Hypnosis suggestions and altered states of consciousness: Experimental evaluation of a new cognitive-behavioral theory and the traditional trance-state therapy of "hypnosis." *Annals of the New York Academy of Sciences, 296*, 430–433. doi:10.1111/j.1749-6632.1977.tb38159.x

Bard, P. (1934). On emotional expression after decortication with some remarks on certain theoretical views: Part I. *Psychological Review, 41*(4), 309–329. http://psycnet.apa.org/doi/10.1037/h0070765

Barnes, J., Dong, C. Y., McRobbie, H., Walker, N., Mehta, M., & Stead, L. F. (2010, October 6). Hypnotherapy for smoking cessation. *Cochrane Database of Systematic Reviews.* Retrieved from http://www.cochrane.org//CD001008/TOBACCO_does-hypnotherapy-help-people-who-are-trying-to-stop-smoking

Bartlett, F. C. (1932). *Remembering: A study in experimental and social psychology.* Cambridge, England: Cambridge University Press.

Baskin, D. G., Figlewicz Lattemann, D., Seeley, R. J., Woods, S. C., Porte, D., Jr., & Schwartz, M. W. (1999). Insulin and leptin: Dual adiposity signals to the brain for the regulation of food intake and body weight. *Brain Research, 848*(1–2), 114–123.

Bassey, E. J. (1998). Longitudinal changes in selected physical capabilities: Muscle strength, flexibility and body size. *Age and Ageing, 27*(Supp. 3), 12–16. https://doi.org/10.1093/ageing/27.suppl_3.12

Baumrind, D. (1964). Some thoughts on ethics of research: After reading Milgram's "Behavioral study of obedience." *American Psychologist, 19*(6), 421–423. doi:10.1037/h0040128

Baumrind, D. (1991). The influence of parenting style on adolescent competence and substance abuse. *The Journal of Early Adolescence, 11*(1), 56–95.

Baumrind, D. (2012). Differentiating between confrontive and coercive kinds of parental power-assertive disciplinary practices. *Human Development, 55*(2), 35–51. doi:10.1159/000337962

Bechara, A., & Damasio, H. (2002). Decision-making and addiction (part I): Impaired activation of somatic states in substance dependent individuals when pondering decisions with negative future consequences. *Neuropsychologia, 40*(10), 1675–1689.

Bechara, A., Damasio, H., & Damasio, A. R. (2003). Role of the amygdala in decision-making. *Annals of the New York Academy of Sciences, 985*, 356–369. doi:10.1111/j.1749-6632.2003.tb07094.x

Beck, A. T. (1976). *Cognitive therapy and emotional disorders.* New York, NY: International Universities Press.

Beck, A. T. (2005). The current state of cognitive therapy: 40-year retrospective. *Archives of General Psychiatry, 62*(9), 953–959. doi:10.1001/archpsyc.62.9.953

Beck, A. T., Freeman, A., & Davis, D. (2004). *Cognitive therapy of personality disorders* (2nd ed.). New York, NY: Guilford Press.

Beck, A. T., & Ward, C. H. (1961). Dreams of depressed patients: Characteristic themes in manifest content. *Archives of General Psychiatry, 5*(5), 462–467. doi:10.1001/archpsyc.1961.01710170040004

Bell, A. P., Weinberg, M. S., & Hammersmith, S. K. (1981). *Sexual preference: Its development in men and women.* Bloomington, IN: Indiana University Press.

Ben-Eliyahu, S., Yirmiya, R., Liebeskind, J. C., Taylor, A. N., & Gale, R. P. (1991). Stress increases metastatic spread of a mammary tumor in rats: Evidence for mediation by the immune system. *Brain, Behavior, and Immunity, 5*(2), 193–205. http://dx.doi.org/10.1016/0889-1591(91)90016-4

Benjamin, E. J., Blaha, M. J., Chiuve, S. E., Cushman, M., Das, S. R., Deo, R.,...Muntner, P. (2017, January 25). Heart disease and stroke statistics—2017 update: A report from the American Heart Association. Dallas, TX: American Heart Association/American Stroke Association. https://doi.org/10.1161/CIR.0000000000000485

Berk, M., Hallam, K., Lucas, N., Hasty, M., McNeil, C. A., Conus, P.,...McGorry, P. (2007). Early intervention in bipolar disorders. *The Medical Journal of Australia, 187*(7), 11–14.

Berkowitz, L. (1978). Aversively stimulated aggression: Some parallels and differences in research with animals and humans. *American Psychologist, 38*(11), 1135–1144. http://psycnet.apa.org/doi/10.1037/0003-066X.38.11.1135

Berkowitz, L. (1986). *A survey of social psychology* (3rd ed.). New York, NY: Holt, Rinehart and Winston.

Berkowitz, L. (1989). Frustration-aggression hypothesis: Examination and reformulation. *Psychological Bulletin, 106*(1), 59–73.

Berkowitz, L. (1993). Towards a general theory of anger and emotional aggression: Implications of the cognitive-neoassociationists perspective for the analysis of anger and other emotions. In R. S. Wyer & T K. Srull (Eds.), *Perspectives on anger and emotion: Advances in social Cognition* (Vol. 6, pp. 1–46). Hillsdale, NJ: Lawrence Erlbaum Associates.

Berndt, T. J. (1982). The features and effects of friendships in adolescence. *Child Development, 53*(6), 1447–1460. doi:10.2307/1130071

Bhattacharyya, S., Khanna, S., Chakrabarty, K., Mahadevan, A., Christopher, R., & Shankar, S. K. (2009). Anti-brain autoantibodies and altered excitatory neurotransmitters in obsessive-compulsive disorder. *Neuropsychopharmacology, 34*(12), 2489–2496. doi:10.1038/npp.2009.77

Binet, A., & Simon, T. (1905). *The development of intelligence in children* (the Binet-Simon scale) (E. S. Kite, Trans.). Baltimore, MD: Williams & Wilkins.

Birger, M., Swartz, M., Cohen, D., Alesh, Y., Grishpan, C., & Kotelr, M. (2003). Aggression: The testosterone-serotonin link. *The Israel Medical Association Journal, 5*(9), 653–658.

Blennow, K., de Leon, M. J., & Zetterberg, H. (2006). Alzheimer's disease. *Lancet, 368*(9533), 387–403. doi:10.1016/S0140-6736(06)69113-7

Bleuler, E. (1950). *Dementia praecox; or, the group of schizophrenias.* New York, NY: International Universities Press.

Bloom, F., Lazerson, A., & Hofstader, L. (1985). *Brain, mind, and behavior.* New York, NY: W. H. Freeman.

Bodamar, M. D., & Gardner, R. A. (2002). How cross-fostered chimpanzees (Pan troglodytes) initiate and maintain conversations. *Journal of Comparative Psychology, 116*(1), 12–26. doi:10.1037/0735-7036.116.1.12

Bombardieri, M. (2005, January 17). Summers' remarks on women draw fire. The *Boston Globe.* Retrieved from http://archive.boston.com/news/education/higher/articles/2005/01/17/summers_remarks_on_women_draw_fire/?page=2

Bond, A. J. (2005). Antidepressant treatments and human aggression. *European Journal of Pharmacology, 526*(1–3), 218–225. http://dx.doi.org/10.1016/j.ejphar.2005.09.033

Borke, H. (1975). Piaget's mountains revisited. *Developmental Psychology, 11*(2), 240–243.

Borovecki, F., Lovrecic, L., Zhou, J., Jeong, H., Then, F., Rosas, H.,... Krainc, D. (2005). Genome-wide expression profiling of human blood reveals biomarkers for Huntington's disease. *Proceedings of the National Academy of Sciences, 102*(31), 11023–11028. doi:10.1073/pnas.0504921102

Bosley, H. & Eagleman, D. (2015). Synesthesia in twins: incomplete concordance in monozygotes suggests extragenic factors. *Behavioural and Brain Sciences, 286*, 93–96. doi:10.1016/j.bbr.2015.02.024

Bouchard, T. J. (1984). Twins reared together and apart: What they tell us about human diversity. In S. W. Fox (Ed.), *Individuality and determinism* (pp. 147–184). New York, NY: Plenum Press.

Bouchard, T. J., Lykken, D. T., McGue, M., Segal, N. L., & Tellegen, A. (1990). Sources of human psychological differences: The Minnesota study of twins reared apart. *Science, 250*(4978), 223–228. doi:10.1126/science.2218526

Bouton, M. E. (2016) *Learning and Behavior: A contemporary synthesis* (2nd ed.). Sunderland, MA: Sinauer Publishers.

Bower, G. H., & Clark, M. C. (1969). Narrative stories as mediators for serial learning. *Psychonomic Science, 14*(4), 181–182. doi:10.3758/BF03332778

Bowlby, J. (1965). *Child care and growth of love* (2nd ed.). Baltimore, MD: Penguin.

Bowlby, J. (1980). *Attachment and loss: Vol 2. Loss sadness and depression.* New York, NY: Basic Books.

Boysen, G. A. (2011). The scientific status of childhood dissociative identity disorder: A review of published research. *Psychotherapy and Psychosomatics, 80*(6), 329–334. doi:10.1159/000323403

Brannon, L., Feist, J., & Updegraff, J. A. (2014). *Health psychology: An introduction to behavior and health* (8th ed.). Belmont, CA: Wadsworth.

Braun, K. A., Ellis, R., & Loftus, E. F. (2001). Make my memory: How advertising can change our memories of the past. *Psychology & Marketing, Jan; 19*(1), 1–23. doi:10.1002/mar.1000

Brecher, R., & Brecher, E. M. (1966). *An analysis of human sexual response.* New York, NY: Little Brown.

Bremer, J. (1959). *Asexualization.* New York, NY: Macmillan.

Bremner, J. D., Vythilingam, M., Vermetten, E., Southwick, S. M., McGlashan, T., Nazeer, A.,... Charney, D. S. (2003). MRI and PET study in deficits in hippocampal structure and function in women with childhood sexual abuse and posttraumatic stress disorder. *The American Journal of Psychiatry, May; 160*(5), 924–932. https://dx.doi.org/10.1176/appi.ajp.160.5.924

Brewster, D. (1854). North British Review. In J. Miller (Ed.), *States of mind (1983).* New York, NY: Pantheon Press.

Briddell, D. W., & Wilson, G. T. (1976). Effects of alcohol and expectancy set on male sexual arousal. *Journal of Abnormal Psychology, 85*(2), 225–234.

Brodbeck, A., & Irwin, O. (1946). The speech behavior of infants without families. *Child Development, 17*(3), 145–156.

Brooks, J. O., & Watkins, M. J. (1989). Recognition memory and the mere exposure effect. *Journal of Experimental Psychology, 15*(5), 968–976.

Brown, R. (1973). Development of the first language in the human species. *American Psychologist, 28*(2), 97–106.

Bruins Slot, L. A., & Colpaert, F. C. (2003). A persistent opioid-addiction state of memory. *Behavioral Pharmacology, 14*(2), 167–171. doi:10.1097/01.fbp.0000063264.43827.d0

Buijs, R. M., van Eden, C. G., Goncharuk, V. D., & Kalsbeek, A. (2003). The biological clock tunes the organs of the body: Timing by hormones and the autonomic nervous system. *The Journal of Endocrinology, 177*(1), 17–26.

Bunker, S. J., Colquhoun, D. M., Esler, M. D., Hickie, I. B., Hunt, D., Jelinek, V. M.,... Tonkin, A. M. (2003). "Stress" and coronary heart disease: Psychosocial risk factors. *The Medical Journal of Australia, 178*(6), 272–276.

Burger, J. M., Soroka, S., Gonzago, K., Murphy, E., & Somervell, E. (2001). The effect of fleeting attraction on compliance to requests. *Personality and Social Psychology Bulletin, 27*(12), 1578–1586.

Burnette, J., Pollack, J. M., & Forsyth, D. R. (2011). Leadership in extreme contexts: A groupthink analysis of the May 1996 Mount Everest disaster. *Journal of Leadership Studies, 4*(4), 29–40. doi:10.1002/jls.20190

Burt, C. (1966). The genetic determination of differences in intelligence: A study of monozygotic twins reared together and apart. *British Journal of Psychology, 57*(1–2), 137–153. doi:10.1111/j.2044-8295.1966.tb01014.x

Buss, D. M. (1989). Sex differences in human mate preferences: Evolutionary hypotheses tested in 37 cultures. *Behavioral & Brain Sciences, 12*(1), 1–14. https://doi.org/10.1017/S0140525X00023992

Buss, D. M., Abbott, M., Angleitner, A., Asherian, A., Biaggio, A., Blanco-Villasenor, A.,... Lohamy, N. E. (1990). International preferences in selecting mates: A study of 37 cultures. *Journal of Cross Cultural Psychology, 21*, 5–47. doi:10.1177/0022022190211001

Buss, D. M., & Shackelford, T. K. (2008). Attractive women want it all: Good genes, economic investment, parenting proclivities, and emotional commitment. *Evolutionary Psychology, 6*(1), 134–146. doi:10.1177/147470490800600116

C

Call, J., & Tomasello, M. (2008). Does the chimpanzee have a theory of mind? 30 years later. *Trends in Cognitive Science, 12*(5), 187–192. doi:10.1016/j.tics.2008.02.010

Calvin, C. M., Fernandes, C., Smith, P., Visscher, P. M., & Deary, I. J. (2010). Sex, intelligence and educational achievement in a national cohort of over 175,000 11-year old schoolchildren in England. *Intelligence, 38*(4), 424–432. http://dx.doi.org/10.1016/j.intell.2010.04.005

Cameron, N. M., Shahrokh, D., Del Corpo, A., Dhir, S. K., Szyf, M., Champagne, F. A., & Meaney, M. (2008). Epigenetic programming of phenotypic variations in reproductive strategies in the rat through maternal care. *Journal of Neuroendrocrinology, 20*(6), 795–801. https://dx.doi.org/10.1111/j.1365-2826.2008.01725.x

Cantor, N., & Mischel, W. (1979). Prototypes in person perception. In L. Berkowitz (Ed.), *Advances in Experimental social psychology* (Vol. 12). New York, NY: Academic Press. doi:10.1016/S0065-2601(08)60258-0

Cardinale, A., & Biocca, S. (2008). The potential of intracellular antibodies for therapeutic targeting of protein-misfolding diseases. *Trends in Molecular Medicine, 14*(9), 373–380. https://dx.doi.org/10.1016/j.molmed.2008.07.004

Cargill, B. R., Clark, M. M., Pera, V., Niaura, R. S., & Abrams, D. B. (1999). Binge eating, body image, depression, and self-efficacy in an obese clinical population. *Obesity Research, 7*(4), 379–386. doi:10.1002/j.1550-8528.1999.tb00421.x

Carlson, N. R. (2010). *Physiology of behavior* (9th ed.). Boston, MA: Allyn & Bacon.

Carlson, N. (2014). *Foundations of behavioral neuroscience* (9th ed.). New York, NY: Pearson.

Carlsson, A. (1977). Does dopamine play a role in schizophrenia? *Psychological Medicine, 7*(4), 583–595.

Carlsson, A., & Carlsson, M. L. (2006). A dopaminergic deficit hypothesis of schizophrenia: The path to discovery. *Dialogues in Clinical Neuroscience, 8*(1), 137–142.

Carlsson, M., & Carlsson, A. (1990). Schizophrenia: A subcortical neurotransmitter imbalance syndrome? *Schizophrenia Bulletin, 16*(3), 425–432.

Carr, P. B., & Steele, C. M. (2009). Stereotype threat and inflexible perseverance in problem solving. *Journal of Experimental Social Psychology, 45*(4), 853–859. http://dx.doi.org/10.1016/j.jesp.2009.03.003

Carrillo, M. R., Ricci, L. A., Coppersmith, G. A., & Melloni, R. H., Jr. (2009). The effect of increased serotonergic neurotransmission on aggression: A critical meta-analytical review of preclinical studies. *Psychopharmacology, 205*(3), 349–368. doi:10.1007/s00213-009-1543-2

Cattell, R. B. (1950). *A systematic theoretical and factual study.* New York, NY: McGraw-Hill.

Cattell, R. B., & Cattell, H. E. (1995). Personality structure and the new fifth edition of the 16PF. *Educational and Psychological Measurement, 55*(6), 926–937.

Cavallaro, S., Schreurs, B. G., Zhao, W., D'Agata, V., & Alkon, D. L. (2001). Gene expression profiles during long-term memory consolidation. *The European Journal of Neuroscience, 13*(9), 1809–1815. doi:10.1046/j.0953-816x.2001.01543.x

Cecconi, J. P., Lopes, A. C., Duran, F. L., Santos, L. C., Hoexter, M. Q., Gentil, A. F.,... Migel, E. C. (2008). Gamma ventral capsulotomy for treatment of resistant obsessive-compulsive disorder: A structural MRI pilot prospective study. *Neuroscience Letter, 447*(2–3), 138–142. doi:10.1016/j.neulet.2008.09.061

Centers for Disease Control and Prevention. (2013, November 21). *Marriage and divorce.* Retrieved from https://www.cdc.gov/nchs/fastats/marriage-divorce.htm

Centers for Disease Control and Prevention. (2015, October 7). *Attention deficit hyperactivity disorder (ADHD).* Retrieved from https://www.cdc.gov/nchs/fastats/adhd.htm

Centers for Disease Control and Prevention. (2016a, March 11). *Alzheimer's disease.* Retrieved from https://www.cdc.gov/nchs/fastats/alzheimers.htm

Centers for Disease Control and Prevention. (2016b, June 13). *Obesity and overweight* [U.S. data]. Retrieved from https://www.cdc.gov/nchs/fastats/obesity-overweight.htm

Centers for Disease Control and Prevention. (2016c, July 18). *Sexual risk behaviors: HIV, STD, & teen pregnancy prevention.* Retrieved from https://www.cdc.gov/healthyyouth/sexualbehaviors/

Centers for Disease Control and Prevention. (2017, January 19). *Mental health* [Fast Stats]. Retrieved from https://www.cdc.gov/nchs/fastats/mental-health.htm

Cesario, S. K., & Hughes, L. A. (2007). Precocious puberty: A comprehensive review of literature. *Journal of Obstetric, Gynecologic, and Neonatal Nursing, 36*(3), 263–274. https://dx.doi.org/10.1111/j.1552-6909.2007.00145.x

Charney, D. S. (2003). Neuroanatomical circuits modulating fear and anxiety behaviors. *Acta Psychiatrica Scandinavica, Supplementum, 417,* 38–50.

Chase, M. H., & Morales, F. R. (1983). Subthreshold excitatory activity and motor neuron discharge during REM periods of active sleep. *Science, 221*(4616), 1195–1198.

Chase, M. H., & Morales, F. R. (1990). The atonia and myoclonia of active (REM) sleep. *Annual Review of Psychology, 41,* 557–584. https://dx.doi.org/10.1146/annurev.ps.41.020190.003013

Chase, T. (1990). *When rabbit howls: The troops for Truddi Chase.* New York, NY: Jove.

Chen, A. (2016, October 4). The DEA just cut opioid production by 25 percent for next year. *The Verge.* Retrieved from http://www.theverge.com/2016/10/4/13166594/dea-opioid-epidemic-manufacturer-2017-substance-abuse

Cheung, Y. L., Molassiotis, A., & Chang, A. M. (2003). The effect of progressive muscle relaxation training on anxiety and quality of life after stoma surgery in colorectal cancer patients. *Psycho-oncology, 12*(3), 254–266. https://dx.doi.org/10.1002/pon.638

Chomsky, N. (1965). *Aspects of the theory of syntax.* Cambridge, MA: MIT Press.

Chomsky, N. (1968). *Language and mind.* New York, NY: Harcourt Brace.

Chomsky, N. (1993). On the nature, use, and acquisition of language. In A. I. Goldman, *Readings in philosophy and cognitive science* (pp. 511–534). Cambridge, MA: The MIT Press.

Chomsky, N. (2011). Language and other cognitive systems. What is special about language? *Language Learning and Development, 7*(4), 263–278. http://dx.doi.org/10.1080/15475441.2011.584041

Clancy, S. A. (2005). *Abducted: How people come to believe they were kidnapped by aliens.* Cambridge, MA: Harvard University Press.

Clark, L., Bechara, A., Damasio, H., Aitken, M. R., Sahakian, B. J., & Robbins, T. W. (2008). Differential effects of insular and ventromedial prefrontal cortex lesions on risky decision-making. *Brain: A Journal of Neurology, 1311*(5), 1311–1322. doi:10.1093/brain/awn066

Clarke, A. M., & Clarke, A. D. (1976). *Early experience: Myth and evidence.* London, UK: Open Books.

Clément, K., Vaisse, D., Lahlou, N., Cabrol, S., Pelloux, V., Cassuto, D.,...Guy-Grand, B. (1998). A mutation in the human leptin receptor gene causes obesity and pituitary dysfunction. *Nature, 392*(6674), 330–401. https://dx.doi.org/10.1038/32911

Cohen, S., & Williamson, G. M. (1991). Stress and infectious disease in humans. *Psychological Bulletin, 109*(1), 5–24.

Cohen-Kettenis, P. T. (2005). Gender change in 46,XY persons with 5a-reductase-2 deficiency and 17beta-hydroxysteroid dehydrogenase-3 deficiency. *Archives of Sexual Behavior, 34*(4), 399–410. https://dx.doi.org/10.1007/s10508-005-4339-4

Collignon, O., Davare, M., DeVolder, A. G., & Poirier, C. (2008). Time-course of posterior parietal and occipital cortex contribution to sound location. *Journal of Cognitive Neuroscience, 20*(8), 1454–1463. doi:10.1162/jocn.2008.20102

Colwill, R., & Rescorla, R. (1986). Associative structures in instrumental learning. In G. H. Bower (Ed.), *The psychology of learning and motivation* (Vol. 20). New York, NY: Academic Press.

Commons, M., & Grotzer, T. (1990). The relationship between Piagetian and Kohlbergian stage: An examination of the "necessary but not sufficient relationship." In M. Commons, *Adult development, models and methods in the study of adolescent and adult thought* (Vol. 2 pp. 205–233). New York, NY: Praeger Publishers.

Conway, A. R., Jarrold, C., Kane, M. J., Miyake, A., & Towse, J. N. (Eds.). (2007). *Variation in working memory* (Vol. 19). New York, NY: Oxford University Press.

Cooper, E. B., Scherder, E. J., & Cooper, J. B. (2005). Electrical treatment of reduced consciousness: Experience with coma and Alzheimer's disease. *Neuropsychological Rehabilitation, 15*(3–4), 389–405. https://dx.doi.org/10.1080/09602010443000317

Cooper, J. B., Jane, J. A., Alves, W. M., & Cooper, E. B. (1999). Right median nerve electrical stimulation to hasten awakening from coma. *Brain Injury, 13*(4), 261–267.

Cooper, J. R., Bloom, F. E., & Roth, R. H. (2003). *The biochemical basis of neuropharmacology,* (8th ed.). New York, NY: Oxford University Press.

Copen, C. E., Daniels, K., Vespa, J., & Mosher, W. D. (2012, March 22). First marriages in the United States: Data from the 2006–2010 national survey of family growth. *National Health Statistics Report, 49.*

Coren, S., & Ward, L. (1989). *Sensation and perception* (3rd ed.). San Diego, CA: Harcourt Brace Jovanovich.

Cornier, M. (2011). Is your brain to blame for weight regain? *Physiology & Behavior, 104*(4), 608–612. doi:10.1016/j.physbeh.2011.04.003

Correia, A. S., Anisimov, S. V., Li, J. Y., & Brundin, P. (2006). Stem cell-based therapy for Parkinson's disease. *Annals of Medicine, 37*(7), 487–98. https://dx.doi.org/10.1080/07853890500327967

Costa, P. T., & McCrae, R. R. (1992). Four ways five factors are basic. *Personality and Individual Differences, 13*(6), 653–665. http://dx.doi.org/10.1016/0191-8869(92)90236-I

Costa, P. T., & McCrae, R. R. (1994). *Set like plaster? Evidence for the stability of adult personality.* In T. Heatherton & J. Weinberger (Eds.), *Can personality change?* (pp. 21–40). Washington, DC: American Psychological Association.

Costa, R. M., Gutierrez, R., de Araujo, I. E., Coelho, M. R., Kloth, A. D., Gainetdinov, R. R., …Simon, S. A. (2007). Dopamine levels modulate the updating of tastant values. *Genes, Brain, & Behavior, 6*(4), 314–320. https://dx.doi.org/10.1111/j.1601-183X.2006.00257.x

Costello, E. J., Sung, M., Worthman, C., & Angold, A. (2007). Pubertal maturation and the development of alcohol use and abuse. *Drug and Alcohol Dependence, 88*(Supp. 1), S50–S59. https://dx.doi.org/10.1016/j.drugalcdep.2006.12.009

Cox, J. J., Reimann, F., Nicholas, A. K., Thornton, G., Roberts, E., Springell, K.,… Woods, C. G. (2006). An SCN9A channelopathy causes congenital inability to experience pain. *Nature, 444*, 894–898. doi:10.1038/nature05413

Craighead, W. E., & Dunlop, B. (2014). Combination psychotherapy and antidepressant treatment for depression: For whom, when, and how. *Annual Review of Psychology, 65*, 267–300. doi:10.1146/annurev.psych.121208

Craik, F. I., & Tulving, E. (1975). Depth of processing and the retention of words in episodic memory. *Journal of Experimental Psychology: General, 104*(3), 268–294.

Crockenberg, S. C., & Leerkes, E. M. (2006). Infant and maternal behavior moderate reactivity to novelty to predict anxious behavior at 2.5 years. *Development and Psychopathology, 18*(1), 17–34. https://dx.doi.org/10.1017/S0954579406060020

Crockenberg, S. C., & Smith, P. (1982). Antecedents of mother-infant interaction and infant irritability in the first 3 months of life. *Infant Behavior & Development, 5*(2–4), 105–119. http://dx.doi.org/10.1016/S0163-6383(82)80021-0

Crook, L. S., & Dean, M. C. (1999). "Lost in a shopping mall"—a breach of professional ethics. *Ethics and Behavior, 9*(1), 39–50. https://dx.doi.org/10.1207/s15327019eb0901_3

Crooks, R., & Baur, K. (2014). *Our sexuality,* (12th ed). Belmont, CA: Wadsworth/Cengage Learning.

Croyle, R., & Cooper, J. (1983). Dissonance arousal: Physiological evidence. *Journal of Personality and Social Psychology, 45*(4), 782–791.

Csikzentmihalyi, M., & Larson, R. (1984). *Being adolescent: Conflict and growth in the teenage years.* New York, NY: Basic Books.

D

Damasio, A. R. (1992). Aphasia. *New England Journal of Medicine, 326*, 531–539. doi:10.1056/NEJM199202203260806

Damasio, A. R. (1995). *Descartes' error: Emotion, reason, and the human brain.* New York, NY: G. P. Putnam's Sons.

Damasio, A. R. (2000). A neurobiology for consciousness. In T. Metzinger, *Neural correlates of consciousness: Empirical and conceptual questions* (pp. 111–120). Cambridge, MA: The MIT Press.

Damasio, A. R. (2001). Fundamental feelings. *Nature, 413*, 781. doi:10.1038/35101669

Damasio, A. R. (2004). Emotions and feelings. In A. Manstead, N. Frijda, & A. Fischer, *Feelings and emotions* (Vol. 413, pp. 49–57). New York, NY: Cambridge University Press. https://doi.org/10.1017/CBO9780511806582.004

Damasio, A. R. (2005). Human behaviour: Brain trust. *Nature, 435*(7042), 571–572. https://dx.doi.org/10.1038/435571a

Damasio, A. R. (2010). *Self comes to mind: Constructing the conscious brain.* New York, NY: Random House.

Damasio, A. R., & Damasio, H. (1992). Brain and language. *Scientific American, 267*(3), 88–95.

Darley, J. M., & Latané, D. B. (1968). Bystander intervention in emergencies: Diffusion of responsibility. *Journal of Personality and Social Psychology, 8*(4), 377–383. http://psycnet.apa.org/doi/10.1037/h0025589

Darwin, C. (1871/2004). *The descent of man.* London, England: John Murray/Penguin Classics.

Darwin, C. (1872/1955). *The expression of emotion in man and animals.* London, England: John Murray.

Davis, C., Kleinman, J. T., Newhart, M., Gingis, L., Pawlak, M., & Hillis, A. E. (2008). Speech and language functions that require a functioning Broca's area. *Brain and Language, 105*(1), 50–58. doi:10.1016/j.bandl.2008.01.012

Davis, D., & Loftus, E. F. (2007). Internal and external sources of misinformation in adult witness memory. In M. Tolgia, J. Read, D. Ross, & R. Lindsay, *The handbook of eyewitness psychology* (pp. 195–237). Mahwah, NJ: Lawrence Erlbaum.

Davis, J. I., Senghas, A., Brandt, F., & Ochsner, K. N. (2010). The effects of BOTOX injections on emotional experience. *Emotion, 10*(3), 433–440. doi:10.1037/a0018690

Davis, M. (1992). The role of the amygdala in fear and anxiety. *Annual Review of Neuroscience, 15*, 353. doi:10.1146/annurev.ne.15.030192.002033

Davis, M., Walker, D. L., & Myers, K. M. (2003). Role of the amygdala in fear extinction measured with potentiated startle. *Annals of the New York Academy of Sciences, 985*, 218–232.

Davis, S. R., & Braunstein, G. D. (2012). Efficacy and safety of testosterone in the management of hypoactive sexual desire disorder in postmenopausal women. *Journal of Sexual Medicine, 9*(4), 1134–1148. doi:10.1111/j.1743-6109.2011.02634.x

de Araujo, I. E., Ferreira, J., Tellez, L., & Ren, X. (2012). The gut-brain dopamine axis: A regulatory system for caloric intake. *Physiology & Behavior, 106*(3), 394–399. doi:10.1016/j.physbeh.2012.02.026

Debiec, J., Bush, D. E., & LeDoux, J. (2011). Noradrenergic enhancement of reconsolidation in the amygdala impairs extinction of conditioned fear in rats. *Depression and Anxiety, 28*(3), 186–193. https://dx.doi.org/10.1002%2Fda.20803

Deierborg, T., Soulet, D., Roybon, L., Hall, V., & Brundin, P. (2008). Emerging restorative treatments for Parkinson's disease. *Progress in Neurobiology, 85*(4), 407–432. doi:10.1016/j.pneurobio.2008.05.001

Dement, W. C. (1972). *Some must watch while some must sleep.* San Francisco, CA: W. H. Freeman.

Dement, W. C., & Kleitman, N. (1957). Cyclic variations in EEG and their relation to eye movements, bodily motility, and dreaming. *Electroencephalographic Clinical Neurophysiology,* 9(4), 673–690. http://dx.doi.org/10.1016/0013-4694(57)90088-3

Denollet, J. (2005). DS14: Standard assessment of negative affectivity, social inhibition, and Type D personality. *Psychosomatic Medicine, 67*(1), 89–97. https://dx.doi.org/10.1097/01.psy.0000149256.81953.49

Denys, D., van der Wee, N., Janssen, J., De Geus, F., & Westenberg, H. G. (2004). Low level of dopaminergic D2 receptor binding in obsessive-compulsive disorder. *Biological Psychiatry, 55*(10).

Depino, A. M., Tsetsenis, T., & Gross, C. (2008). GABA homeostasis contributes to the developmental programming of anxiety-related behavior. *Brain Research, 1210*, 189–199. doi:10.1016/j.brainres.2008.03.006

Deutsch, J. A., & Folle, S. (1973). Alcohol and asymmetrical state-dependency: A possible explanation. *Behavioral Biology, 8*(2), 273–278.

Deutsch, M., & Gerard, H. (1955). A study of normative and informational influence upon individual judgment. *Journal of Abnormal and Social Psychology, 51*(3), 629–636. http://psycnet.apa.org/doi/10.1037/h0046408

Devane, W., Hanus, L., Breuer, A., Pertwee, R. G., Stevenson, L. A., Griffin, G.,...Mechoulam, R. (1992). Isolation and structure of a brain constituent that binds to the cannabinoid receptor. *Science, 258*(5090), 1946–1949. doi:10.1126/science.1470919

Devlin, B., Daniels, M., & Roeder, K. (1997). The heritability of IQ. *Nature, 388*(6641), 468–471. https://dx.doi.org/10.1038/41319

Diamond, M., & Sigmundson, H. K. (1999). Sex reassignment at birth. In S. J. Ceci, & W. M. Williams (Eds.), *The nature-nurture debate: The essential readings. Essential reading in developmental psychology* (pp. 55–75). Malden, MA: Blackwell.

Dickens, W. T., & Flynn, J. R. (2005). Black Americans reduce IQ gap: Evidence from standardization samples. *Psychological Science, 17*(10), 913–920.

Dickstein, S. G., Bannon, K., Castellanos, F. X., & Milham, M. P. (2006). The neural correlates of attention deficit hyperactivity disorder: An ALE meta-analysis. *Journal of Child Psychology and Psychiatry, and Allied Disciplines, 47*(10), 1051–1062. https:/dx.doi.org/10.1111/j.1469-7610.2006.01671.x

Dinsdale, J. E., & Moss, J. (1980). Plasma catecholamines levels in stress and exercise. *Journal of the American Medical Association, 243*(4), 340–342. doi:10.1001/jama.1980.03300300018017

Dollard, J., Doob, L. W., Miller, N. E., Mowrer, O. H., & Sears, R. R. (1939). *Frustration and aggression.* New Haven, CT: Yale University Press.

Donchin, E., & Herning, R. I. (1975). A stimulation study of the efficacy of stepwise discriminant analysis in the detection and comparison of event related potentials. *Electroencephalography and Clinical Neuropsychology, 38*(1), 51–68.

Dourish, C. T., Ruckert, A. C., Tattersall, F. D., & Iversen, S. D. (1989). Evidence that decreased feeding induced by systemic injection of cholecystokinin is mediated by CCK-A receptors. *European Journal of Pharmacology, 173*(2–3), 233–234.

Dowrick, P. W. (1999). A review of self modeling and related interventions. *Applied and Preventative Psychology, 8*(1), 23–39. 10.1016/S0962-1849(99)80009-2

Dowrick, P. W., Kim-Rupnow, W. S., & Power, T. J. (2006). Video feedforward for reading. *The Journal of Special Education, 39*(4), 194–207.

Drevets, W. C., Price, J. L., & Furey, M. L. (2008). Brain structural and functional abnormalities in mood disorders: Implications for neurocircuitry models of depression. *Brain Structure and Function, 213*(1–2), 93–118. doi:10.1007/s00429-008-0189-x

Driver, H. S., Rogers, G. G., Mitchell, D., Borrow, S. J., Allen, M., Luus, H. G., & Shapiro, C. M. (1994). Prolonged endurance exercise and sleep disruption. *Medicine and Science in Sports and Exercise, 26*(7), 903–907.

Dudley, C. A. (2005). Alcohol, sexual arousal, and sexually aggressive decision-making: Preventative strategies and forensic psychology implications. *Journal of Forensic Psychology Practice, 5*(3), 1–34. http://dx.doi.org/10.1300/J158v05n03_01

Dudley, R. M. (1991). IQ and heredity. *Science, 252*(5003), 191–192. doi:10.1126/science.252.5003.191-a

Dufresne, A., Rainville, P., Dodin, S., Barré, P., Masse, B., Verreault, R., & Marc, I. (2010). Hypnotizability and opinions about hypnosis in a clinical trial for the hypnotic control of pain and anxiety during pregnancy termination. *International Journal of Clinical and Experimental Hypnosis, 58*(1), 82–101. doi:10.1080/00207140903310865

Dunham, R. M., Kidwell, J. S., & Wilson, S. M. (1986). Rites of passage at adolescence. *Journal of Adolescent Research, 1*(2), 139–154.

Dunn, M. J., & Searle, R. (2010). Effect of manipulated prestige-car ownership on both sex attractiveness ratings. British Journal of Psychology, 101(1), 69–80. doi:10.1348/000712609X417319

Dunn, R. T., Willis, M. W., Benson, B. E., Repella, J. D., Kimbrell, T. A., Ketter, T. A.,... Post, R. M. (2005). Preliminary findings of uncoupling of flow and metabolism in unipolar compared with bipolar affective illness and normal controls. *Psychiatry Research, 140*(2), 181–198. https://dx.doi.org/10.1016/j.pscychresns.2005.07.005

Durtschi, J. A., Fincham, F. D., Cui, M., Lorenz, F. O., & Conger, R. D. (2011). Dyadic processes in early marriage: Attributions, behavior, and marital quality. *Family Relations: An Interdisciplinary Journal of Applied Family Studies, 60*(4), 421–434. https://dx.doi.org/10.1111%2Fj.1741-3729.2011.00655.x

E

Ebbeling, C. B., & Ludwig, D. S. (2008). Tracking pediatric obesity: An index of uncertainty? *Journal of the American Medical Association, 299*(20), 2442–2443. doi:10.1001/jama.299.20.2442

Ebbinghaus, H. (1913). *Memory: A contribution to experimental psychology* (H. Ruger & C. Bussenius, Trans.). New York, NY: Teachers College (Originally published in 1885).

Eibl-Eibesfeldt, I. (1989). *Human ethology.* Hawthorne, NY: Aldine Transaction.

Eisenberger, N. I., Lieberman, M. D., & Williams, K. D. (2003). Does rejection hurt? An fMRI study of social exclusion. *Science, 302*(5643), 290–292. doi:10.1126/science.1089134

Ekman, P. (Ed.) (1982). *Emotion and the human face: Studies in emotion & social interaction* (2nd ed.). New York, NY: Cambridge University Press.

Ekman, P., & Friesen, W. V. (1984). *Unmasking the face* (2nd ed.). Palo Alto, CA: Consulting Psychologists Press.

Ekman, P., Levenson, R. W., & Friesen, W. V. (1983). Autonomic nervous system activity distinguishes among emotions. *Science, 221*(4616), 1208–1210.

Ekstrand, J., Hellsten, J., & Tingström, A. (2008). Environmental enrichment, exercise and corticosterone affect endothelial cell proliferation in adult rat hippocampus and prefrontal cortex. *Neuroscience Letters, 442*(3), 203–207. doi:10.1016/j.neulet.2008.06.085

Elkins, G., Jensen, M. P., & Patterson, D. R. (2007). Hypnotherapy for the management of chronic pain. *International Journal of Clinical and Experimental Hypnosis, 55*(3), 275–287. https://dx.doi.org/10.1080/00207140701338621

Ellis, A. (1962). *Reason and emotion in psychotherapy.* New York, NY: Lyle Stuart.

Ellis, A., & Dryden, W. (2007). *The practice of rational emotive behavior therapy* (2nd ed.). New York, NY: Springer.

Ellis, A., & Ellis, D. J. (1984). Rational emotive behavior therapy. In R. Corsini (Ed.), *Current psychotherapies* (3rd ed., pp. 151–192). Itasca, IL: F. E. Peacock.

Ellis, L., & Ames, M. (1987). Neurohormonal functioning and sexual orientation: A theory of homosexuality-heterosexuality. *Psychology Bulletin, 101*(2), 233–258. doi:10.1037/0033-2909.101.2.233

Ely, R., Gleason, J. B., MacGibbon, A., & Zaretsky, E. (2001). Attention to language: Lessons learned at the dinner table. *Social Development, 10*(3), 355–373. doi:10.1111/1467-9507.00170

Emory, L. E., Cole, C. M., & Meyer, W. J., III (1995). Use of Depo-Provera to control sexual aggression in persons with traumatic brain injury. *Journal of Head Trauma Rehabilitation. 10*(3), 47–58.

Engle, S., Zhang, X., & Wandell, B. (1997). Colour tuning in human visual cortex measured with functional magnetic resonance imaging. *Nature, 338*(6637), 68–71. https://dx.doi.org/10.1038/40398

Ennis, R. H. (1975). Children's ability to handle Piaget's propositional logic: A conceptual critique. *Review of Educational Research, 45*(1), 1–41.

Epstein, A., & Teitelbaum, P. (1967). Specific loss of the hypoglycemic control of feeding in recovered lateral rats. *American Journal of Physiology, 213*(5), 1159–1167.

Erickson, K. I., Miller, D. L., & Roecklein, K. A. (2012). The aging hippocampus: Interactions between exercise, depression, and BDNF. *The Neuroscientist, 18*(1), 82–97. doi:10.1177/1073858410397054

Erikson, E. (1963). *Childhood and society* (2nd ed.). New York, NY: Norton.

Erkut, S. (1983). Exploring sex differences in expectancy, attribution, and academic achievement. *Sex Roles, 9*(2), 217–231. 10.1007/BF00289625

Erlenmeyer-Kimling, L., & Jarvik, L. (1963). Genetics and intelligence: A review. *Science, 142*(3598), 1477–1479.

Estes, W. (1972). An associative basis for coding and organization in memory. In A. W. Melton, & E. Martin (Eds.), *Coding process in human memory* (pp. 161–190). Washington, DC: Winston & Sons.

Etscorn, F., & Stephens, R. (1973). Establishment of conditioned taste aversions with a 24-hour CS-US interval. *Physiological Psychology, 1*(3), 251–253. doi:10.3758/BF03326916

Ettenberg, A. (2004). Opponent process properties of self-administered cocaine. *Neuroscience and Biobehavioral Reviews, 27*(8), 721–728. https://dx.doi.org/10.1016/j.neubiorev.2003.11.009

Ettenberg, A., Raven, M. A., Danluck, D. A., & Necessary, B. D. (1999). Evidence for opponent-process actions of intravenous cocaine. *Pharmacology, Biochemistry, and Behavior, 64*(3), 507–512. http://dx.doi.org/10.1016/S0091-3057(99)00109-4

Ettinger, R. H. (2017). *Psychopharmacology* (2nd ed.). New York, NY: Taylor and Francis Group.

Ettinger, R. H., Ettinger, W. F., & Harless, W. E. (1997). Active immunization with cocaine-protein conjugate attenuates cocaine effects. *Pharmacology, Biochemistry, and Behavior, 58*(1), 215–220.

Ettinger, R. H., Thompson, S., & Staddon, J. E. (1986). Cholecystokinin, diet palatability, and feeding regulation in rats. *Physiology and Behavior, 36*(5), 801–809.

Evans, F. J. (1989). Hypnosis and chronic pain: Two contrasting case studies. *Clinical Journal of Pain, 5*(2), 169–176.

Everson, C. A., Bergmann, B. M., & Rechtschaffen, A. (1989). Sleep deprivation in the rat: III. Total sleep deprivation. *Sleep, 12*(1), 13–21.

Eysenck, M. W., & Keane, M. T. (2010). *Cognitive psychology: A student's handbook* (6th ed.). New York, NY: Psychology Press.

F

Faymonville, M. E., Meurisse, M., & Fissette, J. (1999). Hypnosedation: A valuable alternative to traditional anaesthetic techniques. *Acta Chirurgica Belgica, 99*(4), 141–146.

Fazio, R. H., & Olson, M. A. (2003). Implicit measures in social cognition research: Their meaning and uses. *Annual Review of Psychology, 54*, 297–327. doi:10.1146/annurev.psych.54.101601.145225

Ferini-Strambi, L., Fantini, M. L., Zucconi, M., Castronovo, V., Marelli, S., Oldani, A., Cappa, S. (2005). REM sleep behaviour disorder. *Neurological Sciences, 26*(Supp. 3), s186–s192. doi:10.1007/s10072-005-0485-7

Ferraro, K. F., Thorpe, R. J., Jr., & Wilkinson, J. A. (2003). The life course of severe obesity: Does childhood overweight matter? *The Journals of Geronotology. Series B, Psychological Sciences and Social Sciences, 58*(2), S110–S119.

Ferster, C. B. (1965). Classification of behavior pathology. In L. Krasner, & L. Ullman (Eds.), *Research in behavior modification (pp. 6–26).* New York, NY: Holt, Rinehart and Winston.

Festinger, L. (1957). *A theory of cognitive dissonance.* Stanford, CA: Stanford University Press.

Festinger, L., Carlsmith, J., & Bem, D. (2007). *Issue 4: Does cognitive dissonance explain why behavior can change attitudes?* In J. Nier (Ed.), Taking sides: Clashing views in Social Psychology (2nd ed ., pp. 74–91). New York, NY: McGraw Hill.

Festinger, L., Schachter, S., & Back, K. (1950). *Social pressures in informal groups: A study of human factors in housing.* Stanford, CA: Stanford University Press.

Fiser, J. (2009). Perceptual learning and representational learning in humans and animals. *Learning and Behavior, 37*(2), 141–153. doi:10.3758/LB.37.2.141

Fisher, S., & Greenberg, R. (1977). *Scientific credibility of Freud's theories and therapy.* New York, NY: Basic Books.

Flannery, D. J., Vazsonyi, A. T., & Waldman, I. D. (2007). *The Cambridge handbook of violent behavior and aggression*. New York, NY: Cambridge University Press.

Fleg, J., Morrell, C., Bos, A., Brant, L., & Talbot, L. (2005). Accelerated longitudinal decline of aerobic capacity in healthy older adults. *Circulation, 112*(5), 674–682. https://dx.doi.org/10.1161/CIRCULATIONAHA.105.545459

Fleischmann, M., & Pons, S. (1989). Electrochemically induced nuclear fusion of deuterium. *Journal of Electroanalytical Chemistry and Interfacial Electrochemistry, 261*(2 Part 1), 301–308. http://dx.doi.org/10.1016/0022-0728(89)80006-3

Ford, C., & Beach, F. (1951). *Patterns of sexual behavior.* Oxford, England: Harper & Brothers.

Forgeard, M. J., Haigh, E. A., Beck, A. T., Davidson, R. J., Henn, F. A., Maier, S. F.,... Seligman, M. E. (2011). Beyond depression: Towards a process-based approach to research, diagnosis, and treatment. *Clinical Psychology, 18*(4), 275–299. https://dx.doi.org/10.1111/j.1468-2850.2011.01259.x

Fox, S. I. (2011). *Human physiology.* New York, NY: McGraw-Hill.

Foxx, R. M. (2003). Treatment of dangerous behavior. *Behavioral Interventions, 18*(1), 1–21. doi:10.1002/bin.127

Franco, P., Szliwowski, H., Dramaix, M., & Kahn, A. (1999). Decreased autonomic responses to obstructive sleep events in future victims of sudden death syndrome. *Pediatric Research, 46*(1), 33–39.

Freedman, J. L. (1984). Effects of television violence on aggression. *Psychological Bulletin, 96*(2), 227–246.

Freedman, J. L. (2002). *Media violence and its effects on aggression: Assessing the scientific evidence.* Toronto, Canada: University of Toronto Press.

Freeman, W., & Watts, J. (1950). *Psychosurgery: In the treatment of mental disorders and intractable pain.* Springfield, IL: Charles C. Thomas.

Freidman, M., & Rosenman, R. H. (1974). *Type A behavior and your heart.* New York, NY: Knopf.

Freud, S. (1900). *The Interpretation of dreams* (3rd ed.). London, England: Hogarth Press.

Freud, S. (1905). *Three essays on the theory of sexuality.* (J. Strachey, Trans.) New York, NY: Basic Books.

Freud, S. (1933). The standard edition of the complete psychological works of Sigmund Freud: Vol. 22. (1932–1936). *New introductory lectures on psycho-analysis and other works* (J. Strachey, Trans.). London, England: Hogarth Press.

Freud, S. (1936). *The problem of anxiety.* New York, NY: Norton.

Fried, I., Mukamel, R., & Kreiman, G. (2011). Internally generated preactivation of single neurons in human medial frontal cortex predicts volition. *Neuron, 69*(3), 548–562. doi:10.1016/j.neuron.2010.11.045

Friederici, A. D., Rüschemeyer, S.-A., Hahne, A., & Fiebach, C. J. (2003). The role of left inferior frontal and superior temporal cortex in sentence comprehension: Localizing syntactic and semantic processes. *Ceberal Cortex, 13*(2), 170–177. https://doi.org/10.1093/cercor/13.2.170

Friedman, H., Newton, C., & Klein, T. W. (2003). Microbial infections, immunomodulation, and drugs of abuse. *Clinical Microbiology Reviews, 16*(2), 209–219.

Friedman, M., & Ulmer, D. (1984). *Treating Type A behavior—and your heart.* New York, NY: Knopf.

Fullerton, H. N., Jr. (1999, December). Labor force participation: 75 years of change, 1950–98 and 1998–2025. Retrieved from https://www.bls.gov/mlr/1999/12/art1full.pdf

G

Gabora, L., Rosch, E., & Aerts, D. (2008). Toward an ecological theory of concepts. *Ecological Psychology, 20*(1), 84–116.

Gais, S., Lucas, B., & Born, J. (2006). Sleep after learning aids memory recall. *Learning & Memory, 13*(3), 259–262. doi:10.1101/lm.132106

Galdi, S., Cadinu, M., & Tomasetto, C. (2014). The roots of stereotype threat: when automatic associations disrupt girl's math performance. *Child Development, 85*(1), 250–263. doi:10.1111/cdev.12128

Gallopin, T., Luppi, P. H., Cauli, B., Urade, Y., Rossier, J., Hayaishi, O.,...Fort, P. (2005). The endogenous somnogen adenosine excites a subset of sleep-promoting neurons via A2A receptors in the ventrolateral preoptic nucleus. *Neuroscience, 134*(4), 1377–1390. https://dx.doi.org/10.1016/j.neuroscience.2005.05.045

Ganger, J. B. (2000). Genes and environment in language acquisition: A study of early vocabulary and syntactic development in twins (Doctoral dissertation). Cambridge, MA: Massachusetts Institute of Technology Dept. of Brain and Cognitive Sciences. Retrieved from http://hdl.handle.net/1721.1/9436

Garbutt, J. C., West, S. L., Carey, T. S., Lohr, K. N., & Crews, F. T. (1999). Pharmacological treatment of alcohol dependence: A review of the evidence. The *Journal of the American Medical Association, 281*(14), 1318–1325.

Garcia, J., & Koelling, R. A. (1966). Relation of cue to consequences in avoidance learning. *Psychonomic Science, 4*(1), 123–124. doi:10.3758/BF03342209

Garcia, J., Kimeldorf, D. J., & Hunt, E. L. (1961). The use of ionizing radiation as a motivating stimulus. *Psychological Review, 68*, 383–395.

Gardner, R. A., & Gardner, B. T. (1969). Teaching sign language to a chimpanzee. *Science, 165*(3894), 664–672. doi:10.1126/science.165.3894.664

Gardner, R. A., & Gardner, B. T. (1975). Early signs of language in child and chimpanzee. *Science, 187*(4175), 752–753. https://dx.doi.org/10.1126/science.187.4178.752

Gardner, H. (1983). *Frames of mind: The theory of multiple intelligences.* New York, NY: Basic Books.

Gardner, H. (1999). *Intelligence reframed: Multiple intelligences for the 21st century.* New York, NY: Basic Books.

Gardner, H. (2006). *Multiple intelligences: New horizons (Rev. ed.).* New York, NY: Basic Books.

Gardner, H. (2011). The theory of multiple intelligences. In M. A. Gernsbacher & J. R. Pomerantz (Eds.), *Psychology and the real world* (pp. 122–130). New York, NY: Worth.

Garlicki, J., Konturek, P. K., Majka, J., Kwiecien, N., & Konturek, S. J. (1990). Cholecystokinin receptors and vagal nerves in control of food intake in rats. *American Journal of Physiology, 258*(1), E40–E45.

Gebicke-Haerter, P. J. (2012). Epigenetics of schizophrenia. *Pharmacopsychiatry, 45*(Supp. 1), S42–S48. doi:10.1055/s-0032-1304652

Gehringer, W., & Engel, E. (1986). Effect of ecological viewing conditions on the Ames' distorted room illusion. *Journal of Experimental Psychiatry, 12*(2), 181–185.

George, W. H., Lehman, G. L., Cue, K. L., Martinez, L. J., Lopez, P. A., & Norris, J. (1997). Postdrinking sexual inferences: Evidence for linear rather than curvilinear dosage effects. *Journal of Applied Social Psychology, 27*(7), 629–648. doi:10.1111/j.1559-1816.1997.tb00652.x

Gershoff, E. T., & Bitensky, S. H. (2007). The case against corporal punishment of children: Converging evidence from social science and international human rights law and implications for U.S. public policy. *Psychology, Public Policy, and Law, 13*(4), 231–272.

Gesell, A. (1926). *Infancy and human growth.* New York, NY: The Macmillan Company.

Giambra, L. M. (2000). Frequency and intensity of daydreaming: Age changes and age differences from late adolescent to the old-old. *Imagination, Cognition and Personality, 19*(3), 229–267.

Gibbs, J. C., Basinger, K. S., Grime, R. L., & Snarey, J. R. (2007). Moral judgment development across cultures: Revisiting Kohlberg's claims. *Development Review, 27*(4), 443–500. http://dx.doi.org/10.1016/j.dr.2007.04.001

Gibson, E. J., & Walk, R. D. (1960). The visual cliff. *Scientific American, 202*, 64–71.

Gibson, J. J. (1979). *The ecological approach to visual perception.* Boston, MA: Houghton Mifflin.

Gibson, J. J. (2002). A theory of direct visual perception. In A. Noë & E. Thompson (Eds.), *Vision and mind: Selected readings in the philosophy of perception* (pp. 77–90). Cambridge, MA: MIT Press.

Gillam, B. (1980). Geometrical illusions. *Scientific American, 242*(1), 102–111. http://psycnet.apa.org/doi/10.1038/scientificamerican0180-102

Gillespie-Lynch, K., Greenfield, P. M., Lyn, H., & Savage-Rumbaugh, S. (2011). The role of dialog in the ontogeny and phylogeny of early symbol combinations: A cross-species comparison of bonobo, chimpanzee, and human learners. *First Language, 31*(4), 442–460.

Gillett, R., & Warburton, F. (1970). Barbiturate blood levels found at necropsy in proven cases of acute barbiturate poisoning. *Journal of Clinical Pathology, 23*(5), 435–439.

Gillie, O. (1976, October 24). Pioneer of IQ faked his research findings. *Sunday Times of London*, H3.

Gilligan, C., & Attanucci, J. (1988). Two moral orientations: Gender differences and similarities. *Merill-Palmer Quarterly, 34*(3), 223–237.

Gistau, V. S., Pintor, L., Matrai, S., & Saiz, A. (2006). Fatal familial insomnia. *Psychosomatics, 47*, 527–528. http://dx.doi.org/10.1176/appi.psy.47.6.527

Gleason, J. B. (2000). *The development of language* (5th ed.). Needham Heights, MA: Allyn & Bacon.

Gleitman, L., & Gillette, J. (1999). The role of syntax in verb learning. In W. Ritchie & T. K. Bhatia (Eds.), *Handbook of child language acquisition* (280–298). San Diego, CA: Academic Press.

Goebel, M. U., Trebst, A. E., Steiner, J., Xie, Y. F., Exton, M. S., Frede, S.,...Schedlowski, M. (2002). Behavioral conditioning of immunosuppression is possible in humans. *The Journal of the Federation of American Societies for Experimental Biology, 16*(14), 1869–1873. https://dx.doi.org/10.1096/fj.02-0389com

Goldman-Rakic, P. S. (1992). Working memory and the mind. Scientific American, 267(3), 110–117.

Goldman-Rakic, P. S. (1999). The "psychic" neuron of the cerebral cortex. *Annals of the New York Academy of Science, 868*, 13–26. doi:10.1111/j.1749-6632.1999.tb11270.x

Goldstein, E. (2010). *Sensation and perception* (8th ed.). Independence, KS: Cengage.

González-Burgos, I., Velázquez-Zamora, D. A., & Beas-Zárate, C. (2009). Damage and plasticity in adult rat hippocampal trisynaptic circuit neurons after neonatal exposure to glutamate excitotoxicity. *International Journal of Developmental Neuroscience, 27*(8), 741–745. http://dx.doi.org/10.1016/j.ijdevneu.2009.08.016

González-Maeso, J., Weisstaub, N. V., Zhou, M., Chan, P., Ivic, L., Ang, R.,...Gingrich, J. A. (2007). Hallucinogens recruit specific cortical 5-HT(2A) receptor-mediated signaling pathways to affect behavior. *Neuron, 53*(3), 439–452. https://dx.doi.org/10.1016/j.neuron.2007.01.008

Gordon, B. A., Rykhlevskaia, E. I., Brumback, C. R., Lee, Y., Elavsky, S., Konopack, J. F.,... Fabiani, M. (2008). Neuroanatomical correlates of aging, cardiopulmonary fitness level, and education. *International Journal of Neuroscience, 45*(5), 825–838. https://dx.doi.org/10.1111/j.1469-8986.2008.00676.x

Gorski, R. (1985). The 13th J.A.F. memorial lecture: Sexual differentiation of the brain: Possible mechanisms and implications. *Canadian Journal of Physiology and Pharmacology, 63*(6), 577–594.

Gosling, S. D., Rentfrow, P. J., & Swann, W. B., Jr. (2003). A very brief measure of the Big-Five personality domains. *Journal of Research in Personality, 37*(6), 502–528. http://dx.doi.org/10.1016/S0092-6566(03)00046-1

Gottesman, I. I., & Shields, J. (1976). A critical review of recent adoption, twin, and family studies of schizophrenia: Behavior genetics perspective. *Schizophrenia Bulletin, 2*(3), 360–398.

Gottesman, I. I., McGuffin, P., & Farmer, A. E. (1987). Clinical genetics as clues to the "real" genetics of schizophrenia. *Schizophrenia Bulletin, 13*(1), 23–47.

Gould, J. L., & Marler, P. (1987). Learning by instinct. *Scientific American, 256*(1), 75–85. doi:10.1038/scientificamerican0187-74

Gould, S. J. (1981). *The mismeasure of man.* New York, NY: W. W. Norton.

Graham, J. M., & Connolly, C. W. (2006). The role of marital attributions in the relationship between life stressors and marital quality. *Personal Relationships, 13*(2), 231–241. doi:10.1111/j.1475-6811.2006.00115.x

Greenough, W., & Green, E. (1981). Experience and the changing brain. In J. March, J. McGaugh, & S. B. Kiesler (Eds.), *Aging: Biology and behavior* (159–200). New York, NY: Academic Press.

Greenough, W., McDonald, J. W., Parnisari, R. M., & Camel, J. E. (1986). Environmental conditions modulate degeneration and new dendritic growth in cerebellum on senescent rats. *Brain Research, 380*(1), 136–143.

Greenwald, A. G., McGhee., D. E., & Schwartz, J. L. (1998). Measuring individual differences in implicit cognition: The implicit association test. *Journal of Personality and Social Psychology, 74*(6), 1464–1480.

Gregory, R. L. (1978). *Eye and brain: The psychology of seeing* (3rd ed.). New York, NY: McGraw-Hill.

Greiss, K. C., & Fogari, R. (1980). Double-blind clinical assessment of alprazolam, a new benzodiazepine derivative, in the treatment of moderate to severe anxiety. *Journal of Clinical Pharmacology, 20*(11–12), 693–699.

Griffitt, W., & Veitch, R. (1974). Preacquaintance attitude similarity and attraction revisited: Ten days in a fall-out shelter. *Sociometry, 37*(2), 163–173. doi:10.2307/2786373

Grilo, C. M., & Pogue-Geile, M. (1991). The nature of environmental influences on weight and obesity: A behavior genetic analysis. *Psychological Bulletin, 110*(3), 520–537.

Grochowicz, P. M., Schedlowski, M., Husband, A. J., King, M. G., Hibberd, A., & Bowen, K. M. (1991). Behavioral conditioning prolongs heart allograft survival in rats. *Brain, Behavior, and Immunity, 5*, 349–356. http://dx.doi.org/10.1016/0889-1591(91)90030-E

Groesz, L. M., McCoy, S., Carl, J., Saslow, L., Stewart, J., Adler, N.,...Epel, E. (2012). What is eating you? Stress and the drive to eat. *Appetite, 58*(2), 717–721. doi:10.1016/j.appet.2011.11.028

Grosser, B. I., Monti-Bloch, L., Jennings-White, C., & Berliner, D. L. (2000). Behavioral and electrophysiological effects of androstadienone, a human pheromone. *Psychoneuroendocrinology, 25*(3), 289–299.

Guilford, J. P. (1967). *The nature of human intelligence.* New York, NY: McGraw-Hill.

Guilford, J. P. (1977). *Way beyond the I.Q.* Buffalo, NY: Creative Education Foundation and Bearly Unlimited.

Guilford, J. P. (1982). Cognitive psychology's ambiguities: Some suggested remedies. *Psychological Review, 89*(1), 48–59.

Guilford, J. P. (1998). Some changes in the structure-of-intellect model. *Educational and Psychological Measurements, 48*(1), 1–4. doi:10.1177/001316448804800102

Gunkelman, J. (2014). Medication prediction with electroencephaly phenotypes and biomarkers. *Biofeedback, 42*(2), 68–73. doi:10.5298/1081-5937-42.2.03

Gusella, J. F., Wexler, N. S., Conneally, M. P., Naylor, S. L., Anderson, M. A., Tanzi, R.,... Martin, J. (1983). A polymorphic DNA marker genetically linked to Huntington's disease. *Nature, 306*, 234–238. doi:10.1038/306234a0

H

Haenisch, B., Bilkei-Gorzo, A., Caron, M. G., & Bönisch, H. (2009). Knockout of the norepinephrine transporter and pharmacologically diverse antidepressants prevent behavioral and brain neurotrophin alterations in two chronic stress models of depression. *Journal of Neurochemistry, 111*(2), 403–416. doi:10.1111/j.1471-4159.2009.06345.x

Haggard, P. (2011). Decision time for free will. *Neuron, 69*(3), 404–406. http://dx.doi.org/10.1016/j.neuron.2011.01.028

Halas, E. S., & Eberhardt, M. J. (1987). Blocking and appetitive reinforcement. *Bulletin of the Psychonomic Society, 25*(2), 121–123. doi:10.3758/BF03330302

Hall, J. (1992, August 8). New theory on the origin of twins. *Science News, 142*, 84.

Halperin, J. M., Newcorn, J. H., Koda, V. H., Pick, L., McKay, K. E., & Knott, P. (1997). Noradrenergic mechanisms in ADHD children with and without reading disabilities: A replication and extension. *Journal of the American Academy of Child and Adolescent Psychiatry, 36*(12), 1688–1697. https://dx.doi.org/10.1097/00004583-199712000-00017

Halpern, G. J., & O'Connell, B. E. (2000). The security circuit: a proposed construct for the central nervous system. *The International Journal of Neuroscience, 102*(1–4), 1–254.

Hamamy, H. A., al-Hakkak, Z., & al-Taha, S. (1990). Consanguinity and the genetic control of Down syndrome. *Clinical Genetics, 37*(1), 24–29.

Hamilton, D. L., Katz, L. B., & Leirer, V. O. (1980). Memory for persons. *Journal of Personality and Social Psychology, 39*(6), 1050–1063. http://psycnet.apa.org/doi/10.1037/h0077711

Hamilton, J. (1943). Demonstrable ability of penile erection in castrated men with low titers of urinary androgen. *Proceedings of the Society of Experimental Biology and Medicine, 54*, 309.

Haney, C., & Zimbardo, P. G. (1974). *The socialization into criminality: On becoming a prisoner and a guard.* New York, NY: Holt, Rinehart and Winston.

Harden, B. (2002, May 14). In fight over turf in Montana Valley, it's man vs. grizzly. *New York Times, 151(52118).*

Hardy, J., Stolwijk, J., & Hoffman, D. (1968). Pain following step increases in skin temperature. In D. Kenshalo, *The skin senses: Proceedings* (pp. 444–454). Springfield, IL: Thomas.

Hare, R. D. (1970). *Psychopathy: Theory and Research.* New York, NY: Wiley.

Hare, R. D. (1975). *Psychophysiological studies of psychopathy.* In D. C. Fowles (Ed.), Clinical applications of psychophysiology (pp. 77–105). New York, NY: Columbia University Press.

Hare, R. D., Frazelle, J., & Cox, D. N. (1978). Psychopathy and physiological responses to threat of an aversive stimulus. *Psychophysiology, 15*(2), 165–172. doi:10.1111/j.1469-8986.1978.tb01356.x

Hare, R. D., & Neumann, C. S. (2006). The PCL-R assessment of psychopathy: Development, structural properties, and new directions. In C. J. Patrick (Ed.), *Handbook of psychopathy* (pp. 58–88). New York, NY: Guilford Press.

Harley, T. A. (2008). *The psychology of language: From data to theory* (3rd ed.). New York, NY: Psychology Press.

Harlow, H. F., & Harlow, M. (1966). Learning to love. *American Scientists, 54*(3), 244–272.

Harlow, H., Harlow, M., & Suomi, S. (1971). From thought to therapy: Lessons from a primate laboratory. *American Scientists, 59*(5), 538–549.

Harlow, H. F., & Zimmerman, R. R. (1958). The development of affectional responses in infant monkeys. *Proceedings of the American Philosophical Society, 102*, 501–509.

Harmon-Jones, E., & Harmon-Jones, C. (2008). Cognitive dissonance theory: An update with a focus on the action-based model. In J. Y. Shah & W. L. Gardner (Eds.), *Handbook of motivation science (pp. 71–83).* New York, NY: Guilford Press.

Harris, I. M., & Miniussi, C. (2003). Parietal lobe contribution to mental rotation demonstrated with rTMS. *Journal of Cognitive Neuroscience, 15*(3), 315–323. doi:10.1162/089892903321593054

Harris, S. (2012). *Free will.* New York, NY: Free Press.

Hartshorne, H., & May, M. (1928). *Studies in the nature of character* (Vol. 1). New York, NY: Macmillan.

Hastings, M. H., Maywood, E. S., & Reddy, A. B. (2008). Two decades of circadian time. *Journal of Neuroendocrinology, 20*(6), 812–819. doi:10.1111/j.1365-2826.2008.01715.x

Hathaway, S. R., & McKinley, J. C. (1942). *Minnesota Multiphasic Personality Inventory.* Minneapolis, MN: University of Minnesota.

Havas, D. A., Glenberg, A. M., Gutowski, K. A., Lucarelli, M. J., & Davidson, R. J. (2010). Cosmetic use of botulinum toxin-a affects processing of emotional language. *Psychological Science, 21*(7), 895–900. doi:10.1177/0956797610374742

Haw, J. (2008). Random-ratio schedules of reinforcement: The role of early wins and unreinforced trials. *Journal of Gaming Issues, 21*, 56–67. doi:10.4309/jgi.2008.21.6

Hawkins, R. D., Abrams, T. W., Carew, T. J., & Kandel, E. R. (1983). A cellular mechanism of classical conditioning in Aplysia: Activity dependent amplification of postsynaptic facilitation. *Science, 219(4583)*, 400–405.

Hayes, C. (1951). *The ape in our house.* New York, NY: Harper & Row.

Hearnshaw, L. S. (1979). *Cyril Burt: Psychologist.* Ithaca, NY: Cornell University Press.

Heath, R. G. (1972). Pleasure and brain activity in man: Deep and surface electroencephalograms during orgasm. *Journal of Nervous and Mental Disease, 154*(1), 3–18.

Hebb, D. O. (1955). Drives and the CNS. *Psychological Review, 62*(4), 243–254. http://psycnet.apa.org/doi/10.1037/h0041823

Heider, F. (1946). Attitudes and cognitive organization. *Journal of Psychology, 21*(1), 107–112. http://dx.doi.org/10.1080/00223980.1946.9917275

Hennenlotter, A., Dresel, C., Castrop, F., Ceballos-Baumann, A. O., Wohlschläger, A., & Haslinger, B. (2009). The link between facial feedback and neural activity within the central circuitries of emotion—New insights from Botulinum toxin-induced denervation of frown muscles. *Cerebral Cortex, 19*(3), 537–542. doi:10.1093/cercor/bhn104

Hermans, E., & Ramsey, N. (2008). Exogenous testosterone enhances responsiveness to social threat in the neural circuitry of social aggression in humans. *Biological Psychiatry, 63*(3), 263–270. https://dx.doi.org/10.1016/j.biopsych.2007.05.013

Hernandez, C. M., & Dineley, K. T. (2012). Alpha7 nicotinic acetylcholine receptors in Alzheimer's disease: neuroprotective, neurotrophic or both? *Current Drug Targets, 13*(5), 613–622.

Heston, L. L., & Shields, J. (1968). Homosexuality in twins. *Archives of General Psychiatry, 18*(2), 149–160. doi:10.1001/archpsyc.1968.01740020021003

Hilgard, E. R. (1975). Hypnosis. *Annual Review of Psychology, 26*, 19–44. doi:10.1146/annurev.ps.26.020175.000315

Hilgard, E. R. (1977). *Divided consciousness: Multiple controls in human thought and action.* New York, NY: Wiley.

Hodgkin, J. (1988). Everything you always wanted to know about sex. *Nature, 331*(6154), 300–301. https://dx.doi.org/10.1038/331300a0

Hodgkins, P., Shaw, M., McCarthy, S., & Sallee, F. R. (2012). The pharmacology and clinical outcomes of amphetamines to treat ADHD: Does composition matter? *CNS Drugs, 26*(3), 245–268. doi:10.2165/11599630-000000000-00000

Hoffman, H. G. (2004, August). Virtual reality therapy. *Scientific American, 291*, 58–65.

Hollon, S., & Garber, J. (1990). Cognitive therapy for depression: A social cognitive perspective. *Personality & Social Psychology Bulletin, 16*(1), 58–73.

Holmes, D., & Jorgensen, B. (1971). Do personality and social psychologists study men more than women? *Representative Research in Social Psychology, 2*(1), 71–76.

Holtzheimer, P. E., & Mayberg, H. S. (2011). Deep brain stimulation for psychiatric disorders. *Annual Review of Neuroscience, 34*, 289–307. doi:10.1146/annurev-neuro-061010-113638

Holway, A. H., & Boring, E. G. (1941). Determinants of apparent visual sight with distant variant. *American Journal of Psychology, 54*(1), 21–37.

Horney, K. (1950). *Neurosis and human growth: The struggle toward self-realization.* New York, NY: Norton.

Hoss, R. A., & Langlois, J. H. (2003). Infants prefer attractive faces. In O. Pascalis, & A. Slater (Eds.), *The development of face processing in infancy and early childhood: Current perspectives* (pp. 27–38). Hauppauge, NY: Nova Science.

Hote, P. T., Sahoo, R., Jani, T. S., Ghare, S. S., Chen, T., Joshi-Barve, S.,...Barve, S. S. (2008). Ethanol inhibits methionine adenosyltransferase II activity and S-adenosylmethionine biosynthesis and enhances caspase-3-dependent cell death in T lymphocytes: Relevance to alcohol-induced immunosuppression. *The Journal of Nutritional Biochemistry, 19*(6), 384–391. https://dx.doi.org/10.1016/j.jnutbio.2007.05.010

Houdini (Version 5) [computer software]. Kessel-Lo, Belgium: Cruxis/Robert Hodart. Retrieved from http://www.cruxis.com/chess/houdini.htm

Hovland, C. I., & Sears, R. R. (1940). Minor studies of aggression VI. Correlation of lynchings with economic indices. *Journal of Psychology. Interdisciplinary and Applied, 9*, 301–310. http://psycnet.apa.org/doi/10.1080/00223980.1940.9917696

Hu, Y., Yu, X., Yang, F., Si, T., Wang, W., Tan, Y.,...Chen, D. (2010). The level of serum brain-derived neurotrophic factor is associated with the therapeutic efficacy of modified electroconvulsive therapy in Chinese patients with depression. *The Journal of ECT, 26*(2), 121–125. doi:10.1097/YCT.0b013e3181c18bbf

Huang, Y.-Y., & Kandel, E. R. (2007). Low-frequency stimulation induces a pathway-specific late phase of LTP in the amygdala that is mediated by PKA and dependent on protein synthesis. *Learning and Memory, 14*(7), 497–503. https://dx.doi.org/10.1101%2Flm.593407

Hubbard, T. L. (1990). Cognitive representation of linear motion: Possible direction and gravity effects in judged displacement. *Memory and Cognition, 18*(3), 299–309.

Hubel, D. H., & Wiesel, T. N. (1979). Brain mechanisms of vision. *Scientific American, 241*(3), 150–162. doi:10.1038/scientificamerican0979-150

Hublin, C., Kaprio, J., Partinen, M., & Koskenvuo, M. (1999). Nightmares: Familial aggregation and association with psychiatric disorders in a nationwide twin cohort. *American Journal of Medical Genetics, 88*(4), 329–336.

Hublin, C., Kaprio, J., Partinen, M., & Koskenvuo, M. (2001). Parasomnias: Cooccurance and genetics. *Psychiatric Genetics, 11*(2), 65–70.

Huesmann, L. R. (2007). The impact of electronic media violence: Scientific theory and research. *Journal of Adolescent Health, 41*(6 Supp. 1), S6–S13. https://dx.doi.org/10.1016%2Fj.jadohealth.2007.09.005

Huesmann, L. R., Moise-Titus, J., Podolski, C.-L., & Eron, L. D. (2003). Longitudinal relations between children's exposure to TV violence and their aggressive and violent behavior in young adulthood: 1977–1992. *Developmental Psychology, 39*(2), 201–221. doi:10.1037/0012-1649.39.2.201

Hull, C. L. (1920). Quantitative aspects of the evolution of concepts: An experimental study. *Psychological Monographs, 28*(Whole No. 123).

Hull, C. L. (1943). *Principles of behavior: An introduction to behavior theory.* New York, NY: D. Appleton-Century.

Hurley, M. J., & Jenner, P. (2006). What has been learnt from study of dopamine receptors in Parkinson's disease? *Pharmacology & Therapeutics, 111*(3), 715–28. https://dx.doi.org/10.1016/j.pharmthera.2005.12.001

Hurvich, L. M., & Jameson, D. (1957). An opponent process theory of color vision. *Psychological Review, 64*(6 Pt 1), 384–404. http://psycnet.apa.org/doi/10.1037/h0041403

Hyde, J. S., & McKinley, N. M. (1997). Gender differences in cognition: Results from meta-analyses. In P. J. Caplan, M. Crawford, J. S. Hyde, & J. T. Richardson (Eds.), *Gender differences in human cognition* (pp. 30–51). New York, NY: Oxford University Press.

Hyde, J. S. (2005). The genetics of sexual orientation. In J. S. Hyde, *Biological substrates of human sexuality* (pp. 9–20). Washington, DC: American Psychological Association. http://psycnet.apa.org/doi/10.1037/11196-002

Hyde, J. S. (2007). New directions in the study of gender similarities and differences. *Current Directions in Psychological Science, 16*(5), 259–263.

Hyde, J. S., & Grabe, S. (2008). Meta-analysis in the psychology of women. In F. L. Denmark & M. A. Pauldi (Eds.), *Psychology of women: A handbook of issues and theories* (2nd ed., pp. 142–173). Westport, CT: Praeger.

I

Isidori, A. M., Giannetta, E., Gianfrilli, D., Greco, E. A., Bonifacio, V., Aversa, A.,... Lenzi, A. (2005). Effects of testosterone on sexual function in men: results of a meta-analysis. *Clinical Endocrinology, 63*(4), 381–394. https://dx.doi.org/10.1111/j.1365-2265.2005.02350.x

Izard, C. E. (1990). Facial expression and the regulation of emotions. *Journal of Personality and Social Psychology, 58*(3), 487–498.

J

Jacobs, G. (1983). Colour vision in animals. *Endeavour, 7(3)*, 137–140.

Jacobson, E. (1932). Electrophysiology of mental activities. *American Journal of Psychology, 44*, 677–694. http://psycnet.apa.org/doi/10.2307/1414531

James, F. R., Large, R. G., & Beale, I. L. (1989). Self-hypnosis in chronic pain: A multiple baseline study of highly hypnotisable subjects. *Clinical Journal of Pain, 5*(2), 161–168.

James, W. (1884). What is an emotion? *Mind, 9*(34), 188–205.

James, W. (1890). *The principles of psychology: In two volumes.* London, England: MacMillan.

Janecka, A., Perlikowska, R., & Fichna, J. (2007). Endomorphin analogs. *Current Medicinal Chemistry, 14*(30), 3201–3208. doi:10.2174/092986707782793880

Janet, P. (1920). *The Major Symptoms of Hysteria: Fifteen lectures given in the medical school of Harvard University* (2nd ed.). New York, NY: Macmillan.

Janis, I. L. (1972). *Victims of groupthink: A psychological study of foreign-policy decisions and fiascoes.* Boston, MA: Houghton Mifflin.

Janis, I. L. (2007). Groupthink. In R. P. Vecchio (Ed.), *Leadership: Understanding the dynamics of power and influence in organizations* (2nd ed.) (pp. 157–169). Notre Dame, IN: University of Notre Dame Press.

Janowsky, J. S. (2006). Thinking with your gonads: Testosterone and cognition. *Trends in Cognitive Sciences, 10*(2), 77–82. https://dx.doi.org/10.1016/j.tics.2005.12.010

Jansen, A., Bollen, D., Tuschen-Caffier, B., & Roefs, A. (2008). Mirror exposure reduces body dissatisfaction and anxiety in obese adolescents: A pilot study. *Appetite, 51*(1), 214–217.

Jacquin, K. M., Harrison, M. L., & Alford, S. M. (2006). Gender and peer presence influence responses to aggressive provocation. *American Journal of Forensic Psychology, 24*(3), 29–44.

Jemmott, J. B., III, & Locke, S. E. (1984). Psychosocial factors, immunologic mediation, and human susceptibility to infectious diseases: How much do we know? *Psychological Bulletin, 95*(1), 78–108. doi:10.1037/0033-2909.95.1.78

Jemmott, J. B., III, Borysenko, M., Chapman, R., Borysenko, J. Z., McClelland, D. C., Meyer, D., & Benson, H. (1983). Academic stress, power motivation, and decrease in salivary secretory immunoglobulin A secretion rate. The *Lancet, 321(8339)*, 1400–1402. http://dx.doi.org/10.1016/S0140-6736(83)92354-1

Jensen, A. R. (1969). How much can we boost IQ and scholastic achievement? *Harvard Educational Review, 39*, 1–123.

Jensvold, M. L., & Gardner, R. A. (2000). Interactive use of sign language by cross-fostered chimpanzees (Pan troglodytes). *Journal of Comparative Psychology, 114*(4), 335–346.

Johnson, M. W., & Ettinger, R. H. (2000). Active cocaine immunization attenuates the discriminative properties of cocaine. *Experimental and Clinical Psychopharmacology, 8*(2), 1–5.

Jones, E. E., Flammer, A., Grob, A., Luthi, R., Augoustinos, G., Swap, W. C.,...Fletcher, G. J. (1989). Attribution Theory. In J. P. Forgas & M. J. Innes (Eds.), *Recent advances in social psychology: An international perspective* (pp. 63–125). Amsterdam, Holland: North-Holland.

Jones, H., & Conrad, H. (1933). The growth and decline of intelligence: A study of a homogeneous group between the ages of ten and sixty. *Genetic Psychology Monographs, 13*, 223–298.

Jung, C. G. (1916). *Analytical psychology* (C. E. Long, Trans.). New York, NY: Moffat Yard.

Jung, C. G. (1933). *Modern man in search of a soul.* New York, NY: Harcourt, Brace & World.

Jung, C. G. (1953). *Collected works (Vol. 13).* Princeton, NJ: Princeton University Press.

K

Kagan, J., & Klein, R. E. (1973). Cross-cultural perspectives on early development. *American Psychologist, 28*(11), 947–961.

Kahneman, D., & Tversky, A. (1973). On the psychology of prediction. *Psychological Reviews, 80*(4), 237–251. http://psycnet.apa.org/doi/10.1037/h0034747

Kales, A., Tan, T. L., Kollar, E. J., Naitoh, P., Preston, T. A., & Malmstrom, E. J. (1970). Sleep patterns following 205 hours of sleep deprivation. *Psychosomatic Medicine, 32*(2), 189–200.

Kallman, F. J. (1952). Twin and sibship study of overt male homosexuality. *American Journal of Human Genetics, 4*(2), 136–146.

Kalmuss, D. (1984). The intergenerational transmission of marital aggression. *Journal of Marriage and Family, 46*(1), 11–19.

Kalueff, A. V., & Nutt, D. J. (2007). Role of GABA in anxiety and depression. *Depression and Anxiety, 24*(7), 495–517. https://dx.doi.org/10.1002/da.20262

Kamin L. J. (1969). Predictability, surprise, attention, and conditioning. In B. Campbell, & R. Church (Eds.), *Punishment and aversive behavior (279–296).* New York, NY: Appleton-Century-Crofts.

Kamin, L. J. (1974). *The science and politics of IQ.* Mahwah, NJ: Lawrence Erlbaum.

Kandel, E. R., & Abel, T. (1995). Neuropeptides, adenylyl cyclase, and memory storage. *Science, 268*(5212), 825–826.

Kandel, E. R., & Hawkins, R. D. (1992). The biological basis of learning and individuality. *Scientific American, 267*, 78–86.

Kanno, T. Y., Yaguchi, T., Nagata, T., Shimizu, T., Tanaka, A., & Nishizaki, T. (2012). Indomethacin enhances learning and memory potential in interacting with CaMKII. *Journal of Cellular Physiology, 227*(3), 919–926. doi:10.1002/jcp.22800

Kaplan, M. J., Lazoff, M., Kelly, K., Lukin, R., & Garver, D. L. (1990). Enlargement of cerebral third ventricle in psychotic patients with delayed response to neuroleptics. *Biological Psychiatry, 27*(2), 205–214.

Kaufman, A. S. (2001). WAIS-III IQs, Horn's theory, and generational changes from young adulthood to old age. *Intelligences, Mar-Apr; 29*(2), 131–167. http://dx.doi.org/10.1016/S0160-2896(00)00046-5

Kaufman, L., Vassiliades, V., Noble, R., Alexander, R., Kaufman, J., & Edlund, S. (2007). Perceptual distance and the moon illusion. *Spatial Vision, 20*(1–2), 155–175.

Kayser, S., Bewernick, B. H., Grubert, C., Hadrysiewicz, B. L., Axmacher, N., & Schlaepfer, T. (2011). Antidepressant effects of magnetic seizure therapy and electroconvulsive therapy in treatment resistant depression. *Journal of Psychiatric Research, 45*(5), 569–576. doi:10.1016/j.jpsychires.2010.09.008

Keating, D. P. (1988). Byrnes' reformulation of Piaget's formal operations: Is what's left what's right? *Developmental Review, 8*(4), 376–384. http://dx.doi.org/10.1016/0273-2297(88)90016-0

Kebbell, M. R., & Wagstaff, G. F. (1998). Hypnotic interviewing: The best way to interview eyewitnesses? *Behavioral Sciences & the Law, 16*(1), 115–129.

Keel, P. K., Mitchell, J. E., Miller, K. B., Davis, T. L., & Crow, S. J. (1999). Long-term outcome of bulimia nervosa. *Archives of General Psychiatry, 56*(1), 63–69.

Kelley, H. (1987). Causal schemata and the attribution process. In E. Jones (Ed), *Attribution: Perceiving the causes of behavior* (pp. 151–174). Hillsdale, NJ: Lawrence Erlbaum Associates.

Kellner, R. (1990). Somatization: Theories and research. *The Journal of Nervous and Mental Disease, 178*(3), 150–160.

Keller, D. M. (2012, April 23). Cingulotomy gives lasting relief to long-term OCD patients. Medscape. Retrieved from http://www.medscape.com/viewarticle/762498

Kellogg, W., & Kellogg, L. (1933). *The ape and the child: A study of environmental influence upon early behavior.* New York, NY: McGraw-Hill.

Kessler, R. C., Berglund, P., Demler, O., Jin, R., Merikangas, K. R., & Walters, E. E. (2005). Lifetime prevalence and age-of-onset distributions of *DSM-IV* disorders in the National Comorbidity Survey Replication. *Archives of General Psychiatry, 62*(6), 593–602. doi:10.1001/archpsyc.62.6.593

Kiefer, J. C. (2007). Epigenetics in development. *Developmental Dynamics, 236*(4), 1144–1156. doi:10.1002/dvdy.21094

Kiehl, K. A., Bates, A. T., Laurens, K. R., Hare, R. D., & Liddle, P. F. (2006). Brain potentials implicate temporal lobe abnormalities in criminal psychopaths. *Journals of Abnormal Psychology, 115*(3), 443–453. doi:10.1037/0021-843X.115.3.443

Kierkegaard, S. (1844). *Enten—eller [Either/or].* Copenhagen, Denmark: University Bookshop Reitzel.

Kihlstrom, J. F. (2004). Implicit methods in social psychology. In C. Sansone, C. C. Morf, & A. T. Panter (Eds.), *The Sage handbook of methods in social psychology* (pp. 195–212). Thousand Oaks, CA, US: Sage Publications.

Kimura, D. (1992). Sex differences in the brain. *Scientific American, 267*(3), 118–125.

Kinsey, A. C., Pomeroy, W., & Martin, C. (1948). *Sexual behavior in the human male.* Philadelphia, PA: Saunders.

Kinsey, A. C., Pomeroy, W., Martin, C., & Gebhard, P. H. (1953). *Sexual behavior in the human female.* Philadelphia, PA: Saunders.

Klaich, D. (1974). *Woman plus woman: Attitudes towards lesbianism.* New York, NY: Simon & Schuster.

Klinesmith, J., Kasser, T., & McAndrew, F. T. (2006). Guns, testosterone, and aggression: An experimental test of a mediational hypothesis. *Psychological Science: A Journal of the American Psychological Society, 17*(7), 568–571. https://dx.doi.org/10.1111/j.1467-9280.2006.01745.x

Klüver, H., & Bucy, P. C. (1939). Preliminary analysis of functions of the temporal lobes in monkeys. *Archives of Neurology and Psychiatry, 42*, 979–1000. 10.1001/archneurpsyc.1939.02270240017001

Knackstedt, L. A., Samimi, M. M., & Ettenberg, A. (2002). Evidence for opponent-process actions of intravenous cocaine and cocaethylene. *Pharmacology, Biochemistry, and Behavior, 72*(4), 931–936.

Kohlberg, L. (1964). The development of moral character and moral ideology. In M. Hoffman, & L. Hoffman (Eds.), *Review of Child Development Research* (Vol. 1, pp. 383–431). New York, NY: Russell Sage Foundation.

Kohlberg, L. (1968). The child as a moral philosopher. *Psychology Today, 2*(4), 25–30.

Kohlberg, L. (1969). Stage and sequence: The cognitive-developmental approach to socialization. In D. A. Goslin (Ed.), *Handbook of socialization theory and research* (pp. 347–480). Chicago, IL: Rand McNally.

Koles, Z. J., Lind, J. C., & Flor-Henry, P. (2010). Gender differences in brain functional organization during verbal and spatial cognitive challenges. *Brain Topography, 23*(2), 199–204. doi:10.1007/s10548-009-0119-0

Koob, G. F., & Le Moal, M. (2008). Neurobiological mechanisms for opponent motivational processes in addiction. *Philosophical Transactions of the Royal Society of London, 363*(1507), 3113–3123. https://dx.doi.org/10.1098%2Frstb.2008.0094

Kotov, R., Gámez, W., Schmidt, F. L., & Watson, D. (2010). Linking "big" personality traits to anxiety, depressive, and substance use disorders: A meta-analysis. *Psychological Bulletin, 136*(5), 768–821. doi:10.1037/a0020327

Kovács, A., Téglás, E., & Endress, A. D. (2010). The social sense: Susceptibility to other's beliefs in human infants and adults. *Science, 330*(6012), 1830–1834. doi:10.1126/science.1190792

Kraepelin, E. (1918). *Dementia praecox and paraphrenia* (R. M. Barclay, Trans.). London, UK: Livingstone.

Krebs, D. L., & Denton, K. (2005). Toward a more pragmatic approach to morality: A critical evaluation of Kohlberg's model. *Psychological Review, 112(3)*, 629–649. https://dx.doi.org/10.1037/0033-295X.112.3.629

Krebs, D. L., & Denton, K. (2006). Explanatory limitations of cognitive-developmental approaches to morality. *Psychological Review, 113(3)*, 672–675. https://dx.doi.org/10.1037/0033-295X.113.3.672

Ku, L., Sonenstein, F. L., Lindberg, L. D., Bradner, C. H., Boggess S., & Pleck, J. H. (1998). Understanding changes in sexual activity among young metropolitan men: 1979–1995. *Family Planning Perspectives, 30*(6), 256–262.

Kuppens, S., Grietens, H., Onghena, P., & Michiels, D. (2009). Associations between parental control and children's overt and relational aggression. *British Journal of Developmental Psychology, 27*(Pt 3), 607–623.

Kuriyama, K., Mishima, K., Suzuki, H., Aritake, S., Uchiyama, M. (2008). Sleep accelerates the improvement in working memory performance. *The Journal of Neuroscience, 28*(40), 10145–10150. https://doi.org/10.1523/JNEUROSCI.2039-08.2008

Kurtz-Costes, B., Rowley, S. J., Harris-Britt, A., & Woods, T. A. (2008). Gender stereotypes about mathematics and science and self-perception of ability in late childhood and early adolescence. *Merrill-Palmer Quarterly: Journal of Developmental Psychology, 54*(3), 386–409.

L

Lacey, S., & Campbell, C. (2006). Mental representation in visual/haptic crossmodel memory. Evidence from interference effects. *The Quarterly Journal of Experimental Psychology, 59*(2), 361–376. https://dx.doi.org/10.1080/17470210500173232

Lai, Y.-Y., Hsieh, K.-C., Nguyen, D., Peever, J., & Siegel, J. M. (2008). Neurotoxic lesions at the ventral mesopontine junction change sleep time and muscle activity during sleep: An animal model of motor disorders in sleep. *Neuroscience, 154*(2), 431–443. https://dx.doi.org/10.1016%2Fj.neuroscience.2008.03.085

Lamb, M. (2005). Attachments, social networks, and developmental contexts. *Human Development, 48*, 108–112. doi:10.1159/000083222

Lambracht-Washington, D. & Rosenberg, R. N. (2013). Advances in the development of vaccines for Alzheimer's disease. *Discovery Medicine, 15*(84), 319–326.

Lamkin, D. M., Sloan, E. K., Patel, A. J., Chiang, B. S., Pimentel, M. A., Ma, J. C.,... Cole, S. W. (2012). Chronic stress enhances progression of acute lymphoblastic leukemia via b-adrenergic signaling. *Brain, Behavior, and Immunity, 26*(4), 635–641. doi:10.1016/j.bbi.2012.01.013

Lang, A. J., Craske, M. G., Brown, M., & Ghaneian, A. (2001). Fear-related state dependent memory. *Cognition & Emotion, 15*(5), 695–703. http://dx.doi.org/10.1080/02699930125811

Lang, P., & Melamed, B. G. (1969). Case report: Avoidance conditioning therapy of an infant with chronic ruminative vomiting. *Journal of Abnormal Psychology, 74*(1), 1–8. http://psycnet.apa.org/doi/10.1037/h0027077

Lange, C. G., & James, W. (1885/1922). *The Emotions.* Baltimore, MD: Williams & Wilkins.

Langlois, J. H., & Roggman, L. A. (1990). Attractive faces are only average. *Developmental Psychology, 1*(2), 115–121.

Langlois, J. H., Kalakanis, L., Rubenstein, A. J., Larson, A., Hallam, M., Smoot, M. (2000). Maxims or myths of beauty? A meta-analytic and theoretical review. *Psychological Bulletin, 126*(3), 290–423.

Langlois, J. H., Roggman, L. A., Casey, R. J., Ritter, J. M., Rieser-Danner, L. A., & Jenkins, V. Y. (1987). Infant preferences for attractive faces: Rudiments of a stereotype? *Developmental Psychology, 23*(3), 363–369.

Lanska, D. J. (2000). George Huntington (1850–1916) and hereditary chorea. *Journal of the History of the Neurosciences, 9*(1), 76–89. https://dx.doi.org/10.1076/0964-704X(200004)9:1;1-2;FT076

Lanzetta, J., Cartwright-Smith, J., & Kleck, R. E. (1976). Effects of nonverbal dissimulation on emotional experience and automatic arousal. *Journal of Personality and Social Psychology, 33*(3), 354–370.

LaPiere, R. (1934). Attitudes vs. action. *Social Forces, 13*(2), 230–237. doi:10.2307/2570339

Lashley, K. S. (1929). *Brain Mechanisms and Intelligence [Monograph].* Chicago, IL: University of Chicago Press.

Lashley, K. S. (1950). In search of the engram. *Symposia of the Society for Experimental Biology, 4*, 454–482.

Latané, B., & Darley, J. (1970). *The unresponsive bystander: Why doesn't he help?* New York, NY: Appleton-Century-Crofts.

Lazarus, R. S. (2001). Relational meaning and discrete emotions. In K. Scherer, A. Schorr, & T. Johnstone (Eds.), *Appraisal processes in emotion: Theory, methods, research* (pp. 37–67). New York, NY: Oxford University Press.

Lazarus, R. S., & Folkman, S. (1984). *Stress, appraisal, and coping.* New York, NY: Springer.

LeDoux, J. E. (1992a). Brain mechanisms of emotion and emotional learning. *Current Opinion in Neurobiology, 2*(2), 191–197.

LeDoux, J. E. (1992b). Emotion and the amygdala. In J. P. Aggleton (Ed.), *The amygdala: Neurobiological aspects of emotion, memory, and mental dysfunction* (pp. 339–351). New York, NY: Wiley-Liss.

LeDoux, J. E., Wilson, D. H., & Gazzaniga, M. S. (1977). A divided mind: Observations of the conscious properties of the separated hemispheres. *Annals of Neurology, 2*(5), 417–421. doi:10.1002/ana.410020513

Lee, D. L., & Belfiore, P. J. (1997). Enhancing classroom performance: A review of reinforcement schedules. *Journal of Behavioral Education, 7*(2), 205–217. doi:10.1023/A:1022893125346

Lehne, G. K., & Money, J. (2000). The first case of paraphilia treated with Depo-Provera: 40-year outcome. *Journal of Sex Education and Therapy, 25*(4), 213–220.

Leinninger, G. M. (2011). Lateral thinking about leptin: A review of leptin action via the lateral hypothalamus. *Physiology & Behavior, 104*(4), 572–581. doi:10.1016/j.physbeh.2011.04.060

Leu-Semenescu, S., Arnulf, I., Decaix, C., Moussa, F., Clot, F., Boniol, C.,...Roze, E. (2010). Sleep and rhythm consequences of a genetically induced loss of serotonin. *Sleep, 33*(3), 307–310.

Levenson, M. R. (2009). Gender and wisdom: The roles of compassion and moral development. *Research in Human Development,* 6(1), 45–59. http://dx.doi.org/10.1080/15427600902782127

Leventhal, H., & Tomarken, A. J. (1986). Emotion: Today's problems. *Annual Review of Psychology, 37*, 565–610. doi:10.1146/annurev.ps.37.020186.003025

Levitan, R. D. (2007). The chronobiology and neurobiology of winter seasonal affective disorder. *Dialogues in Clinical Neuroscience, 9*(3), 315–324.

Lewis, E. R., Baird, R. A., Leverenz, E. L., & Koyama, H. (1982). Inner ear: Dye injection reveals peripheral origins of specific sensitivities. *Science, 215*(4540), 1641–1643.

Lewy, A. J., Rough, J. N., Songer, J. B., Mishra, N., Yuhas, K., & Emens, J. S. (2007). The phase shift hypothesis for the circadian component of winter depression. *Dialogues in Clinical Neuroscience, 9*(3), 291–300.

Lindberg, L. D., Jones, R., & Santelli, J. S. (2008). Noncoital sexual activities among adolescents. *Journal of Adolescent Health, 43*(3), 231–238. http://dx.doi.org/10.1016/j.jadohealth.2007.12.010

Lissek, S., Orme, K., Mcdowell, D. J., Johnson, L. L., Luckenbaugh, D. A., Baas, J. M.,...Grillon, C. (2007). Emotion regulation and potentiated startle across affective picture and threat-of-shock paradigms. *Biological Psychology, 76*(1–2), 124–133. http://dx.doi.org/10.1016/j.biopsycho.2007.07.002

Little, A. C., Jones, B. C., & DeBruine, L. M. (2011). Facial attractiveness: evolutionary based research. Philosophical *Transactions Royal Society B: Biological Sciences,* 366(1571), 1638–1659. doi:10.1098/rstb.2010.0404

Loftus, E. F. (1975). Leading questions and the eyewitness report. *Cognitive Psychology, 7*(4), 560–572.

Loftus, E. F. (1994). The repressed memory controversy. *The American Psychologist, 49*(5), 443–445. http://psycnet.apa.org/doi/10.1037/0003-066X.49.5.443.b

Loftus, E. F. (1997). Creating false memories. *Scientific American, 277*(3), 70–75. doi:10.1038/scientificamerican0997-70

Loftus, E. F., & Bernstein, D. M. (2005). Rich false memories: The royal road to success. In A. F. Healy, *Experimental cognitive psychology and its applications* (pp. 101–113). Washington, DC: American Psychological Association. http://psycnet.apa.org/doi/10.1037/10895-008

Loftus, E. F., & Burns, T. E. (1982). Mental shock can produce retrograde amnesia. *Memory and Cognition, 10*(4), 318–323. doi:10.3758/BF03202423

Loftus, E. F., Garry, M., & Hayne, H. (2008). Repressed and recovered memory. In E. Borgida & S. T. Fiske (Eds.), *Beyond common sense: Psychological science in the courtroom* (pp. 177–194). Malden, MA: Wiley-Blackwell.

Loftus, E. F., & Ketcham, K. (1994). *The myth of repressed memory: False memories and allegations of sexual abuse.* New York, NY: St. Martin's Press.

Loftus, E. F., & Loftus, G. R. (1980). On the permanence of stored information in the human brain. *American Psychologists, 35*(5), 409–420. http://psycnet.apa.org/doi/10.1037/0003-066X.35.5.409

Loftus, E. F., Miller, D. G., & Burns, H. J. (1978). Semantic integration of verbal information into a visual memory. *Journal of Experimental Psychology, 4*(1), 19–31. http://psycnet.apa.org/doi/10.1037/0278-7393.4.1.19

Loftus, E. F., & Palmer, J. C. (1974). Reconstruction of automobile destruction: An example of interaction between language and memory. *Journal of Verbal Learning and Verbal Behavior, 13*(5), 585–589. http://dx.doi.org/10.1016/S0022-5371(74)80011-3

Loomis, A. L., Harvey, E. N., & Hobart, G. A. (1937). Cerebral states during sleep as studied by human brain potentials. *Journal of Experimental Psychology, 21*(2), 127–144. http://psycnet.apa.org/doi/10.1037/h0057431

Lorenz, K. Z. (1937). The companion in the bird's world. The *Auk, 54*(3), 245–273. doi:10.2307/4078077

Lorenz, K. Z. (1974). *Civilized man's eight deadly sins.* New York, NY: Harcourt Brace Jovanovich.

Lu, P. H., Masterman, D. A., Mulnard, R., Cotman, C., Miller, B., Yaffe, K.,... Cummings, J. L. (2006). Effects of testosterone on cognition and mood in male patients with mild Alzheimer disease and healthy elderly men. *Archives of Neurology, 63*(2), 177–185. https://doi.org/10.1001/archneur.63.2.nct50002

Luce, G. G. (1965). *Current research on sleep and dreams* (Health Service Publication No. 1389). Washington, DC: U.S. Department of Health and Education.

Luzer, D. (2013, October 23). Is the gay population a lot bigger than even Kinsey predicted? *Pacific Standard*. Retrieved from https://psmag.com/is-the-gay-population-a-lot-bigger-than-even-kinsey-predicted-7786492b8c3#.jqr0nectf

Lykken, D. T. (1957). A study of anxiety in the sociopathic personality. *Journal of Abnormal Psychology, 55*(1), 6–10. http://psycnet.apa.org/doi/10.1037/h0047232

M

Maccoby, E. E. (2002). Gender and group process: A developmental perspective. *Current Directions in Psychological Science, 11*(2), 54–58.

Maccoby, E. E., & Jacklin, C. N. (1974). *The psychology of sex differences.* Stanford, CA: Stanford University Press.

Machaalani, R., & Waters, K. A. (2008). Neuronal cell death in the Sudden Infant Death Syndrome brainstem and associations with risk factors. *Brain: A Journal of Neurology, 131*(1), 218–228. https://doi.org/10.1093/brain/awm290

Mahowald, M. W., & Schenck, C. H. (1989). REM sleep parasomnias. In M. H. Kryger, T. Roth, & W. C. Dement (Eds.), *Principles and practice of sleep medicine (pp. 897–916).* Philadelphia, PA: Saunders.

Malan, V., Pipiras, E., Sifer, C., Kanafani, S., Cedrin-Durnerin, I., Martin-Point, B.,...Benzacken, B. (2006). Chromosome segregation in an infertile man carrying a unique pericentric inversion, inv(21)(p12q22.3), analysed using fluorescence in situ hybridization on sperm nuclei: significance for clinical genetics. A case report. *Human Reproduction, 21*(8), 2052–2056. https://doi.org/10.1093/humrep/del090

Markman, E. M. (1987). How do children constrain the possible meanings of words. In U. Neisser (Ed.), *Concepts and conceptual development: Ecological and intellectual factors in categorization* (pp. 255–287). New York, NY: Cambridge University Press.

Marler, P. (1967). Animal communication signals. *Science, 157*(3790), 769–774. doi:10.1126/science.157.3790.769

Marmor, J. (1980). *Homosexual behavior.* New York, NY: Basic Books.

Marshall, D. S. (1971). Sexual behavior on Mangaia. In D. S. Marshall, & R. C. Suggs (Eds.), *Human sexual behavior: The range and diversity of human sexual experience throughout the world—as seen in six representative cultures* (pp. 103–162). Englewood Cliffs, NJ: Prentice-Hall.

Marshall, G. D., & Zimbardo, P. G. (1979). Affective consequences of inadequacy explained physiological arousal. *Journal of Personality and Social Psychology, 37*(6), 970–988.

Martin, J. B. (1987). Genetic linkage in neurological diseases. *The New England Journal of Medicine, 316*, 1018–1020. doi:10.1056/NEJM198704163161608

Martin, L. A., Doster, J. A., Critelli, J. W., Purdum, M., Powers, C., Lambert, P. L., Miranda, V. (2011). The "distressed" personality, coping, and cardiovascular risk. *Stress and Health, 27*(1), 64–72. doi:10.1002/smi.1320

Martinez, G. M., & Abma, J. C. (2015, July). Sexual activity, contraceptive use, and childbearing of teenagers aged 15–19 in the United States. National Center for Health Statistics Data Brief, 209.

Maslow, A. (1965). A philosophy of psychology: The need for a mature science of human behavior. In E. Severin, *Humanistic Viewpoints in Psychology* (pp. 17–33). New York, NY: McGraw-Hill.

Masters, W. H., & Johnson, V. (1966). *Human sexual response.* Boston, MA: Little, Brown.

Matlin, M. W. (2008). *Cognition* (7th ed.). New York, NY: Wiley.

Matsuzaki, M., Honkura, N., Graham, C. R., Ellis-Davis, G., & Kasai, H. (2004). Structural basis of long-term potentiation in single dendritic spines. *Nature, 429*(6993), 761–766. doi:10.1038/nature02617

Max, L. (1937). An experimental study of the motor theory of consciousness. IV. Action-current responses in the deaf during awakening, kinaesthetic imagery and abstract thinking. *Journal of Comparative Psychology, 24*(2), 301–344. http://psycnet.apa.org/doi/10.1037/h0057481

Mayberg, H. S., Lozano, A. M., Voon, V., McNeely, H. E., Seminowicz, D., Hamani, C.,... Kennedy, S. H. (2005). Deep brain stimulation for treatment-resistant depression. *Neuron, 45*(5), 651–660. https://doi.org/10.1016/j.neuron.2005.02.014

Mayeux, L., Sandstrom, M. J., & Cillessen, A. H. (2008). Is being popular a risky proposition? *Journal of Research on Adolescence, 18*(1), 49–74. doi:10.1111/j.1532-7795.2008.00550.x

Mazur, R., & Seher, V. (2008). Socially learned foraging behaviour in wild black bears, Ursus americanus. *Animal Behavior, 75*(4), 1503–1508.

Mazzella, F., Cacciatore, F., Galizia, G., Della-Morte, D., Rossetti, M., Abbruzzese, R.,... Abete, P. (2010). Social support and long-term mortality in the elderly: Role of comorbidity. *Archives of Gerontology and Geriatrics, 51*(3), 323–328. http://dx.doi.org/10.1016/j.archger.2010.01.011

McCathren, R. B. (2001). How language comes to children: From birth to two years [book review]. *Early Childhood Research Quarterly, 16*(3), 395–397. http://dx.doi.org/10.1016/S0885-2006(01)00109-0

McCaughey, S. A., & Scott, T. R. (1998). The taste of sodium. *Neuroscience and Biobehavioral Reviews, 22*(5), 663–676. http://psycnet.apa.org/doi/10.1016/S0149-7634(97)00067-5

McClelland, D. C. (1953). *The achievement motive.* New York, NY: Appleton-Century-Crofts.

McClelland, D. C., & Pilon, D. A. (1983). Sources of adult motives in patterns of parent behavior in early childhood. *Journal of Personality and Social Psychology, 44*(3), 564–574.

McClintock, M. K. (1998). On the nature of mammalian and human pheromones. *Annals of the New York Academy of Science, 855*, 390–392. doi:10.1111/j.1749-6632.1998.tb10596.x

McConnell, J. V. (1962). Memory transfer through cannibalism in planarians. *Journal of Neuropsychiatry, 3*(Supp. 1), S42–S48.

McConnell, J. V. (1983). *Understanding human behavior: An introduction to psychology.* New York, NY: Holt, Rinehart and Winston.

McCrae, R. R., & Costa, P. T., Jr. (2008). The five-factor theory of personality. In O. P. John, R. W. Robins, & L. A. Pervin (Eds.), *Handbook of personality: Theory and research* (3rd ed., pp. 159–181). New York, NY: Guilford Press.

McCrink, K., & Wynn, K. (2004). Large-number addition and subtraction by 9-month-old infants. *Psychological Science, 15*(11), 776–781.

McCrink, K., & Wynn, K. (2009). Operational momentum in large-number addition and subtraction by 9-month-olds. *Journal of Experimental Child Psychology, 103*(4), 400–408. doi:10.1016/j.jecp.2009.01.013

McGowan, P. O., Suderman, M., Sasaki, A., Huang, T. C., Hallett, M., Meaney, M. J., & Szyf, M. (2011). Broad epigenetic signature of maternal care in the brain of adult rats. *PLOS ONE, 6*(2). http://dx.doi.org/10.1371/journal.pone.0014739

McGraw, M. B. (1940). Neural maturation as exemplified in achievement of bladder control. *Journal of Pediatrics, 16*(5), 580–589. http://dx.doi.org/10.1016/S0022-3476(40)80187-X

McHugh, M. C., Koeske, R. D., & Frieze, I. H. (1986). Issues to consider in conducting nonsexist psychological research: A guide for researchers. *41*(8), 879–890. doi:10.1037/0003-066X.41.8.879

McLeod, P. J., & Brown, R. E. (1988). The effects of prenatal stress and postweaning housing conditions and sexual behavior of Long-Evans rats. *Psychobiology, 16*(4), 372–380. doi:10.3758/BF03327334

Meade, M. L., & Roediger, H. L. (2002). Explorations in the social contagion of memory. *Memory & Cognition, 30*(7), 995–1009. doi:10.3758/BF03194318

Meaney, M. J., & Szyf, M. (2005). Maternal care as a model for experience-dependent chromatin plasticty. *Trends in Neuroscience, 28*(9), 456–463. https://doi.org/10.1016/j.tins.2005.07.006

Mechelli, A., Price, C. J., Friston, K. J., & Ishai, A. (2004). Where bottom-up meets top-down: neuronal interactions during perception and imagery. *Cerebral Cortex, 14*(11), 1256–1265. https://doi.org/10.1093/cercor/bhh087

Medford, N., & Critchley, H. (2010). Conjoint activity of anterior insular and anterior cingulate cortex: awareness and response. *Brain Structure & Function, 214*(5–6), 535–549. https://dx.doi.org/10.1007%2Fs00429-010-0265-x

Meichenbaum, D. (1993). Stress inoculation training: A preventative and treatment approach. In R. Woolfolk, & P. M. Lehrer, *Principles and practices of stress management* (pp. 497–518). New York, NY: Guilford Press.

Melnick, I. V., Price, C. J., & Colmers, W. F. (2011). Glucosensing in parvocellular neurons of the rat hypothalamic paraventricular nucleus. *European Journal of Neuroscience, 34*(2), 272–282. doi:10.1111/j.1460-9568.2011.07742.x

Meltzoff, A. N., & Moore, M. K. (1983). Newborn infants imitate adult facial gestures. *Child Development, 54*(3), 702–709.

Melzack, R., & Wall, P. D. (1965). Pain mechanisms: a new theory. *Science, 150*(3699), 971–979. doi:10.1126/science.150.3699.971

Mendle, J. (2008). *Association of early pubertal timing with externalizing behavior in adolescent girls.* Charlottesville, VA: University of Virginia.

Messenger, J. C. (1971). Sex and repression in an Irish folk community. In D. S. Marshall, & R. C. Suggs (Eds.), *Human sexual behavior: Variations in the ethnographic spectrum* (pp. 3–37). New York, NY: Basic Books.

Milgram, S. (1963). Behavioral study of obedience. *Journal of Abnormal and Social Psychology, 67*(4), 371–378. http://psycnet.apa.org/doi/10.1037/h0040525

Milgram, S. (1964). Issues in the study of obedience: A reply to Baumrind. *19*(11), 848–852. http://psycnet.apa.org/doi/10.1037/h0044954

Miller, J. D., Maples, J., Few, L. R., Morse, J. Q., Yaggi, K. E., & Pilkonis, P. A. (2010). Using clinician-rated five-factor model data to score the *DSM-IV* personality disorders. *Journal of Personality Assessment, 92*(4), 296–305. doi:10.1080/00223891.2010.481984

Miller, K. J., Siddarth, P., Gaines, J. M., Parrish, J. M., Ercoli, L. M., Marx, K.,... Small, G. W. (2012). The memory fitness program: Cognitive effects of a healthy aging intervention. *The American Journal of Geriatric Psychiatry, 20*(6), 514–523. doi:10.1097/JGP.0b013e318227f821

Miller, M. E., & Bowers, K. S. (1993). Hypnotic analgesia: Dissociated experiences or dissociated control? *Journal of Abnormal Psychology, 102*(1), 29–38.

Miller, N. (1941). The frustration-aggression hypothesis. *Psychological Review, 48*(4), 337–342. http://psycnet.apa.org/doi/10.1037/h0055861

Milling, L. S., Coursen, E. L., Shores, J. S., & Waszkiewicz, J. A. (2010). The predictive utility of hypnotizability: The change in suggestibility produced by hypnosis. *Journal of Consulting and Clinical Psychology, 78*(1), 126–130. https://doi.org/10.1037/a0017388

Mingzheng, W. (2005). The moderator effect of attitude strength on the relationship between implicit attitude and explicit attitude. *Psychological Science, 28*(2), 388–391. Retrieved from http://caod.oriprobe.com/articles/654621/The_Moderator_Effect_of_Attitude_Strength_on_the_Relationship_Between_.htm

Mischel, W. (1968). *Personality assessment.* New York, NY: Wiley.

Mischel, W. (1986). *Introduction to personality* (4th ed.). New York, NY: Holt, Rinehart and Winston.

Mischel, W. (2004). Toward an integrative science of the person. *Annual Review of Psychology, 55*, 1–22. doi:10.1146/annurev.psych.55.042902.130709

Mischel, W. (2007). Toward a science of the individual: Past, present, future? In Y. Shooda (Ed), *Persons in context: Building a science of the individual* (pp. 263–277). New York, NY: Guilford Press.

Moerk, E. L. (2000). *The guided acquisition of first language skills.* (Vol. 20). Stamford, CT: Ablex Publishing.

Moffett, M. W. (1990). Dance of the electronic bee. *National Geographic, 177*, 134–140.

Möhler, H. (2012). The GABA system in anxiety and depression and its therapeutic potential. *Neuropharmacology, 62*(1), 42–53. doi:10.1016/j.neuropharm.2011.08.040

Mohsenin, N., Mostofi, M. T., & Mohsenin, V. (2003). The role of oral appliances in treating obstructive sleep apnea. *The Journal of the American Dental Association, 134*(4), 442–449.

Mols, F., Oerlemans, S., Denollet, J., Roukema, J., & van de Poll-Franse, L. (2012). Type D personality is associated with increased comorbidity burden and health care utilization among 3080 cancer survivors. *General Hospital Psychiatry, 34*(4), *352–359*. doi:10.1016/j.genhosppsych.2012.01.014

Money, J., & Ehrhardt, A. A. (1972). *Man and woman, boy and girl: Differentiation and dimorphism of gender identity from conception to maturity.* Baltimore, MD: Johns Hopkins University Press.

Money, J., Ehrhardt, A. A., & Masica, D. N. (1968). Fetal feminization by androgen insensitivity in the testicular feminizing syndrome: Effect on marriage and maternalism. *Johns Hopkins Medical Journal, 123*(3), 105–114.

Monte-Silva, K., Kuo, M. F., Hessenthaler, S., Fresnoza, S., Liebetanz, D., Paulus, W., & Nitsche, M. A. (2013). Induction of LTP-like plasticity in the human motor cortex by repeated non-invasive brain stimulation. *Brain Stimulation, 6*(3), 424–432. doi:10.1016/j.brs.2012.04.011

Morden, B., Mitchell, G., & Dement, W. (1967). Selective REM sleep deprivation and compensation phenomena in the rat. *Brain Research, 5*(3), 339–349.

Morrison, A. R. (1983). A window on the sleeping brain. *Scientific American, 248*(4), 94–102.

Moshman, D. (2009). Identity, morality, and adolescent development. *Human Development, 52*(5), 287–290. doi:10.1159/000233260

Most, S. B., Simons, D. J., Scholl, B. J., Jimenez, R., Clifford, E., & Chabris, C. F. (2001). How not to be seen: The contribution of similarity and selective ignoring to sustained inattentional blindness. *Psychological Science, 12*(1), 9–17. https://doi.org/10.1111/1467-9280.00303

Mott, F. L., & Haurin, R. J. (1988). Linkages between sexual activity and alcohol and drug use among American adolescents. *Family Planning Perspectives, 20*(3), 128–136.

Moynihan, J. (2003). Mechanisms of stress-induced modulation of immunity. *Brain, Behavior, and Immunity, 17*(Supp. 1), S11–S16. http://dx.doi.org/10.1016/S0889-1591(02)00060-0

Mueller, A. D., Pollock, M. S., Lieblich, S. E., Epp. J. R., Galea, L. A., & Mistlberger, R. E. (2008). Sleep deprivation can inhibit adult hippocampal neurogenesis independent of adrenal stress hormones. *American Journal of Physiology. Regulatory, Integrative and Comparative Physiology, 294*(5), R1693–1703. https://doi.org/10.1152/ajpregu.00858.2007

Mummendey, H. D. (1978). Modeling instrumental aggression in adults in a laboratory setting. *Psychological Research, 40*(2), 189–193. doi:10.1007/BF00308414

Murphy, K., Kubin, Z. J., Shepherd, J. N., & Ettinger, R. H. (2010). Valeriana officinalis root extracts have potent anxiolytic effects in laboratory rats. *Phytomedicine, 17*(8–9), 674–678. doi:10.1016/j.phymed.2009.10.020

Murray, H. (1938). *Exploration in personality: A clinical and experimental study of fifty men of college age.* New York, NY: Oxford University Press.

Murray, R. M., Lappin, J., & Di Forti, M. (2008). Schizophrenia: From developmental deviance to dopamine dysregulation. *European Neuropsychopharmacology, 18*(Supp. 3), S129–S134. doi:10.1016/j.euroneuro.2008.04.002

Mwamwenda, T. S. (1993). Formal operations and academic achievement. *Journal of Psychology, 127*(1), 99–103. http://dx.doi.org/10.1080/00223980.1993.9915547

Mwamwenda, T. S. (1999). Undergraduate and graduate students' combinatorial reasoning and formal operations. *Journal of Genetic Psychology, 160*(4), 503–506. http://dx.doi.org/10.1080/00221329909595563

N

Nandhagopal, R. K., Kuramoto, L., Schulzer, M., Mak, E., Cragg, J., McKenzie, J.,...Stoessl, A. J. (2011). Longitudinal evolution of compensatory changes in striatal dopamine processing in Parkinson's disease. *Brain: A Journal of Neurology, 134*(11), 3290–3298. doi:10.1093/brain/awr233

Nathans, J. (1987). Molecular biology of visual pigments. *Annual Review of Physiology, 10*, 163–194.

National Heart, Lung, and Blood Institute. (2011, December 13). *What is Insomnia?* Retrieved from https://www.nhlbi.nih.gov/health/health-topics/topics/inso

National Heart, Lung, and Blood Institute. (2012, July 10). *What is Sleep Apnea?* Retrieved from http://www.nhlbi.nih.gov/health/health-topics/topics/sleepapnea/

National Institute on Alcohol Abuse and Alcoholism. (2006) *Drinking and Your Pregnancy.* (No. 96–4101). Retrieved from http://pubs.niaaa.nih.gov/publications/DrinkingPregnancy_HTML/pregnancy.htm

National Institute on Drug Abuse. (2016, December). *Monitoring the future survey: High school and youth trends.* Retrieved from http://www.drugabuse.gov/publications/drugfacts/high-school-youth-trends

National Institute of Mental Health. (2016). *Serious mental illness (SMI) among U.S. adults.* Retrieved from https://www.nimh.nih.gov/health/statistics/prevalence/serious-mental-illness-smi-among-us-adults.shtml

National Institute of Neurological Disorders and Stroke. (2016). *Huntington's Disease Information Page.* Retrieved from https://www.ninds.nih.gov/Disorders/All-Disorders/huntingtons-Disease-Information-Page

National Park Service. (2016). *Grizzly bears & the Endangered Species Act.* Retrieved from https://www.nps.gov/yell/learn/nature/bearesa.htm

Navarro Cebrian, A., & Janata, P. (2010). Electrophysiological correlates of accurate mental image formation in auditory perception and imagery tasks. *Brain Research, 1342*, 39–54. doi:10.1016/j.brainres.2010.04.026

Nedergaard, M. & Goldman, S. A. (2016, March). The brain's waste-disposal system may be enlisted in Alzheimer's and other brain illnesses. *Scientific American, 314*(3).

Nemeroff, C. B., Bremner, J. D., Foa, E. B., Mayberg, H. S., North, C. S., & Stein, M. B. (2006). Posttraumatic stress disorder: A state-of-the-science review. *Journal of Psychiatric Research, 40*(2), 1–21. https://doi.org/10.1016/j.jpsychires.2005.07.005

Neto, F., Borges, G., Torres-Sanchez, S., Mico, J., & Berrocosco, E. (2011). Neurotrophins role in depression neurobiology: A review of basic and clinical evidence. *Current Neuropharmacology, 9*(4), 530–552. doi:10.2174/157015911798376262

Neumann, C. S., Hare, R. D., & Newman, J. P. (2007). The super-ordinate nature of the psychopathy checklist-revised. *Journal of Personality Disorders, 21*(2), 102–117. https://dx.doi.org/10.1521%2Fpedi.2007.21.2.102

Nier, J. A. (2007). *Taking sides: Clashing views in social psychology* (Vol. 19, 2nd ed.). Dubuque, IA: McGraw-Hill/Dushkin.

Nisbett, R., Caputo, C., Legant, P., & Marecek, J. (1973). Behavior as seen by the actor and as seen by the observer. *Journal of Personality and Social Psychology, 27*(2), 154–164. doi:10.1037/h0034779

Noell, G. H., Call, N. A., & Ardoin, S. P. (2011). Building complex repertoires from discrete behaviors by establishing stimulus control, behavioral chains, and strategic behavior. In W. W. Fisher, C. C. Piazza, & H. S. Roane (Eds.), *Handbook of applied behavior analysis* (pp. 250–269). New York, NY: Guilford Press.

Norman, W. T. (1963). Toward an adequate taxonomy of personality attributes: Replicated factor structure in peer nomination personality ratings. *Science, 66*(6), 574–583. http://psycnet.apa.org/doi/10.1037/h0040291

North, M. M., North, S. M., & Coble, J. R. (2002). Virtual reality therapy: An effective treatment for psychological disorders. *Studies in Health Technology and Informatics, 44*, 59–70.

Novak, M. A., & Harlow, H. F. (1975). Social recovery of monkeys isolated for the first year of life: I. Rehabilitation and therapy. *Developmental Psychology, 11*(4), 453–465.

Nunn, J. A., Gregory, L. J., Brammer, M., Williams, S. C., Parslow, D. M., Morgan, M. J.,… Baron-Cohens, S. (2002). Functional magnetic resonance imaging of synesthesia: Activation by V4/V8 by spoken words. *Nature Neuroscience, 5*(4), 371–375. doi:10.1038/nn818

Nussbaum, D. A., & Steele, C. M. (2007). Situational disengagement and persistence in the face of adversity. *Journal of Experimental Social Psychology, 43*(1), 127–134. http://dx.doi.org/10.1016/j.jesp.2005.12.007

Nutt, D. J. (2008). Relationship of neurotransmitters to the symptoms of major depressive disorder. *The Journal of Clinical Psychiatry, 69*(Supp. E1), 4–7.

O

Olds, J. (1956). Pleasure centers in the brain. *Scientific American, 193*, 105–116.

Olds, J., & Milner, P. (1973). Positive reinforcement produced by electrical stimulation of septal areas and other regions of rat brain [Commentary]. In E. S. Valenstein, *Brain stimulation and motivation: Research and commentary.* Glenview, IL: Scott, Foresman.

Olds, M. E., & Forbes, J. L. (1981). The central basis of motivation: Intracranial self-stimulation studies. *Annual Review of Psychology, 32*, 523–574. https://doi.org/10.1146/annurev.ps.32.020181.002515

Olsen, J. M., & Stone, J. (2005). The influence of behavior on attitudes. In D. Albarracin, B. T. Johnson, & M. P. Zanna (Eds.), *The handbook of attitudes (pp. 223–273).* New York, NY: Routledge.

Opris, D., Pintea, S., Garcia-Palacios, A., Botella, C., Szamosközi, S., & David, D. (2012). Virtual reality exposure therapy in anxiety disorders: A quantitative meta-analysis. *Depression and Anxiety, 29*(2), 85–93. doi:10.1002/da.20910

Orne, M. T., & Scheibe, K. E. (1964). The contribution of nondeprivation factors in the production of sensory deprivation effects: The psychology of the "panic button." *Journal of Abnormal and Social Psychology, 68*, 3–12.

Ornstein, P., & Naus, M. (1978). Rehearsal processes in children's memory. In P. Ornstein (Ed.), *Memory development in children* (pp. 69–100). Hillsdale, NJ: Erlbaum.

Osaka, T., & Matsumura, H. (1994). Noradrenergic inputs to sleep-related neurons in the preoptic area from the locus coeruleus and the ventrolateral medulla in the rat. *Neuroscience Research, 19*(1), 39–50.

P

Paivio, A. (1971). *Imagery and Verbal Processes.* New York, NY: Holt, Rinehart, and Winston.

Paivio, A. (1991). Dual coding theory: Retrospect and current status. *Canadian Journal of Psychology, 45*(30), 255–87. doi:10.1037/h0084295

Palca, J. (1989). Sleep researchers awake to possibilities. *Science, 245*(4916), 351–352.

Palchykova, S., Winsky-Sommerer, R., Meerlo, P., Dürr, R., & Tobler, I. (2006). Sleep deprivation impairs object recognition in mice. *Neurobiology of Learning and Memory, 85*(3), 263–271.

Palermo-Neto, J., de Oliveira Massoco, C., & Robespierre de Souza, W. (2003). Effects of physical and psychological stressors on behavior, macrophage activity, and Ehrlich tumor growth. *Brain, Behavior, and Immunity, 17*(1), 43–54.

Panjari, M., & Davis, S. R. (2010). DHEA for postmenopausal women: a review of the evidence. *Maturitas, 66*(2), 172–179. doi:10.1016/j.maturitas.2009.12.017

Pardes, H., Kaufman, C., Pincus, H., & West, A. (1989). Genetics and psychiatry: Past discoveries, current dilemmas, and future directions. *The American Journal of Psychiatry, 146*(4), 435–443. doi:10.1176/ajp.146.4.435

Parvizi, J., & Damasio, A. R. (2001). Consciousness and the brainstem. *Cognition, 79*(1–2), 135–160.

Pastorino, L., & Lu, K. P. (2006). Pathogenic mechanisms in Alzheimer's disease. *European Journal of Pharmacology, 545*(1), 29–38. doi:10.1016/j.ejphar.2006.06.078

Patterson, D. R., & Jensen, M. P. (2003). Hypnosis and clinical pain. *Psychological Bulletin, 129*(4), 495–521.

Patterson, K., Vargha-Khadem, F., & Polkey, C. E. (1989). Reading with one hemisphere. *Brain, 112*(1), 39–63.

Penfield, W., & Perot, P. (1963). The brain's record of auditory and visual experience. *Brain, 86*, 595–696.

Pepperberg, I. M. (2002). Cognitive and communicative abilities of grey parrots. *Current Directions in Psychological Science, 11*(3), 83–87.

Pepperberg, I. M. (2006). Grey parrot numerical competence: A review. *Animal Cognition, 9*(4), 377–391. 10.1007/s10071-006-0034-7

Pérusse, L., Rankinen, T., Zuberi, A., Chagnon, Y. C., Weisnagel, S. J., Argyropoulos, G.,...Bouchard, C. (2005). The human obesity gene map: The 2004 update. *Obesity Research, 13*(3), 381–490. https://doi.org/10.1038/oby.2005.50

Peterson, C., Maier, S. F., & Seligman, M. E. (1993). *Learned helplessness: A theory for the age of personal control.* New York, NY: Oxford University Press.

Phelps, J. A., Davis, J. O., & Schartz, K. M. (1997). Nature, nurture, and twin research. *Current Directions in Psychological Research, 6*(5), 117–121.

Piaget, J. (1970). *Piaget's theory.* P. H. Mussen (Ed.), *Carmichael's handbook of child psychology* (pp. 703–732). New York, NY: Wiley.

Piaget, J. (1972). Intellectual evolution from adolescence to adulthood. *Human Development, 15*(1), 1–12. doi:10.1159/000271225

Piaget, J. (1977). *The development of thought: Equilibrium of cognitive structures.* New York, NY: Viking Press.

Pilley, J. W., & Reid, A. K. (2011). Border collie comprehends object names as verbal referents. *Behavioral Processes, 86*(2), 184–195. http://dx.doi.org/10.1016/j.beproc.2010.11.007

Pittenger, C., & Kandel, E. R. (2003). In search of general mechanisms for long-lasting plasticity: Aplysia and the hippocampus. *Philosophical Transactions of the Royal Society of London, Series B: Biological Sciences, 358*(1432), 757–763. https://doi.org/10.1098/rstb.2002.1247

Plack, C. J. (2005). *The sense of hearing.* Mahwah, NJ: Lawrence Erlbaum Associates.

Pliszka, S. R., McCracken, J. T., & Maas, J. W. (1996). Catecholamines in attention-deficit hyperactivity disorder: current perspectives. *Journal of the American Academy of Child and Adolescent Psychiatry, 35*(3), 264–272. https://doi.org/10.1097/00004583-199603000-00006

Plomin, R. (2003). Genetics, genes, genomics and g. *Molecular Psychiatry, 8*(1), 1–5. doi:10.1038/sj.mp.4001249

Plomin, R., & Bergeman, C. S. (1991). The nature of nurture: Genetic influence on "environmental" measures. *Behavioral and Brain Sciences, 14*(3), 373–427. https://doi.org/10.1017/S0140525X00070278

Plomin, R., Kennedy, J. K., & Craig, W. I. (2006). Editorial: The quest for quantitative trait loci associated with intelligence. *Intelligence, 34*(6), 513–526. http://psycnet.apa.org/doi/10.1016/j.intell.2006.01.001

Plutchik, R. (1980). *Emotion: A Psychoevolutionary Synthesis.* New York, NY: Harper & Row.

Plutchik, R. (2001). The nature of emotions. *American Scientist, 89*(4), 344. *http://dx.doi.org/10.1511/2001.4.344*

Pollatos, O., Kirsch, W., & Schandry, R. (2005). On the relationship between interoceptive awareness, emotional experience, and brain processes. *Brain Research, 25*(3), 948–962. http://dx.doi.org/10.1016/j.cogbrainres.2005.09.019

Pomeroy, W. (1965, May). Why we tolerate lesbians. *Sexology,* 652–654.

Premack, A. J., & Premack, D. (1991). Teaching language to an ape. The emergence of language: development and evolution. In W. S. Wang (Ed.), *The emergence of language: Development and evolution: Readings from "Scientific American"* (pp. 6–27).

Premack, D. (1971). Language in chimpanzees. *Science, 172*(3985), 808–822. doi:10.1126/science.172.3985.808

Price, D. D., & Bushnell, M. C. (Eds.) (2004). *Psychological methods of pain control: Basic science and clinical perspectives.* Seattle, WA: IASP Press.

Puka, B. (Ed.) (1994). Moral development: A compendium: Vol. 3. *Kohlberg's original study of moral development.* New York, NY: Garland.

Pylyshyn, Z. W. (1984). *Computation and cognition: Toward a foundation for cognitive science.* Cambridge, MA: MIT Press.

Pylyshyn, Z. W. (2002). Mental imagery: In search of a theory. *Behavioral & Brain Sciences, 25*(2), 182–238.

Pynn, L. (2016, June 3). B.C. will require grizzly hunters to remove meat, predicts wildlife federation. *The Vancouver Sun.* Retrieved from http://vancouversun.com/news/local-news/b-c-auditor-general-to-investigate-grizzly-trophy-hunting

Q

Qiu, M. G., Ye, Z., Li, Q. Y., Liu, G. J., Xie, B., & Wang, J. (2011). Changes in brain structure and function in ADHD children. *Brain Topography, 24*(3–4), 243–252. doi:10.1007/s10548-010-0168-4

R

Rabbitt, P. (2005). Cognitive gerontology: cognitive change in old age. Introduction. *The Quarterly Journal of Experimental Psychology. A Human Experimental Psychology, 58*(1), 1–4.

Rabbitt, P., Ibrahim, S., Lunn, M., Scott, M., Thacker, N., Hutchinson, C.,...Jackson, A. (2008). Age-associated losses of brain volume predict longitudinal cognitive declines over 8–20 years. *Neuropsychology, 22*(1), 3–9. doi:10.1037/0894-4105.22.1.3

Rachlin, H., Logue, A. W., Gibbon, J., & Frankel, M. (1986). Cognition and behavior in studies of choice. *Psychological Review, 93*(1), 33–45. http://psycnet.apa.org/doi/10.1037/0033-295X.93.1.33

Radtke, T., Scholz, U., Keller, R., Knäuper, B., & Hornung, R. (2011). Smoking-specific compensatory health beliefs and the readiness to stop smoking in adolescents. *British Journal of Health Psychology, 16*(3), 610–625. doi:10.1348/2044-8287.002001

Ramachandran, V. S., & Hubbard, E. M. (2003). The phenomenology of synaesthesia. *Journal of Consciousness Studies, 10*(8), 49–57.

Ramsey, J. L., Langlois, J. H., Hoss, R. A., Rubenstein, A. J., & Griffin, A. M. (2004). Origins of a stereotype: Categorization of facial attractiveness by 6-month-old infants. *Developmental Science, 7*(2), 201–211.

Rapoport, J. L. (1990). Obsessive-compulsive disorder and basal ganglia dysfunction. *Psychological Medicine, 20*(3), 465–469.

Rapoport, J. L. (1991). Recent advances in obsessive-compulsive disorder. *Neuropsychopharmacology, 5*(1), 1–10.

Rapoport, J. L., & Fiske, A. (1998). The new biology of obsessive-compulsive disorder: Implications for evolutionary psychology. *Perspectives in Biology and Medicine, 41*(2), 159–175.

Rausch, S. M., Gramling, S. E., & Auerbach, S. M. (2006). Effects of a single section of large-group meditation and progressive muscle relaxation training on stress reduction, reactivity, and recovery. *International Journal of Stress Management, 13*(3), 273–290. http://psycnet.apa.org/doi/10.1037/1072-5245.13.3.273

Recanzone, G., & Sutter, M. (2008). The biological basis of audition. *Annual Review of Psychology, 59*, 119–142. doi:10.1146/annurev.psych.59.103006.093544

Rechtschaffen, A., Bergmann, B. M., & Everson, C. A. (2002). Sleep deprivation in the rat: An update of the 1989 paper. *Sleep, 25*(1), 18–24.

Rechtschaffen, A., Gilliland, M. A., Bergmann, B. M., & Winter, J. B. (1983). Physiological correlates of prolonged sleep deprivation in rats. *Science, 221*(4606), 182–184. doi:10.1126/science.6857280

Reiner, W. G., & Gearhart, J. P. (2004). Discordant sexual identity in some genetic males with cloacal exstrophy assigned to female sex at birth. *New England Journal of Medicine, 350*, 333–341. doi:10.1056/NEJMoa022236

Reinisch, J. (1981). Prenatal exposure to synthetic progestin increases potential for aggression in humans. *Science, 211*(4487), 1171–1173.

Rescorla, R. (1968). Probability of shock in the presence and absence of CS in fear conditioning. *Journal of Comparative and Physiological Psychology, 66*(1), 1–5. http://psycnet.apa.org/doi/10.1037/h0025984

Rescorla, R. A. (1987). A Pavlovian analysis of goal-directed behavior. *American Psychologist, 42*(2), 119–129.

Rescorla, R. A. (1988a). Pavlovian conditioning: It's not what you think it is. *American Psychologist, 43*(3), 151–160. http://psycnet.apa.org/doi/10.1037/0003-066X.43.3.151

Rescorla, R. A. (1988b). Behavioral studies of Pavlovian conditioning. *Annual Review of Neuroscience, 11*, 329–352. doi:10.1146/annurev.ne.11.030188.001553

Rescorla, R. A. (1999). Summation and overexpectation with qualitatively different outcomes. *Animal Learning and Behavior, 27*(1), 50–62. doi:10.3758/BF03199431

Rescorla, R. A. (2007). Renewal after overexpectation. *Learning and Behavior, 35*(1), 19–26. doi:10.3758/BF03196070

Ribble, M. A. (1943). *The rights of infants: Early psychological needs and their satisfaction.* New York, NY: Columbia University Press.

Rice, W. R., Friberg, W., & Gavrilets, S. (2012). Homosexuality as a consequence of epigeneticly canalized sexual development. *The Quarterly Review of Biology, 87*(4), 343–368.

Richards, J. E., & Rader, N. (1981). Crawling-onset age predicts visual cliff avoidance in infants. *Journal of Experimental Psychology: Human Perception and Performance, 7*(2), 382–387.

Richter, L., de Graaf, C., Siegart, W., Varagic, Z., Mörzinger, M., de Esch, I. J.,...Ernst, M. (2012). Diazepine-bound GABAA receptor models identify new benzodiazepine binding-site ligands. *Nature Chemical Biology, 8*(5), 455–464. https://dx.doi.org/10.1038%2Fnchembio.917

Richter, M. A., de Jesus, D. R., Hoppenbrouwers, S., Daigle, M., Deluce, J., Ravindran, L. N.,... Daskalakis, Z. J. (2012). Evidence for cortical inhibitory and excitatory dysfunction in obsessive compulsive disorder. *Neuropsychopharmacology, 37*(5), 1144–1151. doi:10.1038/npp.2011.300

Rimmele, U., Davachi, L., & Phelps, E. A. (2012). Memory for time and place contributes to enhanced confidence in memories for emotional events. *Emotion, 12*(4), 834–846. doi:10.1037/a0028003

Robbins, T. W., & Murphy, E. R. (2006). Behavioural pharmacology: 40+ years of progress, with a focus on glutamate receptors and cognition. *Trends in Pharmacological Sciences, 27*(3), 141–148. https://doi.org/10.1016/j.tips.2006.01.009

Robinson, L. A., Berman, J. S., & Neimeyer, R. A. (1990). Psychotherapy for the treatment of depression: A comprehensive review of controlled outcome research. *Psychological Bulletin, 108*(1), 30–49.

Roediger, H. L., III, & McDermott, K. B. (1995). Creating false memories: Remembering words not presented in lists. *Journal of experimental psychology: Learning, memory, and cognition, 21*(4), 803–814.

Roediger, H. L., III, Meade, M. L., & Bergman, E. T. (2001). Social contagion of memory. *Psychonomics Bulletin & Review, 8*(2), 365–371.

Roediger, H., Rajaram, S., & Geraci, L. (2007). Three forms of consciousness in retrieving memories. In P. D. Zelazo, M. Moscovitch, & E. Thompson (Eds.), *The Cambridge handbook of consciousness* (pp. 251–288). New York, NY: Cambridge University Press.

Rogalsky, C., Matchin, W., & Hickok, G. (2008). Broca's area, sentence comprehension, and working memory: An fMRI study. *Frontiers in Human Neuroscience, 2*,(14). https://dx.doi.org/10.3389%2Fneuro.09.014.2008

Rogers, C. (1987). Sex roles in education. In D. J. Hargraves & A. M. Colley (Eds), *The psychology of sex roles.* New York, NY: Hemisphere.

Rogers, C. R. (1961). *Becoming a person: A therapist's view of psychotherapy.* Boston, MA: Houghton Mifflin.

Rogers, C. R. (1977). *On personal power: Inner strength and its revolutionary impact.* New York, NY: Delacorte.

Rogers, C. R. (1980). *A way of being.* Boston, MA: Houghton Mifflin.

Roggman, L. A. (2004). Do fathers just want to have fun? Commentary on theorizing the father-child relationship. *Human Development, 47*(4), 228–236. doi:10.1159/000078725

Roggman, L. A., Langlois, J., & Hubbs-Tait, L. (1987). Mothers, infants, and toys: Social play correlates of attachment. *Infant Behavior and Development, 10*(2), 233–237. http://dx.doi.org/10.1016/0163-6383(87)90037-3

Rohrbaugh, J. W. (1979). Improving the quality of group judgment: Social judgment analysis and the Delphi technique. *Organizational Behavior & Human Performance, 24*(1), 73–92. http://dx.doi.org/10.1016/0030-5073(79)90017-5

Rolls, E. T., & Baylis, L. (1994). Gustatory, olfactory, and visual convergence within the primate orbitofrontal cortex. *The Journal of Neuroscience, 14*(9), 5437–5452.

Romano-Spica, V., Mettimano, M., Ianni, A., Specchia, M. L., Ricciardi, G., & Savi, L. (2003). Epidemiology of essential hypertension: the role of genetic polymorphism. *European Journal of Epidemiology, 18*(3), 211–219. https://doi.org/10.1023/A:1023360410810

Romeo, R. D., Richardson, H. N., & Sisk, C. L. (2002). Puberty and the maturation of the male brain and sexual behavior: Recasting a behavioral potential. *Neuroscience and Biobehavioral Reviews, 26*(3), 381–391.

Roper, S., & Chaudhari, N. (2010). Taste coding and feedforward/feedback signaling in taste buds. In G. M. Shepherd, & S. Grillner, *Handbook of brain microcircuits* (pp. 277–283). New York, NY: Oxford University Press.

Roper, W. G. (1996). The etiology of male homosexuality. *Medical Hypotheses, 46*(2), 85–88.

Rosch, E. (1975). Cognitive representation of semantic categories. *Journal of Experimental Psychology: General, 104*(3), 192–253.

Rosch, E. (1978). Principles of categorization. In E. Rosch, & B. Llyod (Eds.), *Cognition and categorization* (pp. 27–48). Hillsdale, NJ: Erlbaum.

Rosch, E. (2002). Principles of categorization. In D. Levitin (Ed.), *Foundations of cognitive psychology: Core readings* (pp. 251–270). Cambridge, MA: MIT Press.

Rose, J. E., & Fantino, E. (1978). Conditioned reinforcement and discrimination in second-order schedules. *Journal of the Experimental Analysis of Behavior, 29*(3), 393–418.

Rosenzweig, M. R. (1966). Environmental complexity, cerebral change, and behavior. *American Psychologist, 21*(4), 321–332. http://psycnet.apa.org/doi/10.1037/h0023555

Rosenzweig, M. R., Bennett, E. L., & Diamond, M. C. (1972). Brain changes in response to experience. *Scientific American, 226*(2), 321–332. http://psycnet.apa.org/doi/10.1038/scientificamerican0272-22

Rossi, A., Stratta, P., D'Albenzio, L., Tartaro, A., Schiazza, G., DiMichele, V.,...Casacchia, M. (1990). Reduced temporal lobe areas in schizophrenia: Preliminary evidences from a controlled multiplanar magnetic resonance imaging study. *Biological Psychiatry, 27*(1), 61–68. http://dx.doi.org/10.1016/0006-3223(90)90020-3

Rotge, J.-Y., Langbour, N., Guehl, D., Bioulac, B., Jaafari, N., Allard, M.,...Burbaud, P. (2010). Gray matter alterations in obsessive-compulsive disorder: An anatomic likelihood estimation meta-analysis. *Neuropsychopharmacology, 35*(3), 686–691. https://dx.doi.org/10.1038%2Fnpp.2009.175

Rothbaum, B. O., Hodges, L. F., Ready, D., Graap, K., & Alarcon, R. D. (2001). Virtual reality exposure therapy for Vietnam veterans with posttraumatic stress disorder. *Clinical Psychiatry, 62*(8), 617–622.

Rothblum, E. D. (1988). More on reporting sex differences. *American Psychologist, 43*(12), 1095.

Roy-Byrne, P. P. (2005). The GABA-benzodiazepine receptor complex: structure, function, and role in anxiety. *The Journal of Orthopsychiatry, 66*(Supp. 2), 14–20.

Rubenstein, A., Langlois, J., & Roggman, L. (2002). What makes a face attractive and why: The role of averageness in defining facial beauty. In G. Rhodes, L. Zebrokwitz, & A. Leslie (Eds.), *Advances in visual cognition: Vol. 1. Facial attractiveness: Evolutionary, cognitive, and social perspectives* (pp. 1–33). Westport, CT: Ablex Publishing.

Rubin, J. Z., Provenzano, F. J., & Luria, Z. (1974). The eye of the beholder: Parent's views on sex of newborns. *American Journal of Orthopsychiatry, 44*(4), 512–519. http://psycnet.apa.org/doi/10.1111/j.1939-0025.1974.tb00905.x

Rück, C., Karlsson, A., Steele, J. D., Edman, G., Meyerson, B. A., Ericson, K.,...Svanborg, P. (2008). Capsulotomy for obsessive-compulsive disorder: Long-term follow-up of 25 patients. *Archives of General Psychiatry, 65*(8), 914–921. doi:10.1001/archpsyc.65.8.914

Rumbaugh, D. M. (1977). *Language learning by a chimpanzee: The Lana Project.* New York, NY: Academic Press.

Rushton, J. P., & Jensen, A. R. (2005). Wanted: More race realism, less moralistic fallacy. *Psychology, Public Policy, and Law, 11*(2), 328–336. http://psycnet.apa.org/doi/10.1037/1076-8971.11.2.328

S

Sadker, M., & Sadker, D. (1995). Sexism in the schoolroom of the '80s. In A. V. Kesselman, L. D. McNair, & N. Schniedewind (Eds.), *Women: Images and realities: A multicultural anthology* (pp. 66–70). Mountain View, CA: Mayfield.

Sakai, K. L., Homae, F., & Hashimoto, R. (2003). Sentence processing is uniquely human. *Neuroscience Research, 46*(3), 273–279.

Salvy, S.-J., Mulick, J. A., Butter, E., Bartlett, R. K., & Linscheid, T. R. (2004). Contingent electric shock (SIBIS) and a conditioned punisher eliminate severe head banging in a preschool child. *Behavioral Intervention, 19*(2), 59–72. doi:10.1002/bin.157

Samuels, M. H. (2008). Cognitive function in untreated hypothyroidism and hyperthyroidism. *Current Opinion in Endocrinology, Diabetes, and Obesity, 15*(5), 429–433. doi:10.1097/MED.0b013e32830eb84c

Sandhu, S., Cook, P., & Diamond, M. C. (1986). Rat cerebral cortical estrogen receptors: Male-female, right-left. *Experimental Neurology, 92*, 186–196.

Saunders, N. L., & Summers, M. J. (2010). Attention and working memory deficits in mild cognitive impairment. *Journal of Clinical and Experimental Neuropsychology, 32*(4), 350–357. doi:10.1080/13803390903042379

Savage-Rumbaugh, E. S., Pate, J. L., Lawson, J., Smith, S. T., & Rosenbaum, S. (1983). Can a chimpanzee make a statement? *Journal of Experimental Psychology: General, 112*(4), 457–492.

Savage-Rumbaugh, E. S., Rumbaugh, D. M., & Boysen, S. (1980). Do apes use language? *American Scientist, 68*(1), 49–61.

Savage-Rumbaugh, E. S., Shanker, S. S., Taylor, T. J. (1998). *Apes, language, and the human mind.* New York, NY: Oxford University Press.

Savic, I., Hedén-Blomqvist, E., & Berglund, H. (2009). Pheromone signal transduction in humans: What can be learned from olfactory loss. *Human Brain Mapping, 30*(9), 3057–3065. doi:10.1002/hbm.20727

Sawaguchi, T., Franco, P., Kato, I., Shimizu, S., Kadhim, H., Groswasser, J.,...Sawaguchi, A. (2002). Interaction between apnea, prone sleep position and gliosis in the brainstems of victims of SIDS. *Forensic Science International, 130*(Suppl), 44–52. http://dx.doi.org/10.1016/S0379-0738(02)00138-X

Scammell, T. E. (2003). The neurobiology, diagnosis, and treatment of narcolepsy. *Annals of Neurology, 53*(2), 154–166. doi:10.1002/ana.10444

Schachere, K. (1990). Attachment between working mothers and their infants: The influence of family processes. *Psychological Review, 60*(1), 19–34.

Schachter, S., & Singer, J. (1962). Cognitive, social, and physiological determinants of emotional state. *Psychological Review, 69*(5), 379–399. http://psycnet.apa.org/doi/10.1037/h0046234

Schacter, D. L. (1995). Implicit memory: A new frontier for cognitive neuroscience. In M. Gazzaniga (Ed.), *The Cognitive Neurosciences* (pp. 815–824). Cambridge, MA: MIT Press.

Schacter, D. L. (1999). The seven sins of memory: Insights from psychology and cognitive neuroscience. *American Psychologist, 54*(3), 182–203.

Schacter, D. L., Gallo, D. A., & Kensinger, E. A. (2007). The cognitive neuroscience of implicit and false memories: Perspectives on processing specificity. In J. S. Nairne (Ed.), *The foundations of remembering: Essays in honor of Henry L. Roediger III* (pp. 353–378). New York, NY: Psychology Press.

Schechter, H. (2005). *Savage pastimes: A cultural history of violent entertainment.* New York, NY: St. Martin's Press.

Schiffman, S. S. (2000). Taste quality and neural coding: Implications from psychophysics and neurophysiology. *Physiology & Behavior, 69*(1–2), 147–159.

Schluppeck, D., & Engel, S. A. (2002). Color opponent neurons in V1: A review and model reconciling results from imaging and single-unit recording. *Journal of Vision, 2*(6), 480–492. doi:10.1167/2.6.5

Schum, T., Kolb, T., McAuliffe, T., Simms, M., Underhill, R. L., Lewis, M. (2002). Sequential acquisition of toilet-training skills: A descriptive study of gender and age differences in normal children. *Pediatrics*, 109(3), e48.

Scott, R. M., He, Z., Baillargeon, R., & Cummins, D. (2012). False-belief understanding in 2.5-year-olds: Evidence from two novel verbal spontaneous-response tasks. *Developmental Science, 15*(2), 181–193. doi:10.1111/j.1467-7687.2011.01103.x

Seeman, P. (2002). Atypical antipsychotics: Mechanisms of action. *Canadian Journal of Psychiatry, 47*(1), 27–38.

Seeman, P. (2011). All roads to schizophrenia lead to dopamine supersensitivity and elevated dopamine D2 receptors. *CNS Neuroscience & Therapeutics, 17*(2), 118–132. doi:10.1111/j.1755-5949.2010.00162.x

Segall, M. H., Campbell, D. T., & Herskovits, M. J. (1966). *The influence of culture on visual perception.* New York, NY: Bobbs-Merrill.

Seligman, M. E. (1975). *Helplessness: On depression, development and death.* San Francisco, CA: Freeman.

Seligman, M. E., & Maier, S. F. (1967). Failure to escape traumatic shock. *Journal of Experimental Psychology, 74*(1), 1–9. http://psycnet.apa.org/doi/10.1037/h0024514

Selye, H. (1936). A syndrome produced by diverse nocuous agents. *Nature, 138*(32). doi:10.1038/138032a0

Selye, H. (1956). *The Stress of Life.* New York, NY: McGraw-Hill.

Selye, H. (1974). *Stress without distress.* Philadelphia, PA: Lippincott.

Selye, H. (1976). *Stress in health and disease.* Woburn, MA: Butterworths.

Semple, M. N., & Kitzes, L. M. (1987). Binaural processing of sound pressure level in the inferior colliculus. *Journal of Neurophysiology, 57(4)*, 1130–1147.

Senju, A., Southgate, V., Snape, C., Leonard, M., & Csibra, G. (2011). Do 18-month olds really attribute mental states to others? *Psychological Science, 22*(7), 878–880. https://dx.doi.org/10.1177%2F0956797611411584

Senko, C., Durik, A. M., & Harackiewicz, J. M. (2008). Historical perspectives and new directions in achievement goal theory: Understanding the effects of mastery and performance-approach goals. In J. Senko (Ed), *Handbook of motivation science* (pp. 100–113). New York, NY: Guilford Press.

Seyfarth, R. M., & Cheney, D. L. (1992). Meaning and mind in monkeys. *Scientific American, 267*, 122–129.

Shackelford, T. K., Schmitt, D. P., & Buss, D. M. (2005). Universal dimensions of human mate preferences. *Personality and Individual Differences, 39*(2), 447–458. http://psycnet.apa.org/doi/10.1016/j.paid.2005.01.023

Shapiro, C. M., Bortz, R., Mitchell, D., Bartel, P., & Jooste, P. (1981). Slow-wave sleep: A recovery after exercise. *Science, 214*(4526), 1253–1254.

Shatz, M., & Gelman, R. (1973). The development of communication skills: Modifications in the speech of young children as a function of listener. *Monographs of the Society for Research in Child Development, 38*(5), 1–38. doi:10.2307/1165783

Shea, A. K., & Steiner, M. (2008). Cigarette smoking during pregnancy. *Nicotine and Tobacco Research, 10*(2), 267–278. https://doi.org/10.1080/14622200701825908

Sheffield, E. (1966). A drive induction theory of reinforcement. In R. N. Haber (Ed.), *Current Research in Motivation.* New York, NY: Holt, Rinehart and Winston.

Sheffield, E., Wulff, J., & Backer, R. (1951). Reward value of copulation without sex drive reduction. *Journal of Comparative and Physiological Psychology, 44*(1), 3–8.

Shepard, R. N., & Metzler, J. (1971). Mental rotation of three-dimensional objects. *Science, 171*(3972), 701–703. doi:10.1126/science.171.3972.701

Sherif, M. (1937). An experimental approach to the study of attitudes. *Sociometry, 1*, 90–98. http://psycnet.apa.org/doi/10.2307/2785261

Shettleworth, S. (1983). Memory in food-hoarding birds. *Scientific American, 248*(3), 102–110.

Shiffrin, R. M., & Atkinson, R. C. (1969). Storage and retrieval processes in long-term memory. *Psychology Reviews, 76*(2), 79–193. http://psycnet.apa.org/doi/10.1037/h0027277

Sillitoe, R. V., & Vogel, M. W. (2008). Desire, disease, and the origins of the dopaminergic system. *Schizophrenia Bulletin, 34*(2), 212–219. https://dx.doi.org/10.1093%2Fschbul%2Fsbm170

Simons, D. J., & Chabris, C. F. (1999). Gorillas in our midst: Sustained inattentional blindness for dynamic events. *Perception, 28*(9), 1059–1074. https://doi.org/10.1068/p281059

Singer, D. G., & Singer, J. L. (2005). *Imagination and play in the electronic age.* Cambridge, MA: Harvard University Press.

Skeels, H. M. (1966). Adult status of children with contrasting early life experiences. *Monographs of the Society for Research in Child Development, 31*(3), 1–65. doi:10.2307/1165791

Skinner, B. F. (1953). *Science of Human Behavior.* New York, NY: Macmillan.

Skinner, B. F. (1957). *Verbal Behavior.* Englewood Cliffs, NJ: Prentice-Hall.

Skinner, B. F. (1974). *About behaviorism.* New York, NY: Alfred Knopf.

Skinner, B. F. (1981). Selection by consequences. *Science, 213*(4507), 501–504.

Skinner, B. F. (1987). *Upon further reflection.* Englewood Cliffs, NJ: Prentice Hall.

Slade, A. (1987). Quality of attachment and early symbolic play. *Developmental Psychology, 23*(1), 78–85.

Slotnick, S. D., & Schacter, D. L. (2004). A sensory signature that distinguishes true from false memories. *Nature Neuroscience, 7*(6), 664–672. doi:10.1038/nn1252

Smith, L. M., LaGasse, L. L., Derauf, C., Grant, P., Shah, R., Arria, A.,...Lester, B. M. (2008). Prenatal methamphetamine use and neonatal neurobehavioral outcome. *Neurotoxicology and Teratology, 30*(1), 20–28. https://dx.doi.org/10.1016%2Fj.ntt.2007.09.005

Smith, P. J., Langolf, G. D., & Goldberg, J. (1981). Effect of occupational exposure to elemental mercury on short term memory. *British Journal of Industrial Medicine, 40*(4), 413–419.

Smith, S. M., Brown, H. O. E., Toman, J. E., & Goodman, L. S. (1947). The lack of cerebral effects of I -Tubocurarine. *Anesthesiology, 8*(1), 1–14.

Smith, T. (2012, May 10). Romney's views on gay marriage: Also evolving? *National Public Radio.* Retrieved from http://www.npr.org/2012/05/10/152431577/romneys-views-on-gay-marriage-also-evolving

Snarey, J. R. (1985). Cross-cultural universality of social-moral development: A critical review of Kohlbergian research. *Psychological Bulletin, 97*(2), 202–232.

Snethen, G., & Puymbroeck, M. V. (2008). Girls and physical aggression: Causes, trends, and intervention guided by social learning theory. *Aggression and Violent Behavior, 13*(5), 346–354. http://dx.doi.org/10.1016/j.avb.2008.05.003

Snyder, S. (1984). Drug and neurotransmitter receptors in the brain. *Science, 224*(4644), 22–31. doi:10.1126/science.6322304

Snyderman, M., & Rothman, S. (1987). Survey of expert opinions on intelligence and aptitude testing. *American Psychologist, 42*(2), 137–144.

Söderqvist, S., Bergman Nutley, S., Peyard-Janvid, M., Matsson, H., Humphreys, K., Kere, J., & Klingberg, T. (2012). Dopamine, working memory, and training induced plasticity: Implications for developmental research. *Developmental Psychology, 48*(3), 836–843. doi:10.1037/a0026179

Solomon, R. L. (1980). The opponent-process theory of acquired motivation: The costs of pleasure and the benefits of pain. *American Psychologist, 35*(8), 691–712. http://psycnet.apa.org/doi/10.1037/0003-066X.35.8.691

Solomon, R. L. (1982). The opponent-process in acquired motivation. In D. W. Pfaff (Ed.), *The physiological mechanisms of motivation* (pp. 321–336). New York, NY: Springer-Verlag.

Solomon, R. L., & Corbit, J. D. (1974). An opponent-process theory of motivation. *Psychological Review, 81*(2), 119–145. http://psycnet.apa.org/doi/10.1037/h0036128

Solso, R. L., MacLin, O. H., & MacLin, M. K. (2008). *Cognitive psychology* (8th ed.). New York, NY: Allyn & Bacon.

Sorensen, R. C. (1973). Adolescent sexuality in contemporary America: Personal values and sexual behavior, ages thirteen to nineteen. New York, NY: World Publishing.

Spanos, N. P., Perlini, A. H., & Robertson, L. A. (1989). Hypnosis, suggestion, and placebo in the reduction of experimental pain. *Journal of Abnormal Psychology, 98*(3), 285–293.

Spelke, E. S. (2005). Sex differences in intrinsic aptitude for mathematics and science? A critical review. *American Psychologist, 60*(9), 950–958. https://doi.org/10.1037/0003-066X.60.9.950

Sperling, G. (1960). The information available in brief visual presentations. *Psychological Monographs: General and Applied, 74*(11), 1–29. http://psycnet.apa.org/doi/10.1037/h0093759

Sperry, R. W. (1968). Hemispheric deconnection and unity in conscious awareness. *American Psychologist, 23*(10), 723–733. http://psycnet.apa.org/doi/10.1037/h0026839

Spiro, R. J. (1975). *Inferential reconstruction in memory for connected discourse (Technical Report No. 2).* Urbana, IL: University of Illinois Laboratory for Cognitive Studies in Education. Retrieved from http://hdl.handle.net/2142/17616

Spitz, R. A. (1945). Hospitalism: An inquiry into the genesis of psychiatric conditions in early childhood. The *Psychoanalytic Study of the Child, 1*, 53–74.

Spitz, R. A., & Wolf, K. M. (1946). Anaclitic depression; an inquiry into the genesis of psychiatric conditions in early childhood, II. *The Psychoanalytic Study of the Child, 2*, 313–342.

Srinivasan, V., Pandi-Perumal, S. R., Trahkt, I., Spence, D. W., Poeggeler, B., Hardeland, R., & Cardinali, D. P. (2009). Melatonin and melatonergic drugs on sleep: possible mechanisms of action. *The International Journal of Neuroscience, 119*(6), 821–846. doi:10.1080/00207450802328607

Steele, C. M. (2012). Conclusion: extending and applying stereotype threat research. In M. Inzlicht, & T. Schmader, *Stereotype threat: theory, process, and application* (pp. 297–303). New York, NY: Oxford University Press.

Steele, C. M., & Aronson, J. (1995). Stereotype threat and the intellectual test performance of African Americans. *Journal of Personality and Social Psychology, 69*(5), 797–811.

Steele, C. M., Spencer, S. J., & Aronson, J. (2002). Contending with group image: The psychology of stereotype and social identity threat. In M. P. Zanna (Ed.), *Advances in experimental social psychology* (Vol. 34, pp. 379–440). San Diego, CA: Academic Press. http://psycnet.apa.org/doi/10.1016/S0065-2601(02)80009-0

Steen, R. G., Mull, C., McClure, R., Hamer, R. M., & Lieberman J. A. (2006). Brain volume in first-episode schizophrenia: Systematic review and meta-analysis of magnetic resonance imaging studies. *The British Journal of Psychiatry: The Journal of Mental Science, 188*, 510–518. https://doi.org/10.1192/bjp.188.6.510

Stellar, E. (1954). The physiology of motivation. *Psychological Reviews, 61*(1), 5–22. http://psycnet.apa.org/doi/10.1037/h0060347

Steriade, M., & Timofeev, I. (2003). Neuronal plasticity in thalamocortical networks during sleep and waking oscillations. *Neuron, 37*(4), 563–576.

Stern, J. A., Brown, M., Ulett, G. A., & Sletten, I. (1977). A comparison of hypnosis, acupuncture, morphine, and valium in the management of experimentally induced pain. *Annals of the New York Academy of Sciences, 296*, 175–193. doi:10.1111/j.1749-6632.1977.tb38171.x

Sternberg, R. J. (1979). The nature of mental abilities. *American Psychologist, 34*(3), 214–230. http://psycnet.apa.org/doi/10.1037/0003-066X.34.3.214

Sternberg, R. J. (1980). Sketch of a componential subtheory of human intelligence. *Behavioral and Brain Sciences, 3*(4), 573–584. doi:10.1017/S0140525X00006932.

Sternberg, R. J. (1981). Testing and cognitive psychology. *American Psychologist, 36*(10), 181–1189.

Sternberg, R. J. (1982). *Handbook of human intelligence.* New York, NY: Cambridge University Press.

Sternberg, R. J. (1985). *Beyond IQ: A triarchic theory of human intelligence.* Cambridge, MA: Cambridge University Press.

Sternberg, R. J. (2003). Construct validity of the theory of special intelligence. In R. Sternberg, & J. Lautrey (Eds.), *Models of intelligence: International perspectives.* (pp. 55–77). Washington, DC: American Psychological Association.

Sternberg, R. J. (2005). The triarchic theory of successful intelligence. In D. P. Flanagan & P. L. Harrison (Eds.), *Contemporary intellectual assessment: Theories, tests, and issues* (156–177). New York, NY: Guilford Press.

Sternberg, R. J., & Grigorenko, E. L. (2006). Cultural intelligence and successful intelligence. *Group & Organization Management, 31*(1), 27–39.

Stocks, J. T. (1998). Recovered memory therapy: A dubious practice technique. *Social Work, 43*(5), 423–436. https://doi.org/10.1093/sw/43.5.423

Straus, E., & Yalow, R. (1979). Cholecystokinin in the brains of obese and nonobese mice. *Science, 203*(4375), 68–69. doi:10.1126/science.758680

Suomi, S. J. (1976). Early experience and social development in Rhesus monkeys. *La Psychiatrie de l'enfant, 19*(1), 279–302.

Suomi, S. J., & Harlow, H. (1972). Social rehabilitation of isolation-reared monkeys. *Developmental Psychology, 6*(3), 487–496.

Swaab, D. F., Chung, W. C., Kruijver, F. P., Hofman, M. A., & Ishunina, T. A. (2002). Sexual differentiation of the human hypothalamus. *Advances in Experimental Medicine and Biology, 511*, 75–105.

Swann, W. B., Jr., Wenzlaff, R. M., Krull, D. S., & Pelham, B. W. (1992). Allure of negative feedback: Self-verification strivings among depressed persons. *Journal of Abnormal Psychology, 101*(2), 293–306.

Szymusiak, R., & McGinty, D. (2008). Hypothalamic regulation of sleep and arousal. *Annals of the New York Academy of Sciences, 1129*, 275–286. doi:10.1196/annals.1417.027

T

Tabet, N. (2006). Acetylcholinesterase inhibitors for Alzheimer's disease: anti-inflammatories in acetylcholine clothing! *Age and ageing, 35*(4), 336–338. https://doi.org/10.1093/ageing/afl027

Takahashi, H., Higuchi, M., & Suhara, T. (2006). The role of extrastriatal dopamine D2 receptors in schizophrenias. *Biological Psychiatry, 59*(10), 919–928. https://doi.org/10.1016/j.biopsych.2006.01.022

Takeuchi, T., Ogilvie, R. D., Murphy, T. I., & Ferrelli, A. V. (2003). EEG activities during elicited sleep onset REM and NREM periods reflect different mechanisms of dream generation. Electroencephalograms. Rapid eye movement. *Clinical Neurophysiology, 114*(2), 210–220.

Talarico, J. M., & Rubin, D. C. (2007). Flashbulb memories are special after all: In phenomenology, not accuracy. *Applied Cognitive Psychology, 21*(5), 557–578.

Tausk, F., Elenkov, I., & Moynihan, J. (2008). Psychoneuroimmunology. *Dermatologic Therapy, 21*(1), 22–31. doi:10.1111/j.1529-8019.2008.00166.x

Taylor, S. M. (2008). Electroconvulsive therapy, brain-derived neurotrophic factor, and possible neurorestorative benefit of the clinical application of electroconvulsive therapy. *The Journal of ECT, 24*(2), 160–165. doi:10.1097/YCT.0b013e3181571ad0

Tellegen, A., Lykken, D. T., Bouchard, T. J., Jr., Wilcox, K. J., Segal, N. L., & Rich, S. (1988). Personality similarity in twins reared apart and together. *Journal of Personality and Social Psychology, 54*(6), 1031–1039.

Terman, L. M. (1921). Intelligence and its measurement: A symposium—II. *Journal of Educational Psychology, 12*(3), 127–133. http://psycnet.apa.org/doi/10.1037/h0064940

Terman, L. M. (Ed.) (1925). *Genetic studies of genius: Vol. 1. Mental and physical traits of a thousand gifted children.* Stanford, CA: Stanford University Press.

Terman, L. M. (1954). Scientists and nonscientists in a group of 800 gifted men. *Psychological Monographs, 68*(7), 1–44. http://psycnet.apa.org/doi/10.1037/h0093672

Tesser, A. (1990). Attitudes and attitude change. *Annual Review of Psychology, 41*(1), 479–523. doi:10.1146/annurev.ps.41.020190.002403

Thoman, D. B., White, P. H., Yamawaki, N., & Koishi, H. (2008). Variations of gender-math stereotype content affect women's vulnerability to stereotype threat. *Sex Roles, 58*(9), 702–712. doi:10.1007/s11199-008-9390-x

Thomas, A., & Chess, S. (1977). *Temperament and development.* New York, NY: Brunner/Mazel.

Thompson, R. (1985). *The brain: An introduction to neuroscience.* San Francisco, CA: Freeman.

Thorndike, E. L. (1898). Animal intelligence: An experimental study of the association process in animals [Monograph]. The *Psychological Review, 2*(4).

Thorndike, E. L. (1911). *Animal intelligence: Experimental series.* New York, NY: Macmillan.

Thorndike, R. L., Hagen, E. P., & Sattler, J. M. (1986). *The Stanford-Binet intelligence scale* (4th ed.). Chicago, IL: Riverside Publishing Company.

Thurstone, L. L. (1938). *Primary Mental Abilities.* Chicago, IL: University of Chicago Press.

Thurstone, L. (1946). Comment [Commentary on the paper "The Measurement of Attitudes Toward the Japanese in America" by G. Nettler & E. H. Golding]. *American Journal of Sociology, 52*(1), 39–40.

Tinbergen, N. (1958). *The study of instinct.* Oxford, England: Oxford University Press.

Toates, F. M. (2001). *Biological psychology: An integrative approach.* Reading, MA: Pearson Education.

Tolman, E. C., & Honzik, C. H. (1930). Introduction and removal of reward and maze performance in rats. *University of California Publications in Psychology, 4,* 257–275.

Tolman, E. C., Ritchie, B. F., & Kalish, D. (1946). Studies in spatial learning: II. Place learning versus response learning. *Journal of Experimental Psychology, 36*(3), 221–229.

Treisman, A. M. (1960). Contextual cues in selective listening. *Quarterly Journal of Experimental Psychology, 12*(4), 242–248. http://dx.doi.org/10.1080/17470216008416732

Treisman, A. M. (1964). Monitoring and storage of irrelevant messages in selective attention. *Journal of Verbal Learning & Verbal Behavior, 3*(6), 449–459. http://psycnet.apa.org/doi/10.1016/S0022-5371(64)80015-3

Truchot, D., Maure, G., & Patte, S. (2003). Do attributions change over time when the actor's behavior is hedonically relevant to the perceiver? *Journal of Social Psychology, 143*(2), 202–208. https://doi.org/10.1080/00224540309598440

Truman, J. L., & Morgan, R. E. (2016, October). *Criminal victimization, 2015.* U.S. Department of Justice Office of Justice Programs. Retrieved from https://www.bjs.gov/index.cfm?ty=tp&tid=31

Tulving, E. (1972). Episodic and semantic memory. In I. Janis, *Current trends in psychology* (381–402). New York, NY: Academic Press.

Tulving, E. (1974). Cue-dependent forgetting. *American Scientist, 62*(1), 74–82.

Tulving, E. (1983). *Elements of episodic memory.* New York, NY: Oxford University Press.

Tulving, E. (2002). Episodic memory: From mind to brain. *Annual Review of Psychology, 53,* 1–25. 10.1146/annurev.psych.53.100901.135114

Tulving, E., & Schacter, D. L. (1990). Priming and human memory systems. *Science, 247*(4940), 301–306. doi:10.1126/science.2296719

Turkkan, J. S. (1989). Classical conditioning: The new hegemony. *Behavioral and Brain Sciences, 12*(1), 121–179. https://doi.org/10.1017/S0140525X00024572

Tversky, A., & Kahneman, D., (1981). The framing of decisions and the psychology of choice. *Science, 211*(4481), 453–458.

U

Uddin, L. Q., Rayman, J., & Zaidel, E. (2005). Split-brain reveals separate but equal self-recognition in the two cerebral hemispheres. *Consciousness and Cognition, 14*(3), 633–640. https://doi.org/10.1016/j.concog.2005.01.008

Uddin, L. Q., Mooshagian, E., Zaidel, E., Scheres, A., Marquilies, D. S., Kelly, A. M.,... Milham, M. P. (2008). Residual functional connectivity in the split-brain revealed with resting-state functional MRI. *Neuroreport, 19*(7), 703–709. doi:10.1097/WNR.0b013e3282fb8203

Uecker, A., Reiman, E. M., Schacter, D. L., Polster, M. R., Cooper, L. A., Yun, L. S., Chen, K. (1997). Neuroanatomical correlates of implicit and explicit memory for structurally possible and impossible visual objects. *Learning and Memory, 4*(4), 337–355.

U. S. Census Bureau. (2012). *Statistical abstract of the United States.* Washington, DC: U. S. Department of Commerce.

V

Valenstein, E. (1973). *Brain control: A critical examination of brain stimulation and psychosurgery.* Toronto, Canada: John Wiley & Sons.

Valian, V. (1986). Syntactic categories in the speech of young children. *Developmental Psychology, 22*(4), 562–579. doi:10.1037/0012-1649.22.4.562

van Jaarsveld, C. H., Fidler, J. A., Simon, A. E., & Wardle, J. (2007). Persistent impact of pubertal timing on trends in smoking, food choice, activity, and stress in adolescence. *Psychosomatic Medicine, 69*(8), 798–806. https://doi.org/10.1097/PSY.0b013e3181576106

Vasilevko, V., & Cribbs, D. A. (2006). Novel approaches for immunotherapeutic intervention in Alzheimer's disease. *Neurochemistry International, 49*(2), 113–126. http://dx.doi.org/10.1016/j.neuint.2006.03.019

Visintainer, M. A., Selligman, M. E., & Volpicelli, J. (1983). Helplessness, chronic stress, and tumor development [Abstract]. *Psychosomatic Medicine, 45*(1), 75–76.

Vlassova, A. & Pearson, J. (2013). Look before you leap: Sensory memory improves decision making. *Psychological Science, 24*(9), 1635–1643.

Volkow, N. D., Wang, G. J., Newcorn, J., Telang, F., Solanto, M. V., Fowler, J. S.,... Swanson, J. M. (2007). Depressed dopamine activity in caudate and preliminary evidence of limbic involvement in adults with attention-deficit/hyperactivity disorder. *Archives of General Psychiatry, 64*(8), 932–940. https://doi.org/10.1001/archpsyc.64.8.932

von Békésy, G., & Wever, E. G. (1960). *Experiments in Hearing.* New York, NY: McGraw-Hill.

von Frisch, K. (1974). Decoding the language of the bee. *Science, 185*(4152), 663–668. https://doi.org/10.1126/science.185.4152.663

W

Wade, T. J., Fuller, L., Bresnan, J., Schaefer, S., Mlynarski (2007). Weight halo effects: Individual differences in personality evaluations and perceived life success of men as a function of weight? *Personality and Individual Differences, 42*(2), 317–324. http://dx.doi.org/10.1016/j.paid.2006.07.011

Wagner, D. M. (2002). *The illusion of conscious will.* Cambridge, MA: Bradford Books.

Waldvogel, J. (1990). The bird's eye view. *American Scientist, 78*(4), 342–353.

Walker, S. O., & Plomin, R. (2006). Nature, nurture, and perceptions of the classroom environment as they relate to teacher-assessed academic achievement: A twin study of nine-year olds. *Educational Psychology, 26*(4), 541–561. http://dx.doi.org/10.1080/01443410500342500

Wallace, B., & Fisher, L. E. (1991). *Consciousness and behavior* (4th ed.). Needham Heights, MA: Allyn & Bacon.

Walling, M., Andersen, B. L., & Johnson, S. R. (1990). Hormonal replacement therapy for postmenopausal women: A review of sexual outcomes and related gynecologic effects. *Archives of Sexual Behavior, 19*(2), 119–137. doi:10.1007/BF01542227

Wallner, M., & Olsen, R. W. (2008). Physiology and pharmacology of alcohol. *British Journal of Pharmacology, 154*(2), 288–298. doi:10.1038/bjp.2008.32

Wang, S., Baillargeon, R., & Paterson, S. (2005). Detecting continuity violations in infancy: A new account and new evidence from covering and tube events. *Cognition, 95*(2), 129–173. http://dx.doi.org/10.1016/j.cognition.2002.11.001

Wang, X., Zhang, T., & Ho, W.-Z. (2011). Opioids and HIV/HCV infection. *Journal of Neuroimmune Pharmacology, 6*(4), 477–489. doi:10.1007/s11481-011-9296-1

Wang, Y., Markram, H., Goodman, P. H., Berger, T. K., Ma, J., & Goldman-Rakic, P. S. (2006). Heterogeneity in the pyramidal network of the medial prefrontal cortex. *Nature Neuroscience, 9*(4), 534–542. doi:10.1038/nn1670

Ward, J. (2004). Emotionally mediated synesthesia. *Cognitive Neuropsychology, 21*(7), 761–772. http://dx.doi.org/10.1080/02643290342000393

Wason, P. C. (1960). On the failure to eliminate hypothesis. *The Quarterly Journal of Experimental Psychology, 12*(3), 129–140. doi:10.1080/17470216008416717

Watkins, S. S. (2000). Opponent process and nicotine addiction: Perpetuation of dependence through negative reinforcement processes (Doctoral dissertation, University of California, San Diego). Dissertation Abstracts International. B, *The Sciences & Engineering, 61*, 1689.

Watson, J. B. (1924). *Behaviorism.* Piscataway, NJ: Transaction.

Watters, P. A., Martin, F., & Schreter, Z. (1997). Caffeine and cognitive performance: The nonlinear Yerkes-Dodson Law. *Human Psychopharmacology: Clinical & Experimental, 12*(3), 249–257. doi:10.1002/(SICI)1099-1077(199705/06)12:3<249::AID-HUP865>3.0.CO;2-J

Weaver, C. (1993). Do you need a "flash" to form a flashbulb memory? *Journal of Experimental Psychology, 122*(1), 39–46.

Wechsler, D. (1944). *The measurement of adult intelligence* (3rd ed.). Baltimore, MD: Williams & Wilkins.

Wegner, D. M. (2002). *The illusion of conscious will.* Cambridge, MA: MIT Press.

Weigel, R., & Newman, L. (1976). Increasing attitude-behavior correspondence by broadening the scope of the behavioral measure. *Journal of Personality and Social Psychology, 33*(6), 793–802. doi:10.1037/0022-3514.33.6.793

Weinrott, M. R., Riggan, M., & Frothingham, S. (1997). Reducing deviant arousal in juvenile sex offenders using vicarious sensitization. *Journal of Interpersonal Violence, 12*(5), 704–728.

Welin, C., Lappas, G., & Wilhelmsen, L. (2000). Independent importance of psychosocial factors for prognosis after myocardial infarction. *Journal of Internal Medicine, 247*(6), 629–639.

Wever, E. G. (1949). *Theory of hearing.* New York, NY: Wiley.

Widholm, J. (2010). Extinction learning as a model of drug treatment and relapse: A behavioral overview. *The Open Addiction Journal, 310*(57), 57–62. doi:10.2174/1874941001003010057

Wiederhold, B. K., & Wiederhold, M. D. (2005). Final comments and future directions. In B. K. Wiederhold, & M. D. Wiederhold, *Virtual reality therapy for anxiety disorders: Advances in evaluation and treatment* (pp. 191–196). Washington, DC, US: American Psychological Association.

Wiederhold, B. K., Jang, D. P., Gevirtz, R. G., Kim, S. I., Kim, I. Y., & Wiederhold, M. D. (2003). The treatment of fear of flying: A controlled study of imaginal and virtual reality graded exposure therapy. *IEEE Transactions on Information Technology in Biomedicine, 6*(3), 218–223.

Wikgren, J., Lavond, D. G., Ruusuvirta, T., & Korhonen, T. (2006). Cooling of the cerebellar interpositus nucleus abolishes somatosensory cortical learning-related activity in eyeblink conditioned rabbits. *Behavioural Brain Research, 170*(1), 94–98. https://doi.org/10.1016/j.bbr.2006.02.007

Wiley, J. (1998). Expertise as mental set: The effects of domain knowledge in creative problem solving. *Memory & Cognition, 26*(4), 716–730. doi:10.3758/BF03211392

Wilfley, D. E., Kass, A. E., Kolko, R. P., & Stein, R. I. (2012). Eating disorders and obesity. In P. C. Kendall, *Child and adolescent therapy* (pp. 283–323). New York, NY: Gilford Press.

Wilkinson, L. O., & Jacobs, B. L. (1988). Lack of response of seotonergic neurons in the dorsal raphe nucleus of freely moving cates. *Experimental Neurology, 101*(3), 445–457. http://dx.doi.org/10.1016/0014-4886(88)90055-6

Williams, D. A., Butler, M. M., & Overmier, J. B. (1990). Expectancies of reinforcer location and quality as cues for a conditional discrimination in pigeons. *Journal of Experimental Psychology: Animal Behavior Processes, 16*(1), 3–13.

Wilson, E. O. (1975). *Sociobiology: The New Synthesis.* Cambridge, MA: Harvard University Press.

Wilson, E. O. (1978). *On Human Nature.* Cambridge, MA: Harvard University Press.

Wilson, G. T., & Lawson, D. M. (1976). Expectancies, alcohol, and sexual arousal in male social drinkers. *Journal of Abnormal Psychology, 85*(6), 587–594.

Winterbottom, M. R. (1958). The relation of need for achievement to learning experiences in independence mastery. In J. Adkinson (Ed.), *Motives in fantasy, action, and society* (pp. 453–478). Princeton, NJ: Van Nostrand.

Wolpe, J. (1958). *Psychotherapy by reciprocal inhibition.* Stanford, CA: Stanford University Press.

Wolpe, J. (1985). *The practice of behavior therapy* (3rd ed.). New York, NY: Pergamon Press.

Wolpe, J., & Rachman, S. (1960). Psychoanalytic "evidence." A critique based on Freud's case of Little Hans. *Journal of Nervous and Mental Disease, 131*, 135–147. http://psycnet.apa.org/doi/10.1097/00005053-196008000-00007

Woods, B., Yurgelun-Todd, D., Benes, F. M., Frankenburg, F. R., Pope, H. G., Jr., & McSparren, J. (1990). Progressive ventricular enlargement in schizophrenia: Comparison to bipolar affective disorder and correlation with clinical course. *Biological Psychiatry, 27*(3), 341–352. http://dx.doi.org/10.1016/0006-3223(90)90008-P

Wrase, J., Reimold, M., Puls, I., Kienast, T., & Heinz, A. (2006). Serotonergic dysfunction: Brain imaging and behavioral correlates. *Cognitive, Affective & Behavioral Neuroscience, 6*(1), 53–61. doi:10.3758/CABN.6.1.53

Wysocki, C. J., & Preti, G. (2004). Facts, fallacies, fears, and frustrations with human pheromones. *The Anatomical Record Part A: Discoveries in Molecular, Cellular, and Evolutionary Biology, 281*(1), 1201–1211. https://doi.org/10.1002/ar.a.20125

Y

Yan, L. L., Liu, K., Matthews, K. A., Daviglus, M. L., Ferguson, T. F., & Kiefe, C. I. (2003). Psychosocial factors and risk of hypertension: The Coronary Artery Risk Development in Young Adults (CARDIA) study. *Journal of the American Medical Association, 290*(16), 2138–2148. https://doi.org/10.1001/jama.290.16.2138

Yantis, S. (2001). *Visual perception: Essential readings.* New York, NY: Psychology Press.

Yeo, G. (2012). FTO and obesity: A problem for a billion people. *Journal of Neuroendocrinology, 24*(2), 393–394. https://doi.org/10.1111/j.1365-2826.2011.02254.x

Yerkes, R. M., & Dodson, J. D. (1908). The relation of strength of stimulus to rapidity of habit formation. *Journal of Comparative Neurological Psychology, 18*(5), 459–482. doi:10.1002/cne.920180503

Yomogida, Y., Sugiura, M., Watanabe, J., Akitsuki, Y., Sassa, Y., Sato, T.,...Kawashima, R. (2004). Mental visual synthesis is originated in the fronto-temporal network of the left hemisphere. *Cerebral Cortex, 14*, 1376–1383. doi:10.1093/cercor/bhh098

Z

Zald, D. H., Cowan, R. L., Riccardi, P., Baldwin, R. M., Ansari, M. S., Li, R.,... Kessler, R. M. (2008). Midbrain dopamine receptor availability is inversely associated with novelty-seeking traits in humans. *The Journal of Neuroscience, 28*(53), 14372–14378. doi:10.1523/JNEUROSCI.2423-08.2008

Zelnik, M., & Kantner, J. F. (1977). Sexual and contraceptive experience of young unmarried women in the United States, 1976 and 1971. *Family Planning Perspectives, 9*(2), 55–71.

Zelnik, M., & Kantner, J. F. (1980). Sexual activity, contraceptive use and pregnancy among metropolitan-area teenagers: 1971–1979. *Family Planning Perspectives, 12*(5), 233–237.

Zhu, G., Yan, J., Smith, W. W., Moran, T. H., & Bi, S. (2012). Poles of dorsomedial hypothalamic cholecystokinin signaling in the control of meal patterns and glucose homeostasis. *Physiology & Behavior, 105*(2), 234–241. https://dx.doi.org/10.1016%2Fj.physbeh.2011.08.007

Zikopoulos, B., & Barbas, H. (2007). Circuits for multisensory integration and attentional modulation through the prefrontal cortex and the thalamic reticular nucleus in primates. *Reviews in the Neurosciences, 18*(6), 417–438.

Zimbardo, P. G. (1975). Transforming experimental research into advocacy for social change. In M. Deutsh, & H. A. Hornstein, *Applying social psychology: Implications for research, practice and training* (pp. 33–66). Hillsdale, NJ: Erlbaum.

Zotti, M. E., Replogle, W. H., & Sappenfield, W. M. (2003). Prenatal smoking and birth outcomes among Mississipp. residents. *Journal of the Mississippi State Medical Association, 44*(1), 3–9.

Zuger, B. (1989). Homosexuality in families of boys with early effeminate behavior: An epidemiological study. *Archives of Sexual Behavior, 18*(2), 155–165. doi:10.1007/BF01543121

INDEX

C

D

E

F

G

M

N

Q

R

S

T

U

V

W

Y

Z